Production and Inventory Control Handbook

Second Edition

APICS

Prepared under the Supervision of the
Handbook Editorial Board of the
American Production and
Inventory Control Society (APICS)
Henry F. Sander, C.A.E., Executive Director

James H. Greene, Ph.D., CFPIM

Editor in Chief

McGraw-Hill Book Company

New York St. Louis San Francisco Auckland Bogotá Hamburg
Johannesburg London Madrid Mexico Montreal New Delhi
Panama Paris São Paulo Singapore Sydney Tokyo Toronto

In recent years, the role of women in manufacturing, engineering, and management has seen tremendous growth, and this is indeed desirable. However, the terminology of these fields is replete with such words as "manpower" and "man-hour." In addition, the English language has no neuter personal pronoun. Therefore, when words such as "manpower" or the pronoun "he" are used, we hope that readers will understand them to refer to persons of either gender.

Library of Congress Cataloging-in-Publication Data

Production and inventory control handbook.
   "Prepared under the supervision of the Handbook
Editorial Board of APICS."
   Includes bibliographies.
   1. Production management—Handbooks, manuals, etc.
2. Inventory control—Handbooks, manuals, etc.   I. Greene,
James H. (James Harnsberger)   . II. American
Production and Inventory Control Society. Handbook Editorial
Board.
TS155.P74   1987   658.5   86-7195
ISBN 0-07-024321-2

234567890   DOC/DOC   893210987

ISBN 0-07-024321-2

The editors for this book were William Sabin and Mary Ann McLaughlin, the designer was Mark E. Safran, and the production supervisor was Teresa F. Leaden. It was set in Melior by Saybrook Press.

Printed and bound by R. R. Donnelley & Sons Company.

Dedicated to:

Henry F. Sander
Executive Director of the
American Production and Inventory Control Society

In appreciation for his loyal service to the society.

About the Author

Dr. James H. Green, CFPIM, Professor of industrial engineering at Purdue University, is a consultant in operations management and author of several widely used books in the field.

As a consultant for the European Productivity Agency, he has lectured in England, Ireland, Denmark, and Germany. He has also served as Fulbright Lecturer at Finland's Institute of Technology. And in the United States he has served, among others, the Ford Motor Company, Caterpillar Tractor, RCA, and the Century Geophysical Corporation.

His broad industrial experience spans association with such firms as H. W. Harper, Wyman Gordon, and Brown & Sharpe Manufacturing.

He is a fellow of the American Production and Inventory Control Society and has served on the society's advisory council, accreditation committee, and inventory control committee.

Contributors

Emil Albert, DBA, CPM, Associate Professor of Finance, Indiana University at South Bend, South Bend, Indiana (CHAPTER 6)

Timothy J. Albert, Engineer, Allied Automotive/Bendix Chassis and Brake Components Division, South Bend, Indiana (CHAPTER 20)

Sharon B. Allen, MA, Instructor, Santiago Community College, Santa Ana, California (CHAPTER 27)

Robert G. Ames, Vice President—Administration, California Industrial Products, Inc., Santa Fe Springs, California (CHAPTER 25)

Eugene Baker, President, E. F. Baker & Associates, Northbrook, Illinois (CHAPTER 28)

Gus Berger, CPIM, President, The Gus Berger Group, Inc., Anaheim, California (CHAPTER 27)

Richard B. Black, Chairman of the Board and Chief Executive Officer, Mademont Corp. (Retired), New York, NY (CHAPTER 11)

George Brandenburg, CFPIM, Manager of Materials Management, Johnson and Johnson International, New Brunswick, New Jersey (CHAPTER 3)

Roger B. Brooks, Executive Vice President, Oliver Wight Education Associates, Newbury, New Hampshire (CHAPTER 7)

J. Thomas Brown, CFPIM, Senior Marketing Manager, Manufacturing Systems, Burroughs Corporation, Roswell, Georgia (CHAPTER 11)

Robert G. Brown, CFPIM, President, Materials Management Systems, Inc., Thetford Center, Vermont (CHAPTER 29)

David W. Buker, President, David W. Buker, Inc., Antioch, Illinois (CHAPTER 27)

Fredric E. Bulleit, CFPIM, Vice President and Director, Manufacturing Sciences and Services, Armstrong World Industries, Lancaster, Pennsylvania (CHAPTERS 1 and 2)

Joseph A. Carrano, Assistant Vice President—Distribution, New York City Transit Authority, Glen Cove, New York (CHAPTER 11)

Donald A. Chartier, CPIM, Senior Consultant, Arthur Andersen & Co., Chicago, Illinois (CHAPTER 19)

Lloyd M. Clive, PE, CPIM, Coordinator of Industrial Engineering— Technology Programs, Centre for Integrated Manufacturing, Sir Sandford Fleming College, Peterborough, Ontario, Canada (CHAPTER 17)

Stephen A. DeLurgio, Ph.D., CFPIM, Professor of Operations Management, Division of Business and Public Administration, University of Missouri at Kansas City, Kansas City, Missouri (CHAPTERS 17 and 31)

Jack N. Durben, Director, Materials Management, Consumer Healthcare Division, Miles Laboratories, Inc., Elkhart, Indiana (CHAPTER 21)

Ralph C. Edwards, CFPIM, Industrial Engineer, Leupold and Stevens, Inc., Beaverton, Oregon (CHAPTER 26)

Randall Eldridge, CPIM, Superintendent of Material Control, ICI Americas, Inc. Charleston, Indiana (CHAPTER 26)

Craig R. Erhorn, CPIM, MIS Manager, Matrix Instruments Corporation, Orangeburg, New York (CHAPTER 15)

Dennis Fisher, CPIM, Senior Consultant, The Gus Berger Group, Inc., Anaheim, California (CHAPTER 27)

Donald W. Fogarty, Ph.D., CFPIM, Professor of Operations Management, Southern Illinois University at Edwardsville, Edwardsville, Illinois (CHAPTER 20)

Paul Funk, CPIM, Director of Education, The Gus Berger Group, Inc., Anaheim, California (CHAPTER 27)

Jack Gips, CFPIM, President, Jack Gips, Inc., Chagrin Falls, Ohio (CHAPTER 15)

Walter Goddard, President, Oliver Wight Education Associates, Newbury, New Hampshire (CHAPTERS 4 and 7)

Eliyahu M. Goldratt, Ph.D., Chairman, Creative Output, Milford, Connecticut (CHAPTER 27)

Hank Grant, Ph.D., President, FACTROL, West Lafayette, Indiana (CHAPTER 17)

Robert J. Greene, Principal, Reward $ystems, Inc., Glenview, Illinois (CHAPTER 26)

Timothy J. Greene, Ph.D., Associate Professor, Department of Industrial Engineering, and Operations Research, Virginia Polytechnic University, Blacksburg, Virginia (CHAPTERS 17 and 20)

Frank Gue, Manager, Inventory Programs, Corporate Productivity Services, Westinghouse Canada, Hamilton, Ontario, Canada (CHAPTER 16)

Robert Hall, Ph.D., CFPIM, Professor, Operations Management, Indiana School of Business, Indianapolis, Indiana (CHAPTER 24)

Richard Hansen, CPIM, Manager, Arthur Andersen & Co., Chicago, Illinois, (CHAPTER 19)

Willard R. Hazel, Manager, Systems and Programming, Division of AMF—Potter and Brumfield, Princeton, Indiana (CHAPTER 11)

Ed Heard, President, Ed Heard and Associates, Inc., Columbia, South Carolina (CHAPTER 16)

Julie A. Heard, Executive Vice President, Ed Heard and Associates, Inc., Columbia, South Carolina (CHAPTER 26)

Richard C. Heard, CFPIM, President, R. C. Heard and Co., Inc., Bartlesville, Oklahoma, (CHAPTERS 3 and 15)

Earl W. Hildebrandt, Manager, Production Control, John Deere Company, Horicon Works, Horicon, Wisconsin (CHAPTER 25)

O. John Howard, Senior Manager, Technical Products, McCormick & Dodge, Irvin, Texas (CHAPTER 20)

K. James Hunt, Manager, Special Projects, Arrowhead Metals Ltd., Toronto, Ontario, Canada (CHAPTER 17)

James A. Jacobs, CPIM, Executive Vice President, The Gus Berger Group, Inc., Anaheim, California (CHAPTER 27)

Robert L. Janson, CPIM, Senior Manager, Ernst & Whinney, Cleveland, Ohio (CHAPTER 5)

Henry H. Jordan, Jr., CMC, CFPIM, Managing Partner, Consulting Services, Inc., Stone Mountain, Georgia (CHAPTER 11)

Henry H. Jordan, III, CMC, Executive Director, Center for Inventory Management, Stone Mountain, Georgia (CHAPTER 11)

Mark L. Kornhauser, Manager of Manufacturing Strategic Planning, Black and Decker, Professional Products Division, Hampstead, Maryland (CHAPTER 25)

G. A. Landis, CFPIM, President, G. A. Landis and Associates, Pell City, Alabama (CHAPTER 26)

Raymond L. Lankford, President, R.L. Lankford and Company, Dripping Springs, Texas (CHAPTER 3)

William B. Lee, Ph.D., CFPIM, Partner, Touche Ross & Co., Houston, Texas (CHAPTER 23)

Mitchell Levy, CPIM, Inventory Control Supervisor, Instromedix, Portland, Oregon (CHAPTER 26)

Richard C. Ling, CFPIM, President, Richard C. Ling, Inc., Winston-Salem, North Carolina (CHAPTER 13)

C. H. ("Pete") Link, President, Link and Associates, Arlington, Texas (CHAPTER 10)

Paul Maranka, Corporate Manager, Material Systems, Copeland Corporation, Sidney, Ohio (CHAPTER 16)

André J. Martin, President, André Martin & Associates, Inc., Laval, Quebec, Canada (CHAPTER 22)

Hal Mather, CFPIM, President, Hal Mather, Inc., Atlanta, Georgia (CHAPTER 16)

Tim McEneny, CFPIM, President, Tim McEneny, Inc., Holmdel, New Jersey (CHAPTER 16)

Carol Merritelio, Analyst, Materials Management Systems, GTE Communication Systems, Northlake, Illinois (CHAPTER 12)

Robert D. Miller, Materials Manager, FMC Corporation, Chicago, Illinois (CHAPTER 25)

James L. Morgan, Business Science Specialist, The Dow Chemical Company, Midland, Michigan (CHAPTER 9)

Rod Morris, CPIM, Materials Manager, Joy Manufacturing Co., Africa, Johannesburg, South Africa (CHAPTER 15)

Leroy D. Peterson, CFPIM, Partner, Arthur Andersen & Co., Chicago, Illinois (CHAPTER 19)

Christopher J. Piper, CFPIM, Associate Professor, School of Business Administration, The University of Western Ontario, London, Ontario, Canada (CHAPTER 21)

George W. Plossl, CFPIM, President, G. W. Plossl Company, Inc., Big Canoe, Georgia (CHAPTER 3)

Keith R. Plossl, Vice President, George Plossl Educational Services, Inc., Marietta, Georgia (CHAPTERS 3 and 20)

Arnold O. Putnam, CMC, Chairman Emeritus, Chief Executive Officer, Rath and Strong, Inc., Management Consultants, Lexington, Massachusetts (CHAPTER 8)

Richard E. Putnam, Ph.D., System Analyst, Boeing Computer Services, Seattle, Washington (CHAPTER 20)

Tzvi Raz, Ph.D., Assistant Professor, Department of Industrial and Management Engineering, University of Iowa, Iowa City, Iowa (CHAPTER 30)

Stephen D. Roberts, Ph.D., Professor of Industrial Engineering, School of Industrial Engineering, Purdue University, W. Lafayette, Indiana (CHAPTER 30)

Michael J. Rowney, Ph.D., Director of Productivity and Technology, Omark Industries, Portland, Oregon (CHAPTER 25)

Richard Russell, CFPIM, Vice President, Jack Gips, Inc., Chagrin Falls, Ohio (CHAPTER 15)

Charles Sandlin, CFPIM, President, C. R. Sandlin & Associates, Inc., Northfield, Illinois (CHAPTER 18)

Albert V. Santora, CMfgE, Consultant to Management, Coral Springs, Florida (CHAPTER 10)

F. John Sari, CFPIM, President, John Sari and Company, Winston-Salem, North Carolina (CHAPTER 13)

Spaulding Schultz, P.E., P. Eng., Consultant to Management, Kingfield Farm, Gray, Maine (CHAPTER 21)

Terry R. Schultz, CFPIM, President, The Forum Ltd., Milwaukee, Wisconsin (CHAPTER 14)

Lars O. Sodahl, MYSIGMA Sodahl & Partners AB, Goteborg, Sweden (CHAPTER 3)

Earle Steinberg, Ph.D., Partner, Touche Ross & Co., Houston, Texas (CHAPTER 23)

Michael J. Stickler, CPIM, Vice President, David W. Buker, Inc., Antioch, Illinois (CHAPTER 27)

Lewis E. Stowe, CPIM, Material Manager, Davidson Rubber Company, Ex-Cell-O Corporation, Dover, New Hampshire (CHAPTER 25)

Ernest C. Theisen, Jr., CFPIM, Director of Materials, Micromeritics Instrument Corporation, Norcross, Georgia, (CHAPTER 11)

Robert E. Thiele, Jr., Senior Research Logician (Retired), The Dow Chemical Company, Midland, Michigan (CHAPTER 9)

Kenneth W. Tunnell, President, K. W. Tunnell Company, Inc., King of Prussia, Pennsylvania (CHAPTER 10)

Roswell W. Van Cott (Retired), Timber Pines, Spring Hill, Florida (CHAPTER 10)

Will Wendell, CFPIM, Manager—Materials Management Systems, GTE Communications Systems, Northlake, Illinois (CHAPTER 12)

William A. Wheeler, III, Partner, Coopers & Lybrand, Boston, Formerly Vice President, Rath & Strong, Inc., Boston, Massachusetts (CHAPTER 8)

Richard W. White, Senior Consultant, K. W. Tunnell Company, Inc., King of Prussia, Pennsylvania (CHAPTER 10)

Robert W. Whittaker, Senior Vice President and, General Manager, Steel Heddle Manufacturing Company, Greenville, South Carolina (CHAPTER 11)

Roger G. Willis, Partner, Arthur Andersen & Co., Chicago, Illinois (CHAPTER 19)

Contents

Foreword

This second edition of the *Production and Inventory Control Handbook* reflects the broader thinking of the new professional who is concerned with the integration of the manufacturing functions into a closed-loop manufacturing resource planning and control system that encompasses strategic planning, service parts management, and distribution resource planning.

The scope of production and inventory control has been extended beyond the myopic shop-floor view; today it is used to translate sales predictions into human resources and facility requirements, and its schedules and capacity plans set the tempo for the factory. Its influence traverses the purchasing department to coordinate the vendor's deliveries with production. Computer-aided design and manufacturing promise an even closer relationship between production control, the factory floor, and engineering. Two-way communications exist and are maintained with the quality control department to ensure that the customer always receives the quality product desired, and future satisfaction is assured by coordinating the manufacturing and service departments. By sharing a common information database with accounting, the production and inventory control function assists management in exercising tighter cost control.

Contrary to the popular belief that Just-in-Time production, zero inventory, Kanban, and other efficiency techniques were developed off-shore, in actuality, we have only rediscovered the basics of efficiency upon which industry was built. Value analysis, methods study, system design, simulation, participative management, and other efficiency techniques are but a few elements in our manufacturing inheritance. The motto "keep it simple" must have been as important to Eli Whitney, Thomas Edison, and Henry Ford as it is to any successful manufacturer today. This edition of the Handbook restates the industry's dedication to "keep it simple," efficient, and cost-effective.

Over eighty percent of this edition's contents are new, including such subjects as strategic planning, master production scheduling, capacity planning, distribution resource planning, production activity control, Just-in-Time production, group technology, cellular manufacturing, CAD/CAM, robots, bar coding, and micro- and mainframe computers.

The society membership and I are indebted to all of the past presidents of APICS, but in particular to Roswell W. Van Cott and Al Perrault who pioneered the first and second editions, respectively. Mr. Henry F. Sander, Executive Director of the American Production and Inventory Control Society, is owed a deep debt of gratitude for his encouragement and patience as this edition slowly ground through the stages of development.

The Handbook could not have been produced without the creative and unfailing support of the editorial committee and its chairman, Dr. Emil Albert. The committee members guided the development of the Handbook's structure, made important suggestions, served as a liaison with the chapter editors, and reviewed manuscripts.

I personally would like to thank the chapter editors and their contributors for so graciously and freely giving their expertise. They represent some of the most creative thinkers in the profession. Without their contributions, this Handbook couldn't have been produced. I would be remiss if I did not also thank the secretaries of the chapter editors who often carried my urgent pleas to their overburdened employers. They also sent me manuscripts that often needed little further attention because of their careful preparation.

Miss Joyce Hinds, Mrs. Connie Good, and Mrs. Diane Schafer have all done their part on their word processors. In particular I am indebted to the efficiency, promptness, and incomparable skills of Mrs. Catherine Ralston, who eased the burden of putting this edition into press.

As the editor of this Handbook, I alone take full responsibility for its development and contents.

James H. Greene, Ph.D., CFPIM
Editor in Chief
Professor of Industrial Engineering
Purdue University
W. Lafayette, IN

Preface

In 1957, some twenty dedicated business practitioners founded the American Production and Inventory Control Society. In the ensuing three decades, changes in the field have occurred at an explosive rate and provide us today with a fundamentally expanded management science of techniques, concepts, and applications.

The era of the 1960s was one of education, a sharing of knowledge by practitioners and academicians. Increased productivity was inevitable, and production and inventory control gained respect and legitimacy in the business environment. By the end of the decade, the initial handful of practitioners had expanded to over seven thousand active APICS members. In 1970, the first edition of the *Production and Inventory Control Handbook* joined other APICS efforts in providing members with current state-of-the-art techniques.

During the 1970s and continuing into the early 1980s, the dominant theme of production operations management was material requirement planning. Today, MRP techniques have been adopted by the majority of large manufacturing firms and are being taught and researched in many major universities. What will be the theme of the future that will enable American firms to meet the challenges of tomorrow and maintain an edge over the competition?

Business managers today are faced with a highly volatile set of problems and opportunities. One of the most difficult and yet rewarding continues to be the challenge of learning from the previous experience of others. APICS remains dedicated to the sharing of information and it is with this objective in mind that the second edition of the *Production and Inventory Control Handbook* is published.

Section I provides an overview of the production and inventory management function. This discussion of the function's evolution, current industry basics, and prospects for the future is an introduction to the profession for the novice and a review for the seasoned practitioner.

Section II covers the processes required for implementation of strategic long-range business policy. These plans must be defined in the major areas of marketing, manufacturing, finance, and production before the day-to-day operations can proceed in an orderly manner.

Section III recognizes the need for pre-production information in major strategic areas. Customer service levels, product specifications, process methods, manpower requirements, and inventory investment decisions must be defined for implementation of the business plan to occur. This section identifies techniques in all of these areas.

Section IV outlines the tools required for tactical planning and control. Specific details are presented for the development and implementation of the master production schedule, the material requirements planning system, the capacity requirements planning system, and the activity of production control.

Section V covers the variety of information systems used to support production and inventory control activity. Introduction and selection criteria for the broad spectrum of production support systems, as well as for the computer-integrated manufacturing environment, are provided.

Section VI discusses the special interests of the warehouse and distribution operation. Physical handling and material management systems peculiar to this industry function are provided.

Section VII presents the leading edge philosophy on inventory management. Just-in-time concepts and applications are discussed, as used in managing and ultimately reducing the large financial investment of American business.

Section VIII reviews the management concepts and performance evaluation techniques required for managing the production and inventory control function. System and personnel management and performance techniques are exemplified.

Section IX provides a review of the various quantitative methods widely used in the industrial environment. Specific techniques are provided for adaptation and use of bar coding, inventory theory, management tools, and statistics.

It is with pride that APICS brings you this Handbook. We sincerely hope that you will find it a useful tool as you rise to the challenge of competitive opportunity. We wish to express our sincere thanks to the chapter editors and contributors for their many hours of time spent in sharing with us their wealth of knowledge.

Production and Inventory Management

Professionalism

Editor

FREDRIC E. BULLEIT, CFPIM, Vice President and Director, Manufacturing Sciences and Services, Armstrong World Industries, Inc., Lancaster, Pennsylvania

SCOPE OF THE HANDBOOK

A handbook on production and inventory control (PIC) serves professionals engaged in production and inventory management and control, those studying for professional certification, students of management, and persons designing control systems. More importantly, it is a resource for general managers and chief operating officers, sales managers, and general production managers, whose policy-making decisions impact directly on the inventory investment.

The meaning of the word *control* in the title is much broader than the more common meaning of exercising restraint or direction. It is broader, also, than the definition of controlling, which refers to testing, or verifying by a standard. *Contol,* as used in the title of this book, begins with a plan, which is used as a standard.

A *plan* is a scheme of action for a definite purpose. *Planning* means arranging for work or for enterprise or projecting a course of action. Synonyms of *plan* include *model,* or *system.*

A plan, as a system, broadens the scope of this book. A *system* is an assemblage or a combination of things or parts forming a complex or unitary whole. It is also an ordered, comprehensive assemblage of facts, *principles,* doctrines, or the like in a particular field of knowledge or thought. It is also a coordinated body of *methods,* or a complex scheme, or plan of procedure.

Controls and plans and systems suggest that a method of *managing* is being used, or suggest management itself. To *manage* means to bring about, to succeed in accomplishments, to take charge of, to conduct business or commercial affairs. *Management* is accomplished through an organization. An *organization* is a body of persons organized for some end or work.

This book, then, is about planning, controlling, and managing production and inventories through systems and an organization; applying principles, methods, and models, based on facts, knowledge, forecasts, and predictions to accomplish goals and objectives. This book covers production and inventory control in its broadest sense.

A handbook of PIC must be broad enough to include the large businesses as well as the small. It should cover the process industries as well as the assembly and fabrication industries. It should cover the businesses that produce to order as well as those that ship "off the shelf." It should concern itself with distribution inventories as well as with manufactured inventory, from the simple manufacturing processes to the very complex. This is such a book.

The act of writing a book of production and inventory control implies that a professional field of endeavor exists; and, in fact, it does. But the recognition of the profession is recent, and has resulted from a combination of various actions and extensive work on the part of dedicated people over the past quarter-century.

DEVELOPMENT OF PROFESSIONALISM

Professionalism in PIC most likely developed in industry when the various functions relating to the field were assigned to a single manager. That manager, in that business, became a potential professional when the manager carried the responsibility for controlling production and inventories, in its broadest definition. This consolidation of these functions in a single department began in the 1920s in the automobile industry, a necessary outgrowth of the assembly line, and extended to some other industries in the 1930s. However, this trend was not common or universal. More commonly, the functions were scattered among many departments or staff areas.

Following World War II, three trends began to be noticed. First, many functions relating to scheduling, shop floor control, and inventory control were assigned to a single department, which reported to a general production manager, or plant manager. Second, PIC professionals began to talk with one another, across companies. As an example, the New Bedford Production and Inventory Control Association, located in New Bedford, Massachusetts, began functioning officially in 1946. Other PIC associations, independent of one another, began to be organized in Los Angeles; the Minneapolis/St. Paul area; Louisville, Kentucky; Cleveland, Ohio; and many other places.

Third, after World War II more sophisticated techniques became available to attack the problems of both inventory control and production flow through the manufacturing process. These included the *operations research* techniques, many developed in World War II by the British and Americans. These techniques have names that are quite common today, such *Monte Carlo, queuing,* and *linear programming*. Industrial engineering schools and some business schools began teaching the use of these techniques as well as extending class studies in shop floor control and scheduling. Economical-order-quantity (EOQ) models were studied and used more intensively. Gantt charts and machine loading systems were examined for possible applications.

In 1956, some 26 production and inventory control professionals met in Cleveland, Ohio, many representing local professional associations already functioning. The purpose was to discuss the organization of a national PIC society. In a pioneering spirit, with a strong commitment to professionalism, the American Production and Inventory Control Society (APICS) was formed. And in 1957 the first national conference was held in Cleveland.

By 1960, the fourth national conference had been held, and 47 chapters of the APICS were scattered throughout the country. Approximately 1500 members were listed nationally. Growth during the 1960s was rather slow. Local and regional seminars were held, and national conferences were held annually. Speakers became more professional in knowledge, principles, and applications.

By 1970, 114 chapters existed with a combined membership of 8387. The first handbook of production and inventory control was published. Also in 1970 a milestone decision was reached by the APICS to establish the Curriculum and Certification Council. The first assignment was to develop the criteria for testing an individual's knowledge in PIC and to award a certification of professionalism in that field. Simultaneously, with the encouragement of the council, the APICS began extensive work with universities and colleges through the local chapters and regions to develop curricula and courses for training in PIC. The APICS itself began to expand its training, adding more seminars and course material. The production and inventory technical journal had existed since the early 1960s, and was now recognized as the professional journal in the field of PIC.

In 1971 and 1972, professional examinations were being written and developed by the Curriculum and Certification Council with the assistance of the Educational Testing Service. In the fall of 1972, the first examinations were given. There were four modules in the examination structure: on forecasting, shop floor control, material-requirements planning, and inventory planning. A separate test was used for each.

By 1975, the membership in the APICS had increased to 14,177. More significantly, 91 members had been declared CPIMs (certified in production and inventory management). Also 50 members had completed the examination program at the fellow level. By 1980, membership in the APICS had mushroomed to 41,045 and the number of CPIMs had risen from 91 to 3459, the number of fellows to 916.

Today, a little over 25 years later, there are over 50,000 members in APICS, and 10,000 of those members are certified at the certificate or fellow level. The examination program now covers five separate modules with specific examinations for each: inventory management, production activity control, capacity management, master planning, and material-requirements planning.

When APICS was first formed, there was no well-defined body of knowledge. Today, such knowledge exists, and much of the credit should go to the APICS for its efforts to encourage colleges and universities to pursue education in the field, for its own efforts in developing technical manuals and educational programs, and, finally, for its very fine certification program that continues to stress education and learning as its joint goal with professionalism. Certification has been the rallying point around which so many of these other more important activities have been carried out.

2

Organizing for Profitability

Editor

FREDRIC E. BULLEIT, CFPIM, Vice President and Director, Manufacturing Sciences and Services, Armstrong World Industries, Lancaster, Pennsylvania

Production and inventory control (PIC), in its broadest definition, encompasses functions common to all manufacturing businesses, whether heavy industry or light industry. Variations in the functions being carried out, from business to business, partly reflect the planning horizon used. But the extent to which these functions are recognized and utilized relates to the level in the organization at which the planning and scheduling are performed.

STRATEGIC PLANNING

Corporate Level

At the highest level within a company, the chief planning officer and president are primarily concerned with profitability and growth. Both concerns influence both the direction that the company takes in the various markets which it serves or desires to serve and the requirements for capital needed for equipment, facilities, and current assets (cash, accounts receivable, and inventory). For a corporate strategic plan to be meaningful, normally it is consolidated from forecasts and plans built by various divisions, or units, within the company. This section is about planning carried on in these units.

Business Unit

Strategic planning for a business unit involves the study of future expectations and scenarios, including various courses of action that management can take to help mold the business unit as it moves toward the objectives set by the chief planning officer and the president's office. The *business unit* is defined as the most manageable unit within a company. It can be a single business or a collection of related businesses distinguished by common competitors, common markets, distinctive product line, common distribution, and a common mission. Above all, a business unit is one whose planning and managing are generally the responsibility of one manager.

The planning horizon for a business unit varies from industry to industry and from business to business. Most commonly, the planning horizon for a business unit extends at least 2 years but probably no more than 5 years. But the time frame is not rigid, and variations are normal.

Business-unit strategic planning begins with a forecast of the future. Sales forecasts for strategic planning are based on a variety of analyses, including a history of actual experience and predictions of the economic and competitive environment expected in the future. A business-unit manager first defines the size of the industry in which the business unit is operating, determines the industry's historical growth rates, and projects the future of the industry over the next 3 to 5 years. A prediction is made for the business unit that considers the various markets served. The most important use of the prediction is the development of various strategies to attain the objectives. It is important to determine the life cycle of the business in developing this strategy. Strategic studies cover product development, market development, physical distribution, marketing methods, and pricing policies, all aimed at the business unit's strengths and the competitor's weaknesses.

In business-unit strategic planning, PIC personnel are utilized where their unique knowledge can aid the development process. Areas of assistance might include developing the forecast of final demand over the early part of the planning horizon; determining availability of the production capacity required to meet the forecast; analyzing warehouse capacities and physical distribution networks related to growth or to changes in the distribution system; reviewing raw-material and component-part requirements to aid in analyzing suppliers' capacity and capabilities; assisting the purchasing function in "make or buy" analyses that require additional capital; and reviewing skilled-labor requirements, based on production forecasts, that impact on training and redeployment.

Manufacturing Unit

Closely related to, or possibly synonymous with, a business unit is a manufacturing unit. A *manufacturing unit* may support more than one business unit. However, the strategy planned for a manufacturing unit is related to the manufacturing rather than the marketing aspects and likely uses a shorter planning horizon, extending only 1, 2, or 3 years. The horizon is no farther than is needed to allow the addition of new or modified production capacity and to ensure raw-material or component-part availability. Whether this type of planning is called strategic or tactical depends partly on one's vantage point. The business-unit manager might call this tactical planning rather than strategic planning since it more clearly relates to the tactics of carrying out the strategies of the business unit. To the professional production planner or PIC manager, it is strategic because the functions of the production planner are partly exploratory and do not commit the manufacturing unit to a course of action in the PIC area (although they may commit the manufacturing unit to add manufacturing equipment and facilities).

Strategic planning for a manufacturing unit involves most of the same functions that are carried out in the strategic business-unit plan, but in greater depth. Strategic planning is much more detailed in terms of both time increments and product groupings. Instead of time increments being 1 year, they may be quarterly or monthly, extending to a period of 1 to 3 years. The forecast for the manufacturing unit is divided into major product groupings by production process within each manufacturing unit rather than market groupings, although the original business-unit forecast may have been developed by markets.

Grouping product forecasts by manufacturing unit and production process enables the development of the production plan for a specific manufacturing unit. The product grouping must be an identifiable family of products. This enables major production process capacities to be analyzed. Quarterly increments enable analysis of capacities on a seasonal basis. Seasonal inventory requirements of finished product can be compiled and analyzed in relation to warehouse capacity limitations. Dollar inventory investment requirements will aid in later financial analysis. A rough-cut material-requirements plan can be supplied to purchasing for analysis of supplier's capacity, and will enable the development of purchasing strategies and selection of suppliers. Make-or-buy analysis can be carried out as the material-requirements planning (MRP) process deepens. Finally, labor requirements and the availability of labor skills can be studied in depth for the specific manufacturing unit. A detailed list of the major functions and those activities associated with the execution of the strategic plans is shown in Table 2.1.

TACTICAL PRODUCTION PLANNING—MANUFACTURING UNIT

A *tactical production plan* is sometimes called an *aggregate plan*, a *resource requirement plan*, or a *rough-cut resource plan*. This tactical plan is used to determine the impact of planned production on key resource considerations such as the work force levels, overtime requirements, machine capacity limitations and hours required, finished-inventory requirements, and space availability. Externally, the tactical plan is used to ultimately determine the demand on suppliers for materials and component parts. A tactical production plan commits the PIC people to action.

A tactical production plan also begins with a sales forecast. The forecast may be as detailed as the master schedule (discussed later), but most likely it is only as detailed as necessary to accomplish the purpose just stated. Normally, the forecast detail for tactical planning is by product group, subdivided by each major finishing process. Product groups most likely would exclude the differentiation among finish, color, etc. Packaging sizes might be excluded from consideration unless they involve special processing facilities. Often a forecast is developed by major product groupings and is later subdivided into subgroups, if necessary. It is a top-down forecast rather than a forecast developed by adding the individual pieces. The product groups may be one or two levels higher than the individual stock-keeping unit (SKU) used in the master schedule. Normally, the forecast is developed in monthly increments and extends only as far as needed to consider seasonal impact, new-product introduction schedules, and material-requirements lead times. Pric-

TABLE 2.1 Production and Inventory Control Functions

Strategic Materials Management

Functions	Strategic Planning	
	Business Unit	Manufacturing Unit
Sales forecasting	Broad scope of major product groups; single or related businesses Annual increments 2- to 5-year horizon	Major product groups related to specific manufacturing unit Quarterly or annual increments 1- to 3-year horizon Dollar sales volume
Production planning and scheduling/finished-inventory management	Dollars and units of output required by major product group Annual requirements, inventory requirements, dollars and units	Units of output—major product groups—related to major finishing facility control point Quarterly requirements—1- to 3-year horizon Finished inventory—units required to service
Capacity-requirements planning: Equipment and facilities Work force and overtime Goods in process (GIP) control	General review of total manufacturing facility requirements General review of critical skills	Adequacy of manufacturing facility and equipment capacity and technology level Work force skills, training, and numbers GIP systems and space review
Materials-requirements planning: Raw material and components Interplant requirements Outside purchase Related inventory	Review of significant changes in outside or inside sourcing availability Supplier vs. industry capacity and health Make-or-buy potential	Review of sourcing, supplier health, and purchasing strategy Make-or-buy analysis Review of pricing trends and alternate materials Technological advances
Production activity control	Not applicable	Adequacy of systems, methods, professional skills, and organization
Sales service and customer order processing	General review of system adequacy	Review of adequacy of staffing and systems
Physical distribution	Review of adequacy of distribution system or markets to be served	Review of adequacy of manufacturing finished warehouse facilities and distribution centers and locations

ing moves and competitive actions are given consideration in the forecast. The requirement for customer service may be critical, and inventory positions required to maintain customer service may be a major consideration in converting the forecast of consumer market demand to production requirements.

A tactical production plan developed from the forecast relates to a manufacturing unit or a plant, not a business unit. A tactical plan may bring together similar products that may be sold to different markets and by different business units. Tactical production plans are mostly built around bottleneck operations and finishing or final assembly operations.

This rough-cut tactical production plan can be used in the analysis of the demand forecast and inventory requirements on machine capacities and crewing requirements as well as the probable overtime and machine loading needed to avoid critical limitations later. In practice, the final master schedule (discussed later) may modify the plan as actual production performance and demand are evaluated. Rough-cut material requirements calculated from the plan are passed on to the purchasing department, which allocates and makes commitments to suppliers after the sourcing is determined. These commitments would probably be on a monthly basis, later supported by specific delivery schedules based on the master schedules. Estimates of dollar inventory requirements for finished goods are developed for later use by the financial managers and the business-unit managers.

In many instances, multiple plants are affected by the tactical production plan when one plant supplies another. The MRP developed by the using plant can become the basis for the production plan for the supplier plant. Obviously, where multiple plants produce the same products, the tactical production plan may begin as a master plan, divided further into tactical production plans for each separate plant, allocating production requirements or territory assignments or both, in order to equalize and optimize the production loads among plants.

Clearly this form of tactical planning is crucial and critical to the smooth control of output throughout the operation. The most obvious problem in any production plan, however, is that the plan is based on an estimate of future demand. To some extent, at least, any plan based on an estimate of the future will require adjustment as actual demand varies from that estimated. Consideration should be given to revising the production plan monthly, adding 1 month to the horizon, as each planned month is converted to actual performance. Monthly, rather than infrequent, revisions to plans make it possible to have smaller production adjustments, to react to customer requirements better, and to improve control of the inventories. It also aids in minimizing changes in overtime and workforce requirements, which is critical to the smooth and efficient operation of the plant. As plans are revised and changed from month to month, the raw-material requirement estimates given to suppliers can be adjusted in smaller increments. This can have beneficial effects on the suppliers' plans and schedules and may enable purchasing to do better negotiating. Although making infrequent changes in plans, such as once a quarter, appears to stabilize production, in fact, poor customer service or excessive inventories are a result of prolonged stability, which later results in more drastic changes in operating levels and crewing levels or extensive overtime. Infrequent changes in plans can also cause pronounced changes in raw-material requirements, resulting in delays in deliveries or poorer supplier relations.

MASTER SCHEDULING

A *master production schedule* (MPS) differs from a tactical production plan in that it is a detailed, item-by-item schedule of finished products. It represents what a plant plans to produce, expressed in specific configurations of products or styles or colors or finishes. It specifies the dates on which the material is required and the exact quantity to be produced. The master schedule is usually subdivided in weekly, rather than monthly, time increments. It is generally developed for each specific manufacturing organization where final determination of the finished product is established. In an assembly-type operation, it may be found at the highest or final level in the build, assembly, or finishing operation.

An MPS originates from either a backlog of customer orders or a sales forecast of each finished stock-keeping unit, in the case of an off-the-shelf company. An MPS is built from the bottom up, establishing the priority of each specific configuration, style, design, and color based on the need for finished inventory replenishment or the priority of customer orders. To be valid, an MPS must take into consideration not only the finished-inventory position and the relative priority of each item to be produced but also the availability of capacity and material and component parts. Earlier preparation of the tactical production plan helps ensure that the MPS is realistic and attainable. The aggregate amount of finished production in the build schedule, in weekly increments, should conform to and, if necessary, be restricted to the aggregate amount originally planned in the tactical production plan. This helps ensure that what is scheduled on an item-by-item basis can be produced, since it is based on the rough-cut plan previously established for crewing levels and machine capacities. If the schedule is inadequate to service customer demand, then consideration must be given to increasing the aggregate plan with all the attendant considerations relating to crewing, overtime, machine capacity, and material availability. However, if the MPS reflects increases in finished inventory or undesirable reductions in backlogs (where production is on a to-order basis), then consideration must be given to reducing the aggregate tactical rough-cut production plan. Either alternative can be assessed by a study of the aggregate base inventory level and incorporated in the original tactical production plan.

A tactical production plan and an MPS complement each other. The tactical production plan is used to set the output level that must fit within the MPS. After the specific items to be produced are verified, the MPS is used to verify that the aggregate tactical production plan will cover the demand as it currently appears. MPS quantities may be fixed because of lead-time considerations. Accelerating an MPS may only require advancing the specific schedules by a day, as overtime is added, or increasing machine speeds (if the operation is machine-paced) or crew sizes (if it is human-paced). The amount of production for each lot size can remain constant. The aggregate plan may be fixed for the current month, but the succeeding months are subject to change as expectations, customer demand, and the MPS dictate. The dicipline involved in dovetailing tactical production plans with master production schedules is necessary to minimize short- and long-term capacity problems, labor instability, deterioration in customer service, or excessive inventories. The *top-down plan* and the *bottom-up schedule* are both vital to the smooth operation of the plant.

A detailed list of the major functions and those activities associated with the execution of the tactical production plan and the MPS is shown in Table 2.2.

ORGANIZATIONAL STRUCTURE

A study of the functions of production planning can throw light on those organizational structures that would best enable the functions to be carried out. Changing an organizational structure in an operating company is often traumatic to the individuals involved. It should be done only following an in-depth study of the functions required, the effectiveness of their performance, and possible redundancy or overlap. Assigning responsibility to a single manager of those interrelated functions, however, will prove most beneficial.

A PIC handbook cannot adequately discuss organizational structures without considering the products, processes, markets served, and methods of distribution. In addition, the very size of the company involved (whether a single plant or many plants), whether there are single or multiple markets, and whether the products are similar or diverse must be given considerations. Even given all these variables, some commonality exists among PIC functions regardless of markets, products, and manufacturing units. A review of the functions to be carried out in a small, medium, and finally large organization may provide a perspective helpful in organizing to get the best job done.

Single, Small Manufacturing Facility

First, consider the small, single-plant company. For example, this company might manufacture home furnishing products sold through retail outlets.

In this small, single-plant company, the production plan is developed from a sales forecast. The marketing manager, who reports to the president, develops this sales forecast. The sales forecast is turned over to the production manager, who with the aid of the scheduling department develops a broad, rough-cut production plant. This plan denotes what is to be produced monthly for each major product group. The plan sets the overall operating rate of the plant and determines the operating levels of major machines and the labor force requirements.

Since the finished inventory is kept in the manufacturing warehouse, the inventory level is controlled by the rate of flow of production through the plant in relation to the rate of sales of the major product groups. Effective control of the finished product in inventory is based on the accuracy and adequacy of the sales forecast. In this case, the marketing manager might assume responsibility for the finished inventory since the forecast is her or his responsibility.

The MPS developed by the scheduling department dovetails closely with the production plan and specifies how many of the various products will be produced and when. From this MPS and from an adequate bill of materials, a material-requirements plan (MRP) is developed that can be used to schedule both raw-material deliveries from suppliers to meet the MPS and the component part of subassembly schedule. Raw-material and component-part inventory control is the responsibility of the scheduling department, which, in turn, works closely with the plant purchasing department. If the scheduling department is organized as a part of purchasing's responsibility, a looser control might exist.

The transportation of inbound materials falls under the purview of the purchasing department, again working in close collaboration with scheduling. Outbound transportation, however, which includes negotiating freight rates and routings, falls under marketing and distribution, since the finished-inventory control and distribution are the responsibility of marketing. The computerized information systems for manufacturing are the responsibility of the data processing department working with manufacturing, marketing, and particularly the scheduling department.

The important point is that the major functions have been enumerated in a manufacturing and marketing organization that relate to PIC and to what we might broadly call materials management. But a materials management organization has not been created yet. A variety of departments exist, each performing only some

TABLE 2.2 Production and Inventory Control Functions

Tactical Materials Management

Functions	Tactical Planning and Scheduling for Manufacturing Units	
	Tactical Production Planning	Scheduling
Sales forecasting	By-product group as related to production process Usually monthly increments Usually limited to 12-month horizon Seasonals, promotions, new products	Specific customer orders or specific SKUs Expected demand over production cycle—short term Horizon limited to estimated replenishment cycle
Production planning and scheduling/finished inventory management	Rough-cut resource or production plan in monthly increments, horizon 12 months or less By-product group or subgroup to finishing operation Aggregate base inventory level plus planned or anticipated stock	Master scheduling Specific production requirements by customer orders or individual SKU Lot size and sequence Finite schedule by weekly increments; horizon extended to lead time of material and labor flexibility
Capacity-requirements planning: Equipment/facility Work force/overtime GIP control	Operating levels of all major production lines Overtime and work force levels established GIP inventory levels set for control points Engineering, design, process changes	Specific machine schedules and finite/infinite loading related to customer orders or SKU lot sizes Specific overtime or crewing levels set Specific machine loads/GIP control Engineering, design, process changes
Material-requirements planning and scheduling	Rough-cut monthly requirements from suppliers set in conformance to sourcing strategies Interplant and inplant components plan set	Bill of material Specific release or delivery schedules issued, material-requirements planning application JIT—Kan Ban application

2.8

Production activity control	Engineering, design changes	Raw or component inventory control
		Buy ahead on price increases
		Quantity discount analysis
		Engineering, design changes
	Systems development	Priority control
	Dispatching, releasing, reporting, follow-up systems and organization	Actual control in conformance to schedule or requirements
	Cost measurement systems	Overtime decisions
	Crewing levels set	Crewing changes
		Liaison, control, expediting of inbound material, parts
		Maintenance scheduling
Sales service and customer order processing	Backlog analysis	Specific order releases to shipping
	Customer promise procedures	Specific promises on individual orders
	Liaison with master schedule and finished inventory control	Keep customer informed of order status
	Systems development for order processing	
	Liaison with engineering, design on special orders	
Physical distribution	Establish system for distribution center, inventory management push/pull	Actual inventory replenishment decisions and movements between centers
	Establish reorder point and replenishment quantity control	
	Review replenishment cycles—transportation mode	

aspects of PIC. There is a separate purchasing department. A scheduling department works under the production manager, performing only some of the PIC functions. The marketing department controls the sales forecast and is responsible for finished inventory. The transportation function is carried out by nonprofessionals. Actually, in this organization, the president really is the materials manager since marketing and production report to him or her.

Single, Large Manufacturing Facility

Now assume that this small company is prosperous and continues to grow. The plant has become a large, multiproduct plant. The marketing offices, together with the president's office and immediate staff, have been moved to a new location away from the plant site. More than one type of retail outlet is now served, and specialty products are being produced for the different markets. Following considerable discussion between marketing and manufacturing, it is agreed that the inventory of the finished product located in the plant is governed not only by the sales volume and service required but also by the economics of production and the timing of individual runs. The general level of the finished inventory is controlled by the output of finished product as related to the general forecast. But the minimum base inventory level is governed by the product line, production economics, and service required by the marketing organization for each item. It is also evident to the marketing and production organization that the MPS has a dramatic impact on the service given to customers since it controls the replenishment cycle in the finished warehouse, production economics, and machine and plant capacities.

The MRP developed from the MPS requires an ever-increasing close coordination between scheduling and purchasing in view of the increased complexity of raw-material and component-part procurement. The effectiveness of the production plan depends on continuous updating of the sales forecast as market conditions and new-order receipts fluctuate. The plan is also affected by new-product introductions and product promotions that force unusual demand cycles. As the sales territory covered by the marketing organization expands, the complexity of transporting products to customers increases and freight costs become significant. The close coordination that existed among people when it was a small organization, particularly between marketing and manufacturing, is hindered by the physical separation of the two units and the removal of both the general production manager and the general marketing manager from involvement in much of the forecasting and planning detail.

Considering these problems, the company president decides to make an organizational change. A staff production planning manager is added whose assignment, among others, is to develop the broad sales forecast by major product groups. This manager works in direct consultation with the marketing organization to develop this forecast. The manager's responsibilities are to update, revise, and change the forecast on a routine basis. This follows a review with the marketing organization of such things as the changing business climate, the seasonal and cyclical trend of orders, new-product introductions, promotions, price changes, and other factors over which marketing has direct control. A corollary responsibility is to develop the broad, major product group production plans based on the forecast. These plans set the overall operating levels of the plant and control the finished-inventory level. The production plan is to be developed in close collaboration with the general production manager and staff. Finished-inventory levels are reviewed with both the marketing and production organizations to ensure adequacy of customer service and to keep within the limits imposed by physical facilities and sound economics. The production planning manager also has the primary responsibility for finished inventory, working closely with both the marketing and production manager.

In addition, although the scheduling department reports directly to the manufacturing manager, it has a direct, functional responsibility to the manager of production planning. The manager of production planning also becomes involved with the supervision of the MPS to ensure that it relates closely to the broader production plan. This manager also has functional interest in the material- and capacity-requirements plans developed from the MPS.

The purchasing function continues to be a manufacturing function since there is only one manufacturing plant.

A transportation group is added that has the professional skill for performing rate negotiations aimed at cost reductions. This group also is responsible for establishing routings to customers. The transportation department assists purchasing in working with suppliers to improve freight costs on inbound transportation.

The functions of the data systems department have become more complex as the business has grown. Very close liaisons develop among the production planning manager, scheduling department, manufacturing management, and data systems department to ensure the effective application of more advanced designs and specifications.

This organizational structure might look something like that in Fig. 2.1.

Multiplant Manufacturing—National Distribution

The company continues to prosper. It now has multiple-plant locations. Each plant manufactures some of the product lines produced at other plants, but some specialty items are produced in only a few plants. By now the products are distributed nationwide. The territories serviced by each plant can be shifted to balance the manufacturing load among plants. Some products move between plants so that each customer can buy all products from one location, simplifying customer ordering, improving the customer's frequency of supply, and increasing the size of individual shipments to improve freight economics.

Similarly, some raw materials and purchased parts of an identical nature are required by each plant, with some specialty raw materials needed by only some plants. Uniform purchasing requirements create an obvious opportunity for consolidating purchases among plants. This is done to arrange more favorable contracts with suppliers on a national basis, ensuring that the best supply and price is available to each plant and allowing the best negotiating posture with suppliers.

New-product development activities involving the engineering department, product design, and research and development are located near the corporate headquarters, where the president and general production managers and general marketing managers are based.

The president again examines the organizational structures of the materials management function with a view to improve overall effectiveness in this area. The president broadens the responsibility of the corporate-level production planning manager, who works with the general production managers and the general marketing managers. This manager is responsible for finished-inventory and raw-material inventory management, as well as for developing sales forecasts and the subsequent production plans for the multiple-plant operation. Territory transfers between plants are done to utilize most effectively the multiple plants' overall capacity and to stabilize production as nearly as possible among plants. This same manager works in close collaboration with the transportation department since interplant freight costs have become a significant factor. In addition, freight costs become a factor in territorial transfers to serve national markets. Service to customers is critical, and liaison between marketing and production planning is vital both for sales forecasting and for territorial changes. Occasionally, allocations of production

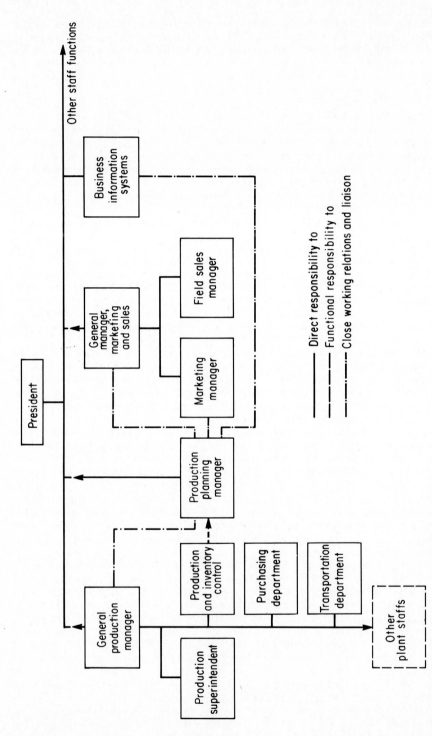

FIG. 2.1 Organization chart for a large single-plant company.

President

Other staff functions

Business information systems

General manager, marketing and sales

Field sales manager

Marketing manager

Production planning manager

General production manager

Production and inventory control

Purchasing department

Transportation department

Production superintendent

Other plant staffs

Direct responsibility to
Functional responsibility to
Close working relations and liaison

2.12

capacity must be made between marketing groups, following consultation with manufacturing and marketing.

The manager of production planning continues to have functional supervision of plant production planning and works closely with each of the multiple-plant production planning organizations and with plant management.

A corporate manager of purchasing is appointed who functionally supervises plant purchasing at each of the various plants. The prime responsibility of this manager is to develop the purchasing strategy and to negotiate with major suppliers on a nationwide basis. Most day-to-day purchasing, including issuing of specific purchase orders or specific material releases, is still executed by plant purchasing.

A central transportation department is established to perform rate negotiations with railroads, truckers, and trucking companies on both inbound and outbound material to obtain the best service and cheapest transportation. The central transportation department must work hand in hand with central purchasing and central production planning to perform this function.

All three functions have a close relationship with the data systems group. Each is a user, and each is involved in the development of advanced systems, both centrally and at plant level. Because of the need to use common information at all plant locations, the development of common data systems becomes necessary.

Finally, to ensure the highest degree of coordination among production planning, purchasing, and transportation, a director of materials management, who reports to the president, is appointed to carry out the combined coordinating functions of purchasing, production planning, transportation, and physical distribution at the corporate level. This organizational structure might look like that shown in Fig. 2.2.

One of the most controversial issues today in many organizations is centralization versus decentralization, particularly as it affects staff functions. The materials management organization discussed earlier appears highly centralized. On the contrary, the intent is to centralize only those functions that can best be done centrally and to move all other functions to the plants. The staff of the corporate production planning department might be only one manager plus the clerical help required. Corporate purchasing is concerned mostly in strategy and major contracts and agreements that move across plant boundaries. It is also a small central organization. Other purchasing functions are decentralized.

Reviewing the functions of PIC, we see that all functions related to the tactical plan and the MPS might best fall under the responsibility of one department head. Also, since PIC decisions affect both marketing and production, and since production and marketing policies set the stage for executing the plans, it seems logical for the head of PIC to report to the general manager who has the responsibility for both the production manager and marketing manager. Whether the manager responsible for PIC should also be responsible for purchasing and transportation depends more on the size of the organization, the number of plants and products. Both functions are professional specialties, and both relate closely to and are contiguous with the PIC function. Nonetheless, a close working and cooperative relationship must exist.

PRINCIPLES AND FUNDAMENTALS OF PRODUCTION AND INVENTORY CONTROL

In an overview chapter on PIC, some discussion must center on basic fundamentals and principles that must be understood to execute the various functions. They

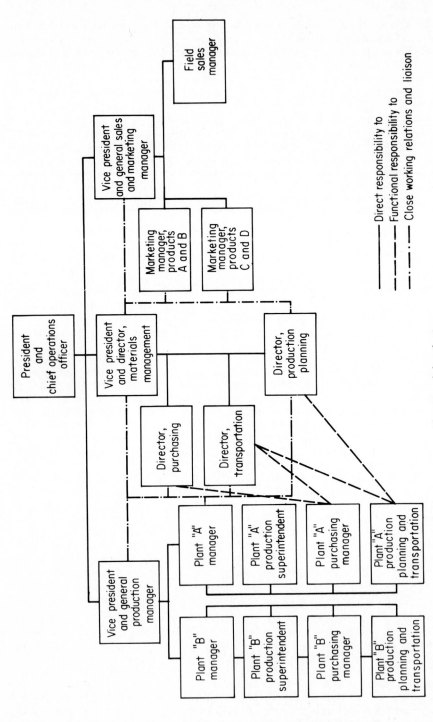

FIG. 2.2 Organization chart for a multiplant company with national distribution.

Direct responsibility to
Functional responsibility to
Close working relations and liaison

should have a relationship to general management objectives and should be compatible with and give assistance to general management in carrying out its objectives. Fundamentals and principles should be applicable regardless of the markets served, the production process, or the size of the organization.

Return on Assets

In analyzing the performance of profit-making organizations, financial and business analysts have developed a variety of financial ratios; many are now commonly used throughout industry. They are used by investors, and they are used internally to compare the performance among divisions or among competitors. Some of these ratios also apply to inventory management, and they have been used as the basis for developing inventory models as well.

The *percentage profit on sales* is the profit (before taxes) divided by the sales income, converted to a percentage.

Turnover, as used by the financial analyst, is the sales income divided by assets (less cash). Cash is usually excluded in internal or competitive comparisons so that the ratio can be used to compare operating results, excluding financial considerations.

Return on assets (ROA) is a simple ratio of profit (before taxes) as a percent of total assets (less cash).

The *return on equity* (ROE) and *return on investment* (ROI) are ratios more commonly used for investment analysis or financial management.

The first three ratios are very closely related, and each has application to inventory management.

$$\text{Return on assets} = \frac{\text{operating profit}}{\text{total assets (less cash)}}$$

$$\text{Percentage profit on sales} = \frac{\text{operating profit}}{\text{annual sales income}}$$

$$\text{Turnover} = \frac{\text{annual sales income}}{\text{total assets (less cash)}}$$

Therefore,

$$\text{Return on assets} = \frac{\text{operating profit}}{\text{sales income}} \times \frac{\text{sales income}}{\text{total assets}}$$

$$= \text{percentage profit on sales} \times \text{turnover}$$

In the last model, return on assets equals percentage profit on sales multiplied by turnover. The analyst's ratio has direct significance to inventory management. Inventory turnover, the annual cost of goods sold divided by the cost of inventory, has always been considered a measuring stick for inventory management. However, most PIC decisions influence profits by their effect on the sales rate or production costs. Inventories are assets, and reducing investment in inventories can have a beneficial effect on ROA. At the same time, it is possible to be trapped into reducing inventories which, in turn, may have a detrimental effect on the ability to service the marketplace and thus have a negative impact on profits. Reducing inventories may improve turnover, but it could also have a negative impact on production costs.

If a management objective of either reducing or increasing inventory levels is to be set, the goal should be a positive effect on the ROA, at least in the long term. Clearly the management ratio of ROA can be applied to, and be a useful concept in, production and inventory control. PIC decisions usually relate to incremental changes in inventory and the effect of incremental changes in inventory on profits or costs. To apply the ROA concept to inventory decisions, we must examine specific incremental changes.

To effectively use the ROA concept, general management should first establish a basic ROA objective. One preliminary criterion is to establish the cost of capital. The *cost of capital* is normally defined as the rate of return an investor would expect to earn in the long term by investing in a specific business, both through the appreciation of capital and through dividends. A before-tax cost of capital in today's market might be in the range of 20 to 30 percent. The cost of capital is greater than is the cost of borrowing money, usually a poor measure of the cost of capital.

After the cost of capital is determined, a rate is usually established for controlling incremental investments within a company. This incremental capital rate is sometimes called a *hurdle rate*. It should be at least as high as the cost of capital. The rule is that investments falling below the hurdle rate should probably not be made. Hurdle rates are used for controlling capital expansion related to either cost reduction or capacity additions. Hurdle rates may be set in excess of a 50 percent annual return before taxes. For short-term incremental investments, such as inventories, a minimum hurdle rate may be as low as 30 percent but likely not less.

Management normally sets an ROA rate for incremental investments in inventories that are common to all facilities even through short-term ROA objectives for the facility or business unit may be lower. This policy helps ensure that the allocation of available capital is based on a common long-term ROA goal. A policy might state the objecive as follows:

> Each decision for an incremental inventory investment opportunity, or an inventory reduction opportunity should be governed by the rate of return on the net asset change. If the ROA target is not equaled or exceeded by the incremental change, the decision should be avoided, normally.

Raw Material and Purchased Parts

When a raw material, part, or component is to be purchased, the question of how much to receive in any one delivery is critical and fundamental to inventory management. If the material is to be used for a particular production run and is not to be reordered, the question is probably academic. But if the material is to be used in manufacturing on a regular basis and in fairly predictable quantities, then buying in larger quantities with less frequent deliveries may enable one to receive quantity discounts because of reduced freight or other cost factors determined by the supplier. Buying in larger quantities, however, results in an increase in the average inventory investment; clearly, an economic decision can be made directly applicable to the ROA principle. Increasing the inventory investment by buying in larger quantities will allow buying at a reduced price per unit and, therefore, increase the profit. Given a hurdle rate of 30 percent for inventories, if the savings converted to an annual rate result in a percentage return greater than 30 percent based on the average added investment, a decision should probably be made to buy in the larger increment.

A simple example is shown in Table 2.3. The minimum quantity possible to purchase is 100 pounds (lb). By purchasing in 1000-lb quantities, the average inventory is increased by $435, generating a savings rate equivalent to $360 per year and a return on the incremental investment inventory of 83 percent. Obviously, this is well above the hurdle rate of 30 percent and a good decision.

Additional discount quantities can also be analyzed. The 1000-lb decision is confirmed as desirable. If the item is bought in 5000-lb quantities, additional savings are available beyond those at the 1000-lb level. For an additional investment of $1815, an additional saving of $600 per year is possible. This gives an additional return of 33 percent. Since this is above the hurdle rate of 30 percent, it is appropriate to make an overriding decision to buy in 5000-lb quantities.

To buy in 10,000-lb quantities gives additional savings. But given the additional investment, the return drops below the 30 percent hurdle rate and the 10,000-lb quantity should be turned down as inadequate.

Note that the return on incremental investment is impacted directly by the usage rate. Doubling the usage rate in the example, bringing it to 24,000 lb/yr, will double the savings in each step and, therefore, double the return, making the 10,000-lb quantity a desirable buy at a 44 percent return.

Fundamentally, one must look at inventories as an investment. Financially, inventories are on the balance sheet as a current asset. A recommendation to increase inventory investment should be accompanied by an improvement in profits from either improved sales or reduced costs, and the improvement should be some rate of return that is adequate from a financial management standpoint. This financial approach sets a policy by which general management can direct the production and inventory control managers to reduce inventories, if needed, based on a hurdle rate. For example, if the hurdle rate were raised from 30 to 40 percent in

TABLE 2.3 Price-Discount Schedule*

Quantity per delivery, lb	100	1000	5000	10,000
Quantity discount per pound	$1.00	$0.97	$0.92	$0.88
Dollar amount of delivery	$100	$970	$4600	$8800
Average inventory investment[†]	$50	$485	$2300	$4400
Average incremental investment over next smaller quantity	—	$435	$1815	$2100
Savings per purchase related to next smaller quantity price[‡]	—	$30	$250	$400
Number of purchases per year[§]	120	12	2.4	1.2
Annual savings rate related to next smaller quantity	—	$360	$600	$480
Return on incremental average investment[¶]	—	83%	33%	23%

* Raw material: Specialty resin B

    Usage rate: 1000 lb/mo planned
                12,000 lb/y estimated

[†] Dollar amount of delivery divided by 2.

[‡] 1000 lb @ $1.00 vs. 1000 lb @ $0.97; 5000 lb @ $0.97 vs. 5000 lb @ $0.92; etc.

[§] Annual usage/quantity per delivery.

[¶] Annual savings/average incremental investment.

the example, the buying quantity for specialty resin B would be reduced to 1000-lb, since that is the only level to exceed the hurdle rate. All purchased items in inventory could be reviewed by using the same criteria. Some items would be affected by the decision of management to increase the hurdle rate; others would not. Management can now begin controlling total raw-material inventory investment by changing policy based on financial constraints, rather than by some arbitrary fiat.

Purchasing Ahead of Price Increases

An extension of the mathematical model just discussed can help determine how much material or how many parts to buy in anticipation of price increases. If a price increase is announced and the supplier has given the customer adequate time, it may be possible to purchase material ahead of the price increase, increasing the inventory and avoiding the high material costs for a time. Again, an ROA analysis should be made. Use the same hurdle rate as before, to determine how much to buy ahead. Theoretically, one additional day's supply might be bought and the equivalent annual rate of return that it would generate determined. Next calculate the return obtained if a second day's supply is purchased. Gradually increase the number of days' supply purchased until the last increment added gives a return of no more than 30 percent. In practice, a week's supply or a month's supply is used to give a reasonably accurate determination. The question then becomes, How much should be bought so that the last weekly or monthly increment added still exceeds the hurdle rate, while the next increment added falls below the hurdle rate?

In a simple example, suppose 1000 lb/mo of resin B is used, and normally it is purchased in 1000-lb quantities. Also suppose a price increase of 5 percent was announced effective 1 month ahead. It was decided to buy an additional one month's supply over and above normal. In this example, 5 percent was saved on the 1000-lb purchase. Since only a 1-month supply was purchased, convert the 5 percent saved to an annual rate by multiplying it by 12 times per year, to get an annual rate of return of 60 percent. If the hurdle rate were 30 percent, obviously it would be desirable to buy at least a 1-month supply.

If it were decided to purchase an additional 1-month supply, making a total supply of 2 months, then the second month would yield only a 30 percent annual rate of return (5% × 12 ÷ 2). The second month's supply also equals the hurdle rate and is acceptable.

If it were decided to examine the alternative to purchase a third month's supply, the third month would yield only a 20 percent return (5% × 12 ÷ 3), well below the hurdle rate.

It is easy to establish a model to determine how many months' supply should be purchased so that the last incremental month added equals the hurdle rate. The equation is

$$M = 12\left(\frac{P}{R}\right)$$

where R = hurdle rate (30% as an example)
      P = percentage increase (7%, as an example)
   12 = 12 mo/yr
    M = month's supply to buy so that last monthly increment equals hurdle rate

As an example,

$$M = 12 \left(\frac{0.07}{0.30} \right) = 2.8 \text{ mo}$$

This is a simple formula to apply. It determines how much to buy ahead while staying within the management policy and financial guideline. In practice, inventories should not be increased ahead of price increases unless management is aware of the possible change in inventory levels.

Purchasing strategies must be taken into consideration in buying ahead of price increases. A price increase may be announced, but later negotiations may establish that the price increase will not stick. Close liaison between purchasing and PIC, as well as with the financial managers, should be maintained to ensure appropriate management concurrence.

Production Run Lengths

Production managers are well known for their desire to increase the production run length, or lot size, of a product because this improves the opportunity for production efficiencies and spreads the setup and startup cost over more units. Setup and startup costs can be quite excessive. In many instances, the level of product scrap is high in the early stages of production. The common solution is to increase the production run length, spreading the startup and scrap cost over a greater number of items to lower the unit cost of production. This is portrayed in Fig. 2.3.

In this particular case, the setup and startup cost per run size is $585. This chart shows that the setup cost per carton of product runs from $1.17 per carton for a production run of 500 cartons to $0.12 per carton for a production run of 5000 cartons.

A company producing to order might set a price-discount schedule based on a decreasing setup cost per quantity ordered with the purchaser making buying decisions on a price-discount schedule similar to one discussed earlier.

However, suppose a company is manufacturing to inventory to service the consumer market. This is an off-the-shelf company with consumers expecting service from inventory on all items. Most of the time, it would be necessary to make some sort of an economic decision on how much to put into inventory. Clearly the production run size determines the setup and startup cost per carton, but the run size also determines the investment in inventory. In Fig. 2.3., neglecting inventory turnover, and looking only at setup costs, one might select an economic run of 6000 cartons, giving a setup cost of only $0.10 per carton. If the unit cost per carton is $6.18, there will be an average total inventory investment of $18,540 (6000 × $6.18/2). If they were selling at a rate of 300 cartons per month, a 20-month inventory would have been produced. However, if they were selling at a rate of 6000 cartons per month, only a 1-month supply would have been produced. The difference is not the setup cost or the investment. What has changed is the turnover rate, and turnover is an important factor in the ROA formula. It is possible to construct a model that reflects turnover and savings potential resulting from the run length and to relate both to the average added inventory investment. Let

R = hurdle rate = 30%
S = setup and startup scrap costs per run = $585
C = unit cost of inventory = $6.18 per carton

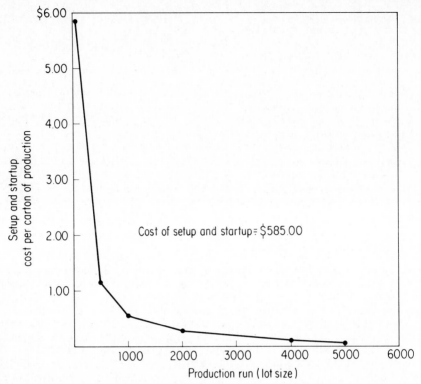

FIG. 2.3   Setup cost per unit of output. The cost of setup and startup per carton of material is $585.00.

$$V = \text{sales volume per month}$$
$$N = \text{optimum number to produce}$$

The model is

$$N = \sqrt{\frac{12SV}{R(C/2)}}$$

For example,

$$N = 6200 \text{ @ sales rate of } 5000$$
$$N = 3900 \text{ @ sales rate of } 2000$$
$$N = 1500 \text{ @ sales rate of } 300$$

This model is comparable to the classical EOQ model. It suggests lot-size production at an optimum run length that will yield an adequate return on assets. The basic policy on inventory investment can be adhered to by utilizing the hurdle rate established by management that fits within the financial policy.

In each of these examples, increasing the run length beyond that calculated as optimum drops the return below 30 percent for all units in excess of the calculated figure. In the calculation of total costs (with the hurdle rate as a cost of capital), the total cost (investment plus setup) per unit increases if we produce either more or less than the N factor or optimum.

Learning to apply the basic EOQ formula is only the beginning in learning to use the model as an inventory investment principle.

Adjusting the ROA Factor (Hurdle Rate).   The ROA factor, or hurdle rate, obviously can be adjusted by a management policy decision. Adjusting the hurdle rate affects the cycle stock inventory, or that portion of the total inventory related to run length decisions generally. Thus it ultimately impacts on the total inventory required in the system. Suppose the average sales rate per SKU in this product group is 2000 cartons per month. Also suppose management changes the hurdle rate in the example from 30 to 40 percent. The average economic run length changes from 3900 to 3370, a reduction of approximately 14 percent. Any time the ROA factor is increased from 30 to 40 percent, a 14 percent reduction in the run length for all items is established, thereby reducing aggregate cycle stocks by 14 percent. A comparable percentage could be developed for any relative changes in the ROA factor. This enables management to influence inventory investment of finished stock based on economic and financial considerations rather than by some arbitrary fiat issued by management.

Storage Costs.   The cost of storage facilities, property taxes, and insurance that relate to the cost of carrying inventory were not included in the ROA factor shown above. Obviously, the ROA factor can be adjusted upward to consider such costs that relate to inventory investment. An alternative exists when the capital cost of warehousing is considered. The inventory value, or C factor, can be adjusted by adding the investment cost in warehousing per unit of inventory. This has positive effects not obtained by merely increasing the ROA factor. As an example, the $6.18 of unit inventory value per carton might relate to a carton of flooring tile. The average investment cost of the building to store a carton of flooring tile might be $2.00 per carton. This could be added to the C factor. In contrast, a carton of empty glass containers, physically the same size as the carton of tile, might have a value of only $0.60. The average investment in the building might still cost $2.00 per carton. Obviously, warehousing investment costs are a much greater factor for the low-value item than for the high-value item and are best handled as an investment cost rather than a percentage increase in the R factor.

Reducing Setup Costs.   The *just-in-time* (JIT) or *zero-inventory* concept has recently become a subject of much discussion in PIC circles. This management approach emphasizes minimizing the cost of setup and startup. The impact of the JIT approach on the traditional EOQ calculation is interesting and deserves serious consideration. The JIT approach does not change the principle of EOQ. That principle still has validity. To the contrary, the investment theory of EOQ has been enhanced by the JIT approach. In practice, instead of ignoring EOQ, the JIT principle suggests that management concentrate its effort on reducing the setup cost. This is not new to all U.S. industry, but too often production management has taken the easy way out and asked that the setup cost be reduced per unit of output by lengthening the production run. Mechanical innovation, computerized processes, training of changeover crews, and quality control techniques have all been used to improve efficiency, reduce downtime, and produce less scrap or offgoods during the startup. The benefits of concentrating on setup costs rather than increasing the run length are impressive. For example, given the original factors in the EOQ example, at a sales rate of 2000 cartons, if the setup cost is reduced by 50 percent, a reduction from the $585 to $292, then the optimum length of run is reduced from 3900 to 2750 cartons. The cost of setup per unit of production is reduced from $0.15 to $0.10 per carton, and the cost of inventory investment at a 30 percent ROA is likewise reduced from $0.15 to approximately $0.10 per carton. This is the best of both worlds—reduction in the unit cost of the product and a reduction in the inventory investment. Computerized process control, robotics, and other automation technologies are part of the answer in reducing setup costs. The other part is the heavy concentration of management attention on making the setup and changeover costs more efficient.

Obsolescence Factors. No formula or mathematical model should be the sole guide to decision making. In the case of EOQ, clearly the potential for obsolescence, because of engineering changes, design changes, style changes, or spoilage, increases as the inventory turnover declines or as the magnitude of the inventory in terms of month's supply increases. So it is always advisable to put some limit on the run length by limiting how long the inventory will last. Given the various risk factors, even arbitrary decisions such as "no more than a 6-month supply" may be appropriate in the absence of a better criterion. Sales forecasts on which economic run decisions are made are also subject to error. Placing a time limit on the quantity to go into inventory can compensate for this risk factor.

Safety Stocks—Safety Time

How the fundamental concepts of safety stocks or safety times are applied should be determined by the cause of the uncertainty and the need to protect against this uncertainty.

If inventory is expected to be available to cover future demand and the demand fluctuates because of changes in the marketplace or the economic environment, then it is called an *independent demand*. If demand changes randomly or is not directly influenced by another controllable or predictable factor, then it is an independent demand. Maintenance, repair, or operating supplies might fall into this category.

However, if demand for an item changes in direct relationship to a change in a production schedule, the demand is called *dependent demand*. A dependent-demand item might be a raw material used in the manufacturing process or a part or a component of a finished assembly.

Independent Demand

The marketplace, or the distribution system, may require that an item be available from inventory in the face of unpredictable or independent demand. How much inventory is required is influenced by the lead time. The *lead time* is the time lapse between deciding to replenish a stock-keeping unit and actually receiving the replenishing supply. The expected demand during the lead time might be the statistical average. If the average is used as the expected demand during the lead time, no safety stock is allowed. However, if greater than the average is used to make the replenishment decision, then a safety stock is created. It is the difference between the average and the greater-than-average demand used in the replenishment decisions.

Statistical methods are most commonly used to determine the reorder or replenishment inventory levels and are discussed in Chaps. 12 and 29.

A basic principle in statistics relates to the frequency of exposure. For example, an item produced to inventory every 4 wks has an exposure to stock-out of 13 times per year. If expected average sales are used to establish the replenishment part, six stock-outs should be expected. In other words, half of the time sales will be greater than the average, causing a stock-out each time. If the service level is measured by the number of weeks out of service of a calendar year, then the service in this example would be 46/52, or 88 percent. If the goal or target service level is set at 95 percent, then a safety stock must be established to reduce the exposure.

On the other hand, if an item is produced to inventory only four times per year (produced in quantities equal to a 13-week supply), then exposure is only four times; and if average sales are used to set this replenishment point, a stock-out frequency of two per year would be expected—a service level of 50/52, or 96 percent. No safety stock is required.

Determining what the market really needs in the way of service may be more critical than the statistical determination of the requirements for safety stock. Some markets and distribution systems can tolerate out-of-stock conditions 2 weeks or even longer. The consumer is accustomed to waiting. Competitive forces allow for stock-outs to occur without a loss of sales. For example, the commercial construction industry expects to place orders with the manufacturer, complying with the lead time of the manufacturer, which may be 3 to 4 weeks. However, immediate service from a manufacturer's or distributor's inventory may be required to serve the consumer market for comparable products. Therefore, each market and competitive situation should be studied extensively before service requirements are established.

Dependent Demand

Raw materials and component parts used in the manufacture of a finished product are utilized in proportion to the finished production schedule, as set by the bill of materials or recipe. The usage depends on the quantity scheduled and the timing of the schedule.

Occasionally a safety stock is carried because of the desire from marketing or manufacturing to create flexibility in the finished production schedule. If the quantities scheduled are changed upward, obviously the supporting raw material or component part must be available, and so a safety stock is required. Establishing a more disciplined MPS with fixed quantities would eliminate the need for this safety stock.

Safety time describes the process of ordering delivery of the desired quantity before it is needed to offset potential delays on the part of the supplier or the transportation system. Safety time also enables a production schedule to be advanced, which is sometimes necessary and desirable to increase the aggregate output.

There appears to be more justification for using the principle of safety time for independent-demand items. Suppliers do fail to deliver on schedule. Developing a close relationship with suppliers by keeping them constantly informed of changes in the rate of flow of the receipts can reduce this uncertainty. Again, JIT principles (with encouragement from management), load leveling, fewer suppliers and long-term arrangements, increased emphasis on quality control by the supplier, and commited transporation systems can all help.

Base Inventory Level

In managing the MPS tactical production planning function, there is a fundamental concept that relates to base inventory levels. The base inventory level is the normal aggregate inventory level, composed of the aggregate of the lot-size inventories, or run length inventories, or cycle stock (these terms are used interchangeably) plus the aggregate of safety stock inventories. The base inventory level is the theoretical inventory level required to maintain the policies established for production run length and to conform to the policies established for service, resulting in safety stock inventories. The base inventory level is applicable when finished production is placed in finished inventory in anticipation of future demand. If items are produced to order with no finished inventory carried, the tactical production plan and MPS are managed from the backlog. In this latter case, base inventory theory either does not apply or has limited application.

The portion of the aggregate inventory that relates to the lot size or run length is normally called the *cycle stock*. For an individual item, the cycle stock fluctuates from a high point immediately following production being placed into finished inventory, to a low point immediately prior to new production entering the inventory system. The average cycle inventory of each SKU is one-half of the run length. Therefore, the average aggregate cycle inventory of all SKUs at any time equals the sum of the normal lot size divided by 2. As discussed earlier, changing the ROA factor, or hurdle rate, can effectively change the theoretical aggregate cycle stock inventory. Changing any other of the factors in the EOQ model can alter the aggregate inventory, such as changing the sales rate or the setup cost.

The portion of the inventory which is the aggregate of safety stocks depends on the service levels determined for each SKU. Service levels are established by a management policy. In earlier sections on safety stocks, 95 percent service policy was set based on the frequency of stock-outs per year. Changing that service level to 90 percent could effectively reduce the aggregate safety stock inventory required on the theoretical basis.

The grand total of the aggregate safety stock and cycle stock equals the aggregate base inventory level. Theoretically, this is the lowest point that the aggregate inventory can, in fact, reach and still enable the PIC manager to maintain the prescribed service level and the optimum economics of lot size that have been established by management policy.

In practice, the aggregate inventory level is affected by the rate of total output and the rate of shipment. Total inventories will decline when the shipment rate exceeds the production rate. Conversely, when the shipment rate falls below the production rate, inventories will increase. Figure 2.4 portrays fluctuations in the aggregate inventory (actual total inventory) based on changes in the shipment rate and the production rate. Theoretically, if the total aggregate inventory is in excess of the base inventory level, the master schedule for finished product can be developed by scheduling the economic runs of those items that are most needed, sequencing the items in the MPS according to priority of need, with all items being produced in adequate time or earlier than needed to maintain the appropriate level of service. If total shipments have exceeded production, the aggregate inventory will drop below the base inventory level. In this case, when the MPS is prepared, it would be evident that there is not enough time in the schedule to produce all items when they are needed, if the economic run policy is to be followed.

If the aggregate inventory is below the base level, three alternatives exist: (1) increase the total output, such as by adding overtime or additional crews, thereby increasing the amount of time available in the MPS and enabling those items to be produced when needed; (2) continue to follow the economic run policies and accept a lower level of service as a policy decision; and (3) reduce the run lengths or lot sizes to squeeze more items into the MPS. All options are possible. In a theoretical discussion, there is no proper solution, since not all the facts are known. However, in real life, it should be possible to make an economic decision, given the needed information. In the first and second alternatives, whether to increase the

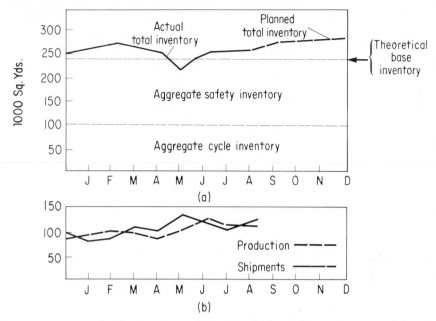

FIG. 2.4 Comparison of theoretical base inventory level and monthly production and shipments. (a) Theoretical base inventory level. (b) Aggregate monthly production and shipments.

aggregate production might hinge on the cost of overtime or the cost of hiring. It would include an evaluation of potential future demand. If demand is expected to fall off seasonally, or if demand is unusually high because of promotions or new-product introductions, then no action to increase production might be taken. In the third alternative, reducing the economic run sizes may help the situation only temporarily and in the long term might impair the ability to keep production rates high and increase the cost of production. The point is that many solutions and alternatives are viable. Given enough information and facts, the best decision can be reached. This is the management aspect of PIC that is so important.

Forecasting

The need to forecast future demand is clear to PIC professionals who manufacture products for the consumer market. The previous example of base inventory planning and management emphasized this need. The need for aggregate forecasting also exists for those manufacturers producing to order. In those industries, backlogs of orders to be produced become the critical barometer to track rather than the aggregate inventory level. Forecasting future aggregate demand may be more difficult for those industries, because real demand is obscured by the process of backlog accumulation.

Aggregate demand forecasting is not a disciplined forecast in most instances. It involves analyzing markets, the economics environment, competitive forces, pricing policies, and new-product introductions. Statistical correlation analysis, trend analysis, and seasonal factors must also be considered in estimating the future.

Aggregate forecasting is a separate, distinct exercise, differing fundamentally from the forecasting performed for the stock-keeping unit.

Forecasting the demand for the individual SKU is done primarily for two reasons. First, it is required for use in the EOQ model. Although accuracy is desirable, the forecast accuracy is critical when the lot size begins to exceed 3 months or more. In many instances, an exponentially smoothed average can suffice quite adequately. Occasionally, the statistical forecast must be overridden because of price increases, promotions, etc., that will distort the future demand from that of the past. Statistical forecasting proves quite inadequate when the demand is erratic or lumpy. Occasionally, judgmental forecasting must be used. Forecasting with exponential smoothing is used to determine the variation in demand that might be expected during the lead time. This variation in demand is required to establish safety stock levels if, indeed, service is important in the marketplace.

Chapter 9 discusses forecasting methods in greater depth. The fundamental principle is that the aggregate demand forecast should *not* be a sum of the statistical forecast used for the stock-keeping unit. The best aggregate demand forecast is made by analyzing marketing and economic factors, points usually given little consideration in the forecast used for stock-keeping units.

The other important principle is that any forecast of the future is wrong to some extent. A regular review of the extended aggregate forecast is appropriate, to update the forecast as market conditions, economic conditions, and other factors change.

TECHNIQUES AND SYSTEMS

Techniques and systems are used to apply fundamentals and principles. A thorough knowledge of principles and fundamentals makes it possible to analyze and selectively use the appropriate techniques and systems to achieve management objectives.

Use of the ROA concept is fundamental to sound business management. This principle can be applied to inventories to make inventory management consistent with general management objectives.

EOQ is fundamental to inventory management consistent with ROA principles. How EOQ is applied, however, may be more closely related to techniques. To be effectively utilized, EOQ must be incorporated in a system.

The concept of safety stocks is basic; the application of which may relate to techniques such as exponential smoothing and may be incorporated in a finish-stock inventory management system.

The concept of aggregate planning and base inventory may be incorporated in systems to effectively execute the plan and manage the inventories.

Some techniques may be widely used by different industries, markets, and manufacturing situations. Not all techniques are applicable in all situations.

Computerized management information systems have grown rapidly in the past decade. Systems for PIC generally must be tailor-made or modified extensively for use from business to business or product to product.

One systems development that is noteworthy is a facet of JIT that uses a Kan Ban system. This very simple card system notifies a supplier or manufacturer that an additional unit of inbound material is required. It can also be used within a manufacturing unit. In an oversimplification, Kan Ban is an extension of the two-bin system used years ago in many manufacturing situations. In the two-bin system, material from one bin is used; when this is empty, material from the second bin is used and material is reordered to fill the first bin. In effect, Kan Ban is similar in concept except there may be more than two bins in the system.

SUMMARY

Production and inventory control is a management department or operation encompassing a variety of functions. It can almost be considered as a third-line function, sitting somewhere between the sales/marketing function and the manufacturing function and working between the two. The decisions emanating from this department have an impact on investment capital, distribution, marketing, manufacturing requirements, and work forces. Recognition of the uniqueness of the PIC function is the beginning of the development of a professionally trained staff, organized for profitability. The primary ingredient is people, aided by systems and techniques. Within this framework management must recognize the principles of asset management, such as reflected in the ROA concept.

BIBLIOGRAPHY

Bulleit, Fredric E.: "Organization Structure: How Important?" *Inventories and Production,* vol. 1, no. 4, September-October, 1981.

Hall, Robert W.: *Zero Inventories,* Dow Jones-Irwin, Homewood, Ill., 1983.

Monden, Yasuhiro: *Toyota Production System,* Industrial Engineering and Management Press, Atlanta, 1983.

3

Perspective

Editor

GEORGE W. PLOSSL, CFPIM, President, G. W. Plossl Co., Inc., Big Canoe, Georgia.

Contributors

GEORGE BRANDENBURG, CFPIM, Manager of Materials Management, Johnson & Johnson International, New Brunswick, New Jersey

RICHARD C. HEARD, CFPIM, R. C. Heard & Co., Inc., Bartlesville, Oklahoma

RAYMOND L. LANKFORD, President, Lankford R. L. and Company, Dripping Springs, Texas

KEITH R. PLOSSL, Vice President, George Plossl Educational Services, Marietta, Georgia

LARS O. SODAHL, Partner, MYSIGMA Sodahl & Partners, AB, Goteborg, Sweden

WHAT IS PRODUCTION AND INVENTORY CONTROL?

History

Production and inventory control (PIC) has developed rapidly from humble beginnings in the early 1900s. Originally used only for clerical help for first-line supervisors, PIC has risen to high organization levels and broad responsibilities in all planning and control activities. It is now recognized as a vital function in all manufacturing, distribution, and servicing of products. Some of its principles and techniques also apply in agriculture and mining, the other sources of real wealth.

Production, Inventory, and Manufacturing Control

PIC is a single, inseparable function although some managers continue to treat it as two different activities—inventory control (office planning work) and production control (plant execution activities). Also misunderstood is its basic purpose, which is *not* to get the right product in the right quantity, time, and place. This goal requires proper execution which is a line function, not the job of PIC. The total task of running a manufacturing operation properly is now called *manufacturing control*, and it requires the coordinated actions of all departments (marketing, engineering, finance, and manufacturing).[1]

The primary objective of PIC is sound planning and control. Planning assigns quantitative measures to future occurrences expected or desired; control measures deviations promptly and accurately by the feedback loops in the system as the plan is executed and highlights significant deviations. Successful PIC develops a viable plan and triggers the need for corrective action to get back on plan or, as a last resort, revise the plan.

Functions

Manufacturing control includes the following:

1. Preproduction, requiring resources within plan horizon
   a. Research and development of new products
   b. Application design, including making prototypes
   c. Tool design, methods, and standards
   d. Equipment procurement
   e. Plant layout and energy needs
2. Operations
   a. Master production scheduling
   b. Capacity planning and control
   c. Priority planning and control
3. Execution
   a. Vendor performance
   b. Plant centers' performance
   c. Equipment and tool maintenance
   d. Problem solving

No PIC system is complete unless it permits the development of a fully integrated plan incorporating all these functions. Clearly this is *not* simply a materials management system. It is a total planning and control system encompassing all resources including people, capital and expense, plant and equipment, and materials.

What Is Inventory?

The full scope of the term *inventory* must be understood. It has meaning far beyond the usually accepted raw materials, work in process, stocked components, and finished goods related to a company's products. For effective control, all items required for manufacture must be included in the planning and control activities. These obviously include tools, fixtures, gages, cutters, test equipment, and similar devices employed in the production processing operations. These cannot be properly managed independent of operating schedules and without utilizing applicable inventory management techniques. Supplies such as lubricants, grinding materials, cleaning and sterilizing compounds, and fuels also must be part of the formal inventory plan.

Equally important and more frequently neglected are the items needed to keep processing equipment and machinery in operation. Unscheduled breakdowns cannot be tolerated. Preventive maintenance based on mean time between failures and scheduled in harmony with production can eliminate such problems.

PIC is only one portion of manufacturing control, albeit a vital part. Clearly, production and inventories can be controlled in any industry, with any type of products and for any processing operations. New success stories appear daily. Some long-held concepts—really misconceptions—have had to be changed to achieve success, however. Inventory is more of a liability than an asset; it has real value only when it is flowing through operations. Manufacturing problems cannot be covered up successfully; they can and must be eliminated. Replanning is admission of failure; it is no substitute for execution. Greater precision in the plan, such as daily time periods, does not make it more accurate. Greater sophistication in the system really provides more opportunities for underqualified people to self-destruct at higher speeds. Systems built around the proper techniques are necessary but not sufficient. Skill in operating businesses with systems determines the success achieved.

TYPES OF PRODUCTION

Facilities Classification

Classification of a particular manufacturing facility depends on equipment configuration, materials movement, and manufacturing processes.

Equipment Configuration. Equipment may be configured three ways: functionally, linearly, or as a combination of these two. Functional configuration groups equipment performing similar operations into work centers or departments, and each performs one basic function—milling, blending, assembly, etc. Linear configuration lines up equipment that performs the specific series of operations to produce a single product or a family of similar products. A manufacturing facility with functional equipment configuration is commonly referred to as a *job shop*, a misnomer that is explained later. A plant composed only of production lines is commonly referred to as a *flow shop*. A facility that combines functional linear equipment configurations at different stages in the manufacturing process is called a *mixed shop*, unless one of the types of configuration is dominant in the determination of materials movement.

Materials Movement.   Material can be moved in discrete batches, it can flow continuously, or it can be moved in some combination of batch and continuous flow. *Pure batch flow* implies that each unique batch is completed in one work center before the entire batch is moved to the next work center. *Pure continuous flow* implies the uninterrupted flow of a single product through a dedicated production line. Pure batch- and pure continuous-flow plants are not common; most plants overlap batches and products in varying degrees.

Most batch-oriented facilities allow for overlapping operations and/or splitting of lots. A single batch can be resident at more than one work center at a time. It can be argued that this subdivision of the original batch simply creates a larger number of smaller discrete batches that move in a pure batch mode. In some production environments this is indeed the case. However, as the batch size approaches 1, batch flow approaches continuous flow. These are referred to as *mixed-mode production environments.*

Most flow-oriented facilities produce a variety of similar products on a single production line. The flow of a specific product in this type of environment is intermittent. Most flow facilities also incorporate discrete batch control at some point in the manufacturing process, most commonly for blending, reacting, materials handling, production reporting, quality assurance, and/or packaging. The existence of these batch characteristics is an important factor in the design of planning and control systems, but it is ignored by the most commonly accepted system of classifying production. Therefore, discretion is advised in using the type of production in the selection of planning and control methodology.

Manufacturing Procedures.   Manufacturing processes can be grouped into two major categories: discrete and process. *Discrete manufacturing processes* produce a single, or discrete, unit of product each time an operation is performed. Machining, fabrication, and assembly operations typify discrete manufacturing. *Process manufacturing* produces a large number of units of product simultaneously. Blending, mixing, and reacting operations typify process manufacturing. Molding operations are a good example of a combination of process and discrete manufacturing in a single operation. Extrusion or rolling operations may produce discrete lengths of product at a relatively slow rate and be classified as discrete. Or they may produce massive lengths of product at very high rates and be classified as process. Other mass production units, such as screw machines, that produce a large volume of discrete units in a very short time are sometimes controlled as in the continuous-flow process, but they are discrete by definition. Categorizing manufacturing processes is often indefinite or misleading, particularly when such categories are loosely or generally applied in the selection of planning and control strategies and techniques.

Production Classification

The common classifications of production are job shop, intermittent, repetitive, and process. Clearly, there will be many exceptions in the application of these categories to the real world of manufacturing. More definitive terms and clearer identification of their characteristics are necessary if planning and control activities are to be effective.

Job Shop Production.   A more definitive term for this category of production is *single job lot.* In the true job shop, each job processed is different, and products are made to order or engineered to order. Examples are tooling, special machinery, custom clothing, and preengineered, prefabricated steel buildings. Equipment is functionally configured, and most machines are the general-purpose type. Material moves from work-center to work-center in discrete batches, and there is very little overlapping of jobs. The routing of each job through the plant is somewhat unique, and the size (unit volume) of each job is normally small, with few exceptions. Inventory is carried only as raw material and work in process. The term *job shop* is often confused with *intermittent*.

Intermittent Production.   A more definitive term for this category of production is *intermittent job lot*. Many jobs are repeated relatively frequently. Products are typically stocked or are of the assemble/blend/finish-to-order variety, with a limited number of made-to-order products. Examples are home appliances, office equipment, hand tools, and electric machinery. Most equipment is functionally configured, although there may be some isolated linearly grouped or flow departments. Individual pieces of equipment tend to be less the general-purpose type and more functionally specific, particularly where automated. Material is moved between work centers in discrete batches and job splitting and/or overlapping is common. There is consistency in the routings among jobs, and batch quantities can vary from a few to many thousands of units. Inventories are carried at all levels of the bills of material, and work in process is usually large.

Repetitive Production.   A more definitive term for this category is *intermittent flow*. The same job runs steadily for a time, and there is very little distinction, if any, between lots. Products are typically of the made-to-stock variety, with a limited number of assemble/blend/finish-to-order products. Almost all equipment is configured linearly, with the exception of a few feeder departments. Individual pieces of equipment are very specialized and product-specific. Material is moved from operation to operation in very small batches which approximate continuous or semicontinuous flow. Jobs are typically grouped to form schedules that are expressed in terms of the rate of product flow over time. The routing for each item produced is almost identical to that of every other item. Inventories comprise finished goods, purchased raw materials, components, and small quantities, if any, of manufactured components. Work in process is low.

Process Production.   A more definitive term for this category is *continuous flow*. Each product is processed by almost identical methods. Products are typically bulk commodities, some of which may be packaged to order, and include chemicals, paint, pharmaceuticals, and foods. All equipment is linearly configured, with the possible exception of material preparation (blending, mixing, and weighing) and packaging. Material flows at a variable, specified rate through production lines from raw material to finished product. Routings are the same for each product processed on a specific facility. Production runs are typically expressed in units per time period for a predefined production rate. Run lengths vary from short periods to continuous operation. Cleanout of equipment between runs of different materials requires a significant amount of work. Only raw-material and finished-product inventories are carried. Work in process is very small. Many, if not a majority, of the process manufacturing environments are intermittent-flow facilities or should be made so. A few process manufacturing environments are found in the job shop and intermittent job lot categories. This fact has contributed to the lack of interaction between the discrete and process manufacturing communities in the development of the current body of knowledge of production and inventory management. Once the semantics smoke screen has been lifted, their similarities far outnumber their differences. The planning and control of manufacturing operations are based on information that depicts the use of facilities and the movement of materials. The structure and use of that information within one of the above categories is impacted very little by the differences between process and discrete manufacturers. Thus there is very little difference between the planning and control systems that are used to manage them.

REQUIREMENTS FOR EFFECTIVE CONTROL

By the mid-1970s all the basic requirements for achieving control of manufacturing operations had been identified.[2] They are a complete, integrated system (with regard to design, installation, and operation); a valid master production schedule; accurate data; qualified people; and organization to execute the plan. The integrated system with its design, installation, and operation of the system is the only one of the five which is primarily technical. The remaining four are primarily people-oriented and as such are much more difficult to achieve.

System

The elements required for a complete system were listed earlier and assumed in Fig. 3.1. The functions to be planned and controlled were also covered earlier. Manual systems are now obsolete; computers are required for the processing speed required and the masses of data involved. Computer hardware and software, however, are now available to any company at an affordable price. These topics are covered in detail in Chap. 19.

The level of sophistication of the system should match the capabilities of its users. The differences required in systems for the varied types of processes and manufacturing lie mainly in formatting the data base and output reports and in the degrees of emphasis on the various techniques. Systems are, and will remain, in a constant state of evolution; the perfect, ultimate system has not been, and will never be, designed and implemented.

Valid Master Production Schedule

In achieving control of manufacturing operations, the master production schedule (MPS) is the most difficult and most important set of numbers to be developed. The commonly recognized and probably most important function of the MPS is to drive the formal planning system to initiate procurement of needed materials, work force, money, and other resources. It has many other uses.[2] The MPS provides the best basis for making valid customer delivery promises, for budgeting inventories (direct and indirect labor requirements), for determining purchase commitments, for scheduling engineering, and for measuring the performance of manufacturing and marketing groups in meeting their commitments to the basic company operating plans. This is covered in detail in Chap. 13.

The greatest difficulty in developing a valid MPS lies in determining the plant's ability to produce the product mix desired. This problem is made more difficult by the proliferation of products and the varieties of technologies employed in the processing. The most successful plants are focused on a limited product line, utilizing relatively few manufacturing operations. Effective use of capacity-requirements planning techniques, covered in Chap. 15, is vital for the development of a valid MPS.

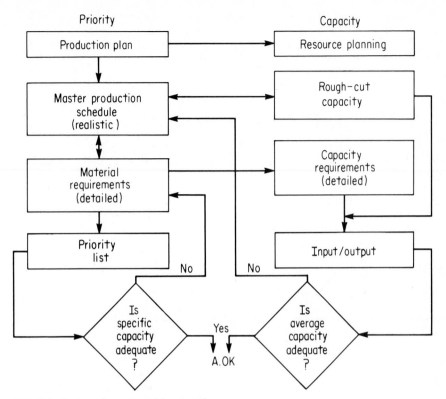

FIG. 3.1 System elements and framework.

The MPS is not intended to be a constraint or a straight-jacket setting a rigid program to be followed at all costs. It is a planning device to initiate the procurement of the necessary materials and other resources. Master scheduling, the development of this set of numbers, should involve the top-level managers in marketing, manufacturing, engineering, finance, and general management. This activity provides the mechanism whereby the conflicting policies and objectives of these people can be reconciled and a consensus developed on an operating plan of the company.

Accurate Data

The 1970s saw dramatic developments in effective work for eliminating record errors. Previously, most managers believed that accurate records would be tremendously expensive, take an inordinate amount of time, and offer little in tangible benefits. The fallacies of these ideas are pointed out later in the chapter, together with the tangible benefits which are very significant.

Fundamental to achieving accurate records is management's intolerance of sloppy data handling and processing. It must be clear to all people handling information that errors cannot and will not be tolerated. Individuals must understand clearly their own responsibilities in this task. Job descriptions should contain specific references to data handled and accuracy levels desired. Performance should be periodically compared to the desired standards. Then these people must be given the necessary tools to do their work effectively, including locked stockrooms, counting scales, checking digits, program editing, etc.; some are physical and others are systems tools.

A recognized management principle states that *you cannot control what you do not measure*; this is equally true of record accuracy. The technique required to do this, *cycle counting*, is now well known and tested. It is far easier to find errors than to find out what caused them, but the elimination of the causes of error is required for high levels of accuracy. Cycle counting, when properly conducted, can help identify such causes, but this requires a thorough understanding of the company's operations and its planning and control system. Eliminating error from records can be a speedy, highly rewarding process. The real tragedy of poor data is that it is unnecessary.

Qualified People

The changing nature of production and inventory control activities follows the reverse of the Peter principle.[3] The job requirements are rising beyond the level of competence of the people holding them. Newer, more sophisticated computer systems embodying new techniques and providing much more information more quickly in an environment of more rapid changes are dictating the need for people with faster and more intelligent response who can operate under severe pressures. The need for adequate preparation of individuals for planning and control jobs was never greater.

Developing qualified people in PIC really involves matching the capabilities of the people to the jobs of the system. This leads to the obvious conclusion that systems improvements must be accompanied by the development of increased understanding and capabilities among the people using them. The possibility of doing this successfully by a system revolution is obviously very small. This subject is discussed in greater detail later in the chapter.

Organization

Effective management of manufacturing operations can result only when sound plans are successfully executed; planning is necessary but not sufficient. Execution requires an organization of people working together effectively toward common goals. Contrast the professional sporting team with the method of operation of the typical management team. Managers must agree not only on company goals but also on the methods of achieving them. This topic is covered later in more depth.

The primary roles of each significant group in a manufacturing organization must be reevaluated. The basic objective of such reevaluation must be to break down the compartmentalization of specialty groups such as purchasing, manufacturing, engineering, and cost accounting and to create instead roles as team members in an organized effort to run a manufacturing company. Operating the total business, not just an individual portion, must be seen more clearly as a primary objective of each group. Sound planning and effective execution make it mandatory that these groups know their real jobs, know how to do them properly, and know when they are and are not performing well. The bulk of this book is developed with a view to detailing these jobs and how to do them well.

THE SYSTEM

Basic Elements

The basic elements of a manufacturing control system are shown in Fig. 3.1. Greatly simplified, this figure highlights the dual functions of priority and capacity planning and control. The production plan and resource planning boxes represent long-range planning, usually 1 to 5 years in the future. Often called *business planning* or *strategic planning*, this long-range planning incorporates management's goals, policies, and strategies for operating the total business. The needed resources of capital, people, materials, and plant and equipment are identified. Production is expressed in value or units of families of similar items. Time periods are varied from monthly, in the near term, to quarterly, semiannually, and annually farther out.

The MPS and rough-cut capacity boxes represent the next level of planning. One important role of the MPS is evident: linking the long- and short-ranged plans. Driven by the MPS, the formal system develops detailed plans and schedules which support the production plan or indicate clearly through feedback that it cannot be supported. Detailed plans and schedules must be realistic and achievable so that individuals can be held responsible for execution. The MPS must be tested for realism via rough-cut capacity analysis, comparison with previous operations, or more detailed evaluations.

The third (and final) phase of planning includes detailed materials and capacity-requirements determinations, as shown in the third set of boxes. Modern formal systems ensure that all details are integrated into a unified whole, so all involved in execution are "singing the same music." The arrows in Fig. 3.1 indicate this complete integration.

The lower right-hand quadrant indicates capacity control activities, which are more important than priority control. Input/output control measures the *flow rates* of work into and out of both vendors and plant work centers to detect significant deviations promptly, so that queues and lead times can be controlled. Average data over moderately long horizons are adequate. This is the "acid test" of the validity of the MPS. With rare exceptions in some industries and countries, most companies try to get adequate capacity to execute the plan set by the MPS. The bypass arrow around the capacity requirements (detail) box conveys an important message: *Input/Output must operate by using only rough-cut capacity data* until more detailed data are available.

The lower left-handed quadrant covers priority control activities. Proper sequences of work established by the materials plan, by using order completion dates and sometimes work content, are communicated to suppliers and plant work centers via lists called variously *daily dispatch*, *order of work*, *work schedules*, etc. Resulting erratic loads must be examined to ascertain whether the short-term capacity permits holding to schedules. Excessive overloads require revisions to the material plan and possibly to the MPS, although the latter should be avoided unless costs are excessive.

Foundations

Sound systems require

- An adequate data base with up-to-date information with *no significant* errors in customer orders, bills of material, on-hand inventory, open purchase and manufacturing orders, processing operations, work standards, tooling, spare parts, equipment specifications, costs, etc.

- Performance measures indicating the health of the system including file data accuracy, number of action messages by category, lists of data omissions, aged transaction errors, etc.
- People to operate the systems whose qualifications match its capabilities. Since businesses change, there will never be an ultimate system; people and systems must evolve together.

Supporting Subsystems

In addition to the basic elements, systems must include many supporting subsystems. Details of these make up the bulk of this handbook. The principal ones include the following:

Demand forecasting	Customer order processing
MPS file	Inventory transactions
Open orders—purchasing bills of material processing	Open orders—manufacturing
	Engineering change control
Process data file	Methods change control
Production reporting	Quality control
Tooling file	Maintenance data
Cost data	Budgets

Variations

The systems framework is essentially identical for all types of production. Figure 3.2 is the framework diagram developed by an APICS workshop group focusing on the process industries.[4] Even a brief study shows that the basic elements are identical to those of Fig. 3.1, and the differences result from added details or missing arrows common to both applications. A similar group within APICS concentrating on the particular interests of the repetitive industries (those producing high volumes at fairly continuous rates) has identified no essential differences in basic control elements. These are common to all; only in their application to specific companies do differences in emphasis and details appear. Experienced professionals recognize these.

Frequency of Replanning

Modern computer-based systems create the "illusion of precision." Neatly tabulated reports, arithmetically perfect, look highly credible; this is enhanced greatly by utilizing shorter time periods. Many believe the ultimate is the bucketless, 1-day period. Computer power and economics make instant (or on line, or transaction-driven) replanning practical. There are two fallacies in such thinking—that planning can be accurate and that replanning improves accuracy and aids execution. Dealing as it does with future activities, planning will never be accurate; the perfect plan will never be made. Replanning is an admission of failure to execute; it should

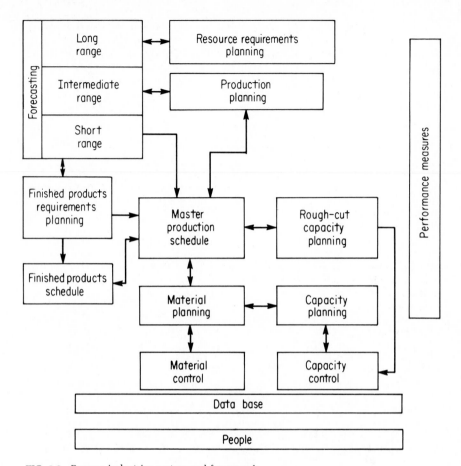

FIG. 3.2 Process industries system and framework.

be used only as a last resort. Weekly planning periods and weekly updating of the plan are satisfactory for practically all companies. Shorter, more frequent planning should be utilized only where significant benefits can be identified.

Use in Planning and Execution

Planning (soft) data, however, should not be confused with execution (hard) data. The former represent future occurrences (dates for completing orders, levels of inventory targeted, etc.), while the latter show realities (amount of inventory on hand now, quantity completed through an operation, etc.). Planning data can be useful if they are updated periodically; hard facts should be up to date *when the user needs them for decision making.* Real-time entry of transactions to adjust hard data is necessary for effective execution.

A key activity in the execution process is problem-solving. This involves analyzing the problem threatening proper execution of the plan. A late component, unusual scrap loss, unexpected tool breakdown, equipment failure, or record error must trigger analysis of formal systems data to decide on corrective actions to get back on plans. Snap decisions made with partial or invalid data create more problems than they solve. The use of systems will occupy more time and be more important in problem-solving than in planning. This fact must be prime consideration in the design of the system, particularly in the selection of "enhancements," which often add sophistication without significantly improving utility.

MASTER PRODUCTION SCHEDULE

The MPS is a statement of when and how much of an item are planned to be produced. Each item in the MPS is described by a bill of materials. With simple products, the MPS item is a finished product, ready for sale. Where option combinations are numerous, the MPS item represents subassembled options or convenient artificial groupings called *modules*.

The MPS is a manufacturing plan, not a sales (shipment) plan. Where modular (planning) bills of material describe the MPS items and where products are assembled or finished to customer orders, the MPS is different from the assembly, finishing, and packaging schedules.

The MPS is not a schedule in the usual sense; it is a *plan* to initiate the procurement and production of the needed materials and capacity, including money. Quantities in the MPS are not orders, but plans to work from. The MPS and supporting formal planning programs provide integrated sets of data from which to determine quantitatively and specifically what materials and work centers are affected when significant changes become necessary.

The MPS is a short- to medium-range plan. The minimum horizon is the longest sum of the lead times required to procure a raw material and process it through various manufacturing operations through all levels of the bill of materials in each product family; a year is most commonly used. Most frequently, a 1-week time period (bucket) is used; longer intervals make the plant too insensitive. One-day time intervals (bucketless) are possible but impractical; they give the illusion of precision to basically inaccurate planning data.

What It Does

The main purpose of the MPS is to "drive" the formal system calculations, both material- and capacity-requirements planning, leading to detailed production schedules and purchases at all levels of the bills and providing capacity data.

Another important function of the MPS is to "lock" the detailed planning to the broader-based, longer-range resource planning of the production plan, as shown in Fig. 3.2, which shows the relationship of the MPS to other major planning and control activities. Other uses of the MPS are to make customer delivery promises, to measure the ability of the factory to execute the plan, to schedule design engineering, and to provide a mechanism for developing a consensus among top-level managers of marketing, manufacturing, engineering, and finance.

Planning versus Execution

The MPS drives the planning process which attempts to provide money, materials, machinery, and people to manufacture the desired products. As stated earlier, the perfect plan will never be made and executed perfectly. The inescapable conclusion is that companies will always need to make something different from what they planned and that the formal plan will never eliminate all shortages. Revising the plan (replanning) can be helpful if adequate time remains to react. Defining *adequate* is difficult.

Fences are needed in the MPS to define the front end of the horizon within which the plan will not be altered. *This does not mean:*

- Make what is planned whether needed or not.
- If they are not planned, items cannot be made.

The fence simply shuts off replanning and activates execution activities. The formal system is used to allocate the sets of components needed to build products desired and can reveal shortages. Each shortage is analyzed to determine whether the material can be obtained in time at reasonable cost. The location of the fence is determined by the time period covered by firm orders, but it should not exceed a few weeks. Finished-product warehouses replenishment orders can be firmed up 2 to 4 weeks ahead and included. Customer orders available well in the future are susceptible to design, option definition, quantity, and delivery date changes, and should not be included.

The proper sequence is as follows:

1. Develop a realistic MPS.
2. Work to improve its validity by cutting lead times, matching customer orders to avoid changing the plan, and weeding out extraneous products from lines.
3. Revise the plan for significant customer-related or design changes.
4. Attempt to execute the plan to obtain components, but expect some shortages.
5. Within the fence period, use allocation routines to determine specific shortages which are preventing completion of desired products *whether planned or not.*
6. Concentrate on filling shortages to enable shipment of a maximum number of desired orders.
7. Identify problems preventing execution of plans and minimize or eliminate them.

The number of shortages uncovered in the allocation phase will be manageable if

- Continual efforts are made to make a better plan.
- Careful attention is given to providing flexibility by means of limited safety stocks, controlled overplanning of option modules, and product component standardization.
- The organization concentrates on eliminating problems interfering with execution of the plan.

ACCURATE DATA

Manufacturing control systems are simply information systems manipulating data on which all manufacturing plans are based and aiding in executing these plans. The plan cannot be more accurate than the data; the system cannot correct errors.

Integrated manufacturing systems pass errors from level to level through the entire product structure and the total system. Common item errors affect many product structures with devastating results not limited to class A or B items. Class C item record errors can also be deadly. The quality of the plan limits the effectivity of execution and, in turn, depends on the credibility of the data.

What Is Required?

High levels of record accuracy are possible. Achieving them is not expensive and can be accomplished in a few months by following these five essential steps[5]:

1. Establish a climate of high expectations.
2. Assign responsibility.
3. Provide adequate tools.
4. Measure record accuracy.
5. Find and correct basic causes of error.

These activities should not be limited to inventory records; they should be applied to all vital records supporting the manufacturing control system. A list of the most important is given here. Additional details are covered in Chap. 19.

Vital Records

- Customers' orders
- Bills of material
- On-hand inventory
- Open purchase orders
- Open manufacturing orders
- Processing routines:
  Work centers
  Standards
  Tooling, equipment
- Costs

Establish a Climate of High Expectations. People want to and will do a good job if they know what is expected of them. Management must make clear its expectations and set high goals for record accuracy. Managers must indicate intolerance of sloppy performance and high incidence of errors. This can be done through meetings, posters, banners, letters, and gimmick programs stressing that bad records must be corrected.

The costs involved in developing this improved climate are minimal; it is impossible to spend much money on this activity. It must be clear to all people, however, that management is serious about eliminating, not just reducing, errors if the balance of the program is to be effective.

Assign Responsibility. Management must identify clearly and assign responsibility for transactions updating record data. This should be detailed in job descriptions, and performance should be measured periodically. It is best if an individual (or two, at most) is assigned specific records. If more than one person is responsible for a segment, no one can be held really accountable. For example, one person should be accountable for individual receipts and issues and the accuracy of balances for specific inventory items in a few aisles or a section of a stockroom.

Material planners should be responsible for open purchase and manufacturing order data on a specified list of items. Design engineering should be responsible for the accuracy of bills of material including phasing in engineering changes. Routings and standards should be the responsibility of manufacturing engineering. Plant engineering should be held accountable for machine data, spares inventories, and utilities information. The cost of assigning such responsibilities and monitoring performance is small. The primary benefit is making clear to each individual what is expected in accuracy of data handling.

Provide Adequate Tools.   Simply understanding and stressing the need for record accuracy is not enough; people must be given adequate tools with which to do their jobs. Tools fall into two categories:

System Tools	Physical Tools
Checking digits	Counting scales
Hash totals	Marking hand counters
Edit checks	Standard containers
Serial numbers	Good housekeeping
Good form design	Locked stockrooms
Documentation	Stamped part numbers

The costs of providing these tools can be significant but are a one-time expense. Some have real fringe benefits; for example, standard containers reduce material handling costs and accidents.

Measure Record Accuracy.   Most companies have no quantitative measures of record accuracy, although good managers know they cannot control what they do not measure. The needed measures are provided by *cycle counts*, a check of the records for a small sample of items against physical counts, visual checks, or cross-record comparisons. The techniques are covered in Chap. 12. They can be applied to all records, not just inventory balances.

Find and Correct Basic Causes of Errors.   Finding and correcting errors will not improve the general level of record accuracy; this requires finding and fixing the causes of errors. These causes are primarily human—carelessness in transcribing data, poor counting, incorrect identification, loss of documents, or mistakes in simple calculations. Poor form design, lack of documentation, and inadequate training also create problems. Education, discipline, and recognition eliminate these problems at little cost. Very few people make errors consciously or deliberately attempt to sabotage records.

QUALIFIED PEOPLE

The biggest problem in obtaining qualified people is to change some of their misconceptions.

Common Misconceptions

Developing qualified people requires imparting new ideas, facts, and other information and correcting existing misconceptions. The latter is by far the more difficult task. These misunderstandings have persisted through many years and are held by people at all levels of the organization. The most insidious include the following.

1. Manufacturing problems cannot be eliminated; cushions of inventory and time must be provided to reduce their harmful effects. In spite of the obvious failure of safety stock and added time to solve the problems, people persist in pursuing this approach. This wastes inventory, makes planning less valid, and actually aggravates the problems. Even worse, it diverts attention from the real solution— eliminating machine and tool failures, scrap and rework effects, equipment breakdown, late vendors, and other interference with executing the plan.

2. More frequent and precise replanning will result in better execution. This myth is exploded in the section "The System" in this chapter. Computer systems can easily handle the revisions and action notices which they generate, but people and plants cannot. Again, the real problem arising from this myth is that efforts to make a more valid plan are neglected. This requires short planning horizons and quick execution.

3. Lead times cannot be controlled; they can only be monitored and adjusted. This fiction, like the others, leads to actions which aggravate the problem. Two truths about lead time must be recognized:

   a. *A difference between planned and measured lead times cannot be eliminated by changing the planned figure.* If the plan is increased, the gap will widen. The vicious cycle thus generated is disastrous for companies, industries, and national economies. Cutting the planned lead times will be less damaging but will not wipe out the difference either. Such differences are caused by incorrect work-in-process levels caused by excess or inadequate capacity and can be eliminated only by cutting or increasing capacity.

   b. *Actual lead times will change with the planned figure.* If the planned lead time is increased, the measured value will increase by at least as much, and vice versa. The truth of this becomes obvious immediately if the inevitable reactions of ordering techniques and people employing them are thought through.

4. Idle time must be prevented. The tangible costs of people or machines being idle are easily calculated, whereas the true total cost of avoiding them are not. Among the latter are excess inventory, commitment of flexible resources to the wrong items, poor reaction to customers' needs, and less valid planning data. Successful companies tolerate some downtime while striving to eliminate the causes.

5. A common misconception is that it is not worth the effort to reduce setup costs. Such costs are usually included in factory overhead, calculated by dividing the setup cost by the standard lot size. Compared to the per-piece material and labor costs and other overhead items, the setup cost appears negligible. Its insidious effect on lead times must be recognized. It has a direct influence on all elements of lead time—setup itself, running time for the batch, move time, and queue time. Cutting setup thus not only shortens the working elements but also makes possible a dramatic reduction in the dominant element, queue time, by smoothing the flow of material through the operations.

Who Must Be Qualified?

The activities of manufacturing planning and control are not limited to any single department; they involve all departments and all levels of management within them. These activities represent the sensory system, the intelligence, the communication media, and the muscles of the organization. No company can realize its full potential if some part of its organization lacks understanding or is mishandling its proper role.

The major concerns of the principal departments in manufacturing firms have little in common. Engineering sees its role as technical, inventing and developing products, improving methods and tooling, and managing the physical plant and equipment. Marketing focuses on defining and meeting the customers' needs through a variety of products and desires flexible response to changes. Manufacturing is preoccupied with stability of operation, level loads, getting the necessary resources, and keeping costs low. Finance concentrates its attention on acquisition of the needed capital, cash flow, budgets, and policing of others' performance. Top management tries to coordinate and direct operations to achieve desired goals. Instead of a management team, they perform as a group of all-star players, often seeming to be playing different games.

The manufacturing control system provides the information all need, ending perennial arguments about whose data are correct. It also provides the mechanism whereby each can contribute to the development of the consensus on how the business will be operated and then can be measured on the effectiveness with which plans are executed.

Professionalism

The day of the amateur has passed. Manufacturing can be controlled, but it takes professionals to do it. Failure to control now means failure to survive in all but a few companies. Chapter 1 details the development of PIC from a collection of loosely related techniques to a recognized profession over the 1960s and 1970s. It has its unique body of knowledge, language, principles, and techniques as well as the requirement of skill in applying these to specific situations. PIC affects the welfare of individuals, companies, industries, and countries as much as any other profession.

In other professions—law, medicine, dentistry, commercial airline flying, engineering, accounting—people cannot practice activities affecting the public without society's sanction through licensing or registration.

It is not yet possible to define rigorously what is required to be a professional manager, but clearly it must include a knowledge of the fundamentals of effective planning and control of manufacturing operations. All managers in positions of responsibility for engineering, marketing, financial, or manufacturing activities should be required to demonstrate their familiarity with these principles.

How to Get Qualified

Several avenues are open to those wishing to become qualified. A very few of the business schools are now recognizing the need to include courses on manufacturing operations in their master's curriculum. Many colleges, particularly in their extension services, are offering courses and some degrees in production management.

The APICS, many private consulting firms, and all computer hardware and software companies offer some courses on various topics. Videotapes, games, books, articles, training aids, and a wealth of published materials are available.

No special skills in mathematics, statistics, computer technology, or other high-level science are required. Few individuals, when given the proper education, have been unable to master the requirements for jobs in the field. Three phases are necessary:

1. Understand the state of the art. This takes an intensive program of indoctrination led by someone with experience and broad exposure to developments in the field and applications in various industries. The objective is to show what professional performance can do.
2. Understand the individual's role. This phase focuses on the support the user needs to give the system and the help the system will provide for the user. It details the ways in which the individual must change his or her way of life and why.
3. Monitor actual performance. Daily on-the-job use of the system and the information it provides must be reviewed to ensure adherence to policies and practices, to prevent backsliding, to ensure adaptation to changing needs, and to handle employee turnover.

ORGANIZATION

Every professional should know and understand how her or his function developed in the organization.

Evolution of Manufacturing Control

Production and inventory control evolved from a simple clerical service to first-line supervisors, such as those handling telephone calls, keeping production records, ordering materials, and chasing after needed tools. Adding the task of coordination of work among supervisors resulted in PIC being elevated in the organization and reporting to superintendents. Other added duties such as interaction with maintenance, quality control, the toolroom, and other departments outside manufacturing made the plant manager's office the right reporting level. In the 1970s, the full scope of manufacturing control was recognized, and PIC became part of a total planning and control effort spanning all activities in all departments, reaching vice-presidential levels in many companies.

Materials Management

During the 1960s materials management was adopted as an organizational form by many companies seeking to improve control. The results rarely lived up to expectations; most companies found that they had simply added another high-level position and pushed the problems down lower in the organization. The real problem was lack of sound planning and control. And its solution was hindered, not helped, by the addition of minor functions such as receiving, shipping, stores, and materials handling to the responsibilities of the manager. The basic idea itself was flawed.

Material is only one of the four classes of resource involved. Too narrow a focus doomed the effort.

External Relationships

The activities of manufacturing planning and control span all departments. Some say that PIC should be part of the chief executive's office if it is to be effective, but this is nonsense. A clear understanding of its relationships with other functions rather than a particular form of organization is needed. In fact, formal organization structure is only a minor factor; it should be developed to utilize the strengths of individuals and to compensate for their weaknesses rather than to suit functions.

When the primary role of each organizational group is properly defined, its interrelationships with other groups are clear. Here is a statement of the primary role of each major unit in a manufacturing company:

1. *Manufacturing planning and control.*   Develop realistic plans for materials, people, money, and physical plant; measure promptly and accurately progress made in executing these plans. Detect and identify significant deviations from the plan, and initiate corrective actions. This role is planning and control, not execution.

2. *Manufacturing.*   Manage plant, equipment, and line personnel to execute the plan, procuring materials and services and converting them to products in support of market needs.

3. *Engineering—design.*   Improve present products and develop new products to serve the markets, utilizing present plant and equipment and informing others via drawings, specifications, and properly structured bills of material of the details they need.

4. *Engineering—manufacturing.*   Improve present methods and develop new methods of processing materials to improve function, quality, and durability of products; to reduce costs; and to smooth out the flow through the plant.[6]

5. *Engineering—plant.*   Arrange and maintain plant buildings, machinery, and equipment; provide energy to ensure continuity of production.

6. *Marketing.*   Identify markets, define customers' needs, establish distribution, get orders, communicate expected customer demand via forecasts, and reconcile the customers' and company's interests. This includes both sales and marketing activities.

7. *Finance.*   Provide capital and operating funds, manage cash and investments, coordinate budgeting and highlight significant variations, assist in financial analyses, and report needed information to managers, stockholders, and the government. This includes cost accounting but should not duplicate physical control activities simply because the unit of measure is money.

8. *Data processing.*   Provide specialized assistance in the application of computers to operations, particularly in setting up a common data base, selecting hardware and software, and providing documentation. This does not necessarily include operating the company's computers.

9. *Purchasing.*   Locate better sources for materials and services; negotiate prices, terms, and conditions; and prepare legal purchase orders and work with suppliers to ensure a smooth flow of quality materials and services in adequate quantities and short lead times. This focuses on capacity, not priority, and frees

purchasing of the trivia of expediting to concentrate on acting as the company's intelligence in the supply marketplace.

10. *Top management.*   Direct and coordinate all activities to achieve the goals and embody the policies of the company. The manufacturing control system is their means of implementing plans and coordinating activities at all levels including line operations in engineering, manufacturing, and sales and not just concentrating on financial results.[7]

Achieving maximum benefits requires the utmost in teamwork. Each group must understand its proper role in the total effort, not just in its specialty. *Managing the total business is properly the primary job of all the managers.*

MAKING IT WORK

Experience has shown that there are five stages in improving performance in PIC. These stages are shown in Fig. 3.3. If the manufacturing control system is not already in place, all these stages will be needed. If the system is in place, planning and implementing the system will have been done, but the other steps will be necessary.

Basic Strategy

With strong words in 1969, Wickham Skinner criticized the management of U.S. manufacturing companies for their failure to integrate manufacturing and corporate

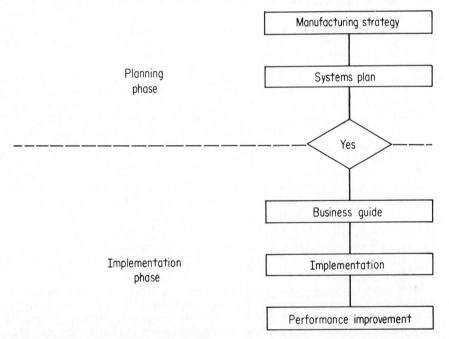

FIG. 3.3 Performance improvement stages.

strategy. He believed that top managers had the wrong perception of manufacturing, that plants were mismanaged, and that business school teachings were faulty.[8] The indictment was both justified and prophetic. At that time two powerful forces were emerging which together would change the course of U.S. industry as no other influence had since the industrial revolution:

1. Abroad, the rising productivity of foreign industry, especially in Japan and West Germany, was eroding the supremacy of U.S. companies in manufacturing technology and management.

2. At home, new concepts of manufacturing planning and control were emerging to join with an increase in capability and availability of computers to create the systems revolution of the 1970s.

From that point onward, the two imperatives of manufacturing management have been to respond to the challenge of foreign competition and to master the use of manufacturing systems as weapons in the competitive struggle.

The requirements for effective manufacturing control covered earlier will not be met nor will companies reach their full potential unless they are directed by a coherent manufacturing strategy. And yet large numbers of companies proceed with the development of PIC systems without considering either the role of manufacturing in corporate strategy or the role of PIC in the performance of the manufacturing mission. They do so, moreover, without developing explicit policies consistent with their strategy to provide operating people with guidelines for using the system. As a consequence, many—perhaps a majority—of newly implemented manufacturing systems either fail outright or do not yield the benefits expected by management at the time the investment decision was made.

How does a viable manufacturing strategy evolve? The total process was described well by Wickham Skinner. The first requirement is a corporate strategic plan. The principal objectives and strategies from this plan are translated to corresponding mandates for manufacturing in the areas of process technology, human resources, and control systems. Invariably, this definition of the manufacturing mission forces resolution of conflicting objectives, such as the trade-off between short lead times and inventory investment. In each case the resolution must be clear, unambiguous, and explicitly stated. The resulting collection of objectives and action plans is the manufacturing strategy statement.

The company strategic plan usually views the business as a group of business segments involving specific products and markets, with strategies for gaining advantages in each individual segment. It is essential to recognize when the several market strategies mandate manufacturing strategies which are inconsistent with one another. An excessive diversity of product lines or manufacturing missions, if imposed on the same production facility, will result in confusion of purpose and suboptimal performance in some of, if not all, the control processes. Failure to achieve "factory focus" will be especially troublesome to the PIC organization and will force degrading compromises in the design of planning and control systems.

The fact that the company produces multiple products with different market requirements of volume, lead time, cost, and quality does not necessarily imply a different plant for each business segment. The object of the focus can be achieved through the concept of a plant within a plant.[9] This will entail dividing the existing facility organizationally and physically into an appropriate number of units, each with its individual manufacturing mission, organizational structure, control systems, and policies.

Once the manufacturing strategy has been made explicit, the elements of the production system must be analyzed, among them production planning and control. The materials management process is examined as to focus, staffing, system capabilities, and functional reliability; and each aspect is judged against the requirements of the manufacturing mission. Finally, adjustments are made to achieve congruence between support elements and production tasks. Frequently, this involves the development or revision of the planning and control system, either in its entirety or in part.

System Development

It is not the purpose of this section to present a manual on system development, However, there is a strong correlation between how well a system works and its process of design and implementation. Incomplete systems do not work. Likewise, trauma in the organization inflicted during implementation can impair system functioning. So the importance of system development must be understood. At the system plan stage of the improvement process, management must be certain that all the necessary PIC functions are considered.

In the first section of this chapter, the basic functions of manufacturing are enumerated. The only workable system is one which includes all these basic functions—preproduction, the master plan, capacity planning and control, priority planning and control, and execution. Omission of one function will result in an unworkable system. As simple as this concept is, it is frequently ignored. In the preoccupation with materials-requirement planning (MRP) in the years following its popularization, most companies adopting MRP neglected either master scheduling or capacity management or, in many instances, both. Frustration and disappointment were epidemic. Thus one of the major landmarks in manufacturing control was the development of the concept of the integrated manufacturing system.

This concept is the antithesis of a historical tendency of practitioners to seek a panacea in some single technique or segment of the total body of knowledge. Indeed, the history of PIC is one of a proliferation of techniques, each with its advocates and detractors, but each adopted by hopeful practitioners who often understood neither the specific tool nor the total process of which that tool was just a single part.

Following World War II the advocates of operations research predicted a major role for quantitative methods in PIC. In the early 1970s some crusaders for MRP emphasized the power of that technique [10] virtually to the exclusion of other system needs. Proponents of simulation, what is now called *operation sequencing*, were similarly enthusiastic. In the early 1980s mathematical optimization techniques again had their advocates. The success of Japanese production techniques had such an impact on U.S. managers that Kanban was thought to be the key to success by many who did not understand the profound philosophical basis, the painstaking preparation, and the meticulous execution of JIT production.[11]

Yet all these techniques have their role in specific production environments, and any may be inappropriate in other environments. It is the responsibility of the qualified practitioner, as discussed earlier, to use those tools most suited to the production tasks.

If the necessary system improvements are implemented in a disciplined way, changes can be effected without trauma to the organization. This requires a well-structured system plan with sound management of the implementation project. That this type of constructive change maximizes the chance of positive improvements in materials management functions has been demonstrated by research into the causes of success or failure in hundreds of companies.[12]

The importance of user preparation in making control systems work cannot be overemphasized. System failure and poor materials management performance have been attributed to a variety of causes, including management indifference, data inaccuracy, and incomplete systems. However, studies have shown that the most frequent cause of poor results is failure to prepare the users adequately in how to use their system to operate the business.[13] The training of operating people in the execution of their specific tasks is a vital part of performance improvement. This training in the specifics of a new system or a proposed change in existing procedures will be more productive if it is preceded by a more general education in the fundamentals of modern materials management. The preparation process is most challenging when a complete integrated manufacturing system is being implemented. In such cases the scope of the changes involved is so broad and the functional interrelationships are so complex that a well-structured approach to user preparation is essential.

User Documentation

The heart of the user preparation process is the development of user system documentation. This is not to be confused with the technical documentation which is prepared by systems technicians as part of the system design and programming process. Technical documentation is concerned principally with program functions and relationships. User documentation is concerned with how the system is used to carry out its *business* purpose. For this reason it is referred to in Fig. 3.3 as the *business guide*.

A business guide contains the following elements for each major system module:

- The *conceptual approach* being taken in the application, for example, the rationale and structure of planning bills of material
- The *functional process* involved in using the system module, for example, converting the sales forecast to the production plan
- The *technical aspects*, for example, data elements, transactions, and reports to be used in specific functional tasks
- The *management policies* to ensure consistent application of manufacturing strategy, for example, the use of MPS
- The *procedures* to be followed in performing functional tasks effectively, for example, engineering change control
- The *measurement criteria* to measure progress in all vital functions, for example, the goal for customer delivery performance

The *business guide* is the application manual for the user department. For maximum effectiveness it should be written within the user department.[14] In addition to providing an immediate and ongoing training resource, the business guide accomplishes two functions vital to making the system work. First, it ensures not only user involvement but also user mastery of system functioning, thereby facilitating confident, purposeful, and skilled planning and control actions. Second, and of equal importance, it forces the confrontation of any unresolved issues or latent tensions which may have been impairing the management process. Moreover, it achieves these fundamentals before the demanding effort of implementation begins.

Even if a totally new system is not involved, some variant of the business guide development process must be followed to *improve performance* in manufacturing planning and control. The key to success is knowing what the organization is trying to do and how it is supposed to do it. For example, companies that have problems with excessive or unproductive inventories usually lack a coherent strategy for deploying the inventory so that it is a competitive weapon for the company; frequently they lack explicit policies governing items and amounts to be stocked.

The business guide is also the vehicle by which the manufacturing strategy of the company is converted to workable tactics of production and inventory management. The correlation between this conversion process and performance is inescapable. Studies have shown that whenever strategic objectives are propagated to all levels of functional management, performance is dramatically better than in companies where such communication is neglected.[15]

Fundamentals for Success

Performance improvement may be gained by attention to other fundamentals. Significant gains can be made before a company's "ultimate" system is put in place. For example,

- An aggressive program to get integrity in all the vital records will produce dramatic operating results with a relatively small investment.
- Better discipline in the management of the MPS will stabilize production operations and improve customer service.
- Queue management through input/output control, accomplished manually if necessary, will shorten lead times and reduce work in process.[16]

It certainly has not been lost on U.S. observers of the Japanese industrial miracle that it was not accomplished through sophisticated computer systems.[17] Rather, the Japanese concentrated on fundamentals of executing production tasks consistent with a coherent strategy. From the beliefs that inventory is an evil and the perfection of the process is possible, the Japanese manufacturing strategy of JIT production and total quality control (TQC) evolved. The concrete embodiment of this strategy in the factory is execution of the myriad of fundamental tasks accomplished through teamwork and attention to detail. The tactics employed to achieve strategic manufacturing objectives include

- Extremely short setup times
- Continuous material flow with short lead time, i.e., lot sizes approaching one
- Simplification of the process and of planning and control activities
- Reliance on self-improvement, not on specialist intervention

Both the strategy—JIT and TQC—and the tactics are applicable to manufacturing anywhere. What are the keys to effective performance in PIC? There are five steps in making it work, and each step must be *managed*:

1. A coherent manufacturing strategy must be an integral part of the company's strategic plan.
2. Planning and control systems must be complete and appropriate to the manufacturing mission.
3. Production and inventory management people must become skilled professionals and must have a clear policy guidance.

4. The implementation of change must be planned carefully and undertaken in the conviction that improvement of the total process is an obligation of everyone in the organization.

5. Performance improvement must be measured against specific goals and must be rooted in a committed and purposeful concentration on doing the fundamental tasks well.

BENEFITS

The tangible and intangible benefits of improved control of manufacturing operations are literally enormous. These benefits are achieved when the operating plan is sound and when concerted actions are taken by all the departments to execute it. No other actions, including investment in new high-technology automated equipment, aggressive marketing programs, or wage and salary incentives, can generate anything approaching these benefits.

Three Objectives

Significant benefits can be achieved in all three areas in which managers struggle in vain and for which they yearn so strongly: (1) better utilization of capital assets, particularly inventory; (2) higher productivity and lower costs; and (3) improved customer service.

Here are the ranges of benefits achieved by actual companies in reductions in specific categories of inventories:

- Raw materials, 20 to 40 percent
- Purchased and manufactured components, 20 to 40 percent
- Safety stocks, 50 to 95 percent
- Work in process, 25 to 75 percent
- Finished products, 10 to 40 percent
- Repair parts (customers'), 25 to 50 percent
- Repair parts (internal), 40 to 60 percent
- Tooling, gauging, etc., 20 to 40 percent
- Obsolete items, 50 to 90 percent

Zero Inventory was the title of an APICS crusade in 1984 and 1985. Like JIT, the term describes a concept, not a technique or objective. Both indicate the *direction* in which companies should move; neither is an immediate goal.

To achieve the higher figures, a company does not have to be poorly managed when it starts these actions. Very few companies are already doing such a good job that high potentials no longer exist. The low end of the range is easy to achieve; the higher numbers take more time and work.

Inventories of internal repair parts, tooling, gauges, fixtures, and the like are very fertile areas for improved inventory management. In very few companies have these items been included in the formal planning and control system. Rarely is such control based on or concerned about operating schedules for the plant, and this is a serious omission.

Raw material, purchased and manufactured components, and finished products can be reduced significantly by the following actions:

- Developing an integrated plan in which materials are procured and manufactured only in time to meet the need for higher-level production
- Eliminating redundant safety stocks at unnecessary levels in bills of material
- Paying constant attention to reducing order quantities
- Eliminating cushions of inventory for protection against unplanned occurrences
- Applying sound inventory management principles to distribution of finished products among branch warehouses

Work in process is technically the easiest inventory to reduce but practically the most difficult to cut. It involves the smallest planning effort but requires the largest execution attention. It is the most visible of wasted inventories and yet the most vitally needed to support a sound plan and execution. It should be the first class of inventory attacked since it comprises half the total of inventories in most companies. Reducing work in process will ease the task of reducing all other classes of inventories. Its elimination will free up additional space for more production equipment, avoid the necessity of expanding plants and buildings, and free up capital for automated equipment.

Benefits in higher productivity and lower costs can be achieved in the following ranges:

- Direct labor productivity, up 10 to 50 percent
- Factory indirect productivity, up 25 to 60 percent
- Office productivity, up 20 to 40 percent
- Unplanned overtime, down 50 to 90 percent
- Alternate operations, down 50 to 85 percent
- Substitute materials, down 50 to 95 percent
- Obsolete materials, down 25 to 80 percent
- Material costs, down 5 to 25 percent
- Storage, interest, and insurance, down 20 to 40 percent

Increasing productivity and lowering other costs may be even more important to a company's survival than reducing inventories. Effective planning and control can develop more significant improvements in productivity and much lower costs than automation requiring high capital investment or work incentive plans requiring higher expenses. Significant gains can be made for direct, indirect, and office workers, although the latter two classes are much more difficult to measure. In a well-planned operation with effective execution, unplanned overtime, alternate operations, and substitute materials will obviously be decreased, but idle time may actually be increased. Some idle time is a measure of tight control and may cost far less than the steps taken and the inventories carried to avoid it.

The ranges of customer service benefits which can be achieved are as follows:

- On-time delivery, 85 to 95+ percent
- Quicker deliveries, 25 to 75 percent
- Excess freight costs, cut 75 to 95 percent

- Internal sales costs, cut 50 to 90 percent
- Sales productivity, up 20 to 40 percent

On-time delivery or a fraction of the product delivered in much shorter than standard lead times can be a major factor in improving a company's position in a competitive industry. Makers of capital equipment can command higher prices when their delivery schedules are reliable. The ability to beat a competitor's delivery time or to react more quickly to customers' changes can provide a major competitive advantage as well as the ability to command premium prices. Penalty clauses in delivery contracts or the cost of premium freight to overcome delays can add tremendously to costs when products are not finished on time. A sales force on the defensive, making excuses for the failure of their plant to deliver past orders, will be severely handicapped in getting new orders.

No Comparable Activities

The management of a manufacturing company can do nothing else to approach the potential benefits, both tangible and intangible, of improved operations planning and control. The successful companies including the Japanese have proved this; success cannot be attributable to better marketing, more cooperative unions, more friendly governments, or unique cultures alone or even in combination. A sound plan followed by effective execution is the key to success. The tools and actions needed to do both jobs are covered in outline form in this chapter and are covered in supporting detail in subsequent chapters.

Reindustrialization?

Industry in North America and Europe has lost control of many markets to successful companies in the Far East including Japan, Korea, and the Malay States, and additional losses can be expected if corrective actions are not taken immediately. The list of such industries is long and growing; it includes steel, fasteners, castings, electronic equipment, optical devices, automobiles, motorcycles, and wristwatches. Computers, medical equipment, and aircraft are in jeopardy.

Many vocal individuals in economics, government, academia, and the media speak glibly about the necessity for abandoning the "smokestack" industries and fostering the "sunrise" companies, meaning those in high technology where we are supposed to retain leadership. Only a little study is required to see that we have lost leadership in markets which, until very recently, were considered high technology—witness the machine tool industry. Also the electronics companies, now the hope of the future, are just not capable of generating the number of jobs already lost or the supporting businesses so necessary to preserving our present standard of living.

The knowledge and resources necessary to reestablish and to maintain our leadership in world markets are available in the professional activities of manufacturing planning and control.[18] This is evident in the performance of the excellent companies everywhere. No new inventions or concepts are needed. A major investment is required, however, in education of managers and workers on the compelling need to change their ways and get their houses in order. There is no better way or any so well proven.

REFERENCES

1. G. W. Plossl, "Opportunity and Mandate to Excel," *Production and Inventory Management*, APICS, First quarter, 1976.
2. H. F. Mather and G. W. Plossl, *The Master Production Schedule: Management's Handle on the Business*, George Plossl Educational Services, Atlanta, 1977.
3. L. Peter and R. Gull, *The Peter Principle*, William Morrow, New York, 1969.
4. S. G. Taylor, S. M. Seward, S. F. Bolander, and R. C. Heard, "Process Industry Production and Inventory Planning Framework," *Production and Inventory Management*, APICS, First quarter, 1981.
5. G. W. Plossl, *MRP and Inventory Record Accuracy*, George Plossl Educational Services, Atlanta, 1973.
6. P. G. Conroy and E. R. Lewis, *The Synthesis of MRP, Group Technology and CAD/CAM*, APICS Conference Proceedings, 1982.
7. G. W. Plossl and W. E. Welch, *The Role of Top Management in the Control of Inventory*, Reston Publishing, Reston, Va., 1979.
8. W. Skinner, "Manufacturing: Missing Link in Corporate Strategy," *Harvard Business Review*, May/June, 1969.
9. W. Skinner, "The Focused Factory," *Harvard Business Review*, May/June, 1974.
10. J. Orlicky, *Material Requirements Planning*, McGraw-Hill, New York, 1975.
11. R. J. Schonberger, *Japanese Manufacturing Techniques*, Free Press, New York, 1982.
12. J. C. Anderson, R. G. Schroeder, S. E. Tupy, and E. M. White, *Material Requirements Planning: A Study of Implementation and Practice*, APICS, 1981.
13. Ibid.
14. B. Thompson and J. R. Walsh, *Implementing a Closed-Loop System in a Rapid Growth Environment*, APICS Conference Proceedings, 1982.
15. F. Rafii and J. G. Miller, *Interfacing Competitive Goals with Manufacturing Strategies*, Boston University School of Management, 1983.
16. R. L. Lankford, *Input/Output Control: Making It Work*, APICS Conference Proceedings, 1980.
17. R. W. Hall, *Stockless Production for the United States*, APICS Conference Proceedings, 1982.
18. O. W. Wight, *MRP II: Unlocking America's Productivity Potential*, CBI Publishing, Boston, 1981.

BIBLIOGRAPHY

Anderson, J. C., R. G. Schroeder, S. E. Tupy, and E. M. White: "Material Requirements Planning Systems: The State of the Art," *Production and Inventory Management*, APICS, Fourth quarter, 1982.

Balot, T.: "Closing the Loop: A Guide to the MRP/Management Marriage," *Production and Inventory Management Review*, January, 1982.

Brenizer, N. W.: "The Odyssey of Inventory Management," *Production and Inventory Management*, APICS, Second quarter, 1981.

Clark, J. T.: *Selling Top Management: Understanding the Financial Impact of Manufacturing Systems*, APICS Conference Proceedings, 1982.

Gue, F. S.: "Control Capacity and Priority," *Inventories and Production*, Part I, May/June, 1981; Part II, Nov./Dec., 1981.

Mather, H. F., and G. W. Plossl: "Priority Fixation vs. Throughput Control," *Production and Inventory Management*, APICS, Third quarter, 1978.

Plossl, G. W.: *Manufacturing Control: The Last Frontier for Profits*, Reston Publishing, Reston, Va., 1973.

———: "Opportunity and Mandate to Excel," *Production and Inventory Management*, APICS, First quarter, 1976.

———: *What We've Had and What's Ahead*, APICS Conference Proceedings, 1978.

CHAPTER 4

Progress*

Editor

WALTER GODDARD, President, Oliver Wight Education Associates, Newbury, New Hampshire

When APICS was started in 1958, computers were just being introduced into manufacturing companies. Both APICS and computers have experienced rapid growth ever since. Material-requirements planning (MRP) was still a decade away. A body of knowledge had not been developed. The process was one of trial and error. Order launching and expediting were the result. There were a number of popular, well-known techniques, but they were so loosely connected that they hardly constituted an operating system. The books, articles, and APICS meetings of the 1960s revolved on reorder points, economical order quantities (EOQ) and machine loading.

The name of the society came from the process in which the typical manufacturing company organized its approach to planning resources and scheduling materials. Typically, there was an inventory control department that ordered materials. Another group, often referred to as *production control*, worried about what was needed. This group expedited the "hot" jobs—those jobs that were causing shortages. Even though these two groups may have reported to a common boss, there was a distinct separation between those who ordered and those who expedited. Only in theory did the two work together.

AN ALTERNATE APPROACH—MRP

There were, however, a number of companies using the computer to perform a different approach to ordering. Instead of using the reorder-point method, these

---

* Ollie Wight was a champion of APICS. He welcomed the chance to write this chapter and had prepared an outline before his untimely death. Walter Goddard, his friend and associate, agreed to complete it.

companies were exploding requirements down through a bill of material. By to-day's standards, it was quite cumbersome and time-consuming. Frequently, it took a month to complete, 1 week for each level in the bill of material was commonplace. It was not until the late 1960s that the term *material-requirement planning* came into being to describe this process.

MRP was first used in J. I. Case, Twin Disc, Black & Decker, and Perkin-Elmer. These were pioneering firms in the creation and development of MRP.* APICS played a decisive role in 1971. A heated debate had sprung up between the advo-cates of the reorder-point approach and advocates of MRP. A small group of APICS members formed the "APICS MRP crusade" to spread the word on the differences between the two and the advantages of MRP.† It would be difficult to find a more successful effort. The APICS MRP crusade literally changed the approach to mate-rial planning in the United States.

ADVANTAGES OF MRP

The success of MRP did not arise from how well it was promoted, but from the results that it has helped generate. Not only does MRP order material at the right time, but also it has the distinct advantage of being the only system available for rescheduling. For each schedule, MRP checks the current due date of material against the current-need date. The due date is the expected completion date. The need date is when there will be a shortage or the safety stock will be used unless existing scheduled materials arrive. Whenever there is a difference between these two dates, MRP generates an action message to alert the user to review the situation. The user must make a decision as to whether the message is significant (requiring action) or insignificant (no effort is required). An example containing a reschedule message is shown in Fig. 4.1 which would be followed by an action message, "Time to Order."

A system that correctly orders and reschedules was a tremendous breakthrough for the field. With MRP, the planning department could do what the expeditors were trying to do—answer the question, When do we really need this? When it is managed properly, not only can MRP predict when each job will be needed much further in advance than an expeditor can, but also it can "unexpedite," i.e., advise what schedules should be rescheduled to a later date. A good scheduling system operates in both directions—some jobs are needed earlier and others are needed later. Only when a company maintains valid dates on all the schedules can it eliminate the hot list, red tags, and expeditors overriding the scheduled dates.

Maintaining valid schedules starts in the planning office but does not end there. If the factory cannot complete the schedules on time, it is irrelevant that the due date is right when it is impossible to meet. It became obvious that feedback was essential to maintaining valid schedules. Vendors and foremen who cannot meet the scheduled dates, for whatever reason (be it lack of capacity, tooling, parts, or scrap, etc.), must feed this information back to the planning department with not only the bad news but also a revised expected completion date. The two-way flow of information between the planning group and the two execution groups is shown in Fig. 4.2.

---

* Individuals such as Joe Orlicky, Jim Burlingame, Bob Maddox, Paul Rosa, and Gaynor Kelley deserve a great deal of credit for demonstrating that this approach is superior to the reorder-point approach.

† In addition to a number of practitioners, major leadership came from Oliver Wight, Joe Orlicky, and George Plossl.

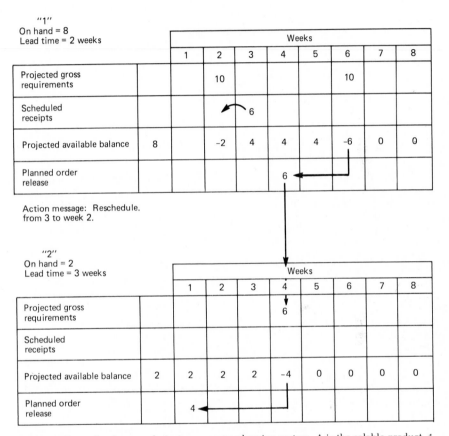

Master Production Schedule for "A"	Weeks							
	1	2	3	4	5	6	7	8
MPS at start date		10				10		

"1"
On hand = 8
Lead time = 2 weeks

		Weeks							
		1	2	3	4	5	6	7	8
Projected gross requirements			10				10		
Scheduled receipts			⬉ 6						
Projected available balance	8		-2	4	4	4	-6	0	0
Planned order release					6 ⬅				

Action message: Reschedule.
from 3 to week 2.

"2"
On hand = 2
Lead time = 3 weeks

		Weeks							
		1	2	3	4	5	6	7	8
Projected gross requirements					6				
Scheduled receipts									
Projected available balance	2	2	2	2	-4	0	0	0	0
Planned order release		4 ⬅							

FIG. 4.1 Example of a manufacturing resource planning system. A is the salable product, 1 is a component of A, and 2 is a component of 1.

CAPACITY PLANNING

Machine loading is as old as the reorder-point approach. The intent of machine loading is commendable; it is to predict the future capacity required in key work centers. But just as the reorder point has problems, so does machine loading. The typical company was not maintaining accurate schedules in the factory, and so the information summarized on a machine load report was not reliable. Usually, it was front-end-loaded, a very large load accumulated as past due, from the jobs ordered

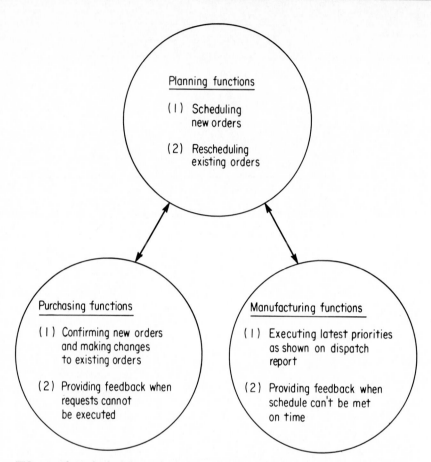

FIG. 4.2 Flow of scheduling information. *Note:* A number of companies have combined the purchasing and planning of purchased material into the same department.

that were not rescheduled correctly. Additionally, machine loading reflected only the scheduled jobs and thus had a very short horizon. Capacity planning requires reliable visibility a long distance into the future, certainly beyond the manufacturing lead time.

MRP contains the solution to both flaws. First, by maintaining correct dates on all shop orders, the information for capacity planning is lined up correctly. Second, the planned orders supply the needed input for calculating future capacity needs. This approach is called *capacity-requirements planning* (CRP). A comparison between machine loading and CRP is shown in Fig. 4.3.

What MRP has done to reorder points CRP has done to machine loading—both the older techniques have faded rapidly.

CLOSING THE LOOP

By tying together MRP, CRP, shop floor control, purchasing, and feedback, another major milestone was reached. The term *closed-loop MRP* was used to describe this

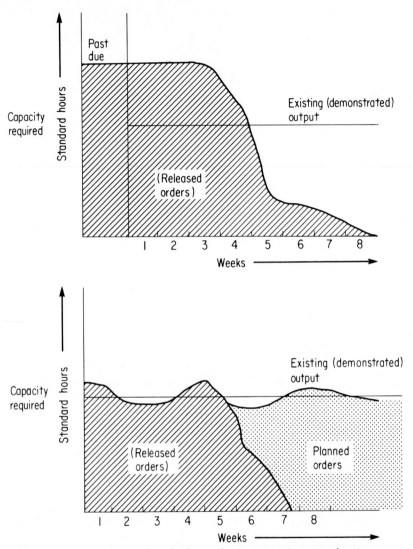

FIG. 4.3 Comparison of machine loading and capacity-requirements planning.

system. A closed-loop system starts with a master production schedule (MPS) and includes maintaining valid schedules in purchasing in addition to the factory. Figure 4.4 displays the functions that make up a closed-loop MRP system.

With a closed-loop system, the profession finally has an operating system that works. It is no longer simply order launching and expediting. By the mid-1970s, we reached the age where we knew how to order material at the right time, maintain valid schedules as the needs of the company change, predict capacity, and coordinate the execution departments (purchasing and manufacturing) with the planning departments (inventory and production control).

However, simply implementing a correct operating system does not yield good results. For the users to make the right decisions, the required data must be accurate.

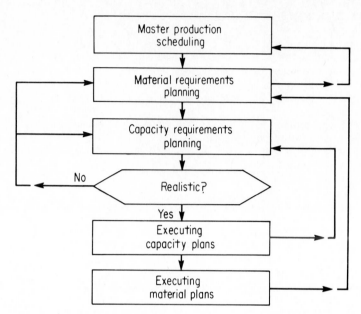

FIG. 4.4   Closed-loop MRP II.

An expeditor does not need accurate inventory balances, accurate bills of materials, or accurate routings. An expeditor works in spite of them, not thanks to them. The odds of a company having extremely accurate data, when it does not help get the job done, are slim. Yet if a formal system lacks reliable data, the decisions are being built on quicksand. The never-ending challenge is to maintain very accurate data in order for a formal system such as closed-loop MRP to work properly.

MASTER OF MRP

Master scheduling was also poorly understood initially. Originally, it was perceived that the input to MRP would be customer orders plus forecasts of what companies expected to sell. Manufacturing professionals quickly realized that there were many significant reasons why a manufacturing company did not make the product in the same way as they sold it. Rather, there is a need to level the load on the factory; sequence the products in an effective manner; and take into account the availability of capacity, tooling, and component parts. Resources are required to support how a company builds its products, not how it sells them. This is what the master schedule must represent.

The MPS is the "master" of both the material capacity needs. If the MPS is not managed well, the other activities will not be able to overcome this weakness. Even today, the typical company with a closed-loop MRP system is apt to have an unrealistic master schedule. Too many companies put their "hopes and dreams," what they would like to do, into the MPS rather than what they can do.

ROLE OF THE PRODUCTION PLAN

In the formative years of MRP, it was popular to say that management's "handle on the business" was the MPS. However, that statement reflected a lack of knowledge as to what a general manager can do as well as what she or he should do. The typical general manager does not have the time, let alone the interest and capabilities, to review every plan for every product. However, the master scheduler's job is not to set strategy or policy.

It is the general manager and his or her staff who must take responsibility for determining rates of output for broad categories of products. Enter the term *production planning*. The production plan determines the rate of output for families of products. It is aggregate planning. All resource planning decisions revolve around the production plan. Material, capacity, direct labor operators, indirect labor operators, engineering, accounting, etc., are required to support this decision.

The production plan is the general manager's vehicle for communicating policy to the master scheduler. The production plan becomes a budget for the master schedulers to spend. The master scheduler's job is to determine the best product mix to meet the requirements of the production plan.

A company's business plan is practically identical to its production plan. Both are aggregate, both look forward in time a long distance, both are the responsibilities of top management, and both are essential to running the business. The major difference is the unit of measure. The business plan represents the expected flow of dollars. It projects what the company expects to sell, to make, and to buy, stated in cost dollars as well as sales dollars. This becomes the basis for determining cash needs, profit projections, and budgets.

In most companies, the business plan is laid out first. Then the production plan is determined. Regardless of the sequence, it is critical that each support the other. Since the sum of the items in the master schedule must equal the production plan for each family, so must the dollars which will be generated from the production plan match the approved business plan. Top management's ongoing responsibility is to review and maintain both the business plan and the production plan. Whenever there is a need to change either, the impact on the other must be evaluated. Usually, this means that a change in one will require a change in the other.

A more powerful system has now been developed. The system is capable of linking policy to detailed planning and scheduling. The general manager could use it to establish a direction for the company with confidence that the system could help people convert this target to the specific action required to achieve it.

FURTHER EXPANSION OF MRP

The next evolution of MRP again came from practitioners. Companies such as Abbott Laboratories of Canada recognized the opportunity to integrate not only their financial planning needs but also the requirements of their distribution system. Andre Martin was the force behind the composite system.

The information for the financial system comes from the operating system. Once the operating system has valid schedules and accurate data, the financial system has excellent input. Without these prerequisites, however, the data from the factory are suspect at best. As a result, the financial people often develop a separate set of books. When the data are right, however, they can be used by the financial group. Data are simply a by-product of the operating system: to the factory, the data are schedules and quantities; to the financial group, the data are dollars and cents.

Distribution resource planning (DRP) is the term that describes how a company should manage its resource needs at the distribution centers and couple this process with resource planning at the manufacturing locations. An example illustrating this connection is shown in Fig. 4.5. DRP is identical to MRP, with all the advantages of MRP, except that it operates above the MPS dealing with finished goods and distribution centers rather than below the MPS dealing with components.

NEW NAME—MRP II

In 1979, *Modern Material Handling* published an article describing how three companies, Tennant Company,[1] Twin Disc,[2], and Hewlett-Packard, [3] were integrating their operating and financial planning systems. The term used in the magazine article was *manufacturing resource planning*, or *MRP II.*

Resource planning is an excellent description. It includes material, capacity, tooling, finance, etc. Yet the term *manufacturing resource planning* and the acronym *MRP II* were not accepted by a number of people. Rather, these people felt that a new term would be more appropriate. However, many supporters felt that a completely new acronym was not needed. These advocates viewed the change as an evolution. MRP had grown to encompass more activities. In their judgment, the acronym *MRP II* was a more logical way to describe this new system. Oliver Wight's support and leadership has led to *MRP II* being the accepted term today.

Unfortunately, MRP II is often translated in a more limited sense than intended. The word *manufacturing* conjures up the idea of factory in many people's minds. They do not initially perceive it as applying to all departments within a manufacturing company.

Figure 4.6 is a schematic which shows the major functions that make up an MRP II system. Material requirements planning was the function put in place first. However, it is not a stand-alone operating system. Until it expanded, both up and down, we lacked the ability to establish a realistic plan and then to convert it to the detailed actions required to carry it out. Those functions that make up a closed-loop MRP system permitted us to do that. The expansion of the closed-loop system to include business planning, production planning, and distribution resource planning allows us to have one system for planning all resources. The one additional characteristic of a good MRP II system is the capability to run simulations to evaluate the consequences of alternative plans and/or trade-offs for determining the best choices when not all choices can be satisfied.

BEYOND MRP II

A number of exciting extensions of MRP II are still occurring. An increasing number of manufacturing companies are providing their suppliers with planned orders to aid the suppliers in doing a better job of managing their businesses. In turn, these companies are expecting more reliable deliveries as well as reduced lead times.

The logical extension of MRP II is to tie in customers. If a customer has a good MRP II system and is willing to share information, that customer's planned orders should become input to the supplier's MPS. This converts independent demand, which must be forecasted, to dependent demand, which can be calculated. Once the ability to manage a company in a better manner occurs, the ability to ship faster and more reliably to customers will follow.

Product "A"

On hand balance = 43
Safety stock = 15
Lead time = 1 week
Order quantity = 20

Chicago distribution center

		Weeks							
		1	2	3	4	5	6	7	8
Forecast		10	10	10	10	10	15	15	15
Scheduled receipts									
Projected available balance	43	33	23	13	23	13	18	3	8
Planned order release			20		20		20	20	

Product "A"

On hand balance = 10
Safety stock = 10
Lead time = 2 weeks
Order quantity = 10

Los Angeles distribution center

		Weeks							
		1	2	3	4	5	6	7	8
Forecast		5	5	3	3	3	3	6	6
Scheduled receipts		10							
Projected available balance	10	15	10	7	14	11	8	12	6
Planned order release		10			10		10		

Demand upon New York manufacturing plant

Product "A"		Weeks							
		1	2	3	4	5	6	7	8
Forecast		8	8	8	8	8	8	8	8
Chicago			20		20		20	20	
Los Angeles		10			10		10		
Total demand		18	28	8	38	8	38	28	8

FIG. 4.5 Relationship between distribution resource planning and manufacturing resource planning.

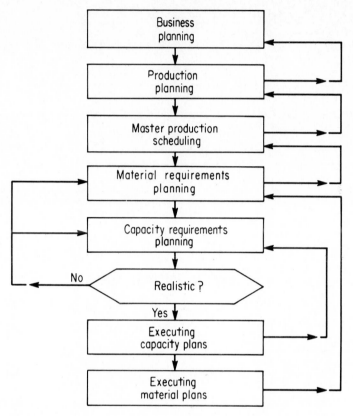

FIG. 4.6   MRP II.

Other candidates for MRP II include the resources needed for maintenance. Some companies plan their materials and labor to maintain key equipment in a manner identical to material and capacity plans for manufacturing product.

Additionally, companies are planning their design engineering and drafting functions as part of the MRP II network scheduling approach. Predicting the capacity needs for these work centers is as crucial as for any other work center in the company. Maintaining valid schedules and priorities in engineering is essential.

Order promising is now perceived as simply a by-product of good master scheduling. The first question the customer wants answered is, When can you ship? To answer this question, you need to know when material and capacity will be available. The answer to these two issues can be found in the MPS. By marrying the two activities, better delivery promises are possible.

The most recent development centers on simulations. Once a company has both an operating and a financial planning system that work, contingency planning becomes practical. Being able to predict the consequences of alternative plans, and being able to answer "what if" questions, becomes an invaluable aid to any manager. Being warned of the consequences ensures that better decisions will be made.

EVALUATING MRP II

Oliver Wight, who helped promote MRP and led its growth into MRP II, also made a major contribution by answering the question of how well a company can use an MRP II system. He established the criteria for evaluating an MRP II system. By answering 25 questions, a company can rate itself as an A, B, C, or D user (Fig. 4.7).

The class D user simply has MRP II running on the computer. Managers are not using the information. Even though this company has expended most of the costs to get it this far, it is getting very little payback.

The class C user orders material, but out in the factory hot lists still exist. The system is simply an order launcher with only limited payback as a result of better ordering.

The class B user not only orders through MRP II, but also is using MRP II to reschedule both the factory and purchase orders. Major improvements in deliveries, inventory turns, and productivity await a company that achieves a class B level.

The class A user has three characteristics beyond a class B user. First, the users have linked the financial planning system to the operating system; second, they have the ability to simulate and evaluate alternate plans; and third, the general manager and staff are using the information from MRP II to help manage the business.

ABCD CHECK LIST

Data Integrity   Yes   No

1. Inventory record accuracy 95% or better.   _____   _____
2. Bill of material accuracy 98% or better.   _____   _____
3. Routing accuracy 95% or better.   _____   _____

Education

4. Initial education of at least 80% of all employees.   _____   _____
5. An ongoing education program.   _____   _____

Technical

6. Time periods for master production scheduling and Master Requirements Planning are weeks or smaller.   _____   _____
7. Master production scheduling and Material Requirements Planning run weekly or more frequently.   _____   _____
8. System includes firm planned order and pegging capability.   _____   _____
9. The master production schedule is visibly managed, not automatic.   _____   _____

FIG. 4.7   ABCD checklist.

10. System includes capacity requirements planning.   _____ _____

11. System includes daily dispatch list.   _____ _____

12. System includes input output control.   _____ _____

Use of the System

13. The shortage list has been eliminated.   _____ _____

14. Vendor delivery performance is 95% or better.   _____ _____

15. Vendor scheduling is done out beyond the quoted lead times.   _____ _____

16. Shop delivery performance is 95% or better.   _____ _____

17. Master schedule performance is 95% or better.   _____ _____

18. There are regular (at least monthly) production planning meetings with the general manager and his staff including: manufacturing, production and inventory control, engineering, marketing, finance.   _____ _____

19. There is a written master scheduling policy which is adhered to.   _____ _____

20. The system is used for scheduling as well as ordering.   _____ _____

21. MRP is well understood by key people in manufacturing, marketing, engineering, finance, and top management.   _____ _____

22. Management really uses MRP to manage.   _____ _____

23. Engineering changes are effectively implemented.   _____ _____

24. Simultaneous improvement has been achieved in at least two of the following three areas: inventory, productivity, customer service.   _____ _____

25. Operating system is used for financial planning.   _____ _____

FIG. 4.7   (continued).

THE NEW CRUSADE

APICS has launched a new crusade—*zero inventories.* Its goal is to raise the performance of manufacturing companies to new heights. By focusing on both the planning process and the execution process, a number of companies have been able to dramatically reduce setup times, order quantities, work-in-process inventories, manufacturing lead times, etc. All contribute to improved inventory turnover, productivity, and customer service.

The zero-inventories crusade, the JIT concept, is a philosophy, a process to eliminate all waste in the process of procuring raw materials, manufacturing components and products, and delivering them to your customers. It is not a set of techniques or an operating system. In fact, those companies who have a class A MRP II system in place are in the best possible position to achieve significant ongoing improvements in their quest for JIT performance.

SUMMARY

As we look at the development of MRP II, it began as a simple alternative to reorder points called material-requirements planning. The technique, in turn, became an operating system, closed- loop MRP. From an operating system, a companywide resource planning system that includes the financial aspects was reached with an MRP II system. Armed with the right system, the thrust is now to use it in the best possible manner. MRP II has become the means for many companies to achieve the goal of continuous improvement.

Wight's words best explain this new way of life:

> Manufacturing resource planning is, without question, the most significant development in the management of manufacturing companies of this decade. In the few companies where it is working, you can see for the first time ever, the full value of the computer as a management tool. Why do I say for the first time ever? Because never before has the computer had in its memory so complete and accurate a picture of what is happening in the manufacturing operations—the heart and soul of a manufacturing company. This makes it possible to plan the resources of the *entire company* with an unprecedented level of confidence.
>
> Further, this exceptionally detailed, timely, and accurate information—which was only until recently the exclusive property of the production and inventory control people—is made easily accessible to people in every function and at all management levels. And they can get what they need in their own "language," their own terminology, and their own context.
>
> Top management can get profit-and-loss projections in a format they are used to, but with an accuracy and precision that cannot be achieved any other way. Financial people can get inventory level data, expressed in dollars, with unprecedented accuracy. Marketing can get cost information so reliable that they can work out pricing strategies with complete confidence, not only with the knowledge that their pricing will produce profit, but also how much profit will be produced.[4]

MRP and MRP II are the tools. Wight gave us the insight. APICS was the catalyst.

Without the proper tools and the skills to use them properly, no group can truly call themselves professionals. A profession is distinguished by its body of knowledge. APICS has grown to this stage. The tools are known, yet enhancements will always be created. The skills have been demonstrated, but there will always be an opportunity and an incentive to improve them. The combination of proven tools and demonstrated skills has caused a revolutionary change in how well we manage manufacturing companies. We have gotten better. However, we have a long way to go.

Wight loved manufacturing; he said, "It's an honorable profession." He knew that the ultimate use of better information was for each of us to be able to do a better job and, in turn, work together as a more effective team. Whenever this occurs, the quality of life improves immensely and working becomes fun. Being productive and enjoying your job are the results. APICS, the computer, MRP, and MRP II have all contributed to this ideal.

REFERENCES

1. "At Tennant—MRP II Gets the 'Impossible' Answers!" *Modern Materials Handling*, September, 1979, pp. 88–91.

2. Oliver W. Wight, "Effective Company Operation as Never Before!" *Modern Materials Handling*, September, 1979, pp. 80–83.
3. "At Hewlett-Packard—A New Level of Management Control," *Modern Materials Handling*, September, 1979, pp. 84–87.
4. Wight, p. 80.

BIBLIOGRAPHY

Berry, William L., Thomas E. Vollman, and D. Clay Whybark: *Master Production Scheduling; Principles and Practice*, APICS, Washington, 1979.

Martin, Andre: *DRP: Distribution Resource Planning: Distribution Management's Most Powerful Tool*, Oliver Wight Limited Publications, Essex Junction, Vt., 1983.

Orlicky, Joseph: *Material Requirements Planning*, McGraw-Hill, New York, 1975.

Wallace, Tom (ed.): *APICS Dictionary*, 5th ed., APICS, Falls Church, Va., 1984.

Wight, Oliver W.: *The Executive's Guide to Successful MRP II*, Oliver Wight Limited Publications, Essex Junction, Vt., 1981.

———: *Manufacturing Resource Planning: MRP II—Unlocking America's Productivity Potential*, Rev. Ed., Oliver Wight Limited Publications, Essex Junction, Vt., 1984.

———: *Production and Inventory Management in the Computer Age*, CBI Publishing, Boston, 1974.

Strategic Business Planning

5

Strategic Market Planning

Editor

ROBERT L. JANSON, CPIM, Senior Manager, Ernst & Whinney, Cleveland, Ohio

Production and inventory control (PIC) personnel have a proprietary interest in strategic market planning (SMP).* All employees in the company want the enterprise to prosper since its success will help them progress in responsibility and thus in income. And at the same time, perhaps the PIC job will be easier if the marketing department is more adept at planning.

The challenge in SMP is twofold: to obtain a workable plan and to see the company reach its objectives. Thus it is somewhat paradoxical to observe senior executives working so hard at planning and then leave the execution to others with little personal follow-up. The challenge is to get away from complicated, numbers-oriented plans and to return to decisions based on human, qualitative data based on selected statistical information.

Three dominant themes exist in strategic planning: (1) efficient use of resources, (2) high productivity of personnel, and (3) continual cost containment. These three items can best be explained by an illustration. Figure 5.1 shows a comparison of a company's profits under two conditions. On the left-hand side of the chart are a typical company's annual 5 percent pretax profits. The right-hand side presents the additional potential profits that can be achieved by reducing operating costs,

* The author wishes to extend his gratitude to Philip J. Kaszar and Denise M. Jaras for their technical and editorial assistance with this chapter.

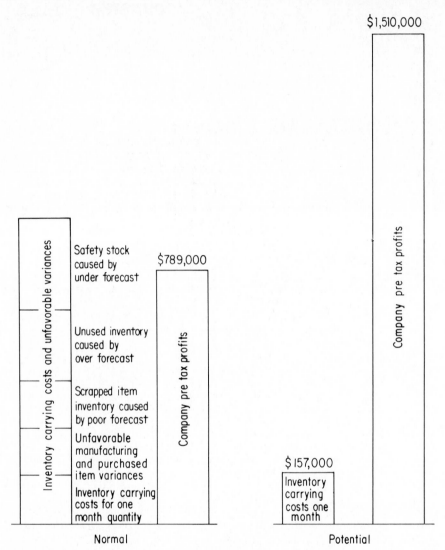

FIG. 5.1 Normal versus potential company profits. *(Source: Ernst & Whinney.)*

cutting inventory to a 1-month supply, and eliminating obsolete items, unfavorable manufacturing, and purchased-item variances. These gains, from a fair 5 percent pretax to a good 10 percent profit, are the result of executing a good SMP.

STRATEGIC MARKET PLANNING INTRODUCTION

The major concept of market evolution and strategic product fit gives us what is called *strategic market planning*. This concept reflects the fact that all markets undergo a series of evolutionary changes regarding customer's needs, technology, competitors, laws, and even distribution channels. The companies that look out of a "strategic window" continually watch these changes, assess the requirements, and modify their SMP as necessary. They note that there is a limited period of fit between the development of a plan and its execution. The *strategic management process* has been defined as "the managerial process of developing and maintaining a viable relationship between the organization and its environment through the development of corporate purpose, objectives and goals, growth strategies and business portfolio plans for company wide operations."[1] These major steps result in the SMP. There are certain important characteristics to this process. For example, successful SMPs exhibit an adaptability to change, a trust in one's associates, an open-mindedness as to the environment, both positive and creative thinking, and an awareness of the interrelationships both intracompany and within the economy. Planners are required who understand the company's strengths and weaknesses and who are adept at listening, observing, and thinking. Last, these persons exhibit an ability to see that their plan is accomplished once it has been developed.

Thus, an SMP is a time-phased written document that recognizes the mission of the firm and its objectives. It identifies the strategies to be used to achieve these objectives, such as the general product or market and growth plans and any competitive advantage anticipated by the company. Normally only one strategic plan and one marketing plan exist at the top level. However, companies that have many product lines and perhaps serve a number of industries may wish to have several marketing plans, one for each product line. Then these individual plans are integrated into the overall master strategic plan.

One compelling reason to draw up these plans is illustrated by the trend in the prime interest rate during the last 30 years. Many managers have forgotten that the prime interest rate hit a low of 3 percent in 1953 and then reached a high of 20.5 percent in 1981, as shown in Fig. 5.2. This dramatic upward trend of the cost of money has placed great emphasis on strategic planning, if only to conserve the resource called cash.

Any strategic plan, for a function such as marketing, considers the following inputs from the executive committee:

- Company purpose or mission, specific as to the business in which it will operate (e.g., product class, customer group, technological field, market need); it may specify, "enter the growing market for minicomputers."
- Objectives and goals—profitability, sales growth, market share improvement, innovation; e.g., "increase return on investment to 7½ percent by the end of next year."
- Growth strategy, which is a method to achieve objectives by selecting a major direction for pursuing objectives, e.g., to increase the sales and profit of a specific product.

MARKETING PERSPECTIVE AND MOTIVATION

Before we explore SMP, some background data may be of value. According to Peter Drucker,[2] marketing was invented in Japan around 1650 by the first member of the Mitsui family to settle in Tokyo as a merchant who opened what might be called the first department store. Two hundred and fifty years before Sears, Roebuck and Co. Mitsui wanted to be a buyer for his customers, to design the right products for them, and to develop production sources. He used the principle of "your money back and

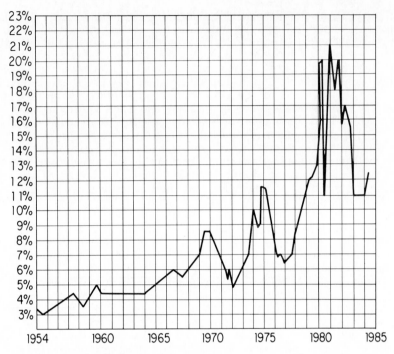

FIG. 5.2 Trend in bank prime interest rates.

no questions asked," and he offered a large variety of products rather than focusing on a single craft, product category, or a process. Drucker notes that the first man in the western hemisphere to see marketing clearly was Cyrus H. McCormick, founder of the International Harvester Company. He invented not only the mechanical harvester but also the basic tools of modern marketing: market research, market analysis, the concept of market standing, pricing policies, the service salesperson, service parts warehouse to supply the customer, and even installment credit. Yet 50 more years had to pass before the term *marketing* first appeared in college courses in around 1900. In 1911 Curtis Publishing Company installed the first marketing department, and subsequently other companies followed this concept.

Over the years various organizational conflicts between marketing and other departments have evolved. Figure 5.3 summarizes some of these conflicts, by department, showing their particular emphasis and the contrasting marketing emphasis.[3] Obviously all these points are considered in preparing the SMP.

Strategic Market Plan Concept

The elements to consider in developing an SMP include these items:[4]

Short-term profits versus long-term growth

Profit margin versus competitive position

Direct sales effort versus market development effort

Department versus Marketing Emphasis

Department	Department's Emphasis	Marketing's Emphasis
R&D	Basic research Intrinsic quality Functional features	Applied research Perceived quality Sales features
Engineering	Long design lead time Few models Standard components	Short design lead time Many models Customer components
Purchasing	Narrow product line Standard parts Price of material Economic lot sizes Purchasing at infrequent intervals	Broad product line Nonstandard parts Quality of material Large lot sizes to avoid stock-outs Immediate purchasing for customer needs
Manufacturing	Long production lead time Long runs with few models No model changes Standard orders Ease of fabrication Average quality control	Short production lead time Short runs with many models Frequent model changes Customer orders Aesthetic appearance Tight quality control
Finance	Strict rationales for spending Hard-and-fast budgets Pricing to cover costs	Intuitive arguments for spending Flexible budgets to meet changing needs Pricing to further market development
Accounting	Standard transactions Few reports	Special terms and discounts Many reports
Credit	Full financial disclosures by customers Low credit risks Tough credit terms Tough collection procedures	Minimum credit examination of customers Medium credit risks Easy credit terms Easy collection procedures

FIG. 5.3 Department versus marketing emphasis.

Penetration of existing markets versus the development of new markets
Related versus unrelated market opportunities as a source of long-term growth
Profit versus nonprofit goals (that is, social responsibilities)
Growth versus stability
"Riskless" environment versus high-risk environment

PLANNING PROCESS

Strategic market planning is one of the six primary aspects of manufacturing resource planning and control, as illustrated in Fig. 5.4. The company's board of directors, president, and/or senior executives develop an SMP that considers the

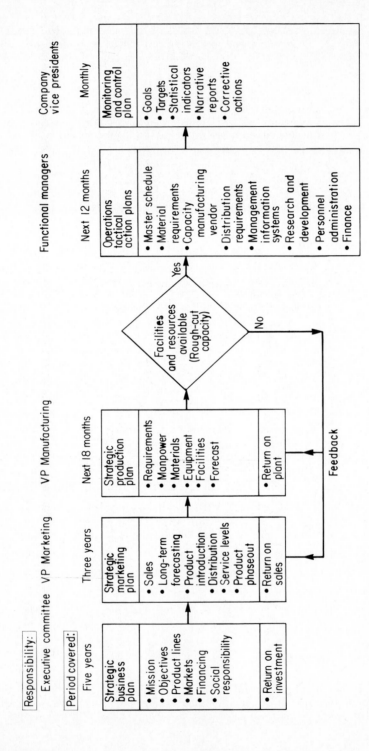

FIG. 5.4 Conceptual flowchart of manufacturing resource planning and control.

overall return on investment (ROI). This plan usually is for the next 5 years. From this mission and objective statement, the marketing function devises its own 3-year SMP by using the appropriate return on sales as well as asset turnover guidance restricted to the perspective of the marketing and sales function. Next, the company's 18-month SMP is developed. The success of this plan is measured by the return on manufacturing assets. Once established, the capacity stated in this plan is compared to the existing capacity of various facilities and resources in a step called *rough-cut capacity planning*. Should there be inadequate capacity, feedback to modify the earlier plans is necessary. Once rough-cut capacity planning is accomplished, several operational tactical action plans, often covering 12 months, are prepared by various company functions and include the master scheduling, material-requirements planning (MRP), management information systems, etc. Last, a monthly monitoring and control procedure is mandatory since these plans, having longer duration, are all dynamic and require continual updating.

Long-Range Planning

Before we discuss this quite involved exercise, some history of planning should be reviewed. Long-range planning, as a business technique, goes back less than 100 years. During the late nineteenth century and as a direct result of the growth of the scientific management movement, the use of planning in U.S. business became popular. The early pioneers of this technique sought to replace rule-of-thumb methods of operating by a more scientific approach. They coined and introduced numerous techniques of planning factory performance and business activities.

Around 1900, long-range planning was an informal organizational arrangement in contrast to today's formalized organizations. The long-range planning at that time relied in great measure on intuitive judgment in contrast to today's systematic approach. It was undertaken by some companies, but few organizations reached a stage of planning that detailed activities over a long range.

What is now known as long-range strategic planning at the turn of the century was composed of two major types. The first was planning for personal growth, which was undertaken by the aggressive business tycoons and the early empire builders. The second was a type of intuitive look-ahead. A president attempted to assess the long-range future to ascertain what opportunities could be exploited by the company. Often this early long-range planning, in addition to being aggressive, was fueled by an intensive personal drive in the hope of obtaining consolidations, a type of vertical integration, and a very rapid expansion of the existing sources and facilities.[5]

Planning in the Early 1900s.   In 1916, a French industrialist, Henri Fayol, referred to five key functions of management: planning, organizing, command, coordination, and control. Fayol commented about planning, "The plan of action is, and one in the same time, the result envisioned, the line of action to be followed, stages to go through, and the methods to be used." In his view, to plan meant "to access the future and make provisions for."[6]

In 1926, in the American Management Association's *Production Executive Series Bulletin*, one author wrote, "The simplest way is to get from the sales department an estimate of what deliveries may be expected to be on each line of product. But what if the sales department cannot give a reliable estimate of what sales will be over the period?" The author, Leonard Tyler, was stating one of the frustrations of management. How do you forecast and make plans for a period longer than just a few months in advance? This was one of the early formal references to the problems of sales forecasting and the attendant long-range planning requirements. Tyler continued, discussing the benefits that could be obtained from any valid attempt to forecast a production program. He thought one should consider the purposes for which a budget or forecast is adopted. These were two:[7]

1. Plan ahead for the volume of work anticipated, so that it may be begun and carried through smoothly and as rapidly as possible.
2. Set up standards, of both performance and cost analysis, by which what is actually done can be checked.

Subsequent authors[8] noted both that the customer was the only person for whom a company exists and that the only true customer a plant has is the sales department. This was a rather revolutionary view at that time. Managers stated that orders should be placed by the sales department, and if the sales people could not dispose of these orders after the goods were produced, it was the fault of the sales department. Many people felt that general management could not hold manufacturing responsible for the creation of inventories if such sales orders were incorrect.

Planning from 1930 to 1945.   In the early 1930s, Professor Paul Holden and two associates of the Stanford Business School surveyed 31 large organizations, concentrating their efforts and attention on the interest of the top managers on planning. This survey disclosed that only two of the companies had formal plans for 5 years ahead, but half or more of the companies had made plans for some of or all their operations up to 1 year in advance. This study left its authors to conclude, "One of the greatest needs observed during the course of this study is for more adequate planning and clarification of future objectives, both near term and long-range."[9]

In 1931, Dean W. B. Donham of the Harvard Business School produced an important contribution to corporate long-range planning. In his book he anticipated some of the business development planning that was to take place in the late 1950s.[10] He commented that the time seemed right to review the whole subject of forecasting, including its limitations. He said that any planning theory should approach the subject from a scientific point of view. Each situation and its potential success would depend on the ability to reduce the number of variables involved to a manageable number. Any theory of forecasting (he referred to it as "foresight") has well-defined characteristics which one must recognize and provide as major elements for the solution of each problem.

In the later 1930s, the Tennessee Valley Authority project utilized some of the newer approaches to long-range planning. Although public power systems were not new, this extensive concentration in one area caused the chairman at the time, David E. Lilienthal, to describe the long-range planning approach as a "unified development" and to say that this was synonymous with long-range planning as performed by corporations.[11]

Planning Following World War II.   With the completion of World War II, a revolution came about in the business community in regard to planning. The extensive conversion necessary from government-oriented production to consumer applications necessitated dramatic changes in many companies. In addition, the emphasis in the late 1940s and 1950s on leveling manpower because of union demands, and on lowering inventories because of the high carrying cost, led to a reevaluation of the current business theories. The thought of using a statistical approach, the possibility of extending the wartime success of operations research (with its new tools such as linear programming), and a general awareness of scientific knowledge in business operations invited new attention and interest in scientific, quantitative analysis as applied to long-range planning.

Planning in the 1970s. A study at this time in a leading magazine, *Business Management*,[12] attempted to answer the questions, What does corporate planning mean to company managers, and how are the various functions delegated? The answers to these questions were most interesting, and indicate the level of long-range planning in U.S. industry today. Some 101 companies were queried, and all but one indicated that they were engaged in some kind of planning. The overall majority (84 percent) established some type of goal for sales, share of the market, and/or return on investment. A majority used planning for only one-time projects. Yet 50 percent of the companies surveyed admitted they were involved in long-range planning to some degree.

One conclusion drawn was that as a company grows, so do its long-range planning activities and its inclination to look to the future. Another major conclusion of this study concerned the participation of operating managers in long-range planning. Of the companies reviewed 92 percent said their operating managers did participate in the planning process. Some paid only lip service to the concept, but a majority submitted some type of departmental long-range plan. A large number based their estimates of work force needs in the future on some type of long-range plan.

Today, detailed, broad-scale, long-range corporate planning is not widespread. However, many companies do agree that they must do some sort of advance looking and managing.

Strategic Planning

This procedure—indeed, it is a most elaborate one—began to receive emphasis in the 1970s. The major change in emphasis went from using the past, called *extrapolative planning*, to attempting to foresee the future by using strategic planning. Although it is long-range in nature, strategic planning permits the setting of goals concerning the overall direction of the company for the next several years.

Of special note is the continuous nature of this planning. As suggested in Fig. 5.4, all the six types of plans interrelate. Specific tasks are performed at designated times during the year, but overlap is common with considerable replanning efforts. The final result, in truth, is never obtained since constant revisions are necessary as economic conditions and markets change.

Four aspects of strategic planning should be noted:

1. It is long-range, depending on the industry, extending from 3 years (for a food processor) to 30 years (for a public utility).
2. It is the responsibility of the company's senior executives representing all the major departments—marketing, engineering, materials, manufacturing, human resources, management information, and finance.
3. Strategic planning is a primary commitment of the necessary resources to develop, critique, and publish the strategic plan.
4. It is performed best in an unstructured creative proactive environment, given a complex array of known and anticipated events, both intracompany and external government, community and environmental factors.

STRATEGIC MARKET PLANNING STEPS

True and effective SMP is a complicated effort requiring considerable expenditure of time and energy, close corporate coordination and communications, and patience. Most work done today under the guise of SMP is really intermediate—or inaccurate long-range planning. True market planning is still a rarity and involves a complicated sequence of activities.

The general steps are the same for almost all industries, but they must be tailored to individual company needs. A definite program must be established after considerable thought, and it must be adhered to with some degree of rigidity. The steps necessary for successful SMP are as follows.

1. *Understand the company's strategic business plan objectives.* The first step in market planning is understanding the company's goals, often called the *objectives* of the business. This involves a review using clear, sharp considerations of past trends, thinking ahead to the desires of the company and anticipating what situations might evolve. This objective is achieved by reviewing business issues, problems, and successes.

   For example, the objectives of one company might include planned investment, turnover desired, and ROI expected. The objectives of the marketing department within this company, as summarized on a worksheet like that shown in Fig. 5.5, might be as follows:[13]

   • Volume of sales desired
   • Growth anticipated
   • Profit percentage by product line
   • Markets to be approached

   The sales department might list their objectives as

   • Net sales
   • Facilities planned
   • Division investment
   • Community and employee relations

2. *Select the personnel to undertake this program.* Of understandable importance is the type of individuals who make the long-range plan. It is possible to take one of several approaches: most smaller companies use an individual either full- or part-time, some use staff specialists, others obtain assistance from outside or internal consultants, and still others use a long-range planning committee. Some larger companies hire a full-time staff to help in the planning analysis. Some companies use their marketing organization chart (Fig. 5.6) as a point of reference. There is no particular best method of selecting the mode of operation for the plan. Judgment is important, and often parallel approaches can be used.

3. *Review available information; then select the method of approach.* In practice, there are two general methods of approaching the market planning task. The first is to study the established corporate goals and then use a long-range plan to understand and reach these goals. The second is for the marketing department to calculate its own future as accurately as it can without regard to other divisions of the company or any particular emphasis on goals. Both approaches have been tried successfully, and there is no right or wrong approach. It is up to the company involved to evaluate both, weigh one against the other to see which has the most desirable pattern, and then fit it into the overall market plan.

   Should the approach be that taken by the marketing department, the method must be consistent with any previously established companywide objectives. By disseminating these data to the individuals involved, the sales manager can transform the broad, long-term company objective to specific plans for the department.

Con-trol no.	Item	19_	19_	19_	19_	19_	19_	19_	19_	19_	19_
	Sales value of 40-hour capacity										
101	Target										
102	Previous target										
	Market										
103	Present estimate										
104	Previous estimate										
	Net sales										
105	Target										
106	Percent of 40-hour capacity										
107	Percent of market										
108	Previous target										
109	Percent of 40-hour capacity										
110	Percent of market										
	Earnings before taxes										
111	Target										
112	Percent of net sales										
113	Previous target										
114	Percent of net sales										
	Facilities program										
115	Capital										
116	Authority expense										
117	Total										
	Average investment										
118	Target										
119	Turnover										
120	Percent of return before taxes										

FIG. 5.5   Worksheet of company objectives. (*Source: American Brake Shoe Company.*)

4. *Establish the marketing department policies to guide the plan.*   The next step in market planning is to establish department policies. Such policies are normally general statements or understandings which will channel the thinking and actions of the entire department into the long-range plan. For members of marketing departments, it often includes a consideration of the production characteristics, the complexity of the manufacturing, the degree of product specialization, the capacity and flexibility of facilities and warehousing, and the quality requirements.

A typical policy statement of a department might include the following:[14]

- A general statement regarding the operations
- The minimum acceptable profits to be expected
- The markets to be developed
- The general rules establishing product lines
- A statement with respect to sources of supply and policies such as reciprocity

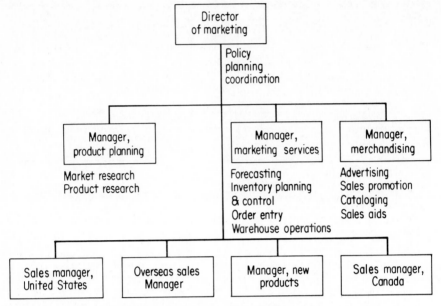

FIG. 5.6 Marketing organization chart. (Source: Ernst & Whinney.)

- A statement with respect to company organization, principles, and practices
- A statement regarding any planned research programs
- A statement regarding finances, including the use of working capital, company debt, and dividend plans
- A statement with respect to personnel policies for all levels and types of employment
- A general statement with respect to public relations

5. *Select the procedures for the course of action.* This step in the SMP includes defining all the elements. These elements may vary considerably from one business to another, but generally speaking they should include the following:

- Procedural and policy plans
- Rapidity of change
- General departmental flexibility
- Accurate delivery promises
- Capital limitations
- Customer buying criteria, such as listed in Fig. 5.7

Outside of the department's control are a number of other elements, such as political climate, economic conditions, speed of technological change, and status of labor. These generalized elements are to be considered in this step.

The SMP should enumerate tangible and intangible items for specific considerations, including

- Sales
- Cost of sales
- Existing capacity
- Administration expenses
- Capital expenses

Customer's Buying Criteria	
Price	Availability of stock vehicles
Product durability	Residual value
Low maintenance cost	Past operating experience
Service parts availability	Manufacturer's image or reputation
Service availability	Lessor financing
Specifications met	Ease of use
Financing	Few breakdowns, low maintenance
Warranty coverage	High quality

FIG. 5.7 Customers' buying criteria. *(Source: Ernst & Whinney.)*

- Research and product development
- Personnel development
- Material requirements or limitations

6. *Establish a budget, including methods of reviewing the program.*   A budget is an integral part of any long-range plan. It can be a statement of expected results in numerical and financial terms, or it can be just a complex set of the expected results of the policies and procedures which would come from long-range consideration. It may include methods of correlating and relating short- and long-range programs. It often includes a flexible timetable which gives the planners an opportunity to make whatever moves might be necessary. One part of the budget is the provision for periodic review. Normally the market plan is analyzed once a year, but it can be done as frequently as every 6 months. Refer to Fig. 5.8 which can be used as a worksheet for a planning budget.

   It is often possible to set up controls on an exception basis. When there is a deviation from a norm, it can be spotted, and its correction becomes a type of review.

   Whatever the approach, it is important to establish the budget, measure the results against this budget (in either numerical or intangible measures), and exercise whatever type of action is necessary for the future.

7. *Select the analytical techniques to guide the plan.*   A number of techniques can be used in the market planning efforts, including such basic techniques as historical statistics, forecasting, and Gantt charts. Intermediate tools include the use of trends, various index indicators, and extrapolations. Advanced techniques include operations research, PERT (Program Evaluation and Review Technique), linear programming, and the technique of simulation. (For details, refer to Chaps. 17 and 31.)

   The actual decision of which technique to use depends on the accuracy required, the complexity of the problem, the validity and accuracy of the input data, and the results desired.

8. *Summarize salient points and conclusions; then present the plan to executive management.*   This step incorporates the most important information obtained and the conclusions drawn from these data. In the market study, these points might include

   - Accomplishments in the marketplace
   - Market share (sales) by product
   - Market and government regulation limitations by type of product
   - Distribution-channel problems and advantages
   - Pricing methods and consumer reaction

| (Control no.) | | | | Estimated costs | | | | |
Step	Task no.	Description	Documents required	Salaries	Expenses	Capital equipment	Target date	Responsibility

FIG. 5.8 The budget. *(Source: Ernst & Whinney.)*

- Competitive position
- Gross margin by product
- Purchase rationale decisions of buyers

Figure 5.9 is a market analysis summary for the R. G. CEPT Company, a fictitious but representative company which illustrates selected market planning steps.

9. *Write a draft of the SMP.*   This draft of the plan—and there must be a tentative document—highlights the initial SMP. Emphasis of the plan should reflect the proposed future distribution network (listed by product market segments), type of product development, investment in customer service inventory, and a mandatory forecast of sales.

10. *Recheck the initial decision for validity.*   Review the efforts and decisions to date; then examine the possibility of alternative courses of action. There is seldom a marketing plan which does not have reasonable alternatives. These should be evaluated and a decision made either to stay on the established course or to change direction. It is necessary to recheck the validity of the sales projection and take whatever corrective action is called for.

11. *Modify the SMP draft and obtain executive approval.*   The marketing department usually sets the tone of the company. Although the SMP should be developed by this department, a thorough executive review usually calls for selective modifications. Some modifications are caused by recent changes in the economic and/or market conditions which have occurred since the preparation of the draft.

    For whatever revisions are made, executive written approval should be obtained. An example of the R. G. CEPT Company revised sales forecast, which reduces sales targets of low-margin products, is furnished in Fig. 5.10.

12. *Issue the modified plan and the reasons for the plan within the company.* Obviously considerable efforts are required in successful SMP. In reality, it involves comprehending the company's objectives and uses techniques which permit it to control the company's future. Companies engaged in this form of planning learn that there is a side benefit when plans including the company objectives, department goals, and so forth are publicized at least in a summary-style document. A new spirit emerges; individuals take the goals as their own or

R. G. CEPT Co. Market Analysis, by Segments

Product Line	Year					Buying Criteria Priorities	Competitive Environment
	1980	1981	1982	1983	1984		
Bicycles:							
Market units sold	801,763	797,623	861,011	901,731	916,471	1. Available in stock	• Wilburn Corporation is traditionally the strongest competitor, but Whitehall has grown recently to near parity with Wilburn. Montford, historically the third major factor in this segment, has lost share in the past year or two.
R. G. CEPT sales	26,192	29,673	24,111	25,371	25,374	2. Price	
Percentage of market	3.3	3.7	2.8	2.8	2.8	3. Company reputation	
Tricycles:							
Market units sold	371,816	367,418	359,714	352,816	341,699	1. Available in stock	• Chief competitor is Montford followed by Wilburn and Bradford. All currently have greater market shares than R. G. CEPT. Wilburn and Bradford have remained in relatively stable market share positions while Montford has experienced rapid growth in this segment over the last several years.
R. G. CEPT sales	18,219	20,943	19,065	17,994	17,061	2. Attractiveness	
Percentage of market	4.9	5.7	5.3	5.1	5.0	3. Price	
CEPTmobile:							
Market units sold	473	861	1,033	1,161	1,342	1. Low maintenance	• R. G. CEPT is the largest supplier in this segment with Oakwood a distant second. No other manufacturer has gained better than 12% share of market on average over the past 7 years. There does not appear to be any significant trend in changes in relative market position.
R. G. CEPT sales	423	700	805	863	954	2. Ease of use	
Percentage of market	89.4	81.3	77.9	74.3	71.1	3. Warranty coverage	

FIG. 5.9 R. G. CEPT Co. market analysis by segments. (*Source: Ernst & Whinney.*)

R. G. CEPT Co./1985 Forecast

Product Line	Original			Revised	
	Units	Sales Value (000)	Gross Margin	Units	Sales Value (000)
Bicycles:					
Single-Speed	19,770	$1,463	8%	7,919	$ 586
3- and 5-Speed	3,532	332	22%	8,478	797
10-Speed	5,122	584	12%	1,851	211
TOTAL	28,424	$2,379	11%	18,248	$1,594
Tricycles:					
Standard	11,647	$ 396	12%	5,235	$ 178
Chrome Seat and Wheels	5,037	272	41%	10,815	584
TOTAL	16,684	$ 668	31%	16,050	$ 762
CEPTmobile:					
Standard	398	$1,216	23%	462	$1,411
Deluxe	383	1,398	28%	437	1,596
CMJ Special	159	819	30%	166	854
TOTAL	940	$3,433	26%	1,065	$3,861
GRAND TOTAL	46,048	$6,480	21%	35,363	$6,217

FIG. 5.10 R. G. CEPT Co. 1985 forecast. (Source: Ernst & Whinney.)

departmental goals and strive to achieve the objectives. There should be no concern that the wrong person might learn of these goals, since generally speaking these are internally oriented. Even if a company's sales or profit objective should become known on the outside, it might not be harmful since it gives a progressive impression of the firm. Once plans are stated, they should be disseminated to all interested parties. The hourly employee within the corporation must be included.

13. *Implement the program, including a schedule of activities.* Implementation of the SMP might seem easy, but it necessitates a great deal of effort. Part of the implementation is to establish a schedule. This schedule is similar to a "budget" of the planned effort, noting various checkpoints to ascertain the progress.

14. *Evaluate progress; replan as necessary.* Experience indicates that the plan is changed more often than it is used without revision. Usually, any change occurs with regard to timing and not in the steps of the action to be taken. Sometimes the loss of a key sales individual or a large surge of business demands that efforts be made in other directions. Should this happen, the plan should not be destroyed, but merely modified for a time.

    During the plan period, a number of problems arise, and a considerable amount of important information is gathered which should be analyzed at the end of the 6-month period. Whatever changes are necessary should be made in the plan. If trouble appears inevitable, corrective action should be taken. If problems emerge, they should be tackled. Ample opportunity must exist to examine the plan and redirect it as necessary.

15. *Use the results and act on the decisions from the plan.* The information gained from the planning must be used, or else too much work will have been wasted (perhaps in exploring new product lines or in relation to manpower additions and training). Irrespective of the information which comes from planning, the data must be gathered, disseminated, and integrated into the company's operations. Increases in the effort of people and monetary investment may be necessary, but they will be for naught if the results are not used. This comment may seem unnecessary, but so few companies have realized the results of their efforts that we stress it here.

A REPRESENTATIVE SMP

Figure 5.11 shows an SMP for the R. G. CEPT Company. This plan considers the company's strategic objectives to establish a market strategy and then develops a method to attain them.

SALES INVENTORY MANAGEMENT POLICY

Guidance should be provided by marketing in terms of an inventory management policy. Most managers realize that inventory systems should answer the three basic questions of what, how much, and when. This is not easy, but it should be done through the establishment of a sales inventory management policy. This policy might include these typical contents:

> We desire to maintain sufficient inventory to meet our customer's requirements at a competitive quality and price. The company further desires to maintain its investment

A Representative Strategic Market Plan, R. G. CEPT Co.

Strategic Objective	Strategy	Plan
1. Meet company return on sales objective of 14%.	Emphasize sales or products with higher gross margin.	Modify original sales forecast, increasing sales targets of CEPT-mobile, decreasing targets of single- and three-speed bicycles and of the standard tricycle.
2. Increase sales of CEPTmobile from last year's $2,976,183 to $3,861,000 this year.	Expand number of distributors for CEPTmobile.	Set up marketing program for southwestern United States. Study feasibilty of using golf club shops in Florida.
3. Reduce cost of producing the standard tricycle.	Seek new sources for purchased materials.	Identify all purchased class A and B parts; then conduct detailed price quotations and negotiations.

FIG. 5.11 A representative strategic market plan for R. G. CEPT Co. *(Source: Ernst & Whinney.)*

in inventories at as low a level as possible but consistent with the customer service requirements. To achieve this objective, this inventory management policy is used as an overall guide to achieve the performance desired in the company. The responsibility to implement this policy is assigned to the inventory coordinator.

To achieve maximum customer service and profits, we utilize the following guidelines:

1. A forecast, developed by the marketing department, is to be used as a guiding factor in inventory investment planning.

2. Inventory stratification will be performed and items controlled based on the ABC classification.

3. Inventory investment dollar and turnover targets will be established based on type (raw material, work in process, finished goods, product line) and ABC classification.

4. Safety stock and order quantities will differ according to the classification. Class A items will be closely monitored, and class C items will have higher safety stock and order quantities with less frequent reorders.

5. Excess and obsolete inventory will be identified, closely monitored, and disposed of rapidly.

6. Substitution of material will be permitted to utilize excess stock or meet customer requirements provided appropriate approvals are obtained.

7. Vendor-rejected material will be debited immediately against the vendor's account and speedily returned.

8. Accuracy of inventory transactions, i.e., counting and posting to records, is of paramount importance to achieve a high level of perpetual record balance and actual stockroom on-hand accuracy.

9. Reports will be submitted monthly, indicating actual dollars and units measured against the previously approved inventory investment targets.

10. Turnover of inventory, in times per year, based on cost of sales should be at least the following:

    a. Raw material   6
         Work in process   4
         Finished goods   4

    b. Class A   6
         Class B   4
         Class C   3

    c. Product 1   3
         Product 2   8
         Product 3   5

11. Service to customers will be based on these levels of stock availability and days to replenish stock-out inventory:

Inventory Class	Stock Availability	Days to Replenish Inventory
A (key items)	98%	3
B	96%	5
C	90%	10

12. Obsolete and slow-moving inventory, compared to the forecast and actual customer orders, shall not exceed a 1-month supply.

13. Accuracy of inventory records, by comparing perpetual book value to actual value, shall exceed the following: class A, 98 percent; class B, 96 percent; and class C, 92 percent.

LONG-TERM SALES FORECASTING

Forecasting is covered in detail in Chap. 9. But since it is an integral part of strategic market planning, a few comments and important observations are made here.

When this type of planning was first used, a monthly, quarterly, and/or annual analysis of sales was often made. From this developed a manufacturing plan to use in the future. The more sophisticated companies would prepare elaborate charts and attempt to determine definite schedules for future periods. In a later period the marketing department would tell the production department what to produce and/or what to keep in stock. Few economic forecasts were available, and often field opinions from sales personnel and executives in the various sales districts resulted in the forecast of the coming year.

More recently, the errors in forecasts have been decreasing,[15] but companies are still misled by dramatic economic changes, kinds of product modifications, customer desires, deviations in production capacity, etc. A point of diminishing returns in forecasting improvement can be reached, so caution is advised before extensive efforts are made to refine these techniques.

The various techniques that can assist in the market plan range from the basic analysis of historical statistics and current bookings to the complicated techniques of linear programming and computer simulation. Any company that plans for the longer range immediately discovers an ardent desire for good historical statistics about the company's activities. Often this information concerning sales, production, shipments, etc., is not available, and the company has to re-create data for the last year or two. Special emphasis should be placed on the most recent year's activities. The importance of historical and continuing statistics cannot be overstressed, for it becomes the historical basis on which to forecast the future. The company must know what has happened in the immediate past, or it must compile the information that is not readily available.

A variety of methodologies are used in producing market forecasts, with the following being the key ones:[16]

Expert Opinion. Knowledgeable people are selected and asked to assign importance and probability ratings to various possible future developments. The most refined version, called the *Delphi method*, puts experts through several rounds of event assessment, during which they keep refining their assumptions and judgments. However, several managers working together can use a worksheet such as Fig. 5.12 to summarize their opinions.

Gantt Charts. Listing information in tabulated form makes it difficult to quickly note highs and lows in any certain pattern. One effective technique to show information graphically is the *Gantt chart*. This graphical presentation is very effective for displaying information. It can be used to indicate forecast, backlogs, production capacity, available workers, and similar factors. The Gantt chart of backlog information, for example, can be used to project an estimated workload and to see where problems are arising and where extra efforts such as overtime, transfer of personnel, etc., will be necessary.

Position	Duties	Type of data	Type and modification	Paper form	Frequency	
Sales engineer	Obtain basic information by sales district Include options and variables Note any trends and potential new customers	Units	None	Memo	Quarterly Monthly if appropriate	Flow of data
District manager	Consolidate district forecast Detail by model plus variables and options	Units and dollars	None	List	Quarterly Monthly if appropriate	
Product sales manager	Recommend and assist in preparation of forecast	Units and dollars	None	Memo	Quarterly Monthly if appropriate	
General sales manager	Determine forecast Publish after approval	Units and dollars	Yes, by percent	Form	Quarterly	
Vice president, manufacturing	Approve forecast	Units	Yes, by history	Form	Quarterly	
Production and inventory control manager	Check forecast	Units	Yes, by judgment	Form	Monthly	

FIG. 5.12 Information sequence for a qualitative forecast. *(Source: Ernst & Whinney.)*

Trend Extrapolation. Researchers fit best-fitting curves (classified as linear, quadratic, or S-shaped growth curves) through past time series to serve as a basis for extrapolation. This method can be very unreliable in that new developments can completely alter the expected direction of movement.

Extrapolations of trends are well suited to manufacturing and its related forecasts, since this approach is adaptable to routine clerical procedures. An extrapolation is made, and an average forecast is determined for a period. This technique has a built-in danger: it assumes the conditions of the past will hold true in the future.

Trend Correlation. Analysts correlate various time series in the hope of identifying lead and lagging relationships that can be used for forecasting.

One type of forecast of demand is to use a trend line. In such a technique, past demands are considered and trend lines established. Control limits can be developed which are based on past fluctuations of actual sales from the trend. Usually a certain percentage (often 95 percent or more) of the demand can be expected to fall within these limits.

Dynamic Modeling.   Researchers build sets of equations that attempt to describe the underlying system. The coefficients in the equations are fitted by statistical means. Econometric models including more than 300 equations, for example, are used to forecast changes in the U.S. economy.

Cross-Impact Analysis.   Market experts identify a set of key trends which are high in importance and/or probability. The question is put: If event A occurs, what will be the impact on all other trends? Then the results are used to build sets of domino chains, with one event triggering others.

Multiple Scenarios.   Researchers build pictures of alternative future conditions, each internally consistent and with a certain probability of happening. The major purpose of the scenarios is to stimulate contingency planning.

Demand and/or Hazard Forecasting.   Researchers identify major events that would greatly affect the firm. Each event is rated for its convergence with several major trends taking place in society. It is also rated for its appeal to each major public segment of the society. The higher the event's convergence and appeal, the higher its probability of occurring. The highest-scoring events are researched further.

Wright's Indicators.   In 1953, a Standard Oil of New Jersey economist, Ashley Wright, developed a device for determining turns in the business cycle. Wright used the normal distribution curve, often called a *bell-shaped curve*, and noted that the upturns and downturns in a large number of business indicators would show such a distribution pattern. By using Wright's theory, a general business cycle can be forecast and used as part of long-range planning. This concept also has applications in utilizing internal corporate statistics.

Linear Programming.   One example of a linear program shows the best balance among production stability, inventory level, and customer service. Factors such as demand characteristics, cost of holding inventory, cost of modifying production levels, etc., can be put together in a whole range of alternatives from which a model can be developed. Linear programming is often based on rather rigid assumptions but has applications in production planning.

Simulation.   One outgrowth of operations research has been simulation, which normally uses computers but sometimes uses manual methods. Through simulation, a whole production complex can be evaluated by inserting a number of variables into a program. Changes in product mix, forecast, delivery, quality, and seasonal effects are examples of variables that can be incorporated. Computer simulation is highly mathematical. And although an exact duplicate of the actual operation is seldom obtained, the results are more than adequate to simulate the factory operations and so estimate the behavior in advance.

New-Product Introduction Coordination

All products have a life cycle, but each varies in its characteristics. The life cycle (refer to Fig. 5.13) consists of five phases: development, introduction, growth,

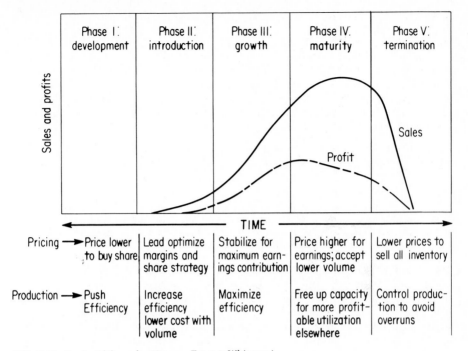

FIG. 5.13   Product life cycle. (*Source: Ernst & Whinney.*)

maturity, and termination. In some of the high-technology products, the entire cycle lasts as little as 1 to 2 years, whereas many customer products live for decades.

Product life cycles can be a key in developing cost, price, forecast, and production strategies for a product line. Life cycles can be constructed for each product line by plotting its known history against time and projecting it into the future. Profits peak during the growth phase, so a wise company closely monitors the profit trend during the maturity phase for guidance concerning dropping a product line.

SALES AND VENDOR CAPACITY PLANNING

Vendor capacity planning is a methodology which expands considerably on the time-tested, blanket-order technique. Thus, the sales department (acting as the vendor) can establish blanket-order contracts with the customer's purchasing department; this greatly facilitates both the company's inventory and production planning. These types of contracts, which are difficult to establish but well worth the effort, have three essential ingredients from the selling company's (vendor) perspective:[17]

1. A company that is willing and able to reserve capacity for its customer's requirements
2. Carefully worded purchase orders with detailed clarification of the contract
3. Monthly releases based on the customer's master schedule which is incorporated into the company's MRP system

You might say that this is one step beyond the traditional blanket order. This contract is characterized by cancellation privileges for either party within a certain time, such as with advance notice of 6 months.

The terminology on the VCP purchase order should be similar to the wording below. You, as the vendor, should carefully review the terminology.

> This purchase order is written to establish a vendor capacity planning blanket order with the Dorshwood Foundry Company. It is valid for 1-year period beginning January 1, 1985. The forgings covered by this contract, along with their minimum monthly schedule and unit prices, are as listed below. Delivery will be FOB at our plant. We will issue forging releases giving you a 30-day shop lead time for all finished requirements and 60-day lead times for raw material. We will also furnish you, at no obligation whatsoever to our company, a forecast of our anticipated requirements for the third, fourth, fifth, and sixth months in the future. Each month's release will average 96,000 pounds (lb) of forgings produced by your company, but individual monthly releases can vary plus or minus 20 percent on a month-to-month basis. You will reserve production capacity each month for approximately 96,000 lb of forgings. We will machine-load the forging work center to this established level, using the production standards that you have previously furnished us.

The supplier reserves an amount of capacity for the customer's needs. The input is in the form of purchase order releases and goes into the work-in-process "load." The output of this backlog or load is equal to the production capacity reserved. When the customer's business increases, more orders are placed and the load increases. Thus, VCP solves problems by establishing a contractual communication between the vendor and the main customers. Follow these steps in establishing VCP:

1. *Select candidates for VCP.*   One rule of thumb is to find out which customers and parts dominate your production. Single-source customers, captive companies, and hard-to-find materials are good starting points for VCP. Parts in high demand that are subject to rejection for quality and raw materials that become critical parts are also candidates. The output of this step is a list of potential sources of parts and customers for a VCP program.

2. *Obtain a forecast of requirements.*   Looking out to a time horizon at least 1 year or preferably up to 3 years, obtain a forecast of the customer's requirements. Rough estimates based on historical usage will suffice. The output is a forecast by monthly periods.

3. *Collect detailed information about possible VCP customers.*   Even though you may have dealt with the company for many years, it is uncertain whether you will have adequate data. Complete a VCP vendor questionnaire (Fig. 5.14) with special emphasis on capacity information. The output is a completed VCP questionnaire.

4. *Interview potential VCP purchasing agents.*   Inquire about their interest and willingness for a VCP arrangement, their credit ratings, freight costs, compatible production facilities, and even management ability. The output is a VCP customer list.

5. *Complete request for quotations.*   Stress that this is a potential VCP contract, and specify quantity price breaks and methods that you use to calculate capacity. The output is a request for quotations.

6. *Select VCP candidates.*   Use a comparative request-for-quotation review matrix, and be certain to structure the capacity data carefully. The output is a comparative summary.

```
Name of potential vendor _____
Prepared by _____ As of _____
```

```
Annual sales                                      _____
Location of plants                                _____
Number of employees                               _____
Type of union                                     _____
Date of last strike                               _____
Number of shifts worked                           _____
Total floor space available                       _____
Type of buildings                                 _____
Date built                                        _____
Type of special equipment                         _____
General housekeeping conditions                   _____
Quality control methods                           _____
Production capacity measure                       _____
Number of machines used for our production        _____
```

FIG. 5.14   VCP survey checklist. (*Source: Ernst & Whinney.*)

7. *Negotiate with the selected VCP customer.*   Use time-honored, face-to-face discussions. Since the quotation is not necessarily the best or final price, this might be determined through further negotiation. The output is a summary of negotiated agreement.

8. *Receive blanket-style purchase orders.*   Stress the production capacity measure, quantity, item specifications, authorized raw-material requirements, and setup/changeover costs. Specify the lead time required by the production department; allow for a certain percentage of product to be rushed, if necessary. The output is the customer's purchase order.

9. *Acknowledge the purchase order.*   Have your customer specify any mandatory requirements on the front of the purchase order, such as timing of order releases and increase or decrease in volume. The output is sales acknowledgment.

10. *Invite the customer's representatives to meet your production employees.*   A long-term relationship should develop. The output is a reference list of people with position titles.

11. *Accept purchase order schedule release.*   This release is usually received from the customer monthly, via buyer or schedulers, and it shows item due dates and any one-time purchases. Use MPSs or the shipping schedules. The output is the monthly release and forecast.

12. *Monitor performance.*   Check the use of capacity reserved, watch customer delivery trends, and monitor late shipments. The output is aggregate inventory commitment. Use reports on requirements using capacity measure; open-stock status for expediting; and backlog, by customer.

13. *Plan for next year.*   Look for new sources, customers, items for VCP, contract improvements, and ways to better customer relations.

Potential VCP contracts, established by your sales and customer purchasing departments, exist today that can reap benefits far in excess of the time necessary to set up the agreement. With increased emphasis on MRP systems, many foresee VCP contracts being used in one-half of the companies in 5 years.

MAKE OR BUY—A COMPLEX DECISION

The principle behind these two choices is to determine the most economical method for a company to obtain production items. Three considerations are when to do it, how to do it, and who can help.

The challenge for the marketing department is to assist in obtaining a rational decision because it is quite easy—by varying certain assumptions, such as the weight of fixed versus variable costs—to prove either a make or a buy decision is correct. Remember that what the company and the customer wish is the most economical overall price consistent with a reliable source of supply. Numerous companies feel they should make all parts themselves. This is a noble concept but often the more costly choice.

Although Fig. 5.15 is a useful worksheet, a number of points merit consideration:

1. The decision should not be made by only one department.
2. It is often false to assume a company can always make an item at lower cost rather than purchase it.
3. Purchasing is responsible for taking the first step in make-or-buy studies.
4. Many companies ignore make-or-buy decisions, but considerable profit improvement may be the result of such work.
5. A good time for these analyses is during the planning of a new product or plant addition.
6. A make-or-buy study must include all possible aspects of costs.
7. Care should be taken in considering overhead costs; some can be very misleading.
8. If you have a seasonal product which ties up production, a buy can have special cost consideration.
9. Use a budgeting committee or a special ad hoc group to help in the make-or-buy decisions.

UPDATING THE STRATEGIC PLAN

From time to time, companies must stand back and critically review their overall marketing effectiveness. This goes beyond carrying out the annual plan, profitability, and efficiency controls. Marketing is one of the major areas in which rapid obsolescence of objectives, policies, strategies, and programs is a constant possibility. Because of the rapid changes in the marketing environment, each company should periodically reassess its overall approach to the marketplace.

Marketing effectiveness is not so simple. Good results may be due to a company's being in the right place at the right time rather than the consequence of effective marketing management. Improvements in one division's marketing might boost results from good to excellent. At the same time, another division might have poor results in spite of the best SMP. Replacing the present marketing managers might only make things worse.

The marketing effectiveness of a company or division is reflected in the degree to

I. Basic information

Prepared by _____ Date _____ Dept. _____

Item no. _____ Description _____ Annual usage _____

Commodity code no. _____ Blueprint no. _____

Present supplier _____ Quotation dated _____

Department _____ Estimate dated _____

Return on investment target _____

II. Calculations of Unit Cost; pro rated

Cost Item or Category	1. Cost to Make	2. Cost to Buy	3. Cost to Lease	Accumulative ± Difference	
				1 to 2	1 to 3
Material Labor Overhead Others: Paper processing Equipment Tools/dies Implementation Subtotal Purchased goods Transportation Inventory carrying Sales of scrap material					
Net Cost Totals					

III. Recommended action: _____ Make _____ Buy _____ Lease _____ By _____

        Approved by _____ Date _____

FIG. 5.15 Make, buy, or lease analysis. *(Source: Ernst & Whinney.)*

which it exhibits five major attributes of a marketing orientation: customer philosophy, integrated marketing organization, adequate marketing information, strategic orientation, and operational efficiency.

Indicators of Progress

Managers have a tendency to become disenchanted because normally market plans do not manifest an immediate return on the efforts invested. Therefore, some indicators of progress will help in not only selling the plan and the continuing efforts, but also giving the individuals involved an idea of the progress:

1. Recognition by key management individuals of the impact of the plan on the company. If agreement is achieved among the management team, there is a much greater opportunity for success.

2. Continuing top management support demonstrated by the use of the SMP. If this support is lacking, it can be taken as a negative.

3. Intelligent and enthusiastic participation of the personnel involved in the SMP. Included also are the integration of the planning system and existing management system and reliable information collected and transmitted for the day-to-day operations as well as for the long-range planning.

4. Decided improvement in the information-gathering, reporting, and decision-making processes. Since the plan itself is slow in developing, more effective management does result from the imposed input of information.

5. Career success of the one person responsible for the long-range plan. This is true whether this person is an individual or the chairperson of the market planning committee. If the efforts are well received for performing certain services, such as feeding back information, it is an indication that effective planning is being achieved.

6. A continuous program of training, indoctrination, and motivation regarding the long-range plan.

7. The use of statistical measures, called *key indicators* (refer to Fig. 5.16), which, by showing monthly progress against preset target goals, indicate through trend-line graphs the results of sales efforts.

Replanning

The plan must include provisions for increases and decreases, both for the department as a whole and for specific aspects of the program. The plan must be flexible because of changes in management concepts and people involved, all of which may have an effect on the initial long-range plan.[18] Someone once remarked that what is needed is a system for changing your system. You need a super system.[19] To a certain extent, this is true of market planning.

Replanning, then, involves looking back at the initial plan and determining where there have been slippages or delays, and whether the plan is achieving the results anticipated, and whether economic or other conditions necessitate a revision.

Reasons for Failure

Why does planning fail? A number of reasons, listed here, can alert you to some of the pitfalls:

1. Failure to adequately explain and sell the importance of the strategic market plan to the executives and managers involved. If an environment of acceptance is not created at the onset, the long-range plan will not have a good chance for success.

2. Failure to plan in advance for a disciplined, step-by-step approach that uses the most modern techniques applicable.

3. Failure to work out in advance the path to follow and a disciplined adherence to this plan as time progresses.

4. Failure of management to recognize the time required by the individuals involved in the long-range plan.

October   Marketing   C.L. Smith

Report no.   Department   Prepared by

#	Indicator	Measure	Target	This month	Progress to date months J F M A M J J A S O N D	Scale	Last year	YTD
1	Shipments (YTD)	Compared with last year	117%	90%		· 120% · 100% · 80%		
2	Backlog of orders (000)	5th month in future	$250	$190		· 350 · 250 · 150		
3	Forecast achievement (dollars)	This month actual shipment vs. Third month previous forecast	90%	74%		· 100% · 85% · 70%		
4	Order entry time	more than 4 days	10%	18%		· 20% · 10% · 0%		
5	Cancellations	Value this month	$20,000	$18,731		· 40,000 · 20,000 · 0		
6	Field complaints	Number received	0	4		· 20 · 10 · 0		
7	Catalog distribution	Number mailed out	610	290		· 750 · 500 · 250		
8	Cost per ad inquiry	Cost of ads divided by number of inquiries	$ 76	$ 93		· 150 · 100 · 50		
9	Delivery performance	On time vs. original promise	95%	90%		· 100% · 90% · 80%		

FIG. 5.16 Key indicator worksheet. (Source: *Ernst & Whinney*.)

5. Failure to put one individual in charge, as a committee chairperson, a coordinator, or the sole person to oversee the planning. Along with this, there is often a failure in the delegation of the work. One person can be in charge in small and medium companies, but this person must be given the privilege of obtaining assistance as necessary.

6. Failure to establish an implementation schedule and to regularly evaluate the progress of the long-range plan; replanning as necessary.

7. Failure to define each problem as it arises and to sort out the symptoms from the causes.

8. Failure of the executive in charge to replace the long-range planning coordinator or committee if this individual or group should fail. Since market planning is difficult, many who assume they have the ability to be the coordinator or chairperson of the committee discover they are not capable of carrying out this challenging assignment. Should this point be reached, the individual must be removed and replaced by a more competent individual.

Criteria for Evaluation

A number of questions serve as a guide to whether the long-range plan is succeeding and enable evaluations to be made:

- Have we achieved an open-minded, enthusiastic attack in the market planning?
- Does the plan evaluate those things influencing the corporate growth?
- Are the strengths and weaknesses of the department adequately analyzed and studied?
- Does the department have capabilities in the various functions to support the long-range plan?
- Is there a good, practical timetable that is also both flexible and enforceable?
- Have provisions been made for alternative courses of action?
- Is one individual or committee specifically charged with the responsibility of developing the market plan?
- Are the key operating personnel committed to the plan?
- Are reviews being made on a continuing basis and roadblocks being removed?
- Have short-term problems been ignored in order to concentrate on longer-range plans?
- Does the department have sufficient courage to stick to the long-range plan in spite of temporary problems?
- Do you have adequate yardsticks to evaluate the performance so you know whether the objectives are being reached?

MARKETING/PRODUCTION AND INVENTORY CONTROL—CONTINUING RELATIONS

Marketing's success in establishing a firm forecast for production to follow is rarely achieved. If for no other reason, economic conditions make a fixed forecast impossible.

The SMP has to be constantly updated, so both marketing and PIC must maintain a continuous dialogue if the enterprise is to succeed.

REFERENCES

1. Philip Kotler, *Marketing Management; Analysis, Planning and Control*, 4th ed., Prentice-Hall, Englewood Cliffs, N.J., 1980, p. 65.

2. Peter F. Drucker, *Management: Tasks, Responsibilities, Practices*, Harper & Row, New York, 1973, p. 62.

3. Kotler, op. cit., p. 593.

4. Robert Weinberg, "Developing Management Strategies for Short-Term Profits and Long-Term Growth," Advanced Management Research, Inc., seminar, Regency Hotel, New York, Sept. 29, 1969.

5. B. W. Scott, *Long-Range Planning in American Industry*, American Management Association, New York, 1965.

6. Henri Fayol, *General and Industrial Management*, Pitman Publishing, New York, 1949.

7. Leonard Tyler, *Forecasting the Manufacturing Program*, American Management Association, Production Executive Series, no. 27, New York, 1926.

8. A. S. Rodgers and Huge Diomer (eds.), *How to Set Up Production Control for Greater Profits*, McGraw-Hill, New York, 1930.

9. P. E. Holden, L. S. Fish, and H. L. Smith, *Top Management Organization and Control*, Stanford University Press, Stanford, Calif., 1941.

10. W. B. Donham, *Business Adrift*, McGraw-Hill, New York, 1931.

11. D. E. Lilienthal, *TVA: Democracy on the March*, Harper & Row, New York, 1944.

12. ———, "How 101 Companies Handle Corporate Planning," *Business Management*, September 1967.

13. ———, "Determining and Reporting Division Objectives," *Guide to Profit Improvement Program*, American Brake Shoe Company, Ernst & Whinney, Cleveland, Ohio, 1959.

14. David T. Kollat, Roger D. Blackwell, and James F. Robeson, *Strategic Marketing*, Holt, New York, 1972.

15. O. W. Wight, "Principles of Production Planning," *Proceedings of Ninth Annual National Conference*, APICS, Philadelphia, September 29, 1966.

16. James R. Bright and Milton E. F. Schoeman, *A Guide to Practical Technological Forecasting*, Prentice-Hall, Englewood Cliffs, N.J., 1973.

17. Robert L. Janson, "Vendor Capacity Planning," *Midwest Purchasing Magazine*, December, 1982.

18. F. R. Denham, "Network Planning Techniques in Manufacturing," *Proceedings of Fifth Annual Seminar*, Canadian Association for Production and Inventory Control, Toronto, May 12, 1966.

19. Ken Leavery, "Managing Systems Change," *Proceedings of Fifth Annual Seminar*, Canadian Association for Production and Inventory Control, Toronto, May 12, 1966.

BIBLIOGRAPHY

Kantrow, A., (ed.): *Survival Strategies for American Industry*, Wiley, New York, 1983.

Kollat, David T., Roger D. Blackwell, and James F. Robeson: *Strategic Marketing*, Holt, New York, 1972.

Kotler, Philip: *Marketing Management; Analysis, Planning and Control*, 4th ed., Prentice-Hall, Englewood Cliffs, N.J., 1980.

Payne, Bruce: "Steps in Long Range Planning," in D. W. Ewing (ed.), *Long Range Planning for Management*, Harper & Row, New York, 1964.

Sherman, P.: *Strategic Planning for Technology Industries*, Addison-Wesley, Reading, Mass., 1982.

Skinner, W.: *Manufacturing in the Corporate Strategy*, Wiley-Interscience, New York, 1978.

Steiner, G.: *Strategic Planning: What Every Manager Must Know*, Free Press, New York, 1979.

Whittaker, James B.: *Strategic Planning in a Rapidly Changing Environment*, Lexington Books, Lexington, Mass., 1978.

Strategic Manufacturing and Financial Planning

Editor

EMIL ALBERT, DBA, CPM, Associate Professor of Finance, Indiana University at South Bend, South Bend, Indiana

Strategic manufacturing and financial policy deal with those specific functional areas of the firm that provide a system designed to carry out corporate objectives in an effective manner. Manufacturing and financial policy is a subfunction of overall corporate strategic planning. This necessarily implies that long-range corporate objectives have already been established for the organization. Although these long-range corporate objectives should be explicit, often they are only implied. Consequently, formalized corporate objectives are established by the functional areas of marketing, finance, and manufacturing rather than at the corporate level.

GUIDELINES FOR DEVELOPMENT OF CORPORATE STRATEGY

Before any effort is expanded in developing and implementing strategic manufacturing and financial policy, it is necessary to develop long-range guidelines. The process should begin with a thorough analysis of market conditions and culminate with the implementation of corporate objectives.

The total sequence of activities to follow in implementing the corporate objectives is illustrated in Fig. 6.1. Each one is identified by a corresponding number:

1. *Corporate objectives.* Define the goals of the organization as a whole.
2. *Corporate strategy.* Establishes a plan by which the corporate objectives are to be achieved.
3. *Functional strategies.* Develop plans under which the major functions of marketing, manufacturing, and finance operate to implement corporate strategies.
4. *Functional policies.* Prepare statements of operating activities to be accomplished by the operating functions.
5. *Operating procedures.* Outline detailed statements regarding methods of implementing corporate objectives.

Corporate objectives relate to strategic business planning. Corporate strategy and functional strategy are discussed in this chapter. Functional policy, along with operating procedures, is partially covered in this chapter and in remaining chapters.

These five activities represent the complete sequence of steps necessary to implement the corporate objectives from inception to final detail. In the hierarchy of corporate planning, these five activities must be accomplished before the overall matter of corporate objectives can be affected. Consequently, the following discussion is provided as supplemental information to assist in establishing a proper framework for the development of strategic manufacturing and financial policy. The following introduction briefly reviews the various aspects of corporate objectives and corporate strategy as they impact on manufacturing and finance. Manufacturing and financial strategies and their corresponding functional policies are discussed in detail in this chapter as well as approaches to long-range planning. The activities involved in developing functional operating procedures are covered in detail in the other chapters.

Corporate Objectives and Strategies

The goals of the organization as a whole are established through a process of corporate strategy development and implementation. The following brief description is included so that the user is aware of the importance of developing a production and financial strategy compatible with the overall corporate objectives. The development of corporate objectives needs to be emphasized. Avoidance of possible conflicts within the hierarchy of activities and functional strategies is important if the production system is to operate effectively.

CORPORATE STRATEGY FORMULATION

The corporate strategy formulation process requires three areas of analysis: external conditions, corporate strengths and weaknesses, and management desires.

External Conditions

External conditions include factors over which the corporation has limited or no control depending on the level of competition in the industry in which the

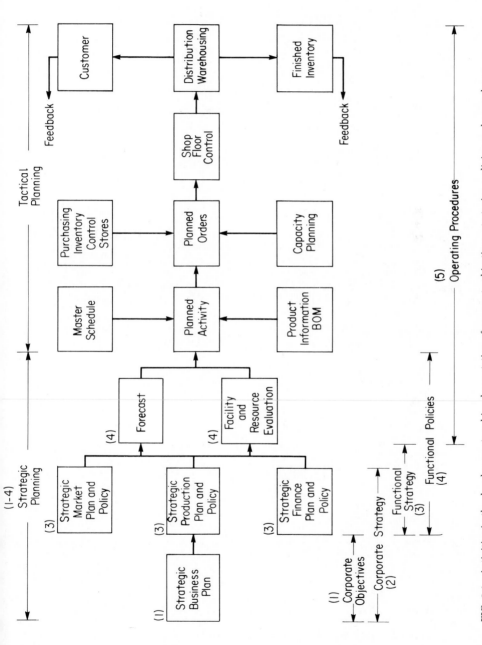

FIG. 6.1 Activities in the development and implementation of corporate objectives, strategies, policies, and procedures.

6.3

firm is operating. These external conditions can be categorized into four areas:

1. Economic conditions which include overall domestic and world economic levels and trends, sources of supply, and markets.
2. Technological developments in the industry ranging from basic research and development to current implementation of product developments. Also, process technology will impact on this area.
3. Government policies including but not limited to regulation of the industry, definition of product specifications, and limitation on foreign trade.
4. Social responsibility either accepted by the corporation as a legitimate responsibility or dictated by society through laws or mores.

Each area noted above requires an in-depth study to provide inputs into the process or corporate strategy formulation and functional strategy development.

Corporate Strengths and Weaknesses

Those capabilities that the firm can depend on or those shortcomings that should be avoided are its strengths and weaknesses. A thorough study of corporate strengths and weaknesses will provide guidance as to what the corporation can do exceptionally well and what it cannot do well from an overall position.

Organizational Attributes. The corporation needs to look at its capabilities and weaknesses, beginning with the following:

- Production, the consideration of which should include the age and location of facilities, technology employed, cost and availability of inputs of labor and material, and overall cost structure.
- Finance, including capital structure, the amount of financial leverage utilized, working capital available, and profitability of the operation.
- Marketing, including the competitiveness of the product or service, quality levels, and acceptance in the marketplace (both production and finance are covered in this chapter).
- Engineering, with emphasis on new-product development.
- Personnel, categorized into three groups: managerial, technical, and operational. Each group is significant to the success or failure of strategy implementation.

Management Desires

If the manager of the organization wants to live in Miami, or Desert Springs, or Phoenix to be able to play golf regularly, the the obvious major criterion in corporate strategy as well as production and financial strategy will be to build a facility in the proper area, close to the country club, with careful financial planning to generate sufficient cash flow to cover green fees. Likewise, other management desires may take precedence. The point is that they may not be correct, but the president does have priority.

Beyond the area of strong personal desires, there are also those personal beliefs and values that impact on the development and implementation of functional strategies. A partial list of specific beliefs and values would include ethics, religion, economics, politics, and education. Each of these impacts on top management's views and must be considered in strategy development. Those individuals involved in the preparation of a production and financial strategy must carefully consider the conflicts and compatibilities that exist among top executives who will ultimately pass judgment on the implementation of that strategy.

The sections which follow deal with formulation of corporate objectives on a limited scale and are based on the assumption that the necessary definition of the corporate objectives has been provided by the chief executive officer of the firm. If corporate objectives have not been clearly stated, effective manufacturing and financial strategy and policy cannot be established. At this point the rule is *Go ask*.

AN APPROACH TO MANUFACTURING AND FINANCIAL POLICY

Since quantitative techniques have limited value in long-range planning, the following sections provide a structured approach to establishing strategic manufacturing and financial policy, beginning with the identification of the determinants of manufacturing and financial policy. Next, a discussion of long-range planning is provided, followed by an approach to industry analysis and a description of manufacturing systems. The final topics deal with manufacturing policy and financial policy determinations as specific activities.

Determinants of Manufacturing and Financial Policy

The first determinant that impacts on strategic manufacturing and financial policy is the structure and age of the facilities in which the organization carries out the production process.

The second determinant is the evolution or life cycle through which a product or service passes from its inception to its termination. This is important because policy must change along with the evolution if the organization is to be effective in the marketplace.

The third determinant policy is the firm's manufacturing characteristics. These may range from a project system, to an assembly line, to a flow process system. It is important to be aware of how changing market conditions demand different manufacturing systems which in turn require different types of labor, material, and facilities to function effectively.

A fourth element in determining a manufacturing and financial policy is the selection of a production inventory management system that facilitates effective performance from the manufacturing system. This subject is of vital importance to manufacturing and financial policy and is covered thoroughly and in detail in other chapters.

A fifth determinant is composed of the primary decisions to be made regarding the purchase of inputs. The consideration here is the form in which inputs are purchased, ranging from basic raw material to finished product. Net-present-value analysis, a quantitative method for analyzing input decisions and cash flows, is outlined later as a method to assist in making financial policy decisions.

LONG-RANGE PLANNING AND FORECASTING

Before financial resources are committed to long-lived assets in a production system, a plan must be developed for correctly applying those resources to attain the objective of the firm. This plan includes decisions regarding facility size, location, type of equipment, and a multitude of detail elements, all of which become part of the operating production system. A long-range plan that is as close to reality as possible is the objective, but this plan is always subject to some degree of variation which may be measurable either statistically or subjectively. Variation is inevitable because we are dealing with future projections and not past events that are known. Long-range planning is, in reality, a projection of future needs expected to develop for a particular product or service, followed by a translation of those projections to physical facilities and production capabilities.

There are a multitude of approaches to long-range forecasting. Each currently in use has some benefit and some drawbacks. So the following discussion of long-range forecasting does not cover all the possible methods of accomplishing this function. Rather, this discussion provides the forecaster with information to assist in preparing an approach specifically designed for a firm's needs and, at the same time, points out possible pitfalls. Remember, once a long-range forecast is cast into manufacturing and financial policy, ultimately leading to brick-and-mortar commitments, the forecaster has given birth to a irreversible process. Although success can mean personal benefits for the forecaster, failure can generate the need for the forecaster to update a résumé quickly.

Approaches to Long-Range Forecasting

Attempts to provide accuracy in long-range forecasting have led to concepts that are very useful if fully understood but, at the same time, yield misleading results if improperly applied.

One example of an approach that is both useful and misleading is trend analysis, a form of regression analysis. It is a method for projecting history into the future by a statistical process. In its simplist form, this procedure assumes that the past is a strong indicator of what will happen.

"Rulist" Trend Approach.   A straight-line projection of the past into the future is identified here as a *rulist approach*. It is assumed that whatever has happened in the past will continue, as illustrated in Fig. 6.2.

A true rulist abhors curves. A French curve may never be used in forecasting. Such strict adherence to an approach can lead to erroneous conclusions from the forecast. One has only to look at some of the projections that have been made in the price and demand for motor fuel in recent years. Realistically, actual demand will seldom (if ever) follow the rulist. Some modification to the rulist approach is needed.

"Curvist" Trend Approach.   A second approach to long-range forecasting is the opposite of the rulist approach. In this approach, demand is expected to follow a well-defined cycle such as might be described by a sine wave. Whatever goes up must come down in a continuous curve. Straight-line demand does not occur, so rulers are not used. This type of forecasting is identified as a *curvist approach*. The curvist approach is illustrated in Fig. 6.3.

Rate-of-Change Approach.   Between the extreme approach of the rulist and curvist approaches is the *rate-of-change approach*. The rate-of-change approach

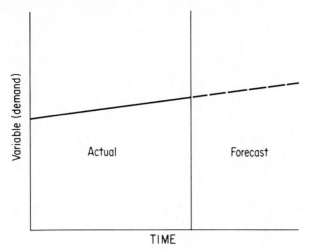

FIG. 6.2 Forecasting model for the rulist trend approach.

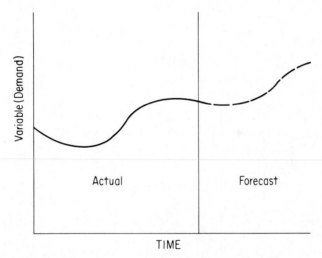

FIG. 6.3 Forecasting model for the curvist trend approach.

uses a concept of calculus, the first derivitive, which measures the slope of the forecast at any particular time. This is a measurement of the rate at which the demand is changing at a specific time. Demand changes can then be divided into six phases:

Increasing at an increasing rate—phase 1

Increasing at a constant rate—phase 2

Increasing at a decreasing rate—phase 3

Decreasing at an increasing rate—phase 4

Decreasing at a constant rate—phase 5

Decreasing at a decreasing rate—phase 6

They are illustrated and identified by phase number in Fig. 6.4.

The rate of change identifies the direction of change in the long-range forecast and the rate at which the forecast is changing. An example of the concept is illustrated in Table 6.1; the data are adjusted for seasonal variations and number of working days per month.

During February and March, sales increased at an increasing rate (phase 1), followed by a period from April to June during which they increased at a decreasing rate (phase 3). From July to November sales decreased at an increasing rate (phase 4). Finally, in December sales improved, to show a continued decrease but at a decreasing rate (phase 6). By measuring rate of change, it is possible to project what is going to happen to absolute levels, for the rate of change precedes changes in the absolute level by one-quarter cycle. For example, if the rate of change goes from an increasing to a decreasing rate of increase, this indicates that if business were to continue along the same path, then within one-quarter cycle the absolute level of demand would reach a peak and start to decline. Using rate of change makes this much easier to ascertain than trying to determine when the absolute level has peaked. In addition, there is one-quarter cycle advanced warning during which corrective action can be taken.

Product Cycles

The objective of life-cycle forecasting is to gather information which will lead to the selection of methods to develop a life cycle of the product or service being forecast.

Life Cycles.   A simple version of the life cycle would appear as the very familiar curve illustrated in Fig. 6.5. Initially, as a new product or service is introduced to the market, it is subjected to substantial changes to conform to expected markets as identified by a specific form of market forecasting. At the end of this introduction, the product enters the beginning of phase 1 as demand starts to increase at an increasing rate. During phase 1, it is difficult to satisfy demand because production is rapidly increased to meet the ever-increasing demand growth rate. As the growth

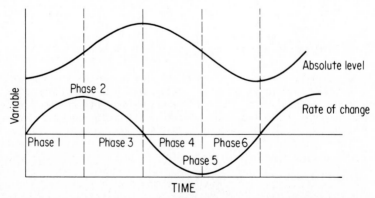

FIG. 6.4   Relationship of absolute levels of demand and the rate-of-change forecasting model.

TABLE 6.1   Rate of Change of Daily Sales

Month	Average Daily Sales, Units	Volume Change, Units	Percentage Change	Phase
January	10,000			
February	11,000	1,000	+10	1
March	12,500	1,500	+13.6	1
April	13,800	1,300	+10.4	3
May	14,600	800	+5.8	3
June	15,000	400	+2.7	3
July	15,000	0	0	
August	14,000	1,000	−6.7	4
September	13,000	1,000	−7.3	4
October	11,500	1,500	−11.5	4
November	9,500	2,000	−17.4	4
December	9,000	500	−5.3	6

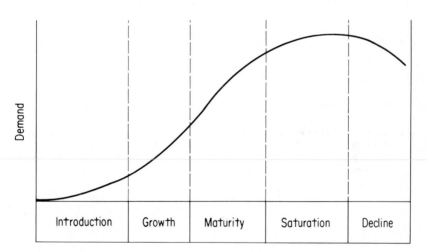

FIG. 6.5   The classical life-cycle demand curve model.

rate slows, the cycle enters a transition period from phase 1 to phase 2 and ultimately phase 3. Demand has now matured, and it is still increasing, but at a decreasing rate. Later, a further transition occurs as supply saturates the market, and demand growth has declined appreciably. Finally, demand levels off and may start to decline as it enters phase 4. Whether the last two phases are significant will depend on what steps the firm takes to revive or eliminate the product or service.

Throughout the life cycle, demand for the product or service will change, and subsequently the characteristics of the product or service will change. Different customers come into the market at different times. Also, manufacturing and financial policy emphasis change as the demand changes and other competitors enter the market. The changing characteristics of the product during the various phases are summarized in Table 6.2.

TABLE 6.2   Changing Life-Cycle Characteristics of a Product

Cycle Stage	Volume	Design	Price	Profit Margin
Introduction	Low	Unique	Very high	Loss
Growth	Low	Variable	High	High
Mature	Medium	Limited	Medium	Medium
Saturated	High	Rigid	Low	Low
Declining	Low	Variable	Medium	High

As Table 6.2 indicates, the product starts out as a low-volume, unique, high-priced product available on only a limited basis to consumers who are willing to pay the high price. As the cycle proceeds from this to a high-volume, low-priced standard product which is widely available, the characteristics change. Consequently the manufacturing and financial policy must also change in order for the production system to function effectively in the environment. This changing product characteristic places extreme demand on the production system and financial resources. Sooner or later the system is no longer efficient and must be corrected. The more rigid the system, the shorter the effective life of the production system.

Evolutionary Cycles.   A more involved and realistic approach to life-cycle analysis is the concept of a continuous evolutionary cycle, rather than a single life cycle. Figure 6.6 illustrates how the product demand follows the familiar cycle described above in the initial stages. As the rate of change in demand reaches a point of changing from phase 1 to phase 2, elements are introduced to create an increase in demand to force the demand back into phase 1. The changes that are introduced can take many forms, from minor changes in design, packaging, and price to major changes in policy and design.

Each evolutionary change has a ratchet effect. In the early stages of life cycle, the changes have the effect of moving the life cycle from phase 2 back to phase 1. Later, it becomes more difficult to keep the product's life cycle in phase 1, so the changes become more involved with moving the cycle from phase 3 back to phase 2. Ultimately, the product will proceed through the balance of the phases, finally becoming obsolete. An increase in the economic value of the facilities is accomplished since the life cycle of the product is adjusted to the life of the facilities used to produce it.

Long-Range Consideration of Risk and States of Nature Forecasting

Risk must be considered in long-range forecasting. It is not a case of whether or not to consider risk, but rather a case of the degree of risk to be considered. Along with risk, one also needs to identify conditions that exist which will affect the forecasting and, subsequently, the degree of risk involved. These conditions that are involved in forecasting but over which one has no control are usually referred to as states of nature. Both risk and states of nature are important to the long-range planning process.

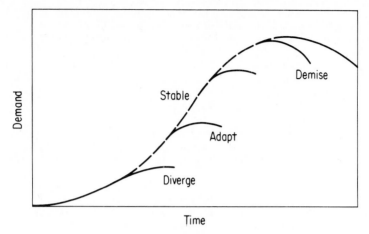

FIG. 6.6   The evolutionary life-cycle demand model.

Degrees of Risk.   Risk can be classified into three categories. These are:

1. Certainty—which exists when future results can be predicted with close to 100 percent certainty.
2. Risk—which exists when results can be forecast with a relatively high degree of probability.
3. Uncertainty—which exists when future results cannot be predicted with any degree of accuracy.

States of Nature.   States of nature are conditions in the environment and the market that affect the forecast but over which control cannot be exercised. As a simple example, the number of individuals in a specific age group who are potential customers will affect a forecast, but the firm will have no control over the size of the group.

The various states of nature that might exist can be classified in a number of ways. In this material only four states, ranging from a simple single state to a completely unknown state, are used. The classification of the states is not as important as knowing that they exist and that they form the continuous pattern over the range described above. The four states used here and their descriptions follow:

1. A single state occurs when only one condition is expected to exist over the life cycle of the product or service being forecast. This state is expected to remain rigid during the cycle.
2. A rigid multistate occurs when more than one state can exist, but the number of states and the time when they will occur are known with a high degree of accuracy or near certainty.
3. Evolving multistates exist whenever more than one state can occur, as in item 2; the probability of each state's occurrence can be forecast, but the time of occurrence is not known.

4. Unknown states exist whenever either the possible specific states or the probabilities of their occurrence are not known. This would include the worst case where nothing is known about a proposed new product or service.

There is a strong relationship between states of nature and levels of risk. This relationship follows a relatively stable pattern, as illustrated in Table 6.3. The information in Table 6.3 should be viewed as a continuous flow from the upper left to the lower right rather than a series of distinctive steps.

Summary of Long-Range Planning and Forecasting.   Successful long-range forecasting requires the ability to correctly identify expected future states of nature relative to the product or service along with their expected probabilities of occurrence. The forecaster also needs to determine the degree of risk associated with the forecast. The third area of concern to the forecaster is the development of the expected evolutionary cycle for the product or service.

In this discussion, no attempt was made to identify specific techniques that the forecaster should use to develop a long-range forecast. These specific techniques are numerous and specialized and are discussed in detail elsewhere in this book. Rather, at this point, the forecaster must first develop an overall procedural framework into which specific approaches can fit. Once the framework and an understanding of the market have been established, appropriate techniques can be selected which will improve the probability of success in long-range forecasting.

TABLE 6.3 Relationship between
Degrees of Risk and States of Nature

Degree of Risk	States of Nature			
	1	2	3	4
Certainty	X			
Risk		X	X	
Uncertainty			X	X

INDUSTRY ANALYSIS

An industry analysis is a complete study of all aspects of the particular industry in which the firm operates. This analysis should be carried out as a phase of strategic manufacturing and financial policy to provide a thorough understanding of what states of nature currently exist and what states might be expected. Once an industry analysis has been done, it should be kept current by adding any new information. This industry analysis is a valuable tool for long-range planning purposes.

The following is a cookbook approach to developing an industry analysis, what specific areas to research, and what sources of information might be available to provide specific details of what is going on in the industry.

Background

Tracing development of an industry from its inception to the present is often an invaluable source of information regarding what has transpired and what might transpire. These specific areas are of prime importance:

- Which were the initial firms in the industry, what families controlled those firms, and what banks provided the financial resources?
- What new firms were born from the original firms, where did they locate, and why?
- How did the original firms control the market, supply, and pricing? How did they control the entry of new firms?
- What relationships did the original firms have with foreign firms, and what relationships exist today?
- How, if at all, has government been involved in the industry?
- Was the original industry development affected by activity other than economic? If so, what were the patterns of these activities?

This list could be expanded to include many other possibilities. The main objective is for the researcher to obtain pieces of information that can be fitted together to provide a detailed understanding of how the specific industry functions. Bear in mind that there are few, if any, purely competitive industries in the world, and so collusion is not impossible.

Development of a Macroindustry Model

The macroindustry model traces the flow of material from its basic state to final consumption. This model indicates the various processes, their sequence, inventory points where material is stocked, and any recycling steps that occur in the process.

A macroindustry model can best be explained by an example, provided in Fig. 6.7. This is a complete macromodel of the aluminum industry. It shows the flow of the basic ore, processing of the ore, conversion of the oxide to pure metal, processing of the pure metal into usable forms, and finally the manufacture of products usable by the consumer. Information to prepare such a model can be obtained partly from the historical background study and partly from an engineering evaluation. Also shown are the various inventory points, the reclamation process, and import-export aspects, all factors that impact on the industry.

Microanalysis

A microanalysis is concerned with the internal workings of the firm as well as the internal steps of other firms in the industry in cases where close coordination is required. An example would be when molten metal is transferred from one firm to another or where firms are attempting to install just-in-time (JIT) inventory systems. This microstudy provides an understanding of what is available within the firm and what is required for the firm to function effectively.

The microanalysis of the firm can be divided into two areas. One deals with the physical characteristics of the firm. The second deals with quantitative and financial characteristics.

Physical Characteristics. The purpose of a complete examination of the physical characteristics of a firm is to determine the age and health of the facilities. If a firm is in the wrong age bracket or has gotten "fat and flabby," it will not be able to compete with a young, "lean" organization. This is the point where we determine what the firm has and does not have as far as physical characteristics are concerned. Match-

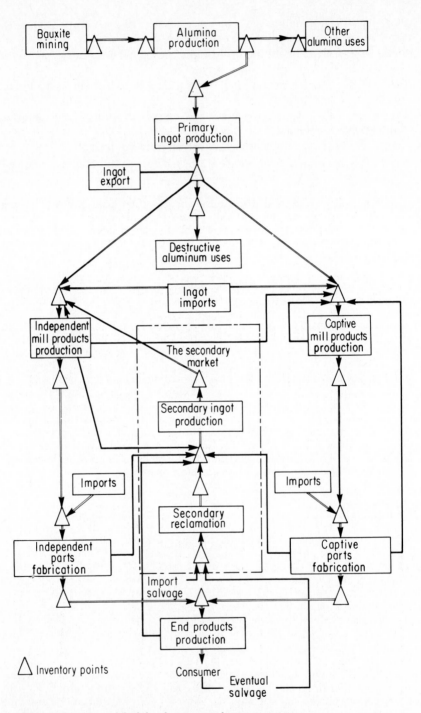

FIG. 6.7 A macromodel of the aluminum industry operations.

ing the firm's life cycle with the product's life cycle is the objective of the analysis.

Facility Layout and Capacity   A number of characteristics of a firm can be determined by a thorough examination of the facility layout. First, determine the general age of the buildings and equipment. Note that old age does not necessarily condemn a facility. Second, determine the type of facility layout—whether it is project-, process-, or product-oriented. Third, get specific information about the equipment. This information should indicate age, general maintenance, whether it is general- or special-purpose equipment, and its productive capacity limitations.

Processes and Procedures   A microanalysis of the processes and procedures used should cover details regarding individual operations performed. This includes what is normally considered to be the process planning activities of work place layout, motion and time study, tool planning, and standards.

Planning and Control Activity   How to measure planning and control activity is covered in detail in Chap. 27. For purposes of strategic policy formulation, this information will help determine what the firm is capable of performing effectively and the degree of flexibility of the production system.

Quality Analysis   The objective of an analysis of the quality capabilities of a firm is to determine what can be accomplished compared to what is being done. Every individual piece of equipment has a limit on the level of quality that can be produced. A part of strategic manufacturing and financial policy requires establishment of a quality-level goal. Once that goal is established, the system is expected to perform at that level. Unfortunately, too often the quality goals and the capability of the system are not properly coordinated. A system that produces below the required level is costly in that it produces excessive scrap. And a system that produces above the required level is also inefficient in that costs are higher than necessary.

Labor Force Analysis   An analysis of the labor force provides information regarding the potential of the workers. There is a need to determine not only their current capabilities but also their unused potential. A *skills inventory* should be performed to identify the labor force capabilities. This inventory is accomplished by a complete review of the educational and performance records of each individual in the organization. A system should be established which maintains this information in a readily available place so that it can be accessed when a particular skill is needed. A computer record of individuals and their skills in the labor force could be very effective in this case.

Quantitative and Financial Capabilities.   This part of the microanalysis of the firm consists of three parts: a time-series analysis of sales, shipments, and production; a cost structure analysis; and an analysis of working capital.

Time-Series Analysis   It is recommended that a time-series analysis be performed that covers, as a minimum, the preceding 10 years. This should include a relevant measure of production, sales, and inventory levels. A detailed description of how to perform a time-series analysis is available in Chap. 9. The purpose is to identify the three variations common in a time-series analysis—the seasonal, cyclical, and the trend conditions that existed in the market. In addition, a fourth variation that a trend analysis will often indicate is when irregular fluctuations have occurred.

A key benefit of the time-series analysis is the identification of these irregular fluctuations, which, once identified, can often be explained. For example, a particular analysis showed what was thought to be an irregular fluctuation. As it turned out, it was a 60-day cycle occurring at the end of each year. December shipments always showed a substantial increase over November shipments, followed by a large drop in January. A thorough investigation revealed that January business was moved back into December via early shipment to make the preceding year's forecast appear better than it actually was. Investigations of this type often provide similar explanations for previously unexplained fluctuations.

A word of caution is necessary when a time-series analysis is performed. Be sure to use a constant unit of measure such as shipments per workday or production per day. If a constant unit of measure is not used, completely erroneous results will develop. A classic example is the researcher who arrived at the momentous result that business was improving because March shipments were 8 percent higher than February shipments. Actually sales were declining because March has 10 percent more days than February.

Cost Structure Analysis   A cost structure analysis serves two purposes in a microanalysis. First, it provides information regarding a firm's operating leverage; second, it indicates the amount of value a firm adds to a product or service.

For purposes of clarification, it is necessary to establish definitions of fixed and variable costs. Fixed costs are associated with the physical facilities which enable productive capacity. The fixed costs, once committed, continue regardless of whether any product or service is provided. Variable costs are associated with activities to put the facilities into operation. Variable costs such as labor, material, and some power are incurred as a product is manufactured. The rate of usage of the facilities will vary directly with the incurrence of variable costs.

First, consider the *operating leverage* as the relationship between fixed and variable costs. If a firm has low capital investment and consequently low fixed costs, most of the product cost is variable in the form of labor and material. Such a firm tends to operate on a variable, or "chase," schedule with production closely following demand. This allows the firm to reduce inventories and to enhance cash flow. However, a firm that has high capital investment and thus high fixed cost and low variable cost is probably more concerned with maintaining production to absorb fixed charges. Such a firm would probably follow a stable production policy, using fluctuations in inventories to absorb variations in demand.

Second, the value added indicates the importance of a specific firm in the macromodel and consequently the importance of that firm to the overall product cost. There is a direct relation between value added and economic strength in an industry. The firm that controls the major part of the cost, usually through high capital investment, is the firm that will determine how a given industry will operate. The smaller firms, providing little value added, will have to follow the lead of the dominant firms.

An example will clarify the effect of operating leverage and value added. A basic metal is processed from an ore into a pure metal in a capital-intensive refining process. The metal is further processed into sheet stock, again in a capital-intensive firm. Following the processing, the material is formed into stampings on punch presses, delivered to an assembly plant, and finally assembled into consumer durable goods. Assuming that each process stage is independently owned and operated, each firm in the macromodel will function differently. The expected activity is summarized in Table 6.4.

The cost structure analysis indicates the conditions faced by a specific firm and the effect of these conditions on manufacturing and financial policy. Only by closely coordinating the potential of the firm with what is possible in the industry will the firm be able to perform efficiently and profitably.

Working-Capital Analysis   Working capital consists of cash, accounts payable, accounts receivable, inventory, and short-term sources of funds along with routine financing. With the exception of inventories, these factors are often overlooked in determining manufacturing policy. This results in situations where manufacturing sets policy relative to inventories; finance sets policy in cash management, short-term sources of funds, and accounts payable; and marketing establishes policy

TABLE 6.4   Macromodel Activity

Stage	Activity	Cost Structure	Value Added	Operating Pattern	Economic Strength
1	Refining	High fixed, low variables	High	Stable	High
2	Alloying process	High fixed, low variables	High	Stable	High
3	Stamping	Medium fixed, medium variable	Low	Chase	Low
4	Assembly	Low fixed, high variable	Medium	Modified chase	Medium

relative to accounts receivable. In each case, the policies become functionally oriented rather than organizationally oriented. Consequently, they do not operate as a benefit to corporate, long-range strategy. In this type of a situation, strategy development has been pushed too far down in the organization.

One specific area of consideration is accounts receivable terms and manufacturing policy. If more lenient terms are allowed, sales should increase, placing a heavier demand on production. If the firm is using a level production plan, additional inventories must be financed to support these sales, and additional capacity might even be added. In this case, a marketing decision impacts heavily on manufacturing and finance with surprising and costly results.

Numerous other similar examples related to working capital are possible. The policymaker must evaluate the impact on the organization of each working-capital decision. If variable decisions are to be allowed, manufacturing and financial policies must provide for the necessary flexibility in the original construction of the system.

Sources of Data

Obtaining the information required in the preceding steps can be done with varying degrees of ease. In some industries, such as coal, large amounts of information are available. In other industries, for instance, platinum, very little information is readily available. It boils down to trying numerous sources to obtain whatever information is available. As clues to where to look, check the cities where the industry started, the families who run the firms, newspapers in those cities, unions involved, etc. Table 6.5 provides possible sources of information and data. It is not exhaustive, but it provides the researcher with a good start.

An Industry Analysis Checklist

A thorough industry analysis should provide substantial assistance for long-range forecasting and the development of manufacturing and financial policy. The pitfalls of the past can be avoided, and some advantages for the future may be identified. The following list is provided for that purpose:

1. Historical analysis

   What family, industry, and foreign relationships exist?
   In what life-cycle stage is the industry?
   How has the industry grown?

2. Macroindustry model

What is the material flow?
What are the inventory characteristics?
Where are the materials stocked?
What are the critical processing steps?
What reprocessing steps are used?
What are the relationships of capacity between stages?
What product substitutes are there?

3. Microanalysis

What are the physical characteristics relative to plant layout, processes and procedures, planning and control activity, quality analysis, and labor force analysis?

Has adequate quantitative and financial analysis been performed relative to time-series analysis, cost structure analysis, and working-capital analysis?

What are the international characteristics of the industry, such as net importer or exporter, development of consortia, and preempting local markets?

Extensive research has lead to the conclusion that many similarities exist within and between industries. Leading managers move to different firms and carry ideas with them. The ideas are tried in the new situations. Sometimes the ideas succeed, and sometimes they fail. By identifying these successes and failures, better manufacturing and financial policy can be established.

TABLE 6.5 Sources of Micro- and Macroindustry Information

Information Sources	Type of Information
Annual reports	Production, financial, and marketing data plus historical information concerning the specific firm
Bureau of Mines	Mineral industry surveys (monthly and annually); industry data, domestic and foreign; historical information
Bureau of Labor Statistics and Department of Commerce	Labor statistics by industry current industry reports, business statistics
Industry associations	Historical information and current data regarding the specific industry
Technical journals	Technical, historical, and operating data on a particular industry
Newspapers	Current information

CHARACTERISTICS OF MANUFACTURING SYSTEMS

Manufacturing systems are characterized by the rigidity that becomes inherent in the system upon the expenditure of funds and installation of facilities, equipment, and tooling. In addition to the rigidity inherent in bricks and mortar, there is also considerable inflexibility that limits the range of system application. A system designed for mass production is not efficient for low-volume specialty production or vice versa. The following description of the various types of production systems reveals their rigidity.

Project Systems

A project system is set up to produce a single item or group of items at one geographic location within a limited time. Examples are battleships, buildings, and dams. The project system is unlike any other in that it is assembled at the job site, the product or service is provided, and the system is dismantled and moved to a new job site.

Job Shop Systems

A job shop system is well suited to low-volume production where early life-cycle characteristics require constant design changes to meet consumer demand. This system is organized as a process system where like activities or processes are grouped in departments.

Inputs to this system consist of highly skilled labor that can be utilized in a number of different tasks. The facilities are usually small. Equipment is general-purpose, as are the materials. Usually only general-purpose tooling is used. The highly skilled labor is expected to perform complicated tasks and use minimum tooling and equipment. The advantage of this arrangement is flexibility at the expense of volume. This system is not well suited to produce at a high relative volume.

Such a system has low operating leverage, for there is a minimum use of fixed assets and hence fixed costs while variable costs are high. This arrangement allows a firm easy entry and exit from a market. If the product or service fails, the firm can easily get out of the market. If the product or service is successful, the firm will have to create a more sophisticated system if it expects to remain competitive.

The type of cost structure appropriate in this case is illustrated in the break-even analysis in Fig. 6.8. Here fixed costs are relatively low while variable costs are high.

Intermittent Production Systems

Some characteristics of an intermittent production system are very similar to those of a job shop system. The intermittent system is also organized as a process system, grouping like activities in a departmental arrangement. Variations include larger size, the utilization of less skilled labor for repetitive tasks, the inclusion of some more sophisticated tooling to increase productivity, and standardization at increased volume levels as the product or service moves into the early growth stage of its life cycle.

The operating leverage of an intermittent production system is higher than a job shop system because of the higher concentration of fixed costs in equipment and tooling. Variable costs should be lower because less skilled labor can be used for the repetitive tasks. The repetitive system still retains a relatively high degree of flexibility, although flexibility needs to be sacrificed to some extent to provide an increase in volume. Also, the sacrifice is necessary to provide reduced unit costs to meet competition.

Assembly Line and Flow Process Systems

A major difference between an assembly line and a flow process system is that the latter is product- rather than process-oriented. Thus the plant and equipment layout is such that efficient product flow is the major criterion. The product or customer

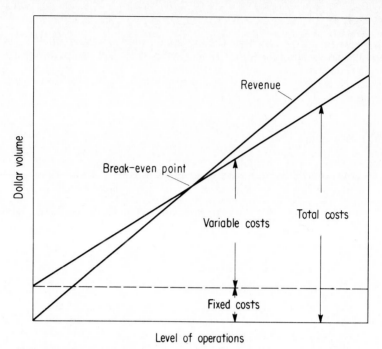

FIG. 6.8 A break-even chart for a low-fixed-, high-variable-cost operation.

moves from operation to operation along a preestablished, fixed path. Essential equipment is provided at each sequential step to ensure that deviations from the path are unnecessary.

The inputs to a flow process system or assembly line are substantially different from those used in a job shop or intermittent system. This results from a product-oriented system which is designed to be most effective for a product moving into its mature stage. Specifically, the product is characterized by being well defined and designed for high volume and a low selling price in a competitive market. This situation is well suited to a manufacturing system using extensive tooling and special equipment plus materials specially developed for the "mature" product.

Labor inputs to an assembly line can be much less skilled because the tooling and equipment provide the technical results in accordance with the product's specifications. A frequent problem is that as many firms move from a process- to a product-oriented system, they have more skilled labor than necessary. The higher-skill workers end up doing tasks that could easily be done by less skilled workers at a much lower cost. So labor costs are higher than necessary to meet competition, especially foreign competition.

The cost structure of an assembly line is more efficient at high levels of facility utilization because it tends to have high fixed and low variable costs. Figure 6.9, a break-even analysis, indicates the relationship between the high-fixed- and low-variable-cost structure of an assembly line. High levels of operation generate substantial profit margins. Of course, low levels of utilization also lead to high losses. The high fixed costs in the system result from special machinery, robots, and special tooling to minimize the content and skill level of labor.

A summary of costs for the continuous production system would include mini-

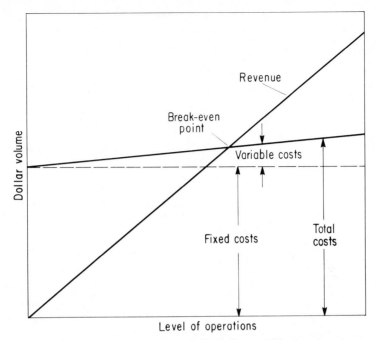

FIG. 6.9 A break-even chart for a high-fixed-, low-variable-cost operation.

mum material costs resulting from thorough engineering design, low labor costs resulting from the use of reduced skill levels and special equipment, and high relative fixed costs resulting from extensive facility costs. Such a system must operate at high-volume levels to be profitable.

MANUFACTURING POLICY DETERMINATION

Manufacturing policy is the result of translating corporate strategy to a long-range plan for the production function of the firm. The policy should be developed in conjunction with marketing strategy, as discussed in Chap. 5, and financial policy, summarized later in this chapter. Manufacturing policy should not be established without a complete system analysis in association with these other corporate functional areas.

Goal of Manufacturing Policy

The goal of manufacturing policy is the establishment of a production system which can carry out corporate objectives in the most effective manner over the longest period, thus providing the firm with the largest possible net present value in the long run. This establishment of a production system requires extensive researching of the industry, environment, and potential markets. Specifically, the firm has to address a number of factors as elements of its manufacturing policy.

One factor is how to minimize long-range costs as they relate to the product life cycle. It would be advantageous to have a facility that wore out at the same time as the product demand stopped. In the past it often was possible to extend a product's life cycle to get greater utilization from a facility. But in today's market, competition and new-product development have all but eliminated this possibility. So the first objective of manufacturing policy is to develop a system with a projected life equal to the product life.

A second goal of manufacturing policy is to provide a system with flexibility. The greater the flexibility, the greater the expected life, but only at a cost. Providing flexibility will mean the inclusion of system costs for facilities, equipment, tooling, and work force that will reduce profits in the short run but will improve the overall net present value of the manufacturing system. As a goal priority, flexibility should be given preference over short-range profitability.

A third goal is to minimize the system's sensitivity to changes in inputs. Avoidance of complete dependence on one source of supply, or a single power source, or a single transportation system, is very important. Some of the benefits of current efforts toward single sourcing must be weighed against the risks of dependence on the single source. Likewise, dependence on unusual labor skills should be avoided, as should restrictive labor contracts. The list can become endless. Every potential input must be carefully analyzed relative to its current cost and long-range benefit. A slightly higher current cost can be justified if the system's sensitivity to that input can be reduced.

Research for Manufacturing Policy

Earlier in this chapter, a number of research subjects were explained in detail to provide a basis for the establishment of an effective manufacturing policy. These subjects are summarized here.

Background. The background study provides information on how a specific industry originated, who were the initial leaders, how and where the competition developed, and how the market was developed and controlled. Successful activities tend to be repeated. The historical background provides information on past successes and failures.

Macroindustry Model. This model illustrates material flow patterns, critical processes, inventory points, and the relationships among the various process stages. This provides information about the controlling stages in the industry.

Microanalysis. The microanalysis provides both knowledge relative to the internal physical characteristics of the industry processes and quantitative and financial aspects relative to trends, cost structure, and working-capital resources.

Product-Life/Evolutionary Cycle. A study of the life/evolutionary cycle of a product or service provides an analysis of what the future might be regarding time and volume, what changes might be expected, and what the current controlling element might be relative to design, cost, demand, or production difficulties.

Summary of Production System Characteristics

The following is a brief summary of the various types of production systems.

Project Systems.   A project system produces a single product or a few products at one location before the production system is moved to a new location. This system uses highly skilled labor for most tasks, general-purpose machines and tools, and both standard and special materials.

Job Shop Production Systems.   A job shop system is organized according to activities and is especially suited for low-volume specialty production or service. Inputs include highly skilled labor, general-purpose equipment machinery and tools, and general-purpose common materials.

Intermittent Production Systems.   This system is also organized according to activities with like activities grouped in departments. This system is larger and better suited for medium-volume business with limited repetitiveness. The intermittent system uses both high- and low-skill labor as needed. Also, some special equipment and tooling are substituted for general-purpose equipment whenever volume and produce life dictate. The same is true as far as material is concerned; special-purpose material is used if it is economically feasible.

Assembly Lines and Flow Process Systems.   These systems are product-oriented and are organized to minimize material flow time and maximize throughput. The product or service follows a consistent flow pattern through the system. Low-skill labor is widely used to reduce labor costs. Most of the equipment and tooling are special-purpose to provide for quality and volume control. Special materials are also widely used.

Coordination of Product and System Life Cycles

The degree of manufacturing policy effectiveness results from the degree of success that management has in coordinating the product requirements with the capabilities of the manufacturing system. In a sense, the product and the manufacturing system should be "born" at the same time, they should grow together, and they should "die" at the same time. By this it is not meant that the firm should go out of business; rather, the firm should plan its manufacturing policy so that the manufacturing system will be appropriate to meet market requirements. The system should change to meet market changes.

An overview of generally valid market conditions and systems requirements is provided in Fig. 6.10. The product life-cycle approach with system characteristics superimposed provides a picture of the matching of the product or service market with the production system.

No single manufacturing system is appropriate to meet the needs of a product or service throughout its entire life. In the initial stage, the market is interested in supplying the needs of the consumer who wants the innovative, new product or service. The system must provide the consumer with what is desired. Costs are irrelevant. The manufacturing system must be designed to produce the special product or service. The best system would be a job shop, furnished with standard equipment, and staffed by highly trained and skilled employees. A rigid, continuous production system would not be able to accomplish this objective effectively, although it might be able to produce. The same argument could apply to the other stages of a product or service life cycle.

A firm that wishes to function in all stages of product life cycle must have a manufacturing policy that provides a system appropriate for every stage of the product life cycle. Thus a series of facilities are necessary to carry the product or

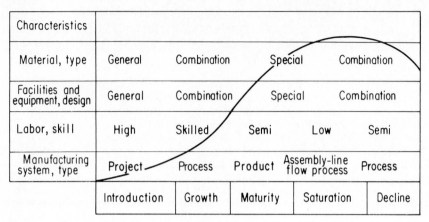

Characteristics					
Material, type	General	Combination	Special	Combination	
Facilities and equipment, design	General	Combination	Special	Combination	
Labor, skill	High	Skilled	Semi	Low	Semi
Manufacturing system, type	Project	Process	Product	Assembly-line flow process	Process
	Introduction	Growth	Maturity	Saturation	Decline

FIG. 6.10 Characteristics of inputs relative to life-cycle stages.

service through the cycle, beginning with a job shop and progressing to an assembly line or continuous production system. The alternative is for the firm to select a highly efficient system for a single stage and then choose or purchase products or services that fit into the production system. When the product passes the stage that is appropriate for the firm's system, the product can be dropped or sold to another firm, to be replaced by another product or service just entering the effective range of the firm's manufacturing system.

Methods of Adjusting Manufacturing Policy

Manufacturing policy adjustments, which are long-range, require the physical change of facilities in the form of layout and location. All firms eventually reach this position. The only alternative is to build new facilities, install new equipment, or do some combination of the two. Any firm that fails to make a major policy adjustment as necessary will eventually face bankruptcy.

In the short range, a number of policy adjustments can be made:

- Price adjustments to force demand up or down.
- Inventory adjustments to absorb deviations between efficient production rates and demand. In a high-fixed-, low-variable-cost structure, this is an effective tool. In a low-fixed-, high-variable-cost structure, this is not effective since most costs are out of pocket.
- Work period adjustments can be used to change the rate of output. The alternatives are overtime or undertime, changes in number of shifts, or a complete shutdown.
- Work force adjustments are a way to make small incremental adjustments to policy. This approach has a seldom recognized detrimental effect in that it generates imbalances in the work flow. The worst case is the assembly line where a rebalance is necessary to provide equal workstation labor content.
- Customer order backlogs can provide a form of manufacturing policy adjustment if the customers are willing to extend the waiting period before they take delivery of the product or service.

- Policy adjustments may be made by either increasing or decreasing performance through the selection of inputs of differing efficiency. As an example, the use of higher-skill labor may provide a higher quality level; and as long as a marginal analysis shows that the net result is an increase in system performance, manufacturing policy will have increased the effectiveness. Numerous other possibilities exist and should be evaluated in each instance on a marginal basis.

Conditions That Affect Manufacturing Policy Implementation

Every condition within the production operation, marketing, and finance will have some effect on policy implementation. It is a matter of degree. The same applies to all external conditions. The following is not an exhaustive list but summarizes what the policymaker should evaluate as potential conditions impacting on implementation efforts.

The implementor should consider these questions:

Is manufacturing policy explicitly and clearly communicated?

How will learning affect implementation? (See learning curves, as described in Chap. 11.)

Have priorities during the implementation process been developed? A useful tool for this is PERT or CPM, discussed in detail in Chap. 17.

Have decisions regarding computer systems and software been made?

What control system will be used in cost, quality, inventory, and production?

Performance Evaluation

Measuring how well a manufacturing system is doing on a strategic manufacturing and financial policy level is not easy. Using single criterion such as return on investment (ROI) is inadequate. Likewise, using only quantitative measures is not acceptable.

A series of criteria should be used to assess how well a manufacturing system is doing relative to established policy. Table 6.6 includes the minimum criteria recommended.

Using the matrix approach requires first the determination of objectives for each criterion. As Table 6.6 shows, the firm's product is in the mature stage of the life cycle, and so market risk is determined to be low in a competitive market. Given these conditions, we would expect to be using a facility with high fixed costs, low variable costs, and relatively little flexibility. These conditions are indicated by X's in Table 6.6. After the criteria are determined the actual conditions of the firm being evaluated can be marked on the matrix and the variance (the difference between desired and actual) can be estimated. A comparison of the variance between the desired and actual conditions provides a basis for evaluation of the specific production system.

Final determination of how well a manufacturing system is performing relative to the goal is primarily a subjective judgment and not a numerical comparison. The quantitative measures, such as ROI and profit margins, should be viewed as variances from desired levels rather than deviations from absolute levels.

TABLE 6.6 Manufacturing Policy Performance Evaluation Matrix

Criteria	Low ←————————— Comparative Scale —————————→ High		
Life-Cycle Stage	Introduction		Decline
Fixed costs			X
Variable costs	X		
Flexibility		X	
Profit margin			
Labor skill			
Quality			
Service level			
ROI			
Market risk	X		
Working capital			
Other			

FINANCIAL POLICY DETERMINATION

When to buy, sometimes referred to as a *make-or-buy decision*, is a problem of determining the most efficient form in which to purchase inputs for the production system, since all inputs into the production system are purchased in some form. Some are bought as completed subassembly components. In other situations, a firm may purchase natural resources and process them completely. The whole range of extremes is also available. The differences lies in whether the buyer or seller owns the real assets, such as machinery, equipment, etc., that do the processing, and how payment for the use of the real assets is made. The customers can pay for either the use of the assets in the purchase price of the product or their use through depreciation.

An additional consideration in manufacturing and financial policy determination is the problem of finding the most efficient operation in the various stages of the industry macromodel. That is, what individual firm can do a specific operation best in the creation of the product or service? If a combination can be put together which includes the most efficient producing steps given all the costs, then the lowest cost and consequently the most profitable when-to-buy decision will have been made. The following material is intended as a guide to assist the decisionmaker in making better when-to-buy choices.

Elements of a When-to-Buy Decision

A thorough when-to-buy analysis consists of a series of decisions. For the buyer, the first step requires an analysis of the market for the product or service for which the input is to be used. As discussed earlier, this is the most important step. It requires decisions about the market, production process, and type of inputs, along with a careful determination of the life-cycle stage of the product or service.

A second step involves an engineering analysis to determine what processes are feasible alternatives to accomplish the objective. This entails a microanalysis, as described previously.

The third step in the financial analysis is to determine projected cash flows which are expected to occur in the long-range future of the process. This financial forecasting involves varying degrees of inaccuracy depending on the states of nature experienced and information shortcomings that may be experienced. Note that this process is based on forecast, not explicit data. Completely accurate results cannot be expected.

Market Analysis.   Techniques for both macroforecasting and detailed microforecasting are discussed extensively in Chap. 9. The importance of accurate forecasting for when-to-buy decisions is that it provides a basis for determining expected cash flows. Profitable cash flows into the business will provide funds to pay for the needed inputs into the system. The greater the accuracy of the forecast, the more assurance there will be that a correct financial policy decision was made. At the same time, incorrect decisions and their consequence can be expected.

Engineering Analysis.   The engineering analysis step provides detailed information regarding the production process, including equipment of the proper capacity and the cost delivered, installed, and tested along with auxiliary equipment, power, and support equipment such as material-handling and storage items. The site of the equipment itself must be checked. Nothing can be more decisive in determining an individual's future than to have a project slowly sink into quicksand under the equipment foundation. Besides equipment selection, special personnel to operate and maintain the process must be available. Future maintenance and repair costs must be included. These costs should be assigned to time periods. Some will be incurred at the time of installation, and others will be incurred during future time periods.

If the need for working capital changes, it must be included in the considerations. The change might involve additional inventory, accounts receivable, accounts payable, etc. These should be treated as additional initial investments which may be recovered when the project is terminated.

Determination of Cash Flows.   Expenditures associated with any buying decision must be made strictly on a cash flow basis, not on an accounting basis. Accounting statements contribute information to determine levels of profit, depreciation, and taxes. For this purpose the accounting statement should not be used in an unadjusted accrued accounting format; rather, they need to used on a cash flow basis. In addition, cash flows should be viewed in two separate categories: those that are known and those that are projected.

Cash flows that are known and firm are those associated with an initial decision to make a certain purchase. For example, if a firm wants to evaluate a decision to purchase a component in raw-material form, the firm will incur certain initial costs. Assume that the firm fabricates the component from the material and has to install $60,000 in equipment. The firm will also incur $10,000 in tooling costs. The equipment is subject to a 10-year life with a 10 percent investment tax credit. For the purpose of simplicity, straight-line depreciation with no salvage value is used. Federal taxes are 46 percent. (Refer to current accounting practices and government regulation for details in handling depreciation and taxes.)

Known Cash Flows   Based on the above information, the known cash flows are

Cost of equipment	+$60,000
Cost of tooling	+10,000
Investment tax credit	−6,000
Net known cash flow	$64,000

This is the net amount that will be paid at the time of installation. It constitutes actual dollars departing from the bank account.

Projected Cash Flows   The accuracy of these projections will depend on how accurate a job has been done in forecasting market requirements, changes in demand, the product life cycle, and changes in costs. The projected cash flows are

Estimated annual savings from project	$20,000
Depreciation per year	−6,000
Taxable savings	$14,000
Tax @ 46%	6,440

$$\text{Net cash flow} = 20,000 - 6,440 = \$13,560$$

An annual net cash flow benefit of $13,560 is expected. Note that depreciation was used to determine how much tax liability existed. The net estimated cash flow is the estimated net annual savings less the amount that must go to the government for taxes. The analysis is a cash flow analysis, not an accounting analysis.

Analysis Techniques

A number of techniques have been developed to assess whether a project is worthwhile, including payback, average rate of return, internal rate of return, and net present value. Of these, only the last two are correct because they consider both the life of a project and the time value of money. Of the last two, the net-present-value approach is better for three reasons. First, it is more conservative; second, it is easier; and third, it is a correct approach because it considers the time value of money.

Net-Present-Value Approach.   The following discussion provides sufficient information to apply the net-present-value approach as a decision-making tool. Those users desiring a complete description of the technique along with theoretical discussions are directed to one of the many excellent corporate financial management or capital budgeting textbooks listed in the Bibliography. This discussion is based on one premise: *there is no free lunch.*

An important aspect of net present value is understanding compounding, discounting, and annuities.

Compounding   The process of determining the future value (FV) of something that is owned today is called *compounding.* One dollar in the bank at 10 percent annual interest will be worth $1.10 in 1 year. That $1.10 will be worth $1.21 in 2 years, and so on. Thus

$$FV = PV(1 + r)^n$$

where FV = future value at end of n periods
   PV = present value at beginning of periods
   r = interest rate per period
   n = number of periods
   $1 + r$ = compound factor

Discounting   The opposite process from compounding is *discounting.* This method is used to determine the present value of something that will be received in the future. Solving the previous equation for present value gives

$$PV = \frac{FV}{(1 + r)^n}$$

An Annuity   A stream of payments that are received regularly over a number of time periods is an *annuity*. In essence, it is a series of present values all strung together. An annuity is special in that the future values being discounted are all equal. In the projected cash flow example, a series of future values of $13,560 are to be received at the end of each of the next 10 years of the project life.

To find the present value of an annuity which is a series of period payments, use the following formula:

$$PVA = PP \times PVIFA$$

where   PVA = present value of annuity
          PP = period payment
   PVIFA = present value interest factor for annuity

$$= \frac{1}{r}\left[1 - \frac{1}{(1 + r)^n}\right]$$

Defining r, the interest rate per period, is easy but r is rather difficult to determine. It is the required rate of return for an investment of equal risk as determined in the marketplace. Practically, it is established by management to reflect the rate of return that needs to be achieved for a project of equivalent risk so that stockholders earn an adequate ROI.

Determining the net present value, the amount by which present value differs from the initial investment, is a matter of combining the components described above:

Net present value = present value of period payments − investment
or   NPV = PV − I
Thus   PV = PVA = PP × PVIFA

Here I is negative because it is a payout, and PV is positive because it is a receipt. Solving, we find

$$I = \$64{,}000$$

and

$$PP = \$13{,}560$$

Assume that r has been established at 15 percent. Then

$$PVIFA = \frac{1}{0.15}\left[1 - \frac{1}{(1 + 0.15)^{10}}\right] = 5.019$$

and

$$PVA = \$13{,}560 \times 5.019 = \$68{,}058$$

So

$$NPV = PV - I$$
$$= \$68,058 - \$64,000$$
$$= \$4058$$

Because the net present value is positive, the actual rate of return exceeds the required rate of return of 15 percent. Thus the project should earn a greater return than required. If the investment had been greater than the present value of the period payments, it would not have been worthwhile and other alternatives would have to be examined.

Two points need to be emphasized. First, the net-present-value approach does not say that the proposed project is best. It says only that the proposed project is good enough to meet the management objective of a 15 percent required rate of return. Other projects may be better, so keep looking. Second, if the period payments are not the same each period as in the example, then the annuity approach is not correct. When each payment is different, each period must be discounted separately, and then they must be summed to find the present value of the period payments. A simple example, shown in Table 6.7, illustrates the procedure:

TABLE 6.7   Unequal Payments

Period	Period Payment	Compound Factor	Present Value
Year 1	$9,000	1.15^1	$7,826
Year 2	8,000	1.15^2	6,049
Year 3	7,000	1.15^3	4,603
			$18,478

$$\text{Present value} = \frac{\text{future value}}{\text{compound factor}}$$

FINANCIAL POLICY—WORKING-CAPITAL MANAGEMENT

Funds used to purchase a manufacturing system in essence provide available manufacturing capacity to produce for the marketplace. The manufacturing system does not perform until working capital is applied to utilize that capacity. Until then, the facility is a bare skeleton.

Putting the system into operation requires the assignment of cash, accounts receivable, inventory, and accounts payable. These areas are the responsibility of financial management, but they impact directly on manufacturing policy. This impact is in direct conflict with goals in the functional areas of finance, marketing, and production. An increase in one area reduces resources available for another area.

Cash

Cash reserves provide flexibility in manufacturing policy. The greater the cash reserve, the more actual production can vary from the plan. This allows production the luxury of taking advantage of situations which will use funds to provide a net gain for the firm. A specific case might be overproduction of an item in anticipation of higher-than-forecast sales. Numerous examples arise daily. Each, by itself, probably has little significance as a single tactical decision, but a large number of such advantages will lead to improved profitability.

Accounts Receivable

Marketing decisions regarding credit terms will determine the level of business activity, and ultimately this will determine manufacturing policy. Marketing should not be allowed to make independent changes in credit terms without considering the impact on other working-capital areas, cash and inventory, and capacity utilization. If funds are used to build up accounts receivable, they will not be available to purchase material and pay workers to operate the facility.

If credit terms are loosened, sales will increase, requiring additional production. But at the same time production will be limited to the extent that funds for inventory and accounts payable are reduced.

Inventory and Accounts Payable

Levels of inventory are discussed extensively in Chaps. 12, 21, and 29. The assignment of working capital to finance inventories is an integral part of manufacturing and financial policy. Releasing funds to pay for the material through accounts payable is also a crucial step. Not taking discounts and "stretching" accounts payable are methods that all companies are likely to use occasionally to generate additional funds. Such tactics cause little damage. *Stretching* is a process in which the buying firm delays payment beyond the invoice due date to use the funds for a longer time and thus avoid having to borrow additional funds. If financial policy is to continually stretch the account payables, then manufacturing policy will suffer from higher material costs, less reliable suppliers, and less flexibility in inputting material. If stretching is the financial policy, then plan for it in the manufacturing policy. Establish plans to counter the problems cited.

Risk in Working-Capital Policy

There is an inverse relationship between levels of working capital and profitability. The more working capital assigned at a given level of production, the less risk the firm faces and the lower the potential profit, because of the greater amount of assets used. Obviously, the opposite would lead to greater risk and greater potential profits. When manufacturing and financial policy is created, the policymaker must evaluate the use of working capital on a net-present-value basis to determine an appropriate level of working-capital utilization.

SUMMARY

Manufacturing and financial policy is part of an overall hierarchical decision system. The decision system begins with corporate objectives, which define the goals of the organization. Corporate strategy and functional strategies follow the establishment of corporate objectives. Proceeding from functional strategies are functional policies. Finally, operating procedures can be established.

Manufacturing and financial policy is determined by the physical facilities utilized, the product life/evolutionary cycle, the type of manufacturing system utilized, the production and inventory management system, and financial decisions relative to system inputs.

Corporate strategy formulation can be developed from a thorough analysis of environmental conditions under which the firm operates and the strengths and weaknesses of the firm.

The process of policy formulation requires a long-range plan and forecast. An effective method of doing this is the rate-of-change approach combined with a life/evolutionary cycle analysis of the product or service produced by the firm. The long-range planning and forecasting are subject to varying degrees of risk and changing states of nature.

An industry analysis is a useful tool to prepare for effective long-range planning and forecasting. An industry analysis begins with an extensive historical background study. It also includes a macro- and a microanalysis of the industry and the specific firm.

Different types of manufacturing systems have different characteristics, ranging from project systems designed to produce a single unit of a product or service at a site to highly specialized, high-volume flow process systems. Each of these manufacturing systems has a special place in the life/evolutionary cycle of the product or service.

Manufacturing policy is the result of translation of corporate strategy to a long-range plan for the production function of the firm. Manufacturing policy is determined by the application of the processes described in this chapter.

Financial policy is, in a similar framework, a translation of corporate strategy to a long-range plan for the when-to-buy decisions, based on a net-present-value approach to financial analysis. Financial policy determination also includes coordinated decisions regarding working-capital management.

BIBLIOGRAPHY

Albert, Emil: "Aluminum Ingot Market, 1959–1968," unpublished dissertation, Michigan State University, 1971.

Brealey, Richard, and Stewart Myers: *Principles of Corporate Finance*, McGraw-Hill, New York, 1981.

Chase, Richard B., and Nicholas J. Aquilano: *Production and Operations Management*, 3d ed., Irwin, Homewood, Ill., 1981.

Christensen, C. Roland, Norman A. Berg, and Malcolm S. Salter: *Policy Formulation and Administration*, 8th ed., Irwin, Homewood, Ill., 1980.

Harris, Roy D., and Richard F. Gonzalez: *The Operations Manager: Role, Problems, Techniques* West, St. Paul, 1981.

Harvey, Donald F. : *Business Policy and Strategic Management*, Merrill, Columbus, Ohio, 1982.

McNichols, T. J. : *Executive Policy and Strategic Planning*, McGraw-Hill, New York, 1977.

Patterson, Charles: "Formulating and Implementing Business Strategy," paper presented at Education Liaison Workshop, St. Charles, Ill., June 1981.

Schmenner, Roger W.: *Production/Operations Management*, Science Research, Chicago, 1981.

Sherman, P. M.: *Strategic Planning for Technology Industries*, Addison-Wesley, Reading, Mass., 1982.

Skinner, Wickham: "Manufacturing—Missing Link in Corporate Strategy," *Harvard Business Review*, May–June 1969, pp. 136–145.

————: *Manufacturing in the Corporate Strategy*, Wiley, New York, 1978.

Steiner, G. A. : *Strategic Planning: What Every Manager Must Know*, Free Press, New York, 1979.

Tellis, Gerard J., and C. Merle Crawford: "An Evolutionary Approach to Product Growth Theory," *Journal of Marketing*, Fall 1981.

Van Horne, James C.: *Fundamentals of Finance Management*, 5th ed., Prentice-Hall, Englewood Cliffs, N.J., 1983.

Wheelwright, Steven C.: "Reflecting Corporate Strategy in Manufacturing Decisions," *Business Horizons*, February 1978, pp. 57–66.

7

Strategic Production Planning

Editor

WALTER E. GODDARD, President, Oliver Wight Education Associates, Newbury, New Hampshire

Contributor

ROGER B. BROOKS, Executive Vice President, Oliver Wight Education Associates, Newbury, New Hampshire

Production planning is as old as the pyramids. All manufacturing companies do it. They may not call it by that title, or it may be done informally, but it is an inescapable function. This chapter describes the information and procedures that need to be in place, plus what the managers of the business must do, in order for the production planning process to operate effectively.

The production plan establishes the manufacturing rates for running the company. As defined in the *APICS Dictionary*, the production plan is "the function of setting the overall level of manufacturing output."[1] The day the founder started the business and hired some people to make products, the founder made a production plan. When more people were added to increase the output, the production plan was revised. This is the process of production planning— determining the rate of output by broad categories extending a long period into the future.

It is an extremely critical function for all manufacturing companies. The production plan represents the company's aggregate, strategic plan for servicing the marketplace. From it come the needs for material, capacity, money, space, tooling, direct labor operators, indirect labor operators, staffing, etc. A company requires each of these resources to support the rates of output. Thus, the production plan becomes the determining factor for calculating all the resources needed by a manufacturing firm.

Since production planning is such an old and important function, it would be logical to assume that companies do production planning well. That certainly is the case for many companies; for them, it is a smooth-running, standard operating procedure.

Other companies, however, have a weak spot in this area. One possible explanation is that for the last 20 years the attention within the American Production and Inventory Control Society (APICS) has centered largely on specific techniques, not on aggregate planning. Practitioners have been immersed in reorder points versus material-requirements planning (MRP), net change versus regeneration, single- versus full-level pegging, critical ratios versus operational dates, exponential smoothing versus weighted averages, dynamic versus fixed lot sizing, etc. As a result, a number of companies have concentrated on the details too much and so need to step back and take a broader view.

There is another reason why some companies lack an effective production plan. Until a company has an operating system that includes both aggregate, strategic planning and detailed, specific planning, there is less incentive to do one well. Today such a system exists. Manufacturing resource planning (abbreviated MRP II) is the link from front-office planning all the way to the factory floor. In fact, MRP II cannot operate properly without the framework established by top management through the business plan and the production plan.

WHO IS RESPONSIBLE?

Because of the importance of the production plan, it is the responsibility of the general manager to approve it. Staff members contribute to the plan's contents and are accountable for its execution. The final accountability for production planning, however, lies with the boss. That person has various titles from one company to the next—president, managing director, chief executive officer, chief operating officer, executive vice president, group vice president, etc. Regardless of the title, the responsibility lies with the person to whom these four functions report: marketing, manufacturing, engineering, and finance. In this chapter, the title *general manager* is used. This person must take the leadership role for production planning.

Additionally, the term *production planning* is not universally used. It accurately describes the end result of the process but does not make clear who is involved in the process. Some people interpret production planning as involving only manufacturing. However, without marketing, engineering, finance, and the other key functions reporting to the general manager, the production planning process cannot be done properly. Some companies have changed the name of this process to the *sales and operating plan*. Although titles are important, it is too late to change. The term *production planning* has become standard in the field.

Relationship to the Business Plan

The production plan and the business plan are mirror images of each other. The business plan is maintained by the same group of people—the general manager and staff. It is also grouped into broad categories and extends far into the future. Its unit of measure is always dollars. This is a distinguishing characteristic between the two. Later the unit of measure typically used in the production plan is discussed.

A great many companies start the planning process with the business plan. They forecast what they expect to receive for new customer orders, predict what they expect to ship, calculate what they expect to have in finished-goods inventory or backlog of customer orders, and determine their profit projections and cash flows—all in dollars. The business plan becomes the basis for determining the budgets of all departments within the company.

If a company lays out the business plan first, the goal of production planning is to determine the rates of output required to support the targets established by the business plan. Some companies, however, reverse this process. They begin by determining the rates of output thought to best serve the company. Then these plans are converted to the dollar consequences and become the business plan.

It is not necessary to worry about which of these two critical plans comes first. It is important to recognize that they must be done in lockstep. No company can afford to have a production plan that does not support the business plan, or vice versa. Invariably, a change in one requires an adjustment in the other.

General Manager's Role

Why must the general manager assume responsibility for both the production plan and the business plan? Part of the answer lies with the need to reach a consensus. It is very difficult for marketing, manufacturing, engineering, and finance to resolve differing opinions without the guidance of the boss. Companies that try to resolve these differences without the guidance of the general manager typically find that the situation turns into a power struggle. Each side protects its own needs. Each becomes convinced that the others do not appreciate why. This degenerates into a lack of teamwork.

The other reason why the general manager should assume responsibility is even more important. Once the production plan has been approved, it is the basis for determining all the resource needs of a manufacturing company. As stated previously, materials, capacity, money, tooling, direct labor operators, indirect labor operators, and staffing all revolve on the level of business at which you are going to operate. Increasing or decreasing the level of output determines the need for greater or less resources. The end result is that this is the very essence of managing the business. General managers should never delegate this critical function. It is their job. Every person on the general manager's staff has a two-way role: determining what the plan should be and then supporting it. Each should be held accountable for doing both, as described in detail later.

Relationship to Detailed Plans

One of the most important objectives of a good operating system is to break down the aggregate plans to the detailed plans, to convert general strategies to specific tasks, and to coordinate long-range plans and the day-to-day planning. For example, the daily dispatch list is the culmination of breaking down the business plan and the production plan into what job is to be done next. Only when this process is done properly can the general manager lay out a plan, confident that it will be implemented. If the several activities involved are not linked together properly and/or used correctly, there is great risk that what the general manager is determining through the business plan and the production plan will not, in fact, be implemented.

When MRP first became popular in the early 1970s, the relationship between this function and the general manager's job was not clearly understood. Many companies had an MRP system without a good master production schedule (MPS) and/or an MPS that was not coordinated with the production plan. Such a system may yield improved results compared to what it replaced but it certainly does not meet today's standard of a good operating system. Various chapters in this book explain these other important functions.

The art of managing a manufacturing company has matured to the point where there is a cause-and-effect relationship—good information generates correct action. For example, the general manager who can see the consequences of various plans is able to make a smarter choice. If the selected plan can be converted to the detailed task required to execute it, the general manager can have confidence that his or her decision will be executed. If a problem or an opportunity develops either inside or outside the company, the general manager needs to reassess the current plan. This sequence is a never-ending process. The production plan is a vital part of this process.

Make-to-Stock Example

The easiest aspect of production planning is the arithmetic. The formulas are simple, and there are only two, one for make-to-stock products and another for make-to-order products. Each is illustrated with an example.

Assume that a company has a family of products that consist of standard, ship-off-the-shelf products. The marketplace is serviced from finished goods. Additionally, assume the need to plan for the next 12 months. To calculate what the factory needs to produce for this category, three pieces of data are needed: the forecast of what is expected to be sold for the next 12 months, the desired finished-goods inventory at the end of 12 months, and the starting finished-goods inventory. This formula is shown in Table 7.1. The inventory in the formula is strictly finished goods; it does not include component inventories or work in process. The example indicates that the factory must make 1100 units of this family given a forecast of 1000 for the year and the goal of raising finished-goods inventory from 100 to 200.

The formula could not be easier. The challenge, however, is to supply the forecast and to determine the ending finished-goods inventory target.

Forecasting is both unreliable and, in many companies, painful. Too often marketing has been taken to task for its inaccurate guesses and so will not volunteer to supply this number. The general manager's reaction to inaccurate forecasts has much to do with marketing's willingness or unwillingness to participate. If the general manager blames marketing for errors, marketing will either reluctantly commit itself or, worse still, not offer this information. By default, some other group must do the forecasting job. Equally bad is a general manager who believes that overselling the forecast is good but underselling is bad. Understandably, marketing will provide a figure that it expects to exceed. Accuracy for the forecast is desirable: inaccuracy in either direction is undesirable. Honesty, however, is essential. The general manager should insist on honesty. Otherwise, everyone will second-guess the forecast, and the production planning process will lose its effectiveness.

As difficult as it is for anybody to predict the future with confidence, it is an unavoidable task for make-to-stock products. Marketing's major contribution to both the business plan and the production plan is to supply this information. With this job also comes accountability. Marketing should be measured by the accuracy of its forecast.

Agreeing on the desired ending finished-goods inventory is also a challenge. A company is apt to get as many different recommendations for this figure as there are

TABLE 7.1 Example for Make-to-Stock Family

Formula
Production plan = forecast + (desired ending finished goods inventory − starting finished goods inventory)

Example
Given: Forecast = 1000 for 12 months
desired ending finished goods inventory = 200
starting finished goods inventory = 100
Then: Production plan = 1000 + (200 − 100) = 1100

Inventory Expressed in Time

$$\text{Average monthly sales} = \frac{\text{Annual forecast}}{12} = \frac{1000}{12} = 83$$

$$\text{Months of inventory} = \frac{\text{Inventory level}}{\text{average monthly sales}} = \frac{200}{83} = 2.4$$

people on the general manager's staff. Generally, marketing advocates higher values whereas finance usually recommends lower ones. Perhaps these are unfair stereotypes. Yet, they do reflect the individual's worries.

No person on the staff wants to hurt the company. None will simply defend his or her parochial interest. Each needs to be able to recommend what he or she feels is the best, knowing all of the consequences, not just those in the area. After listening to all sides, the general manager must cast a vote. Sometimes that vote counts more than all the others combined.

The starting finished-goods inventory position is clean-cut. It reflects where you are today—good, bad, or indifferent. You may not be happy with the situation, but this is reality.

Many companies express the inventory figures in terms of time—days, weeks, or months. Many executives are more comfortable evaluating inventory levels in terms of time rather than quantity. It might be misleading, for example, to say that the total finished-goods inventory is going to be higher when, in fact, it is decreasing in terms of how many days worth of inventory it represents. Many executives can sense where too little inventory begins or where more than enough starts. The term *forward coverage* is often used to describe this concept, i.e., how long will the inventory last? In the example in Table 7.1 the ending finished-goods inventory would represent a 2.4-month supply based on average sales.

Since many companies do not sell at a level rate during the year, it is important to view the finished-goods inventory levels on a month-by-month basis rather than simply considering the end figure. With a highly seasonal product, a month-by-month survey could easily point out interim problems. For example, for several months a company is building far more than it is selling: this may reflect a severe space or cash flow problem. However, if the high-selling season occurs at the beginning of the planning process and the starting point is a low inventory, the company may have a severe back order problem because sales are exceeding production.

Make-to-Order Example

The formula for make-to-order products is similar but not identical to that for make-to-stock products. *Make-to-order products* are either products that are going to be finished to a customer's specification or highly engineered orders that are designed after receipt of a customer's order. A company that has finished-to-order products starts making the product based on a forecast and manufactures components up to a certain level. The company would not complete the assembly until a customer order arrived. The customers typically select features, options, attachments, and accessories. For a highly engineered product, two events must occur before anything is bought or made. First, a company has to win the order; second, the design engineers must tell purchasing and the factory what they need to buy and make. All the purchasing and manufacturing activities are being carried out to the specific customer's specifications.

Obviously, in both make-to-order categories the expectation is to have no finished-goods inventory. Rather, the term *backlog* is appropriate. Backlog is equal to all customer orders received and not yet shipped. Although the term *backlog* is common, some companies use it differently. To them, it includes only those customer orders that should have been shipped prior to today, i.e., those that are past due. That is not how it is used in this chapter. Here backlog orders include those customer orders that are past due and all future-dated ones. Some companies describe the backlog as representing their "order board."

Table 7.2 shows the formula for determining how much the factory needs to produce for a make-to-order category. Again, it requires from marketing a forecast of new orders expected in the next 12 months (in this example). To that figure, add the difference between the starting backlog and the desired ending backlog. If marketing expects 100 new orders to arrive and the company's goal is to cut the backlog in half, from 40 to 20, then the factory needs to produce 120 in the next 12 months.

The formula is simple, and the arithmetic, once provided, does not require a computer to solve. The challenge is to supply the forecast and to get a resolution on the desired ending backlog.

The figures for the formula are as important and as difficult to provide as in the make-to-stock environment. Generally, marketing advocates less backlog. Marketing is the first to foresee the problem of getting new customer orders if the company takes longer to ship its product than its competitors do. Thus, from marketing's point of view, the ideal backlog would be less than that of the competitors. When a company is considering buying new capital equipment and/or expanding the plant,

TABLE 7.2   Example for Make-to-Order Family

Formula
Production plan = forecast + (starting backlog − desired ending backlog)

Example

Given: Forecast = 100 for 12 months
         desired ending backlog = 20
         starting backlog = 40
 	
Then: Production plan = 100 + (40 − 20) = 120

Backlog Expressed in Time
$$\text{Average monthly sales} = \frac{\text{annual forecast}}{12} = \frac{100}{12} = 8.3$$
$$\text{Months of backlog} = \frac{\text{backlog level}}{\text{average monthly sales}} = \frac{20}{8.3} = 2.4$$

however, the existence of a decreasing backlog will certainly make the top manufacturing person and others very nervous. Often, manufacturing would like an increasing backlog since it reflects, to them, a more secure figure on which to base plans. As a result, a heated discussion is not uncommon. At the appropriate point the general manager must decide which plan to follow.

As with finished goods, many companies express backlog in terms of days, weeks, or months. The size of the backlog itself is not as important as what it represents in terms of how long a customer has to wait. In fact, from marketing's point of view, it would be ideal to have sales increase while the company can ship faster to customers (because the rate of output is greater than the booking rate). And even if a competitor's total backlog is not known, generally this information can be discovered by asking customers how long it takes a competitor to ship new orders. In many industries, standards develop over time, representing what the customers will accept. If the company is able to maintain a figure close to the standard, it is competitive in terms of delivery.

Output versus Goals

The two formulas reflect a fundamental relationship. For make-to-stock products, if the goal is to build inventory, then the output from the factory must exceed the incoming customer orders. For make-to-order products, in order to decrease the backlog, the output from the factory must be greater than the incoming customer orders. To achieve the opposite ending positions, the output must be less than the incoming orders. If a company believes its current level of either finished goods and/or backlog to be correct and wishes to end at the same level, then the company is striving to balance the outgoing and the incoming.

To express what manufacturing must produce as a rate, the total output should be divided by the available workdays over the planning horizon. The formula for calculating output rates is shown in Table 7.3. It is assumed that 250 workdays are available. If a new rate represents a significant increase from the current level and if the factory cannot implement it immediately, a stepped production plan is required. An example of this is also shown in Table 7.3.

Relationship with the Master Production Schedule

The production plan is the means by which the general manager communicates policy to the master schedulers. The MPS defines what products a company expects to build, how many, and when. The production plan becomes a budget for the master schedulers to spend. The plan reflects management's policy by family; the schedulers, in turn, convert this plan to considerably greater detail. For example, the master schedulers define what is to be built in terms of specific configurations (end items, modules, or planning bills), which can be analyzed via a bill of materials. Additionally, the production plan is normally expressed in broad categories of time, i.e., by month. Scheduling by month is too broad for priority planning, so the master scheduler must schedule in intervals of weeks or less.

In essence, the master scheduler's job is to take the approved production plan and to convert it to specific product plans. The master scheduler determines the best mix of products which, when totaled, equals the production plan. No master scheduler should have the authority to submit a plan that exceeds or understates the production plan. The scheduler's job is to execute the plan by scheduling the best product mix within the budget.

TABLE 7.3 Example of Rates of Production

Formula	

$$\text{Rate of production} = \frac{\text{Production plan}}{\text{Available workdays}} = \text{Daily output}$$

Example

Given: Made-to-stock production plan = 1100
(see Table 7.1)
Available workdays   = 250

$$\text{Then: Daily output} = \frac{1100}{250} = 4.4$$

Example of Stepped Production Rates

Given: 60 days at current rate of 3.4
Remaining workdays to meet target of 1100 are $250 - 60 = 190$
Then: $60 \text{ days} \times 3.4 = 204$ (total output at current rate)
$1100 - 204 = 896$ (required total output for remaining 190 days)
New rate $= \dfrac{896}{190} = 4.72$ (to be effective in 60 days)

However, when the master schedulers do not agree with the budget, they should speak up. They should predict the consequences of following the current plan and recommend a better plan. In turn, the general manager owes the master scheduler two things: consideration of the master scheduler's prediction and recommendation and a decision. Given this new information, the general manager must choose to change the plan or to continue with the existing plan.

This process is a closed-loop process. See Fig. 7.1. It must be in place and working smoothly for a company to get the full benefit from both production planning and master scheduling. Each function benefits from the other. The master schedulers need to understand management's goal. It is not enough to say, "Have enough but not too much" or "Do a good job." The master scheduler will never succeed in carrying out those instructions. But a master scheduler can understand and work with a goal of "build at the rate of 4000 per month." Note that the general manager needs to know that the sum of the individual decisions of the master schedulers totals the approved plan. Additionally, the MPS should be converted to dollars, and the total dollars should equal the business plan. If there is a variance, it should quickly surface and be resolved.

DESIGNING THE
PRODUCTION PLANNING PROCESS

Production planning is critical and simple, and it should be straightforward to implement and easy to operate. Only a few issues need to be resolved. The balance of this chapter describes these issues, how the process should be designed, and how the process should be managed.

Who is responsible for the production plan? As explained earlier, it is the general manager's responsibility. If this question is not answered properly, the rest of the

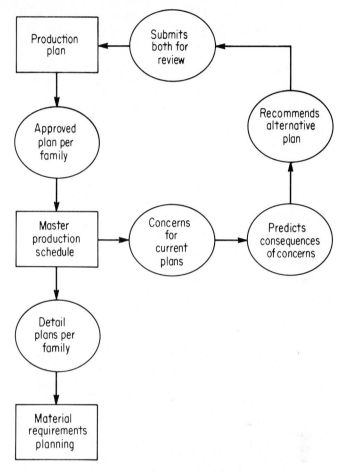

FIG. 7.1 Closed-loop process. Production plan with the MPS.

items on the checklist will have little value. The general manager must recognize that this is her or his responsibility.

A lot of information is required for production planning. Although not responsible for all the gathering and analyzing of these data, the general manager must know what information is important, who should be responsible for supplying it, and how the information can be utilized. Definitions of family, correct planning horizon, and right unit of measure are three design issues that must be agreed upon to make the production planning process effective.

Definition of Family

The goal is to define the family as broadly as possible, yet have each family related to a manufacturing process. Unfortunately, there is no formula to reach this goal.

Fortunately, however, it is a very forgiving issue; it is not like pouring concrete. Rather, companies that do not, at first, define a family properly can easily change the definition. If too many are created, group some. If there are too few, subdivide and create more.

Although judgment is necessary, there are two reliable guidelines to follow. First, begin by defining a family as broadly as possible. Note the similarities among the products and processes rather than the differences. The end result is more accurate forecasts, more reliable planning, and less work.

If too few families are designated, the second guideline applies in the discussion among marketing, manufacturing, and engineering. If marketing, manufacturing, and engineering are not able to communicate, if they cannot relate to the family, a frown caused by the confusion will be evident.

For example, picture an office furniture manufacturer that produces and sells desks, filing cabinets, and chairs. If this company lumped all three categories of products under one large family called *office furniture*, a communications problem would occur. Marketing might predict sales to increase next year by 30 percent and ask manufacturing if this can be handled. The vice president of manufacturing might shrug her shoulders, frown, and ask, "Are sales going to go up 30 percent in each of the categories—chairs, filing cabinets, and desks?" It is possible that next year's sales could go up 50 percent in one category and 10 percent in another and stay flat in the third category, resulting in an overall 30 percent gain in sales of office furniture. If this were to occur unexpectedly, the vice president of manufacturing probably would not support this change. The skills and equipment needed to make chairs are not transferable to filing cabinets or to desks. Thus, to say that office furniture sales are going to go up or down is not meaningful. That family is too broad. To relate to the manufacturing process, three families need to be reviewed.

In most companies, product lines correspond to manufacturing processes. In the example of the manufacturer of office furniture, it is a one-on-one relationship. At times, however, marketing has more product lines than manufacturing has processes. For example, if marketing has a separate sales force for different industries, farming versus manufacturing or original equipment products versus replacement products, marketing may treat these as separate categories, each with its own forecast. However, if the products in each category follow the same flow in the factory, these forecasts should be consolidated and discussed in terms of their total impact.

Unfortunately, sometimes the product lines and the manufacturing families are intertwined. It is not a straightforward consolidation. Where this exists, the choices may be difficult, but they are not numerous. One group has to learn how to relate to the other group's definition or else develop tables to convert forecasts.

Although they are not applicable to all manufacturing companies, other families are possible. Some companies review their need for repair parts and service parts in the same manner as regular products. Similarly, some review the resources needed for scrap, shrinkage, and rework. Also, whenever engineers use production equipment for research and development work or to make prototypes, certain resources are required, as with regular products. However, in other companies these categories are not elevated to the production planning function, but are included as part of the detailed planning functions. The decision of how to treat them should be based on the importance of each category in each company. The decision is also influenced by the need of the general manager and staff to review these categories or consider a resolution from a lower level.

Having a family called *emergency business* is helpful for a number of companies. It addresses the need to respond immediately to urgent customer demands. If these types of orders are a routine part of the business, they should be accommodated without jeopardizing existing commitments or generating constant overtime. To do so, this category should be identified as a separate family. It should have a forecast and a production plan to ensure that sufficient capacity and other resources are available.

In summary, start with as few families as possible and reluctantly add more. Since this does not lend itself to arithmetic, many companies debate for long hours, trying to find the best definition of a family. It is not worth it. It is better to get a rough estimate, start using it, and judge it by hindsight. If it is working, fine. If it is not working, then adjust it accordingly.

Planning Horizon

How far out should the production plan extend? Many companies think in terms of their fiscal year. Typically, the financial planning horizon is a year to establish budgets, review cash flow, and predict profits. Yet, from an operating point of view, it would be a coincidence if the production planning horizon also required 12 months.

To judge this issue for a company, four activities must be analyzed, all of which depend on a production plan to be handled properly. These four activities are material planning, capacity planning, purchasing visibility, and "what if" simulations. That function which requires the longest look ahead, i.e., the longest lead time, holds the answer. The production plan has to extend at least that far into the future to support this activity.

Material planning is the least likely to be the longest. The longest total time for material planning is determined by that product with the longest cumulative lead time. An example is shown in Fig. 7.2. Here the production plan and the MPS must extend at least 32 weeks in order to do MRP properly. If the production plan and thus the MPS were to extend out less than 32 weeks, purchasing would not have adequate time to procure the long lead-time components. The buyers would be starting their activity late, and so they would be expediting, not planning, in an attempt to bring the material in on the required date.

Invariably, however, capacity planning requires a longer look ahead because it involves dealing with some highly skilled operators, design engineers, etc., and some typically complicated long-lead-time capital equipment. Additionally, a plant or a division within a large corporation must consider the bureaucratic time required to get approval for any costly capital expenditure.

Purchasing visibility is a critical function that may require an even longer look ahead. Take an example where the cumulative material lead time is 32 weeks. If purchasing wanted 50 weeks of planned orders (the visibility) for that 30-week lead-time component, then the MPS would have to extend out 82 weeks to provide this information. No doubt, it is extra work for the top managers, but it is worthwhile if there are high paybacks from more effective negotiations with suppliers.

One of the most dramatic changes that will occur in the future is the use of simulations in the front office. The typical general manager, once given a simulation capability, will exercise it frequently. This has been a promise since the advent of computers in manufacturing companies. Yet, very few companies have the necessary ingredients in place to provide the capability. It requires a valid operating system, accurate data, software to process the request without disturbing the current operating data, and a terminal that is used conveniently by a general manager.

In the near future, many companies will have these elements, and their general managers will be able to make better decisions by knowing the consequences of various alternatives. Predicting the consequences of various plans does not eliminate surprises, but certainly a manager armed with pertinent information is better

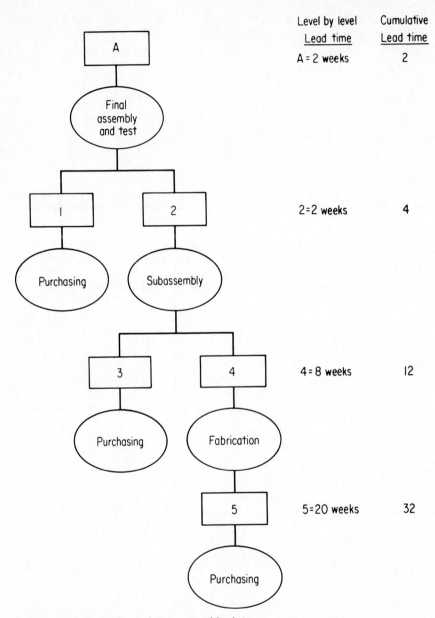

FIG. 7.2 Example of cumulative material lead time.

off than one using strictly past experience. Generally, simulation requires the longest look ahead. That is, how far out would the general manager like to evaluate alternate strategies, such as plan A versus plan B versus plan C? An example showing alternative plans is given later. Once the length of the planning horizon is determined, it becomes a rolling horizon. As a period goes by, another period must be added.

Finally, a system should be designed with growth in mind. It is better to have a system that can accept growth and not use it than to design a system for today's needs and discover later that more is needed.

Unit of Measure

Without a doubt, the worst unit of measure that marketing could use in giving manufacturing a forecast is sales dollars. Everybody knows that next year could bring more sales dollars and simultaneously require fewer people in the factory. A combination of two events will do it—an increase in selling price combined with selling more products that require fewer factory hours than current products. Although the sales barometer is pointing up, a layoff is coming.

Pieces or units of measure in many companies are satisfactory. If the labor content is very similar from one piece to another, then pieces or units are an excellent choice. Where there is variety from one piece to another but a high volume of sales, a company can often use a representative piece. This represents a weighted average for the whole family. A number of companies have developed conversion tables of weighted averages which allows a forecast from marketing to be expressed in one unit of measure and presented to the manufacturing and engineering groups in terms of standard hours.

OPERATING THE PRODUCTION PLAN

Having the families defined properly, the unit of measure agreed upon, and the length of the planning horizon resolved is important. Every company must answer these questions, or else confusion will result. Yet, having the answers to these problems is not sufficient. The general manager and staff must develop an ongoing ability to maintain an effective production plan. That is what this section addresses—how to operate the production planning function.

Frequency of Review

Typically, companies review the production planning process monthly. No doubt, one contributing reason is that financial reviews occur monthly. Managers get in the habit of reviewing the financial report card to see how well they are doing. Reviewing the production planning process monthly also has other logic behind it. Most manufacturing companies consider a week insufficient time to spot a trend. Adding people or laying them off is a serious decision. More time has to elapse before a trend requiring some adjustment in the rates of output is apparent.

Even though there are ups and downs from one week to another, most companies sit back and watch the trends. They absorb small changes by letting finished goods grow or shrink or by letting the backlog expand or contract. Most do not immediately start working overtime, adding people, or laying them off to correct what may be a mere fluctuation.

On the other hand, a company can wait too long to review the rates of output. Quarterly meetings, for example, are generally too infrequent. It is better to have a short, 5-minute meeting and reconvene a month later than to put off a meeting and have a major problem. Holding frequent meetings does not prevent problems from occurring. Rather, it catches the problem before the crisis stage is reached.

Equally important as determining the frequency of meetings is having the dates of future meetings on everybody's calendar. Otherwise, availability of key people becomes a hit-or-miss affair. If the marketing manager has had to leave town on an important sales call, a product manager can represent marketing. Similarly, if the manufacturing manager is visiting another factory, a plant manager can be sent instead. This is not to demean middle managers. What this means is that the vital function of production planning is delegated to middle managers as opposed to company leaders. The best way to make sure all the right people are present is for the general manager to announce, "It is absolutely essential that the top leaders of the business be present."[3] Everybody will be there if it is that important to the boss.

Agenda for the Meeting

Some executives resist having an agenda for a meeting. They see it as too confining and unnecessary. A problem caused by not having an agenda is that the production planning meeting can deteriorate into a "crisis of the hour" meeting.

The production planning meeting should look at the forest, not the individual trees. An agenda helps ensure that time is being spent productively on the right issues. The agenda should spell out who is going to attend the meeting, what they are going to bring with them, what is going to be talked about, and what the objectives are. Run the production planning meeting according to this agenda, and then adjourn to talk about other issues. Avoid mixing the issues.

Measurements

Typically, a company starts the meeting with a review of the production plan. It looks backward to see what has been done to execute the current plan. Everyone can learn through hindsight and so plan ahead with greater confidence.

The key is to have three figures laid out for all members of the general manager's staff: what they have agreed to do, what their performance is measured against, and a tolerance level to determine whether the performance was satisfactory. Table 7.4 shows an example.

Marketing should be measured by how the incoming orders match the prediction, i.e., bookings versus forecast. In addition to this tracking on a period-by-period basis, it is important that the data be analyzed on a year-to-date basis. Performance in any area is apt to be off in any one period, but over several months the random ups and downs should cancel. However, if performance is out of control, an explanation should be forthcoming. This is another way of focusing on those areas that warrant it.

Manufacturing should be measured by actual versus expected factory output, engineering by the number of hours or jobs completed versus those projected, finance by its support of cash needs, distribution by actual versus planned inventory in the warehouses, and purchasing by its ability to bring in sufficient amounts of key commodities.

By reviewing each performance in such a manner, the general manager can determine who is doing a good job and who needs help. Measurements are necessary to assess performance. By reviewing how well each person is executing the plan, a common mistake is avoided. Whenever the boss asks whether something can be handled, the temptation is to say yes even though facts dictate otherwise. Without measurements it becomes difficult later to find out what actually happened and who caused it. In short, do not make promises that cannot be kept.

TABLE 7.4 Example of Measuring the Production Plan

Marketing[a]

	Period	Forecast	Actual	Difference	Forecast	Actual	Cumulative Difference[b]
					Last 6 periods		
History	1	100	95	−5	600	610	+10
	2	110	95	−15	610	605	+5
	3	120	100	−20[c]	630	600	−25
Future	4	110					
	5	100					
	6	100					

Manufacturing[d]

	Period	Planned Production	Actual	Difference	Cumulative Difference[e]
History	1	105	104	−1	−1
	2	105	104	−1	−2
	3	105	104	−1	−3[f]
Future	4	105			
	5	105			
	6	105			

[a] Tolerances individual period = ±18.
[b] Tolerance cumulative = ±12.
[c] Denotes out-of-tolerance.
[d] Tolerance individual period = ±4.
[e] Tolerance cumulative = ±2
[f] Denotes out-of-tolerance.

The general manager is also responsible for a key item in each product family. In a make-to-stock family, the general manager should assume responsibility for the size of the finished-goods inventory. Once the general manager approves the plan, attaining its parameters becomes the goal. If the goal is not reached, then obviously the plan was not successful. It should be easy to look at what happened and find out the reason for the failure. Nonetheless, the general manager must accept responsibility for the team not performing to its expectations.

If the product family is a make-to-order item, the general manager's responsibility is the desired ending backlog figure. Here again, not achieving it means that the team was unsuccessful in that plan. Again, the general manager will be able to quickly find the explanation. Regardless of the outcome, the general manager must take full responsibility.

Proposed Changes

Having looked backward to evaluate how well each function is doing against the current plan, the company then discusses the need to alter the current plan. The meeting becomes a forum in which members of the staff, including the general manager, submit changes. The economy changing differently than expected, competitor doing something unexpected, a new product selling faster than expected, or the impact of a sales change or promotion being more successful than expected could require a different rate of output.

The proposal for a change should offer both an explanation of why it is necessary and a prediction of the consequences if the change is not made. To the extent that there are alternatives, each should be spelled out. Evaluating the alternatives then becomes the central issue. What if we do not change? How quickly do we have to change? Are there some trade-offs that could be considered?

Each answer may generate a series of questions. After the choices and their consequences have been aired, a decision must be made. The general manager and staff have been trained and are expected to make this decision.

Information helps. When the choices are laid out so that each alternative can be compared, the decision-making process is improved. Figure 7.3 is an example. It shows a product line with a high seasonality. Plan A reflects a level manufacturing rate. For several months the plant's output exceeds sales, and inventory is building; later the opposite occurs, and inventory is depleted. This plan would generally be favored by the manufacturing vice president since it is the most stable one. The financial manager might object because it requires money to be tied up in inventory. Plan B reflects a changing manufacturing rate that leads the sales curve. Even though the vice president of finance would prefer this plan, without a doubt, the vice president of manufacturing would object strenuously. The third choice, plan C, is a compromise: a 20 percent boost in outputs occurs in the spring, and a corresponding 20 percent drop occurs in the fall. If another family existed whose manufacturing needs were the reciprocal of the first one—more people required in the fall and fewer in the spring and summer—plan C might be an excellent choice.

But to complicate matters and yet reflect reality, perhaps the vice president of marketing is going to revise the sales forecast upward and needs to know whether manufacturing can support the revision with output. If manufacturing is having difficulty supporting the third plan, certainly it will not be able to simply say yes without more review. How much more product is needed? How quickly is it needed? Also purchasing, engineering, and other contributors will need to discuss the situation in terms of being able to support each alternative or explaining why if they cannot.

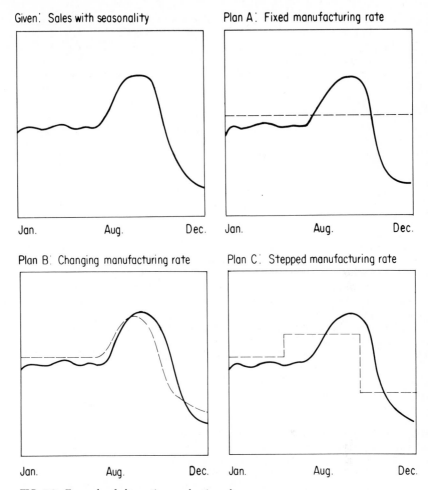

FIG. 7.3 Example of alternative production plans.

Ideally, one plan will surface that is the best choice. Often, however, this is not the case. Rather, the pros and cons of each plan are significant. Here the general manager is tested. After an appropriate amount of discussion, a resolution must be achieved. For each family there has to be one agreed-on plan all parties recognize, support, and measure themselves against.

Planning Aids

As an aid to the general manager and staff, many companies develop a *resource-requirements planning* capability, also known as *rough-cut capacity planning*. It represents a profile of the probable impact on key resources for each family. In manufacturing terms, this would represent the key work centers; in engineering terms, the key design and drafting work centers; in financial terms, the probable cost dollars as well as sales and profit dollars. These profiles permit the group to assess the likely impact of a change up or down and offer a better basis for judging its feasibility.

An example of a resource requirements profile is shown in Table 7.5. The vice president of manufacturing has identified three work centers as being critical and has estimated the number of standard hours required to produce one product in a specified family. If currently 1000 units of this family are produced weekly and the request is to increase it by 30 percent in 12 weeks, the vice president of manufacturing could use this rough-cut planning to gauge the hours required for each work center.

The real value of resource-requirements planning is seen whenever a combination of changes is being discussed. It is important to be able to estimate the *net* impact on key resources. Simply addressing the proposed changes one at a time, without realizing their interaction, can be misleading. Occasionally a confident answer cannot be supplied in this meeting. On such occasions, it is usually better to avoid agreeing or disagreeing. Rather, discuss how long it will take for the assessment and postpone the final determination until that time.

Changes in the production plan can always be carried out given sufficient time and/or money. The size of the change and existing conditions dictate how long and/or how expensive it will be. Guidelines, however, have proved helpful for many companies. These companies develop "time fences" as an aid for managing changes. The intent is to introduce changes in an economical manner by planning ahead. For example, one company's time fence stated that in the first 60 days, overtime was the most practical way of reacting to the need for greater output; from 60 to 120 days, a 20 percent change could be implemented; beyond 120 days, almost any size change could be handled. The capacity constraint was usually labor, and a minimum of 3 to 4 months was needed to add to the labor force. Obviously, if the labor market is tight at any particular time, more time could be needed. Additionally, if key commodities cannot be procured, more output will not be generated even though operators could be added.

Minutes of the Meeting

Each company has its own style of conducting meetings. Some are structured, others are more informal. Many companies do not take minutes of meetings. The risks can be serious. Each person may be confident as to what was agreed on, but this may not match another person's confident memory of the same meeting. When

TABLE 7.5   Example of Resource Requirements Profile*

Critical Work Center[†]	Labor/Machine Content per Unit, Hours	Offset from Completion Week
1. Final assembly	2	Needed in final week
2. Rough grind	14	Needed 4 weeks prior to final week
3. Turning	32	Needed 8 weeks prior to final week

* Given: for family "X," 3 critical manufacturing work centers.

† Proposal: to increase weekly output of family "X" by 30 percent, from 1000 to 1300, in 12 weeks, and then impact on critical work centers:
1. Final assembly needs 600 additional hours starting in 12 weeks.
2. Rough grind needs 4200 additional hours starting in 8 weeks.
3. Turning needs 9600 additional hours starting in 4 weeks.

there is confusion, the penalty is enormous. To avoid this, companies should take careful minutes of the meeting and publish them.

Preliminary Effort

To make the production planning meeting as effective as possible, some companies do their homework. Publishing the data a few days in advance of the meeting is one way to do this. Then everybody can review what is to be discussed in the meeting.

Another aid, with the same purpose in mind, is preliminary meetings. In one company a materials manager conducts two "smaller" meetings. To gather information, the manager meets separately with marketing and the vice president of manufacturing to review specific problem areas. Then the materials manager works with both groups in an effort to come to the main meeting with alternatives laid out. The materials manager in this company is a facilitator.

A third aid is to have a special section on each agenda for additional issues. Prior to the meeting, the general manager asks all staff members whether any other issues, not normally discussed in the production planning meeting, need to be brought up. This gives staff members the feeling that it is their meeting and is an excellent way to ensure good communications. Some topics, however, are not appropriate for the meeting. For example, any topic that does not concern all staff members, relates to specific product parts, or concerns a personality problem would not qualify for the agenda of the next meeting.

Resolving Conflicts

With control come difficult decisions. With difficult decisions comes a crossroad for every general manager. Will the general manager face up to reality and make the hard decisions or turn away, hoping that ignoring the situation will make it go away? Production planning gives excellent visibility to the top management team. But good visibility often shows that the general manager cannot do everything that she or he wishes. After agonizing over the practical alternatives, the general manager makes the final trade-offs during the production planning process.

For example, if business is increasing for both a make-to-stock and a make-to-order product family faster than the factory can expand capacity and/or purchasing can produce commodities, then a difficult decision has to be made. To which category should capacity be allocated? Or should some capacity be given to each, though not enough to either? Avoiding this tough decision will only force it to be made at a lower level, in reaction to the complaints that are bound to occur.

Similarly, sometimes a viable plan cannot be executed because of an unavoidable problem. Perhaps a key supplier had a major catastrophe or a wildcat strike, a major problem has developed with equipment in the factory, new equipment has not come on line as expected, or a quality problem unexpectedly developed in the field which causes a corrective action in the factory. These are painful crises that unfortunately every company encounters. Sometimes the ideal plan cannot be met even with the best effort. As soon as this becomes apparent, the bad news must be fed back to the general manager—what is wrong, what caused it, what is being done to correct it, how long it will take, and what are the choices for a new plan.

If an uncorrectable problem occurs and the general manager refuses to change the plan, an obvious and serious follow-up problem will develop. The general manager will be disappointed when the unrealistic plan is not achieved. All the other people in the company will be disappointed that the general manager is not accepting reality.

SUMMARY

With the business plan and the production plan, the general manager can direct the company. Without them, the general manager may be going through the motions but will be relying on good fortune, not good tools, to be successful. The recommended actions that the general manager should initiate to ensure proper design and operation of the production plan are shown in Table 7.6.

In some companies, however, the general manager expects that the operating system can achieve the desired objectives without a formal business plan and production plan. In essence, he or she has spelled out the goals in such broad terms as "do whatever it takes to hit the profit goal." In the ideal situation, the general manager recognizes and is prepared to do the job. The ideal general manager gives his or her best and expects everyone else to do the same. In these companies the business plan and the production plan operate in a well-organized manner.

For companies not having a good operating system in place today and/or implementing an improved one, the production planning function can be implemented quickly with significant benefits. Even though it may not mesh smoothly with the existing system, by providing direction in the form of rates of output, the existing scheduling system will, undoubtedly, give better control.

One of Oliver Wight's many insights was that all manufacturing companies are similar. He delineated this in his fundamental manufacturing equation: "What are we going to make? What does it take to make it? What have we got? What do we have to get?"[4] Every manufacturing company must answer these questions regardless of size, type of product, or type of process.

When they are viewed in the aggregate, these questions become the basis of both the business and the production plan. The question of what to make is solved by

TABLE 7.6 Summary Checklist

Category	Action
Most Important Issue	
Responsibility	Understood and accepted
Design Issues	
Families	Defined
Unit of measure	Agreed upon
Planning horizon	Established
Operating Considerations	
Frequency of review	Scheduled
Agenda	Laid out
Measurements	Determined
Alternative proposals	Expected
Resource-requirements profiles	Available
Time fences	Developed
Minutes	Published
Homework	Identified
Conflicts	To be resolved

looking at forecasts and inventory backlog and determining the desired finished goods and/or the size of the ending backlog. What is needed to make the product is answered by manufacturing, engineering, finance, and purchasing, which translates the proposed rate of output into specific goals. "What have we got?" is answered by knowing the current number of workers, machine availability, inventory, vendor status, engineering status, finances, etc. "What we have to get" is the difference between what it takes and what we have.

These four fundamental questions, answered for each product, become the basis for the MPS function. When they are answered for each component, it makes up the function called MRP; when they are answered for each work center, it constitutes the function called capacity-requirements planning. The questions are simple, logical, and necessary steps for handling these functions correctly.

When functions are managed well, they make up an effective operating system. "Elegant simplicity" is how one general manager described the end result. When each person does his or her job well, the result is excellent teamwork. The combination of the right operating system and of people doing their jobs efficiently produces predictable results.

Running a manufacturing company is not easy, and no one wants to make it tougher than it has to be. Having a production plan that is properly designed and operated does not mean all of the decisions will be the right ones. It simply means that the company will be far better off making decisions by design, armed with good information, rather than by default.

The production planning function in the hands of a skilled general manager enables him or her to be in control of the business.

REFERENCES

1. Thomas F. Wallace (ed.), *APICS Dictionary*, 5th ed., APICS, Falls Church, Virginia, 1984, p. 24.
2. "Control of the Business," *1985 Newsletter*, The Oliver Wight Companies, Newbury, New Hampshire, 1985, p.8.
3. David Rucinski, "Game Planning," *Production and Inventory Management Journal*, First quarter, 1982, p. 67. Quote from Milton J. Henrichs, Vice President and Division President of Abbott Laboratories.
4. Oliver W. Wight, *Manufacturing Resource Planning: MRP II—Unlocking America's Productivity Potential*, rev. ed., Oliver Wight Limited Publications, Essex Junction, Vermont, 1984, p. 47.

BIBLIOGRAPHY

Wallace, Tom (ed.): *APICS Dictionary*, 5th ed., APICS, Falls Church, Virginia, 1984.

Wight, Oliver W.: *Manufacturing Resource Planning: MRP II—Unlocking America's Productivity Potential*, rev. ed., Oliver Wight Limited Publications, Essex Junction, Vermont, 1984.

Information Requirements

CHAPTER 8

Customer Service

Editors

ARNOLD O. PUTNAM, CMC, Chairman Emeritus and Chief
Executive Officer, Rath & Strong Inc., Management Consultants,
Lexington, Massachusetts

WILLIAM A. WHEELER, III, Formerly Vice President, Rath &
Strong, Inc., Lexington, Massachusetts. Presently a partner with
Coopers and Lybrand, Boston, Massachusetts

Since the last edition of this book a major breakthrough has occurred—the development of *just-in-time* (JIT) technology. This topic is covered in Chapter 24, so it is not repeated here. The impact of JIT technology on customer relations does not make the ordering logic wrong, but it makes many of the factors previously considered less important.

The thrusts of JIT technology are as follows:

- It reduces setup costs, so lot sizes can become very small—frequently only a single day's supply.
- It makes job shops perform as production or flow shops by the use of group technology.
- It achieves defect-free products, so zero inventories are required in receiving, in process, or before final assembly.

This chapter discusses lot sizing, ordering quantities, and inventories with the appropriate logic. The seriousness of deviating from the calculated value may not be as great as was assumed in the past. Because inventory levels are so much lower with JIT operations, reducing them by another 50 percent does not produce spectacular savings.

PROOF OF QUALITY, ON-TIME SHIPMENTS

The rapid adoption of JIT techniques affected the vendor-customer relationships in the automotive industry. After considerable vendor education, the automobile manufacturers expect the vendor to furnish *statistical proof* of process quality with each shipment and proof that it will arrive exactly on the day needed. For some vendors this has meant major quality improvements as well as holding of inventories for exact-day shipment. The vendors incur excessive costs doing this until their own JIT capabilities are in full operation, after which there should be a cost savings.

COOPERATIVE VERSUS ADVERSARY ROLES

Historically, customers in the United States have held vendors in an adversary relationship and frequently kept many sources of supply to maintain competition. As a result, vendors subdivide the business so that the threatened loss of a customer does not mean much compared to the vendor's receiving all or 50 percent of the customer's business. In Japan, the one or two vendors per item, or type of item, has become the rule. The larger orders created a greater interest on the part of the vendor to please the customer and to hold and expand the business. The customer and vendor developed a relationship of cooperation rather than continuing as adversaries. From this relationship clearly both can gain:

CUSTOMER	VENDOR
Gives vendor larger orders over longer periods.	Gains greater knowledge of customer's product and processes.
Keeps vendor informed of quantities and scheduled needs.	Makes recommendations about product or parts that improve quality and/or reduce cost.
Reviews vendor's facilities and processes and recommends ways to improve quality and costs.	Experiences improved gauge control and coordination.
Has greater assurance of excellent ongoing source of supply.	Has shared investment in future improvements.
Incurs lower cost in providing products.	Has greater assurance of an ongoing business.
Enjoys less paperwork and overhead in getting shipments, adjusting schedules, etc.	Incurs lower cost of selling the product.
	Releases for shipment against contract.

Some U.S. manufacturers are concerned about vendor dependency and the risk of strikes or unforecasted disruptions of service. This may mean that U.S. manufacturers will always have more vendors for each part than their Japanese counterparts. All the same, the trend to cooperative customer-vendor arrangements will expand rapidly, for the economic justification is too great to resist.

FORECASTS

JIT technology has a large impact on forecasts and forecast accuracy. The reduction of lead time due to smaller lot sizes and zero inventory for receiving, work in process, and assembly protection may be as much as two-thirds; thus 9 months becomes 3 months, 6 months becomes 2 months, etc. It has always been the longer lead time that adversely affects forecast accuracy as well as directly affecting the amount of safety stock needed for any given level of customer service.

Generally, under contract purchasing there is a long-term quantity estimate covering the length of the contract period, usually a year. This quantity establishes the price for the shipment releases during the year. If, at the end of the year, a lower quantity has been used, the price at the final volume level is computed, and the customer pays the vendor for the difference.

The second forecast level includes the customer's lead time and the vendor's lead time needed for ordering raw material. When the forecast is not extended this far forward, the vendor has to carry raw material as determined by the annual forecast.

The third forecast level includes the final adjustments because the vendor can expect actual releases to come in somewhat different quantities and at slightly different release dates than indicated in the forecast. This forecasting procedure is more complicated than might be expected under the older noncontract noncooperative arrangements.

These forecasting arrangements become more acute when the product is unique to the customer and has no other use. Conversely, the arrangements can be loose where the product is used by many other customers. Even so, the cooperative customer is interested in protecting his or her delivery position and probably will follow some forecast connections with the common-parts vendor.

OVERVIEW OF CUSTOMER SERVICE

The objective of the inventory, production control, and distribution function is to get the right goods at the right place at the right time to maintain the desired level of customer service at a minimum total cost. How this objective is carried out varies tremendously from industry to industry and even within each industry because of different needs. Before we consider the relationship of inventory and production control to customer service, and specific functions of shipping, transportation, and warehousing, it seems best to consider some variables that make one industry different from another and the variations within each specific industry.

Type of Product

Products vary from those that are standard and satisfy the needs of many customers to those that are completely special. Obviously the inventory, production, and distribution policies required to support these two different types of products are substantially different.

Standard Products.   Standard products are those made to final, exact specifications for a multitude of customers against a forecast, or rate of sale, and with relatively little risk of obsolescence. Random or trend variations in sales may require some more or less inventory at certain times. For all practical purposes, obsolescence need not be considered too seriously. With standard-type products the main consideration is the amount of money invested in inventory related to the desired customer-service rate. Standard-type products, as shown later, lend themselves to less sophisticated inventory and production control systems.

Standard Plus Specials. There are many companies whose products are in the standard-plus-specials category. This means that many of the assemblies and components going into the particular end product may be made from a forecast of stock with relatively little risk of obsolescence and also with improved delivery performance and customer relations. In addition, special items may be required. If these special features have sufficient volume in themselves, they can be made and attached later at a final assembly, such as special seats in a new automobile. If the volume of the special item is so small that it has to be made after the receipt of the order, this may control the lead time for delivery and customer service.

Some types of standard parts are handled in the standard-plus-specials category but are really a refinement of the standard-type products. For example, in the oil-pumping equipment business it is frequently possible to assemble a unique pump for a customer's order within 24 to 48 hours from different size A frames, reduction gears, motors, and level arms. This rapid delivery service is possible even though the exact combination is in stock as a final assembly. The building of the special is the controlling factor in customer service. Inventory of standard products should be maintained at a high enough level to ensure that all the attention can be devoted to specials.

Special Products. Special-type products are typical of those ordered on government contracts to support the development of unique defense weapon systems prior to production in mass quantities. In most cases a company cannot risk production until the actual contract or order is received. Consequently the order is always in a back-order position, and good performance against schedule is necessary to satisfy the customer. In some cases, plants have to combine special and standard products on common production facilities.

Therefore, a universal type of production control system is necessary to keep the demands properly balanced and scheduled. Even for orders of special types of products, a company can protect itself by placing orders of intent with vendors to reserve certain types of standard raw materials, hardware, and component parts prior to the actual contract ordering. However, adequate escape clauses should be provided in the agreement in case the order fails to materialize. Where there are common parts among a number of specials in a company's business, it may be possible to borrow back and forth between the projects to meet the lead-time commitments.

COOPERATIVE CONTRACTING

Cooperative contracting is a type of customer-vendor relationship whereby each strives to improve synergistically its operations. The basis of this type of agreement is shared common elements previously reserved for each member's internal organization, but rarely promulgated outside the organization, such as

Shared communications

Shared objectives

Shared strategies

Shared decisions

Shared opportunity realization

Real customer service improvement cannot be achieved without a mutual policy of continuous improvement which requires that all these elements be reviewed constantly. In most cases cooperative contracting results in consolidating the procurement of items from many sources to one or two for each group of items. The concept that many competitors lead to lower prices and better services gives way to another idea. The vendor says, "A larger volume makes you more important to me, so I can afford to offer you the best price and service. Your future success also becomes more important to me, and I want to help you with product design, cost savings, service, etc."

The easiest way to comprehend cooperative contracting is to address common material-procurement principles and to explain how cooperative contracting optimizes this precept: *The supplier knows more about the product than the customer does.* This intimacy applies not only to the scheduling process but also to the manufacturing, the designing for optimal cost effectiveness, and the control of the process. Therefore, the customer's responsibility is to clearly communicate what is needed in these areas. The cooperative vendor must assume absolute responsibility for applying his or her expertise to the customer's requirements.

One of the most important applications of the vendor's expertise is the contribution to the "fitness for use."[1] When a customer's design engineers specifically detail the component's configuration, they may be mainly concerned with the product's end use. They often overlook the contribution that the vendor can make to manufacturing, maintenance, and cost reduction. Every aspect of the potential synergy must be exploited, from the duplication of drawings of each part to the application of joint-value analysis.

The major difference between a normal customer-vendor relationship and a cooperative relationship is the degree of intensity of vendor involvement. The following principles illuminate these differences.

(1) *Forecasts are usually wrong.* Cooperative contractors recognize this principle and seek to neutralize the consequences by minimizing the degree of error. It is commonly accepted that forecasts are more accurate if made for a short period close to the time needed and at a level of aggregate commodity rather than specific part number. Therefore, replenishment signals to the vendor are given at the last possible moment. This moment takes into account the shortest throughput time for manufacturing. Lead times and queue management thus become critical to the contract formulation.

Additionally, cooperative contracts are established at a commodity level and not for specific part numbers, as with blanket contracts. Based on the assumption that a vendor can only apply resources to a relatively fixed amount of a commodity per day, the vendor's resource requirements are relatively constant as long as the delivery lot sizes are minimal.

To ensure a relatively smooth supply, specific part numbers cannot be contracted with one vendor or even different manufacturing facilities of the same vendor. Some customers choose to split purchased items on a fixed percentage basis among two or more vendors. This approach is acceptable as long as each vendor manufactures each item within the commodity group and at about the same time intervals.

As an example, assume that the quoted lead time for a simple forging or integrated circuit is 16 weeks. Yet the actual manufacturing and delivery time is 1 week, which assumes good vendor queue management. The customer's production plan indicates a required daily consumption level of 10 units. Therefore, the specific configuration of the 50 units is relayed to the vendor 1 week before planned consumption. The capacity required to manufacture the 50 units is "pre-reserved" via the production plan or forecast, which must have a horizon beyond 16 weeks.

The specific item configuration is not firm at the forecast time. Thus the forecast is far more accurate 1 week before the time of use than 16 weeks before. Therefore, the vendor's resources are applied to what is really needed. Figure 8.1 shows that most businesses use only a small portion of commodity resource buying. So customers cannot regulate the suppliers' resources to meet changes in customer needs. Figure 8.2 shows that the greater the number of different parts on order, the poorer the on-time performance becomes because of the conflict of demands. When a contract is made for a number of dedicated machines, the parts with top priority can be produced on schedule.

In a true JIT supply environment, the customer's actual demand horizon may be less than the manufacturing or delivery horizon. In this case, some form of contingency stocking and indemnification procedure must be agreed upon. However, it is incumbent upon both parties to strive to eliminate the surplus stock via improved JIT management techniques and communications.

(2) *Anybody, anything, or any movement that does not add value to the products in the integrated supply chain should be eliminated or, at best, minimized.* Some examples include eliminating the requisition, purchase order, planning signals, incoming inspection, etc. Exactly how each function tolerated previously is eliminated depends on the creativity of the cooperative contracting team.

The ultimate goal is a replenishment signal from the user, receipt of perfect parts at the point of use, and payment triggered by a shipment release document. Figures 8.3 and 8.4 compare the usual long replenishment and the shortened cooperative cycles.

(3) *Quality rejections interrupt the supply chain.* Because quality rejections cause some form of rescheduling or justifying of inventory, an additional cost is incurred by both parties. Cooperative contracting seeks to jointly eliminate the cause for quality rejections. The quality improvement program must be a joint effort by customer and vendor. Most rejections and/or quality problems are caused by

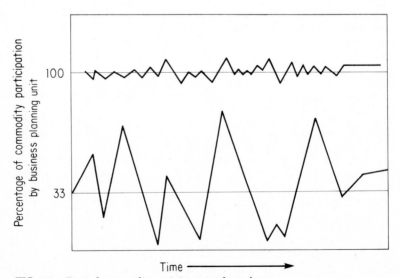

FIG. 8.1. Typical commodity activity to total purchases.

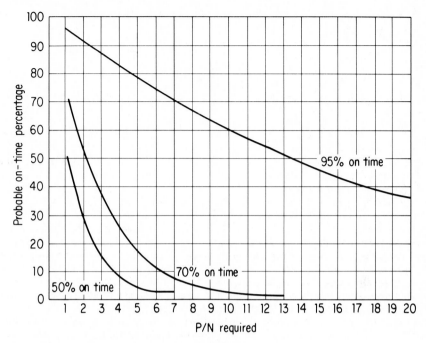

FIG. 8.2. On-time expectancy versus P/N required.

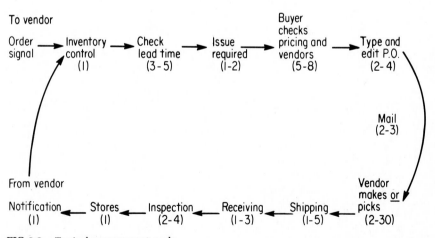

FIG 8.3. Typical procurement cycle.

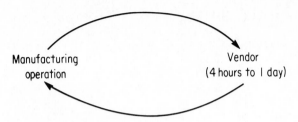

FIG. 8.4. JIT procurement cycle.

both parties. Therefore, an aggressive improvement program should be one of the first cooperative steps taken.

The ultimate goal is to have *no* incoming inspection, *no* need for proof of compliance, and deliveries made to the point of use at the time of use.

(4) *Adopt a habit of mutual continuous improvement.* This form of cooperative agreement becomes almost symbiotic. In a well-executed cooperative contract, each party depends on the other for growth and profitability. Therefore, agreed-on cost-reduction goals should be established and incorporated into the long-range price structure. Figure 8.5 shows a 25 percent cost reduction over the longer period, but the producer's margin remains about the same. This can be accomplished only if the producer also applies JIT cost reduction in the plant.

Cooperative contracting, then, becomes a means of defining a journey that both parties must traverse to obtain the components of improved customer relations.

Table 8.1 summarizes the differences between the traditional approach to contracting and the cooperative approach.

SPARES, OR REPAIR-PART CONSIDERATIONS

It may also be necessary to provide parts for repair or spares in addition to those going into the new products. Most companies do not reserve spare parts because the reservation would be of short duration before it was cleared by a shipment. Companies that do reserve spares may have difficulty in making the stockroom personnel respect the reservation if the spare and production items are combined in a storage area. Therefore, some companies physically separate and account for the spares stock separately. Theoretically such an approach requires more inventory for maintaining the same level of customer service, but its justification may be the elimination of confusion. Where spares are stocked in more than one location, they are usually treated separately. An important part of customer relations is the maintenance of proper service and spare parts while at the same time the new-product customers are receiving their products satisfactorily.

When a model is discontinued, there is the problem of maintaining adequate supplies of parts that are likely to wear out. In many cases, a company is happy to maintain adequate stocks as long as the usage or wear-out rate is high and the continued production of spare items is a profitable venture. Unfortunately, in almost every situation, some items tend to malfunction only occasionally. In such cases the maintenance of adequate service stocks for customer satisfaction costs more. Where a great number of parts and an extensive investment are involved, management is wise to consider the proper balance between inventory investment and the risk of customer dissatisfaction.

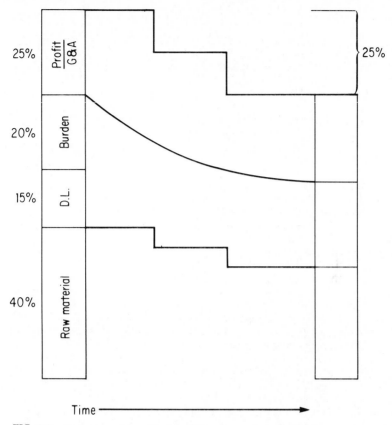

FIG. 8.5. Improvement in costs from JIT program.

TYPES OF SERVICE

Historically, the type of service in many industries is dictated by what has been established by competition and what the customers have been led to expect. However, in some industries there is a chance of varying the type of service. In other cases a combination of types of service is required to give customer satisfaction.

Retail Service

Although everyone is aware of the retail methods that bring products to the market-place, few are aware of the various ways in which the retailer is maintained and supported. In some types of retail business, the inventory is maintained on a unit basis. When the inventory is sufficiently depleted, an order goes directly to the wholesaler or to the factory, depending on the support network. Often the inventory items are not replenished by the retailer's buyer or section manager, except as the result of a periodic review or when the particular item size or style happens to be a

TABLE 8.1   Comparison of Traditional and Cooperative Purchasing

Factor	Traditional	Cooperative
Order cycle	Long	Short (1–3 days)
Quality	Acceptable quality level (AQL) tolerated	Zero rejected
Price	By part number	By predetermined formula
Order signal	Purchase order or release	Signal from point of use by operator
Term of agreement	Order or quantity length	"Indefinite"
Engineering design	By customer	Participative with vendor leading
Sources	Many	One or few
Professional's duties	Quasi-clerical	Management
Price forecast	Increasing	Decreasing
Raw-material inventory	High, "just-in-case"	Very low or none
Receiving inspection	100% or sample	None or few audits
Information loops	Poorly defined or by inquiry	Open and necessary
Performance tracking	Informal or inaccurate	Mandatory/critical path
Redress support	When requested	Automatic
Payables	Per invoice	By statement or backflush

stock-out. Although this method is gradually being replaced, it is still the predominant one in many retail-type industries.

Another type of retail service is often maintained by the distributor or the manufacturer of the particular line of products. In this situation a distributor's representative goes to the retail establishment, reviews the adequacy of the stocks, and orders those items that are too low for the desired service. The recommended order is written up by the representative and approved by the customer. Thus inventory levels are maintained at the desired level.

Retail businesses are exploring an automated type of inventory support. When the major packages are opened at the retail establishment, direct entry is made to the communications network and a supply is sent forward more or less automatically.

These are some highlights of the types of service supporting the retail activities. All these should be considered in planning an efficient inventory, production, and distribution control system. By using such a thorough approach, the optimum degree of customer service can be achieved at the right cost.

Distribution Service

Distributors serving retailers frequently perform an important service when the purchased quantity is considered insufficient to justify shipping directly from the producer to the retailer. The distributer combines products from many producers. Thus, manufacturers can save transportation costs by shipping a full truckload of products to a distributor, who in turn distributes them to a number of retailers. The distributor can combine the products of several manufacturers in one large shipment to a retailer, thus saving money and time.

With the use of split shipments and faster transportation, the volume of products going directly from the factory to the ultimate retailer and bypassing the distributor is increasing. It is wise, however, to consider carefully in each situation whether the distributor has an important role to play in customer service. Frequently a combination of direct shipments to the retailer in some areas and the use of distributors for others makes the most efficient type of service.

Warehouse Service

For some products, particularly semiconsumer type of products, the existence of warehouses for service and distribution to the customer is very important. Typical of this type of product might be industrial tools; some might be sold directly to factories and others to retailers, who in turn sell to individuals. Discussed later is the consolidation of inventory into a smaller number of warehouses, which may permit a high degree of customer service at reduced inventory levels. In some cases, warehouse personnel do some repair work or make some final modifications of the product to make it satisfactory and acceptable for all the customers.

Factory Service

A great many industries with either heavy or unique products require direct shipments from the factory to the ultimate user without the use of a distributor or warehouse. Many products supplied to the original equipment manufacturer (OEM) for incorporation into its products are shipped from the factory to the OEM customers. These same products may be available to users of smaller quantities through distributors. Typical of the factory-f.o.b. type of shipments would be industrial equipment and machine tools. These products may have a back-order schedule ranging from 1 or 2 weeks to years, depending on the lead time and engineering requirements of the special modifications in the products involved.

Combination-Service Considerations

As already pointed out, goods may require direct delivery in some markets. These same goods might also be sold through warehouses or distributors to other types of markets. Thus many kinds of products require more than one type of distribution method to meet the total needs of the marketplace.

COMPETITIVE FACTORS

Regardless of the type of product in a particular distribution situation, management must appraise its position in relation to its competitors. Analysis shows that distribution patterns for industrial products are sometimes determined historically rather than logically. If traditionally the industry has been supplied by a large number of small manufacturers, customers may expect to receive shipments directly from the factory. If a few big factories are in the business, they may have numerous warehouses close to the customers, making it necessary for other manufacturers to follow suit. Regardless of economic analysis, management must always consider the position of the competitor.

Service Rate for Off-the-Shelf Shipments

Retail outlets, warehouses, distributors, and the factory can each have a stock-item service rate. These are calculated as a percentage of times that the items are not available. For example, the factory has a 5 percent stock-out rate to the region warehouse, the region warehouse has a 7 percent stock-out rate to the distributor, the distributor has a 3 percent stock-out rate to the retailer, and the retailer has a 1 percent stock-out rate to the customer.

If the various points in the distribution chain are all controlled by a single management, it is best to calculate the effectiveness of the system rather than to rely on the off-the-shelf service at each point in the total distribution chain. The equal distribution of most of the stock in the areas closest to the point of retail sale always creates the possibility of extra cost of shipments between warehouses or a higher stock-out risk. Mathematically, it is better to hold a larger portion of the stock in a central or reserve warehouse if rapid transportation permits its distribution to support the random sales demands at various outlying points.

Many textbooks indicate that the percentage of the zero-stock balances is not the best indicator of service level. However, it is used frequently because it is so convenient to obtain. There is no real evidence that the number of zero balances indicates that the demand against these items will occur while there is zero stock. The actual number of demands against the zero balances and the period of time to fill orders comprise a more complete measure. However, the statistics can never be complete for this type of calculation. Once a supply system begins to fail, the number of successive demands may be limited by some customers turning to other alternatives and so not showing the demand on the record. Regardless of their complexity, as long as such calculations are approximate and consistent, they can guide management into thinking logically about the service rate in relationship to competition. Such indicators will be a substantial improvement over "seat of the pants" controls of the past.

Normal Transit Time

Each industry has certain guidelines for shipping stock and special items. In recent years many industries have made a substantial improvement in the response rate for both stock and special items. A significant improvement has been made by a straightforward simplification in the paperwork of the order-entry procedures. The order is sent to the stockroom and the shipping room with minimal delay. In some cases, data transmission networks between outlying regions and warehouses and the central factory or office have been added.

In many companies reduced inventories and improved inventory service at the final transfer point have resulted from using round-the-clock truck service or air freight. All the transit-time considerations figure in the calculation of ways to meet the competitive situation. In some cases reducing the transit time can offset the advantage of a larger number of warehouses used by competitors.

ORDER-ENTRY PROCEDURE

The relationship between the customer and the manufacturing organization typically begins when an order is received. Depending on the type of product involved, there may be some contact between the customer and the company prior to the order entry, but such contact is often on an exploratory basis. For the products that might be classified primarily as *special*, or in some cases *standard plus special*, there may be written quotations and perhaps letters of intent prior to the order itself. The quotation does not establish a commitment on the part of the customer, so usually it has no impact on the manufacturing operation. Only when a quotation is accepted and the customer places an order does the commitment become firm on both sides.

The procedure followed for entering the order has considerable impact on production control and scheduling as well as customer relations. In a computerized integrated system, key information about the products required and the customer is captured at the order-entry stage. Recently the tendency has been to pass as much work as possible back to the salesperson and sometimes to the customer. Again, the kinds of products being handled affect how far back the paperwork can be passed. If, for example, a company is making standard products which are sold to distributors, either wholesale or retail, often it is possible to leave an order form listing all the company's products with catalog numbers. The customer fills in the order form with the quantities of each product required. In some cases, the customer can order from a catalog or an order sheet by placing a number that can be read by a sensor or input at a direct-entry terminal. In such cases or when keypunched cards are used, the order may go directly to the manufacturing company by telephone or telegraph lines. However, the customer can mail in a partially prepared order sheet to the company. In many cases, customers can telephone in orders, and an order clerk will fill in the form for the customer.

When the order comes in on a form prepared by the customer or is telephoned in and prepared by the order clerk, perhaps on forms that are predesigned with numbers for product names, typically it is scrutinized by an *order editor* and then entered in the system through prepared punch cards or by direct entry. If the order has been received by telephone or telegraph, it can go directly to the computer. A hard copy may be generated for editing purposes.

Customer order-entry and follow-up procedures are described for two types of orders: orders that are normally filled from stock with unavailable items back-ordered or canceled, shown in Fig. 8.6, and orders that are normally back-ordered and contain some of or all special manufactured items.

Orders normally filled from stock are as follows:

1. *Customer orders.*   Customers' orders usually come in on their own *purchase order* forms, though some vendors have convinced customers to make direct entry and/or releases against orders in compliance with the vendor's data processing system. The data cover "bill to" information as well as "ship to" information if these are different. The order notes the quantities, part numbers, description, prices, and totals. The totals may include or exclude freight charges depending on vendor terms.

   In some companies there is an *order log* showing the order number, customer, time in and time out, and back-order data. In many companies having little or no back-ordering, the log is omitted. In this case, orders pending shipment may be filed alphabetically by customer in case a customer follows up.

2. *Sales orders.*   The sales order is typed into an order set or is keyed directly into the computer. In the latter case, much of the standard data come from the computer memory. If the sales order is typed, the item number and description, unit price, terms, and credit should be checked. Usually the shipping costs are left for final invoicing, unless they are paid by the vendor.

3. *Acknowledgment.*   The acknowledgment is usually omitted if the goods will be sent within a day or two; longer delays and back orders almost always get an

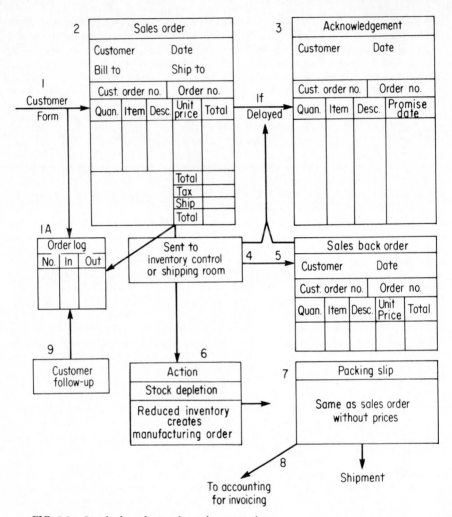

FIG. 8.6. Standard products sales order processing.

acknowledgment and a promised shipment date. The order is usually logged out when it leaves the order-entry section, but some organizations wait to note any back-order condition.

4. *Inventory control and/or shipping room.* In companies where all inventory supports distribution and direct shipment, these functions are combined. In companies where inventories also support in-house assembly activities, the functions may be separate; the parts are removed from the inventory (and the inventory records) and sent to the shipping room with the sales order copies.

5. *Sales back order.* If there is insufficient stock to fill all items to the ordered quantity, anything still due is placed on a new order (back-order form). Usually the order log also shows this status change. If a typed order set is used, the form has to be returned to sales order entry for retyping. If a computer program is used,

the back order can be prepared automatically by keying in the proper instruction. The customer gets a copy of the back order with the new promise date.

6. *Manufacturing action.*   If the stock issued for the order brings the balance on hand below the reorder point, a new factory order is created. In some companies this is not necessary because the order may be generated by sales or requirements forecasting, and the reorder point may be only an expedite signal upon orders already outstanding.

7. *Packing slip.*   The packing slip of goods actually sent accompanies most shipments—usually without prices. In some cases a copy of any back order is included.

8. *Invoicing.*   A copy of the packing slip notifies accounting of the need to debit the customer's account. Invoicing may be by each order or for all orders within an agreed period. In computerized systems much of this status and invoicing takes place automatically at planned cycle times.

9. *Customer follow-up.*   Usually there is little follow-up if an order from stock business is running with a few back orders. The inquiries usually come to customer service. If there is a manual or a computer order log, the reply can be given directly. Where such data do not exist, the status has to be traced to shipping control where it may be in alphabetical sequence awaiting handling and shipment.

The following discussion applies to sales orders that are routinely backordered.

Special sales orders that are normally back-ordered, shown in Fig. 8.7, are as follows:

1. *Customer data.*   Frequently, the final order for special products is not determined until the sales specification is completed, showing the standard and special requirements needed for the customer. Sometimes after the specification sheet is completed, a proposal is typed in detail, copied by the customer, and recopied as the final sales order by the vendor. Obviously computers greatly facilitate this process.

  Order log.   In almost all these types of companies, a complete log of customer orders is kept. The promise date and any revisions are always useful. As the delivery date draws near, the customer service representative may be in continual contact with the factory about last-minute delays and missed schedules.

2. *Engineering and pricing.*   In some companies cost estimation is done by the engineering department, and in others it is a separate function. Engineering may take a few days to several months to design and integrate the special requirements. During this time purchasing may get estimates on special requirements from vendors, and the standard parts and assembly pricing can be developed. The final price and lead-time estimate may come from manufacturing engineering and production.

3. *Proposal and/or sales order.*   Depending on the detail furnished in the proposal, more or less work has to be added to get the final sales order typed. This order may specify test and acceptance conditions as well.

  Acknowledgment copy.   The customer receives a copy of the sales order with a promise date from the master scheduler.

4. *Master scheduler.*   Where a master scheduler does not exist, the promise date usually comes from production control. Whoever supplies the date is usually

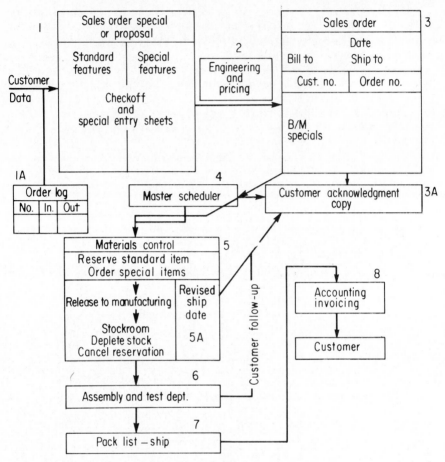

FIG. 8.7.   Special products sales order processing.

responsible for its revision and is the source of information for customer service inquiries.

5. *Materials control.*   Materials control checks the availability of standard items and reserves or places them in a time-phased requirements chain in a full materials-requirements planning (MRP) system.

   Materials control releases all special orders to manufacturing and procurement.

   When the order is ready to be assembled, materials control may advise the master scheduler and/or customer service of shortages, quantity, or other problems that could delay assembly or shipment. On issue to assembly, materials control adjusts the stock record and is responsible for the ongoing supply of standard parts.

6. *Assembly and test.*   During this phase production and engineering usually monitor the order's progress, and they may be in touch with customer service if problems or delays arise. In some cases a customer visit is necessary to clarify needs.

7. *Pack and ship.* This is routine except for special air shipments made to compensate for delays. The packing list and instruction booklets go with the product and notification to accounting for invoicing.

Various practices are followed at the time of card punching or direct input. In almost all cases some hard copies are generated. The order copy varies with different products and the problems encountered in generating invoices, shipping tickets, and bills of lading at the same time. If it is possible to ship the product out of stock or to send it as one shipment after manufacturing, the invoice should be prepared when the order is received. If there are split shipments, because of back ordering, it may be desirable to delay the preparation of invoices. The copies should be prepared as needed, not as a complete packet as they used to be.

Products Shipped from Stock

If it is reasonably certain that a shipment can be made immediately with material out of stock, the following procedure may be desirable. The order is checked first against the master customer file, to verify the name and address and to obtain standard shipping and invoicing and discount instructions. The order is entered into the system by transferring the information to the computer. The orders are checked against the master inventory file to make sure there are products on hand. If all the required products can be filled from stock, the inventory is reduced accordingly and picking tickets, shipping papers, and invoices are prepared. The picking tickets and shipping papers are sent to the warehouse. When the copies indicating that shipment has been made are returned to the accounting department, the invoices are dispatched.

If checking the orders against inventory reveals that it is impossible to ship some items, back orders are prepared immediately. Only those items available in stock are designated for picking and shipping. Invoices are prepared for these designated items. Costume jewelry is a typical product that might be handled in this way. Orders are received, filled out of stock, and shipped by parcel post to the customer. Such a procedure requires very accurate inventory records; otherwise, items will be back-ordered that are actually on hand.

Sometimes products are available in inventory, but the order must wait several days because shipments are pooled in a single truck to get the most economical rate. In such cases, inventory may have been reserved for a particular order that is held in the shipping room waiting for a truck. Meanwhile, a second customer may require the same merchandise. In such a case, neither customer would get the merchandise immediately, the first because the merchandise was waiting for a truck and the second because the computer showed no inventory on hand. If a company such as a frozen foods company has many problems of this nature, it is probably better not to prepare invoices and to deplete the inventory until the shipment has been made.

Although inventory records may be maintained on a computer, they may not be kept up to date, minute to minute, but may be handled on a batching basis. Under such circumstances products can be depleted in a warehouse before they show up as out of stock on the computer record. If such a batching procedure is followed, it may be desirable to prepare the picking papers but wait to prepare the back orders until evidence of shipment is received.

Instead of using an order form designed for easy keypunching, a company warehousing a standard product may rely on a tub file of *product cards* to generate an order. When the customer's order comes on his or her own form, order clerks select prepunched product cards and feed them into the data processing machine along with a prepunched header card containing the customer's name, address, and shipping instructions. Variable information is added to obtain hard copies of all the necessary forms for filling, shipping, and (in some cases) invoicing the order. This procedure is being replaced by directly keying in the variable data to a menu on a screen that is used to complete the order forms and related documents.

Products Ordered in Advance

Sometimes companies in a seasonal business receive orders several months in advance of shipment. Then the invoice should be written when the shipment is made, so that decisions on back orders versus cancellation of the order balance can be made properly. Many times if the order cannot be filled completely, no back order is made. The company waits until the customers decide whether they wish to place another order.

Nonstandard Products

A somewhat different procedure is likely to be followed by companies making products that are not standard and so cannot be filled from stock on hand. Often an order must go to engineering first. In some cases the product is not completely designed at the order stage. The order may be a blanket order indicating the general magnitude of the expected price, but the final price depends on design and engineering costs. Or the price may be firm, but the specific components required as attachments or integral parts of the product may necessitate engineering decisions. Whenever it is impossible to determine the precise nature of the product or the selling price, orders should be cleared through engineering before data enter the system and influence inventory and production scheduling. Only after engineering has determined precisely what is to be made to satisfy the order should the data enter the total system. For such products partial shipments are not unusual. It is not desirable, therefore, to prepare an invoice when the rest of the documents are prepared.

Advising the Customer

Whatever the nature of the product, the manner in which the order is entered and the subsequent steps taken have a vital impact on customer relations. If the product can be shipped from stock, it is essential that the order processing be as fast as possible and that shipment to the customer be made quickly. If any delay is expected, the customer must be notified of when shipment is expected. This applies to both a standard product that is temporarily out of stock and a special product that must be manufactured. In each case the customer should be told to expect receipt of the merchandise.

If the order takes time to fill, the customer should be told both when to expect the order and when the shipment is made. If a partial order is shipped and a back order is entered, the customer should be advised. The invoices should be tied into the customer's order and to the shipments made in such a way that the customer knows the charges exactly.

Automatic Replenishment

In most cases, order placement is the first step in getting merchandise to a customer. Sometimes when customers maintain stocks of standard items, the order-entry system has been scrapped entirely in favor of automatic replenishment. In such cases, the supplier maintains a record of the customer's inventory. All withdrawals from the inventory are transmitted by telephone or telegraph line directly to the supplier's computer where they are recorded. Automatic reordering rules are programmed into the computer. When the customer's inventory reaches the reorder point, an order is automatically generated and the customer's inventory is resupplied.

Many such systems exist, and probably this type of relationship between customer and supplier will continue to expand. The relationship is extremely close in this kind of a situation. Nonetheless, it may be some time before most companies are able to tie in their customers' inventories with the computer at the source. However, such companies may establish automatic reordering procedures for their own warehouses. For many manufacturers with extensive inventories located in warehouses or retail stores, the major customer is the warehouse organization. In such cases, procedures should be created to track final demand. This final demand should be related to economic shipping quantities and economic manufacturing order quantities. Where final demand is tracked, procedures for producing the merchandise and resupplying the warehouses can be integrated to optimize cost for both the manufacturing and the distributing organization.

ROLE OF INVENTORY IN CUSTOMER RELATIONS

Customer relations, from the point of view of production planning and control, involve (1) getting the order into the system as quickly and accurately as possible, (2) advising the customer of the action taken, and (3) supplying the merchandise as quickly as possible. The first two involve the design of the order-entry system and the communication network. The third is related to the inventory maintained, production's response time (where applicable), and the efficiency of shipping.

The cost of shipping merchandise and the speed with which the customer must be supplied are usually functions of the location of the inventories relative to the customer. In some situations a customer may expect to be supplied within a few hours or even to be able to drive to the warehouse to pick up the merchandise. Where such service is required, inventory stocks must be kept close to the customer. This may indicate the use of distributors, who maintain inventories, or an extensive network of branch warehouses.

The second important factor affecting the location of inventories is the cost of shipping the merchandise. Generally the larger the quantity of merchandise to be shipped to a particular place, the cheaper the shipping cost per item. It is necessary, therefore, to determine whether it is cheaper to maintain a supply of merchandise in a warehouse in a particular location where sales are high and supply it by truck or railcar, or to incur high individual shipping costs and eliminate the cost of maintaining warehouses.

In the past many companies maintained inventories in a number of private or public warehouses throughout the country. In recent years analysis of warehousing versus shipping costs has suggested that it is cheaper to cut down on the number of warehouse points. Two factors have influenced the trend in this direction: a better understanding of the nature of the costs incurred, particularly the cost of maintaining the extra safety stock required for multiple warehouse location, and faster transportation by truck and plane.

Lot-Size Policies

JIT technology reduces setup costs and order costs by using *releases* for the full cost of a new purchase order. However, other factors have to be evaluated—shipment and/or freight costs may increase with smaller shipments and create an increasing need for attention to a greater number of individual transactions. For example, vendor shipments could be made every hour rather than daily, or daily rather than weekly, where the extra receipts do nothing to further efficiency or output.

The economic order quantity (EOQ) rules still apply, but the values used should be those reduced by JIT technology applications:

$$EOQ = \sqrt{\frac{2U(S + O)}{IC}}$$

where U = usage of item per month by customer

$S + O$ = constant portion of freight cost, often a minimum, plus cost of handling release for shipment and related paperwork

I = value of money in investment, frequently about 2% per month

C = unit value of each item

EOQ = final order or shipment quantity

When many parts are involved in the release and they are shipped as a single delivery, group lot-size calculations should be used. With group lot-size rules, the average value and total usage have to be expressed to calculate the frequency of shipment.

Master Production Scheduling—In Customer Relations

The customer's master production schedule (MPS) should be directly related to the forecast, from the one that supports the annual forecast to the revised MPS that supports the shipment release against the customer's order. The vendor's MPS may show the specific customer's time-phased demand if the items are unique. If the items are common, more likely the total customer demand or the part will be aggregated into a demand summary.

Work Authorization

For standard items, there is no work authorization from the customer other than the contract purchase order and releases for shipment against such orders.

In ordering specific parts, the annual contract implies an obligation for parts within a specified lead time. Frequently, in the automotive companies, the final month's schedule is 100 percent payment guaranteed, while work-in-process and material costs are guaranteed for the second month and raw material only for the third month. In annual contracting, it is important that these arrangements be specifically defined.

Stock-Out Policy and Safety Stocks

A company's relationship to its customers depends on the kinds of products it makes. If the company is making special products which must be engineered, the customer will not expect rapid delivery. The customer knows that the articles must be manufactured specially and is prepared to wait. For standard products the customer expects to obtain quick service.

Companies have found it difficult to apply a value to stock-out costs because they are not sure whether the stock-out means a lost sale or loss of a customer. It is possible, in most cases, to assign a cost to preventing stock-outs. It is possible to determine how much safety stock is required to provide various degrees of protection against stock-outs. The average daily use of a product, variation in use per day, average time to replace stock in a warehouse, and variation about the average replacement time are known.

Assume that warehoused TV sets cost $160 per unit and sell for $200, returning a profit of $40. Also assume average sales of 30 units per day with an average of 10 days to replace the stock after an order is issued. The variation in sales per day is shown on graph a of Fig. 8.8. Graph b shows the variation in time to replenish, and graph c represents the combined variation, i.e., the variation in number of units required to cover orders during a replenishment period. Note that two somewhat skewed distributions, a and b, combine to make one that is adequately represented by the well-known bell-shaped normal curve.

Histograms a and b are constructed by taking actual samples from historical data. Each X represents a reading in the appropriate value range shown on the horizontal axis. The average sales per day multiplied by the average lead time (30 units per day × 10 days) equals the average usage, 300 units, during the 10-day replenishment period. Histogram c is calculated by considering the variations in both sales and lead time. It shows the probable variation in sales during a replenishment period. Graph c is obtained by considering the interaction in graphs a and b.

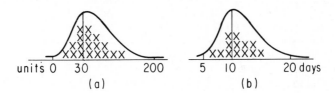

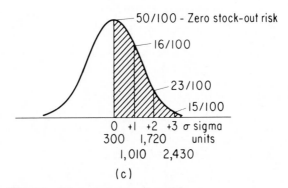

FIG. 8.8.   Safety stocks at various risks.

If each quantity is extended by its corresponding replenishment days, the resulting data can be used to calculate the standard deviation, or sigma (σ):

$$\sigma = \sqrt{\frac{\Sigma(X - \bar{x})^2}{n}}$$

Or sigma is the square root of the sum of the deviations from the average $\bar{X}$ squared of all readings divided by the number of readings.

By definition, half of the time the sales or lead time is less than average, so a reorder point of 300 would provide inventory during this 50 percent of the time. Half of the time the combination of sales or replenishment time is greater than average, so unless the reorder point is raised above 300, stock-outs occur 50 percent of the time. It can be seen from the normal curve that the probability of a stock-out is reduced substantially by raising the reorder point from 300 to 1010, providing a safety stock of 710 units. A safety stock of 710 is the statistician's one standard deviation, called *sigma*, for this particular case. At the one σ point, the normal curve has its point of inflection; that is, it stops curving downward and starts to flatten. Each equal increment of safety stock beyond gives less additional protection to the company than the previous increment. Table 8.2 shows what happens in the example under discussion.[2]

This example is designed to dramatize the small return on excessive investments in safety stocks. The investment is constant because extra units of all items have to be added since demands come at random times on random items. Although many companies have product lines which cost much less per unit, the cumulative effect can be similar to that shown above. In this example it was assumed that sales are lost when there is a stock-out. It is possible that the customer will wait and business will not be lost. An example of this type, however, indicates the cost of providing safety stock against stock-out and gives the sales manager a basis for making judgments of the protection needed to maintain good customer relations.

Undoubtedly a sales manager would decide that the same rules did not apply to all products. For products where the marginal contribution to profits is high, more protection may be desired because the cost of stock-outs in terms of lost sales is

TABLE 8.2   Cost of Stock-Out Protection

Reorder point	300	1,010	1,720	2,430	3,140
Standard deviations	—	$+1\sigma$	$+2\sigma$	$+3\sigma$	$+4\sigma$
Stock-out risk	50%	15.9%	2.3%	0.135%	0.003%
Average monthly demand	600	600	600	600	600
Lost sales	300	95	14	.8	0.018
Lost profit	$12,000	$3,800	$560	$32	$1
Incremental gain	—	$8,200	$3,240	$528	$31
Inventory investment	—	$113,600	$113,600	$113,600	$113,600
Return on Investment					
Monthly	—	7.05%	3.03%	0.47%	0.02%
Annual	—	85%	36%	6%	0.2

Source: Arnold O. Putnam, E. Robert Barlow, and Gabriel N. Stilian, *Unified Operations Management*, 2d ed., Rath & Strong, Inc., Lexington, Mass., 1969, p. 240.

greater than for products with a relatively low contribution. Various other factors may enter into the situation. For example, if there there is a good backup stock in a central warehouse or at the plant, merchandise can be sent to a customer very quickly by air but with an increased transportation cost to the company. If an analysis of customer's requirements indicates that rapid air shipment is as satisfactory as supplying from a local warehouse, the cost of protection against stock-out compared to cost of premium transportation can be considered. To take advantage of premium transportation, backup stocks must be available.

Backup Stocks Improve Customer Relations

It can be demonstrated that, to give the same degree of protection, less safety stock must be maintained in one location than when several locations are used. Four warehouses with a safety stock of 40 units each, for a total of 160 units, would give the same assurance as one warehouse with 80 units (Fig. 8.9). This assumes that the same items are involved and there is no inventory-time loss due to transportation. This can be seen clearly by comparing 100 items stored in one location and sent by air mail and 1 item stored in 100 different places. A second demand in each place will cause a stock-out, whereas 101 demands on the central warehouse are needed to produce a stock-out. The standard deviation at the central warehouse is

$$\sigma_n = \sqrt{\sigma_a^2 + \sigma_b^2 + \sigma_c^2 + \sigma_d^2 + \cdots}$$

In Fig. 8.9 the four equally sized warehouses have 40 units of safety stock each, to obtain the same stock-out protection provided by the single warehouse with only 80 units, or half as much investment.[3] This fact can be used to reduce safety stock in any warehouse as long as merchandise can be shipped quickly from the central

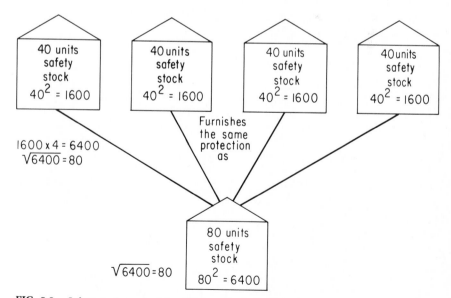

FIG. 8.9.   Safety stock required for different numbers of warehouses.

warehouse. The total safety stock required to give protection to customers is reduced with either a central warehouse or backup point at the factory.

Companies with a central warehouse and an extensive branch warehousing system are likely to find that the major demands on manufacturing and production control come from replenishing their own distribution system. The factory would be faced with large and infrequent demands if manufacturing did not track customer demands at the point of entry into the system but waited until demand was placed on the factory by the central warehouse. Data representing demand by the central warehouse upon the factory would give an entirely false picture of the real demand. In the typical situation, the central warehouse would show little use for 2 months, and then a large order would occur, followed by no use. The actual demand for the product, as represented by customers' orders at the branch warehouses, might indicate a regular, predictable demand. So manufacturers must track customer demand rather than replenishment demand for the central warehouse.

Some companies with large warehouse systems also supply customers directly. In this situation, it is not uncommon for production control to give priority to a customer's order. Production control is likely to state that the warehouse system orders represent no particular customer, and no real pressure is brought to bear by outsiders to get the orders out. Therefore, customers who have placed orders directly and who are likely to be putting pressure on production control for delivery get preference. Distribution personnel quickly become aware of the situation and are likely to place orders sooner because they fear a long lead time. The net result is an increasing backlog of orders.

If the distribution system is ordering sensibly according to a well-designed formula, its orders should be treated on an equal basis with direct customer orders. Presumably warehouses are set up to provide good service to customers on products that they are expected to need. If production control fails to give the warehouse organization good service, the customers in turn will not get the service for which the system was designed. Production control needs a system to track demand at the consumer level and to translate this demand to manufacturing orders while providing the most economical service to the company and to the customer. This need can be filled by the critical-ratio system for distribution.

Critical Ratio for Distribution[4]

A variation of the critical-ratio technique now widely used in manufacturing operations can be applied to reduce distribution costs and improve service. Daily warehouse usages at all points are provided to the manufacturing organization through telecommunications, and with a computer the needed shipping quantities can be determined.

Each day, or less frequently if desirable, information on usage and inventory levels at all points in the system is subjected to predetermined computer formulas which indicate the item and quantities to be shipped to each distribution point. These are some assumptions implicit in the application of critical-ratio techniques to distribution:

1. The priority ranking for shipping each item from one point to the next can be expressed mathematically by considering the risk of running out of stock before the regular shipment is received.

2. The amount of each item to be shipped can be determined initially by economics related to order cost versus inventory level.

3. The initial economic order shipment (EOS) can be decreased mathematically if conditions indicate that the backup stock should be used sparingly.

4. The safety stock at both the distribution point and the factory can be raised or lowered to balance performance service level against investment.

The first step is to determine the expected amount of merchandise to be supplied to customers from a particular warehouse during the year. This can be translated to truckloads or freight-car loads. The total number of truckloads per year can be expressed as the number of truckloads per month or per week. Assume that the cheapest method of shipping is to send all merchandise to the warehouse from the central warehouse or the plant in truckloads. Then the schedules for trucks going to the warehouse can be worked out.

Assume that in a particular analysis the optimum number of truckloads is about 50 per year, or 1 per week, and all items on the truck should cover at least a 1-week supply, to eliminate the need to ship the next truck early or to avoid a stock-out. Dividing the available quantity [i.e., the on-hand amount (OH) less safety stock (SS)] by the smoothed usage (SU) at a warehouse gives the best estimate of anticipated stock of each item in terms of *days of supply* (DS). Thus,

$$DS = \frac{OH - SS}{SU}$$

and

$$CR = \frac{DS}{LT + LTR}$$

where CR = critical ratio, LT = lead time, and LTR = lead time remaining.

If the days of supply do not cover the lead time remaining, a stock-out is anticipated before the next shipment. If the item is not on the next shipment, then the days of supply must cover the lead time also. Thus, any item with a critical ratio less than 1.0 should be shipped on the next trip. But if critical ratio is greater than 1.0, the forecast indicates the item can be deferred until the next economical trip (Fig. 8.10). Thus, a computer program is designed to do the calculations for each item and list line items in order of criticalness.

For the normal shipment of an item from backup stock, the shipping quantity

Item	On hand	S.S.	Available	SMU	D.S.	L.T.	LTR.	Ratio
A	150	50	100	50	2	10	2	2/12=0.167
B	2000	800	1200	100	12	10	2	12/12=1.00

FIG. 8.10. Distribution planning report. The next truck goes in 2 days. With only 16.7% of item A above the safety stock, it must go on the truck. If item A misses the next truck, there will be only 2 days of supply left before the arrival of trucks 12 days later, or only 16.7% of the average stock required. Item B has just enough stock to cover the next 12 days. SS = safety stock; available = on hand minus safety stock; SMU = smoothed usage; DS = days of supply, LT = lead time between shipments; and LTR = lead time remaining before next shipment.

should never be less than the usage during the lead time. However, if every item of a large multiproduct inventory had to be shipped every trip, the paperwork plus the cost of picking and putting away would be excessive.

The economic-order-quantity (EOQ) formula can be applied in a modified form to balance the cost involved. Thus

$$\text{EOS} = \sqrt{\frac{2uo}{ic}}$$

where u = usage during reorder period

      o = cost of ordering, including paperwork, picking, counting, receiving, and storing

      i = carrying charges, expressed as percentage in time period equivalent to usage period

      c = direct cost effect on inventory level per unit involved

The cost value c requires specific analysis of each case, since it could range from the full manufacturing cost of the item for the period to an amount as low as the added value created by the transportation commitment.

Another important factor relates to reducing the amount of each shipment if the stock availability at the higher level is threatened during the lead time remaining before the next replenishment. The availability can be calculated. First the days of supply are obtained by dividing the on-hand inventory at the central or backup point by the smoothed usage per day for that specific stream of goods. The days of supply divided by the lead time remaining to replenish the central stock give the *index of criticalness*. If this index is less than 1.0, all shipments of that item are reduced to the index level; i.e., a 0.5 index equals 50 percent of the EOS. Expressed in a formula, the on-hand central supply divided by the smoothed-usage total equals days of supply (DS). The critical ratio equals DS/LTR (lead time remaining for supply from factory). The procedure prevents a common distribution problem of shipping too many of some items to branch warehouses in one week, which results in stock-outs caused by demands from other branch warehouses in the next week. The controls should also minimize the cost of any warehouse shipments to cover imbalances.

The critical ratio of all items could be calculated daily and ranked according to criticalness. All items with a critical ratio less than one have to be shipped on the next truck. If all such items did not represent a full truckload, then the next items on the critical list would be selected and shipped. With such a system it would be possible to reduce the inventories in the distribution system significantly and maintain stock-out at any risk level desired.

The system not only keeps the branch warehouses supplied, but also provides for the resupply by production control of the backup warehouse.

SUMMARY

Good customer relations can exist only if customers obtain the products they want when they need them. Although the sales department is responsible for direct contacts with customers, the maintenance of good customer service requires smooth functioning of many operations, including order entry, production control, inventory control, warehousing, and shipping. The definition of adequate customer service differs from company to company depending on the nature of the products and the competitive situation. The requirements vary from providing the customer with the product immediately out of warehouse stock for standard products to delivery in months or years for special products built to customer specifications.

New statistical techniques and computer assistance can be used to cut costs and improve service for almost every variation of product and customer requirements. These opportunities can be seized by first determining the desired level of customer service and then tracing through the whole system from inventory to final shipment to determine the needs at each stage, the alternatives available, and the relative cost-service advantages.

Finally, the JIT technique enables planning on defect-free deliveries almost the instant the customer wants them. This requires that the vendors know their process capabilities and how to keep control.

REFERENCES

1. J. M. Juran and Frank M. Gryna, Jr., *Quality Planning and Analysis*, 2d ed., McGraw-Hill, New York, 1980.

2. Arnold O. Putnam, E. Robert Barlow, and Gabriel N. Stilian, *Unified Operations Management*, 2d ed., Rath & Strong, Lexington, Mass., 1969, p. 240.

3. R. Everdell and Arnold O. Putnam, *A Practical Approach to Scientific Inventory Management*, 4th ed., Rath & Strong, Lexington, Mass., 1961.

4. Arnold O. Putnam, "Managing Distribution and Inventories for Profit and Reliable Customer Service," *APICS Quarterly Bulletin*, vol. 6, no. 4, October, 1965.

CHAPTER 9

Forecasting

Editors

JAMES I. MORGAN, Business Science Specialist, The Dow Chemical Company, Midland, Michigan

ROBERT E. THIELE, JR., Senior Research Logician, The Dow Chemical Company, Midland, Michigan

Effective planning for production and inventory control requires some means of resolving the uncertainty of the future. A necessary part of this resolution is some guess, estimate, prediction, or forecast of the future. The term *forecasting* is used here to characterize the mechanism of arriving at measures for planning the future.

Before we get our hopes too high, it is important to realize that we cannot resolve all the uncertainty of the future. We can only attempt to reduce some of it. Also, no forecasting mechanism is suitable for all situations. This chapter makes no pretense of presenting a general-purpose forecasting procedure.

It is possible in this chapter to develop but a few of the many forecasting methods available. Approaches to forecasting have been developed in statistics, econometrics, control theory, system dynamics, production planning, marketing research, and technological forecasting. Only recently has an attempt been made to draw from these separate areas to form a new discipline. The International Institute of Forecasters has annual meetings and publishes two journals.[1] Through its activities, cross fertilization of concepts is occurring. Although there may never be one general forecasting approach of which every technique is a special case, efforts to relate different approaches have had some success.

CONSIDERATIONS IN FORECASTING

Realizing that we must forecast to plan, what do we need to know about forecasting? Of interest are the more obvious questions of why, what, and how; but also involved are such questions of frequency, time horizon, precision, and what constitutes a good forecast.

Why Forecast?

The question of why is answered simply: to plan the future. A basic axiom of planning is that it cannot be done without some forecast of the future.

What to Forecast?

As to what to forecast, a concise answer is everything we need to know to plan the future. This covers such things as product demands and supplies, costs, prices, and lead times. In this chapter we do not discuss all these things; rather we limit ourselves to the key factor in most production and inventory control systems—the demand for an item. In any case, it is generally not feasible or economical to forecast everything in actual situations.

In every system, there is an uncontrollable *triggering event* whose magnitude determines what happens in the rest of the system. In an inventory system or a production scheduling system, the triggering event is the demand for an item. The better we are able to determine future levels of this demand, the better we can control the system and, consequently, the better we can maximize the system's effectiveness. Thus, *demand for a physical product triggers the system.* The better we can estimate this demand, the better we should be able to plan.

Under the question of what to forecast, the problems of item mix are important. Few companies use one raw material or supply item or have just one product to distribute. Therefore, many items may have to be forecast. In many situations it may be hard to define an item and hence to determine what items to forecast. How we distinguish or delineate an item largely depends on what we are trying to plan. In other words, we must answer the question, What is the purpose of the forecast?

If we are planning how much stock to carry, we must do our planning at the finest distinction by which a customer requires an item. If customers want a particular size, package, color, formulation, physical property, or finishing, we must stock their needs if we are to get their business. In some cases, it may be possible to substitute an item with similar attributes (retail stores seem to be best able to get away with this), but this is an exception rather than the rule.

The lowest common denominator by which we distinguish one stock item from another is commonly called the *stock-keeping unit* (SKU). Effective planning of inventory stock levels must be done through forecasts of each SKU. Unfortunately, when possible combinations of attributes are considered, the number of SKUs increases enormously, thus creating special forecasting problems.

However, if we are planning new or leased physical facilities months to years in the future, we seldom need detailed SKU forecasts. We are more interested in aggregate rather than individual movements—the degree of aggregation depending on our needs. In many cases product obsolescence may make it foolish to attempt long-term forecasting on an SKU basis.

Another consideration of what to forecast is location, or geographical area. Seldom in physical distribution systems do we distribute through one location, hence the need for area forecasts. How the area is delineated depends again on the purpose of the forecast. The possibility of transshipment when one area is short of a given item adds another complexity. Clearly, adding geography to product definition increases by severalfold the number of items which must be forecasted.

Another aspect of what we are forecasting is the time period. We generally think of demand per time; hence we have to determine the time period. Because we can readily convert from one time basis to another, the time period is not as critical as product mix or geographical considerations. However, if the time period is repetitive (that is, we are not making a one-time estimation), then we have a *time series*. In such a series, the demand can take on different values in successive and equal time periods. A vast collection of methods for time-series analysis has been developed, several of which are given in this chapter.

How to Forecast

Now the big question: How? Here we are interested in questions such as

What are the different methods?

Which are the practical methods?

How are these methods applied?

What are the limitations of each method?

Unfortunately there are probably as many methods—and then some—as there are people who forecast. Many of the methods are valuable in certain situations; however, as yet, no foolproof methodology has been developed.

The ideal way to estimate future demand for a product is to first determine the customers, their uses for the product, how much is needed for each use, how and when each customer will order the material, and any other relevant information and then develop a computational system or mathematical model to relate the demand to the factors. Because of the vast number of factors and interrelationships, a complete model is seldom, if ever, possible. Approximate models, however, have been developed and used in many practical situations.

Assembly parts demand a bill-of-materials explosion, and models come close to being causal relationship situations; nevertheless, even with them, an end product must be forecast. Where dependent relationships can be established, it is helpful to break the forecasting problem into dependent and nondependent components.

Causal models must be developed for a specific situation and so may be time-consuming to develop and to use and hence expensive. Of course, if possible benefits outweigh costs, then causal models are desirable. The development of these models is a field in itself and beyond the scope of this chapter.

Because of the difficulty of developing more complete models, it is necessary to rely on other, less scientific means of estimation. Later in this chapter we attempt to answer the questions posed above. First, some other questions must be answered.

Distinctions between Forecasting Methods

One important question is: Are there different types of forecasts? Most certainly some distinctions should be mentioned.

Forecasts or Predictions. In estimating demand it is helpful to consider two classes of factors which generate the future. One class contains the factors which have generated the demand in the past; the other class contains the factors which influence demand for the first time. Brown refers to estimates of the first class as *forecasts* and to estimates of the second class as *predictions.*[2]

By examining the past, we should be able to get a feel for the effects of factors of the first class. The statistical tools of time-series analysis provide one means of anticipating the future on the basis of the past. These techniques assume that relationships which held in the past will continue in the future. Anticipating the effects of the second class of factors is not readily handled by statistical means. Here, knowledge, experience, judgment, and intuition are important in making predictions. The past is generally the first place we look when we want to know the future. A good forecasting technique should effectively use the past provided that the past has meaning to the future.

Single-Point or Frequency Distribution.   A forecast may be strictly a one-value estimation, or it may be one or more values in which some frequency distribution is involved. In Chap. 30, the principles behind frequency distributions are discussed, and so we do not go into them here. A later section of this chapter further discusses the use of distributions.

In general, a single-valued forecast is generally unsatisfactory in inventory control work. Some kind of a frequency distribution is called for, even though this may be nothing but an estimate of the highest and lowest values of demand in a time period. When a range is given, it is assumed that the actual value will fall with equal frequency anyplace between the high and the low point of the range. This is referred to as a *uniform distribution.*

Related to the problem of a single-value versus a frequency-distribution forecast is the distinction which must be made between discrete and continuous values. In many cases, a helpful estimate may be obtained by *bounding,* that is, estimating the highest and/or lowest value that the forecast value might reasonably be.

Repetitive or One Time.   Another distinction is whether the forecast is made for a single situation or whether it is to be made over and over again. The techniques used in either case can vary. Time-series analysis becomes more important with repetitive situations. Repetitive situations are usually better structured than one-time situations and thus are more amenable to mathematical treatment.

Quantitative or Qualitative.   A *qualitative* estimation states whether the value is expected to go up or down. A *quantitative* estimation states an amount. In many cases, a mere qualitative estimation of direction is as desirable as an estimation of magnitude. Qualitative techniques are usually easier to carry out and are generally more successful. In production planning and inventory work, however, we need quantitative estimations.

Long or Short Range.   These types of estimation are relative to each other. The relativeness depends on the nature of the variable. For instance, an estimate of sales for one year in advance would be considered short range, whereas an estimation of the operation of a particular machine for one year would be considered long range. The techniques of estimation used in both cases are usually different. The long-range estimations are generally less scientific.

Subjective or Scientific.   The distinction here is one of degree. A subjective estimation gives values based solely on intuition or other unscientific characteristics. When a good amount of judgment and experience form part of the hunch, the estimates may be good. They may even be better than scientific estimates. The scientific estimation involves a more organized study of the factors involved. It attempts to determine the factors which affect the variable, how the factors affect the variable, and how these relationships change with time. It attempts to completely explain the variable. Ideally, it is the only sound method. Because of the complexity of the factors involved, the lack of scientific methodology, and/or time and expense, it is seldom possible to make a complete scientific model to estimate the variable. As a result, a scientific study may not always be successful. It is the ideal, however.

Outline of Methods

It seems safe to say that with all these distinctions there must be many forecasting methods. Indeed there are. In fact, the literature on forecasting methods is so voluminous that it is hopeless to try to survey all the methods in this chapter. No doubt we have omitted many successful techniques. Even when forecasters agree on a forecast, they are apt to reach common conclusions for different reasons. Even when forecasters are right, they are frequently right because of reasons or conditions they did not anticipate.

The following outline summarizes the spectrum of forecasting techniques. The distinctions mentioned above may be found in these techniques.

I. Unscientific techniques
  A. Guesses
  B. Hunches based on intuition
  C. Hunches based on experience, judgment, and commonsense reasoning
II. Quasi-scientific techniques
  A. Intrinsic
    1. Persistence: The same value which occurred last period will occur next period.
    2. Trajectory: The trend of the past data is fitted to a mathematical curve by least-squares or other techniques. It is assumed that future values will follow the same trend. The trends may be short or long range.
    3. Cyclical: These techniques are similar to trajectory except that cycles are examined and are assumed to hold for future periods. The values for future periods are correlated to values in a previous cycle. The cycles may be seasonal, business, etc. The use of the value for same period last year fits into this category.
    4. Use of averages
      a. The arithmetic average of all past data gives the estimate for the next period.
      b. The arithmetic average of most recent data gives the estimate. Data may be over a finite number of most recent periods (moving average) or a fixed period such as last year.
      c. A weighted average of all or part of past data gives the estimate. Exponential smoothing fits into this category.
    5. Correlative: An estimate is developed from an autocorrelation function which relates estimate to finite number of preceding values.

6. Random: A probability distribution is obtained from past data or assumed by subjective means. Estimates of future values are obtained by Monte Carlo methods. The probability may be the variation from one period to the next, the variation from the average, the variation from trend, the variation from a cycle, etc. Coin tossing might be used to predict either an upward or downward change.

7. Studies of previous forecasts: These techniques involve obtaining relationships between the actual values and the values estimated from some method. These relationships are then used to adjust future values estimated by this method. These techniques are often valuable in removing bias or accounting for factors which the given method has omitted. Many so-called adaptive methods fall into this category.

B. Extrinsic

1. Correlative

   a. Leading time series: A time series of an index or some factor may be affected by the same components which affect the value being studied. A mathematic equation relates the estimate to past values of leading time series.

   b. Analog: The characteristics of some other factor may be such that it can be used to estimate the value under study. These techniques are especially valuable when no historical data are available.

2. Causation

   a. Leading time series: These techniques are the same as 1(*a*) except that the factors are related causally.

   b. Comparative pressures: A ratio or difference may reach a specified value which may be an indication that a change is imminent which will affect the value estimated.

C. Combinations: Weighted or unweighted averages of any of the above unscientific and quasi-scientific estimates. Opinion polls and surveys are estimates of this type. The classical analyses of time series fall into this category.

III. Scientific: Methodology which develops a scientific model that relates the estimate to all factors influencing it. Causal relationships are quantitatively enumerated.

The technique used in a particular situation depends on many factors. One is the ability to interpret the factors influencing the variable in question. Available historical data and what data can be generated are also important. The time available to make studies is another.

Later sections of this chapter introduce some of the more practical techniques in production and inventory control and summarize an approach to undertaking a forecasting problem. First, however, let us answer some further questions.

How Frequently to Forecast?

There is no pat answer to the question of how frequently to forecast. In repetitive situations, two possibilities exist: on some periodic basis or whenever some new historical data are available. Often new data are available periodically (such as monthly demand recaps), so these possibilities may be identical.

In real-time control systems, it is frequently desirable to make a forecast whenever a new demand (new history) is received. Thus, an item is looked at only when some new action transpires. (The term *transaction* is often used to describe control systems of this type.) These systems generally have to have some periodic means of "cleaning out" dead items, however.

With periodic systems, a balance must be made between the benefits of a new forecast and the cost of obtaining it. Because a forecast is by nature inaccurate, it is often of little benefit to update a forecast just because new data are available, especially when the new forecasts may be expensive to obtain. Quite often forecasts for monthly planning made quarterly or even yearly are satisfactory. Such tools as ABC (item-volume) analysis can be helpful in determining how frequently to forecast (often for A items, less often for C items).

An important consideration in using past data is how current the data are. Information systems may give a lag between the transaction and its recording in the data bank where it is available for use in making forecasts. Time is necessary to assemble, condition, and aggregate data. This information lead time can lead to failure to pick up marked changes in demand which may make forecasts (based on "old" data) unreliable. Often, the information lead time can be overcome with a costlier information system. Nevertheless, the cost of the information system must be balanced against the benefits received.

What Time Horizon to Forecast?

The time horizon to forecast is dependent on the reason for forecasting. Unless seasonality or supply capacity is important, inventory control forecasts generally are short term—one period in the future. Production planning forecasts, especially when supply constraints or seasonality are present, may be over a longer term, say months for the coming year. Facilities planning forecasts are of even longer term, say 5 to 10 years in the future. Some techniques are generally better for short-term forecasting (moving average), others for medium-term (seasonality adjustments to averages), and still others for longer-term (trend lines). Forecasts for all time horizons do require judgment, with judgment perhaps being most critical to longer-term forecasts.

How Precisely to Forecast?

Important to the question of precision is the value of an item. With a high-value item, such as a jet or ocean vessel, it is fairly important to be precise in demand forecasts. However, with nail demand, precision is not too important (unless, of course, your entire business is distributing nails). Such tools as ABC (item-volume) analysis can be helpful in determining how precisely to forecast. (Concentrate on the big items with more sophisticated methods; use less sophisticated methods on the small.)

What Is a Good Forecast?

An important consideration is how to determine whether a forecast is good, or what makes one forecast technique better than another. It is not possible to give pat answers here. The answer depends on what we are forecasting. In general, however, the factors of error and bias are important.

A difficulty with error is that there are several ways of measuring it. Examples are sum of deviations, average (mean) absolute deviation, standard deviation of errors, and percentage of demand variation explained by a functional equation. It may be necessary to consider several of these measurements when the best forecasting technique is selected.

The problem of bias (whether the demand is actually consistently higher or lower than the forecast) is often overlooked. One reason is that there is no generally accepted measurement of bias. You can have low error but high bias. In some cases, such as inventory control, bias is important. In other cases it is not.

Other considerations are richness (does the forecast resemble history, possibly showing some of the same oscillations?), parsimony (are there few parameters to estimate?), and simplicity (can the forecast be readily interpreted and explained?).

The best test of a forecast technique is to try it out on history. This may not be possible if reliable past data are not available. If the forecast mechanism depends on history and if data are available, then it is good practice to develop forecast mechanisms on the first half of available history and test them on the second half. This is simple enough, but it seems as if few forecasters bother with this simple test.

A major difficulty with using history is that the demand history we have is generally sales or shipment history rather than demand. This history reflects not what was actually demanded, but what was shipped. It fails to consider lost demand because of product unavailability, delayed shipments, substituted product, or transshipments.

This lack of correspondence of shipments with demand is a major problem in inventory forecasting. Modern electronic data processing systems help alleviate this problem, as they allow us to store more historical information such as date requested, date promised, and date shipped. However, not until we have customers' computers ordering upon suppliers' computers will we be able to solve this problem.

Aggregation of Forecasts

If many items at different levels of detail are forecasted, then an important consideration is whether the sum (aggregate) of the forecasts of a group of items is equal to an independent forecast of the group as a whole. If planning in an organization is integrated or if for some reason a forecast for the total is believed to be superior, it may be desirable to "force" the various subforecasts to equal the total, so that there is internal integrity. A number of approaches can be used to force a one-number system. Muir discusses some methods and special considerations.[3] Because of variance reduction, forced forecasts are often better than unforced forecasts. In general, aggregate forecasts are more accurate than individual item forecasting because variations of one item are offset by variations of others.

PRACTICAL METHODS WITH APPLICATIONS AND LIMITATIONS

The forecasting methods which have found widest application in production and inventory control utilize historical data. They are based on the assumption that the past history of a time series is rich in information concerning its future behavior. History tends to repeat itself in that patterns observed in the past may recur in the future. By careful analysis of the past, we can observe these patterns and thus predict the future. These are methods for forecasting the expected (most likely) value of the time series. A glossary of the symbols used in describing the methods is given at the end of the chapter.

In the sections which follow, we give a variety of forecasting methods based on the general categories of moving average and equation fitting. Since many methods consider not only past history but also past performance, a section on error statistics precedes the sections on moving averages and equation fitting. In a following section, we present some forecasting methods based on measuring how a time series is changing over time. Then we cover an integrated approach to forecasting which considers error measurements, moving averages, equation fitting, and change measurements.

ERROR STATISTICS

The basic assumption of the methods which follow is that an observed value is determined by some explained pattern plus some unexplained random influences. That is,

$$\text{Actual} = \text{Pattern} + \text{Randomness}$$

The forecast attempts to give the pattern. The randomness is the error which the forecast cannot explain. The goal of forecasting is to explain as much of a time-series behavior as possible so as to minimize the randomness and hence the error.

By taking the pattern to be the forecast and randomness to be the error, rearrangement of the above equation gives

$$\text{Error} = \text{Actual} - \text{Forecast}$$

In mathematical terms this basic error equation is

$$e_t = X_t - F_t$$

where e_t = forecast error for period t
X_t = actual sales for period t
F_t = forecast sales for period t

To test how well a particular model is predicting the series, it is necessary to have a statistic which reflects this error over time. One statistic is the sum of errors from the time the forecast was initiated (or some other starting point):

$$E_t = e_1 + e_2 + \cdots + e_N$$

where N is the number of observations. Mathematically, the sum of errors is expressed more succinctly by use of a summation sign

$$E_t = \sum_{i=1}^{N} e_i$$

where i is an index which takes values that increase as they go back in time. This statistic is sometimes called *CUSUM*, for cumulative sum of errors.

Because e can be positive or negative, the sum of the forecast errors can fluctuate around zero. Its use is to test bias, or whether the forecast system is out of control. Error measurements which consider the sign effect are the sum of absolute errors $\Sigma abs\ e$ and sum of squared errors Σe^2. Measurements which average the error are average (mean) error $\Sigma e/N$, mean absolute error $\Sigma abs\ e/N$, and mean squared error $\Sigma e^2/N$. Measurements which consider the relative magnitude of the error are relative error $\Sigma(e/X)$, mean relative error $\Sigma(e/X)/N$, and mean absolute relative error $(abs\ e/X)/N$.

Other measurements use percentages rather than relative ratios and medians rather than means. Other statistics are the square root of the mean squared error (SE)—equivalent to the standard deviation of the forecast error and sometimes referred to as the *root mean squared error*—and the geometric root mean squared error. Other measures are the coefficient of variation, SE/average of data; the unexplained variation, SE/variance of data; and the coefficient of determination. The mean squared error and the root mean squared error are probably the most commonly used measurements.

MOVING AVERAGES

Many common forecasting methods come under the general category of moving averages. These techniques *average*, or *smooth*, past data in some way.

Simple Averages

If historical data are the basis for a demand forecast, a simple forecast is to take the actual demand from the preceding period. Since most time series experience variations in demand (often called *noise*, or *disturbance*), better estimates are generally possible by smoothing the history through averaging. In mathematical terms, the simple average of demand for 2 periods (which we designate by the symbols 1 and 2) is given by

$$A = \frac{X_1 + X_2}{2}$$

where X_1 = sales in period 1
$\quad\quad X_2$ = sales in period 2
$\quad\quad A$ = 2-period average demand

For example, if the demand in period 1 is 100 ($X_1 = 100$) and the demand in period 2 is 150 ($X_2 = 150$), then the 2-period average is

$$A = \frac{100 + 150}{2} = 125$$

The general formula for calculating an average of N periods (where $N = 12$ for a 12-month average, for example) is

$$A = \frac{X_1 + X_2 + \cdots + X_N}{N}$$

$$= \frac{\displaystyle\sum_{i=1}^{N} X_i}{N} \tag{9.1}$$

This method is commonly applied by taking an average over some fixed period. For example, the average monthly sales for last year might be the forecast for each month of the current year.

Because of its ease of understanding and application, this method is used often. Its major difficulty is its slower response to demand pattern changes.

Simple Moving Averages

Contrasted with a fixed-period average is a moving average in which the average is taken over a period which changes with time. For instance, the forecast for a given month would be the average monthly sales over the immediately preceding 12 months rather than the 12 months of last year. This moving of the base period makes the forecast respond more rapidly to demand than with the simple fixed-period forecasts.

In mathematical terms, a moving-average forecast for an arbitrary period $t + 1$ based on history through time t would be

$$F_{t+1} = A_t = \frac{X_t + X_{t-1} + \cdots + X_{t-N+2} + X_{t-N+1}}{N}$$

$$= \frac{\displaystyle\sum_{i=t-N+1}^{t} X_i}{N} \tag{9.2}$$

where
$$A_t = \text{average through period } t$$
$$F_{t+1} = \text{forecast for period } t + 1$$
$$X_t = \text{sales in time period } t$$
$$X_{t-1} = \text{sales in time period } t - 1$$

In this symbolism, the values of the index i increase with time. In practice, the moving average for a period is often calculated by taking the previous average, adding the proportionate part of the latest value, and subtracting the proportionate part of the value dropping out of the base period. Hence the calculation is

$$A_t = A_{t-1} - \frac{X_{t-N}}{N} + \frac{X_t}{N} = A_{t-1} + \frac{X_t - X_{t-N}}{N} \tag{9.3}$$

There are two types of moving averages. The formula above is based on a trailing moving average. For analytical purposes, such as correlating one time series with another, centered moving averages are often used. In this type of average the referenced time period is the *middle* period of the average. For instance, the formula for a 3-month centered average is

$$A_t = \frac{X_{t+1} + X_t + X_{t-1}}{3}$$

Special adjustments are needed for centered moving averages for even-numbered periods.

By definition, centered moving averages cannot be used for direct forecasting unless the forecasted time series is related to the averaged series by a lagged relationship.

For a stationary series (i.e., no significant trend up or down over time), a long-term moving average would give best results. Here a 12-, 15-, or even 18-month trailing moving average would be used. Examples of products suitable to this approach might be commodities such as soap, flour, or washing machine assembly parts.

However, if sharp changes in demand level are to be expected, short-term moving averages will better detect these changes. Three-month moving averages might better be used for products such as popular phonograph records, books, or dye (color) stocks. An extreme example would be the weather which, it is said, is best predicted with a 1-day moving average (i.e., the weather tomorrow will be the same as today).

Weighted Moving Averages

The averages discussed so far give equal weights to the historical data. For instance, Eq. (9.2) could be written

$$A_t = \frac{1}{N}X_t + \frac{1}{N}X_{t-1} + \cdots + \frac{1}{N}X_{t-N+1}$$

where $1/N$ is the weight given to each value.

The sum of the weights is 1. With this type of mechanism, each past period is assumed to be equally important. In many situations, especially if the time series is not stationary, it may be desirable to give more weight to most recent data. For instance,

$$A_t = 0.7X_t + 0.3X_{t-1}$$

might be used to make a weighted forecast based on two periods of history. In this case, more weight is given to X_t, the more recent history.

The corresponding unweighted (or, in reality, the equally weighted) forecast would be

$$A_t = 0.5X_t + 0.5X_{t-1}$$

In more general terms, the forecast formula can be written as

$$A_t = \alpha X_t + (1 - \alpha)X_{t-1} \tag{9.4}$$

where α is a weighting factor.

For N periods, the general equation is

$$A_t = w_t X_t + w_{t-1}X_{t-1} + \cdots + w_{t-N+1}X_{t-N+1} \tag{9.5}$$

$$= \sum_{t=1}^{N} w_i X_{t-i-1}$$

where w_t is a weighting factor for time t and

$$w_t + w_{t-1} + \cdots + w_{t-N+1} = 1$$

Weighted moving averages have been extensively used in inventory forecasting. The multiplicity of possible formulas is subject to the forecast designer's imagination.

A particular type of weighted moving average, exponential smoothing, has found extensive use in inventory applications with a huge body of literature being developed about it. It is discussed in detail later.

Seasonality Factors

Where seasonality can be reasonably measured, better forecasts generally are possible by including factors which adjust for it. For series with regular, repetitive variations over L periods ($L = 12$ for seasonal monthly data), a seasonal multiplier, or factor, can be used in an equation such as

$$SF_{t+1} = F_{t+1}S_{t+1}$$

where SF_{t+1} = seasonally adjusted forecast
  F_{t+1} = unadjusted forecast
  S_{t+1} = seasonal multiplication factor

Forecasts can also be adjusted by an additive factor

$$SF_{t+1} = F_{t+1} + S_{t+1}$$

where S_{t+1} is the seasonal additive factor.

There are several methods for determining a seasonal adjustment factor. The most common method for determining a multiplication factor is to take the ratio of the actual demand in the corresponding period of the last cycle to the average demand over the cycle. That is,

$$S_{t+1} = \frac{X_{t+1-L}}{SA}$$

where X_{t+1-L} = demand in period $t + 1 - L$
  SA = average demand
  L = cycle period

The value of SA can be determined from Eq. (9.1) or (9.2).

A seasonal factor obtained in this way is simply one estimate of the seasonality. The seasonal factor itself can be forecasted by averaging methods.

A major problem with the use of seasonal factors is that several cycles of history are needed to get meaningful estimates. Further, the use of seasonality factors increases the amount of data handling and calculations. Further, the existence of trend, other cyclical factors, and random factors can complicate the determination of seasonal factors. Therefore, it is important to ascertain that seasonality really exists and that the use of seasonality forecasts will significantly improve the forecasts. The data-handling problems can be alleviated somewhat if the seasonality factors apply to several contiguous periods, i.e., a quarterly factor for monthly forecasts. Subjective estimates often exaggerate the magnitude of seasonality. Also what appears to be seasonality may actually be induced by control mechanisms. See Harrison for a discussion of seasonality in forecasting and some methods for making seasonal estimates.[4] There are several methods of testing the significance of seasonality, of which the analysis of variance is the most common (see Chap. 30).

Of course, the simplest seasonal forecast is

$$F_{t+1} = X_{t+1-L}$$

That is, the forecast is the actual demand for the same period in the last cycle.

Census Method

One of the more developed moving-average techniques is the $X-11$ version of the Census Method II procedure.[5] This method was developed by the Bureau of the Census to forecast economic time series. It is often called the *Shiskin decomposition method* (for Julius Shiskin, the statistician responsible for its development). This method was an outgrowth of Census Method I, which was the computerization of standard methods of time-series analysis. For details of time-series analysis methods, see Croxton and Cowden.[6] Method II takes fuller advantage of the capabilities of the electronic computer, adding many adjustments and other features. The method would be infeasible without a computer.

The method is quite complex as far as the number of steps required. We do not give a detailed presentation here. McLaughlin gives a detailed discussion.[7] In any case, packages for executing the method are available on a number of computer systems and have been used widely. Thus the user is spared the necessity of doing the multitudinous calculations.

Basically, the method assumes a demand series X composed of four components:

$$X = T \times C \times S \times I$$

where T = trend component
$\quad\quad\ \ C$ = cyclical component
$\quad\quad\ \ S$ = seasonal component
$\quad\quad\ \ I$ = irregular component

It decomposes the series into three components:

$$X = TC \times S \times I$$

where TC is the combined effect of trend and cycle components. The components are estimated as follows:

1. Estimate TC component via a moving average of X.
2. Estimate SI as ratio of X to TC.
3. Adjust SI for extreme points (find extreme points and round by moving average).
4. Estimate S by an averaging of SI.
5. Estimate TCI by ratio of X to S.
6. Estimate I by ratio of TCI to TC.

Several steps are repeated more than once for refinements.

The procedure is not a forecasting method directly; however, the procedure gives data which can be the basis for a forecast. One simple approach is to base forecasts on

$$F = TC \times S$$

with I giving a measure of variation. In this equation, the seasonal factors are extrapolated.

Plots of the trend-cycle curve are useful in tracking trends and estimating turning points. Figure 9.1 shows the raw, seasonally adjusted, and trend-cycle curves for a time series. Because of the heavy computer requirements, the method is limited for SKU forecasting. A certain amount of aggregation is usually desirable when this method is used. It is also limited to products with a fair amount of history (at least 3 years of monthly data). Its principal uses in production and inventory planning are in monthly forecasting for a seasonal major product over the coming year and in analyzing trend and seasonal factors for use in other forecasting methods.

Extensions and adaptations to the X-11 procedure have been developed. Levenbach and Cleary summarize the Seasonal Adjustment–Bell Laboratories (SABL) decomposition program which has alternative methods of smoothing, summarizing, and displaying data.[8] See also Dagum.[9]

Exponential Smoothing

The use of exponential smoothing in inventory forecasting was introduced by Brown. This method combines the moving-average features with minimal data storage requirements.

Basic Model. Basically, exponential smoothing is a moving average in which different weights are given to past data. The weights are set so that they decrease as they go back in time. Thus greater significance is given to more recent history. (By contrast, the average monthly demand for the past 12 months would be a 12-month trailing moving average with equal weights given to each of the 12 months.)

To forecast with this method, we first need some past knowledge of the system. Assume an average of past values which can be used as the forecast for the current period. For illustrative purposes, let this average be 100. Now assume that we experience a demand of 120 in the current period, and we are interested in calculating a new average which can be used as a forecast for the next period. We want to take advantage of our latest experience to make our new forecast. Since 120 is higher than 100, we logically want to make our forecast higher than 100. The question is, How much higher? In other words, how much weight do we want to give to our new experience? Exponential smoothing makes a forecast by saying that we want to add to (subtract from) our previous forecast a fraction of the amount by which the demand this period exceeds (is below) the previous forecast. That is,

New forecast = old forecast + α(new demand − old forecast)

where α (Greek letter alpha) is an arbitrary smoothing constant between 0 and 1. Its value depends on how much weight we want to give to our new experience—the higher the value, the greater the weight. If alpha were 1, we would give all our weight to the latest value while ignoring the old average. If alpha were 0, we would

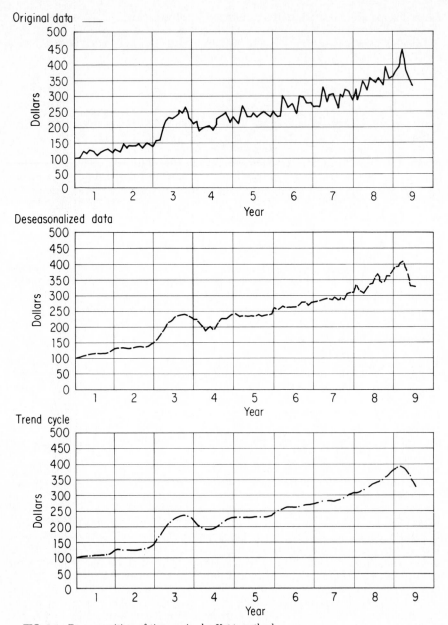

FIG. 9.1 Decomposition of time series by X-11 method.

ignore the latest value. If we took alpha as 0.25, then the new forecast in the example would be

$$\text{New forecast} = 100 + 0.25(120 - 100)$$
$$= 105$$

Mathematically, the relationship is

$$F_{t+1} = A_t = A_{t-1} + \alpha(X_t - A_{t-1}) \qquad (9.6)$$

where F_{t+1} = forecast for next period $t + 1$
A_t = exponentially smoothed average through period t
A_{t-1} = exponentially smoothed average through $t - 1$ (previously calculated average)
X_t = actual demand in current period t
α = smoothing constant $(0 \leqslant \alpha \leqslant 1)$

The preceding relation can be rearranged to give

$$A_t = \alpha X_t + (1 - \alpha)A_{t-1} \qquad (9.7)$$

which is the basic equation of simple exponential smoothing. Then we can take this value of A_t as the old average in the calculation for the next time period. That is,

$$A_{t+1} = \alpha X_{t+1} + (1 - \alpha)A_t$$

Thus, one of the principal advantages of a simple exponential smoothing over other types of moving averages is that only two values have to be carried from period to period. To make a forecast for the next period, all that is necessary is the value for α (the smoothing constant), the more recent data point, and the last forecast.

When Eq. (9.7) is applied successively backward in time to some initial average A_0, the exponential smoothing model becomes

$$A_t = \alpha X_t + \alpha\beta X_{t-1} + \alpha\beta^2 X_{t-2} + \cdots + \alpha\beta^{t-1}X_1 + \beta^t A_0 \qquad (9.8)$$

where $\beta = 1 - \alpha$. The "exponential" part of the name is derived from the exponents of β. Since α is less than 1, the coefficients of the past-demand terms decrease going back in time. Since β is the factor which causes the coefficients to decrease, β is sometimes called the discount rate. Also the coefficients sum to 1, so the model is a weighted moving average.

Another way of looking at exponential smoothing is as follows. Suppose that just before the current data point became available, a catastrophe in the data storage system left us with only the current average A_{t-1}. One proposal for obtaining a forecast for the next period might be to assume that the data point N periods ago was A_{t-1}. That is, $X_{t-N} = A_{t-1}$ in Eq. (9.3). The current average then becomes

$$A_t = A_{t-1} - \frac{A_{t-1}}{N} + \frac{X_t}{N}$$

or

$$A_t = \frac{1}{N}X_t + \left(1 - \frac{1}{N}\right)A_{t-1} \qquad (9.9)$$

If $1/N$ is replaced by α and $1 - 1/N$ by $1 - \alpha$, then

$$A_t = \alpha X_t + (1 - \alpha)A_{t-1}$$

which is Eq. (9.7). Note that this equation is equivalent to Eq. (9.4) with

$$A_{t-1} = X_{t-1}$$

As we can see from Eq. (9.9), the weighting or smoothing factor α is related to N, the number of periods in a moving average. Since the relationship is inverse $(\alpha \sim 1/N)$, small α values should be used where large N values are effective. The two systems would be exactly equivalent except for the fact that where data points are eliminated from consideration after N periods in moving-average calculations, they are theoretically never "forgotten" in exponential smoothing calculations. Brown relates α and N by

$$\alpha = \frac{2}{N + 1} \tag{9.10}$$

Hence where the data points in a 12-month moving average would all be weighted $\frac{1}{12}$ or 0.0833, for 12 past periods (and 0 for anything older than that), an equivalent exponential smoothing system in the sense of average age of data would have a smoothing constant of $2/(12 + 1) = 0.154$. The weights in Eq. (9.8) would be 0.154, 0.130, 0.110, 0.0932, etc., decreasing exponentially. (An earlier name, *exponentially weighted moving averages*, expresses this more precisely at the expense of being wordier.) Figure 9.2 illustrates the weights for some representative smoothing constants.

Another way of understanding the significance of the smoothing constant is to compare what proportion of the total weight is given to a specific number of periods. A value of 0.5 gives over 90 percent of the total weight to data from the last

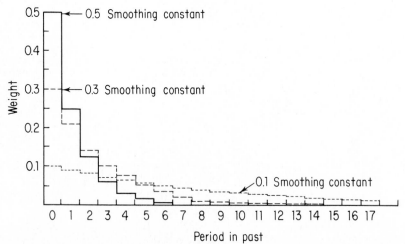

FIG. 9.2   Exponential smoothing weights: weights given to previous periods for different smoothing constants.

4 periods, whereas a value of 0.1 gives the same proportion of weight to data from the last 22 periods.

The necessary information to start such an exponential smoothing forecasting system includes

1. Some initial estimate X_0 of the level (usually an average of historical data)
2. A value for the smoothing constant α

Because of the difficulty of choosing alpha and because of the possibility that varying values of alpha may be appropriate at different times, several methods have been developed which allow alpha to change based on certain criteria. Some of these methods are discussed later. Bretschneider and Gorr illustrate the relationships of some of the newer approaches.[10]

The initial estimate can be one data point or an average. Because of decreasing weights, the influence of the initial estimate on the forecast decreases with time; therefore, the initial choice is not overly critical.

One way of starting a system is to assume an alpha of 1 for the first period (all the weight is applied to the only piece of history—the single bit of history is the forecast), an alpha of ½ after the second period, an alpha of ⅓ after the third period, and so on until the alpha is no longer greater than the long-term desired smoothing constant. In mathematical terms,

$$\alpha = \frac{1}{N} \qquad \text{if} \qquad \alpha > \alpha' \qquad \text{else} \qquad \alpha = \alpha'$$

where N = number of periods of history
       α' = long-term (steady-state) smoothing constant

This method does require carrying over an additional piece of data—the number of periods of history N.

In a manner analogous to how the length of time included in the moving average varies with the series type, the smoothing constant in exponential smoothing also varies with series type. For a relatively stationary series, α could range from 0.1 to 0.15, corresponding to 18 to 12 period moving averages, while for series with sharp level changes α may vary from 0.2 to 0.5, equivalent to 9 to 3 period moving averages. Figure 9.3 is a nomograph which can be used to test the significance of alpha. Lacking any other information, an alpha of 0.1 is a reasonable choice for a reasonably stable series, whereas a value of 0.2 is a good starter for an uncertain series. For a series with wide fluctuations, epitomized by alternating high and low values, a smaller alpha (0.05 to 0.1) is generally a good selection. Likewise, a low alpha is usually best for so-called lumpy demand—many periods with zero demands. Higher values of alpha are generally best when short runs (trends or cycles) are possible.

Smaller alphas are usually more appropriate with shorter periods (day or weeks, compared to quarters or years) because they have relatively greater fluctuations than longer periods. Likewise, individual SKUs may have greater relative fluctuations than aggregate items and so call for smaller smoothing constants.

Figure 9.4 shows the response of the simple exponential smoothing model to several standardized inputs. The *impulse* might represent the effect of random noise. The simple model reacts proportionally to α in the next period and then resumes tracking the true value. The *step* illustrates a basic nonstationary series.

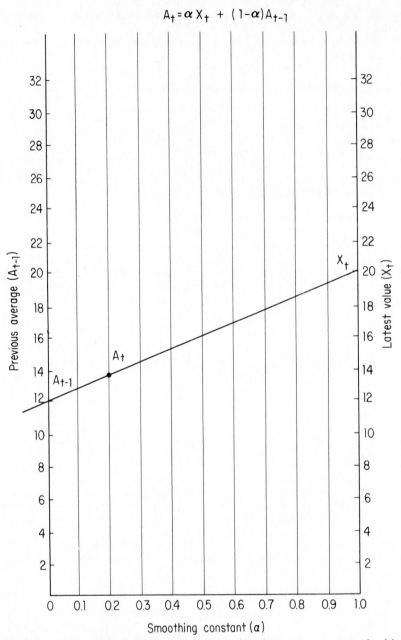

$$A_t = \alpha\, X_t + (1-\alpha) A_{t-1}$$

FIG. 9.3 Exponential smoothing nomograph (graph to determine new average for different smoothing constants). Procedure: Locate X_t and A_{t-1} on respective axes. Draw line connecting these points. Read A_t on vertical scale as intersection of drawn line with vertical line for desired smoothing constant.

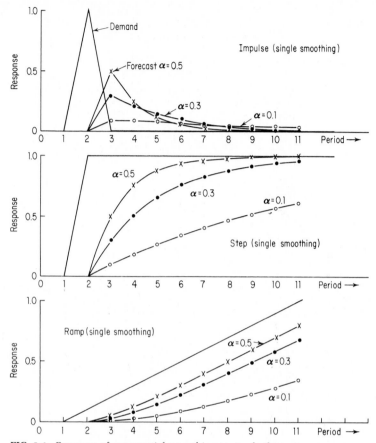

FIG. 9.4   Response of exponential smoothing to standard inputs.

The simple model's speed of response is directly proportional to the value of alpha. In the case of *ramp* or trend, the simple model eventually has the correct slope, but *always* lags the true value, the lag being inversely proportional to alpha.

Multiple Exponential Smoothing.   Because of the lag inherent in simple exponential smoothing, higher-order models have been developed and used. The basic equation of multiple exponential smoothing is

$$A_t^n = \alpha A_t^{n-1} + (1 - \alpha)A_{t-1}^n \qquad (9.11)$$

where A_t^n = nth-order smoothed average. In the equation, n is a designator of the order rather than a power term. The A's are a function of the demand X with

$$A_t^0 = X_t$$

by definition.

Thus, the first three orders of exponential smoothing are

$$A'_t = \alpha X_t + (1 - \alpha)A'_{t-1} \tag{9.12}$$
$$A''_t = \alpha A'_t + (1 - \alpha)A''_{t-1} \tag{9.13}$$
$$A'''_t = \alpha A''_t + (1 - \alpha)A'''_{t-1} \tag{9.14}$$

where the prime sign is used to indicate the order of smoothing. Orders higher than 3 have found little practical use. Brown covers higher-order smoothing in more detail, giving the background for the equations.[11] Double smoothing would be used if a trend were believed to exist, whereas triple smoothing would be used if the trend changed with time.

A double-smoothed forecast consists of two components:

$$F_{t+1} = A_t + R_t$$

where A_t = average demand at period t
$\quad\quad R_t$ = trend at period t

The components are estimated from

$$A_t = 2A'_t - A''_t$$
$$R_t = A''_t - A''_{t-1}$$

where A'_t and A''_t are determined by Eqs. (9.12) and (9.13), respectively. The forecast, by substitution, is then

$$F_{t+1} = 2A'_t - A''_{t-1} \tag{9.15}$$

Hence to forecast by double exponential smoothing, three values must be carried from month to month: the smoothing constant and the single- and double-smoothed averages, A' and A''.

The equation for forecasting more than one period in advance is

$$F_{t+u} = A_t + uR_t$$

where u is the lead time of the forecast.

Double smoothing, at the expense of having extra calculation and data storage requirements, gives more response to demand changes than single smoothing. There is a lag; however, its magnitude decreases with time under steady-state conditions. Because of the greater response, smaller values of alpha give the same significance to history. For instance, a smoothing constant of 0.1 with double smoothing is approximately equivalent to an alpha of 0.2 with single smoothing.

Winter's Modified Model.   In an attempt to account for seasonality and trend while still using relatively simple exponential smoothing techniques, a model was proposed by Winters.[12] It consists of a multiplicative seasonality factor and an additive trend factor, each smoothed separately. Its form is

$$F_{t+1} = A_t = \alpha \ \frac{X_t}{S_{t-L}} + (1 - \alpha)(A_{t-1} + R_{t-1}) \tag{9.16}$$

where S_{t-L} = seasonal factor
$\quad\quad R_{t-1}$ = trend factor

The trend factor is updated by

$$R_t = \delta(A_t - A_{t-1}) + (1 - \delta)R_{t-1} \tag{9.17}$$

where δ = smoothing constant $(0 \leq \delta \leq 1)$.
   The seasonal factor is updated by

$$S_t = \gamma \frac{X_t}{A_t} + (1 - \gamma)S_{t-L} \tag{9.18}$$

where γ = smoothing constant $(0 \leq \gamma \leq 1)$.
   The forecast for u periods in the future is then

$$F_{t+u} = (F_t + uR_t)S_{t-L+u} \tag{9.19}$$

One advantage of using seasonal and trend factors in an exponential smoothing model is that forecasts can be made for months beyond the current forecasts.
   With this model, the problem of choosing a smoothing factor is threefold, since theoretically values for α, δ, and γ must be selected. In practice, however, since trend and seasonality are not subject to step changes very often, smoothing factors between 0.1 and 0.2 are often assigned based on experience.
   A careful examination of the exponential model and its response to various inputs leads to the notion that if somehow α could be adjusted or updated, the model might track more closely the underlying series to be forecast. Several directions have been followed in research on this problem.

Brown's General Models.   Brown proposed many exponential smoothing models, including polynominals, exponentials, sinusoids, sums, and products of such functions.[13] In summary, the models are exponential smoothing based on *discounted multiple regression*; the effect of using them approximates moving the time-axis origin to the most recent data point. These models require more storage and manipulation for each series than simpler exponential smoothing systems.
   Brown's basic trend correction model is

$$F_{t+u} = A_t + uR_t \tag{9.20}$$

where $A_t = A_{t-1} + R_{t-1} + \alpha(2 - \alpha)(X_1 - F_t)$
          $R_t = R_{t-1} + \alpha^2(X_t - F_t)$

He recommends a smoothing constant of 0.05.

Error Tracking.   In theory, the selection of a smoothing constant should be based on which constant gives the lowest error by one of the statistics mentioned earlier. In practice, however, a plot of error versus the smoothing constant gives a curve with a flat minimum (see Fig. 9.5). As a result, it is difficult, by this approach alone, to justify that one smoothing constant is significantly better than another.
   In exponential smoothing, a useful statistic is the *mean absolute deviation* (MAD), which is defined as the smoothed absolute value of the error. Its calculation is

$$P_t = \eta \text{ abs } e_t + (1 - \eta)P_{t-1} \tag{9.21}$$

where P_t = mean absolute deviation at period t
η = smoothing constant $(0 \leqslant \eta \leqslant 1)$
abs e_t = absolute value of e_t

In most practical systems, $\eta \approx 0.1$ (assuming no radical swings in absolute deviation).

Another related statistic is the *smoothed average deviation* (SAD), called Q here. It is calculated similarly as

$$Q_t = \eta e_t + (1 - \eta)Q_{t-1} \tag{9.22}$$

Here again a practical value of η is 0.1.

In measuring the suitability of a particular model to a particular time series in a multiple forecasting environment, the assumption is made that the errors actually are independent random values, normally distributed with zero mean. If this assumption is granted, then something like control limits could be estimated for these errors. To do this, some measure of how the system is following or tracking the actual data is needed. Since, if the above assumption is made, P can be shown to approximate (or at least be proportional to) the root mean square error, it could be included as one factor in such a tracking signal. Now if the random-error assumption is correct, the sum of such errors E_t should also oscillate around zero. If, however, some change has occurred in the basic character of the series, E_t will accumulate above or below zero. Therefore the ratio

$$TS_t = \frac{E_t}{P_t} \tag{9.23}$$

should remain inside the limits. This ratio is commonly called a *tracking signal*. The most commonly used control-limit values are ± 4.0. If TS passes these limits for, say, two consecutive periods, E is reset to zero. If, within some short period (say, 6 time units), the same control value is again violated, this is a good indication the basic series has undergone a change in character. If no further violations are observed in this period, it is assumed that some short-term aberration affected the series.

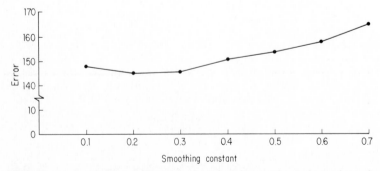

FIG. 9.5 Error related to smoothing constant (based on a 36-period test of actual product).

In a similar way, the tracking signal could be calculated by

$$TS_t = \frac{Q_t}{P_t} \tag{9.24}$$

Here the theoretical limit of the ratio is ± 1.0. The approximate ± 2 "sigma" tracking signal limit (TSL) is

$$TSL = \frac{2.4\eta}{[\eta(2 - \eta)]^{0.5}} \tag{9.25}$$

For $\eta = 0.1$, this is ± 0.55. A similar control-by-exception system to that above would serve to warn of changes in the characteristics of the series.

Adaptive Models.   Research in exponential smoothing forecasting systems has led to the development of models in which the smoothing factor is not constant but is adjusted based on current performance of the model. Some representative adaptive systems that have been used in actual situations are discussed here.

Trigg and Leach Modification   A simple modification of single smoothing has been proposed by Trigg and Leach.[14] They point out that since the Q/P (SAD/MAD) ratio has limits of ± 1.0, its absolute value could be used directly as an adaptive α. In their evaluation of the response of such a system, they show good results for step and ramp functions. The response, or rather overreaction, to impulses suggests that this method should not be used where large random fluctuation may be encountered. They also suggest that, because of the magnification of effect, this adaptive α be used only in the equation for single exponential smoothing.

Burgess Model   Burgess proposes the use of a second-order model with seasonality factors and an adaptive smoothing constant determined by statistical tests.[15] The basic formula for a next-period forecast is

$$F_{t+1} = S_{t+1-L}(A_t + R_t) \tag{9.26}$$

with the formula for u periods in the future as

$$F_{t+u} = S_{t+u-L}(A_t + uR_t) \tag{9.27}$$

The smoothing constant is obtained by the following logic: The mean absolute deviation P_t, the smoothed absolute deviation Q_t, the tracking signal TS_t, and TSL are calculated by using Eqs. (9.21), (9.22), (9.24), and (9.25), respectively. A parameter H is calculated from

$$H = \frac{1 - \alpha}{\alpha}$$

where α is the previous smoothing constant. If the tracking signal is greater than the tracking signal limit (abs $TS_t > $ TSL), then set $H = H - r$, or else set $H = H + 1$. In mathematical terms,

$$H = \begin{cases} H - r & \text{if abs } TS_t > TSL \\ H + 1 & \text{otherwise} \end{cases}$$

The parameter r is a reduction factor set high (that is, $r = 10$) for a fast response to control-limit breakthroughs and low (that is, $r = 2$) for slow reaction. The smoothing constant is then calculated from

$$\alpha = \frac{1}{H + 1}$$

To keep the value of the smoothing constant within a reasonable range, limits are set on the values of H. For instance, to keep α within the range of 0.05 and 0.5, the maximum and minimum values of H would be 19 and 1, respectively.

With this approach to changing alpha each period, a high value such as 0.5 can be used as the initial value (given 0.5 as the starting value, H can be interpreted as the count of the number of periods since forecasting commenced). As the series shows more stability, the value of alpha is automatically reduced. Unless some deviation occurs which throws the smoothed forecast errors out of a control limit, the value of alpha will reach a steady-state value of the lower limit.

The value of A_t in Eq. (9.26) is then obtained as follows. The single-smoothed average is calculated by

$$A'_t = \alpha \frac{X_t}{S_{t-L}} + (1 - \alpha)A'_{t-1}$$

The double-smoothed average A''_{t-1} is calculated by Eq. (9.13). A current trend estimate is calculated by

$$T_t = \frac{A'_t - A''_t}{H}$$

A trend signal is found from

$$RS_t = \text{abs } \frac{T_t}{P_t}$$

A trend control limit is given by

$$TL_t = 0.625k\alpha^{1.5}$$

where k is a factor to give the desired level of probability significance. (It is analogous to $k = 3$ sigma limits in quality control.) If the mean value of the trend signal is within the trend control limit, then the average in the forecast equation is the single-smoothed average; otherwise, it is the double-smoothed forecast of Eq. (9.15). That is,

$$A_t = \begin{cases} A'_t & \text{if } RS_t < TL_t \\ 2A'_t - A''_t & \text{otherwise} \end{cases}$$

The trend component R_t in the forecast equation is determined from

$$R_t = \begin{cases} 0 & \text{if } RS_t < TL_t \\ T_t & \text{otherwise} \end{cases}$$

Likewise, a significance level can be placed on the seasonality factor. A seasonality limit is given by

$$SL_t = \frac{\psi \; abs \; (X_t/A_t - S_{t-L})}{S_{t-L} + (1 - \psi)SL_{t-1}}$$

where ψ is a smoothing constant for which Burgess suggests a value of 0.3. If the limit is greater than 1, then seasonality is not significant and no seasonal adjustment is made. The seasonal factor S_t is calculated by Eq. (9.18).

In mathematical terms,

$$S_t = \begin{cases} 1.0 & \text{if } SL_t > 1.0 \\ S_t & \text{otherwise} \end{cases}$$

This model overcomes many of the difficulties with simple exponential smoothing at the expense of being complex and requiring more data storage. The values of Q, P, α, A', A'', SL, and S must be carried over from period to period for each item as compared with just A and α for single smoothing. So the user must carefully judge whether this violation of the principle of parsimonious parameterization produces significantly better forecasts.

Dudman Model Starting with Winter's model as a basis, Dudman developed a model which automatically adjusts smoothing constant, trend, and seasonality.[16]

The smoothing constant is determined from a ratio of an autocovariance estimate to a variance estimate. That is,

$$\alpha = \frac{W_t}{V_t(1 + \xi)}$$

where W_t = autocovariance estimate
V_t = variance estimate
ξ = factor to dampen effect of autocorrelation

The variance estimates are

$$W_t = \rho e_t e_{t-1} + (1 - \rho)W_{t-1}$$
$$V_t = \rho e_{t-1}^2 + (1 - \rho)V_{t-1}$$

where the e's are the appropriate forecast errors and ρ is a smoothing constant.

The current average and trend equations are, respectively,

$$A_t = A_{t-1} + R_{t-1} + \alpha e_t$$
$$R_t = \delta(A_t - A_{t-1}) + (1 - \delta)R_{t-1}$$
$$= R_{t-1} + \alpha \delta e_t$$

The seasonal factor for the current period j of the cycle is updated by

$$S_{j,t} = \gamma \frac{C}{A_{t-1} + R_{t-1}} S_{j,t-1}$$

where $S_{j,t}$ is the seasonal factor for cycle period j calculated at time t. The seasonal factors (a total of $L - 1$) for other than period j are normalized by the relationship

$$S_{i,t} = \frac{S_{i,t-1}(L - S_{j,t})}{L - S_{j,t-1}}$$

so that the summation of the factors over the cycle time L is equal to L.
The forecast is

$$F_{t+u} = (A_t + uR_t)S_{t+u,t}$$

Dudman recommends values of 0.15, 0.15, and 0.20 for δ, ξ, and γ, respectively. She also proposes that during the course of a cycle, the sum of the absolute deviations be calculated for the case where seasonal factors are used and for the case where seasonal factors are 1.0. If at the end of a cycle the former is less than 85 percent of the latter, then the seasonal factors are used over the next cycle; otherwise, they are not.

EQUATION FITTING

Up to this point the methods presented have smoothed or averaged the random factors in a series of historical data points. In some cases, this may be taken care of in another way. For instance, if only annual data are available, the monthly fluctuations for a year are essentially absorbed in the single yearly value. For very new (or fast-decaying) products, the random fluctuations may be less important.

For series where some pattern seems to emerge from the randomness of the data, a correlation of the data with time, with past values of the series, or with some other series may yield a mathematical curve or relationship which can be used for forecasting by extrapolation. The most commonly used statistical approach to curve fitting involves regression by maximum-likelihood criterion. Chapter 30 covers the subject in detail, so we discuss it only briefly here. A more detailed presentation is given by Draper and Smith[17] and others.

Curves fitted by maximum-likelihood regression have the property of *least squares*. The fundamental concept of least squares involves selecting the coefficients of an equation so that the sum of the squares of the deviations of the calculated values from the data points is minimized.

Mathematically, minimize

$$\sum_{i=1}^{N} (X_i - Y_i)^2$$

where X_i = actual value in period i $(i = 1, 2, \ldots, N)$
Y_i = value calculated by fitted equation

In the symbolism of this section, Y represents a value obtained by a curve fit. Thus, the forecast would be

$$F_t = Y_t$$

where F_t = forecast for period t.

Intrinsic Factors

Two types of intrinsic curve fitting are commonly used. In one type, autoregression, the predicted value is related to past values of the series. In the other, the predicted value is related to time. Least-square methods are most commonly used to fit these types of curves; however, other techniques are also used, and some are mentioned here. Regression analysis computer packages are common, thus freeing the forecaster from the drudgery of making calculations.

Autoregression.   The basic concept of autoregression is to correlate a current value of a time series to previous values. This approach can be used if a time series is influenced by recent past values. The most obvious relationship of this type would be $Y_{t+1} = X_t$; that is, the forecast is the last value of the series. Other common relationships are

$$Y_{t+1} = X_t + a$$
$$Y_{t+1} = aX_t$$
$$Y_{t+1} = a_0 + a_1X_t$$
$$Y_{t+1} = a_0 + a_1X_t + a_2X_{t-1}$$

The general linear equation is

$$Y_t = \delta + \sum_{i=1}^{p} \phi_i X_{t-i} \tag{9.28}$$

where p = the number of past-value terms (order of autoregression).

The coefficients may be obtained by the linear multiple-regression techniques. See Chap. 30. Meaningful correlations can be obtained only if p (number of terms in the equation) is less than N (number of historical data values used).

Seasonality can be introduced into an autoregression function by having one of the terms include the corresponding value from the previous cycle.

Time-Dependent Correlations.   The spectrum of possible models in which a time series can be related to time is limited by the forecaster's ability to formulate the model and solve for its coefficients. We discuss some of the more common models.

Linear   The most familiar model is the linear, or straight-line, model:

$$Y_t = a + bt \tag{9.29}$$

In this equation, the coefficient b represents the linear trend. The coefficient a is a position coefficient. For the determination of coefficients a and b, the data X_t for periods 1 to N are required. The equations for determining the coefficients are

$$a = A \times S_1 - B \times S_2$$
$$b = -B \times S_1 + C \times S_2$$

where

$$A = \frac{2(2N + 1)}{N(N - 1)}$$

$$B = \frac{6}{N(N - 1)}$$

$$C = \frac{12}{N(N^2 - 1)}$$

$$S_1 = \sum_{i=1}^{N} X_i$$

$$S_2 = \sum_{i=1}^{N} iX_i$$

X_i = given data for period i (i = 1 for oldest observation)
N = number of values of data

This model may also be used for a nonlinear series if the data can be transformed to a linear form. For instance, if

$$X'_i = f(X_i)$$

where f is some mathematical operation such as taking a logarithm, then X'_i can be substituted for X_i in the above equations.

With this model, projections can be made by extrapolating the model in time beyond the given data set. Care must be taken in this extrapolation, however, because the confidence interval widens as the curve projects in time. Figure 9.6 is an example of a fitted curve which is projected in time.

Polynomials Polynomials in time are sometimes helpful but are much more sensitive to minor fluctuations in data. The general equation is

$$Y_t = a_0 + \sum_{i=1}^{M} a_i t^i \tag{9.30}$$

where M = number of time-dependent terms. If M = 1, then the linear equation of the previous section results. If M = 2, then a second-order equation of the form $Y = a_0 + a_1 t + a_2 t^2$ results. The second-degree equation can be used if there is an acceleration in the trend.

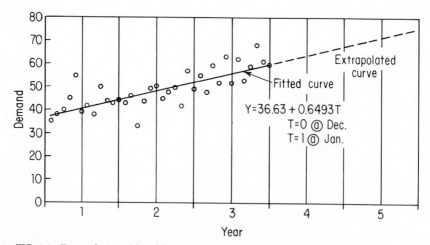

FIG. 9.6 Extrapolation of fitted linear curve.

The coefficients of each term can be determined by the linear multiple-regression techniques shown in Chap. 30. Note that the term *linear* here refers to the coefficients and not the time variables.

Care must be taken in using these equations as they can give very extreme forecasts in long-range projections. Their use should be based on a thorough appraisal of the past data and should comprise very short-term forecasts at best.

Sinusoids　Equations such as

$$Y_t = a \sin \omega t + b \cos \omega t \tag{9.31}$$

are called *sinusoids* since they involve sine functions. They can be used to represent cyclic, or recurrent, patterns when these appear to be the dominant factor. The parameter ω gives the period of the cycle. Regression analysis of Y_t with $\sin \omega t$ and $\cos \omega t$ yields the coefficients a and b.

Exponential Curves　One family of commonly used curves involves the use of the exponential function e, or exp. The most common equation is

$$Y_t = a \exp bt \tag{9.32}$$

where a and b are coefficients and exp represents the exponential-function base (exp = 2.71828). This equation assumes that the series is growing at a constant rate $\exp (b) - 1$. For a growing series b will be positive; for a decaying series, negative. The coefficient a is a location parameter.

This equation may be linearized by the natural logarithm transformation

$$\log Y_t = \log a + bt$$

Hence the formulas for the linear model may be used to obtain a fit by substituting $\log X_i$ for X_i. The resulting coefficients are $\log a$ and $\log b$. Figure 9.7 is an example of a fitted curve.

This curve can also be expressed by

$$Y_t = aB^t$$

where $B = \exp b$. The linearization form is then

$$\log Y_t = \log a + t \log B$$

These constant-rate growth curves are primarily for long-term forecasting. Care, however, should be exercised in using them for too long a forecast horizon.

S-Type Growth Curves　A family of curves has the characteristic that the rate of change is a prime characteristic of the curve. The increment of growth declines with time approaching zero as a limit. These curves are sometimes called S *curves* because they usually start with a small slope (when plotted on constant scale paper), sweep upward in midarea, and flatten out as they approach a maximum value. Their first stage represents a period of experimentation; the second stage, the rapid exploitation of the product; and the third, the leveling off of growth with the saturation of demand. They are also sometimes referred to as *asymptotic* growth curves because each approaches an upper limit.

The two most common types of S curves are the *Gompertz* curve (see Fig. 9.8)

$$Y_t = ka^{b^t} \tag{9.33}$$

and the *Pearl-Reed*, or logistics, curve

$$Y_t = \frac{1}{k + ab^t} \tag{9.34}$$

For the Gompertz curve k is the upper limit. For the logistics curve the upper limit is $1/k$. Their main difference is the point of inflection, the Gompertz reaching the inflection earlier.

Since neither curve can be linearized directly, they cannot be solved directly by linear regression techniques. One approach to solution involves splitting the historical data of N values into three equal parts and taking partial totals of the appropriate function of the data. For the Gompertz, the function is the natural logarithm

$$S_1 = \sum_{i=1}^{N_1} \log X_i \qquad S_2 = \sum_{i=N_i+1}^{N_2} \log X_i \qquad S_3 = \sum_{i=N2+1}^{N} \log X_i$$

Where $N_1 = N/3$ and $N_2 = 2N/3$. For the logistics, the function is the reciprocal $1/X_i$.

The coefficients for the Gompertz can then be obtained by solving the following equations:

$$b^{N1} = \frac{S_3 - S_2}{S_2 - S_1}$$

$$\log a = \frac{(S_2 - S_1)(b - 1)}{(b)(b^{N_1} - 1)^2}$$

$$\log k = \frac{S_1 \times S_3 - (S_2)^2}{(S_1 + S_3 - 2 \times S_2)N_1}$$

For the logistics, a and k are substituted for $\log a$ and $\log k$, respectively, in the above equations.

Another approach for determining the Gompertz curve coefficients is to first transform the equation to the form

$$\log Y_t = \log k + b^t \log a$$

Then select an arbitrary value of b (some value between 0 and 1) and take a regression between $\log Y_t$ and b^t, calculating the sum of squares of the residuals or errors. Repeat, using other values of b until a value is obtained which gives the lowest sum-of-squares values. The values of k and a are coefficients obtained by this regression.

For the Pearl-Reed model, first transform the equation to

$$\log \frac{1 - kY_t}{Y_t} = \log a + t \log b$$

Then select a value of k (an approximate upper bound on k is the reciprocal of the highest data value), and take a regression of the left-hand term of the equation

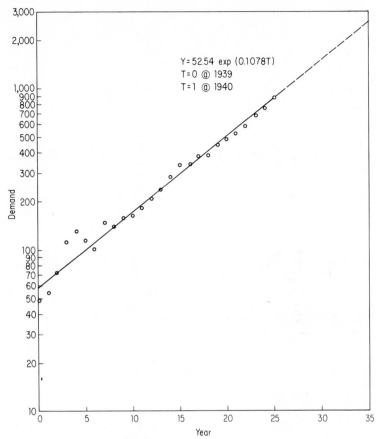

FIG. 9.7   Fitted exponential curve.

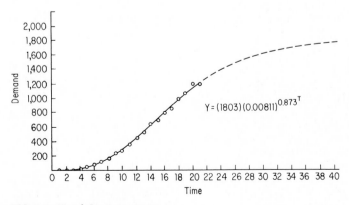

FIG. 9.8   Fitted Gompertz curve.

9.33

versus t. Repeat the iterative process with different values of k until no significant reduction in the sum of squares of the residuals is obtained.

Care must be taken in the use of these curves. Data should include history of the item from its inception. There should be reason to believe the growth rate is decreasing with time and that the series is apt to reach a saturation point. For a fuller discussion of the use and fitting of these curves, see Croxton and Cowden. Cleary and Levenbach discuss a more general type of growth curve useful for long-term forecasting.[18]

Use of Regression Models.   Some points need to be emphasized on the use of a fitted curve, particularly in regard to data selection and model projection.

A careful perusal of the time-series data before the regression analysis is done may eliminate causes of later difficulty. When a rough plot of the data is examined to determine a fitting model, extraneous data should be removed or smoothed. Such data might be early information with an obviously different trend or individual points which are evidently random impulses. This "hand smoothing" will precondition the data for better use of regression analysis. (Further discussion is given later in this chapter.)

The base period (time span on which the regression is based) of the historical data can have a major influence on the coefficient obtained. The inclusion of one additional data value may give quite different coefficients if that data point is unusually high or low. To get away from the ambiguity of base-period selection, although not necessarily away from the problems, a moving base-period fit can be used. For example, a regression may be done each period by using the last 12 periods as the base period.

Another approach to selecting a base period is to take a regression for all possible base periods (above a minimum high enough to cover any cycles) and then select the base period that gives the highest coefficient of determination (or some other degree of fit measurement).

When regression models are projected into the future as a forecast mechanism, two major factors should be considered in regard to the confidence placed in the extrapolated points. First, how good is the model at fitting the past? This can be judged by measures such as those discussed in the error statistics section. Even if the correlation is excellent, extrapolation of the fit is into an area of widening confidence limits (see Fig. 9.9). A second factor to consider is the relationship of the forecast extrapolation period to the base period. Intuitively, you would not project more than one period if you only had two periods' data. (Hopefully, you would not project anything at all!) Similarly, if you had a model which gave a good fit for a long period (60 to 96 periods), you would project it for 6 to 12 periods with reasonable confidence. You might be more confident still if you had used 48 periods (of 60) to build the model and had gotten good results predicting the remaining 12 points of the history.

In using curves, especially growth curves, for longer-range forecasting, it is helpful to compare the curve for an item with the curve for the set of which the item is a part, for instance, comparing the curve of apples and the curve for fruit. It is quite possible to fit curves in which the growth of apples is greater than the growth of fruit so that in some future period the forecast demand for apples is greater than the forecast demand for fruit. Judgment is continually called for in forecasting.

The discussion so far has assumed, for the most part, the use of linear regression techniques in curve fitting. This approach uses a least-squares criterion. This criterion may not necessarily be the best. For one thing, least-square fits may give undue weight to unusually high or low values (outliers). As a result, a number of other mathematical approaches to curve fitting are used. Two of these approaches come under the headings of linear programming and nonlinear programming.

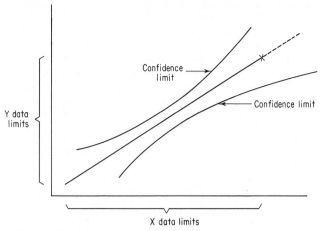

FIG. 9.9 Confidence limits of fitted curve.

Linear Programming Curve Fitting.   Techniques of linear programming may be used to fit linear-coefficient curves by criteria other than least squares. Linear programming techniques are well developed, and computer packages are readily available. The trick is to formulate the criterion and its restrictions in such a way that a standard linear programming algorithm can be used to determine the coefficients.

One criterion amenable to this approach is the minimization of the sum of absolute errors. To use this criterion for the linear curve $Y = a + bt$, each historical value is assumed to be determined by

$$X_i = a + (b - c)i + d_i - g_i$$

where $a, b, c, d,$ and g are coefficients. The latter two coefficients represent the error and thus are different for each period. The doubling of the coefficients (b and c) is necessary because of the nonnegativity constraint in linear programming. If only positive coefficients are desired, c would be removed. A similar argument explains the double error terms, d_i and g_i. In both cases, only one coefficient will be greater than zero for any solution.

The linear programming model is then

$$\text{Minimize} \quad \sum_{i=1}^{N} (g_i + d_i)$$

subject to the above set of equations and to all coefficients being greater than or equal to zero.

Another criterion is to minimize the maximum deviation (minimax). The objective here is to minimize d subject to all coefficients being greater than or equal to zero, where d is the maximum deviation. The equations for the linear curve are

$$X_i = a + (b - c)i + d - f_i$$
$$X_i = a + (b - c)i - d + g_i$$

Again, double coefficients are necessary where both positive and negative coefficients are possible. Also note the necessity for doubling the number of equations (data sets) to allow for a negative maximum deviation. The particular nature of this criterion calls for extra judgment in the use of curves derived from it for forecasting.

Another feature of regression by linear programming is the ability to add constraints to any variable. As noted, the coefficients can be selectively limited to positive values. In addition, the coefficient values may be bounded, the regression line may be forced through the origin (0,0) by elimination of the free term a, or any other constraint of the variables which can be expressed as a linear inequality may be used. This makes the two regression schemes based on linear programming very flexible indeed. The main difficulty with using linear programming is the complexity of the calculations, making a computer a necessity. Klein[19] and Bracken and McCormick[20] give a more detailed discussion on curve fitting by linear programming.

Nonlinear Programming Curve Fitting.   For the fitting of curves in which the coefficients are nonlinear and also for cases where a nonlinear criterion is used, several nonlinear programming techniques have been used. See Bracken and McCormick, Wilde and Beightler,[21] and Draper and Smith[22] for an introductory discussion. Nonlinear techniques are more complicated mathematically and are not as standardized as linear programming; so we do not delve into them here.

Extrinsic Factors

Almost every time series is influenced by other factors, although it may not be known exactly how. The most rigorous model, mathematically speaking, would be the causative-factor type in which relationships between the forecast variable and the extrinsic factors are explicitly spelled out. Construction of such a model would involve examining the system for the true underlying causes for demand and then building equations composed of the relationships between the forecast variable and the causative factors. Such models may be involved and relatively expensive; consequently, the value of the resulting forecast would have to justify the effort.

For cases where explicit causative models are not feasible, and for cases where causal relationships are believed to exist but their exact nature is not known, regression techniques are commonly used to fit forecasting equations. The techniques are used also to relate time series where "nonsense" correlations exist. That is, two series may react similarly, but there is no logical explanation as to why.

While these correlations are relatively easy to make by using computers, they are sensitive to changes in relationships. They should be periodically reevaluated to see whether the relationships are still valid.

Correlations.   Extrinsic techniques utilize past relationships between the forecast variable and one or more extrinsic factors. A simple example is the fitting of the curve

$$Y_t = a + bZ_t$$

by least-squares techniques. Here Z_t is the value of an extrinsic time series for period t. For this equation, the equations to determine the parameters are

$$a = \frac{\Sigma Z^2 \ \Sigma X - \Sigma Z \ \Sigma ZX}{N \ \Sigma Z^2 - (\Sigma Z)^2}$$

$$b = \frac{\Sigma X - Na}{\Sigma Z}$$

where the summations are over periods 1 to N. The value of the variable Z_t may be smoothed or adjusted before the fit is made.

Any number of extrinsic variables could be included in the equation. Likewise, more than one term could be included for each variable (a variable could have both a linear and a second-order term). A problem with using this approach is determining which variables and which terms to include. Stepwise regression techniques which selectively analyze the significance of each term are helpful in determining which factors and terms to include in the equation. Methods for fitting multiple-variable and multiple-term equations are discussed in Chap. 30.

The equation above assumes that forecast period values of the extrinsic factor are available. This situation is generally not possible; nevertheless, forecasted values, with their increased uncertainties, are often available. In this latter situation, however, the correlations should be made by using the historical forecasts rather than the actual values.

When many variables are involved, such as in the national economy, it is necessary to use sets of regression equations (which are not necessarily linear). Many techniques in the field of econometrics have been developed to handle sets of simultaneous equations.

Leading Series.   Rather than making correlations between coincident periods, forecast correlations may be made between the forecast variable and a past-period value of the extrinsic variable, such as

$$Y_t = a + bZ_{t-3}$$

This type of correlation is called a *leading-series correlation*. As with the equations mentioned in the preceding section, multiple variables and terms may be included in the equation. Both current and leading variables may be included in the same equation.

With this type of correlation, the problem is thus the quest for *leading* series. The Department of Commerce has extensively studied time series which affect the national economy in its search for leading series. It publishes the commonly referenced *Index of Leading Indicators* plus many other time series which might be leading indicators. Also many computer data bases have series which can be tested for lead traits.

CHANGE ANALYSIS

In forecasting the movement of a time series, we have an interest not only in the current level of the variable but also in how the level of the variable is changing over time. Measurement and analysis of differences, rate of changes, growth rates, and trends are an integral part of many forecasting methods. These determinations are a part of the general category of change analysis.

As we have seen, the determination of a trend can be a part of both moving-average and equation-fitting techniques. In many situations, particularly in long-range forecasting, an estimate of a growth rate may be more important than actual time-value estimates. Also, the rate-of-change curve for one variable may be a leading indicator of the movement of another variable. In general, evaluation of differences and rate of changes can give early warnings of significant changes in a variable. Such evaluation may indicate when to change production and inventory levels.

Change Measurement

Change is a comparative relationship between a *current* measurement, or value, and a *base* measurement. Change may be measured in a number of different ways:

$$\text{Difference (absolute change)} = \text{current} - \text{base}$$

$$\text{Relative (proportionate ratio)} = \frac{\text{current}}{\text{base}}$$

$$\text{Relative \% (proportionate \%)} = \frac{\text{current}}{\text{base}} \times 100$$

$$\text{Proportionate change (differential ratio)} = \frac{\text{current}}{\text{base}} - 1$$

$$\text{Percentage change (differential \%)} = \left(\frac{\text{current}}{\text{base}} - 1 \right) \times 100$$

For instance, if the base value is 100 and the current value is 110, then

$$\text{Difference} = 110 - 100 = 10$$

$$\text{Relative} = \frac{110}{100} = 1.1$$

$$\text{Relative \%} = \frac{110}{100} \times 100 = 110\%$$

$$\text{Proportionate change} = \frac{110}{100} - 1 = 0.1$$

$$\text{Percentage change} = \left(\frac{110}{100} - 1 \right) \times 100 = 10\%$$

If the difference is above zero, then there is growth. Similarly, positive values for the proportionate change and percentage change indicate growth. For growth, the relative must be over 1.0 and the relative percentage must be over 100.

In any case, all ways of measuring change or growth involve some relationship between two values: current and base. Many of the comments which follow apply to each of the different ways.

Change analysis can be applied not only to raw historical data but also to conditioned data. Because actual data tend to be erratic from period to period, it is often advisable to adjust the data by averaging or smoothing techniques. For instance, the methods of handling trends in exponential smoothing models involve averaged data. Adjustments for seasonality may be appropriate, too.

Differencing. Successive differencing of the history of a time series is when the base measurement immediately precedes the current measurement. This differencing helps in specifying parameters to certain forecasting models and can give guides to making subjective forecasts of the series.

The first difference of a time series at any time t is

$$D'_t = X_t - X_{t-1}$$

The second difference is

$$
\begin{aligned}
D_t'' &= D_t' - D_{t-1}' \\
&= X_t - X_{t-1} - (X_{t-1} - X_{t-2}) \\
&= X_t - 2X_{t-1} + X_{t-2}
\end{aligned}
$$

Similarly, higher differences can be generated.

A plot of the first differences can tell much about the series. If the values are consistently above zero, then a trend is indicated. A forecast model should consider this trend. If the first differences are randomly above and below zero, with the deviation following a normal distribution, then the series is said to be *stationary*. If there are runs of positive and/or negative values, then there may be serial or autocorrelation.

Second differences measure changes in trends. They indicate an accelerating or decelerating growth.

Relative Change.   If the historical data are available for a time horizon over which there is some growth, it is more advisable to study relative changes than differences. The relative change from one period to the succeeding period is

$$
\mathrm{ROC}_t = \frac{X_t}{X_{t-1}}
$$

where *ROC* is the relative change, sometimes called rate of change. The ROC for any past period is

$$
\mathrm{ROC}_{t:i} = \frac{X_t}{X_{t-i}}
$$

where i is the lag. The ROC may also be expressed as a percentage by multiplying by 100.

Periodic Change.   If the series is periodic, such as monthly or quarterly, then the difference between the current value and the corresponding value one period ago is of interest. For instance,

$$
D_{t:L} = X_t - X_{t-L}
$$

where L is the period (that is, $L = 12$ for monthly data). The corresponding ROC equation is

$$
\mathrm{ROC}_{t-L} = \frac{X_t}{X_{t-L}}
$$

Corresponding period evaluations are common in that they give a quick reading of the instantaneous growth rate, and they implicitly consider the effects of seasonality.

Growth Rates.   The proportionate change is sometimes called the *growth rate*. It is related to the relative change (rate of change) by

$$g_t = \text{ROC}_t - 1$$

It may be expressed as a percentage by multiplying by 100.

If the data are yearly, then g_t is an annual growth rate. If the data are monthly, then the following equation gives a simple annualized growth rate:

$$g = 12g_t = (12)(\text{ROC}_t - 1)$$

If data were quarterly, then 4 would be substituted for 12. The above equation does not consider compound growth. The compounded annualized growth rate is

$$g = \exp(12 \log \text{ROC}_t) - 1$$

Growth rates derived from the above equations are essentially instantaneous. A long-term growth rate can be derived by the linear regression (least-squares) method of Eq. (9.32) by taking a point-to-point estimate (by ratioing values at two points over a time horizon) or by an eyeball fit of a straight line drawn through raw data plotted on a graph with a log scale. The least-squares growth rate is derived from the coefficient b fitted to Eq. (9.32). The deriving relationship is

$$g = (\exp b) - 1$$

To derive an annualized growth rate from a least-squares equation fitted to monthly data, use

$$g = \exp[12 \log(1 + b)] - 1$$

Care must be taken in using growth rates calculated by regression equations. Extreme values may distort the results. Also, using different ranges of historical values can give dramatically different results. Techniques of exclusion, discounting, or averaging can be used to adjust for extreme values. Splitting the data in different time horizons and calculating growth rates for each horizon can often alleviate distortions caused by time-horizon selection.

The annualized growth rate for a point-to-point estimate is

$$g = \exp(\log \text{ROC}_{t:L}/L) - 1$$

where L is the lag period expressed in the same time frequency as the data. The point-to-point estimate is easier to calculate than a regression estimate; however, its meaningfulness for planning purposes depends on whether the two values are representative of the data.

The growth rate for the eyeball fit would be obtained by taking the values of two points on the fitted straight line and using them and the time differential value in the above point-to-point equation.

Rate-of-Change Analysis

The plotting of different ROC curves over time has proved to be a useful tool in anticipating cyclical changes in a time series and in comparing two time series. In these analyses, there is a constant time interval from the current and the base measurements, so a running comparison is made. Any time interval may be used, but the most common ones are the last period and the corresponding period 1 year ago.

Essentially two components are involved in an ROC analysis: the method of averaging the raw data and the period of the lag. Since the method of averaging can vary and the period of lag can vary, certain terminology is commonly used to identify a particular rate-of-change curve. The format is

Source identification/Lag period

where source identification refers to the type of moving average. For a simple trailing moving average, a number is used that gives the periods in the average. A moving average of 1 is the raw data. Thus a $\frac{1}{12}$ rate of change for monthly data is a comparison of the current month to the 12-month previous value (same month last year). Other common curves are

$$\frac{1}{1} \qquad \text{current period to previous period}$$

$$\frac{3}{12} \qquad \begin{array}{l}\text{trailing 3-period average to} \\ \text{trailing 3-period average} \\ \text{12 periods ago}\end{array}$$

$$\frac{12}{12} \qquad \begin{array}{l}\text{trailing 12-period average to} \\ \text{trailing 12-period average} \\ \text{12 periods ago}\end{array}$$

For monthly data, a $\frac{12}{12}$ rate of change is a moving year-to-year comparison. For quarterly data, a $\frac{4}{4}$ rate of change is also a moving year-to-year comparison. A $\frac{3}{3}$ rate of change for monthly data is equivalent to a $\frac{1}{1}$ for quarterly data.

In the Census Method II X-11 Shiskin statistical decomposition, a trend-cycle (TC) curve is generated. This curve may be used in ROC analysis. The most common trend-cycle ROC curves are

$$\frac{TC}{1} \qquad \text{current period to previous period}$$

$$\frac{TC}{12} \qquad \text{current period to same period last year}$$

A $\frac{1}{12}$ rate of change is the latest measurement of year-to-year change; however, it tends to be very volatile. A $\frac{12}{12}$ change measurement is more stable; however, it lags the general change level. A $\frac{3}{12}$ measurement is a compromise although it has a lag of a couple months.

To remove the volatility of the $\frac{1}{12}$ curve while maintaining its currentness, some smoothing method may be used. One approach is a trailing 3-month moving average of the $\frac{1}{12}$ curve. Another approach is the trend-cycle curve from the X-11 analysis to give a same-month-last-year comparison.

ROC curves can give early warnings of changes in the basic movement of a time series. A downward movement indicates a declining growth and thus should be a yellow light. The point at which a curve levels after an upward movement should be noted.

Some analysts use the point at which the ¹⁄₁₂ curve crosses the ¹²⁄₁₂ curve as a warning signal. Figure 9.10 shows the TC/12 curve superimposed on the ¹²⁄₁₂ curve. The TC/12 is a smoothed alternative to the ¹⁄₁₂ curve. Downward cross points are noted in years 3, 5, 6, 8, and 10. Years 3 and 8 cross points did give some leads on subsequent downturns. The year 5 cross point was at the trough of a minor dip.

A comparison of the TC/12 curve with the trend-cycle curve shows that generally the peaks and valleys of the two coincide. However, the TC/12 peaked in late year 7, some 5 months before the trend-cycle curve.

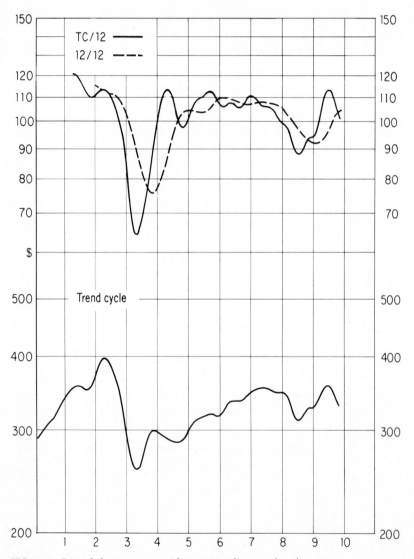

FIG. 9.10 Rate-of-change curves with corresponding trend-cycle curve.

ROC values can also give some simple forecasting methods. For instance,

$$F_{t+1} = (X_t)(\text{ROC}_{t+1-L:1})$$
$$= X_t \frac{X_{t+1-L}}{X_{t-L}}$$

This equation takes the forecast as the latest period value adjusted for the $\frac{1}{12}$ ROC value for the same period one cycle ago.

UNIFIED AUTOREGRESSION AND MOVING AVERAGES

In general, the techniques described so far have just assumed a model and then analyzed the fit of the data (time series) to that model. Box and Jenkins have developed a unified forecasting system which includes the determination of not only model parameters but also a model.[23] The methodology also provides estimates of confidence limits for forecasts.

The Box-Jenkins philosophy is that forecasting models should be based on summary statistics of the historical data rather than assumptions based on abstract theory. The models should be arrived at in a systematic pattern rather than by trial and error.

The methods developed by Box and Jenkins are commonly called *ARIMA* (for autoregressive integrated moving average). The approach requires at least 30 values of history (preferably more) for good results. Because it requires extensive calculations, it does not lend itself to SKU forecasts. It is possible, however, to assume a derived model is valid for many related SKUs. The method also is limited to long-term forecasting since a forecast tends to dampen to a long-term mean (or to a long-term trend if one exists). The method continually redetermines the average and/or trend, however. The method also requires some experience in subjectively evaluating statistics and in setting model parameters. Even though the method is complex, many computer software packages are available which simplify its use.

The methods proposed by Box and Jenkins combine several techniques in an approach to model specification, parameter estimation, diagnostic checking of the model, and subsequent forecasting from the specified model. Basically they surmise that projections of a time series will depend on the length and type of "memory" inherent in the series. Some series "remember" only their prior values (autoregressive). Others remember shocks or random noise values (moving averages). Still others remember both and so are a combination of autoregressive and moving averages. The techniques proposed attempt to determine which type or types of memory are exhibited by a time series and then specify the model using the *least* number of parameters (parsimonious parameterization) which adequately describes the data. The residual portion (differences between predicted values in the past and actual series data) is then used to characterize the unpredictable nature of (the "random noise" affecting) the series. With the model specified and the noise characterized, both point forecasts and confidence limits may be projected.

Moving Average

The moving-average model assumes that the time series has a mean μ and that all values are normally distributed about this mean in a random sequence over time.

The basic equation is

$$Y_t = \mu + a_t$$

where a_t is the deviation from the mean. The deviation is

$$a_t = X_t - \mu$$

The model attempts to capture shocks, disturbances, or spikes to this basic model by adding terms to the basic equation. If only one past value is captured, then

$$Y_t = \mu + a_t - \theta_1 a_{t-1}$$

where θ is a coefficient. Although this equation is analogous to the basic exponential smoothing equation, it allows the coefficient to be positive or negative. The above equation is called a *first-order moving-average process* and is abbreviated MA(1).

The model can be extended to include any number of terms. Its general equation is

$$Y_t = \mu + a_t - \sum_{i=1}^{q} \theta_i a_{t-i}$$

where q is the order (number of terms). The above equation is symbolized by MA(q). In contrast to moving-average models discussed earlier, the coefficients do not necessarily sum to 1.

Autoregression

The autoregression model is an extension of the general autoregression equation

$$Y_t = \delta + \sum_{i=1}^{p} \phi_i X_{t-1} + a_t$$

where a_t is the error term, p is the order (number of terms), and δ and ϕ are coefficients. AR(p) represents the above equation. The AR(1) model is

$$Y_t = \delta + \phi_1 X_{t-1} + a_t$$

Autoregression—Moving Average

Combining the two models gives

$$Y_t = \delta + a_t + \sum_{i=1}^{p} \phi_i X_{t-1} - \sum_{i=1}^{q} \theta_i a_{t-1}$$

The general symbolism is ARMA(p,q).

Integrated Autoregression—Moving Average

The ARMA model is meaningful only if the data are stationary. A series is stationary if its statistical properties do not vary over time. For instance, the series has a constant mean and variances. A stationary series thus tends to wander more or less uniformly about some fixed level. The Box-Jenkins method provides a model-building block to convert most nonstationary behavior (such as trends and seasonal patterns) to stationary behavior. Box and Jenkins do this integration through the process of differencing (converting the differences between successive values to a series). In some cases, it may be necessary to do a prior transformation (such as taking the logarithm of an exponentially increasing series) before the differencing process is attempted.

The need for differencing can be detected by calculating the autocorrelation function of the variable with itself for a range of lagged time periods. Many computer programs automatically generate a graph (*correlogram*) of the autocorrelation functions for visual examination. If their autocorrelations dampen to zero, there is little gained by differencing. If the autocorrelations are all the same sign, then there may be a trend which can be removed by differencing.

The general symbolism for the integrated model is

$$\text{ARIMA } (p,d,q)$$

where p = degree of autoregression
  d = degree of difference
  q = degree of moving average

In general, the degree refers to the number of terms.

In most practical cases, the derived degrees of autoregression, differencing, and moving averages will be small, typically of an order to 0 to 2. The MA(1) and AR(1) models then become special cases. For instance, MA(1) is equivalent to ARIMA (0,0,1), and AR(1) is equivalent to ARIMA(1,0,0).

Confidence Limits

An advantage of the Box-Jenkins method is that it provides formulas for setting the confidence limits of forecasts. These formulas are based on the variance of the error or disturbance term. They reflect changing confidence as the forecast horizon increases. The formulas depend on the particular model and the length of the forecast. They are part of computer software packages, so we do not discuss them here.

Steps

There are three principal steps in a Box-Jenkins analysis: identification, estimation, and forecasting. In the identification, or specification, step, summary statistics of autocorrelation and partial autocorrelation relationships are generated. These statistics may indicate that differencing or other transformations of data should be made. The step can then be repeated with data transformed by one or more degrees of differencing. The statistics also indicate appropriate degrees of autoregression and moving-average specification. The purpose of this step is to tentatively identify an initial model and its appropriate differencing, autoregression, and moving-average structure.

The second step is to estimate the parameters in the tentative model via a minimization-of-errors technique. The estimated errors are then checked by goodness-of-fit criteria. If necessary, reidentification and reestimation may be done until a model and parameter are achieved which meet requirements of being stationary and having low error.

The final step is the forecasting by using the derived model. Evaluation of forecasting results may require further recycles of the previous steps.

Extensions

The Box-Jenkins method provides ways of handling seasonality. There may be different degrees of autoregression, differencing, and averaging, so a more general model is

$$\text{ARIMA } [(p,d,q) \times (P,D,Q)]$$

where P, D, and Q are the respective seasonality orders.

The Box-Jenkins methods described so far handle the intrinsic relationship of a variable with itself. There are methods for including the effects of external variables through techniques of multivariate ARIMA. Here, multiple-regression techniques are integrated with ARIMA techniques.

As with exponential smoothing, there are methods for adaptively adjusting the ARIMA equation coefficients.

The Bibliography gives many references to the Box-Jenkins method.

IMPLEMENTING A FORECAST

This chapter has introduced the problems of forecasting, presented points to be considered in forecasting, and outlined some of the different methods. We have discussed some of the more practical methods with some mention of how they are applied and their limitations. In this section, we expand on these latter two subjects as we concern ourselves with the problems of implementing a forecasting procedure.

In approaching a forecasting problem, the reader must answer the questions stated in the beginning of this chapter. In answering the question how, he or she must be aware of the distinctions mentioned in the beginning of the chapter. The forecaster must ask what part subjective factors will play in the forecast. He or she must ascertain what part history will play in deciding the forecasting mechanism. Another concern is that the product of forecasting is often the understanding of relationships rather than the particular numbers involved.

Influence of Subjective Factors

There is no such thing as a completely objective means of determining a forecast. No matter how sophisticated the statistics and mathematics involved in a forecasting scheme, there is much subjective judgment in determining which model or equation to use, which variables should be a part of the model, and what data should be used in determining the model coefficients.

One question which should be answered is, Should a scientific or quasi-scientific method be used at all in preference to a nonscientific method? In many cases, this question is answered by the huge volume of forecasts which must be made. In other cases, a scientific forecast can be used as a check on a nonscientific forecast, and vice versa, since no scientific forecast should be accepted blindly without some subjective reasoning.

One of the most intriguing areas of forecasting is how to combine subjective considerations (such as special knowledge about a new customer or other kinds of marketing intelligence) with a scientific forecast. Often this can be done by building into a forecasting system an additive special-knowledge factor. For example,

$$F^* = F + SK$$

where F^* = forecast after special knowledge
      F = forecast before special knowledge
      SK = special-knowledge factor

There is danger, however, in overdoing special knowledge, especially when forecast deviations are a part of the forecast system. This danger can be overcome, by including the special-knowledge factor if the factor is, say, greater than some measure of the forecast error. For example,

$$\text{If} \quad SK > k \times SE \quad \begin{array}{l} \text{then} \\ \text{else} \end{array} \quad \begin{array}{l} F^* = F + SK \\ F^* = F \end{array}$$

where SE = standard deviation of forecast error
      k = control factor (such as 1.5)

One practical example of how a statistical forecast could be combined with a nonstatistical prediction is to see whether the single-value prediction fell within plus or minus some control limits (in the quality control sense) of the single-value statistical forecast. The control limits would be some measure of the forecast error, which would be based on history. If the prediction fell outside the control limits, the person making the prediction would be asked to reevaluate the estimate. Figure 9.11 is an example of comparing a statistically derived forecast with a prediction.

One way of combining statistical and nonstatistical forecasting is to take a weighted average of the two, the weighting factors measuring how much confidence is placed in each of the methods. For instance, the confidence might be based on error measurements. Also forecasters have found that averages of forecasts derived by different statistical methods may perform better than individual forecasts.[24]

Use of Statistical Distributions

An important question is whether the forecast is single-valued or described by a distribution. The use of the latter is becoming more common because

1. Single-valued forecasts are limited in trying to describe an event which is not known with certainty.

2. Inventory control methods have shown how measurements of uncertainty are vital in determining such things as safety stocks.

3. Business has become sophisticated in the use of quantitative methods.

Subjective methods can be used in obtaining distributions (this is indeed a necessity if no history exists). However, history is often of more value in determining the distribution than in determining the single-point expected value estimate. Forecasting systems in which the single-point estimate is obtained by subjective judgment and the distribution is obtained from statistical analysis of history are quite common.

A difficulty with multipoint or distribution estimates is that more data are involved, thus making forecasting and bookkeeping more difficult. Thus the benefits of the more detailed forecasts must be balanced against the costs of obtaining them.

One approach to determining a probability distribution of a sales estimate is given by this example. The customers or users are enumerated, and three estimates of their requirements are made—an expected maximum (optimistic), the most likely, and an expected minimum (pessimistic). A model is constructed in which these values are parameters to an assumed distribution such as beta, uniform, or triangular. By using Monte Carlo simulation, a number of forecasts are made which are then fitted to a distribution.

Use of History

Even if an item's history is not used in developing the forecasting technique, its study is important in giving insight into the item's demand characteristics and in understanding the factors influencing the item's demand.

In determining the importance of history in influencing the item's future de-

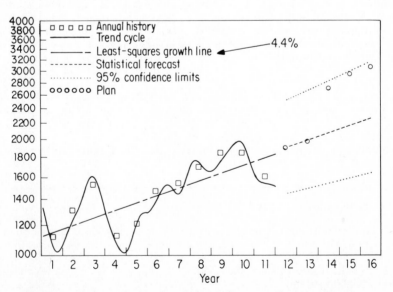

FIG. 9.11 Comparison of predicted plan with statistically derived forecast.

mand, consideration must be given to what internal factors are at work trying to change the history. There may be factors such as sales promotions, product improvements, developments of new uses, etc. which are under the control of the forecasting organization and which the organization is trying to exploit. Change is inherent in business, and the forecaster must be cognizant of efforts effecting this change.

After it is decided that history is to be a part of a forecast, the question arises as to how to analyze it. The following approach can be used. (A computer program could be written to do the same analysis described here and more.) If there is much data, the question of how much to use arises. Generally it is best to use as much as possible, discarding some as the analysis proceeds. The general problem is not enough data rather than too much. The amount of data is especially important in fitting curves by regression analysis as the results may be very sensitive to the period of fit.

Table 9.1 gives some data which are analyzed for illustrative purposes.

A. *The data should be plotted on coordinate graph paper in time sequence.* Many computer programs are now available to do plotting automatically. This plotting assumes data are given in demand units per time period. The time period should correspond to the forecast period. Special graph papers are available which have a time axis. See Fig. 9.12 for a scatter diagram of the data of Table 9.1.

Scaling of the vertical axis is important, for it may affect the data interpretations. The zero value should be indicated, at least on the initial graph.

Points to observe are as follows:

1. Do values tend to follow either an upward or a downward trend? If so, can a line or curve be drawn through the data points to represent the trend? The slope of the line can indicate whether the trend is significant enough to be considered further. If the variation of data points about the fitted line is high (especially in relationship to the trend), then the use of a mathematically fitted curve may not be of much value in developing a forecast mechanism. If the fitted line is a straight line, then a linear model may be the best fit. If the line is a curve, some other equation might be appropriate, and the use of curve-fitting techniques may find a mathematical curve which gives a reasonable fit.

2. Are the data such that later values are a multiple of 10 or 100 of earlier values? If so, an exponential growth curve may exist, and the plot should be made

TABLE 9.1 Data for Analysis

As Given		Sequenced				
Period	Demand	Demand	Frequency	Cumulative Frequency	Cumulative Proportion	Cumulative Percentage
1	11	10	0	0	0	0
2	18	11	1	1	0.1	10
3	15	12	2	3	0.3	30
4	19	13	1	4	0.4	40
5	13	14	0	4	0.4	40
6	12	15	3	7	0.7	70
7	15	16	1	8	0.8	80
8	15	17	0	8	0.8	80
9	12	18	1	9	0.9	90
10	16	19	1	10	1.0	100
		20	0	10	1.0	100

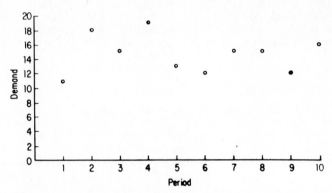

FIG. 9.12   Scatter diagram. Scaling of the vertical axis is important, since it may affect the data interpretations. The zero value should be included, at least on the initial graph.

on a graph paper whose vertical axis has a logarithmic scale. (This growth in the series might be obvious from the data; if so, the plot can be made first on a log scale.) A log transformation of the data may make it more tractable.

3. Is there much variation about the average or trend line? This gives a measure of the noise which the forecast method should reduce. What are the magnitude and significance of this variation in relationship to the average?

4. Are there extreme values which can be explained by unusual circumstances? These values (outliers) might be eliminated from further analysis or else smoothed (averaged) or discounted in some way.

5. Do the data run in cycles? If so, do these cycles have a common periodicity? Is there seasonality? Identifying the phase of the cycle and basing the forecast on the corresponding phases of the cycle may help.

6. Do the data appear to be one population or several? That is, are there breaks in the data (such as a sudden jump or step, or a change in trend)? If so, perhaps only the latest population (set of data) should be analyzed. If trends, seasonality, or other measurable factors affect the demand, then measures of these factors should be obtained (such as determining the trend from a fit of a linear curve or determining seasonality by some measure). The X-11 method, if available, is most helpful at this stage. The data should be adjusted by these measures before the following steps are done. In practice, these adjustments would be part of the forecasting mechanism. Step B should be done with both unadjusted and adjusted data to see the effects of the adjustments. The significance of the adjustments can be measured by comparing the adjusted variance against the unadjusted variance.

7. Are the data sporadic or lumpy? Aggregating the data into a less detailed time period or trying to identify the data as part of a cycle may help. Sometimes the data should be adjusted before analysis. For instance, the variation in the number of working days in a month may be significant enough to warrant adjustment, although this factor may be considered in the seasonal factor. Likewise, strikes or other shutdowns may be significant. If data are in dollars, it may be critical to convert to a volume measurement by price deflation.

   B. *Common statistical averages should be taken.*   These include the average (mean)

$$\mu = \frac{\sum_{i=1}^{N} X_i}{N}$$

the variance

$$V = \frac{\sum_{i=1}^{N} (X_i - \mu)^2}{N}$$

the standard deviation

$$\sigma = \sqrt{V}$$

and the range

$$RG = X_{max} - X_{min}$$

where the X values are the highest and lowest, respectively.

The variance can also be calculated from

$$V = \frac{\sum_{i=1}^{N} X_i^2}{N} - \mu^2$$

that is, mean of the squares minus the square of the mean.

Note that the above formula gives the variance of the given data. If the given data are considered as a sample of the general population of data, then the following formulas should be used if the sample size N is small:

$$V = \frac{\sum_{i=1}^{N} (X_i - \mu)^2}{N - 1} = \frac{N \sum_{i=1}^{N} X_i^2 - \left(\sum_{i=1}^{N} X_i\right)^2}{N(N - 1)}$$

If the sample size $N \leq 10$, then the sample standard deviation can be approximated by

$$\sigma = \frac{RG}{\sqrt{N}}$$

The graph of Fig. 9.13 can be used in roughly determining the standard deviation for monthly data.

C. *A histogram of demand variation should be made.* Figure 9.14 is an example. The data are broken down into classes. The frequency with which the data fall within each class is tabulated and plotted. If the data are discrete rather than continuous (such as some small number of orders per day), then each demand level (number of orders) is a class.

Points to observe are:

1. Is the frequency uniformly distributed between the highest and lowest value? If so, a uniform distribution may describe the demand.

2. Does the frequency peak near the center? If so, a symmetric distribution, such as a normal distribution, may describe the demand.

3. Does the frequency peak but not near the center? If so, the distribution is biased, and some unsymmetric distribution such as lognormal may describe the demand.

4. Are data discrete with the mean approximately equal to the variance? Then the Poisson distribution may describe the demand. To use this distribution, there should be some logical justification for the arrival of demand orders being independent of one another.

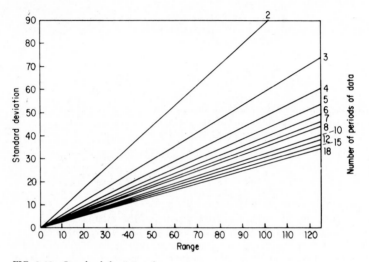

FIG. 9.13   Standard deviation from range.

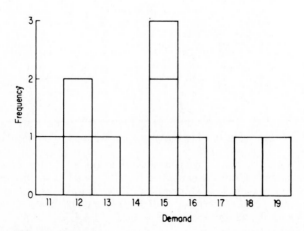

FIG. 9.14   Histogram.

An alternative approach to showing a demand distribution is to make a box plot such as Fig. 9.15. The box shows the interquartile range (middle 50 percent of the data). The tails show the entire range. The line in the box is the median, or 50th percentile point. The circle is the mean. Box plots are particularly useful to represent the distribution of monthly values when yearly history is plotted over time. See Cleary and Levenbach for more detail.[25]

D. *A cumulative frequency-proportion plot should be made.*   See Fig. 9.16 for a plot on rectangular paper. The cumulative plot aids testing of whether the distribution follows certain special mathematical functions. Special graph papers are available to test plots against normal and lognormal distributions. The cumulative frequency plot is also valuable for giving measures such as what proportion of the

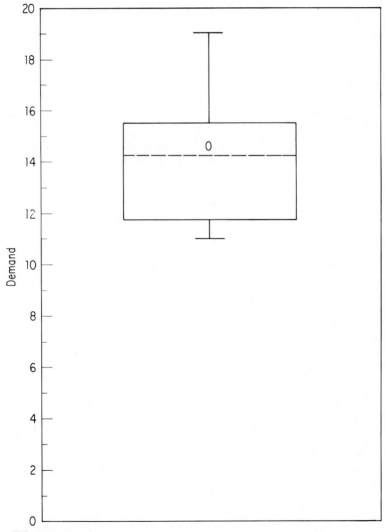

FIG. 9.15   Box plot.

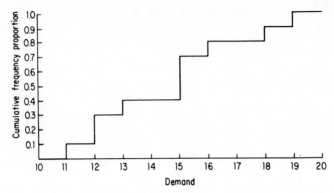

FIG. 9.16 Cumulative frequency plot.

time periods the demand will be over a given amount. If random sampling is done with Monte Carlo methods, then the cumulative frequency plot is needed to give the demand corresponding to a selected random number.

Figure 9.17 is an example of a cumulative frequency plot of the given data on normal probability paper. An eyeball straight line has been drawn through the plotted points. The intersection of the line with the 0.50 point on the vertical axis gives the fitted estimate of the mean. The intersection of the line with the 0.84 point* gives the 1-standard-deviation intersection. The fitted standard deviation is then determined by

$$\sigma = 0.84 \text{ intersection} - 0.50 \text{ intersection}$$

Similarly, an estimate of the standard deviation can be obtained from the 0.16-point intersection. If the fitted straight line gives a reasonable fit to the plotted points, and the fitted mean and standard deviation approximate the calculated values, then the normal distribution can be assumed to approximate the given data.

The normal distribution is frequently used to approximate the distribution of demand data primarily because it is relatively easily understood and the mathematics and tables for its use are well developed. In practice, few demand populations are "normal"; nevertheless, the normal distribution is used because no other distribution gives a reasonable fit.

One difficulty with using a normal distribution is that it allows demand to fall below zero, a situation which is usually unrealistic. The lognormal distribution is sometimes used in preference to the normal distribution because it has no below-zero values; however, the mathematics is more complicated.

To study change, many of the above steps can be repeated for the period-to-period differences of the time series.

The analysis of history by using these steps can give some feel for whether there are patterns which can be used in a forecasting procedure. This analysis can give some feel as to whether there might be other extrinsic factors (such as national economy) to which the given time series can be related by correlation analysis. This analysis of extrinsic relationships is generally not worth the effort with individual stockkeeping units, but is often extremely valuable for forecasting a business for

---

*The cumulative probability at 1 standard deviation above the mean is 0.8413. See Chap. 30.

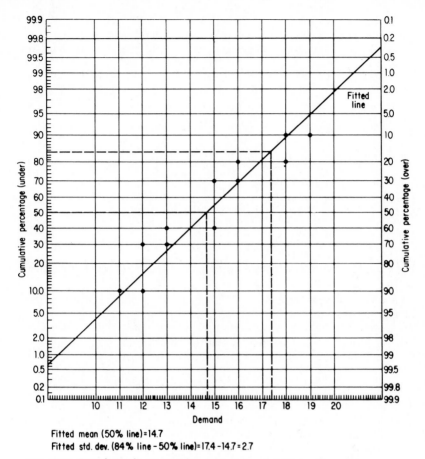

FIG. 9.17   Cumulative frequency plot on normal probability paper.

longer-term planning. When combined with subjective estimation of the factors difficult or impossible to determine from history (such as new markets), this analysis can tell whether curve fitting and/or correlative relationships are significant enough to be used.

In initial explorations of a variable, the elementary plotting of points is very useful. It is preferred over sophisticated mathematical methods unless the researcher has some a priori basis for choosing a specific method.

Use of Sophisticated Methods

Unsophisticated methods fail to furnish a clear explanation of phenomena under investigation; nevertheless, they are desirable in a first look at a problem. Even sophisticated models yield unreliable results if they are employed without careful planning, without understanding the phenomena, and without understanding the technique of analysis.

A look at the management science literature on forecasting—especially some of it on exponential smoothing—may give the impression that the management scientists feel compelled to increase the complexity of all models on the assumption that intricacy and sophistication are correlated with usefulness. This premise is valid for some systems; nevertheless, the simpler approaches frequently serve as well or almost as well. Elaborate models are worthwhile only if they have been adequately researched.

Choice of Method

The requirements of a good forecasting method are

1. It should state intended use.
2. It should state assumptions.
3. It should not be too restrictive.
4. It should state possible range of error.
5. It should be easy to understand.
6. It should have a mechanism for showing when it is out of balance and provide a means for rectifying this situation.
7. It should be easy to explain.
8. It should work.

In choosing among the methods described, the following points need consideration in addition to which method gives the best forecast:

1. Amount of calculation
2. Amount of computer storage
3. Hand versus machine calculations
4. Ability to initiate system
5. Ability to "tune up" system
6. Ability to maintain system

The amount of calculation and amount of storage affect whether calculations are by hand or machine or some combination of the two. Hand calculations can make use of nomographs and tables. Many machines from desk calculators to on-line computers are available.

Timeliness of the forecast is important in choosing whether a computer is to be used. Batch processing of data by computer may require only seconds of actual computer time but may require lengthy periods to condition data for the computer and to get the results back from the computer.

The various methods have their advantages and disadvantages. The simple-average model does not react to changes. Simple moving-average methods require considerable data storage, but do not readily react to changes and have the problem of choosing the length of the average. Basic exponential smoothing has low data storage, reacts to changes although with a lag, and has the problem of choosing a smoothing constant. Adaptive exponential smoothing models correct somewhat for the problems of lag and the choice of smoothing constant, but they are more complex and require more calculations. They tend to be heuristic or pseudostatistical. Exponential smoothing is generally more suitable to stockkeeping-unit forecasts than for aggregate-item forecasts.

In general, curve-fitting methods are used for longer-range forecasts. Curves are more apt to be fitted to yearly rather than weekly or monthly data because of the increased randomness which tends to appear in shorter periods. Fitted curves can, of course, be adjusted by seasonal factors.

Intrinsic correlation models require much data storage, may require frequent extensive calculations, and have the problems of choice of curve (model), selection of period over which to fit data, and selection of fitting criterion. Extrinsic correlation models may improve forecasts over intrinsic forecasts by relationships with causative factors. However, the problems exist of which factors to include and whether the relationships will continue to hold.

In general, the average methods are more applicable when many items are to be forecast routinely, whereas the curve-fitting methods are more appropriate when a single occasional forecast is to be made.

When many items are forecast at the same time, consideration must be given to whether the same method is used for all items or different methods are used for various classes of items. The concept of ABC analysis is important in answering this question. Even when the same method is used for many items, questions arise as to whether each item will have its own parameters in its equations or whether some parameters can be used over many items. For instance, common seasonality and/or trend factors may be used for many items. Or with exponential smoothing, the same smoothing constant may be used over many items. All time-series models are limited by the basic assumption that historical patterns will continue in the future.

The ultimate criterion as to which is the best forecasting technique or which is the best parameter in a forecasting model should be not which technique or parameter gives the best forecast by some error criteria, but rather which technique or parameter minimizes the cost associated with production and inventory planning and control. These costs include not only inventory, production, and customer service costs, but also system costs—the costs of forecasting. The costs of forecasting include the cost in developing, testing, and selling the technique; the cost of using; and the cost of maintaining. The cost versus the value of the forecast is often overlooked, but it is extremely important.

Use of a Computer

The computer has had a dramatic effect on the development of forecasting methods. Methods that were formerly prohibitive are now feasible. Many new methods have been developed. One advance has been the development of forecasting modules which can be built into inventory control and production scheduling systems. These modules eliminate the need for reprogramming the forecasting model every time a control system is developed.

The other progression has been the development of computer program packages which permit the forecaster to try out different methods on historical data. Most computer manufacturers and software companies offer these packages, and many companies now have developed their own. These programs permit the forecaster to very rapidly simulate how well a given technique works with actual data.

The computer does have some very definite advantages. It has tremendous calculation and storage capabilities which save processing time over hand calculations, facilitate the use of methods otherwise impractical, and allow the handling of many items. The computer can give fancy printouts including graphical output. But computers can be costly, and many forecasting methods can tax the capabilities of a computer, especially when many items are forecast. With computers, human judgment is not a part of the calculations, thus causing forecasting to be "automatic."

There is no forecasting method that can effectively handle all contingencies, and the intervention of human judgment is often extremely valuable.

Another difficulty is that people tend to ignore the fact that some mathematical method is used in developing a computer-derived forecast. They become result-rather than method-oriented. Because they do not have to perform the calculations themselves, they often do not understand the method. More important, they may not understand the limitations of the method and thus the limitations of the results. Finally, the results from a computer depend on the input data with the GIGO (garbage in/garbage out) principle in effect. Conditioning sales history by computer can be an extremely difficult job.

Summary

The following points summarize the factors to consider in the search for techniques:

1. There are no infallible ways to forecast the future. No technique works for all situations, and more than one technique may work for a given situation.
2. A forecast should recognize that there is no certainty. Therefore, a forecast is expected to be wrong on occasion. Even though there is this uncertainty, we should use good methods.
3. Conditions change so that we must have some way of adapting our forecasts to these changes.
4. Even though many forecasting techniques may be quite scientifically sound, there is much judgment in
    a. Use of techniques
    b. What data to use
    c. How data are conditioned
    The forecaster is more important than the method.
5. The forecaster should not be technique-oriented.
6. Precision is seldom important in a forecast.
7. Elements which determine the best method include:
    Purpose
    Money—potential benefit
    Timeliness

GLOSSARY OF SYMBOLS

The following is a list of the mathematical symbols used in this chapter, with a brief definition of each. Indexes, coefficients in equations, and intermediate values used in simplifying formulas are not included.

Symbol	Definition
a_t	Deviation from mean for period t
A	Average demand
A_t	An average demand as of time period t

Symbol	Definition
A'_t	Single-smoothed average for period t
A''_t	Double-smoothed average for period t
A'''_t	Triple-smoothed average for period t
C	Cyclical component in a time series
d	Order of differencing
D'_t	First difference for period t
D''_t	Second difference for period t
e_t	Forecast error for period t
E_t	Sum of forecast errors through period t
F	Forecast of time series
F_t	Forecast demand for period t
F^*	Special-knowledge adjusted forecast
g_t	Growth rate at period t
I	Irregular component in time series
k	Safety or significance control factor
L	Time periods in cycle
M	Number of terms in equations
N	Number of periods in history
p	Order of autoregression
P_t	Mean absolute deviation (MAD) at period t
q	Order of averaging
Q_t	Smoothed average deviation (SAD) at period t
r	Reduction factor
R_t	Trend at period t
RG	Range
$ROC_{t:i}$	Rate of change for period t for lag i
RS_t	Trend signal at period t
S	Seasonal component in time series
S_t	Seasonal adjustment factor for period t
SA	Average demand over a cycle
SE	Standard deviation of forecast error
SF_t	Seasonally adjusted forecast for period t
SK	Special-knowledge factor
SL_t	Seasonality limit for period t
t	Time period
T	Trend component in time series
T_t	Trend estimate for period t
TC	Trend cycle
TL_t	Trend control limit at period t
TS_t	Tracking signal at period t
TSL	Tracking signal limit
u	Lead time of forecast (periods)

Symbol	Definition
V	Variance
V_t	Variance estimate at period t
w_t	Weighting factor for period t
W_t	Autocovariance estimate at period t
X	Actual demand
X_t	Actual demand in period t
X'_t	Transformed demand in period t
Y_t	A demand for period t estimated by a curve
Z_t	Value of external factor in period t
α	Demand smoothing constant
α'	Long-term demand smoothing constant
β	Discount rate ($=1 - \alpha$)
γ	Seasonality smoothing constant
δ	Trend smoothing constant/equation coefficient
η	Error smoothing constant
μ	Mean
ξ	Autocorrelation damping factor
ρ	Variance smoothing constant
σ	Standard deviation
ψ	Seasonality limit smoothing constant
ω	Cycle period in sinusoidal functions
ϕ	Autoregression equation coefficients
θ	Moving-average equation coefficients

REFERENCES

1. *Journal of Forecasting*, Wiley & Sons, Limited, Chichester, United Kingdom and *International Journal of Forecasting*, Elsevier Science Publishers, Amsterdam.

2. R. G. Brown, *Statistical Forecasting for Inventory Control*, McGraw-Hill, New York, 1959.

3. J. W. Muir, *The Pyramid Principle*, American Production and Inventory Control Society, 22d Annual Conference Proceedings, Washington, 1979, pp. 105–107.

4. P. J. Harrison, "Short-Term Sales Forecasting," *Applied Statistics*, vol. 14, 1965, pp. 102–139.

5. J. Shiskin, A. H. Young, and J. C. Musgrave, U.S. Bureau of Census, *The X-11 Variant of the Census Method II Seasonal Adjustment Program*, Tech. Paper no. 15, GPO, 1967.

6. F. E. Croxton and D. J. Cowden, *Applied General Statistics*, 2d ed., Prentice-Hall, Englewood Cliffs, N.J., 1955.

7. R. L. McLaughlin, *Time Series Forecasting*, American Marketing Association, Chicago, 1962.

8. H. Levenbach and J. P. Cleary, *The Beginning Forecaster: The Forecasting Process through Data Analysis*, Lifetime Learning Publications, Belmont, Calif., 1981, pp. 248–274.

9. E. B. Dagum, *The X-11-ARIMA Seasonal Adjustment Method*, Statistics Canada, Ottawa, 1980.

10. S. I. Bretschneider and W. L. Gorr, "On the Relationship of Adaptive Filtering Forecasting Models to Simple Brown Smoothing," *Management Science*, vol. 27, August, 1981, pp. 965–969.

11. R. G. Brown, *Smoothing, Forecasting and Prediction of Discrete Time Series*, Prentice-Hall, Englewood Cliffs, N.J., 1963.

12. P. R. Winters, "Forecasting Sales by Exponentially Weighted Moving Averages," *Management Science*, vol. 6, March, 1960, pp. 324–342.

13. Brown, *Smoothing, Forecasting and Prediction of Discrete Time Series*.

14. D. W. Trigg and A. G. Leach, "Exponential Smoothing with an Adaptive Response Rate," *Operational Research Quarterly*, vol. 18, March, 1967, pp. 53–59.

15. J. T. Burgess, "Adaptive Forecasting," paper presented at 13th annual meeting of The Institute of Management Science, Philadelphia, September, 1966.

16. R. S. Dudman, "Forecasting with Three-Factor Adaptive Smoothing," paper presented at 13th annual meeting of The Institute of Management Science, Philadelphia, September, 1966.

17. N. P. Draper and H. Smith, Jr., *Applied Regression Analysis*, 2d ed., Wiley, New York, 1981.

18. J. P. Cleary and H. Levenbach, *The Professional Forecaster: The Forecasting Process through Data Analysis*, Lifetime Learning Publications, Belmont, Calif., 1982, pp. 78–88.

19. M. Klein, *Rational Approximation via Minimax Linear Programming Regression*, Proceedings of the 23d National Conference of the Association for Computer Machinery, Brandon Systems Press, Princeton, N.J., 1968, pp. 79–84.

20. J. Bracken and G. P. McCormick, *Selected Applications of Nonlinear Programming*, Wiley, New York, 1968.

21. D. J. Wilde and C. S. Beightler, *Foundations of Optimization*, Prentice-Hall, Englewood Cliffs, N.J., 1967.

22. N. P. Draper and H. Smith, *Applied Regression Analysis*, Wiley, New York, 1967.

23. G. E. P. Box and G. M. Jenkins, *Time Series Analysis Forecasting and Control*, rev. ed., Holden-Day, San Francisco, 1970, 1976.

24. S. Makridakis and R. L. Winkler, "Averages of Forecasts," *Management Science*, vol. 29, September, 1983, pp. 987–999.

25. J. P. Cleary and H. Levenbach, *The Beginning Forecaster: The Forecasting Process through Data Analysis*, Holden-Day, San Francisco, 1981, pp. 81–83.

BIBLIOGRAPHY

Abraham, B., and J. Ledolter: *Statistical Methods for Forecasting*, Wiley, New York, 1983.

Aiso, M.: "Forecasting Techniques," *IBM Systems Journal*, vol. 12, 1973, pp. 187–209.

Anderson, O.D.: *Time Series Analysis and Forecasting—The Box-Jenkins Approach*, Butterworth, London, 1976.

Anderson, T. W.: *The Statistical Analysis of Time Series*, Wiley, New York, 1971.

Armstrong, J. S.: *Long-Range Forecasting: From Crystal Ball to Computer*, 2nd ed., Wiley, New York, 1985.

Ascher, W.: *Forecasting: An Appraisal for Policy-Makers and Planners*, Johns Hopkins, Baltimore, 1978.

Bails, D. G., and L. C. Peppers: *Business Fluctuations: Forecasting Techniques and Applications,* Prentice-Hall, Englewood Cliffs, N.J., 1982.

Bartlett, M. S.: *An Introduction to Stochastic Processes,* 2d ed., Cambridge University Press, Cambridge, Mass., 1966.

Bean, L. H.: *The Art of Forecasting,* Random House, New York, 1969.

Bloomfield, P.: *Fourier Analysis of Time Series—An Introduction,* Wiley, New York, 1976.

Bowerman, B. L., and R. T. O'Connell: *Time Series and Forecasting: An Applied Approach,* Duxbury Press, North Scituate, Mass., 1979.

Brillinger, D. R.: *Time Series: Data Analysis and Theory,* Holt, Rinehart and Winston, New York, 1981.

Brown, R. G.: *Materials Management Systems: A Modular Library,* Sec. 2, Wiley, New York, 1977.

Butler, W. F., R. A. Kavesh, and R. B. Platt (eds.): *Methods and Techniques of Business Forecasting,* Prentice-Hall, Englewood Cliffs, N.J., 1974.

Chambers, J. C., S. K. Mullick, and D. D. Smith: *An Executive's Guide to Forecasting,* Wiley, New York, 1974.

Chatfield, C.: *The Analysis of Time Series: An Introduction,* 2d ed., Chapman & Hall, New York, 1980.

Chisholm, R. K., and G. R. Whitaker, Jr.: *Forecasting Methods,* Irwin, Homewood, Ill., 1971.

Cleary, J. P., and H. Levenbach: *The Professional Forecaster: The Forecasting Process through Data Analysis,* Lifetime Learning Publications, Belmont, Calif., 1982.

Dauten, C. A., and L. M. Valentine: *Business Cycles and Forecasting,* 5th ed., Southwestern, Cincinnati, 1978.

Draper, N. R., and H. Smith: *Applied Regression Analysis,* 2d ed., Wiley, New York, 1981.

Eby, F. H., Jr., and W. J. O'Neill: *The Management of Sales Forecasting,* Lexington Books, Lexington, Mass., 1977.

Enrick, N. L.: *Market and Sales Forecasting—a Quantitative Approach,* Krieger Publishing, Huntington, N.Y., 1979.

Fels, R., and C. E. Hinshaw: *Forecasting and Recognizing Business Cycle Turning,* National Bureau of Economic Research, Columbia University Press, New York, 1968.

Fildes, R., and D. Woods (eds.): *Forecasting and Planning,* Saxon House, Farnborough, England, 1978.

Firth, M.: *Forecasting Methods in Business and Management,* Edward Arnold Ltd., London, 1977.

Fuller, W. A.: *Introduction to Statistical Time Series,* Wiley, New York, 1976.

Georgoff, D. M., and R. G. Murdick: "Managers' Guide to Forecasting," *Harvard Business Review,* Vol. 64, January/February, 1986, pp. 110–120.

Gilchrist, W.: *Statistical Forecasting,* Wiley, New York, 1976.

Gordon, G., and I. Pressman: *Quantitative Decision Making for Business,* 2d ed., Prentice-Hall, Englewood Cliffs, N.J., 1983.

Granger, C. W. J.: *Forecasting in Business and Economics,* Academic, New York, 1980.

Granger, C. W. J., and P. Newbold: *Forecasting Economic Time Series,* Academic, New York, 1977.

Gross, C. W., and R. T. Peterson: *Business Forecasting,* 2nd ed., Houghton Mifflin, Boston, 1983.

Hanna, E. J.: *Multiple Time Series,* Wiley, New York, 1970.

Harrison, P. J., and C. F. Stevens: "A Bayesian Approach to Short-Term Forecasting," *Operational Research Quarterly,* vol. 22, 1971, pp. 341–362.

Harvey, A. C.: *The Econometric Analysis of Time Series*, Halsted Press, New York, 1981.

Hirsch, A. A., and M. C. Lovell: *Sales Anticipations and Inventory Behavior*, Wiley, New York, 1969.

Hoff, J. C.: *A Practical Guide to Box-Jenkins Forecasting*, Lifetime Learning Publications, Belmont, Calif., 1983.

Intriligator, M. D.: *Econometric Models, Techniques, and Applications*, Prentice-Hall, Englewood Cliffs, N.J., 1978.

Introduction to Sales Forecasting, STSC, Inc., Rockville, Md., 1985.

Jenkins, G. M.: *Practical Experience with Modelling and Forecasting Time Series*, Gwilym Jenkins, Lancaster, United Kingdom, 1979.

Jenkins, G. M., and D. G. Watts: *Spectral Analysis and Its Applications*, Holden-Day, San Francisco, 1968.

Jones, H., and B. C. Twiss: *Forecasting Technology for Planning Decisions*, Macmillan, New York, 1978.

Kendell, M.: *Time Series*, Hafner Press, New York, 1976.

Klein, L. R., and R. M. Young: *An Introduction to Econometric Forecasting and Forecasting Models*, D. C. Heath, Lexington, Mass., 1980.

Levenbach, H., and J. P. Cleary: *The Beginning Forecaster: The Forecasting Process through Data Analysis*, Lifetime Learning Publications, Belmont, Calif., 1981.

Lewis, C. D.: *Industrial and Business Forecasting Methods*, Butterworth, Sevenoaks, Kent, England, 1982.

Lewis, C. E.: *Demand Analysis and Inventory Control*, Saxon House/Lexington Books, Lexington, Mass., 1975.

Mabert, V. A.: *An Introduction to Short-Term Forecasting Using the Box-Jenkins Methodology*, Production Planning and Control Monograph Series, no. 2, American Institute of Industrial Engineers, Atlanta, 1975.

McLaughlin, R. L.: "A New Five Phase Economic Forecasting System," *Business Economics*, vol. 5, September, 1975, pp. 49–60.

McLeod, G.: *Box-Jenkins in Practice*, Gwilym Jenkins, Lancaster, United Kingdom, 1983.

Makridakis, S., and S. C. Wheelwright (eds.): *The Handbook of Forecasting*, Wiley, New York, 1982.

Makridakis, S., and S. C. Wheelwright (eds.): *Forecasting*, North-Holland, Amsterdam, 1980.

Makridakis, S., and S. C. Wheelwright: *Interactive Forecasting, Univariate and Multivariate Methods*, 2d ed., Holden-Day, San Francisco, 1978.

Makridakis, S., S. C. Wheelwright, and V. E. McGee: *Forecasting Methods and Applications*, 2d ed., Wiley, New York, 1983.

Malinvaud, E.: *Statistical Methods of Econometrics*, 3d ed., North-Holland, Amsterdam, 1980.

Michael, G. C.: *Sales Forecasting*, American Marketing Association, Chicago, 1979.

Milne, T. E.: *Business Forecasting—A Managerial Approach*, Longman Group, London, 1975.

Montgomery, D. C., and L. A. Johnson: *Forecasting and Time Series Analysis*, McGraw-Hill, New York, 1976.

Moore, G. H.: *Business Cycles, Inflation and Forecasting*, 2d ed., Ballinger, Cambridge, Mass., 1983.

Muir, J. W.: *Without a Forecast You Have Nothing*, American Production and Inventory Control 25th Annual Conference Proceedings, APICS, Washington, 1982, pp. 554–557.

Murdick, R. G., and A. E. Schaefer: *Sales Forecasting for Lower Costs and Higher Profits*, Prentice-Hall, Englewood Cliffs, N.J., 1967.

Nelson, C. R.: *Applied Time Series Analysis for Managerial Forecasting*, Holden-Day, San Francisco, 1973.

Nerlove, M., D. M. Grether, and J. L. Carvalho: *Analysis of Economic Time Series*, Academic, New York, 1979.

Nickell, D. B.: *Forecasting on Your Microcomputer*, Tab Books, Blue Ridge Summit, Penn., 1983.

O'Donovan, T. M. (ed.): *Short-Term Forecasting: An Introduction to the Box-Jenkins Approach*, Wiley, New York, 1983.

Pankratz, A.: *Forecasting with Univariate Box-Jenkins Models; Concepts and Cases*, Wiley, New York, 1983.

Parzen, E.: *Empirical Time Series Analysis*, Holden-Day, San Francisco, 1970.

Pindyek, R. S., and D. L. Rubinfeld: *Econometric Models and Economic Forecasts*, McGraw-Hill, New York, 1981.

Plossl, G. W.: "Getting the Most from Forecasts," *Production and Inventory Management*, vol. 14, 1973, pp. 1−15.

Rao, P., and R. L. Miller: *Applied Econometrics*, Wadsworth, Belmont, Calif., 1977.

Rao, V. R., and J. E. Cos, Jr.: *Sales Forecasting Methods: A Survey of Recent Developments*, Marketing Science Institute, Cambridge, Mass., 1978.

Rothermel, T. W.: "Forecasting Resurrected," *Harvard Business Review*, vol. 60, March/April, 1982, pp. 139−149.

Sales Forecasting, The Conference Board, New York, 1978.

Singhvi, S. S.: "Financial Forecast: Why and How?" *Managerial Planning*, vol. 32, March/April, 1984, pp. 32−41.

Smith, B. T.: *Focus Forecasting Computer Techniques for Inventory Control*, CBI Publishing, Boston, 1978.

Spencer, M. H., C. G. Clark, and P. W. Houget: *Business and Economic Forecasting*, Irwin, Homewood, Ill., 1961.

Stekler, H. O.: *Economic Forecasting*, Praeger, New York, 1970.

Sullivan, W. G., and W. W. Claycombe: *Fundamentals of Forecasting*, Reston Publishing, Reston, Va., 1977.

Techniques for Forecasting Product Demand, American Institute of Certified Public Accountants, New York, 1968.

Tersine, R. J.: "Logic for the Future: The Forecasting Function," *Managerial Planning*, vol. 31, March/April, 1983, pp. 32−35.

Theil, H.: *Principles of Econometrics*, Wiley, New York, 1971.

Thomopoulos, N. T.: *Applied Forecasting Methods*, Prentice-Hall, Englewood Cliffs, N.J., 1980.

Vandaele, W.: *Time Series Models for Business Decisions*, Academic, New York, 1983.

Wheelwright, S. C., and S. Makridakis: *Forecasting Methods for Management*, 4th ed., Wiley, New York, 1985.

Wolberg, J. R.: *Prediction Analysis*, Van Nostrand, Princeton, N.J., 1967.

Wonnacott, R. J., and T. H. Wonnacott: *Econometrics*, 2d ed., Wiley, New York, 1979.

Woods, D., and R. Fildes: *Forecasting for Business*, Longman, New York, 1976.

CHAPTER

Product and Process Information

Editor

KENNETH W. TUNNELL, President, K. W. Tunnell Company, Inc., King of Prussia, Pennsylvania

Contributors

C. H. "PETE" LINK, President, Link and Associates, Arlington, Texas

ALBERT V. SANTORA, C.Mfg. E., Consultant to Management, Coral Springs, Florida

ROSWELL W. VAN COTT, Retired, Spring Hill, Florida

RICHARD W. WHITE, Senior Consultant, K. W. Tunnell Company, Inc., King of Prussia, Pennsylvania

Product and process data are an essential foundation on which every manufacturing control system is constructed. These files, currently and accurately maintained, are required for a materials management system to function effectively. These data are used in planning, scheduling, and controlling the manufacturing function of a company.

This chapter is devoted to identifying the various types of product and process information, defining how it is maintained, and discussing its relationship with manufacturing systems.

DEFINITIONS

Product data consist of information that accurately and precisely defines a part, subassembly, raw material, or end item. They also consist of a *bill of materials*, which is a list of all the subassemblies, parts, and materials that go into an assembled product with the quantity of each required to make one assembly. These subassemblies and parts together can generally be categorized as components. Bills of materials can be grouped into three types of formats: product summary form, product structure form, or matrix form. Bills of materials for items having common components can also be structured in a where-used form.

Process information or routings determine on which machines a particular job will be manufactured based on the route sheet. At one time routing was frequently performed by the same group that handled production control. Today, this is seldom the case, although many production control departments do determine on which specific machine centers a job will be done within the general route sheet specifications.

The *route sheet* specifies each operation on a part and the sequence of these operations with alternate operations and routings wherever feasible. It is prepared by process engineers when the part is first put into production. Other processing specifications included on a route sheet are the material requirements; machining tolerances; tools, jigs, and fixtures required; and time allowance for each operation.

IMPORTANCE OF PRODUCT AND PROCESS INFORMATION

Every manufacturing concern is faced with the critically important task of defining its current product. The complexity of the task varies considerably from company to company depending on the product, the nature of the manufacturing resources, and the management policies. For example, the manufacturer producing 50 standard items has a much different product definition requirement than the manufacturer of automobiles producing a number of standard products but with many options and accessories.

The advent of the computer has permitted the application of profitable production and inventory control (PIC) techniques, such as material-requirements planning (MRP). These techniques require an accurate data base, including routings and product structures, as well as the ability to quickly and accurately provide specific product definition with every requirement that is to be produced.

Product and process information is necessary to a manufacturing company for the following reasons:

- This information is used to identify the product.
- A formal system such as MRP demands accurate product and process information. For instance, the bill of material is essential in calculating requirements for each item and developing the master schedule.
- Cost accounting uses this information to calculate product costs.
- Production planning uses the information to plan capacity requirements and calculate requirements for the thousands of components that can be derived from a few hundred items in the master production schedule (MPS).

- Purchasing uses the information to identify and correctly order components and raw materials.
- Manufacturing uses this information to identify the components and raw materials that must be issued from the stockroom and to correctly fabricate parts and build the various assemblies and end products.

PRODUCT STRUCTURE

The product structure lists all the subassemblies, components, and materials that go into an assembled product with the quantity of each required to make one assembly. In other words, it defines the structural relationship between the different items in a manufacturing operation.

Types

Within the manufacturing industry, the term *product structure* may be referred to in a variety of ways:

- Bill of materials
- Formula
- Recipe
- Specifications
- Parts list

The term *bill of materials* is probably the most commonly used.

A typical bill of materials is shown in Fig. 10.1. Information that is normally contained in the bill of materials includes the following:

- Part number
- Description
- Item class
- Quantity per assembly
- Level code

The bill of materials may contain additional information such as source code, effective date, and effective change order number.

A *part number* is a number that uniquely identifies a component; in many instances, products and raw materials are also assigned numbers loosely referred to as part numbers. A *description* is a statement that identifies the part number. The *item class* is a code that identifies the part number as to make (manufactured) or buy (purchased). The *quantity per assembly* is the quantity of that part number required to produce the assembly. The *level code* denotes the structure of a product. Level 0, for example, is the final assembled product. Level 1 is all the components that go into the final assembly. Level 2 is all the components that go into the level 1 subassemblies, and so forth.

PARENT

PARENT ITEM NUMBER	ITEM DESCRIPTION	ITM TYP	ITM CLS	ITEM STAT	ITEM UM	ENG REV	MFG REV	DEM CTL	ISS CTL	DSGN SRCE	DWG NUMBER	DWG SIZE
40600412	PACKAGED TRUCK HEATER 6 CYL GM,FMC	1	1	2	EA	E	C	2	1			M

FIND NO	COMPONENT ITEM NUMBER	ITEM DESCRIPTION	ITM CLS	Q T	QTY	UM	COMP TYP/U	OP	SC	L/T OFF	WORK CNTR	DEM OPER	ISS	CTL	EFFECT	REV LVL	ECO NUMBER	BAS DATE
001	9600606	ADAPTER-HTR UNIT(FORMED)	I	1	1	EA	1	00	00	000		2	1	IN	76-089	A	0001	76-009
002	32408602	POWER CORD ASSY	B	1	1	EA	1	00	00	000			1	IN	76-089	A	0001	76-100
														OUT	76-101	B	1001L	
002	324110	POWER CORD	B	1	1	EA	1	00	00	000			1	IN	76-101	B	1001L	76-100
003	106026	ENGINE BLOCK ADAPTER PLAT	B	1	1	EA	1	00	00	000			1	IN	76-089	A	0001	76-095
														OUT	76-145	D	3003	
004	111018	GASKET	B	1	1	EA	1	00	00	000			1	IN	76-089	A	0001	76-095
005	308001	CORD PLUG PROTECTOR	B	1	1	EA	1	00	00	000			1	IN	76-089	A	0001	76-089
006	702004	LIFETIME GUARANTEE CARD	B	1	1	EA	1	00	02	001			2	IN	76-089	A	0001	76-095
007	703042	INSTRUCTION SHEET	B	1	1	EA	1	00	00	000			1	IN	76-089	A	0001	76-105
														OUT	76-105	C	2002E	
007	703043	INSTRUCTIONS HEATER	B	1	1	EA	1	00	00	000			1	IN	76-105	C	2002E	76-105
008	704001	INDIVIDUAL BOX	B	1	1	EA	1	00	00	000			1	IN	76-089	A	0001	76-089
009	704022	MASTER CARTON(34 HTRS)	B	1	.03	EA	1	00	00	000			1	IN	76-089	A	0001	76-089
010	70504401	LABEL	B	1	1	EA	1	00	00	000			1	IN	76-164	E	4004	76-105

FIG. 10.1 Single-level bill of materials.

Coding and Classification

All products must be accurately and precisely defined from the product end item level through subassemblies down to component and raw-material levels. *Product end items* are those items which are typically shipped to customers, as distinguished from either spare parts or accessories.

Part numbers relate to each of the following conditions:

1. Every item, whether purchased or manufactured, that is scheduled to satisfy customer orders or sales forecasts should have a unique part number and be included in the bill of materials.
2. Every part that is sold for service or replacement should have a unique part number even though it may be purchased and not manufactured.
3. Every product that is returned from a customer and disassembled and returned to inventory should have a unique part number for each component and/or subassembly.
4. Each subassembly or group of parts that is put together but never placed in inventory should have a unique part number, commonly called a *phantom*. This is discussed later.

Part numbers may be significant or nonsignificant. A *significant* part number is intended to convey certain information such as the source of the part, the material in the part, the shape of the part, etc. A *nonsignificant* part number is assigned to each part but does not convey any information. Part numbers are identifiers, not descriptors. The part number should be as short as possible to minimize errors in transacting receipts, reporting production, etc. Significant part numbers, because of their descriptive characteristics, tend to be long part numbers.

Parts are usually classified. The following additional kinds of data are usually required to adequately define the part.

ABC Code.   The ABC classification places inventory items in decreasing order of annual dollar volume. This array is then split into three classes, called A, B, and C. Class A contains the items with the highest annual dollar value and receives the most attention. The medium class B receives less attention, and class C, which contains items with low annual dollar values, is controlled routinely. The ABC coding thesis is that effort saved through relaxed control of low-value items can be applied to reduce inventories of high-value items.

Unit of Measure.   The unit of measure is normally the unit in which purchasing buys the part or in which manufacturing makes it. The vast majority of parts are coded "ea" for "each," but there are exceptions. Some other common units of measure are foot, ft; gram, gr; and inch, in.

Buyer/Planner Codes.   This code identifies the buyer or planner who is responsible for planning the part. Each buyer or planner should have a unique code.

Class Code.   This code groups related parts and is often used to sort and produce reports in specific classes. Here is an example:

10	Parts made in machine shop
20	Parts made in subassembly
30	Purchased parts
40	Parts made in wiring

50   Parts made in printed-circuit fabrication

60   Parts requiring special attention

Commodity Code.   This code enables the grouping of like commodities. A typical example is

01   Steel

02   Abrasives

03   Hardware

04   Chemicals

05   Motors

06   Compressors

Inventory Code.   This code typically identifies the inventory level in which the item would be stocked. Here is an example:

0   Raw material

1   Semifinished parts

2   Subassemblies

3   Finished goods

4   Finished parts

5   Expensed material

Order Policy Code.   This code identifies how the item is manufactured or purchased:

Fixed order quantity

Fixed period quantity

Lot for lot

Economic order quantity (EOQ)

Least unit cost

Least total cost

Part period balancing

The types and uses of these codes vary from industry to industry and company to company. They may be revised, replaced, or substituted based on the individual needs of each business.

Parent-Component Relationships

Each component used in a bill of materials is assigned a level code that identifies the lowest structure level in which the component is used. In a computerized bill-of-materials system, the level number is an internally generated code used to control the explosion process and product structure integrity. Low-level codes are used in the MRP process and are also used to prevent assigning parts to produce themselves.

The relationship of each part number within a bill of materials can be described in terms of a parent or component. An item with no components is assigned the highest level number in the structure. The level number of any other item in the structure is then computed as one number below the highest level number of its own call-out.

The end products are always at the lowest level number, usually zero, in any product structure. The best way to understand the definition of this relationship is to give an example of a bill of materials.

How to Structure a Bill of Materials

A motor assembly is produced by combining three subassemblies (A, H, N) and one part (Z). The true structure diagram for the motor assembly might look like Fig. 10.2. The structure can be defined by specifying five parent and component levels. For example, subassembly A consists of subassembly B plus parts I and P. Subassembly H consists of subassembly F and part G, and so on.

A partial listing of the structure might look like this:

Parent	Component	Parent	Component
X	A	H	F
X	H	H	G
X	N	N	P
X	Z	N	Q
A	B	N	R
A	I	N	S
A	P		

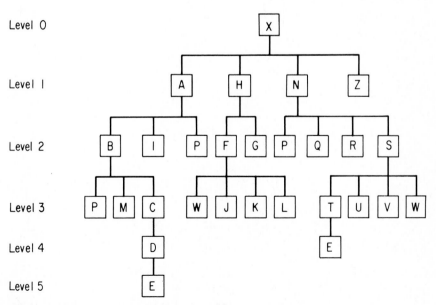

FIG. 10.2 Structure diagram for motor assembly.

Phantoms

A *phantom* is an item, not a bill of materials. A phantom can exist at any level in the bill of materials, is actually built, is rarely stocked, and is usually a subassembly. MRP will drive requirements straight through the phantom item to its components (blow-through), but will net against any occasional inventories that may exist.

A phantom identifies any group of parts that can be assembled but are not usually placed in inventory. These subassemblies exist for only a short time during the manufacturing process. They are transient and may exist at any level in the bill of materials.

For example, assume that a motor assembly is put together on an assembly line. Workers are stationed at different points on the assembly line to add subassemblies and components. At the same time, other people are assembling subassemblies on feeder assembly lines. These subassemblies are consumed into the final assembly as part of the production process. They are not sent back into inventory. If they were sent back to inventory, they would have to be quickly withdrawn, which would result in multiple receipt and issue inventory transactions. The subassemblies are phantoms that are built, quickly consumed, and not usually put in the stockroom.

There is some confusion in identifying phantoms. Some companies have called phantoms *pseudo bills, blow-through bills, transient bills,* or *self-consumed bills.* The definition and use of the terms are not consistent from one company to the next.

When a phantom is used in a bill-of-materials structure for processing in a computerized MRP system, the following steps should be taken:

1. Lead time should be set to zero.
2. Order policy should be lot for lot.
3. Phantom should be coded as such.
4. Phantom should be bypassed unless the on-hand quantity is greater than zero.

Phantoms should not appear on any *pick lists* but should be indicated on printouts of the bill of materials. Phantoms should be used in the following situations:

1. Residual inventory of a subassembly built on a feeder line frequently occurs, and it is forwarded to inventory.
2. It is important that a group of parts be identified and added to the bill-of-materials structure even though they are not assembled and put into inventory.
3. The bill-of-materials structure must be modularized, and groups of parts that are commonly used when an option is specified must be identified.

Planning Bills

A *planning bill,* sometimes called a *pseudo bill,* is a parent item which describes an artificial grouping of items which will never be built. Here are examples:

The superbill (S bill) is a generic number at the highest level (lowest level number) which ties together modular bills and possibly a common parts bill in order to define an entire product or product family.

The *kit number* (K number) is a number assigned to a group of small loose parts.

The *modular bill* is a number assigned to a set of components relating to a product module or option. A modular bill scrambles the parts at the same level in the product structure and regroups them. Groups related to the same option are identified with a phantom. The modular bill provides a means of pulling together all the phantoms, subassemblies, and components for a given product. This bill of materials identifies all options and major subassemblies that will make a final assembly.

Planning bills do not require the creation of a different product structure. They are made up of the same phantoms, subassemblies, and components that are in the bill-of-materials files. They are generally used as an aid in forecasting master schedule items by permitting the percentage of accessories and options needed based on historical usage. The percentages are expressed in decimals and loaded into the quantity-per-assembly field in the bill-of-materials file. Then the forecast for each accessory or option can be calculated by exploding the MPS for the final product by the planning bill percentages.

Types of Reports

The six most popular bills of materials generated from a bill-of-materials file are the following:

1. A *single-level bill of materials* (Fig. 10.1) lists the direct components for an assembly. It is a single-level list in that only the components called out directly by the assembly are listed.

2. An *indented bill of materials* (Fig. 10.3) lists the components on all lower levels. The number of levels is indicated in the report by an indentation of component item numbers under the respective item number.

3. A *summarized bill of materials* (Fig. 10.4) lists all components for a given assembly with the gross quantities required to satisfy the manufacture of the component's parent.

4. A *single-level where-used bill* (Fig. 10.5) lists all parents in which the component is used.

5. An *indented where-used bill* (Fig. 10.6) traces usage of a given component in its parent and, in turn, the parent's parent, until the end item is reached. The indentations signify levels.

6. A *summarized where-used bill* (Fig. 10.6) is an expanded where-used list including all the components and a total of the quantities used in each of the higher-level assemblies.

Responsibility for Product Information

The responsibility for the release of product information varies from industry to industry. In the process, fabrication, and assembly industries, the responsibility lies with the engineering function. In the style goods business (decals, cards, etc.), the product release is made by the art department. In the garment industry, product release is accomplished by manufacturing in accordance with specification established by marketing or by a design function. In the pharmaceutical industry, the laboratory is responsible for the development of product specifications.

These departments generally have the following responsibilities:

- To create new products that allow the company to penetrate new markets and increase market share

A20112223 DATA

REQUESTOR ID RER

OPTIONS- EFFECTIVITY 3

INDENTED BILL OF MATERIAL   60600612

PARENT ITEM NUMBER	ITEM DESCRIPTION	ITM TYP	ITM CLS	ITEM STAT	ENG REV	MFG REV	DEM CTL	ISS CTL	DSGN SRCE	DWG NUMBER	DWG SIZE
60600612	PACKAGED TRUCK HEATER 6 CYL GM,FMC	1	I	2	E	A	2	1			N

LEVEL ....5....10...15	FIND NO	COMPONENT ITEM NUMBER	ITEM DESCRIPTION	ITM CLS	QTY TYP	QTY UM	COMP TYP/U	OP SC	DEM CTL	ISS CTL	EFFECT	REV LVL	ECO NUMBER
1	001	90600606	ADAPTER-HTR UNIT(FORMED)	I	1	1 EA	1	00 00	2	1 IN	76-089	A	0001
2	001	90601406	STANDARD HTR UNIT	I	1	2 EA	1	00 00	2	1 IN	76-089	A	0005
3	001	105069	ADAPTER	B	1	2 EA	1	00 05	1	1 IN	76-089	A	0006
3	002	32204206	FORMED ELEMENT	C	1	1 EA	1	00 02	1	1 IN	76-089	A	0006
4	001	32700101	ELEMENT ASSY (ANNEALED)	B	1	1 EA	1	00 00	1	1 IN	76-089	A	0020
5	001	301001	ELEMENT ASSY	E	1	1 EA	1	00 00	1	1 IN	76-089	A	0026
6	001	326001	HELIX COIL ASSY	E	1	1 EA	1	00 00	1	1 IN	76-089	A	0035

7	001 504009	RESISTANCE WIRE	A	1	4.07 FT	1	00 00	1	IN 76-089	A 0042
7	002 304016	UPPER TERMINAL PIN	B	1	2 EA	1	00 00	1	IN 76-089	A 0042
7	003 304017	LOWER TERMINAL PIN	B	1	2 EA	1	00 00	1	IN 76-089	A 0042
6	002 110012	PLASTIC CUP	B	1	2 EA	1	00 00	1	IN 76-089	A 0035
6	003 110013	PLASTIC WASHER	B	1	4 EA	1	00 00	1	IN 76-089	A 0035
6	004 505001	MAGNESIUM OXIDE SAND	A	1	.01 LB	1	00 00	1	IN 76-089	A 0035
	003 506001	SOLDER	A	3	0 LB	1 F	00 00	1	IN 76-089	A 0006
3	004 505002	GLYPIAL	A	3	0 QT	1 F	00 00	2	IN 76-089	A 0006
3	005 110012	PLASTIC CUP	B	1	1.00 EA	1	00 00	1	IN 76-100	B 1023
3	007 110019	PLASTIC WASHER	B	3	0 EA	1	00 00	1	IN 76-105	C 2034
1	002 324110	POWER CORD	B	1	1 EA	1	00 00	1	IN 76-101	B 1001L
1	003 106026	ENGINE BLOCK ADAPTER PLAT	B	1	1 EA	1	00 00	1	IN 76-089	A 0001
									OUT 76-145	C 3003
1	004 111018	GASKET	B	1	1 EA	1	00 00	1	IN 76-089	A 0001
1	005 308001	CORD PLUG PROTECTOR	B	1	1 EA	1	00 00	1	IN 76-089	A 0001
1	006 702004	LIFETIME GUARANTEE CARD	B	1	1 EA	1	00 02	2	IN 76-089	A 0001
1	007 703043	INSTRUCTIONS HEATER	B	1	1 EA	1	00 00	1	IN 76-118	C 2002E
1	008 704001	INDIVIDUAL BOX	B	1	1 EA	1	00 00	1	IN 76-089	A 0001
1	009 704022	MASTER CARTON(36 HTRS)	B	1	.03 EA	1	00 00	1	IN 76-089	A 0001

FIG. 10.3 Indented bill of materials.

A20112231 DATA

REQUESTOR ID RER   SUMMARIZED BILL OF MATERIAL   GROUP ID CCC

OPTIONS- EFFECTIVITY 1

PARENT

ITEM NUMBER	ITEM DESCRIPTION	UM	ITEM TYPE	ITEM CLASS	ITEM STAT	ENG REV	MFG REV	DSGN SRCE	DWG NUMBER	DWG SIZE	QTY	EFF	OPTION
60600612	PACKAGED TRUCK HEATER 6 CYL GM,FMC	EA	1	I	2	E	A			N	100	1	
90601406	STANDARD HTR UNIT TRUCK HTR MODEL 1600 - 18	EA	1	I	2	C	B	DR	10728-A	E	5000	1	

COMPONENT

ITEM NUMBER	ITEM DESCRIPTION	UM	ITEM CLASS	MAKE BUY	UNIT COST	TOTAL QTY	TOTAL COST
105069	ADAPTER	EA	B	2	0.5000	10920	5,460.0000
106026	ENGINE BLOCK ADAPTER PLAT	EA	B	2	1.0000	100	100.0000
110012	PLASTIC CUP	EA	B	2	0.0500	15808	790.4000
110013	PLASTIC WASHER	EA	B	2	0.0500	31616	1,580.8000
111018	GASKET	EA	B	2	0.0500	100	5.0000
301001	ELEMENT ASSY	EA	E	1	2.0000	5304	10,608.0000

302044	GROUND STRIP	EA	C	1	0.3000	200	60.0000
304016	UPPER TERMINAL PIN	EA	B	2	0.0200	10608	212.1600
304017	LOWER TERMINAL PIN	EA	B	2	0.0200	10608	212.1600
308001	CORD PLUG PROTECTOR	EA	B	2	0.0800	100	8.0000
32204206	FORMED ELEMENT	EA	C	1	3.5000	5304	18,564.0000
324007	CORD SET	EA	B	2	0.5400	100	54.0000
32408802	POWER CORD ASSY	EA	B	2	1.0000	100	100.0000
326001	HELIX COIL ASSY	EA	E	1	1.0000	5304	5,304.0000
32700101	ELEMENT ASSY (ANNEALED)	EA	B	2	2.5000	5304	13,260.0000
503007	#260 Brass Alloy	LB	A	2	0.6200	42	26.0400
504009	RESISTANCE WIRE	FT	A	2	0.0135	21587	291.4245
505001	MAGNESIUM OXIDE SAND	LB	A	2	0.2500	53	13.2500
05002	GLYPTAL	QT	A	2	10.4000	0	0.0000
06001	SOLDER	LB	A	2	12.0000	0	0.0000
702004	LIFETIME GUARANTEE CARD	EA	B	2	0.0500	102	5.1000
703042	INSTRUCTION SHEET	EA	B	2	0.1250	100	12.5000
704001	INDIVIDUAL BOX	EA	B	2	0.0500	100	5.0000
704022	MASTER CARTON(36 HTRS)	EA	B	2	1.1500	3	3.4500
90600606	ADAPTER-HTR UNIT(FORMED)	EA	I	1	13.0000	100	1,300.0000
90601406	STANDARD HTR UNIT	EA	I	1	5.0000	5200	26,000.0000

FIG. 10.4 Summarized bill of materials.

A20112222 DATA

REQUESTOR ID RER SINGLE LEVEL WHERE-USED 110013

OPTIONS- EFFECTIVITY 4

COMPONENT ITEM NUMBER	ITEM DESCRIPTION	ITM TYP	ITM CLS	ITEM STAT	UM	ENG REV	MFG REV	DEM CTL	ISS CTL	DSGN SRCE	DWG NUMBER	DWG SIZE
110013	PLASTIC WASHER	1	B	2	EA			1	1	DR	10585	8

FIND NO	PARENT ITEM NUMBER	ITEM DESCRIPTION	ITM CLS	QTY TYP	QTY	UM	COMP TYP/U	-PCT- OP	-PCT- SC	DEM CTL	ISS CTL	EFFECT	REV LVL	ECO NUMBER	DWG NUMBER	DWG SIZE
003	301001	ELEMENT ASSY	E	1	4	EA	1	00	00	1	1	IN 76-089	A	0035		M
002	90100501	TANK(WELDED) 850W-120V	D	1	1	EA	1	00	00	1	1	IN 76-095	B	0023		M
006	90601406	STANDARD HTR UNIT	I	1	2.00	EA	1	00	00	1	1	IN 76-100	B	1023	10728-A	E
												OUT 76-105	C	2034		
002	90804401	F.P. 'A' SUB-ASSY	E	1	1.00	EA	2	00	00	1	1	IN 76-095	B	5555555		M
002	90804501	F.P. 'A' ASSY	E	1	2.00	EA	1	00	00	1	1	IN 76-095	B	00200		M
003	301011	ELEMENT ASSY	E	1	2	EA	1	00	00	1	1	IN 76-105	B	2065		M
006	301011	ELEMENT ASSY	E	1	2.0	EA	1	00	00	1	1	IN 76-105	B	2065		M
												OUT 76-110	C	3078		

FIG. 10.5 Single level where used.

- To create the documentation for the products to enable them to be efficiently and effectively manufactured
- To keep the product documentation representative of the way it should be manufactured through change and configuration control
- To maintain the necessary spare-parts lists so that inventories can be maintained to support the product in the field
- To provide proper documentation, instruction manuals, application support, and design feedback

The production of any new product requires a system of engineering releases to inform all functional departments of the data pertinent to producing the product. These data are used with the issued drawing as authorization for purchasing materials, writing process sheets, designing tools, and recording design progress leading toward release for initial production.

The new-product instruction checklist shown in Fig. 10.7 and the engineering release form shown in Fig. 10.8 are useful forms for coordinating new-product activities.

The engineering release form should contain all the essential information required when a new or existing item is released. After the initial design has been approved, drawings produced, and the final design determined, the engineering release form is issued. The engineering release procedure is explained in detail later.

Summary

A bill of materials should be structured as follows:

- It should lend itself to the forecasting of optional product features
- It should permit the MPS to be stated in the fewest end items.
- It should lend itself to the planning of subassembly priorities.
- It should permit easy order entry.
- It should provide the basis for product costing.
- It should be usable for final-assembly scheduling.
- It should lend itself to efficient computer file storage and maintenance.

PROCESS AND ROUTING INFORMATION

Although product and process information is being described as being sequential in development, ideally those persons responsible for developing the process of manufacture should be involved during the design stage, prior to product release. Close liaison with design engineers can reduce endless delays and complications in moving a product from the design stage to production. Such liaison ensures that the product as released will be produced economically in the manufacturing facility with few product changes as manufacturing and/or cost problems arise. This is particularly critical when complex products or difficult manufacturing operations are involved and when the product is to be produced in more than one manufacturing facility, perhaps in different countries.

A20112224 DATA
REQUESTOR ID RRF
OPTIONS- EFFECTIVITY 3

INDENTED WHERE-USED

304016

COMPONENT ITEM NUMBER	ITEM DESCRIPTION	ITM TYP	ITM CLS	ITEM STAT	UM	ENG REV	MFG REV	DEM CTL	ISS CTL	DSGN SRCE	DWG NUMBER	DWG SIZE
304016	UPPER TERMINAL PIN	1	B	2	EA	1	1					N

LEVEL ....5....10....15	FIND NO	PARENT ITEM NUMBER	ITEM DESCRIPTION	ITM QTY CLS	TYP	QTY	UM	COMP TYP/U	OP	SC	-PCT- DEM SC	ISS CTL	EFFECT	REV LVL	ECO NUMBER
1	002	326001	HELIX COIL ASSY	E	1	2	EA	1	00	00	1	1	IN 76-089	A	0042
2	001	301001	ELEMENT ASSY	E	1	1	EA	1	00	00	1	1	IN 76-089	A	0035
3	001	32700101	ELEMENT ASSY (ANNEALED)	B	1	1	EA	1	00	00	1	1	IN 76-089	A	0026
4	001	32204206	FORMED ELEMENT	C	1	1	EA	1	00	00	1	1	IN 76-089	A	0020
5	002	90601406	STANDARD HTR UNIT	I	1	1	EA	1	00	02	1	1	IN 76-089	A	0006
6	001	90600606	ADAPTER-HTR UNIT(FORMED)	I	1	2	EA	1	00	00	2	1	IN 76-089	A	0005
7	001	60600612	PACKAGED TRUCK HEATER	I	1	1	EA	1	00	00	2	1	IN 76-089	A	0001

REQUESTOR ID RER
SUMMARIZED WHERE USED
GROUP ID EEE

OPTIONS- EFFECTIVITY 1

COMPONENT ITEM NUMBER	ITEM DESCRIPTION	UM	ITEM TYPE	ITEM CLASS	ITEM STAT	ENG REV	MFG REV	DSGN SRCE	DWG NUMBER	DWG SIZE	COST CHANGE	EFF	OPTION
110012	PLASTIC CUP	EA	1	B	2			DR	10584	B	0.0700		2
110013	PLASTIC WASHER	EA	1	B	2			DR	10585	B	0.0500		1

PARENT ITEM NUMBER	ITEM DESCRIPTION	UM	ITEM CLASS	TOTAL QTY	COST CHANGE
301001	ELEMENT ASSY	EA	E	6	0.3400
32204206	FORMED ELEMENT	EA	C	6	0.3400
32700101	ELEMENT ASSY (ANNEALED)	EA	B	6	0.3400
60600612	PACKAGED TRUCK HEATER	EA	I	18	1.0336
90100501	TANK(WELDED) 850W-120V	EA	D	1	0.0500
90600606	ADAPTER-HTR UNIT(FORMED)	EA	I	18	1.0336
90601406	STANDARD HTR UNIT	EA	I	9	0.5168

FIG. 10.6 Indented where used and summarized where used.

	Begin	Complete	Man-hours	By
Part A. Design				
1. Obtain development authorization				Engineering
				Sales
				Planning
2. Obtain marketing authorization				Engineering
				Sales
3. Prepare manufacturing drawings				Engineering
				Drafting
				Planning
4. Interim planning and cost estimating				Planning
				Cost
				Engineering
5. Make necessary drawing revisions and				Drafting
subassembly drawings				Engineering
				Planning
6. Manufacture samples				Model shop
7. Test samples				Engineering test
8. Release design and specifications				Line engineer
Part B. Planning				
1. Final planning				Planning
2. Issue tracings				Drafting
3. Establish standard costs				Cost
4. Review and approve				Products task force
5. Establish packing method and label design				Engineering
				Planning
Part C. Tooling and production				Sales
1. Plant equipment appropriation				Planning
2. Tool drafting				Planning
3. Order tools				Planning
4. Tool and equipment procurement				Planning
5. Approve one part from each major tool				Planning
(prior to production release)				Engineering
6. Order material for units including				Production
packing material				
7. Release production schedule				Production
8. Produce at planned rate				Production

FIG. 10.7 New-product instruction checklist.

Release No. _____   ENGINEERING RELEASE   Part no._____
Supersedes _____   Date_____   Assembly no. _____
Machine no. _____   Part name_____
Quantity per assembly_____   Assembly name _____
Drawing date_____   Prints issued _____
Material specifications _____

Raw material	Purchased part	Casting
New_____ Active_____	New_____ Active_____	Pat. no. _____
No. _____	Vendor _____	Est. weight _____
Size_____	No. and spec. _____	_____

Field replacement _____   Ref. dwg. change no._____
                          Supersedes drawing_____
Remarks _____

Issued by	Approved by	

FIG. 10.8 Engineering release form.

Although process definition is a must for an effective PIC system, it is also essential data for many other systems in the company. Decisions as to what information is needed to satisfy these companywide requirements demands careful analysis and understanding by all the functions of the business involved. This ensures that key data elements are properly identified and that responsibilities for both development and input to the data base are firmly established. Although this is true regardless of the type of system(s) used, it is vital to the success of data base, communication-oriented computer systems.

Process information necessary to support operating systems varies greatly from company to company depending on the complexity of the business itself, i.e., how the company is organized and how it plans to efficiently manufacture, market, distribute, and service the product once it is in the field.

The complexity of the operating philosophy of a business, as it relates to required process information, is determined by a number of factors. Listed are some processing data required to develop the information to support the operating systems:

1. Number and type of products manufactured
2. Number of individual parts in the product
3. Number of operations and complexity of operations required to make a part
4. Commonality of parts across total product line
5. Lead time required to make the part and, in turn, the final product
6. Amount and complexity of tooling and/or equipment required
7. Commonality of tooling—same tools make a number of parts
8. Size and length of production runs
9. Stocking philosophy—how product is to be made available to customer
   a. Made only to order
   b. Stocked complete either in house or in a distribution point against forecast
   c. Stocked partially assembled with final assembly to customer specifications after receipt of order
10. Variations of a standard product offered to customer, e.g., options, attachments, etc.
11. Service-part requirements
12. Number of different manufacturing facilities involved

Relatively little unique process information is required to support the operating systems in a one-process industry, such as a chemical operation. The process and its required equipment are defined and developed in detail by engineering personnel prior to the construction of the facility. Operating control is almost entirely a matter of equipment performance and maintenance.

Most other types of industrial and service operations require a greater amount of process detail to plan and control operation on a continuing, effective basis. The actual amount of such detail varies considerably even within similar industries; there are no standard rules which can be applied across the board. A complete understanding of the specific needs are a prerequisite to the development of the operating control system.

Process information and definition are what permits an effective process control of the operation to be obtained and maintained. Given the extreme variability of the potential requirements, the objective here is to illustrate the major types of process information applicable to a typical, but somewhat complex, manufacturing operation. The reader can develop the specific information required to best control a given facility.

Make or Buy

Probably the first process information required by PIC, after the release of the product by engineering, is the identification of which parts or assemblies are to be made by the plant and which are to be purchased, either partially or totally.

In some instances, this decision has been answered by engineering in the product design and is so stated in the engineering release. In others, there are options and a decision has to be made as to how the item is to be obtained. This is generally an economic decision derived from a make-versus-buy analysis of the options. Since there are multiple options, this is generally done by a *make/buy committee* of representatives from various functions of the company. After a review of the item as released, the members supply data to be considered in the decision which are then evaluated in financial terms. The PIC considerations involved in making this decision should be represented on this committee.

Information used for this analysis is added to the product data base, where it is readily available for everyday use and provides an easy means for further analysis. A make decision, for example, could be changed to a buy decision at a future date if capacity considerations warranted, or vice versa.

Types of Process Information

The final bill of materials for a product, as released from engineering and modified by the make/buy analysis, defines and documents the active product components. It does not define and document how the various components of the product are to be made and actually put together in manufacturing. A production control system, regardless of its degree of computerization, should have the capability to develop a satisfactory manufacturing plan, implement that plan into production, execute the plan within some acceptable control limitations, and monitor, measure, and report the results.

To accomplish this requires some information within the system as to how the product itself will be produced and how the production of this product relates to all other products the plant is being called on to produce at a scheduled rate. Obviously, the system needs considerable detailed information about the facility itself, its capabilities, and the effect of these capabilities on each individual production requirement.

The actual data elements required to adequately support the production control system and how they are input, stored, and maintained within the system vary depending on the complexities of the system being used. The types of process data required to fit all systems and manufacturing environments can be defined in general terms and fall into these broad categories: work center data, tooling data, routing data, and operational data.

Work Center Data

These data reflect the various resources that make up the production facility. A work center can be an individual machine, a group of machines, a work station, an individual or group, or any subdivision of the facility to be specifically identified and controlled. The data may be created for other physical or functional areas where work is to be performed and the activity is to be scheduled and controlled, such as engineering, subcontracting, and materials storage.

Work center data are used to develop information for scheduling, capacity planning, routing, performance reporting, as well as labor reporting, cost analysis, etc. It is usually desirable to define and describe all the unique work centers through which work must flow.

A unique work center can be established based on a variety of criteria. Once established, it is assigned an identification number for control and reporting purposes. Typical examples of data used to describe such work centers are as follows:

1. General data
   a. Work center description and identification
   b. Foreman identification
   c. Department
   d. MPS resource center
   e. Fixed burden rates
   f. Variable burden rates
   g. Queue and move time standards
2. Machine data
   a. Identification of all machines in center
   b. Identity and number of machines capable of doing the same work
   c. Identification of labor required to operate the machine
3. Resource data
   a. Employees in the center—name, job classification, labor grade
   b. Number of shifts to be scheduled
   c. Shift length
   d. Overtime days
   e. Additional overtime hours
4. Capacity data
   a. Loading percentages
   b. Performance factor
   c. Reserve factor
   d. Maximum capacity hours

In summary, data elements loaded into this category are those required to develop the process information for control and the performance reports used in a given company which are based on work center knowledge.

Tooling Data

Tool control is a key requirement for successful manufacturing. The problem of control can be simple or extremely difficult depending on the type and complexity of the manufacturing process involved. Meeting production control objectives depends on the availability of proper tooling, in condition to be used, when the work is scheduled to be run. This gives production control a vested interest in tooling information even though data required to develop this information are generally created in other functional areas.

Data in this category define the tooling, how the tooling is used, maintenance requirements, and availability status. Following are some of the typical data elements which might be required for adequate control:

1. General data
   a. Category: special or general purpose
   b. Identity number
   c. Description
   d. Capital investment/depreciation
   e. Permanent storage location
   f. Tool group
   g. Date of update to new engineering change
2. Where-used data
   a. Part number(s) and change levels using tool
   b. Operation numbers
   c. Identification of other tools required to complete tooling
   d. Machine where tools are used
3. Maintenance data
   a. Preventive maintenance schedule
   b. Standards for pulling tools for repair
   c. Date tool is due for repair
   d. Where tool is to be repaired (in house or outside)
   e. Time required for repair
   f. Usage data
   g. Maintenance history
   h. Current status
4. Availability data
   a. When scheduled to be used
   b. Current availability status
   c. Anticipated delays

In summary, these data are of interest to many functional areas of the business. Ease and timely availability for numerous users can be critical to satisfactory scheduling and cost control. It is a procedure often neglected and underestimated.

Routing and Operations

All factory products (parts, subassemblies, assemblies) are produced and changed into their final form in a series of individual and sequential steps called *operations*. Product information, as released, must be translated to a series of instructions describing each operation for every item the plant produces. A considerable mass of detailed information results. This can be compared to a road map showing the route each manufactured item is to follow in progressing from original to final form, together with technical data as to how each operation is to be performed.

This translation is referred to under the broad heading of *routing*, and the file where such data are stored is the *routing file*. The routing file is an important part of production control information without which the production control system could not function. The routing file may be manual or part of a computerized manufacturing data base, but regardless of the storage method it must be readily accessible for use by the production control system.

Routing is closely related to product design. How the factory plans to make the product should be a significant consideration in the initial design decisions. Routing decisions should be fed back to change initial design decisions when desirable. Many times less costly manufacturing processes can be used if certain acceptable design changes can be made.

Routing decisions are nearly always related to volume. Large production quantities of a given item will justify larger initial capital investments in the process, to speed up production and reduce the unit cost. Low production quantities do not normally justify this type of investment.

Routings vary considerably from company to company, product to product, and even within companies making the same type of product. Data in the routing file, while usually considerable in volume, can be classified, more or less, as fixed data. Once the initial processing of an item is complete and entered to the file, frequent changes are not usually necessary.

Operation Description

Normally, a standard routing is developed for each item that the plant produces, and it describes the following:

- The actual sequence of operations required to fabricate or assemble an item.
- The general information required to define the operation to be performed: the department to do the work, the machine(s) on which the work is to be performed, the number and job classification of the operators needed, the tooling required, description of any special material-handling equipment needed, preplanned operation splitting, etc.
- The technical information and references required by manufacturing to properly execute the operation. This includes such data as the feeds and speeds of the machines involved in the operation, setup times, run times per piece or for some given quantity of pieces, loss factors or expected yield percentage, drawing numbers, special description and control information, etc.
- Reference information related to the operation required to perform it properly: specific quality or inspection references, special engineering references, special drawing references, government specification references, etc.

Alternate Operations

Routing and operation files, or data bases, generally describe the standard processes by which the product is expected to be made. From these data, the production control system develops the information required for the planning, scheduling, and monitoring of production, and the costing system develops the standard product costs and other financial information and controls.

There are many times when, for any number of valid reasons, it is impossible for the plant to use the standard processing. At times it also may be undesirable to use the standard processing because of load conditions or similar reasons.

When this occurs, it is a common procedure to develop alternatives to the standards either by rerouting the work to another work or machine center or changing the operation to be performed or both. Although this is a common approach, it often creates problems in departmental performance, labor reporting, factory payroll, maintenance of adequate product cost control, and performance reporting. Since the situation is normal and always occurs, a method to keep it under control is required.

To maintain control, the alternate routings and operations should be entered in the system's data base so that the system can perform in a normal manner. It can be a difficult and sizable problem to establish the disciplines necessary to ensure that the alternate operation data are placed in the data base routinely.

The problem of maintaining plant control is minimized when

- Alternative decisions are made in advance of a problem situation, possibly even at the time of initial processing, and are loaded into the system to be used as a routine scheduling option for the standard process.
- The decisions are made in anticipation of a plant problem situation. The data are loaded properly into the system, but alternate processing is not a routine scheduling option and is used only if and when the plant's anticipated problem actually exists.

The problem of maintaining plant control is maximized when alternate processing decisions are made on a crash basis if an unexpected problem situation occurs in the plant. Many times such decisions are made on the floor, perhaps by the supervisors themselves. In such cases, it might be a one-shot deal to solve an immediate situation, only to be dealt with by the system after the work has been performed. Once used, such alternate processing may or may not be maintained in the system for any potential future use. To be realistic, the process should be designed with this alternate in mind.

The planning and scheduling of production, particularly in the more complex manufacturing environments, cannot always be based on the clear distinction between using a standard versus an alternate operation.

It is critical that the system data base correctly reflect what operations were actually made and the machine centers where they were performed. The more timely and easier such inputs are to make, the more accurate and usable the results will be.

Lead-Time Elements

There have been many articles in the production control literature and discussions held at seminars on the subject of lead times and their effect on production control systems. However, lead times still remain somewhat misunderstood. The *lead time* is the total span of time required to perform an activity and the activity in question is normally the procurement of materials and/or products either from an outside supplier or from one's own manufacturing facility.

Four definable lead-time elements relate directly to plant activities once an order for some quantity of product is placed on the plant: move time, queue time, setup time, and run time.

Move Time.   A certain time is consumed from when a given production lot in an operation is completed to when it has been moved and enters the queue of the next operation. In this frame of reference, we can include the time from release of the original material from stores until the job is in the queue for the first operation and the time from the completion of the final operation until the finished parts are received in stores or on the assembly line. This portion of the total required manufacturing lead time is called *move time.*

Move times are developed during processing as a planned or an acceptable standard time allowance covering all the various factors considered part of move time. These data are developed for movements between each operation. Separate factors might be considered in developing a move-time allowance for a given factory-produced item:

1. The trucking time is an allowance for physically moving the parts to the location of the next operation (to another cost center, to the shipping room if the next operation is outside the plant, to another machine in the same center, to stores, etc.).

2. The vendor lead time, if the next operation is outside the plant, includes the in-plant time of packing, shipping, incoming inspection, and transit times.

3. The work-in-process or final inspection time, if necessary and not included in the run time, is for the operation itself.

4. The administrative time is the time to do the routine paperwork, data entry, reloading, etc., which might be necessary before the work is sent to the next operation.

5. The receiving time is the time for the next cost center to receive, check, make the data entry, etc.

6. The lot splitting time is that needed for dividing lots into smaller production lots for subsequent operations.

These data elements are usually developed by use of generalized, realistic rules in that they represent an average. Here are examples: If the job has to be moved to another machine group in the same center, allow 0.5 day for trucking; if the job must go to another work center for the next operation, allow 2 days for trucking and 0.5 day for dispatching, and so forth. These will allow the system's buildup of the total move time by operation when production requirements for the items are loaded into the system.

Such data are relatively fixed and not often subject to change. Obviously, all such rules should be measured against actual experience, and when the times are outside an acceptable range, they should be changed to better fit actual conditions.

Queue Time.   The second element of the total manufacturing lead time is queue time. In the processing of a plant-supplied item, it is the amount of time allocated for a production lot to wait in the queue with all other lots which are scheduled for the next machine.

Here again, we are dealing with a standard, or average, queue-time factor. This factor is generally established by the work center where the operation is scheduled to be performed. Each operation on all items processed requires that each work or machine center be given the same queue-time factor.

Using an unrealistic queue time factor during processing will distort subsequent reports generated by the system, particularly the loading and capacity-related reports. So care must be exercised in the development of the factor.

While the queue-time factor is also semifixed data in the data base and not subject to numerous changes, it should be reviewed periodically. If it is found to be unrealistic, in terms of actual plant experiences, it should be changed. Such changes can obviously affect many records in the data base.

The combination of move and queue times is the total allocated time between the completion of one required operation and the start of the next on an in-house manufactured item.

Setup Time.   The third element of total manufacturing lead time is *setup time*. This might be more accurately called *make-ready time* since factors other than pure setup can be included in this time allowance.

The main portion is setup time. It differs from the other lead-time elements described in that it is not an average or a time allocated to all operations. It is, instead, an industrial engineering type of decision, an estimate of how long it actually takes to prepare the machine(s) to perform the operation. Even when the same machines are involved, obviously there are wide variances in how long a setup will take, depending on the operation itself, the complexities of the operation, the specific tooling and fixtures involved, the tolerances to be maintained, etc.

These are other elements which consume time, in some cases considerable time, which can be included with the estimated pure setup time to form total make-ready time:

The inspection time (for first-piece inspection or more involved quality restrictions) can cause lost machine time while workers wait for a quality acceptance and the authorization to run the production lot. In some cases, this loss is significant, and an estimate of such loss should be included in the setup allowance.

The tear-down time is the time needed to remove tooling, fixtures, etc. from the machine for the previous job. This also can cause a substantial amount of lost machine time, and an allowance should be included in the total setup time. Since it is not generally known at the time of processing what specific part will be run immediately ahead of the item being processed, a standard time for tear down can be allocated, when considered necessary, to all operations processed through a given center.

Run Time.   The final element of total manufacturing lead time to be considered during processing is the *run time*, the time during which the machine performing the operation is actually producing products. This is also an industrial engineering type of decision, based on the actual operation being performed and the machine performing the operation. Once run time is calculated and loaded to the data base, it is not changed unless the operation itself changes or the calculation proves to be in error.

Run time is usually shown as the running time of the operation per piece produced or as some multiple number of pieces produced. This could be the running time, for one piece, per 100 pieces produced, per 1000 pieces produced, or per any multiple considered proper for the part, the operation involved, and/or the anticipated production volume of the part.

Lead-Time Rollup

When the processing of an item to be produced in the plant has been completed, a *rollup*, or summary, of the total manufacturing lead time required to complete the item can be made. This is usually a system-generated calculation based on the data elements loaded into the data base during processing.

An illustration of the lead-time rollup and the loading of a production order can be seen in Table 10.1. The item, as processed, requires only four production operations, each of which involves the four elements of manufacturing lead time.

The total-hours line reflects the summary of the four lead-time elements through the four manufacturing operations. Run time has been calculated as the running time per piece produced.

For illustrative purposes only, not as a normal processing step, the effect of placing a production order for 1000 pieces of the item is shown. This reflects only in the running time (time per piece times number of pieces); other lead-time elements remain constant.

For ease of explanation, given an 8-hr production day, which is not a normal loading assumption, the 1000-piece order would require 86.5 production days to complete.

TABLE 10.1 Lead-Time Rollup

Operation	Move, hr	Queue, hr	Setup, hr	Run, hr
10	48	16	4	0.10
20	24	8	4	0.15
30	16	4	8	0.05
40	32	12	16	0.20
Total hours	120	40	32	0.50

$$\text{Lead time for 1000 pieces using 8-hr day} = \frac{120}{8} + \frac{40}{8} + \frac{32}{8} + \frac{0.5(1000)}{8}$$
$$= 15 + 5 + 4 + 62.5$$
$$= 86.5 \text{ days}$$

Types of Reports

There are some informational and control reports in general use in most manufacturing environments based on processing data. Availability of specific reports and the flexibility of report format and content are system-dependent, whether the system is computerized, manual, or some combination of both.

A mass of detailed data are generated during the initial processing of a production item, and a certain amount of additional data are generated later as processing changes take place. If the plant makes hundreds or thousands of different parts, each with an average or above-average number of manufacturing operations, the amount of processing data in the files will be huge and presents a sizable data management problem.

Production control, among other plant functions, must obviously be able to recapture and use data from the files quickly and accurately. This need is best considered when the basic system specifications are developed and when the software used to operate the system is chosen. To obtain a new or revised report which was not included in the original system specifications can be difficult, cost-prohibitive, or even impossible after the system is running, even though the data needed to develop the wanted report are in the files.

Process Sheet

One of the most useful and important reports using processing data is the *process sheet*. In one form or another it is in general use in all manufacturing environments. This form is also known as the *route sheet, operation sheet* or *chart routing card*, or *manufacturing data sheet*.

There is a process sheet on file for each item produced in the plant and the capability to issue the information to the plant when required. The process sheet can be "hard" copy for duplication, as used in a manual system, or can be stored in a computer, brought up as needed, and issued to the plant in the form of printout or through terminals.

The process sheet is a comprehensive report containing considerable information about an item, with many user options as to its exact content. When the process sheet is issued to the plant, it contains detailed manufacturing instructions. Three types of information are contained in this report:

1. *Fixed information:* Part nomenclature and identification, engineering change levels, effective date, where-used data, drawing references, material used (type, description, quantity).

2. *Routing information:* Operations to be performed, sequence of operations, work centers performing operations, machine identification, move and queue times, and, where feasible, alternate operations and routings with similar information.

3. *Operation detail information:* Descriptions, drawing references, feeds, speeds, tools, fixtures, machining detail and tolerances, standard setup and run times, quality references, and numerical control tape codes.

When issued to the plant, the process sheet can contain specific details relative to the production order with which the process sheet is being issued.

A typical example of manufacturing information documentation in support of a predominantly manual system is illustrated in Fig. 10.9. This particular example considers the basic information requirements not only for manufacturing but also for scheduling, loading, material control, quality control, and cost accounting. In addition, it provides identification and separation of both fixed standard information and the variable lot information.

An example of a computer-prepared process sheet is shown in Fig. 10.10. In this example, only the fixed processing and routing data have been extracted from the data base.

RESPONSIBILITY FOR PROCESS
AND ROUTING INFORMATION

The responsibility for the process and routing information depends on the organization, functions involved, and processing cycle.

Organization

The organizations responsible for development, maintenance, and control of process information differ widely. It would be impossible to pinpoint a specific organizational structure and claim that it could be used across all industries. There

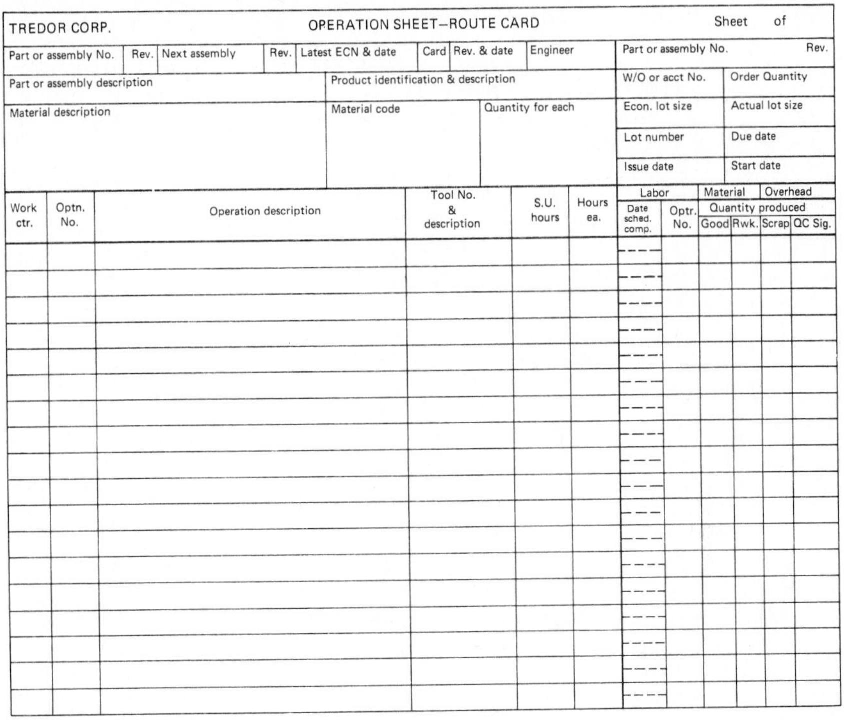

TREDOR CORP.				OPERATION SHEET—ROUTE CARD						Sheet of	
Part or assembly No.	Rev.	Next assembly	Rev.	Latest ECN & date	Card	Rev. & date	Engineer	Part or assembly No.			Rev.
Part or assembly description				Product identification & description				W/O or acct No.		Order Quantity	
Material description				Material code		Quantity for each		Econ. lot size		Actual lot size	
								Lot number		Due date	
								Issue date		Start date	

Work ctr.	Optn. No.	Operation description	Tool No. & description	S.U. hours	Hours ea.	Labor		Material	Overhead		
						Date sched. comp.	Optr. No.	Quantity produced			
								Good	Rwk.	Scrap	QC Sig.

FIG. 10.9   Operation sheet—route card.

is no such thing as a typical organization. Too many variables affect the possible structure of such an organization.

Size.   Companies vary from a small one where one person does everything to the very large where a department of many specialized people exists, with each doing some portion of the process function. There are unlimited possibilities in between.

Types.   Given even a commonality of size, process, and routing, organizations in a high-volume assembly plant, in a job shop or made-only-to-order plant, or in a highly specialized plant such as a stamping plant can be different.

Systems.   Organizational needs in support of a largely manual system will be different from one in support of a computerized system. And they can vary even further depending on the type, size, and complexity of the computer system being used.

Management.   Top executives have their own individual preferences as to how they want an organization to be structured and where in that organization specific functions will be performed.

In addition, there is the problem of what to call people performing these responsibilities. Methods engineers, process engineers, production engineers, manufacturing engineers, and industrial engineers are all used. Each company has its own

ITEM NUMBER		ITEM DESCRIPTION	UM	ITEM CLASS
23327		VALVE BODY VS100M 67.0	EA	E
OPN NUMBER	WORK CENTER	LN OPERATION DESCRIPTION	TOOLS	
0010-0-0	1080-08005	INSPECT FOR SAND FINS OR 01 EXCESS MATL IN CORED 02 GROOVES		
0020-0-0	2010-01450	MILL BOTTOM HOLE 2 1/2 01 TO CENTER OF CORED HOLE	23150	
0030-0-0	1010-01035	MILL TOP 5.00 DIM 01 TO BE 5.005/5.010	20730	
0040-0-1	1012-17005	DRILL + CBORE BOTTOM 01 .105 DIM TO BE .110	20449,20041	
0040-0-2	1012-17005	DRILL + TAP TOP 25/32 01 TO BE .781/.785	20042,20909	
0050-0-0	2010-01405	MILL ENDS 1.560	20737	
0060-0-0	1030-0300	DRILL + TAP ENDS + SIDES 01 BORE CBORE 2 HOLES - 02 1.999/2.001, 1.996/1.997	20450 20041	
0070-0-0	1010-01140	HONE INSPECT 100%	22972	
0080-0-0	1010-01025	FINISH GRIND 01 TOP + BOTTOM HOLE .105		
0080-1-0	1010-01030	FINISH GRIND 01 TOP + BOTTOM HOLE .105		
0080-2-0	1010-01040	FINISH GRIND 01 TOP + BOTTOM HOLE .105		

FIG. 10.10   Computer-prepared process sheet.

definitions, and there is considerable overlap as to how the responsibilities are defined and performed under these engineering job titles.

Although it is impossible to define the organizational structure, we can break down the functions performed on a common basis. The functions themselves are performed somewhere in the total company structure where they best fit the local situation.

We can also, for purposes of understanding, simplify the total problem while knowing the function is called any number of titles in various companies. Although the technical aspects are industrial engineering by nature, here we combine all the functions under the broader title of *manufacturing engineering*.

Functions

The functions responsible for process and routing information development, maintenance, and control can be seen in Fig. 10.11. They can be defined broadly as follows:

ITEM STAT	DWG NUMBER			DWG SIZE	ENG REV	MFG REV	PRS DATE
2	2602-1515			A	B	A	80-122
	MOV HR	QUE HR	SETUP HR	RUN HR	STD CDE	LBR GRD	PRS DATE
			.0	.008	1	A	80-122 80-122 80-122
			1.8	.178	1	B	80-122 80-122
			.6	.12	1	B	80-122 80-125
			2.4	.39	2	C	80-122 80-122
			2.4	.40	2	C	80-122 80-122
	8	8	2.7	.23	1	B	80-122
			6.0	1.10	2	B	80-122 80-122 80-122
			3.3	.541	1	B	80-122
			.5	.215	1	C	80-122 80-122
			1.0	.215	1	C	80-125 80-125
			.5	.275	1	C	80-125 80-125

1. *Tooling:* Design of original tooling and modifications to existing tooling, specification of tool maintenance requirements, and tool control.

2. *Processing and routing:* The actual development of how and where production items are to be made, including alternate operations and routings.

3. *Engineering liaison:* The necessary prerelease liaison between design and manufacturing engineering and the constant necessary follow-up liaison relative to a released product.

4. *Record and systems:* This is a basic function, often not fully recognized and sometimes taken for granted, regardless of the type of system being used. Obviously, as the system becomes more complex, the more critical the function becomes. The responsibility includes the accuracy and timeliness of the input as well as the information issued and distributed that is needed to operate the plant. The development of needed system requirements is included in this function.

5. *Work measurement:* The responsibility for the necessary review and evaluation of plant and worker performance, as well as development of actions and programs to correct problems and improve performance.

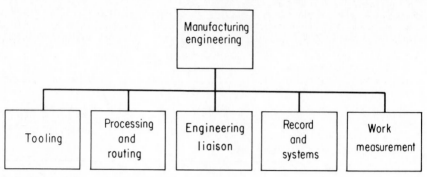

FIG. 10.11 Functional chart—process and routing.

But these are not the only functions that might be included under the industrial engineering-manufacturing engineering umbrella. Only the process information portion of the specific activity has been discussed.

Processing Cycle

Product processing and the development of process information are a continuing activity that occurs both when a product is first released and throughout the life cycle of the product. In some industries it continues beyond the production life of the product and includes the service life of the product in the field.

Preproduction. This portion of the processing cycle deals with the activity between the design and manufacturing engineering activities. The aim is to move a product into production as quickly and as effectively as possible, so it can be manufactured in the facility, at the lowest possible cost, at a quality level consistent with marketplace requirements.

In some types of businesses, such as automotive, preproduction processing is a major and critical phase of the total activity and involves both the supplier and intercompany production. Although in other businesses it is not as critical, preproduction processing should be recognized as a required aspect of the total activity.

Initial Production. This has been described in considerable detail. It involves that portion of the responsibility dealing with the initial data processing of a released product. It includes the development of process and routing data and loading them into the data base for future use.

Maintenance. Without a continuing processing effort, processing and routing data in the data base become more and more inaccurate, and the resulting control and information reports become more and more unreliable. Employees will rapidly work around the system when this happens.

Often the extent of maintaining processing information is underestimated, and too often sufficient resources are not allocated to properly perform this activity. Care must be taken that the maintenance activity is performed in an acceptable and timely fashion and resources promptly added as necessary.

Service.   There are often unique processing considerations where there is a requirement to supply service parts. Although it is common to take service parts from production lots, in some cases there are valid reasons not to do so, and special processing is needed because of the volumes, special packaging requirements, etc.

When an item is no longer to be made as a current production item but is to remain as a service item, there are usually new processing considerations affecting production control. The planning for supplying service parts is another critical dimension in the total processing effort.

RELATIONSHIP OF PRODUCT
AND PROCESS INFORMATION TO MRP II SYSTEMS

Manufacturing resource planning (MRP II) is a formal system within which top management can communicate business objectives to the entire organization. Top management develops business, sales, and production plans and communicates these to the operating management. These plans are used to create the MPS by using the bill of materials, routings, work centers, and inventory data to plan material and capacity requirements.

The material requirements are then communicated to purchasing and the shop floor. The capacity requirements are reviewed so that sufficient capacity is available in each work center.

Feedback is given to top management in terms of performance measurements so that actual versus planned performance comparisons can be made by top management. As a result, top management can continuously review performance, directing resources to each area of the business to meet the planned objectives. This process is shown pictorially in Fig. 10.12.

Accurate, complete, and standardized documentation of all product and process information is essential to the successful use of MRP II.

Item Master

The *item master* contains comprehensive information about each part including accounting, engineering, and planning data. The type of information contained in the item master was discussed earlier. Responsibility for maintaining this information is normally shared among several departments—accounting, engineering, and planning, to name a few.

Master Production Schedule

The bill of materials is important for the master scheduling function because MPS drives the entire manufacturing control system. The purpose of the MPS is to state material and capacity requirements in terms of the bills of material.

Master production scheduling will normally accommodate three types of planning situations involving product information: master scheduling end items, master scheduling a pseudo or phantom part number for the purpose of identifying groups of parts required to build an option or variant, and master scheduling at two levels. When end items are found on the master schedule, they, in turn, call out components that are processed in material-requirements planning (MRP).

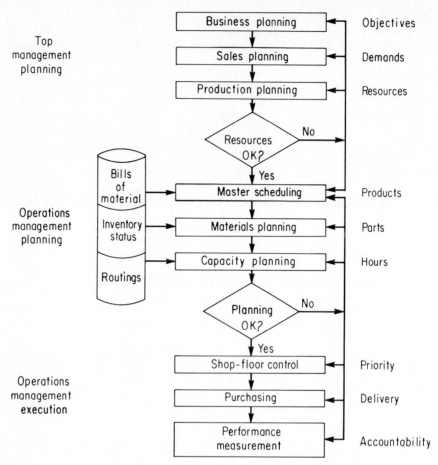

FIG. 10.12   Manufacturing control system.

The MPS incorporating a phantom part number consists of a structure in which several items are members of a product family. This type of product structure is used to handle the planning of product options and variants and is usually called a *planning bill*. The use of a planning bill permits ordering materials based on a sales forecast and actual customer orders. This is accomplished by master scheduling a generic model, for example, determining the percentage of each of various options for an automobile based on sales history. This is accomplished by exploding the generic forecast into individual forecasts based on a historical ratio of the product mix.

MPS items may appear at many levels in the bill of materials. An example might be a chemical manufacturer which sells its product in bulk or in individual product packages.

Material-Requirements Planning

Component requirements are determined by exploding the MPS items against the bill-of-materials structure and creating the associated demands. The MRP system repeats the process for all affected component items, computes the time-phased inventory requirements, and then explodes to the next lower level generating purchasing requirements. This procedure continues, level by level, throughout the product structure.

Capacity-Requirements Planning

The calculation of capacity requirements is accomplished by scheduling each released and unreleased work order into work centers, using the standard times from routings to determine the load requirements by time period, for each work center. After the load profiles have been calculated, the resource requirements for each work center are compared with the production capacity available. Comparing the current and projected workload against available capacity permits the manufacturer to analyze the shop's ability to perform and make adjustments in capacity if necessary.

The capacity-requirements planning module of an MRP II system uses the process information contained in the routing file to make its calculations. Without this process information, capacity calculations could not be made.

Shop Floor Control

The shop floor control module of an MRP II system usually releases work orders to the shop floor, provides the capability of recording production feedback by operation to permit the determination of work-order status, and provides various production reports. This module depends on the bill of materials and routing information contained in the data base.

The structure of the bill of materials normally determines the number of work orders released. The work order also provides a routing, and the routing displays the sequence of operations, their locations, and any memorandum, material, or tooling data that have been included in the standard routing. The routing permits the feedback of production information by operation which, in turn, allows querying of work-order status.

Data Collection

Ever-increasing numbers of companies are using magnetic or bar codes to collect data from the shop floor. Typical applications might include time and attendance reporting, labor reporting, shop floor control, inventory recordkeeping, shipping and receiving, and serial number control on such things as motors and compressors. The information on the document being scanned comes from the data and process information contained in the computer data base.

A variety of documents can be magnetically encoded or bar-coded such as identification labels, shop orders, move tickets, and shipping tickets. A typical application could be in shipping where data collection is used to record product movement. Captured information at the point of transaction permits bills of lading and invoices to be generated that are based on actual quantities shipped.

Magnetically encoded labels identifying each lot of material could be attached to a container as the material is processed through each station, the code is read, and the results are transmitted to the host computer.

RELATIONSHIP TO THE CAD/CAM SYSTEM

Changes in engineering tend to be slow and evolutionary, but CAD/CAM (computer-aided design/computer-aided manufacturing) is exploding in every corner of the profession as nothing before. If there was ever anything in engineering and manufacturing that could be classified as a revolution, this is it.

CAD/CAM is magnifying the power of the human mind just as the industrial revolution expanded the strength of human muscles. This new wave of change depends not on exhaustible natural resources but on the limitless human creativity. We are just now seeing the beginning.

Engineers trying to learn about CAD/CAM often run into problems. There are mountains of literature on specific systems, but little advice exists about how to bring these systems together in CAD/CAM. It is difficult to pinpoint all the diverse areas of CAD/CAM and see how they fit together. A lot of confusion exists about CAD/CAM terminology because CAD/CAM means many different things to people. Confusion and lack of clear definition are the most pressing problem of today's CAD/CAM technology.

Interactive Graphics

CAD/CAM has developed so rapidly that it is difficult to understand. Not many years ago, computers cost millions of dollars and filled entire rooms with electronic gear. Moreover, they could be operated only by those familiar with programming and computer technology. Lengthy numerical printouts were tedious and time-consuming to interpret. Now, computers with comparable power can fit on a desktop and are affordable. More importantly, the mystique and wizardry that once surrounded computers are now being removed by new user-friendly, interactive graphics systems that use visual displays and require no knowledge of programming or computer system operations.

As the user creates the CRT image with any of these devices, the coordinate data are stored in the computer memory. The computer then manipulates, reorganizes, or otherwise analyzes the data in many ways. The output is displayed graphically on a screen. The cross section of a diesel piston, for example, can show stress levels in various colors, so the designer can see high-stress areas without wading through reams of computer printouts.

Graphics Applications

This new generation of friendly, affordable equipment puts increasingly powerful computers within the reach of an expanding range of users. The electronics industry was the first to make wide-scale use of interactive computer graphics for designing complex circuits. The success of computer graphics in this industry prompted its use in many other applications to manipulate data and present information pictorially for ready evaluation.

Design and Manufacturing

There are many applications for computer graphics, but the areas that have grown most rapidly are mechanical design and manufacturing. Since the mid-1970s, mechanical CAD/CAM has been the largest application area, and its continued skyrocketing expansion is predicted.

CAD/CAM frees engineers from tedious, time-consuming chores that have little to do with technical ingenuity. These systems speed design and manufacturing, stripping away much of the paperwork and drudgery that hamper engineering productivity and creativity. According to the National Science Foundation Center for Productivity, CAD/CAM has more potential to radically increase productivity than any development since electricity.

CAD/CAM Functions

CAD/CAM systems have such power because of the broad range of tasks they handle. Generally, CAD encompasses five distinct functional areas: geometric modeling, analysis, testing, drafting, and documentation. A particular system may not perform all these functions. In fact, most systems handle only a few. Understanding these areas is necessary to comprehend the full potential of computer-aided design.

The computer-aided manufacturing side of CAD/CAM represents great economic potential for improving manufacturing productivity. It also presents more difficult technical challenges because shaping or assembling, maneuvering and/or controlling a part, or assembly on the shop floor is more difficult than creating and moving an image on a CRT. Consequently, CAM has traditionally lagged CAD technology, and development work is aimed at closing this technical gap. Developments for systems in CAM are in four main areas: numerical control, robotics, process planning, and factory management.

A key concept behind CAD/CAM is that these individual functions are not only computerized but also tied together through a shared data base in computer memory. In an idealized system, the user interacts with the computer through a graphics terminal, designing and producing a part or assembly from start to finish, with information for each activity stored in the computer data base. Some present systems have many CAD functions interfaced, and a few have limited numerical control capabilities. Other CAM functions are still in the early stages of development and usually are performed apart from the CAD system, such as robot programming and process planning. Cooperative efforts are underway on several fronts to integrate these separate areas into unified CAD/CAM systems.

Geometric Modeling

In geometric modeling, the user creates a description of part geometry. This so-called geometric model is a mathematical representation, both in size and in shape, of a part or assembly in computer memory. The ease and speed with which users enter and extract data graphically from computers have made CRT geometric pictures virtually synonymous with the geometric models they represent. Experts consider the model to be one of the most important elements of CAD/CAM because so many other design and manufacturing functions, such as finite-element analysis, automated drafting, and numerical control, use these geometric data as a starting point.

Most geometric modeling today is done with *wire frames* that represent part shapes with interconnected line elements. Wire frames are the simplest models to create, and they use relatively little computer time and memory. They provide precise information about the location of surface discontinuities on the part. However, wire frames contain little, if any, information about surfaces themselves, and they do not differentiate between the inside and outside of objects. Thus, wire frames can be ambiguous in representing complex structures.

Many of these ambiguities are overcome with surface models. These models are built from extensive menus of surface features. The plane is the most basic surface element. More complex shapes are represented by tabulated cylinders, ruled surfaces, surfaces of revolution, sweep surfaces, and fillet surfaces. Sculptured surfaces are the most general representation.

Through techniques such as hidden-line removal, surface models can easily be made to appear solid. In computer memory, surface models represent only an envelope of part geometry. Their inability to represent the solid nature of parts leads to difficulties in calculating parameters such as weight, volume, and moments of inertia.

The highest level of sophistication in geometric modeling is three-dimensional solid modeling. Solid models may be created by using a surface representation to define the boundary of an object. Another approach uses combinations of elementary cubes, spheres, and other so-called primitives to create complex solid models. Or a combination of these two techniques may be employed. These models allow the solid nature of an object to be represented in the computer, facilitating the calculation of mass properties and the representation of internal details.

In a typical solid modeling process, a conventional wire frame model is first created of, for example, a disk brake rotor assembly. Computer software then converts this wire frame to a solid model, displayed with color and shading. Cross sections may be cut from the model to reveal cooling fin cavities, wheel studs, and other internal details, and exploded views may be generated to show component assemblies.

Analysis

After a geometric model is created, some CAD systems allow the user to move directly to analysis. Through simple keyboard commands, the computer can calculate such characteristics as weight, volume, surface area, moment of inertia, or center of gravity.

Some CAD systems also have kinematic capabilities for designing and analyzing complex mechanisms. Before the advent of computer graphics, engineers designing mechanisms had to grind through lengthy mathematical equations or build physical models for trial-and-error development. Now, computer graphics systems do the difficult work required for complex mechanisms, ranging from nuts and bolts to aircraft landing gears.

One of the most powerful and widely used computer techniques for analyzing a structure is the *finite-element method*. This technique determines characteristics such as deflections and stresses in a structure otherwise too complex for closed-form mathematical analysis. The structure is divided into a network of simple elements, each of which has stress and deflection characteristics easily defined by classical theory. Determining the behavior of the entire structure then becomes a task of solving the resulting set of simultaneous equations for all elements. The network of simple elements is called a *mesh*, or *grid*, with elements connected at *nodes*. The total pattern of elements is referred to as a *model*. The simultaneous equations describing the model usually number in the hundreds or thousands, so a computer and specialized data-handling programs are required to implement the method.

In integrated CAD systems, the user can call up a geometric model of the part and then use automatic node and element generation capabilities to create a finite-element model of, for example, a steam generator housing. Once a part is modeled, the user can specify loads and perform an analysis. With graphics postprocessing, the computer condenses the output and presents it in graphic form for quick evaluation. Output data, for example, may be displayed as a deflected shape, perhaps superimposed over the original model, with deflections exaggerated to aid interpretation. In the analysis of a dish antenna, for example, the deformed shape produced by a simulated load is displayed in white, superimposed on the blue undeformed structure. Stress levels over the structure may be indicated in color-coded plots, with red indicating the highest stress concentrations.

Testing

A computer-based testing technique frequently used with CAD systems is *model testing*. In this approach, a prototype is driven by a forced vibration, and the resulting data are fed into a computer-based system. A graphic display shows animated mode shapes as the structure deforms at various frequencies. Observation of the mode shapes allows areas of excessive deflections to be identified.

Dynamic testing of structural model characteristics, a tedious and time-consuming procedure, has recently become more practical. This advancement comes primarily from development of mini computer-based vibration analysis systems.

The first step in model testing is the creation of a computer model, a pattern of interconnected points representing the basic shape of the structure. This model may be developed from the prototype itself or from existing geometric model data in computer memory.

After the model is completed, a driving force is applied to the actual structure. As the structure is vibrated by the driving force, signals from accelerometers on the structure are fed into the model analyzer. From these data the equipment pinpoints the structure's natural frequencies and graphically displays the displacements to show how the structure deforms at these frequencies. This animated mode shape shows how the structure bends, twists, and rocks at various frequencies. Because the actual displacements are comparatively small and rapid, the deformation is exaggerated and the action is slowed considerably.

Drafting

Automated drafting produces engineering drawings and other hard-copy documentation. In fully integrated systems, drawings are produced by plotting various views of the geometric model. Users not needing the capabilities of a fully integrated system may produce drawings with stand-alone, computer-assisted drafting systems.

New drawings may be produced on these less expensive units just as models are created with a full CAD system. Points and lines are specified with a device such as a stylus, joystick, or thumbwheel. The drawing process is aided by function menus that construct basic drawing elements from simple pushbutton commands.

Most automated drafting systems also have a large digitizing tablet that resembles a conventional drafting board. In the digitizing process, the cursor is placed over a point on the drawing, and a key is pressed to enter the position. In this manner, the user specifies the points and lines that make up a drawing. This procedure enters an idealized form of the sketch into the computer, which "cleans up" the drawing by straightening lines, smoothing curves and arcs, and orienting lines at proper angles.

Generally text is placed rapidly on drawings through an alphanumeric keyboard. Most systems automate much of the dimensioning. Some systems also provide a number of editing commands to copy, scale, delete, rotate, and move portions of the drawing.

Numerical Control

Probably the most mature of CAM technologies, *numerical control* (NC) refers to the technique of controlling machine tools with prerecorded coded information. These automated machines drill, torch-cut, punch, mill, turn, bend, and form raw material into finished parts.

In the most basic NC systems, programmed instructions stored on punched paper tapes are placed on electromechanical tape readers connected to the machine tool. More advanced systems use *computer numerical control* (CNC), in which the machine is controlled by a dedicated minicomputer with NC instructions stored in its memory.

The most sophisticated systems use *direct numerical control* (DNC). In a DNC system, individual manufacturing units are connected to a central mainframe computer that supplies instructions. These systems are also called *distributed numerical control*, in that machine control is distributed among a network of minicomputers or mainframes. Instructions for these NC systems used to be prepared manually. The programmer calculated coordinates for the entire tool path and then coded these data into an alphanumerical format for direct entry into the machine control unit. This process was tedious and error-prone and required extensive testing on the machine tool to make the program run properly.

NC instructions are now prepared more quickly and with fewer errors with special programming languages used in computer-assisted systems. The part programmer enters statements identifying machining parameters, part shape, and tool type. Then the computer automatically calculates the tool path required to produce the shape.

In a step beyond computer-assisted programming, a new generation of software uses the CAD geometric model stored in the data base to automatically produce NC instruction. The programmer does not have to enter data manually. The computer prompts with questions displayed on a terminal screen. Most of these NC programming packages also display simulated tool paths to check the program.

These computer-based programming systems speed the generation of NC programs. Perhaps more significantly, the user need not be intimately familiar with the intricacies of programming languages or tool-path generation. As a result, engineers designing parts can now do their own NC programming, provided they have at least minimal knowledge of machining.

Work is now underway to develop a fully computerized processor capable of generating NC instructions automatically for generalized part shapes. Ultimately, via *generative programming*, the processor will automatically recognize the solid model of the part, identify the material to be removed from raw stock to produce the part, select the tools required, determine machining parameters such as feed rates and spindle speeds, establish the proper sequence of work elements, and determine optimum tool paths to fabricate the part while avoiding special tooling clamps and fixtures.

A key factor in the development of generative NC programming is the ability to accommodate complex sculptured surfaces. These are made of arbitrary, non-analytical contours that may not obey mathematical laws and were formerly considered to be impractical to machine with NC.

Efforts are underway to develop a program for defining arbitrary shapes and manufacturing them on NC machine tools. Complex surfaces are represented by a network of interconnected patches in this program. After the surface is modeled, the program output can generate NC machining instructions.

Robots

Automated manipulator arms, or industrial robots, are used to perform various materials-handling functions in CAM systems. Robots may select and position tools and workpieces for NC machine tools. They may use their hands, called *end effectors*, to grasp and operate tools such as drills.

Robots typically repeat sequences of programmed movements over and over, rapidly and precisely. They are well suited to repetitive tasks such as welding and spray-painting automobiles, appliances, and other high-volume items. This consistent performance in mass production increases productivity dramatically, and a robot typically pays for itself in less than 2 years.

The earliest way to program robots was by manual teaching, which remains the predominant method today. In this approach, the user leads the robot through the required motions, which are recorded in memory. Teach-mode programming requires relatively little operator training and typically can be performed by shop floor personnel. Also, the cost of teach-mode robots and the associated maintenance are generally much less than for more sophisticated robots. However, manual teaching is time-consuming and error-prone for complex processes. Production facilities usually must be tied up during programming. In addition, modifying some of the steps in the program usually requires the entire program to be retaught.

Off-line languages make robot programming faster and more accurate, and changes can be made readily. The program is documented more completely, and sensor data and adaptive control are more effectively utilized.

Process Planning

Whereas NC is concerned with controlling the operation of a single machine, process planning considers the sequence of production steps required to make a part from start to finish. Basically, the goal is to develop a procedure for making the part as quickly and inexpensively as possible. Thus, the process planner must take into account both the state of the workpiece at each work station and the physical routing of the part around the shop floor.

Process planning has been a part of manufacturing operations for some time. Recently, the computer has been brought to bear on this activity, mainly because of the increase in low-volume manufacturing operations. Currently, most industrial parts produced in the United States are made in small lots of 50 pieces or less. In contrast to rigid mass-production operations, these batch-type shops frequently change part-routing and machine operations. As a result, the production sequence is often less than optimal. In batch-type metalworking shops, for example, 95 percent of the total production time is spent moving and storing workpieces, 3.5 percent is spent in secondary operations such as setup and loading, and only 1.5 percent is spent actually cutting metal. Computer-assisted process planning is seen as the best approach for increasing this productivity by standardization of process operations, tools, materials, and techniques.

Group Technology

Most current process planning systems use a retrieval technique based on group technology. This is a manufacturing philosophy that takes advantage of similarities among parts and processes. Parts are organized into families according to similar shape or common manufacturing operations. Standard plans stored in computer memory contain menus of operational codes for fabricating each part family. A customized process plan for a new part is developed by editing this standard plan. In this manner, a retrieval-type process planning system uses computer memory of operational sequences to replace human memory, with the user providing all data relevant to the specific part.

Future process planning systems are expected to have increased capability to provide more data on fabricating parts and will aid in decision making. Ultimately, the computer will generate its own process plans from memory data, internal computations, and independent decision-making ability. In these generative systems, process plans will be produced directly from the geometric data base with almost no human assistance.

Factory management systems under development typically rely heavily on group technology, with families of similar parts fabricated in individual manufacturing cells. As factories become more automated, these cells are expected to contain increasing numbers of robots and NC machines. Eventually cells will be linked together and controlled by a unified computer system, paving the way for overall factory automation. Forecasts indicate that factories totally automated by computer will be a reality before the end of this century.

Benefits and Cost

Computer graphics allow designs to be developed much faster and more accurately than traditional manual methods. As a result, the user gains dramatically increased productivity as well as many other intangible benefits. CAD/CAM is expensive. Even the simplest system can cost well over $100,000. A more sophisticated system with multiple work stations can cost more than $500,000. Thus, managers choosing a computer graphics system need to consider carefully whether the benefits are sufficient to justify the high cost of the system.

With mechanical CAD/CAM, overall productivity in design generally increases 2:1 during the first year of operation in comparison with manual methods. After the first year, the improvement typically levels off at about 3:1 or 4:1, depending on the application. Some users report productivity increases as high as 30:1, especially in the electronics industry. NC operations generally reach 3:1, and computer-aided process planning 10:1, although 20:1 has been reported.

In addition to measurable increases in productivity, CAD/CAM also produces certain intangible benefits that are not readily quantified. For example, engineers may be able to produce designs closer to an optimum because of rigorous computer analysis such as the finite-element method. Redundant efforts are eliminated when a CAD/CAM data base is used. Automated drafting capabilities allow the user to quickly generate isometrics, perspectives, and other difficult views. Another drafting benefit of CAD/CAM is increased drawing accuracy which results from the system's capability to automatically perform tasks such as dimensioning. In addition, CAD/CAM also promotes standardization by storing frequently used symbols. Perhaps the greatest (and most subtle) benefit of CAD/CAM is enhanced creativity of the user, resulting from the rapid exchange of data between the user and computer in pictures rather than cumbersome raw printouts.

Staffing

Successful implementation of a CAD/CAM installation depends on many technical factors involving system hardware and software. A computer graphics system is virtually useless, however, without qualified people to run it, so staffing considerations are important. Operators must be carefully selected, training programs must be established, and the psychological impact of switching people from drawing boards to CRT screens must be considered.

A typical novice operator passes through four stages of training during the first 30 months of system operation. During the first 3 months, no significant productivity occurs as the operators familiarize themselves with the equipment and procedures. From 3 to 9 months, productivity increases modestly as operators become reasonably familiar with the equipment and common languages. From 9 to 15 months, operators are up to full speed and completing even the most complex drawings with relative ease. After 15 months, there is some further increase in design turnaround time as operators learn how to organize tasks and perform additional functions on the system.

Operators for NC machines and robots can be trained by the companies supplying the machines. A few trade and technical colleges offer courses as well as the Numerical Control Society. Maintenance personnel must be trained well ahead of the actual installation of equipment. NC tool setters and part programmers also require substantial training. Usually, the best NC programmers are former general machinists with some college-level education in mathematics and a desire to get into the white-collar ranks.

ENGINEERING-CHANGE SYSTEMS

Engineering changes for current product models are essential for design improvement. The development and incorporation of changes in design can, and do, affect the marketability and profit contribution of a product. New products are very often old products which have been continually changed over the product life cycle.

Design changes and/or engineering document changes occur for many reasons, all of which, when properly administered, make for an improved product. Changes often reflect market or customer requirements and in general represent the manufacturer's concept of "a better mousetrap." Marketing and sales groups often play a major role in the announcement of major model changes, which they frequently treat as a new-product release.

The finished-goods inventories in warehouses and on dealers' shelves can become obsolete upon the announcement of a major model change. Moreover, sudden dips in new orders for the current model can affect factory inventories severely and at great cost. Therefore, in many cases engineering changes must be planned carefully, and inventory strategy, including factory inventories, must be considered in the timing of product change release to the marketplace.

Frequently, slow-moving products can be "turned around" and sales improved through a model design change. Although sales and marketing groups are prone to quick announcements in such cases, inventory strategies must be carefully worked out. Detail factory-cost analysis must be made before a model change occurs.

Many changes in design are forced on the factory, sometimes *before* and many times *after* a product has reached the marketplace. These changes are more plentiful in more complex products and in the early stages of production than in less complex products and in the later stages of production. Changes forced on the factory usually deal with function, customer specifications, and occasionally safety. It is not uncommon in certain product lines to test and inspect prior to shipment and have the product reported as "dead on arrival" when it is examined by the customer. A minor change in dimensions or specifications may make the product functional again. These kinds of changes are mandatory and must be incorporated at the production line at once.

Frequently, sales-oriented managers request that changes be incorporated into the product at once for reasons which are nonfunctional. *Competitive position* is the more frequently used term. This term may be translated to mean, "Our competitor has better features in his similar but better model this year." The term can also mean, "A change will give something better than the competitor, and thus a better position in the marketplace."

Careful analysis of inventories, lead times, and production schedules must be made before a decision is made to change. Usually this kind of decision must be made at a high level of management.

Many changes in design are incorporated for purposes of cost reduction. These changes are initiated very often at the manufacturing stage and sometimes at the suggestion of a supplier or vendor.

Still other changes, which are considered minor or routine, may involve simple changes in hardware or drafting corrections, sometimes spelling corrections to a drawing or parts list. These may not affect "form, fit, or function" of the product and may not affect inventories. Therefore, simple changes of this type can be incorporated at once.

Regardless of the type or kind of change in design or engineering documentation, an orderly method or system of recording and communication must be developed and implemented. A method of change analysis approval, incorporation, and control must be devised, and this procedure followed. Means of monitoring and checking the system must be developed. Finally, the system must respond rapidly and reflect the good judgment of the people working with it.

An understanding of the impact of change is essential prior to the development of engineering-change systems. Depending on the kind and type of engineering change contemplated, varying effects on the entire organization will take place. A whole series of events and activity resembling a chain reaction evolves.

The greatest impact of engineering change is felt in the PIC function. Inventory quantities and values including finished goods, work in process, finished parts, and raw materials must be determined. Further determinations must be made as to disposition of parts changed or deleted.

Parts, materials, or assemblies must be scrapped or reworked. Therefore, production control must be certain that all parts, material, or assemblies to be changed or deleted are accumulated from various manufacturing departments, stores, and subcontractors. Rework or scrap orders must be published and distributed. Perhaps the most critical part of the entire procedure is to ascertain that all parts or subassemblies to be changed have been accumulated and changed. Failure to accomplish this task effectively may result in old parts or subassemblies being used in the final assembly. If the nature of the change will permit the assembly of these parts, then the consequence may be a malfunction at test or inspection of the product.

Schedules must be redeveloped for current orders, and changes in customer or warehouse delivery must be communicated to the sales department. The redevelopment of new schedules will require research and follow-up of engineering, tooling, standards, methods, and procurement lead times.

Machine loads and schedules must be reviewed and adjusted. Rework orders will require new schedules.

Drawings, shop orders, and manufacturing specifications, including operation sheets, must be physically accumulated and destroyed or changed. Consideration for parts changed which are used on other products is important. Should the engineering change require a deletion of the part from one product and not from others, the accumulation of physical parts is more complex. Then only a partial amount of the parts in the manufacturing area will have to be removed to stores or disposition areas. Should a change be required where reworking can be performed, instead of scrap or deletion, production control must be certain that the part number is changed. This kind of situation can be a problem if the new part and the old part are similar, since there is a good possibility of mixing the two parts in stores or in manufacturing areas of the plant. This problem can be avoided by good part-numbering and identification plans.

Frequently, a bill of materials needs to be changed as a result of a part change. To determine whether a bill of materials needs to be changed, use the "form, fit, or function" test. That is, if a part change does not change form, fit, or function, then it can be interchangeable with the old part. Hence, the bill of materials need not be changed. Conversely, if a part does change the form, fit, or function, then the part may not be interchangeable with the old one and so will change the bill of material.

Some companies change the part number by advancing the revision letter one position, for example, part AR12345-201E to AR12345-201F, regardless of the type change. Other companies change the body of the part number only if the form, fit, or function is modified. Where the form, fit, or function is not modified, the revision letter is changed.

Part-numbering schemes and systems are important to the efficiency of the planning and engineering people who work with part numbers each day. Therefore, systems and schemes should be standardized and adhered to at all times.

Production control must also make certain that the new change has been considered in inventory control. Frequently, the addition of a part to a model will change the inventory class of the part. If, as a result of a change, the anticipated usage of a part is increased substantially, the part may move from a C classification to a B classification or from a B to an A classification. Likewise, the deletion of a part from a model may change the part classification from A to B or from B to C.

Where-Used File

The where-used file can simplify the determination of where a part is used. The where-used file contains all part numbers used in manufacturing. The end-product number is posted along with the quantity per unit for each product model. This file must be corrected or updated each time an engineering change is published.

The where-used file can be a computer-produced record or a simple card file organized by part-number numerical order. The use of the where-used file can eliminate the burdensome task of searching through all bills of materials.

Finally, production control must determine the effective date of the change. The effective date is the date, lot number, or serial number of the change incorporated into the product. The effective date is determined from schedule and lead-time information which has been confirmed by manufacturing, procurement, engineering, and industrial engineering. The effective date may be transmitted to all concerned, including engineering, quality control, configuration control, and the customer through the sales department or contract administration. The effective date may be published and distributed to repair depots and/or service centers. Many government contracts make effective dates mandatory.

Establishing effective dates is often very difficult, but it must be done as accurately as possible. Although engineering-change effective dates are considered a planning function, they are better described as a forecasting function and usually are given by the PIC department.

The forecaster must establish, from the data gathered regarding the part to be changed and the classification of the change, when a change is to be implemented. For example, if a part change has been designated "next time ordered," then the MRP system should be used to determine both when the part will be ordered and the number of parent assemblies that can be made with the quantities of old parts available (both on hand and on order). With this information, the forecaster can determine the actual setback time required for the new part (because the lead time may change) as well as establish the effective date on the shop floor.

Note that the effective date recorded in the computer system (bill-of-materials module) reflects the date to be implemented on the shop floor. This implies that the bill-of-materials (product structure) file will maintain both the old and the new part number. The new part number is not used, however, until the effective date (which is embedded) has come to pass. This technique ensures that in reprocessing of the MRP (usually weekly) the old part number is not inadvertently dropped prematurely, hence incorporating the new part number prematurely and creating a false shop floor shortage.

Although not all changes have the same impact on an organization, all changes have some impact. The following is a checklist of items or documents that may be affected by an engineering change. The checklist is not all-inclusive. It demonstrates the volume of activities affected by an engineering change in product design or documentation. The production control department should prepare its own checklist tailored to its own product line and organization.

Checklist of Items Affected by Engineering Change

I. Inventories

    A. Finished goods

        1. Warehouse

        2. Distribution

        3. Dealers

    B. Work in process

        1. Major assembly

        2. Subassembly

        3. Parts production

            a. Manufacturing

            b. Subcontract

    C. Finished parts

        1. Stores

        2. Assembly area

        3. Repair depots

        4. Warehouse

        5. Open orders with suppliers

    D. Raw materials

        1. Stores

   2. In process
   3. Open order with suppliers
II. Industrial engineering
   A. Tooling
      1. In process
      2. Design lead time
      3. Tool-making lead time
         a. Materials
            (1) Stores
            (2) Open order or lead time
   B. Operation sheets
   C. Time standards
   D. Audiovisual production aids
   E. Make or buy
   F. Assembly-kit lists
III. Production control
   A. Production schedules
   B. Lead time
      1. Engineering
      2. Tooling
      3. Methods, standards, kitting
      4. Procurement
   C. Shop and machine loading
   D. Interchangeability and substitutions
   E. Classification of inventory
   F. Effective date
   G. Disposition of goods deleted or changed
   H. Rework orders
   I. Disposition of drawings, shop orders, etc.
   J. Where-used file
   K. Inventory class
   L. EOQ change
IV. Cost estimating and accounting
   A. Prices
      1. Customer open orders
      2. Open proposals
      3. Future proposals
   B. Cost
      1. Change of product cost
      2. Obsolete parts and material

      3. Tooling

         a. Capital investment

      4. Scrap

    C. Engineering

      1. Design

      2. Drafting

      3. Clerical

V. Engineering

    A. Drawings

    B. Bills of materials

    C. Parts lists

    D. Product specifications

    E. Where-used file

    F. Handbook and instruction manual

    G. Schematics

    H. Customer requirements

VI. Sales

    A. Catalogs

    B. Price lists

    C. Handbook and instruction manuals

    D. Spare-parts provisioning

    E. Service centers and repair depots

    F. Products in the field (customers, dealers, etc.)

    G. Customer requirements and specifications

Clearly engineering changes can present a burdensome task to the entire manufacturing organization. Cost is always involved in design change, although the type and kind of change will dictate the order of magnitude. Therefore, the basic step in organizing for an engineering-change control system is to develop a strategy for evaluating changes.

Policy Development

Development of engineering-change policy will depend very largely on specific product lines and methods of sales and distribution. The relationship of manufacturing and final delivery of the product to the customer is important to the policy. The answers to these questions will classify the problem at the start:

- Is the product manufactured to stock?
- Is the product distributed through warehouses and dealers?
- Is the product manufactured to stock and shipped directly from factory to customer?
- Is the product a standard item which is modified to customer specifications?

- Is the product manufactured completely to customer specifications?
- Is the product a commercial item or manufactured under government contract?

   In most cases, these questions can be answered affirmatively. Moreover, in most plants the answers are different for various product lines. A standard engineering-change control system must apply to all product lines. Where a product is manufactured repetitively, regardless of whether the method is considered mass production, many changes can be incorporated in future production lots as opposed to the current production lot. The manufacturing group will hope for no changes at all during a production run. Although it is desirable to "freeze the design" during a production run, it is not always possible. Every effort must be made, however, to minimize changes during a production run. Only mandatory changes should be incorporated during a production run. Mandatory changes are those needed for function or customer requirements, which sometimes include essential quality and reliability improvement. All other changes should be incorporated in subsequent production runs.

Engineering-Change Considerations

Although we know that to freeze a design can result in a freeze in sales, we must be prepared to weigh the costs of change against the market probabilities. The total impact of change on the factory and customer deliveries must be measured.
   These questions should be answered prior to approval of a change:

- Is the change necessary?
- What are the total costs of change?
- Can the change be incorporated in the next or subsequent runs?
- Will the change halt production? For how long?
- Will schedules and customer delivery be jeopardized?
- Have inventory positions been analyzed?
- If the change is requested for purposes of improving manufacturing methods, can the ease of manufacture balance the costs of change and schedule jeopardy?

Engineering-Change Classifications

Engineering changes should be classified or coded to indicate the extent and significance of change. An example of such a classification of change is shown below, from the U.S. Air Force-Navy Aeronautical Bulletin 445.
   CLASS I DEVIATION: Any change affecting fit, form, or function of an item or, more specifically, affecting one or more of the following configuration features:

- Contract specifications, price, weight, delivery, or schedule
- Contract reliability and/or maintainability
- Interchangeability
- Electrical interference to communications equipment or electromagnetic radiation hazards

- Safety, performance, or durability
- AGE/SE, trainers, training devices, or GFE

CLASS II VARIATIONS: Any change not falling within the class I category. Changes may be further classified to indicate incorporation policy.

Example 1

MANDATORY: Must be incorporated into current production run.

ROUTINE: Incorporate in next production run.

Example 2

CLASS A: Incorporate into all products including units in the field through revision AA1.

CLASS B: Incorporate into all unpacked units including units in assembly and subassembly.

CLASS C: Incorporate into all unassembled units.

CLASS D: Incorporate next time ordered.

Example 3

CLASS A: Scrap

CLASS B: Rework

CLASS C: Use up current materials

CLASS D: Next time ordered

Design Review Procedure

Engineering design or documentation changes occur more frequently in the early stages of production. Figure 10.13 shows a schematic of this procedure. It is not uncommon in some industries to anticipate these changes and to accept the problem. Many manufacturing companies maintain special areas where reasonably short runs are made as production pilot runs. During this stage of development, design and manufacturing methods can be tested and changes made at will. This pilot run can serve as the final design review before establishment of a baseline configuration. The policy provides for any change to be made during the pilot production run, which culminates in a complete design review and implementation of all changes. This point is frequently referred to as *baseline design* or *configuration*. After the establishment of baseline design, only mandatory changes affecting function and/or customer requirements may be incorporated.

Engineering changes can be requested from any department within the company and frequently from suppliers or vendors. The *request for change* is usually a printed form which, when properly approved, also serves as an engineering-change notice. Engineering-change requests (ECRs) are sometimes referred to as *engineering-change proposals* (ECPs). Engineering-change notices (ECNs) are sometimes called *engineering-change orders* (ECOs) or *engineering-change authority* (ECA).

An ECR must have proper approvals, and then an ECN is initiated. Frequently, the same form with multicopies is used as the ECR and converted upon approval to

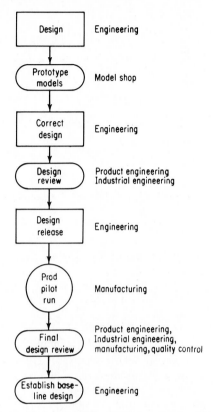

FIG. 10.13 Pilot run and final design review procedure.

an ECN. ECNs and ECRs must be numbered and logged for control. Should a request be rejected for any reason, the requester is notified and given an opportunity to represent his or her request at a higher level of management.

Figure 10.14 illustrates the format for a multipart ECO system, while Fig. 10.15 can be used both as an ECR and subsequently as an ECN. Figure 10.16 is an engineering authorization which is used for new-product release and an engineering-change order (ECO).

Sample Engineering-Change Procedure

   I. *Purpose:*   To provide a procedure for processing and controlling engineering changes.

  II. *Scope:*   This procedure applies to all engineering changes and includes the procedure for requesting engineering changes.

 III. Definitions:

   A. *Document* is any drawing, parts list, or product specification used to define a product.

Variation_____. Deviation_____
If deviation, check out characteristics affected

Interchangeability_____ Performance_____ Safety_____

Weight _____ Maintenance handbooks _____

Contract No. _____

Contract change No. _____

Name_____ Date_____

Process charts affected					
Number	Sh.	Number	Sh.	Number	Sh.

Reference ECO numbers

Sheet ___of___ Sheets

Proposed by _____

Advance copy   Yes ☐   No ☐

	Date
Changed by	
Checked by	
Engineering approval	
Product eng. approval	
Factory approval	
Customer review	

ECO No.

	A	B	C
Class change			

Drawing number

Change letter	From	To

	Name	Date
Change issued		

Eng. data review	Chge. letter	Drawing number
	From	To	

FIG. 10.14 Multipart ECO system.

B. *Deviation class 1 change* is any change in fit, form, or function specifically affecting one or more of the following configuration features:
  1. Specifications, price, weight delivery, or schedule
  2. Reliability and/or maintainability
  3. Interchangeability
  4. Safety, performance, or durability

C. *Variation class 2 changes* are all other changes not classified as class 1.

D. *Mandatory changes* are those necessary to the function and operation of the product or specifically required by the customer. Mandatory changes must be incorporated in current production runs.

E. *Routine changes* are those that do not necessarily affect function or operation and can be incorporated in the next or subsequent production runs. These changes can include those intended for cost reduction, product improvement, ease of manufacture, and quality improvement.

F. *Engineering-change request* (ECR) is the form used for officially requesting a change.

G. *Engineering-change notice* (ECN) is the authorization for changing engineering documents.

IV. ECR

  A. Any department may initiate an engineering-change request. The filled-out ECR form must include
    1. Drawing number
    2. Title
    3. Reason for change
    4. Effectivity date
    5. Sign

  B. Department head must approve and sign ECR.

  C. Forward ECR to change control administrator (CCA).

  D. The control administrator will check the ECR and classify the change.

  E. The ECR shall be forwarded to the project engineer for disposition.
    1. If the request is rejected, the ECR with the engineer's reason for rejection is returned to the requester via the CCA.

☐ Engineering channel request
☐ Engineering change notice
 CM No. _____
 Engineering change No. _____
 Project No. _____ ☐ Class I (deviation)
 Sheet ____ of ____ ☐ Class II (variation)

Dwg. no.

Drawing No. _____ Unit No. _____ Present revision _____

Rev. no.

Title _____

Reason for change	Type of Change	Effectivity	Material disposition
☐ Error	☐ Mandatory	☐ Immediate	☐ None
☐ Additional information	☐ Elective	☐ Next time ordered	☐ Use up stock
☐ Design improvement	☐ Routine	☐ (See remarks)	☐ Order as required
☐ Vendor required	☐ Emergency		☐ Scrap
☐ Customer required			☐ Rework
☐ Latest process			☐ Use elsewhere
☐ Clarification			☐ (See remarks)
☐ Cost reduction			
☐ (See remarks)			

Description of change   From   To

Remarks

Change requested by _____   Approved by   Date

Date originated _____   Department head

Effective date _____   Project engineer

Change rejected by _____   Manufacturing engineer

Reason _____   Director of engineering

_____   Quality control

_____   Government agency

Draftsman _____ Drafting supervisor _____ Checker _____
Date _____ Date _____ Date _____

FIG. 10.15 Combined ECR and ECN.

2. If the request is approved, copies of the ECR are distributed to industrial engineering, PIC, quality control, and the CCA.

F. Industrial engineering reviews the ECR and evaluates costs, schedules, and technical feasibility. Considerations for cost include capital investment required, tooling, facility change, methods, etc. These costs and considerations shall be defined and recommendations indicated.

 1. Copies of the ECR shall be forwarded to the CCA and the cost accounting and estimating group.

Used on: Drawing No._____
                                                                    Rev_____
        Title:

DESIGN ENGINEERING

1. Classification
   - ☐ Class I   ☐ New part   ☐ -New assemblies
   - ☐ Class II   - Revision requiring no disposition of parts or assemblies
   - ☐ Class III   - Change to be made as soon as practical
                    ☐ Balancing of parts required
   - ☐ Class IV   - Change to be effective immediately
                    Completed parts   Completed assemblies

                    ☐ Use as is   ☐ Use as is
                    ☐ Alter or scrap   ☐ Alter or scrap

2. The following parts are affected by the above change:

   _____ _____   _____ _____   _____ _____

3. Type of change   (Give description and reason of change, special instructions, etc.)
                     ☐ Design   ☐ Cost reduction
                     ☐ Shop request   ☐ Sales request   S.O. _____

   Description:_____
   _____
   _____
   _____

   Reason: _____
   _____
   _____

   Prepared by_____ Date_____ Approved by_____ Date_____

PRODUCTION ENGR

1. Estimated monthly requirement _____

2. Tooling information
   ☐ Tooling required   ☐ New   ☐ Alteration
   ☐ Tooling is available   ☐ Temporary   ☐ Permanent
   ☐ Tooling is not required
   Remarks:_____

                              Approved by_____ Date_____

METHODS DEPARTMENT

1. Source   5. Special instructions
   ☐ Purchase part   _____
   ☐ Shop part   _____
2. Required tools   _____
   ☐ Alteration   Date available_____ _____
   ☐ New   Date available_____ _____
3. Stock status   _____
   Completed parts   _____
   ☐ Use as is   _____
   ☐ Alter or scrap   _____
   Completed assemblies   _____
   ☐ Use as is   _____
   ☐ Alter or scrap   _____
4. Material   _____
   ☐ Standard   _____
   ☐ Special
                                        Prepared by:_____
                                        Date:_____

FIG. 10.16 Engineering authorization.

G. Production and inventory control will review the ECR and evaluate costs, schedules, and lead times. Cost considerations include all inventories affected. Effect of change on current schedules is evaluated, and effective dates are forwarded to the CCA and cost accounting and estimating.

H. Quality control reviews the ECR and evaluates costs, schedules, and quality considerations. Recommendations are made and copies forwarded to the CCA and the cost accounting and estimating group.

I. Cost accounting and estimating reviews ECRs received from industrial engineering, PIC, and quality control and prepares a report and recommendation considering total cost of change. Cost consideration includes all inventories, capital investment, tooling, etc. The summary report reflects new pricing and consideration for open orders and proposals and is forwarded to the engineering department with copies of ECRs from industrial engineering, quality control, and PIC.

J. The engineering department evaluates the cost and pricing reports along with recommendations from quality control, PIC, and industrial engineering and approves or rejects the ECR.
  1. The controller and marketing department are to be consulted.
  2. If the request is rejected at this step, the requester is advised.

K. Engineering assigns an ECN number to the ECR and forwards it to the CCA.

L. The CCA records the ECN number and releases it to drafting and engineering for processing.
  1. Copies of ECNs are distributed to departments concerned (production control, manufacturing inspection, quality control, engineering, industrial engineering, etc.). The ECR procedure is shown in Fig. 10.17.

V. ECN:

A. Upon receipt of the ECN, PIC will
  1. Issue appropriate stop-work orders
  2. Physically accumulate parts and materials, drawing shop orders, and assembly work orders for scrap, rework, or other dispositions
  3. Prepare inventory reports for the accounting write-off
  4. Place new orders or rework orders for items changed
  5. Determine available schedule times for materials, components, etc.
  6. Develop schedules and effective dates (adjust master schedules)
  7. Communicate dates to sales
  8. Determine extent of tooling changes and obtain schedules
  9. Provide new machine loads as required
  10. Adjust inventory records including planned available balances
  11. Adjust where-used file
  12. Adjust interchangeability and substitution files
  13. Adjust inventory classification files
  14. Adjust EOQ values
  15. Establish follow-up dispatch plans

B. Industrial engineering, upon receipt of the ECN, will
  1. Evaluate tool changes and establish tool schedules
  2. Prepare necessary tool stop-work orders
  3. Design new tools or changes
  4. Evaluate change or establish new methods and operation sheets
  5. Evaluate time-standard changes and implement new standards as required
  6. Determine make-or-buy policy as required
  7. Review and correct assembly kit lists
  8. Change audiovisual aids as required

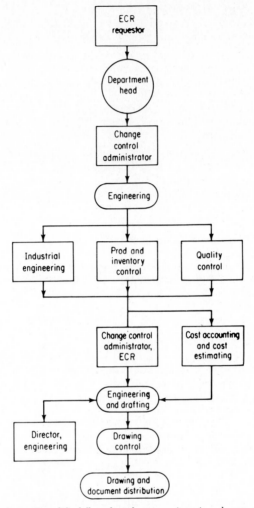

FIG. 10.17 Simplified flowchart for an engineering-change system.

Conclusions

Although control of engineering changes is very difficult even in a class A MRP system shop, it is essential and can be performed effectively in many companies. Some of the essential elements of effective engineering control are

- Well-defined engineering change procedures
- Education programs to properly train all planners, expeditors, schedulers, shop supervisors, etc., in the proper use of the system
- Established effective dates
- Clear objectives for those who determine that changes will or will not be made
- Logs and reports to accumulate costs of scrap and rework of inventory

PRODUCT STANDARDIZATION

Standardization is the process of establishing basic product specifications for commonly used characteristics of size, shape, and performance. The use of standard components and material is more economical than the use of nonstandard components and materials.

In designing finished goods, standard components should be designated wherever practical. Standardization reduces the kinds, types, and sizes of raw materials and components which have to be purchased, fabricated, and inventoried. Large quantities of the required sizes can be purchased or fabricated at lower cost, through quantity discounts or larger production runs. In addition, fewer blueprints, books, and manufacturing instructions are required.

Disadvantages

Standardization programs do have some disadvantages. In some cases, a part may be easier to install and more effective in operation even though it may be more expensive to purchase. Another disadvantage of standard parts is that they may inhibit progress. Attempts may be made to standardize parts too soon, before an effective design has been developed. Sometimes established standards present an obstacle to change; yet improvements must be made if progress is to continue.

Standardization Programs

A number of standardization programs have been established outside the individual firm. Often, standards have been enacted into law for safety and health reasons. Examples are automobile seat belts and windshield safety glass. In some cases, codes have been established to regulate electric wiring, plumbing, and other types of construction activity. In any of these, standards have been established through the cooperation of industry members via sponsorship of industrywide or professional associations or government agencies.

Self-imposed industrywide standardization programs are sometimes only partially successful. Standardization programs tend to favor the larger companies which, because of the quantities produced, tend to realize the greater benefits. The smaller firms which cannot afford the high costs of their larger competition may offer nonstandard models at a slightly higher cost, thus undercutting the initial purpose of the industrywide standardization program.

Project Organization

The heart of the standardization program rests with engineering design. It designs new products from information supplied by other sources and should make a continued effort to use standard components.

The sales department should continually monitor sales activity and recommend the discontinuance of items that fail to generate sufficient sales. Sales should work closely with engineering design in the development of new products which may not be standardized in final appearance but could be made from standard components. Finally, the sales department should continually review existing designs to ensure that existing models and sizes do not proliferate and that existing models are continually improved.

The materials management department should supply engineering design with information on slow-moving materials and components which are likely candidates for elimination and possibly could be utilized in a future design or a revision of a design.

PART-NUMBERING SYSTEMS

The choice of the proper part-numbering system not only establishes a code for identifying the item but also facilitates the processing of data on modern electronic computers. The establishment of part numbers should take into consideration the following elements: expandability of categories, flexibility for new items on file, ability to be sorted into required categories or fields, minimum number of characters consistent with overall company requirements, and convenience of assignment.

There is a large reliance on the assignment of proper part numbers in electronic data processing. The overall operating efficiency of such systems may be directly related to a good or bad part-numbering system.

Types

A part number is any number which uniquely identifies a component. In many instances, products and raw materials are also assigned numbers loosely referred to as part numbers.

There are essentially three types of part-numbering systems:

1. *Significant:* All characters in the numbering system are significant, i.e., represent a dimension, type of material, color, or some other factor.

2. *Semisignificant:* Some of the characters in the numbering system are significant; the balance are not and do not represent a group or other factors.

3. *Nonsignificant:* None of the numbers assigned have any significance. There are no classifications of groups in the part number. Classifications of groups would have to be accomplished by use of a commodity code or some other coding scheme.

Typically, significant part numbers are considerably longer than nonsignificant numbers.

The selection of a numbering system is generally governed by the type and variety of products produced. In some companies where there is a limited product line or where classification is vital, it may be practical to use a fully significant part-numbering system.

As an example, assume that a company producing tubing allows two or three digits to identify the material, and the remaining portion of the part number defines inside and outside diameters and the length of the item. If the tubing manufacturer expands its product line into various shapes (such as squares, oblongs, or rods) and adds various threadings or punchings, clearly these new conditions could strain even the best significant part-numbering system.

The following reasons indicate the practicality of using a nonsignificant part-numbering system:

1. A nonsignificant system functions independently of classifications and standards. Any or all may be updated, revised, or changed, as circumstances dictate.

2. A nonsignificant numbering system of any group of digits can identify more parts with greater flexibility than any significant system.

3. A single nonsignificant system can cover all types of numbering, including standard hardware and all product classes, whereas a significant system could possibly cause duplication.

4. Sheer volume alone defeats the prime advantage of a significant system—operating people memorizing the meanings of the part numbers.

5. A nonsignificant system cannot run out of numbers or break down through diversification of new products, sizes, finishes, materials, etc.

A compromise between a significant and a nonsignificant part number could be the use of a semisignificant part-numbering system. If only one, two, or three digits of the part number were made significant, we would not be testing completely the five advantages of utilizing a nonsignificant system. By letting the two or three digits represent major product lines or classes of products, the assignment of other codes (e.g., commonality code) will enhance the sorting of data and preparation of summaries.

In using the semisignificant approach, we have to expand what is basically a nonsignificant number by the additional semisignificant digits. But often this cost is outweighed by its usefulness and better acceptance by the operating people of this type of system. When a limited amount of significant numbers are introduced to a system to cater to a particular need, care must be taken not to open the door to a rash of additional suffixes, prefixes, letters, etc., which would tend to contradict the worth of this system and would lead back to an unwieldy significant number with all its inherent deficiencies.

Once a particular part-numbering system is chosen, care should be taken that the procedures governing its use are clear, concise, and enforced. The administration of the system should rest with one group to preclude any chance of error. If part numbers need to be assigned at remote locations, the administrating group could assign a block, insisting on proper feedback for the maintenance of the central control.

SUMMARY

The continuing evaluation of sophisticated manufacturing control systems makes the design and maintenance of product and process information a vital factor in the operation of the business. Although the materials management department does not create the data base, it cannot successfully fulfill its mission without this information. However, the materials management department normally has the responsibility for setting such things as order-policy codes, purchased lead times, lot sizes, etc.

It is imperative that materials management coordinate the introduction of new-product releases and engineering changes with the various engineering departments. Also they must take steps to ensure the integrity of the data base. To achieve all this, materials management must establish a harmonious and close working relationship with not only engineering and industrial engineering, but also with the entire manufacturing function.

BIBLIOGRAPHY

American Production and Inventory Control Society, Inc.: *25th Annual Conference Proceedings*, Falls Church, Va., 1982.

————: *APICS Dictionary*, Falls Church, Va., 1984.

Carson, Gordon B., Harold A. Bolz, and Hewitt H. Young: *Production Handbook*, Wiley, New York, 1972.

Deis, Paul: *Production and Inventory Management in the Technological Age*, Prentice-Hall, Englewood Cliffs, N.J., 1983.

Garwood, Dave: *How to Successfully Structure Bills of Material*, R. D. Garwood, Atlanta.

Guess, Vincent C.: *Engineering the Missing Link in MRP*, Vanard Lithographs, San Diego, 1979.

Janson, Robert L.: *Production Control Deskbook*, Prentice-Hall, Englewood Cliffs, N.J., 1975.

Mather, Hal: *Bills of Materials—Recipes and Formulations*, Wright Publishing Company, Atlanta, 1982.

11

Manpower Information*

Editor

HENRY H. JORDAN, Jr., CMC, CFPIM, Managing Partner, Consulting Services Incorporated, Stone Mountain, Georgia

Assistant Editor

HENRY H. JORDAN III, CMC, CFPIM, Executive Director, Center for Inventory Management, Stone Mountain, Georgia

Contributors

J. THOMAS BROWN, CFPIM, Senior Marketing Manager, Manufacturing Systems, Burroughs Corporation, Roswell, Georgia

JOSEPH A. CARRANO, Assistant Vice President—Distribution, New York City Transit Authority, New York

WILLARD R. HAZEL, Manager, Systems and Programming, Potter & Brumfield, Princeton, Indiana

ERNEST C. THEISEN, Jr., CFPIM, Director of Materials, Micromeritics, Stone Mountain, Georgia

ROBERT W. WHITTAKER, Senior Vice President and General Manager, Steel Heddle Manufacturing Company, Greenville, South Carolina

*The editors wish to acknowledge the contributors to the original version of this chapter: W. Neil Benton, Richard B. Black, Walter Cloud, Dr. Robert C. Klekamp, J. Clifford Kulick, Leo A. Smith, David D. Swett, and Dennis B. Webster.

MANPOWER INFORMATION

A key factor in the success or failure of the manufacturing operation is the planning and control of manpower. It is certainly as important as having the right parts at the right time.

Master Production Schedule

Proper planning and control of manpower needs begin with the master production schedule (MPS) (see Fig 11.1), which quantifies the products to be manufactured during specific time periods to meet the demands of customers. Through the use of time standards or historical profiles, the time-phased units of measure for each product are converted to man-hours or some equivalent meaningful factor for calculating manpower requirements.

Numerous factors directly or indirectly affect the development of the MPS and cannot be ignored if manpower planning and control is to be handled properly. These factors are shown in Fig. 11.2, along with the actions that follow as a result of the MPS.

Manpower Capacity

The term *capacity* by itself can be misleading. In fact, calculations of available capacity and required capacity must be made in manpower planning. *Available capacity* indicates the current availability of such resources as manpower, equipment, and facilities under normal operating conditions. *Required capacity* refers to the capacity needed to meet company goals of optimum customer service, inventory levels, and manufacturing efficiency in light of customer order/forecast requirements. Logically, required capacity is calculated first and then compared with available capacity to determine whether the latter should be, and can be, adjusted to meet the forecasted demand.

In most companies, available manpower capacity is somewhat flexible because new hires assigned to open work stations or equipment can increase capacity while layoffs or departmental transfers can decrease capacity. In fact, many options are available to adjust manpower capacity:

- Working overtime
- Adding a second or third shift
- Hiring new employees
- Laying off employees
- Reducing the workweek
- Adding new equipment
- Increasing subcontracting
- Reducing subcontracting
- Improving production methods

Successful manpower planning and control must also take into account the learning curve, the effect of adding new hires, quality of workers already in place, fatigue factor caused by working longer hours for extended periods, deteriorating equipment, etc.

	Weeks							
Product	1	2	3	4	5	6	7	8
A 2001	20	20	20	20	20	20	20	20
B 1742	100		100		100		100	
C 4019	1500	1500	1500	1600	1600	1600	1700	1700
D 6730			10			10		

FIG. 11.1   Master schedule.

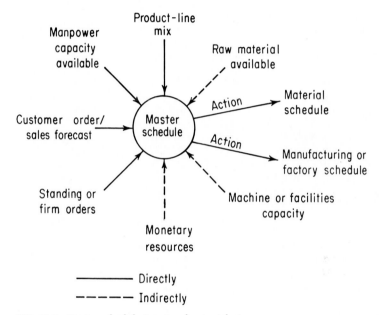

FIG. 11.2   Master schedule input and output factors.

Customer Order/Sales Forecast

In those companies with large customer order backlogs, the development of an MPS and resultant manpower plan is eased somewhat because they are not subjected to the vagaries of forecasting.

When manpower planning is based on a forecast, in lieu of firm customer orders, it is important that the planning team understand forecasting techniques and their differing degrees of accuracy. Usually, by testing various techniques against historical demand, forecasting methods can be selected that give the "least wrong" results, thus minimizing the actual demand surprises which can force replanning of manpower requirements. Various forecast techniques are discussed elsewhere in this book.

Cyclical and Seasonal Considerations

Cyclical or seasonal sales patterns present a different challenge to manpower planning and control. A management decision must be made between a relatively stable workforce accompanied by fluctuating inventory levels and a fluctuating workforce with relatively fixed inventory levels. These decisions are usually dictated by the skill levels required to manufacture the product and the availability of workers with the corresponding skill levels in the communities surrounding the manufacturing facility.

Figure 11.3 shows an example of a level manpower plan versus a seasonal sales forecast. Production planned on the leveling method minimizes manpower fluctuations but accentuates inventory accumulation, as shown by the crosshatched area. The minimum manpower cost resulting from a constant level of production must be balanced against the increased cost of carrying inventory during the periods of slack customer demand.

Figure 11.4 illustrates a situation in which a trained labor force is readily available, or the labor skill required is low, resulting in low training costs. The planned production level is changed in a step manner to closely anticipate customer demand. An addition to the workforce would result in increased production; conversely, each decline would be accomplished via layoffs, shorter workweeks, or other decreases in available manpower capacity.

Some companies with the highly skilled labor needed to fabricate component parts and the easily available semiskilled labor used in assembly of the final product use both methods of manpower planning in a seasonal or cyclical environment. The skilled manpower is planned at the level rate, building up the less expensive component inventory during the off season, while the semiskilled labor fluctuates closer to the customer's demand for the finished product, thus keeping this more expensive level of inventory relatively low.

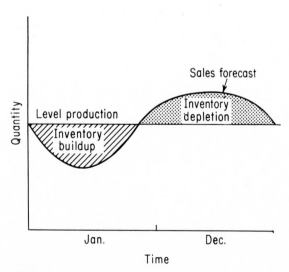

FIG. 11.3 Level workforce.

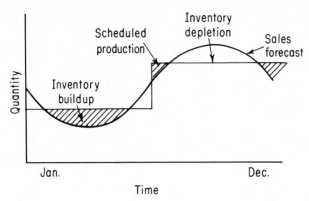

FIG. 11.4 Variable workforce.

Product-Line Mix

Variations in demand for different product lines made in the same plant must be taken into account in the manpower planning process. Variations to consider include skill levels needed to manufacture, material content, size of the product, high versus low volume, and contribution to profit. It is often necessary to regard each product line in the mix as a separate entity and to plan accordingly.

The problem of product mix is accentuated when the customer order/forecast demands more capacity than can be made available. For example, suppose product line A demands 60 percent of the available capacity; product line B, 30 percent; and product line C, 35 percent. Then current capacity has to be increased by 25 percent. If after all methods have been used to expand capacity, such as overtime, additional shifts, adding people, subcontracting, etc., there is still a shortfall of capacity, then the alternative is to delay or stretch out customer order/forecast requirements and quote longer lead times to customers. It might be feasible to load the available capacity with the higher-profit product lines and to fill out the balance with product lines in descending order of profit contribution. However, customer satisfaction and future product potential must be carefully weighed when this decision is made.

Standing Orders, or Firm Business

Many companies are fortunate to have firm customer orders covering long periods in the manufacturing cycle. This firm business, sometimes called *standing orders*, enables planners to assign manpower on a continuing basis to a core of work that is relatively permanent. This enables planning for a basically permanent workforce to handle the firm business, with the concentration of manpower planning performed on the other-than-firm segment of the business. Surges in the latter category are handled via overtime, temporary hires, additional shifts, etc.

Control of Manpower

To control manpower requires monitoring, measuring, and comparing it with the manpower plan created earlier. Just as sales demand will vary around the manpower plan, so will production vary around the manpower plan. A certain amount of variation is considered normal, so it is wise to establish tolerances, or plus-and-minus ranges within which no change in manpower planning would be required. Any deviation from these predetermined ranges would trigger replanning via overtime, layoffs, etc. Inherent in planning is the necessity to predict and prepare a manpower plan under conditions of great uncertainty. Successful control requires corrective action be taken as soon as possible when actual conditions fall outside the tolerances of the manpower plan. Numerous methods of reporting and measuring are used to compare actual performance against the plan. As part of an overall management information system, reports should be developed showing the number of employees, number of absentees, frequency of absenteeism, layoffs, transfers, new hires, types of skills, and skill levels.

Measures of productivity efficiency indicate output per unit of manpower. Measurement might be in dollars or units of output per man-hour, man-day, etc. Other useful ratios are the number of direct to indirect man-hours, direct labor man-hours to idle man-hours, direct labor man-hours to machine-hours, overtime hours to straight-time hours, piece-rate workers to day workers. Each ratio measures actual performance against the plan, to trigger corrective action and bring results back to the planned norms. Without this type of comparison there would be no knowledge of either efficent or inefficient use of manpower.

Long-Range Manpower Planning

Although most manpower planning is relatively short-range, as compared to facilities planning, there is an important need for periodic long-range planning. This need is apparent where the demand for skilled labor is projected to increase but the available supply is constant or decreasing. This situation might require upgrading existing manpower through various training programs, such as apprentice programs to supply skilled toolmakers or machinists, formal on-the-job training programs, technical-school sessions, tuition-refund plans for technical training courses, etc. Attention to long-range manpower planning might dictate the relocation of a plant to an area with a surplus of the labor type required. Long-range manpower planning should be part and parcel of any company's projections which are greater than a year into the future.

MANPOWER LOADING

Manpower loading, also called *labor loading*, is a process which compares expected labor requirements with the available capacity of that labor. Many techniques are used in manpower loading but all perform three basic functions:

1. Estimate the manpower resources required to accomplish a specific production schedule. This production schedule may be a long-range production plan, a medium-range MPS, or a short-range schedule of manufacturing operations.
2. Project the manpower resources that will be available to meet the production schedule. This projection of manpower availability must span the time horizon stated in the production schedule and must include the labor skills specified in the requirements definition.

3. Provide visibility of current or anticipated imbalances between labor requirements and capacity. These imbalances are analyzed, and actions are planned to
match labor resource availability and labor requirements for each period.

This process may seem familiar. It is just one of the forms of capacity or resource
management. It is different from other forms of capacity management in that it
specifically addresses only manpower capacity. The focus on manpower resources
in managing capacity is necessary because people are the most important resource.

Effective management of the production process requires a knowledge of what
labor skills are needed, how much labor is required to meet production objectives,
when that labor is needed, and how much of the needed labor skills will be
available. The techniques of manpower loading are used to assist the capacity
planner in answering these questions, arriving at a sound manpower plan, and
monitoring operations to ensure successful execution of the plan.

Manpower versus Machine Capacity

Managing the capacity of a manufacturing process requires that both labor and
machine resources be considered. Obviously each is essential for production.
Manpower capacity should be adequate to support the planned rate of production
and should be balanced with the capacity of the equipment resources. A commonly
used technique for simplifying this procedure is to group as many machines and
operators as possible into work centers. Through this technique, the work center is
viewed as a single man-machine capacity unit. The work center serves as a resource
load center where the required production is converted into the required work
hours. The assumption for manpower loading is that manpower load hours are the
same as work center load hours. This approach of using work centers to load
manpower requirements works well in most direct labor situations; however, some
exceptions must be considered when this approach is used.

It is important to provide the capability to change the capacity of the work center
in the future. The capacity of a work center may increase or decrease depending on a
number of variables. Many production processes allow for changes in overall
capacity by changing the utilization of manpower resources while maintaining a
constant level of machine capacity. In this situation the work center's capacity is a
function of manpower assignment, and the manpower loading system should provide effective data indicating when a change in manpower capacity is to occur.

The process of combining resources into work centers assumes that all machines
and personnel in the group are interchangeable with respect to work assignments.
Each is assumed capable of performing any job and at approximately the same rate.
This assumption can cause problems in both machine and manpower loading. If a
particular job requires a specialized machine or a worker with an advanced skill
level, this job should be loaded to a special work center designated for this purpose.
This allows special jobs to be handled by exception without having to load each
individual machine or labor skill level separately.

Manpower and Machine Data

The proper selection and definition of work centers for manpower and machine
loading is crucial. The following three-step procedure identifies those factors
which indicate logical work center groups and define the work center's manpower
and machine capacity.

Step 1. Identify the important resource attributes.

	Manpower	*Machine*
Resource function	Labor type	Machine type
	Operator	Drill
	Setup	Mill
	Inspector	Grinder
Resource rating	Skill level or grade	Size or speed
Alternate resource	Skill level or grade	Machine or work center

Step 2. Specify relationships between scheduled items and productive resources.

	Manpower	*Machine*
Standard times	Setup labor hours	Setup machine hours
	Labor time per unit	Machine time per unit
	Teardown labor hours	Teardown labor hours
Planned allowances	Fatigue	Adjustments
	Delay	Tooling changes
Efficiency Factor	*Labor Efficiency*	*Machine Efficiency*
Actual performance versus standard times	Standard labor hours produced per hour worked	Standard machine hours produced per hour worked

Step 3. Estimate actual resources available in future periods.

	Manpower	*Machine*
Gains/losses	Hiring/layoff plans	Purchase plans
	Training plans	Rebuild plans
	Turnover percentage	Divestiture plans
Availability	Absentee rate	Repair downtime
	Holidays/vacations	Preventive maintenance
	Training/administrative time	Fuel/power shortage
Utilization Factor	*Labor Utilization*	*Machine Utilization*
Actual time worked versus scheduled	Production hours worked per hour scheduled	Hours operated per hour scheduled

Planning the Load

Many techniques can be used to project manpower requirements. The selection of the proper technique depends on the time horizon of the manpower plans being made and data availability. Three of the most commonly used techniques for manpower loading are presented here. This is, by no means, a complete list of all the techniques that have been successfully applied. However, most manpower loading techniques employ variations of the examples shown here.

Rough-Cut Manpower Loading

This technique, abbreviated RCML, is used to provide early warning of long-range labor imbalances. It is not a technique for detailed manpower planning. RCML verifies that adequate levels of the critical labor resources are available. RCMP is accomplished by converting the production plan or MPS to labor requirements by use of a bill of labor.

A *bill of labor*, shown in Table 11.1, is a statement of the key labor resources required to manufacture a fixed number of units of a specific item or a given mix of a family of items. The last column in the bill of labor shows the month in the production process during which that labor activity will most likely take place. The calculation of average standard hours used for a product group is typically accomplished by a weighted-average technique. This technique is demonstrated for assembly labor in Table 11.2. This product group is composed of four items whose projected product mix and standard hours are used to find the average standard for each labor type.

The RCML plan is developed by multiplying the MPS quantities for each product group and the labor standards listed in the bill of labor. An example of an RCML plan for assembly labor, Table 11.3, shows the requirements for this labor type for each product group by monthly period, the total labor required, the projected labor available, and the projected difference between requirements and availability.

Capacity-Requirements Planning

Capacity-requirements planning (CRP) is a detailed, analytical approach for medium- to short-range capacity planning. It is as valuable as a manpower loading technique as it is for machine loading. The long-range, rough-cut manpower plans are not detailed enough to support the decisions which must be made concerning work assignments, the use of overtime, or reduction of shift hours. The distinguishing feature of CRP, then, is its attention to detail. Each item, including all subassemblies and component parts, is "backward-scheduled," and the required load is placed on the appropriate work centers in the proper time period.

TABLE 11.1 Bill of Labor, Product Group A

	Average Standard Hours per 100 Units	Month
Design engineers	10.8	1
N/C programmers	6.5	2
Machinists	30.0	3
Welders	12.2	3
Assembly	24.7	4

TABLE 11.2 Assembly Labor, Product Group A

Item	Product Mix (A)	Standard Assembly Hours per 100 Units (B)	A × B
1	0.20	27.6	5.52
2	0.13	31.4	4.08
3	0.42	21.3	8.95
4	0.25	24.6	6.15
	1.00		24.70

TABLE 11.3 Rough-Cut Manpower Load Plan, for Assembly Labor

	January	February	March
MPS			
Product group A	14,400	17,000	15,000
Product group B	9,100	13,000	9,400
Manpower load hours			
Product group A	3,557	4,199	3,705
Product group B	1,911	2,730	1,974
Total	5,468	6,929	5,679
Available labor hours	6,350	6,000	6,100
Variance	+882	−929	+421

Because of the detail involved, CRP is rarely performed manually. Generally CRP begins with the material-requirements planning (MRP) system output and loads the work centers shown in the routing file without considering capacity constraints (infinite loading). The load is assigned to the appropriate time period based on a calculated operation time for the lot and standard queue and transit times for the work center. The data required for this process come from the detail plant schedule or MRP, the routing file for each part, and the work center file for each load center. The output of CRP is a work center load profile which shows the load, time period, and source of that load.

Regression Analysis

In job shops where each part is engineered and produced to customer specification, it may be difficult to estimate labor requirements because of the variety of parts produced and the absence of historical data on a specific part. In fact, it is often necessary to estimate manpower requirements before the engineering department has completed the design process.

The experience gained in the past on parts with similar characteristics may be used to estimate requirements for a new part. This is done by using a technique known as *multiple linear regression*. By examining a representative sample of parts produced in the past, each with varying dimensions and characteristics, an estimating formula can be derived by using regression analysis that predicts the labor required to perform the major manufacturing operations. For example, a statistically significant relationship may be found that links four part variables X_i to the time Y needed for a drilling operation.

$$Y = T_0 + T_1X_1 + T_2X_2 + T_3X_3 + T_4X_4$$

where X_1 = alloy type code
X_2 = largest diameter
X_3 = number of holes
X_4 = weight of part

Multiple linear regression is used to derive estimates for the coefficients T_i, to verify statistically the validity of the variables and the overall predicting equation, and to estimate the range of expected errors.

Analyzing the Load

The steps in manpower loading covered thus far involve selecting appropriate capacity load centers, obtaining the necessary capacity data to define required and available capacity, and using these data with a production schedule to calculate the load on manpower resources. The next step in manpower loading is to compare the manpower capacity required with available resources. The imbalances must be analyzed to determine what actions need to be taken.

Graphing Techniques

The actual comparison of available manpower capacity to required capacity is best accomplished by using graphing techniques. In analyzing load problems, a picture is worth 1000 words and probably 10,000 numbers. The use of graphs makes analyzing the load easier, quicker, and more accurate because the planner can recognize the particular problem and separate true capacity problems from random variations. The particular technique used is not important. Some prefer bar charts while others favor line chart representations. The important point is to use some form of graph to assist in seeing the true load problems.

Period versus Cumulative Loading

When a manpower load profile such as the one shown in Table 11.4 is analyzed, two basic questions must be answered: What are the capacity imbalances for each period? What is the total imbalance for all periods? Random fluctuations in load often create what appear to be serious problems.

On closer comparison of the cumulative capacity required versus that available in the example, the analyst observes that the level of manpower resources is actually well matched to the total requirements. The random variations in load can be smoothed by a modification to the schedule if necessary.

The best method for analyzing manpower is to use graphs for both cumulative and noncumulative loading. The two graphs in Figs. 11.5 and 11.6 illustrate this point. The first is a bar chart for the data previously presented in the load profile table for work center 760. Note in the first graph the magnitude of the load imbalances by time period. Obviously, the required hours in periods 29 and 32 exceed available capacity, and a rescheduling of at least part of this overload to periods 28, 30, and 31 is indicated. The second graph, which shows the cumulative load, indicates that there is no need for additional manpower since the total available additional manpower capacity is adequate.

TABLE 11.4 Load Profile for Work Center 760

		Week Number				
	Past Due	28	29	30	31	32
Required man hours	80	245	449	273	208	537
Available man hours	0	360	360	360	360	360
Variation	+80	−115	+89	−87	−152	+177
Cumulative variation	+80	−35	+54	−33	−185	−8

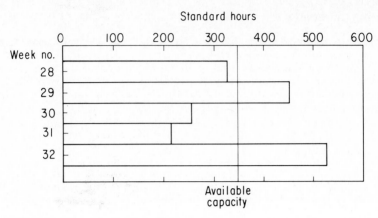

FIG. 11.5 Manpower load profile.

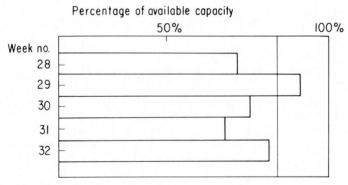

FIG. 11.6 Cumulative manpower load profile.

Manpower Load Control

Earlier we discussed the techniques of loading used in developing the manpower plan. The next step is to establish acceptable input and output performance ranges, to measure actual load inputs and outputs, and to take corrective actions when the limits are exceeded.

Input/output control uses the manpower load plan to determine the average load expected to arrive (input) and the load expected to be completed (output) at each work center for each time period in the short range. For manpower control the units used to measure input and output are standard man-hours.

Tolerance limits are set for acceptable variations in inputs and outputs by considering the degree of uncertainty (scrap, machine failures, etc.) in the manufacturing process. A statistical investigation of queue lengths can be an extremely valuable method for both setting planned queue lengths and determining the degree of variation considered as normal random occurrences. Actual queue lengths are monitored, and order releases are timed to keep queue lengths within established limits.

An input/output report is shown in Table 11.5. This report shows a situation in which the input to work center 124 is within the established tolerance limits. However, the output level is far below the planned level. The cumulative deviation of the actual to planned output is 34 standard labor hours, and the control limit is set at 25. The cause of this problem lies within work center 124, and corrective actions are needed to get the queue back into control and the actual output up to an acceptable level.

Direct and Indirect Labor

Most methods of manpower loading deal almost exclusively with direct labor. However, the amount of indirect labor used in many manufacturing operations is very significant, and because of increased automation, the trend is toward increased levels of indirect labor personnel. Good manpower management today must deal with planning and controlling indirect labor.

The most widely used method for indirect labor loading is known as *ratio-trend analysis*. In this method, the historical ratio between the number of direct and indirect workers in a plant or department is studied. A forecast of the future ratio is made that makes allowances for changes in organization or methods. In Table 11.6 the forecast of 320, 280, and 270 direct production employees was derived by using the RCML techniques previously described. The inspector forecasts of 36, 33, and 34, respectively, were computed by applying the forecast ratio to the direct production employee forecasts. This technique, although crude, is easy to understand and use.

A more analytical approach requires a study of all indirect labor jobs and the factors that affect them. The number of floor sweepers, for instance, is determined by the floor area to be cleaned, not by the level of production or the number of direct labor employees. The number of security guards required is a function of the number of unmanned shifts and the area to be patrolled.

When the number of indirect labor employees involved is small, note that the need for additional personnel is a step function. An example of this step-function behavior illustrates this point. Suppose each material handler is assigned to cover 10 machines. Presently, five material handlers cover 48 machines. If one or two machines are added, then the current level of five personnel should be adequate to handle the additional load.

TABLE 11.5 Input/Output Report for Work Center 124 in Standard Man-Hours

Week No.	Planned Input	Actual Input	Cumulative Deviation (Tolerance +25)	Planned Output	Actual Output	Cumulative Deviation (Tolerance + 25)	Work in Process Beginning
12	100	97	−3	100	94	6	33
13	100	102	−1	100	86	20	49
14	100	96	−5	100	91	29	54
15	100	109	4	100	95	34	68
16	100			100			
17	100			100			

TABLE 11.6 Ratio-Trend Forecast—Inspectors

		No. Employees		Ratio
	Year	Production	Inspectors	Inspector:Production
Actual	−3	240	24	1:10
	−2	300	30	1:10
	−1	350	39	1:9
Forecast	Next year	320	36	1:9
	+2	280	33	1:8.5
	+3	270	34	1:8

TECHNIQUES OF WORK MEASUREMENT

To be proficient in planning and controlling production and inventory facilities, it is important to be able to schedule and evaluate plant operations. This can be accomplished only through the use of accurate time estimates. Thus it is important to know how to construct these time measurements and to realize their strengths and weaknesses.

Time estimates are used in two basic ways: for planning and evaluation. The planning estimate is used to schedule production and delivery dates, plan personnel requirements, plan for the arrival of incoming materials, and estimate costs. The evaluation estimate is used as a basis for wage-incentive plans or standard cost systems. For these reasons, the planning estimate may be called a *forecast*, and the evaluation estimate may be called a *standard*.

With all these different uses for time estimates, clearly any one measurement technique may not meet all the objectives required for each estimate. Various applications may require different accuracies in the estimates, and it is important to be able to select the tool that satisfies the intended need. However, analysis of the method should precede the application of a technique whenever it is to be used as a time standard.

A number of techniques have been developed. Methods are available that give highly accurate estimates where precision is required, and others give crude approximations where only ballpark figures are desired.

Estimates Based on Past Experience

This technique of obtaining time estimates is often used in practice but is rarely advocated in texts. Certainly, this method should not be employed unless time, resources, or needs permit no other technique to be used or unless the estimates need to be little more than approximate figures. Sometimes, however, even given these limitations, this technique may be the only way to obtain an estimate for an operation that has never been performed.

In the application of this procedure, past performances of similar jobs are often kept in the same file. Whenever an estimate of a particular task is needed, performance measures are available for reference for that or similar jobs. If a number of performance measures are available for the same task, an average or some other combination may be used, perhaps with some changes made based on modifications of other variables in the task. If there are no past records, an estimate of the time necessary for the task under consideration is often made by individuals familiar with the task, such as foremen or production personnel. Several of these people may discuss the task and arrive at a value judgment, or one individual may estimate the time.

Estimates from past experience should not be used for a critical, short-range purpose such as wage payments, but they may be very effective for highly repetitive, moderate, or long-range tasks, especially if the personnel are experienced and no better technique is available.

Stopwatch Time Study

One of the most common and accurate methods for obtaining time estimates is the stopwatch time study. Time study was originated by Frederick W. Taylor in the machine shop of Midvale Steel Company around 1881, but Ralph M. Barnes is often given credit for being a pioneer in the full development of this tool of management.

The objective of a time study is to develop a standard time for a particular task. *Standard time*, in this instance, is time (usually expressed in minutes per part) required to perform a task by a person possessing a moderate degree of skill, using a prescribed method, and working at a "normal" pace (i.e., a pace that will cause no harmful effects to the individual).

To obtain a standard time, some concept of a normal pace must exist, in order to arrive at a performance rating for the worker. In rating performance, one judges the performance as a percentage, in comparison to the expected performance of a trained individual working at the company's specified normal pace. For example, if a worker is judged to be working at only 80 percent of normal, the rating is 0.80; if the individual is working 20 percent higher than normal, the rating is 1.20. (Note, however, that the rating measures the worker's performance in terms of both speed and skill as contrasted to pace rating, which judges an individual's performance in terms of speed only.)

Also, tasks are not generally timed for a whole day, so other variables have to be considered in the estimate, such as personal needs and delays inherent in the task. The standard time allotted for a task must reflect these unavoidable delays and workers' needs that may be unrelated to the task.

The equipment used by a time-study analyst frequently consists of only a clipboard to which a decimal stopwatch and data sheets are attached. For the study, the analyst is positioned so as not to be distracting to the worker but where both the individual performing the task and the watch and board can be seen easily. Many variations in the method of conducting a time study exist (see Fig. 11.7). This is one accepted procedure:

1. Observe and record job conditions.
2. Establish the elements of the job.
3. Time the elements.
4. Determine the normal time.
5. Calculate the standard time.

Step. 1. Observe and record job conditions. The analyst should observe the job for a time and then discuss the task with both the supervisor and worker to become as familiar with the task as possible. All conditions surrounding the task should be recorded in a neat, orderly, and systematic manner, so that the job could be reconstructed if the need arose.

Study No. ___10045___　　　　STOP – WATCH OBSERVATIONS　　　Time began 1:30 Time ended 2:00
Production during study

No.	Description	R*	T	2 R	T	3 R	T	4 R	T	5 R	T	6 R	T	7 R	T	8 R	T	9 R	T	10 R	T	Ave. elem. time	Rating	Normal time	Allow	Std. time
1	Reach for assembled part and box-place box at side of paper and the part in the paper	120	03 3	100	21 4	110	38 4	100	56 3	120	74 3	100	92 3	100	12 5	100	35 3	100	52 3	80	72 4					
2	Wrap part	120	07 4	100	25 4	110	43 5	100	61 5	120	79 5	100	96 4	100	17 5	100	39 4	100	57 5	80	76 4					
3	Reach for box; Place wrapped part in individual box	120	11 4	100	29 4	110	47 4	100	64 3	120	83 4	100	99 3	100	23 6	100	43 4	100	61 4	80	79 3	Standard time – minutes/piece Foreign elements				
4	Close lid and aside individual box to carton	120	17 6	100	34 5	110	53 6	100	71 7	120	39 6	100	07 8	100	32 9	100	49 6	100	68 7	80	86 7					

	Total	Average (hundreds of minutes)	Average rating	Normal time
Element 1	3 5	35/10 = 3.50	1.03	.0361
Element 2	4 5	45/10 = 4.50	1.03	.0464
Element 3	3 9	39/10 = 3.90	1.03	.0402
Element 4	6 7	67/10 = 6.70	1.03	.0690
				.1917 total normal time

Standard time = normal time + (normal time x allowances)
minutes/part
= .1917 + (.1917 x .12)
= 0.2147 minute/part

Details of allowances —

Minimum delay	2%
Personal	4%
Fatigue	5%
Cleanup	1%
	12%

*R= rating, T= time.　　　　　　(a)

FIG. 11.7　Stopwatch observation sheet (*front*).

Step 2. Establish the elements of the job.　For repetitive tasks, the job is broken into "timetable" elements, and the elements may be described on the data sheets before the study begins. Elements should have definite beginning and ending points. Machine elements should be separated from worker-controlled elements. For nonrepetitive tasks, the job elements may be longer and not as easily anticipated as in the repetitive tasks. This may necessitate a "write as you go" type of study. Nonproductive and productive work should be separated.

Step 3. Time the elements.　A number of observations should be recorded for each element. During these observations, the analyst should judge and record the worker's performance rating. For highly repetitive tasks, one rating may apply to an entire cycle; but for long or nonrepetitive tasks, a rating is generally applied to each element studied.

This step of the procedure is a sampling technique, and as such, enough samples must be taken to represent the population. Determining the number of samples is a statistical problem, but recognized texts dealing with management or industrial engineering practices give procedures, tables, or charts which can be used to determine the number of readings required for a desired level of accuracy.

Step 4. Determine the normal time.　Depending on how the rating procedure was performed in step 3 (by element or cycle), the ratings should be multiplied by the recorded time to calculate the normal time required for the task. If a rating is given for each element, the procedure should be to first normalize each element by multiplying the element's recorded time by its rating and to then add all elements for the task, to obtain a total normal time for the task. If a rating is given for each

TIME-STUDY SHEET

Operation	Packing ball-stud scope mount		Oper. No.	46

Mach. type __None__ Mach. No. _____ Dept. __Final assembly__

Part name __Ball-stud scope mount__ Part No. __1440__ Operator __John Steele__

Study No. __10045__ Analyst __James Smith__ Date __5/20/86__

Elem No.	Left-hand description	Right-hand description	Machine element	Speed	Feed	Std. time
		Written standard practice				
1	Reach for assembled part, grasp, and return, placing part on stack of tissue paper	Reach for individual box, grasp, and return, placing box at right side of tissue paper				
2	Wrap part in paper	Using the thumb, separate two layers of the paper and wrap the part				
3	Reach, grasp, and hold box	Reach, grasp, and hold box; transfer to the left hand and release; reach and grasp part, move part to box, position and place wrapped part in box				
4	Release and return, alternately aside individual box to carton, position and place box in carton	Close lid; alternately aside individual box to carton, position, and place box in carton				

Standard production — pieces/hour		Standard time — minutes/piece	

Sketch of work place

Setup, tools, jigs, fixtures, gauges —

Legend:
1. Assembled parts in tote box
2. Individual boxes
3. Tissue paper
4. Cartons
5. Workman (seated)

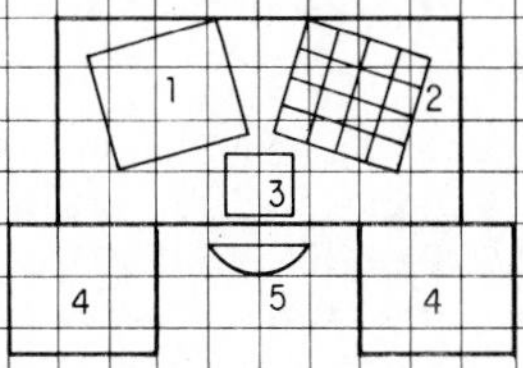

(b)

FIG. 11.7 (Back).

cycle only, add the recorded times for all elements of the task and then normalize the total recorded task time by multiplying the total recorded time by its rating.

Step 5. Determine the standard time.   By using the normal time developed in step 4, allowances (usually expressed as a percentage of normal time) for rests, personal delays, and unavoidable delays are added to increase the normal time to the standard time for the task. The standard time is the estimate that is often used for scheduling and incentive-pay plans.

To recapitulate, the method and equations used to obtain the standard time from the recorded times of a task are as follows:

1. Recorded time × rating = normal time
2. Normal time + (normal time × allowances) = standard time

Work Sampling

Work sampling, sometimes called *ratio delay*, is another method of direct observation for estimating the time to perform a task by using a sampling procedure. It can be used to develop allowances in time studies or to determine standard times for jobs.

Work sampling has the advantages over other types of work measurement of being inexpensive, requiring little training for the observers, using no timing device, collecting data in simple terms, and simultaneously including many workers and machines in the data collection process. A high degree of accuracy may be obtained by using work sampling. In fact, sometimes it may be more accurate than methods using continuous observation.

The simplest work-sampling study consists of using a number of randomly selected observations and noting whether the individual on the task under study is either working or not; if the individual is working, a judged performance index is noted. The observations, therefore, are dichotomous and follow a binomial distribution. Frequently, a normal approximation to the binomial can be used, and normal-curve tables are searched to find the required number of observations for a desired level of accuracy. Any good reference text dealing with management or industrial engineering practices gives procedures or tables and charts which explain how to calculate the required number of observations.

The standard time for a job may be calculated by

$$\text{Standard time (time units/part)} = \frac{\text{total time (time units)} \times \text{working time (percent)} \times \text{performance index (percent)}}{\text{total number of pieces produced}} + \text{allowances (time units/piece)}$$

Of the estimates needed to determine the standard time, only the percentage of working time and the performance index must be provided by the work-sampling study. The total time can be found in the company's time-card records. The total number of parts produced can be obtained from production records. Allowances are the result of company-union negotiations or past practices and are readily available.

To determine the standard time for a task, do as follows:

1. Select the task(s) to be studied. Estimate the percentage of working time that can be expected to be observed on the task, from past records, if available. For this percentage, approximate the number of observations required for the desired accuracy level.

2. Divide the working time on each task into time increments, usually minutes, and number them consecutively. Using a random-number table, select the instants that an observation should be taken by choosing random numbers that correspond to the numbered time increments over the range of working times. The period of the sampling study should be long enough to allow the workers to become accustomed to the observer's presence and so less likely to feign activity and bias the results.

3. Begin making the observations as determined in step 2. Periodically check the percentages of working and idle times, and recalculate the number of readings that should be obtained.

4. Continue to collect data until the desired number of observations has been obtained. Calculate the standard time, using the equation given.

Predetermined Motion-Time Systems

The use of predetermined motion-time systems to calculate a time estimate is one of the most refined techniques of work measurement. As opposed to the techniques of time study or standard data, the time units are basic motions of much shorter duration in a predetermined motion-time analysis.

A number of predetermined motion-time systems have been formulated since the early 1940s. They are available under such names as *methods time measurement* (MTM), *motion-time analysis* (MTA), *work factor* (WF), *motor-time standards* (MTS), *basic motion-time* (BMT), and *Maynard operation sequence technique* (MOST). Generally, for these systems the times associated with the basic motions have been normalized, but no allowances have been added.

The basic motions contained in a predetermined motion-time system are very small elements upon which extensive time data have been collected and analyzed by such techniques as time-study and motion-picture analysis. To estimate a time for a task requires that the job be synthesized from the basic motions and the times accumulated for each of the motions included. Allowances are then added to determine the standard time for the task. In this manner, the methods and times for jobs can specified even before the job is actually performed by an operator. The application of this technique necessitates the use of a well-trained analyst.

Standard Data

In the process of time-studying a number of similar tasks, it may become obvious that there are elements common to many jobs. If these elements are identical for each task, the time values obtained could be collected from all the jobs studied and averaged for a more accurate estimate than could be obtained from just the study of one task. This is exactly how standard data, or elemental times, are developed. Data on elements common to a family of jobs are gathered, from which standard times may be synthesized for other tasks containing these elements. In effect, it is a form of predetermined time system, but the elements are not as minuscule and generally are developed within the framework of one plant's operations. However, some industries, such as the metalworking industry, have developed standard data for industry-wide use.

Element types generally encountered during standard data compilation are (1) identical from job to job; (2) similar in nature, but the times vary because of differences in a particular variable (size, weight, etc.) involved in the task; and (3) times controlled by the physical or technical characteristics of the material and process.

Elements of the first type are easy to handle. To ensure that a representative time is obtained, a sufficient number are collected and averaged. Elements of the second type are a little more difficult. Sufficient studies have to be made to ascertain the relationship between the varying characteristic of the element and the performance time, so as to develop a series of time values that vary with the characteristic.

Generally elements in the third group can be calculated from physical data, such as the feeds, speeds, and depth of cut in the machining task discussed above.

Problems in Using Work Measurement Techniques for Production Control

A basic problem exists in using these methods of work measurement for production control. Except for the past-experience method, these techniques are used most often to determine standard times for incentive-pay systems. Time estimates for production control are also needed for planning and scheduling purposes. An incentive-pay system is generally set up so that an average-skill employee working at a normal pace will earn 25 to 30 percent incentive pay, i.e., will be performing the task in 25 to 30 percent less time than the standard allows. Thus if the standard time is used for scheduling purposes, the jobs will be completed, on average, in 25 to 30 percent less time than the schedule permits and will greatly increase the likelihood of creating idle time on production facilities.

Before standard times are used for scheduling, therefore, the times should be adjusted to account for this discrepancy. This can be done separately by job, if it is known who the workers will be and their average performance indices; or by department, by using an average factor to account for the differences between the standard and expected times. Sometimes, however, this difference is ignored, the attitude being that the scheduling plan is so loose that this additional error will make little difference in the plan's overall effectiveness.

PRODUCTION PROGRESS FUNCTION

Anyone who has observed a repetitive task, whether it was simple, involving the performance of only a few operations, or complex, requiring many operations, probably noted the improved proficiency as frequency increased. That is, the operator has "learned" the task as he gained experience with it. The scale on which task proficiency was measured might have been based on any number of criteria, such as time to perform the task, accuracy of performing the task, or cost of performing the task. Nevertheless, the relationship between the proficiency measure and the number of times the task was performed probably appeared as shown in Fig. 11.8. In the typical learning curve, task proficiency is shown to be low initially, to increase rapidly as the task is repeated the first few times, and to continue to increase but at a slower and slower rate as the number of repetitions becomes greater. So the learning curve is typically exponential and can be represented by

$$Y = KX^n$$

where Y = proficiency measure
K = constant
X = cumulative number of task repetitions
n = exponent of curve

The phenomenon of the learning curve is familiar to individuals within the production planning and control organization concerned with the management of direct labor. It has long been recognized that human learning must be accounted for

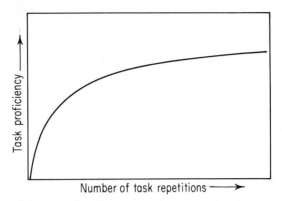

FIG. 11.8 Typical learning curve.

in setting time standards for manual operations, and a new employee should not be assigned to a paced task where the pace has been based on fully learned performance.

Human learning is not the only type of learning that should concern the production planning and control organization, however, because production processes, in the aggregate, also are subject to learning. Just as human performance tends to improve as individuals repeat tasks, so the performance of complete production processes tends to show improvement as time passes and manufacturing continues. This process improvement manifests itself as a decrease in the number of man-hours required to produce a unit of product. Although a large part of the improvement is the result of direct labor learning, a significant contribution to the total is made by improvement in supporting operations. For this reason, when reference is made to total-process learning, the phenomenon is sometimes called the *time-reduction curve, experience curve, startup curve, production progress function,* and *production-acceleration curve.*

A number of factors contribute to the ability of a manufacturing process to improve. If prior to production a large amount of effective engineering effort is expended on the problems of product design, tooling and equipment selection, work-method design, and personnel selection and training, then the opportunity for learning, or improvement, is reduced. Once production has begun, advances in the state of the art, tooling and work-method changes, quality improvements (resulting in less scrap, rework, and inspection), effective work-simplification programs, and human performance learning will all enhance process improvement. It is imperative that individuals using the production-acceleration curve as a planning tool understand that many factors contribute to the improvement.

Development of the Curve

The production progress function was first used for production planning in the airframe industry during the 1940s. The form of the equation used to model the improvement phenomenon was a negative exponential rather than the positive one given above, since the variable of interest was the number of man-hours required to produce each airframe. A variation of the original model commonly used today is

$$Y = KX^{-n}$$

where Y = cumulative average man-hours per unit after X units have been produced

   K = number of man-hours required to build first unit

   X = cumulative number of units produced

   n = exponent of curve

A typical curve is plotted in Fig. 11.9. Note that in some applications of the progress function Y is defined as the actual number of man-hours required to build a unit after X units have been produced, rather than the cumulative average man-hours per unit. The definition of Y which should be used in a particular situation depends on the situation itself. Cumulative average man-hours are used here since its use is perhaps most common.

The model describes constant percentage reduction. Each time the cumulative production is increased by a constant percentage, the cumulative average man-hours per unit are decreased by a constant percentage. This characteristic can be illustrated as follows. Take any two points in production, say X_1 and X_2, where X_2 is greater than X_1. Define the ratio of X_2 to X_1 as the production ratio, and call this quantity C. Application of the model indicates that the cumulative average man-hours per unit at X_1 are $Y_1 = KX_1^{-n}$ and similarly at X_2 it is $Y_2 = KX_2^{-n}$. Next form the ratio of Y_2 to Y_1:

$$\frac{Y_2}{Y_1} = \frac{KX_2^{-n}}{KX_1^{-n}} = \frac{X_2^{-n}}{X_1^{-n}} = \left(\frac{X_2}{X_1}\right)^{-n} = C^{-n}$$

Since Y_2 is less than Y_1, the quantity C^{-n} lies between 0 and 1. Rearranging the previous equation gives $Y_2 = Y_1 C^{-n}$.

From this we see that if the production ratio between any two points in production is a constant C, then the cumulative average man-hours per unit at the second point will be a constant percentage C^{-n} of what it was at the first point.

In practice, the production ratio usually is $C = 2$. Thus each time production is doubled, the cumulative average man-hours per unit are reduced to 2^{-n} percent of the previous value. Values of the exponent n for various percentage curves can be

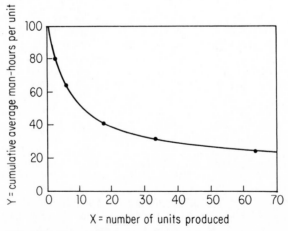

FIG. 11.9   The production progress function.

calculated quickly. For example, if the cumulative average time was reduced to 80 percent of its previous figure when production doubled, then $Y_2 = Y_1(0.80)$ or $C^{-n} = 0.80$. Since $C = 2$, thus $2^{-n} = 0.80$ and n is easily found to be 0.322. Values of n for several learning percentages are presented below for ready reference. Note that a learning percentage of P percent implies that when production doubles, the cumulative average man-hours per unit are reduced *to* P percent of the initial value, not reduced *by* P percent.

Learning percentage	n
95	0.074
90	0.152
85	0.234
80	0.322
75	0.415
70	0.515
65	0.622

The value of the constant K is defined as the number of man-hours required to manufacture the first production unit. This result is obtained in the following manner. Let Y_1 equal the cumulative average man-hours per unit after the first unit has been reproduced, that is, at $X = 1$. Note that the cumulative average time is equal to the unit production time when only 1 unit has been produced. Application of the model illustrates that K is equal to Y_1, which is the unit production time of the first unit.

$$Y = KX^{-n}$$

$$Y_1 = K(1)^{-n} = K$$

Example

The production progress function can be applied in the following situation. A firm has recently accepted a contract to build twenty 35-ft boats for a sport fishing charter outfit operating throughout the Caribbean. The first two boats have been completed, taking 7000 and 4900 man-hours, respectively. Estimate how many man-hours will be required to produce all 20 boats and how many boats will be completed before the man-hour requirement per boat is 3000 hr or less.

In approaching this problem, first determine the percentage learning in effect in order to know what value of the exponent n to use in the progress function equation. Since production has doubled from unit 1 to 2, the correct learning percentage can be determined by forming the ratio for the cumulative average time at unit 2 to the cumulative average time at unit 1:

Y_1 = cumulative average time at first unit = 7000 man-hours

and

Y_2 = cumulative average time after second unit = $(7000 + 4900)/2$
= 5950 man-hours

so

$$\frac{Y_2}{Y_1} = \frac{5950}{7000} = 0.85$$

Thus the cumulative average time after unit 2 has been produced is 85 percent of what it was at unit 1, and the correct value of n is found in the table to be 0.234.

Now the total number of man-hours required for all 20 boats can be estimated. The total time required at any point in production is equal to the cumulative average time at that point multiplied by the number of units produced. Thus

$$\begin{aligned} T &= \text{total time} = YX \\ &= (KX^{-n})(X) \\ &= KX^{1-n} \end{aligned}$$

So the total time for all 20 boats is

$$\begin{aligned} T &= \text{time for 20 boats} = K(20^{1-n}) \\ &= 7000(20^{0.766}) \end{aligned}$$

This equation can be solved directly if a scientific calculator is available or by converting to logarithms. Solution by logarithms is used here:

$$\begin{aligned} T &= KX^{1-n} \\ \log T &= \log K + (1-n)(\log X) \\ &= \log 7000 + 0.766 \log 20 \\ &= 3.84510 + 0.766(1.30103) \\ &= 3.84510 + 0.99659 \\ &= 4.84169 \\ T &= 69{,}454 \text{ man-hours} \end{aligned}$$

To find the production unit on which the time per boat goes below 3000 man-hours, we again use the total-time equation. The unit time for any particular unit X can be found by subtracting the total time at unit $X-1$ from the total time at unit X. That is, unit time for $X = T_X - T_{X-1}$. To find the point in production where the unit time is equal to some specified number of hours, in this case 3000, we first guess at the point and then make successive unit-time calculations until the desired point in production is reached. This procedure is shown here, where the initial guess was that the unit time would be less than or equal to 3000 hr on unit 12:

$$T = KX^{1-n} = 7000X^{0.766}$$

Unit No.	Total Time	Difference = Unit Time
11	43,934	—
12	46,962	3028
13	49,932	2970

Thus the unit time goes below 3000 man-hours on unit 13.

To get a close initial guess, take the first derivative of T with respect to X and solve for the value of X for which the derivative is equal to the desired number of hours. For the current example, the calculations would be

$$\frac{dT}{dX} = (1 - n)KX^{-n}$$

$$= \text{estimate of man-hours required per unit}$$
$$3000 = (1 - 0.234)(7000)(X^{-n})$$
$$= (0.766)(7000)(X^{-n})$$
$$= 5362(X^{-n})$$
$$\log 3000 = \log 5362 - 0.234 \log X$$
$$3.47712 = 3.72933 - 0.234 \log X$$
$$\log X = \frac{3.47712 - 3.72933}{-0.234}$$
$$= 1.07782$$
$$X = 11.96 = 12$$

This method does not give an exact answer because X is a discrete rather than a continuous variable. But it becomes an increasingly better estimate as X increases, since the progress curve becomes flatter with increasing X.

This example demonstrates the type of planning information that can be obtained through application of the production progress function. Such information can be useful in scheduling production, estimating delivery dates and production budgets, and performing break-even analyses and estimating man-hour requirements. The user may wish to actually draw the progress curve for the particular process for ready reference. This can be done rather quickly by calculating a few points on the curve and drawing the curve through these points:

Point in Production	Cumulative Average Man-Hours
Unit 1	$Y_1 = K$
Unit 2	$Y_2 = K \, (\% \text{ learning})$
Unit 4	$Y_4 = K \, (\% \text{ learning})^2$
Unit 8	$Y_8 = K \, (\% \text{ learning})^3$
Unit 16	$Y_{16} = K \, (\% \text{ learning})^4$
etc.	etc.

Note that if the progress curve is plotted on log-log coordinate paper, the resulting curve is linear with slope equal to $-n$. Many people may find the linear curve easier to interpret than the exponential one, and so at least consider using it.

For the example the progress curve can be plotted from the following data:

Point in Production	Cumulative Average Man-Hours
Unit 1	$Y_1 = K = 7000$
Unit 2	$Y_2 = K \, (0.85) = 5950$
Unit 4	$Y_4 = K \, (0.85)^2 = 5058$
Unit 8	$Y_8 = K \, (0.85)^3 = 4299$
Unit 16	$Y_{16} = K \, (0.85)^4 = 3654$

The curve is plotted on log-log coordinates in Fig. 11.10.

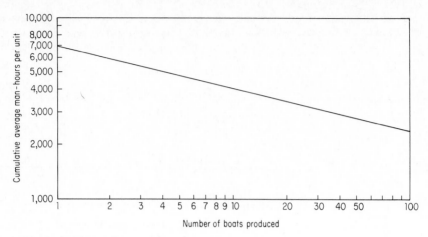

FIG. 11.10   The production progress function, log-log.

Some Cautions in Applying the Production Progress Function

Probably the greatest problem that confronts the potential user of the production progress function is estimation of the correct value of n to use in the calculations. One common error is to assume that an n value which has been found to be appropriate for one industry or one class of products will be appropriate for other industries or other products. All too often the aerospace industry's characteristic improvement of 20 percent with its corresponding n value of 0.322 has been carried over to other applications with no justification for doing so. Several procedures can be used to estimate the value of n in any particular situation. A few are given here with the caution that each has its limitations and potential sources for error:

1. Assume n is the same as in previous applications with the same industry.
2. Assume n is the same as in previous applications with the same or a similar product.
3. **a.** Evaluate the status of production variables that affect the ability of the process to improve.

   b. Compare the current status of the variables with that existing during previous production of a similar product.

   c. Given n from the previous production situations, estimate the new n by comparison of (a) and (b).
4. Wait until 2 or 4 units have been produced, and estimate n from these data, as was done in the example.

Even if a good estimate of n has been obtained, there are several application errors to guard against. If elemental time data are used in calculating the expected value of K, so the model can be used before production begins, one must know whether the elemental data apply to a learned or unlearned process. If the data came from a learned process, perhaps the user should inflate the estimate of K as determined by the elemental data. Do not forget that the improvement percentage applies to the aggregate production process and that the same percentage may *not* apply to individual components of the process. Nor should it be assumed that multishift situations give the same results as single-shift operations in determining the value of X to use in the model calculations. Finally, do not ignore the effects of labor force changes, production interruptions, or new-equipment installations, since these may result in a period of either relearning or unusually accelerated learning. If one is careful in estimating the values of n and K and keeps in mind the various factors that can affect production progress calculations, so as not to apply the model blindly, reliable information can be obtained for planning purposes.

ROBOTS IN MANPOWER MANAGEMENT AND CONTROL

Over the past two decades, robots have gradually infiltrated the industrial environment. Spurring them on have been miniature computers, rising labor costs, and declining productivity. Management has used these drones to make repetitive, time-consuming, and hazardous tasks more efficient and profitable.

There are currently about 300 types of robots ranging in price from $1500 to $250,000, with installations costing from $50,000 to millions of dollars. In the United States, it is estimated that 5000 robots are being used actively in industry, while Japan has at least 10 times as many. One factor contributing to Japan's competitive position is automation, including expertise in "making robots work." By 1990, U.S. industry is expected to respond aggressively to this imbalance and have 100,000 robots in operation.

Robots, sometimes called *flexible automation*, enable diverse mechanical activities to be automated through their programming feature. Their popularity and use have risen sharply, since these "steel-collar workers" have the capabilities of speed, efficiency, and reliability, all contributing to increased productivity and greater profits.

Applications and Implementation

Applications of robots involve tasks or processes which are tedious, repetitive, boring, or hazardous and which present excellent opportunities for improving output. Typical implementations of robots include welding, paint spraying, machining operations, loading and unloading, filling, parts picking and transfer, and inspection.

When a robot installation is considered, apply the following implementation guidelines:

1. Obtain top management policy guidance, active participation, and support in accordance with corporate objectives.
2. Prepare a short- and long-range plan of company automation needs and goals.
3. Perform a thorough industrial engineering study, identifying specific robot application needs.
4. Research the robot manufacturer's capabilities to meet application requirements.
5. Begin with applications where the risk of failure is lowest, i.e., the most obvious and simplest application, with emphasis on operations which are physically hazardous.

6. Work with a robot manufacturer that understands the company's manufacturing operation and processes.

7. Educate manufacturing management and provide for their supervision in the use of robots. Achieve participation in selecting, developing, and installing the automated system. This will ensure acceptance and successful installation of robots.

Materials Management

Because of the high efficiency and almost perfect performance of robots, materials management, including MRP, inventory control, and materials handling, is critical to optimum production flow. The planning, movement, and supply of materials to the production line require exacting fulfillment of quantities, phasing, and timing requirements. Since robots usually do exactly what is expected, in terms of finite output and quality, material supply must be equally efficient, or else bottlenecks will occur.

Robot efficiency can be a major contributing factor in achieving significant reductions of work-in-process queues, an increase in inventory turns, which results in greater return on investment and profit.

Work Measurement and Efficiency

Compared to humans with regard to work measurement and efficiency, robots offer exciting features such as exacting specifications, standard times, practically perfect performance, instantaneous reporting, and reduction in time and costs. And the task is performed with 100 percent available active working time free of personal time and breaks. Robots promote increased standardization of similar parts and processes, further increasing unit efficiency without demanding overtime or increased pay. Since their capacity is stable, scheduling and loading are always valid and dependable.

It is essential that the surrounding work area, support personnel, and equipment be made equally efficient to avoid an overload and promote a uniform increase in efficiency. The increased output, improved quality, and reduced labor costs are the primary advantages of an efficient operation.

Labor and Management

Robots are viewed by management quite positively as a way of establishing a competitive edge through reduced costs and prices. However, some general ground rules should be followed to promote a smooth interface with labor:

1. Present the personal advantages to the workers and the union.
2. Forewarn workers and unions of installation to minimize apprehension and resistance.
3. Selling the foreman is essential to perpetuate the philosophy.
4. Publicize the fact that the robots are replacing hazardous, tedious, and uncomfortable human tasks.
5. Accomplish job elimination by normal attrition.

Experience has shown, especially in giant corporations, that success was based on these ground rules. Labor, including unions, has realized that robot installation has made the workers' lives less dangerous and more comfortable, meaningful, and enriched in general. Workers have also experienced greater job security and financial success. This has been made possible by robots being successfully assimilated into the company. Robots have taken on the undesirable tasks and directly contributed to increased efficiency. This has paved the way for companies to maintain their competitive edge while promoting profitability.

MAKE-OR-BUY ANALYSIS

The decision to make or buy is based on two basic considerations, which are separate and distinct and should be kept completely independent: reduced costs and additional capacity.

Reduced-Cost Consideration

If the supplier and the purchaser have nearly equivalent capabilities in terms of manufacturing processes, it is rarely cheaper to buy than to make. This may seem heresy to many accountants or purchasing executives, but it can be proved. The key factor, of course, is identification of fixed versus variable costs. Most large companies have high fixed costs as a result of rental or depreciation of equipment, salaries, taxes, and the like.

Make-or-buy decisions should be made on the basis of variable or incremental cost. In other words, ask how much extra it will cost to produce the units in question, never what the unit cost of producing the parts is, including full burden, administrative cost, and overhead.

Often one hears the phrase, "We can buy them much cheaper than we can make them," which may be true in a strict accounting sense. The following example, however, illustrates the principle involved. An article or part can be manufactured as follows:

Direct materials	$0.80
Direct labor	0.10
Factory overhead—fixed	0.40
Factory overhead—variable	0.05
General and administrative	0.60
Total factory cost	$1.95

The purchasing agent may easily locate a supplier who will furnish the part for $1.50. The vendor, while paying the same or even more for direct labor and materials and variable overhead ($0.95), can make a profit, since fixed costs may be much less as a result of limited overhead, general, and administrative expenses. The purchaser, however, may not be maximizing profits at this price because his fixed costs are ongoing.

Capacity Balance

Many firms purchase items they could make themselves, on the basis of balancing plant capacity. Cost is a factor here as is profit, but the decision is based on utilization of capacity in a long-term sense rather than a simple unit-cost concept. Firms must maintain a high utilization of equipment to keep costs low. Idle plant and equipment can be very costly. Therefore, where demand varies, wise management staffs and equips to a minimum point and absorbs fluctuations through purchase of fabricated items. This is an intelligent approach and is a real cost saver for several reasons:

- It cuts down on training costs for new employees—employees who produce the most scrap and are the least productive.
- It permits maximum output with minimum investment.
- It enables the plant to run with stable workforce and stable output.
- It reduces overtime.

The ability to level production by purchasing items depends on a company's ability to project production and predict shop loads accurately. The steps in the process are as follows:

1. Establish sales forecast or production needs for a period well in advance of purchase lead times.
2. Reduce sales and production forecasts to requirements for specific items of manufacture.
3. Use accurate work standards to project hours of work for each machine center of the plant.
4. Compare the workload for each section with optimum, stable levels desired for plant operations.
5. Contract with suppliers to furnish all items which would create excessive workloads.
6. Schedule and maintain machine loads for each machine center to dovetail with receipts of purchased items.

Other considerations in conjunction with make-or-buy decisions are quality control requirements and diversification of supply to protect plant assembly schedules.

Quality Control

The production of items adhering to exact specifications requires time and organization. This fact should be seriously considered in make-or-buy decisions. A company may have gained a high degree of skill and in-plant experience which permits manufacturing items easily to exact specifications. A supplier who has not made a similar part may have difficulty initially in meeting specifications. It takes time to develop skills.

Diversification of Supply

Protection of assembly schedules through multiple sources can be a factor in the make-or-buy decision. Suppliers may be shut down by strikes over which a customer has no control. This dictates more than one supplier of critical items or splitting the requirements between the customer's own plant and a supplier. This approach may require some extra tooling but may be less costly than a production stoppage.

MULTIPLE SHIFTS AND OVERTIME CONSIDERATIONS

The question of whether to operate on a multiple-shift basis, to work overtime, or to expand single-shift operations is primarily economic. However, there are many other considerations, such as availability of labor, equipment, and supervision.

On one hand, there are series of continuous process-type operations such as in steel mills, refineries, and power plants where there is rarely any alternative to a full-time operation of three shifts, 7 days a week. Such operations are much more costly to shut down than they are to run on a continuous basis.

On the other hand, there are a few traditionally one-shift operations where no one would even consider working more than one shift. One is garment plants where the sewing machine operator has a machine which has been coddled and adjusted until it does everything just the way the operator wants it to—it "feels" right. No one else can run this machine, and only certain mechanics are allowed to put a screwdriver to it. That some stranger would come in and actually touch the machine at night is unthinkable.

In between these two extremes there is a larger body of industry where a change in shift operation as conditions vary may or may not be necessary and advisable.

Cost of Capital Investment

Where the cost of capital equipment is high, there are economic reasons why it must be operated at the highest possible degree of utilization. Textile factories are an example of this heavy investment in capital equipment.

The economics are simple. The depreciation costs are fixed, since the equipment will likely be obsolete in 5 to 10 years. With total fixed costs amounting to 30 to 40 percent on some operations, the equipment must operate no less than 24 hours per day since dropping two shifts will increase fixed costs to 40 to 50 percent.

Aside from the depreciation which must be carefully and accurately taken into consideration for cost purposes, there is, of course, the original cost of equipment acquisition. No company could afford to purchase three times as much equipment for a single-shift operation as the competitor who is using it on a three-shift basis. However, there are those operators, usually small, who have an abundance of fully depreciated equipment and therefore are not affected by original cost.

Availability of Equipment

When companies are forced to expand production on relatively short notice, often they cannot get additional equipment quickly enough. So they have no alternative but to run a second shift. This situation is frequently encountered when a single, specialized piece of equipment constitutes a bottleneck. Basically this is a short-term problem since in the long run additional equipment can be procured as warranted by other considerations.

Availability of Personnel

The availability of personnel may also affect decisions on shift operation. At times people may be available for first-shift work but not for second or third shifts. But there may be people available for second or third shifts but not the first. In this latter category are many people working at a second job, students who attend classes during the day, a parent who cannot leave the children except when the spouse or some other person who works days is available.

Availability of Supervision

Many times it is possible to recruit personnel for second- and third-shift work if adequate supervision can be provided. Where the technical qualifications required of supervision are high, this can be difficult.

Comparison of Quality and Performance by Shifts

In some plants and companies, performance relative to both quantity and quality is always higher on the second than on the first shift. Various explanations have been advanced for this. It has been said—facetiously, of course—that things are better on the second and third shifts because there are not so many members of management around to bother the workers. Strange as this may seem, there are good reasons why it is so:

The average experience may be higher on the later shifts if the company makes a practice of training on the first shift and putting more experienced workers on night. Obviously sometimes the reverse is true, and the new employees are all concentrated on the second shift.

Second-shift workers may be more professional in their approach to the job. Especially in banks where clearing activities are usually done at night to reduce float time, the best workers and highest performances tend to be at night. There may be fewer distractions at night, so workers can concentrate on the job at hand.

The second shift may not be loaded as fully, by having a smaller workforce or a smaller load per work station. Accordingly, there are fewer bottlenecks and problem areas.

INDUSTRIAL RELATIONS AND EFFECT ON MANPOWER

Industrial relations includes both the individual employer-employee relationships and the employer-union relationship. Although industrial relations is a highly specialized staff function, the primary responsibility for the effective use of the assigned workforce belongs to the line supervisor.

Employee Relations

The degree to which employee relations contributes to the successful operation of a company may be measured by the respect that labor and management have for each other. This respect is built up over the years by an intelligent and realistic approach to personnel administration and labor relations.

Selection and Training of Employees

The word *selection* as applied to new employees indicates that several applicants are available, and a selection can truly be made. If this is not the case in your company, examine carefully your wage levels, company policies, and working conditions.

Supervisory training is more important than employee training. The ratio of supervisors to employees may average 1:10. Nevertheless, supervisory skills will provide a climate where 10 well-supervised employees will outperform 10 others.

The well-trained supervisor analyzes the employee-training requirements and lays out long-range plans. He writes job descriptions and checklists for new employees. He has a step-by-step procedure for introducing new employees to the job. This procedure should be coordinated with the personnel department.

Employee training does not stop with the new employee's understanding of his first job. He must be measured against known standards for each job. There is also the continuous task of training employees for transfer or promotion.

Collective Bargaining

The sessions where labor and management sit together to negotiate new labor agreements are known as the collective-bargaining process. But it is not just the session where new labor agreements are negotiated. It is any discussion throughout the year between management and labor of common problems. Any discussion between a supervisor and a worker in reality constitutes collective bargaining.

Wage and Salary Administration

Sound management practice dictates that the administration of wages and salaries should be standardized. A clock is a very poor tool to measure work performed. Two employees on the same job seldom turn out identical rates of production unless the production rate has been standardized in some way. Management realized this fact many years ago and so established a variety of piecework, incentive-rate, or bonus plans. These could be group or individual plans. They have one thing in common: Any change in material or equipment or method makes the old standard invalid. How much change? If you say "any change at all," it will take an army of industrial engineers to keep up with all the changes. If you say "any change that the supervisor determines is sufficient cause," you have a variety of incentive plans in effect at the same time.

Modern management practice tends toward measured-daywork systems. This puts the burden on the supervisor and on other management personnel to meet the standard. Management sets the standard without any negotiation with labor. The standard provides predetermined costs for budgeting and for pricing. No change of methods or materials will affect an employee's pay. Therefore, management can make changes which affect production rates at its own discretion. In addition, sound standards provide the data necessary for equipment and crew scheduling and lead to lower costs.

Records, Reports, and Research

Record keeping starts when a prospective employee applies for work. All application blanks should be retained. The applicant's files should be cross-indexed by name and job. Successful applicants will have added to their file copies of numerous government forms, health and insurance forms, union checkoff authorization, etc.

However, suppose personnel turnover has become a problem in your company. Research is required, and some special reports should be issued for a stated time. Determine your plant's percentage of labor turnover by dividing the number of separations by the number of employees on the payroll, and multiply the answer by 100. Compute this percentage for a number of past periods. Plot the results on a graph. Analyze separately the reasons for employees being laid off and for voluntary separations. Make allowances for, but do not disregard, unavoidable separations. Set a goal for the labor turnover rate which will be acceptable. Change policies to correct the reasons for a high rate of separation. Measure progress toward the goal, and make special reports to management on this progress. Discontinue the reports when the goal is reached or when turnover is no longer a problem.

The same approach should be applied to any other personnel problem.

Coordination with Industrial Relations

The impact of personnel problems on production output cannot be overemphasized. No attempt is made here to offer specific guidance to the production and inventory control manager in the solution of such problems. However, a yardstick is provided to measure the effectiveness of industrial relations in the company and thus act as a constructive force in the coordination of personnel actions affecting manpower.

ORGANIZATION FOR MANPOWER MANAGEMENT

Because of the quick response in today's competitive business environment, the effective management of manpower resources has become both increasingly complex and critically important. The most effective organization to manage manpower planning and control both specifically assigns responsibility for achieving results and inspires active participation and cooperation among line manufacturing, production and inventory control, sales, and finance functions. Whether its prime focus is a production planning committee or an individual manufacturing manager, the importance of coordination between the numerous interrelated responsibilities and functions outlined in the next section should be recognized.

Line and Staff Responsibilities for Manpower Planning and Control

Responsibilities for manpower planning and control can be divided into three important task areas: planning, acquiring and training, and control. The importance of the responsibilities within each area varies considerably depending on the company size, growth pattern, product-design stability, cyclical pattern of business, types of manufacturing, and labor skills required.

Table 11.7 enumerates many of these responsibilities, defines the line or staff nature of each, and suggests the department or function in the company to which the responsibility would probably be assigned.

Using Consultants

A consultant may be called on to define any of the planning and control responsibilities previously outlined, recommend policy and organization structure, or even write operating procedures. In using a consultant, however, remember that in most cases he will not expound new truths but will more likely bring into the open the thinking within the organization, catalyzing it into meaningful policies or plans.

Even with a reputable firm, a bitter experience can occur if the individual assigned to the project uses less than extreme care in evaluating the problem. Therefore, the choice is critical, and the client must make a comprehensive review of the qualifications of potential consulting firms. The following minimum considerations should guide the investigation:

1. Evaluate the background and experience of the consulting company's principals.
2. Compare the firm's experience with the project at hand.
3. Question former clients regarding work assigned, performance, personnel, action taken on the recommendations, and repeat work performed.

Upon completion of the preliminary investigation and prior to making a final selection, the client should request of one or more firms a written proposal clearly defining

- The objectives of the assignment
- The work to be accomplished and the approach to be followed
- The involvement and coordination required of the client
- Possible difficulties that might hinder success in achieving the objectives
- The experience of the personnel to be assigned to the project and the role of each
- Statement of fees and the basis on which they are to be paid

It is important to realize in reviewing a formal proposal that the use of a consultant does not permit management to abrogate its responsibility for making decisions, adopting a course of action, and obtaining results.

MANPOWER DATA COLLECTION AND ANALYSIS

Management decisions should be based on accurate, up-to-date, and factual information. The techniques which should be used to obtain and process such information depend on the kind, volume, and time increments of information required. The kind of data refers to information such as employee, shop order, product or part, operation, quantity produced, and time worked as well as any other data considered necessary for manpower planning and control. The volume of data is a function of

TABLE 11.7 Manpower Planning and Control Responsibilities

Task Area	Responsibility		Department or Function* (Line or Staff Responsibility)
	Planning		
Long range	Establishing company performance objectives		Gmnfs
	Developing long-range sales forecasts		Gfs
	Inventory-level planning		Gsf
	Production planning		CMnf
	Broad manpower-level planning:	Direct	CMnf
		Indirect	CGmfs
Resource planning (shorter range)	Sales forecasting		Scfm
	Inventory-level and production plan balancing		Cmnfs
	Determination of manpower and machinery requirements		Mnf
	Simulation techniques (with or without computer)		Cfn
	Resource balancing:		
	"Normal man per work center" definition		Nf
	"Normal" machine utilization		Nf
	Work center resource targets		
	Manpower targets		Nf
	Machine utilization targets		Nf
	Establishment of work center manpower plan		Mnfc

Acquiring and training	Determination of lead time required for skills needed (availability in area, extent of training required, etc.)	Pm
	Attention to company's local competitive position in acquiring workers	Pm
	Review and analysis of interviewing, testing, and other hiring procedures to maintain their relevance in meeting company's manpower needs	PM
	Training programs (on the job, special technical, etc.)	Mpn

Control

Measurement	Work measurement programs (timed standards, standard data, estimated standards, ratio, delay studies, etc.)	NMpf
Information processing, analysis, and reporting	Coordinating objectives of programs	Cf
	Development of meaningful control reports for line managers and supervisors to show performance against these targets and objectives	MFC
	Establishing definitive feedback information for revisions to resource and long-range plans	CFmn
Supervision and control of manpower	Direct and indirect	M
	Coordination with planning and other control functions	Mfc

* Lowercase letters denote staff responsibilities, and uppercase letters denote line responsibilities: Cc, production control; Ff, finance; Gg, general management; Mm, manufacturing; Nn, manufacturing support (industrial engineering, manufacturing engineering, etc.); Pp, personnel; Ss, sales.

the amount of information collected for each transaction and the number of transactions that require collection. The time increments of data should relate to the intended usage and can be expressed in seconds, minutes, hours, days, weeks, months, or any other measurable time period. Manpower data collection and reporting systems can become unduly complicated and expensive, so system costs should be evaluated with respect to the value of information produced. Generally, manpower data collection and analysis techniques can be classified as either manual or automated systems.

Manual Data Collection

Manual techniques are normally utilized whenever the information to be collected is minimal (low volume) and time requirements are such that it can be collected and processed in a timely manner or the resources required for other collection methods are not available. When properly designed, manual systems can be effective and economical. They are used widely and are applicable for many small shops in operation today. However, for medium- and large-scale operations, the potential disadvantage of not having timely information is an important consideration.

Automated Data Collection

When data collection requirements are too complex for a manual system, use of an automated system should be considered. The degree of automation necessary to satisfactorily meet the information requirements can vary greatly and thus can play a significant role in determining costs associated with the system.

Data Collection Methods

Design and manufacture of data collection equipment is a dynamic activity. The introduction of computer terminals and electronic data collection devices in manufacturing has had a dramatic impact on the techniques of data collection, volume of data available, and timeliness of gathering shop floor control information.

The most commonly used technique to capture shop floor control information is to report progress as each step in the manufacturing or processing cycle has been completed for a predetermined grouping such as an order, a release, a batch, or some other meaningful reporting entity.

Early systems required experienced data entry or keypunch operators to convert information contained on labor tickets, labor logs, or tear sheets to computer-readable format, such as punched cards, for further processing.

The most desirable types of preprinted documents are those which can be easily and inexpensively prepared, withstand exposure to a manufacturing environment, and then be read by automated equipment, on the shop floor, which will interface directly with a computer.

Computer Terminals

Computer terminal data collection systems have proved effective tools for increasing productivity in many wide-ranging retail and industrial applications.

Terminals display information in predetermined formats via either a cathode-ray tube (CRT) or a printer and include a keyboard that allows the operator to modify or add predetermined information during the data collection process. Computer terminals have become inexpensive, which allows their installation on the shop floor, as required, for data collection devices. Properly designed systems require a minimum effort for data entry and ensure accurate information through preprogrammed validating or editing procedures.

Bar Coding

Bar-code data collection systems have also proved effective tools for increasing productivity in many different retail and industrial applications. Bar codes can be printed by specialized, high-speed machines in conjunction with human-readable documentation such as pull lists, process routing sheets, move tickets, and various other kinds of shop paperwork. Then the bar-coded information can be read by portable, handheld wands, or scanners placed in fixed positions to automatically collect information. More advanced scanning devices have keyboards and on-line interface capability with computers which allow them to be used in a manner very similar to computer terminals. Bar codes allow rapid, accurate, and reliable data collection for processing by computer.

Electronic Scales

Electronic scales that have been available for a number of years now offer a versatility which makes them even more useful to industry. In addition to their CRT displays, remote capabilities, and simultaneous weighing and counting, they are programmable with computer interface capability, which allows them to be incorporated into the total inventory and production control system of a company. Through computer interface, electronic scales can provide accurate and instantaneous updating of inventory and production counts. Additionally, scale systems can be used as stand-alone applications to meet the needs of special counting or weighing purposes anywhere within the plant.

Data Processing Systems

Modern data processing equipment is capable of converting vast quantities of information to meaningful management reports at an extremely high speed. However, the information must first be converted to computer-recognizable form through data entry procedures in the data processing department or through the use of equipment installed directly in the departments where the information originates.

Information Processing

The method of data collection can be a critical factor in the timeliness of information processing and reporting. So it is important to match the data collection technique with the processing method needed to obtain the reporting at the time desired.

Off-Line Data Collection

This method can be used for collecting data whenever the additional processing capability provided by a central computer is not required. Whenever this approach is used, the delay between collecting and processing data cannot be avoided; however, it can be controlled.

On-Line Data Collection

This method is used for collecting data whenever control of additional processing capability by a central computer is desired. When this approach is used, the operator can access the central computer, thereby allowing the data to be entered directly into the computer for further processing.

Batch Processing

Data are collected and accumulated for predetermined time frames, such as a production shift, and then processed by the computer in a single update run. Either the time frame or the frequency of processing by the computer can vary, if required. Both manual and automated data collection systems can operate in a batch processing environment.

Real-Time Processing

Data are collected by an on-line data collection terminal or device and are processed by the computer immediately so that the results are available in time to influence the process or operation being monitored or controlled. This approach allows information to be continuously updated throughout the day and eliminates the need for batch update computer runs. On-line data collection systems are required for operation in a real-time processing environment.

Production and Time Reporting

To properly control a manufacturing organization, it is necessary to know how effectively the production plan is being executed. The two major areas of concern are production progress and employee efficiency. Production progress is needed to identify those activities which have not been executed as planned. Time reporting is needed to monitor the efficiency of production employees during plan execution.

At the employee level, production and time reporting systems require virtually the same basic information, such as shop order number, operation number, and quantity completed. The additional basic information required to determine employee efficiency is simply the time required to produce the quantity reported as completed. It may not always be desirable or realistic to combine the data collection systems for production progress and employee efficiency reporting. But the key point for consideration is that, with today's data collection and data processing technology, the potential combination of these systems is a realistic objective that will eliminate the collection of a significant amount of redundant data.

Management Reporting

Successful manufacturing organizations must be able to produce a quality product, on time, at a competitive price while making an acceptable profit. To accomplish these objectives, management must have accurate, current, and concise information. The information requirements vary for each company; however, production planning and control must supply management with realistic master schedules so that the total factory manpower and machine capacity can be evaluated. Then exception reports must be available to draw attention to potential problem areas, so corrective actions can be planned and initiated. Through the proper use of modern manpower data collection and analysis techniques, the planning and control systems needed can be successfully developed and utilized.

MANPOWER COST TECHNIQUES

No techniques, whether for manpower cost control or for any other aspect of business, offer a "control" or "determine implications" of a situation or ultimately "make decisions." Properly designed, these techniques provide timely and accurate information which intelligent management uses as a basis for decision making. That is, solutions to problems are derived from proper analysis and evaluation of facts provided by the technique and are executed by the manager. These cost techniques provide management with the tools it requires to properly determine costs and evaluate the return on investment and profit.

Estimating Manpower Costs

From time immemorial estimators have had little black books in which they collected secret formulas, rules of thumb, and innumerable other devices for estimating labor costs. Management demanded estimates on which to base price quotations, plan personnel buildup, and schedule deliveries. Any standard was better than no standard, so almost any figure could be used that seemed halfway reasonable. The standard technique of the estimator was to explain why the estimate was wide of the mark. Changed methods or specifications were a convenient alibi and were equally hard to prove or disprove. Thus, the "guesstimator" made his way.

In the aircraft industry, during and after World War II, estimates were commonly made by the pound. The relative size, complexity, or type of aircraft was not a part of the formula: only the calculation of the weight and the hours and cost were derived automatically.

Things are not so simple today. Considerable sophistication has been introduced to cost estimating, so accuracy is considerably improved and the results are much more dependable. Accurate cost estimating is possible today through the use of scientifically developed standard data, which actually are so developed that the term *estimating* is no longer appropriate. Rather, standard data applications have superseded estimating per se and have a completely different implication.

The accuracy with which standard data can be applied is entirely a function of how precisely the method of production can be defined. If the exact method is known, the exact time is also known. When the number of unknowns increases, accuracy decreases since successive assumptions, whose validity is always subject to question, must be made.

To illustrate the method of cost calculation and the typical problems encountered, the following process may be useful. The development of costs for a single part is included with the understanding that the procedure would be the same for all parts and eventually for complete assemblies.

The first step is to list the processes by which the part is made. This involves decisions as to whether a casting or raw stock will be used and a list of the operations and inspections necessary to produce the finished part.

Here is a typical list of operations:

Operation	Machine or Process
1. Cut raw stock to length	Do-all saw
2. Turn to shape	Engine lathe
3. Grind to final dimension	Centerless grinder
4. Drill and ream	Drill press
5. Plate	Chrome plate process
6. Inspect	

The next step is to develop the detail for each operation to the depth necessary to apply data. A word of explanation is necessary here concerning the different degrees to which data synthesis can be carried and their effect on the accuracy of results and the time necessary to apply the data. The number of variables considered determines the accuracy of measurement and the time necessary to apply data. The degree to which details are taken into account is normally a function of the number of items to be produced. High volumes require greater accuracy and, as a result, more data, which permits consideration of a great many variables. On the other hand, making one part may allow the consideration of very few variables.

To illustrate how this works, we consider operation 4, drill and ream, for the hypothetical part. We list the variables:

1. *Fixture.*   If a tool drawing is available, exact data may be obtained of how the piece is placed and removed from the fixture and the type and number of clamps. This information together with the dimensions and weight of the piece makes possible an exact time value. If a fixture is to be used, but no drawing is available, assumptions must be made about the fixture and the data applied on the basis of these assumptions, with a corresponding degree of uncertainty and loss of accuracy for the final result.

2. *Material specifications.*   If the precise material from which the part is made is known, the exact drilling feed, speed, and time are known. However, if this has not been determined, an educated guess must be made and the data applied accordingly.

3. *Hole diameter and depth.*   Usually this information is readily available, so an accurate time and cost can be determined if the material is known. However, for very rough standards, such as might be used for maintenance parts, any hole up to ½ by ½ inch might be considered as one standard and up to 1 by 1 inch as a multiple thereof, to reduce the calculations and hence the time to arrive at the cost.

4. *Materials handling.*   To arrive at a completely accurate standard, the type and size of container in which the parts are delivered for the operator should be known. If the data are not certain, assumptions based on the usual shop practices must be made.

5. *Lot size.* This factor has an obvious effect on setup times, which are constant per lot rather than per piece. It also influences the degree of proficiency operators can attain in making a particular piece. If there are few pieces, the operator may not develop his full production potential, especially if tooling and fixtures are complex.

The use of standard data for calculations, rather than estimating manpower costs, is preferred to all other methods. Even if a few variables are defined, all costs will have a known degree of accuracy depending on the refinements built into each standard.

This method of determining manpower costs has led to standard data developers and standard data applicators, who have replaced cost estimators. The standard data developer must be familiar with work measurement techniques. The standard data applicator, on the other hand, must know the processes, such as drilling and milling, and must be able to predict each move the operator will make to produce the piece. Knowing each move, he can apply the data accurately.

Overhead Rates

The method of determining overhead rates is one of the most controversial areas of cost accounting. Too many cost accountants have fixed ideas about the subject.

How Many Cost Centers?   The best answer is: as few as possible consistent with accurate and realistic accounting. Keep in mind that the only reason for having more than one cost center is to distinguish between costs of items passing through one center as opposed to another. If the costs are not different in each center, there is no justification for differentiation at all. To say it another way, the reason for isolating a cost center is to ensure that a product will not be unjustly burdened or too lightly burdened with overhead costs.

Cost centers are often referred to as *responsibility* centers, and this may be a valuable key to how the plant should be divided for calculation of overhead rates. If one supervisor or manager can be identified with a center, that is progress.

Also watch for a process which utilizes special equipment that is very costly, takes an inordinate amount of space, or, like plating, uses unique and costly materials. Any item not passing through these areas with their cost characteristics should not be burdened with their costs. The costs should be absorbed by only those items which incur them.

If, however, flow is uniform so that all products go through two areas, each having widely different cost characteristics, there is no real reason to separate them. Only when some products do and others do not pass through such areas should different cost centers be maintained.

Expense Distribution.   The next step is to distribute all plant overhead expense to each cost center. The basis of distribution can be simple or varied depending on the nature and magnitude of the expense. Some common expense items and suggested bases for distribution follow in Table 11.8.

Indirect Centers and Redistribution.   Some responsibility centers, such as maintenance, shipping-receiving, stockrooms, toolrooms, and personnel department, occupy space, have supervision and indirect labor, use heat, light, and power, but *do not produce anything*. Good practice usually indicates that original expense distribution be made to these centers just as with the direct production centers. The expenses of these indirect centers are then redistributed to the direct centers on

TABLE 11.8

Item	Basis of Distribution
Heat and light	Floor space occupied
Power	Installed horsepower*
Depreciation	Actual machines installed
Supervision	Actual supervisors assigned or part thereof
Indirect labor	Direct labor hours
Supplies	Direct labor hours
Indirect materials	Actual utilization
Real estate taxes	Space occupied
Social security taxes	Payroll dollars
Vacation and holiday pay	Payroll dollars

*If metered separately; otherwise, estimate percentage of total expense for light and power separately.

some logical basis. For example, personnel department expenses might be distributed on head count or direct labor hours, shipping and receiving expenses by pounds processed, and toolroom expenses to applicable departments on an actual record basis. The exact basis of distribution is usually not of paramount importance if it is fairly realistic and logical. For example, whether expense is distributed by head count, labor hours, or payroll dollars, the final results will not differ significantly.

Excess Direct Labor Costs.   Excess labor costs do exist, and they must be absorbed in standard costs or else the plant will go out of business. Make it a rule to include in overhead rates a reasonable amount of excess direct labor cost. The standard cost, or overhead rate, should be reasonably attainable.

Calculation of Overhead Rate.   Following distribution of all shop expenses plus planned excess indirect labor to cost or responsibility centers, the overhead rate for each cost center can be established. The rate can be established per machine hour, direct labor hour, or some unit of production such as pounds, tons, yards, etc.

Of all the possible bases for expressing the rate, the direct labor hour method is probably the most widely used and the most accurate for most situations.

Machine hours are used where the process is primarily machine-controlled, such as with spinning in textiles, and the direct labor hour is somewhat nebulous. Machine hours are also used in certain process industries. The unit of production is closely related to machine hours for most products, and for any given item one can convert from one to another. The selection of one or the other is largely a matter of convenience.

Whichever basis of expression is used, the projected activity of the cost center, expressed in direct labor hours, machine hours, or pounds, yards, etc., is divided into the allocated expense to obtain the overhead rate.

Budgets for Direct Manpower.   The development of budgets for direct manpower can be as accurate as the ability to forecast the volume of production and product mix that will evolve as sales for the period are realized. Budgets can be established in a number of ways, but the preferred way is through the application of standards to accurately forecast production. Of course, this is not always possible or practical. And many firms develop budgets by taking the trend of actual expenses for the past several years and extrapolating on for the next year as a basis for an educated guess. This unscientific but sometimes accurate approach to budgeting needs no further analysis here, since the techniques are fairly obvious and self-explanatory.

Budgets for direct manpower have several purposes and connotations for different people. The purposes of budgeting might be classified as profit planning and forecasting, forecasting manpower requirements, and control of manpower costs.

A budget is a planning and cost control tool, and every company should use one to maximize profits. Budgeting as related to profit planning starts with a sales forecast, which combined with selling prices results in the income plan, or budget. When all cost items, including manpower costs, are deducted from income, a profit for the year is obtained. The more detailed and accurate the sales forecast of item quantities and product mix, the more accurate the budget becomes. Operating with a budget implies management's resolve to keep all costs in line with the plan. If the profit objectives are to be met, sales that fall off must be stimulated and costs that fail to develop as planned must be brought into line. Control mechanisms, to keep management advised of each part of the plan, are necessary if the planned profit is to be realized.

The forecasting of manpower requirements is an outgrowth of the budget. If increased sales are forecast and manpower needs are planned accordingly, management is given the lead time necessary to recruit and train personnel. Given the time necessary to develop people for each phase of the production process, a schedule for hiring and training can be developed to meet future needs.

The concept of budgeting used as a control mechanism is considerably more complex and introduces the idea of a flexible budget. In this context, the flexible budget tells management how much manpower and associated cost are required for various forecast levels. Although the fixed budget, based on a forecast, works well when sales are as expected, it lacks flexibility and hence usefulness when the volume becomes either more or less than was forecast. For example, if the volume of production is less than was forecast, the budgeted expenditures for manpower should be less. On the other hand, if sales and production increase, a comparison with the budget may be unsatisfactory because it appears that more manpower is being used than anticipated, while in reality, the opposite may be true.

The flexible budget is not directly related to the forecast and is only indirectly related to profit planning. More accurately, the flexible budget reflects current performance and thus is most valuable as a control mechanism. Flexible budgets, which contract as output contracts and increase when production increases, compare predicted performance against actual units produced and are more realistic and valuable than fixed budgets.

To be wholly effective and accurate, flexible budgets should be based not only on units shipped or transferred to finished stock, but also on the actual production achieved at each operation during the productive process. Otherwise, changes in "in-process" inventories will distort the flexible budget and produce a false reading. For example, if in-process inventory is reduced, the count of finished units produced will be too high. Conversely, if in-process inventories are being increased, much useful work will be accomplished without actually producing finished units.

To illustrate the development of a manpower budget using standards and a production forecast, the following simplified examples are used.

Example

Assume that the monthly sales forecast for the five products manufactured by a company are as follows: product A, 100; product B, 500; product C, 50; product D, 800; product E, 950. The standard cost sheet (Table 11.9) shows, among other things, the following labor and materials requirements for product A. Similar cost sheets exist for products B, C, D, and E.

The application of the standards to the production forecast, simplified to illustrate the process, is shown in Table 11.10. The resulting calculations show the authorized manning for each department, based on the forecasted production requirements. Control reports which show the relationship of the forecast to the actual mix indicate the validity of the original budget.

The illustrated budget is valid, provided that the departments operate at standard, which, of course, is not always the case. If the actual productivity levels are substantially different from standard, the manpower figures can be prorated for planning purposes. For cost control the variance from standard may be highlighted.

Indirect Manpower Budgets.   The term *indirect labor*, or *manpower*, is widely used in a number of different senses. In the narrowest sense it is labor which does not contribute anything to the value of the product, and it includes materials handling, service personnel, inspection, and operations such as mold cleaning and shake-out in foundries. This strict definition serves no useful purpose and seems to confuse the issue and budget concepts discussed here.

At the other extreme is the concept often associated with the aircraft and aerospace industries, where manpower is considered indirect if it cannot be identified with a given contract. Under this very loose definition almost any function such as stockkeeping, maintenance, personnel, purchasing, and design can be classified as direct if the people perform their functions for only one contract. This definition is too broad and is useful only for invoicing against a cost-reimbursement type of contract.

TABLE 11.9   Standard Cost Sheet

Standard Cost Calculation for Product A			
I. Materials			
A. Steel sheet 1040 A	100 lb/unit		
B. Wire, copper no. 10 regular	50 ft/unit		
C. Paint, industrial enamel	0.50 gal/unit		
II. Direct labor	Hours	Rate	Cost per
A. Cutting	unit	hour	unit
1. Do-all saw	0.2650	9.75	2.5838
2. Shear	0.4078	10.05	4.0984
3. Brake	0.2160	9.90	2.1384
B. Assembly			
1. Subassembly 1	0.5065	9.60	4.8624
2. Subassembly 2	0.7862	9.60	7.5475
3. Final assembly	1.6035	10.20	16.3557
C. Finish and pack			
1. Spray paint	0.1345	9.84	1.3235
2. Touch up	0.0756	9.45	0.7144
3. Pack	0.6300	9.30	5.8590

TABLE 11.10 Development of Manpower Budget: Direct Labor

Product	Cutting Department			Assembly			Finish and Pack			Total
	Saw	Shear	Brake	Subassembly 1	Subassembly 2	Final	Paint	Touch up	Pack	
A 100	26.50	40.78	21.60	50.65	78.62	160.35	13.45	7.56	63.00	462.51
B 500	—	—	—	—	—	—	—	—	—	—
C 50	—	—	—	—	—	—	—	—	—	—
D 800	—	—	—	—	—	—	—	—	—	—
E 950	—	—	—	—	—	—	—	—	—	—
Total man-hours/month	753.25	835.56	685.60	940.36	1260.50	2580.36	436.12	350.48	1080.31	8922.54
Employees required	4.38	4.86	3.99	5.47	7.33	15.0	2.54	2.04	6.28	51.88
Manpower budget		13.23			27.80			10.86		

For budgeting and control purposes, these are definitions: *Direct labor* is any labor activity which varies directly with the volume of output. *Indirect labor* is any labor activity which does not vary directly with the volume of output.

These definitions result in some activities, such as inspection and materials handling between processes, being classified as direct labor. There is no problem for there is no reason not to establish standards per unit of output for these activities and control them as conventional direct labor, which varies directly with output. For budgeting purposes these may be treated exactly as direct labor.

With indirect labor, which includes labor activities that do not vary directly with volume, the budgeting problems are more clearly defined. Examples of such indirect labor items are maintenance workers, oilers and cleaners, stockroom attendants, inventory control clerks, tool-crib attendants, shop clerical employees, and janitors.

Some may argue that some manpower is more indirect than others, and this is true. Even indirect labor bears some relationship to volume of output. But in the instances given, the relationship is not direct, and so it is correctly classified as indirect.

Budgets for indirect manpower (and incidentally indirect costs) must be related to a given volume of output. Therefore, when sales and output have been forecast and the direct manpower has been established, indirect labor may be predicted.

In comparing actual indirect labor to budgeted labor (as opposed to direct labor to budgeted labor), the variances must be expressed in two ways. First, clearly if the number of units produced are reduced, the earned budget for indirect expenses will also be reduced if the flexible budget approach is maintained. This produces a volume variance which is actually the result of change in output. A second type of variance comes about when volume is actually as forecast, but the expenditures are more or less than contemplated in the budget. This variance is rightly termed *performance variance* and must be expressed independent of the volume variances.

In actual practice, it is common for one variance to offset the other, one being negative and the other positive. The following examples illustrate the interaction of volume and performance variances and the significance of each.

Example A

Plant activity (volume of output)	80 percent
Budgeted indirect manpower at 100 percent	$8,500/month
Flexible budget at 80 percent activity	$6,800/month
Actual expenditure	$8,500/month
Volume variance (negative)	$1,700/month

Example B

Plant activity (volume of output)	120 percent
Budgeted indirect manpower at 100 percent	$8,500/month
Flexible budget at 120 percent activity	$10,200/month
Actual expenditure	$9,000/month
Performance variance (negative)	$500/month
Volume variance (positive)	$1,700/month
Net variance (positive)	$1,200/month

The above approach to indirect manpower budgets is an interesting exercise in algebraic addition and compares actual performance with a budget and with a planned profit. It shows why profit objectives may or may not be realized and in this sense is a control mechanism. However, it is not the complete answer to control since there is no indication of what management is actually getting for the amounts expended. Supervisory appraisal is the only assurance that control is maintained. A department may be well within budget but way out of line in relation to actual work accomplished.

The answer is a budget within a budget in which indirect activity is measured and evaluated on the same basis as direct labor. By definition, an activity is indirect when it is not related to units produced or sold. For example, the floor must be swept once a day regardless of the volume of units produced. Measuring and controlling an indirect labor activity can ensure that the hours of work paid for match the work actually accomplished, even if it is completely unrelated to the profit plan.

Order Costs versus Standard Costs

Job-order costs versus standard costs is synonymous with saying actual costs versus standard costs. From a modern control technique viewpoint, job-order costs per se serve a historical purpose only. As history is evolved, job-order costs provide a continuous stream of information, but for control purposes this is of little value.

In this context, job-order costing implies identification of various costs with a job order and the collection of these costs to obtain the total cost of the job. The process starts with the requisitioning of materials from stock. Material requisitions contain job-order numbers, and costs are posted on the job-order cost card (cost-accumulation sheet).

For factory labor, each operator records the hours worked for each job, which are extended and posted to each job-order cost-accumulation sheet. When a job is finally completed and shipped, the costs entered on the cost-accumulation sheet are summarized and compared with an estimate of budget. Subsequently, this record is useful in estimating future jobs, and a complete cost history is obtained.

The difference between the standard cost approach and the job-order cost approach is that the latter provides no frame of reference or anchor point to tell management where the performance was good or bad. Past records are available, and comparisons with estimates are possible and useful. However, there is no qualitative determination, i.e., whether the performance was what it should be or could be and whether it was good or bad in an absolute sense.

Good labor standards are a prerequisite to a standard cost system. To try to install a standard-cost system without them is to perpetuate the job-cost system. Standards should be established on an engineered basis, with setup standards separately identified.

With labor standards available, they are naturally used for both control and cost purposes. This implies that operators will report the time and units of production. The comparison of each individual's performance against the standard is made daily or weekly for control purposes.

For controlling individual performance, it is usually advisable to segregate operation standards, which vary with the number of units processed, as opposed to setup standards, which vary per batch, per shift, or on some basis other than units produced. This prevents variances over which the individual operator has no control.

At times standards used for control purposes are applied on an "as incurred" basis, such as placing cobbles on a cold reduction mill. This is the best way to determine and control the performance of individuals. For cost purposes, however, these as-incurred standards, such as setup, batch, and lot constants, must be included in unit standard costs on a standard, or average-frequency, basis.

Another significant difference between job-order and standard costs is in the way in which excess costs for delays, breakdowns, etc. are customarily handled. Under the job-cost system, excess labor costs usually get charged to the job being worked on at the time. This may produce significant variations in individual job costs. Under the standard cost system, however, there is usually provision for charging delays, breakdowns, interruptions, etc., as "off standard time." These charges find their way into overhead and are applied to all jobs rather than falling randomly to a particular job.

Another problem involves differences in skill and effort of various individuals in the shop. Under the job-shop, or actual-cost, system, a new operator assigned to a job is unduly penalized. Under the standard cost system, a job has only one standard regardless of the person to whom it is assigned. Variances from standard or losses through failure to make standard are not all loaded onto a particular job, but are absorbed evenly by all jobs.

To summarize, standard costing is more refined than job costing because it establishes a "should be" cost on an absolute level. It is also more equitable because excess costs for delays and substandard performance are absorbed by all jobs rather than by one or two jobs selected on a random basis.

SUMMARY

Efficient manpower planning may be the deciding factor in the success or failure of a manufacturing operation. Responsibility for efficient manufacturing makes it imperative that production and inventory control personnel be fully acquainted with master scheduling, manpower capacity, manpower loading, work measurement, production progress functions, make-or-buy analyses, industrial relations, manpower data collection, and manpower costs. Only by an intelligent application of these techniques is efficient manufacturing possible.

BIBLIOGRAPHY

Andress, F. J.: "The Learning Curve as a Production Tool," *Harvard Business Review*, January-February, 1954.

Armstrong, M., and J. F. Lorentzen: *Handbook of Personnel Management Practice*, Prentice-Hall, Englewood Cliffs, N.J., 1982.

Barnes, R. M.: *Motion and Time Study—Design and Measurement of Work*, 7th ed., Wiley, New York, 1980.

Beach, D.: *Personnel—The Management of People at Work*, 4th ed., Macmillan, New York, 1980.

Chamberlain, N. W., and J. W. Kuhn: *Collective Bargaining*, 2d ed., McGraw-Hill, New York, 1965.

Clark, J. T.: *Capacity Management, Part Two*, 23d Annual Conference Proceedings, APICS, 1980.

Clark, W.: *The Gantt Chart*, Sir Isaac Pitman & Sons, London, 1938.

Dickie, H. F.: "Six Steps to Better Inventory Management," *Factory Management and Maintenance*, August, 1963.

Fogarty, D. W., and T. R. Hoffman: *Production and Inventory Management*, Southwestern, Cincinnati, 1983.

Greene, J. H.: *Production Control Systems and Decisions*, rev. ed., Irwin, Homewood, Ill., 1974.

Hannon, J. W.: "New Approaches to Employee Training," *Business Management*, June, 1967.

Jordan, H. H.: "Graphic Capacity Planning," *Inventory Management Newsletter*, vol. 9, no. 1, Center for Inventory Management, Stone Mountain, Georgia, January, 1981.

Jucius, M. J.: *Personnel Management*, 9th ed., Irwin, Homewood, Ill., 1979.

McCormick, E. J.: *Human Factors Engineering*, 4th ed., McGraw-Hill, New York, 1976.

Niebel, B. W.: *Motion and Time Study*, 7th ed., Irwin, Homewood, Ill., 1982.

Personnel Audits and Reports to Top Management, National Industrial Conference Board, Studies in Personnel Policy, no. 194, New York, 1964.

Personnel Practices in Factory and Office, National Industrial Conference Board, Manufacturing Studies in Personnel Policy, no. 194, New York, 1964.

Personnel Procedures Manuals, National Industrial Conference Board, Studies in Personnel Policy, no. 180, New York, 1961.

Rice, W. B.: *Control Charts*, Wiley, New York, 1955.

Robbins, S. P.: *Personnel: The Management of Human Resources*, 2d ed., Prentice-Hall, Englewood Cliffs, N.J., 1982.

Salvendy, Gavriel: *Handbook of Industrial Engineering*, Wiley, New York, 1982.

Wright, T. P.: "Factors Affecting the Cost of Airplanes," *Journal of Aeronautical Sciences*, February, 1936.

Zollitsch, H. G., and A. Langsner: *Wage and Salary Administration*, 2d ed., Southwestern, Cincinnati, 1970.

12

Inventory Information*

Editor

WILL WENDELL, CFPIM, Manager, Materials Management System, GTE Communication Systems, Northlake, Illinois

Contributor

CAROL MERRITELLO, CPIM, GTE Communication Systems, Northlake, Illinois

Inventories represent stocks of raw materials, work in process, and finished goods that are held for a short term before being converted into sales dollars. Inventories are one of the most active elements of a business operation and appear on the balance sheet, the manufacturing statement, and the profit-and-loss statement. Inventories are of vital interest not only to management but also to the stockholders, who are concerned about any drastic changes that might occur from time to time.

Inventories have a two-way effect on the financial health of the firm. On the one hand, inventories are an asset and therefore represent stored value that, when sold, will generate revenue and hopefully profit; on the other, inventories are usually a major investment and are financed by equity or debt. Therefore, inventory levels directly affect the return on investment. *Return* is reduced by the cost of capital (debt interest), while *investment* is increased by inventory. Thus, unnecessarily

---

* Parts of this chapter appeared originally in the first edition in chapters edited by Jack N. Durben, Miles Laboratories, Elkhart, Indiana, and Oliver Wight, Oliver Wight Inc., Newbury, New Hampshire.

high inventory levels have a double negative impact on the return on the investment.

WHY INVENTORIES?

Inventories are nonproductive assets which earn no return and which are subject to loss, pilferage, obsolescence, and taxes. Since inventory represents waste, why have any inventory at all? Inventories exist solely to cover discontinuities in the supply-demand relationship, which can be discussed in two major categories: lot-size inventories and anticipation inventories.

Lot-Size Inventories

Lot-size inventories are created whenever it is more economical to produce or move products in batches rather than continuously.

Purchasing places orders for batch deliveries on a one-time or delivery schedule basis to minimize order-processing costs, take advantage of price breaks or quantity discounts, or meet the vendor's minimum order requirements.

Transportation moves materials from the vendor to the customer in batch quantities. This allows full loads or consolidation of shipments and the more efficient use of containers.

Manufacturing produces parts and products in lot sizes to achieve manufacturing efficiencies. These show up both in the stockroom and on the factory floor, where there are shorter queues between work centers and fewer setups.

Anticipation Inventories

Anticipation inventories, as the term suggests, arise in anticipation of a mismatch between supply and demand.

Sales and distribution keep inventories on the shelf to satisfy anticipated, but variable, customer demand. The exact demand pattern is not known with certainty, and products are therefore stocked to cover that uncertainty.

Marketing requires adequate inventory for a new-product promotion campaign. Safety stocks will be required in order to cover demand that exceeds forecast. The safety-stock inventory level is a function of the anticipated forecast error and the number of stock-outs that can be tolerated.

Purchasing, marketing, or sales may stockpile inventory in anticipation of supply disruptions, such as strikes or plant closings.

Manufacturing may generate substantial inventories to cover seasonal demand while maintaining reasonably smooth production rates. This demand pattern results in an inventory buildup followed by a rapid inventory depletion.

Business-cycle studies indicate a correlation between (1) business cycles and (2) production and inventory control practices. If too much inventory exists, production will be reduced until the excess inventory is consumed. Conversely, if shortages exist, production has to be stepped up to replenish supplies.

Despite this clear correlation and despite the large-scale computer models that exhaustively simulate entire national economies, the cause-effect relationships of the production-consumption imbalance have not been completely predictable.

Classes of Inventory

There are three basic classes of inventory:

Raw materials are those items purchased to be processed further. They may be chemicals, fabrications, metals, packaging, etc., to be stored for future use and manufactured into finished goods. The items may be purchased from outside or may be supplied from another division. *Components* or *assemblies* purchased outside may be classified separately but are often considered as raw materials.

Work-in-process inventories are raw materials that have had some labor and burden added to them and are awaiting further processing into finished goods.

Finished goods are those products available for delivery. They may be carried in inventory or may be shipped upon completion.

Companies frequently have other categories of inventory. These include supplies absorbed through overhead, such as cutting oil and small tools. Service parts are considered a classification when they are an important part of a company's business.

SIMPLIFICATION AND STANDARDIZATION

As a firm grows, it continues to develop new products and to revise the old ones. These product changes (which are made in order to meet marketing demands) are healthy but leave potential inventory problems in their wake because new products make others obsolete. Revised designs replace old components and materials. Eventually, this obsolete material tends to increase the cost of manufacturing.

Simplification is the elimination of all extraneous or marginal product lines, but not necessarily in any logical fashion.

Standardization of materials means determining their fixed sizes, shapes, quality, and dimensions. Standardization follows a more scientific plan than simplification of inventory does. Inventory control alone cannot directly accomplish the standardization of materials, but it can encourage the use of standards. When specifications are issued, every effort should be made to designate the accepted industry standards.

Value-analysis techniques can be used as a before-the-fact purchasing tool to implement simplification and standardization, both of which can produce savings by reducing inventory, inventory storage space, obsolescence, and handling costs and by improving product quality.

CLASSIFICATION AND CODING

Before a useful coding method is selected and applied, it is necessary to establish the data classification plan and identify the data items within it. All uses to which the data are to be put must be considered in the development of the classification plan in order that as many major classifications and subdivisions may be devised as are necessary.*

During the identification procedure, it is advisable to record a *dictionary of standard nomenclature* for items within each classification subdivision so that uniformity may be maintained for all future usage. This dictionary serves as a reference guide for the identification and classification of new items and should be maintained on a current basis as long as the data file is in use.

After the classification plan has been completed and the data items have been identified within that plan, the coding method is selected. The particular method selected should be:

Expandable.   The code must provide space for additional entries within each classification for new items. There must also be capacity to expand existing classifications and add new ones to take care of future changes.

Precise.   The code structure must be such that only one code may be correctly applied to a given item.

Concise.   The code should require the least possible number of digits that would adequately describe each item.

Convenient.   The code must be easily understood by each user and simple to apply, whether encoding or decoding.

Meaningful.   If possible, the code itself should indicate some of the characteristics of the items.

Operable.   The code should be adequate for present and anticipated data processing machine methods as well as for manual reference.

The coding method having these qualities will be an efficient implement with which to accomplish the data-handling objectives.

Coding Methods and Their Uses

Sequence Codes.   The sequence method of coding is the simplest to use and apply. It is the assignment of consecutive numbers, beginning with 1, to a list of items as they occur, just as man-numbers might be assigned to employees as they are hired. This is the method preferred by some computer companies:

Code Number	Employee Name
1	George Adams
2	John Beldon
3	Arthur Brown
4	John Callahan

Block Codes.   Block coding is a minor refinement of the simple sequence code. A series of consecutive code numbers is divided into blocks, each block of numbers

---

* Material in this section is abstracted from *Coding Methods*, IBM Manual F20-8093, IBM Corporation, White Plains, N.Y.

being reserved for the identification of groups of items having some common characteristics. Block coding provides a data-classification system that uses a few code digits to identify each item. Expansion of the code to include additional items within each block is confined to those numbers left unassigned when the plan is originally established:

Code Number	Data Item	
1	Razor blades—packed 10	Codes 1 through
2	Razor blades—packed 25	5 reserved for
3	Razor blades—packed 50	blades
4		
5		
6	Safety razor—gold	Codes 6 through
7	Safety razor—silver	12 reserved for
8	Safety razor—chrome	safety razors

Group-Classification Codes. Group-classification codes are those which designate major and minor data classifications by successively lower-order groups of code digits:

	Major Group	Intermediate Group	Minor Group
Code digits	XX	XXX	XX

Significant-Digit Codes. Significant-digit codes are those in which all or some of the code digits describe weight, dimension, distance, capacity, or other characteristics of the items themselves. The code for a specific item is therefore determined by, and signifies, the physical makeup of the item itself:

Code	Description
TT 670 15 B 1	Tube type, size 670 × 15, blackwall, 1st line
TT 670 15 W 1	Tube type, size 670 × 15, whitewall, 1st line
TT 710 15 B 1	Tube type, size 710 × 15, blackwall, 1st line

Decimal Codes. The decimal method of coding is used primarily for indexing libraries or classifying written correspondence. It is a subject classification and coding system:

Decimal Code	Subject
520.	Astronomy
530.	Physics
531.	Mechanics
531.1	Machines
531.11	Lever and balance
531.12	Wheel and axle

Mnemonic Codes. Mnemonic code construction is characterized by the use of letter and number combinations that describe the items coded, the combinations having been derived from descriptions of the items themselves. The combinations are designed to be an aid to memorizing the codes by associating them with the items they represent:

Code Number				Item Description
Item	Size	Color and Style	Mfr.	
BY	010	RB	01	Bicycle, 10″, red, boy's, Comet
BY	010	RB	02	Bicycle, 10″, red, boy's, Red Star
BY	020	RB	01	Bicycle, 20″, red, boy's, Comet

Consonant Codes. Consonant codes are made up of abbreviations of the alphabetic data items themselves. The initial letter is always retained, but all subsequent vowels are dropped (including W and Y under special circumstances). Codes derived in this fashion from the different item characteristics will be unique to the items and may be used for sorting procedures:

Consonant Code	Item Name
JNS	Jones
PMPHNDLS	Pump handles
SMTH	Smith
SNDL	Snodel
SNWLY	Snowley
TRCK MTRL	Track material

Example of a Workable Code System. The raw-material and supply code described here meets the criteria of flexibility, expansion, machine compatibility, and convenience. It is a code currently in use by a large manufacturer. Processing is performed on both manual and large-scale data processing equipment.

This coding system consists of a nine-digit code that has most amply satisfied the user's need. While the nine digits may seem excessive, the degree of identification given to the individual item outweighs the processing disadvantage.

The coding structure is divided into two basic parts—raw materials and supplies. *Raw-Material Coding.* For raw materials, the code is as follows:

1	2	3	4	5	6	7	8	9	
									Number
X	X								Class
		X							Form or shape
			X	X	X				Chemical composition
						X	X	X	Size

0	6	4	0	6	1	0	9	2	Nine-digit code
0	6								Carbon steel
		4							Strip
			0	6	1				AISI C-1010 analysis—cold-rolled
						0	9	2	Assigned arbitrarily

Supplies Coding. In the supplies category fall the following: small hand tools, small machine tools, and supplies. The coding structure is as follows:

1	2	3	4	5	6	7	8	9	
									Number of digits in code
X	X								Class
		X	X						Kind
				X	X				Type
						X	X	X	Size

INVENTORY CONTROL PROCEDURES

Seldom will you see the inventory control department in the simplified organization chart, yet no other single department affects the destiny of the rest of the firm so much.

The demands that inventory hears from other departments include "Eliminate overtime," "Reduce inventory investment 7 percent," "Incorporate these product revisions in next week's production," "Sustain a 27 percent sales increase with no back orders," and "Balance the workload in the finishing department."

Because of the extensive volume of communication and interdependence with other departments, inventory control must keep the problems in proper perspective by using an efficient system.

Basic Control Systems

The inventory control system follows a basic cycle regardless of the firm's size: It begins by determining the production needs and is completed by filling the customer's order. Records and information will flow from similar sources, although the timing, accuracy, frequency, and completeness will be a function of the firm's size and its reliance on data processing systems. The basic information is contained on several records:

The Part Master Record. This includes a description of the part and of the planning and ordering rules—such as the lot size, manufacturing and cumulative lead times, planner codes, source codes, standard costs of material, labor, and burden and inventory balances for on-hand, in-inspection, in-transit, and floor stock.

Bill of Materials. This record contains the product structure by the relationships of the part numbers. By describing the successive single-level relationships, the entire multilevel product structures are described for all assemblies and subassemblies. This information can then be manipulated to determine the number of components required at each level to produce the final product. Conversely, the parent products that use a given component can also be determined.

Engineering-Change Records.   These contain past, present, and future engineering changes to the bills of materials. These changes are effective as of a given date, parent serial number, or order number; they may be changes in the quantity of a component per parent or may be the substitution of one component for another. This information is used to plan and execute changes in the product structure by making changes in the components required to build a parent. Information is retained for some specified period to provide a complete record of the part's engineering evolution.

Routing Records.   These contain the manufacturing-process information used to make a part. They relate the processes for the part in the sequence in which they take place as well as the special tools and time required. This time may be subdivided into move, queue, setup, and run times expressed in hours, with adjustment factors for efficiency, shifts worked, crew size, etc. This information is used to route manufacturing orders through the production facility and to plan the labor and machine time that will be required to attain the production schedule.

Routing-Change Records.   These contain past, present, and future versions of the routing for any given part. They are used to change the routing on the date, the serial number, or the order's effective date. The process and/or routing changes can include the substitution of one operation for another, a change in the setup or run time for a part, etc. This information is used to plan and execute changes in the processes used to manufacture a part.

The basic data records described above are used in various combinations to plan and control production schedules and inventories. This information is only part of the total data base used to support an integrated manufacturing control system and its links to other corporate systems. Not every company will have all the elements described here.

Inventory Records

The *perpetual inventory record* is a continuous account of the incoming materials, outgoing materials, and the balance on hand. It may be the part master or it may be a card record system, a page in a ledger book, a visual control board, or a tag tacked to the bin where the material is stored. A simple card record will be discussed here, since the same ideas apply to the other forms of recording inventory information.

At practically any instant, the perpetual inventory record should give the balance on hand and the activity for any particular inventory item. The record has two sections: a *heading*, where the permanent information is to be found, and the *body* of the card, where the changing information occurs.

The heading should contain the *part number* and *part description*. It is also the place to record the reordering information, such as the *reorder point*, *reorder quantity*, and sometimes the list of vendors and their *vendor rating*. Part location is also placed on the inventory record at times, as are part numbers that might be used as substitutes. Any other useful information may be added, but the card should not contain useless information.

In the basic inventory record (see Fig. 12.1), there will be three columns in the body; they contain information about receiving the material, issuing the material, and the remaining balance. These columns should be further divided so that each transaction can be traced. For example, the "received" column should have the document number (perhaps the receiving-report number), the date, and the quantity. Raw-materials records will have transaction information which is entirely different from that in finished-goods records.

This basic inventory record with just three columns often does not present sufficient information for adequate control. When the ordering cycle is long and there are apt to be several orders out at one time, it may be desirable to add another column showing what is "on order." This will help prevent duplicating orders; however, because it adds to the confusion of keeping the records, it should not be included in the system unless absolutely essential.

An "allocated" column might also be added to the record. This is used in circumstances when it is desirable to allocate material to customers and to orders awaiting production.

Bin Tags. Some inventory control systems are operated with a perpetual inventory card attached to the bins. At times such a card system has been operated in conjunction with a perpetual-inventory-record system.

Bin tag systems are not always satisfactory. The cards are apt to get dirty, and the stores clerks are often careless in how they fill out the record—frequently neglecting to do so at all.

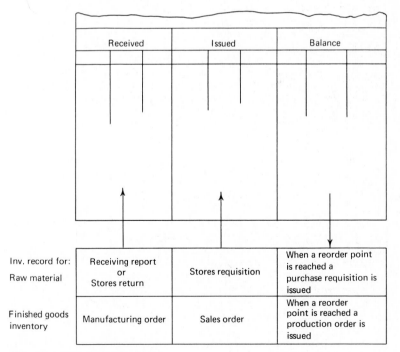

FIG. 12.1 Basic inventory record.

Basic Storeroom Operation

There are four basic storeroom operations: receiving, storing, issuing, and returning. (See Chapter 21.) The complexity of each operation will vary according to the size and type of business, but all four operations must be performed. The inspection function is not included, since it is a function of quality control.

The layout of the stores area is a function of space available, size of materials, part-number systems, material similarities, and special considerations.

Centralized stores provide the advantages of fewer personnel, less space requirement, less dated inventory, better record control, and less record duplication. The case against centralized stores is that the time required to move materials to the using areas is lengthy, involving added labor and handling equipment.

Certain low-value materials are better controlled by no control. The change of an inventory item to an expendable supply item without a requisition reduces the overhead associated with that item, and inventory control effort may thus be placed where control is needed.

Protection or security of inventory is especially important when the items stored may have value or may be used elsewhere. Shortages can shut down production when material is available only "on paper."

Storeroom Security. The first step in developing an efficient inventory control system is to limit access to the storage areas so that only authorized personnel are permitted to enter. This may mean enclosing the area with fences and installing locked gates. Controlled receipts and issues and a locked storeroom are basic to the implementation of a successful cycle-counting program. Not only will easy access to the stockroom contribute to the possibility of parts being removed without the proper paperwork, but responsibility for accuracy will not be accepted by the stockroom personnel. A concerted company effort must also be made to ensure that all paperwork is handled on a timely basis and that errors are corrected quickly. Effective controls must be established and understood so that the stockroom personnel and the rest of the organization are convinced that any inventory errors will have widespread effects. Unauthorized people must not be permitted to submit inventory transactions or adjustments directly into the records. It is not uncommon for companies to bond their stockroom employees to ensure against any losses caused by thievery.

ABC INVENTORY ANALYSIS

The ABC technique is an analytical management tool for focusing attention on and applying effort in the area that will give the greatest results. While the ABC technique has universal application in many areas of human endeavor, this discussion will concern only its use in inventory control.

The creation of inventory results from ordering material for both known and forecasted requirements. When orders are issued for known requirements, the tightest degree of ordering control can be achieved. This may be designated as *required* (or *unique*) inventory. The ABC technique of ordering control does not apply to this low-risk inventory.

When material for stock is ordered based on forecasted requirements, inventory is created in anticipation of needs. This can create high inventory values, so there must be a technique available that is capable of applying the greatest effort to the high-annual-usage-value items.

From a control viewpoint, the value of an item can be defined by its *annual usage value*. This is calculated by multiplying the quantity used in a year (in terms of usage past or forecasted) by the unit cost of the item. The *dollar value of annual usage* is the common factor for categorizing the inventory items.

Without its dollar value, annual usage gives no meaningful common factor for making comparisons. For example, the same attention may unwisely be given to ordering 500 screws as is given to ordering 500 electric motors, yet the order value for the screws may be only $20 as opposed to $10,000 for the order value of the electric motors.

The importance of the ordering decision should not rest only on inventory investment considerations. Since the order is being issued for material in anticipation of needs, the accuracy of the forecast becomes a very important consideration in minimizing inventory risk for high-value items.

Steps for an ABC Analysis

First, consider all the stock items in Table 12.1 and determine their annual usage value (column 3 times column 4 equals column 5). Next, arrange the items in descending order in accordance with their annual usage value (column 6), which is developed by adding the value of each successive item.

The data include 19,840 items ordered for stock, and their total annual usage value is $76,366,187. A review of the data quickly reveals that there is a wide range of values for the items ordered for stock. However, approximately 3000 of the items constitute about 90 percent of the total value. These data can be most clearly represented in chart form.

Figure 12.2 shows the accumulated annual usage value in chart form. The purpose of the chart is to give visual impact to where the logical breaks occur in the curve. Generally, one can expect to find that approximately 10 percent of the items will constitute 75 percent of the total value and that 75 percent of the items will constitute only 10 percent of the value. This is a typical distribution; however, each inventory analyzed will deviate from it.

In practice, one must apply judgment to determine the two points on the curve that divide the inventory into the three ABC categories. Usually, the points are selected by observing where the curve seems to change shape.

In this particular analysis, the first 1231 items, which are 6 percent of the total, account for slightly over $61 million, or about 80 percent of the total accumulated annual usage. Judgment dictates the exact control point at which the high-value A inventory limit is set. The fewer the number of A items there are, the greater the amount of individual attention that can be applied. Considerable latitude can be exercised to round out the control point conveniently. For instance, a point was selected on the curve to limit the A items to the first 1231 high-value items. It would have been just as logical to set the limit at 1000 items.

The next logical break in the curve appears to fall between the first 2500 to 3500 items in the sequence. The point chosen in this analysis is after the 2841st item. The balance of 16,999 items, which are 86 percent of the total items, accounts for nearly $7 million, or about 9 percent of the total value. These items, having the lowest annual usage value, are classified as the C inventory. For controlling an individual item, these are given the least attention.

The middle-value items, resulting from setting the lower limit for A items and the higher limit for C items, are identified as the class B inventory. The B inventory group in this analysis would consist of 1610 items, representing 8 percent of the total items. The annual usage value would be $8,714,604, or 11 percent of the total value.

TABLE 12.1 Selected List of Inventory Items Ranked by Annual Usage Value

Item Number* (1)	Part Number (2)	Cost per Unit, Dollars (3)	Annual Usage (4)	Annual Usage Value, Dollars (5)	Accum. Annual Usage Value, Dollars (6)
1	FD-101	0.175	10,601,733	1,855,303	1,855,303
2	D-5102	1.184	1,318,779	1,561,434	3,416,737
3	D-28462	0.968	1,186,456	1,148,489	4,565,226
4	D-3837	0.644	1,349,578	869,128	5,434,354
5	FD-102	0.180	4,023,976	724,316	6,158,670
10	D-5216	0.237	2,166,712	513,511	8,982,966
15	D-4665	1.160	341,307	395,916	11,081,861
20	D-4619	0.261	1,343,610	350,682	12,877,146
25	D-437	0.225	1,406,582	316,481	14,520,424
250	WA-101	10.062	5,262	52,946	40,216,073
500	D-28306	0.132	200,441	26,458	49,557,607
750	D-15006	0.277	62,339	17,268	54,897,995
1000	D-5805	0.105	116,294	12,211	58,527,225
1231	FD-100	1.190	8,034	9,560	61,004,981
1250	D-6882	0.356	26,394	9,396	61,184,819
1500	FD-400	278.330	27	7,515	63,302,335
1750	MC-4225	0.830	7,534	6,253	65,014,705
2000	D-4241	0.488	10,535	5,141	66,433,279
2250	D-28188	0.471	9,131	4,301	67,607,577
2500	D-6765	0.084	43,424	3,648	68,593,110
2750	GB-1013	0.007	448,772	3,141	69,437,792
2842	MP-600	0.097	30,930	3,000	69,719,585
3000	D-15017	0.002	1,377,559	2,755	70,174,851
3250	D-28550	0.610	3,929	2,397	70,819,676
3500	H-88085	2.421	863	2,089	71,378,523
3750	GB-1014	0.007	265,461	1,858	71,872,492
4000	D-9406	0.210	7,812	1,641	72,307,554
4250	H-88473	0.141	10,462	1,475	72,696,462
4500	D-2707	3.370	384	1,294	73,042,385
4750	D-7157	0.113	10,323	1,116	73,349,007
5000	D-28131	0.838	1,244	1,042	73,623,828
5250	D-6770	0.060	15,769	946	73,871,584
5500	FD-106	0.200	4,253	851	74,096,117
5750	H-88660	0.910	843	767	74,298,016
6000	FD-10	0.650	1,049	682	74,478,735
6500	H-88033	0.202	2,796	565	74,788,851
7000	D-28408	0.024	19,523	469	75,046,820
8000	D-49002	0.669	475	332	75,442,845
9000	D-78077	0.365	636	232	75,722,325
10000	H-88549	0.513	329	169	75,920,932
19840	H-8896	0.006	57	1	76,366,187

* Note: These are only representative items.

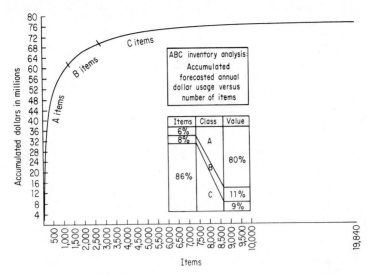

FIG. 12.2   ABC analysis.

The data discussed in the last three paragraphs are summarized in Fig. 12.3, which shows the ABC distribution. In addition to charting this accumulated annual usage, it is also convenient to chart the annual usage value for each item, as illustrated in Fig. 12.4.

The purpose of the following chart is to allow the proper ABC identification of the annual usage limits on a per-item basis. Item 1231 has an annual usage value of $9,560, and this becomes the lower-limit value for a class A inventory item. Item 2842 has an annual usage value of $3,000, and this becomes the upper-limit value for a class C inventory item. A class B inventory item would have an annual usage value ranging between $3,001 and $9,559.

| Category | Usage Range | | Number of Parts |
	Lower Limit	Upper Limit	
Class A	$9,561	None	1,231
Class B	3,001	$9,560	1,611
Class C	0	3,000	16,998

THE ANNUAL PHYSICAL INVENTORY

The annual physical inventory is a big, complex job involving a lot of people, many departments, and many activities, and it is usually rushed because it involves a costly plant-shutdown period. The problems typically are poor preparation, improper counting procedures, failure to account for paperwork, and ineffective checking of significant discrepancies.

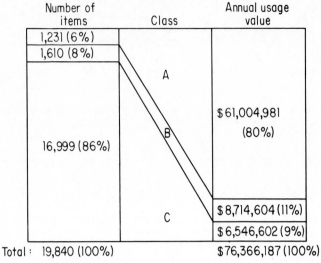

FIG. 12.3   ABC summary.

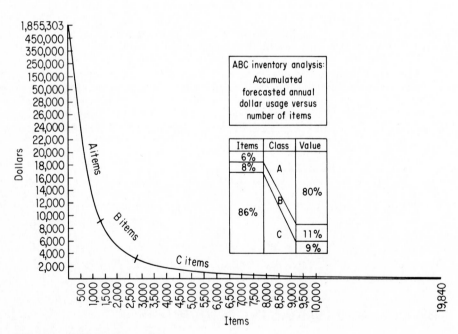

FIG. 12.4   ABC inventory analysis.

1. *Preparation.* Getting ready to take a physical inventory involves four phases:
   a. Housekeeping. Getting materials located and arranged properly so that they can be inventoried easily.
   b. Identification. Ensuring that each part to be inventoried is correctly identified. Errors in counting affect only one record, but errors in identification make two records wrong.
   c. Instruction. Reviewing detailed inventory-taking procedures with all key personnel immediately prior to taking inventory. The answer to this problem is not always detailed written instructions. The best approach is meetings with the responsible department heads and supervisors so that the important elements of inventory taking can be identified and responsibility assigned.
   d. Training. Here actual practice is recommended in taking physical inventory, especially where counting scales and mechanical hand counters are likely to be used and familiarity with their proper operation is essential.

2. *Counting Procedures.* Accurate counting is difficult under the best of circumstances. An *inventory team* is recommended, consisting of one or two counters, a checker, and a writer. The counters are usually factory workers who do the actual work of handling, identifying, and counting the material. A foreman, inspector, or production control person checks the count and item identification.

   Many auditing firms permit the omission of low-value items from the count if adequate substitutes for valuing such items have been agreed upon. Some companies establish a percentage of the total inventory value for these inexpensive items. Others accept a fixed dollar total for a low-value inventory, and this helps a great deal since such items usually represent a large percentage of the total number of parts. Eliminating their counting can greatly reduce the cost of the physical inventory, and more attention can be paid to the more important high-value items.

   There is always a temptation to allow the continued movement of materials, at least on an "emergency only" basis. This is an invitation to errors, and few companies have been able to do this and maintain inventory accuracy. The best approach is to *seal off an area while it is being inventoried* until it has been checked by both groups of auditors and also by those following up major discrepancies between records and physical counts.

3. *Inventory Paperwork.* Serially numbered inventory cards may be used to ensure that all items counted will be accounted for. Many companies use a prepunched deck of tabulating cards primarily to assist in speeding up the processing of inventory data after the actual counting has been done. This also makes it possible to reduce the number of inventory errors by minimizing handwritten information. When using this approach, however, it is important to decide how many cards are necessary for each item at each location, to avoid physical damage to the cards, and to devise suitable means for locating the proper inventory card quickly.

   One of the biggest problems is clearing the normal paperwork channels prior to taking the inventory of all issues, receipts, uncashed requisitions, scrap reports, etc. Here is where systems people, people who really understand the paperwork flow, can assist. Never forget to count materials in the shipping dock, export holding areas, returned-goods departments, marketing displays, and the like. Of course, the computer room itself should not be overlooked for records, and once operations have been resumed, editing stations should be set up with individuals cautioned to look for paperwork that might have gotten through with dates prior to the physical inventory so that corrections can be handled speedily.

4. *Recognition of Significant Variances.* Get the inventory information posted to the production control records *quickly*. Even if this has to be done manually, it is essential if the physical inventory is going to be accurate. The essence of record verification is *timeliness*. The audit team should check any discrepancies before material starts to move again.

Schedules and Instructions for Physical Inventory

It is difficult for one person to keep the physical inventory procedure in mind from year to year, and changes in personnel can cause a severe break in continuity, causing the procedure to become lost. To overcome these difficulties, it is imperative that a written standard procedure be prepared that can be referred to year after year. This does not mean that the system is rigid and cannot be adjusted from year to year. An example of a schedule and instructions for physical inventory are given in Table 12.2. This is one company's standard procedure, but it can be modified to fit any situation.

CYCLE COUNTING

The once-a-year physical inventory reduces the production capacity during the time the facility is shut down. It does not necessarily reduce errors, mistakes in part identification, or record inaccuracies. Consequently, the implementation of a cycle counting, which is a technique for counting the program inventory and verifying the records throughout the year, can be justified on a cost-benefit basis.

A properly managed, well-executed, efficient cycle-counting program can deliver significant benefits at a very low cost. Records that are very accurate can reduce shortages, late orders, and obsolescence costs and can improve customer service and factory morale. Accurate records are the cornerstone of successful production and inventory control.

Classifying the Inventory for Cycle Counting

An effective cycle-counting process requires a counting priority system in which critical items are controlled more tightly than others. For example, items with high-value balances are financially more important than those with low-value balances, and high-usage items are more susceptible to inventory errors than are those with low usage. All part numbers may be placed in at least three categories: A, B, and C. Class A items, the most critical, are counted perhaps 6 times a year; class C items, the least critical, are counted only 2 times a year.

A part which has a low dollar value and a low usage but which is vital to the production of a finished product and is not easily obtained in a short time should be categorized as a Class A part. Consideration should also be given to other situations, such as long lead time, and to multiuse parts that might disrupt production if a shortage occurred. Their priority category should be weighted accordingly. Another consideration is the potential for pilferage; those items which could be stolen should be controlled and placed in a secured stockroom, and a company may want to count them more frequently.

TABLE 12.2 Schedule and Instructions for Physical Inventory

Feb. 26
  I. Order the blank inventory and *precount the cards.*
 II. Remind all people who are doing the ordering not to schedule anything for delivery between June 14 and July 15 unless urgently needed.

Apr. 25
  I. Get the master inventory cards ready to be reproduced.
    A. Delete cards where necessary.
    B. Add cards where necessary.
    C. Add new items.
      1. Make a data processing run on new items:
        a. Items with inventory—add to inventory deck.
        b. Items with no inventory—reproduce deck.
          (1) Original deck—add to inventory deck.
          (2) Duplicate deck—hold until items are checked out.
    D. Add blank cards.
    E. Load header cards.

May 6
  I. Instruct the duplicating department to produce inventory cards to be used for storage areas, and precount the cards for both the storage areas and the work in process.

May 8
  I. Load the header items for the inventory cards on the computer.

May 13
  I. Instruct data processing to reproduce onto the new inventory cards the following information:
    A. Reproduce the part number in card column 1−6 from the master inventory card deck and keep in sequence. (Do not punch the old sequence number.)
    B. Punch the description in card column 7−38 from the computer.
    C. Sequence new inventory cards in card column 74−79.
      1. Start the sequence number with X00000. (X refers to the year.)
    D. Interpret part number (column 1−6), description (7−38), and sequence (55−60).
 II. Reproduce the inventory card's information on the bin identification card.
III. Interpret the identification cards.
 IV. Inventory cards are in card sequence. Print out a list showing the sequence number, part number, and description on four-part narrow paper.
  V. Sort the inventory cards into part-number sequence after step IV is completed. Print a list showing the part-number description and the sequence number on four-part narrow paper.
 VI. Collate the new inventory cards with the bin cards. The inventory card is placed first in the sequence.

May 23
  I. Instruct data processing to return one collated set of inventory cards and two printed lists.
 II. The fourth copy of the printed sequence-number list should have the sequence numbers deleted. Add the following heading and duplicate:

For dept.———				
Seq. No.	Part No.	Description	Location	Assigned to

12.17

TABLE 12.2 *(Continued)*

      1. Distribute list and blank inventory cards.
        a. One to storage area.
          (1) It is best to give out one sheet at a time with its blank cards.
        b. One copy stays in production control as a master list for blank numbers.
          (1) As lists come back from the shop, the master list should be checked.
III. Distribute printed inventory card listings (one by part number and one by sequence number).
    A. One to cost department.
    B. One to department.
    C. One to department.
    D. One (copy with blank numbers missing) to storage area.
IV. Cancel header items that were loaded on computer inventory records.

May 25
  I. Production control starts placing bin cards into stock bins.
    A. Pull all old bin cards and extra checkouts.
    B. To prevent losing the inventory cards, slip them into boxes.
    C. Use status sheets as a guide.
    D. Put the part number on blank bin cards.

May 30
  I. Order the rubber date stamps that are needed for inventory.

June 3
  I. Inventory crew to start count.
    A. Put inventory quantity in "count" column on cards.
    B. As parts are received for use, quantities should be posted to inventory cards.
    C. If there is no inventory card in bin, use precount card.
    D. Be sure to record the number of containers or bins involved if more than one is inventoried and recorded on one inventory card.
  II. Separate voided inventory cards that are returned.

June 14
  I. Discontinue the issuing of purchase orders.

June 18
  I. Run the work orders for assemblies that may be required shortly after the inventory period. These will include:
    A. Assemblies that have the fewest items backlogged.
    B. Assemblies for which parts will be available shortly after inventory.
    C. Assemblies for which parts will be made in June.
      1. Write red X on bills of materials so that the multilith department will know which bills of materials and routing cards are to be returned to the expediters.
  II. Use data processing to sequence old input cards for bills of materials for regular orders and subassemblies.
  III. Stop all warehouse orders unless items are urgently needed. Box and label the cards until the notice to scrap them comes from production control.
  IV. Continue to allocate and ship as long as orders are received.

June 19
  I. Stop all component-part orders unless they are urgently needed. Box and label the cards until the notice to scrap them comes from production control.
  II. Have the expediters send enough work to the assembly departments so that the lines will be supplied until 1 week after shutdown.
    A. Remind the assembly department to start supplying the lines ahead so that all parts will be *pulled* before the storage areas are closed.

June 20
  I. Stop generating bills of materials unless urgently needed (the urgent items will be specified by production control).
  II. Stop processing 30-day checkout cards (discard cards).
  III. Make sure that all stationery supplies have been ordered for inventory before the stationery stores are closed.

When to Count

Despite the benefits, cycle-counting the entire inventory can be expensive, but the cost can be minimized by selecting the most efficient time to count. Techniques that can reduce the cycle-counting times are discussed here.

Opportunity Counts.   Opportunity counts should be generated when inventory quantities are at a low level. One option is to generate a count when the inventory stock level is less than a certain number of weeks of stock on hand, such as 4 weeks of stock on hand. Another option is to count the stock when it is at a low level compared to the average on-hand balance, such as 20 percent of the average on-hand balance. If the cycle-count interval is 90 days, the program might be set up to start looking for a low balance anytime between 70 and 90 days. If an opportunity balance is detected during that period, a cycle count would be generated; if not, then the normal count would be generated on the 90th day. In either case, the next cycle-count date would be set to day 180 to preserve the planned cycle-count frequency of 4 times per annum.

Low-cost Counts.   Low-cost counts may or may not be system-generated. They capitalize on the facts that the part is going to be handled by a stockkeeper anyway, either to pick the part or to put it away, and that it costs very little extra to perform a count at the same time. The count is recorded on a card that has a box to check for an out-of-stock condition and a line for writing in the stock balance. If the stockkeeper uses the remaining stock to fill an issue, the out-of-stock box is checked. If the stockkeeper notes that there are only a few items left in stock when filling an issue, the quantity remaining is entered. If the stockkeeper sees, when processing a receipt, that there is no inventory on hand, the quantity of the receipt is entered.

Date and Time Reconciliation.   It is very easy to get into a situation in which the reconciliation effort consumes more time and resources than the count itself. The reality is that paperwork cutoffs are not always clean. It is not always possible to freeze the records, let alone the stockroom activities. The objective is to manage the reconciliation and adjustment process in an orderly fashion. As consistent performance improvement is achieved, accuracy goals can be set higher accordingly.

This difficulty may be overcome by recording the time and date of every stockroom activity, including the cycle count. When this is done, all transaction records are dated in exactly the same sequence as the activities occurred. This can be done by writing the date and time on all transactions or by using time clocks, similar to those used for employee time cards. Better still is a hand-held computer terminal or a portable, programmable bar-code reader. These units can date- and time-stamp all transactions. Once date- and time-stamped, the transactions can be processed in sequence and "automatically" reconciled.

Containerization and Visual Controls.   Using standard-quantity containers improves the counting process. In this "egg carton" concept, one merely observes visually that all slots are filled. The same concept can be applied to almost any stockroom situation. For example, small parts can be kept in premarked tubes containing 25 parts each, and large subassemblies can be kept in compartmentalized totes containing 10. To maximize the benefits, all activities should take place in multiples of the standard container sizes. For example, if each assembly uses four of the small parts and one subassembly, then for an order of 200 parent pieces the stockroom would pick 32 tubes and 20 tote pans and, upon completion, would receive 20 totes of the finished assembly. It is far easier and more accurate to hand-count standardized tubes and totes than to weigh-count or hand-count individual pieces.

A further extension of the visual control concept is to arrange the standardized containers into standard arrays. For example, tubes stored in bulk can be grouped in sets of 40 each, or 1000 pieces. Stockroom parts can then be counted, issued, and received rapidly and accurately by simple visual control.

Cycle counts can be matched against the inventory record as it stood when the cycle count was performed. Counts with plus or minus the part's tolerance are processed without adjusting balances. Parts that are outside the tolerance bandwidth are placed in sequence according to the size of the difference between the physical count and the record. Parts with major discrepancies (expressed in dollars, units, or percentages) can be segregated so that no adjustment takes place until a recount is performed. Moderate discrepancies can be adjusted on the spot, but this might require a written report on the reason for the error and on the corrective action taken. Minor discrepancies, say below $50 and/or below 5 percent, might generate a record adjustment without further investigation.

Special counts may be necessary under the following conditions:

- Unexpected inventory outages or a negative on-hand inventory are sure signs of a record error and should trigger an immediate special count.
- If a cycle count results in a major discrepancy, it is usually best to leave the record unadjusted and call for an immediate special count. This count should be conducted very carefully to check for stock that is out of its proper location, for misplaced paperwork, etc. Only after a thorough investigation should the record be adjusted. The same approach should be used if paperwork is inexplicably missing.

Parts that are declared obsolete by engineering should be counted immediately so that the analysis of whether to scrap or to rework them is based on an accurate balance. Once the scrap ticket or rework order is issued, the parts must be physically removed from the stockroom.

Transaction Cutoffs

Manufacturing companies are constantly moving, receiving, and issuing stock throughout the factory, and it must be known when these activities occurred in relationship to the cycle count. Without this knowledge, unnecessary adjustments will lead to major operating problems. Cycle counting is a waste of resources unless the counts can be compared to the inventory records at the correct point in time.

There are two methods recommended to achieve clean transaction cutoffs so that the inventory record agrees with what is physically present at the time the cycle count is performed.

The first method is to freeze stockroom transactions. It may be the most difficult to initiate, but it is the easiest to maintain and will result in the fewest errors. Also, it is suitable for a three-shift operation. The freeze may include either all items in a stockroom or a block of items as described:

- A list of the items to be counted is generated, sorted, and sent to the stockroom.
- The count is to be made at a specified time near the end of a shift. All stockroom receipts and issues are cut off prior to this time.
- All items specified on the list or cards are counted by stockroom personnel.

- Production control gathers the paperwork in order to update the inventory records.

This method will only be effective if the stockroom and production control personnel make sure that all paperwork transactions have been entered into the records before cycle counting.

Another option is to identify and put a transaction freeze on a block of items to be counted. This can be done by manually tagging the items in one or more stockroom locations or by placing a freeze on the item transactions.

The second recommended method is to count the inventory during a nonoperational shift. For companies not working three shifts, this is probably the best method of ensuring an accurate data base. The cycle counts are performed on a shift when the people in the area to be audited are not working. The main concern in using this approach is to ensure that any physical transactions that have taken place have been transferred to the perpetual records before the counting begins. Because some documents may be hidden on worktables and desks, some transactions may be delayed in being recorded, so a date and time stamp should be placed on all issues, receipts, moves, and cycle counts. Entries on the records should also identify the time the transaction was recorded.

Cycle-Counting Control Group

The cycle-counting *control group* is a set of part numbers that are counted at regular intervals, such as once a week. This provides information for two critical problems: It indicates the level of processing accuracy currently maintained, and it helps identify problems that are contributing to inaccuracies. These problems must be analyzed and corrected if the cycle-counting program is to be effective. The sample should include raw materials, components, subassemblies, and finished products and should also include a cross section of different part types.

The procedure is to count and recount the control group to correct the causes of errors in the stockroom and in the cycle-count reconciliation process. Since errors always tend to creep into any process, this is a never-ending task; it should be a permanent part of any effective cycle-counting program. A control group consists of about 20 parts from various representative part categories, such as purchased parts and manufactured parts, that are counted by different counting processes, such as hand counting and scale counting. These 20 parts are counted every week and are gradually combined with the other 180 parts that are being cycle-counted during their normal interval (every 3 months, every 6 months, etc.).

When an error is detected in the record for a member of the control group, every transaction can be exhaustively examined to find the cause of the error, because transactions for only 5 days have taken place since the last count, and the audit trail can be followed. There is no way to do this with a regular maintenance cycle count, which takes place every 4 to 6 months. The items in the control-group population should be slowly rotated so that they do not become well known or are no longer representative of the total population.

The control-group procedure will identify any current process errors, their cause, and the rate of improvement. The combination of the rate of improvement and the elapsed time to cycle through the population will establish the expected accuracy in the future. For example, if the counting is improving 5 percent per week on average from a starting point of 50 percent accuracy, it will take at least 10 weeks to get the process under control; therefore, it will take at least 3 months until the cycle counts can be expected to reach 100 percent.

It is not unusual to start a cycle-counting program gradually and count only a few part numbers to determine any causes for errors that might affect all items in the inventory. After any causes for errors are rectified, more part numbers are included in the cycle count until the entire inventory is being cycle-counted.

Counting Tolerances and Accuracy

A record is considered accurate if it is within the established tolerance bandwidth, which is a function of the counting method used, the inventory's availability, the handling method, and usage. For example, if 2000 parts are scale-counted on a scale that is accurate to plus or minus 1 percent, the tolerance bandwidth will be plus or minus 20 pieces, or 1980 to 2020. The record is considered correct if it is within this range, and incorrect if it is above or below the range. A large, valuable, hand-counted part would have a zero tolerance since it can and should be counted exactly. Another cheap part, readily available and having a high usage, might be counted within a 2 percent tolerance. The establishment of proper tolerances will provide a correct performance measurement and will avoid useless adjustments of records that are within tolerance.

The first step in setting accuracy goals for the cycle-counting program is to establish the existing accuracy by counting representative parts. This sets the starting point.

Storeroom Cycle-Counting Problems

Many companies use random stockroom locations to optimize the use of available space. This means that a given part inventory may be found in more than one place. If location information is missing from the inventory records, or if stock is not in the locations as stated in the records, the inventory will be lost until the records are corrected. Stock handlers will not find the parts, the cycle count will have discrepancies, and incorrect write-offs will be made. In view of the potential consequences of incorrect locations, it is important to conduct a location cycle count, which is a comprehensive cross-check between the records and the physical locations.

The first step is to select a group of locations, such as one or more aisles or bays within a stockroom. Next, a list of all parts that are supposed to be in these locations is produced in location sequence from the records. Finally, every location on the list is cross-checked against every location in the area being cycle-counted. Every location on the list and every physical location in the area must be checked off. This ensures that every part is where it belongs and that there are no parts physically present that do not belong in the area.

Personnel Requirements

Some managers decide against implementing a cycle-counting program, believing that the stockroom personnel are not capable. However, a rapid identification of problems, together with efficient training, will make the program succeed. Training produces a program that efficiently uses a few experienced people throughout the year, whereas an annual inventory procedure inefficiently uses inexperienced people in a short, hectic period once a year.

Effective counting results in the timely identification and correction of the cause of errors, reduces the loss of production time, and results in a systematic improvement of record accuracy. Often the personnel will be given an acceptable error tolerance and will be required to meet it. Cycle-counting personnel are sometimes divided into teams by storeroom areas so that they can compete on the basis of accuracy; as an incentive, their records are posted in a prominent place.

The number of personnel required for a cycle-counting program can be determined by the following procedure:

1. Determine the number of counts required per day:
   a. Determine the number of counts per year for each inventory category. For example, 500 class A parts counted per quarter for four quarters equals 2000 counts per year. Do the same for each class, and total them.
   b. Add an estimate of special counts, recounts, negative- and zero-balance counts, and opportunity counts. Remember that some of these counts will replace the maintenance counts. Include the count made by the maintenance control group.
   c. Divide the total count by the working days to obtain the counts per day.
2. Determine the number of cycle counts that can be done by an average person per hour and per day. Variables include the type of product and containerization, the centralization of stockrooms, and the arrangement of shelves and bins.
3. From the counts required per day and the count that a person can do in a day, calculate the number of personnel required per day to produce the cycle-count lists. Incidentally, the part numbers should be listed in a sequence that will minimize the travel time by the cycle counter.

CONTROLLING INDEPENDENT INVENTORIES

Material-requirements planning is an acceptable way of controlling *dependent inventory* items (Chapter 14). However, there are many situations in which *independent inventory* items must be controlled, and it is this category which is discussed here.

The importance and necessity of inventories are well-established, but the function that they should serve is not so well established. Typically, the salespeople feel that inventories provide a means for giving good customer service; therefore, they would like plenty of everything to be available at all times. On the other hand, the part of the organization that is concerned with the financial aspects of the business regards inventories in an entirely different light; it views them as tying up the working portion of the current assets (circulating capital) and thus feels that inventories should be maintained at a minimum in order to increase capital turnover.

Those connected with production have still another point of view. They would like long production runs with a minimum number of setups. Therefore, production people consider inventories as a means for obtaining an efficient plant operation.

From this discussion, it appears that inventories should be planned so that good customer service is achieved, the inventory investment is kept at a minimum, and the most efficient plant operation results. It is apparent, however, that these are opposing objectives. This means that inventories must be planned according to what is best for the company rather than to what is best for a particular department.

The inherent dangers in planning inventories by an intuitive approach should also be emphasized. As the word *intuitive* implies, the company using this method tries to gain a quick and ready insight into the problem based on the knowledge of the individual who is planning the inventories. However, such individuals will be biased by the traditional thinking of that part of the organization to which they have belonged; although their intentions will be good, it is doubtful that they will be looking at the problem from the proper perspective.

Inventories have a profound effect on the movement of money within an organization. A company cannot afford to plan its inventories in a haphazard manner if it expects to prosper. Neither can it afford to plan its inventories from a partisan point of view. Effective planning demands analyzing the problem as a whole.

There are basically two questions that must be answered: (1) *When* should the inventory be replenished? (2) *By how much* should the inventory be replenished? Given that there are opposing objectives that must be considered before answering these questions, it is not surprising that there are opposing costs that correspond to these objectives, that is, as some costs are reduced, the costs associated with other objectives will increase. The answers to the two questions above should be such that the total cost of the inventory is at a minimum. Needless to say, such an analysis must be carried out formally. It entails too many considerations to arrive at good results by an intuitive approach.

The Basic EOQ Model

The formal analysis of inventories is referred to as *scientific inventory control*. The idea is to construct a mathematical model that represents the interaction of the opposing costs that are related to the inventory. The model that has received by far the most attention is the basic economic order quantities (EOQ) model, and with good reason.

The basic EOQ model has been used more than any other model. With slight modifications, it is used by nearly all companies that calculate economic order quantities. The model is an extremely simplified representation of actual inventory situations; however, in many cases it gives good approximations to more complex models. Its simplicity also makes the calculation of EOQs relatively easy.

The basic EOQ model is used almost exclusively by authors as a foundation upon which to build a more complex inventory theory. (See Chapter 29.) The simplicity of the model makes it ideal for illustrating the philosophy behind inventory models. It is also important because several of the more complex models are nothing more than refinements or extensions of the basic model.

The basic EOQ model assumes that the inventory situation can be represented as in Fig. 12.5. It is apparent that this is quite a simplified representation of the inventory for an actual stockkeeping item. It is assumed that the demand is known and that stock is withdrawn continuously at a constant rate. It is also assumed that the inventory can be replenished instantaneously; that is, it takes zero time to replenish the stock. A third assumption is that the inventory is replenished when the stock on hand drops to zero. No stock-outs or back orders are allowed to occur. The inventory is replenished by the same amount, q, each time. Since the sawtooth inventory pattern has been assumed, the average inventory on hand will be $q/2$. Therefore, the average inventory depends directly on the order quantity.

Notice in Fig. 12.5 that there is a relationship between the order quantity and the time between replenishments. The order quantity q is equal to the demand rate D times the replenishment cycle t. That is, $q = tD$. Hence, the size of the order affects the number of times that the inventory must be replenished.

The effect of varying the size of the order quantity can be seen by considering Fig. 12.6. If the order quantity is cut to one-third the original quantity, the average inventory is only one-third as large. At the same time, the replenishment cycle is

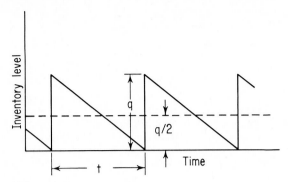

FIG. 12.5 Inventory pattern.

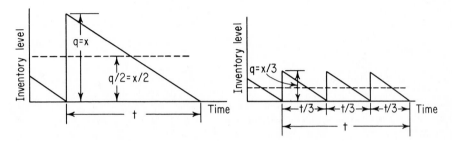

FIG. 12.6 Effect of order-quantity size.

only one-third as long, and hence the inventory must be replenished 3 times as often. The same idea can be extended for reducing the quantity by any fraction.

To determine the best order quantity, the costs associated with the stockkeeping item must be considered. These costs may be placed in three broad categories according to their effect on the size of the order quantity:

1. Costs that tend to increase the order quantity
2. Costs that tend to decrease the order quantity
3. Costs that have no effect on the order quantity

The first group of costs consists of those connected with the replenishment of the inventory. Suppose that it costs R dollars to replenish the inventory 1 time. The number of times it must be replenished is equal to the demand D divided by the order quantity q. Therefore, in general, the cost of replenishing the inventory every year is $R \times D/q$. An increase in the order quantity decreases the number of times the inventory must be replenished. Therefore, the cost of replenishing the inventory is also reduced by using larger order quantities. This can be seen from Fig. 12.7.

Those costs which tend to decrease the order quantity are associated with holding the inventory in stock. Included in this second group are:

Cost of obsolescence

Cost of depreciation

Taxes

Insurance

Interest on capital invested

Cost of storage facilities

Handling costs

These cost elements are referred to compositely as the *inventory carrying charge*. Typical values in application tend to fall somewhere between 15 and 35 percent, but this need not be true in every case. Each company should thus establish its own estimate for the inventory carrying charge and not use handbook values. For example, suppose that the cost of holding one unit of an item per time period is I; the cost of carrying the item in inventory will be I times the average inventory, which was seen to be $q/2$. The fact that the cost of carrying inventory tends to decrease the order quantity can be seen from Fig. 12.8.

The third group of cost elements has no direct bearing on the size of the order quantity and is referred to as *fixed costs*. These costs are shown graphically in Fig. 12.9.

All the costs can now be added together to obtain the total cost for the stockkeeping item. The result is shown in Fig. 12.10. The graph of the costs for a stockkeeping item will always have the same general appearance regardless of the value of the parameters.

The original objective of developing the model was to obtain that order quantity which minimizes the total cost for a stockkeeping item; therefore, from Fig. 12.10, the optimum order quantity q^* is chosen that corresponds to the minimum total cost T^*. Several conclusions can be drawn from this figure:

1. The optimum order quantity q^* will be the same regardless of the value of the fixed cost. The only effect the fixed cost has is that it raises or lowers the base upon which the variable costs are added.

2. The optimum order quantity q^* occurs when the cost of carrying inventory is equal to the replenishment cost; that is, when $Iq^*/2 = RD/q^*$.

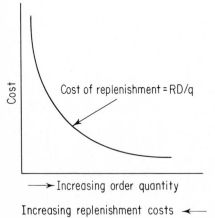

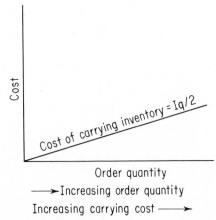

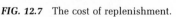

FIG. 12.7 The cost of replenishment.   **FIG. 12.8** The cost of carrying inventory.

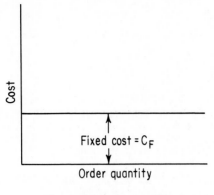

FIG. 12.9   Fixed cost.

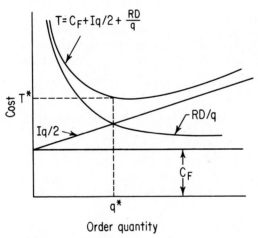

FIG. 12.10   The total cost of an item.

3. The curve for the total cost is relatively flat near the optimum order quantity. Thus, there can be some error in the order quantity without significantly affecting the total cost.

From the first conclusion, it is evident that only the replenishment cost and the cost of carrying inventory need be considered in order to determine the optimum order quantity. Therefore, the problem can be reduced to that shown in Fig. 12.11. From the second conclusion, the optimum order quantity can be found analytically. Since q^* occurs when $Iq^*/2 = RD/q^*$,

$$q^* = \sqrt{\frac{2RD}{I}}$$

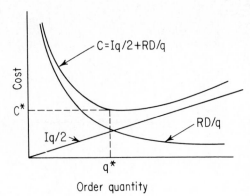

Order quantity

FIG. 12.11 The total variable cost.

It can be seen from the figure that q^* does in fact give a minimum cost.

The relationship between the minimum variable cost C^* and the optimum order quantity q^* can also be determined from the second conclusion. The variable cost is

$$C = \frac{Iq}{2} + \frac{RD}{q}$$

The minimum cost can be found by substituting q^* into the cost equation:

$$C^* = \frac{Iq^*}{2} + \frac{RD}{q^*}$$

However, the second conclusion says that $Iq^*/2 = RD/q^*$; therefore,

$$C^* = \frac{Iq^*}{2} + \frac{Iq^*}{2}$$

or
$$C^* = Iq^*$$

This says that the minimum variable cost is directly proportional to the optimum order quantity and, further, that the constant of proportionality is simply the inventory carrying charge. This result can be extended to solve for C^* directly:

$$C^* = Iq^*$$

but
$$q^* = \sqrt{\frac{2RD}{I}}$$

Hence
$$C^* = I\sqrt{\frac{2RD}{I}} = \sqrt{2RDI}$$

For those who are more comfortable with more rigorous mathematical approaches, the following development is extended. The total variable cost for a stockkeeping item has been shown to be

$$C = \frac{Iq}{2} + \frac{SD}{q}$$

The calculus can be used to determine the order quantity as follows: Take the first derivative of C with respect to q and set it equal to zero.

$$\frac{dC}{dq} = \frac{I}{2} - \frac{RD}{q^2} = 0$$

Then

$$\frac{I}{2} = \frac{RD}{q^2}$$

$$q^2 = \frac{2RD}{I}$$

and

$$q^* = \sqrt{\frac{2RD}{I}}$$

which is the same result obtained before. This can then be substituted into the cost equation to obtain the minimum variable cost:

$$C^* = \frac{I}{2}\sqrt{\frac{2RD}{I}} + \frac{RD}{\sqrt{2RD/I}}$$

$$= \sqrt{\frac{RDI}{2}} + \sqrt{\frac{RDI}{2}}$$

$$= 2\sqrt{\frac{RDI}{2}} = \sqrt{2RDI}$$

Again the result is the same as obtained before. The proportionality of C^* and q^* can also be shown by

$$\frac{C^*}{q^*} = \frac{\sqrt{2RDI}}{\sqrt{2RD/I}} = I$$

or

$$C^* = Iq^*$$

To be mathematically complete, the second derivative should be taken in order to be sure that C^* is in fact a minimum and not a maximum. Doing this,

$$\frac{d^2C}{dq^2} = \frac{2RD}{q^3}$$

The result is positive, and, therefore, C^* is a minimum variable cost.

Equations have been developed here to calculate both the optimum order quantity and the total variable cost for a stockkeeping item. Thus, the question of *how much* has been answered. It remains to determine *when* an order should be placed.

To do this, consider again the assumed inventory pattern in Fig. 12.12. According to the assumptions of the model, the inventory is to be replenished at exactly the time when the stock is depleted. Since it takes time to replenish the inventory, the order must be placed ahead of this time.

The time from when it is realized that the inventory must be replenished until the stock is added to the inventory is called the *lead time*. The lead time is made up of such activities as processing the order, setting up for the production run, and manufacturing the item. The lead time is shown as T.

The lead time must now be expressed in terms of the inventory level, since this is the information that appears in the inventory records. The inventory level at which an order should be placed is referred to as the *reorder point*. The reorder point is determined by multiplying the lead time T by the demand rate D. The reorder point is shown as L. An order is placed when the inventory level drops to L.

Sensitivity of Model.   So far, it has been assumed that the demand, the inventory carrying charge, and the replenishment cost can be estimated exactly, but this is not true in practice. Therefore, it is important to understand the sensitivity of the model. It was noted that the cost curve is relatively flat at the bottom. This indicates that some error can be made in determining the optimum order quantity without significantly affecting the cost.

This conclusion can be extended. Suppose that the order quantity found is in error by 100p percent. That is, suppose that the optimum order quantity is determined to be $(1 + p)q^*$. The effect that this error has on the variable cost can be determined from Fig. 12.13:

1. Find p on the bottom scale.
2. Move vertically up the curve.
3. Move horizontally from the curve to the vertical axis.
4. Read the effect on the variable cost from the vertical axis.

It also happens that the variable cost is equally sensitive to the demand, the inventory carrying charge, or the replenishment cost. The effect of an error in one of these parameters can also be found from Fig. 12.13. Suppose that a parameter is in

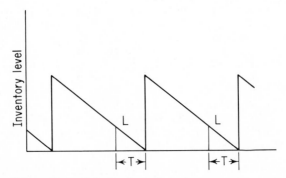

FIG. 12.12   Lead time and reorder point.

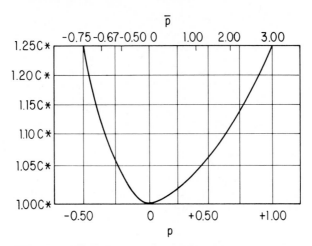

FIG. 12.13 Effect of error on the variable cost.

error by $100\bar{p}$ percent. Find $\bar{p}$ on the top scale and the effect can be read from the vertical axis.

Manufacturing versus Buying.   Although purchased inventories and manufactured inventories present entirely different problems from an operating point of view, both can be represented by the basic EOQ model. The only difference comes when the cost elements are determined for the replenishment cost.

In the first case, the replenishment cost is composed of the variable costs connected with placing and receiving an order, and it is generally referred to as the *procurement cost.* For the case of manufactured inventories, the replenishment cost is made up of the variable cost elements associated with setting up for a production run, and it is usually referred to as the *setup cost.*

Methods for Determining the Order Quantity.   In computer applications of the basic EOQ model, the square-root equation $q^* = \sqrt{2RD/I}$ is usually solved directly. There are situations, however, when limited computer memory can be a problem. In this case, one possibility of reducing the storage requirements is to group the items according to their replenishment costs. Then an average replenishment cost $\bar{R}$ can be used to calculate the order quantity for all items in a group. This eliminates the need for storing the replenishment cost for each item.

This method should be used only when it is absolutely necessary, because accuracy is lost. When using this method, extreme care should be taken when establishing the range of replenishment costs that should be included in a given group. Appropriate ranges and the effect on the variable cost can be determined from Fig. 12.13.

In manual applications, the square-root equation can be solved directly; but if the number of stockkeeping items carried in inventory is large, the task becomes quite burdensome. For this reason, many companies use tables, graphs, nomographs, or special slide rules.

Tables for Inventory Decisions.   Tables work best for families of stockkeeping items that have only one parameter that varies: for example, suppose that a group of items has the same inventory carrying charge I and the same replenishment cost R;

that is, only the demand rate D varies. When more than one parameter varies, tables can also be used by making separate columns for different values of the second parameter: for example, suppose that only I is the same for all items and that R and D both vary; this situation requires a table such as Table 12.3.

Graphs for Inventory Decisions. The same information can be represented more compactly on a graph than in a table. Graphs have another advantage over tables in that the need to interpolate between values in the table is eliminated. As shown in Fig. 12.14, the lines on the graph are not straight. If the information is plotted on log-log paper, the lines will be straight. Choosing between the use of graphs plotted on coordinate paper and graphs plotted on log-log paper is simply a matter of preference.

Nomographs for Inventory Decisions. Another popular method of solving the equation is by the use of nomographs. They are particularly useful where the ranges of the parameters make tables or graphs impractical and cumbersome. It is also possible to have the nomographs printed on the backs of the production order or other documents so that the calculation of the order quantity becomes a part of the permanent records.

Slide Rules for Inventory Decisions. Special slide rules for solving the square-root equations are also available commercially.

With perhaps some slight variations, the above procedures indicate what is available in order to reduce the mechanical difficulties of obtaining order quantities.

TABLE 12.3   Typical Order-Quantity Table Where
$I = 0.20$

Annual Usage, Dollars, D	Order Quantity, Dollars		
	R = $6.40	R = $10.00	R = $16.70
10	26	32	41
25	40	50	65
50	57	71	92
75	70	87	112
100	80	100	129
250	126	158	204
500	179	224	289
750	219	274	354
1,000	253	316	408
2,500	400	500	646
5,000	566	707	914
7,500	689	866	1,120
10,000	800	1,000	1,290
25,000	1,260	1,580	2,040
50,000	1,790	2,240	2,890
75,000	2,190	2,740	3,540
100,000	2,530	3,160	4,080

Source: W. Evert Welch, *Tested Scientific Inventory Control*, Management Publishing Corporation, Greenwich, Conn., 1959.

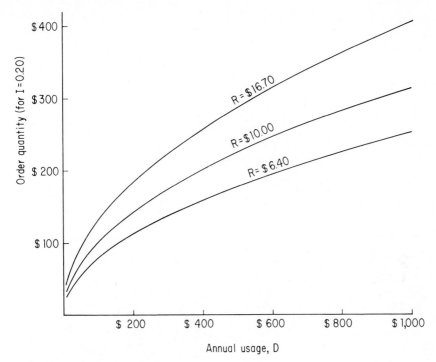

FIG. 12.14 Inventory graph.

Practical Considerations.   The basic EOQ model is a fairly simplified representation of real-world inventories. Therefore, difficulties may be encountered in applying the model.

Finite Production Rates.   The basic EOQ model assumes an instantaneous replenishment rate. However, this is not actually the case in practice. It takes time to produce parts, move them into storage, etc. A better approximation of the actual case is shown in Fig. 12.15. In the figure, the replenishment rate is shown to be P and the demand rate D. Since stock is being added to and taken from the inventory at the same time, the net effect is that the inventory level increases at a rate of $(P - D)$ while it is being replenished.

If the replenishment rate is relatively large, the situation approaches that of the basic EOQ model. However, as the replenishment rate becomes smaller, the variable cost can be affected significantly and the order quantity should be adjusted accordingly. As a rule of thumb, if the ratio $D/P \leq \frac{1}{3}$, the effect can be neglected. If, however, $D/P > \frac{1}{3}$, the optimum order quantity should be adjusted. In this case, the order quantity becomes

$$\text{Optimum order quantity} = \frac{1}{\sqrt{1 - D/P}} q^* = \frac{1}{\sqrt{1 - D/P}} \sqrt{\frac{2RD}{I}}$$

Price Discounts.   The basic EOQ model assumes that the cost per unit for a stockkeeping item remains constant. It does not account for the possibility of price

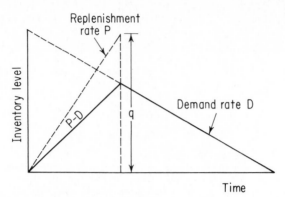

FIG. 12.15 FInite production rate.

discounts. If it were known in advance what price range the order quantity would fall into, the cost could be used in the equation and all would be well. However, there is no easy way to obtain the appropriate price range a priori. Since the price per unit will have an effect on the order quantity, additional calculations must be made to arrive at the best answer.

Unwanted Increases in Inventory Investments. Another problem that may be encountered is an unwanted increase in the inventory investment. There are two reasons why such an increase can occur when the basic EOQ model is used.

First, there may be too much error in the estimates of the demand, the inventory carrying charge, and/or the replenishment cost. Naturally, such errors will affect the order quantities, and if the errors are large enough, the order quantities may be unreasonable.

Another possibility is that the estimates are correct but that the company is not in a financial position to carry out the optimum policy indicated by the equations. The model does not consider the financial condition of the company. Also, when the model is used, the order quantity is determined for each stockkeeping item as if it were completely independent of the other items in the inventory. The model gives no consideration to the aggregate results.

If there is an indication that the model will cause large, undesirable increases in the inventory, it may be necessary to incorporate techniques that give consideration to the aggregate results.

Choosing, Testing, and Using a Model. The basic EOQ model is the most explored model, but it is not the only one available by any means. The literature abounds with models that have been proposed to solve inventory problems; and, of course, it is entirely possible to construct an original model. In choosing, developing, or refining a model, there is a prime requirement that should not be lost sight of: *The model must be justified economically.*

Remember that the more elaborate a model is, the more time and money will be required to calculate the order quantities and the reorder points. It does not make sense economically to spend additional money refining the model and calculating order quantities if that money cannot be returned in cost savings.

The model that is proposed for use should also be tested. Regardless of how much care has been expended in formulating or choosing the model, there is still a chance that it will not yield "workable" order quantities. The time to find out that a model will not work is *before* large amounts of time and money have been spent installing it.

There is another important point regarding the use of inventory models: *The model is not the decision maker; it is an aid to the decision maker.* A practical model cannot be constructed that will handle all the peculiar situations that may occur. There will be times when the model does not come up with the right answers. The inventory system should have *management by exception* built into it.

Inventory models can be a great asset to management and can result in substantial savings. However, models must not be used blindly. Management should understand the model and its weaknesses thoroughly before putting it into practice.

Statistical Order-Point Determination

The concept of the order point can be explained best by starting with a rather ideal item, as illustrated in Fig. 12.16. In this example, the future usage for the item is assumed to be exactly 100 per week, and the lead time is assumed to be exactly 3 weeks. If an order is placed when the available inventory reaches 300, the item will arrive in exactly 3 weeks (lead time) and the usage during the 3-week order cycle will be exactly 300. Therefore, just as the last unit is consumed, the replenishment order will arrive. This would be a perfectly managed inventory that has only working or cycle stock. An equation for this relationship is

Order point (OP) = anticipated usage during lead time

However, since neither the demand nor the lead time is usually known precisely, the formula could be altered to:

OP = anticipated usage during anticipated lead time

Since actual demand should exceed the average demand 50 percent of the time, the order point would result in a stock-out during 50 percent of the reorder cycles. Therefore, to maintain a high service level when there is an uncertain demand, the reorder system cannot permit the inventory level to drop as low as the average usage during the lead time before an order is placed. Therefore,

Order point = anticipated average usage during lead time + safety stock

This safety stock is referred to by various names, such as *reserve stock, buffer stock,* or *protective stock.* Whatever the terminology, its purpose is to provide a high level of service where the expected demand and/or lead times are uncertain.

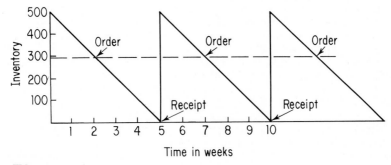

FIG. 12.16   Order-point concept.

It is the intent of the order point to provide a reorder signal in time to replenish the inventory and still meet the expected demand during the next replenishment lead time. The order point allows safety stock to provide a contingency for uncertainty in demand and lead time. It is most important to note that the demand in the order point is the expected demand during the next lead time; therefore, an order-point system must have the provision for *forecasting* the expected demand during the lead time.

The Concept of Forecast Error.   The key reason for safety stock is the presence of *forecast errors*. Many inventory systems have fallen far short of their potential savings because safety stocks were based on a fixed rule and not on the forecast error for each item. No forecast is likely to be perfect, and in any inventory system in which there is uncertainty in demand, it is important to measure the forecast error and provide protection against it. Error is inherent in forecasts, but lead-time variations *should* be controllable through better production control or better vendor follow-up (or perhaps better choice of vendors). For this reason, most well-designed systems try to *control* lead times and *protect* against forecast errors.

A dynamic inventory management system therefore has four basic steps:

1. Selection of an appropriate forecast model
2. A means of updating the forecasts of average usage on a routine basis
3. A means of measuring forecast errors so that reserve stocks can be calculated for each item rationally
4. A means of updating the estimate of forecast error so that reserve stocks will reflect current forecasting ability

If the order point is not revised upward as demand increases, orders will not be placed on time and excessive stock-outs will result. If the order point is not revised downward as demand drops off, an order will be placed before required and an excessive inventory will be built up while demands are actually dropping off.

Selection of Forecasting Model.   In forecasting the demand for most items for the coming lead time, the use of the intrinsic approach is recommended. *Intrinsic forecasting* is the projection of information contained within the product's past history into the near future, whereas *extrinsic forecasting* is the use of such external indicators as the Federal Reserve Board index, new housing starts, and gross national product to forecast the use of an item.

The first step in intrinsic forecasting is to find the past pattern of demand. Pattern identification is most often referred to as *forecast-model selection*. A discussion of the demand for the items shown in Table 12.4 will illustrate the process of forecast-model selection; the demands for items A, B, and C were made artificially stable to make the model, or pattern, selection easier.

Intrinsic forecasting is the extension of the past pattern into the future. An extension of the exact horizontal pattern for item A would produce a forecast of 17 units for month 6. Note that all five demands fit exactly on a horizontal line which has a "height" of 17, and this item would thus require a horizontal model. An extrapolation of the pattern for item B produces a forecast of six units in month 6; the demand pattern, or model, for item B is "trend." An extrapolation of the demand for item C produces a forecast of three units for month 6; the demand pattern for item C is "seasonal."

The pattern and forecast for item D is more difficult to recognize. The selection of the forecast model is difficult because, in this more realistic example, the demand varies erratically and more data are required in order to determine whether a horizontal trend or a seasonal model best applies. An analysis of the demand for a similar item shown in Fig. 12.17 will illustrate the problem; this is the plot of 2 years of demand recorded in 4-week periods. A close examination of this demand indicates that there is little or no significant trend. The peaks and valleys of demand cannot be reliably attributed to seasonal effects since the peak in one year occurs three periods earlier in the following year. The figure indicates that the pattern (or model) is simply a horizontal one, with the horizontal line representing the average demand of 100. The demand does *vary* significantly about the horizontal line, but its variation would be wider about a trend line or a seasonal pattern. This brief exercise in forecast-model selection with realistic data indicates the complexity of the job, particularly when it must be done for thousands of individual inventory items. To assist in this analysis, some computer software companies supply programs that analyze past data, screen out unusual demands, and select the most

TABLE 12.4   Demand Models

Months	Item A	Item B	Item C	Item D
1	17	1	1	120
2	17	2	3	83
3	17	3	1	107
4	17	4	3	90
5	17	5	1	95
6	?	?	?	?

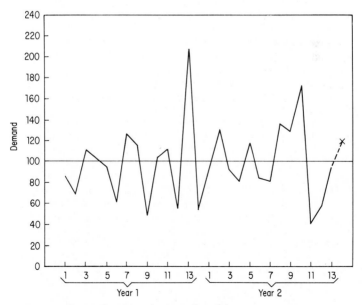

FIG. 12.17   Demand pattern—horizontal model.

appropriate forecast model. The best forecasting model produces the least average forecast error and requires the least safety stock.

The next element required is a forecast-updating technique. This updating technique must be a compromise, since as we have seen in Fig. 12.17, the best forecast for this erratic demand pattern is 100. Nevertheless, a good forecasting technique should be sensitive enough to react to a real increase or decrease in demand that persists. At the end of year 2, the best forecast is still 100 units. Assume that the demand in the following period is 120. A logical series of steps in updating, or correcting, the old forecast of 100 might be

$$\text{New forecast} = \text{old forecast} + \text{correction}$$

or

$$\text{New forecast} = \text{old forecast} + \text{forecast error}$$

or

$$\text{New forecast} = \text{old forecast} + (\text{demand} - \text{old forecast})$$

For example,

$$\text{New forecast} = 100 + (120 - 100)$$
$$\text{New forecast} = 120$$

This means that we have corrected the forecast by the full amount of the forecast error, thus reacting dramatically to the forecast error. A better approach that would meet the requirements for a compromise between reacting and overreacting would be to correct the old forecast by a fraction of the forecast error; the formula would then be

$$\text{New forecast} = \text{old forecast} + \alpha \,(\text{demand} - \text{old forecast})$$
$$\text{New forecast} = 100 + \alpha \,(20)$$

The value of α would be 0.10 if it is decided to correct the forecast by 10 percent of the difference between current demand and the old forecast. In this example, the new forecast would be 102 units.

This technique of forecasting is known as *exponential smoothing*. This particular technique employed for the horizontal item is known as *first-order*, or *single*, *exponential smoothing*; the term *single* is used because the technique revises the single point (average) which designates a horizontal line. The percentage adjustment of the forecast error is called *alpha* (α). We used 0.1, which will react roughly equivalent to a 19-period moving average. A higher alpha would react more quickly to changes in demand (0.2, for example, would react like a 9-period moving average) but would result in a more erratic forecast. There have been articles and textbook chapters dedicated to the selection of alpha; today, however, most authorities recommend against elaborate research to determine an optimum alpha.

Using the single-order exponential smoothing formula to forecast all items, however, could be disastrous. Figure 12.18 shows a different type of demand pattern. A horizontal line will not accurately represent the demand for this item. This is a trend item, and a trend forecast model would work here. A trend line can be represented as two points or as a point and a slope. The technique for forecasting the item with a two-point model is known as *double smoothing*, which is really single smoothing with a trend correction.

Using double smoothing, the forecast is made up of two parts, usually designated as A and B:

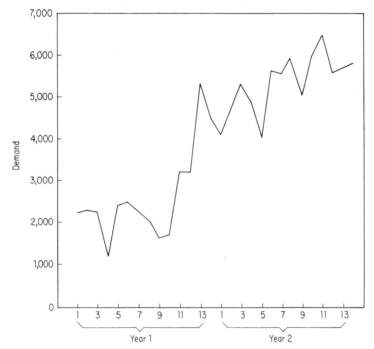

FIG. 12.18 Demand pattern—trend model.

$$A = \text{old forecast} + \alpha\,(\text{demand} - \text{old forecast})$$
$$B = \text{old } B + \alpha\,(\text{new } A - \text{old } B)$$

The first part, A, is simply single exponential smoothing as given before. B provides a point against which trend can be measured. This correction is made by adjusting the first point A by the difference between A and B.

$$\text{New forecast} = A + (A - B)$$
$$\text{New forecast} = 2.1 - B$$

This is the proper forecasting formula when exponential smoothing is to be used to update the forecast for a trend item. The key element here is that the trend item can be forecast just as accurately as the horizontal item if the right technique is selected. This means that the trend item could have the same service level with the same approximate ratio of safety stock to sales. High forecast errors mean high safety stocks; low forecast errors mean low safety stocks.

Figure 12.19 is a classical example of a seasonal item. A horizontal or a trend model would not work well in forecasting an item of this type.

Companies sometimes say that they have tried exponential smoothing and that it has failed. In many cases, the failure was due to using single smoothing on either a trend or seasonal item or to using trend forecasting on a seasonal item.

There are forecasting techniques that fit the seasonal item. The simplest of these is to use some sort of seasonal index or percentage. If the year were divided into 13 four-week periods, for example, an *average* period would be one-thirteenth of the year's sales, or 7.7 percent. If demand in period 13 is normally 12.0 percent of the

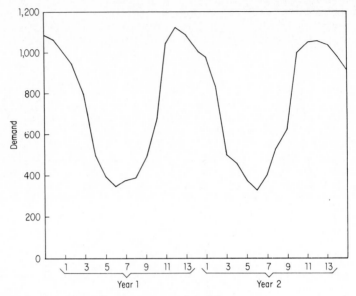

FIG. 12.19 Demand pattern—seasonal model.

year's sales, then in forecasting sales for that period they would be adjusted upward to reflect this. For example, if the exponential-smoothing forecast was 700 units per period and the forecast was being made for period 13, the following calculation would be involved:

1. Forecast for an "average" period (7.7 percent) = 700
2. Adjustment for period 13 = 12.0/7.7 × 700
3. Forecast for period 13 = 1091

   Incoming demand data are *deseasonalized* in the same manner, making the data equivalent to an average month's sales before they are entered into the exponential smoothing formula.
   Exponential smoothing is a simple and well-accepted method for updating item forecasts. The four basic forecast models that could be applied using the forecast-updating techniques discussed above are:

1. Horizontal model: single exponential smoothing
2. Trend model: double exponential smoothing
3. Horizontal-seasonal model: single smoothing with seasonal adjustment
4. Trend-seasonal model: double smoothing with seasonal adjustment

Measuring and Updating Forecast Errors. No forecast will ever be perfect. Forecast error is inherent in every forecast. To set the minimum safety stock for a desired level of customer service, safety stocks should be established based on forecast error. Techniques for measuring forecast error and updating these measures of error are discussed here.
   In Table 12.5 the sum of the algebraic forecast errors is zero, as it should be if the

TABLE 12.5 Exponential Smoothing

Period	Old Forecast	Demand	Forecast Error	New Forecast
1	100	120	+20	102
2	102	92	−10	101
3	101	81	−20	99
4	99	119	+20	101
5	101	111	+10	102
6	102	82	−20	100

correct forecasting technique is being used. There are two common statistical techniques used to calculate the average dispersion (forecast error here) in such a way that the positive values will not cancel the negatives:

1. Square the forecast errors, sum the squares, and divide by the number of errors to give the average squared error. Then take the square root. This calculation is called the *standard deviation*, and the formula is

$$\text{Standard deviation} = \sqrt{\frac{\sum (\text{forecast error})^2}{\text{number of errors}}}$$

The precise calculation of the standard deviation to give an *unbiased* sample would require that the denominator read "number of errors minus one." For simplicity, this minus one has been ignored in this chapter.

2. Take the absolute value (treat all values as positive) of each error, sum the absolute (that is, ignoring plus and minus signs) value, and divide by the number of errors. The result, which can be used to approximate the standard deviation, is known as the *mean (average) absolute deviation (MAD)*. The formula is

$$\text{MAD} = \frac{\text{sum of absolute errors}}{\text{number of errors}}$$

Table 12.6 illustrates this calculation and is taken from the example in Table 12.5.

More powerful computers may reduce the importance of MAD. MAD is recommended because it is easier to calculate than other techniques and it has more practical meaning. It is theoretically less precise than the standard deviation but close enough for most inventory applications. MAD and standard deviation have a numerical relationship for the normal distribution:

$$\text{Standard deviation} = 1.25 \text{ MAD (approximately)}$$

The above relationship makes it easy to convert established statistical tables or the standard deviation so that they can be used with MAD.

Using Forecast Error in Calculating Order Points. Earlier, it was stated that an order point is equal to the forecast of demand over lead time plus safety stock. Using MAD as the measurement for forecast error, the order point (OP) becomes:

OP = anticipated average usage during lead time plus safety stock

Safety stock = anticipated error for the forecast of usage during lead time (MAD) multiplied by a service factor

This service factor is obtained from standard statistical tables (like that shown in Table 12.7) and is usually designated k. Larger values of k will result in more safety stock and a higher level of service, as discussed in the following section. The safety stock (SS) can then be expressed as

$$SS = k \times MAD_{LT}$$

and the order point becomes

$$OP = forecast_{LT} + k \times MAD_{LT}$$

Note that the forecast and MAD are for the *lead time* (LT). The order point can be described as the *maximum reasonable demand for the lead time*; that is, the order point is the expected lead-time usage plus enough safety stock to cover the additional demand up to a maximum economical level. The forecast and MAD for each item are normally calculated for an even time interval, such as 1 week, 4 weeks, or 1

TABLE 12.6 Standard Deviation and MAD

Forecast Error		Squared Error		Absolute Error
	+20	400		20
	−10	100		10
	−20	400		20
	+20	400		20
	+10	100		10
	−20	400		20
Sum	0	6	1800	6	100
Average			300		16.67

1. Standard deviation = $\sqrt{300}$ = 17.32
2. MAD = 16.67

TABLE 12.7 Safety Factors for "Order-Cycle"

Safety Factor, k	Percent of Order Cycles with No Back Order or Stock-Out
0.00	50.00
1.00	78.81
1.25	84.13
2.00	94.52
2.50	97.72
3.00	99.18
3.75	99.87

month. The calculated forecast and MAD must then be projected to cover the lead time.

For a horizontal item, the lead-time forecast is

$$\text{Forecast}_{LT} = (\text{forecast}) \left(\frac{\text{lead time}}{\text{forecast interval}} \right)$$

Example

$$LT = 6 \text{ weeks}$$
$$\text{Forecast interval} = 4 \text{ weeks}$$
$$4\text{-week forecast} = 100 \text{ units/week}$$
$$\text{Forecast}_{LT} = (100)(6\!/\!4) = 150$$

The extrapolation of the trend item is more complicated because the trend for the forecast interval must be added. The formula is

$$\text{Forecast}_{LT} = (\text{forecast})(T) + (T) \frac{(T + 1)}{2} \text{ trend}$$

where $T = $ lead time $\div$ forecast interval. This last equation is exact where T is an integer and is a close approximation where T is not an exact integer.

In extrapolating the forecast for a seasonal item, the seasonal effect must be added for each period contained in the lead time.

It is logical that the average percentage of forecast error for a 1-week forecast will be higher than the percentage of error in an annual or a monthly forecast. Therefore, MAD for 4 weeks will be less than 4 times MAD for 1 week.

Selecting Safety Factors.   The three elements of the order point in the equation are forecast, k, and MAD. The selections above have described the theory and techniques for calculating the forecast and MAD. The discussion below explains some useful techniques for selecting the safety factor (k) once the desired definition and the service level have been specified.

Two of the most frequently used definitions of the *item service level* are:

1. Percentage of order cycles with no stock-outs

2. Percentage of dollar demand filled off the shelf (without back orders)

For an item, the dollar service level and unit service level are identical. The above two measurements are the two that can be set easily when using statistical tables directly.

In using either of the two definitions of service mentioned above, both a stock-out and a back order are a *disservice*; that is, if the quantity desired is not on the shelf at the time the order is entered, there is a disservice by the definition of statistical service. It will also be assumed that *forecast errors* (not demand) are normally distributed. If the correct forecasting technique is used, this assumption can be used safely (even though it is not always theoretically correct) for all items except those with demand characterized by extreme variations and frequent zero demand, often called "lumpy" demand.

The measure of service based on order cycles is the simplest service measure. If k were zero, the safety stock would be zero and an order would be placed when the available inventory reached the forecasted usage for the lead time. Normally, the demand will exceed the forecast and result in a stock-out in 50 percent of the order cycles. It is most important to remember that the stock-out occurs in 50 percent of the order cycles, not specifically in weeks, months, or years. If the order quantity is a 1-week supply, 26 stock-outs are expected in a year with zero safety stock. If the order quantity is a 2-year supply, only one stock-out every 4 years will result, since a stock-out will be likely to occur only every other order cycle.

For the selection of k, refer to Table 12.7, which is an excerpt from the normal-distribution tables with the k's adjusted to act as the MAD multiplier instead of the usual standard-deviation multiplier.

Problem   Select k and set the safety stock and order point where

$$\text{Forecast}_{LT} = 200$$
$$\text{MAD}_{LT} = 50$$
$$\text{Desired service} = 97.72$$

Solution   From Table 12.7, a k of 2.50 is selected to meet the specified service level of 97.72 percent; thus

$$k = 2.50$$
$$SS = k(\text{MAD})_{LT} = (2.5)(50) = 125$$
$$OP = \text{FCST}_{LT} + SS = 200 + 125 = 325$$

In the problem, an item with an order quantity (OQ) of 1 week's supply will fill all demand during 97.72 percent of the weekly order cycles, or result in approximately one stock-out per year. An item with an OQ of 1 year's supply would theoretically be out of stock only 2.28 $(100 - 97.72)$ times in 100 years. Note that if the same percentage service level were specified for all items in inventory, the result would be a high service to the low-dollar-volume items (large time supply OQs) and a low level of service to the high-dollar-volume items (small time supply OQs). To use this service measure properly, service should first be established in terms of the number of stock-outs per year that can be tolerated; this should be expressed as a service percentage, and then the value of k should be obtained from the table.

Assume a service level set at one stock-out per year in the examples below.

Example A
1. OQ = 1-week supply
2. 52 reorder cycles or chances for a stock-out
3. 51 out of 52 cycles per year with no stock-out = $\frac{51}{52}$ = 98 percent
4. k = 2.5 (from Table 12.7)

Example B
1. OQ = 6-month supply
2. Two reorder cycles per year
3. One out of two cycles with no stock-out = $\frac{1}{2}$ = 50 percent
4. k = 0 (from Table 12.7)

To use the service measure based on the percentage of unit or dollar demand filled instead of on reorder cycles, a calculation must be made before the statistical tables are used. This calculation is called the *service-function g* calculation, and the equation is

$$g(k) = \frac{\text{usage during order cycle} \, (1 - p)}{MAD_{LT}}$$

where p = desired service level expressed as a decimal.

If the item has a standard order quantity, this quantity is the usage during the order cycle, and the equation becomes

$$g(k) = \frac{OQ}{MAD_{LT}} \times (1 - p)$$

Use Table 12.8, which is a condensed service-function table.

Problem   Select k and calculate the safety stock and order point:

$$FCST_{LT} = 800$$
$$OQ = 600$$
$$MAD_{LT} = 200$$

Desired service = 95 percent. Thus,

$$g(k) = \frac{OQ}{MAD_{LT}}(1 - p) = \frac{600}{200}(1 - 0.95)$$
$$= (3)(0.05) = 0.15$$

The safety factor for a $g(k)$ of 0.15 in the table is 1.0. Thus,

$$\text{Safety stock} = (1.0)(MAD_{LT}) = 200$$
$$\text{Order point} = FCST_{LT} + SS$$
$$= \ \ 800 + 200 = 1000$$

The selection of the service level usually ends up being a management decision. It is strongly advised that a study covering 6 to 8 weeks be made to establish the present service level to be used to select a k to start. It is important that the statistical measure of service be equated to management's concept of service before installing a statistical inventory control system.

TABLE 12.8 Safety Factors for
Unit Service

Safety Factor k	Service Function $g(k)$
2.0	0.0294
1.6	0.0600
1.4	0.0829
1.2	0.1131
1.0	0.1510

The findings of studies to determine the optimum service level based on a "stock-out cost" have usually been overruled because it is almost impossible to determine customer dissatisfaction and the future costs of present lost sales. The best technique for selecting a service level is to show management the present service level and the inventory levels that will be required for various service levels and to have them select the level. The inventory management programs available from various computer manufacturers can be used to develop the type of curve, as shown in Fig. 12.20.

The curve clearly shows that the marginal cost of service rises sharply as the service is raised above 95 percent. Management cannot be told what the service level should be, but it can be shown the amount of inventory required to give the service level it selects.

Demand Filters and Tracking Signal.   If extreme demands are used to update the forecast and MAD, the forecasts will lose their stability. The safety stock might be greatly increased because of one nonrandom demand event, such as a sales promotion. All forecasting systems should pass the current demand through a *filter* before using it to revise a forecast.

A *high filter* and a *low filter* can be designed. The equations for the filters are:

$$\text{High filter} = \text{FCST} + (N)(\text{MAD})$$
$$\text{Low filter} = \text{FCST} - (N)(\text{MAD})$$

N is selected from the normal tables based on the degree of certainty desired in saying that the demand is nonrandom and can be rejected. For example, if $N = 3$ is chosen from Table 12.7, there is only a 0.82 percent $(100 - 99.18)$ chance that a

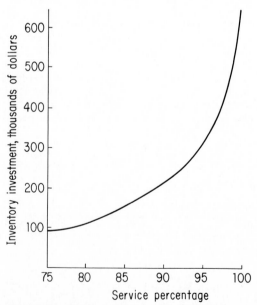

FIG. 12.20   Inventory investment versus service.

demand outside of either of the two filter limits is actually random. That is, it would generally be wise to toss out such a demand on the basis that it was created by some nonrepetitive cause.

Example

$$FCST = 300$$
$$MAD = 90$$
$$N = 3$$
$$\text{High filter} = 300 + (3)(90) = 570$$
$$\text{Low filter} = 300 - (3)(90) = 30$$

The demand would be used to revise the forecast if its value were between 30 and 570. The forecast, MAD, and order point would *not* be revised for a demand greater than 570 or less than 30. Obviously, the filters must consider the seasonal effects for a seasonal item.

The demand filter is used to screen out unusual demand, and an additional "quality control" technique is required to determine whether the forecast errors have a directional bias. This second technique is called a *tracking signal*.

If the correct forecasting technique is being employed for an item, the algebraic sum of the forecast errors should tend to zero. An extreme buildup of forecast errors for an item in either the positive or negative direction is a statistical indication that the system is no longer properly forecasting the item demand. The reason might be a change in forecast model, a sharp but permanent change in demand level, or poor initial values for the forecast or MAD. It *does not* indicate that the current value of alpha is wrong. The tracking signal is normally calculated as

$$\text{Tracking signal} = \frac{\text{algebraic sum of forecast errors}}{\text{MAD}}$$

When the tracking signal for an item exceeds a predetermined level, it is said to "trip." Exception reports can then indicate only those items which have tripped the signal and require attention.

In specifying the value of the tracking signal that requires action, it must be remembered that there will sometimes be some random buildup of errors sufficient to cause a trip. The idea then is to set the limit at a level that will hold the random trips to a workable level and still indicate the items in trouble.

Statistically, there is a calculation problem: The standard deviation required for calculating reasonable limits around the tracking signal must consider the distribution of error *sums,* and this value is not the same as the regular normal-distribution table used above. The relationships for error sums in terms of alpha and MAD are shown in Table 12.9, which shows the number of MADs required for specified percentages of random trips for single smoothing.

An example of the meaning of Table 12.9 is:

1. An inventory manager is willing to look at 6 percent *chance* (random) trips. For items using an alpha of 0.1 for single smoothing, limits of plus or minus 5.38 MADs will produce 6 percent random trips.

2. If an alpha of 0.2 is used, the limits would be 3.72 MADs.

3. If, for an alpha of 0.1, the load of random trips should be lightened to 2 percent because the inventory manager finds too many items tripping the signal, the limits should be raised to 6.66 MADs.

TABLE 12.9   Tracking Signal Limits

Percent Trips	Number of MADs for α = 0.1	Number of MADs for α = 0.2
10	4.72	3.27
8	5.01	3.47
6	5.38	3.72
5	5.61	3.88
4	5.86	4.06
3.6	6.00	4.16
2	6.66	4.61

Table 12.9 can be used for double smoothing by first doubling the alpha before referring to the table. If an alpha of 0.05 were used and 4 percent random trips were allowable, the limits would be plus or minus 5.86 MADs. (The alpha of 0.05 was doubled, giving 0.1, so that the "α = 0.1" column was used in the table.)

The tracking signal is a management tool and should be used accordingly. The number of random trips allowed should be a balance between workload and sufficient reaction to out-of-balance conditions. Accordingly, the limits should be managed to meet these requirements. It is recommended that low limits be set for the class A items by dollar volume. A somewhat higher level should be set for the class B medium items, and a still higher limit for the class C items.

An example of this strategy for an alpha of 0.1 is:

1. Limits of plus or minus 5 MADs for the high-dollar items would produce 8 percent random trips in the high 10 percent.

2. Limits of plus or minus 5.9 would give approximately 4 percent random trips for the medium items.

3. Limits of plus or minus 6.7 MADs would give approximately 2 percent random trips for the slow movers.

The same tracking-signal limit for all items would mean that the inventory manager would spend much more time examining low-dollar items than high-dollar items. This is a clear violation of the principles of ABC.

A tracking-signal trip indicates that the item must be examined to determine the cause and that corrective action must be taken. It does not mean that the alpha should be changed.

A forecasting system without demand filters and tracking signals will eventually lose its accuracy and reliability. No forecasting system is complete without both.

Periodic-Review Systems.   In the order-point-quantity system, as usage varies, the timing of order placement varies. Another approach can be used where it is more practical to vary the quantity and keep the time constant. Where it is desirable to reorder material every 2 weeks, for example, a system could be designed to review inventory every 2 weeks and order each item up to a predetermined level, usually called an inventory "target" or "order up to" level. Using this approach, as usage fluctuates, the quantity rather than the timing of order placement is the variable. The target inventory level is the sum of:

1. Anticipated demand during lead time

2. Anticipated demand during review time

3. Safety stock based on forecast error over lead time plus review time

Lot sizes can be rounded off to approximate multiples of demand during the review period and minimum order quantities set. This means that some items will be reordered every second or third review period.

The principles explained above for use with an order-point system apply to the periodic-review system equally well. It can embody techniques like exponential smoothing and the use of MAD in calculating safety stocks to make the system more efficient than one that uses inventory targets established on a "judgment" basis.

SUMMARY

It is important that the practitioner understand the importance of inventories and the organizational structure designed to control them. The physical inventory and cycle-count techniques must be understood by all inventory control personnel.

Both the ABC concept, answering what, and the economic lot size, answering how much, have been available to practitioners for many years. They are based on sound principles and can be applied very successfully as long as the practitioner understands the principles involved and does not follow the techniques blindly.

The concept of statistical inventory control has been discussed in the literature for many years. With the advent of computers, it has become a practical reality and is applied in many companies. Statistical inventory control provides a rational method for updating forecasts and allocating reserve stock based on forecast error. If used properly in a system, significant reductions in inventory or improvements in customer service should result. This is because the system sets reserve-stock levels rationally and has the capability of updating the forecasts and reserve stocks on a regular basis. Two important points should be kept in mind if real success is to be achieved with these techniques: The practitioner must understand the principles behind the techniques and must use the proper technique in the proper application.

BIBLIOGRAPHY

American Production and Inventory Control Society (APICS): *Inventory Planning*, APICS, Washington, D.C., 1978.

Ammer, D. S.: *Materials Management and Purchasing*, 4th ed., Irwin, Homewood, Ill., 1980.

Batlersby, A. A.: *Guide to Stock Control*, 2d ed., Pittman, London, 1970.

Brown, Robert G.: *Decision Rules for Inventory Management*, Holt, Rinehart & Winston, New York, 1967.

———: *Materials Management Systems*, Wiley, New York, 1977.

Dickie, H. Ford: "ABC Inventory Analysis Shoots for Dollars," *Factory Management and Maintenance*, July 1951.

Elsayed, A., and Thomas O. Boucher: *Analysis and Control of Production Systems*, Prentice-Hall, Englewood Cliffs, N.J., 1985.

Fogarty, Donald W., and Thomas R. Hoffman: *Production and Inventory Management*, South-Western, Cincinnati, 1983.

Graham, G.: *Automated Inventory Management for the Distributor*, CBI, Boston, 1980.

Greene, James H.: *Production and Inventory Control: Systems and Decisions*, Homewood, Ill., 1974.

Hax, Arnaldo C., and Dan Candea: *Production and Inventory Management*, Prentice-Hall, Englewood Cliffs, N.J., 1984.

IMPACT Advanced Principles and Implementation Manual, no. E20-0174, IBM Corporation, White Plains, N.Y., 1971.

Jordan, H.: *Cycle Counting*, APICS, Washington, D. C., 1976.

Love, S. F.: *Inventory Control*, McGraw-Hill, New York, 1982.

Naddor, E.: *Inventory Systems*, Wiley, New York, 1982.

Plossl, George W.: *Production and Inventory Control: Principles and Techniques*, 2d ed., Prentice-Hall, Englewood Cliffs, N.J., 1985.

Thomas, A. B.: *Inventory Control in Production and Manufacturing*, Cohners, Boston, 1980.

Vollman, Thomas E., William E. Berry, and D. Clay Whybark: *Manufacturing Planning and Control Systems*, Irwin, Homewood, Ill., 1984.

Welch, W. Evert: *Tested Scientific Inventory Control*, Management Publishing Corporation, Greenwich, Conn., 1959.

Wight, Oliver W.: *Production and Inventory Management in the Computer Age*, 1974.

Tactical Planning and Control

CHAPTER

13

Master Production Schedule

Editors

RICHARD C. LING, CFPIM
RICHARD C. LING, Inc.
Winston-Salem, North Carolina

F. JOHN SARI, CFPIM
John Sari and Company
Winston-Salem, North Carolina

Second to making a sale, probably no activity is more important for a manufacturing firm than those planning activities that go into creating the master production schedule (MPS). The real importance of the MPS emerged in the mid-1970s as material-requirements planning (MRP) became more widely used and understood. It became obvious that a more formalized tool had to be the "driver" of this powerful MRP system. This tool is the MPS.

The American Production and Inventory Control Society's *Master Production Scheduling: Principles and Practice* offers a comprehensive treatment of the MPS.[1] It presents the MPS in a standard framework and examines eight companies relative to this framework: Hyster, Black & Decker, Dow Corning, Tennant, Elliott, Pfizer, Abbott Laboratories Limited, and Ethan Allen. Each had developed effective approaches to master scheduling. This same standard MPS framework, which is shown in Fig. 13.1, is the framework for this chapter. A reprint of Chapter 2 of *Master Production Scheduling: Principle and Practice*, appears at the end of this chapter.

The *APICS Dictionary* gives the following definition:[2]

MASTER PRODUCTION SCHEDULE (MPS). For selected items, it is a statement of what the company expects to manufacture. It is the anticipated build schedule for those selected

Master Production Schedule Framework

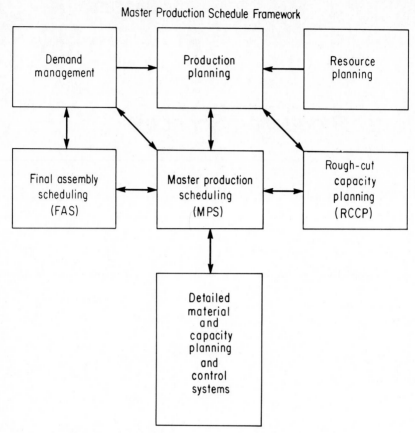

FIG. 13.1   MPS standard framework.

items assigned to the master scheduler. The master scheduler maintains this schedule and, in turn, it becomes a set of planning numbers which "drives" MRP. It represents what the company plans to produce expressed in specific configurations, quantities, and dates. The MPS should not be confused with a sales forecast which represents a statement of demand. The master production schedule must take forecast plus other important considerations (backlog,management policy and goals, etc.) into account prior to determining the best manufacturing strategy. Syn: master schedule (cf. closed-loop MRP).

The lengthiness of this definition is understandable when one considers the many MPS interfaces and their tremendous importance in manufacturing companies.

It is assumed that the reader has a basic overall knowledge of manufacturing resource planning as well as access to *Master Production Scheduling: Principle and Practice*. This chapter does not attempt to duplicate that reference. It does provide a current, overall perspective of the master production scheduling process and outlines significant techniques that various companies utilize to implement and manage that process.

The reader may wish to read the reprint of Chapter 2 of *Master Production Scheduling: Principle and Practice* at the end of this chapter before proceeding.

PRODUCTION PLANNING

Production planning is a formalized, management planning process which directly drives the MPS. Through production planning, operating management reviews and revises aggregate rates of manufacture for the various families, or classes, of products which comprise the business. The executive who has profit-and-loss responsibility for the business operation—the divisional president, general manager, etc. —presides over the formal production planning review meeting. Thus the production plan truly represents top management's "handle" on the business.

The *APICS Dictionary* defines production planning as follows:

> PRODUCTION PLANNING. The function of setting the overall level of manufacturing output. Its prime purpose is to establish production rates that will achieve management's objective in terms of raising or lowering inventories or backlogs, while usually attempting to keep the production force relatively stable. The production plan is usually stated in broad terms (e.g., product groupings, families of products). It must extend through a planning horizon sufficient to plan the labor, equipment, facilities, material, and finances required to accomplish the production plan. Various units of measure are used by different companies to express the plan such as standard hours, tonnage, labor operators, units, pieces, dollars, etc. As this plan affects all company functions, it is normally prepared with information from marketing, manufacturing, engineering, finance, materials, etc. In turn, the production plan becomes management's authorization for the Master Scheduler to convert into a more detailed plan. Syn: production program (cf. business plan, closed-loop MRP).

The Production Plan versus the MPS—An Example

The production plan developed by operating management is the primary driver of the MPS, yet the two are distinctly different in many important respects. Let us use automobiles as an example. Consider the hypothetical M-body family of cars seen in Fig. 13.2.

The M-body family is one of several families produced by Acme Motors, yet it is distinguished from the others by several factors. The M-body sells in a certain price range and thus competes for an identifiable market niche. All M-cars share certain major components—chassis, body, engines, etc. They are assembled in certain specified facilities.

Each month, Acme management formally reviews the M-body, its status in the marketplace, and its production plan for the months ahead. The key to this plan is the marketplace. Historically, Acme knows that a 60-day dealer inventory of-M bodies is desirable. A stock of this size provides a wide variety of product configurations which, in turn, means customers usually can quickly get an M-body which meets their needs. A 60-day stock is also financially manageable by Acme dealers. It provides a buffer between the sales rate and the production rate which does permit some leveling of Acme's labor force.

Every 10 days, dealers report sales statistics and inventory positions. Acme analyzes these and each month formally updates the M-body sales forecast. Using this forecast and the current inventory position, Acme calculates the days of supply of M-bodies in dealer stock.

During periods when sales run heavier than expected, the days-of-supply number falls below the 60-day target. Acme management responds by scheduling assembly overtime within the constraints of major component supplies (engines, transmissions, chassis), labor contracts, etc. If the strong sales situation appears to be long-term, Acme considers other major capacity adjustments such as converting

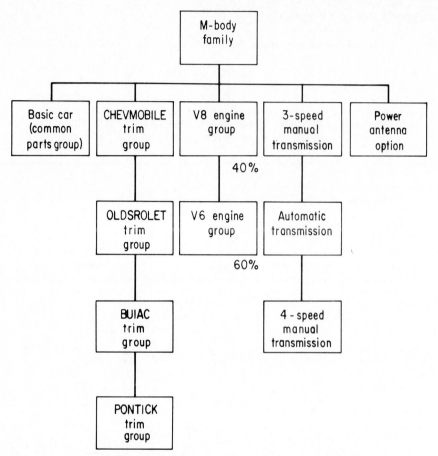

FIG. 13.2 M-body family of cars.

facilities to M-body production, adding shifts, etc. During periods of slow sales, Acme may respond with sales promotions, reduced-rate financing, temporary lay-offs, and other moves to adjust an 87-day dealer inventory downward.

In either case, the desired adjustment to dealer inventory cannot be made instantaneously. Acme management is thus revising overall production rates for M-bodies for the next few months to get back to the historical 60-day target.

Two major decisions typically result from this formal production planning process: (1) Agreed-to rates of manufacture for the family, for example 4000 units per week for the next 4 weeks because of material constraints and 4400 units per week for the next 8 weeks, etc., and (2) an agreed-to sales split which controls the amount of M-body output that will be Chevmobile, Oldsrolet, etc.

These agreements drive the MPS process. The aggregate rates exactly define the numbers of common parts required. The forecasted mix of options is used to revise the master schedules for engine groups, transmission options, etc. Master schedulers are responsible for this planning. They disaggregate the production plan and detail it in terms of the MPS items.

Acme executives discuss the M-body family, aggregate rates of sales and manufacture, and monthly plans during production planning. Master schedulers detail those plans in terms of specific MPS items, considering the weekly and daily rates of manufacture. They take into account such factors as desirable lot sizes and vendor sources which are not normally considered during production planning.

Business Plan versus Production Plan

Many manufacturing companies have formal annual business planning processes which set boundaries on the production plan. The two processes have a relationship which is important to understand. It is also important to know the differences between the two and how the ongoing production plan serves to support the business plan.

In general, the business planning process is much more financially oriented than production planning and includes more far-reaching strategic implications. Business planning deals with investment planning, profit planning, asset planning, and capital planning. It includes product and market strategies such as market share, new-product planning, analyses of competition, distribution strategies, and product positioning to meet customer service objectives. Business planning is concerned with major capital expenditures for new facilities, new technologies, new processes, and the like. These plans usually cover a 3- to 5-year planning horizon.

Certain aspects of business planning cover manufacturing plans. Aggregate inventory objectives such as planned levels and turnover objectives are included. Aggregate rates of manufacture are planned. Capacities required are planned including overall work force plans as well as needed plant and equipment.

The first year of a typical 3- to 5-year business plan generally represents the set of operating plans and budgets against which company performance is measured. There frequently are midyear, or perhaps quarterly, reviews of operations. This budgetary aspect of business planning is the main area of overlap with the ongoing, monthly production planning process. The business plan can be viewed, in some senses, as establishing objectives, targets, and the strategies designed to accomplish them. The production planning process is then viewed as the ongoing review and refining of tactics necessary to meet the targets. Most businesses find themselves at variance with the operating plan and budgets at some time during the fiscal year. Continuous, midcourse adjustments are thus made through the production planning process.

Business plans can be distinguished from production plans in several important ways. Business plans are normally expressed in dollars whereas production plans are convertible to dollars but usually are expressed in other terms—units, tons, dozens, square feet, or other measures. Production plans also express monthly rates of manufacture by families of products whereas business plans often express annual objectives for the overall business, market segments, or other high-level groupings.

Production planning focuses on managing rates of manufacture to meet targeted inventory and/or backlog levels, which is only one aspect of business planning. Make-to-stock businesses target finished-goods inventory levels to maintain desired levels of customer service. Make-to-order businesses target backlog levels (all unshipped customer orders on hand, not necessarily past due) to maintain desired customer service levels. In the latter case, these are usually expressed as desired lead times to the customer, and there is a recognized need to offer competitive lead times.

In both types of businesses, the aggregate forecast of sales normally drives the production plan. During periods of scarce capacity, the production plan drives the sales forecast. At times, it becomes necessary to revise targeted inventory and/or backlog levels because of marketplace or manufacturing conditions.

Production Plan Formats and Mechanics

Figure 13.3 illustrates a typical production plan format and situation. The display shows 3 months of history in order to gain a better historical perspective and to clearly see how the current situation was reached. The 5-month picture in the future is shown here instead of the normal 12- to 24-month picture.

The original plan developed 3 months ago planned manufacture to exceed the forecasted rate of sales in order to increase inventory to a targeted position of 1 month's sales (or 30-day supply). Actual sales and manufacture for the last 3

PRODUCTION PLAN WORKSHEET

Make-to-Stock — Target: One Month Inventory

Marketing

(Months)		-3	-2	-1	Today	Current	+1	+2	+3	+4
Forecast		120	120	120	Original	120	120	120	120	120
Actual		109	137	133	Revised	130	130	130	130	130
Difference		-11	+17	+13						
Cumulative difference			+6	+19						

Manufacturing

Planned		125	125	125	Original	125	120	120	120	120
Actual		121	118	119	Revised	125	130	135	135	135
Difference		-4	-7	-6						
Cumulative difference			-11	-17						

On hand — Inventory

Planned			106	111	116	Original	121	121	121	121	121
Actual		101	113	94	80	Revised	75	75	80	85	90
Difference			+7	-17	-36						

FIG. 13.3 Production plan worksheet—make to stock. Target is 1-month inventory.

months have varied somewhat from those planned. Sales have exceeded forecast by 19 units in the last 3 months, or approximately 5 percent (19/360). Manufacturing missed planned production by 17 units, or 5 percent (17/375). Inventories thus are 36 units, or 31 percent (36/116), under plan.

The production plan worksheet shows the composite results of the production planning process. Sales and marketing have revised the sales forecast. A best-efforts manufacturing plan has been put forth by the manufacturing manager. Although material and capacity constraints exist in both the current month and month +1, the plan has been increased in month +1. This is based on the expected resolution of a material or capacity problem which was principally responsible for the manufacturing shortfall of 17 units over the last 3 months. Beginning in month +2, manufacturing rates of 135 per month are being recommended to improve the inventory position. This strategy will not achieve the 1-month inventory goal by month +4. To do so would require a significantly higher manufacturing rate than 135 per month. Judgment has suggested a course of action that, on balance, increases capacity and hiring but temporarily sacrifices target inventory goals. The key is that agreement was reached and communicated.

The example illustrates a typical compromise proposal which will not fully satisfy any one member of the management team. Sales may not be happy because of the inventory position. Manufacturing is being challenged since they have not consistently produced to plan in the past, and this revised plan calls for yet more output.

The example illustrates the formal process used to review the production plan each month:

1. Sales forecasts are reviewed and revised.
2. Current inventory and/or backlog positions are documented.
3. Demonstrated capacities are documented.
4. Production rates are revised within the constraints of both material and capacity availability.
5. Projected inventory and/or backlog positions are calculated and compared to targets.
6. Contingency plans are developed based on reasonable variations of sales and manufacturing from plans, e.g., optimistic and pessimistic alternatives.
7. Alternatives are presented for top management discussion, review, and approval.

Note that in the example, substantial communication and preparation took place prior to the formal review for management approval. In most companies, this is the case. Middle management discusses and prepares alternatives for review and agreement. Usually, a formal planning cycle is defined in a policy which outlines the process, specifying the information which must be communicated by certain working days of the month to meet the formal review meeting schedule. On occasion, the top management approval meeting will initiate yet another plan revision.

Figure 13.4 illustrates a typical situation for a make-to-order family of products. In this example the target is expressed as a desired backlog level of 2 months. This could be expressed as a 2-month delivery lead time provided all orders are delivered on a first-come, first-served basis.

Normally, make-to-order forecasts project *bookings*, or order receipt rates. The manufacturing plan expresses the projected rates of shipment since each product is produced in response to a firm customer's order. The time difference between the booking and the shipment is often expressed as a *booking-to-shipment curve*, or *ratio*. Figure 13.5 illustrates such a ratio. Of $10,000 booked this month, $2170 will

PRODUCTION PLAN WORSHEET

Make-to-Order   Target: Two Month Backlog

Marketing

	(Months)	-3	-2	-1	Today	Current	+1	+2	+3	+4
Forecast		30	30	30	Original	30	35	35	35	35
Actual		32	32	35	Revised	— NO CHANGE —				
Difference		+2	+2	+5						
Cumulative difference			+4	+9						

Manufacturing

		-3	-2	-1		Current	+1	+2	+3	+4
Planned		35	35	35	Original	35	35	35	35	35
Actual		33	32	33	Revised	— NO CHANGE —				
Difference		-2	-3	-2						
Cumulative difference			-5	-7						

Backlog   Beginning Backlog   Backlog

						Current	+1	+2	+3	+4
Planned		86	81	76	Original	71	71	71	71	71
Actual	91	90	90	92	Revised	87	87	87	87	87
Difference		+4	+9	+16						

FIG. 13.4   Production plan worksheet—make to order. Target is 2-month backlog.

ship this month, $1850 will ship in month +1, and so on. This ratio, which varies according to marketplace conditions, is used to translate the bookings forecasts to shipment forecasts.

Figure 13.6 depicts a consolidated format which includes both make-to-stock and make-to-order conditions. It combines the two previous examples of the production plan worksheets.

Note the shipments line which did not appear in the previous figures. Projected shipments appear as the marketing forecast line of the make-to-stock worksheet for the stocked portion of the family and, as noted, in the manufacturing planned line for the make-to-order portion. The shipments line consolidates these two.

Production Planning Families and Units of Measure

It is sometimes difficult to define families for purposes of production planning. It is desirable to limit the number of families in order to streamline the top-management

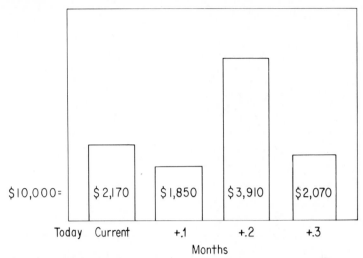

FIG. 13.5 Booking-to-shipment ratio.

review process. However, this may be difficult to do in firms with diverse product lines.

The overriding objective is to structure families to facilitate marketing-manufacturing communications. On one hand, sales and marketing must be able to forecast marketplace demand. On the other hand, manufacturing must be able to translate proposed production rates to required capacities.

In many instances, such as the automobile M-body noted earlier, the family structure serves both needs. Demand can be forecast for the M-body because it serves an identifiable market niche. The planned production rate is straightforward in terms of planning needed capacity. In other instances, a communications gap exists. A hand-tool company with a family of wrenches in its product line including Allen, pipe, open end, and socket wrenches illustrates the problem. The different wrenches require quite different manufacturing processes. It may be possible to adequately forecast the demand for wrenches. However, unless this demand can be translated smoothly to the expected mix of basic types of wrenches, manufacturing may be unable to determine staffing and equipment capacities needed to manufacture the product.

The unit of measure used to state the sales forecast rate and the manufacturing rate bears on this problem. In marketplace-oriented families such as the wrench family noted above, units of measure such as "each" lose meaning. Dollars become the only common denominator in which communication can occur. In other instances, the family structure serves both marketing and manufacturing and permits units of measure such as units or "each," pounds, tons, square feet, dozens, yards, and the like to be used. Hours are an appropriate unit of measure in some businesses, especially with engineered-to-order products.

Marketplace-oriented families may require the use of rough-cut capacity planning (RCCP). To directly relate family rates of manufacture to needed capacities, RCCP load profiles which assume typical, or average, mixes are then used to determine rough-cut capacities. In similar fashion, even though given families may relate directly to some required capacities, RCCP may have a role in production

PRODUCTION PLAN WORKSHEET

Make-to-Stock and Order

Marketing

Marketing	(Months)	-3	-2	-1	Today	Current	+1	+2	+3	+4
Forecast		150	150	150	Original	150	155	155	155	155
Actual		141	169	168	Revised	160	165	165	165	165
Difference			-9	+19	+18					
Cumulative difference				+10	+28					

Manufacturing

		-3	-2	-1		Current	+1	+2	+3	+4
Planned		160	160	160	Original	160	155	155	155	155
Actual		154	150	152	Revised	160	165	170	170	170
Difference			-6	-10	-8					
Cumulative difference				-16	-24					

Inventory/backlog

						Current	+1	+2	+3	+4
Inventory	101	113	94	80		75	75	80	85	90
Backlog	91	90	90	92	Revised	87	87	87	87	87
Shipments		142	169	166		165	165	165	165	165

FIG. 13.6   Production plan worksheet—make-to-stock and order.

planning. For example, the M-body family of cars might compete for stamping plant capacity with other families. Then RCCP would be useful in reviewing that competition for capacity.

DEMAND MANAGEMENT

Managing demand helps to manage supply. The capacity needed to meet current customer demand is lost when the wrong product is produced. Capacity is lost when excessive schedule changes ripple through a manufacturing process.

MRP systems respond to forecasts of demand, and the better the forecast, the better the resulting customer service. MRP's rapid replanning ability must be controlled. The better managed the reaction to changing marketplace conditions, the better the overall performance in customer service, inventory, and productivity.

The activities which link sales and marketing to manufacturing and the needs of the marketplace to manufacturing plans are encompassed by the demand management process. *Demand management* is an umbrella term first publicized in the APICS text *Master Production Scheduling: Principle and Practice*. The current APICS *Dictionary* definition reads as follows:

> DEMAND MANAGEMENT. The function of recognizing and managing all of the demands for products to insure that the master scheduler is aware of them. It encompasses the activities of forecasting, order entry, order promising, branch warehouse requirements, interplant orders, and service parts requirements (cf. manufacturing production schedule).
> The related definitions of Demand(s) are:
> DEMAND. A need for a particular product or component. The demand could come from any number of sources, i.e., customer order, forecast, interplant, branch warehouse, service part, or to manufacturing the next higher level. At the finished goods level, "demand data" are usually different from "sales data" because demand does not necessarily result in sales, i.e., if there is no stock there will be no sale (cf. dependent demand, independent demand).
> DEPENDENT DEMAND. Demand is considered dependent when it is directly related to or derived from the demand for other items or end products. Such demands are therefore calculated, and need not and should not be forecast. A given inventory item may have both dependent and independent demand at any given time (cf. independent demand).
> INDEPENDENT DEMAND. Demand for an item is considered independent when such demand is unrelated to the demand for other items. Demand for finished goods, parts required for destructive testing and service parts requirements are some examples of independent demand (cf. dependent demand).

Several chapters of this book discuss aspects of demand management—forecasting, distribution resource management (of branch warehouse requirements), and sales order entry among others. The discussion which follows focuses on the important interfaces between the demand management functions and the other planning processes which compose the MPS framework of Fig. 13.1. Figure 13.7 identifies these major interfaces.

Forecast Interfaces: Aggregate versus Item Forecasts

A forecast is a formal request from sales and marketing to manufacturing to have product *or* capacity available to meet perceived demand. With few exceptions, forecasts are driving forces in MRP. Most firms rely on forecasts of expected business to plan major aspects of both material and capacity, although some companies, e.g., defense contractors, have sufficient backlogs of firm orders with which to plan both capacity and material requirements. Figure 13.8 describes the interface aspects of forecasts.

Aggregate family forecasts drive the production planning process. These forecasts, along with management decisions to increase or decrease inventories or backlog, establish the planned *volume* of production. Supporting item forecasts establish the planned *mix* through the MPS.

Good planning communications at this level require the two aggregation-disaggregation processes shown. The forecasting process should provide the ability to aggregate the item forecasts to ensure consistency with the family forecasts. Conversely, it is necessary to be able to disaggregate a family forecast into item forecasts. Companies derive forecasts both ways. Some begin at the item level and aggregate to

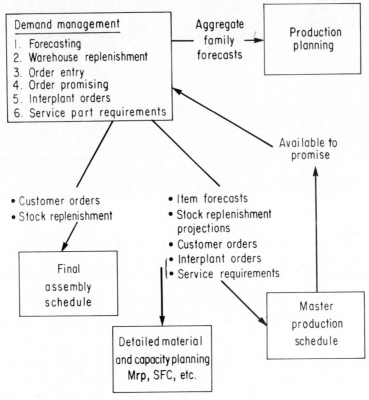

FIG. 13.7 Demand management interfaces.

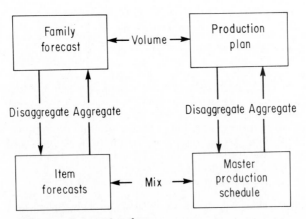

FIG. 13.8 Forecast interfaces.

the family. Others forecast the family and disaggregate to the items. Either way, it is important to have consistency.

A similar aggregation-disaggregation process exists between production planning and the MPS. The agreed-to family rate of manufacture must be disaggregated to the item detail of the MPS. *Superbills*, or *planning bills of materials*, often serve this purpose. Bottom-up MPS summaries are used to aggregate the MPS to ensure that it agrees with the production plan within reasonable tolerances.

Forecasts of lower-level demands often interface directly to MRP, especially in companies with significant service-parts activity or interplant supply activity. Aggregate forecasts, usually expressed in dollars and/or hours, are used for production planning and RCCP. The item forecast detail may interface to the MPS but more commonly interfaces to MRP. MRP interfaces are needed with items which have both *dependent* (i.e., used on high-level items) and *independent* (e.g., service-parts sales) demands.

Forecast Interfaces: Forecast Consumption

In any given period, rarely does actual demand agree with forecasted demand, either in aggregate or by item. This fact, combined with the rapid replanning capabilities of MRP systems, leads to the need for *forecast consumption*—the process of replacing the forecast with customer orders, or other actual demands, as they are received. The examples which follow illustrate some of the issues.

In Fig. 13.9, an original sales forecast of 20 per month has been smoothed to 5 per week to present demand uniformly to the planning system. If no sales occur in period 1, that is, actual demand is less than forecast, the planning system requires some reasonable rules with which to proceed, or it may react too nervously. Figure 13.10 shows two possible solutions for 1 week later.

Choice 1, dropping the unrealized forecast which has gone past due, will generate a reschedule-out (deexpedite) recommendation since the projected available balance of 31 in period 5 indicates the MPS quantity of 30 in period 5 is no longer needed. Choice 2, carrying forward the unrealized forecast into period 2, maintains the original projected available balance projection. No rescheduling action is recommended.

The choice of procedure is an important one. In any given period (week, month), one would expect demand to be less than forecast on half of the MPS items and exceed the forecast on the other half. Thus, there is a large potential for planning

		Period							
		1	2	3	4	5	6	7	8
Forecast		5	5	5	5	5	5	5	5
Projected available balance	21	16	11	6	1	26	21	16	11
Master production schedule						30			

FIG. 13.9 Smoothed forecast.

Today

Choice 1

		Period						
		2	3	4	5	6	7	8
Forecast		5	5	5	5	5	5	5
Projected available balance	21	16	11	6	31*	26	21	16

*Recommends reschedule out (De-expedite)

Choice 2

Forecast		10	5	5	5	5	5	5
Projected available balance	21	11	6	1	26	21	16	11

Master production schedule					30			

FIG. 13.10 Forecast consumption alternatives.

nervousness, i.e., reschedule-in and reschedule-out recommendations. A master scheduler could spend quite a bit of time reviewing reschedule recommendations and deciding what, if anything, to do.

A visible, easily managed alternative to choice 2 is to define a cumulative *forecast adjustment* field which maintains a running total of the difference between actual demand and forecast. Figure 13.11 shows the operation of the forecast adjustment field after week 1 with no sales. If actual demands exceed forecast over time, the forecast adjustment field will turn negative.

In use, the forecast adjustment dampens reschedule recommendations to the master scheduler as actual demand varies from forecast. Thus, forecast adjustment should be monitored and managed by a responsible individual in sales or marketing as well as the master scheduler.

A common rule is to consume forecasts within the forecast interval and not to expect them to be accurate in any smaller period. Many companies forecast monthly, spread forecasts weekly for scheduling purposes, yet consume forecasts quarterly. The cumulative forecast adjustment capability is especially useful for sporadic-demand items. It is frequently used for service demand for lower-level items handled by MRP in order to prevent excessive nervousness.

A forecast consumption process is required at several levels—in aggregate for production planning and at item levels in MPS and MRP. The MRP systems are capable of very rapid replanning. Forecast consumption processes permit people to exercise judgment and control.

Defined time fences (see the "MPS Mechanics" section) are another tool for managing the rate of change to schedules. Eventually manufacturing activity must react to changing marketplace needs. Time-fence policies define when and how.

	Forecast adjust-ment	Period						
		2	3	4	5	6	7	8
Forecast	+5	5	5	5	5	5	5	5
Projected available balance	21	16	11	6	1	26	21	16	11
Master production schedule						30			

FIG. 13.11   Forecast adjustment field.

Order-Entry and Order-Promising Interfaces: Available to Promise

The demand management function of order entry is the process of accepting and translating a customer order to the internal language and definition used by the manufacturer. This can range from translating a verbal description to a part number to a protracted engineering process.

The order-promising function assigns delivery dates to the order. Available-to-promise (ATP) tools and procedures provide the necessary information to make good customer promises. ATP mechanics are discussed, with examples, in the "MPS Mechanics" section.

ATP tools essentially compare actual demands to MPS items on hand or scheduled. The uncommitted portion of the inventory or planned production is "for sale." Time-phased ATP tools, frequently updated, provide up-to-date delivery possibilities.

In the past, many companies quoted standard delivery lead times to their customers. These were reviewed periodically and changed with backlog conditions. ATP information is much more timely and better reflects the dynamics of customer orders.

Although the arithmetic of ATP techniques is quite simple, ATP status has become a sophisticated tool in practice. Firms producing optionalized products, e.g., automobiles, have ATP tools which can base the customer order promise on the gating option. For example, the engine and transmission ordered may have ATP status, but the requested sunroof option may not have ATP status to match.

Another adaptation of ATP tools involves promising an order with several line items. An order for a suite of office furniture might include desk, chair, credenza, and filing cabinets. Many of these could be optionalized products. The ATP status for the order reflects the ATP status for each line item. Transportation schedules become another consideration.

Capacity-managed businesses such as foundries (see the "MPS Environments" section) and engineered-to-order companies may base customer order promises on ATP capacity. Incoming orders are converted to capacity demands through an estimating process. These demands compete for ATP capacity with other demands.

Order-Promising Interfaces: Abnormal Demands

Closely associated with both consuming forecast with actual demands and ATP status is the need to manage abnormal demand conditions. Figure 13.12 shows the

		Period							
		1	2	3	4	5	6	7	8
Forecast		3	3	3	3	3	3	3	3
Production forecast									
Actual demand									
Projected available balance	13	10	7	4	1	23	20	17	14
Available to promise		13	13	13	13	38	38	38	38
Master production schedule						25			

FIG. 13.12   Managing abnormal demand. Promising an order for 24.

status of an MPS plan at the time an ASAP (as soon as possible) delivery order for 24 is received. Procedures and guidelines are needed to properly manage this type of situation. Clearly, a customer promise needs to be made since the 13 on hand will not satisfy the order for 24. Several important questions need to be addressed before that promise is made:

1. Should the future forecast be increased? Is this a new, continuing customer or a source of demand?
2. Is this a truly abnormal demand? Should the order be treated as a one-time deviation (increase) to the forecast?
3. Is this order merely the forecast coming true? Is this item normally ordered in large quantities? This occurs if the normal practice is to spread the forecast uniformly while actual demand tends to be lumpy.
4. Should the total shelf stock be used to satisfy part of this order, or should some be held back to service other customers?
5. What is a realistic promise for this order? The portion of the order not shipped from on-hand inventory may be satisfied by the replenishment of 25 due to stock in period 5. Alternatively, it may be best to give this order full lead time in order to obtain enough product to satisfy this abnormal demand plus the forecast.

A procedure used in many businesses is to establish a maximum order size by item which can be satisfied from shelf stock. The intent of this guideline is to prevent depletion of on-hand stock by exceptionally large orders. To do so frequently leads to poor service levels for the normal customer order pattern.

Maximum-order-size parameters are analogous to the demand filters used in some forecasting models. Demand filters are tripped when demand in a period differs from that forecast by a specified number of mean absolute deviations.

A reasonable set of rules is needed to manage unusual incoming demands. Normally, such rules are not unduly sophisticated. People make the final determination. Computer logic and procedures are used to identify abnormal conditions.

LONG-RANGE RESOURCE PLANNING AND RCCP

The comprehensive discussion of contemporary capacity planning tools in Chap. 15 should be reviewed. Two of these are considered parts of the overall framework of master scheduling: long-range resource planning and RCCP.

The *APICS Dictionary* provides the following definitions:

> LONG-RANGE RESOURCE PLANNING. A planning activity for long-term capacity decisions, based on the production plan and perhaps on even more gross data (e.g., sales per year) beyond the time horizon for the production plan. This activity is to plan long-term capacity needs out to the time period necessary to acquire gross capacity additions such as a major factory expansion.
>
> ROUGH-CUT CAPACITY PLANNING. The process of converting the production plan and/or the master production schedule into capacity needs for key resources: manpower, machinery, warehouse space, vendors' capabilities and, in some cases, money. Product load profiles are often used to accomplish this. The purpose of rough-cut capacity planning is to evaluate the plan prior to attempting to implement it. Syn: resource requirements planning (cf. capacity requirements planning).

In contemporary practice, long-range resource planning is associated most closely with the strategic aspects of longer-range business planning. Many companies develop annual business plans, projecting several business objectives over a 3- to 5-year horizon. This exercise usually takes into consideration the following types of items:

1. Financial plans—investment, profit, asset, and capital objectives and requirements
2. Market and product plans—market strategies, product and technology plans, sales rates, customer delivery objectives, etc.
3. Manufacturing plans—planned shipments, inventory and backlog levels, annual production rates, aggregate capacities, etc.

The long-range resource planning aspects of this process are used to examine major capacity considerations, such as new facilities and overall staffing levels, which have significant capital budget implications. Computer-assisted techniques such as modeling, probability analysis, and financial analysis are sometimes used in this planning process. Periodic, less comprehensive plan updates may occur semiannually or quarterly.

RCCP is most closely associated with the ongoing production plan and/or the MPS. These planning horizons are shorter than those of the annual business plan and are more product-specific. RCCP provides a reasonability test of capacity needed to accomplish these plans at intermediate levels of detail (i.e., more specific than the annual plan but less detailed than the routing/work center detail of capacity-requirements planning).

RCCP techniques vary among companies, but most involve two essential ingredients: identified *critical resources* and *load profiles.*

Critical resources are company-specific. They normally include bottleneck factory processes, both equipment and labor, constraining vendor capacities, engineering capacities, quality assurance or test facilities, and so on, the critical few resources which truly dictate overall throughput rather than the large number of specific capacities.

Load profiles identify the loads placed on critical resources as production planning families of products or specific MPS items are planned. They are developed by summarizing the detailed routings used to produce the various components of a product and by analyzing cost data or labor reporting. Or they may simply be estimates prepared by knowledgeable individuals.

Through experience, companies develop a proper level of RCCP *precision* appropriate to their needs. Many companies perform RCCP at overall family rates of manufacture as stated in the production plan. Once satisfied, such companies proceed to develop detailed component plans through MPS and MRP. Other companies make a more precise RCCP analysis by evaluating item-specific plans as stated in the MPS before proceeding to the detailed component planning processes.

A tool manufacturer might illustrate this precision issue. A family of open end wrenches could be rough-cut as a family if all open end wrenches followed essentially the same manufacturing process and generated similar loads for critical resources. However, a broader production planning family of wrenches which included both open end and socket wrenches might be rough-cut at an MPS item level since the different style wrenches impact on very different critical resources.

RCCP tools are designed to permit a rapid analysis of how reasonable the production plan and/or MPS is in light of demonstrated capacities. Highly interactive, computer-assisted RCCP is very desirable. What-if questions abound in most manufacturing companies, and RCCP is a major what-if evaluation tool. It is used whenever changes of consequence are proposed in production plans and/or the MPS. It is also used to evaluate high-impact customer orders and in myriad other situations.

MPS ENVIRONMENTS

The overall framework for developing and controlling the master scheduling process is described at the beginning of this chapter. The specific MPS approaches and techniques in use vary from firm to firm, although the objective and purpose of the MPS remain the same. To repeat, for *selected items*, the MPS is a statement of what the company expects to manufacture. It is the *anticipated build* schedule for those selected items assigned to the master scheduler. The master scheduler maintains this schedule, and it in turn becomes a set of planning numbers which drives MRP.

One way to categorize this variety of master scheduling environment techniques is to examine the various *competitive* environments in which they are utilized. Current APICS terminology provides the following definitions:

> MAKE-TO-STOCK PRODUCT.   The end item is shipped from finished goods, "off the shelf" and therefore is finished prior to a customer order arriving.
> MAKE-TO-ORDER PRODUCT.   The end item is finished after receipt of a customer order. Frequently long lead time components are planned prior to the order arriving in order to reduce the delivery time to the customer. Where options or other subassemblies are stocked prior to customer orders arriving, the term "assemble-to-order" is frequently used.

The term *make to order* is probably too broad. For the purposes of this chapter, *make to order* is subdivided into several, more descriptive categories:

> *Make-to-order products.*   Materials are purchased and capacity is committed after receipt of customer order. No stocking is done prior to receipt of order. For repeat business, the product is preengineered.

Finish- or assemble-to-order products.   Options, subassemblies, or other component materials are stocked prior to customer order. For assembled products, both options and end items are usually preengineered.

Engineer-to-order products.   Significant aspects of the product are undefined at receipt of customer order. Some lower-level, common materials may be stocked prior to receipt of customer order.

Capacity-managed products.   In businesses such as foundries and contract machining shops, capacities are planned prior to receipt of orders. Upon receipt of the customer's order, capacity is committed to manufacture in order to meet the required date.

Although these categories are somewhat arbitrary and imprecise, they do provide a more convenient breakdown of make-to-order businesses for the purpose of describing contemporary master scheduling techniques.

Implicit in both definitions is the competitive nature of the market. Companies must maintain an acceptable delivery lead time for the customer. Admittedly, in make-to-stock businesses, delivery off the shelf may not result solely from competitive pressure, but it certainly is a primary factor. Manufacturing processes, efficiencies, seasonality, load leveling, and other variables contribute to a decision to stock at various levels in anticipation of customer orders. Figure 13.13 illustrates the role of the MPS in controlling the competitive lead time offered to the customer. It

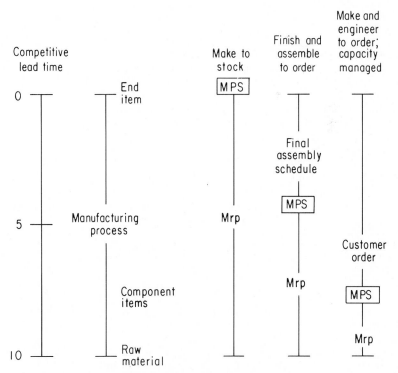

FIG. 13.13   Role of MPS in controlling competitive lead times.

depicts the level of completion through the manufacturing process at which the MPS stages material and/or capacity prior to receipt of the customer order. The higher this MPS level, the shorter the competitive or delivery lead time to the customer.

Although any such generalization is subject to many exceptions, Fig. 13.14 describes commonly used MPS techniques in various environments. Where needed, the techniques themselves are described in the section "MPS Mechanics."

It is common to find many variations and clever uses of these various MPS techniques, so do not assume that the techniques apply only in the listed environment.

Multiple-level MPS processes are also common, for example, when a manufacturing facility logically breaks down into different processes. Suppose that a bulk pharmaceutical manufacture has batch-process characteristics requiring one set of MPS criteria. The finishing or packaging process with line orientation is subject to another set of scheduling considerations. In such circumstances, two separate but related, person-controlled "master schedules" may be in use.

A multiple-level or two-level MPS is utilized in assemble-to-order businesses where the production plan sets the rate of manufacture for the family, which also

MPS Environments		
	MPS Item	MPS Techniques
Make to stock	• End item	• End item forecasts • End item safety stocks • End item bills of material (BOM)
Finish and assemble to order	• Options, accessories, attachments, intermediates • Common parts BOM	• Option forecasts • Planning BOM as aid • Modularized BOM with or without end item BOM • Phantoms and pseudo planning items • Option overplanning (in lieu of safety stock) • Available to promise material

Make to order	• Customer orders
	• Management authorizations of:
	  – Long-lead-time component items
	  – Speculative items
		• Customer intelligence forecasts
		• Replacement of authorizations with customer orders
		• Customer commit fences
		• Manufacturing cycle promising

Engineer to order	• Customer orders
	• Management authorizations of:
	  – "Generic" BOM
	  – Long-lead-time component items
		• Customer intelligence forecasts
		• Engineering scheduling systems
		• Engineering/manufacturing cycle promising
		• Rough-cut capacity planning of both engineering and manufacturing capacities

Capacity managed	• Capacity representations	• Forward loading based on available to promise capacity • Raw/intermediate materials on order points or time-phased order points

FIG. 13.14 MPS techniques for various environments.

specifies the need for common parts. In addition, the second level, or option level, is also governed by the MPS, because of the wide variation of end configurations and the difficulty of forecasting and scheduling at the end configuration level. This is discussed in more detail in the discussion of planning bills of materials.

Another multiple-level MPS example occurs with major subassemblies or component items subject to capacity constraints. Although normally planning occurs at MRP levels, it may be necessary to state a schedule with firm planned orders in order to recognize the constraints. This schedule then places significant constraints on the higher-level, possibly end-item, MPS. Even though the lower-level item is technically an MRP item, it is given the same degree of attention and the same amount of human control as an MPS item.

Capacity-managed businesses—foundries, contract machining firms, etc.—are noted for their strong orientation to capacity management first, with secondary consideration for material needs. Frequently, incoming customer orders are converted to capacity requirements and forward-scheduled based on both ATP capacity (load) and customer request date. Materials needed are often secondary considerations. Many plastics business, e.g., injection molding, are similar, especially those working with common compounds and other materials.

The concept of a master scheduling process strongly oriented to capacity management with secondary consideration to material management is perhaps another way to categorize various MPS environments. The early MRP pioneers tended to be job shop, assembled-products manufacturers who focused planning processes initially on materials needed and derived capacity needs from them. Repetitive manufacturers and process industries commonly proceed in reverse fashion. With more dedicated, flowlike manufacturing processes, decisions on the use of capacity dictate the materials needed. In the more general-purpose job shop environment, the decision on what to make, stated in terms of materials needed, dictates capacities needed.

For some of these same reasons, process and flowlike industries often utilize operations research techniques, e.g., linear programming, to optimize schedules for their facilities. Since these industries are usually capital-intensive and normally less constrained by material considerations, their planning systems emphasize efficient utilization of facilities and capacity.

ROLE OF THE BILL OF MATERIAL IN MASTER SCHEDULING

There is a relationship between the structure and form of the bills of materials and the master scheduling approach within a company. Given the various categories of MPS environments outlined earlier, the format of the bills of materials most commonly in use is as follows:

Master Scheduling Environment	Bill-of-Material Form	Engineering Status
Make to stock	End item	Preengineered
Finish or assemble to order	Modular	Preengineered
Make to order	End item	Preengineered
Engineer to order	End item	Engineered to order
Capacity managed	End item (if there is one at all)	Usually engineered if not a repeat order

The *APICS Dictionary* provides the following definitions:

END ITEM.   A product sold as a completed item or repair part; any item subject to a customer order or sales forecast. Syn: finished product.

OPTION.   A choice or feature offered to customers for customizing the end product. In many companies, the term "option" means a mandatory choice—the customer must select from one of the available choices. For example, in ordering a new car, the customer must specify an engine but need not necessarily select an air conditioner (cf. accessory, attachment).

ACCESSORY.   A choice or feature offered to customer for customizing the end product. In many companies, this term means that the choice does not have to be specified prior to shipment but could in fact be added at a later date. In other companies, however, this choice must be made prior to shipment (cf. attachment, option).

ATTACHMENT.   A choice or feature offered to customers for customizing the end product. In many companies, this term means that the choice, although not mandatory, must be selected prior to the final assembly schedule. In other companies, however, the choice need not be made at that time (cf. accessory, option).

MODULAR BILL (OF MATERIAL).   A type of planning bill which is arranged in product modules or options. Often used in companies where the product has many optional features, e.g., automobiles (cf. planning bill, common parts bill, super bill, option).

PLANNING BILL (OF MATERIAL).   An artificial grouping of items, in bill of material format, used to facilitate master scheduling and/or material planning (cf. common parts bill, modular bill, super bill).

SUPER BILL (OF MATERIAL).   A type of planning bill, located at the top level in the structure, which ties together various modular bills (and possibly a common parts bill) to define an entire product or product family. The "quantity per" relationship of super bill to modules represents the forecasted percentage popularity of each module. The master scheduled quantities of the super bill explode to create requirements for the modules which also are master scheduled (cf. planning bill, modular bill, common parts bill).

COMMON PARTS BILL (OF MATERIAL).   A type of planning bill which groups all common components for a product or family of products into one bill of material (cf. planning bill, modular bill, super bill).

TRANSIENT BILL OF MATERIAL.   A bill of material coding and structuring technique used primarily for transient (non-stocked) subassemblies. For the transient subassembly item, lead time is set to zero and lot-sizing is Lot-For-Lot. This permits MRP logic to drive requirements straight through the transient item to its components, but retains its ability to net against any occasional inventories of the subassembly. This technique also facilitates the use of common bills of material for engineering and manufacturing. Syn: phantom bill of material, blow through.

PSEUDO BILL (OF MATERIAL).   See: planning bill.

PHANTOM BILL (OF MATERIAL).   See: transient bill of material.

The sheer number of bill-of-material terms here should forewarn the reader that there is much to consider in relating the MPS approach to the structure of the underlying bills of materials.

Modular Bills of Materials

Modular bills are the natural choice in firms producing products such as automobiles. Because of the very large number of possible end items in a family, end item needs cannot be forecast. It is practical, however, to forecast and include in the MPS options, accessories, and attachments. For similar reasons, such firms may not develop maintained-item bills of materials. Since a particular configuration may be produced only once, a *one-time* bill of material is constructed for the customer or final-assembly order. The one-time bill lists the options, accessories, etc., required to produce the end item and serves as the historical record of what was produced.

The groups of component parts which constitute the option and accessories' bills of materials are often artificial groups. The power- and manual-steering options of an automobile illustrate the situation. Those related steering parts which are used on all cars of the family, regardless of the power- or manual-steering choice, are structured in a common-parts group. Those related solely to power steering (hydraulic pumps, hoses, etc.) are structured into power-steering-option bills of materials. Similarly, those related solely to manual steering go into a manual-steering-option bill of material. This organization of the bills of materials often results in planning items, e.g., common-parts group, power-steering group, which cannot be assembled but can be planned as a matched set of parts. It requires a common-parts group *and* a power-steering group *or* a manual-steering group along with all other specified options, to actually assemble the completed product.

Many of the terms defined here developed in environments similar to this automobile example. The *superbill* type of planning bill is often used for forecasting options via percentage mix relationships. Specifics of superbills are discussed in the "MPS Mechanics" section.

Although modular bill concepts are generally discussed in the context of assembled products such as automobiles, they can be useful in planning for a wide variety of products. Apparel manufacturers, e.g., men's dress shirts, frequently produce large numbers of end items or stockkeeping units (SKUs) because of the permutations of style, size, and color. Modular bills might be useful to plan common items such as yarn or thread and optional items such as dyes or labels. Specialty metals manufacturers may employ modular bill concepts to plan intermediate levels of metals in basic alloys and forms but then fabricate or finish to customer specification.

The reader is cautioned to thoroughly study this relationship between the MPS approach and bills-of-materials structures. Bills of materials are cornerstone documents in a manufacturing company that have broad implications. Business procedures which may be impacted by the structure of the bill of material include

- Order-entry and promising procedures
- Produce costing procedures
- Invoicing procedures
- Engineering drawing systems and change procedures
- Forecasting processes
- Manufacturing instructions and documentation such as pick lists, material issue procedures, and routing instructions
- Bill-of-material maintenance procedures

Custom, New, and Engineered Products and the Bill of Material

Engineered-to-order firms, firms producing custom or special products, and firms introducing new products frequently utilize the bill of material as a capacity planning mechanism and a type of project management tool. In many environments, new, custom, and engineered products evolved from previously produced products. It is often possible to categorize these with *generic bills of materials*, which are used for two purposes. (1) Generic bills identify major components, subassemblies, and materials needed to produce the product. Artificial part numbers are used for this purpose, along with estimated lead times based on past experience. (2) Again by using artificial part numbers, design and development activities may also be incorporated into these generic bill structures with both design work force estimates and estimated lead times required to accomplish design activities. In many regards, such bill-of-material structures resemble PERT (program evaluation and review technique) or critical-path networks used to plan and control project activities. The critical path of a CPM (critical path method) network is analogous to the cumulative lead-time path(s) of a bill-of-material structure. These generic bills of materials serve as a point of departure for both production planning and master production scheduling. The mechanics of the technique are discussed in the "MPS Mechanics" section.

A variation of this technique employs generic bills of materials along with generic routings and work centers. The bill of material is used to identify major materials needed. Routings and work center relationships are used to describe the design and development processes. Operation steps and associated work centers can be defined in the detail required—electrical engineering, mechanical, etc. This approach permits standard MRP scheduling tools such as dispatch lists to be used to schedule various development activities.

THE FINISHING OR FINAL-ASSEMBLY SCHEDULE

The finishing or final-assembly schedule (FAS) is the specific schedule of end items to be produced. For make-to-stock businesses, this schedule replenishes finished-goods inventory. In make-to-order businesses, it states the specific schedule for satisfying customer orders. It schedules the operations required to complete end items from the MPS level.

The term *final-assembly schedule* is in common use because many of the earliest companies to apply MRP techniques were assembled-products manufacturers. The term *finishing schedule* is probably a better generic term and has gained acceptance more recently because it better describes many companies using MRP that do not produce assembled products, e.g., textiles, metals, chemicals, etc. Synonymous terms include *packaging schedules, blending schedules,* and others.

In many companies, the finishing schedule plays a role distinctly different from that of the MPS, although the two plans are closely related. The MPS provides materials for use in finishing and is used to plan aggregate finishing capacities. Despite this relationship, the identifiable differences are many.

Items Scheduled Differ between the MPS and the FAS

In many businesses, notably make- and assemble-to-order companies, the types of items scheduled in the FAS differ from those scheduled by the MPS. Capital equipment such as machine tools and automobiles are classic examples. Assembly schedules are often stated in terms of customer orders which define the precise configurations of end items to be produced. The MPS, however, is expressed in terms of a plan for the mix of product options, parts groups, subassemblies, or other lower-level component items.

In such environments, the FAS is easily visualized as the relief mechanism for the MPS. Stated in terms of end items or customer orders defining end items, the FAS draws on and relieves the product options made available by the MPS plan.

Different Time Frames

To provide adequate forward visibility, cover cumulative manufacturing and procurement lead time, and plan needed capacities, the MPS may extend 12 or more months into the future. The associated finishing schedule may extend only a few days or weeks with firming of the schedule taking place at the last possible moment in order to take maximum advantage of available material and capacity.

Different Time Increments

The MPS and finishing schedule may be stated in quite different time increments. A typical MPS may be stated in weekly priorities (buckets) whereas the finishing schedule may be stated by shifts within the week, by day, by hour, or in other increments (e.g., the automotive industry states assembly schedules by the minute or less).

Control of Material Issues

The finishing schedule frequently is used rather than the MPS to control the issuing of material to specific finishing work areas. A typical example is found in a pharmaceutical manufacture with multiple packaging lines. The MPS provides both bulk and packaging materials without regard to packaging line while the packaging schedule controls the quantity and timing of material issues to specific lines. In major capital equipment assembly, material is frequently issued directly to the proper manufacturing step or routing operation under the control of the assembly schedule.

In make-to-stock businesses utilizing end-item-oriented master schedules, the distinction between the FAS and the MPS may be unclear because both schedules represent statements of end items to be produced. Where a formal FAS is in use, it usually represents a refined MPS plan which considers specific assembly lines or assembly areas to be used, more specific timing of production, and control of the material issue process. The MPS itself is usually not sufficiently detailed for these purposes.

Interfacing the FAS with the MPS

It is often necessary to create interfacing procedures between customer orders as entered and the underlying MPS in order to state or define the finishing schedule. A good example occurs in office furniture manufacture. A customer order specifies a catalog number which identifies a double pedestal desk with a locking center drawer, specific drawer arrangements in each pedestal, a modesty panel, a certain finish for the top, etc., which is one of several thousand possible configurations. Order-entry interpretation procedures, manual or automated, are used to translate the customer order to the product options (pedestals, drawers, desktops, locking parts, etc.) scheduled in the MPS. This interpretation process establishes the customer's actual demands which are used to calculate ATP dates from the MPS. The process also identifies component materials which must be issued to the assembly department in order to satisfy the order.

In other companies, e.g., automobile manufacturers, the customer order details a series of line items which specify the end-item configuration. No catalog number or other permanent reference identifies the end item. The customer or assembly order itself serves as a one-time bill of materials. It is also the basis for historical records of what was produced, i.e., warranty and necessary safety records for automobiles.

Because a wide variety of mechanics are used to state, plan, and control finishing and final-assembly operations, significantly different requirements exist in different companies. Very sophisticated, computer-assisted tools are necessary in many firms. Manual schedules work well in others.

Anticipating Potential Delays

Preexpediting tools, such as potential assembly delay reports shown in Fig. 13.15, are frequently used for the near term to check availability of materials in the quantities needed to maintain trouble-free finishing operations. Such tools are used in lieu of physically staging materials prior to actual need. Even with MPS and MRP delivery performances of 95 percent and better, near-term follow-up is needed to prevent material shortages and improve on assembly performance.

In the example, 30 of assembly 3503642 are to be assembled under manufacturing order 16649. This job is due to be issued (pulled) October 3 and requires 17 component items, 3 of which can cause potential delays—the motor, bracket, and bearing. *Potential* delays exist because the current on-hand balance will not cover this requirement plus all other requirements for the item in the specified 4-week horizon.

The follow-up message on the motor indicates that there is an existing purchase order on vendor 10124 which, if received on time, will cover this requirement. However, a vendor scheduler should be in contact with the vendor and working to ensure the delivery. Contrast this with the assumptions of MRP. Since the requirement is covered by a properly timed scheduled receipt, MRP assumes everything is fine and flashes no warning. In the near term, that is usually not acceptable. People need to be actively working to prevent shortages on the factory floor.

The term *paper staging* is sometimes used for this process of anticipating potential delays. The technique only works, of course, with accurate on-hand and on-order records. If these records are not sufficiently accurate, physical staging or advance pulling usually results since it is the only true way to determine what material is on hand.

MPS MECHANICS

A large body of fairly standard MPS mechanics has developed as the master scheduling process evolved. The major techniques are discussed in this section.

Standard MPS Format

An important advance has been a standardized report or display format, as seen in Fig. 13.16, which evolved from the MRP display, as seen in Fig. 13.17.

Many early implementations of MRP simply drove a sales forecast into the projected gross requirements line of MRP as a way to state what was needed. This initiated the MRP process and did develop the component-material plan much as it is done today.

Before long, however, many people began to recognize the need to "uncouple" the sales forecast from the stated rate of manufacture. With MRP's rapid replanning

Assembly no. 3503642   Job no. 16649

Horizon = 4 weeks
Date 9-28-86

Component part	Description	On Hand	Assy quantity	Other Requirements	Quantity short	Scheduled receipt	Quantity remaining	Date required	Vendor	
1012413	Motor	0	30	0	30	21413	80	10-3	10124	Follow-up
1513164	Bracket	20	60	40	80	32141	60	10-3	Shop	Follow-up
						32215	60	10-24	Shop	Reschedule in
207531	Bearing	35	30	30	25	31014	100	10-3	11028	Follow-up

FIG. 13.15 Potential assembly delay report.

13.29

			1	2	3	4	5	6	7	8
A	Forecast				— Independent demand forecast					
B	Production forecast				Dependent demand forecast					
C	Actual demand				Customer orders					
D	Projected available balance				Line D = (on hand + line F) − (line A + B + C)*					
E	Available to promise				On hand + MPS − actual demand of line C†					
F	Master production schedule				Released + firm planned orders					

*Assumes forecast consumption by actual demand.
†See sample calculations later in this section.

FIG. 13.16 Standard MPS format.

Material requirements plan

	1	2	3	4	5	6	7	8
Projected gross requirements								
Scheduled receipts								
Projected available balance								
Planned order release								

FIG. 13.17 Material-requirements planning format.

capability, it was frequently impossible for manufacturing to react to changes in plans caused by forecast changes. This uncoupling process sowed the seeds for some very important MPS mechanics.

The standard MPS illustrates the uncoupling as well as the basic information used to develop the MPS. Lines A and B (Fig. 13.16) provide two means to state forecasted requirements. Line A, the forecast, usually states independent demand forecasts for MPS items. Line B, the production forecast, states forecasts *dependent* on popularity of options, accessories, and attachments for a family (or model) of products. (See the treatment of planning bills of materials for additional discussion.) Line C, actual demand, summarizes current demand for this item.

Line D, the projected available balance, is the difference between total demand (both forecasted and actual) and total supply (on hand plus MPS on order). This triggers the logic generating reschedule recommendations (expedite, deexpedite, cancel, etc.). The uncoupling of the sales rate from the manufacturing rate is very visible with the rise and fall of line D. For any number of valid reasons, the MPS may differ from the forecasted requirements for the item. Line E, ATP status, is the difference between *firm* actual demands (line C) and total supply (on hand plus

MPS on order). Line F, the MPS, states the manufacturing and/or procurement rate in terms of released (inside manufacturing or vendor lead time) and firm planned orders.

Figure 13.18 illustrates the various calculations. The item is a stocked, purchased subassembly with two sources of demand. It is a product option used to produce parent items (winches) of certain configurations. As such, it has a production forecast, line B, representing this forecasted parent-item usage. It is also sold independently as a service or repair part and has an independent demand forecast, line A, representing this usage.

Note that Fig. 13.18 displays ATP data as both a noncumulative and a cumulative number. A more complete explanation of ATP calculations appears later.

Firm Planned Orders

The *firm planned order* (FPO) is an item build or buy schedule which is fixed in both quantity and due date. Computer logic does not automatically change FPOs. Rather, the standard time-phased logic of master production scheduling and materials-requirements planning which calculates the projected available balance critiques the schedule of FPOs and recommends changes. Any change, however, is the responsibility of the master scheduler for that item. The FPO is the normal method of stating the MPS, and use of the FPO ensures a stable (not changed by the computer) MPS that may differ from the forecasted demand for the item.

By stating the MPS in terms of FPOs, the master scheduler has the opportunity to answer several important questions before actually changing either the quantity or the timing of the MPS: Is material available to support the change? Is capacity available to support the change? Is the change practical? Is the change too costly? Is there a real need to change the plan? (For example, if the recommended change results from actual sales differing slightly from forecast, there may be no real need to change the build plan.)

G 1 0 2 Gearbox			1	2	3	4	5	6	7	8
A	Forecast (service demand)		8				10			
B	Production forecast		0		4		12		15	
C	Actual demand		14		10		2			
D	Projected available balance	25	3	3	29	29	5	5	30	30
E	Available (noncumulative) to promise		11		28				40	
	Available (cumulative) to promise		11	11	39	39	39	39	79	79
F	Master production schedule				40				40	

FIG. 13.18 Example of an MPS format.

Time Fences

Time fences are means of recognizing the degrees of stability required in the MPS. Frequently, they are merely statements of policy, as noted in the *APICS Dictionary*:

> TIME FENCE. A policy or guideline established to note where various restrictions or changes in operating procedures take place. For example, changes to the master production schedule can be accomplished easily beyond the cumulative lead time whereas changes inside the cumulative lead time become increasingly more difficult to a point where changes should be resisted. Time fences can be used to define these points.

In this context, time fences formalize points in time dictating the types of changes which may occur to the FPOs composing the MPS. A typical policy statement is illustrated in Fig. 13.19.

Too frequently, time fences are established based on cumulative lead times for both manufacturing and procurement material. In many companies, the constraints of capacity availability may be more severe than those of material availability. A truly comprehensive time-fence policy reflects the firm's ability to flex capacity as well as material availability. In many engineered-to-order companies, for example, engineering capacity is usually a major constraint, and the lead times required to make significant increases can be substantial. The same is often true in process or capacity-managed businesses.

In addition to time-fence policy statements, some companies incorporate time-fence logic into their MPS formats. See the section "A Master Production Schedule Example" for a representative example.

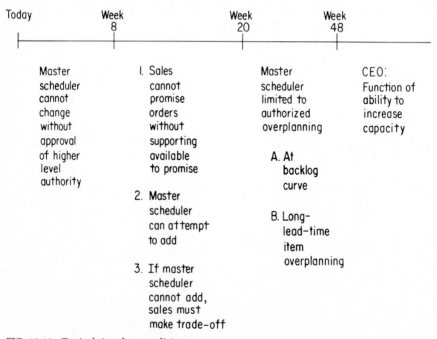

FIG. 13.19 Typical time-fence policies.

Customer Order Promising—ATP Data

As mentioned in the earlier discussion of sales and marketing inputs to, and outputs from, the MPS, the ATP information is an important contribution to marketing-manufacturing communications and is critical to quality customer promises.

ATP status is calculated by comparing the actual demand to the on-hand plus MPS. Figure 13.20 shows a typical situation with a cumulative display of ATP data. Five are considered ATP in the current week (week 1). Although 23 are on hand, 18 customer commitments exist, 11 in week 1 and 7 in week 2, which must be satisfied from that 23. Customer commitments of 11 exist in weeks 3 and 4 which can be satisfied from the 40 scheduled due in week 3. This leaves 29 of the 40 available to promise plus 5 from previous weeks for the total shown of 34.

Weeks or perhaps months ago, the MPS was stated with FPOs in order to cover forecasted demands. As time passes, actual demand materializes, but it rarely ever agrees exactly with the forecast. The ATP figure thus shows the current picture of product available to customers based on current customer commitments and current build plans. Many companies rely on this information for quoting delivery dates instead of quoting standard delivery lead times.

Many forms of make-to-order businesses routinely employ customer promising based on ATP data because they are continuously dealing with changing backlogs of customer orders scheduled for future shipments. Make-to-stock firms building to forecasts normally view on-hand shelf stocks as ATP. However, when they are back-ordered on an item or when customer orders are requested or scheduled for future shipment, make-to-stock firms require similar time-phased ATP information. It is important to protect existing customer commitments when new customer orders are promised.

Planning Bills of Materials

Although planning bills or superbills of materials were defined earlier, the use of the planning bill in master scheduling requires some additional discussion.

			Period							
			1	2	3	4	5	6	7	8
A	Forecast									
B	Production forecast			2	4	5	10	10	10	10
C	Actual demand		11	7	6	5				
D	Projected available balance	23	12	3	33	23	13	3	33	23
E	Available to promise (cumulative)		5	5	34	34	34	34	74	74
F	Master production schedule				40					40

FIG. 13.20 Available-to-promise display.

Planning bills of materials are commonly found in companies that finish or assemble to order. In many instances, many possible configurations of end items that go into the assembly can be produced from a small number of subassemblies, parts groupings (modules), and common-component parts. Classic examples include automobiles, machine tools, and electronic equipment. Figure 13.2 shows a typical planning bill for a hypothetical automobile family.

In most instances, planning bills grow out of the need to simplify forecasting problems. Often it is virtually impossible to forecast the finished end-item configurations which will sell, but it is possible to forecast, with workable accuracy, the mix of product options, accessories, and attachments which will then be configured into the end item by the customer order. The percentages of the planning bill detail this forecast of option mix. The term *two-level forecasting* is sometimes used to describe the process: level 0 forecasts for the forecast family (M body) and level 1 forecasts for the percentage popularity of the product options (common-parts group, V8 group, V6 group, etc).

The term *dependent forecast* is used to describe the forecast for a given option. For example, if the plan for the M-body family is 500 per week, the dependent forecast for the 60 percent V6 engine group is 300 per week. Since 300 per week is calculated by multiplying by a percentage, it is termed *dependent* in the same sense that gross requirements for an MRP component are dependent demands calculated by multiplying quantities according to the relationships in a bill of material.

Planning bills of materials are very powerful MPS tools. They have a number of purposes beyond simplifying the forecasting problem: They aid in production planning, reduce mismatched options, aid in rescheduling MPS options, aid order promising, and control forecast consumption for MPS options.

Aid in Production Planning. Very often the planning families organized into planning bills are the same families reviewed by the production planning group. In the hypothetical M-body family of automobiles, the production planning group, faced with dwindling dealer stock, might agree to a rate of manufacture which is designed to increase dealer stocks to a target level over time. This rate of production clearly must exceed the expected rate of sales by dealers during this period in order to increase dealer stocks. It is this agreed-to production plan for M bodies which is then used to drive the master scheduling of options through the planning bill of material. It is for this reason that line B of the standard MPS format (Fig. 13.16) is often labeled *production* forecast.

Reduce Mismatched Options. The option mix contained within the planning bill is reviewed frequently. Based on the historical mix, the mix of the current backlog, and marketing insight into future trends, these percentages are modified as needed. Any such changes immediately initiate the rebalancing of MPS options. Some companies have found it helpful to time-phase percentages in planning bills so that varying option mixes can be used at different times.

Aid in Rescheduling MPS Options. Over time, actual demand probably will occur in about the expected mix. In any given week or month, however, the actual mix varies from the forecasted mix. As this occurs, appropriate rescheduling recommendations are made on those MPS options impacted. (The forecast consumption discussion which follows details some of the specifics of how this happens.)

Aid in Order Promising. Frequently, the planning bill is integrated directly into the customer promising function of order entry. In the M-body example, a customer or dealer order might call for a special model with a V6 engine, automatic transmission, and power antenna. The promise for the order would be based on the ATP conditions of the selected options. In concept, the gating or pacing ATP data would dictate the delivery date.

Control Forecast Consumption for MPS Options.   A variety of techniques are used to control forecast consumption for MPS options with planning bills. Some common approaches are discussed through a series of examples.

The classic example used in the literature is a hoist (Fig. 13.21), popularized by Orlicky, Plossl, and Wight.[3] With 2400 possible combinations of modules (options, features, attachments, etc.), planning bills are very useful for forecasting and master scheduling this product.

Figure 13.22 illustrates the typical three-zone MPS of make- and assemble-to-order companies. The planning process involves setting a production plan (40 per month) for hoists which considers marketplace needs, desired backlog levels, staffing required, etc. With a forecasted split of 50/50 between pendants 1 and 2 (P1 and P2), the second-level forecast for P1 and P2 becomes 20 per month, or 10 every other week, as shown. (The examples all assume 4-week months for simplicity.)

Zone 1 covers weeks 1 to 3, in which hoists are completely sold out. Second-level mix forecasts for P1 and P2 are no longer needed in zone 1 since actual backlog fully describes the P1/P2 mix. Zone 3 covers weeks 7 and beyond. There is no customer backlog beyond week 6, and the plan must be based on pure two-level forecasts. Zone 2 is in the middle, weeks 4 to 6, where the plan must deal with a mixture of backlog and actual demand.

The actual demand indicates the 50/50 forecasted mix is not bad. Of 36 hoists sold through the fourth week, 19 used P1 and 17 used P2.

Three basic types of mechanics are used to control consumption of option forecasts. Type 1 planning bill mechanics (Fig. 13.23) explode the ATP data of the hoist family. In week 4 (zone 2), 16 of 20 hoists have sold and 4 are available to promise for a customer. Of the 4 ATP hoists, a good estimate of option mix is 50/50, that is, two P1's and two P2's. In week 2 (zone 1), this approach produces a zero second-level forecast, which is desirable. In week 8 (zone 3), it produces the desired 10.

This approach of exploding family ATP data is responsive to a changing mix of actual demand but does create the potential for "planning nervousness" with each sale in zone 2 of the MPS. In week 4, the original forecast of 50/50 has now been changed to a 45/55 percent split between P1 and P2. The combination of the remaining P1 forecast of 2 and the actual P1 demand of 7 totals 9. And 9 of 20 is 45 percent. A responsive MPS tool might be to recommend a reschedule or de-expedite of P1 material in week 4 since the original forecast of 10 has been reduced

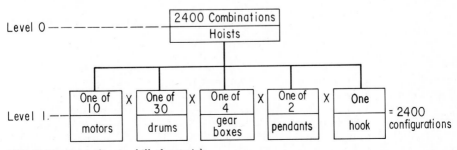

FIG. 13.21   Hoist planning bill of materials.

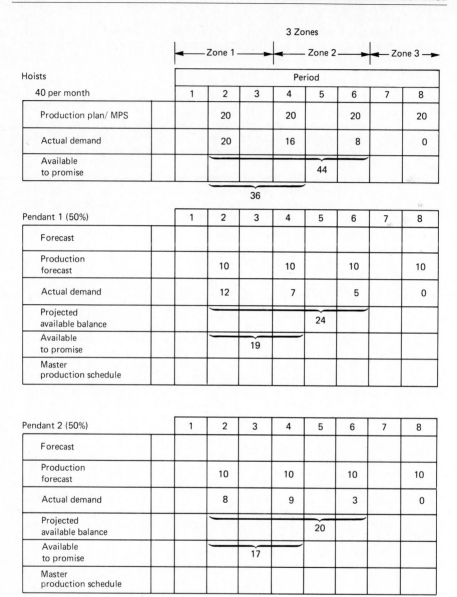

3 Zones							
◄— Zone 1 —►			◄— Zone 2 —►			◄— Zone 3 —►	

Hoists
40 per month

	1	2	3	4	5	6	7	8
Production plan/ MPS		20		20		20		20
Actual demand		20		16		8		0
Available to promise					44			

36

Pendant 1 (50%)

	1	2	3	4	5	6	7	8
Forecast								
Production forecast		10		10		10		10
Actual demand		12		7		5		0
Projected available balance					24			
Available to promise			19					
Master production schedule								

Pendant 2 (50%)

	1	2	3	4	5	6	7	8
Forecast								
Production forecast		10		10		10		10
Actual demand		8		9		3		0
Projected available balance					20			
Available to promise			17					
Master production schedule								

FIG. 13.22 Three-zone MPS.

to 9. The opposite is true in week 6 for P1. The original forecast of 10 has been replaced by requirements for 11 (6 remaining forecast and 5 actual demand).

People who understand the probability theory of flipping coins prefer type 1 planning bills. Sixteen tosses have been made in week 4. Four tosses remain. The best estimate of results in those four tosses is a 50/50 split.

Type 2 planning bill mechanics (Fig. 13.24) consume option forecasts week by week with actual demand. Originally, all P1 forecasts were 10. Since 7 sold in week

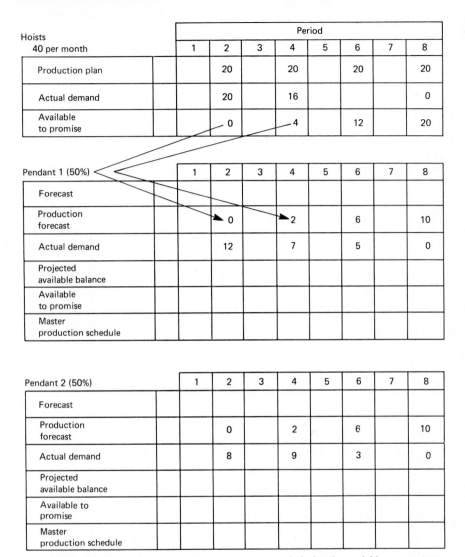

Hoists 40 per month		Period							
		1	2	3	4	5	6	7	8
Production plan			20		20		20		20
Actual demand			20		16				0
Available to promise			0		4		12		20

Pendant 1 (50%)		1	2	3	4	5	6	7	8
Forecast									
Production forecast			0		2		6		10
Actual demand			12		7		5		0
Projected available balance									
Available to promise									
Master production schedule									

Pendant 2 (50%)		1	2	3	4	5	6	7	8
Forecast									
Production forecast			0		2		6		10
Actual demand			8		9		3		0
Projected available balance									
Available to promise									
Master production schedule									

FIG. 13.23 Consuming MPS option forecasts, type 1, explode family available to promise.

4, of the 10 forecast 7 were consumed, leaving 3. In week 2, all 10 were consumed by actual demand of 12, etc.

Type 2 mechanics must deal with the P2 situation in week 2. Even though only 8 sold, the unconsumed forecast of 2 must be eliminated. Otherwise, the MPS would call for 10 sets of P2 material, 2 of which are not required. Type 2 mechanics must also deal with situations where forecasts and the actual demands do not fall in the same week.

Hoists 40 per month	Period							
	1	2	3	4	5	6	7	8
Production plan		20		20		20		20
Actual demand		20		16				0
Available to promise								

Pendant 1 (50%)	1	2	3	4	5	6	7	8
Forecast								
Production forecast		0		3		5		10
Actual demand		12		7		5		0
Projected available balance								
Available to promise								
Master production schedule								

Pendant 2 (50%)	1	2	3	4	5	6	7	8
Forecast								
Production forecast		2		1		7		10
Actual demand		8		9		3		0
Projected available balance								
Available to promise								
Master production schedule								

FIG. 13.24 Consuming MPS option forecasts, type 2, current period forecast consumption.

Type 2 planning bills do a better job of protecting the original 50/50 forecast split than type 1 bills. The assumption made is that 20 hoists will sell 50/50 in the end.

Type 3 planning bills (Fig. 13.25) extend the thought process of type 2. For example, examine P1. Type 3 mechanics recognize that through week 4, of the original 20 forecast for P1, 19 have sold and 1 unconsumed forecast remains in week 4. Through week 6, 24 of 30 have sold and 6 remain—1 in week 4 and 5 in week 6. Type 3 tries to hold to the projected 50/50 split on a cumulative basis. It potentially generates less MPS nervousness than either type 1 or 2. Type 3 is also slowest to respond to a changing mix.

Hoists 40 per month		Period							
		1	2	3	4	5	6	7	8
Production plan			20		20		20		20
Actual demand			20		16		8		0
Available to promise									

Pendant 1 (50%)		1	2	3	4	5	6	7	8
Forecast									
Production forecast			0		1		5		10
Actual demand			12		7		5		0
Projected available balance									
Available to promise						Σ 24 of 30			
Master production schedule				Σ 19 of 20					

Pendant 2 (50%)		1	2	3	4	5	6	7	8
Forecast									
Production forecast			0		3		7		10
Actual demand			8		9		3		0
Projected available balance					Σ 20 of 30				
Available to promise			Σ 17 of 20						
Master production schedule									

FIG. 13.25 Consuming MPS option forecasts, type 3, cumulative forecast consumption.

Cautionary Notes on Planning Bills of Materials. Any discussion of planning bills would be incomplete if it did not include two notes of caution on planning bills. Planning bills work well under certain business conditions. Planning bills work well for families of products with reasonable sales volumes, fairly stable mix conditions, large numbers of customer orders for small quantities, and smooth customer demand patterns. As these conditions change, results become mixed.

Major customers who buy products in certain configurations, e.g., a fleet buyer of automobiles that are all equipped with power steering, can disrupt a planning bill forecast which assumes a standard option mix. Lumpy demand patterns can vary substantially from the smooth pattern projected by planning bills. Planning families with small sales volumes or a small percentage of options are difficult to handle since any sale, in itself, represents a significant portion of the forecast and any variation from either forecast totals or mix will be significant.

The second cautionary note regards the general application of planning bills. Today's literature, including the discussions of this section, describes planning bills as useful for planning families of finish-to-order products—automobiles, hoists, etc. Planning bills have also found use in many other planning situations. For example, when end items produced to stock are planned, aggregate forecasts of family sales can be apportioned to individual items by the percentages of a planning bill.

Another variation found in some companies is a planning bill which forecasts raw- and intermediate-material needs in the intermediate to long horizon of the MPS. As these forecasted needs reach specified decision points or time fences in the MPS, the plans are converted to firm planned orders which define the specific end items to be produced. A firm making a family of handsaws might utilize this technique. Beyond some specified time, a planning bill could be used to forecast blade steels in some mix. As it came time to commit to specific end items, this planning bill would be replaced by end-item-specific FPOs. Many process industries with relatively few common raw materials operate in a similar manner.

Custom, New, and Engineered Products and the MPS

Earlier the use of generic bills of material was discussed in firms producing engineered-to-order and custom products as well as firms managing significant amounts of new-product introduction. These generic bills are used to estimate levels of design and development activity as well as schedule that activity to meet required dates.

Both production planning and master scheduling have a strong capacity orientation initially. In the intermediate- to long-range planning horizon, the primary need is to plan adequate staffing capacities to meet expected business levels. Various categories of products and projects represented by generic bills are forecast. Expected rates of business are expressed with artificial family or item numbers in the production plan and MPS. Then MRP explosions of generic bills are used to calculate time-phased staffing requirements.

Customer orders, when received, are assigned the appropriate generic bill of materials. Assigned a completion date, the customer-specific bill is then used to schedule design and development activity. Long lead-time items are customarily designed first. As the specifics of the design progress, the artificial part numbers of the generic bill are replaced by "real" part numbers. Routings and work center assignments are added by manufacturing or industrial engineering. In concept, the generic bill progressively evolves to the actual bill of materials.

Conventional MRP logic is used with the progressing design to plan component-material priorities. The generic bill-of-materials structure with estimated lead times which exists above the real components serves to time-phase priorities until the design is complete. Should customer-required dates change, MRP replanning is automatically initiated for all components and remaining development activities.

New-product development activities are often managed in a similar manner. Although new products are usually not tied to customer orders, the generic bill-of-materials structure serves as a project planning and control device.

PERT and CPM tools are effective as single-project planning and control tools.

The generic bill-of-materials approach outlined above is effective because it is useful in the *multiple*-project circumstances found in many companies. In engineered-to-order firms, each customer order in house is a "project" competing for common resources. MRP logic thus becomes useful in planning and scheduling that competition for capacity.

Option Overplanning

Option overplanning is a master scheduling technique used to manage a sophisticated form of safety stock. It is most commonly associated with finish- or assembly-to-order firms although, once again, variations on the technique also apply in other master scheduling environments.

Given the hoist with pendant 1 or pendant 2 options introduced earlier, Fig. 13.26 displays the mechanics of option overplanning. Zone 2 of the MPS begins in week 4. This is the point where the customer backlog curve declines. Customer orders on hand are less than the total number of hoists to be manufactured.

Only 20 pendants are required in week 4 since the overall production plan is set to produce 20 hoists, each requiring one pendant. The MPS, however, calls for a total of 22 pendants in week 4—10 P1's and 12 P2's. The excess of 2 represents a mix hedge in zone 2 of the MPS. This is the first point of exposure to possible variation in option mix demand.

In the fourth week, 4 hoists remain to be sold (20 hoists planned minus 16 firm customer orders). These appear as ATP hoists. Normally, these 4 would split 50/50 between P1 and P2. The number of ATP hoists for P1, however, is 3 in week 4, since 7 actual customer demands exist for the 10 in the MPS. In week 4, similarly, 3 P2's are available to promise (9 actual demands versus 12 in the MPS). The extra pendants, i.e., option overplanning, provide a 75/25 percent mix protection either way on the two pendants. Of 4 hoist orders 3 could call for either pendant, and sufficient components would be available. If perfect mix protection were desired, the MPS would read 11 in week 4 for P1 with 4 available to promise and 13 in week 4 for P2, also with 4 available to promise.

Figures 13.26 and 13.27 illustrate the management of option overplanning as hoist bookings materialize. Effectively, once 4 additional hoist orders are committed in week 4, zone 1 moves out and now includes weeks 4 and 5. In Fig. 13.27, of the 4 orders received, 3 specified P1 and the other specified P2. Under these circumstances, the extra two pendants visible in Fig. 13.26 are P2's. Since these are obviously no longer required in week 4, the MPS is now changed in two positions: the 12 P2's in week 4 of Fig. 13.26 are reduced to 10, leaving none available to promise, and the 10 P2's in week 6 of Fig. 13.26 are changed to the 12 of week 6 in Fig. 13.27. Through this rolling-out process, the master scheduler attempts to maintain a measure of protection against customer order mix by managing extra options in the early periods of zone 2 of the MPS.

In the example, two extra (i.e., above the original forecast) P1 options have been committed to customer orders in weeks 2 and 4. The master scheduler must now consider material lead times and capacity constraints before increasing some future MPS plan to restore some option overplanning for P1. Conceptually, the MPS plan would be increased in the period just beyond the cumulative lead time for P1's.

Rolling the unused options forward as illustrated for the P2 option creates the potential for planning nervousness within MRP. The original gross requirements pattern of 12 and 10 in weeks 4 and 6, respectively, has been changed to a 10 and 12 pattern on each component of the P2 option. If some of these components are planned using discrete lot size rules, such as lot-for-lot sizing rules, then a de-

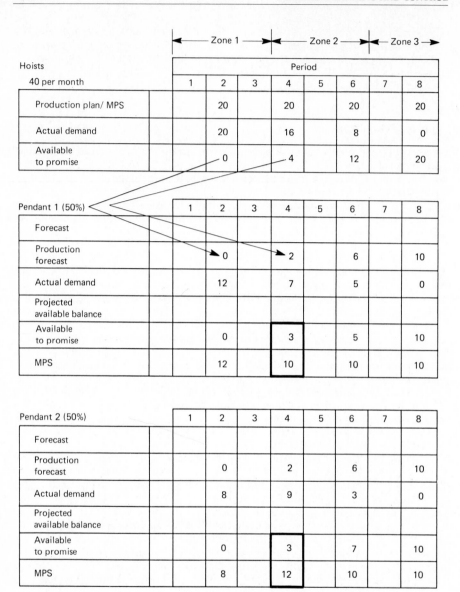

Hoists 40 per month	◄— Zone 1 —►◄— Zone 2 —►◄ Zone 3 → Period							
	1	2	3	4	5	6	7	8
Production plan/ MPS		20		20		20		20
Actual demand		20		16		8		0
Available to promise		0		4		12		20

Pendant 1 (50%)	1	2	3	4	5	6	7	8
Forecast								
Production forecast		0		2		6		10
Actual demand		12		7		5		0
Projected available balance								
Available to promise		0		3		5		10
MPS		12		10		10		10

Pendant 2 (50%)	1	2	3	4	5	6	7	8
Forecast								
Production forecast		0		2		6		10
Actual demand		8		9		3		0
Projected available balance								
Available to promise		0		3		7		10
MPS		8		12		10		10

FIG. 13.26 One example of MPS option overplanning.

expedite or reschedule-out recommendation may result. As a practical consideration, however, this potential nervousness is often dampened by the MRP lot-sizing rules in use. For example, the change in the gross requirements pattern might have no effect on a component produced in lot sizes of 50.

Option overplanning has decided advantages over conventional MRP safety stock techniques. It is consciously managed by master schedulers whereas standard

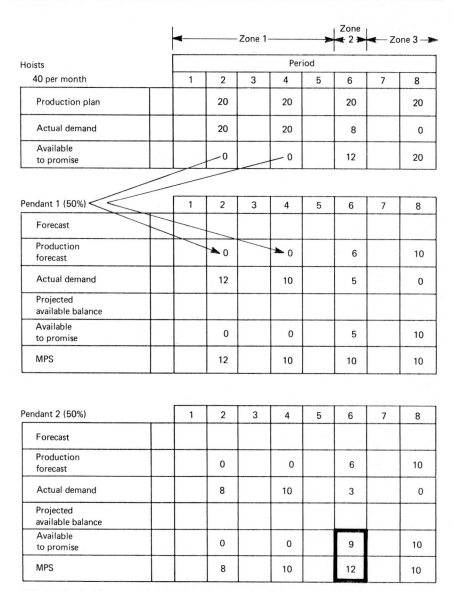

Hoists		Period								
40 per month		1	2	3	4	5	6	7	8	
Production plan			20		20		20		20	
Actual demand			20		20		8		0	
Available to promise			0		0		12		20	

Pendant 1 (50%)		1	2	3	4	5	6	7	8
Forecast									
Production forecast			0		0		6		10
Actual demand			12		10		5		0
Projected available balance									
Available to promise			0		0		5		10
MPS			12		10		10		10

Pendant 2 (50%)		1	2	3	4	5	6	7	8
Forecast									
Production forecast			0		0		6		10
Actual demand			8		10		3		0
Projected available balance									
Available to promise			0		0		9		10
MPS			8		10		12		10

FIG. 13.27 Another example of MPS option overplanning.

safety stock provisions are controlled automatically by computer logic. In periods of scarce capacity, for example, a person will react by cutting back on such overplanning. By contrast, standard computer logic without intervention will continue to plan to replenish safety stock and give safety stock equal priority to firm, committed customer requirements.

MRP safety stock logic also continuously attempts to maintain materials on hand and thus in inventory, unlike option overplanning techniques. A manufacturing company with a firm 12-week backlog (zone 1 of the MPS) illustrates this difference.

Components of a P2 option with cumulative lead times greater than 12 weeks must be on order or in-process to support P2 option overplanning in week 13 of the MPS. Other components with lesser cumulative lead times may not even be on order. Standard safety stock logic, however, would try to maintain all specified components in inventory regardless of their lead times.

Most important, however, option overplanning in the MPS works to create safety stocks in *matched sets of parts*. To achieve the same effect by using MRP-level safety stocks, the safety stocks specified on the various component items would have to be carefully coordinated. In general, managing option overplanning in the MPS will more consistently create the necessary matched sets of parts.

Frequently, master schedulers who lack contemporary MPS tools resort to overstating the planning percentages in the planning bill of materials as a way to provide option mix protection. For example, one might specify 55 percent option forecasts on both P1 and P2 options in Fig. 13.26, totaling 110 percent. This forecasts a total of 22 pendant options for every 20 hoists planned. The shortcoming, however, in this approach is that it projects requirements at a 110 percent rate through *all* periods. By contrast, the option overplanning technique overstates the needs for P1 and P2 *only* in the early periods of zone 2.

On balance, option overplanning is a valid technique for managing safety stocks. Users of the technique must be aware of its potential to cause MRP nervousness as well as the level of effort required by master schedulers to properly manage option overplanning.

A GENERAL MASTER PRODUCTION SCHEDULING* FRAMEWORK

The framework shown in Fig. 13.28 is used in describing the operating features of MPS systems discussed here and in understanding the common elements in the practice of master scheduling in any firm. This figure depicts the elements in manufacturing planning and control systems that relate directly to master production scheduling. The arrows indicate the flows of information among these elements. The activities contained in each element are defined and discussed in this chapter.

Demand Management

The demand management block represents the *forecasting, order-entry, order-promising,* and *physical distribution activities in a company.* This block includes all the activities that place demands (requirements) for products on manufacturing. These *demands* may take the form of actual and forecast customer orders, branch warehouse requirements, interplant requirements, international requirements, and service part demand. Clearly, some categories may take on more or less importance in particular companies. That is, the manufacturing output at some firms may be

---

*The following is a reprint , modified slightly to conform with McGraw-Hill house style, of Chapter 2 of W.L. Berry, T.E. Vollman, and D.C. Whybark, *Master Production Scheduling: Principle and Practice.* Reproduced by permission of the American Production and Inventory Control Society, Falls Church, Va., 1979.

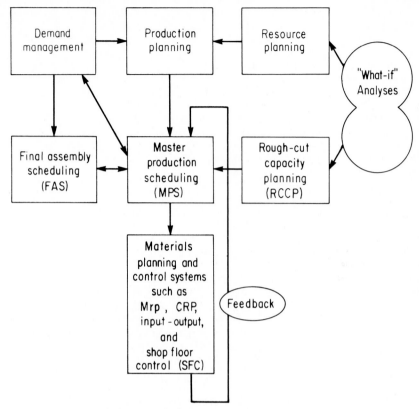

FIG. 13.28 Master production scheduling planning framework.

entirely directed toward the replenishment of distribution warehouses, while at other firms the production output may be solely to satisfy individual customer orders. At still other firms, manufacturing may have to satisfy demand from both sources.

A key aspect of demand management involves the interfunctional coordination of various demands placed on manufacturing. That is, manufacturing needs to be closely coordinated with other functional areas within the company (e.g., marketing and distribution) in processing detailed customer orders, preparing forecasts of production requirements, and coordinating the restocking of warehouses. This coordination is more than simply improving interfunctional communications. It is necessary to establish detailed computer data bases and to clearly define functional responsibilities for transactions and updates to the data bases. Examples include forecast data that are updated by actual customer orders, clear definitions of when a product is shipped, and how title passes for inventory moving from manufacturing work in process to finished goods.

Figure 13.28 indicates that the demand management activity influences three other manufacturing planning and control elements: production planning, master scheduling, and final-assembly scheduling. The forecasts prepared as a part of the demand management activity are used in preparing overall production plans and provide an estimate of the requirements for individual product items for use in preparing the MPS. Likewise, the order-entry and order-promising activities provide requirements information for individual products directly to the MPS as well as to the final-assembly schedule.

In a similar fashion, the demand management function coordinates requirements from the field warehouse with the preparation of the MPS or the FAS. Again, the particular interface between demand management and the other manufacturing planning and control activities may vary from company to company, and each of the related information linkages may take on more or less emphasis.

Production Planning

The production planning block represents the activities involved in preparing an overall production plan for the business. Such a plan represents a *strategic game plan* for the company which *reflects the desired aggregate output* from manufacturing. In some firms, the production plan is simply stated in terms of the monthly or quarterly sales dollar output for the company as a whole or for individual plants or businesses. In other firms, the production plan is stated in terms of the number of units to be produced in each major product line monthly for the next year. The *units of manufacturing activities* used in preparing the production plan vary considerably among companies. In addition to sales dollar output and the overall units per month for major product groupings, measures such as direct labor hours, pounds of product produced, etc., are used.

The production plan is a top-management responsibility, representing management's control over the business. It provides guidelines and constraints within which manufacturing is expected to operate. The production plan represents an agreement among marketing, manufacturing, and finance as to what (in aggregate) will be produced and made available for sale to the customers. This agreement forms the basis for budgetary and market planning for the company. A change in one aspect of a company's strategic plans, such as the sales plan, the production plan, or the financial plan, necessarily implies a change in the other two plans. Once the production plan is set, manufacturing has its task clearly defined—to achieve the goals of the production plan. In many firms, the production plan is a key yardstick for measuring the performance of the plant managers. Likewise, once the production plan is established and agreed to by top management, sales has its work defined—to meet the sales budget. A sales budget that is not met (or is exceeded) means that unplanned finished-goods inventory (or excessive back orders) will be created.

The production planning activity at some firms is a highly structured process, often conducted on a monthly basis. This process often begins with the creation of a new sales forecast covering a year or more. Next, any increases or decreases in inventory or backlog levels are decided on in order to determine total production requirements. Once the total demand to be placed on manufacturing is determined, the way in which manufacturing will meet this demand, i.e., the production plan, can be decided. Note that the production plan should equal the sales forecast in total over a designated period, perhaps a year. However, the timing of production may vary considerably from the sales forecast, creating planned increases (or decreases) in inventory levels. The steps involved in preparing the production plan occasionally span several weeks or more, involving the top executives—the president, the vice president of manufacturing, the vice president of marketing, and the vice president of finance.

The production planning block feeds directly into the master production scheduling activity. The production plan provides the guidelines within which the master production scheduling process takes place.

Resource Planning

The resource planning block shown in Fig. 13.28 represents the process of determining the *long-range capacity needs of the business.* This activity involves translating the long-range sales forecasts and production plans, covering the next 1 to 10 years, to the *required manufacturing facilities.* The time horizon considered reflects the lead time required to acquire new facilities. In some firms, the resource plan is stated in terms of the number of machine hours required per year for individual machines and work centers to meet the planned annual production rate. At other firms, the resource requirements may be stated in terms of the number of pounds of output required per year for specific manufacturing processes. Other measures are used as well.

The resource planning block is directly related to the production planning block. This indicates that *resource planning sets the capacity limits within which the production planning activity must operate.* To the extent that the resource planning activity is performed using the same units as those considered in production planning, improvement in communication and operation performance can result. Although it is not shown in Fig. 13.28, the resource planning activity often provides the basis for the capital budgeting activities in a company.

Final-Assembly Scheduling

The final-assembly scheduling activity serves as the basis for planning and controlling the final-assembly and test operations in manufacturing. The preparation and execution of the FAS is separate from master scheduling. The MPS represents the *anticipated* build schedule for a firm's products, covering the time span between raw-material acquisition and the delivery of the component items to the inventory just before final assembly. The FAS specifies the actual build schedule covering a period that begins when all the component items are available for final assembly and ends when the products are shipped to customers. Thus, it serves to accumulate necessary component parts and to schedule final assembly, testing, and packing operations.

The FAS represents a commitment to the production of specific end-product configurations. If customer orders are not on hand for these items, they will become a part of the firm's finished-goods inventory. Thus, the decision of what items to put into finished-goods inventory becomes a part of the final-assembly scheduling process. In make-to-order firms, where sufficient customer orders exist in an order backlog, the FAS is simply a commitment of when to produce each customer order.

In assemble-to-order and make-to-stock firms, it is desirable to hold off on the commitment of when to produce specific final product configurations until the last possible moment that still allows time for order picking, final assembly, and test operations. By holding off as long as possible in firming up the FAS, component items can be used to produce actual customer orders as opposed to forecasts of customer orders likely to be received. Thus, simultaneous excess inventories of finished products and assembly shortages are minimized. Because of the endless variety of final product configurations in most assemble-to-order firms, the assembly scheduling process is perhaps most critical in these companies.

The FAS is often stated in terms of the number of units of each end-product catalog item to be produced. However, in make-to-order firms, the FAS may be stated in terms of individual customer orders. Another variant of the FAS is found in assemble-to-order firms. The FAS is frequently identified by an assembly order number and is stated in terms of the quantities of individual product options that are to be grouped and assembled as a unit.

The FAS can serve an additional purpose in manufacturing firms where not all the items required to produce an end product are under the control of the MPS. In many firms, inexpensive hardware items and short lead-time components are scheduled and controlled via the FAS. Similarly, some component items are far too bulky or expensive to produce in advance of assembly; these items can sometimes be under the control of the FAS instead of the MPS, with timing carefully controlled by the FAS.

The flow of information into the FAS block comes from two sources: demand management and master scheduling. Actual customer orders come from the order-entry activity under demand management, and the production schedule for individual product configurations comes from the MPS function.

Rough-Cut Capacity Planning

The RCCP activity involves an analysis of the MPS to determine the existence of critical manufacturing facilities that are potential bottlenecks in the flow of production. Such analysis is typically made during the MPS review or whenever adjustments are made to the MPS. Every firm has several critical steps in the production process that need to be carefully monitored as changes in product mix occur in the MPS. At some firms, final-assembly or finishing operations represent the critical operations to be closely watched. In other firms, the critical operation involves a key machine that is operating on a three-shift basis. At still other firms, the critical operation may be a vendor who supplies a key raw material not readily available from other sources. RCCP identifies the impact of the MPS on these critical operations.

The RCCP analysis is typically performed much less frequently and covers a longer time span than the weekly shop load reports produced from capacity-requirements planning (CRP) systems using shop floor control and MRP data. The RCCP analyses also involve the use of simpler capacity planning techniques and far less detailed information than the CRP analysis. That is, RCCP typically involves the use of bills of capacity or simple planning factor estimates instead of time-phased MRP and routing file data. The simpler procedures, though less accurate, permit a quick analysis to indicate whether the MPS is feasible in view of the current capacity of the company. They also permit a rapid analysis of several alternatives that may be posed by top management in reviewing the MPS. Such an analysis sometimes leads to a decision to change the MPS to accommodate the capacity limitations of the key facilities or to maintain the MPS and implement adjustments to capacity involving overtime, subcontracting, alternate routing of work, employment level changes, and so forth. These changes are often planned over a considerable time, covering a quarter or more into the future.

The RCCP block is shown in Fig. 13.28 as feeding information into the MPS function. This reflects its basic objective of keeping the MPS realistic in terms of available capacity.

Master Production Scheduling

The master production scheduling block shown in Fig. 13.28 covers the variety of activities involved in the preparation and the maintenance of the MPS. The MPS is a statement of the anticipated build schedule for a company's products. This schedule is stated in specific product configurations, and typically it indicates the quantity to be produced in weekly buckets (priorities) during the next 6 to 12 months or longer. The product unit that is selected for master scheduling, however, varies considerably among firms. For example, in the make-to-stock company, the MPS is often stated in terms of end-product items. It can also be stated in terms of lower-level items such as a major assembly or component part or unpackaged bulk product. In some make-to-order firms, the actual customer order is used as the master scheduling unit. Assemble-to-order firms have a very complex problem in defining a master scheduling unit. In this case, their master scheduling unit may not be a buildable end item, but rather units of a planning bill that facilitates the scheduling of production and relies on the FAS to make a salable product. This could involve master scheduling at the option level if it reduced the number of items planned on the MPS. As an example, the MPS in an assemble-to-order firm may be stated in terms of customer options such as horsepower and rear-axle gear ratios on trucks. One criterion in selecting the master scheduling unit is to minimize the number of items in the MPS. By reducing the number of items considered in the MPS, improved forecasting accuracy and reduced administrative costs are gained.

The MPS is a statement of production and not a forecast of market demand. That is, the planned production level may vary considerably from the actual pattern of market demand. The MPS reflects manufacturing's strategy (as stated in the production plan) for meeting the market demand, given such factors as production capacity limitations, raw-material availabilities, and production economics.

Another characteristic of the MPS is that it represents a disaggregation of the production plan into individual product items. In particular, the MPS represents the *first* time that the production plan is disaggregated into specific product units, while the FAS represents the *final* disaggregation of the production plan into specific buildable end products. This characteristic has two important implications. First, if the MPS represents a disaggregation of the production plan, then the reverse must also be true. That is, the MPS must always aggregate back to the production plan in order for it to remain consistent with the overall business plan. Second, the MPS represents a *forecast* of what products will be built (anticipated build schedule), while the FAS specifies *exactly* what end products will be produced. The MPS represents a management commitment authorizing only the procurement of raw material and the production of component items. The FAS represents a management commitment to deliver specific end products to either the customers or the finished-goods inventory.

The firm planned order is a key concept in master production scheduling. The FPO clearly separates the demand for a company's products from the schedule for producing the products. It makes it possible to manage the MPS while accounting for capacity, demand, product mix, and other important variables. The FPO introduces stability into the schedule and provides the basis for accountability in managing the schedule. In addition, it provides the communication link with the MRP system to explode component requirements.

The master scheduling block shown in Fig. 13.28 represents the focal point of all the production planning and control activities shown. For example, demand management supplies all the demand requirements and customer orders to the MPS. Likewise, production planning indicates the operating constraints within which the MPS function must work. Furthermore, the RCCP activity indicates bottleneck work centers or production facilities that are likely to be roadblocks in meeting the MPS. The MPS framework also indicates the flow of information away from the MPS activity. Scheduling information is provided for the preparation of the FAS. Finally, the MPS model shows the flow of information back from the MRP, CRP, and shop floor control systems to the MPS. This feedback is useful in indicating material and capacity unavailabilities, thereby keeping the MPS realistic.

What-If Analysis

Another element in the MPS model is what-if analysis. From time to time, top management may be concerned with the ability of the company to respond to certain changes in the production plan or the MPS. Sometimes these changes involve the addition of products not currently included in the MPS. That is, marketing may want to know the impact on the current delivery commitments to customers if a large order is accepted or if the delivery date on an order for an important customer is advanced. Likewise, a potential strike at an important supplier may concern top management. Thus, an important element of the MPS system is the ability to simulate changes in the MPS or the production plan and to rapidly assess the subsequent effects.

Many computer-based MPS and production planning systems have the capability to answer what-if questions. Such systems have special features to ensure that the data files are not altered permanently to reflect the what-if analysis conditions, but are returned to reflect the current conditions. Flexibility, rapid turnaround, and easy access to the data are all important in providing this capability.

Materials Planning and Control Systems

Certain aspects of a production planning and control system have been deliberately excluded from the MPS model shown in Fig. 13.28 because they were not within the scope of this study. The materials planning and control systems block represents the MRP, CRP, shop floor control, input/output systems, etc. Although these systems are quite important in executing the MPS, they do not receive major emphasis in either the MPS framework or its subsequent use in analyzing the practice of master scheduling at the eight firms reported in this book.

SAMPLE MPS REPORTS

The principal output of the MPS system is the MPS plan report (Fig. 13.29). This report or video display shows the current data about an item on the MPS: the forecast(s) of independent demand, current actual demands, the computer-calculated projected available balance and ATP information, and the MPS planning for the item.

The report is used by the master scheduler to manage the MPS. The new MPS is input to and drives MRP. By controlling the MPS in this manner, unnecessary nervousness is taken out of the MRP system, thus minimizing unnecessary exceptions and changes in MRP. The report is also the vehicle for promising sales order availability by using the ATP line.

The report contains four distinct sections: A, indicative item information; B, planning horizons; C, MPS detail; and D, actual demand detail. Sections C and D are

MASTER PRODUCTION SCHEDULE

MASTER SCHEDULER A1   DATE A2   PAGE A3

PART NUMBER	PRIMARY DESCRIPTION	ITEM STATUS	FAMILY	STND. COST	SELLING PRICE	FORECAST SOURCE	FORECAST CONSUMPT.	LOAD PROFILE	CRITICAL RESOURCES					
									RES.	QTY.	RES.	QTY.	RES.	QTY.
A4	A5	A6	A7	A8	A9	A10	A11	A12	A13	A14	A13	A14	A13	A14

	LOT SIZE		SAFETY STOCK		TIME FENCES			LEAD TIME	CUMUL. L.T.	SPECIAL INSTRUCTIONS	ACTIONS RECOMMENDED		
	1	2	POLICY	FACTOR	1	2	3				WEEK	QTY.	RES.
BALANCE ON HAND	A16	A17	A18	A19	A20	A20	A20	A21	A22	A23	A24	A24	A24
A15													

WEEK									WEEK
SERV. FORECAST									B1
PROD. FORECAST									B2
ACTUAL DEMAND									B3
PROJ. AVAIL. BAL.									B4
AVAIL.-TO-PROMISE									B5
MPS									B6
									B7

WEEK
SERV. FORECAST
PROD. FORECAST
ACTUAL DEMAND
PROJ. AVAIL. BAL.
AVAIL.-TO-PROMISE
MPS

WEEK
SERV. FORECAST
PROD. FORECAST
ACTUAL DEMAND
PROJ. AVAIL. BAL.
AVAIL.-TO-PROMISE
MPS

WEEK
SERV. FORECAST
PROD. FORECAST
ACTUAL DEMAND
PROJ. AVAIL. BAL.
AVAIL.-TO-PROMISE
MPS

MASTER SCHEDULE DETAIL

REQUIRED DATE	ORDER NUMBER	LOT NO.	ORDER QUANTITY	ORDER TYPE	STATUS	RECOM. ACTION
C1	C2	C3	C4	C5	C6	C7

ACTUAL DEMAND DETAIL

REQUIRED DATE	ORDER QUANTITY	REFERENCE NUMBER	ORDER NUMBER	TYPE	CODE	
D1	D2	D3	D4	D5	D6	D7

FIG. 13.29 MPS example.

13.51

generally available on inquiry when video displays rather than printed reports are used.

Indicative Item Information

A1. *Master Scheduler*—master scheduler code for the person responsible for this item. The report is sequenced by master scheduler code so that it can be distributed to the scheduler responsible for a certain group of master scheduled items.

A2. *Date*—the date the report was generated by the system.

A3. *Page*—a sequential page number assigned within master scheduler code.

A4. *Part Number*—the unique identification assigned to the master scheduled part or item.

A5. *Primary Description*—a brief description of the item. A secondary, more extensive description is also maintained.

A6. *Item Status*—a code indicating the stocking status of the item:

STK—The item is either manufactured or purchased and is stocked in usable form.

PHAN—Phantom or transient assemblies which are immediately used to manufacture a higher-level item. These items are planned in order to provide matched sets of component parts.

PSDO—Psuedo planning items which define matched sets of component parts. These items do not exist as manufactured entities.

A7. *Family*—a user-maintained field which identifies a group, family or model of product. This designation may be used for Production Planning or to identify a planning bill of materials for the item.

A8. *Standard Cost*—the current standard cost of the item.

A9. *Selling Price*—the current selling price of the item.

A10. *Forecast Source*—the source from which the forecast was derived:

STATIS—Derived from a statistical forecast.

JUDMNT—A manually input judgmental forecast.

PLANBL—Developed through an explosion of a forecast (projected usage) relationship of a planning bill of material.

A11. *Forecast Consumption*—user-specified control over the process of consuming (or netting) forecast by actual demand:

ADJUST—The cumulative, + or − difference between actual demand and forecast. A "+" adjustment indicates demand was less than the original forecast; a "−" indicates demand exceeded forecast.

PLANBL—The Production Forecast of master scheduled items, options, or features is calculated by exploding the percentage relationships in the planning bill of material.

A12. *Load Profile*—the identification of the load profile used to develop Rough-Cut Capacity Plans for this item.

A13. *Critical Resource*—user-maintained identification of critical resources required by this item. May be critical work centers, skill classifications, or other specified resources.

A14. *Critical Resource Quantity*—the amount of the specified critical resource required to complete one of the items.

A15. *Balance on Hand*—the quantity of the item in inventory.

A16. *Lot Size 1*—the preferred ordering practice for the item:

"P.O.Q."—Specified when periods or weeks of supply replenishment is preferred.

"FIXED"—Specified when fixed quantity planning is preferred.

"L-F-L"—Specified when lot-for-lot or discrete planning is preferred.

A17. *Lot Size 2*—a quantity or time factor used in conjunction with Lot Size 1 specification:

"P.O.Q."—Contains number of periods to be combined for suggested replenishment quantity.

"FIXED"—Contains suggested fixed order quantity.

"L-F-L"—Lot Size 2 is not required.

A18. *Safety Stock Policy*—the preferred method for providing safety stock of the item:

"NO"—No safety stock is planned.

"QTY"—A safety stock quantity is desired. Although included in projected available balance, safety stock quantity will be netted for planning.

"TIM"—A safety time or weeks of supply safety is preferred. If used, system planned quantities will be recommended for both order release and order receipt the specified number of periods earlier than actually required.

A19. *Safety Stock Factor*—the quantity or time factor used in conjunction with Safety Stock Policy:

"QTY"—The quantity of the item reserved for safety stock.

"TIM"—The number of periods of safety time to be applied.

A20. *Time Fences*—three interchangeable fields used by the Master Scheduler to denote material and capacity constrained times within the planning horizons. The first position of each field is used to indicate the type of time fence in use.

"P"—Planning Time Fence—the number of planning periods, beginning with the current period, in which the MPS will not be altered by the system. Recommendations to reschedule, cancel, etc., will be displayed for the Master Scheduler but no planning quantities or dates will be automatically changed. Beyond this fence, the system will compute recommended plans based on the specified lot size policies. When necessary to state the entire MPS horizon in person-controlled firm planned orders, this fence is established at the full planning horizon.

"R"—Release Fence—the number of periods, beginning with the current period, in which the MPS should contain *released* replenishment orders. An unreleased manufacturing or purchase order encountering this fence will generate a "time-to-release" notification.

"M" or "C"—managed changed fence for Material ("M") or Capacity ("C")—user-maintained reference which permits further definition of the nature of the planning constraints for the item.

A21. *Lead Time*—the planning lead time, in working days, established for the item. It is used to offset in time requirements to the next level for MRP. For stocked items, it would reflect the time required between the release of an order and the receipt of the item to stock.

A22. *Cumulative Lead Time*—the longest lead time leg (or critical path) for the components of this item.

A23. *Special Instructions*—a user-maintained area used to communicate notes or other information.

A24. *Action Recommended*—summary recommendations to the Master Scheduler appear here.

"RESC-I"—One or more scheduled plans are planned later than actual need.

"RESC-O"—One or more scheduled plans are planned earlier than actual need.

"CANCEL"—One or more scheduled plans are not required within the lead time for the item.

"PLAN"—One or more system-computed plans falls within one period of the "P" (Planning) time fence and should be scheduled with a firm planned or released order.

"REDUCE"—One or more scheduled plans contains *sufficient* excess Projected Available Balance to warrant reducing the planned quantity. This condition can occur when overplanning options and model sales meet the original forecast mix. Option overplanning can then be reduced or rolled-out in time. This condition also is recognized by comparing a user-specified cost of ordering with the cost of carrying the excess Projected Available balance.

"RELEAS"—One or more firm, but not yet released, plans falls within one period of the Release Fence or within one period of lead time if no Release Fence is specified.

"NEGATP"—A negative available to promise condition exists. This occurs whenever actual demand exceeds the master scheduled supply of material.

B. Planning Horizons

B1. *Week*—the beginning date for each period.

B2. *Service Forecast*—the quantity of service or other independent demand forecasted for the item shown in the period that it is required. These forecast quantities are allocated to unshipped service demand and consumed by shipped service demands.

B3. *Production Forecast*—the quantities directly forecasted for the item or the result of forecasted requirements from a top-level model or family planning bill of material exploding "dependent" forecasted requirements for this item.

B4. *Actual Demand*—summarized actual requirements for this item from sales or service orders are displayed on this row. They are shown in the period that they are required.

B5. *Projected Available Balance*—the quantity calculated to be available at the end of each planning period. Beginning Projected Available Balance equals Balance-on-Hand. For each subsequent planning period, it equals Previous Projected Available Balance + MPS Scheduled Quantity – Unconsumed Forecasts – Actual Demand. This Projected Available Balance is used to determine if scheduled MPS lots should be rescheduled, reduced, or cancelled. It also is used to determine when additional MPS should be planned.

B6. *Available-to-Promise*—the quantity of this item that is available to sell (i.e., is not required to satisfy another demand). It is equal to balance-on-hand plus MPS quantity less actual demand. An available-to-promise quantity is calculated for each MPS lot and, at user option, does or does not accumulate to the next available to promise quantity. Safety stock is considered available to promise.

B7. *MPS (Master Production Schedule Quantity)*—the quantity that is scheduled, consisting of released or firm planned orders within the planning time fence or system-planned orders outside the planning time fence. MPS quantities are displayed in the period in which the orders are due.

C. Master Schedule Detail

This section of the Master Schedule report displays the details of each released or firm planned order as well as system planned orders that are due to be scheduled. Each line represents an order. Action messages are printed for any order that requires scheduling, re-scheduling, or cancellation, etc.

C1. *Required Date*—the date that the order is currently scheduled to be complete or received. This date is the one used to place the quantity in the MPS (Master Production Schedule Quantity) row of the planning horizon.

C2. *Order Number*—the number assigned by the scheduler to released and firm planned orders to identify the order.

C3. *Lot Number*—a number assigned with order number to further define the order number by lot or run or the unique identifier for master schedule lots.

C4. *Order Quantity*—the quantity remaining open on the order.

C5. *Order Types*—a code indicating the type of order:

MFG—Manufacturing Order.

PUR—Purchase Order.

BLK—Blanket Purchase Order Release.

REQ—Requisition.

MPS—Master schedule lot (pseudo and phantom items).

C6. *Order Status*—a code indicating the status of the order:

RLSD—Released Order.

FIRM—Firm Planned Order or MPS lot.

AUTH—Requisition with paperwork awaiting purchase order release by purchasing or planner release to manufacturing.

C7. *Recommended Action*—suggested action messages printed according to the planning logic and the Projected Available Balance quantity in each period:

R/I-99—Reschedule in the number of periods following R/I.

R/O-99—Reschedule out the number of periods following R/O.

CANCEL—Cancel.

PLAN—A system-planned order falls in the period just outside the planning time fence. The system recommends that the master scheduler firm up this plan by establishing a firm planned or released order.

REDUCE—The excess projected available of this order should be placed on a separate, later order.

RELEASE—The firm order falls within one period of the release fence or within one period of lead time if no release fence is specified.

D. Actual Demand Detail

This section provides detailed information on the actual demand summarized in the Actual Demand planning horizon.

D1. *Required Date*—the ship date or final assembly start date (depending on which date is being used to synchronize the planning) for the customer order.

D2. *Order Quantity*—the quantity remaining open on the order.

D3. *Reference Number*—an abbreviated customer name or other reference information.

D4. *Order Number*—the order number requiring the item.

D5. *Demand Type*—the type of demand.

"A"—Customer order for an assembled or made-to-order item.

"C"—Customer order for a stocked item.

"S"—Service order for the item.

"R"—Distribution or warehouse replenishment order.

"F"—Finished-goods inventory replenishment order.

"I"—Interplant order.

D6. *Demand Status*—a code which indicates the status of the demand and/or the status of the upper-level order requiring the item.

"R"—Released requirement or demand. Occurs when the direct order for the item has been released for manufacture (final assembly). Indicates stock withdrawal authorizations are outstanding.

"F"—Demand has been generated from an upper-level order which is firm planned, but not yet released for manufacture or shipment.

"Q"—Customer order is in quotation status.

"H"—Customer order is on hold for credit check or other reasons.

"S"—This item is itself shippable, but other items on the order are held up.

"I"—The demand has been partially issued.

D7. *Demand Code*—an indicator that the demand is unusual and will be treated as an addition to the forecast. This occurs because of one-time, special orders (frequently promotions) or with orders which exceed a maximum order size guideline.

"A"—Abnormal demand, not part of the forecast.

Blank—Normal demand which consumes appropriate forecast.

A MASTER PRODUCTION SCHEDULE EXAMPLE

The G102 gearbox example of Fig. 13.30 is a purchased subassembly with two demand streams:

1. It is an MPS option with a 30 percent option forecast against the planned production rate of a family of winches. The production plan equals 400 per week through the week beginning December 1, 1984, 420 per week until January 12, 1985, and 440 per week afterward.

2. The gearbox has a service forecast of 20 per month which appears in the first calendar week of each month. Month to date is October 1984; 12 of the forecast of 20 have been consumed—7 represented by customer order C1834 required October 31, 1984, and 5 others which have already been shipped. This consumption of service forecast is separate and distinct from the MPS option forecast consumption of the gearbox. That process uses type 1 mechanics (explode family available to promise) described earlier.

Abnormal levels, i.e., over and above forecast orders, exist in orders C1813 and C1801. Neither has consumed forecasts.

MASTER PRODUCTION SCHEDULE

MASTER SCHEDULER A2

Header data

PART NUMBER	G102
PRIMARY DESCRIPTION	4FPM GEARBOX
ITEM STATUS	STK
FAMILY	WXYY
TIME FENCES (1 / 2 / 3)	P12 / / 3
BALANCE ON HAND	320
LOT SIZE (1 / 2)	FIXED / 500
SAFETY STOCK (POLICY / FACTOR / QTY)	1 / 2 / 100
STND COST	
LEAD TIME	60
CUMUL LT	12
SELLING PRICE	
FORECAST SOURCE	PLANBL
FORECAST CONSUMPT	PLANBL
LOAD PROFILE	WFPM
CRITICAL RESOURCES (RES / QTY)	GBA / 4, GBM / 7.5
SPECIAL INSTRUCTIONS	WXYY-30% OPTION

Weekly grid — Block 1

	PAST DUE	10/13/4	10/20/4	10/27/4	11/03/4	11/10/4	11/17/4	11/24/4	12/01/4	12/08/4	12/15/4	12/22/4	01/05/5
SERV FORECAST								20					20 P
PROD FORECAST				80	20	120	120	120	120	126	126	126	105 P
ACTUAL DEMAND	8			77									80 P
PROJ AVAIL BAL		189	79	422	291	171	51	411	271	145	619	493	288 P
AVAIL TO PROMISE				423				480			520		
MPS				500				500			600		

Weekly grid — Block 2

	01/12/5	01/19/5	01/26/5	02/02/5	02/09/5	02/16/5	02/23/5	03/02/5	03/09/5	03/16/5	03/23/5	03/30/5	04/06/5
SERV FORECAST				20				20					20
PROD FORECAST	129	132	132	132	132	132	132	132	132	132	132	132	132
ACTUAL DEMAND	159	395		243	111		347	195	431		299	167	515
PROJ AVAIL BAL	527					479				563			
AVAIL TO PROMISE	500					500				500			500
MPS	500					500				500			500

Weekly grid — Block 3 & Block 4 (dates 04/13/5 →, blank)

ACTIONS RECOMMENDED

RESC-I

WEEK	RES	QTY
01/05/5	20, 105 P, 80 P, 288 P	
04/06/5	20, 132, 515, 500, 500	

MASTER SCHEDULE DETAIL

ORDER NUMBER	LOT NO	ORDER QUANTITY	ORDER TYPE	STATUS	RECOM ACTION	REQUIRED DATE
4228	005	500	PUR	RLSD	R/I-01	10/27
4228	006	500	PUR	RLSD	R/I-01	11/24
4756	001	600	PUR	RLSD		12/15

ACTUAL DEMAND DETAIL

REQUIRED DATE	ORDER QUANTITY	REFERENCE NUMBER	ORDER NUMBER	TYPE	CODE
10/13	60	WA01	M0814	F	R
10/13	45	WA04	M0815	F	R
10/13	15	ALLEN MFG	C1802	A	R
10/20	60	WA06	M0819	F	A
10/20	30	TORO MFG	C1819	A	F
10/20	15	GEN ELEC	C1825	A	F
10/27	5	ALLIS CHAM	C1831	F	F
10/27	60	WA01	M0820	F	F
10/27	10	DUKE PWR	C1837	A	S
10/31	7	LIFTUM-HI	C1834	S	S
11/28	20	GSA	C1813	S	F
01/05	80	AT&T	C1801	A	A

FIG. 13.30 Master production schedule example.

REFERENCES

1. W. L. Berry, T. E. Vollman, and D. C. Whybark, *Master Production Scheduling: Principle and Practice*, American Production and Inventory Control Society, Falls Church, Va., 1979.
2. Thomas F. Wallace, *Dictionary*, 5th ed., APICS, Falls Church, Va., 1984.
3. Joseph A. Orlicky, George W. Plossl, and Oliver W. Wight, "Structuring the Bill of Materials," *Production and Inventory Management*, vol. 13, no. 4.

BIBLIOGRAPHY

APICS Training Aid—Master Production Scheduling, APICS, Falls Church, Va., 1984.

W. L. Berry, T. E. Vollman, and D. C. Whybark: *Master Production Scheduling: Principle and Practice*. APICS, Falls Church, Va., 1979.

Dave Garwood and John Civerolo, *Production Planning Starter Kit*, R. D. Garwood, Inc., Atlanta, 1984.

F. John Sari, "The MPS and the Bill of Material Go Hand-in-Hand," Richard C. Ling, Inc., Winston-Salem, N.C., 1981.

Oliver W. Wight, *Manufacturing Resource Planning: MRP II*, rev. ed., Van Nostrand Reinhold, New York, 1984.

14

Material Requirements Planning

Editor

TERRY R. SCHULTZ , CFPIM, President, The Forum Ltd., Milwaukee, Wisconsin

Material requirements planning (MRP) is a time-phased priority planning system that calculates material requirements and schedules supply to meet changing demand.* Figure 14.1 presents an overview with the three prerequisite inputs for making MRP work clearly visible: MPS (what is planned), bill of material (how it is done), and inventory status (what has been done). With these three inputs, MRP can determine what needs to be done in terms of what, how much, and when.

MRP LOGIC

The logic of MRP can be illustrated by using simple arithmetic and Fig. 14.1:

$$D = A \times B - C$$

where A = MPS quantities
       B = bills-of-material quantities

---

* The source for this material is Terry R. Schultz, *Business Requirements Planning, BRP, The Journey to Excellence*, The Forum Ltd., Milwaukee, Wis., Aug. 1984. Permission has been granted.

C = inventory quantities

D = action needed

How accurate is D, the action needed? The answer is, just as accurate as A, B, and C. If MRP does not work, it is because $A \times B - C$ is not equal to D. In other words, there is no valid MPS or accurate bill of materials or inventory status. If A, B, and/or C are inaccurate, D will not be accurate. MRP is a powerful tool, but it depends on people—people to maintain the MPS, bills of materials, and accurate inventory records and people to take the required action.

Independent versus Dependent Demand

Independent demand is forecast and specified on the MPS. Dependent demand can be calculated based on the bill-of-materials relationships of the products. The power of master production scheduling and MRP is that matched sets of components can be calculated very precisely.

For example, if 2 B's and 3 C's are required to make A, and 100 A's are scheduled to be produced, then a total of 200 B's plus 300 C's is required (see Fig. 14.2). MRP can also determine timing. If the schedule for A is changed, MRP will reschedule the requirements for B and C accordingly.

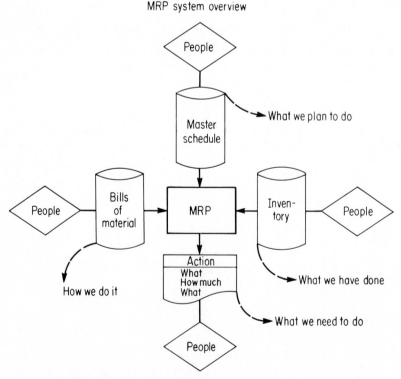

FIG. 14.1 MRP system overview.

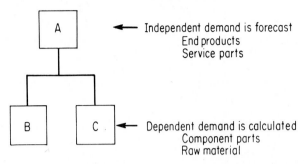

FIG. 14.2 Independent versus dependent demand.

In historical systems based on order points, there was no visibility of future demand. If the schedule for A changed, it would not directly affect B and C in terms of date or quantity. Order points are part-oriented, and it is only by coincidence that B's and C's might be on hand to support A. Master production scheduling and MRP are product-oriented. That is the right approach since customers want products, not parts in a bag with a set of assembly instructions.

MRP was defined as a time-phased priority planning system. Notice in Fig. 14.3 that the basis for time-phased planning is the *cumulative product lead time*, which is the total time it takes to purchase raw materials, manufacture component parts, build subassemblies, and assemble end products.

Independent demand for end products is listed on the MPS at level 0 in the bill of materials. The MPS is then exploded down to level 1 to reflect the demand for assemblies. MRP now checks the current status of the number of assemblies in inventory. If there are enough, it stops right there. If there are not enough, MRP subtracts available inventory from demand to find out how many assemblies are needed. It then offsets the assembly lead time and calculates the demand for component parts at level 2. MRP again checks the inventory status and subtracts to see whether there is enough. If there is, that level is OK. If not, MRP offsets the lead time needed to make the component parts and calculates the demand for raw material at level 3. Again, inventory is checked to see whether there is enough. If not, MRP offsets the lead time needed to order raw material so purchasing can order what is needed in January to produce end products by July.

This is an illustration of the overall time-phased planning involved in a good MRP system. Now examine how the scheduling logic of MRP keeps supply and demand in balance for each part and raw materials. In MRP terms, requirements are demand, and orders are supply. MRP compares the statement of demand requirements directly to the statement of supply orders. It then looks for imbalances and recommends the appropriate order—defer, expedite, or cancel action. Figure 14.4 illustrates examples of each action.

The first example shows a requirement for 10 in period one. MRP has balanced that with an order for 10 in period one and recommends an order. By doing so, supply and demand would be in balance. The customer would be served, inventory would be zero at the end of the period, and the shop's productivity would be OK (assuming an appropriate lead time).

The second example involves periods 2 and 3, where there is a requirement for 10 in period 3 and an order for 10 currently scheduled in period 2. MRP recognizes

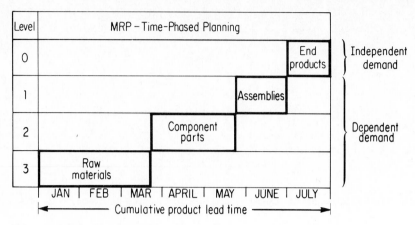

FIG. 14.3   MRP: time-phased planning.

MRP schedules orders
to meet requirements

	Time Periods					
	1	2	3	4	5	6
Reqmts	10		10	10		
Orders	10	10			10	10

	Order	Defer	Expedite	Cancel
Example:	1	2	3	4

FIG. 14.4   MRP examples.

the imbalance and recommends deferring the order from period 2 to period 3. If the order were not deferred, what would happen to inventory? It would go up. Inventory would be in excess for at least a week, perhaps for a month or longer.

The third example is in period 4. There is another requirement for 10. There is an order for 10 currently scheduled in period 5. MRP recognizes the imbalance and recommends expediting the order from period 5 back into period 4. If this part went into an assembled product involving many other parts and were not expedited, what would happen to inventory? Again, it would go up. All the other parts would come into work in process, waiting for the shortage to arrive.

The fourth example is in period 5. The requirement has dropped away for some reason, but there is still an order scheduled in period 6. MRP again recognizes the imbalance and recommends canceling that order. If it were not cancelled, what would happen to inventory? Again, inventory would go up.

In fact, every time there is an imbalance between supply and demand, it must be paid for with inventory. This is true not only for products but also for every part and raw material in the system. That is why MRP's ability to schedule orders is so powerful. It can satisfy changing requirements from marketing by maintaining valid due dates for both purchasing and manufacturing. It helps reduce shortages to improve productivity on the shop floor and minimize excess inventory.

MATERIAL PLANNING PROCESS

Before we go through the planning process, we list six MRP prerequisites: a valid *master schedule* that supports the production plan, structured *bill of materials* that reflects the manufacturing process, accurate and timely *on-hand* and *on-order* inventory status, and *order policies* and *lead times* for purchased and manufactured parts. The materials planning process is composed of four steps that use these six prerequisites to determine the action required to balance supply and demand for each part.

1. Calculate the gross requirements, and ask, Is the total demand OK? *Gross* means without regard for inventory. To answer the question, the MPS quantity of products is multiplied by the quantity of each part required in the bills of materials. The entire process is repeated for all parts by exploding down through the bills of materials level by level.

2. Project the on-hand inventory to answer the question, Is the net demand OK? At this step, the on-hand balance and scheduled production and purchase orders are subtracted from the gross requirements to determine whether enough inventory is available. If there is, MRP can stop, since no more material needs to be ordered.

3. Reschedule open orders, in anticipation of the question, Is the current schedule OK? Here is where MRP looks for imbalances between supply and demand and recommends the appropriate expedite, defer, or cancel action. Note that MRP will reschedule previously released orders before it will plan new orders.

4. Plan new orders and ask, Is the total supply OK and in balance with total demand? To plan new orders, MRP uses order policies to calculate order quantities, and lead times to calculate due and release dates for each order. It then recommends that the planner order.

By answering yes to each question in the materials planning process, MRP can prepare the reports that tell the planners what action is required in terms of what, how much, and when, to make the MPS a reality.

Example of MRP Process

Here the MRP process is followed in detail, with an actual product. Walking through each step will take the mystery out of MRP. The product is introduced so that you are familiar with it and can go through each step. Figure 14.5 shows a relatively simple bill of materials in which the end product is A. Here A is made up of C plus B, and B, in turn, is made up of 2 C's plus D. For simplicity, D is eliminated from consideration here to allow concentration on A, B, and C. First, a master schedule of independent demand for product A is developed. Then it is exploded through the bill of materials, level by level, to calculate the dependent demand for parts B and C. Then the supply orders for parts B and C needed to satisfy the MPS for product A are scheduled.

To do that requires the use of low-level codes. Low-level coding is a simple technique that assigns a code for the lowest level of usage of each part. Since they

Product A

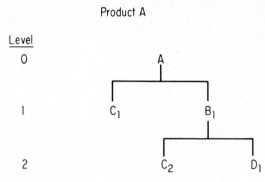

FIG. 14.5   Bill of materials.

are at the highest level of use, end products are given a low-level code of 0. In the bills of materials, each part is given an assignment according to its lowest level of use. In the example, part B is used nowhere else in the total product line, so it is assigned a low-level code of 1. Part C, however, is used at level 1 on A and again at level 2 on B. Therefore, its low-level code assignment is 2. MRP will process each part in low-level code sequence to be sure that all upper-level demand for each component has been summarized.

Calculate Gross Requirements.   The first step is to calculate the gross requirements by using the MPS, bills of materials, and quantity per for each component part. Since product A is made up of B and C, and B has a low-level code of 1, it is the first part to process.

Figure 14.6 shows that MPS to produce 10 A's in period 1, 15 A's in period 3, and 15 A in period 5. Since A can be produced in less than a day, no lead-time offset is required when A is exploded down to the lower-level components. Now multiply the MPS and the bill-of-materials quantities. One B is needed to make each A. The results of this multiplication equal the gross requirements (or total demand) for B. They are a direct reflection of the MPS: 10 A's require 10 B's in period 1; 15 A's require 15 B's in period 3, and likewise in period 5. That is relatively straight-forward.

Project On-Hand Inventory.   Step 2 checks whether there is enough inventory to cover the total demand. To project on-hand inventory, two additional prerequisites are used, as shown in Fig. 14.6 The first is the on-hand balance of B, which is 10. Those 10 are in the stockroom. The other prerequisite is the current status of released orders due. In the same figure, there is a released order for 10 due in period 3 out in the shop. The bill of materials shows that B is made up to two components and is a manufactured assembly. And C is not made up of any components and so comes from outside suppliers and is a purchased part. In this example, the released order for B is being assembled, and the necessary components to produce that order have already been issued.

Now the on-hand inventory can be projected. Starting with the balance on hand, the time-phased schedules for supply and demand are used to project future inventory. Gross requirements are demands; released orders are supply. Requirements decrease inventory; orders increase inventory.

The beginning balance on hand is 10, and the projected on-hand balance in

Step 1   ① Calculate gross reqmts

A		On hand	1	2	3	4	5
Master schedule			10		15		15
B					Explode ↓ BOM		
① Gross reqmts			10		15		15

Step 2   ② Project-on-hand inventory

A		On hand	1	2	3	4	5
Master schedule			10		15		15
B					Explode ↓ BOM		
① Gross reqmts			10		15		15
Released orders—due					10		
② Projected on hand		10	0	0	−5	−5	−20

Step 3   ③ Schedule orders

A			On hand	1	2	3	4	5
Master schedule				10		15		15
B	Order qty 10	Lead time 2			Explode ↓ BOM			
① Gross reqmts				10		15		15
Released orders—due						10		
② Projected on hand			10	0	0	−5	−5	−20
Planned orders—due						10		10
③ Planned orders—release				10		10		

FIG. 14.6 MRP process.

period 1 is 0. The gross requirements of 10 consume the entire beginning stockroom balance. There is no activity in period 2. In period 3, 15 are required and an order is released for 10. Subtracting supply from demand results in −5. There is going to be a shortage unless something is done. There is no additional activity in period 4, so that projected on-hand balance remains −5. In period 5, another 15 are required, resulting in a cumulative projected on-hand balance of −20, that is, a projected shortage of 20.

At this point, it would be helpful to make a comparison between MRP and a shortage list. If you understand how a shortage list works, you will understand MRP. In a typical situation, a production order is released with the order number, date, and quantity on top. The order quantity is extended by the quantity of each component on the bill of materials, and somebody goes to the stockroom and tries to pull those parts.

One of two things happens: (1) there is enough of the component, and it is put on a skid and sent out to assembly; or (2) there is not enough, and the component is written on the shortage list. It is a fail-safe system for finding shortages and is used by most companies in the world today. There is one catch: The shortage is discovered too late. The shortage is discovered just when it is time to build the product.

MRP projects shortages in the future so that something can be done about them. Look at period 3 in the example, If the lead time for B were less then 3 weeks, would there be a problem? No, because there is enough time to recover. The shortage could be prevented by releasing another order or increasing the current order. MRP projects shortages in time to prevent physical shortages. That is the key to MRP's success.

Schedule Released and Planned Orders.   Step 3 in the process is to reschedule released orders and/or plan new orders. MRP first looks at the released order line and asks, Is the current schedule OK? In other words, is the released order currently scheduled in period 3 in the right time period? The answer is yes. It is not enough in total quantity, but it is not necessary to expedite or defer it.

However, is the total supply OK? The answer is no. The first shortage appears in period 3, and the total shortage is −20 in period 5. MRP must now plan new orders to cover those shortages. MRP has determined when a new planned order is due, which is period 3, the first period in which there is a projected shortage.

At this point, the last two prerequisites, order quantity and lead time, are used. Figure 14.6 shows the order quantity for B is 10 and the lead time is two periods. These tell MRP how much and when to order. Is 10 sufficient to cover the shortage of −5? Yes. So MRP plans to have an order due in period 3 to cover that shortage. The next question is, When should it be released? Look at the lead time; it is two periods. MRP offsets the lead time as the arrows indicate and releases an order for 10 in period 1 to satisfy the projected shortage of −5 in period 3.

MRP assumes that order will be released and the projected on-hand balance will increase to +5 on the basis of the planned receipt in period 3. In period 4 the projected on-hand balance is also 5. But in period 5, the 15 required will result in a shortage of 10. MRP continues the process and asks, How much still needs to be ordered? The answer is to plan another new order for 10. Will 10 satisfy the projected shortage? Yes. What is the lead time? MRP will again offset the lead time of 2 weeks and plan to release the second order in period 3 to satisfy the shortage of 10 in period 5.

Now each step in the overall process has been completed. MRP exploded the MPS through the bills of materials to calculate the total gross requirements. It projected the on-hand inventory, checked the schedule for open orders, and planned any new orders necessary. The planning for B is completed, and supply and demand are in balance at that level. MRP does this on a level-by-level basis. It is time to start all over again at the next level with part C.

Summarize Gross Requirements.   There are several sources of demand for C. One is direct from the MPS. Another is planned orders from any higher-level parts in the bill of materials above C. The third source is any open requisitions from released orders of parts above C in the bill of materials. The released order for B is being worked on, and component C has been issued from stock to the floor. Therefore, there are no longer any open requirements or allocations against the inventory of C for that order.

Figure 14.7 shows how MRP calculates the requirements for C from A and B. The requirements from A equal the MPS value for A times C. That results in 10 C's required in period 1, 15 C's in period 3, and 15 C's in period 5. The requirements from B come from B's planned order-release line. That is where MRP projects the need to issue C to support the planned production of B. MRP will plan C's to be available by multiplying B's planned orders times 2 C's, resulting in 20 C's required in periods 1 and 3. MRP now asks if there are any other usages for C. The answer is no. That means it is at the lowest level of use, and MRP can summarize the total gross requirements for C, which are 30 in period 1, 35 in period 3, and 15 in period 5.

Repeat MRP Process. Now that the total demand is OK, MRP can repeat the rest of the process for C. To project the on-hand inventory, MRP needs to know the current inventory status of C. Figure 14.8 indicates there are 25 C's on hand and two released orders for 20 C due to arrive in periods 1 and 4.

The projected on-hand inventory for C equals the beginning balance of 25 plus the scheduled release in period 1 of 20, which is 45. Subtracting the 30 required results in an ending balance in period 1 of 15. With no activity in period 2, the projection remains 15. However, in period 3 there is a total demand of 35 against a projected balance of 15. That is a shortage of 20 in period 3. There is no demand in period 4. However, a release is scheduled to come in at the end of period 5, so the projected on-hand balance will be 0. There is zero inventory available in period 4, in which 15 more are required. That results in a projected shortage of 15 at the end of that period.

Before planning any new orders, MRP asks, Is the current schedule of released orders OK? The released order in period 4 could be expedited to period 3 to cover the projected shortage. MRP takes the appropriate action and recommends to expedite. MRP will not do it, but it will make the recommendation. MRP must plan new orders to cover the ending shortage of 15. It looks at the order quantity put in by the planner and orders 20 to be due in period 5. The release date is based on the lead time, which is three periods. MRP offsets that lead time from period 5 to schedule the planned order release of 20 in period 2.

MRP has now balanced supply and demand and determined what actions are

MRP process
(★) summarize gross requirements

A		On hand	1	2	3	4	5
					Time periods		
Master schedule			10		15		15
B					Explode ↓ BOM		
Planned orders—release			10		10		
C					Explode ↓ BOM		
Reqmts from A X 1C =			10		15		15
Reqmts from B X 2C=			20		20		
(★) Gross reqmts for C			30		35		15

FIG. 14.7 Gross requirements summary.

			On hand	Time periods				
				1	2	3	4	5
A								
Master schedule				10		15		15
B	Order qty	Lead time		Explode ↓ BOM				
	10	2						
① Gross reqmts				10		15		15
Released orders—due						10		
② Projected on hand			10	0	0	−5	−5	−20
Planned orders—due						10		10
③ Planned orders—release				10		10		
C	Order qty	Lead time		Explode ↓ BOM				
	20	3						
Gross reqmts				30		35		15
Released orders—due				20			20	
Projected on hand			25	15	15	−20	0	−15
Planned orders—due								20
Planned orders—release					20			

FIG. 14.8   MRP process is as simple as 1-2-3.

required for parts B and C to meet the MPS for A. Analyzing more closely, one can see what action is necessary (to order, defer, expedite, or cancel).

MRP should be run at least weekly because the changes that take place in a normal manufacturing environment require rebalancing supply and demand at least that often. Therefore, one necessary action is to order everything that needs to be released in period 1. Looking only at parts B and C, we see an order for B needs to be released in period 1, due in period 3. No other orders need to be released at this time. Orders should not be released early because they are subject to change.

However, any orders to expedite, defer, or cancel should be processed. For part C, there is an expedite condition. A released order is due in period 4 but needed in period 3. Therefore, the other action to take is to expedite that released order for C. Looking at the whole planning horizon, MRP plans the release of another order for 10 B's in period 3, due in period 5, and another order for 20 C's to be released in period 2, due in period 5.

MRP Order Action.   The whole MRP report is not needed to identify order action. The MRP order action report highlights exactly what action is required for parts B and C and includes recommendations for part D (Fig. 14.9). The order action report answers the questions of what, how much, and when to order.

The order action report should separate manufactured and purchased parts and be sequenced by the planner. Order, expedite, defer, and cancel actions can also be grouped separately so the most important actions can be taken as quickly as possible. However, it is important to realize that the planners must defer and cancel orders, as well as expedite them, to maintain valid schedules.

What happens if each of the actions is taken? Remember, MRP is just recommending them at this time. MRP's job is to project shortages in time to prevent physical shortages, but planners are still needed to take appropriate action. If the planners can execute each action, then the projected shortages should disappear.

In Fig. 14.10, the planner has released the two planned orders for B, and the

MRP order action report						
Part no	Order no	Order qty	Current		Revised	Action
			Release	Due	Due	
B	Plan	10	1	3		Order
B	Plan	10	3	5		Order
C	12345	20		4	3	Expedite
C	Plan	20	2	5		Order
D	23456	25		3	5	Defer
D	34567	25		6		Cancel

What   How much   When

FIG. 14.9 Order action report.

				Time periods					
A			On hand	1	2	3	4	5	
Master schedule				10		15		15	
B	Order qty 10	Lead time 2	Explode BOM						
① Gross reqmts				10		15		15	
Released orders–due						20		10	
② Projected on hand			10	0	0	5	5	0	
Planned orders–due									
③ Planned orders–release									
C	Order qty 20	Lead time 3	Explode BOM						
Gross reqmts				30		35		15	
Released orders–due				20		20		20	
Projected on hand			25	15	15	0	0	5	
Planned orders–due									
Planned orders–release									

FIG. 14.10 Results after order action.

14.11

projected on-hand balance line shows that all the shortages have been eliminated. Supply and demand are in balance for B. The customers have been satisfied, the ending inventory balance is 0, and the shop had sufficient lead time to produce the B's.

You might ask, Where did the planned orders go? They do not show up as planned orders any more. When the planner authorized and released them, they appeared on the released order line. The quantity of released orders has increased from 10 to 20 in period 3, and the released order for 10 also shows up in period 5.

For part C, the projected on-hand balance line is all positive—no shortages. The planner made the expedite order from period 4 to period 3, resulting in the projected on-hand balance of 0, and released that order for 20 due in period 5. Since the order quantity was higher than the actual quantity needed, the short planning horizon of five periods ended with a projected balance in inventory of five pieces. Now, total supply and demand are in balance, and the MPS is satisfied.

ORDER SCHEDULING AND CONTROL

MRP systems should provide three status codes for order scheduling and control:

Order Status	Quantity/Date	Requirements
1. Released	Firm	Firm
2. Firm Planned	Firm	Planned
3. Planned	Planned	Planned

Released order schedules are controlled by planners and are used to authorize the purchase of material and the production of products. MRP will recommend expedite, defer, or cancel action, but the planner is responsible for taking the action necessary. The firm order quantity will increase the projected on-hand inventory. The firm requirements are calculated based on the bill of materials in effect on the actual release date for each order.

Firm planned order schedules are also controlled by the planners and are used to firm up an order's date and/or quantity based on future material or capacity availability. MRP will still recommend order action, but the planner may override that action to maintain the desired schedule. The firm order quantity will increase the projected on-hand inventory. The planned requirements are calculated based on the bill of materials in effect on the planned release dates for each order.

Planned orders are automatically scheduled and controlled by MRP. They are used to plan future material requirements at each level in the bills of materials. MRP will recommend order action, but the planner is again responsible for converting each planned order to a firm-planned or released order. The planned order quantity will not increase the projected on-hand inventory. The planned requirements are calculated based on the bills of materials in effect on the planned release date for each order.

PEGGED REQUIREMENTS

There are really two parts to the overall MRP process. The first is to go through the bills of materials and determine what is required at each level to satisfy the MPS.

The second is to look at the action required and decide whether it can be done. If it can, everything is fine. The MPS is met, the product is shipped, and the customer is satisfied.

But in real life, that does not happen every day. What if it is not possible to take the actions recommended by MRP? A lot of planners would say, "Tell me where the part is used, so I can go back up the bill of materials and get the problem solved." Identifying the source of requirements by using the single level where-used capability from the bill of materials is called *pegged requirements*.

In Fig. 14.11, C is used on A and B. By looking up the bill of materials, the sources of requirements and what amount came from each source can be identified. Here A contributed 10 C's of the total required in period 1, 15 C's in period 3, and 15 C's in period 5. And B contributed 20 in period 1 and 20 in period 3, resulting in total requirements of 30 C's in period 1, 35 C's in period 3, and 15 C's in period 5. If the total requirements for C cannot be met, alternative solutions include partial shipments, alternate suppliers, material substitution, subcontracting, and/or changing the demand schedules for B and A. The problem should be solved at the lowest level possible to minimize changes. Therefore, changing the MPS should be the last resort.

All this MRP information is very helpful, but it has been spread across three separate reports. There was the horizontal MRP report which showed the logic of MRP in quantitative form. From that the order action report and the pegged requirements report were extracted. It is quite a job to manually cross-reference all these reports. Fortunately, they can all be merged into one time-phased vertical report.

Figure 14.12 shows all the same information for part C but displays the results vertically instead of horizontally. Here C has an order quantity of 20, a lead time of 3, and a beginning on-hand balance of 25. In the center of the vertical report are the requirements and the orders for C in date sequence. In the right column next to the projected inventory available is the necessary order action. The left column shows the sources of requirements, or single-level pegging. This report gives the planner an excellent picture of what must be done to manage each part's supply and demand.

This report especially lends itself to display on a cathode-ray tube (CRT). Planners today can look at their CRTs and call up each part they are responsible for managing. At the end of the day, when they have gotten their shortages covered, the managers can go home. They can immediately update supply-and-demand balances and know they have gotten their jobs done.

An accurate data base is the foundation for manufacturing planning and control systems (Fig. 14.13). To support MRP, the MPS file, part master file, and product structure file are needed to calculate requirements level by level. MRP also needs to

Pegged requirements

C		1	2	3	4	5	BOM
Source of reqmts		Single-level where used					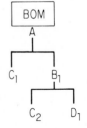
A		10		15		15	
B		20		20			
Total reqmts		30		35		15	

FIG. 14.11 Pegged requirements.

MRP report – vertical

Part no	Order policy	Order qty	Lead time	On hand	Description
C	EOQ	20	3	25	Example
		Requirements / orders			
Source	Order	Date	Qty	Avail	Action
	P1234	1	20	45	
A	M1234	1	10	35	
B	PLAN	1	20	15	
A	M2345	3	15	0	
B	PLAN	3	20	20–	
	P2345	4	20	0	Expedite–3
	PLAN	5	20	0	Order–2
A	M3456	5	15	15–	

Single-level pegging   Projected inventory Order defer Expedite cancel

FIG. 14.12 Vertical MRP report.

Data-base overview

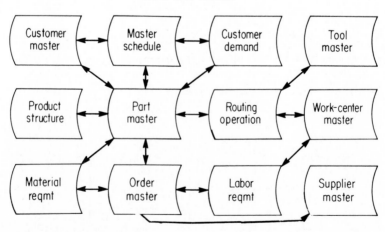

FIG. 14.13 Data base overview.

know what is on order for both purchased and manufactured parts. The scheduled purchase and shop orders are stored in the order master file. Material required for those orders would be in the material requirements file. By using the material requirements and order master files in date sequence, the vertical time-phased supply-and-demand report shown can be prepared.

SUMMARY

The MRP system checklist (Table 14.1) summarizes what is required to make MRP work. First, it is necesary to establish a written and approved production plan. Otherwise, the master scheduler is really running the company. Unfortunately, the master scheduler has not been given the direction needed to do the job.

A written and approved production plan provides the guidelines to set up a valid MPS. The master scheduler and management need to work together to manage change. To do that, they need time-fence policies based on the cumulative product lead time. They also need the capability to do rough-cut capacity planning. This process provides a quick look at whether there is enough capacity to meet the MPS.

Without a bill-of-materials accuracy of 98 percent or greater, the right requirements cannot be exploded down through the lower levels. In fact, if a part is not on the bill of materials it will not get planned and will show up as a shortage. Inaccurate bills of materials generate inaccurate requirements.

The same is true for inventory accuracy. A good MRP system needs an inventory record accuracy of 95 percent or better. These disciplines count. Managing a formal system by the numbers should not be too much of a challenge because those disciplines are internal. Customers do not make the inventory or bill-of-materials accuracy low. These are things that companies can control themselves. It is up to management to decide that they will run by the numbers with the formal system.

In addition, order policies and lead times are needed to plan new orders. Scrap and shrinkage factors are necessary to adjust order quantities to reflect the real world, where 100 percent perfect parts are not made every time. As pointed out, order action and pegging capabilities are recommended so that planners have a

TABLE 14.1 MRP System Checklist

	Yes	No
Written and approved production plan	————	————
Valid MPS	————	————
Time-fence policies	————	————
Rough-cut capacity planning	————	————
Bill-of-materials accuracy 98%+	————	————
Inventory record accuracy 95%+	————	————
Order policies	————	————
Lead times	————	————
Scrap and shrinkage factors	————	————
Order action and pegging capability	————	————
Run at least weekly	————	————
Ongoing education and training	————	————

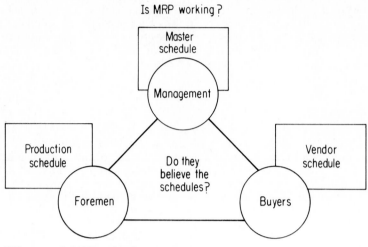

FIG. 14.14 Is MRP working?

good idea of how to schedule parts. MRP needs to be run at least weekly to rebalance supply and demand, and time periods should be a week or less. Last, ongoing education and training are needed to maintain the understanding of why and how the formal system provides a better chance to make the business plan a reality than the informal system does.

When it comes to the bottom line, how can you know whether MRP is really working in the company? Ask yourself, Do they believe the schedules? (Fig. 14.14). Does management believe the MPS is valid and can be made? Do the foremen believe the production schedule? Are they working to that schedule as opposed to the shortage list? Do the buyers believe the vendor schedule? Are they directing the suppliers to bring in the parts that support MRP and the MPS? If everyone believes the schedules, MRP is definitely working.

If it is, the company has clearer priorities of what to do, improved delivery to customers, reduced lead times, lower inventories, fewer shortages, increased productivity, lower total costs, and improved equipment utilization. Most important is the improvement in quality of life. A special spirit of confidence comes from believing you can get the job done, as part of a winning team in a "can do" company.

MRP helps plan material. If everything works right, will the MPS be satisfied, or is there something more to check? Yes, check that there is enough capacity at each work center to support the materials plan, to meet the MPS, and satisfy the business plan.

Capacity Planning

Editor

JACK GIPS, CFPIM, President, Jack Gips, Inc., Chagrin Falls, Ohio

Contributors

CRAIG ERHORN, CPIM, MIS Manager, Matrix Corporation, Orangeburg, N.Y.

RICHARD C. HEARD, CFPIM, President, R. C. Heard & Co., Bartlesville, Oklahoma

ROD MORRIS, CPIM, Materials Manager, Joy Manufacturing Co. (Africa),PTY Limited, Johannesburg, South Africa

RICHARD RUSSELL, CFPIM, Vice President, Jack Gips, Inc., Chagrin Falls, Ohio

DEFINITION OF CAPACITY PLANNING

All manufacturing companies, regardless of products and processes, require material and capacity to produce their products. In some companies the process takes one or more raw materials and performs some manufacturing operations to convert the materials to finished goods. Other companies may buy several materials or components and assemble them into finished products. Still others may buy raw materials, convert them to manufactured components, and then assemble the manufactured components with other manufactured and purchased components into subassemblies. These subassemblies may then be assembled with other components and subassemblies to make a finished product. In all these cases, it is necessary to plan both purchase orders for raw materials or components and manufacturing orders for the manufacturing operations that occur in the production of components, subassemblies, and final assemblies.

The process of scheduling these orders and ensuring that material is available whenever needed in the manufacturing process is addressed in the planning process called *material-requirements planning* (MRP) and by other similar scheduling processes. These approaches try to ensure that the right components and materials are available at the right time in the manufacturing process to satisfy the schedules for finished goods. These approaches consider existing inventories, manufacturing orders, and purchase orders currently in process and help determine when additional future orders should be placed or what changes should be made to the dates and quantities of those existing orders.

The capacity required to perform all the manufacturing operations to make the components, subassemblies, and finished goods scheduled is addressed by several different capacity planning techniques. In essence, these techniques look at the plans for producing the components, subassemblies, and finished goods or final assemblies and convert these plans to a measurable workload for each of the manufacturing processes involved in the production. The purpose of this chapter is to show the thought processes and techniques that must be utilized to make valid capacity decisions in manufacturing companies.

Capacity

The *APICS Dictionary* defines capacity in the following terms: "In a general sense [capacity] refers to an aggregated volume of work load. It is a separate concept from priority."[1] In the second definition, capacity is "the highest sustainable output rate which can be achieved with the current product specifications, product mix, work force, plant, and equipment." These two definitions refer to capacity from two different viewpoints. The first definition looks at capacity as a requirement on manufacturing, that is, the amount of work to be done. The second definition views capacity as a measure of what the manufacturing organization in its environment can produce. Because capacity must be viewed from both angles, the term *capacity* can easily be confused in its meaning, and capacity decisions can become very difficult. So it is important to add to the term *capacity* some adjectives that define more specifically which viewpoint is being used. In this chapter the following definitions are used consistently:

> *Required capacity.*   When manufacturing orders or rates of manufacturing subassemblies or finished goods are converted to measurable units (such as standard hours) to predict the need for capacity in different parts of the manufacturing process, the resulting numbers are the *required capacity.*

> *Demonstrated capacity.*   This is the currently accepted rate of output demonstrated by an individual work center, or group of work centers, that can be accepted by the organization as its current capability based on current levels of staffing, efficiency, work schedules, etc.

> *Maximum capacity.*   This is the highest sustainable output rate which can be achieved with the current product specifications, product mix, work force, plant, and equipment.

This chapter describes several techniques used to evaluate the need for capacity, consistent with the production plans, that can be compared with the demonstrated and maximum capacities to highlight capacity decisions which must be made to meet those plans.

Capacity Planning Tools

This chapter focuses on the following major capacity planning processes: rough-cut capacity planning (RCCP), capacity-requirements planning (CRP), and input/output control. The *APICS Dictionary* defines these terms as follows. RCCP is "the process of converting the production plan and/or master production schedule into the impact on key resources, such as man hours, machine hours, storage, standard cost dollars, shipping dollars, inventory levels, etc." CRP is "the function of establishing, measuring, and adjusting limits or levels of capacity that are consistent with a production plan. The term *capacity requirements planning* used in this context is the process of determining how much labor and machine resources are required to accomplish the tasks of production." Input/output control is "a technique for capacity control where actual output from a work center is compared with the planned output developed by capacity requirements planning. The input is also monitored to see if it corresponds with plans so that work centers will not be expected to generate output when jobs are not available to work on." One other term that requires immediate definition, because of the frequency with which it will be used, is *work center*, which the *APICS Dictionary* defines as "a specific production facility consisting of one or more people and/or machines which can be considered as one unit for purposes of capacity requirements planning and detailed scheduling." Because, in individual companies, this term is often used interchangeably with *work station, equipment, machine, workbench,* etc., we standardize on the term *work center* and expand it to mean not only production facilities but also any other area or group of people for which we wish to plan capacity. A work center may be a group of people who perform a specific manufacturing function or a related function that affects manufacturing such as a quality control operation, an engineering operation, and a storeroom operation, as well as a piece of machinery.

HOW CAPACITY PLANNING FITS INTO THE MANUFACTURING SYSTEM

The capacity planning tools just defined are used to support various segments of a complete manufacturing system. The RCCP is used to identify capacity constraints during the production planning process. Capacity checks at this point help to develop an achievable production plan. The CRP is used to identify capacity constraints in the current material plan. Analyzing the capacity requirements and solving future capacity problems help to ensure that the material plans are achievable. The input/output report is used to make sure capacity is actually delivered as planned. This is a vital step in the process because today's capacity problems, when left unsolved, become tomorrow's shortages. The master production schedule (MPS) summary is another important capacity planning tool not previously mentioned. It is discussed in the section "Other Capacity Planning Tools." Briefly stated, this report provides a way for the master scheduler to ensure that the master schedules have remained within the capacity limitations defined by the production plans.

GOAL OF CAPACITY PLANNING

One major difference between planning material and planning capacity is that material is more tangible. If material is available, one knows it because one can walk into the plant and see it. If it is required in a particular spot in the plant, one can pick it up and carry it there. However, capacity is more of a notion or assumption than something you can touch. Certainly, one can walk through the plant and see machinery that represents capacity. But depending on the product mix one is planning to produce and the many other factors that can affect capacity, both the required capacity and the demonstrated capacity are assumptions based on fact. Last week's output numbers, based on last week's levels of efficiency, absenteeism, and machine downtime, may be useful to predict next week's capacity. However, there is no guarantee that these factors will be exactly the same from week to week. Therefore, because capacity is somewhat abstract, the capacity planner must make some assumptions, take the necessary actions, and then measure continuously to ensure that the assumptions are coming true and the actions are providing the expected results. The goal of capacity planning can best be stated in the following way:

Required capacity − Demonstrated capacity = Capacity actions

This equation states that once the required capacity is determined, it must be compared with the current level of demonstrated capacity to see whether capacity actions are required to alter the demonstrated capacity to match the required level. If the required and demonstrated capacities are equal, then no capacity actions are required. If the demonstrated capacity is lower than the required capacity, some actions must be taken to increase the demonstrated capacity. If the demonstrated is higher than the required capacity, some action should be taken to reduce the demonstrated capacity to the level of the required. In either case, the most desirable action is usually to change the demonstrated capacity. If, for some reason, altering the demonstrated capacity is not practical or is not economically feasible, then the only choice may be to alter the required capacity to bring it to the level of the demonstrated capacity. This implies changing management's plans because the level of capacity will not be adequate to accomplish them.

The management of a manufacturing company requires the following information from capacity planning:

- Are the production plans that management desires to produce within the capacity of the plant?
- If not, what actions are required to bring the capacity of the plant to the level of those plans? How much will they cost?
- If it cannot be done, what is the best set of plans that can be achieved within the capacity of the plant?
- Is there a danger of exceeding the maximum capacity in any of the work centers in the immediate future?

Given this information, management can make good decisions about adjusting the plant capacities (such as buying machinery, increasing the size of the plant, working overtime, subcontracting, etc).

The key to all capacity planning is to make the necessary capacity decisions in advance, to ensure that the capacity requirements and demonstrated capacity remain consistent with each other. The failure of many companies in planning capacity is that they wait until the discrepancy that exists between demonstrated and required capacity creates a backlog or out-of-work condition severe enough to cause the action. In this case, capacity actions occur too late, and the company must suffer the symptoms of poor capacity planning before solving the problem.

CAPACITY ACTIONS

Where a discrepancy exists between required and demonstrated capacity, three courses of action can be taken to resolve the discrepancy:

1. Increase or decrease the demonstrated capacity by taking specific actions related to the work centers.
2. Increase or decrease the capacity requirement by adjusting the schedules.
3. Do some combination of the above.

Which action is appropriate is determined by the significance of the discrepancy and the significance of the impact of the capacity action on the company's production plans and business plans. For example, suppose the discrepancy between demonstrated and required capacity exists only in a few work centers and in certain periods. Then the two easiest solutions may be to take a small capacity action, such as working overtime to increase the demonstrated capacity, and to make a minor adjustment to some component schedules to smooth out the workload so that it can be handled by the existing demonstrated capacity.

However, if the discrepancy is significant enough to cause the company to miss its production plans, customer deliveries, and business plans, then the first choice is usually to find some way to change the demonstrated capacity so that the original plans can be met. If this cannot be done or if it is not economically feasible, then the choice of last resort may be to accept the fact that the plans will be missed and alter the plans. Depending on the circumstances, any of these choices can be a valid decision. The only decision that is always incorrect is the decision not to adjust either the demonstrated or the required capacity, to allow the schedules to be implemented with the discrepancy, and to hope that the product will come out as planned in the end. Because capacity decisions are somewhat subjective, it is easy to convince oneself that this is a good approach.

CAPACITY DECISIONS TO BE MADE

As discussed earlier, several capacity actions are possible. The capacity decision depends, in part, on the nature of the capacity discrepancy and its impact on the business plans. The appropriate action also depends on the planning time frame. In the long term, the impact on capacity of new products, markets, or businesses must be considered. Of equal importance are plans to eliminate old products or to exit from existing markets. Appropriate capacity decisions at this level center on plant and equipment issues.

In the medium term, a company is operating within an existing business plan that integrates plans for sales and marketing, engineering or R&D, manufacturing, and finance. Capacity decisions made during this time frame focus on meeting the goals of the business plan by achieving the production plan and staying within the manufacturing budgets. Appropriate decisions include increasing or decreasing labor force in selected work centers, adding or eliminating shifts, establishing or eliminating subcontract programs, and load leveling by manufacturing in advance of requirements.

The emphasis in the short term is to make the decisions needed to meet the due dates of master schedules and component orders. At this point, the options are somewhat limited because of the need to implement the action very quickly.

Typical short-term decisions include working overtime, using alternate work centers, and adjusting the labor force levels of the temporary work force. The time frame involved also determines which capacity planning tool is most appropriate. Fig. 15.1 illustrates which technique is used for each planning horizon and highlights the overlap that exists.

HOW CAPACITY PLANNING VARIES AMONG COMPANIES

The nature of the production environment influences the focus and use of the capacity planning techniques. Table 15.1 identifies some of the differences in material planning and manufacturing that have a bearing on the approach to capacity planning.

ROUGH-CUT CAPACITY PLANNING

Rough-cut capacity planning (RCCP), sometimes referred to as *resource requirements planning,* is the process of determining the long-range capacity a resource must provide. These resources include labor force and/or machines. RCCP is integrated with the production planning process. Production planning has five major functions:

1. Determine rates of output required for broad categories of products.
2. Allocate production capacity to products.
3. Communicate the output goals to the organization.
4. Authorize resources, in terms of material and labor, to support the output goals.
5. Serve as input to the financial plans.

RCCP supports the production planning process by analyzing various alternatives for capacity constraints as well as allocating capacity by product. RCCP is an iterative process of trying to balance the demonstrated capacity with the required capacity. The RCCP techniques used for validating the production plan are also very valuable when contingency or various long-range plans are developed. Used in this way, the rough-cut capacity plan is a "what if" simulator. As such, it must have the capability of being generated very quickly. The rough-cut capacity plan is used to identify the capacity actions necessary to bring the demonstrated capacity into

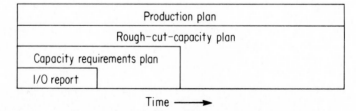

FIG. 15.1 Capacity planning horizons.

TABLE 15.1 How the Production Environment Affects Capacity Planning

Production Process	Production Environment		
	Job Shop or Batch Manufacturing	Repetitive Manufacturing	Process or Continuous Flow
Material planning	Many levels in bill of materials, material planning is complex	Few levels in bill of materials, material planning is less significant	Few levels in bill of materials, material planning is less significant
Manufacturing	Many different routings and work centers, products compete for capacity of work centers, long lead times	Dedicated facilities, lines, fewer scheduling points, similar/identical routings, short lead times, higher degree of automation	Dedicated facilities, lines, fewer scheduling points, similar/identical routings, short lead times, changeover time is significant, higher degree of automation
Capacity planning	Rough-cut capacity plan, master schedule summary, capacity requirements plan, input/output report, capacity constraints could involve people or equipment	Rough-cut capacity plan, master schedule summary, input/output report, capacity constraints usually involve equipment only	Rough-cut capacity plan, master schedule summary input/output report, capacity constraints usually involve equipment only

the "ballpark" with the capacity required to support the production plan. Note that this is not a replacement for the fine-tuning capability provided by CRP.

The rough-cut capacity plan is the major report. These steps are followed to calculate this report:

1. Select typical product structure.
2. Identify the critical resources.
3. Calculate the product load profile.
4. Calculate the rough-cut capacity plan.

Steps 1, 2, and 3 are discussed in detail in the section "Data Required."

The key ingredient in generating the rough-cut capacity plan is the product-load profile, which is a statement of the resources needed to produce 1 unit of product. Once these load profiles have been established, generating the plan is simply a matter of extending the profile by a proposed production plan. Table 15.2 is an example of a basic rough-cut capacity plan. It shows the total capacity required for each work center by product. It also compares the demonstrated capacity with the total capacity required for each work center and calculates the capacity actions in terms of hours. An important factor is service demand. If the service requirements use a significant amount of capacity, they must also be included in the rough-cut capacity plan.

Manufacturers with long lead times require rough-cut capacity plans produced in a time-phased format. An example is provided in Table 15.3. It shows a summary of the capacity required by product by month. It also includes the capacity required for service. The demonstrated capacity is compared to the total capacity required by month, and the capacity actions are calculated. For example, January's production plans generate capacity requirements in the mill three months earlier in October.

Horizon for Use

The length of the time period to the horizon for RCCP depends on the resources being analyzed but should be at least as long as the lead time needed to acquire the resources. As shown earlier, the rough-cut capacity plan horizon extends beyond the horizon for CRP to the end of the production planning horizon, which is typically 12 to 24 months.

Who Uses It?

As described earlier, the rough-cut capacity plan is used to validate the production plan. Development of the production plan is the responsibility of the general manager but also of executives from manufacturing, marketing, materials, engineering, and finance. A key component of the process is the production planning meeting. For most companies, the meeting is held monthly. At the meeting, the management team reviews past performance, looks at the forecast, discusses the need for changes, and reviews the alternatives. RCCP is used to identify the allocation of capacity to products and to highlight any resource constraints. The primary people involved in the RCCP process are the master scheduler, who is often responsible for maintaining changes to the production plan, and the manufacturing manager, who is responsible for making changes to capacity. The result of this process is an agreed-on company game plan which has been checked for validity.

TABLE 15.2 Rough-Cut Capacity Plan

| Work Center | Production Plan | | | Service | Required Capacity (hr) | Demonstrated Capacity (hr) | Capacity Action (hr) |
	Product X 10/mo	Product Y 20/mo	Product Z 30/mo				
001 Final assembly	800	500	300	0	3200	3000	−200
002 Mechanical subassembly	600	800	850	250	5000	5200	200
003 Electrical subassembly	200	320	400	150	2800	2900	100
004 Mill	500	200	200	450	3000	3000	0

· · ·

TABLE 15.3   Rough-Cut Capacity Plan with Time Phasing

Product	Production Plan					
Family	Jan.	Feb.	Mar.		Dec.	Totals
X (units)	1	1	1		0	10
Y	2	2	2		1	20
Z	1	1	1		0	10
. . .						
. . .						
. . .						

Rough-Cut Capacity Plan Work Center: 004 Mill						
Product Family	Oct.	Nov.	Dec.		Sep.	Totals
X (hr)	50	50	50		0	800
Y	50	50	50		25	500
Z	30	30	30		0	300

Product totals (hr)	350	400	375		360	4700
Service totals	50	75	65		40	800
Required capacity	400	475	440		400	5500
Demonstrated capacity	450	450	450		450	5400
Capacity action	50	−25	10		50	−100

Resultant Actions

When the required capacity exceeds the demonstrated capacity, the first choice is to take the actions required to increase the demonstrated capacity. Consider the example in Table 15.4. In this example, the company has three products, X, Y, and Z, and a service parts business.

The first five work centers shown are all overloaded. Possible solutions are increasing manpower, adding machines, shifting manpower, adding a shift, or subcontracting. Assuming that each worker can produce 2000 standard hours per year, the problems in final assembly and mechanical subassembly are minor and could probably be solved with overtime. An increase of one person should be planned in electrical subassembly. The overload in the mill does not justify additional manpower in itself, but a person could be hired if a similar overload exists in another work center where the person could be shifted as needed.

At first glance, the problem in the small turret lathes, work center 005, looks as though it could be solved by overtime. However, further inspection shows a better solution would be to transfer some work from the small to the large turret lathes where there will be excess capacity.

The problem in the special mill, work center 007, cannot be solved by hiring an additional person. In this work center, they are already working three shifts per day, 7 days per week. If additional capacity cannot be obtained when needed, then actions to reduce the required capacity should be considered. These include off-loading work, changing make-versus-buy decisions, or, as a last resort, changing the production plan. When changes to the production plan are considered, the rough-

TABLE 15.4 Sample Rough-Cut Capacity Plan with Overloaded Work Centers

Work Center	Production Plan (Units)			Service	Required Capacity	Demonstrated Capacity	Capacity Action
	Product X 10/mo	Product Y 20/mo	Product Z 10/mo				
001 Final assembly (hr)	1,800	1,500	1,300	0	4,000	4,600	−600
002 Mechanical subassembly	1,600	1,800	1,850	1,250	6,500	6,000	−500
003 Electrical subassembly	1,200	2,320	1,400	1,150	6,070	4,000	−2,070
004 Mill	1,500	1,200	1,200	1,450	5,350	4,000	−1,350
005 Small turret lathe	630	1,065	695	710	3,100	2,650	−450
006 Large turret lathe	665	940	760	105	2,470	3,250	780
007 Special mill	520	3,730	590	140	4,980	3,850	−1,130
⋮	⋮	⋮	⋮	⋮	⋮	⋮	⋮
⋮	⋮	⋮	⋮	⋮	⋮	⋮	⋮
⋮	⋮	⋮	⋮	⋮	⋮	⋮	⋮
Totals	12,600	12,750	9,985	7,500	42,835	− 42,510	−325

cut capacity plan is a key tool since it identifies the allocation of capacity by product. However, this particular mill has some special features that are needed. Jobs routed to this machine cannot be run on any other mill in the plant. There is a 1-year lead time to get a new machine from the manufacturer, and it will take 8 months to get into a subcontractor's schedule. In this case, the production plan must be changed. The rough-cut capacity plan highlights the need to change the production plan for product Y. Making this change would affect marketing, finance, materials, engineering, and manufacturing. Obviously, this problem should be solved at the production planning meeting where all functions are represented.

Frequently, there is a tendency to avoid giving any details to top management. Simply providing the management team with plant summaries, however, can be very misleading. For example, Table 15.5 shows that 42,835 hr are required plant-wide to support the production plan. The total demonstrated capacity is 42,510. This gives the illusion that there are no capacity problems when, in fact, some work centers have serious problems. On the other hand, supplying management with the details of a few hundred work centers can be equally ineffective. The key is to provide a sufficient level of detail for the significant areas, which are the critical resources.

When the required capacity is less than the demonstrated capacity, the first choice is to take the actions required to reduce the demonstrated capacity. This example shows several work centers in an underloaded situation. Appropriate actions could include planning to shift manpower, reducing the work force, or eliminating a shift. A layoff of one worker in electrical subassembly might be planned first. Layoffs of one in both final assembly and mechanical subassembly would be planned for some point during the year. The decision at the mill is not as clear-cut. Suppose another mill work center has an overload. In this case, a layoff would not be planned. Instead, a shift in manpower would be planned as required. What if it were highly undesirable to lose the critical skills of the mill operators? Then actions to increase the required capacity would be considered, including changing the subcontract decision, releasing work early, changing the make-versus-buy decision, or changing the production plan.

Data Required

Generating the rough-cut capacity plan requires the establishment of a product-load profile. To build these profiles, a company must first select a typical product structure and identify the critical resources.

Selecting a Typical Product Structure. A typical product structure can be defined by using a standard configuration plus the popular options, planning bills of materials, or the most popular end item. Planning bills are used by make-to-order and assemble-to-order companies to forecast top-level components. Planning bills consist of all top-level components with the corresponding quantity per and planning percentage. This percentage represents the forecasted popularity for the component. Table 15.6 gives an example.

Identifying Critical Resources. Those resources which usually become overloaded when the schedule is increased or run out of work when the schedule is reduced are *critical resources*. These work centers represent the major constraints

TABLE 15.5   Sample Rough-Cut Capacity Plan with Underloaded Work Centers

Work Center	Production Plan				Required Capacity	Demonstrated Capacity	Capacity Action
	Product X 10/mo	Product Y 20/mo	Product Z 10/mo	Service			
001 Final assembly (hr)	1,800	1,500	1,300	0	4,600	6,000	1,400
002 Mechanical subassembly	1,600	1,800	1,850	1,250	6,500	8,000	1,500
003 Electrical subassembly	1,200	2,320	1,400	1,150	6,070	8,000	1,930
004 Mill	1,500	1,200	1,200	1,450	5,350	6,000	650
⋮	⋮	⋮	⋮	⋮	⋮	⋮	⋮
⋮	⋮	⋮	⋮	⋮	⋮	⋮	⋮
Totals	12,600	12,750	9,985	7,500	42,835	50,000	7,165

TABLE 15.6 Planning Bill of Materials

Part Number	Description	Quantity per	Planning Percentage
Product Family X			
5020A	Common parts	1.0	100
6801A	Case	1.0	80
6801B	Case	1.0	20
7525A	Motor	1.0	40
7525B	Motor	1.0	50
7525C	Motor	1.0	10
.	.	.	.
.	.	.	.
.	.	.	.

to changing the plans and usually are reviewed first. Work centers could be a constraint for one or more of the following reasons:

- Subcontracting is difficult and costly.
- New equipment is costly or has a long lead time.
- Skilled operators are not readily available.
- Work centers are bottlenecked under normal conditions and always require overtime.
- Alternate routings are not available or have significant cost or schedule implications.
- There is a proprietary or sole-source process or operation.

Critical resources do not have to be limited to work centers. They could also include other resources that vary with volume such as engineering, numerical control programming, or storage space.

Calculating the Product-Load Profiles.   The rough-cut capacity plan is calculated by using a product-load profile. Synonymous terms include *bill of labor, bill of capacity,* and *bill of resources*. In its simplest form, the product-load profile may be created manually from estimated times and include only critical work centers. Or it may be constructed with computerized methods by utilizing a typical product structure and time standards on the routings. Here is the logic for calculating the product-load profile:

1. Process each part in the product structure on a level-by-level basis.
2. For each part, calculate the setup per piece by dividing the setup time by the standard lot size.
3. Compute the total time per piece by adding the setup time per piece and the run time per piece.
4. Extend the total time per piece by the total quantity required on the bill of materials.
5. Summarize the hours by work center.

Consider the following example. Figure 15.2 shows the product structure for product X. The numbers in parentheses are the quantity of each item used to make 1

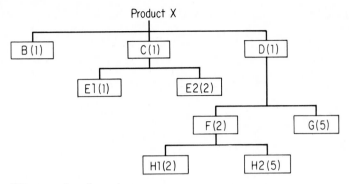

FIG. 15.2 Sample product structure.

unit of its parent item. In this example, part numbers B, G, and H2 are routed over the mill, work center 004. The routings for these parts are shown in Table 15.7.

In this example, the setup time per piece for part number B in the mill is 2.50 divided by the standard lot size of 10, or 0.25 hr. Adding the run time per piece of 10.00 hr yields a total per piece of 10.25 hr. It takes one B to build 1 unit of product X. This requires 10.25 hr for the mill, work center 004. For part number G, the setup time per piece is 1.25/5, or 0.25 hr, and the run time per piece is 2.5 hr for a total time per piece of 2.75 hr. The milling time required for part number G is calculated from the quantity per (5) times the total time per piece (2.75), or 13.75 hr. To calculate the hours of milling required for part number H2, each level of the bill must be processed first to determine the total quantity required. By examining the product structure, it can be seen that 10 of part number H2 are required to build 1 unit of product X (that is, 2 of part number F are required, and each F requires 5 of H2). The setup time per piece for part number H2 is 5.00/50, or 0.10 hr, and the run time per piece is 2.50 hr for a total of 2.60 mill hr per piece. Multiplying by the total quantity required (10) gives a total of 26 mill hr required. This process is continued for each part number on the routings. Then the totals by work center are calculated to give a product-load profile. For product X, there are 10.25 + 13.75 + 26.00 hr required on the mill, or a total of 50 hr as shown in Table 15.8.

Manufacturers with long lead times require the use of product-load profiles with lead-time offsets to facilitate time-phased planning capability. This requires a change in the logic to calculate the product-load profiles. Back-scheduling logic can be modified to determine a lead-time offset for each operation on the routing. Standard back-scheduling logic begins with the last operation and works back to the first operation, calculating when each operation will take place. The calculation considers move time and queue time as well as the setup time and run time. The *move time* is the time required to move pieces between operations. The *queue time* is the time that pieces are planned to wait at a work center before work is initiated. Referring to the routing for part number B, Table 15.9 shows the back-scheduling detail for each operation. Note that the quantity of B required to make 1 unit of product X would be 1. All times are expressed in hours.

Part number B is used in the final assembly of product X. The final assembly requires 2 weeks; therefore, operation 030 has an offset of 3 weeks. In other words, operation 030 must take place 3 weeks prior to shipping product X. The offset for operation 020 would be 4 weeks. And finally, the offset for operation 010, at the mill, would be 5 weeks. The offsets are calculated for each operation of every part

TABLE 15.7 Sample Routings

Operation		Work Center	Department	Setup Hours	Run Hours
		Part Number B	Standard Lot Size: 10		
010	Mill	004	02	2.50	10.00
020	Grind	008	02	1.50	10.50
030	Inspect	100	10	4.00	8.00
		Part Number G	Standard Lot Size: 5		
010	Saw	011	02	.50	2.75
020	Lathe	015	02	3.30	4.85
030	Mill	004	02	1.25	2.50
040	Grind	008	02	1.15	8.55
050	Inspect	100	10	3.20	4.75
		Part Number H2	Standard Lot Size: 50		
010	Saw	011	02	.75	3.15
020	Mill	004	02	5.00	2.50
030	Grind	008	02	2.25	7.75
040	Inspect	100	10	2.10	3.50

TABLE 15.8 Product-Load Profile

		Product		
	Work Center	X	Y	Z
001	Final assembly (hr)	80	25	30
002	Mechanical subassembly	60	40	85
003	Electrical subassembly	20	16	40
004	Mill	50	10	20
	.			
	.			
	.			

TABLE 15.9 Example of Lead-Time Offset Calculation

	Element of Lead-Time	Hours	Lead-Time Offset (Weeks)
Final assembly lead-time	Assembly	40	1
	Assembly	40	2
	Move	8	
	Operation 030	12	3
	Queue	20	
	Move	4	
Part number B lead-time	Operation 020	12	4
	Queue	24	
	Move	6	
	Operation 010	12.50	5
	Queue	22	

number through each level in the product structure. The hours are then summarized by work center by week. Table 15.10 gives an example of a product-load
profile with lead-time offsets. Note that the hours in a work center may fall in more
than one week. Many times the production plan is specified as a monthly rate. In
that case, lead-time offsets can be calculated in months instead of weeks.

Accounting for Service.   If a forecast of service demand by part number is available, it can be extended by the routings for each item in the product structure to give
the capacity required by work center. Sometimes a unit forecast is not available. In
this case, various techniques can be used to estimate the capacity required for
service. One method is to build a load profile based on dollar volume. Table 15.11
shows an example of such a profile. The capacity required for service parts is
calculated simply by extending the planned dollar volume at cost by this profile.
The hours for this special profile can be estimated by calculating the load hours for a
sample of popular service parts.

CAPACITY REQUIREMENTS PLANNING

Capacity planning in the medium range is a much more detailed process than the
rough-cut process described earlier. In the medium range, capacity requirements
can be calculated from released and planned manufacturing orders rather than the
approximation techniques of RCCP. Attempting to balance demonstrated capacity
with required capacity through the use of capacity actions is still the goal. With
CRP, the plans are further refined. Using CRP to make fine-tuning adjustments to
capacities or schedules requires that the demonstrated capacity be in the ballpark
with the capacity required to support the production plan. Management uses
rough-cut techniques to achieve this balance. Attempting to make major changes
based on the capacity requirements plan in the short to medium range is both very
difficult and expensive.

Capacity is used in both productive and nonproductive ways. Capacity utilized
for productive purposes is typically measured in standard hours of output, because
standard hours represent a good common denominator. For instance, if a work
center produces many different types of products or components, measuring in
units of product input or output could be very misleading. If, however, a work
center always produces the same product, capacity could be measured in product
units. Nonproductive capacity drains include downtime, operator breaks, inspection time, delays, absent time, operator inefficiency, scrap, and rework. By measur-

TABLE 15.10   Product-Load Profile with Lead-Time Offsets

Work Center	Lead-Time Offset (Weeks)						17	18	19	20
	1	2	3	4	5					
Product Family X										
001 Final assembly	40	40								
002 Mechanical subassembly			30	20						
003 Electrical subassembly			20							
004 Mill			10	40	12					
.										
.										
.										

TABLE 15.11 Product-Load Profile
for Service Parts

Work Center	Hours per $1000 Sales
002 Mechanical subassembly	100
003 Electrical subassembly	95
004 Mill	88
.	
.	
.	

ing in standard hours, these variables can be excluded from the process. Utilizing standard hours also facilitates having a consistent measure between input and output.

An example of a CRP is given in Table 15.12. This report summarizes by work center all the scheduled hours needed to produce the orders currently released to the shop and those that are being planned. The data are displayed in a weekly time-phased format. The scheduled hours are also graphed as a percentage of demonstrated capacity. The X's represent that portion of the load which is derived from released orders while the **X**'s indicate the percentage of capacity needed for planned orders. When adjustments are considered, the details of the capacity requirements are needed. The system should enable the facility to view the details of any selected week.

Table 15.13 shows the part number/order number detail associated with the week of October 27. When this report is used, it is important to remember that it shows scheduled hours. There is no guarantee that the hours will actually happen this way. Feeding work centers determine when the load will actually occur. In the example, 150 hr is shown in the week of October 27, and 850 hr is shown the following week. It is more likely that work will flow at 500 hr/wk because feeding work centers are more likely to produce at a steadier rate than the way the work is scheduled. Work-in-process reporting makes it possible to exclude work which has already been completed. Calculating scheduled hours for planned orders can be accomplished by back scheduling them in the same way the released orders were scheduled.

Horizon for Use

The length of the horizon for CRP depends on the length of the manufacturing lead times. Typically, this horizon is 3 months to 1 year. As shown earlier, the CRP horizon covers the short and medium term, whereas the horizon for RCCP extends to the end of the production planning horizon.

Who Uses It?

The capacity requirements plan is used by shop management to help execute the plans on a timely basis. The key users of the capacity requirements plan are the capacity planners or shop planners and the shop supervisors. When changes to the capacity requirements are needed, the shop planners must also communicate with the material planners and/or master schedulers. A crucial part of the process is the weekly capacity meeting. Prior to the meeting, the shop planners should review the

TABLE 15.12 Example of a CRP

Demonstrated Capacity: 500 Standard hr/wk.

Week	Hours	0%	100%	200%
Past due	150	XXX*		
9/15	550	XXXXXXXXXX**XX**		
9/22	600	XXXXXXXXX**XXXX**		
9/29	500	XXXXXXXX**XXX**		
10/6	400	XXXXXX**XX**		
10/13	550	XXXXX**XXXXX**		
10/20	250	XXX**XX**		
10/27	150	XX**X**		
11/4	850	XX**XXXXXXXXXXXXXX**		

* X = released order load; **X** = planned order load.

TABLE 15.13 Example of CRP Detail Display

Workcenter BHJ, Department 038

Week	Hours	Part Number	Order Number	Type
10/27	21.3	7-1007	101	REL
10/27	36.9	8-8162	123	REL
10/27	19.2	7-2152	118	REL
10/27	14.6	6-3894	134	REL
10/27	26.8	4-9833	115	REL
10/27	31.2	2-1102	999	PLN
	150.0			

REL = released order; PLN = planned order.

capacity requirements plan and identify future capacity problems. They should also work with the shop supervisors to develop potential capacity actions. At the weekly capacity meeting, the shop planners can review the future capacity problems with the manufacturing manager and shop supervisors and, as a group, agree on action plans to solve the problems. As a part of the meeting, they can also measure the results of previous capacity actions.

Resultant Actions

The rough-cut techniques of capacity planning allow the firm to make the longer-term plant and equipment decisions. These techniques also facilitate the development of general plans for additional shifts, overtime, subcontracting, etc. Since CRP is using more precise data, the tentative capacity plans can be further refined. The goal in CRP is to balance blocks of capacity requirements with blocks of demonstrated capacity. The capacity requirements are analyzed on a cumulative basis in Table 15.14. Reviewing this report reveals that management has done a good job of providing enough capacity to support the plans. Even though the weekly display of these same capacity requirements illustrated in Table 15.12 shows some peaks and valleys, over the next 8 weeks the required and demonstrated capacities are in balance. Based on these reports, no capacity actions would be taken.

Now review the capacity requirements plan shown in Table 15.15. Assume this work center is currently working one 8-hr shift per day. The data indicate the need

TABLE 15.14 Example of Capacity Requirements Shown on a Cumulative Basis

Demonstrated Capacity: 500 Standard hr/wk

Week	Cumulative Hours	0%	100%	200%
Past due	150	XXX*		
9/15	700	XXXXXXXXXXXXXX		
9/22	1300	XXXXXXXXXXXXX		
9/29	1800	XXXXXXXXXXXX		
10/6	2200	XXXXXXXXXXX		
10/13	2750	XXXXXXXXXXX		
10/20	3000	XXXXXXXXXX		
10/27	3150	XXXXXXXXX		
11/4	4000	XXXXXXXXXX		

* X = released order load; **X** = planned order load.

TABLE 15.15 Overloaded CRP

Demonstrated Capacity: 500 Standard hr/wk

Week	Hours	0%	100%	200%
Past due	1000	XXXXXXXXXXXXXXXXXXXXX*		
9/15	700	XXXXXXXXXXXXX		
9/22	850	XXXXXXXXXXXXXXXX		
9/29	1050	XXXXXXXXXXXXXXXXXXXXXX		
10/6	800	XXXXXXXXXXXXXXX		
10/13	1050	XXXXXXXXXXXXXXXXXXXXXX		
10/20	850	XXXXXXXXXXXXXXXX		
10/27	700	XXXXXXXXXXXXX		
11/4	1000	XXXXXXXXXXXXXXXXXXXX		

* X = released order load; **X** = planned order load.

to add a second shift or implement a subcontract program. Actually, a two-phased plan might be used. Since it may take some time to add a shift or implement a plan to subcontract, overtime may be used in the interim. If a subcontract program were used, the CRP detail report would identify specific orders as candidates for the program.

Next, consider the cumulative plan in Table 15.16. Clearly the demonstrated capacity is too high and should be reduced. In this one, the second shift would be eliminated.

The example shown in Table 15.17 is for a gateway work center. It appears that this work center will run out of work next week. Further inspection, however, shows an overload the following week. The overload is coming from orders that have not yet been released to the shop. They are still in a planned state. The appropriate action, in this case, is to release some of these planned orders 1 week early. The capacity planner would use the CRP detail report to make selections and then would review this plan with the appropriate master scheduler or material planner.

TABLE 15.16   Underloaded CRP

Demonstrated Capacity: 1000 Standard hr/wk

Week	Hours	0%	100%	200%
Past due	150	XX*		
9/15	550	XXXXXX		
9/22	600	XXXXXX		
9/29	500	XXXX**X**		
10/6	400	XX**XX**		
10/13	550	XXX**XXX**		
10/20	250	X**XX**		
10/27	150	X**X**		
11/4	850	XX**XXXXXXX**		

* X = released order load; **X** = planned order load.

TABLE 15.17   Example of Early Release

Demonstrated Capacity: 500 Standard hr/wk

Week	Hours	0%	100%	200%
Past due	150	XXX*		
9/15	550	XXXXXXXXX**XX**		
9/22	150	XX**X**		
9/29	850	XXXXX**XXXXXXXXXXXX**		
10/6	400	XXXX**XXXX**		
10/13	550	XXXX**XXXXX**		
10/20	250	XX**XXX**		
10/27	600	XXXX**XXXXXXXX**		
11/4	500	XX**XXXXXXXX**		

* X = released order load; **X** = planned order load.

Data Required

To accomplish CRP, the following information must be available.

Routings.   The manufacturing routing describes the manufacturing process required to produce a component, or product. As a minimum, it defines the basic manufacturing operations or steps, the work centers where those operations are performed, and the time required to set up and complete each operation. Sometimes the routings contain information about the tools required for each operation or alternate routing information. The setup and run times can be expressed as standard times or may represent estimated times.

The manufacturing routing information is stored in the routing file. Then these data are used to calculate the timing of the capacity requirements and to identify the work centers in which the required capacity is scheduled. These data are also used by the shop floor control system to calculate the operation start and due dates for each operation. The detailed scheduling process is called *back scheduling* since the process begins with the order due date and calculates backward from the last operation to the first, accounting for the move, queue, setup, and run times. A copy of the routing and the result of this calculation are stored in the work-in-process file. This file is used for tracking an order through the manufacturing process. Since it contains the information about all uncompleted operations for released shop orders, it is also used to calculate the capacity requirements for these orders.

For planned orders, the routing file is also used in combination with the back-scheduling logic to calculate a temporary shop order detail file. This file is used to calculate the remainder of the capacity requirements.

Time Standards.   Many companies question the accuracy of their standard times and wonder whether they are sufficient. Typically, companies track a *productivity ratio* that measures standard hours produced per clock hour. This ratio can be very helpful for capacity planning. Assume a given work center has a productivity ratio of 0.75. This means that for every clock hour, this work center produces three-quarters of a standard hour. This could be the result of inaccurate time standards, machine downtime, or other delays. This ratio reflects the sum of all the possible reasons. If the capacity requirements were 180 standard hr/wk higher than demonstrated, then this work center would need an additional 240 clock hours (that is, 180 standard hours per week ÷ .75). This ratio varies by work center and represents an average of all jobs produced at each. For this ratio to be a valid technique to compensate for inaccurate standards, the standards must be set consistently. It is also vital to have a complete set of standards.

INPUT/OUTPUT CONTROL

In the short range, capacity management is concerned with measuring the flow of work into a work center and actual output delivered, comparing them to planned levels, and taking short-term capacity actions. Input/output control is the technique used for this purpose. The input/output report is a control device used to monitor the flow of work through the shop. It is an excellent tool for determining bottlenecks. This report provides a way to measure work center performance in terms of how well the actual amount of work that arrives in a work center compared to plan and the actual amount of work completed at a work center compares to its plan.

Initially, plans for input and output are developed for each work center. Then actual data are collected for input and output. These deviations to input and output are then calculated and compared to predefined tolerances for each. Work centers that are out of tolerance should be reviewed for possible capacity actions or scheduling changes.

The input/output report should also list the status of the backlog. This backlog of orders at a work center is called the *queue*. The *total queue* is the total amount of work available to be processed regardless of priority or schedule dates. This work may be located in or near the work center or elsewhere. The *planned queue* is the number used in the scheduling system to represent the expected time an on-schedule order will wait in the work center before processing. This figure is also used to calculate manufacturing lead times. The *current queue* is the amount of work available to be processed that is prioritized ahead of the order that enters the queue right on schedule. The current queue is calculated by totaling all the work that is available and scheduled prior to the current date plus the number of planned queue days for the work center.

The objective for queues is for the planned and total queue to be as small as possible without losing capacity because of a lack of work. The queues represent a buffer to prevent work centers from running out of work owing to material-handling problems, missed delivery dates from vendors and feeding departments, changing master schedules, quality problems, unavailable tooling, etc. Actual queues are a result of how well capacity is planned and how well the capacity plans are executed. If the input to a work center exceeds the output for any reason, the queue in the work center will grow. Input will exceed output under the following conditions:

- The input plan is not valid and is understated (poor plan).
- Actual input exceeds a valid plan (poor execution).
- The output plan is not valid and is overstated (poor plan).
- Actual output is less than a valid plan (poor execution).

It is important to measure input, output, and queues continuously to identify problems quickly and keep queues under control.

Horizon for Use

The input/output report provides a snapshot of recent history to show what actually happened. Typically, companies look back 4 to 8 weeks. The future input and output plans are generally developed for a 6- to 8-week horizon.

Who Uses It?

As with CRP, the key users of the input/output report are the shop planners and foremen. The input/output reports are used in combination with the capacity requirements plans to identify capacity actions. A key part of the process again is the weekly capacity meeting. Prior to the meeting, the shop planners and shop supervisors review out-of-tolerance work centers identified by the input/output report. At the meeting, the problem work centers are discussed, capacity actions are determined, and warnings are given to related work centers that might also be affected. This meeting is usually attended by the manufacturing manager, the capacity planner or shop planner, and the shop supervisors.

Resultant Actions

The input/output report is the major tool for making short-term capacity actions. Look at the capacity requirements plan shown in Table 15.18. Based on this report alone, overtime would be scheduled. If the corresponding input/output report looked like the one shown in Table 15.19, this would be a good decision. However, if the input/output report looked like the one shown in Table 15.20, then the overtime decision would not be appropriate. The capacity requirements plan reflects the hours scheduled in this work center, not the load that is actually in the work center. The last input/output report shows that the actual input has not arrived. The problem in this case is coming from a feeding work center.

On the other hand, the capacity requirements plan shown in Table 15.21, makes it appear that no capacity actions are needed. However, the corresponding input/output report shown in Table 15.22 makes it clear that an output problem has existed for several weeks and if output is not increased quickly, a significant backlog will result. Overtime might very well be used to stay on schedule. Even though the capacity requirements plan shows no serious problem, the input/output report is an early warning that one will occur.

TABLE 15.18   Example of Front-End-Loaded Capacity Requirements

Demonstrated Capacity: 450 Standard hr/wk

Week	Cumulative Hours	0%	100%	200%
Past due	270	XXXXXX*		
9/15	720	XXXXXXXXXXXXXXXX		
9/22	1260	XXXXXXXXXXXXXX		
9/29	1620	XXXXXXXXXXXX		
10/6	1980	XXXXXXXXXXXX		
10/13	2475	XXXXXXXXXXX		
10/20	2700	XXXXXXXXXX		
10/27	3465	XXXXXXXXXXX		
11/4	3600	XXXXXXXXXX		

* X = released order load; **X** = planned order load.

TABLE 15.19   Example of an Output Problem

Input/Output Report, Department 038, Dispatch Center BHJ, 9/15

	8/18	8/25	9/01	9/08	9/15	9/22	9/29
			Tolerance: ±80 Std. hr				
Planned input	450	450	450	450	450	450	450
Actual input	480	440	490	460			
Deviation (accum.)	+30	+20	+60	+70			
	Tolerance: ±50 Std. hr		*Std. queue: 270*		*Actual queue: 520*		
Planned output	450	450	450	450	450	450	450
Actual output	380	410	390	430			
Deviation (accum.)	−70	−110	−170	−190			

TABLE 15.20   Example of an Input Problem

Input/Output Report, Department 038, Dispatch Center BHJ, 9/15

	8/18	8/25	9/01	9/08	9/15	9/22	9/29
			Tolerance: ±80 Std. hr				
Planned input	450	450	450	450	450	450	450
Actual input	420	390	400	380			
Deviation	−30	−90	−140	−210			
	Tolerance: ±50 Std. hr		*Std. queue: 270*		*Actual queue: 30*		
Planned output	450	450	450	450	450	450	450
Actual output	460	430	360	340			
Deviation	+10	−20	−110	−220			

TABLE 15.21 Example of a Work Center with an Output Problem

Demonstrated Capacity: 500 Standard hr/wk

Week	Hours	0%	100%	200%
Past due	400	XXXXXXXX*		
9/15	850	XXXXXXXXXXXXXXXX		
9/22	600	XXXXXXXXXXXX		
9/29	250	XXXXX		
10/6	500	XXXXXXXX**XX**		
10/13	150	X**XX**		
10/20	550	XXXXXXXX**XXX**		
10/27	150	X**XX**		
11/4	550	X**XXXXXXXXXX**		

* X = released order load; **X** = planned order load.

TABLE 15.22 Example of an Output Problem

Input/Output Report, Department 038, Dispatch Center BHJ

	8/18	8/25	9/01	9/08	9/15	9/22	9/29
	Tolerance: ±80 Std. hr						
Planned input	500	500	500	500	500	500	500
Actual input	510	485	530	490			
Deviation (accum.)	+10	−5	+25	+15			
	Tolerance: ±50 Std. hr		*Std. queue: 270*		*Actual queue: 520*		
Planned output	500	500	500	500	500	500	500
Actual output	420	460	450	390			
Deviation (accum.)	−80	−120	−170	−280			

Data Required

Developing Planned Input and Output.   Input plans are based on capacity requirements, work center queue targets, demonstrated capacity, and special considerations such as vacations, shut-down periods, rework history, etc. These figures are calculated by using a 4- to 12-week average of capacity requirements. The planned input numbers should be supplied by the capacity planner or shop planner. Planned output is based on demonstrated capacity plus any capacity actions needed to satisfy the capacity requirements. For example, suppose a work center has a demonstrated capacity of 72 standard hr/wk. There are two people who work 40 hr/wk, and their historical productivity ratio is 0.9. If a third person of equal capability were to be added as a capacity action, planned output would be 72 standard hr/wk plus 36 standard hr/wk from the new person (that is, 40 hr/wk × 0.9 demonstrated productivity), or 108 standard hr/wk. The planned output figures should be supplied by the shop supervisor who is responsible for achieving them.

Measuring Work Center Input and Output.   The shop floor reporting transactions are used to update the actual input and output totals. Specifically, the material arrival or movement transaction is used to update the actual input, and the operation completion transaction updates the actual output. The same standard hours must be used in both cases. These totals are then stored in the work center file.

Setting Tolerances. The purpose of establishing tolerances on input and output is to help identify problem situations that might require capacity actions or scheduling changes. Once these tolerances are established, control of the number of exceptions can be maintained by adjusting them. Higher tolerances reduce the exceptions to the worst cases. These tolerances are established by reviewing what has happened to each work center during a period of schedule stability. A level can be set that represents the normal ups and downs to be expected in both input and output. The key is to set the tolerance so that it identifies work centers that should be reviewed for capacity actions. The tolerances can vary among work centers because of the nature of each. The tolerances can be different for input and output of the same work center, because the reasons that cause input variances are different from those that produce output variances. For instance, the input rate of a work center can be erratic because of feeding work centers, while the output rate of the same work center depends on its scrap rates, absenteeism, time spent waiting for tools or materials, etc.

OTHER CAPACITY PLANNING TOOLS

MPS Summary

The MPS summary is a rough-cut tool used to ensure that the MPS is within the capacity allocated during the production planning and RCCP processes. An example of the report is shown in Table 15.23. MPS summaries are produced for each product family in the production plan. The report contains a monthly summary of the master schedules for every item in each product family. The MPS summary for a given product family is then compared to the corresponding production plan. If the MPS summary exceeds the production plan, then the capacity required to support the MPS will be greater than that specified in the rough-cut capacity plan. This can happen as a result of missed shipments carried over, safety stock applied to the MPS, lot sizing, or the accumulation of several individual master scheduling decisions. Through the normal course of business, new orders are taken, others are canceled, and reschedules are made. These decisions are made on an individual basis without a view to the total impact. The MPS summary brings together the resulting schedules for comparison to management's plans.

TABLE 15.23 Example of an MPS Summary

Product Family: Hook Assemblies (Units)

Item	Jan.	Feb.	Mar.	Apr.
H-2001	5,000	5,000	5,000	5,000
H-2522	2,500		2,500	3,500
H-3353		6,000		
H-4441	7,000		5,000	5,000
Total MPS	14,500	11,000	12,500	13,500
Production Plan	11,000	11,000	12,000	13,000

Finite Loading

The capacity planing approach called *finite loading* is defined by the *APICS Dictionary* as " . . . a computer technique that involves automatic shop priority revision in order to level load operation by operation." The process begins similarly to CRP by using the operation schedule dates calculated from back scheduling the released and planned shop orders. But as all capacity requirements are summarized, a comparison is made to the work center capacity. Whenever the work center capacity is exceeded, the system reschedules the load for future periods. After this process has been completed, shop order due dates may be scheduled out beyond the original due dates provided by the MRP system. It is also possible that these changes would necessitate changes to the MPS.

The concept of this approach, as stated in the *APICS Dictionary*, is to put " . . . no more work into a factory than the factory can be expected to execute." The use of this approach in a job shop environment is severely limited by the ability to accurately predict job arrivals. The actual input to a downstream work center depends on the output of feeding work centers. Problems such as scrap, rework, absenteeism, lack of material or tooling, lack of skilled operators, and equipment considerations can cause changes in the sequencing of jobs, and so the actual arrivals can differ from the predicted arrivals. The problem is magnified by the number of work centers and part numbers usually found in this environment. These inherent difficulties have resulted in a very limited application of the finite loading techniques.

Handling Specials

It is very important to handle specials and rework consistently among the planned and actual input and output totals. Two approaches are possible. The first is simpler and more common. In this case, hours for rework or specials are ignored in the plans or actual data. Since the capacity requirements plan does not reflect plans for these hours, it can be used as the primary source of information, as described earlier in developing the input plans. Care must be taken, however, that *both* input and output totals do not include reporting of specials. In this way, only standard hours for planned work are developed and tracked.

The second approach attempts to plan for specials and then includes them in the tracking. The process of developing the input plans begins in the same way, by calculating an average of capacity requirements. Since this does not include any hours for rework or specials, an adjustment must be made. This adjustment is based on an historical percentage for each work center. With this approach, the shop floor reporting transactions for specials are used to update actual input and output totals. Companies that choose this approach spend a significant amount of time on this type of work and usually have an adequate historical base from which to plan.

PLANNING CAPACITY IN INDIRECT AREAS

As mentioned earlier, critical resources being planned do not have to be limited to direct areas, but can be for other resources as well. Capacity requirements can also be developed for any indirect area. For instance, suppose quality control represents a significant portion of the lead time. Further suppose that bottlenecks in this area are a frequent source of missed due dates. After inspection operations are added to the routings, capacity requirements can be calculated, and capacity requirements plans can be generated for quality control work centers.

By having quality control operations on the routings, they also become a part of the work-in-process file that is created for released shop orders. Shop floor control transactions then update actual input and output totals for these work centers, and input/output reports can be prepared. Any area that can be a serious bottleneck in the manufacturing process is a candidate to be handled in this manner. Other possibilities include production control, the stockroom, receiving, tool supply, and engineering.

CAPACITY PLANNING ORGANIZATION

Capacity planning responsibility traditionally has been divided among several positions within the manufacturing organization. The rough-cut capacity plan and the MPS summary are tools used primarily by the master scheduler. The capacity requirements plan is used primarily by the shop planner, and the input/output report is a tool for the shop supervisors and dispatchers. A new trend is now emerging where a position of capacity planner is given responsibility for ensuring that capacity is considered in the decision-making process at all levels. This position generally reports to the manufacturing manager and works closely with top management, the planning organization, and the shop management to plan and control capacity.

MAKING CAPACITY PLANNING HAPPEN

Approaches to managing capacity have evolved very rapidly in recent years, and few companies have operated with all four of the capacity planning techniques (rough-cut capacity plan, MPS summary, capacity requirements plan, and input/output report). Many times, capacity policies are missing, responsibilities are not defined, and operating procedures are not complete. The following steps are crucial to effectively overcome these and other implementation problems:

1. Educate those involved in the concepts of capacity planning.
2. Define levels of authority and responsibility.
3. Install all four techniques.
4. Publish policies on the use of the capacity planning techniques.
5. Ensure accountability through the use of effective management involvement.
6. Define the necessary procedures. Be sure to consider handling of rework, specials, split lots, etc.
7. Establish formal capacity meetings to review capacity problems, agree on capacity actions, and measure prior actions.

REFERENCES

1. Thomas F. Wallace (ed.), *APICS Dictionary*, 5th ed., APICS, Falls Church, Va., 1984.

BIBLIOGRAPHY

Berry, William L., Thomas E. Vollmann, and D. Clay Whybark: *Master Production Scheduling*, American Production and Inventory Control Society, Falls Church, Va., 1979.

Capacity Planning and Control, APICS, Falls Church, Va., 1975.

Gips, Jack: *The "How to" Course of Shop Floor Control and Capacity Planning*, Jack Gips, Inc., Chagrin Falls, Oh., 1985.

Rao, Ashok: *Capacity Management*, APICS Training Aid. APICS, Falls Church, Va., 1982.

Production Activity Control

Editor:

HAL MATHER, CFPIM, President, Hal Mather, Inc., Atlanta, Georgia

Contributors:

FRANK GUE, Manager, Inventory Programs, Corporate Productivity Services, Westinghouse Canada, Hamilton, Ontario

ED HEARD, CFPIM, President, Ed Heard and Associates, Inc., Columbia, South Carolina

PAUL MARANKA, CFPIM, Corporate Manager, Material Systems, Copeland Corporation, Sidney, Ohio

TIM McENENY, CFPIM, President, Tim McEneny, Inc., Holmdel, New Jersey

A routing system contains the detailed plans of how to process work through a factory. These plans are created for all items from completion schedules, the process specifications or routings, and the detailed scheduling system.

A dispatching system authorizes production of specific items and collects data about their production. These two systems, the routing and scheduling, interact so that changes in scheduling and routing result in items being dispatched in their correct sequence. The dispatching feedback loop compares the actual production against the routing system plan and creates management performance reports highlighting out-of-control or problem areas.

Routing and dispatching systems must cope with the changes that are a way of life in manufacturing companies. Materials may need to be processed differently because they are not to specification or because the regular processes are overloaded with more urgent work. Machines break down, scrap occurs, rework needs to be scheduled, etc. Each disruption has an impact on the planned flow of production. Decisions that minimize the disruption that these unplanned events cause are largely based on the information provided by the routing system. The routing system in turn must be updated with these decisions so that it remains current and can support correct dispatching activities.

Company resources, including materials, direct labor, and machines, are committed through routing and dispatching systems. Specific items to be produced are selected and released to the starting operations by a work authorization step. What items to produce and their sequence at the secondary work centers are controlled through dispatching. Commitment of a company's resources to specific products is crucial to the success of the whole manufacturing enterprise.

Actual production data are collected and used to update the routing system and create various reports. Data collection methods can range from verbal notifications to the use of sophisticated computer terminals and scanning devices. To make good dispatching decisions, the speed and formality of data collection must match the type of routing system and the timing of the data used.

Reports from the system must consider both the need for inquiry, for example, the status of a particular job, and the need to highlight the unusual, for example, a work center with inadequate capacity. These reports must be easily aggregated to provide the proper degree of detail for all management levels to assist them in developing the right corrective action to ensure that most production is completed on schedule.

EXECUTION PHASE OF PLANNING

Routing systems are the basis for the actual execution of activities. As such, they must link to the various plans created earlier in the planning and control process. This linkage is shown schematically in Fig. 16.1. The inventory planning process selects the items to be produced based on their characteristics and the degree of manufacturing sophistication available.

A master production schedule (MPS) driving material-requirements planning (MRP) will create planned orders for all dependent demand items in a product's bill of materials. When the start date for a planned order item approaches today's date, it is a candidate for release to the factory. A list of all the items with current start dates becomes an input to the routing system (Table 16.1).

For make-to-stock products or service parts, actual warehouse replenishment is often controlled through a time-phased order-point system. This is similar to MRP except it is for independent demand items. Planned orders are generated based on a forecast of sales netted against warehouse inventory. These planned orders become candidates for the routing system in much the same way as those for MRP. But now the planned orders are for final assembly, packaging, or finishing only.

Some companies use a standard order point for inventory replenishment. In this case, items become candidates for production only when the inventory level drops below the order point. Some companies schedule items based on the ratio of available inventory to the order point, which provides better visibility for the routing system and assists in leveling the flow of work to the plant (Table 16.2). Candidates for release are those items with a ratio close to 1.00.

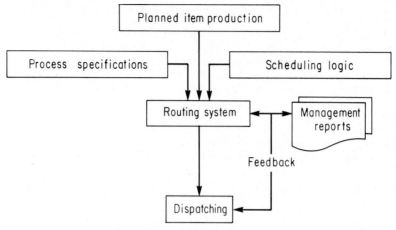

FIG. 16.1 Routing and dispatching relationship.

TABLE 16.1 Planned Production Order Release

Planned Order Release, Release Period 1

Part Number	Quantity	Period Due
1234A	60	6
2354A	175	8
1434A	225	7
4321B	90	6

TABLE 16.2 Order-Point Items for Release

Part Number	Available	Order Point	Ratio	Lot Size
39762	964	1020	0.95	500
42354	345	315	1.10	200
61729	563	510	1.10	150
10438	796	695	1.15	1000

The specifications to make each item define the amount of each production resource required. Specifications can include labor skills, machinery, tooling, and even the materials or parts required. All items to be produced need detailed schedules for checking their progress through the factory. These are developed from the logic built into the scheduling subsystem. The result is operation dates for all jobs to be run.

The routing system is now complete. It is a data base of jobs authorized to be produced, with each process step dated. The standard process specifications may need to be overridden to relieve machinery overloads, cope with offspec materials, or to handle rework. These overridden standard process specifications must be entered into the routing system to create a complete picture of the upcoming production activities.

Dispatching concerns itself with the release of work to the factory and its progress through the various steps in the process. The sequence of work released and the determination of their subsequent priority at secondary work centers come from the routing system details. A key ingredient of dispatching is the feedback of actual production information to the routing system. Actual production steps completed, scrap generated, hours worked, and so on are used to update the status of all work in process. Performance and status reports are a natural result of comparing actual production to the plan.

The financial system is often tied directly to the routing and dispatching system. Work-in-process inventory values are determined from the up-to-date routing information. Job costs, variances, and labor distributions are calculated by comparing actual production activities with the standard. The results are a complete picture of the financial aspects of the factory operation.

WORK AUTHORIZATION

All production should be authorized in such a way that company resources are spent only on needed items. This is usually done by inventory planners, who review the candidates for production and select only those actually needed. In small companies, the authorization can come from the owner, manager, or supervisor.

Order Release

Someone has to decide that the production of a specific quantity of an item is needed by a certain date. The candidates for production come from

- The need for an item to support a customer's order
- An item appearing on a planned-order report initiated by a material-requirements plan or a time-phased order-point calculation
- An item that has tripped its reorder point, or the ratio of the available quantity to order-point quantity is close to 1.00

In any case, the item cannot be automatically released to the factory floor. Parameters in the planning system could be faulty, causing the appearance of a need to order that is untrue. Maybe capacity, tooling, or materials are not available to produce the item at this time. This means a review must occur before the order is released to the routing system, especially if items are candidates for order release from the last two causes. Capacity, tooling, and materials must be checked and adjustments made to the process specifications, order quantities, or completion dates, if needed. Only when the review process is complete should the order be released to the routing system.

Job Shops

The typical result of the inventory planner's review process is the creation of a shop order authorization form (Fig. 16.2). This form is then sent to the department

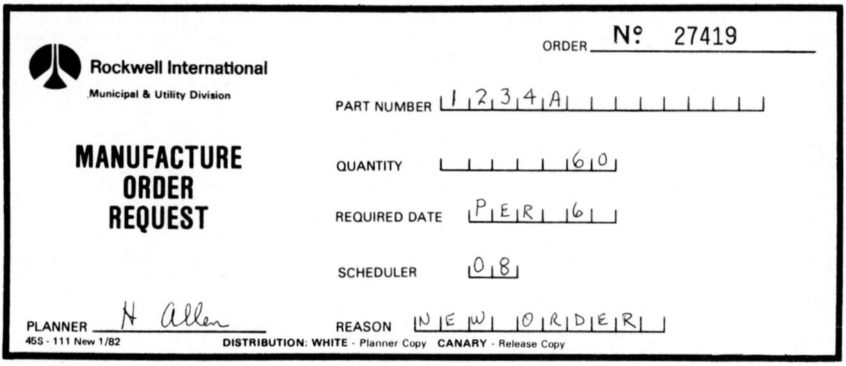
ORDER Nº 27419

Rockwell International
Municipal & Utility Division

MANUFACTURE ORDER REQUEST

PART NUMBER 1 2 3 4 A

QUANTITY 6 0

REQUIRED DATE P E R 6

SCHEDULER 0 8

PLANNER H Allen

REASON N E W O R D E R

45S - 111 New 1/82 DISTRIBUTION: WHITE - Planner Copy CANARY - Release Copy

FIG. 16.2 Shop order authorization. (*Courtesy: Rockwell International.*)

responsible for issuing the shop floor order paperwork. Where on-line entry systems are available, the same information can be entered directly into the system, and the shop floor paperwork can be prepared automatically.

The function responsible for coordinating work performance within an organization must have control of the authorization of work. If it is necessary to bypass formal authorization for some jobs, control over the amount of such work must be established. The materials function or the production and inventory control department is usually given the responsibility for work authorization.

Repetitive Production

This is the fabricating, machining, assembling and testing of discrete, standard units produced in volume. There are unique physical characteristics of repetitive manufacturing:

- Capacity is dedicated, and tooling is likely to be specialized for building a specific type of product.
- Routings are usually fixed, and manufacturing work centers are arranged in sequence. Balancing the production rates at each work center on the line is important.
- Processing cycle time is short. Queues of parts between work centers are not very large.
- There is usually a direct transfer of parts from one work center to another.

For comparison purposes, note that work in job shops is normally authorized by written work orders that identify the work centers through which material must be processed. Work in repetitive environments is frequently authorized by issuing daily, weekly, or monthly schedules. In most cases, the schedule is related to the finishing operation.

Table 16.3 is an example of a schedule authorizing the production of garden and farm tractor electric clutches. Authorization to produce component parts is derived from the *authorized production schedule*. It is unlikely that formal work orders with a job number, a specific production quantity, and a written routing will be used for component-part manufacture in a truly repetitive environment.

TABLE 16.3 Clutch Schedule: Clutches, Tractor Lines, Two Weeks Starting 2/13

Date	Part Number	Customer	Order Quantity	Quantity Complete	Order Due Date	Comments
		Line A Production Rate: 540 Clutches per Shift Shifts Operating: 1				
2/13–2/16	1096-14	J. Deere	5,000	2,850	3/2	
2/17–2/22	1240-01	M. Ferguson	2,000	0	2/24	
2/23–3/8	1050-10	Stock	6,000	0	3/30	Use as fill-in only.
		Line B Production Rate: 1200 Clutches per Shift Shifts Operating: 2				
2/13–2/14	1220-01	Simplicity	6,000	1,800	2/15	
2/14–2/22	5400-03	I.H.	15,000	0	2/24	
2/23–2/28	1500-20	J. Deere	10,000	0	3/16	

Process Manufacturing

For the purpose of this discussion *process manufacturing* deals with changes in fluids, powders, foods, primary metals, and processes involving chemical change. As with repetitive manufacturing, the process is relatively fixed, and management needs to communicate only the desired production rate as an official authorization of production. Specific item planning is accomplished with the MPS and the finished-product schedule. These plans and schedules are detailed specifications of what is required, when it should be produced, and where it should be produced. Table 16.4 shows a work authorization schedule for a food processing company producing canned vegetable products.

Specials

The production of special components for a specific customer order is authorized with a slight variation. The need to make a particular component part is not known until the engineering department has reviewed the customer's requirements, designed the product, and then released engineering drawings illustrating and identifying the needed parts. A planner reviews the engineering specifications and identifies all components to determine whether they are stock or nonstock. Stock items are authorized for production through the inventory management process previously mentioned, and the planner notes stock items on the work document. For nonstock items, a request is made for the necessary work authorization documents on a form similar to the shop order authorization form shown, but without the preprinted order number. In some organizations, the engineering drawing or blueprint is marked with the quantity required and the required manufacturing completion date. The engineering documents are then signed and forwarded to the department responsible for issuing the shop order package.

COMMUNICATING THE WORK AUTHORIZATION

Some organized method must be used to communicate the work authorization to the factory supervisors as well as to the individual workers. They must be told what

TABLE 16.4 Work Authorization Schedule

Form M-426, Run PPS160, Production Schedule: Kansas City Factory, Date Produced 11/04/83[a]

Variety Number[b]	Variety Description[c]	Fiscal Production Year to Date[d]	Remaining Balance[e]	Month[f]												12-Month Total[g]
				Nov.	Dec.	Jan.	Feb.	Mar.	Apr.	May	June	Jul.	Aug.	Sept.	Oct.	
300100	Canned creamed corn	60.0	50.0	25.0	0.0	5.0	5.0	10.0	5.0	15.0	10.0	15.0	5.0	15.0	5.0	115.0
300200	Canned whole corn	50.0	40.0	20.0	0.0	5.0	5.0	5.0	5.0	10.0	10.0	5.0	5.0	10.0	5.0	85.0
300300	Canned green beans	15.0	10.0	5.0	0.0	5.0	0.0	0.0	0.0	0.0	5.0	0.0	5.0	0.0	0.0	20.0
300400	Canned creamed peas	10.0	5.0	0.0	5.0	0.0	0.0	0.0	0.0	0.0	0.0	0.0	0.0	0.0	5.0	5.0
300500	Canned sliced carrots	15.0	15.0	0.0	5.0	0.0	0.0	0.0	5.0	5.0	5.0	0.0	5.0	5.0	0.0	30.0
300600	Canned whole beets	20.0	15.0	5.0	0.0	5.0	0.0	0.0	0.0	5.0	5.0	0.0	0.0	5.0	5.0	35.0
300700	Canned sliced beets	0.0	10.0	5.0	0.0	5.0	0.0	0.0	0.0	0.0	5.0	0.0	0.0	0.0	5.0	20.0
300800	Canned spinach	15.0	15.0	10.0	0.0	0.0	0.0	5.0	0.0	0.0	0.0	0.0	0.0	10.0	10.0	25.0
300900	Canned sweet potatoes	25.0	15.0	5.0	5.0	5.0	0.0	5.0	0.0	5.0	5.0	5.0	0.0	0.0	0.0	30.0
301000	Canned whole peaches	20.0	15.0	5.0	5.0	5.0	0.0	5.0	0.0	5.0	0.0	5.0	0.0	0.0	5.0	30.0
031100	Canned whole pears	25.0	0.0	0.0	0.0	0.0	0.0	0.0	0.0	0.0	0.0	15.0	0.0	0.0	5.0	20.0
301200	Canned sliced peaches	20.0	0.0	0.0	0.0	0.0	0.0	0.0	0.0	0.0	0.0	0.0	5.0	15.0	0.0	20.0
301300	Canned tomatoes	10.0	5.0	5.0	0.0	0.0	0.0	0.0	0.0	10.0	0.0	0.0	5.0	0.0	0.0	15.0
301400	Canned yams	10.0	5.0	5.0	0.0	0.0	0.0	0.0	0.0	0.0	0.0	0.0	5.0	0.0	5.0	15.0
301500	Canned pumpkin mix	5.0	10.0	5.0	5.0	0.0	0.0	0.0	0.0	0.0	0.0	0.0	0.0	15.0	5.0	20.0
	Total 275 050	300.0	210.0	90.0	15.0	40.0	15.0	30.0	15.0	40.0	55.0	35.0	45.0	75.0	55.0	495.0
	Total 275	300.0	210.0	90.0	15.0	40.0	15.0	30.0	15.0	40.0	55.0	35.0	45.0	75.0	55.0	495.0

[a] Indicates date of this computer printout. Printed after the close of each fiscal month.
[b] Company identification code used on every variety produced.
[c] Title of each variety as carried on all company records to identify contents of pack.
[d] Fiscal year is May 1 through April 30 of any given 12-month period. This indicates production received on each variety since fiscal year began.
[e] Balance of production by variety required for remaining months of fiscal year.
[f] Required production by month in proper shift quantities.
[g] Total of production indicated on the 12 individual months on this report.

to make, how much to make, and when it is to be completed. The degree of communication necessary is a function of three basic variables.

1. People
   a. *Organizational.*   How many people have to know about various aspects of the manufacturing process?
   b. *Skill level.*   What level of skill is required by the workers? Theoretically, the more they are expected to know, the less they need to be told.
2. Type of product
   a. *Product complexity.*   Is the product highly technical with many individual operations?
   b. *Part proliferation.*   Are many different parts scheduled to be worked on at the same time?
3. Manufacturing process
   a. *Job shop.*   Are there a number of machine tools on the shop floor that require scheduling?
   b. *Repetitive manufacturing.*   Are there fixed production lines for the highly repetitive work?
   c. *Process manufacturing.*   Is an inherent amount of control already in place because of the manufacturing process?
   d. *Group technology.*   What degree of group technology is being used?
   e. *Subcontracted manufacturing.*   Are there significant amounts of processing done outside the primary manufacturing facility?

MANUAL METHODS

In many small companies, work is still authorized manually. This eliminates the cost of computers as well as their benefits. However, today, manual work authorization is still common.

Verbal Authorization

Verbal instructions from the business owner or production manager, accompanied by a drawing or sketch of the part desired, often suffice to authorize production. An informal note is preferred since it provides a written record to identify the part required and specify the quantity needed and due date. Some shops use a drawing or sketch on which to indicate the quantity to be made. The customer's name, shipping address, and order number might be added. This becomes a valid work authorization document when it is signed by someone with the proper authority. Typically, this manufacturing environment has some or all of the following characteristics:

- Few people are involved.
- The workers are very skilled.
- The product is not complex.
- There are few component parts or raw materials.
- Manufacturing cells are used.

- The environment has a high degree of process orientation.
- The process sequence is repetitive.

In a company without at least some of these characteristics, verbal communications used to initiate work may still be acceptable, but control of work in process will deteriorate.

In environments where verbal communications are sufficient to initiate and complete work on the shop floor, a computer is not needed to authorize production. In fact, it is highly unlikely that the shop disciplines necessary to use a computer are in place.

Work Order

A work order is most often used in a job shop. It frequently incorporates a copy of the routing with space to record the actual production. In some cases a copy of the bill of materials is part of the work order and is used as a *picking-list*. Space is provided to record the actual materials issued. The operational steps on the routing are dated with start and stop times based on the due date for the item and simple scheduling logic. Some companies issue a copy of the routing to all work centers where the work is to be performed; others route a master work order file with each job.

A record is kept of all the orders issued, when they were issued, date and quantity completed, and other important information such as the amount of scrap, problems encountered, and miscellaneous comments. The closed work order is filed for reference when the next lot of these parts is used. A master copy of the work order is usually kept in the production control office or dispatch area. It is updated when production quantities are reported, to provide a concise picture of the status for each job. See the dispatching section for more details.

Schedules

Many companies, for example, repetitive manufacturers and process industries, do not use work orders. Instead they issue schedules of the production needed by each machine and production line. These schedules perform the same function as a work order—they authorize production. In this case the schedule is developed by considering both the capability of the machine as well as the items produced and when they are needed.

The schedule is updated with actual production information in much the same way as work orders. Picking lists or material-need lists can also be a part of the schedule packet.

COMPUTER METHODS

The manufacturing environment that requires a formal work order to authorize production is aided considerably by the use of a computer.

Three data files are used by most companies in their routing system. One is a record of the materials or parts needed to produce an item. These data come from the standard bill of materials plus any modifications necessary for this particular production lot. Modifications could be caused by the correct materials not being available or materials that are off-spec. Consequently, changes in materials are needed. When this data is printed out in a format similar to Table 16.5, it becomes a *material picking list* and authorizes the issuing of these materials to the factory.

The second set of data is the standard routing for an item with any modifications required for this lot. In this case, modifications could be caused by the material changes mentioned or because of overloaded machines. Typical data are shown for a given assembled part (Table 16.6) and for a piece part (Fig. 16.3).

The third data file is a record of each work order that has been authorized and is still open. The record contains a summary status of the order relative to its completion.

Additional documents are sometimes included in the work order packet, for example, move tickets, engineering drawings, raw-material cutting orders, and labor reporting tickets. These are all created at the time of the work order authorization.

Repetitive and process industries rarely issue a work packet. They create the same data files as mentioned earlier and issue a schedule to production. Actual production updates the schedule and provides individual item status reports.

Batch

In a batch environment, the data files mentioned previously are updated periodically. Transactions used to create and maintain the files are accumulated during the workday and then submitted in batches to file maintenance computer runs, usually

TABLE 16.5 Storeroom Picking List*

Report ID P4416		*Rockwell International*		*Run Date 10/07/83*	
		M&U Division		*Page 1*	
		Planner 2A Issue Date 10/07/83			
		Packing List for Manufacturing Order S22952 Part 00620-403-04000 Qty: 95			

From	To	Part Number and Description	U/M	Quantity Required	Picked
	423-0922	00000-009-04320 Dowel pin $\frac{1}{8}$ Dia. $\times$ $\frac{1}{2}$ Steel	Each	95	
	423-0922	00000-009-50196 O-Ring #113 523 Du or Equivalent	Each	95	
	423-0922	00000-009-50197 O-Ring #232 523 Eu or Equivalent	Each	95	
	423-0922	00620-003-02000 Top plate TPL9W/ext lube	Each	95	
	423-0922	00620-135-01000 TPL-9 Turbo oil tube	Each	95	
	423-0922	00620-244-00000 Mag well and post assembly	Each	95	
				Mfg. order S22952	

*Courtesy: Rockwell International Corp.

TABLE 16.6 Assembly Routing*

Part Number 0062040304000
Size:

Routings by Part Number
Description TPL9 Top Plate Assembly with External Lube Drawing: C19507

| | | Routing Description | | | Type OCC | |
| | | C W S | | | B W S | |
OP ALT	Department Machine	W/C Run Rate	Run Hours	Department Machine	W/C Run Rate	Run Hours
0005	Assemble magnet assembly—O rings and pin					
	423	0922				
0010	Hydrostatic Test TPL9			423	0922	
	430	0819				
0015	Assemble pin and oiling tube			430	0819	
	423	0922				
0020 AD	Assemble, water test, disassemble			423	0922	
	425	0814		425	0814	

* Courtesy: Rockwell International Corp.

Rockwell International

Manufacturing Order M1111

MANUFACTURE FOR	PROD. CD.	PART DESCRIPTION		PART NUMBER
RDA REQST	2249	TOP PLATE 1440LB T-140 A-J		00641-003-80000
	DRAWING/REVISION	ORDER QUANTITY	REJECT QUANTITY	PLNR/SCHR.
	E-19865	23		2/2B
			ISSUE DATE	DUE DATE
			10/14/83	

REMARKS

W/C MACH	OPER. No.	DESCRIPTION	COMP. QUANTITY	COMP. DATE	S/U HRS.	HRS/PC PCS/HR	C O D E	LAB GRD	QUANTITY COMPLETE	QUANTITY SCRAPPED
420	0230	005 FACE BOTTOM			0					
		00641-003-80001 EA	23							
		TOP PLATE ROUGH 1440LB								
420	2110	010 RGH MILL TOP TO 050 OVERSIZE FOR K&T			0					
420	0104	015 SP DR, DR, SPT FACE, CHF BOTH SIDE, TAP 2			0					
420	2133	020 MILL TOP-BOSSES-DR-RM C/HOLE PULSE			0					
420	0108	021 BTMDR-CHF-REAM-BURNISH .500 HOLE			0					
420	0106	067 DR-CHF-TAP 2-8-32 HOLES			0					
430	1702	070 WASH			0					
430	0819	075 HYDROSTATIC TEST			0					
425	1202	080 PAINT PRIMER			0					
425	0814	092A0 ASSEM-WT-DISASSEM			0					

TOTAL STANDARD HOURS

PLANT	RUN DATE	PART NUMBER	MFG. ORDER	PAGE
DUBOIS	10/14/86	00641-003-80000	M1111	2

FIG. 16.3 Manufacturing work order. (Courtesy of Rockwell International Corporation.)

processed before the start of the next workday. Orders released for production on the authorization form shown previously will have shop packet information created overnight by the computer and ready for delivery to the shop floor in the morning.

The bill-of-materials and routing information is updated prior to the order-release run, so the very latest information is available. When the shop packet information is generated for each new order, a record is created in the *open-order file*, indicating general information about the order. Detail information is also included concerning each routing operation step. This record base is updated as labor and material transactions are reported during the manufacturing process. The manufacturing work order shown previously is an example of the kind of information found on a computer-generated manufacturing routing for a part that must be routed to various pieces of equipment in a machine shop.

After the file is updated, the information is available in two different ways. It can be printed on reports at the same time as the batch processing is accomplished. It can also be accessed in a *read-only* mode via cathode-ray terminals (CRTs). The significance of batch processing lies not in how the data base is viewed but rather in how and when the data base is updated and accessed.

On-Line Environment

In an on-line environment, the intent is to have the personnel interactive with the file data. File information is updated via a CRT or other on-line input terminal as the information is available. The update does not have to wait for a batch processing computer run. Another feature of the interactive mode is that printed reports and other paper are reserved for only the essential hard-copy requirements. This means that documents such as printed routings, move tickets, material cutting orders, and labor reporting documents are not created. Any needed information can be looked up on a CRT display, and any data that must be recorded can be entered directly into the system. Items such as engineering drawings may still need to be provided on hard copy, but with the advances being made with computer-aided design (CAD), this also will be replaced in the future with CRT inquiry.

To authorize an order for production, a material planner needs only enter the requirement on the CRT. In most cases, the authorization form shown previously is not required. Proper computer linkages access the latest bills of materials and routing files and generate an open-order record. A material authorization is generated, and if a hard copy is necessary for part picking, it will appear on a printer located in the storeroom. Each operation on the routing is reflected on the schedule that will appear on the CRT located at the respective work center. All the information required by the machine operator is available on the CRT, and its presence on the schedule is the production authorization.

Batch versus On-Line Processing

The need for on-line update and data retrieval is a function of the frequency of change in the work-in-process data base and the importance placed by operating management on the need to have instantaneous knowledge about the changes. Modern shop floor control systems are being built with on-line capability. This, with the decreasing cost of computers, is making the difference between batch and on-line processing unimportant.

Distributed Data Processing

Distributed data processing is a term sometimes associated with production and inventory control systems. In essence, it is used to define where the actual data processing is done. A system is said to be *distributed* if the manufacturing unit has its own capability to process data by using a microcomputer, minicomputer, or small mainframe. A tie to a central computer exists for control purposes and possibly additional processing. Figure 16.4 shows one example of a distributed data processing configuration in which all the processors are independent, self-sufficient data processing systems. In this example, the lower-level processors X, Y, and Z are designed for routine repetitive operations such as order entry, shop floor control, inventory, and so on. Processor A, a higher-level machine, is an *information* system, installed at a head-office location. It is designed to answer queries from management, strategy and planning staff, forecasters, product designers, and so on. All the data in processor A are obtained from processors X, Y, and Z. However, in processor A the data are summarized, edited, and reorganized to facilitate instantaneous management use.

ROUTING SYSTEMS

Routing systems provide the necessary bridge between planning and execution. They create the records against which feedback is reported as work takes place on the factory floor. Open-order records are created immediately following work authorization, maintained as long as the order is part of work in process, and eliminated or placed in a history file upon completion.

Work is normally authorized for a manufactured component under specific conditions:

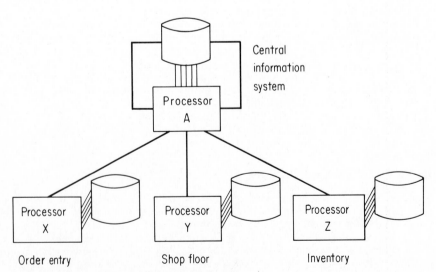

FIG. 16.4 Distributed data processing configuration.

- Additional units are required to meet projected needs.
- A planned-order quantity or a production rate requirement exists.
- Blueprints and bills of materials have been prepared.
- Materials are available and have been allocated.
- A standard routing or process sheet has been prepared.
- Tooling availability has been verified.

Depending on the work-in-process control system's level of sophistication, there may be one, two, or three different types of records for each open order. Virtually every system requires shop order summary records, and each may serve several purposes. They clearly identify the individual unit of work (work order, lot, block, etc.) and its current status. While the order is open, the shop order summary record reflects the number of units authorized or planned, time remaining until the due date, total quantity completed to date, total quantity scrapped to date, total balance due, and the total quantity disbursed.

The individual shop order summary records may be supplemented by operational detail and material detail records. The relationships among the three records and manufacturing charge records is portrayed in Fig. 16.5.[1] The operational detail records provide the specific information needed to track actual versus planned operation performance. During the time the order is open, the operation detail records for each operation show

- The operation number
- Earliest, latest, and actual start dates
- Planned versus actual setup hours
- Planned versus actual run hours
- Quantity reported complete
- Quantity reported scrapped
- Balance to be completed

Taken together, the due date from the order summary record, the start dates from the operation detail records, and the planned setup and run times make up a complete schedule of what is supposed to be done, where it is supposed to be done, and how long it is supposed to take. This information is used as the plan against which actual performance is plotted, based on the input from the shop floor operations.

The material detail records provide the specific information needed to track planned versus actual material performance. During the time the order is open, the material records for each material or component used shows

- Total quantity required
- Standard unit of measure
- Stock location
- Date by which components are required
- Operation for which components are needed

The material detail record provides a complete bill of materials, and when it is combined with the operation detail record the result is a complete parts consumption schedule for the manufacturing order. The schedule describes what parts are

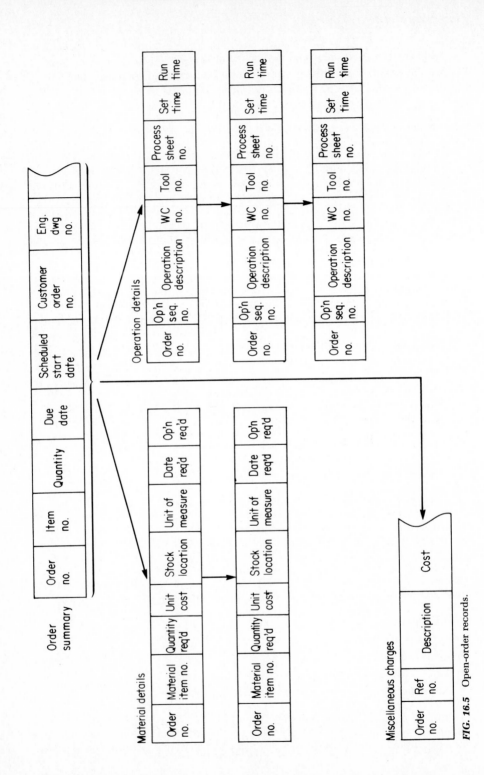

FIG. 16.5 Open-order records.

needed, how many are needed, and when they should be needed by both the calendar and operation sequences. This information is the plan against which performance will be measured based on input from the shop floor and storeroom operations. For further information concerning the open-order records, see the COPICS manuals.[2]

Standard unit-cost data for individual operations may be incorporated into the records described. Whether they are incorporated depends on the degree of integration between the manufacturing and cost accounting systems. If the records include standard unit costs, they can be multiplied by the quantities to be produced to provide a "budget" for each cost component. For example, each material used, the setup and run costs for each operation, and the total material and labor cost for the order are all calculated. These costs serve as a plan against which actual performance can be measured, based on input from the shop floor and storeroom operations.

Types of Plants

Routing system requirements are dictated, to a certain extent, by the specific manufacturing environments. Three key dimensions can be used to characterize and differentiate among manufacturing environments: process continuity, flow homogeneity, and product variety (Fig. 16.6).

Process continuity refers to the degree of manufacturing process fragmentation. Continuous-flow production represents one extreme in this dimension. In such an environment, the materials are loaded into one end of the transformation process and are worked on continuously until they come out the other end as finished products with no waiting, no loading and unloading. Intermittent production represents the opposite extreme of the continuity dimension of manufacturing processes. Material is loaded to an individual machine for one or a few operations and then unloaded and moved to some other machine. The cycle is repeated until all required operations have been completed.

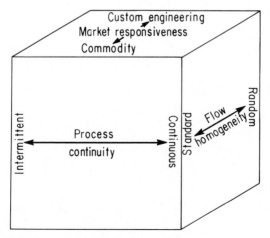

FIG. 16.6   Manufacturing characteristics.

Flow homogeneity refers to the degree to which material flows are standardized. The extremes are complete standardization, such that materials follow a single route through the manufacturing process, to complete randomization, where no two routings are alike. Although flow homogeneity and process continuity are different concepts, they are often confused. The confusion probably results because truly continuous processes are limited to a standard routing. But substantially fragmented processes are the rule, not the exception. Managing materials that follow a standard path through a fragmented process is much simpler than managing those following a variety of different routings—hence the need to differentiate manufacturing environments in terms of process continuity and flow homogeneity.

Product variety is simply a means of characterizing the degree of responsiveness to market requests for product variations. One extreme on this dimension is a single standard product, and the other is complete customization.

Taken together, the three dimensions can be used to characterize virtually any manufacturing situation. Although two plants may appear to be very different, they may occupy near-identical positions on the three continuums described. If so, the same types of routing systems are probably useful for both.

Certain types of manufacturing environments are more common than others; consequently, their similarities have been identified. The most common ones are job shop, repetitive production, and process industry plants.

Job Shops

The term *job shop* is often mistakenly used to describe a wide range of manufacturing situations. In the strictest sense, job shops manufacture batches of nonrepetitive items requiring dissimilar routings through highly fragmented manufacturing processes. Although few plants approach this extreme, large numbers have somewhat similar characteristics. These "near job shops" produce repetitively a relatively broad variety of products that require many different fabricated components having widely varying routings. Not surprisingly, the manufacturing process in such plants usually consists of functionally organized work centers.

Because of the nonrepetitive nature of their product offerings, true job shops cannot prepare planned routings and bills of materials until customer specifications have been received. Once customer specifications have been received and design engineering has accomplished its task, planned routings and manufacturing bills of materials must be developed for each component of the custom product. The necessary routings and bills of materials are typically developed by a process planning group in manufacturing engineering. Route sheets like the one shown in Fig. 16.7 are prepared for all fabricated and assembled items. Planned routings usually include a list of the individual operations needed and indicate the sequence in which they should be performed. Additional information about each operation is also presented:

- Description
- Machine or work center number
- Standard or estimated setup time
- Standard or estimated run time
- Specific tooling requirements
- Machining tolerances
- Material specifications

	ROUTE SHEET												

Part Description: PUMP HOUSING **Part No.** EPH6631PC

Material Per attached drawing

Sheet 1 of 1
Order No. 2504
Quantity 25
Sch. Comp. Date 2/20

Operation No.	Operation Description	Work Center	Machine No.	Tools Required	Standard Time			Finish Date	Inspection			
					Set-up	Per Unit	Per 100		Number		Date	Inspector
									Inspected	Rejected		
10	Mill & Finish	422	4222	A13/C20	3	5	500					
20	Bore	428	4281	A5	2	4	400					
30	Drill	380	3803		4.5	2	200					
40	Face	410	4102	C17/B22	3	2	200					
50	Drill	380	3801		4.5	2	200					
60	Face	410	4102	C17/B22	2	2	200					
70	Inspect	999	N/A	D928/930		12	1200					

FIG. 16.7 Manual routing.

16.19

Theoretically work can be authorized before a routing has been completed, but the actual work cannot start until the details of what is to be done where have been established. Once the routing and bill of materials are available and any necessary tooling is acquired, the process of work authorization can be completed. For each component manufactured, production control normally creates a work order and the necessary records for the open-order file. When a work order is written, the planned routing is the starting point for the routing system, and the first step is the scheduling of each operation.

The production planner reviews the results of the scheduling process in light of information about the current and projected status of machines, work centers, etc. If certain resources are not expected to be available when needed, alternates may be defined or the order may be rescheduled. The net result of this review and scheduling process is a detailed description of where and when the necessary work must be done. Once developed, the order schedule information is added to the open-order summary and operation detail records.

In small, true job shops using handwritten routings, a copy of the work order issued to the floor may serve both the summary and operation detail functions. The open-order file in this case is simply copies of open work orders. Nevertheless, the hard copy of each work order still represents a plan against which actual performance can be plotted. This is done by periodically posting the various labor and material transactions reported from the floor and storeroom operations. In larger, more sophisticated, but still true job shops, process planners may prepare planned routings by using interactive computer software on remote terminals or small business computers. Similar methods may be used to modify the routing as necessary, schedule each work order operation, and enter the resulting information in the order summary and operation detail records.

In near job shops, the degree of repetition of certain fabricated parts and assemblies is sufficient to warrant the creation and maintenance of permanent standard routing files. Once a route sheet for a manufactured item has been added to the permanent file, it can be retrieved and duplicated or printed depending on the form of the data storage in use. Information from it can be transferred either electronically or manually to produce work orders (Fig. 16.8). But once the initial route sheet has been created, reviewing it for problems, providing alternate operations as necessary, scheduling individual operations, and entering all the information into the open-order file take place as described previously.

In some plants, with highly sophisticated communication and information processing facilities, hard copies of work orders are not used. Instead, whenever the information normally found on the work order is needed, shop floor operating personnel consult a computer terminal located in the work area.

Repetitive Production

In repetitive production plants, the product variety is quite limited. Although the plant may offer several variations of its product, these variations tend to be standard configurations produced in very high volumes. On the process continuity dimensions, the manufacturing processes in repetitive production plants tend to be much less fragmented than in job shops. Large segments of the process are organized into continuous-flow units based on the operation sequence required by the components produced and the products assembled. However, flows between the large segments of the process tend to be intermittent. With respect to flow homogeneity, repetitive production is much closer to standardization than job shop production. Low volumes for any given routing are extremely unusual in repetitive manufacturing. Automotive and household appliance manufacturing are often cited as excellent examples of repetitive production.

Planned routings are also developed by process planning groups in repetitive production plants. Although planned routings in a repetitive production situation might look very much like ones from a near job shop, there is a difference in emphasis. The highly repetitive nature of all operations tends to emphasize the development of sophisticated tooling and ideal processing methods. Also, multi-decimal-place accuracy for run and setup time standards become important. Because so many of the individual machines and processes are linked into continuous manufacturing units, the question of where to send the materials after each operation is predetermined. Several sequential operations for a particular component are typically carried out in the same work place. As a result, the where-done column of the planned routing for a component shows very few unique entries compared to the number of operations.

Batch sizes tend to be large, and material flows relatively straightforward in repetitive production plants. As a result, record keeping and performance evaluation are somewhat simplified. Labor for all operations in a work unit may be lumped into a single plan, and the actual labor expended by the entire unit is compared to it for evaluation purposes. Material counting at checkpoints, sometimes called *milestones* and so identified on the routing, may be used instead of production counting at every operation. Consequently, operational detail records are usually somewhat abbreviated in the repetitive production open-order files. Routing systems for repetitive production are usually designed to facilitate the rapid authorization of standard items.

Because production is repetitive, batch sizes tend to be constant, and the work order authorization frequently requires nothing more than the retrieval of a "pre-written" work order from a computer system. In general, the task of the order writer and the routing system is simpler in repetitive operations than in job shops. The substitution of alternate operations is highly unusual in the repetitive environments, so usually the routing systems are not designed to easily accommodate them. In the rare cases when alternate operations are required, manual overrides are used to enter them into the system. The same is not necessarily true for material substitutions. Repetitive production routing systems tend to facilitate material changes.

Historically, process sheets were often permanently stored in the individual work areas in repetitive production facilities as opposed to traveling with individual batches or lots. This is feasible since each work area usually processes a relatively small number of components. But with the presence of computer terminals in individual work areas backed up by sophisticated information retrieval software, this practice is no longer necessary or prevalent. No matter how or where the actual work order information is stored, it tends to be retrieved as required in repetitive production plants as opposed to traveling with the lot or batch.

Process Industry

Process industry plants add value to materials by mixing, separating, forming, chemical reaction, etc. They represent extremes on two of the three dimensions used to differentiate manufacturing environments. With respect to process continuity, many are almost totally continuous, so that raw materials are fed into one end of the process and finished product comes out the other end. Although not all plants in this category are straight-through processors, the number of branch points in the process is usually quite small. Paint manufacturers, refineries, liquid fertilizer and artificial fiber production are examples of process industry plants. The flow pat-

KDX 18 SCH J DEPT 6480

DIV 09
WORK ORDER
PAGE 1

DISP 141 03/31/86 BM2009

WORK ORDER
NUMBER   QUANTITY   PART NUMBER   DESCRIPTION
09743658   100   03551-46794   2 IN KNOB

NOTES:

—	—	MATERIALS REQUIRED —	—	—	DRAWINGS REQUIRED	DIST
					A-03551-46794-1	Y
					A-03551-46794-2	N

MATERIAL	QUANTITY	MATERIAL	QUANTITY	MATERIAL	QUANTITY
5080-9873	100	*5874-4647	55	6473-3637	100
78938-46373	200	8654-8903	100	*9943-0924	1

SEQ-OPR DEPT MACH
005 791 6480 79101   SANDBLAST
                     SANDBLAST FOR 3 TO 5 MINUTES. BE
                     SURE TO PROTECT UNDERSIDE OF CAP.
                     *TOOL 631013 - RACK FIXTURE
                     *DO NOT CHARGE LABOR TO THIS OPERATION

                     SETUP   RUN   TOTAL
                     0.00   0.6670 66.700

010 792 6490 79203   DRILL AND TAP
                     DRILL .063 DIAMETER HOLE IN BUSHING
                     PER DRAWING. TAP AFTER DRILLING
                     USING .063 TAP.
                     *TOOL T183454 - TAP GUIDE
                     *ALTERNATE LOAD MEASURE+ 1.0000
                     *STANDARD YIELD= 86 PERCENT

                     0.15   0.0443 100.000

16.22

```
015 793 6490   LATHE                                    0.50   0.0500   5.000
               *SUBCONTRACTED-1. LEAD TIME=  5 DAYS

020 794 6490   ASSEMBLY                                 0.00   0.0350   3.500
               ASSEMBLY CAP, BUSHING AND DECAL.
               EPOXY CAP TO BUSHING PER DRAWING.
               REMOVE ALL EXCESS EPOXY FROM CAP AND
               BUSHING. USE VACUUM PROBE TO PLACE
               DECAL ON CAP.
               *TOOL   79401 - VACUUM PROBE TIP
               *USE    1.5  PEOPLE PER   100  PARTS
               *OPERATION OVERLAP=  50 PERCENT

025 036 2110   VAPOR DEGREASE            *76191*        0.00   0.0001   0.010

                           - - - END - - -
```

FIG. 16.8 Standard routing.

16.23

terns of all materials introduced into the process tend to be similar. Not only are there very few interruptions after processing begins, but also there are very limited where-to-next options. On the product variety dimension, process industry plants may produce one product continuously, process standard batches repetitively, or offer customized processing services.

Production output and resource consumption in process plants are usually planned and measured in terms of rate per unit time, that is, gallons per hour, tons per day, etc. The types of routing systems used by process industry plants depends almost totally on their respective position on the product variety spectrum. A straight-through process plant continually producing a single standard item has no need for a routing system. Instead, there is a master routing that specifies process operations, times, pressure settings, temperatures, and any other relevant parameters. Once the single, standard product, stipulation is dropped, the situation changes drastically. Open-order records must exist so that actual schedule and resource performance can be compared to the plan. The routing system requirements and operation in process plants producing a limited set of standard products are very much like those in repetitive production processing plants.

In a custom processing environment, the routing must be developed by the process planning group before the work authorization can be completed. The requirements and operation of the routing system in this type of plant are similar to those in a pure job shop. Sometimes, because of the nature of the materials, work orders may be attached to the batches themselves. In other cases, attaching work orders is impossible, and copies of the work orders must be transmitted in hard copy or via computer terminals to the appropriate work areas. In either case, work orders are coordinated with run schedules so that performance measurements can be taken at appropriate points and reported against the correct open orders.

Plant Layout Considerations

As described earlier, flow homogeneity refers to the degree to which material flows are standardized in a given manufacturing environment. Likewise, continuous-process layouts were described as the sequential linking of machines and processes based on the operation sequence so material movement is minimized. Clearly the where-to-next problem diminishes to the extent that flows are standardized and a continuous-process organization is utilized. On the face of it, limited product variety, continuous-process organization, and standardized material flow patterns seem to go hand in hand. However, many plants have standard products, homogeneous flows, and functional plant layouts. In those plants, routing problems continue to be quite complex and require the kinds of sophisticated routing systems described earlier.

Group technology is one method that can be used to convert functionally arranged repetitive production plants to process layouts. The basic idea is to take continuous-layout principles that have been used for years to set up assembly lines and apply them at the component level (Fig. 16.9). Components and machinery are grouped according to the similarity of the sequence of required operations. The efficiency of the method is undeniable, and it is responsible to some extent for the widely acclaimed achievements of Japanese manufacturers. Although there have been notable successes in the United States and in other Western countries, the practice has still not gained widespread acceptance, as evidenced by the large numbers of functionally arranged repetitive production plants that still exist.

Despite the attractiveness of group technology, there are several reasons why it has not been widely used. Equipment within cells must be dedicated to a limited

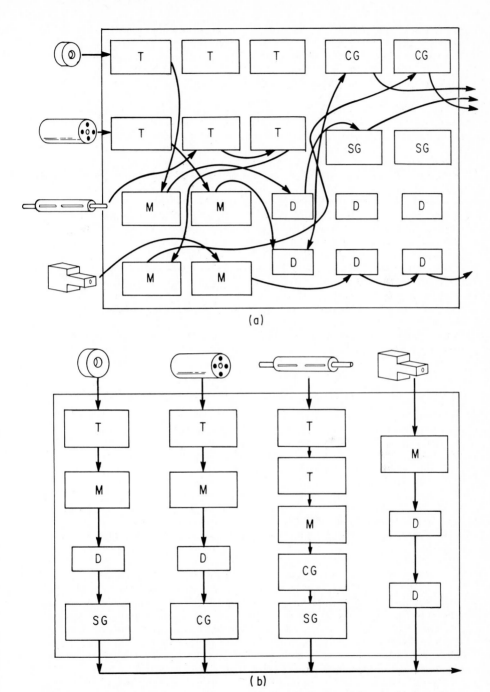

FIG. 16.9 Functional layout versus group layout. (a) Functional layout; (b) group layout (flow-line cell).

number of components. Unfortunately, most machinery does not come in infinitely divisible units. Consequently, high component volumes, relative to the capacity of the equipment, are absolutely necessary. This phenomenon, coupled with an apparently universal commitment to "bigger is better" capital equipment acquisition policies, frequently defeats attempts to convert from functional to group technology layouts.

When some portions of a functionally arranged plant are converted to group technology cells, routings must be rewritten to indicate that multiple operations now occur in the same physical location. To the extent that individual group technology cells are operated as miniature process plants, routing systems must be able to establish plans and measure performance on a rate basis, as described earlier. In a sense, the routing system requirements for a mixed-process plant are more stringent than any discussed because the system must be capable of handling job shop and process operations simultaneously.

The trend toward flexible manufacturing cells also has implications for routing systems. In general, these cells are quite large, their production capabilities are substantial, and their flexibility allows them to be used to produce many different components. When flexible manufacturing cells are interspersed with ordinary equipment, scheduling problems become considerably more complex. The cells are used to process many different components. What happens is that so much material must be routed through the cells it is necessary to plan and control operation start dates much more precisely. Likewise, unexpected downtime on flexible manufacturing cells creates severe scheduling jams. Because of such eventualities, the need to accommodate substitute alternate operations while the order is in process becomes pronounced.

Optimized Scheduling

Manufacturing control software offerings have increased in recent years. Most have emphasized priority and capacity planning and control for the entire plant. The exception has been a thrust that emphasizes network flow optimization. The primary example is optimized production technology (OPT) from Creative Output, Ltd. Its developer correctly recognized that bottlenecks control the rate of manufacturing throughput. Consequently, the system attempts to optimize flow through the bottlenecks. It then derives schedules for all the other work areas needed to support the bottleneck schedule. Except for one system feature, OPT presents no particular problem for the types of routing systems previously discussed.

In functionally organized plants, a batch size for a given component is determined prior to order release. Subsequently, the entire batch is run through each work center on the job routing before any of it is moved to the next. The use of split lots to move a small portion of the batch quickly through the plant is an exception. It is very seldom that batches of the same components are combined during operations. Consequently, manufacturing control software typically keys routing and data collection information to batches and, in some cases, to partial batches. By contrast, OPT produces schedules indicating that the batch sizes of individual components should vary in both directions during processing. The first operation may be scheduled in lots of 50, the second in lots of 125, and the third in lots of 40. The large lots are used at bottlenecks to ensure their full utilization.

It is not clear how the necessary aggregation and disaggregation are to take place on the floor. But it is clear that the routing system is affected. In a conventional system, partial batches are treated as exceptions. Once a batch has been split into partial batches and that information transmitted to the routing system, duplicate open-order records are created, and the split batches are treated as separate entities. Since OPT plans the variable batch quantities prior to release to the floor, the problem can be at least partly solved by keying the open-order records to the largest batch quantity for a particular part. Smaller quantities at other operations can be handled by duplicating the open-order records for the largest quantity.

Taking this approach to its logical extreme implies that the routing system must have enough "intelligence" to direct floor feedback to the appropriate open-order record. This, in turn, implies a need for the ability to aggregate and disaggregate the planned and actual performance to accommodate OPT's variable lot sizes. Finally, the routing system must not override OPT's scheduled operation dates since OPT schedules small run quantities to be accumulated to run through bottlenecks at the same time.

Alternate Operations

Regardless of the information storage and communication media in use, the manufacturing order provides the information base used to answer where-to-next questions on the shop floor. The work order typically specifies in which work center or processing area each operation is to be done. In some cases, the routing system specifies alternate work centers or processing areas in advance because of schedule conflicts. In other cases, shop floor problems or opportunities are not recognized until after an order has been released. Routings are sometimes for the specific machine but more often are only restricted to machine groups, work centers, or processing areas. Consequently, once the job or lot arrives at the work area called for on the work order, another decision must be made. To which machine will the work be assigned? That issue is addressed in the dispatching section.

When a where-to-next decision must be made on the shop floor, the location shown on the work order is always the first choice. But several factors can cause an alternate route to be used. If the machine is broken down or the queues at a primary work center are extensive and a secondary work center is underutilized, routing the job or lot to the alternate location is logical. If the priority on a job or lot is extremely high and the batch run time is extensive, part of the batch may be routed to a secondary work area to speed the completion of the entire batch. Regardless of the reason, the need to deviate from planned primary routings can and does occur during shop floor operations. When it does, production control personnel must be able to access the routing system and manually override the originally specified routing. This is the only way record keeping and performance evaluation can be meaningful. This may trigger rescheduling of subsequent operations, either entered manually or generated by the scheduling system.

Alternate routings can be employed most effectively when they are permanently recorded in a data base which is readily accessible for production control personnel. Note that such a system also lends itself to abuses, so there must be checks and balances to keep alternate routings from being overused. For coordination and control purposes, all shop floor routing changes should probably be channeled through a centralized transaction center staffed by production control people.

Data Storage

A variety of different methods are used to store routing data. Perhaps the most basic method used by small job shops is simply to file handwritten routings in file cabinets. As manufacturing plants gain sophistication, the emphasis shifts toward typed routing masters stored in retrievable filing systems. When routings are needed for actual work orders, it is a simple matter to produce the necessary number of copies by using readily available copying equipment. Some firms producing thousands of components have found microfilm or microfiche storage advantageous. Special machines can quickly create full-size copies of routings or bills of materials for use in the work packet.

Route sheets can be entered into computers from hand-coded versions prepared by process planners. More recently it is possible for process planners to prepare routings while sitting at a computer terminal but using traditional approaches. Currently, focus is shifting toward computer-aided design and manufacturing. In the early versions, the design engineer used a computer terminal for design, and the process planner in turn accessed the design data base to prepare routings in the traditional fashion. In later versions, some of the traditional process planning functions are taken over by the computer itself. The next step, which is already underway, is for the computer to do all the above and to program numerically controlled equipment to execute the necessary processing operations. The process of retrieving the routing and bill-of-materials information and transferring the necessary elements to manufacturing orders and open-order records has kept pace with these developments.

From a shop floor control standpoint, automation of the process planning function is not very significant. The same problems remain. Certain information still has to be collected about the production activity. When components are finished with processing at one work area, they still have to be routed to the next one. The real breakthrough was the ability to store and retrieve work orders in a computer to input, aggregate, and evaluate work order performance data. Thus, it became possible to produce hard copies of work orders on demand. Hard copies can be requested at the time the work is authorized and can be used as routers on the shop floor. The order can then accompany the job or lot on its way through the plant or can be transmitted in advance. Both are common practices.

Another advantage of computerized storage is its ready accessibility. The work order can be called up on remote terminals virtually anywhere in the plant, thus eliminating dependence on hard copy. Likewise, performance data can be input from different locations in the plant. The independence from hard copy promotes routing flexibility, since it is not necessary to chase shop floor routers whenever an alternate routing needs to be used, but at the same time increases the need for centralized control of transactions affecting open work orders.

Handling Special and Rework Orders

There are two keys to handling special and rework orders. First, the responsibilities for them must be clear-cut. This can be achieved by using a product manager to shepherd them through the plant or by clearly specifying manufacturing supervision, manufacturing control, and materials-move control responsibilities. Second, the number of special and rework orders must be tightly controlled lest they become the rule rather than the exception.

No matter how sophisticated the system, exceptions always occur and seem to occupy a disproportionate amount of the available management time and talent. There is a great temptation to deliberately design routing systems to accommodate special and rework orders. Unfortunately, that is probably the most effective way to encourage their proliferation. Therefore, routing systems should not attempt to obscure the uniqueness of special and rework orders but should emphasize it.

Exceptions require special handling. If the special order is not expected to occur again, a handwritten routing and bill of materials is sufficient to create a manufacturing order. If the routing system permits, the work order data may be entered into the computer, based on the handwritten information. Although the special order should not become part of the permanent data base, the need to schedule operations and record performance suggests that open-order records should be created for it. Probably the most straightforward approach involves manually scheduling each operation and loading the schedule, time estimates, etc., to the open-order file.

If a company has a computerized routing and dispatching system, special orders should be entered into it. This ensures that all needs for production are visible in the system and that special orders take their correct priority in the plant. Failure to do this means the formal system will quickly deteriorate, allowing informal practices and poor management control to occur.

Rework can be handled by a similar approach; a rework order can be constructed based on the necessary sequence of operations. But, here again, those operations need to be scheduled and the performance recorded. The solution is the same as that for handling special orders: to manually schedule each operation and load the schedule, time estimates, etc., to the open-order file. The desirability of this approach for rework and special orders is that it allows cost accumulation and performance evaluation and provides a clear picture of all the work in the plant using the conventional system while being awkward enough to discourage special handling proliferation.

DISPATCHING

When orders are released to the shop, scheduled start and finish dates have been developed for each order. To satisfy the customer, the scheduled finish date must be met. However, to meet the scheduled finish date, detailed schedules must be developed for each work center in the routing to indicate when a given order should be completed in that work center.

If each work center completes its operations on schedule, the order will be completed on time. This is the purpose of dispatching—to ensure timely completion of every order at every work center in the shop.

Assigning Work

When an operator or machine becomes available, a decision must be made as to which item to process next. This decision logic varies depending on whether the machine is a gateway work center or a secondary one. The decision is complicated when a large number of jobs are in contention for production. Complete systems are needed to help make the decision. These will be only marginally successful because of the large amount of data, long lead times, and hence variable priorities.

The best method of resolving which job to produce next is to reduce the number of items contending for production. The ideal is only one job in a work center. Priority decisions are automatic in this case. Hence the primary role of dispatching is to control and keep queues of work small. Low work-in-process inventory is another way of accomplishing the same thing. Control of the gateways, the real way to control queues, is of utmost importance.

Gateway Centers

A *gateway center* is a starting work center. Generally, the assignment of work to a starting work center should be more tightly controlled than the assignment of work at subsequent or downstream operations. The production control department controls the release of work into a starting work center. Thus there is a known requirement for the order at the time of release, and the flow of work into the starting work center can be regulated easily.

Since work is flowing into the starting work centers from only production control's decisions, the amount of work flowing into the work center is easily controlled. One method of regulating flow is input/output control. The principle of input/output control is that the amount of work flowing into a work center should never exceed the amount of work flowing out of the work center. By following this principle, the queue at a work center can never increase

An example of an input/output control form is shown in Table 16.7. In this example, the input is planned at a rate of 270 standard hr/wk of work. The output is planned at 300 hr/wk for weeks 9 through 12 and 270 hr/wk afterward. If these plans are achieved, the queue will reduce by 30 standard hr/wk for 4 weeks, or 120 standard hr. Hence the decisions of which job to run next will be easier with fewer jobs in contention.

During week 10, however, the actual output fell below the plan by 40 hr for a cumulative negative deviation of 35 hr. The production control department cut back the input in week 11 to 230 hr to compensate for this reduction in output. This was done to control the size of the queue. After week 12, the output was 60 hr below plan and the input 55 hr below plan. Hence the queue was at 155 hr versus a plan of 150 hr. The principle here is this: Reduce the input by the amount of the shortfall in output to keep the queues at a manageable level. Scheduling the work center to operate at a level of 300 hr in weeks 13 and 14 will get the below-plan hours produced and allow the input to catch up to the plan.

The input/output control technique allows production control to smooth out the peaks and valleys in the order release pattern suggested by the inventory planning system. Inventory planning systems do not consider capacity or the need for level loads in a factory. They plan orders solely based on quantity needed. Hence the

TABLE 16.7   Input/Output Control

Work Center 103, All Data in Standard Hours

	Week						
Input	9	10	11	12	13	14	15
Planned	270	270	270	270	270	270	260
Actual	275	265	230	255			
Cumulative development	+5	0	−40	−55			
Output							
Planned	300	300	300	300	270	270	270
Actual	305	260	280	295			
Cumulative development	+5	−35	−55	−60			
Queue							
Planned (150)	240	210	180	150	150	150	150
Actual (270)	240	245	195	155			

candidates for production must be evaluated against the need for a level release of work. Some orders need to be released earlier and others later than their planned start dates to achieve the level load.

There are other considerations in selecting which orders to start at the gateways. Is a critical downstream work center running low on work? If so, select an order to move quickly into the work center. Can setup or changeover times be minimized? Selecting parts that share similar setups, either at the gateway or at secondary centers, could be beneficial. Are all the materials needed to produce the order available? Allocation routines built into the inventory planning system can check this thoroughly. Is tooling available? Some tools can make a variety of parts, so the needed tool could be producing another part. Maybe the tools are broken or at another facility producing the same item. It makes no sense to assign work to a work center if all the resources are not available to produce it. This applies as much to gateway work centers as to those downstream and must be an integral part of the dispatching function.

Table 16.8 shows the candidates for release to the gateway center 103 as dictated by an MRP explosion. Table 16.9 shows a similar report for order-point control items. In both cases, selecting items to be released is based on the considerations just mentioned.

Downstream Centers

Work assignment is not as easily controlled at downstream centers as in the starting work centers. The task becomes increasingly complex in job shops where the input to downstream work centers comes from a number of feeding work centers. Thus the input will be more erratic with more peaks and valleys in the workload.

Aside from the "random input" problem, the closer a work center is to the finishing operations, the more likely it is to feel pressures from personnel in the "informal system." Assembly supervisors and marketing people, among others, have been known to communicate parts requirements directly to the supervisors responsible for downstream work centers. This further complicates the job of work assignment in these areas.

TABLE 16.8 MRP Order Release Candidates

Week 8, Work Center 103, Planned Rate = 270 hr, Total Backlog = 270 hr

Part Number	Planned-Order Release	Order Quantity	Order Hours	Cumulative Scheduled Hours
52	Week 9	450	37	37
18	Week 9	610	113	150
72	Week 9	315	48	198
36	Week 10	580	77	275
41	Week 10	220	53	53
23	Week 10	1100	127	180
45	Week 10	725	85	265
68	Week 10	500	23	23
53	Week 11	150	62	85

TABLE 16.9 Order-Point Release Candidates

Week 8, Work Center 247, Planned Rate: 120 Hr

Part Number	Total Inventory	Order Point	Total Inventory / Order Point	Order Quantity	Order Hours	Cumulative Scheduled Hours
83	192	250	0.76	500	56	56
72	4080	3350	1.22	1000	35	91
91	8771	6250	1.40	500	39	130
58	5963	4200	1.42	1000	27	27
42	2175	1500	1.45	2500	46	73
77	9984	6800	1.47	2250	35	108
86	4817	2700	1.78	1500	51	159

The trick here, for the person responsible for the dispatching function, is to gain physical control of the work. The dispatcher who has "ownership" of the material or the needed paperwork can gain control of work assignments. This physical control can be accomplished by using the control center concept. A *control center* is a designated area in the plant where in-process materials are temporarily stored. When an order is completed at an operation, it is not moved directly to the next operation, but rather is moved to a control center where the material is counted and then dispatched to the subsequent operation. In some companies the material is not physically moved to the control center. Only the paperwork authorizing the subsequent operation stays in the control center. This provides the dispatching function with the necessary control to assign work properly.

Priority Rules

A major objective of a dispatching system is to develop the relative priority of every order in a work center. Once the orders have been ranked from the most to the least urgently needed order, the physical assignment of work to a given operator or machine can proceed. These methods are used to rank work:

First In/First Out (FIFO) Method.   This is the simplest priority rule. The rule is this: The first order to enter a work center is the first one to be worked on. The advantage of this rule is that is does not require a computer system or complicated controls. The weakness of the FIFO method is that it assumes all orders have the same relative priority. It does not allow an order that may have been released late to jump ahead of other orders in the schedule.

Nonetheless, FIFO can be a very good priority rule in a flow shop or for process industries. For example, a company making printed-circuit boards uses FIFO very effectively. Each order goes through drilling, copper plating, photographic processing, testing, coating, and milling. After the drilling department completes an order, it is sent to the copper plating department, where it goes to the back of the line of orders waiting to be plated. The plating operators work on the orders at the front of the line. This system works effectively because this company has used input/output control to shrink queues and lead times to the point where all work flows at a rapid rate. There is no justification for altering the FIFO flow. All orders are completed in less than 10 days.

Slack-Time Rules.   Minimum slack time was developed to assign relative priorities to jobs in queue at the various operations. The *slack time* is defined as follows:

$$\text{Slack time} = \text{Due date} - \text{Today's date} - \text{Processing time remaining}$$

Slack time is what is left after removing the remaining processing time from the total time left until the due date.

The first version of the rule ranked jobs in priority solely by the slack time remaining. However, if two jobs have the same slack time, the job with the most operations remaining is the more critical. Hence, the rule may be modified:

$$\frac{\text{Slack time per}}{\text{remaining operation}} = \frac{\text{Due date} - \text{Today's date} - \text{Processing time remaining}}{\text{No. of operations remaining}}$$

Consider this example:

Order No.	Slack Time	Operations Left	Slack Time per Operation
1	10 days	5	2
2	10 days	10	1

Order number 2 takes priority over order number 1 based on the lowest slack time per operation.

Critical-Ratio Rule.   This priority rule has most of the properties of the slack time per operation rule. The critical ratio rule differs from the slack time rule in that it looks at the sum of *standard* move and wait allowances for each remaining operation. The critical ratio is computed as follows:

$$\text{Critical ratio} = \frac{\text{Due date} - \text{Today's date}}{\text{Lead time remaining}}$$

and

and

$$\frac{\text{Lead time}}{\text{remaining}} = \frac{\text{Processing}}{\text{time}} + \frac{\text{Setup}}{\text{time}} + \frac{\text{Move}}{\text{time}} + \frac{\text{Queue}}{\text{time}}$$

For example, say today's date = shop date 205, due date = shop date 215, and lead time remaining = 20 days. Then

$$\text{Critical ratio} = \frac{215 - 205}{20} = 0.5$$

Any order with a critical ratio of less than 1.0 is behind schedule. An order with a critical ratio of more than 1.0 is ahead of schedule. An order with a critical ratio of 1.0 is right on schedule.

By using the critical ratio priority rule, orders with the lowest value are the highest-priority jobs. Orders with higher critical ratios are the lowest-priority jobs.

Queue Ratio.   The queue ratio is calculated by dividing the hours of slack time left in the job by the queue time originally scheduled between the start of the operation being considered and the scheduled due date. The ratio decreases as the job becomes late. That is,

$$\text{Queue ratio} = \frac{\text{Slack time remaining}}{\text{Original queue time}}$$

where

Slack time remaining = Due date − Today's date − Processing time remaining

$$\text{Original queue time} = \text{Due date − Scheduled start date − Processing time remaining}$$

Informal System. Companies without a formalized priority system use manual or visual methods of communicating priorities. The infamous "hot list," shortage list, and expedite tags are a few such methods of determining priorities.

Although these approaches to priority planning are widely used, they usually are ineffective methods of determining priorities. There are exceptions, however. Simonds Cutting Tools has a "black tag" system for urgently needed orders. If an order is determined to be critical, a black tag is placed on the material. Any order with a black tag gets first priority in every work center. And it works because only six black-tag jobs are allowed in the plant at any time. Simonds found that if more than six black tags were permitted in the shop at any time, the urgent jobs could not get the immediate attention of the shop floor supervisors. The principle is: If everything is urgent, then nothing is urgent.

Priority rules, especially the mathematical ones, are somewhat limited in scope. They consider the mathematical priority but ignore many other factors, for example, capacity, whether the job is a stock or customer order, how important the job is to meet the shipping budget this month, whether the requisite skills are available, etc. Most companies, after a short love affair with mathematical scheduling rules, realize their shortcomings and either provide more information to the supervisor and dispatcher, so a good decision can be made, or realize that the problem is solved the day there is very little work in process, so there are few choices to make. Aggressive control of the work released and a dedicated attention to a smooth flow of work can reduce queues by a factor of 10, making the work assignment question rather straightforward.

METHODS

The method of dispatching depends on the type of production (whether it is a job shop, process, or repetitive manufacture) and the degree of sophistication of the planning and control system.

Verbal/Visual

The oldest form of dispatching is a verbal work assignment. The person responsible for making a work assignment simply tells the supervisor or operator which job to work on next. It is a straightforward method but one based on limited information and subject to loss of control. This form of dispatching generally relies on expediting to get critical jobs through the plant. Jobs that are not critical have a tendency to sit in the corner of the plant until they become critical.

Work Order Release

In most manufacturing companies, work orders are used to authorize and track the production of parts and products through the shop. Companies call these *shop* orders, *manufacturing orders,* or *jobs.* If production control releases an order number 2638 for 1000 units of part number 123, then the paperwork or shop packet, which includes routing sheets, prints, material requisitions, etc., is sent to the stockroom, and enough raw material or component parts to produce 1000 units are sent to the first operation. This work order is manufacturing's authorization to produce 1000 units of part number 123. All labor, scrap, and rework are then reported against order number 2638.

In many systems, every work center called for on the routing receives a document at the time the order is released indicating, for example, that 1000 units of part number 123 will be coming through that work center. This gives each dispatcher the visibility of what work to expect in the near future. This information can be used for planning manpower, setups, machine loads, etc. When the order is released, the scheduled order completion date can be written on the work order. Further, the operation due dates can be communicated to the work center dispatchers. Once the order physically enters a particular work center, it is added to that work center's dispatch list in date sequence.

When a computer is used to create dispatch lists on a frequent, regular schedule, dates are not normally shown on the work packet. Instead, the dispatch list shows the priority order for which job to work on next. This is due to the difficulty in making changes in the need dates for items. If there is a need to reschedule and the dates are on the work orders, then all copies must be found and dates changed. With a dispatch list, simply recalculating the new priority based on the latest information for an order puts the job in its relative position according to its importance compared to all other jobs. There is no need to change the paperwork.

The dispatch list shown in Table 16.10 shows the part number, description, order number, quantity, number of standard hours required, priority rank of the order, and where the order goes after it is completed at this work center. In this example, only work physically in work center 139 at the time the dispatch list was run is displayed. Many companies also display all orders scheduled to enter a work center over a predetermined horizon. This can include released orders currently in gateway work centers as well as planned orders from the inventory planning system. The dispatcher can now plan labor, material, and machine requirements in advance of physically receiving the order.

The priority rank shown on the dispatch list can be based on any of the priority rules previously discussed or on the start or finish date for the operation. These dates are generated by the forward or backward scheduling techniques. As mentioned earlier, it is useful to show these dates on the dispatch list with any other

TABLE 16.10 Dispatch List

Work Center 139, Date: 10/3, Capacity: 298

| Part | | Order | | | Prior | |
Number	Description	No.	Quantity	Hours	Rank	Goes to
117175	Sleeve	841A	1500	22	1	106-1
276112	Gear	920E	300	13	2	110-2
523153	Housing	663B	120	8	3	106-4
319181	Frame	717C	165	10	26	108-2

Total hours in 103 = 287 hr

pertinent information about these orders that will allow the supervisor and dispatcher to apply judgment in assigning work.

The dispatch list need not be followed exactly. The supervisor should be given the latitude to run jobs slightly out of sequence to save setups and minimize changeover time, as long as the completion dates for jobs can be met. The dispatch list is a statement of relative priority and does not consider production efficiencies. People must superimpose their knowledge of the shop on the dispatch list if they are to satisfy on-time delivery and efficiency objectives.

The dispatch list must be updated on a regular basis. Some companies have tried to update it weekly, but this has proved inadequate for most businesses. As work flows in and out of a work center, the dispatch list becomes outdated. A dispatch list generated on the weekend and sent to the shop floor on Monday morning may show 10 orders in a particular work center. On Monday, 7 new orders enter the work center, and 5 are shipped out. Only 5 of the 12 orders in the center on Tuesday morning will appear on the dispatch list. This makes it virtually useless.

The velocity of material movement is an important factor in determining how frequently the dispatch list must be updated. The faster material flows, the more frequently the dispatch list must be updated. Generally, it should be updated at least daily. In plants where material flows very rapidly, it probably needs to be updated at least every shift. Many plants now have the capability to update the dispatch list in the computer as material movements occur. This is referred to as a *real-time dispatch list*.

Companies in repetitive manufacturing or process environments do not use work orders to track material movement on the shop floor. Instead they issue daily or weekly schedules to each supervisor. The schedules show part number, item, and quantity to be produced during a given period. It then becomes the supervisor's responsibility to requisition the needed material and assign the work to the operators. In these environments, there is no need for a dispatch list. The supervisors simply produce to a schedule.

Computer Inquiry

Generating a dispatch list and updating it on a regular basis require computer assistance in most medium to large manufacturing plants. There are different ways to use the computer to aid the dispatching function.

The first alternative is to update the dispatch list in *batch mode*. Transactions needed to update the dispatch list are keypunched every night and then processed through the computer system. The dispatch lists take into account all activity through the first shift of the previous day and are printed and distributed to floor supervisors and dispatchers the next morning.

The second alternative is to key in the transactions via a CRT as they are generated during the day and then update the dispatch list at night. The output can be either printed or displayed on a CRT the following day. This is referred to as *on-line data entry with a batch update*.

The third alternative is to enter data as the transactions become available and update the dispatch list immediately after the transaction is entered. This is called *on-line, real-time updating*. The dispatch list, available immediately on a CRT or printer, is a mirror image of what is happening on the floor at all times. Priority lists can be as up to date as the last input transaction.

The method selected depends on the frequency of update required and the data processing resources available (hardware, software, etc.). The batch update is not as current, is most subject to error, but is less expensive than the on-line, real-time approach. Conversely, the on-line, real-time update is current, is subject to fewer errors, but requires a larger investment in hardware and software. In high-volume, high-velocity plants, on-line, real-time systems are almost a necessity to keep track of work orders and communicate up-to-date priorities and schedules to the shop floor. There is less need for this approach in a job shop with long lead, run, and setup times.

ORGANIZATION

Two of the most common forms of manufacturing organization are shown in Fig. 16.10. The advantage of alternative one is that the objectives of the dispatching function are more closely aligned with those of production and inventory control. The dispatchers are under less pressure to minimize setup costs, release orders to keep people busy, release more orders that run efficiently, etc. There is better coordination among dispatchers in this form of organization. The dispatchers must still be capable of working hand in hand with the shop supervisors, however, if this form of organization is to be effective.

The advantage of alternative two is that the dispatchers gain a better knowledge of shop operations and have a tendency to work more closely with the shop people. The disadvantage is that decisions favoring operating efficiencies are more likely to be made over customer service and inventory investment objectives with the dispatchers reporting to manufacturing supervisors.

Regardless of where the dispatching function resides, the dispatcher's responsibilities include the following:

- Provide order status reports to manufacturing.
- Highlight past-due orders.
- Communicate due date changes.
- Act as a liaison between manufacturing and the production planning/inventory control department.
- Work with other dispatchers to ensure flow of materials on time.
- Work with the supervisor on work assignment.

Manufacturing's primary responsibilities include the following:

- Assign work to a specific machine or operator.
- Communicate anticipated delays to the dispatcher.
- Report labor, scrap, rework, etc. accurately and on time.
- Produce in accordance with the due dates, schedules, or dispatch list.

To summarize, the dispatching function is a scheduling and coordinating function. Manufacturing's responsibility is to execute the schedules and feed progress back on a timely basis.

FEEDBACK

The purpose of feedback is to provide a scorecard on how well the actual production met the plan and to enable management to quickly view the status of any job.

Alternative 1

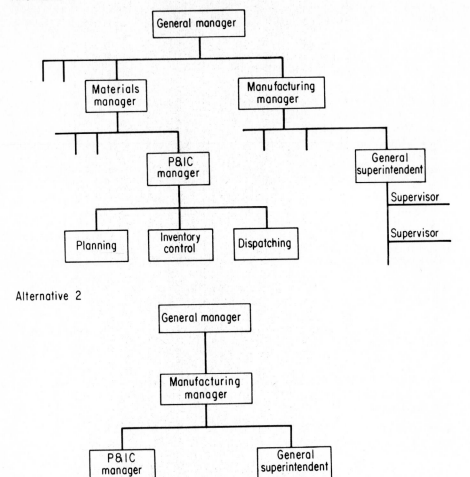

Alternative 2

FIG. 16.10 Two forms of the dispatch organization.

The first is to assist in managing a complex process; the second is to provide information to those needing it.

Schedule Updating

The schedules in a plant need updating for two reasons. The first comes from the actual execution of the schedule, and the second comes from changes caused by the need for items or because of unexpected disruptions.

Actual execution of the schedule must be reported to the routing system personnel. Operations completed, scrap generated, and time spent on each operation are examples of the feedback information used for job status, shop floor control, and financial reports which are available to the management team.

Schedule changes caused by quantity revisions for an item usually come from the inventory planning system. Inventory planners, after reviewing the change requirements for various items, release revised due dates for jobs to the routing system. The scheduling system redates all affected operations, and priorities are revised accordingly.

Changes resulting from unexpected disruptions are usually entered directly into the routing system. Machine breakdowns, overloaded machines, or scrap all require changed plans. Alternate machines, subcontracting, or a rush order to replace the lost material must all be reflected in the routing system. Changes are usually done manually, especially in batch operating systems. On-line systems can accommodate changes more readily and include them in the routing system immediately.

Methods

A variety of feedback methods are possible. To select the correct one, consider the speed of material flow, what decisions will be made based on the timeliness of the data, and the costs of the feedback process. The correct balance of these three will provide the best feedback solution.

Manual Forms

Using a manual system, the direct labor operator fills out a form upon completion of an operation. This form usually contains the part number, operation number, quantity produced, number of hours worked, etc. The form is then routed through production control, on its way to accounting, so the schedules and the work-in-process reports can be updated. Figure 16.11 shows the production reporting form used by DME/Fairchild.

Some companies use a separate material movement document for feedback purposes. The material movement form is generally filled out when all operations performed in a given work center are completed. The move form updates the routing system. Order tracking and scheduling are done on a work center basis rather than by operation. This is especially useful in companies where multiple operations are performed in rapid succession. It is impractical and unnecessary to schedule and report production by each operation.

The disadvantage of using a material movement rather than a labor transaction to update the dispatch list is that it leads to two separate systems for work-in-process management, one for the accounting department and one for manufacturing and

D-M-E COMPANY
A Fairchilds Industries Company

PRODUCTION REPORTING FORM - COMPLETE DAILY

NAME _____ DATE _____ PLANT _____ SHIFT _____ SUPERVISOR _____ EMPLOYEE NO. _____

S.O. NUMBER OR JOB NUMBER	S.O.# PROD. CODE	PROD. TYPE	STEEL TYPE	SIZE/SERIES	THICKNESS(ES)	PROD. CODE ITEM	OPER./ ROUTE CODE	QTY. COMPLETE	WORK STATION	DEPT. NO.	ACC'T. NO.	OTHER	ELAPSED TIME	TIME
													OUT IN	
													OUT IN	
													OUT IN	
													OUT IN	
													OUT IN	
													OUT IN	
													OUT IN	
													OUT IN	
													OUT IN	
													OUT IN	
													OUT IN	
													OUT IN	
													OUT IN	
													TOTAL TIME	

MANUFACTURING PART NUMBER

SUPERVISOR _____

FIG. 16.11 Production reporting form. (Courtesy of A. Fairchilds Industries D-M-E Co., A. Fairchilds Industries Co.)

16.40

materials management. The accountants are unlikely to recognize a material movement transaction in their inventory accounting or costing systems. Their system tracks labor costs, and the routing system tracks pieces. This leads to two sets of records—neither of which is accurate.

There are now two choices. One is to use one transaction to update both systems, and the other is to create a reconciliation process between the two systems.

The obvious choice is one system, but this is easier said than done. The labor transaction, especially in an incentive shop, is mandatory for the accounting system. However, labor transactions are rarely accurate or timely enough to update a routing system. Only with a well thought-out program with very stringent controls on the data will this choice be successful.

The second choice, of having two systems operating in parallel, may be the only choice if the labor transactions cannot be made accurate and timely enough. The two systems can be reconciled at a count point, for example, the stockroom, to make sure the financial and physical systems stay in step.

Cards

Preprinted cards can be used to update schedules and work-in-process reports. When an order is released, a card containing part number, order number, quantity, etc., is created for each operation on the routing sheet. When that order physically enters a particular work center, the card is placed in a rack in priority sequence. This in essence becomes the schedule for that work center. As orders are completed, the cards are removed from the rack.

The preprinted cards can be sent to keypunch and entered into the system for a daily or weekly update of the work-in-process system and the dispatch lists. In many companies, batch updating does not provide timely enough information. The time to keypunch and process the data is usually in excess of 24 hr, and this can mean that the schedules and work-in-process reports reflect 2-day-old information when they are finally sent to the shop floor. In high-volume repetitive manufacturing environments in particular, this is inadequate.

Some companies use prepunched cards to expedite the keypunch process. When an order is released to the shop floor, each work center in the routing receives a number of cards with the part number, order number, work center, and operation already punched in the card. When activity occurs on that order, only the variable data, such as quantity, operator number, hours, etc., are punched into the card. This is sometimes done on the factory floor or in the dispatch area. All the needed data are now on the card in machine-readable form and ready for processing. This speeds up the flow of information and allows for a more timely dispatch list.

Data Collection Terminals

To provide more timely information, data collection terminals can be located on the shop floor to collect and process data on the spot. Data may be entered by using prepunched cards, magnetics, bar codes, or operator keying.

The data collection approach provides two advantages over the card and manual systems. First, work-in-process reports and schedules can be updated instantly. Second, the system can edit transactions to ensure valid part number, order number, unit of measure, etc. If any of the input data are invalid, a message appears or a bell rings, indicating that some data elements are incorrect. The person entering the data must try again. Since the feedback is immediate, a properly trained person has an excellent chance to analyze the data input problem and correct it on the spot. This type of editing is difficult, if not impossible, with manual and batch update systems.

Bar coding provides a method for entering data quickly with a minimum of operator input. By passing a wand, or bar-code reader, over a bar-code label containing the part number and order number, the system reads and records this information, which eliminates the need to "key" it into the system. This greatly reduces the possibility of error and speeds the flow of information. Bar-coding systems can require a significant investment, however, and have a limited application in shops where material is being transferred from one container to another, such as in heat treating, machining, etc.

One of the age-old questions related to data collection is, Who should enter the data? The alternatives include the operator, a designated person in each work center, or centralized input. Table 16.11 shows a comparison of these three alternatives.

The biggest advantages of operator input are speed and ease of error correction. However, a large investment in data collection devices is required, direct labor people are used for the data entry activity, and the training effort is significant. On the other end of the continuum, centralized input requires fewer data input devices, and fewer people have to be trained in data entry procedures. Because the individuals entering the data may have little or no knowledge of the shop, they have no way of correcting errors on their own. They must consult someone in the shop after the fact to make the correction. This makes it difficult, if not impossible, to know what really happened.

There are different approaches to centralized data entry. These include centralized key punching, keying data onto a diskette, and on-line data entry. The first two alternatives do not edit data until after the fact. The third method, on-line entry, allows editing of part number, quantity, order number, etc., for faster error correction.

Some companies expedite the flow of information to the centralized input area by using verbal communications from the shop floor to the data entry area. For example, Simonds Cutting Tools in Fitchburg, Massachusetts, uses an intercom type of system to communicate transactions to a centralized area.

TABLE 16.11 Data Entry Alternatives

Data Entry Responsibility	Number of Data Input Devices Required	Timeliness	Training Required	Error Correction Capability
Operator	High	Excellent	High	Excellent*
One person per work center or department	Medium	Good	Medium	Good
Centralized input	Low	Fair	Low	Poor

* This is true of the fixed data, such as the part number or order number. It is not so true of variable data, for example, quantity completed. The corrections for this depend on the previous operator, whether the operations are performed out of sequence, etc. One designated person per work center or centralized input has access to the total job picture and therefore can often catch quantity errors more effectively than can operators.

FREQUENCY AND ACCURACY

Shop floor reporting is used not only to update schedules, work-in-process reports, and dispatch lists but also as the input to payroll, efficiency reporting systems, and costing systems. The acronoym *SCOPE* describes the uses of shop floor reporting:

S	Scheduling
C	Costing
O	Order tracking
P	Payroll
E	Efficiency

The frequency of updating must satisfy each of the five functions. Generally speaking, the payroll, efficiency, and costing functions are satisfied with a weekly update. This usually is inadequate for scheduling and order tracking purposes, however.

The frequency of updating depends on the lead time to build the product and the velocity of the material movement on the shop floor. For example, a make-to-order product taking 20 weeks to build may not require an on-line scheduling system. Weekly schedule updates may be sufficient. A high-volume product with a lead time of 3 weeks requires a more dynamic system, however.

The schedules must be updated frequently enough to ensure the system is a working tool for the shop floor personnel. If updating is not done frequently enough, people will work around the system and not within the system. Eventually the system will deteriorate, and people will revert to the informal system to get the product shipped.

The system is only as good as the input data. To improve record accuracy, management should follow a five-step program:

1. Create a climate of high expectations with regard to record accuracy.
2. Assign specific responsibilities to maintain accurate records.
3. Provide shop floor personnel with the tools to improve record accuracy. These include weighing scales, counters, nesting containers, etc.
4. Measure the accuracy of data input through an auditing or cycle program.
5. Identify and eliminate the causes of record errors.

If implemented, such a program will dramatically improve the quality of shop floor reporting, which in turn will improve the quality of the scheduling system.

REPRIORITIZING THE PLANT

The following is a partial list of events which can change priorities on the shop floor.

Forecast changes

Customer order promise date changes

MPS changes

Late vendor delivery

Scrap

Absenteeism

Machine breakdowns

Engineering changes

Planned lead-time changes

Order-size changes

Routing changes

Methods changes

Quality problems

The system must be capable of communicating these changes to the dispatcher and ultimately to the supervisor.

A very dangerous practice is to let the computer system automatically change due dates of orders that are on the shop floor. This causes tremendous "nervousness" in the system and may result in unrealistic demands being put on manufacturing. Due dates must be updated to reflect true needs, but only after a planner has communicated with the supervisor or manufacturing manager to find out whether the new due date is realistic. This means checking capacity, tooling, material availability, etc., to see whether the new due date can be met. Only if it can be met should the change be entered into the system. This will result in a change in the relative priority of orders on the dispatch list. To close the loop, the results of this investigation must be fed back to the planner and/or the master scheduler for review.

If a problem such as machine downtime or lack of tooling jeopardizes the completion of an order on time, the shop supervisor should communicate the difficulty by an "anticipated delay" report. At this point the dispatcher and planner should change the due date of the order for that work center and, if necessary, the due dates for each subsequent work center. If the completion date for the order jeopardizes the start date for the next higher-level assembly, its lead time must be compressed as much as possible to support the next higher level.

As a last resort, if all lead times have been compressed as much as possible and the MPS is no longer workable, then it should be changed. This should be done only after each level in the bill of materials has been replanned and can no longer support the MPS. This is referred to as *bottom-up planning.*

PROGRESS REPORTING

A plant must measure flow rates and schedule adherence on all jobs. But customers, production control personnel, master schedulers, and factory managers want progress information on specific jobs. Thus, manufacturing progress reports view progress in two perspectives: by individual orders and by factory work centers in producing their overall load in the correct sequence.

This is an important distinction. Exceptions such as shortages, breakdowns, and customer inquiries raise questions about specific orders in the first perspective. Routine manufacturing is successful when capacity and priority are controlled in the second perspective. Efficient manufacturing systems must routinely yield both kinds of information.

Progress by Order Number

Table 16.12 shows part of a report dealing with an assembly schedule, as can be seen by the presence of three levels shown in the symbol column. Orders exploded from a master schedule are usually for components and so typically have only one line per order. Pegging information makes it possible to trace upward through the structure to determine the impact of shortages, etc.

Continuous or repetitive production firms will tend toward reporting cumulative progress by a finished-goods identification number. An example is the manufacture of light bulbs, made by the thousands per day. Counting points are established which are generally mechanized and tied directly to a computer. Controlling sequence (priority) requires little attention, while control of capacity and shrinkage becomes vital. Table 16.13 illustrates a cumulative production shrink report. It is most commonly displayed on a computer CRT screen, since printed reports are too slow to be helpful.

Style A2013C is near target, as shown by the *off-objective* figure of −11, while C4309F is below plan owing to production being slower than planned and scrap (shrink) at the sealing machine. The cumulative period for such reports should be kept short, since errors in continuously open orders make lot control difficult.

Progress by Work Center

These reports make control and coordination of a factory possible without item-by-item expediting. The shop floor control system is fed actual production information which is compared to records of how the jobs were planned. This yields readings on both adherence to priority (job sequence) and balancing of load to capacity. Table 16.14 shows a Pareto type of distribution for work centers by sequence of priority adherence. The worst is at the top, so prompt action can be taken where the sequence problems are most acute.

Report Frequency

Weekly reporting is often sufficient, especially in slow-moving production without a large number of status inquiries. However, as competitive and financial pressures impose a need for shorter cycle times, daily or even more frequent reporting is necessary. Table 16.15 shows this faster-paced reporting intended to focus on capacity control.

This report shows figures for planned hours per day and per week, hours reported so far in the week, and cumulative hours as well as an off-objective figure. Such reports are helpful if they are accurate and up to date, which requires data collection by bar-code or similar rapid reporting methods.

On-line systems eliminate the need for voluminous reports produced for reference, and the cost of producing, distributing, filing, and disposing of reports is saved. The information is up to date, and inquiries tie up only one person, rather than two. Modern software enables users to answer the numerous one-time questions which would otherwise require a painstaking combing through of reports. This increases the span of control of shop personnel.

Frequency of reporting is intimately tied in with the recycling intervals in batch systems. It is not much help to report on-line if the data are not updated more than once a day. Builders of equipment requiring long cycle times should note that the system cycling frequency must match the rate at which production events occur,

TABLE 16.12 Order Progress Report

Schedule Summary, Day 960, Mail to:

Shop Order	Symbol	Drawing Item	Description	CWS	Date Start	Finish	Operation	Operation To Go	Hours to Go
12P113949	1	P1341	HSB MTR FR	14201	955	959	01	03	3.8
12P113949	11	12P1139H01	Stator Assembly H	14249	949	955	07	01	.4
12P113949	12	12P1139P01	Rotor Assembly HS	14251	953	955	01	02	1.6

TABLE 16.13 Cumulative Production Shrink Report

Style No.	Production Plan Daily	Cumulative	Cumulative Units Past Mount	Seal	Shrink, %	Test	Shrink, %	Off Objective
A2013C	240	2440	2450	2441	0.4	2429	0.5	−11
C4309F	400	4067	3998	3930	1.7	3918	0.3	−149

TABLE 16.14 Work Center Priority Control Report

Work Center	Name	Priority Index	Weeks Overdue	Days Late
23134	Circle shear	4.5	0.6	2.3
23102	Subassembly	3.1	1.3	5.9
23136	Bath press	1.7	0.4	1.5

TABLE 16.15 Capacity Control Report, Department 145

			Hours of Actual Production Reported					
Work Center	Planned Week	Hours per Day	Mon.	Tues.	Cumulative	Off Objective	Wed.	Thurs.	Fri.
01	25	5	8	4	12	+2			
03	300	60	54	48	102	−18			

not the rate at which products are shipped. Long-cycle products have thousands of events scheduled between start and finish, and it is essential that the system track these as they occur and base outputs on a faithful model of the shop as it is now, not as it was thought it might be several weeks before.

Capacity versus Priority Control

The distinction between the two sort sequences of the same information shown in the work center, priority control report, and the work center capacity control report is essential to low-cost, high-reliability control of work flow. The actions needed to control capacity are different from those to control priority. These two reports give a useful emphasis to this difference.

Highlighting the Unusual

Well-designed reports attract attention to the unusual. The Pareto-like sort shown in the work center priority control report is an example because the work centers having the greatest priority control troubles are at the top. The worst sequencing problems, with the highest priority index, are at the circle shear, where production control and supervisory attention are needed to physically organize the input queues, train the operator in following dispatch sequences, and solve similar sequence disrupters.

In firms with customer order assembly schedules above the MPS level, one must know when an order will finish if nothing else goes wrong. The program can add remaining time on the original schedule to "today" to develop a predicted completion date, in a column titled *computed promise*. If this is outside some tolerance, the item must be flagged for attention. Try these techniques for exception reporting:

1. Sorting is simplest and best. Sort in descending order of days late, or some other meaningful number from the data base.

2. Minimize the repeating of sorting and reporting by providing columns on the report which are intended to be blank unless a problem exists, such as a purchase order with a late promise date.

3. Spare the user the comparing of numbers, mental computing, etc. Reduce complex situations to a single number, such as priority index, which has its own meaning (e.g., a large number is more important than a small one).

PERFORMANCE REPORTING

Performance reflects the attainment of the factory's two standing objectives, control of priorities and control of capacity. Performance reports tell how well this has been done lately and what may have to be done soon.

By this procedure one can find bottlenecks of two kinds: chronically critical work centers that are historically short of skilled workers or machine capacity and transient bottleneck work centers resulting from such things as random changes in product mix. The chronic bottlenecks are usually the work centers around which the plant's key planning numbers, such as customer delivery promises and maximum production rates, are built.

Transient bottlenecks are invisible until they create assembly delays and stock shortages. A few days' overload has the potential to ripple into other areas and persist for weeks. Good performance reporting helps to identify these problems in advance.

Flow Management

Visualize the manufacturing schedule as a scroll, winding off a *future* roll, to a window marked *now*, and onto a *past* roll.[3] Marketing, planning, design, and industrial engineering mark this scroll with work orders which, if they have been planned correctly, make a flow of scheduled activities passing the now window.[4] Shop floor control has three objectives:

1. See that products scheduled *now* are done *now*.

2. Ensure that products scheduled for the *future* are not done *now* without good reason.

3. Accelerate products that are past due, or use them intelligently in a reschedule order.

Flow management is a bulk manufacturing decision-making technique in which one good capacity decision replaces many expediting emergencies.

Flow does not imply a level load.[5] One can cope with overloads or underloads of products as they flow without permitting them to pile up and become overdue. This is discussed under corrective action.

Flow management is supported by information on the load summary such as *target hours* and *weeks overdue at average rate*. The program assists in determining the skills needed, where, and when—and, equally important, what skills are not needed, where and when. However, the program makes no staffing decisions, which are best left to those responsible for them.

Flow management, then, is directed at planning and executing short-term rates to which resources will be applied. Different rates are required at a given work center. The common practice of establishing a level working rate by letting overdue orders fluctuate causes a vicious amplification of lumpy loads.[6]

Closing the Loops

Passage of time makes plans obsolete. Completion of planned actions and the intrusion of unplanned events must be fed back to the system and blended with fresh inputs such as new orders, dates, and engineering changes. This is called *closing the loops*, and it is part of the net-change logic.[7,8] Ideally, the system, which is a model of the factory, records each latest event. This is possible with real-time or fast-cycling systems. The reports to be discussed are based on the closed-loop, net-change logic and systems.

Sample Reports

Table 16.16 shows a combination report displaying both recent performance and short-range future requirements. It is a load summary similar to those in many plants, but with important additions.

Here are explanations of the report headings. *Reported last week* is standard hours of work produced last week. *Average past 3 weeks* is the moving average of the reported hours for 3 weeks, that is, the demonstrated capacity. Unless action is taken, next week's output will be similar. *Overdue at average rate* is overdue orders divided by demonstrated capacity or the time to work off overdue orders at the current rates. This key measure *identifies bottlenecks*. And *target hours, no overdue* is a rough guide for the average hours per week required to carry the load of the next 4 weeks, with overdue orders excluded. (Some prefer overdue orders included.) Note the hazards of averaging; a misguided effort to work only average hours per week will result in the work center's carrying insufficient load 50 percent of the time and being overstaffed 50 percent of the time. This figure is for labor planning, not for labor deployment week to week.

Average days late is how much behind or ahead of schedule, on average, reported operations were during the period. And *priority index* measures schedule keeping. Average days late does not tell the distribution of early and late orders caused by departure from schedule sequence. Minor reasons include the effects of a catch-up of overdue orders and normal load fluctuations. These departures form a distribution for which a standard deviation can be developed by the computer at the same time as it records the labor reports. The standard deviation is a priority index.

TABLE 16.16 Load Summary for a Single-Machine Work Center

Load Summary for Work Center 12345, 100 mm DE GIL HBM

Reported last week	22 hr	Target hours, no overdue	48
Average past 3 wk	36 hr	Average days late	8
Overdue at average rate	0.8 wk	Priority index	9

				Week Beginning								Total Excluding
Overdue	022	027	031	036	041	046	051	056	061	066	Future	Future
30	70	18	56	46	48	49	63	15	53	23	8	471

Its statistical meaning is that 68 percent of the labor operations were within a band equal to the average days late plus or minus 9 days, as shown.

This report is one key to shop floor control. If schedule keeping is poor, many overdue orders will stay on the schedule, which looks like a capacity problem. But there are also many underdue orders with operations done ahead of schedule. The work center may be carrying its overall load adequately because it has enough manpower, but is not working on the right things. It is a priority problem not a capacity problem. Accurate segregation of capacity from priority problems and application of the right solutions make for effective shop floor control. A priority index, and a weeks overdue figure almost completely define the performance of the work center in handling the planned work flow. Working the right number of hours is reported by weeks overdue, while working the right hours is reported by the priority index.

Level of Aggregation

In large plants, there are supervisors, superintendents, and managers, each with a span of control. All need performance reports, in the same format, but with figures aggregated for their respective level. Figure 16.12 illustrates this for three levels. At

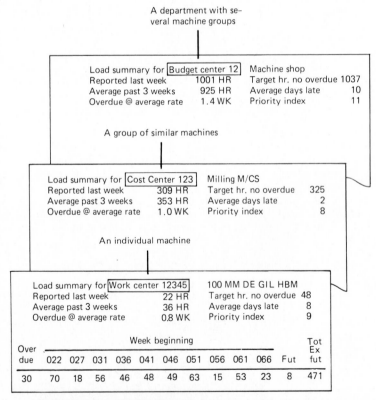

FIG. 16.12 Aggregation for three levels of shop load summaries to the superintendent and shop manager level from the workstation level.

the lowest level, there is one summary per work center. The superintendent can apply similar information across cost centers. The manufacturing manager's information is aggregated at the plant level, where similar corrective action can be applied across departments. As can be seen in the figure, the manager is responsible for 1001 hr/wk, the superintendent for 309 hr/wk, and the supervisor for work centers from 15 to 41 hr/wk. This aggregation aids in putting responsibility where it can best be acted on, exposing higher-level personnel to broader pictures while protecting them from detail. Each report is the exact same program algorithm applied to progressively broader groups of productive facilities.

CORRECTIVE ACTION

If the planning is good, then the shop has two main tasks: (1) work the right number of hours and balance the load to capacity and (2) work the right hours and control priority (sequence).[9] Thus one expects the combined system of the factory with its staff and control programs to control the load balance and sequence.

Why Correct?

Consider two work centers, each off schedule, running early or, more typically, late. Being late to schedule is obviously serious. Work centers being late by different amounts is also serious but perhaps not so obvious. Figure 16.13 explains why.

One could develop the curves by putting an X on coordinate paper according to the days each labor operation is late. After many X's are plotted, a rough bell curve will probably develop, with an average (average days late) and a distribution around the average, expressed by its standard deviation, or priority index. By inspection, it can be seen that the following are true: (1) Assembly can start no sooner than permitted by deliveries from work center 1. (2) Work center 2's production is idle for at least the days between the two averages and usually much more, because the tail to

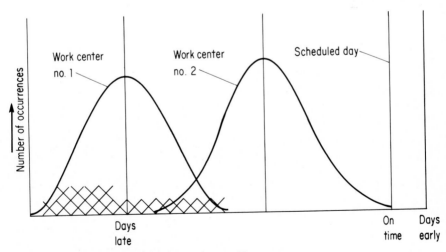

FIG. 16.13 Two work centers feeding one assembly.

the right of the curve for the distribution of work center 1 will control when matching parts are available.

Assuming that one work center feeds the other, instead of them both feeding assembly, does not change the problem. Shipments are made only when the latest work center permits. Since assembly gets parts directly or indirectly from most of the work centers in the plant, the output of the plant is set by the latest work center. Hence, that is an important conclusion: One of the main purposes of corrective action is to find and eliminate the bottlenecks in the plant.

One needs the system's help to avoid these obstacles:

1. Bottlenecks that migrate in response to changes in mix and random events such as illness and parts shortages.

2. Identification of bottlenecks. One operator with 25 hr overdue is worse off than 20 operators with 250 hr overdue.

3. Loss of priority control. Working out of sequence broadens the base of the bell curves, indicating bottleneck symptoms because so much work is overdue. The work center may be working ample hours to carry the load, if only they were the right hours. Overtime usually makes things worse by generating still more wrong parts. The system needs sharp selectivity to separate capacity from priority trouble.

It is necessary to have accurate pointers to loss of load to capacity balance and loss of priority control so that the right corrective action can be applied. This prevents a capacity solution, such as overtime, being applied to a priority problem of working on the wrong things.

When to Correct

The more time that passes, the harder correction becomes. Drift in either the capacity to load balance or the schedule must be corrected immediately; otherwise, the entire factory slows down to the pace and priority of the work center in trouble. But corrective action applied hourly may introduce a destructive nervousness. Most plants use a compromise such as to correct the course weekly and follow up daily.

How to Correct

There is invariably one work center in a department with the most overdue work, shown by weeks overdue at average rate, and one with the least overdue work. The ideal solution to a capacity problem is to take manpower from the work center with the least overdue work and apply it to the one with the most overdue work. Interchangeable skills, liberal labor contracts, and staffing flexibility are needed to make it happen, but it is the most effective solution. Costs that do arise, such as paying an operator above the job classification, are small compared with the alternatives, such as shipping late or paying overtime in the overloaded work center while underloaded ones continue making unwanted parts. Whenever overtime is needed somewhere, excess time is available somewhere else. These two should be considered together, never separately.

The objective is to have equal days late or early across all work centers although peak loads predicted for the future may suggest working ahead to create time in the schedule to handle the peak load and consequently deliver on schedule.

In balancing load to capacity, two useful indicators are weeks overdue and average days late. One should control by the weeks overdue but also monitor the average days late. Great divergence between the two means that some work on the schedule is not being done perhaps because it is not really needed. What is on the schedules must be what is genuinely needed in the sequence shown.

To select work centers for corrective action, arrange them by descending weeks overdue. From this and from the loads expected in future weeks, select a target number of hours this week for each work center. The closer it is to the top of the list, the more augmenting a work center gets, e.g., overtime, shifts, subcontracting. See the work center capacity control report.

Corrective action via input/output control is best. See the capacity control report, Table 16.15, for which the needed data can be collected either manually or by a real-time reporting system. Work center 01 is close to the objective cumulative hours as of Tuesday night, but work center 03 appears to be slipping badly. This may be a true picture (manpower unavailable) or an illustration of the hazards of averaging. Work center 03 may have a peak load in the last 3 days of the week for which supervision is prepared, and there may be no cause for concern. Assume, for the moment, that there is a real problem and that the overdue orders from work center 03 must be expedited. Recalling the one-to-one relationship between overtime and undertime, one should look for extra manpower in the work center exceeding its objective. These questions must be answered: Are the manhours available? Are the skills available? In a well-managed shop, both time and skills can be redeployed on short notice, so the work center running ahead can be slowed down and the one running late can be speeded up.

This approach challenges the traditional thinking of factory personnel. To slow down a work center, even though it may be running late, is nearly unheard of in most plants. Yet it must be routine for shop management whenever the bottleneck is being augmented. Many problems of good shop floor control are emotional, political, and psychological—not technical. The production control staff must be prepared.

How to Correct Lost Priority Control

Consider the reasons why the bell curves go so wide:

1. Operator and supervisory preference to make changes based on incentive pay, available skills, length of run, etc. There is no place for preferences, and the sequence of work must be done as on the schedule.
2. *Materials handling.* Materials movement should be locked into the schedule so that a work center's output is moved on schedule and not moved if not due. Better still, the material should not be moved until it is called for, as in the Kanban system.
3. *Physical layout of input queues.* First in/last out (FILO) materials movement must be overcome with devices such as color-coding floor areas by date. If parts are flat, store the parts vertically so that they can be grabbed easily. Use short conveyors to force adherence to sequence. The plant and its part feeder systems dictate the queue input, but thought must be given to avoiding FILO.
4. *Shortages of two kinds.* Genuine shortages of parts coming in the door or those caused by scrap and shortages from earlier bottlenecks or working out of sequence. The first needs legitimate expediting. But in most factories, the second reason is the main cause of shortages, and expediting is self-defeating, creating

as many problems as it solves by disrupting work flows and applying priority cures to a capacity problem.

Steps in Correcting Priority Problems

First, distinguish priority problems from capacity problems. They look similar. Begin with a Pareto sort, as illustrated in the work center control report. The objective is to make all the indices small. But with limited production control manpower, one must concentrate on the biggest payoff problems. "How small is small" is set by the plant environment. It is like product costs—no matter what it is, it is too high.

Assign a task force to fix work centers with high-priority indices soon—that is, before next week. The group should always consist of production control personnel, augmented one week by purchasing and receiving, perhaps next week by engineering and the drafting department, and the week after that by tool design. These functions must be coordinated.

Some problems are temporary, such as incoming trucks of material being held up, but others are long-standing, such as the tool designers never having a work schedule. The latter are the truly important problems, but once they are fixed, they stay fixed.

Who Should Take Corrective Action?

Factory supervision and production control share the responsibility for taking corrective action. Here are two one-sentence job descriptions for these functions: *Factory supervision* should direct the efficient performance of eligible work according to the schedule sequence and at a sufficient rate. *Production control* should ensure that work which should be done can be done, i.e., ensure a flow of eligible work to work centers.

To do this, production control and supervisors must agree on a short-range plan by a procedure broadly similar to the following:

1. Use current load summaries to agree on the short-term deployment of labor among the work centers, in view of past performance indicators such as weeks overdue, oncoming loads as displayed in the body of the load summary, and known changes such as vacations, retirements, machine maintenance, and directives from management on overall working rates, which result from a review of aggregate load summaries. Record this figure in a short-range plan such as shown in Table 16.15, the capacity control report.

2. *Review priority indices.* Decide where there is a priority control problem, how it shall be handled, by whom, and when.

3. Implement the plan and follow up on where the greatest threats to on-time shipment exist in the feeder and final-assembly line.

4. Repeat this process when current performance information and load summaries are available.

Information Sources

A closed-loop system can signal the weeks of work that are overdue. The information comes from the data stream in the feedback loop from "execute capacity plans" to "capacity requirements planning" in conventional models of such systems.[10] Software programs include a standard-deviation routine, which computes the priority index and average number of days late. Thus all key information can be obtained from a closed-loop system. The system must retain with each labor record its scheduled date and its parent order by pegging, so that the priority can be maintained and controlled. This is especially important when work is behind schedule.[11]

What to Do with a Manual or Inadequate System

If the system will not support the procedure described, use the following principles to obtain improvement:

1. *Make bottlenecks visible.*   Set up an exit storage area per work center. Be sure nothing is removed until it is called for by the next work center. After running a short time, those storage areas that are full are work centers with overcapacity. These should be stopped. Those that are empty are the bottlenecks.

2. *Adjust work center capacities.*   Move personnel from the full-output queue work centers to where the work center output queues are empty. Be sure skill interchangeability and labor contractual matters are solved first.

3. Concurrently with items 1 and 2, ensure that the dating system gives accurate priorities and that the schedule contains only wanted work.[12] Otherwise, action 2 will cause trouble. The clogged exit storage space will contain parts that are not wanted.

4. Each problem solution reveals the next level of improvement needed. Do not shut down the shop, but sell the improvements to coworkers and management. Be prepared to act promptly on problems.

Although the principles discussed are more reaction than action, they will help to make shipments on time with minimum work-in-process and the least labor cost.

Manual Card Systems

If the production is sufficiently repetitive and the product uses many common parts, the manual "pull" Kanban system is ideal.[13]

Handling Overdue Work

Overdue work is either overdue but not wanted or overdue but still wanted and in the same priority. In the first case, its priority has changed, and the work should be rescheduled. In the second case, the work should stay in the same sequence, to be moved either to a customer or to the next work center. The work must not be rescheduled. The system must retain priority information regardless of overdue status. If the desired sequence of shipment has not changed, the priority of work with respect to other work has not changed. The whole schedule is seldom late—only parts of it are. As parts of a job are delayed, they float to the top of the work schedule at the work center. This is a powerful form of simple, automatic priority enhancement. It does in an orderly, consistent way what expediting does in a destructive way.[14]

A Closing Observation

The above principles of performance reporting and corrective action apply to any factory having significant load and mix variations over a time span of a few weeks or days. This covers 70 percent or more of Western factories. The programs outlined can be applied intensively in firms that make products with these characteristics: long manufacturing cycles, multilevel products using parts and assemblies, many routing points, significant mix and activity changes, labor-intensive nature, made-to-order status, and customer options.

REFERENCES

1. Neville May, *Shop Floor Controls—Principles and Use*, American Production and Inventory Control Society (APICS) Conference Proceedings, 1981.
2. *IBM COPICS Manual*, vol. 3, IBM Corporation, White Plains, N.Y., 1972.
3. Jan B. Young, *Practical Dispatching*, APICS Conference Proceedings, 1981.
4. G. W. Plossl and O. W. Wight, *Production and Inventory Control, Principles and Techniques*, Prentice-Hall, Englewood Cliffs, N.J., 1967.
5. May, op. cit.
6. Ibid.
7. Stephen C. Galligan and Panna Hazarika, "Shop Floor Control in a Continuous Production Flow Environment," *Production and Inventory Management*, fourth quarter, 1982.
8. *IBM COPICS Manual*.
9. Plossl and Wight, op. cit.
10. Galligan and Hazarika, op. cit.
11. Plossl and Wight, op. cit.
12. Ibid.
13. Donald E. Ramlow and Eugene H. Wall, *Production Planning and Control*, Prentice-Hall, Englewood Cliffs, N.J., 1967.
14. Plossl and Wight, op. cit.

BIBLIOGRAPHY

Fox, Robert: "OPT—An Answer for America," *Inventories and Production Magazine*, July–Aug. 1982 through Mar.–Apr. 1983.

Galligan, Stephen C., and Panna Hazarika: "Shop Floor Control in a Continuous Production Flow Environment," *Production and Inventory Management*, fourth quarter, 1982.

Gue, F. S.: "Controlling Capacity and Priority—Manufacturing's Potent Pair of Principles," *Inventories and Production Magazine*, May–June, Nov.–Dec. 1981.

———: *Increased Profits through Better Control of Work in Process*, Reston Publishing, Reston, Va., 1980.

Hall, Robert: *Zero Inventories*, Dow Jones-Irwin, Homewood, Ill., 1983.

IBM COPICS Manual, vol. 7, IBM Corporation, White Plains, N.Y., 1972.

May, N.: *Shop Floor Controls—Principles and Use*, APICS Conference Proceedings, 1981.

Orlicky, J.: "Net Change vs. Regenerative Systems," *IBM Systems Journal*, vol. 12, no. 1, 1973.

Plossl, G. W., and O. W. Wight: *Production and Inventory Control, Principles and Techniques*, Prentice-Hall, Englewood Cliffs, N.J., 1967.

Ramlow, Donald E., and Eugene H. Wall: *Production Planning and Control*, Prentice-Hall, Englewood Cliffs, N.J., 1967.

Wallace, Thomas F. (ed.): *APICS Dictionary*, 5th ed., APICS, Falls Church, Va., 1984.

Young, Jan B.: *Practical Dispatching*, APICS Conference Proceedings, 1981.

17

Scheduling and Loading Techniques*

Editor:

TIMOTHY J. GREENE, Ph.D., Associate Professor, Department of Industrial Engineering and Operations Research, Virginia Polytechnique University, Blacksburg, Virginia

Co-Editors:

LLOYD M. CLIVE, P.E., CPIM, Coordinator of Industrial Engineering—Technology Programs, Centre for Integrated Manufacturing, Sir Sandford Fleming College, Peterborough, Ontario

STEPHEN DE LURGIO, Ph.D., CFPIM, Professor of Operations Management, University of Missouri at Kansas City, Missouri

HANK GRANT, Ph.D., President, FACTROL, West Lafayette, Indiana

K. JAMES HUNT, Manager, Special Projects, Arrowhead Metals, Ltd., Toronto, Ontario

---

* This chapter includes excerpts from chapters appearing in the first edition, edited by George W. Plossl and Richard E. Edgerton.

Scheduling and loading are so important to manufacturers, as well as some non-manufacturers, that they have developed and implemented sophisticated computerized systems for production control. Hospitals do not have production control departments, but they do schedule operating rooms, laboratories, and other facilities. Radio and television broadcasters schedule commercials. Colleges and other schools schedule classes. Whatever their product, they face competition, necessitating looking into the future and gaining control over production.

TYPES OF PRODUCTION SCHEDULING

The distinguishing feature of process-type production is that work flows through a fixed and continuous manufacturing process. This differs from a job shop, where work is processed intermittently by job order or lot. Examples of continuous-process-type manufacturing are to be found in the chemical, food, and paper industries.

Continuous-Process Manufacturing

Since work flows through a continuous manufacturing process, production control in this type of industry is often called *flow control*. The rate of flow can usually be varied, although there are processes in which the rate can be varied little if at all.

The importance of production control and scheduling in a continuous manufacturing process is directly proportional to the ease and the amount by which the flow may be varied. If the rate of flow can be varied easily and significantly, management is more apt to vary it. The more it is varied, the more effort is required to keep the system under control and the greater the need for the production control function.

There are different ways to vary the production rate in continuous-process production:

The line equipment may be operated for more or fewer hours.

The line may be operated with more or fewer personnel.

The line may be operated intermittently, with the personnel doing other work.

The line may be operated in two or more stages by pulling the partially completed product from the line and accumulating an in-process inventory. After this inventory is built up to a certain point, the first phase of the process may be shut down and the second phase operated by feeding in the in-process inventory. The same personnel would be used in both phases.

Continuous-process manufacturing has an advantage over intermittent production in that feedback, the comparison of what was scheduled versus what was actually produced, is easier. Since there is a "flow" of material, it is usually possible to utilize some means of automatically and continuously measuring the flow in terms of pieces, gallons, feet, pounds, etc. Feedback, of course, is required in order to maintain the scheduling process.

Generally, scheduling a continuous manufacturing process is easier than scheduling an intermittent manufacturing process. However, there is often enough difficulty so that computers and modern scheduling techniques have been successfully applied.

Intermittent Production

Intermittent production is defined in the *APICS Dictionary* as "a production system in which jobs pass through functional departments in lots." A plant with production of this type is usually called a *job shop*. A home kitchen can be thought of as a job shop, with the refrigerator representing one department, work counters a second, and the stove a third. Contrast this with a cannery where tomatoes are fed into one end of a processing line and continuously processed until they emerge from the other end in cans.

Anyone scheduling and controlling intermittent production is faced with several types of problems. One of these is the requirement for data on the status of the system. Such questions as these are common: "When will order 4763 be done?" "Is it behind schedule?" "Where is it?" "How long will it take to fill this rush order?" "Where can we make this new product?" "How long will it take to make it?" "A machine is down, a product was scrapped, a key employee is absent, what does this do to our schedule?" "Why do you change the schedule so much?" "Why didn't you tell us yesterday that we must work overtime today?"

An associated problem is that much of the data pertaining to the production system are not available, not readily available, unreliable, or reliable for only a short period of time. Thus, many decisions must be based on insufficient data, and consequently performance is often not what it could or should be. The cost of obtaining better data may be prohibitive, however.

Another basic problem is deciding what to schedule and how to schedule it. Should *products* be scheduled or should *machines* be scheduled? What about a combination of these? Should all products or machines be scheduled or just some of them? Should departments or work centers be scheduled? What are the scheduling rules? How should they be applied?

There is little or no problem involved in determining the objectives for a production-scheduling system. The problem is to achieve them. A good production-scheduling system should give a smooth, efficient, profitable, low-overall-cost operation with minimum inventories of production materials, in-process materials, and finished goods. It should be reliable, deliver orders on time with minimal lead times, and have fast reaction times to sudden status changes due to breakdowns, rush orders, late arrival of materials, and employee absences. Finally, it should give an objective, clear-cut feedback of results.

Repetitive Manufacturing

Repetitive manufacturing is the production of discrete units, planned and executed by a schedule, usually at relatively high speeds and volumes, with the material tending to move in a sequential flow. Typical repetitive manufactured products include electrical appliances, toys, and some types of clothing.

The authority for production in repetitive manufacturing is the daily-run schedule, and the feedback information for control is the number of items that pass a control point.

Project-Type Manufacturing

Project-type production relates to the production of a unit or a small number of units that are managed by a project team. Paper machines, some large machine tools, marine diesel engines, and ships are all typical products made in a project-type production situation. The program evaluation review technique (PERT) and the critical-path method (CPM) are typical of the scheduling techniques developed for project-type production.

SCHEDULING PRINCIPLES

To do production scheduling, the production control department must know:

What to make

When to make it

Where to make it

How to make it

What to make it of

How much time is necessary to make it

When it is due

Since production is often for inventory, sales forecasting is usually very important in providing input data to a production control–scheduling system. Although the sales forecast may extend for planning purposes into the distant future, scheduling is usually done for only the near future of perhaps one or two weeks. Established company policy will usually require the production control department to schedule production to meet the requirements of the forecast. In some companies, however, production control is allowed to second-guess the forecast. Actually, there is some second-guessing in either case, in that production control may revise the schedule to use overtime or may increase the rate of production, if necessary, to meet the forecast or to meet actual sales.

Once production control knows what to make, it must know the materials required to make the product. That information should be available from a bill of materials. A bill of materials shows the structure of the product (see Chapter 10).

Frequently, not even stock chasing begins until jobs have failed to meet their shipping date. A better approach is to establish schedule dates by operations and to review jobs that are due to ship this week and next week, as well as those that are past due, to determine what problems are causing delays. Table 17.1 shows this type of *production schedule review*, which can be very effective if used in conjunction with an operation-scheduling system to detect delays. The sales department can then be informed which jobs will be shipped on time and which will not, thus providing it with the means of telling customers ahead of time if their jobs will not be shipped as promised.

Operation-Time Scheduling

Table 17.2 lists the steps in scheduling operations. The first is to provide data for the scheduling system; this data must include the operation sequence, or factory routing. Figure 17.1 is a typical manufacturing order; it includes the operation sequence and shows the setup hours and running time required. Running hours have been calculated by multiplying the quantity on the order (expressed in thou-

TABLE 17.1   Production Schedule Review

Customer	SO	Past Due	This Week	Next Week	Nearest Lot Loc.	Nearest Lot Qty.	Next Lot Loc.	Next Lot Qty.	Remarks
Stalco	17,624	577			D 32	1,150			Will ship next week
Chambers	11,318			40	D 40	94			On salvage (?)
Trild Inc.	10,628		1,100		D 29	1,000		NA	Call complete
Morton	10,959		1,780	2,500	D 32	5,200			Balance 6040 stock
Padsing	11,003		7,000		D 22	7,500			OK
Pennbush	11,004			20,000	D 22	10,750	D 2	10,750	Will ship 10M balance 3/26
Stalco	11,008			7,000	D 40	8,240			OK

TABLE 17.2   Scheduling Steps

1. Provide data
   a. Operation sequence
   b. Standards, engineered or estimated
2. Develop system
   a. Shop calendar
   b. Scheduling rules
3. Choose scheduling method
   a. Backward scheduling
   b. Forward scheduling
4. Schedule
   a. Multiply order quantity by time per operation
   b. Add transit time
   c. Add allowance for delays

sands) by the time figure shown in the column headed "Running Hours/1000." This order is designed to travel with the work through the factory so that the operators can note their time and quantities directly on it. In some companies, this operation sequence is maintained on a master form, which can be reproduced when repetitive orders for the same product are run. In others, this type of routing is maintained in a computer disk file, which can in turn produce hard copy or a readout on a terminal. When the manufacturing order is printed out, a card may be made for each operation, to be used by the machine operator to report the time. By itself, the traveling order does not usually provide the means to report an operator's time and quantity to the timekeeping department.

Time standards, either engineered or estimated, are essential to any scheduling system. Since there will always be orders for new items that have to be scheduled into production before engineering standards have been developed, some means of estimating these standards in either the industrial engineering or the production control department is necessary. Accuracy is not vital, but consistency is important.

Figure 17.2 shows a shop calendar used by many companies on which each *working day* is numbered consecutively; in some cases, the consecutive numbering

Part name Pinion spindle			Drawing No. E-17352	Used on Frame assembly E-oo14		Date wk. 21	Order 2,950		Qty. 5,000	

Material
  Steel bar stock—0.500″
    Spec. A-407
				Remarks
				Note thread is left-hand						

Dept.	Mach. group	Op. No.	Operation description	Set- up hr	Run hr/ 1,000	Run hr this lot	Man No.	Qty. comp.	Qty. scrap	Qty. salv.	Insp.
040	Truck	01	Draw bar stock from stores								
517	14	02	Make pinion spindle on screw machine	14.5	3.1	15.5					
319	18	03	Mill slot to B/P	1.3	9.5	47.5					
771	42	04	Tumble for burrs			2.0					
624	06	05	Drill hole for pin	0.2	4.C	20.0					
771	40	06	Degrease			0.5					
771	43	07	Plate — dull zinc			4.7					
009	04	08	Inspect			AQC 403					
040	Truck	09	Deliver to stock			—					

FIG. 17.1   Typical manufacturing order.

covers a period of 4 years. This enables the scheduler to establish dates without correcting for weekends, plant shutdown periods, or holidays.

Some simple scheduling rules are shown in Table 17.3. These are oversimplified but illustrate the type of rules that must be developed before scheduling can begin.

Block Scheduling

Many companies use general rules, such as the block-scheduling rules shown in Table 17.4, to estimate the amount of time required for each part. These save computation time but usually result in extremely long lead times.

Table 17.5 shows two ways of scheduling the manufacturing order shown previously. Both cases show backward scheduling from the required date (week 51 or day 445). Block scheduling with completion dates by week numbers results in a total of 14 weeks' lead time. Operation-time scheduling requires 44 working days, or about 9 weeks to complete; in the computation, the transit time is added to the next operation. For example, operation 7 must be completed on day 440 in order to allow 3 days of transit time and 1 day of running time at operation 8. Transit time is used to cover the following elements:

1. Time waiting to be picked up for movement out of the department—*wait time*
2. Time actually in transit—*move time*
3. Time waiting to be started at the next machine center—*queue time*

Setup time has also been taken into account. In operation 2, for example, one extra operating day is included because of the setup time required on the screw machine.

JUNE

Wk No.	Sun.	Mon.	Tues.	Wed.	Thurs.	Fri.	Sat.
22	May 24	25 / 347	26 / 348	27 / 349	28 / 350	29	30
23	31	June 1 / 351	2 / 352	3 / 353	4 / 354	5 / 355	6
24	7	8 / 356	9 / 357	10 / 358	11 / 359	12 / 360	13
25	14	15 / 361	16 / 362	17 / 363	18 / 364	19 / 365	20
26	21	22 / 366	23 / 367	24 / 368	25 / 369	26 / 370	27

JULY

Wk No.	Sun.	Mon.	Tues.	Wed.	Thurs.	Fri.	Sat.
27	June 28	29 / 371	30 / 372	July 1 / 373	2 / 374	3	4
28	5	6 / 375	7 / 376	8 / 377	9 / 378	10 / 379	11
*29	12	13	14	15	16	17	18
*30	19	20	21	22	23	24	25

*Vacation weeks are subject to change.

AUGUST

Wk No.	Sun.	Mon.	Tues.	Wed.	Thurs.	Fri.	Sat.
31	July 26	27 / 380	28 / 381	29 / 382	30 / 383	31 / 384	Aug. 1
32	2	3 / 385	4 / 386	5 / 387	6 / 388	7 / 389	8
33	9	10 / 390	11 / 391	12 / 392	13 / 393	14 / 394	15
34	16	17 / 395	18 / 396	19 / 397	20 / 398	21 / 399	22

FIG. 17.2 Shop calendar.

TABLE 17.3   Simple Scheduling Rules

1. Mutiply hours per thousand pieces by number of thousands on order.
2. Round up to nearest 8 hrs, 16 hrs, 24 hrs depending on number of shifts and express time in days; round down to nearest day when excess hours are less than 10 percent of total; minimum of 1 day for operation.
3. Allow 5 days to withdraw stock from stockroom.
4. Allow 1 day between successive operations within the same department.
5. Allow 3 days between successive operations in different departments.
6. Allow 1 day for inspection.
7. Allow 1 day to get material into stockroom.
8. Allow 2 extra weeks for screw-machine parts.

TABLE 17.4   Block-Scheduling Rules

1. Allow 1 week for releasing order and drawing material from storeroom.
2. Allow 6 weeks for screw-machine operations.
3. Allow 1 day for each 400 pieces in the milling department; round upward to next full week.
4. Allow 1 week for drilling and tapping, burring, and similar operations using minor equipment.
5. When operations are very short, combine within the same week.
6. Allow 1 week for inspection and delivery of completed material.

Backward and Forward Scheduling

There are two principal scheduling methods:

Backward Scheduling.   Starting with the date on which the order is required to be completed, calculate backward to determine the proper release date for the order. This assumes that the finished date is known, and the start date is desired.

Forward Scheduling.   Starting with either today's date or the first open time at the first operation, compute the schedule date for each operation to determine the completion date.

Forward scheduling is most frequently used in companies such as paper and steel mills, where the product is bulky but requires few components. The scheduler will probably check the customer's order, and if the requested date and the required date are far enough away, the order will not be scheduled until necessary. In effect, this is really combining backward scheduling with forward scheduling.

Backward scheduling is typically used where components being manufactured to go into an assembled product have different lead times. After determining the required schedule dates for major subassemblies, the scheduler uses these as the required dates for each component and works backward to determine the proper release date for each component's manufacturing order.

TABLE 17.5 Block and Operation-Time Scheduling

Operation No.	Block Scheduling		Operation-Time Scheduling	
	Time Allowed	Week	Time Allowed	Day
Release date		37		402
01	1 week	38	5 days	407
02	6 weeks	44	12 days $T^* =$ 3 days	419
03	3 weeks	47	3 days $T =$ 3 days	425
04	1 week	48	1 day $T =$ 3 days	429
05	1 week	49	2 days $T =$ 3 days	434
06	} 1 week	50	1 day $T =$ 1 day	438
07			1 day $T =$ 3 days	440
08	} 1 week	51	1 day	444
09			1 day	445
Date required		Week 51		Day 445

*T = transit time.

Sequencing Similar Orders

Substantial advantages can be gained by processing similar orders in their proper sequence:

- Setup times on screw machines, punch presses, etc., can be reduced by running families of parts that require only minor changes to convert the setup.
- Cleanout and changeover times can be reduced by running lighter-colored batches of paints, chemicals, etc., before darker ones.
- Raw material can be saved by combining corrugated box sizes, textile patterns, etc., when cutting from continuous sheets.

Inventory records are coded to identify all members of the significant families or preferred sequences. Listings can be used for periodic review to ensure consideration of all items in the groups. The family or group can be considered as one item when determining (economic) order quantities. The total for the family is then distributed among its members so that all will run out or reach the reorder point at about the same time and the family will again be ready for processing.

Scheduling Considerations

1. Select the input to meet the planned production rate. If the plant is not actually producing to meet this plan, the amount of work released into starting operations should not exceed actual capacity.

2. Keep backlogs off the shop floor wherever possible, because they:
   a. Are more difficult to control.
   b. Make engineering changes more expensive to implement.
   c. Generate more expediting.
   d. Create physical problems (newer jobs pile up in front of old work that gets pushed back into corners).
3. Sequence orders based on latest requirements rather than on required dates established when the order was first released. The computer (which can compare changing inventory requirements for many items with production requirements) and the introduction of such techniques as critical-ratio scheduling make it possible to review and revise desired schedule dates periodically.
4. Schedule only those items which the factory can make; planners or schedulers should not release orders for which raw materials, components, tools, or other necessary materials are not available. This will clearly define where the basic problem lies in getting work completed. There are some exceptions to this rule. Where a finished product takes 3 weeks to assemble and the missing component is one added at the last operation, assembly orders can be issued if the scheduler is confident that the missing component will be available when needed. In the drug, electronic, and similar industries, it is sometimes impossible to determine before a schedule is released whether the product can actually be produced.
5. Schedule to a short cycle (weekly or even daily). This not only helps to get the latest and most accurate requirement dates on the orders scheduled but also assists in controlling the orders flowing through the factory.

   An interesting fallacy that has gained wide recognition is that the schedule period must equal the lead time. Even in the extreme example of a company with a 9-month lead time required for a sequence of 50 different operations, someone must make a decision practically on a daily basis as to which items will be started in the first operation. A firm 9-month starting schedule is not required. A weekly starting schedule based on the latest available information on customer requirements, inventory status, and plant workload is practical and effective.

Scheduling Assemblies

Two factors vital in scheduling assembly operations are *component availability* and *assembly-capacity rates*. Parts flow must support assembly rates. Where components are common to many products, the order-point/order-quantity inventory control system is generally used. When unique to one product, a part in a complex assembly of many components with different lead times should be controlled by a materials plan.

Scheduled assembly rates can be held close to actual capacity since component availability is known. Staging or laying out sets of parts in advance of assembly should be held to a minimum. Increasing these advance supplies as a means of gaining information sooner on shortages is poor practice because:

1. Component inventories will be increased.
2. More space will be occupied.
3. Additional records of shortages in each kit will be required.
4. Components in short supply will become more critical.
5. Record errors increase through shifting components from one layout to another.

6. Stockroom workload increases.

7. Control of assembly priorities diminishes.

Scheduled assembly work should equal available capacity. Capacity usually varies with the mix of individual products requiring different assembly times. *Line balancing* is used to develop schedules of balanced loads of available capacity, utilizing the line flexibility by shifting work among work stations for economical assembly.

LOADING PRINCIPLES

There are two techniques for controlling a production system. One of these is scheduling; the other is loading. Of the two, loading is easier to do, but scheduling can give more control. Loading, however, can be very useful.

A *load* is the amount of work assigned to a facility, and *loading* is the assignment of work to a facility. Loading does not specify the sequence in which the facility is to do the work or when it is to do it. The facility may be a machine, a group of machines, a department, and so forth.

Loading is the aggregate assignment of jobs to specific work centers. Inputs necessary for loading include:

1. Routing

2. Standard hours per operations or work center

3. Gross machine or man-hours available

4. Efficiency factors

5. Due date

Loading is closely tied to capacity planning in the sense that loading is the first indication that capacity levels need adjusting.

Steps in the Loading Procedure

Typically, the loading process can be considered a six-step procedure (Table 17.6). Steps 1 through 4 are managerial decision steps that usually do not change week to week or month to month. The last two steps are required on a periodic basis as an input to scheduling.

The first step in machine loading is to choose the load centers. Some companies load by department only if all the machines in a department are interchangeable. When different machine centers within the department have different capabilities (as in a general machine department), the technique is to break the machines down into similar machine groups. All 24-in boring mills, for example, might be included in the same group if jobs are interchangeable among the machines. In some instances—for example, a screw machine with a milling cutter attachment but otherwise identical with other machines in the group—coding should be set up so that an individual machine can be singled out if a job can be done only on it. Group as many machines together as possible, since this will reduce the work and tend to stabilize the load.

The second step is to develop *efficiency factors* by load centers. A load center with two people is capable of 80 hr of production per week, but actual output might

TABLE 17.6 Loading Steps

1. Choose load centers	4. Choose loading method
a. Department	*a.* To infinite capacity
b. Group	*b.* To finite capacity
c. Machine or workstation	*c.* Combination
2. Develop efficiency factors by load center	5. Load scheduled orders into load centers
3. Determine capacity by center	6. Unload completed hours

be considerably less than 80 hr if time is spent on setup work and indirect activity. If they are working on incentive, however, they could be turning out more than 80 "standard hours" of production.

The third step is to determine the gross capacity by load center. This capacity is either man- or machine-dependent. A center is machine-dependent if all machines have at least one operator assigned. A center is man-dependent if there are fewer people than machines and machines stand idle while all workers are busy. With the number of people or machines as an input, the gross capacity is the gross number of hours that the resources (people or machine) are available per planning period. The center's capacity is then the gross capacity times the efficiency factor.

The fourth step is to choose the loading method, which may be either to finite or to infinite capacity. *Infinite-capacity loading* means showing the work for a work center in the time period required, regardless of the work center's capacity. *Finite-capacity loading* means putting no more work into a work center than it can be expected to execute.

The fifth step is to load the scheduled orders into the load centers while at the same time considering the capacity and other restrictions.

The sixth step is to select the unloading technique. *Unloading* is the process of removing work from the load as jobs are partially or totally completed. Manual systems may require shortcuts, such as considering a job to be completed when the first lot of pieces is reported; this saves posting many partial lots and recalculating load balances, but the load is always understated by the number of hours remaining on jobs unloaded. Another shortcut relieves the load only when the last lot is completed, giving a load constantly overstated by the hours completed but not removed.

The numbers of hours to be unloaded must equal the number of hours loaded for each job. For example, if 12 standard hours have been loaded and the job is completed in 9 actual hours, 12 hr must be relieved from the load.

A machine load, based on the actual work orders released, is a good short-term technique for highlighting underloads or overloads on work centers and showing the need for overtime, temporary transfers, subcontracting, or other short-range adjustments. It is seldom adequate for long-term capacity planning.

Loading Concepts and Problems

Why use loading? The major reason is that it can predict some future events. A chart, instead of the late orders, tells of an overload, and it tells this in advance. This same chart can warn of excess capacity before the machines and workers are idle. Therefore, loading is most useful to dispatchers, supervisors, and production schedulers scheduling shopwork. Loading can be used to smooth the workload from month to month or between machines. It is an aid in identifying the critical departments or machines and in judging the effect of breakdowns, rush orders, and new products. It is also useful for documenting the requirements for more or less capacity.

When using infinite loading to create the schedule, it is necessary to check the load to determine whether there is sufficient capacity available in the time period in which the work is required. Loading to finite capacity by operation is more complex than infinite-capacity loading. A facility activity that does not go according to schedule may require that the load be recalculated, and therefore loads will fall in different time periods. Finite-capacity loading also requires that the schedules establish a priority for loading the jobs.

In practice, finite-capacity loading by itself is unsatisfactory, since it assumes that present capacity is all that is available and does not show the time period in which overloads will occur if an attempt is made to meet desirable schedules. Without the latter information, action cannot be taken to improve the plant's performance in meeting customer requirements.

A good machine-loading system involves a combination of both techniques. Orders are first scheduled and loaded to infinite capacity to see where overloads will occur, then rescheduled to level the load based on available capacity after corrective actions have been taken wherever possible.

An effective production-capacity plan must extend far enough into the future to cover the time required for hiring and training the needed production and service employees, obtaining the necessary equipment and materials, and operating long enough at higher capacity to be worthwhile. The backlog of open orders in the machine load rarely covers this much lead time.

Companies have successfully used *simulated* machine loads over longer planning periods to assist capacity planning. Forecasts of individual finished products to be manufactured during this period can be exploded into detailed requirements of production hours on each major work center. While actual production of individual items can be expected to vary greatly from such long-range forecasts, increases in one item will tend to be offset by decreases in another, and the aggregate hours will be reasonably accurate. Machine loads based on these aggregate hours will indicate developing trends toward underload or overload and will give dependable data on the average capacity required to meet the forecasted demand on manufacturing facilities.

The work may be assigned by the nature of the job. If the work can be done by more than one facility, it must be assigned to just one. If it can be done by only one facility, there is no alternative but that one facility. If the work is drilling a hole and there are three drill presses, assignment must either be made to one of them or the three of them can be considered as one facility. The work may be assigned on an individual-job basis, but if the jobs are repetitive, they may be assigned on a standard basis by the use of routings. *Standard routings* show, for each part or assembly, all the operations that must be done to make that part or assembly. In addition to the operations required, the routings also usually show the facility that performs the operation and the standard time required to perform it.

If standard routings are not available, someone must assign the individual jobs to the facilities and must estimate the work content of the assignments. This work content must be in terms that are comparable between jobs. Measures that may be used are hours, pieces, pounds, batches, gallons, etc., per hour, per shift, per day, etc.

Work assignments must be accumulated by facility in order to calculate the load on each facility. One method is to use a ledger in which the job numbers and job loads are entered for each facility. When a job is completed, it is marked off. The jobs are then added periodically to obtain the load on the facility.

Another method is to accumulate the assignments in "buckets"—one bucket for each facility. The bucket may be a box, a file, a peg, etc. A ticket is prepared for each job assigned to the facility and is placed in the box, in the file, or on the peg. A perpetual total of the facility load may be kept for each bucket. Job tickets, as they are added to the bucket, are added to this total. When completed and removed from the bucket, they are deducted from the total. If a computer is available, the buckets may be a computer file. If standard routings are available, these can also be kept in computer files. Then only the part numbers and the quantity need be entered for each job, and the computer can extend the quantities, make the assignments, and calculate the load.

SHORT-INTERVAL SCHEDULING

Short-interval scheduling is intended for the control of manpower-dependent processes in which, there is typically, (1) variation between jobs and (2) worker independence which prohibits setting standard times. In essence, short-interval scheduling is an employee-by-employee first-in-first-out queue system in which jobs are placed in the queue based on the scheduler's priority. The employee draws from the queue the next job to be processed, usually logging in when the job is started and when it is finished; this log provides feedback to the supervisor regarding employee performance. Employees can draw from a group queue or may have an individual queue.

Obviously, short-interval scheduling is scheduler-dependent. The scheduler must determine who should receive what work on a very short time-interval basis. In addition, the scheduler needs to have an intuitive feel for the expected operation time because the expected time has to be compared to the actual operation time in order to measure employee performance.

The productivity of clerical activities can be improved 30 to 50 percent through the allocation, assignment, and control of work in small increments. Short-interval scheduling has also been applied to maintenance, mail rooms, tool and die making, construction, and similar nonstandardized activities. Other advantages include improved control of backlogs, better attention to job priorities, earlier detection and identification of problems, more equitable work distribution, and improved discipline.

The system can be applied to short, repetitive operations reasonably uniform and constant in work content. Since the supervisors handle and distribute all work at frequent intervals and maintain the necessary control records, they must remain in the department almost constantly.

The benefits of short-interval scheduling are that it:

- Reduces volume fluctuations by regulating all work coming into this system, controls backlogs by dispatching only the planned amounts of work, and regulates the sequence of processing.
- Provides for handling nonroutine or exceptional work outside the system.
- Identifies all operations and changes the sequence to get the best possible work flow.
- Improves methods and layout to get the best possible performance.
- Estimates or measures all operation times.

- Determines the capacity of each work center and provides adequate, flexible staffing.
- Determines the overall timetable for the entire process.
- Determines the time interval for dispatching batches of work.
- Establishes one or more dispatching points under a supervisor to release work in the proper amounts, time, and order.
- Follows work in process to see that the schedule is being met.

Forecasting and planning for work expected and manpower required for a future time period is necessary. Long-range forecasts by management provide overall manpower, space, and equipment requirements. Short-range forecasts by the supervisor provide the basis for day-by-day assignment and control of work, using the batch or tally systems. For project work, it is normal week by week to plan 3 months ahead.

Short-interval scheduling relies on adequate work-measurement techniques; however, precise work measurement is not necessary. Supervisors should know or develop the level of performance that they can expect from their people with the standards available.

Management should receive regular reports highlighting present performance and trends. Periodic audits of the system should be made by an independent function (systems department or controller's auditor) to be sure that the system is being used properly, that standards are up to date, and that service is adequate.

The three types of short-interval scheduling systems in use are batch, tally, and project. Differences between the three types occur in length of scheduling increment, homogeneity of tasks to be performed, relative location of individual workstations, responsibility for recording work done, and degree of built-in control.

The *batch* system is the most positive. It includes, for each work center and work input station, a means for distributing batches of work to the employees, for keeping track of work assignments and completion, and for moving completed work to its next work center. At the input station, the work scheduler sorts incoming work into convenient homogeneous batches approximating 1 hr of work and attaches a batch ticket (as in Fig. 17.3), indicating to whom the work has been assigned and the number of units of work included. Batches are stored in trays or bins to be distributed in the desired priority. The employee initials the ticket and indicates the time that he or she completed the work.

The sign-out sheet (Fig. 17.4) shows the department's planned production target for the day. This provides a measure against which the supervisor can compare overall actual performance; it also indicates trouble spots developing either externally or internally. The supervisor notes the number of units of work assigned to each employee. At the end of each time period, the supervisor can determine incomplete assignments and distribute additional batches. The employees do not have to worry about work priority and can also be shown that work is being distributed fairly. As work batches are completed, the time period is noted on the sign-out sheet and the employee credited.

The *tally* system is used where employees work in scattered areas and/or where the work does not lend itself readily to batching. The work may go directly to the employee or it may be received into an input station, sorted, and distributed. The supervisor controls the distribution of work to the individual employees. The backlog is kept at the work input station, where the supervisor may determine its quantity and assign priority. Unlike the batch system, the tally system requires that the supervisor review work accomplished during the day at the individual work-

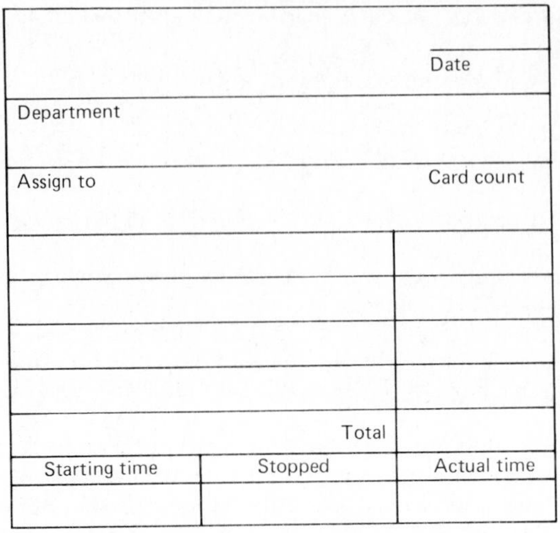

		Date	
Department			
Assign to		Card count	
	Total		
Starting time	Stopped	Actual time	

FIG. 17.3 Batch ticket.

stations. The tally system takes more diligent supervision. Spot checks of employees' tally sheets over long periods have revealed that actual productivity is often 10 to 15 percent less than that reported.

The *project* system is used for controlling the work of professional staff personnel, including engineers, accountants, and researchers, and focuses on the major phases of the project set up to accomplish specific objectives. One day each week, individuals and their supervisors review the progress of work against the previous week's schedule, including project hours to date, hours remaining, and whether or not the project is on schedule. They plan the hours to spend on each project and on other activities during the coming week. As the week progresses, the employees record the actual time spent each day on each project and other activities. Their supervisors periodically check the progress against the plan.

CRITICAL-RATIO SCHEDULING

Critical-ratio scheduling is a technique for use in production scheduling to establish and maintain relative priorities among jobs.* The priority is based on a combination of when the completed job is required and how much time is required to complete it (see Fig. 17.5). The job farthest behind schedule is that which proportionately (1) has the earliest due date, based on up-to-date knowledge of requirements, and also (2) has the longest time required for its completion, based on knowledge of lead times and routing.

---

* Based on APICS National Training Kit No. 2, by Arnold O. Putnam, President, Rath & Strong, Inc., and Robert Cronan, Principal, Rath & Strong, Inc.

Department _____ Division _____ Unit _____ Supervisor _____ Date _____

Forecast and daily plan comparison

	Starting carryover		Planned production			Ending carryover			Percent productivity			Hours required			Hours available			Out hours		
Hours received	Plan	Act.	Plan	Act.	Diff.	Plan	Act.	Diff.	Plan	Act.	Diff.	Plan	Act.	Diff.	Plan	Act.	Diff.	Plan	Act.	
Name / Asgm't																				Comp. Prod.
Assg'd																			C/O	
Sched.																				
Actual																				
Assg'd																				
Sched.																				
Actual																				
Assg'd																				
Sched.																				
Actual																				
Totals																				Comp. Prod.
Actual																			C/O	
Plan																				Tot. Plan
Cumulative difference																				

FIG. 17.4 Sign-out sheet.

17.17

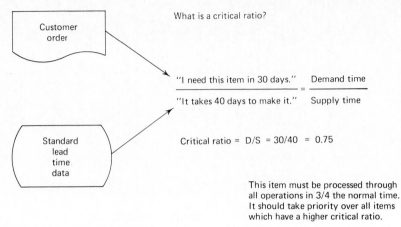

FIG. 17.5   What is critical ratio?

Critical ratio converts the *time* relationship between supply and demand into an index number:

$$\text{Critical ratio} = \frac{\text{demand time}}{\text{supply time}}$$

This makes all jobs, at any point in the process, directly comparable, regardless of the date they are needed or the date they will be completed.

Critical ratio can be used in applications that require economic grouping or sequencing of jobs in order to minimize setup or changeover costs. This requires a two-step procedure. The first step groups or sequences like sets of jobs, as required, within specified delivery restraints. Then critical ratios establish the relative priorities of the respective sets.

Critical ratio is a dynamic system, utilizing frequent feedback of both supply and demand information. In a stock-replenishment application, for example, regular reporting of updated on-hand balances enables the critical ratio to expedite those items for which demand is higher than normal. Equally important, the remaining items (for which demand is less than normal) are automatically "set aside" to permit critical jobs to move faster.

Critical-Ratio Applications

The critical-ratio technique can be incorporated into most production scheduling systems to:

- Determine the status of a specific job.
- Establish relative priorities among jobs on a common basis.
- Provide the ability to relate both stock and make-to-order jobs on a common basis.
- Provide the capability of adjusting priorities (and revising schedules) automatically for changes in both demand and job progress.
- Permit dynamic tracking of job progress and location.

- Eliminate the expediting functions of job-progress lookup, redating of all associated documents, special hand-carrying, etc., by providing supervisors and dispatchers with proper job sequence based on most current information.
- Provide basic data for overall queue control and manning decisions.

Critical-Ratio Formulas for Production Scheduling

The general supply and demand time relationship is developed as follows:

$$\text{Critical ratio (CR)} = \frac{(\text{date required}) - (\text{today})}{\text{days required to complete job}}$$

If CR > 1.0, the job is ahead of schedule. The date on which it will be available is earlier than the date on which it is required.

If CR = 1.0, the job is on time.

If CR < 1.0, the job is behind schedule (critical). Based on its standard lead time and normal rate of progress through the manufacturing process, it will take longer than the required date to obtain it. The lower the critical ratio, the more critical (farther behind schedule) the job is.

Stock-Replenishment Formula.   If the job is for a stock item's replenishment the due date (measured from today) is equal to the days of supply of stock remaining in inventory, assuming average daily usage. Normally, actual usage varies from the average. Critical ratio takes this into account. Whenever usage is below average, CR increases in value, and delivery of the job can be delayed by producing other, more critical jobs in the queue first. Conversely, whenever usage is greater than average, CR decreases in value, and the job moves faster through the process by taking a higher position in the queue.

Prior to implementing the formulas presented below, a decision must be made regarding the use of safety stock. Should the replenishment order be continuously monitored to time its arrival when:

On hand = safety stock?

On hand < safety stock, but > 0?

On hand = 0?

The alternative selected would depend on the nature of demand (large, sporadic demands versus small, frequent demands) and the nature of the manufacturing process (flexible and responsive versus costly and time-consuming to make changes).

1. The equation that includes a safety stock is

$$CR = \frac{(\text{OH} - \text{SS})/\text{ADU}}{\text{LTR}}$$

where   OH = inventory on hand
          SS = safety stock
        ADU = average daily usage
        LTR = standard lead time remaining

2. The equation for reserving a declining safety-stock balance is

$$CR = \frac{[OH - (SS)(LTR/LT)]/ADU}{LTR}$$

where LT = total standard lead time (all operations).

This formula schedules the stock-replenishment order to arrive after some of the safety stock has been used but before the stock on hand falls to zero. The amount of safety stock reserved is directly proportional to the time remaining to complete the job (LTR/LT). It should be noted that LTR never reaches zero, so some safety stock is always reserved. Use of a proportional reduction is based on the ability of critical ratio to accelerate delivery into stock if an unusually high variation in usage occurs.

Note that the safety stock in this formula yields a higher CR than without the safety stock and that a job becomes critical only when actual usage is greater than the sum of average usage plus the allowed safety-stock depletion.

3. No safety stock reserved. Whenever zero is substituted for safety stock in either of the above formulas, the result is the schedule receipt of the order when OH = 0.

This alternative would be satisfactory *only* if management were willing to accept a high level of stock-outs (although the duration of stock-outs would be relatively short).

4. Make-to-Order Formula. For make-to-order items, the requirement date equals a predetermined delivery date rather than a calculated stock-depletion date (Fig. 17.6). The delivery date may be the customer shipment date or, by explosion, the date that a component must be delivered to a stock point for use in a higher-level assembly. Frequently, this date must be changed between the original release of the order and its completion. All such changes must be kept current in order to calculate accurate critical ratios.

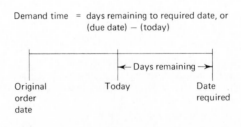

Demand time = days remaining to required date, or
(due date) − (today)

Original   Today   Date
order   required
date

Required date, though subject to change, represents a
"firm" commitment:
for assembly schedules
for customer shipments

Time is measured in working days.

FIG. 17.6   Critical-ratio demand: make-to-order items.

The formula is

$$CR = \frac{due\,date - today}{LTR}$$

where all days are working days.

The standard lead time remaining is the common denominator in all variations of the CR formula. It is defined as the expected *elapsed* time required for the job to pass through predetermined work centers from its present location to job completion. Since our concern is *time* remaining, not *work* remaining, the LTR is more than just the sum of setup and run times for all remaining operations. The LTR is equal to the total lead time minus the lead time for operations completed. The elapsed time, or standard lead time, for any specific work center is described by the formula

$$LT = SQ + \frac{SU + (Q \times R)}{H \times E}$$

where SQ = standard queue allowance in days
SU = setup time in hours
Q = lot size
R = run time in hours
H = hours worked per day
E = percent effectiveness in meeting standards

Note that the queue allowance is included and that the daily production rate is adjusted to represent a realistic estimate of what can be produced. When expanded, this formula is used to calculate the total lead time for any item:

$$LT + O + \Sigma \left[\frac{SQ + SU + (Q \times R)}{H \times E} \right] + \Sigma T$$

where O = order preparation time
T = added allowance for transit time between operations, where applicable

It is possible to simplify the above formulas in cases where the setup and run times are short (hours rather than days) and the queues relatively long (several days per operation). That portion of the formula dealing with work remaining can be set equal to zero, leaving

$$LT = O + \Sigma(SQ + T)$$

In addition to knowledge of total lead times, which is required for every production and inventory control system, critical-ratio scheduling requires:

1. Knowledge of operation lead times
2. Elemental breakdown into queue, setup, and run times
3. Definition of "standard" queue allowances

Use of Queue Allowances

The optimum queue is the minimum amount of work that will satisfy the above objectives. It is sufficient that a standard (not necessarily an optimum one) be defined. The critical ratio can be used to:

1. Sequence jobs (or economic groups of jobs) according to criticality.
2. Summarize the work in queue to determine whether delivery dates can be met.
3. Summarize the total shop load to determine whether changes in the overall production rate are necessary.

Critical ratio operates by changing the relative positions of jobs in queue. It is effective to the extent that job sequence is variable and that individual jobs can be accelerated or delayed in the process. Critical-ratio queue and load analysis provide the basic information for controlling overall lead times.

Summary Critical-Ratio Load Report. One method of consolidating and integrating this information is illustrated in the report format shown in Table 17.7. Each column is numbered to correspond to the following numbered paragraphs, which describe the content and relationships:

1. Identification of work center.
2. New orders written during the current period (week, month, etc.).
3. Long-term average of new orders during past periods. Large random variations in demand will be revealed in comparing columns 2 and 3.
4. Current-period production. Comparison with column 2 will reveal likely changes in critical queue at present or in the near future.
5. Long-term average production rate is a measure of capacity. Comparison with column 4 may signal significant production problems. Comparison with column 3 will reveal the need for adjusting production rates to maintain lead times.
6. Standard queue allowance.
7., 8., and 9. Hours actually in queue and the degree of criticality. The queue is out of control when more than the standard queue is less than 0.8 or greater than 1.2. The nature and extent of corrective action can be determined from the earlier comparison of receipts and production.
10. Total load is the sum of the work required for all orders in the "house regardless of their present location.
11. Average total load is another measure of "normal conditions" and comparison of columns 10 and 11 frequently provides advance information for decision making.
12. This column should be used to indicate conditions which require action.

TABLE 17.7 Summary Critical-Ratio Load Report

Work Ctr. 1	Curr. Rets. 2	Ave Rets. 3	Curr. Prod. 4	Ave. Prod. 5	Std. Queue 6	Actual Queue			Total Load 10	Ave. Load 11	Comts. 12
						<0.8 7	<1.2 8	>1.2 9			
A											
B											
C											
Total											

Critical Ratio for Purchase-Order Follow-up

While standard lead times for purchased items are generally known, there is frequently no elemental breakdown into checkpoints, comparable to production work centers, for reporting progress and determining the lead time remaining. Once such a breakdown is made, the same critical-ratio formulas used in production scheduling can be applied to purchase-order follow-up.

Some or all of the following checkpoints should have standard times associated with them and should have automatic feedback for status reporting:

1. Requisition forwarded to purchasing
2. Purchase order forwarded to vendor
3. Vendor acknowledgment received; promised shipping data compared with lead time and LTR adjusted accordingly
4. Vendor shipment made
5. Order received
6. Material inspected and approved
7. In stock, available for use

Although critical ratio is a very powerful scheduling technique, it is relatively simple and straightforward to use. Its biggest advantage is that it converts the time relationship between supply and demand into an index number that makes all jobs comparable. It can readily be used with a computer to handle a large number of orders.

OPTIMIZED PRODUCTION TECHNOLOGY

Optimized production technology (OPT) is a computer-packaged software system that addresses the variability in an operational facility. Although the batch-size algorithms are proprietary, the general rules used to determine the various batch sizes are presented here*:

1. Do not balance capacity—balance the flow.
2. The level of utilization of a nonbottleneck resource is determined not by its own potential but by some other constraint in the system.
3. Activating a resource (making it work) is not synonymous with utilizing a resource.
4. An hour lost at a bottleneck is an hour lost for the entire system.
5. An hour saved at a nonbottleneck is a mirage.
6. Bottlenecks govern both throughput and inventory in the system.
7. The transfer batch may not and many times should not be equal to the process batch.
8. The process batch should be variable both along its route and in time.
9. Priorities can only be set by simultaneously examining all of the system's constraints. Lead time is a derivative of the schedule.

---

* Optimized Production Technology is a proprietary system of Creative Output, Milford, Connecticut.

OPT provides a new perspective on the traditional methods of planning and scheduling, but it is more of a philosophy than a technique.

OPT has been compared to material requirements planning (MRP), and it is claimed that the two conflict with each other. The two techniques are not mutually exclusive. The fundamental logic of time-phased orders still applies and is incorporated in OPT; however, the order in which the information is processed is different from that in traditional MRP systems. OPT begins with a model of the resources available and converts the conventional bills of materials, routings, etc., into a product-process network. By identifying the critical, or bottleneck, resources, it produces an optimum schedule for these resources.

OPT applies Pareto's law to the selection of orders and resources in that it schedules the orders by priority until most of the resources have been allocated. By working on the vital few first and not worrying about the trivial many until later, a solution is obtained faster. This schedule, which is like a master schedule to OPT, is then used to plan the use of the noncritical resources. Different parameters can be emphasized to improve operating efficiency, reduce inventories, or increase delivery performance, whichever is most critical. The noncritical resources are scheduled below capacity to allow for a safety capacity to exist at all times.

OPT recognizes only one goal for manufacturing—to make money. OPT's goal is simultaneously to reduce operating expense and inventory and to increase throughput (Fig. 17.7).

OPT investigates five areas: variability, bottlenecks, setups, lot sizes, and priorities.

Variability. Most scheduling methods attempt to balance resources. The number of workers will be constantly adjusted to balance machine capacity with worker capacity, and the plans for the subsequent work will utilize these resources at the capacity required to meet demand. It has been shown through mathematical simulation that a balanced plant cannot exist in the presence of variability. Variability in dependent work centers will cause schedules to be missed, resulting in decreased throughput, increased inventory, and increased operating costs.

OPT rules are based on the realization that the constraints on an operation often exist outside the operation. The variability within an operation not only affects that operation but all subsequent operations, especially with bottleneck resources. Therefore, OPT's first rule is: Do not balance capacity—balance the flow.

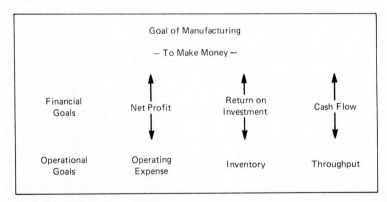

FIG. 17.7 Goal of manufacturing.

Bottlenecks and Nonbottlenecks. A *bottleneck* is exactly as the term implies, a restriction or constraint in the flow of material through a resource. A *resource*, in this case, is any element needed to make a product, whether it be a machine, a person, or space. A resource is considered a bottleneck when it is required to operate at 100 percent capacity to meet the present schedule. As the schedule changes or the product mix changes, different resources may become bottlenecks.

To illustrate the interaction between bottlenecks and nonbottlenecks, four different cases are presented in Fig. 17.8; they represent virtually all the possible combinations of interaction. In the examples, a certain product is manufactured that requires the use of two resources, X and Y. This is the simplest case and can, of course, be expanded for multiple resources. Demand for this product places different time requirements on the two resources, and an imbalance occurs. X denotes a bottleneck resource that has a market demand of 100 hr per week; it also has a capacity of 100 hr per week. (The habit of demanding more from a resource than it is capable of producing will not be discussed.) Y denotes a nonbottleneck resource that has a market demand of 75 hr per week and a capacity of 100 hr per week. These two resources can only interact in four ways.

In case 1, all product flows from X to Y. In this case, resource X has a requirement of 100 hr per week and is fully utilized, but resource Y has only 75 hr of work and is therefore underutilized. The output from X starves Y.

In case 2, all product flows from Y to X can again be utilized 100 percent of the time; however, if Y is activated 100 percent of the time, too much product will be produced for resource X. This will increase work-in-process inventory, consume resources, and not increase throughput. To balance the flow, Y needs to be activated only 75 percent of the time.

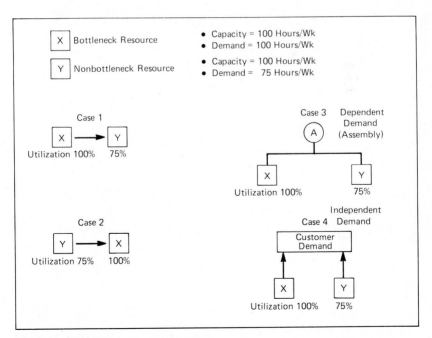

FIG. 17.8 Interaction between resources.

In case 3, X and Y both feed a common assembly. Having worked through cases 1 and 2, we can see that X will be utilized 100 percent of the time to meet the market demand; however, activating Y 100 percent of the time will exceed the demand for this resource and will again build work-in-process in front of the assembly.

In case 4, X and Y both feed independent customer demand and are not interrelated. Activating X 100 percent of the time will exactly meet customer demand. Activating Y 100 percent of the time will exceed the customer demand; this will build inventory, make poor use of the resource, and not increase throughput. Y need only be activated 75 percent of the time. Note that in this case the market has become the constraint.

In all four cases the same results were obtained. X was always active, a good indication of a bottleneck. Y could not be activated more than 75 percent of the time, or one or more manufacturing goals were contravened. From this example comes OPT's second and third rules: The level of utilization of a nonbottleneck resource is determined not by its own potential but by some other constraint in the system, and activating a resource (making it work) is not synonymous with utilizing a resource. All nonbottleneck resources must therefore be scheduled not on the basis of their constraints but on the basis of the system's constraints.

Setups.   The available time at a bottleneck resource can be divided into two categories: processing time and setup time. If an hour of setup is saved at a resource, an hour of processing time is gained. However, if OPT's first two rules are considered, the outcome of the hour saved at a bottleneck not only affects the bottleneck but also affects the nonbottleneck resources. Also, activating nonbottlenecks does not necessarily increase the facility's overall productivity. At nonbottlenecks, a resource can have three categories of time: run time, setup time, and idle time (Fig. 17.9). Changing the lot size at the nonbottleneck will not affect the lot's processing time (since this is constrained from outside the resource) unless the idle time is exceeded in additional setups. These concepts lead to OPT's fourth and fifth rules: An hour lost at a bottleneck is an hour lost for the entire system, and an hour saved at a nonbottleneck is a mirage.

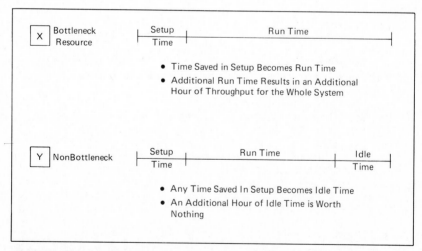

FIG. 17.9   Resource activities.

It is important that setups be saved at the bottlenecks, since time spent not producing affects the entire system. The system will move toward larger batch sizes at the bottlenecks than traditional lot-sizing techniques would indicate. The cost of a setup at a bottleneck resource must also include the cost associated with a loss in throughput for the whole system and is therefore very high.

However, at the nonbottlenecks there may be no gain in avoiding setups. Therefore, smaller batches are run; this does not increase throughput but can reduce inventory and operating expense. There are also advantages in maintaining the required workload below capacity in a nonbottleneck in order to avoid the possibility of constraining bottlenecks.

Lot Sizes. When the activity of a part moving through a production facility is viewed from the perspective of the part, there are only four stages in the job's life: setup, process, queue, and wait. To distinguish between queue and wait, *queue* is the time that the part is waiting for the machine that will process its batch (while the machine is occupied with something else), and *wait* is the time that the part waits in front of assembly for another part.

Typically, the setup and process times are a small portion of the total elapsed time. Some estimates place the percentage of active time at less than 20 percent; therefore, 80 percent of the time the part is waiting or in queue. In either case, the time a part spends in the production facility is determined by the bottleneck. The time that parts spend in the facility also determines the total inventory in the system. From this logic, the sixth rule is derived: Bottlenecks govern both throughput and inventory in the system.

The logic of rules 4 and 5 causes traditional lot-sizing rules to be very difficult to apply. As a batch moves through a facility, it encounters both bottleneck and nonbottleneck resources, and the question arises as to whether a batch should be subdivided or remain a single entity. To resolve the dilemma of whether the batch should be considered of size one or infinity, two different types of batches must be considered in manufacturing:

1. *Transfer batch.* The lot size viewed from the standpoint of the part.

2. *Process batch.* The lot size viewed from the standpoint of the resource.

The economic order quantity (EOQ) model maintains a balance between inventory costs and setup costs. In the case of a bottleneck, the setup cost is viewed from the perspective not only of the resource but of the entire system. An hour lost at a bottleneck is an hour lost for the whole system. This leads to the seventh rule of optimized production technology: The transfer batch may not and many times should not be equal to the process batch.

Since a batch moving through manufacturing will encounter both bottleneck and nonbottleneck operations, all with varying setup and run times, the parameters used in establishing a lot size for the batch must be examined for validity. Normally, batches launched on the shop floor are split, combined, and overlapped to meet the demands of the schedules. The simplicity of EOQs cannot accommodate the complexities and reality of multiple work centers in a manufacturing environment, and it should not be expected that one batch size for a product moving through many work centers should always be the same. This can be stated clearly as OPT's eighth rule: The process batch should be variable both along its route and in time.

Priorities. Many rules exist to determine the sequence in which orders should be run. The most widely accepted rules consider the amount of time remaining to complete the order and the time available to complete the order, or the time to due date.

MRP logic looks at the priorities of an item based on the required due date and the lead-time offset of components. This initial rough cut does not consider capacity constraints and results in a plan that requires reworking until feasible. In effect, MRP looks at priorities and then sees if they fit the capacity. Invariably, however, conflicting priorities result, since two or more different jobs will require processing at the same work center at the same time. To satisfy capacity constraints, one job must be processed first and the subsequent job(s) delayed. Since delay has occurred, the lead time has been affected.

The lead time of a job is thus affected not only by the capacity of the various work centers but by the priority of other jobs. This leads to the ninth rule: Priorities can only be set by simultaneously examining all of the system's constraints. Lead time is a derivative of the schedule.

GANTT-CHART SCHEDULING

The Gantt chart is a graphical method of scheduling activities. The horizontal axis is divided into time increments or production units. The vertical axis contains a row for each activity to be scheduled.

Without a doubt, the Gantt-chart principles are the most extensively used scheduling techniques. They may be used with a simple chart drawn on graph paper or with one dressed up in some of the commercial display panels available. The purpose here is to discuss only the principles, not the applications.

There are advantages to be found in the Gantt chart that can be found in none of the other techniques. These can be briefly stated as follows:

- A plan has to be made. Often this is the most important advantage of any scheduling technique.

- The chart shows the work that is planned and when it is to start and end. At the same time, it also shows the work that has been accomplished.

- Gantt charts are easy to understand and work.

- The Gantt chart is dynamic. It shows a moving picture of what is being planned and accomplished.

- Gantt charts require very little space, considering the amount of information displayed.

Like most of the other scheduling techniques, the Gantt chart requires an understanding of a certain language, or set of symbols. These are illustrated at the bottom of Fig. 17.10. The two inverted L's indicate when a task is to begin and end. The light line connecting these two L's shows what is to be accomplished. This line may be scaled in units of either time or production. The progress of the work is indicated by a heavy line. A "today" line must be placed on the chart to show when it was last brought up to date. In the example, a caret is used. Other symbols may be added to the chart as desired. For example, a crossed-out entry might indicate that a machine is down for repair.

There are two ways of entering information: Start with the present time and work *forward*, or start with some future date and work *backward*. The choice will depend upon the cost of the product as well as upon the availability of transportation, storage, and capital and other considerations.

For scheduling manufacturing, there are two choices in the way the chart is constructed. If getting production out is the important problem, the chart will be constructed in terms of manufacturing orders, as shown in Fig. 17.10. However, if keeping the machines loaded is of paramount importance, the chart should be constructed as shown in Fig. 17.11. Notice that in the former figure the manufacturing orders are listed in the left-hand column, while in the latter the machines or work centers are listed.

In operating the chart, it is essential that information such as move orders or time cards be available to serve as *feedback* for updating the chart. Operating the chart

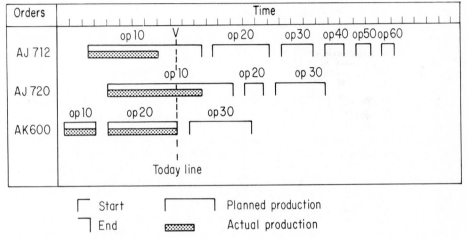

FIG. 17.10   Schedule chart by order number.

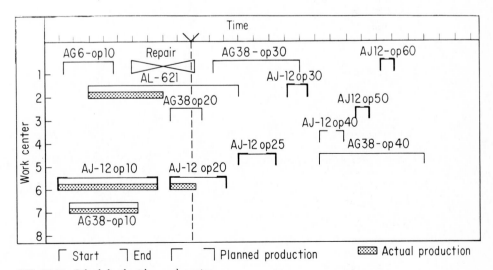

FIG. 17.11   Schedule chart by work center.

successfully requires a person with a certain type of personality, a person willing to accept changing conditions and able to work with details.

Reading the chart is relatively simple. For example, in Fig. 17.10:

1. AJ720 is ahead of schedule
2. AK600 is on schedule
3. AJ712 is behind schedule

You will notice in Fig. 17.11 that a number of jobs are shown for each work center. If each work center is manned, the scheduler will probably want to keep all the vacant spaces filled, which will mean a more efficient plant. The scheduler will have to be flexible and willing to adjust the schedule from time to time. For example, it appears that order AG38, operation 20, is not going to be started before the time it is to be completed. This will require a reshuffling of the operations for AG38.

These are the basic principles of the Gantt chart. From here, one can make modifications to fit the particular situation.

LINE OF BALANCE (LOB)

This is a manual, graphical technique for planning, scheduling, and monitoring progress of simple to complex projects. These may be products assembled over a moderate time period against a firm schedule, a development program for a complex assembly, or a research and engineering project. The project is represented by a network showing the relationship in time among the various milestones (such as receipt of finished components or completion of testing) that make up the project.

The discipline required to set up the chart can help to ensure thorough planning. The schedule of critical activities can be developed accurately (depending on the accuracy of the data on required lead times) and the actual progress monitored. The technique permits showing the following simultaneously on one chart:

1. Source of each component element (purchase, manufacture, assembly, test, etc.)
2. Sequence of assembly, including subassembly, testing, inspection, packaging, shipping, and related activities
3. Comparison of scheduled versus actual finished-product deliveries
4. Comparison of scheduled versus actual component-element completions, showing present and potential shortages or delays

The technique is expensive to set up, increasingly so as the number of components and control points increases. It is inflexible and expensive to revise in terms of schedule changes, variations in elements, or revisions in elemental lead times. Analysis of project status requires accumulating data on all elements simultaneously.

LOB is a network planning technique similar to PERT, CPM, precedence lists, etc., but it lacks their flexibility, versatility, and scope. A Gantt chart should be considered before applying LOB; it will be considerably less expensive and may produce equal results.

LOB has been most frequently applied to complex assemblies built for the U.S. Navy, whose contracts have required using the chart to report status to government inspectors.

Line-of-Balance Charts

Commercial and industrial applications of LOB as an operating technique are extremely rare. Its major application is in planning, scheduling, and controlling the production of complex, assembled products.

An LOB chart consists of three sections (Fig. 17.12): the production plan, the objective chart, and the progress chart. The lower half is the production plan; inaccuracies in it will be reflected throughout the LOB chart. It is a "key" components product tree, with time represented on the horizontal axis. The length of each product-tree bar denotes the lead time required to produce one batch of that component or assembly; the overall product-structure length is the total product lead time. For example, purchased part 1 requires 12 working days' lead time (24 minus 12), and the total product lead time is 24 days.

To construct a production plan, first select those components (from the bill of materials) or events (from the route or process sheets) whose timely completion is important to the project. Relatively unimportant components are lumped together ("All Hardware"). Second, obtain or estimate the lead times for each batch of the selected key components; these should be the most likely time, inclusive of processing, movement, and waiting time. Third, draw the chart by starting from the right with the completion day, week, or month as zero and working to the left, "branching out" as assemblies become subassemblies, and subassemblies become components. Fourth, connect all component horizontal lead-time bars with a vertical line where subassembly or assembly occurs, forming an interconnected network. Select a time scale in units suitable for effective monitoring. Fifth, mark the start of each key component or event line with a control-point number, commencing from the top left and moving to the bottom right. Intermediate events should be given a number only if they are to be monitored. Always number the completion of the project. Symbols indicating the type of component (raw material, purchased part, manufactured part, subassembly, etc.) are helpful, and color coding increases the ease of interpretation. Descriptions of components or events can be shown on the chart. The selection of key components and events, the assignment of control-point numbers, and the use of descriptions must be dictated by the economics of over- or undercontrolling the project's progress.

Using Line-of-Balance Charts

The completed production plan could be used like a Gantt chart for monitoring one project by assigning specific dates to the horizontal time scale and recording actual progress on individual bars of the chart where few or no partial lots of the total order are expected at any control point. Where individual lots are scheduled over several periods, the Gantt chart is difficult to adapt, and the LOB progress chart makes it possible to record the control-point completion status against the schedule.

The upper left portion of Fig. 17.12 is the *objective chart*. It is the cumulative contract delivery schedule plotted vertically against the time plotted horizontally. The cumulative actual delivery schedule is plotted as the project progresses. The horizontal axis is divided into time intervals most closely approximating the delivery schedule. Frequently, both scheduled and actual deliveries in each interval are posted below this axis as a summary of project status. The vertical axis shows units of delivered end product.

The functions of the objective chart are:

1. To show the quantity of end product ahead of or behind schedule by the vertical

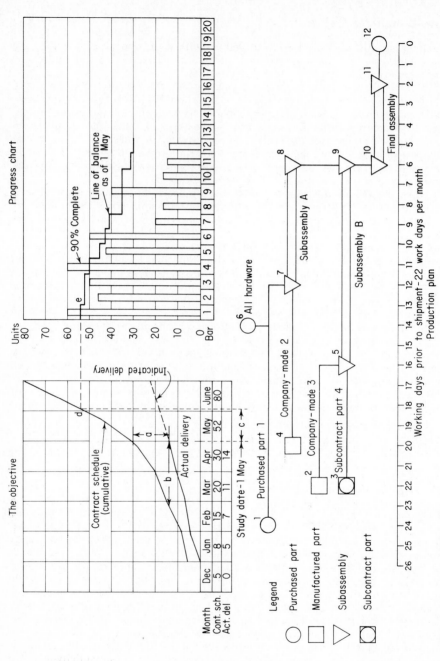

FIG. 17.12 Line-of-balance chart.

17.32

gap between the two curves (a) and by the scheduled and actual totals summarized below the horizontal axis.

2. To show the number of time periods ahead of or behind schedule by the horizontal gap between the two curves (b).

3. To indicate the production rates by the slopes of the lines. Extending the actual line ahead on its historical trend can yield estimates of future production.

4. To provide the basis for drawing the line of balance on the progress chart where control-point completion status is measured.

The upper-right portion of the figure is the *progress chart*. The length of the vertical bars represents the actual quantity of end-product sets of each component or event completed at the study date. The bars are numbered horizontally for each control point on the production plan. The vertical scale shows end-product sets (more than one component may be required per end product). The progress chart shares this scale with the objective chart. The length of the bars increases as progress occurs at each control point. The most important benefit is the measurement of control-point status against plan and is obtained by striking the line of balance—the minimum quantity of each control-point element required to support the end-product delivery schedule as of the study date.

To strike the line of balance:

1. Start with the study date (May 1 on the horizontal axis of the objective chart) and mark off to the right (c for control point 1) the number of lead-time periods required for each control point in advance of end-product completion. This lead-time information is obtained from the production plan. For example, control points 8, 9, and 10 must be completed 6 working days in advance of shipment; control point 3, 2 months in advance, and so on.

2. Draw a vertical dashed line from the lead-time termination until it intersects the cumulative delivery schedule as at d.

3. From the point of intersection, draw a horizontal dashed line to the corresponding control-point bar on the progress chart (e). This is the *balance quantity* or the minimum control-point quantity required to support the end-product delivery schedule.

4. Repeat this procedure for all control points on the production plan.

5. Join the balance quantities to form one staircase-type line of balance across the progress chart.

Bars above the line indicate control points ahead of schedule. Those ending below the line show control points short of quantities required.

The LOB chart is read as a book—from upper left to lower right. First, the objective chart is checked; if the schedule is being properly met, no further reading is required. If the program is significantly behind schedule, the progress chart is checked to determine the control points that are behind schedule. Since the completion of some control points is dependent upon earlier control points, the true problem control point(s) must be located by referring to the production plan.

The chart also shows (1) the amount of off-schedule deliveries in units and periods of time, (2) the indicated future deliveries based on actual delivery-curve trend, and (3) whether the off-schedule or imbalance is caused by a common source type, such as subcontracted or raw materials.

PROJECT MANAGEMENT WITH PERT/CPM

The original program evaluation review technique (PERT) was developed in the late 1950s as a method of planning and controlling the Polaris ballistic missile program for the U.S. Navy. At about the same time, the critical-path method (CPM) was developed by Du Pont, Remington-Rand, and J. E. Kelly in order to manage chemical-process-plant shutdowns better. PERT and CPM are graphical, network methods to organize and schedule projects that have activities of substantial duration—days, weeks or months. Today there are many PERT/CPM software systems that are relatively inexpensive and include extensive graphical, cost-accounting, decision-support, and resource-allocation modules.

PERT/CPM applications include: managing the combined manufacturing lead time (that is, the critical path) for the purchase, fabrication, and assembly of products; the production of make-to-order tools and equipment, such as die sets and lithography plates; the design and implementation of new production information control systems; and the construction and move to a new facility.

Some important project characteristics that assist in determining when to use PERT/CPM include:

- The objective is to minimize times, costs, or resources.
- It is necessary to know which events are on the critical path.
- It is necessary to coordinate many activities.
- There are complex activity interrelationships and interdependencies in parallel and in sequence.
- It is necessary to meet contractual or promised due dates.
- There are long lead and activity times.
- There are limited resources involved in multiple activities or projects.
- Periodic reporting, budgeting, or billing based on project completion is required.
- Several different organizations (such as suppliers) are involved.
- There is uncertainty concerning activity times and delivery dates.
- There is a need for graphic representation of project progress, using Gantt, PERT, work-center load profiles, cash flow, or percent completion charts.
- Several organizations or departments require coordination.

Introduction to PERT/CPM Diagrams

Figure 17.13 illustrates three different project activity structures. All three structures are *activity-on-arrow (arc) diagrams*, in which the arrows (sometimes called *arcs*) represent activities and the circled nodes represent precedent relationships between activities. There is a second type of PERT/CPM diagram, *activity-on-node*, in which the nodes represent activities and the arrows represent precedent relationships.

Activities are specific tasks that require time and resources to complete. Frequently, several activities compete simultaneously for the same human or material resources; therefore, a rational method of allocating these scarce resources is necessary.

For an activity-on-arrow diagram, nodes (or *milestones*) mark the completion of all tasks preceding it. In Fig. 17.13c, for example, activity (3−4) cannot begin until

(a) Parallel Activities (e.g. parallel assembly lines)

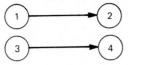

(b) Sequential Activities (e.g. a flow shop or repetitive processing)

(c) Interrelated Activities (e.g. a product scheduled through a job shop or project)

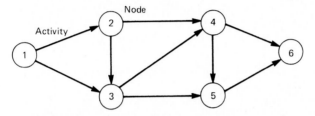

Activity (2-3) cannot begin until activity (1-2) is complete.
Activities (3-4) and (3-5) cannot begin until activities (1-2), (1-3), and (2-3) are complete.

FIG. 17.13 Simple activity-on-arrow precedent structures.

activities (1−2), (1−3), and (2−3) are complete. Similarily, activities (2−4) and (2−3) cannot begin until activity (1−2) is complete.

Diagram Construction

The basics of project management using PERT/CPM are illustrated by a simple example of a wholesaler selecting, purchasing, and implementing a new finished-goods inventory control system. Because the PERT/CPM diagram is the priority planning document that drives resource and capacity acquisition and allocation, a properly constructed network diagram is critical for successful project management. The following five steps are necessary in constructing a PERT or CPM network diagram.

Step 1: Define Major Milestones. For the example, the following major milestones are:

1. Project started.
2. Selection complete.
3. Operator training complete.
4. System installation complete.

Each of the four milestones has several activities that must take place to achieve the final milestone. In defining milestones, however, it is important to keep the level of detail the same for all. It is inappropriate to list a minor milestone, such as "flow chart completed," with a major milestone, such as "system installed."

Step 2: Define Activities.   It is necessary to define all activities that must be completed before each major milestone occurs and then to rank them in approximate order of occurrence. In this simplified example, the following activities are defined:

(1–2) Define the system and select a cost-effective, "canned" inventory control system.

(1–3) Educate the operating personnel in the theory and tools of finished-goods inventory control systems.

(2–3) Document the new system for clarity, maintenance, user reference, and standardization of procedures.

(2–4) Install and check out the system, including the hardware, software, and interfaces to the new inventory control system.

(3–4) Train the operators before going on line with the new system.

To assist in identifying project activities, a hierarchical structure can be generated, as is done with a bill of materials. The bill of activities, or work breakdown structure (WBDS), shows low-level activities that are components of higher-level, general activities (Table 17.8).

Step 3: Define Precedence Relationships.   The precedence relationships that exist among events and activities need to be defined next. To define the precedence relationships, one must identify all activities that occur before each subsequent activity can begin. Those activities which are at the beginning or end of the project are the easiest to define. An initial pass at precedences can begin by using a simplified, indented activity list of work breakdown as shown in Table 17.8. However, network construction and revision are continuing processes requiring the same attention to detail, accuracy, and data integrity as a complex bill of materials.

There are several useful ways to display precedence relationships through *precedence-planning documents*. These include work breakdown structures, Gantt charts (Fig. 17.14), and precedence lists. A *precedence list* is simply a vertical list of all activities associated with each activity; a list of (1) all activities that must be completed before that activity can start, (2) all activities that cannot start until the activity is completed, and (3) all other activities that are not affected. Just as the bill of materials is essential to MRP, the WBDS is essential in defining precedences, dependencies, project structure, and detailed work assignments. Gantt charts are useful for simple project or activity structures. Because they are so easily understood, they can provide operating personnel at all levels with graphic WBDS information, but they may not adequately represent all dependencies of a realistic project.

Step 4: Construct Diagram.   From these precedence-relationship aids, the network diagram can be constructed. The diagram can be either an activity-on-arrow (arc) diagram, which is also known as an *i–j diagram* (Fig. 17.15), or an activity-on-node diagram, also known as a *precedence diagram*. While activity-on-arrow diagrams can be slightly more difficult to construct than activity-on-node diagrams, their graphical representation of the project is easier to understand and use after construction. Because of this reason, the activity-on-arrow representation is chosen here.

TABLE 17.8 Work Breakdown Structure (WBDS) for Inventory Management Systems: Indented Activity Levels

1						INVENTORY MANAGEMENT SYSTEM SELECTION AND IMPLEMENTATION
	2					(1−2) *System definition and selection*
		3				*Define desired system*
			4			Define system requirements
				5		. . .
			4			Prepare functional specifications
				5		. . .
			4			Prepare system specifications
			4			Prepare system flowcharts
			4			Design forms and reports
			4			Define system computations
		3				*Select best available system*
			4			Analyze existing software
			4			Financial analysis
			4			. . .
			4			. . .
	2					(1−3) *General education of operating personnel*
		3				APICS certification classes
			4			Inventory management certification module
			4			. . .
				5		. . .
	2					(2−3) *Documentation of new system*
		3				. . .
			4			. . .
	2					(2−4) *Installation and checkout of system*
		3				. . .
			4			. . .
	2					(3−4) *Systems training of users*
		3				. . .
			4			. . .
				5		. . .

Activity-on-node diagrams (Fig. 17.16) are an efficient method of representing a network and are often used in computer software. This type of diagram has several advantages for the experienced PERT/CPM user that make it the preferred method. Fortunately, after understanding one method, it is relatively easy to convert to the other.

Constructing an activity-on-arrow diagram begins on the far left with a single start node. All initial activities that do not have other activities taking precedence emanate from the start node. At the end of an activity arrow, another node is constructed. Activities that must succeed the previous activity emanate from this node. Note that it is feasible that two or more activities connect two nodes (parallel activities). Also note that all activities that must precede an activity X must route through the node from which activity X starts.

Step 5: Estimate Activity Times. Once the precedence network is defined, project planning continues toward determining the critical path and critical resources. Before making these determinations, it is necessary to estimate activity times (Table 17.9). To model the time relationships of a project, individual activity times must be estimated by people knowledgeable and experienced in each activity. The decision maker assumes that adequate resources (such as personnel, equipment, and material) are available for the activity, without regard to other activity demands.

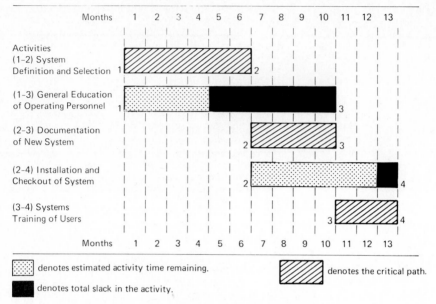

FIG. 17.14 Initial Gantt chart of inventory control system project.

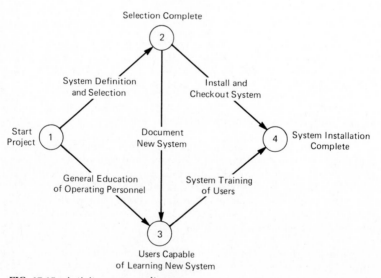

FIG. 17.15 Activity-on-arrow diagram.

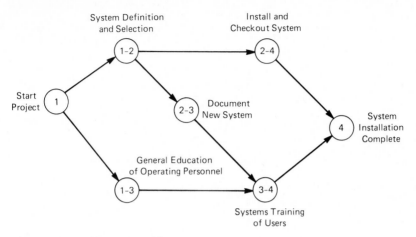

FIG. 17.16 Activity-on-node diagram.

The activity completion times are estimated by using objective or subjective data. When the activity times are relatively certain, a single activity time is estimated. CPM assumes a single, mean activity time ET_{i-j}. However, if the activity time estimates are uncertain, probability distributions are used, and the network diagram becomes a PERT diagram. Herein is the essential difference between CPM and PERT; CPM uses a single, mean activity time while PERT uses a probability distribution.

Specifically, PERT uses three estimates to calculate a mean activity time and a probability distribution; these are a, m, and b (defined in Table 17.9). These time estimates can be based upon objective historical data of similar tasks; if these are unavailable, subjective estimates are used. Some individuals have difficulty in estimating the times because they are subjective; however, it is far better to include a guesstimate of activity time ranges than to ignore variability.

From the three estimates (a, m, b), a mean activity time ET_{i-j} and a variance σ^2_{i-j} can be calculated, using the assumption that the activity times form a beta distribution. The mean of the beta distribution is

$$ET_{i-j} = \frac{a + 4m + b}{6}$$

while the variance (the standard deviation squared) is

$$\sigma^2_{i-j} = \frac{(b - a)^2}{6}$$

The developers of PERT chose a beta distribution to represent activity times because, depending on a, m, and b, it can approximate a wide variety of other probability distributions. While few activity times theoretically match a beta distri-

TABLE 17.9 Notation and Rules of PERT/CPM

$(i-j)$ is used to identify activity $(i$ to $j)$ from start to finish. In this example, activity $(1-2)$ is the "system definition and selection" activity.

Estimated by Decision Makers

a = an optimistic estimate of activity time. This or a shorter time will occur only 1 out of 100 times the task is completed.

m = the most frequent (modal) time to complete an activity. Out of 100 repetitions of the activity, this time will occur most frequently.

b = a pessimistic estimate of an activity time. This or a longer time will occur only 1 out of 100 times the task is completed.

Calculated Activity Times

ET_{i-j} = the *expected* (mean) *time* to complete activity $(i-j)$.

σ_{i-j} = the standard deviation of activity time $(i-j)$.

Calculated Dates Going Forward

ES_{i-j} = the *early start* date of activity $(i-j)$ = maximum EF of preceding (incoming) activities (see rule 2 below).

$EF_{i-j} = ES_{i-j} + ET_{i-j}$, which is the *early finish* date of activity $(i-j)$.

Calculated Dates Going Backward

LS_{i-j} = the *latest* date on which activity $(i-j)$ can be *started* without increasing the duration of the project = $LF_{i-j} - ET_{i-j}$.

LF_{i-j} = the *latest* date on which activity $(i-j)$ can be *finished* without increasing the duration of the project. This equals the minimum LS of the successor (outgoing) activities of activity $(i-j)$.

Calculated Activity and Project Times

$TS_{i-j} = LS_{i-j} = ES_{i-j}$ = the total slack time of an activity. An activity can be delayed this amount without increasing the duration of the project.

ET_p = mean (expected) project time = sum of ET along critical path.

σ_p^2 = variance of project time = sum of the variances along critical path.

Network Computational Rules

Rule 1: All activities leading to an event must be completed before the event occurs and succeeding activities can begin.

Rule 2: When working forward in time at an event, always take the highest EF of preceding (incoming) activities as the ES for succeeding (outgoing) activities.

Rule 3: When working backward in time at an event, always take the lowest of LS of outgoing (successor) activities as the LF of incoming (preceding) activities.

bution, most activities can be adequately represented by it from a practical standpoint. When an activity time can be better represented by another distribution (such as normal or exponential), it can easily be incorporated in the network. Table 17.10 lists a, m, and b for each of the activities of this example. The mean and variance times for activity (1−2) are

$$ET_{1-2} = \frac{a + 4m + b}{6} = \frac{1 + 4(6) + 11}{6} = 6$$

$$\sigma^2_{1-2} = \frac{(b - a)^2}{6} = \frac{(11 - 1)^2}{6} = 16.67$$

Utilizing the PERT/CPM Diagram

Now that the PERT/CPM network diagram has been constructed and the associated activity times determined, the diagram can be used to analyze and control the project.

TABLE 17.10 PERT Statistics for Inventory Control System Project

Activities	a	m	b	Exp. Time (ET)	σ^2 (ET)	Early Start (ES)	Early Finish (EF)	Late Start (LS)	Late Finish (LF)	Total Slack (TS)
(1−2) System definition and selection	1	6	11	6	16.67	0	6	0	6	0
(1−3) General education of operating personnel	2	4	6	4	2.67	0	4	6	10	6
(2−3) Documentation of new system	1	4	7	4	6.0	6	10	6	10	0
(2−4) Installation and checkout of system	2	5	14	6	24.0	6	12	7	13	1
(3−4) Systems training of users	1	3	5	3	2.67	10	13	10	13	0

Activity Start and Finish Dates.   There are several steps in calculating the project activities' start and finish dates. To distinguish between times and dates, a *date* is the day, week, or month on which an activity starts or finishes, while a *time* is the duration of the activity (such as ET_{i-j} and σ_{i-j}). In PERT/CPM calculations, one first works forward to calculate early start (ES) and early finish (EF) dates and then works backwards to calculate late finish (LF) and late start (LS) dates. (When performing these calculations, refer to Tables 17.9 and 17.10 and Fig. 17.15 or 17.16.)

Early start is the date an activity begins if all activities are completed in their expected times (ET). Similarly, *early finish* is the date an activity finishes if all activities are completed in their expected times. The first activities of a project begin on the first date of the project. In this case, it is assumed that the starting date is time zero, but in general the first period will be the shop calendar date. In Table 17-10, early starts (1–2 and 1–3) are both zero; therefore,

$$EF_{1-2} = ES_{1-2} + ET_{1-2} = 0 + 6 = 6$$

$$EF_{1-3} = ES_{1-3} + ET_{1-3} = 0 + 4 = 4$$

Activities succeeding events 2 and 3 cannot begin until all activities leading to them are completed:

Rule 1. All activities leading to an event must be completed before the event occurs and succeeding activities can begin.

Activities (2–3) and (2–4) can begin as soon as (1–2) is complete, while (3–4) cannot begin until both (2–3) and (1–3) are complete. The ES_{2-3} and ES_{2-4} are equal to the EF_{1-2}, which is 6; therefore,

$$EF_{2-3} = ES_{2-3} + ET_{2-3} = 6 + 4 = 10$$

Now that the EF_{2-3} is known, rule 2 is used to choose the ES_{3-4}:

Rule 2. When working forward in time at a node, always take the highest EF of preceding (incoming) activities as the ES for succeeding (outgoing) activities.

The ES_{3-4} is quite logically the maximum EF of all preceding activities. In this case, ES_{3-4} is the maximum of either $EF_{1-3} = 4$ or $EF_{2-3} = 10$, which is 10; therefore, EF_{3-4} is $10 + 3$, or 13. The EF_{2-4} is $ES_{2-4} + ET_{2-4}$, which is 12. Node 4, which is the project's completion, cannot occur until both (2–4) and (3–4) are complete; therefore, the EF of the project, denoted by EF_p, equals the maximum of either EF_{2-4} or EF_{3-4}. In this case, $EF_p = 13$ months, since it is the largest value. The expected completion date of the project is the end of month 13. This completes the forward calculation of early dates. The next phase calculates the latest dates by working backward from the end of the project.

The backward calculation of the late start (LS) and late finish (LF) times is designed to determine how late the activities can start and finish without delaying the project's completion date.

LS_{i-j} = latest date on which activity (i–j) can be started without increasing the duration of the project = $LF_{i-j} - ET_{i-j}$

LF_{i-j} = latest date on which activity $(i-j)$ can be finished without increasing the duration of the project = minimum LS of the successor (outgoing) activities of activity $(i-j)$

The LF and LS dates are important in identifying the critical and near-critical path activities and their completion dates. By convention, the late finishes of the project and the ending activities $(2-4)$ and $(3-4)$ are assigned the early finish EF_p of the project, in this case 13. Each activity terminating at node 4 [that is, $(2-4)$ and $(3-4)$] is assigned the LF of 13. These LFs denote that if activity $(2-4)$ or $(3-4)$ finish later than 13, then the project will be delayed. Logically, the LS of each activity is LF − ET; for example,

$$LS_{3-4} = LF_{3-4} - ET_{3-4} = 13 - 3 = 10$$

$$LS_{2-4} = LF_{2-4} - ET_{2-4} = 13 - 6 = 7$$

The LF_{2-3} is equal to LS_{3-4} = 10. When a node has more than one activity leading back to it, then according to rule 3 of Table 17.9, the LF of activities leading into an event is the minimum of the LS of those activities leaving the event.

Rule 3. When working backward in time at a node, always take the lowest LS of outgoing (successor) activities as the LF of incoming (preceding) activities.

For example, LF_{1-2} is the minimum of LS_{2-4} = 7 and LS_{2-3} = 6; therefore, LF_{1-2} = 6. That is, if activity (1−2) is completed after month 6, then the project will be delayed. This procedure continues until all LSs and LFs have been calculated. Fig. 17.17 gives the results for the example.

Slack and the Critical Path.   The critical path (longest path) may be evident by inspection; however, it is typically more difficult to determine in a larger project. Total slack (TS) is used to identify the critical path. The difference between LS and ES or LF and EF is TS.

$$TS_{i-j} = LS_{i-j} - ES_{i-j} = \text{total slack time of an activity}$$

An activity can be delayed this amount without increasing the duration of the project.

For activity $(2-4)$, this difference is 7 − 6 or 13 − 12, which is 1 month; therefore, activity $(2-4)$ can be delayed 1 month without delaying the expected completion date of the project. In contrast, TS_{2-4} is 10 − 10, or zero months. There is no slack in activity $(3-4)$; therefore, a delay in this activity will delay the project. Logically, those activities on the critical paths $(1-2)$, $(2-3)$, and $(3-4)$ have zero slack. The expected completion date of the project equals the sum of the ETs of these activities; 6 + 4 + 3 = 13. Because these activities determine the project time, management should not permit their delay.

In a large project, there may be more than one critical path and several near-critical paths. For example, TS_{2-4} of activity $(2-4)$ is only 1 month; therefore, the project will be delayed if activity $(2-4)$ is delayed more than a month. Consequently, all activities should be managed so as to minimize costs and meet project due dates. Also, if resources for an activity with considerable slack [such as activity

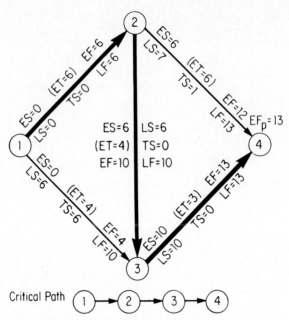

FIG. 17.17   Completed PERT/CPM diagram.

$(1-3)]$ can be transferred to an activity on the critical path [such as $(1-2)]$, then the length and cost of the project may be decreased.

Probabilistic Estimates of Project Completion Dates.   Using the central limit theorem of statistical analysis, it is possible to estimate the probability distribution of project completion dates. The mean (expected) project completion is equal to the length of the critical path (or month 13). Because this is a mean there is a 50 percent chance the project will be completed before this date and a 50 percent chance after this date. Just as in forecasting, a single quantity is much less useful than a range and its probability. Assuming that the activity times along the critical path are independent of each other, the central limit theorem denotes that the project's completion time approximates a normal distribution, with a mean ET_p equal to the critical path time and a variance σ_p^2 equal to the sum of the variances along the critical path.

ET_p = mean (expected) project time = sum of ETs along critical path

σ_p^2 = variance of project time = sum of variances along critical path

In the example,

$ET_p = ET_{1-2} + ET_{2-3} + ET_{3-4} = 6 + 4 + 3 = 13$ months

$\sigma_p^2 = \sigma_{1-2}^2 + \sigma_{2-3}^2 + \sigma_{3-4}^2 = 16.67 + 6.0 + 2.67 = 25.34$ months

Using these approximate relationships, it is possible to calculate probability estimates for project completion times. Using the characteristics of the normal distribution, there is a 68 percent chance that the project will be completed in approximately 8 to 18 months (that is, the mean plus and minus 1 standard deviation, or 13 plus and minus 5.034). Also, there is a 2.5 percent chance that the project will take more than 22.9 months (the mean plus 1.96 standard deviations).

There is considerable uncertainty in the estimated completion times of this project because activity $(1-2)$ has such a large variance. If the estimated time of this activity could be better defined (that is, have a lower variance), then the range of project completion times would be narrower.

Dependence of Critical Paths. In calculating the critical path's mean and variance, it was assumed that critical path $(1-2-3-4)$ was the only possible critical path; however, path $(1-2-4)$ has a very high probability of becoming critical. Path $(1-2-4)$ is expected to be completed at the end of month 12; however, the variance of this path is quite high. In this case, the variance and standard deviation of path $(1-2-4)$ are 40.62 $(16.62 + 24.0)$ and 6.4 months, respectively. The probability (without showing the calculation here) that path $(1-2-4)$ will take longer than 13 months is about 44 percent. Also, there is a 68 percent chance that path $(1-2-4)$ will be completed in 5.6 to 18.4 months (the mean plus or minus 1 standard deviation) and a 2.5 percent chance that path $(1-2-4)$ will take more than 24.54 months (the mean plus 1.96 standard deviations). Consequently, this path has a high probability of being the critical path and should therefore be monitored carefully.

ET_p and σ_p are only approximations because it is assumed that the critical-path time of $(1-2-3-4)$ is independent of other paths; the independence assumption is theoretically wrong and at times misleading. The project duration depends upon the joint probability of completing all possible paths: $(1-2-3-4)$, $(1-2-4)$, and $(1-3-4)$. Fortunately, some PERT/CPM software packages do not make the independence assumptions; they use the more complex and valid joint probability estimates of project completion times. From a management standpoint, it is important to understand the assumption of independent critical paths and to interpret it cautiously.

Because the uncertainties in a project are many and complex, the probability distributions of project and activity times may not be adequately represented by the simple joint probability rule. In such situations, Monte Carlo simulation has been found to be valuable. Computer simulation of projects is being applied more and more frequently, and specialized computer languages have been developed to assist in network simulations.

Dummy Activities. The construction of activity-on-arrow networks may require the introduction of artificial events and activities called *dummies*. For example, as shown in the diagrams below, if two activities have the same beginning event (1) and the same ending event (3),

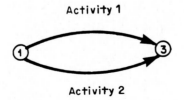

Activity 1

Activity 2

then it is necessary to introduce a dummy event (2) and a dummy activity $(2-3)$ to identify each unique activity.

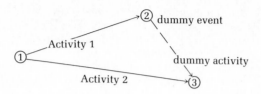

Dummy activities require no time resources and are typically represented by dotted lines, as is done above, or by thinner lines than those for the actual activities.

Resource-Constrained Project Scheduling

The previous section emphasized time analysis. No costs or resource availabilities were included in the analysis; that is, all times were estimated on the assumption that adequate resources were available. However, different activities may compete for the same resources during the same time period; if they do, then the results of PERT-TIME analysis may be too optimistic (that is, too short). Fortunately, PERT-COST and resource-constrained methods exist to make cost and resource trade-offs part of PERT/CPM analysis.

PERT-COST. PERT-COST is a method used to reduce project costs by modeling the relationships between activity times and costs. In estimating activity costs, a normal and a crash time and their resulting costs are often considered. The normal schedule is that of the mean time ET_{i-j}, while the crash cost occurs when the activity time is expedited (crashed) by allocating more resources to it.

Referring again to Fig. 17.17, the crash and normal costs for activity (1−2) are as illustrated in Fig. 17.18. As shown, the activity time can be reduced from 6 to 3 months by incurring an additional $60,000 cost. It is assumed that the relationship is linear; therefore, each month of reduction in the activity time costs $20,000. Nonlinear costs can be included through piecewise approximations. This crash cost per month is important in deciding which activity time is to be reduced. Only those activity times on the critical path need be reduced to decrease the project length. The current critical path is (1−2−3−4); therefore, it is logical to crash that critical path activity which has the lowest crash cost per month.

Table 17.11 illustrates the crash times, costs, and crash rates of all activities in the project. As shown in the right-hand column, activity (3−4) has the lowest expediting rate of $4,000 per month on the critical path. The project duration can be

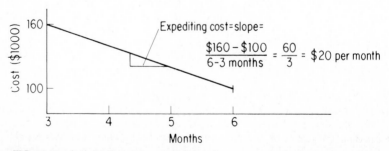

FIG. 17.18 Activity time versus activity cost.

TABLE 17.11 Normal and Crash Activities Times and Costs

Activities	Time		Cost in $1000		Crash Rate, in $1000 per Month
	Normal	Crash	Normal	Crash	
(1−2)	6	3	100	160	20
(1−3)	4	2	32	48	8
(2−3)	4	3	32	54	22
(2−4)	6	4	100	140	20
(3−4)	3	2	32	36	4

reduced by 1 month by reducing activity (3−4) by 1 month. Assume that the indirect costs (indirect labor and overhead) of the project are $7,000 per month; therefore, the project costs can be reduced if the crash cost is less than $7,000 per month. Such trade-offs can be developed into tabular form for easier management decisions. The cost of reducing the project duration from 12 to 11 months is the difference between the activity costs of $20,000 and the project's indirect costs of $7,000; from a cost-minimization standpoint, it costs $13,000 ($20,000 − 7,000) to reduce the project's duration from 12 to 11 months.

For large projects, the crash procedure may be difficult to do manually. Fortunately, heuristic and linear programming methods can be used to solve this problem easily for large projects. Such methods can provide valuable information for the decision maker. Unfortunately, as discussed below, the general project cost-minimization problem under conditions of resource constraints is extremely difficult to solve, but there are a few heuristic methods available for some specific applications.

Constrained-Resource Problem. While it was implied that the previous schedules had sufficient resources, resource availability was not explicitly included in the solution methodology. However, resources are almost always limited and must therefore be scheduled and coordinated in order to achieve project objectives. In general, the coordination of resources is a very difficult part of project management. A large project may have 40 or more different types of resources. In a realistic project, the possible combinations of resources and times are extremely large—so large that it makes a solution by mathematical programming infeasible. However, heuristics exist to assist in allocating human, material, equipment, and financial resources.

Project management objectives related to resource availability include: (1) leveling the resource requirements, subject to meeting the due dates when assuming unlimited resources; (2) minimizing the project's duration, subject to constrained resources; and (3) minimizing the project's cost, subject to the project's due date, indirect costs, resource costs, and resource constraints. Relatively successful heuristic techniques exist to achieve objectives (1) and (2) satisfactorily, and these are briefly discussed below. Unfortunately, there are no efficient heuristics for objective (3): minimizing project costs subject to resource availability in a realistic project.

The first step in achieving resource allocation or leveling is to determine the types and number of resources required by each activity. The WBDS described previously is an important document in this initial step. The WBDS is used to generate Table 17.12, which gives a simplified resource-requirements profile for each activity and resource. This table is combined with the project network to yield the load profile in Fig. 17.19.

A leveling of resource requirements can be accomplished by using trial-and-error heuristics. These heuristics use slack in the noncritical paths to reschedule activity start and finish dates within the early and late time differences. When considerable slack exists, there is considerable flexibility in rescheduling start and

TABLE 17.12 Activity Resource Requirements for Normal Time Schedule

		Resources: Planned versus Available					
		Systems Analysts (man-months)		Educators/ Consultants (man-months)		Systems Users (man-months)	
Activities	Duration (months)	Plan	Avail	Plan	Avail	Plan	Avail
(1−2) System definition and selection	6	24				12	
(1−3) General education of operating personnel	4			8		4	
(2−3) Documentation of new system	4	2		8		2	
(2−4) Installation and checkout of system	6	24		6		6	
(3−4) Systems training of users	3	6				6	

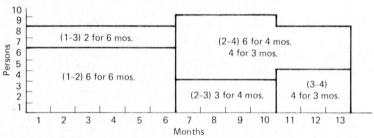

(b) Level Load Profile for Personnel

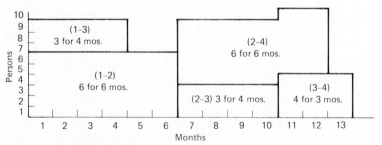

(a) Normal Load Profile for Personnel

FIG. 17.19 Load profile.

considerable slack exists, there is considerable flexibility in rescheduling start and finish times so that the resource profiles will be more level. For example, in Fig. 17.19*a* the personnel demands vary from 4 to 10 persons; in contrast, the personnel demands of Fig. 17.19*b* vary smoothly from 8 to 9 persons. This smoothing was accomplished by extending two noncritical path activities to consume the total slack. The resource demand in activity (1 – 3) was leveled by increasing that activity time from 3 to 6 months and by extending activity (2 – 4) from 6 to 7 months. When heuristics are used to achieve a lower level of one resource, the schedules of other resources will commonly have to be changed. As the number of resources increases, the complexity of this problem increases tremendously. Fortunately, computer software exists that uses a variety of heuristics to provide resource leveling.

Project Duration Research. Research has addressed mathematical programming approaches aimed at minimizing the duration of a project that is subject to constrained resources, but it has not generally achieved useful algorithms for realistic problems. However, a number of successful heuristic methods have been incorporated into computer-based project management systems; these methods employ priority rules for determining which jobs are to be scheduled. The rules include: the least slack, the greatest total resource demand, the shortest activity duration, and the greatest demand for critical-path resources. Wiest (1900) developed a simple heuristic approach based upon the following rules:

1. Starting at the beginning of the project, first schedule those activities with the least slack and the highest resource demand.
2. Allocate resources to those activities with the least slack.
3. Reschedule jobs with slack so that resources are available for critical-path activities.

Integrated Project Management Software. It is not necessary to use an elaborate computer program to receive many of the benefits of PERT/CPM, although many effective computer-based project management programs exist. Approximately 100 microcomputer packages are currently available, ranging substantially in quality and cost. A well-designed project management computer program should:

- Assist in constructing and maintaining the PERT/CPM network diagram on-line and in real time.
- Provide integrated graphics, Gantt charts, bar charts, calendars, resource profiles, and work breakdown structures.
- Support interactive analyses, including all PERT/CPM statistics.
- Assist in resource allocation and resource leveling, using histograms of specific work centers, workers, etc.
- Provide time-cost information.
- Provide accounting and financial budgeting, planning, execution, and control information, including pro forma cash flow, inventory, and labor reports.
- Include data-base management and master files, including past WBDS information, activity times and costs, equipment times and costs, and material costs.
- Be user-friendly, supporting interactive simulation and what-if analysis.
- Include both activity-on-node and activity on-arrow diagrams.
- Support on-site data collection for budgets and activity control.

The American Production and Inventory Control Society (APICS), the Project Management Institute, and others publish surveys of project management computer-based systems to assist in software selection.

LINEAR-DECISION RULES

Linear-decision rules are an operations research–based modeling method for making aggregate decisions. Specifically, a linear-decision model is a set of linear equations which, when solved, simultaneously provide either a single solution or a feasible solution space.

The alternative ways to schedule production to meet fluctuating demand are:

1. Vary production to match the demand. The variation can be obtained by:
    a. Adding people to the productive force or laying them off.
    b. Working short shifts or overtime to vary the work hours of a constant labor force.
    c. Subcontracting work to outside companies.
    d. Some combination of a, b, and/or c.
2. Hold production constant and let inventories of products take care of demand fluctuations.
3. Hold production constant and let backlogs of unfilled customers' orders take care of the fluctuations.
4. Some combination of 1, 2, and/or 3.

TABLE 17.13 Costs of Hiring and Laying Off, Company A Linear-Decision Rule

No. Workers per month*	Total Cost
1	$ 150
2	400
3	700
4	1,000
5	1,500
6	2,000
8	2,800
10	4,000
12	5,000
15	7,000
20	10,000
25	$13,500

* Net additions to (hired) or reductions from (laid off) the work force during the month.

TABLE 17.14 Inventory Carrying Costs, Company A Linear-Decision Rule

Net Inventory, Thousands of Gallons	Monthly Cost
−200	$7,000
−150	5,000
−100	3,500
−50	2,250
0	1,600
50	1,000
100	600
150	400
200	450
250	800
300	1,250
350	1,900
400	2,800
450	4,000
500	$6,000

Each of these major alternatives and subalternatives has costs associated with it. The problem of selecting that combination of alternatives which results in the lowest total cost of operations with relatively unknown future demand and performance is a formidable task. *Linear-decision rules* have been developed that can give *optimal* (or near-optimal) solutions to this problem for certain well-defined assumptions about the related costs. An example will illustrate the form and use of a simple linear-decision rule.

Company A manufactures glue, using a semicontinuous process. Regular payroll costs are known, as are overtime premium payments. The costs associated with hiring and laying off employees are shown in Table 17.13.

Inventory carrying costs are also studied and are determined to be as shown in Table 17.14. Negative inventory (back orders) is believed to be very undesirable, and high costs are associated with being out of stock.

Two equations are developed to yield minimum cost decisions on manpower and production rates for the glue company. These are:

$$M_{Jan} = 2.09 + 0.743\ M_{Dec} - 0.010\ I_{Dec} + \begin{cases} 0.0101\ D_{Jan} \\ +0.0088\ D_{Feb} \\ +0.0071\ D_{Mar} \\ +0.0054\ D_{Apr} \\ +0.0042\ D_{May} \\ +0.0031\ D_{June} \\ +0.0023\ D_{July} \\ +0.0016\ D_{Aug} \\ +0.0012\ D_{Sept} \\ +0.0009\ D_{Oct} \\ +0.0006\ D_{Nov} \\ +0.0005\ D_{Dec} \end{cases}$$

$$P_{Jan} = 153 + 0.993\ M_{Dec} - 0.464\ I_{Dec} + \begin{cases} 0.463\ D_{Jan} \\ +0.234\ D_{Feb} \\ +0.111\ D_{Mar} \\ +0.046\ D_{Apr} \\ +0.013\ D_{May} \\ -0.002\ D_{June} \\ -0.008\ D_{July} \\ -0.010\ D_{Aug} \\ -0.009\ D_{Sept} \\ -0.008\ D_{Oct} \\ -0.007\ D_{Nov} \\ -0.005\ D_{Dec} \end{cases}$$

where M = man-load, number of workers employed
I = inventory, gallons of glue in thousands
D = forecasted demand, gallons ordered in thousands
P = production, gallons of glue in thousands

Using these two equations, simple calculations each month will determine the most economical man-load and production rate for the following months, based on forecasts of demand for the next 12 months. For example, suppose that the data at the end of December were

$$\text{Man-load} = M_{\text{Dec}} = 80 \text{ workers}$$

$$\text{Inventory} = I_{\text{Dec}} = 300{,}000 \text{ gallons}$$

Demand (in gallons) for the next year is forecast as

$D_{\text{Jan}} = 380{,}000$	$D_{\text{July}} = 565{,}000$
$D_{\text{Feb}} = 370{,}000$	$D_{\text{Aug}} = 430{,}000$
$D_{\text{Mar}} = 528{,}000$	$D_{\text{Sept}} = 360{,}000$
$D_{\text{Apr}} = 720{,}000$	$D_{\text{Oct}} = 750{,}000$
$D_{\text{May}} = 420{,}000$	$D_{\text{Nov}} = 683{,}000$
$D_{\text{June}} = 800{,}000$	$D_{\text{Dec}} = 546{,}000$

Solving the two equations for January operating data gives

$$\text{Man-load} = M_{\text{Jan}} = 82 \text{ workers (2 more than in December)}$$

$$\text{Production} = P_{\text{Jan}} = 426{,}000 \text{ gallons}$$

The inventory will increase by the difference between production and demand $(426{,}000 - 380{,}000 = 46{,}000 \text{ gallons})$. The planned inventory at the end of January will then be $300{,}000 + 46{,}000 = 346{,}000$ gallons. This can be calculated in one step, using the equation

$$I_{\text{Jan}} = I_{\text{Dec}} + P_{\text{Jan}} - D_{\text{Jan}}$$

Some interesting observations can be made about the application of such equations to the real business world:

- A practical management would want to test the equations' effectiveness by simulating what would have happened if the equations had been used in the past and comparing this against the actual results.
- Because of the complexity of the mathematical deviations, it is not possible to determine the effect on the decisions of changes in costs without deriving new equations.
- Factors not included in the original derivation might become important, and it may be difficult or impossible to include them in new equations.
- The equations assume a specific amount of production per worker. The actual number of people employed or the hours worked would have to be increased if this productivity were not met.

It is important to expand on the first observation. Linear-decision rules can be applied to nearly any set of linear variables that are interrelated, but the model's results ignore any outside influences not captured by the model's variables; therefore, the results have to be tempered with logic. In addition, these models are very aggregate, not depicting variations due to time or outside perturbation. Hence, the results provide only general solutions, which may need to be adjusted.

Linear-decision rules have real potential for assisting management toward controlling production-level changes on a rational basis. The great danger lies in assuming that management can be relinquished to such rules and that it can handle all significant changes that may occur. It cannot! Applied properly, linear-decision rules result in improved control over production levels when compared to intuitive or irrational approaches. The results would certainly be more stable and consistent as long as no major variations occurred in those factors which affect the basic assumptions used in the derivation of the equations.

SIMULATION

Digital simulation uses a mathematical model to represent a real or hypothetical physical system. A computer simulation model of a physical system provides a laboratory in which alternative designs can be explored and analyzed (see Chapter 31). Simulation is discussed in this section for loading and scheduling applications. The program, executed on the computer, is a replica of the manufacturing system and is controlled so that the system's behavior can be studied and analyzed. Decisions can be made concerning production alternatives. For example, adding a new lathe can be considered without disrupting the actual physical system.

Simulation depends on describing a system in terms acceptable to the computer language used. To do this, it is necessary to have a system-state description, which is typically characterized by a set of state variables included in the computer program that make up the simulation model. The various combinations of values that these variables can take on characterize the unique states of the system. Sufficient variables must be defined to represent all of the pertinent details of the system. As the values of the variables are changed, the system effectively moves from state to state. The process of building a simulation model consists of defining the state variables of the system and the operating procedures that cause the state variables to change over time. Simulation is then the process of moving the system from state to state according to the rules that characterize the operational procedures of the system.

There are two basic methods of managing the variable changes as they occur over time:

- The *discrete-event approach* makes the assumption that the system's variables change in value only at specific events. Each event and the operating rules which cause the system's status variables to change in value are incorporated in the computer program. The simulation moves through time from event to event, characterizing the system dynamics.

- The *fixed-time-interval approach* assumes that the system will be evaluated at regular, fixed time intervals. At the end of these intervals, the system status variables are updated according to a fixed set of rules, and then the system status is evaluated to determine if an event has occurred.

The discrete-event approach is used when the state variables change at irregular time intervals, such as in the manufacturing industry, which deals with discrete parts. The fixed-time-interval approach is typically used in systems having state variables of a continuous nature such as found in chemical process industries.

Specially designed computer simulation languages provide many features for managing the updating of the state variables and advancing time. They also provide features for recording system performance statistics and for generating random numbers to introduce system randomness.

Simulation Languages

The lowest level of computer language typically used is FORTRAN or BASIC. This requires that the simulation process be coded, which is labor-intensive. High-level languages, such as SLAM, SIMSCRIPT, and GPSS, facilitate simulation because they provide subroutines for time advancement, entity maintenance, and statistic collections. Higher-level simulation languages are designed for special purposes; MAP/1, SPEED, and MAST are three designed for the simulation of manufacturing systems. Table 17.15 lists some of the various computer simulation languages available for factory equipment.

Simulation Applications in Industry

Computer simulation has two important applications in industry: design and control. In design, the typical application is for analyzing a production system. Simulating a design is appealing because the components of the model are well-detailed and have a one-to-one correspondence to the physical system. Because there are very few theoretical considerations, the model can represent many of the subtle system nuances; and with such a detailed model, the analyst can gain the confidence of the people using the simulator. Performance measurements, such as the number of parts passing through the system per day, can give an insight into the system's dynamic operation.

Some simulation languages can produce animations. This permits the simulation to be illustrated graphically on a computer terminal so that the analyst can see the system in action and observe its interactions and behavior, a visual function beyond the scope of standard reporting technique. For example, TESS (a software program) provides animation, as well a model-building and output analysis capabilities, for the SLAM simulation language.

When simulation is used as a control aid, it is used to generate and analyze possible production schedules. Since simulation models are used based on very accurate predictions of system behavior, it is logical to use these powerful predictive techniques to develop precise schedules. Highly complex operating rules can be implemented in a model and then downloaded to the shop floor in the form of production schedules with operation start and end times.

There are a few turnkey products available for production scheduling based on-line simulation scheduling. An example of such a software system is SCHED/SIM, which is designed to address the problems of the of the shopfloor supervisor. SCHED/SIM controls the factory floor by providing a computer model of the manufacturing system and interfaces with the shopfloor supervisor, who simulates production situations and generates schedules that are achievable. This makes complex simulation algorithms available to the production supervisor. SCHED/SIM interacts with existing MRP and shopfloor data-collection systems to download schedules with due dates to the scheduling workstation. It also automatically loads this information into the simulation data base to update the information on which to base the schedule. This makes simulation on a day-to-day basis practical.

LINE BALANCING

The term *line balancing* applies to assembly-line operations in which a crew performs sequential operations. The objective of the balancing effort is to distribute the work as evenly as possible for maximum output and economy.

TABLE 17.15 Simulation Systems

Simulation Language	Capability	Availability
INTERACTIVE	A user-friendly simulation language for the evaluation of process-oriented manufacturing systems, inventory policies, etc.	Micro Simulation
INTER-SIM	A discrete-event, visual, interactive simulation package.	Decision Computing
MANIP	An interactive modeling and simulation system.	A. Symons or R. Rijke
MAST (Manufacturing System Design Tool)	A simulation language for flexible manufacturing systems.	CMS Research, Inc.
Materials Processing Flow Simulator	A finite-element simulation of fluid flow and heat transfer, axial symmetry, and steady flow.	B. Caswell
MAXISIM—FLOW SHEET SIMULATION	An interactive process simulator with full recycle capability.	Oklahoma State University
MAXISIZE—EQUIPMENT SIZING	A modular set of routines for sizing and weight estimation of major processing equipment.	Oklahoma State University
Micro NET™	A network-based discrete-event language that operates on microcomputers.	Pritsker & Associates, Inc.
Q-GERT	A network simulation language.	Pritsker & Associates, Inc.
SCHED/SIM	An interactive on-line system for shopfloor scheduling and control.	FACTROL, Inc.
Scheduling Simulator	Designed to simulate the orders being processed in a job-shop environment such that trial schedules may be run and analyzed.	Lionel Poizner
SIMAN Simulation	A general-purpose simulation language with special manu-facturing-system features.	Systems Modeling Corp.
SIMSCRIPT 11.5	A high-level language for discrete systems simulation.	C.A.C.I.
SLAM II™	Permits discrete-event, continuous, and networking modeling.	Pritsker & Associates, Inc.
SPEED II™	An input-driven modeling tool that is manufacturing-oriented.	Horizon Software, Inc.
TESS	An integrated simulation support system, with data-base and graphics capabilities.	Pritsker & Associates, Inc.

Simulation, October, 1984, vol. 43, no. 4. (Courtesy: The Society for Computer Simulation.)

In actual practice there are many kinds of line balancing (which is to say that the line-balancing principle may be applied to a number of varied operations). Consequently, there are actually several different approaches to line balancing, each being applicable to a particular set of conditions.

For lines to be balanced effectively, reliable predetermined time data should be available. The problem with using stopwatch time studies is that, when making changes and testing different line balances, one does not always have the time-study element for the particular work element desired. Therefore, the method must actually be performed by someone and new time studies made to develop the correct standard time. The advantage of predetermined motion times, such as methods time measurement (MTM), is that the time for any conceivable method can be predetermined to develop the best line balance without a series of trial-and-error attempts. The savings in the time and effect of changes can be easily predicted. The following illustrates the use of a predetermined time standard applied to line balancing.

The two most common line types are the rigidly paced and spaced conveyor assembly lines, such as automobile assembly lines or the more flexible flat belts. The process of balancing these lines is basically one of determining the work content for each station on the line and organizing the work crew in the most effective manner. To accomplish this, the following steps are suggested:

1. Determine the output required per time period. It may be as small as an hour or as long as a day.

2. Determine the total man-hours work required per unit of output as standard operating efficiency.

3. Multiply the output required per period by the work standard to determine the total hours of work per period.

4. Divide the total hours by the number of hours in the normal work period at standard operating efficiency to find the number of crew members required to produce the necessary output.

5. Divide the total work per unit by the optimum crew size to arrive at the theoretical work cycle for each crew member per unit of output.

Example: Assume a production requirement of 5000 pairs of heels per 8-hr shift. Assume 0.385 min per heal total true work. Therefore, 5000 pairs × 2 × 0.385 = 3850 min of work per shift. 3850 ÷ 480 min per shift = 9.6, or approximately 10 crew members. 0.385 ÷ 10 = 0.0385 min, the approximate ideal work cycle per heal.

Divide the total work so that each operator on the line will have approximately a 0.0385-min work cycle.

There are several alternatives for balancing the line. All 10 members of the crew may be placed on the same side of the belt and perform the work sequentially with an approximate cycle time of 0.0385 min.

On the other hand, it may be desirable to have five members on each side of the belt performing the same operation, having a cycle time of 0.077 min. A third alternative would be to have one member of the crew feed the belt, another take off, and four members on each side of the belt, each having approximately a 0.77-min work cycle.

The above illustrates the seemingly endless variations possible when balancing lines. Some of the considerations that could have been used to determine which of these combinations to use might be as follows:

- *Difference in job rate.* Line feeders and line emptiers are often paid less than assemblers. Therefore, two crew members could have lower-paying jobs, reducing the total cost, other things being equal.
- *Long-cycle elements.* There may be an indivisible element longer than the desired work cycle. This requires two identical work cycles performed on the same or possibly on opposite sides of the belt.
- *Floor space and layout limitations.* Possibly, the belt is not long enough to have 10 members working on the same side, so the crew members must sit on both sides of the belt.
- *Right- versus left-handedness.* In many cases, an element of work performed on one side of the belt with work coming toward the operator's left side may be completely different when the situation is reversed and the work approaches the right side. Sometimes the operators can be trained to work either way, but in other cases extra movements and hence extra time may be involved.

Testing the Balance

With short, rigidly defined cycles, it is probably never possible to balance the line exactly; that is, not every operator can be assigned exactly the same amount of work. Therefore, since the pace is that of the slowest or longest cycle, there is a certain degree of imbalance that cannot be eliminated. To test the amount of imbalance and establish acceptable criteria for acceptance or rejection of the balance, the following procedure can be used: A rule of thumb is that the line balance is acceptable when the peak cycle, multiplied by the number of operators, is less than the total true work plus 25 percent.

Station	Option 1	Option 2
1	0.050	0.042
2	0.035	0.040
3	0.039	0.036
4	0.030	0.038
5	0.045	0.040
6	0.030	0.035
7	0.037	0.037
8	0.040	0.039
9	0.029	0.040
10	0.050	0.038
Total work	0.385	0.385
True work + 25%	0.481	0.481
Peak	0.050	0.042
Peak × 10 =	0.500	0.420
	(Breakdown not acceptable)	(Breakdown acceptable)

Incentive Payment for Balanced Lines

The decision to accept or reject a given balancing solution should be made on the same basis, regardless of whether the operation is paid day work or is paid on an incentive basis.

For lines of the type indicated above, the incentive payment, if any, must be paid on the basis of the peak cycle just as if everyone had the same amount of work. This is a group incentive system, and all members of the crew must produce the same number of units. One operator's pace cannot be different from another's except as caused by differences in assigned work over which the individual operator has no control whatever.

Machine-Oriented Line Balance

The considerations so far pertain to balancing lines which are primarily geared to labor distribution and which have fairly uniform work cycles and tasks. Other considerations are encountered when lines are machine-oriented and labor may not be the most important criterion. Such a case is encountered at steel plant blooming mills where the line that is to be balanced extends from the soaking pits to the slab yard. In this instance, each position on the line will have a different workload, depending upon the shape rolled. The question of balance now becomes simply one of how many workers are needed in each position to keep the mill running at top efficiency and what their workload is when doing so. There is little that can be done about balance. The issue is merely one of whether or not to add another worker.

BIBLIOGRAPHY

General

Chase, R. B., and N. J. Aquilano: *Production and Operations Management*, 4th ed., Irwin, Homewood, Ill., 1985.

Fogarty, D. W., and T. R. Hoffman: *Production and Inventory Management*, South-Western, Cincinnati, 1983.

Greene, J. H.: *Operations Management for Productivity and Profit*, Prentice-Hall, Englewood Cliffs, N.J. 1984.

———: *Production and Inventory Control: Systems and Decisions*, Irwin, Homewood, Ill., 1974.

Janson, R. L.: *Production Control Desk Handbook*, Prentice-Hall, Englewood Cliffs, N.J., 1975.

O'Brian, J. L.: *Scheduling Handbook*, McGraw-Hill, New York, 1969.

Plossl, George W.: *Production and Inventory Control: Principles and Techniques*, 2nd ed., Prentice-Hall, Englewood Cliffs, N.J., 1984.

Vollman, Thomas E., William E. Berry, and D. Clay Whybark: *Manufacturing Planning and Control Systems*, Irwin, Homewood, Ill., 1984.

Scheduling

APICS Certification Program Study Guide: "Capacity Planning and Master Production Scheduling," *Production and Inventory Management*, vol. 20, no. 2, 1979, 85–102.

Bedworth, David D., and James E. Bailey: *Integrated Production Control Systems, Management, Analysis, Design*, Wiley, New York, 1982.

Berry, W. L., T. L. Vollman, and D. C. Whybark: *Master Production Scheduling: Principles and Practice*, Washington, D.C., 1979.

Bestwick, P. F., and K. G. Lockger: "A Practical Approach to Production Scheduling," *International Journal of Production Research*, vol. 17, no. 2, 1979, 95–110.

Conway, R. W., W. L. Maxwell and L. W. Miller: *Theory of Scheduling*, Addison-Wesley, Reading, Mass., 1967.

Dempster, M. A. H., J. K. Lenstra, and A. H. G. Rinnosy Kan, *Deterministic and Stochastic Scheduling*, Reidel, Boston, 1982.

Hershauer, J. C., and R. D. Eck: "Extended MRP Systems for Evaluating Master Schedules and Material Requirements Plans," *Production and Inventory Management*, vol. 21, no. 2, 1980, 53–66.

Holt, Jack A.: "A Heuristic Method for Aggregate Planning: Production Decision Framework," *Journal of Operations Management*, vol. 2, no. 1, 1980, 41–51.

Muth, J. F., and G. L. Thompson: *Industrial Scheduling*, Prentice-Hall, Englewood Cliffs, N.J., 1963.

Proud, J. F.: "Controlling the Master Schedule," *Production and Inventory Management*, vol. 22, no. 2, 1981, 78–90.

Short-Interval Scheduling

Behan, Raymond J: *Cost Reduction Through Short Interval Scheduling*, Prentice-Hall, Englewood Cliffs, N.J., 1969.

Smith, M. R.: *Short-Interval Scheduling*, McGraw-Hill, New York, 1968.

Critical-Ratio Scheduling

Putnam, Arnold O.: *APICS National Training Kit No. 2*, APICS, Washington D.C.

———, E. Robert Barlow, and Gabriel N. Stilian: *Unified Operations Management*, McGraw-Hill, New York, 1963.

Optimized Production Technology (OPT)

Arnold, J. R., and L. M. Clive: *Introduction to Materials Management*, Sir Sandford Fleming College, Peterborough, Ontario, 1982.

Fox, Robert E.: *OPT(imizing) Just in time, Leapfrogging the Japanese*, APICS International Conference Proceedings, 1984.

Goldratt, Eliyahu: *The Unbalanced Plant*, APICS International Conference Proceedings, 1981.

Line of Balance

Finck, N. E.: "Line of Balance Gives the Answer," *Systems and Procedures Journal*, July–Aug. 1965.

Line of Balance Guide for System and Subsystem Acquisition, a Management Procedure for Production Planning and Control, Aeronautical System Division, Air Force Systems Command, Wright-Patterson AFB, Ohio, AFSCM 174-1, Apr. 6, 1964.

Line of Balance Technology, Office of Naval Material, Department of the Navy, NAVEXOS PI851 (rev. 4-62).

PERT/CPM Project Management

Cleland, D. I., and W. R. King: *Analysis and Project Management*, McGraw-Hill, New York, 1975.

Gido, Jack: *Project Management Software Dictionary*, Industrial Press, New York, 1985.

Kerzner, H.: *Project Management for Executives*, Van Nostrand Reinhold, New York, 1982

————, and H. Thamhain: *Project Management for Small- and Medium-Size Business*, Van Nostrand Reinhold, New York, 1984.

Moder, J. J., C. R. Phillips, and E. W. Davis: *Project management with CPM and Pert*, 3d ed., Van Nostrand Reinhold, New York, 1983.

Project Management Institute (PMI): *Survey of CPM Scheduling Software Packages and Related Project Control Programs*, PMI, Drexel Hill, Pa. 1980.

Smith, L. A., and S. Gupta: "Project Management Software in P&IM," *Production and Inventory Review*, June 1985.

Wiest, J. D.: "Heuristic Programs for Decision Maker," *Harvard Business Review*, Sept.–Oct. 1966, pp. 129–143.

————, and F. K., Levy *Management Guide to PERT/CPM*, Prentice-Hall, Englewood Cliffs, N.J., 1977.

Linear-Decision Rules

Holt, Charles C., Franco Modigliani, John F. Muth, and Herbert A. Simon: *Planning Production, Inventories, and Work Force*, Prentice-Hall, Englewood Cliffs, N.J., 1960.

Simulation

Kiviat, P. J., R. Villaneuva, and H. Markowitz: *The SIMSCRIPT II Programming Language*, Prentice-Hall, Englewood Cliffs, N.J., 1969.

Law, Averill M., and W. David Kelton: *Simulation Modeling and Analysis*, McGraw-Hill, New York, 1982.

Miner, Robin J., and Laurie J. Rolston: *MAP/1 User's Manual*, Pritsker & Associates, West Lafayette, Ind., 1983.

Payne, James A.: *Introduction to Scheduling*, McGraw-Hill, New York, 1982.

Pritsker, A. A. B.: *Introduction to Simulation and SLAM II*, 2d ed., Pritsker & Associates, West Lafayette, Ind., and Wiley, New York, 1984.

————: *The GASP IV Simulation Language*, Wiley, New York, 1974.

————: *Modeling and Analysis Using Q-GERT Networks*, Halstead Press, New York, and Pritsker & Associates, West Lafayette, Ind., 1977.

Schriber, T.: *Simulation Using GPSS*, Wiley, New York, 1974.

Standridge, Charles R., et al.: *TESS User's Manual*, Pritsker & Associates, West Lafayette, Ind., 1984.

Assembly-Line Balancing

Dar-El, E. M., and Y. Rubinovitch: "MUST—A Multiple-Solutions Technique for Balancing Single-Model Assembly Lines, *Management Science*, vol. 25, no. 11, 1979, 1105–1114.

Faouf, A., C. L. Tsui, and E. A. El-Sayed: "New Heuristic Approach to Assembly-Line Balancing," *Computers and Industrial Engineering*, vol. 4, no. 3, 1980, 223–234.

Fisk, J. C., and A. Solano: "Production Scheduling for High-Volume Assemblies—A Case Study," *Journal of the Operations Research Society*, vol. 31, no. 9, 1980, 781–789.

Johnson, R. V.: "Assembly-Line Balancing Algorithms: Computation Comparisons," *International Journal of Production Research*, vol. 19, no. 3, 1981, 248–255.

Kao, Edward P. C., and Maurice Queyranne: "On Dynamic Programming Methods for Assembly-Line Balancing," *Operations Research*, vol. 30, no. 2, 1982, 375–390.

Kottas, John F., and Hon-Shiang Lau: "A Stochastic Line-Balancing Procedure," *International Journal of Production Research*, vol. 19, no. 2, 1981, 177–193.

Pinto, P. A., D. G. Dannenbring, and B. M. Khumawala: "A Heuristic Network Procedure for the Assembly-Line Balancing Problem," *Naval Research Logistics Quarterly*, vol. 25, no. 2, 1978, 229–307.

Sadowski, R. P.: "Manpower Scheduling Method Simplifies Production-Line Assignments Through Graphics," *IE Magazine*, vol. 23, no. 8, 1981, 34–41.

——, and R. E. Jacobson: "Scheduling Algorithms for the Unbalanced Production Line: An Analysis and Comparison," *AIIE Transactions*, vol. 10, no. 1, 1978, 31–39.

Schofield, Norman A.: "Assembly-Line Balancing and the Application of Computer Techniques" *Computers and Industrial Engineering*, vol. 3, no. 1, 1979, 53–69.

Manufacturing Information Systems

Basic Manufacturing Systems

Editor

CHARLES R. SANDLIN, CFPIM, C. R. Sandlin and Associates, Inc.,
Northfield, Illinois

This chapter describes methods that can be used to implement a manual closed-loop manufacturing system. While the introduction of the microcomputer continues to bring the cost of computerized systems down dramatically, many companies will continue to utilize manual systems for all or part of the planning and control function. Manual systems are appropriate for:

- *Small companies or divisions with a limited product line, a small number of components, and very low volumes.* Often the accounting functions operate on a computer system while the material control systems are manual.

- *Moving from an informal environment to a computerized closed-loop system.* Formal manual systems can be used to develop the controls and disciplines needed to implement sound computerized systems. During the phased implementation of a computerized closed-loop system, a well-designed manual system can be used effectively to operate the functions not yet implemented.

- *The company that may have special system needs that are not met by standard computer software.* Where the cost of developing specialized software exceeds the cost of operating a manual system, the manual system is appropriate.

It is important to recognize that the manual system must provide all of the control functions required. In the smaller company, lines of responsibility and function are not well-defined since most people wear many hats. Often, business strategies

strategies are developed informally since the information needed is readily available, and decisions based on experienced judgment are effective and efficient. While many of the planning functions may be informal, key record-keeping and operational activities require formal systems to provide accurate planning and financial data. Specifically, inventory, production work-order, and purchase-order information must be formally maintained. Usually, accurate bill-of-materials routing, and cost data are also required in order to operate effectively.

The major trade-off in a manual system is finding the proper balance between the cost of gathering and reporting information and the benefit of the additional data. Computer systems are viewed as the only means of gaining access to the benefits of closed-loop systems, but they cannot always be cost-justified. As a result, many tools that could be used to improve operations are ignored by the manual user since they are thought to be too complicated or costly to utilize. However, a combination of simpler methods, which have little utility in a computerized system, and the intelligent adaptation of methods usually associated with computerized systems can be a sensible compromise. Visual inventory methods, simplified planning and scheduling techniques, and similar means can often be used effectively to control smaller operations at a minimum cost while gaining most of the benefits of a formal closed-loop system. Additionally, it may be appropriate to utilize techniques such as material requirements planning (MRP) on a limited basis to gain control of a major product line or of key components.

This chapter discusses the trade-offs to be made in selecting techniques and provides simplified approaches where applicable. It describes manual record-keeping equipment and methods for the first-time user. Additionally, it presents methods for using microcomputers with spreadsheet and word processing systems to support the manual system. The chapter is organized into four major sections, which parallel the closed-loop system chart previously presented, and also offers a section on equipment and microcomputers.

BASIC INFORMATION RECORDS

Most companies must maintain master records that indicate the materials and procedures required to produce a product. These records are often used as masters to prepare shop paperwork and material requisitions. Therefore, it is critical to keep these records current and to control access to them.

Part-Numbering Systems

The part number is usually the common identification element used to tie all of the information together. Part-numbering systems come in an infinite array of structures and approaches. A good numbering system can be an aid to the material control function, while a poor one can cause problems. The following comments are a general guide to part numbering that the manual-system user should consider.

- Keep the number as simple as possible. Use the fewest characters that will provide adequate flexibility for expansion.
- Keep the numbers consistent if at all possible. Use the same number of characters. Do not mix alphabetical and numerical characters in the same position. Try to avoid using several different numbering schemes.

- Use a descriptive numbering scheme where the scheme is simple and provides a useful identification tool. Manual systems do not provide ready access to descriptive information as computerized systems do. The descriptive number can be used effectively. Remember to keep the scheme simple; no one will be able to use the scheme effectively if the number is too long and complicated.
- Control the assignment of numbers to avoid duplication.
- Require that everything has a part number, with the exception of low-value parts, supplies, etc.
- Establish a number-assignment procedure and a part-number log.

Engineering Drawings

The simplest form of record is the engineering drawing. Experienced shop personnel can use it to determine the materials and procedures required to build or produce an item. A copy of the latest drawing is usually included in the shop-order packet.

In most cases, a drawing should relate to a single part or component. Although this approach typically requires more drawings, it provides for better configuration control and it simplifies the development of bills of materials and routings. Composite drawings are used to provide assembly views and instructions.

In the manual system, drawings should always contain a list of the materials and/or parts required to produce the item being described. They should also include a history of changes that have been made, thus providing simple configuration control.

Bill of Materials

A bill of materials (B/M) is required when the product being produced has components and subassemblies. The B/M should include a list of the parts, components, subassemblies, raw materials, etc., required to produce the item. The amount required to produce the item, all production-loss factors, and the component's unit of measure should also be shown on the B/M. Another section should be set aside on the B/M to show where the item is used.

There are two methods of maintaining B/Ms that should be considered:

- The B/M can be a single-level B/M (Fig. 18.1a) that lists only the materials that are directly used in the item. By establishing a single-level B/M, it is possible to build a multilevel B/M from the single-level B/Ms. Where-used information can be entered on the single-level B/M to aid in planning. The single-level B/M approach is most useful where components are used on many different products. It also can easily be used for creating material requisitions to be issued in the shop-order packet. The B/M may be placed on the drawing to reduce paperwork.
- An alternative method of B/M recording is to maintain the entire structure for a product (Fig. 18.1b). This method is applicable to situations in which there is little or no commonality of parts across products. The entire B/M is issued with the shop-order packet in this case. It is more difficult to trace where-used information using this method.

Routings

Process routings are maintained for parts that require many steps to produce. Both assembly and production routings may be maintained. The routing may be in the form of a manufacturing order (Fig. 18.2) to simplify the reproduction and issuance of shop orders. The routing should identify the operations required to produce an item and the work center to be used for each operation. It should also contain a detailed description of the work to be performed and provide special instructions, tolerances, and inspection guidelines.

Work Center Records

Records that describe each work center's capability, standard rates, efficiency factors, manning levels, capacity, and special characteristics should be maintained.

Bill of Material				Sheet _1_ of _1_
Assembly No. 10-1048	Description _Motor Mount_			Prepared by _AS_ Approved by _CS_
Unit of Measure Part/Assembly No.	Description	Qty. Rqd.	u m	Comment
40-1412	Bracket - Left	1	ea	Cad Plate
40-1413	Bracket - Right	1	ea	Cad plate
70-8474	Plate - Mounting	1	ea.	
50-2714	Bolt - 3/8" x 5"			
	Hex Head - 2" thread	3	ea.	
90-0047	Hardware Kit	1	Kit	

Where Used List					
Assembly No.	Qty.	Comment	Assembly No.	Qty.	Comment
10-7147	1		10-8014	2	
10-7150	1		10-8015	2	
10-7271	1				
10-7451	1				

FIG. 18.1(a)   Single-level bill of materials;

		Number 9 Pinup Lamp			
Mfg. code 1020314				Date 8/18/___ Approved AES	
Level 1 component number	Level 2 component number	Description	Quantity required	Source	Remarks
X18		Switch	1	Purch.	
Y2L		Socket	1	Mfg.	
	Y2L-S	Shell	1	Mfg.	
	Y2L-B	Base	1	Mfg.	
	Y2L-SI	Shell Insulator	1	Purch.	
	Y2L-BI	Base Insulator	1	Purch.	
	Y2L-XI	Screw stem	1	Mfg.	
9P		Shade	1	Mfg.	
414		Hanger	2	Mfg.	
4107		Cord set	1	Purch.	

FIG. 18.1(b) Indented bill of materials.

Special machine characteristics, scheduling requirements, and crew sizes should be included in the work-center record. Alternate work centers and/or routings that can be used in special circumstances should also be identified.

Product Cost

The cost-accounting department will usually maintain the product-cost records. Material control needs to understand the major components of the cost of an item in order to make daily scheduling decisions and to set production plans.

Quality Control Records

Most companies will find a need to maintain a history of quality control inspections on most material. One approach is simply to file inspection reports. Another is to maintain a summary inspection record that provides a quality history of the item.

PLANNING

The planning process starts with establishing a business plan. In smaller companies the business plan may be developed rather simply, but it must still answer the basic questions of what, when, and how much to produce. The business plan is then used to prepare a production plan that addresses inventory changes and capacity requirements.

The planning process in the nonautomated system is very close to that of a computerized system, with one major exception—the computerized user has access to detailed data that can be summarized into meaningful groupings. The planning techniques described in this handbook are all valid in the nonautomated system,

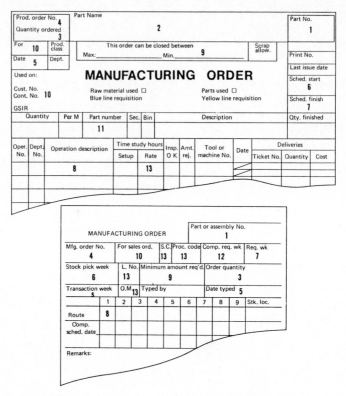

1. Part or assembly number
2. Part name
3. Quantity
4. Manufacturing order number
5. Date written or issued
6. Start date
7. Required completion date
8. Routing or operations sequence
9. Minimum amount required
10. Sales order number or customer reference
11. Raw material quantity or parts required
12. Raw material or component
13. Various significant code number or abbreviations for accounting or control purposes

FIG. 18.2 Process routing and manufacturing order.

but adjustments must be made to recognize the lack of and/or difficulty in obtaining detailed data. The trade-off is one of precision versus practicality.

Business Plan

The business plan should clearly define the product lines and market segments that the business expects to address in the future. Usually, the plan is developed in dollars, covers a 1- to 2-year horizon, and may correspond to the annual budgeting process. The more precise this definition is, the more definitive the downstream planning process can be. Although a lack of precision is fairly common at this level in smaller, more flexible companies, minimal plans that can be used to set initial budgets and production plans are required.

Sales forecasts are a key part of the business plan. The forecast must be made in adequate detail to allow the development of production plans. At the minimum, the business plan must provide an annual dollar sales forecast by product line.

Most companies do a relatively good job of estimating annual sales dollars, but few are able to forecast when the sales will occur or in what products or product lines. A number of factors impact on the timing of sales, including seasonality, sales promotions, product availability, competitive activity, business reporting requirements, bonus and/or commission periods, and short-term business cycles. Past history is one of the most useful tools for predicting the relative level of sales for a specific time period. The sales department should provide the past sales and order history required to establish a sales baseline. The sales data should be provided in as much detail as possible for each product or product line; ideally, monthly units and dollar data should be provided. The details can be used to detect trends and seasonal effects. Care must be taken to judge the impact of back orders and cancellations on the actual sales information. The timing of a sale is also important. In a backlog-type business, it is important to track the size of the backlog as well as actual sales in order to correlate a sale with the production lead time.

Forecasting

The technique used to develop a sales forecast adequate for production planning is not important as long as the results are usable. In many situations, a monthly index can be calculated quite simply and applied to the total sales forecast to get a good period-by-period approximation. The impact of product promotions and special situations must be factored out of the data before the index is calculated. It is usually wise to compare the indexes for several years of history in order to identify major pattern changes and/or potential data errors. A graph of adjusted monthly indexes for several years is useful for identifying monthly characteristics. The final index selected is often judgmental. It should also be noted that the index is more accurate when applied to groups of products with like characteristics. This tends to minimize the impact of random variations on the final index.

Once a base forecast is calculated, promotion plans, new product introductions, etc., should be factored in. It is a good idea to keep a sales diary that records special situations (such as promotions, out-of-stock situations, and large orders) to aid in setting indexes and/or estimating detailed sales activity.

Forecasting in the smaller company is often simple and difficult at the same time. It is simple in that there are few products or lines to consider. It is difficult because variations can be very large, given that the company is usually close to the market and that large orders can create significant short-term impact. This is often used as an excuse for avoiding demand tracking and planning to a forecast.

Basic forecasting starts with collecting organized demand information. While collecting detailed data may not be possible, collecting history by category or product line, etc., is simpler and may well provide the data required to prepare production plans and set long-term capacity.

A number of formal forecasting methods have been developed in recent years, but most depend on computer support. Most of the Focus Forecasting methods available are not really feasible for the manual user because of their computational requirements. However, single-order exponential smoothing and a 3- or 4-term moving average can be used effectively. A simplified exponential smoothing formula can be used that actually makes this method operate with the least effort:

New forecast = old forecast + adjustment

By using an ordinary calculator, this becomes a 5- to- 10-s calculation. Recalculating the forecast for 500 parts would thus take 1 to 2 h. A forecast tracking chart such as that shown in Fig. 18.3 could be used for each item or category being managed.

An advantage of the manual system is that it gives the forecaster an opportunity to review the new forecast and alter it to fit existing conditions quickly and easily. At the very least, a comparison of forecast and actuality has the utility of presenting the data required to identify trends and significant directions. The critical function is the comparison of data over time.

One of the best ways to compare information is graphically. The use of simple line graphs will show seasonal and trend patterns when data for several years is compared.

Using the techniques described, any number of things can be forecasted and planned, including order backlogs, inventory levels, and the input and output of work centers.

Production Plan

Once a detailed sales forecast is developed, it can be converted into a production plan that balances market demand with company resources. The effort required to do the calculation can be significant in a nonautomated system, so it is important to develop methods and factors that can be used to reduce this effort. It is important to provide production plans that are adequate to operate the production facility effectively while meeting company objectives.

Item Number __107745__   Description _X- Powder - 450z_

% Error Factor: _25% starting period 7 due to - trend._

New Forecast = Old Forecast + Error Factor (Actual−Old Forecast)

Period	Actual	Forecast	Error	
1	195	200	−5	
2	173	199	−26	
3	201	196	−5	
4	168	197	−29	
5	114	194	−80	
6	142	186	−44	
7	128	175	−47	
8	159	163	−4	
9		162		

FIG. 18.3 Forecast tracking chart.

The methods used in any specific situation will vary considerably depending on the characteristics of the situation and the needs of the company. The following discussion is intended to be a starting point for developing your own methods rather than an exhaustive list of the methods available.

Step 1. The first step is to convert the sales forecast into a form that can be used for production planning. This could be as simple as dividing the monthly dollar forecast by the unit price to determine the number of units. However, most business-plan forecasts are by product line, making the task more complicated than would normally be the case.

To solve this problem, determine a standard unit for the product line based on average characteristics of the individual products in the line. Standard units can be almost anything (pieces, cases, pounds, feet, gallons, etc.). More than one standard unit may be used for a product line in order to determine capacity requirements and apply inventory. The average characteristics of the individual products might include previous years' sales adjusted for additions and deletions to the line, price increases or decreases, and such other factors as capacity characteristics and inventory use. Once the standard unit is determined, it should be used consistently and monitored for relative accuracy. The method used to determine a standard unit can vary by product line.

Once the forecast is converted into standard units, gross production requirements will have been established.

Step 2. The next step is to produce a production plan that considers inventory, capacity, management constraints, and objectives established by the business plan.

The application of inventory is usually the most difficult step in determining net production requirements. The available stock must be converted to standard units and deducted from the gross requirements. Care must be taken to exclude obsolete and damaged inventory that is not useful for meeting the sales forecast. Often, based on experience, a percentage of the on-hand inventory is used to make this adjustment. The difference between gross production requirements and inventory will be the net production required.

The capacity requirements can be determined from the net production requirements. The gross capacity needed is determined by converting the standard production units into capacity units. Again, there are many valid methods to use. In the simplest situation, the number of hours to produce a standard unit can be used. In other situations, it may be necessary to convert the standard units to a capacity-related standard unit; this is most often the situation when several product lines utilize common resources. It may be feasible to convert to a common measure, such as pounds, hours, feet, or gallons. Work-in-process may need to be applied by converting open jobs to standard units and estimating the percent-complete status of the jobs and the time period in which they will be available. The capacity already consumed by the open jobs is deducted from the gross capacity requirement to determine the net capacity required. In most situations, however, the work in process can be ignored at this planning level. The net capacity required is compared with the available capacity to determine the period-by-period differences and the cumulative effect.

Step 3. The final step is to develop a capacity plan that best balances requirements with constraints. The capacity plan can be converted into standard production units to establish a production plan. Once the production plan is set, an inventory plan for the product line can be calculated in standard units and dollars. Obviously, this process is iterative since a number of constraints must be met. For example, the best capacity plan may result in higher inventories than desired, so one or more passes may be required in order to revise the capacity plan.

To be an effective tool, the production plan should be recalculated at least quarterly and extended to cover 12 months. A sample form is shown in Fig. 18.4.

EXECUTION

Once the production, inventory, and capacity plans are set, it is the responsibility of materials management to implement the plans and control operations to meet the plans. This includes:

- Developing master schedules that detail the production plan into smaller time periods and adjusting for actual demand and/or order backlogs.
- Developing short-term work-center capacity plans and loading jobs into the work center.
- Using inventory control methods to plan the short-term replenishment of parts and raw materials.
- Physical control of inventories.
- Dispatching and controlling the production activity.
- Purchasing and receiving material.

Production Plan for __Z Powder__

Product	Conv. Factor	PD April FCST	S.U.	PD May FCST	S.U.	PD June FCST	S.U.	PD July FCST	S.U.	PD Aug FCST	S.U.	PD FCST
4.5 oz	0.64	5000	3200	5000	3200	—	—	—	—	—	—	—	—
7.0 oz	1.00	2000	2000	3000	3000	9,500	9500	9,500	9500	1500	1500	2000	2000
11.0 oz	1.57	1200	1884	1200	1884	900	1413	900	1413	900	1413	1000	1570
14.0 oz	2.00	900	1800	900	1800	2500	5000	2500	5000	400	800	400	800
21.0 oz	3.00	150	450	150	450	400	1200	400	1200	50	150	50	150

Total Forecast		9334	10334	13300	17113	3863	4520
Total Production Plan		10,000	10,000	15000	15,000	5000	5000
Inventory Impact		+666	-334	+1,700	-2113	1137	480
Planned Inventory		3666	3332	5032	2919	4056	4536
Capacity Requirements		4 Shifts	4 Shifts	6 Shifts	6 Shifts	2 Shifts	2 Shifts

FIG. 18.4   Production plan in standard units.

The execution process involves detailed control of operations and requires detailed records updated at least daily. This section will consider the flow of information required and the records that must be kept. A discussion of the equipment that can be used for record keeping is presented in a later section of this chapter.

Master Production Schedule

The master production schedule (MPS) is used to implement the production plan and provides the basis for scheduling the materials and capacity required to support the plan. The MPS must break the production plans for product lines down into item-level detail. It should cover a long enough time horizon to allow for procurement of materials and for component production.

In general, the MPS techniques presented in Chapter 13 are applicable to the nonautomated system; however, the level of detail and the time horizon of the MPS must be reduced. Additionally, the techniques used to plan the materials and capacity to support the MPS are based on the characteristics of the products, such as the depth of the bill of materials and the routing complexity. The MPS is also revised less frequently in a nonautomated system; often, this means that the MPS is reviewed weekly and minor adjustments made, but it is only completely revised monthly. In some situations, the distinction between the production plan and MPS may be quite blurred and the two may really be one and the same.

A key function of the MPS is to break the product-line production plan down into a schedule for each of the items in the line. The most common approach is to use a percentage of the plan for each item. In fact, the concept of planning bills of materials was developed to implement this traditional method of allocating the production plan.

Once the plan is allocated, the actual sales and/or orders should be reviewed and the plan adjusted to the current situation. The final adjustments must be based on the availability of materials and on the status of open production orders. The master scheduler must set a doable schedule; this task is more difficult in a nonautomated than in an automated system because of the difficulty of gathering the needed support information. Care must be taken to collect the facts before revising the MPS; this means that the MPS will be slower to react to existing conditions. More dependence must be placed on using safety stocks, lead-time safety factors, etc., to smooth out the short-term fluctuations.

Another important step is to make sure that the master production schedule is doable from a capacity standpoint. The MPS should be converted into capacity requirements for key work centers. Either standard hours per operation or a general conversion factor can be used, depending on the situation. The actual product mix being scheduled could well result in deviations from the production plan on a short-term basis. The MPS may need modification if there are obvious overloads or underloads detected at this point. In computerized systems, this step has become known as *rough-cut capacity planning*.

Selecting the proper time horizon for planning is an important decision. In the manual system, this decision must be based in large part on the amount of calculation effort required to plan in detail. There is often enough commonality of material to allow procurement and component production to be planned by using the product-line production plan. The MPS is used to make final assembly or production schedules and to release orders for special materials.

Available-to-promise (AVP) and planned inventory levels can be calculated for each product in the detailed planning horizon. Beyond this horizon, the AVP can be based on consuming the schedule for the entire product line by converting orders to standard units. Obviously, this can lead to temporary overloads that must be managed by the master scheduler. This calls for closer communications between the order department and the materials manager.

The characteristics of smaller companies or of less complicated product lines allows the use of manual MPS methods. Communications between departments is usually quicker, and the personnel are more experienced. In this environment, experienced judgment can go a long way toward making the use of MPS methods feasible.

The forms to use for master scheduling can vary widely, depending on the individual situation. However, the following must be provided for in some manner:

- The form should provide a means of identifying the product or product line and the production plan to be implemented. If a product line, the individual items in the line should be presented.
- The actual order and/or sales and the schedule horizon are entered for each item on the form. Past activity is only needed when sales are from finished goods.

Inventory Planning and Control

Inventory control has two major functions: (1) planning and controlling inventory levels and (2) the physical control of inventories from the time of receipt until issuance for production or shipment to the customer.

The methods used to plan and control inventories must be carefully coordinated to meet the needs of the business and must be based on the characteristics of the operation. An important fact to recognize in the nonautomated system is that the investment in inventory will be higher than that of a comparable automated system. More inventory must be carried in the form of safety stock because of the lack of detailed planning and the slower response times of manual systems. In many situations, the additional inventory cost may be minimal due to the ability of the people operating the system to fine-tune it by using their judgment. The trade-offs in technique can be in the level of detail attempted, the use of less sophisticated techniques, and/or the frequency of review.

In many cases, the manual-system user may be able to gain a large portion of the benefits of advanced techniques by applying them where they can do the most good. MRP can be used for planning major products, planning one or two levels in the B/M, or planning specific components rather than all materials. Other techniques, such as reorder point and visual replenishment, can be used for controlling the balance of materials.

The balance of this section addresses manual MRP and other inventory planning methods, inventory record keeping, and physical control.

Material Requirements Planning (MRP)

Although MRP is usually identified with computer systems, it is practical to use it on a limited basis in a manual system. Obviously, the MRP method is the most desirable to use in a dependent demand environment. Just as obviously, it is an extremely time-consuming method to perform manually. Therefore, it may be practical to use MRP for specific product lines, for one or two levels into the B/M, or on an infrequent basis.

Manual MRP requires the accumulation of gross requirements, on-hand inventory, and open-order information onto a form like the one shown in Fig. 18.5. The requirements section of the form provides an area for entering the net requirements generated by higher-level items. Requirements can be generated by planned orders or master schedule for higher-level items and by customer orders and/or forecast for the items. Care must be taken to enter requirements into the proper time period that reflects lead-time offsets.

The total requirements for each period are entered in the appropriate period on the gross-requirements line. Open orders and current on-hand inventory must be entered on the appropriate line. Then a projected on-hand inventory can be calculated for each period. When the projected on-hand inventory is below zero, or the safety-stock level, a planned order for a lot size is entered on the planned-order line in the period it will be due. The projected on-hand inventory is increased by the planned-order amount. The best procedure is to calculate a projected on-hand inventory for each period, based on the gross requirements and open orders, and then to adjust the open-order due dates and determine the planned orders. Production orders or purchase requisitions can be issued for planned orders within the lead time. The planned orders can be used as requirements for lower-level item planning, using MRP, or as a forecast for determining reorder points.

Note that all the information needed to plan the item is contained on the form. A master form is maintained for each item and copied when needed.

Lot Sizing.   Determination of the best order quantity is an important inventory planning function that has been addressed extensively in the literature. Economic order quantities (EOQs) should be calculated to provide a guideline for setting lot sizes. It is important to use a fixed lot size where there is real value to be gained by balancing the setup and carrying cost. In other cases, it is better to group the requirements into orders by judgment. Lot sizes should be reviewed and changed if necessary at least once a year and whenever a major factor (such as standard cost, forecast, setup cost, or machine capability) changes. The calculated EOQ is often used as a minimum run size and as a basis for setting a standard cost. Any time that a run is larger due to actual requirements, a positive manufacturing variance will be generated. Limits—such as a maximum day's supply or a maximum run quantity—should be used (1) to ensure that run sizes are not artificially inflated to get good manufacturing variance reports and (2) to avoid tying up critical work centers for extended periods of time.

Capacity Requirements

The use of a manual system almost prohibits the detailed calculation of capacity requirements, given the numerous calculations required. If manual MRP techniques are being used, it is feasible to add to the form a capacity line for key work centers. The capacity required can be calculated on the MRP worksheet and transferred to a summary worksheet for each work center.

Even if manual MRP is being done, there will probably be other inventory control systems in use; thus, the capacity requirements calculated from the MRP worksheets will only be part of the total requirement. The other inventory systems will generate orders due within a lead time, so the total load profile will be for the short term only. However, this is better than nothing, and it can be used to verify that the

Searle and Co.
MRP System—Manual
RAW Material—Workshop

	Initials	Date
	Cat	6/15
	Sa.	6/17

Date issued 7/8/XX
Printout Dated 7/1/XX
Prod. Sched. Dated 7/2/XX

Part No. 174061   Description Cornstarch

Sum _____ Standard Cost _____ ABC _____

	Past due	Current month	2	3	4	5	6	7	8	9	10	11	12
Projected Gross Requirements	—	340	500	740	230	840	—	140	500	430	—	640	
Scheduled Receipts 11		7/15 500		9/15 500									
Scheduled Receipts 12													
On Hand (740)		900	400	760	530	-310	-310	-450	-950	-1380	-1380	-2000	
Planned Order				500		500	500	500		1000			

Requirements

Product	1	2	3	4	5	6	7	8	9	10	11	12
1701	40		40	40	40	40	40		40		40	
1703	100		100	100	100		100		100		100	
1705				90					90			
2701	200				200				200			
2705		500	500		500			500			500	
Total	340	500	140	230	840	—	140	500	430	—	640	

Product Data

Order Qty. 500
Lead Time 8 wks.
Scrap Factor NONE

Prod.	Qty./Lot	Prod.	Qty./Lot
1701	40	2701	200
1703	100	2705	500
1705	90		

FIG. 18.5 Manual MRP form. (Courtesy: G. D. Searle and Co., Skokie, Illinois.)

capacity plan's development as part of the production-planning process is still valid. It also provides the scheduler with the information needed to adjust work-center capacity on a short-term basis. Deviation to the capacity plan can well be expected in the short term.

Reorder Points

Often the best compromise for determining order quantities in a nonautomated system is to use reorder point based on replenishment methods rather than the MRP system. The reorder-point method is most applicable for low value parts, raw materials, and parts that are widely used. Safety stocks can be used to protect against variations in demand due to MPS, forecast error, and longer review periods.

Reorder points are based on the forecasted requirements during replenishment lead time plus a safety stock. A detailed item forecast is required in order to use a reorder-point system properly. The lead-time–requirements forecast is based on adjusting the item-demand forecast to the lead-time period. For example, the lead-time forecast for an item with a monthly demand forecast and a 2-week lead time would be one-half of the monthly demand forecast.

Any forecast can be used for this purpose, but a weekly or monthly item forecast provides the best information. The moving-average and single-order exponential smoothing techniques described earlier in this chapter are excellent tools to use for this type of forecasting. As in all forecasting, experienced judgment should be added to the mathematical formulas where possible.

Safety Stock. The other part of the reorder-point formula is safety stock. The method used for setting it should be based on the purpose of safety stock. Judgmental safety stock should be used when there are extended planning cycles, variations in demand due to dependent requirements, or judgmental forecasts. Safety stocks of this type are usually based on providing extra time in the replenishment cycle and are expressed as safety lead time: for example, adding 2 weeks to the lead time. Care must be taken to identify the safety lead time separately from other lead-time components.

When a statistical forecasting method is used and safety stock is used to protect against forecast error, a statistical method may be in order. A simplified safety-stock calculation is shown in Table 18.1. The safety stock should be recalculated frequently to respond to actual forecast error.

Using the Reorder Point. When the available inventory is less than the reorder point, a replenishment order should be placed. *Available* is defined as the amount on hand plus on order:

$$\text{Available} = \text{on hand} + \text{on order}$$

The available inventory is often determined by deducting the reservations for open shop orders or customer orders:

$$\text{Available} = \text{on hand} + \text{on order} - \text{reservations}$$

This approach works well when work orders are dispatched properly and reservations represent short-term issues. This also helps to identify and respond to large requirements due to dependent demand. When dispatching is poorly managed, deducting the reservations will result in excess inventories.

TABLE 18.1 Manual Safety-Stock Calculation

Safety-Factor Table	
Desired Service Level (%)	Rule-of-Thumb Safety Factor
90	1.6
95	2.0
98	2.5
99	3.0

Simplified statistical safety-stock method:

Safety stock = MAD* × Safety factor

MAD = (0.9 × old MAD) + (0.1 × absolute forecast error)

The absolute forecast error is always a positive number.

* MAD (mean absolute deviation).

The posting of manual inventory records also provides an opportunity to detect potential shortage situations. A sound posting procedure is to check open-order due dates whenever the actual inventory on hand (or on hand less reservations) is less than the forecasted lead-time requirements.

Periodic-Review System.   A periodic review system is often a sound alternative to MRP or reorder point when the lead time to resupply quantities is very short, such as 1 or 2 weeks, and the material is readily available. Many commodities fall into this category, and special purchasing arrangements can be made to ensure that vendors will carry a readily available stock at a good price. Another opportunity exists when a capacity to convert raw material into the needed parts is readily available, the process lead time is a few days, and the setup penalties are low. This method is also very useful for items that have mostly dependent demand. Maximum levels can be set, based either on past usage or on expected requirements calculated infrequently by using MRP. Another reason to use this technique is when there is limited space to store the item. The maximum can be set to equal the space allocated to the part.

In a periodic-review system, a maximum level is set and the difference between the on-hand and maximum inventory is ordered every time the item is reviewed. The maximum level is set equal to (1) the forecasted requirement during the review period plus (2) a safety stock.

The review period is usually weekly, but any period up to a month can be used. The maximum level is usually reviewed quarterly or when experience indicates a need. Another good time to review the maximum level is when the requirements are calculated by using manual MRP. The amount to order is reduced by the amount on order; however, when a periodic review is used, there should not be any material on order. A simplified version of the periodic-review calculation is shown in Table 18.2.

Visual Review.   Items that are hard to count, of low value, and easy to replenish are good candidates for visual review systems. The two-bin approach is often used effectively for parts of this type.

Another visual method is to place a visible mark on the storage area and to order a standard quantity when the on-hand inventory drops below the mark. This method is often used for liquids stored in a tank, for powder material stored in large holding containers, and for corrugated cardboard. The visual reorder level is set to

TABLE 18.2 Simplified Periodic-Review Calculations

PERIODIC-REVIEW CALCULATIONS
Maximum level = forecast during review period + safety stock
For simplicity, let the forecast period be the same as the review interval.
Safety stock = MAD × safety factor
See Table 18.1 for proper calculations
Note: The actual safety-stock formual is

$$SS = MAD \times \text{safety factor} \times \sqrt{\frac{\text{review period} + \text{lead time}}{\text{forecast period}}}$$

If the forecast period and review period are equal and the real lead time is less than 1 week, the square-root part of the formula can be ignored.

provide enough material to meet usage needs during the replenishment cycle. While this level can be calculated, it is usually set on the basis of experience. Disciplined reporting is actually more important than the level selected. A variation of this method is to check visual materials frequently to see if they need to be ordered, a kind of periodic visual review system. Floor stocks can be controlled very well using visual review systems.

Continuous Replenishment. Many smaller companies have a limited number of critical materials that can be planned with periodic delivery. In fact, many companies will have storage space or capital limitations that dictate the use of frequent replenishment.

Physical Control

Basically, all of the practices described for physical control in other sections of this handbook apply in a nonautomated system. Limited access to the storeroom and disciplined use of inventory documents are required in order to maintain accurate on-hand balances. Locator files, where required, will be maintained manually. Frequently, fixed-located storerooms are used to facilitate location control.

Manual requisitions and receiving and adjustment documents are used in the nonautomated system. All are usually designed to be turnaround documents, to be routed to the inventory record-keeping function for updating of the perpetual inventory records. To maintain accuracy, cycle counting should be practiced where appropriate.

The simplest solution is to maintain a cycle-count log that groups items by frequency and allows one to record when the material is counted and the results. A log of this type can be quite useful for identifying problem items, groups, storerooms, etc.

Physical inventories are basically manual procedures. The cycle-count log, if in use, should be updated and adjusted according to the quantities in the physical inventory as well as in the perpetual inventory record.

Inventory Records

The inventories controlled may be of many types. The categories of material usually controlled are: raw materials and purchased parts, semifinished and finished components, and finished goods.

In addition, some systems control work in process, using a perpetual inventory record. This record seldom shows a significant balance, as the inventory is not held and stored at this stage. However, the record may be useful for:

- Keeping track of overruns and underruns.
- Furnishing a complete history of component activity.
- Recording component control information.
- Interfiling basic information, such as bills of materials and route sheets.

Functions of Perpetual Inventory Records.   There are only three basic functions of the perpetual inventory record. The record should contain information used to:

- Show material availability for use on incoming orders.
- Signal when to order.
- Determine how much to order.

These three basic functions are carried out through decision rules and through the comparison of control quantities (units or time) with various inventory balances. In addition, the inventory record can perform several corollary functions useful in handing exceptions. All additional functions require more posting effort and hence more cost.

Information Recorded and Its Purpose

Table 18.3 lists the information recorded on perpetual inventory record cards and explains its purpose in helping to fulfill the basic functions of the record. In actuality, owing to posting costs, redundancy, and other local considerations, few records would contain all the information shown in the table. Figure 18.6 illustrates a record-keeping format.

The important job of the system designer is to relate the additional cost of more record keeping to the return expected. In this regard, the number of transactions and balances required to support various basic perpetual-inventory-record balances is an indication of cost, whereas the return expected is the record's ability to perform adequately the basic functions usually required of the perpetual inventory record. For example, low-value material, material with little obsolescence, or material without significant lead times may yield little return from the additional record-keeping cost.

The relative ability of the basic balance and various balance combinations, interacting with control quantities guided by decision rules, to perform the functions of the perpetual-inventory-record system is shown in Table 18.4.

Record-Keeping Efficiencies

The proper selection of information and balances to be included in the perpetual-inventory-record design has been discussed without consideration of record-

TABLE 18.3 Information Recorded on Perpetual Inventory Records and Its Purpose

Information	Purpose
1. *Identifying information:*	
Material or part name and number	
Specifications or descriptive ordering information	
Final assembly, next assembly, or other where-used information and quantity	Aids in estimating future usage and in phasing products in and out.
Unit of measure and conversion factors	
Location in stock room	Eliminates the need for locator records.
Phase-out and obsolete information	
2. *Control Order quantities:*	Determines how much to order.
Reorder point	Signals when to order.
Expedite point	Signals expediting or order-increase desirability.
Safety stock	Used in calculating reorder point.
Lead time	Used in calculating reorder point.
Maximum point	When exceeded, signals desirability of open-order delay, decrease, or cancellation
Historical usage information ⎫ Seasonal and trend factors ⎬	Forecasts expected usage.
Other control data—unit cost; setup cost; carrying percent; A, B, C, category; service level; forecast error; labor leveling factor; scrap rate	Are all useful in setting control quantities.
3. *Balances:*	For comparison with control quantities. When the control quantity is passed by the balance quantity, action is usually required.
On-hand balance	The actual physical quantity in the storeroom. Transactions affecting: + receipts, − issues.
On-order balance	The net quantity on open order. Transactions affecting: + orders, − receipts.
Available balance	The quantity remaining when on-hand and all open orders are reduced by reservations. Transactions affecting: + orders, − reservations.
Reserved balance	The net quantity on open order, that is, unissued reservation. Transactions affecting: + reservations, − issues.
Free-stock balance	That portion of the physical on-hand balance which is not reserved. Transactions affecting: + receipts, − reservations.
4. *Transactions:*	For updating balances and furnishing factual historical data.
Orders—information recorded: date posted, entry reference, quantity ordered, required or promised date, date received complete or check mark (√) to indicate receipt	Date-received-complete or checkmark (√) postings are helpful in causing adjustments to the available balance if receipts vary from orders, in identifying open orders for changes thereto, and in aiding in physical inventory reconciliation. Re-

TABLE 18.3   (Continued)

Information	Purpose
	quired dates are used to anticipate timing of future balances, a start toward time-phased balances.
Receipts—information recorded: date posted, entry reference, quantity received or returned	Updates several balances.
Reservations (syn. assignments, allocations)—information recorded: date posted, reserving order number, quantity reserved, date reserved quantity is needed, date issued complete or check mark (√) to indicate issue	Ability to indicate future usage. Date-issued-complete and checkmark (√) postings are helpful in causing adjustments to the available balance if issues vary from reservations, in selecting reservations not covered by stock on hand for release, and in aiding in physical inventory reconciliation. Required dates are used to anticipate timing of future balances, a start toward time-phased balances.
Planned reservations (quantities, required for orders not on hand but forecasted)	This provides a good indication of future usage and is often used in time-phased balances as calculated by exploding a forecast.
Issues (syn. withdrawals, disbursements)—information recorded: date posted, entry reference, quantity	Updates several balances. Issues can be posted when the reference document is sent to the storeroom (called *preposting* or *planned issues*) or following storeroom disbursement (called *post posting*) or a combination of the two.
Adjustments (returns to stock, scrap, inventory write-off or write-on)—information recorded: date posted, entry reference, quantity	Updates several balances.

keeping alternatives and other efficiencies. There are often effective alternatives, lowering the record-keeping costs while at the same time retaining much of the control:

- *Combinations with other records.* (a) Traveling requisition (TR), purchase-history record, and order-and-receipt record. This combination can eliminate posting receipts and orders to the perpetual inventory record if the TR is filed with this record. If vendor and price information is carried, the purchase-history record can be eliminated. (b) Storeroom records. Quantity-in and -out records in the storeroom are seldom justifiable, as they duplicate the perpetual inventory record.

- *Visible aids on record cards.* Visible aids incorporated into the record card are limited only by the designer's imagination. Generally, the gain must be carefully evaluated where visibility requires additional posting, filing, or tab setting beyond the basic record-balance requirements.
    Some of the more successful visible aids are: (a) Color; for example, the presence or absence of a color-coded record card. (b) Visible balance; for example, control balance and control quantity showing in a margin. (c) Filing sequence.

- *Record-card access and posting efficiency.* Efficient card design should consider: (a) a minimum of hand movements for each access to the record; (b) lines and columns of adequate size; (c) card size to enable lines to be followed easily from left to right; and (d) fixed or semipermanent information on a separate card to prevent recopying information.

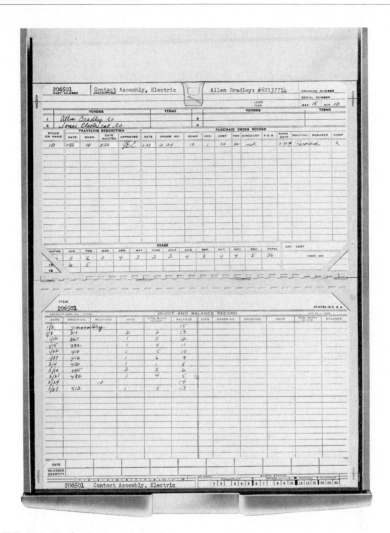

FIG. 18.6 Kardex inventory record.

- *Elimination of records.* This is usually done on items of low unit value or annual cost where costs of control cannot be justified. Here, physical control is used to replace paper control through: *(a)* physical reorder point, using a two-bin system or other segregated reorder point; *(b)* physical inventory on a fixed-time-interval basis; *(c) kitting* by physically reserving material in advance of expected issue.

Production Activity Control

Production activity control (PAC) involves issuing production orders and supporting documents, scheduling work centers, and controlling production activities to accomplish the master production schedule.

TABLE 18.4 Relative Abilities of Basic Perpetual Inventory Records to Perform Certain Functions

Basic Perpetual-Inventory-Record Balances	Functions Performed by Perpetual Inventory Records										Relative Cost (in posting required)	
	Present Balance			Future Balance‡		Ease and Flexibility of Maintenance and Use						
	Stock Position (on hand)	Free-Stock Position (on hand − reservation)	Stock Position (available)	Usage Forecast	Physical Inventory Reconciliation	Evaluating Orders for Qty. or Sched. Change*	Comparing Balance to Reorder Point (ROP)	Properly Calculating ROP to Suit Balances§	Relieving Back-Ordered Reservation	Keeping Balances Accurate*,†	Transactions	Balances Carried
1. On-hand balance	Exc.	...	...	Poor unless predictable usage—then good	Exc.		Poor unless no open orders	Exc.	...	Exc.	2	1
2. Available balance	...	...	Good	Good	Poor*†	Fair	Exc.	Fair	...	Fair	2	1
3. On-hand−available balance	Exc.	...	Good	Good	Exc.	Fair	Exc.	Fair	Fair	Fair	4	2
4. On-hand−available−free-stock balance	Exc.	Exc.	Good	Good	Exc.	Fair	Exc.	Fair	Fair	Fair	4	3
5. On-hand−on-order−free-stock balance	Exc.	Exc.	Fair, must add balances	Good	Exc.	Good	Fair, must add balances	Fair	Fair	Fair	4	3

* Check marks can be placed next to an order-and-receipt transaction indicating complete receipt. This is helpful in making adjustments to the available balance if receipts vary from orders, in identifying open orders for quantity or schedule changes, and in aiding in physical inventory reconciliation. All ratings are improved by this technique.

† Check marks can be placed next to a reservation-and-issue transaction indicating complete issue. This is helpful in making adjustments to the available balance if issues vary from reservations, in selecting back-ordered reservations for release upon material receipt, and in aiding in physical inventory reconciliation. All ratings are improved by this technique.

‡ The relative abilities assigned in these columns assume a significant and largely predictable time lapse between reserving and issuing.

§ The problem here is that reservations are made in advance of issue and cause the available balance to be reduced as if the issue had occurred. Unless the reorder point is adjusted for this difference reservation and issue, the lower available balance will cause premature ordering.

Shop-Order Packet.   Once the production requirements have been determined, production orders are required in order to initiate and control production. The first step is to prepare an order packet that provides the information required to produce the order. The order packet may consist of several different documents, including:

Shop Order/Work Order.   The shop order, also called a *manufacturing order*, authorizes production, indicates how much to produce, and provides a reference for collecting labor, material, and other cost data. It should have a unique number that can be used for reference and identification throughout the PAC and cost systems.

Bill of Materials.   The bill of materials, which is a list of the materials and the quantity of each required to produce the part or component on the shop order, may be a separate document or may be incorporated into the shop order.

Route Sheet.   The route sheet specifies the operations required to produce the part or component, the sequence to be followed, and the work centers or machines required. In addition, it provides tooling, tolerance specifications, quantity specifications, special procedures, etc., and can also provide the standard setup and operation time for each operation. The route sheet may be a separate document or integrated with the shop order.

Material Requisitions.   Material requisitions (Fig. 18.7) are prepared documents used to withdraw material from stores. The material requisition may be a multipart form, with one copy used to update inventory records and another to provide cost data.

Labor Tickets/Job Time Card.   These are for recording actual labor expended on the shop order (Fig. 18.8). Usually, one or more tickets are provided for each operation. The ticket may be a multipart form, with one copy used for payroll, another for updating job status, and a third for cost data.

Move Tickets.   Move tickets (Fig. 18.9) are used to control the movement of materials within a plant, identifying their origin and destination and any special handling instructions. A multipart form can be used, with one copy being used to update the order status.

Blueprints.   Many order packets will contain the latest revision of the blueprints (engineering prints) provided by the engineering department.

A shop order based on the master production schedule and/or customer orders is prepared for each item to be produced. Masters may be stored for the shop order, bill of materials, and route sheet so that copies may be made when creating another

				Req. No. 014673	
		Material requisition			
Deliver to *Press*			Charge to	Order No.	
				Acct. No. *10-4579*	

Quan.	Part No. Code No.	Description	Price	
			Unit	Total
2700 ft.	L-401	asbestos ⅛"	.743	2006.10
1700 lbs.	S-702	Core steel .010	.641	1089.70

Stores: Issue exact quantity requested. If out of stock, draw line through item.	Approved by *CaH.* ___ Date *10/2*
	Issued by *CL.* ___ Date *10/2*

FIG. 18.7   Material requisition.

Employee's Name *a. armstrong*			Clock No. *174*		Job Time Card		
Department *17*		Work Center *141*			Machine *O1*		
Part Number *2733 PT*		Part Name *Gasket*			Account No. *171*		
Operation Number *50*		Operation Name *Flatten*			Sequence No.		
Order Number *10-4579*		Lot Number —			Pieces Produced *7521*		
Order Quantity *7500*		Lot Quantity —			Total	Good	Reject
Start	Date *10/8*	Time *8:00 a.m.*		Std. Cost Per 100 Pcs. *2,815*	*7521*	*7521*	
						$	
Stop	Date *10/8*	Time *4 p.m.*		Employee's Hourly Rate *$ 14.75*	Favorable ✓		Unfavorable
Elapsed Time *lunch 15 — 7.5 hrs.*				Employee's Earnings *$ 103.25*	Approved by: *a.a.*		

FIG. 18.8 Job time card.

From *23*			Move Ticket		To *17*		
Department No. *23*				Department No. *17*			
Work Center No. *154*				Work Center No.			
Machine No.				Machine No.			
Last Operation No. *30*				Next Operation No. *50*			
Released By *CL*				Received By *af*			
Date *10/7*				Date *10/7*			
Containers				Description			
Number	Type	Quantity	Unit	Part Number	Order Number	Lot Number	
2	*PB*	*1750*		*7733 PT*	*10-4579*		
1	*PB*	*1200*		*7733 PT*	*"*		

FIG. 18.9 Move ticket.

order packet. Material requisitions, labor tickets, and move tickets are standard forms used in any shop order.

Dispatching.   Shop orders must be released to production on the basis of a pre-pared schedule. The release of work to production must be carefully controlled to avoid overloading or underloading specific work centers. Also, it is best to keep the "backlog" of shop orders on the scheduler's desk to facilitate maintaining priority control.

Steps must be taken to make sure that material and capacity are available before the shop order is released to production.

Material availability may be checked by using the inventory records and by recording the reservations. Another method of checking parts availability and of reserving them at the same time is to pull all of the parts for an order ahead of the issue date. *Kitting*, as this procedure is known, has been a mainstay for years and is still useful in the manual system. It should be used for special materials ordered for a specific job. Kitting should be done far enough ahead to provide time to expedite shortages, but not so far that parts are unnecessarily tied up and other orders are delayed.

Capacity availability depends on work-center loads and on the manning level established for the work center. It makes little sense to release a shop order which cannot start for several days or which may have to wait during the process for a critical work center. Releasing shop orders prematurely adds to the confusion and can result in the use of critically short materials on the wrong shop order.

Load Tracking. Detailed load tracking can require significant effort. Consider that 1000 items with an average of 10 operations per item will generate 10,000 operations if ordered once per year, or 50,000 operations if ordered 5 times per year. The effort required to calculate detailed work-center loads and to update load charts can quickly become uneconomical in most situations. Satisfactory control results can usually be obtained by loading only the starting and critical work centers. Shop orders that sit longer than a specified number of days at a work center can be identified by using exception reports and can be rescheduled where required to get them completed on time. Work centers that have significant setup-time requirements must also be scheduled and loaded carefully to make sure that output stays at the proper level.

Work-Center Scheduling. Whether dispatching should be centrally controlled or decentralized depends upon the size of the plant, the volume of the parts and products flowing through it, and the type of communications used in the system. Generally, small- and medium-size plants will have strong central control of machine loads and will issue instructions to foremen for the assignment of jobs to workers and machines. Larger plants usually have decentralized control, with a dispatcher in each department carrying out all the functions.

Input/Output Control. One of the most important scheduling functions is to control the input of work into and the flow of production out of a work center. If the capacity-planning function has been performed properly, the required output from the work center is known. It is the responsibility of the scheduler to provide the proper amount of work in a good mix and to assign priorities that will ensure that production management staffs the work center to produce the required output. A daily report of the hours in the work-center backlog and of the hours of production is required. A weekly review of the capacity plan is required in order to determine whether overtime or other capacity-adjustment alternatives should be utilized to adjust out-of-tolerance situations.

Reporting. Collecting and summarizing actual production data can be time-consuming. Usually, labor tickets or time cards must be summarized manually to gain the needed data. This also provides needed order-status information to the scheduler. Control boards (Fig. 18.10) can be used as a visual means to track the order status and to identify problems.

Frequency of Reporting. Work progress information is useful for production control only to the extent that the information transmitted is timely. There can be no control over past events, only over those which are likely to occur if preventive action is not presently taken.

There are two basically different methods of establishing the time and frequency of progress reports: (1) at fixed time intervals and (2) at the completion of assigned

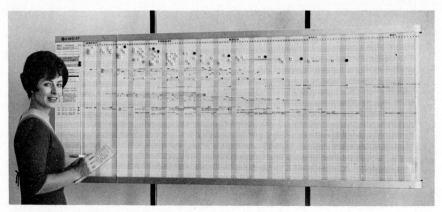

FIG. 18.10 Control Board. *(Courtesy of William Steward Co.)*

tasks. In the continuous type of manufacturing process (or mass-production industries), daily or even hourly reports are necessary in order to maintain production schedules on a current basis. Fixed-interval reporting is also the rule in some job shops that manufacture standard or stock items. However, in most job shops, because of the diversity of production and the conflicting process requirements, it is more common to make reports at the completion of each operation on each manufacturing order. In this way, prompt action can be taken on the tooling and scheduling problems that are more likely to occur in this type of plant. Prompt reporting and corrective action are particularly important where the product is made for customer orders.

The latter type of progress reporting, of course, does not preclude the making of fixed-interval reports as well. In most job shops, daily reports are also made on the status of the jobs still in process.

Purchasing/Receiving

The purchasing functions in the nonautomated system are the same as in any other system. However, the large volumes of paperwork generated by purchasing cause special problems for determining open-order status, dollar commitments, vendor performance, etc.

Purchase Requisition.   A requisition should be used to start the purchasing process. The requisition should identify what material (or supply) is required, how much, and when. Provision should be made for proper authorizations, location to deliver to, budget and/or account assignments, etc. The requisition should be prenumbered for control purposes.

Traveling Requisition.   The use of a *traveling requisition* is strongly recommended for ordering inventory items and regularly ordered supplies. The traveling requisition, which is also used as the perpetual inventory record, minimizes paperwork and provides a purchase history. All of the information needed to place an order is contained on the traveling requisition (Fig. 18.11).

The procedure for using a traveling requisition is quite simple. Inventory control keeps the traveling requisition on file. When an order is to be placed for an item, the

Traveling Requisition

Buyer_____Code No._____ Part No._____

Description _____

_____

_____

Inv. Code_____ Acct. No. _____ Plant No. _____ Dept. No._____

Class

For Resale _ _ _ _ _ ☐   _____ Unit of Measure _____ Maximum_____

Not for Resale _ _ _ _ ☐   Weight _____ Multiple Units _____ Minimum_____

Vend. Code	Vendor's Name	Vendor's Part No.	F.O.B. Point	Freight Allowed on	Terms	Ship via	Lead Time	Transit Time	Economic Quan.	Price

| | | Requisition Record | | | | | | | Purchase Record | | | |

| Date | Total Quan. | Delivery Schedule | | | | | | | Plan App. | Date | Vend. Code | P.O. No. | Pur. App. | Unit Price |
		Date	Quan.	Date	Quan.	Date	Quan.							

FIG. 18.11 Traveling requisition.

traveling requisition is pulled, and the amount required and the due date are entered. The amount ordered can be adjusted to take advantage of any price breaks, etc., noted on the traveling requisition. The completed traveling requisition is then routed through the appropriate authorization procedure and signed off where required. Once the traveling requisition reaches purchasing, the buyer can select a vendor from the ones listed on the traveling requisition in accordance with any special instructions. Once the order is placed, it is noted on the traveling requisition along with any changes in quantity, due date, etc. Price changes, etc., are also updated so that the information on the traveling requisition is current. Then the traveling requisition is returned to inventory control for filing.

When material is received, the traveling requisition should be updated with the date, quantity, price, and quality control comments. When this information is kept current, the traveling requisition contains a complete purchase history of the item and vendor performance reports.

Effective use of the traveling-requisition method depends on good discipline in the purchasing department and in the departments ordering materials. More important, careful attention must be paid to the number of steps and the time required to process a traveling requisition. Excessive handling can result in extending order lead times and in the loss of the traveling requisition.

The traveling-requisition concept is easily applied to any repetitive ordering situation, such as maintenance repair order (MRO) items. Any department could have its own traveling requisition file, but it is a good idea to limit the number of files for control purposes. If there are several files, different-colored card stock should be used to identify the various departments, etc.

Purchase Order.   Once a decision has been made to buy, a purchase order is required. The purchase order is usually a typed, multipart form. A copy of the purchase order is distributed to a number of departments to provide a control record:

Department	Use
Receiving	Identify incoming material. Assign to purchase order.
Accounting	Update cost data. Enter into accounts payable.
Inventrol control	Update open-order status file.

The number of purchase-order file copies should be held to a minimum since the cost of keeping them up to date can become expensive. Since most manual purchase-order files are not updated with current information, either incorrect information is issued or everyone winds up calling purchasing for current status anyway.

Purchasing should maintain a master purchase-order (PO) file and ensure that the information contained in this file is up to date. Access to this file should be severely limited, and any POs removed should be identified by using an *out-of-file card* that notes who is responsible for returning the master copy. A better idea is to provide *copies* of the master PO rather than the PO itself.

Communicating changes to update the PO status can generate more paperwork than the original purchasing process if not carefully controlled. Changes should be categorized, and only the affected area should be notified. A *change-notice slip* is often used to provide a formal record for attachment to the PO copy.

Change requests are generated by the requisitioner and usually involve quantity, due date, or cancellation. A change-request form should be used to provide control. The form should provide a means of confirming to the originator that the change has been made. A copy of the completed request is attached to the master PO.

Receiving.   The receiving department should maintain a file of open POs. Any changes in due date and/or quantity must be routed to receiving. When material is received, it is up to the receiving department to match the material to a PO. The PO number is usually all that is required, but often the vendor part number, description, etc., must be used. Once material is identified, counted, and routed, a receiving report (Fig. 18.12) must be prepared and forwarded to purchasing and other interested departments, such as inventory control and accounting. There are two basic approaches to the receiving report—either use the PO copy or prepare a separate report. The best method to use is based on the characteristics of the company.

Using the receiving copy of the PO as a receiving report works best when all of the material on a PO is received at the same time. The amount received, its

RECEIVING REPORT

Date rec'd _10/12_ No. pckg's _2_ Weight _17_ Pro/car No. _____

Prepaid ☑   Collect $_____ Complete ☑   Partial ☐

Rec'd at ☑ Dock   ☐ Bldg. 12   ☐ Steel shop   ☐ Yard   ☐ _____

Rec'd via _UPS_____ ☐ Parcel post   ☐ Our pickup   ☐ Dodge truck
                Carrier
P. O. date _10/1/XX_   ☐ Express   ☐ Their delivery ☐ _____

                         Delivered to ☑ Receiving insp. ☐ Department indicated

Ordered .
from .   Acme Electric   _____
                                                  Received from
                                              _____
                                                 Shipping point
                                              _____
                                               Received by_____

    Via .

Please direct any questions relative to this order to attention of indicated buyer.

Account number	Charge number	Requisitioned by	Buyer	For department
10-1476	—	ASA	RB	Boards

Quan. rec'd	
3	Electric Boxes 7½" X 12" X 2"
12	Auto Reset Switches

Remarks:

Boxes oversize, Authorized by RB.

Box number		Run letter		Complete	✓	Partial		

FIG. 18.12 Receiving report.

condition, etc., are noted on the PO copy and the copy returned to purchasing if the order is considered complete. If a partial order is received, a copy of the receiving report marked "partial" is sent to purchasing. Receiving will often have a multipart receiving copy of the PO so that a receiving copy can be forwarded to other departments (such as inventory control) at the same time. This ensures that status information is made available on a timely basis to other departments at the lowest clerical cost.

A separate receiving report should be used when there are many receipts for one PO and/or there are many recipients of the receiving report. Companies that use blanket orders or POs with many lined items with different due dates will find a separate receiving report more effective. The separate report can be in the form of a report with many receiving entries or a receiving slip for each receipt. The receiving-slip approach is often used when there is an inspection process required for most incoming material. The slip can be a multicopy form that is used for notification of receipt and clearance from inspection. In any case, it is important that the receiving report be filled out and sent to the recipients at least daily, if not 2 times per day. It is also usual for the receipt amounts to be recorded on the receiving copy of the purchase order. Receiving can determine when a purchase order is complete and forward it to purchasing to be filed with the copy of the master purchase order.

The purchasing and inventory control departments should obtain a receiving date as soon as possible. Complete and timely data minimize status calls to vendors and allow better control of operations.

Open-Order Status.   One of the most difficult tasks to accomplish in a manual system is preparing open-purchase-order status and commitment reports. Inventory control usually wants to see the report in past-due sequence, while accounting wants to see it in due-date sequence to determine cash-flow requirements.

Follow-up.   An important purchasing function is the follow-up and expediting of orders. Often an expedite file containing a copy of the purchase order is maintained by date sequence. Another method is to maintain a simple list of purchase orders by due date. The list or file must be updated to reflect changes in due date, cancellation, etc.

FEEDBACK

All plans must be reviewed on a regular basis and adjusted where required to meet actual conditions. The feedback loop in the closed-loop manufacturing system provides the information flow required to support the review process.

The timeliness of feedback information must be such that the data can be used effectively to adjust plans and operations. There are basically two reporting streams that need to be considered: execution and planning.

Execution Feedback

Daily and weekly information is required to support the execution functions. Daily information includes the reporting of shop-order and purchase-order status. Weekly feedback usually consists of a consolidation of the daily data to provide an overall picture of operations. It is used to adjust the master production schedule and short-term work-center capacity plans. Reporting of this type has been covered in the sections that address production-activity control and purchasing.

Planning Feedback

The feedback information required to support planning is oriented to overall performance measures that cover longer periods of time, such as months, quarters, or years. The goal of planning feedback is to provide trend information that can be used to revise business and production plans. It also provides the information needed for top management to evaluate the operating units.

Planning feedback must be summarized into groups that are comparable with the production plan. Sales data should be summarized into the same product lines used for production planning. If a standard unit is used, sales or order data should be reported in raw units and converted to standard units. Inventory status should be reported in the same manner. Production performance should be in terms of hours—plus the standard capacity units, if used. Utilization and performance should be reported for each key work center or facility used to develop the production plan.

One of the most important functions of planning feedback is to provide a means of checking the factors used for planning against the actual results. Factors such as dollars per hour or hours per pound are powerful planning tools. A small percentage error in one of the factors can have a major impact on the overall accuracy of the production plan. Explainable, nonrecurring deviations, however, should not automatically be included in the factor. Situations that cause this problem include the use of alternate procedures due to major machine breakdowns or to lack of material.

A number of other performance measures can be implemented, depending on the individual situation. One of the most useful is a purchasing-performance measurement of vendors that tracks on-time delivery, quality, and actual price compared to quote.

RECORD-KEEPING EQUIPMENT

Inventory Records

The most practical and efficient method for keeping manual inventory records is the Kardex file. Each item has a card with the required identification, planning, and status information. The cards are placed in a pocket that is hinged at the top. The bottom margin of each card is exposed, providing for fast recognition of the record desired. Record posting is accomplished by sliding the tray out of the cabinet without removing it, resting the tray edge on a horizontal surface, and using the exposed margin to flip open the cards. Posting is done directly, without removal of the card record. Though time is saved in not removing the record, the posting position of the record and its distance from the information to be posted must be considered in an evaluation of the equipment. In addition, the time to remove and refile individual records when required is relatively long.

Slides may be fitted to the exposed margin of the card, which, when set, may indicate inventory quantity, workload, backlog, open-order status, and so on. When open, a tray can be reviewed at a glance by noting the positions of the visible slides.

Records can also be stored in hinged panel files (Fig. 18.13) that have trays, panels, or other record-holding devices attached at the inside edge, much like leaves of a book. Cards are retained in the trays as in the tray file. Other holding devices contain strips of data or receive a die-cut card. Modifications of the hinged panels to resemble a large book are almost invariably desktop types and do not post easily without record removal. The individual strips of data are very popular for cross-reference files, and when the leaves are hung vertically, accessibility to data is rapid.

FIG. 18.13 Hinged-panel file. *(Courtesy: Acme Visible Records.)*

An almost limitless number of configurations of drawers, shelves, pockets, tubs, and other types of record holders are available.

Scheduling Tools

A number of sophisticated schedule boards have been developed over the years but have rarely found wide use. Two of the simplest yet most effective solutions are the porcelain whiteboard and the strip board.

Porcelain Whiteboard. The whiteboard is coated with a baked-on enamel finish that can be written on with special marker pens that come in a wide variety of colors. A wide range of board shapes are available and can be either prelined or divided by the user. The best whiteboards will allow the use of magnetic strips that can be written on with the same marker pens. Boards of this type provide flexibility and can accommodate a large amount of information. When magnetic strips are used, it is relatively easy to rearrange the sequence of jobs or to track their location by work center, etc. Information must be manually transferred from the board to paper.

Strip Boards. When there is a large number of jobs or details to track, strip boards can be useful. Information is entered on a strip that is inserted into two parallel tracks. The strips are narrow and cannot carry a large amount of data, but up to 32 strips may be placed on a board. Each board is 8½ × 11 in, so it can be handled easily and copied quickly. Strips can be moved around easily to reflect schedule or status changes. Different-colored strips can also be used. Boards with magnetic backing can be attached to control boards (whiteboards, for example) that will display several strip boards. Hinged stands for the boards are also available.

DUPLICATING METHODS

Office copying machines provide the most cost-effective means of reproducing schedules, shop orders, bills of materials, etc. New tear-resistant papers can be used for masters.

The equipment used for reproducing engineering prints (blueprints) can also be used effectively in many situations.

MICROCOMPUTER APPLICATIONS

In many situations, a combination of manual and computer-supported systems will best meet a company's needs. One or two functions may justify the use of a computer—such as a great volume of transactions to be processed or a need to summarize and report large amounts of data quickly—while the balance of the operation uses manual systems. In these situations, microcomputers provide an effective, low-cost solution that can easily be integrated with manual systems.

Microcomputers are well-suited to limited, stand-alone functions since they are self-contained units that accept, process, store, and display data. A wide range of software packages are available that meet many manufacturing-system needs, including word processing and spreadsheet software, single-function accounting packages, and complete closed-loop manufacturing systems.

Several microcomputers may be networked together to share data. When operating in this mode, a microcomputer can be used to process a local function and share the results with other microcomputers that are used to process other functions. For example, a microcomputer used to control inventory can communicate the receipt of purchased material to the microcomputer running accounts payable to facilitate invoice matching. In this situation, there is little or no need to send a receiving report to the accounting department.

It is becoming more difficult to draw the line between manual and computerized systems. The best microcomputer packages are composed of several integrated modules that may be implemented independently. This allows the implementation of only the required modules to operate in conjunction with manual procedures.

More important, the combination of microcomputer flexibility and software availability allows the smaller company to implement computerized systems where and when needed. There is no need to computerize all functions just because one or two require computer support.

The microcomputer-system approach also keeps the information processing function under the direct control of the user. Applications and software operation are better understood by the users, leading to more effective implementation of fully computer-supported systems.

The simplest, cheapest, and quickest way to use a microcomputer to support a function is through the use of productivity aids, such as word processing and spreadsheets. These tools may be used for a variety of purposes by several different departments. Computer support for accounting is usually the first specialized application installed. Since accounting functions are relatively standard, there are many such software packages available for microcomputers.

Operations-oriented applications, such as inventory control or order entry, are usually the last to be computerized. These applications are the least standard, and the specifics vary from company to company. While there are a number of software packages available, probably none will exactly fit the methods in use. Therefore, either the procedures or the software, or both, require modification before computerizing an operating function.

Word Processing

Word processing software provides a means of entering text information into a microcomputer and then printing it out in various formats. The software provides a means of easily reformatting the text or merging several text files to produce the finished output. For example, word processors can be used to store and print shop-order, routing, and bill-of-materials masters. Updating the master is a simple process, and new documents can be printed quickly on demand.

Word processors can also be used to prepare purchase orders when the number of vendors and items is limited. Both the vendor's address and the item's descriptive information can be stored as text files. When a PO is created, the word processing operator merges the vendor data into the PO format and then merges the descriptive data for the item to be ordered. Prices and quantities are entered by the operator. For repetitive orders, a PO master can be set up and the quantity, due date, etc., entered when the order is prepared.

Some word processors will allow simple calculations to be stored in the text. This allows the user to do extensions, such as calculating the material and hours required to produce the quantity ordered on a shop order. This facility can also be used effectively to prepare and extend purchase orders.

Spreadsheets

Spreadsheets can be used in a wide variety of situations, including planning, scheduling, inventory control, budgeting, and financial control. They can even be used (in much the same way as the word processors described above) for preparing shop orders, purchase orders, and other documents.

The most common use of spreadsheets is for production planning. It is quite simple to set up a series of columns that represent months or weeks and to establish the calculations required to convert sales forecasts to production units and so forth. The flexibility of spreadsheet software allows it to be adapted to almost any situation. More important, spreadsheets make it feasible to adjust plans more frequently and to plan in more detail. The software will accept changes and automatically reevaluate the impact. This also allows testing several alternative plans to find the best solution.

Spreadsheet software can also be used to track inventory, prepare shop orders and purchase orders, and perform other similar functions. The more advanced spreadsheet systems have built-in word processing and data-base functions that can be used to track information about several items and sort and summarize the data for reporting purposes.

While spreadsheet software is powerful and easy to use, it has certain characteristics that limit its use. First, all of the data accessed by a spreadsheet must usually reside in the computer's memory. If many items are involved, a very large memory will be required. This implies that the processing time for the spreadsheet will be slow. Also, it can be very cumbersome to locate and update information for a specific item in an extremely large spreadsheet.

Second, spreadsheets provide little if any data-input audit or control. Maintaining accuracy is totally up to the user. There is no way to record the updates made and thus no way to trace back to locate a problem.

Third, it is extremely easy to alter a spreadsheet and thereby cause dependent calculations to be incorrect. This could be as simple as accidentally replacing a formula in one cell with a constant value. The result would be to use an incorrect value for all of the ensuing calculations. In a large spreadsheet, a mistake of this type can easily go undetected.

Accounting Software

The most common use of microcomputers in small companies is for collecting and reporting financial data. Accounts receivable, accounts payable, and job costing not only usually involve the processing of large amounts of data but also provide the key data required to control cash flow and costs. Once having computerized one or more of these systems, it typically makes sense to add a general-ledger module to provide an integrated financial-reporting capability. The general-ledger module will allow the preparation of monthly financial statements and budget comparisons to provide better financial control. Payroll is also often computer-supported either by using an outside service or a microcomputer.

Accounting software is well-developed on microcomputers since most of the requirements are standard from company to company. Hundreds of software packages are available, and it is quite simple to interface them with manual manufacturing control systems. Vendor invoices and copies of receiving reports are used to enter accounts-payable data, copies of customer invoices can be used for accounts receivable, and time cards can be used for payroll input. Often little or no change is required in order to interface a manual manufacturing control system with a computerized accounting system.

Operational Applications

Productivity and accounting applications are most commonly implemented on microcomputers, but the most significant benefits can be gained in supporting operating functions. Typically, specific operating functions will generate large numbers of transactions that must be processed quickly to provide customer-service and/or management information. Included in this category are order entry and invoicing, inventory control, and production-activity control.

Order entry and invoicing are good candidates for microcomputer support when a company's order volumes and customer-service needs are high; a company that processes only a few production orders may nevertheless process a large number of customer orders. A company may also need to track open-order backlogs for an extended period of time or to ship and invoice materials quickly. Most companies have unique requirements relating to discount policies, commission and billing methods, and back-order policies, but if an acceptable system were found, a microcomputer could provide order-status data quickly and efficiently for planning and scheduling. A computerized accounts-receivable system could also be integrated or interfaced with a manual system to record goods received when the invoices were prepared, and a computerized inventory control system would make it possible to update the on-hand inventory when the material was shipped.

The tracking and reporting of on-hand inventory status is another likely area for microcomputer support, particularly given a large number of items, locations, and/or updates. Several inventory control packages are available that provide standard functions. Most allow multiple locations, reorder points, order quantities, and other control parameters. The better systems make it easy to determine the cost of on-hand material based either on the standard average actual or last actual cost. Many support both last-in/first-out (LIFO) and first-in/first-out (FIFO) accounting and may be integrated with the general-ledger, order-entry, and job-costing modules.

In make-to-order companies, job costing is an important function that is often computerized, especially when the collection of labor and material costs requires a large number of transactions and when it is important to compare estimated to actual costs as the job progresses. Microcomputers are suitable both for custom make-to-order and for repetitive job-shop systems. The software packages usually provide order-entry and inventory functions, as well as some accounting functions. The better packages provide totals for complete accounting and for capacity reporting and scheduling. With one or two microcomputers, small job shops can use such software to completely automate their operations.

Manufacturing Systems

A number of manufacturing software systems are available for microcomputers. These systems provide complete bill-of-materials, routing, inventory-tracking, and MRP functions. Many provide production-activity control and capacity-planning functions that may be used to implement a computer-supported closed-loop manufacturing control system. In a few cases, the packages are integrated with full-function accounting and order-entry/invoicing modules.

Two characteristics of integrated manufacturing systems on microcomputers make them especially appealing to the small user. First, the hardware and software involved can be extremely low in cost. A stand-alone microcomputer with hard-disk storage and a printer can be purchased for less than $5000. Second, the software is usually modular and can be purchased and implemented in pieces. Systems of this type often average $2500 per module, but the complete system will cost less than $15,000 if purchased at one time. The small user can choose either to implement only the modules needed or to buy the complete system.

While integrated manufacturing software can be a good solution, the small company should be careful about jumping in too quickly, for these packages generally provide a limited set of standard features that provide only a part of the typical user's needs. Special requirements are difficult, if not impossible, to add to the standard package. The prospective user must therefore be extremely careful to match needs to the package features. A small missing element may make the computerized system less effective than a manual procedure.

The system documentation for integrated manufacturing packages is usually complete and usable; however, the user must be able to understand how microcomputers work and how the software is to be used in order to implement it successfully. In most cases, the small user will be relatively on his or her own in choosing the features and options to use and in adjusting existing procedures to interface with the new computer system. It may thus be necessary to educate company personnel or even to use outside consultants during the implementation, and consulting costs can equal or exceed the purchase price of hardware and software. The combined cost of hardware, software, and support may make the project uneconomical.

The user of a microcomputer manufacturing system should not expect local software support. There is not enough profit built into the software price to provide for support offices and personnel; consequently, software support is provided by telephone. Telephone support will be adequate in many cases, but in others it can mean a delay in solving a problem, in which event one's operations can be adversely impacted.

The foregoing discussion points to the often overlooked fact that the real cost of a computer system can be 2 to 4 times more than just the cost of hardware and software. The total cost will depend on the ability of the company's personnel to understand the application and to adjust to new methods of operating. Therefore, the smaller company is urged to use caution when embarking on a computer-system implementation.

Bar Coding

Recent advances in microcomputer and bar-code data-collection technology (see Chapter 28) have opened the door for the smaller company to take advantage of the potential in bar-code data collection. The cost of microcomputers and bar-code equipment can be expected to decline in the future, and inexpensive bar-code data-collection systems are now available for microcomputers. These elements allow the small company to use bar coding for inventory control, labor reporting, and other related functions. It will be feasible to use bar-code data collection as part of a manual system or to integrate it with computerized parts of the system. Chapter 28 provides a more detailed explanation of bar-coding techniques.

BIBLIOGRAPHY

Baker, Eugene F.: *Industry Shows its Stripes—A New Role for Bar Coding*, American Management Association, New York, 1985.

Berry, W. L., T. E. Vollman, and D. C. Whybark: *Master Production Scheduling: Principles and Practices*, APICS, Washington, D.C., 1979.

Fogarty, D. W. and T. R. Hoffman: *Production and Inventory Management*, South Western, Cincinnati, 1983.

Greene, J. H.: *Operations Management for Productivity and Profit*, Prentice-Hall, Englewood Cliffs, N.J., 1984.

Greene, J. H.: *Production and Inventory Control Systems and Decisions*, Richard D. Irwin, Homewood, Ill., 1974.

Janson, R. L.: *Production Control Desk Handbook*, Prentice-Hall, Englewood Cliffs, N.J., 1975.

Orlicky, Joseph: *Material Requirements Planning*, McGraw-Hill, New York, 1975.

Plossl, George W.: *Production and Inventory Control: Principles & Techniques*, 2d ed., Prentice-Hall, Englewood Cliffs, N.J., 1984.

Vollman, Thomas E., William E. Berry, and D. Clay Whybark: *Manufacturing Planning and Control Systems*, Richard D. Irwin, Homewood, Ill., 1984.

Wight, Oliver: *Production and Inventory Management in the Computer Age*, CBI, Boston, 1974.

CHAPTER 19

Computer-Integrated Manufacturing Systems

Editors

RICHARD M. HANSEN, CPIM, Manager, Arthur Andersen & Co., Chicago, Illinois

DONALD A. CHARTIER, Senior Consultant, Arthur Andersen & Co., Chicago, Illinois

Coeditors

LEROY D. PETERSON, CFPIM, Partner, Arthur Andersen & Co., Chicago, Illinois

ROGER G. WILLIS, CFPIM, Partner, Arthur Andersen & Co., Chicago, Illinois

Information systems are the lifelines of production and inventory control operations. Evolving from stand-alone, batch, card-oriented systems, advanced information systems are now fully integrated and operate in an on-line, real-time environment. Today's challenge is to integrate production and inventory control systems across multiple locations, connecting with suppliers and customers and incorporating engineering and production technology. This is necessary to meet ever-increasing demands for improved quality, productivity, and cost containment. In such environments, information systems significantly impact the daily activities of all managers and manufacturing personnel involved with production and inventory control.

The systems concept known as *computer-integrated manufacturing* (CIM) encompasses the entire scope of activities conducted by a manufacturing organization. Its purpose is to transform product ideas and raw materials into high-quality, salable goods at a minimum cost and in the shortest possible time. Unlike traditional manufacturing system approaches, however, the process in a CIM system begins with the design of a product and ends with the creation of that product. With CIM, the customary split between the design and manufacturing functions disappears.

CIM AND OTHER MANUFACTURING CONCEPTS

CIM is just one of many concepts being applied to a manufacturing environment to improve productivity. It is important to understand how CIM relates to these other concepts in order to assess its applicability to a given manufacturing environment. Figure 19.1 describes four stages of manufacturing productivity and the techniques used to achieve them. Although some overlap exists between stages, each successive stage typically follows in numerical sequence.

Automating a production process without streamlining its essential elements and eliminating process problems will only result in the problems also being automated. Similarly, integrating automated processes that have not been fully debugged will not be successful.

Stage 1, or traditional manufacturing, uses manufacturing resource planning (MRP II) to plan and control production, produces in large lots to minimize the effects of setup costs, and carries buffer inventories that result from producing large lot sizes. This inventory helps smooth out imbalances in production rates of the various work centers. Machines are grouped by function; thus, parts must travel long distances throughout the factory to receive all the necessary operations to be performed on them.

Stage 2, or just-in-time (JIT) manufacturing, has the objective of reducing inventories and manufacturing lead times to the lowest level possible. As opposed to traditional manufacturing, it groups dissimilar machines in U-shaped cells that perform various operations on a workpiece to produce a finished part. Travel distances between machines are greatly reduced, which in turn reduces or elimi-

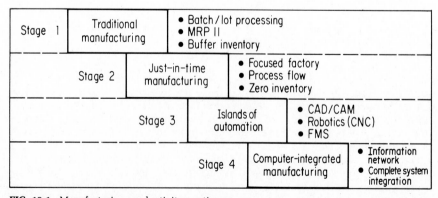

FIG. 19.1 Manufacturing productivity continuum.

nates the need for forklift trucks or sophisticated material-handling equipment. Lot sizes are much smaller because of the concentrated efforts to decrease setup times. This approach not only reduces lead times and inventory investment but also has a very favorable impact on product quality.

Stage 3 is typified by "islands of automation." Once portions of the production process have been made to flow smoothly by using JIT manufacturing techniques and few, if any, improvements in manual procedures can be achieved, it is appropriate to automate selectively. This islands-of-automation technology could be added in the form of robots, computer-aided design (CAD), flexible machining systems, and other systems and technologies that essentially function independently but lead to productivity gains in specific areas. Selective use of automation can further reduce lot sizes and inventories, while enhancing product quality and the workers' quality of life. In many cases, tedious and even hazardous tasks can be transferred from workers to automated systems.

Stage 4, CIM, links the islands of automation. Prior to this stage, engineering technologies, such as computer-aided design/computer-aid manufacturing (CAD/CAM), and production technologies, such as planning and control systems, were essentially separate. *Information technologies* bring the two technologies together, hence the term computer-*integrated* manufacturing. Such systems allow the information used to define the product and process to be automatically employed to manufacture the part and control the process with the speed of the computer. As a result, the ideal lot size of 1 can be achieved. Lot-size reduction, of course, is not the only improvement. Total lead time, meaning the time it takes to design a product *and* manufacture it, is also reduced dramatically through the coordination of all components of the design, manufacturing, and planning and control process.

CIM, which clearly surpasses traditional information systems, is highly technology-oriented. The elements of CIM can be classified as engineering technology, production technology, and information technology. Engineering technology includes CAD, computer-aided engineering (CAE), CAM, computer-aided process planning (CAPP), and group technology. Production technology includes a wide range of hardware and software, including process control, inspection and quality control devices, robotics, computer numeric control (CNC) machines, automated storage and handling, flexible manufacturing systems, and bar-code devices. Information technology includes both old and new technology, such as computer hardware and software, data base management systems, communications, information centers, artificial intelligence, decision support, and simulation.

CLOSED-LOOP MANUFACTURING SYSTEMS

Although the development of many new technologies continues to broaden the scope of CIM, the center of a production and inventory control information system environment is still a closed-loop manufacturing system (MRP II).

A closed-loop manufacturing system is a process that converts top-management directives to operational plans. The plans are executed, and the results provide feedback for updating the planning activities. Because results are used as feedback and incorporated into future input, these activities form a cycle, or closed loop. The goal of a closed-loop manufacturing system is to deliver the right products to the right customers in the right quantities at the right time. If this goal is achieved, the company can obtain the maximum return on investment.

Companies use the closed-loop concept for two reasons. First, the closed loop does not just address manufacturing issues and activities. Rather, it offers a total management system that integrates all company activities, from top-management plans to the final product delivery to the customer. Second, the closed-loop concept is necessary in a dynamic environment. Because most companies operate in industries where business situations and events change rapidly, the analysis of results and application of feedback are critical to the continued success of such firms. For example, if a customer changes a sales order or if plant personnel change production schedules, the company needs a method of communicating the changes. A closed-loop system facilitates that communication by performing periodic checks and providing feedback to appropriate personnel.

A closed-loop manufacturing system includes three major types of activities: top-management planning, operations management planning, and operations management execution. Each type of activity is shown in Fig. 19.2.

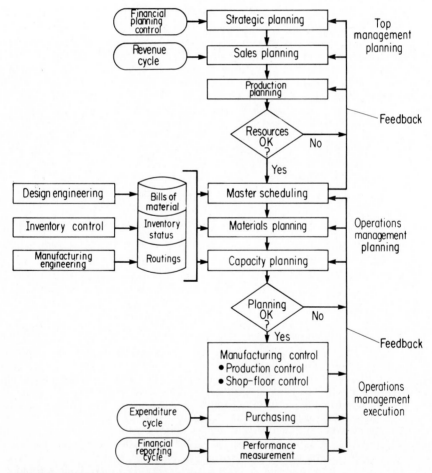

FIG. 19.2 Closed-loop manufacturing systems.

Top-Management Planning

Major activities included in top-management planning are strategic planning, sales planning, and production planning. *Strategic planning* establishes a company's long-term direction, objectives, and strategies. For example, a goal in a strategic plan might be to achieve a 15 percent return on investment. Strategic planning is closely related to financial planning and control functions because many company goals and strategies are financial (such as return on investment). Therefore, it is important to have a strong interface between strategic and financial planning activities.

Sales planning determines the sales rates the company must maintain for its product lines to meet the strategic plan. For example, a materials-handling equipment company may determine that it has to sell $20 million of conveyors to obtain the desired 15 percent return on investment. Actual sales data are used as a source for estimating future sales and determining the accuracy of forecasts currently in effect.

Production planning defines the rates at which the plant should produce goods. The production plan must take into account projected sales from the sales plan and desired inventory levels. The company's manufacturing capacity must also be considered as a constraint. Accordingly, the production plan for the materials-handling equipment company specifies how and when the $20 million in conveyors will be built.

Operations Management Planning

Operations management planning activities address master production scheduling, material-requirements planning (MRP), and capacity-requirements planning (CRP) issues.

The master production scheduling (also called *master scheduling*) activity establishes the quantity of each product to be produced each week. To do this, managers use the production plan to develop a detailed production schedule that defines the quantities to be produced for each product. Weekly or daily quantities are usually planned for each product. This detailed schedule, or master production schedule (MPS), is used to control all production activities and serves as the basis for planning material, labor, and equipment requirements.

For the MRP activity, managers refer to the MPS to determine when the material needed to build products is required. The actions required to ensure availability of both the needed purchases and manufactured parts, in the right quantities and at the right times, are planned in this activity. The MRP process essentially identifies what is needed to make 1 unit of a product and multiplies those requirements by the number of units of that product to be produced for a given week. Then a summary is prepared to show how many individual parts are needed to meet the schedule for the week.

Managers accomplish the CRP activity by interpreting the information in the MPS to define the workload in terms of personnel or equipment hours. For example, one may discover that it takes 8 machine hours to build 100 conveyors. Thus, one must make sure that 8 hr of machine time will be available at the appropriate times. At the same time, capacity problems (both over- and underutilization) can be identified to enable management to take appropriate corrective action.

Operations Management Planning Data Base. Three major types of information are required to perform operations management planning activities. The three activities, which supply and maintain these types of information, are described.

Design engineering prepares and maintains bills of materials, which define the purchased manufactured parts used to build a company's product. This information provides the "recipes" of the parts and materials needed to build the products. The bills of materials support the master scheduling and MRP activities because they identify the items needed to build the product. For example, the bill of materials lists all the parts and the quantity of each needed to make one conveyor.

Inventory control maintains the inventory status data. The inventory records contain information regarding what material is on hand or on order. MRP uses these inventory data to determine material requirements by checking whether any of the parts are available or on order before requirements for additional parts are generated.

Manufacturing engineering develops and maintains routing information. Routings specify each operation that is performed to build the product and the standard time required to perform those operations. As implied by their name, routings also specify the machines to be used and the sequence in which the operations are to be performed.

Operations Management Execution

Operations management execution activities execute and monitor the plans developed in operations management planning. Those activities include manufacturing control, purchasing, and performance measurement.

Manufacturing control involves the activities performed to balance the conflicting objectives of minimum inventory investment, maximum customer service, and low-cost plant operation. Such activities include initiating actual production on the manufacturing floor (production control) and monitoring the status of the production process (shop floor control).

Purchasing is the activity responsible for acquiring purchased material used in the manufacturing process. It places orders with vendors to meet these material requirements.

Performance measurement provides management with a way of measuring the operational plans. Actual costs and other results are determined and compared to expected results. Management then analyzes any differences and takes appropriate action.

CIM FRAMEWORK

The actual application of the CIM concept varies from environment to environment. The following represents a framework for a typical CIM system.

Pyramid Concept

In the ideal CIM environment, the activities of the manufacturing enterprise are performed by several organizational entities but coordinated through various levels of management. Figure 19.3 identifies the five levels of activity that CIM typically addresses. These five levels form the CIM hierarchy. Each level has its own activities, as well as its own inter- and intralevel communication needs, to perform those activities.

FIG. 19.3   CIM pyramid.

1. The *factory level* corresponds to those organizational units responsible for managing a company's overall operations. Activities supported at this level include those performed by the plant manager and other functions concerned with the organization as a whole, such as accounting and long-range planning.

2. The *center level* in manufacturing refers to major portions of the plant such as a line or department. Activities supported at this level include daily scheduling and the overall monitoring and control of the manufacturing cells.

3. A *manufacturing cell* is a group of machines organized to work together and managed as a unit in matching manufacturing capacities to production requirements.

4. A *manufacturing station*, or workstation, is the lowest level at which the manufacturing center operates. Typically, the workstation consists of one or more machines and material-handling equipment within a manufacturing cell.

5. A *manufacturing process* is an operation performed on material at a workstation in the course of production. Examples include milling, drilling, cutting, and assembly.

For each of the five levels of the CIM hierarchy, the activities involved must be conducted in a responsive time frame and be accurately supported by information systems. In addition, a successful CIM system must support effective communication among the various levels.

Information Architecture

An information architecture represents the data and data relationships necessary to support a CIM system at all levels of the CIM hierarchy. The purpose of an information architecture is to combine the data requirements of each separate system (CAD, inventory control, MRP) into an integrated conceptual data model. Each data requirement that can be included in this corporate or enterprise model helps to ensure overall data integrity throughout the company. Although total data integration is the ultimate objective of all systems in a corporate environment, it is *required* in a CIM environment.

The information architecture depicted in Fig. 19.4 is a conceptual, or theoretical, view of data rather than an illustration of a physical or logical data base. As such, the model identifies various data entities (represented by the boxes) and the relationships among those entities.

Factory Automation Architecture

Together, hardware, software, and communications links form a factory automation architecture for a CIM system. One possible technical architecture is found in Fig. 19.5. Note that the following three networks are included in this architecture: business and engineering, production, and office information management network.

Business and Engineering Network.   The business and engineering network consists of the mainframe computer and super minicomputers that support the high-level business, manufacturing, engineering, and shop data collection applications of CIM. These computers are linked by a data communications network that offers the ability to transfer data between applications on the different computers.

A mainframe computer supports most production operations management systems, the financial systems, and the design and manufacturing engineering systems. It requires an operating system that supports high-volume, on-line, and batch processing, as well as a data base management system and a teleprocessing monitor. Personal computers are frequently connected to the mainframe as well.

For shop floor data collection, a fault-tolerant minicomputer may be needed. Alternatively, networks of microcomputers and file servers can be used. Both configurations are designed to support applications with large on-line transaction loads that require distributed processing and extremely high reliability.

Additionally, one or more super minicomputers are used to support the CAD/CAM subsystems. These computers must provide the suitable speed and precision to support engineering functions. These systems can also run on the mainframe computer.

The business and engineering network links the mainframe and minicomputers through a communications network. A standard communications protocol, such as the manufacturing automation protocol (MAP) that has been proposed by General Motors, and a standard local area network, such as the industrial local area network (ILAN), are necessary to interface devices made by different vendors.

Production Network.   The production network is comprised of the computers, application software, and communications links that support operations on the factory floor. Typically, the users of the production network are foremen, machine operators, and inspectors.

Several components can make up the network, with the most common being a shop floor supervisor minicomputer, which is used for direct numeric control (DNC) and real-time control of shop floor operations, including robots and material-handling devices. Frequently, computer numeric control (CNC) machine tools are attached to a production network and directed by programs developed on the engineering super minicomputer. The programs are then downloaded and stored on the shop floor supervisor minicomputer and programmable controllers.

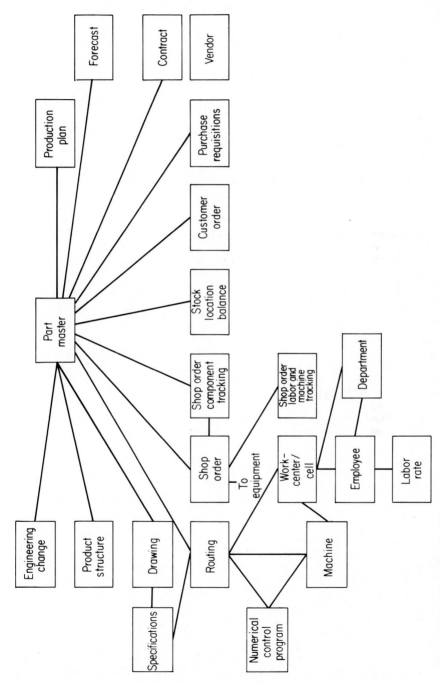

FIG. 19.4 Basic CIM data model.

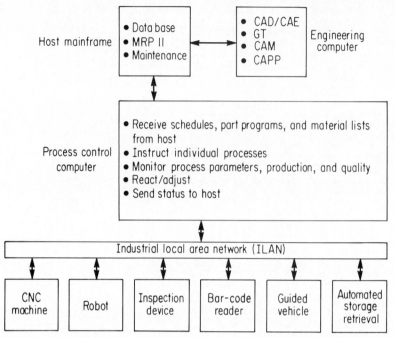

FIG. 19.5   Factory automation architecture.

Stacker cranes, which store and retrieve parts, are often used in automated warehouses along with robots and flexible manufacturing systems. All these components are controlled by the shop floor supervisor minicomputer.

Communications are handled in much the same manner as the business and engineering network, by using MAP and ILAN.

Office Information Management Network.   The office information management network is a configuration capable of supporting both computer-based and stand-alone word processing functions, connected through a dedicated communications network. A minicomputer is used to run a comprehensive word processing system and may allow for document storage which can be shared by all users.

Multifunction workstations are primarily used for word processing but may include select graphics capabilities as well. Other components of an office information management network range from high-resolution graphics terminals and letter-quality character printers to high-quality graphics plotters and color graphics plotters. Communications are supported by any one of several base-band or broad-band local area networks that have been designed for the office environment.

SYSTEMS DESCRIPTIONS

Because CIM is an all-encompassing concept, a wide range of functions are covered by CIM systems and subsystems. These systems can be classified according to three groups: computer-aided engineering and design (CAED), production operations management, and interfacing systems. The following paragraphs present conceptual models of the various systems that comprise the CIM concept.

Computer-Aided Engineering and Design

A CAED system is a comprehensive support tool for all design, drafting, process planning, and industrial facilities planning activities in a manufacturing organization. Extensive on-line graphics facilities enable product and tool designers, drafters, engineers, and facilities planners to document the designs on computer files, forming a central engineering data base. This data base provides key information to all other engineering functions. Product designs supplied by product engineers from customer companies can also be captured on this system. This model includes the following six CAED components:

1. Computer-aided design (CAD)
2. Computer-aided manufacturing (CAM)
3. Group technology coding (GTC)
4. Computer-aided process planning (CAPP)
5. Design engineering (DE)
6. Manufacturing engineering (ME)

The first four systems support the engineering function. A description of each system follows. Design engineering and manufacturing engineering are the bridge from engineering to production and inventory control. These systems are described in detail.

CAED has generally been one of the first information systems that manufacturers implement to develop a CIM environment. Many organizations have followed this trend for two reasons. First, the potential for productivity gains is perceived to be high. Second, CAED systems are perceived as providing relatively easy solutions to productivity problems because of the availability of commercial packages.

The first observation is usually accurate; the second is not. Realizing the benefits of converting to a CAED environment requires, as a minimum, sufficient computer capacity, workspace, and dedicated advocates. It also requires management's commitment to train and retrain engineering and drafting personnel and to adapt regular work habits for a computerized environment.

A CAED system is much more than a graphics workstation or an automated drafting board used to draw sophisticated curves and perform finite-element analyses. To reap the full benefits of CAD, CAM, and the other elements of CAED, the organization must be supported by an integrated engineering and manufacturing data base and by procedures and software intended to maintain the integrity of these data and keep them up to date. Unless engineers and drafters can easily classify, access, and reuse common designs and toolings, they will sacrifice many of the potential productivity gains of CAED. Accurate designs must be easily converted to workable process plans if engineering and manufacturing activities are to function in a coordinated, integrated fashion. Thus, the key obstacle to avoid is installing and using individual CAED systems in a vacuum, without planning and coordinating the systems and procedures used to support plant operations.

Computer-Aided Design. A CAD subsystem provides interactive graphics facilities that assist engineers in product and tool planning, design, drafting, design revisions, process planning, facilities planning, and design optimization (see Fig.

19.6). Most importantly, it is used to maintain bill-of-materials and engineering revision information. In a traditional manufacturing planning and control system, these data are maintained by the design engineering module. In a CIM environment, they are provided by the CAD subsystem.

Computer-Aided Manufacturing.   A CAM subsystem automatically generates numeric control (NC) programs for parts manufactured with NC machine tools, as shown in Fig. 19.7. These programs are based on the geometry of the parts and tool paths, both of which are captured by the CAD subsystem described above. CAM serves as the primary automated communications link between the engineering and shop floor functions of a company, thus integrating design and manufacturing activities.

Group Technology Coding.   The group technology coding subsystem provides a classification scheme, or taxonomy, for parts and tools. This taxonomy supports process planning, retrieval of designs stored in the data base, and tool selection. Items (parts, products, tools, or maintenance parts) classified in this manner include both purchased and manufactured parts, as well as cutting tools, jigs, and fixtures. Group technology coding also provides interactive computer facilities and hard-copy reports that enable users to classify, code, and retrieve these items (see Fig. 19.8). These capabilities allow a company to exploit similarities in the design, manufacture, and use of parts, thereby reducing engineering and manufacturing costs and lead times.

The parts are classified, or *coded*, by their physical attributes, such as length, width, thickness, and tolerance, or their manufacturing attributes, such as drill, mill, and tap specifications. Once a large subset of parts is coded in this manner, designers of new parts or tools can quickly determine whether a similar part already exists in the data base. If an existing part meets the designer's requirements closely enough, that part can be used in the new design, avoiding unnecessary duplication of effort. However, if an existing part is similar but not identical, its specifications can be easily copied and then modified by using CAD.

Computer-Aided Process Planning.   A CAPP subsystem produces both variant and generative process plans for parts, tools, jigs, and fixtures based on the group technology codes. This subsystem automates the process planning task as much as possible and, in turn, reduces engineering lead times and ensures the quality of the resulting plans. It also supports the use of similar manufacturing operations for similar parts, in accordance with the goals of group technology. CAPP supplies the same routing information as a conventional manufacturing engineering module provides; CAPP may also perform much of the work needed in setting time standards for individual operations. Figure 19.9 illustrates the key elements of this subsystem.

Design Engineering.   The design engineering function develops and maintains the material specifications required for the design and manufacture of a company's product. The main objectives of this function are to develop accurate and timely engineering information for new products, maintain engineering changes for existing products, minimize obsolescence, and reduce production costs through effective control of engineering changes and part standardization.

A design engineering subsystem supports this function by defining, organizing, and maintaining the design engineering data required for each unique part and bill of materials. Also provided in a design engineering subsystem are functional facilities to maintain part planning information for the purchasing, production, and

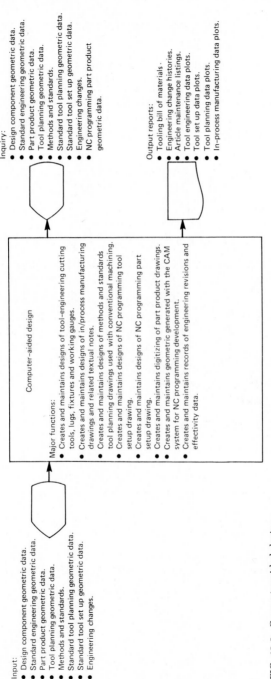

Input:
● Design component geometric data.
● Standard engineering geometric data.
● Part product geometric data.
● Tool planning geometric data.
● Methods and standards.
● Standard tool planning geometric data.
● Standard tool set up geometric data.
● Engineering changes.

Computer-aided design

Major functions:
● Creates and maintains designs of tool-engineering cutting tools, lugs, fixtures and working gauges.
● Creates and maintains designs of in/process manufacturing drawings and related textual notes.
● Creates and maintains designs of methods and standards tool planning drawings used with conventional machining.
● Creates and maintains designs of NC programming tool setup drawing.
● Creates and maintains designs of NC programming part setup drawing.
● Creates and maintains digitizing of part product drawings.
● Creates and maintains geometric generated with the CAM system for NC programming development.
● Creates and maintains records of engineering revisions and effectivity data.

Inquiry:
● Design component geometric data.
● Standard engineering geometric data.
● Part product geometric data.
● Tool planning geometric data.
● Methods and standards.
● Standard tool planning geometric data.
● Standard tool set up geometric data.
● Engineering changes.
● NC programming part product geometric data.

Output reports:
● Tooling bill of materials.
● Engineering change histories.
● Article maintenance listings.
● Tool engineering data plots.
● Tool set up data plots.
● Tool planning data plots.
● In-process manufacturing data plots.

FIG. 19.6 Computer-aided design.

19.13

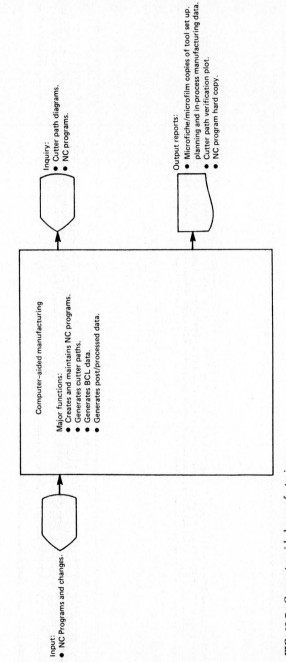

Input:
• NC Programs and changes.

Computer-aided manufacturing

Major functions:
• Creates and maintains NC programs.
• Generates cutter paths.
• Generates BCL data.
• Generates post/processed data.

Inquiry:
• Cutter path diagrams.
• NC programs.

Output reports:
• Microfiche/microfilm copies of tool set up, planning and in-process manufacturing data.
• Cutter path verification plot.
• NC program hard copy.

FIG. 19.7 Computer-aided manufacturing.

19.14

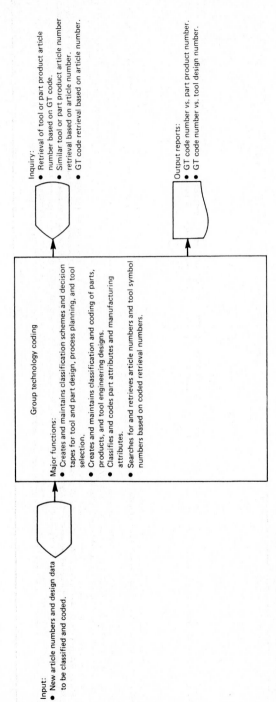

FIG. 19.8 Group technology coding.

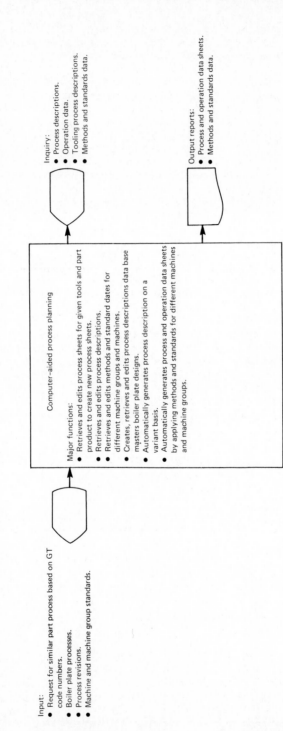

Input:
• Request for similar part process based on GT code numbers.
• Boiler plate processes.
• Process revisions.
• Machine and machine group standards.

Computer-aided process planning

Major functions:
• Retrieves and edits process sheets for given tools and part product to create new process sheets.
• Retrieves and edits process descriptions.
• Retrieves and edits methods and standard dates for different machine groups and machines.
• Creates, retrieves and edits process descriptions data base masters boiler plate designs.
• Automatically generates process description on a variant basis.
• Automatically generates process and operation data sheets by applying methods and standards for different machines and machine groups.

Inquiry:
• Process descriptions.
• Operation data.
• Tooling process descriptions.
• Methods and standards data.

Output reports:
• Process and operation data sheets.
• Methods and standards data.

FIG. 19.9 Computer-aided process planning.

inventory control areas. As such, the design engineering subsystem establishes the information foundation for the production operations management system that is necessary for an integrated manufacturing system.

The design engineering subsystem interfaces with the inventory control subsystem by transmitting the changes to the part master data that may affect the projected inventory. It also interfaces with the MRP subsystem by transmitting the changes to part master data that affect the calculation of planned-order or demand quantities or by conveying changes in lead time that will affect the offsetting of component demands. Other interfaces are with the product costing subsystem, which receives part master data changes that affect costs, and with the master scheduling subsystem, which receives part master changes that affect planned-order quantities and lead-time changes that affect the offsetting of component demands.

Design engineering is integrated with the CAD and group technology subsystems, which provide the information required to maintain part master and product structures. A conceptual overview illustrating many of the key elements of the design engineering subsystem is shown in Fig. 19.10.

The major users of design engineering include engineers who develop specifications for new parts, for engineering changes, and for similar parts on the system. It is also used by engineers to reference tolerance information or material standards and by company buyers to purchase parts and negotiate contracts.

The benefits that these users realize from an interactive design engineering subsystem include

- Reduced lead time to develop part master information and product structures. This improvement is possible because of subsystem features that permit on-line access to information for parts already in the data base, on-line update with validation for all data base maintenance, access to common data for all departments involved in new-part development, and integration with computer-aided subsystems (CAD and group technology).

- Improved accuracy and integrity of design engineering data. This improvement results from the use of on-line validation of all data and segregation of update transactions by responsible functional area.

- Reduced clerical effort associated with adding engineering information. On-line updating capabilities and the ability to copy similar existing product structures and modify them in designing new products produce these reductions.

To achieve these benefits, however, a design engineering subsystem requires certain pieces of information. The data bases used by design engineering include

1. *Part master,* which contains all the information required to define and describe parts, products, and tools
2. *Product structure,* which contains all the parent-component relationships and is used to plan the configuration of manufactured parts
3. *Engineering change,* which defines engineering revisions that result in changes to a part's configuration

Manufacturing Engineering. The manufacturing engineering function provides the interface between the design and the actual manufacture of the product. This function, in conjunction with industrial engineering, develops and maintains the process methods and labor standards required to manufacture a company's products. The main objectives of this function are to develop and maintain routing operation specifications, including sequence, methods, tooling, machines, and

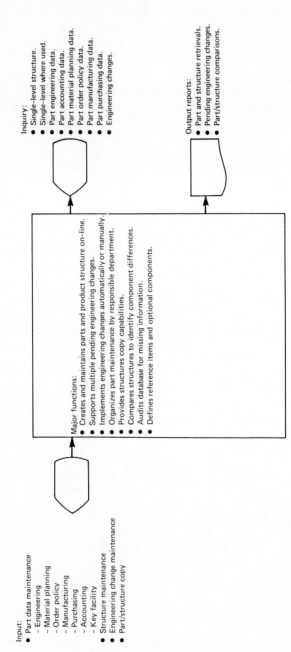

Input:
● Part data maintenance
  - Engineering
  - Material planning
  - Order policy
  - Manufacturing
  - Purchasing
  - Accounting
  - Key facility
● Structure maintenance
● Engineering change maintenance
● Part/structure copy

Major functions:
● Creates and maintains parts and product structure on-line.
● Supports multiple pending engineering changes.
● Implements engineering changes automatically or manually.
● Organizes part maintenance by responsible department.
● Provides structures copy capabilities.
● Compares structures to identify component differences.
● Audits database for missing information.
● Defines reference items and optional components.

Inquiry:
● Single–level structure.
● Single–level where used.
● Part engineering data.
● Part accounting data.
● Part material planning data.
● Part order policy data.
● Part manufacturing data.
● Part purchasing data.
● Engineering changes.

Output reports:
● Part and structure retrievals.
● Pending engineering changes.
● Part/structure comparisons.

FIG. 19.10 Design engineering.

time standards; to organize plant facilities into work centers; and to minimize production costs through effective control of methods and standards changes and make-or-buy decisions.

A manufacturing engineering subsystem supports this function by defining, organizing, and maintaining the manufacturing engineering data required for routing operations and work centers.

A manufacturing engineering subsystem interfaces with the MRP subsystem by transmitting the lead-time changes that affect the offsetting of component demands. It also interfaces with the product costing subsystem by transmitting the changes in routing data that affect costs.

The manufacturing engineering subsystem is integrated with group technology, CAM, and CAPP, which use and maintain process information contained within the manufacturing engineering subsystem. A conceptual overview illustrating many of the key elements of a manufacturing engineering subsystem is shown in Fig. 19.11.

The major users of manufacturing engineering include process planners, who are responsible for maintaining work center characteristics, routings, and part data; methods and standards engineers, who are responsible for establishing setup and run time standards; and cost-estimating personnel, who are responsible for extending the structure and process to develop cost estimates. Other users of a manufacturing engineering subsystem are the inspection personnel who define inspection operations for the routing.

These users realize important benefits from the subsystem:

- Expanded use of engineering data through the subsystem's on-line inquiry capabilities for part and routing data.
- Reduced production costs through more effective control over engineering changes.
- Reduced lead time to develop work center information and routings. This is possible through manufacturing engineering because of the automatic creation and maintenance of process sheets.
- Improved accuracy and integrity of manufacturing engineering data. This improvement results from the subsystem's on-line validation of all data and segregation of update transactions by responsible functional area.

To achieve these benefits, however, a manufacturing engineering subsystem requires information and data from a variety of places. The data bases used by ME include

1. *Routing,* which contains all process operations required to manufacture parts
2. *Work center or cell,* which contains all information required to define work centers, such as capacity.
3. *Part master,* which contains all information required to define and describe parts, products, and tools
4. *Engineering change,* which defines engineering revisions that result in changes to a part's manufacturing process

Production Operations Management

The production operations management system is an integrated manufacturing planning and control system. The production operations management system pro-

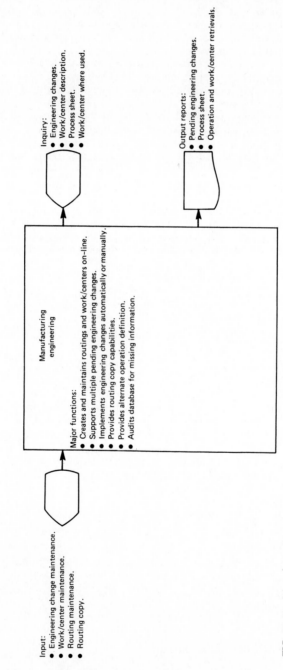

Input:
● Engineering change maintenance.
● Work/center maintenance.
● Routing maintenance.
● Routing copy.

Manufacturing engineering

Major functions:
● Creates and maintains routings and work/centers on-line.
● Supports multiple pending engineering changes.
● Implements engineering changes automatically or manually.
● Provides routing copy capabilities.
● Provides alternate operation definition.
● Audits database for missing information.

Inquiry:
● Engineering changes.
● Work/center description.
● Process sheet.
● Work/center where used.

Output reports:
● Pending engineering changes.
● Process sheet.
● Operation and work/center retrievals.

FIG. 19.11 Manufacturing engineering.

vides effective systems tools for managing manufacturing resources, materials, labor, and other costs.

The key to a successful production operations management system is integration. The production plan and MPS set the overall manufacturing level of activity. Based on the MPS, the material and load requirements for all material levels (assemblies, components, and raw materials) are planned. Capacity must be checked at various stages within this planning process to ensure that sufficient resources exist to meet the demand being placed on the facility. Planned orders and requirements are later converted to actual customer orders, shop orders, and purchase requisitions. Through an integrated production operations management system, the status of these actual orders is tracked, and the inevitable changes are controlled. This enables the system to closely monitor quality and produce analysis reports with timely feedback. The process continues as orders are completed, and various performance reports are generated. Actual results serve as input into the overall planning process; then the cycle is repeated. Throughout the effort to complete and ship products, equipment must be continually maintained to minimize breakdowns.

When fully implemented, a production operations management system yields significant benefits that include overall productivity improvements. Inventory levels can be decreased, freeing capital and reducing inventory obsolescence. At the same time, more orders should be completed on time while overall manufacturing lead times decrease. Finally, all resources can be used more effectively, as requirements are closely monitored against capacity, and preventive maintenance is performed to keep machines running.

An effective production operations management system is composed of the following subsystems:

1. Inventory control
2. Shop floor control
3. Master scheduling
4. MRP
5. Capacity planning
6. Purchasing
7. Product costing
8. Quality reporting
9. Distribution and shipping
10. Inventory accounting
11. Direct numeric control

Inventory Control. One of the primary functions of an inventory control function is to maintain accurate and timely on-hand and on-order balances of materials and parts. In a production operations management system, the inventory control subsystem supports this function by interactively defining and processing all the transactions necessary to control on-hand and on-order balances. It provides on-line inquiry; prepares stock status, production, and purchase order status reports; and highlights surplus, past-due, and obsolete inventory conditions. Shop paperwork is prepared, and the status of component requirements (issues pending) is maintained for each production order to provide component availability checking and to measure material substitution and usage variances.

Inventory control receives requisition status information from the purchasing subsystem and tracks current activity to reconcile quantity balances for inventory accounting. It also supports the MRP subsystem by determining future inventory plans and supports the purchasing subsystem by sending material requisitions.

Inventory control is integrated with CAED function through the design engineering system, which maintains the part and product structure data bases. Inventory control also may send requests for parts to automated material-handling systems and receive issue and receipt transactions. A conceptual overview illustrating many of the key elements of the inventory control subsystem is shown in Fig. 19.12.

The major users of the inventory control subsystem include material control personnel, who requisition material and plan and release orders, and storeroom personnel, who in turn issue material and tools to the floor. Other users of the subsystem include quality assurance management personnel, who must determine the status of material awaiting disposition.

The benefits that these users realize from an interactive inventory control subsystem include

- Improved and more efficient inventory control. This improvement results from inventory control features that perform system maintenance functions (adding orders, issuing or receiving parts, etc.) on-line; analyze the relative (ABC) value of all parts, to establish degrees of control over material and order tracking; and maintain stock balances by user-specified classifications.

- Reduced manual and clerical effort. These benefits are realized through the inventory control subsystem's ability to automatically track inventory within cribs and produce order status reports.

- Reduced overall lead times and minimal schedule delays. An inventory control subsystem prepares component availability reports to help expedite parts with shortages and to control the release of production orders. It also prepares production orders and picking lists, which helps minimize schedule delays.

Before a company can experience the benefits of an inventory control subsystem, however, users must understand its data requirements. The data bases used by inventory control are as follows:

1. *Part master*, which contains inventory control data for each part, including ordering information for purchase and make parts.

2. *Product structure*, or *bill of materials*, which contains parent and component relationships used to determine material requirements for an order.

3. *Stock location balance*, which contains inventory balances for each stockroom location of a part. These balances may be reserved for a particular order.

4. *Shop order*, which contains data regarding a shop order, such as quantity and due dates.

5. *Shop order component tracking*, which contains the planned and actual material components required to complete an order.

Shop Floor Control.   The shop floor control function encompasses the major areas of production order scheduling, shop floor data collection, order status reporting, scrap-performance reporting, and direct and indirect labor performance reporting. It provides order prioritization techniques to aid in scheduling and dispatching production orders that, in turn, minimize total schedule delays. Also the shop floor control function provides timely reporting of schedule delays. The function isolates

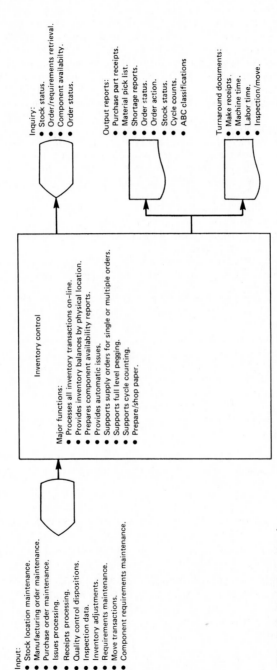

Input:
- Stock location maintenance.
- Manufacturing order maintenance.
- Purchase order maintenance.
- Issues processing.
- Receipts processing.
- Quality control dispositions.
- Inspection data.
- Inventory adjustments.
- Requirements maintenance.
- Move transactions.
- Component requirements maintenance.

Inventory control

Major functions:
- Processes all inventory transactions on-line.
- Provides inventory balances by physical location.
- Prepares component availability reports.
- Provides automatic issues.
- Supports supply orders for single or multiple orders.
- Supports full level pegging.
- Supports cycle counting.
- Prepare/shop paper.

Inquiry:
- Stock status.
- Order/requirements retrieval.
- Component availability.
- Order status.

Output reports:
- Purchase part receipts.
- Material pick list.
- Shortage reports.
- Order status.
- Order action.
- Stock status.
- Cycle counts.
- ABC classifications

Turnaround documents:
- Make receipts.
- Machine time.
- Labor time.
- Inspection/move.

FIG. 19.12 Inventory control.

scrapped and reworked materials by labor operation and monitors and evaluates direct and indirect labor performance.

A shop floor control subsystem supports this function by defining, organizing, and maintaining the labor operations required to complete a manufacturing order. On-line inquiry and production order status reports provide the information necessary to monitor production progress, whereas scrap performance reports provide operating tools that measure quantities scrapped at each work center.

The subsystem also prepares plant, work center, and employee performance reports, which compare actual labor activity reported in shop floor control with preestablished standards. This information helps control labor costs and monitor productivity by work center.

The shop floor control subsystem interfaces with the quality reporting subsystem by transmitting inspection operation results. Shop floor control also may transmit order schedules to programmable controller or flexible manufacturing systems to indicate what parts or products to produce. This subsystem receives shop floor activity transactions as they occur through a variety of data collection devices, including cathode-ray tubes (CRTs), bar-code readers, optical character recognition devices, and voice recognition equipment. A conceptual overview illustrating many of the key elements of the shop floor control subsystem is shown in Fig. 19.13.

The major users of shop floor control include factory personnel, who rely on the dispatch list and order status inquiries to schedule jobs within a work center, and methods and standards engineers, who monitor the accuracy of standards and evaluate the impact of engineering changes on existing shop orders. The benefits that these users realize from an interactive shop floor control subsystem include

- Improved shop floor control. This subsystem feature tracks material sent to quality assurance by original part and operation, monitors direct labor activity, and tracks commingled stock within cribs. Much of the improved control results from the on-line, real-time data collection process (through the devices mentioned) and the ability to revise schedules and process plans as required.

- Reduced manual and clerical effort. Shop floor control features automatically generate all required shop documentation, material requisitions, and material issue tickets.

- Reduced overall lead times and minimal schedule delays. The shop floor control subsystem allows operation splitting and overlays as well as the regeneration of shop orders when a change is made.

To achieve these benefits, however, a shop floor control subsystem requires certain pieces of information. These data bases are used:

1. *Routing*, which details the process operations required to manufacture parts. This data base is used to determine labor requirements for an order.
2. *Shop order labor and machine tracking*, which contains the planned and actual resources (work center, machine, or labor) required to complete an order.
3. *Work center and cell*, which contains work center and cell data, such as size and capacity. It is used to schedule orders through work centers and to report performance.
4. *Part master*, which contain shop floor control data for each make part.

Master Scheduling.   A company's master scheduling function determines what products will be manufactured, when they will be produced, and in what quantities

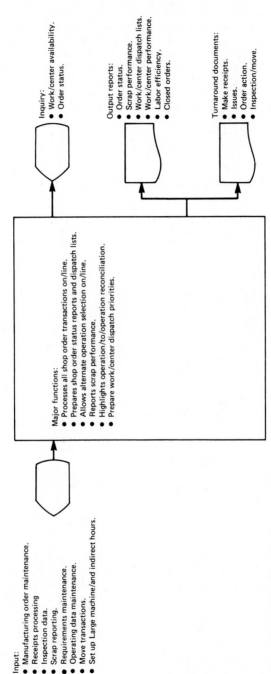

Input:
- Manufacturing order maintenance.
- Receipts processing
- Inspection data.
- Scrap reporting.
- Requirements maintenance.
- Operating data maintenance.
- Move transactions.
- Set up Large machine/and indirect hours.

Major functions:
- Processes all shop order transactions on/line.
- Prepares shop order status reports and dispatch lists.
- Allows alternate operation selection on/line.
- Reports scrap performance.
- Highlights operation/to/operation reconciliation.
- Prepare work/center dispatch priorities.

Inquiry:
- Work/center availability.
- Order status.

Output reports:
- Order status.
- Scrap performance.
- Work/center dispatch lists.
- Work/center performance.
- Labor efficiency.
- Closed orders.

Turnaround documents:
- Make receipts.
- Issues.
- Order action.
- Inspection/move.

FIG. 19.13 Shop floor control.

they will be produced. This information becomes the basis for scheduling all production and procurement activities. Thus the development of a realistic MPS is critical in formulating a company's overall manufacturing plan. The MPS must consider total demands on plant resources, including finished-inventory product sales, inventory build schedules, spare-part requirements, plant capacity, and vendor capacity. Rough-cut capacity planning (RCCP)information helps management to plan long-term labor requirements, monitor utilization of available capacity, adjust planned resource capacities appropriately within economical and practical limits, and develop long-range production load and capacity projections which address effective capital equipment planning and budgeting objectives.

A master scheduling subsystem supports master scheduling personnel in developing a realistic and comprehensive MPS. It maintains product forecasts, desired inventory levels, planning work centers, and planning routings for end items and major subassemblies. It then combines these forecasts with demands (customer orders and interplant orders) to generate an initial master schedule which will meet all stated demands. The order and safety stock policies defined for each part are applied for parts that will be included in the MPS. The RCCP portion of the MPS then uses the planning routings and planning work center information to check key production resources that may limit the company's ability to meet the MPS. A summary load report highlights key capacity problems, and a detailed load report identifies specific orders contributing to the overload.

Personnel responsible for master scheduling then review the suggested MPS and the resource requirements reports to make adjustments and release the firmed MPS for MRP processing. MRP, in turn, is used to explode the MPS into distinct component demands and generates the manufacturing and purchase orders needed to meet these demands.

The basis for the MPS is the forecast. Typically, the marketing group is responsible for forecasting the future demand for various finished products. One approach is to forecast the demand for each end item; this, however, can be a tedious process if the company's product line includes a large number of items. One solution is to group products into families and then specify the percentage of the family associated with individual products or options. Then the production plan is entered for the family, and the system calculates the detailed plan for each item in the family.

The master scheduling subsystem interfaces with order entry, which sends customer orders to be recorded in the MPS, and with MRP, which receives requirements for parts listed on the MPS. This subsystem is integrated with both the CAED system and other subsystems within production operations management. These subsystems include design engineering, which creates the part master and product structure data bases used by master scheduling, and manufacturing engineering, which automatically maintains the manufacturing lead-time factors used by master scheduling. A conceptual overview illustrating many of the key elements of a master scheduling subsystem is shown in Fig. 19.14.

The users of a master scheduling subsystem include material control personnel, who are responsible for order planning and capacity planning; factory personnel, who are involved in capacity overload decisions; and facilities planning personnel, who project machine requirements. These users reap these benefits:

- Improved management planning and responsiveness to change. This improvement results from the subsystem's ability to perform on-line inquiries that access all critical information, to simulate what-if changes to the MPS, and to highlight actions required because of schedule changes.

- Improved customer order delivery performance. This improvement is possible through on-line access to inventory availability information for customer order promising.

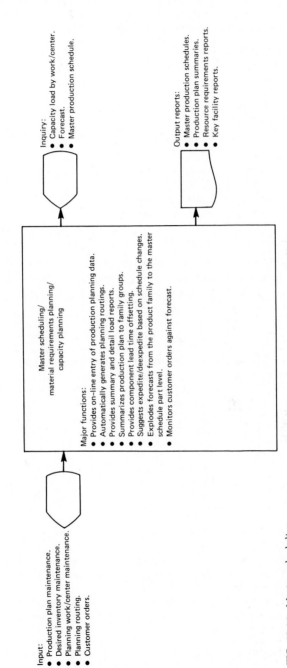

Input:
• Production plan maintenance.
• Desired inventory maintenance.
• Planning work/center maintenance.
• Planning routing.
• Customer orders.

Master scheduling/
material requirements planning/
capacity planning

Major functions:
• Provides on-line entry of production planning data.
• Automatically generates planning routings.
• Provides summary and detail load reports.
• Summarizes production plan to family groups.
• Provides component lead time offsetting.
• Suggests expedite/deexpedite based on schedule changes.
• Explodes forecasts from the product family to the master schedule part level.
• Monitors customer orders against forecast.

Inquiry:
• Capacity load by work/center.
• Forecast.
• Master production schedule.

Output reports:
• Master production schedules.
• Production plan summaries.
• Resource requirements reports.
• Key facility reports.

FIG. 19.14 Master scheduling.

- Reduced overtime. Early visibility of alternative work centers and labor requirements lead to this important reduction. A realistic MPS decreases periods of idle time, which also reduces employee overtime.

To achieve these benefits, however, a master scheduling subsystem requires data from a variety of sources. The data bases most often used by master scheduling include

1. *Routing*, which contains the operations required to manufacture a part and to determine load projections
2. *Customer order*, which contains order requirements and is created by master scheduling as new orders are received
3. *Production plan*, which contains anticipated production levels of a part for the planning horizon used to set the MPS
4. *Forecast*, which contains projected sales over a specified time horizon and is used as an input to the production plan
5. *Shop order*, which contains data on a planned or released shop order, such as quantity and due date
6. *Part master*, which contains order planning parameters for each part
7. *Product structure*, which contains all parent and component relationships
8. *Work center or cell*, which contains information used in capacity load projections

MRP. Time-phased MRP is designed to determine what, how much, and when to order material required to support the MPS. It is one of the most effective inventory management and scheduling tools available to management. The inventory and operations management benefits derived from MRP are a direct function of how well the MPS, bills of materials, on-hand status, on-order status, order quantity policies, and lead times are maintained.

The MRP subsystem that supports this function explodes the MPS generated in the master scheduling subsystem through the bills of materials, to develop component-material requirements by time period. These gross requirements are then netted by applying available, on-hand, and on-order inventory to determine manufacturing and purchase orders needed to meet requirements.

The MRP subsystem interfaces with master scheduling by receiving requirements for parts listed in the MPS and with purchasing by transmitting requirements for purchased parts. Integrated with the CAED system, the MRP subsystem uses the product structure and routing information that is created and maintained there. The MRP subsystem is also integrated with inventory control, which contains order policies and on-hand and on-order inventory information, and capacity planning, which develops the load for each work center created by planned, released, and firm orders. A conceptual overview illustrating key elements of the MRP subsystem is shown in Fig. 19.15.

The users of an MRP subsystem include material control personnel, who are responsible for order planning and order dispatching. They benefit from an MRP subsystem in a number of ways:

- Improved management planning and responsiveness to change. This improvement results from the subsystem's ability to replan all manufacturing and purchase orders based on changes to customer orders and product design.

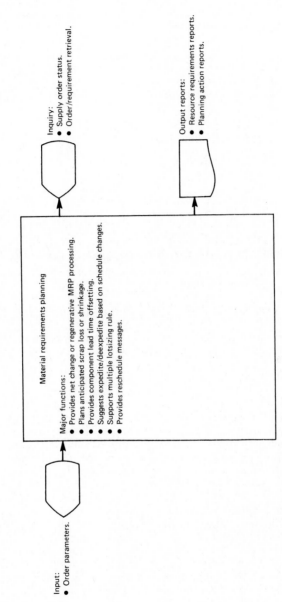

Input:
• Order parameters.

Material requirements planning

Major functions:
• Provides net change or regenerative MRP processing.
• Plans anticipated scrap loss or shrinkage.
• Provides component lead time offsetting.
• Suggests expedite/deexpedite based on schedule changes.
• Supports multiple lotsizing rule.
• Provides reschedule messages.

Inquiry:
• Supply order status.
• Order/requirement retrieval.

Output reports:
• Resource requirements reports.
• Planning action reports.

FIG. 19.15 Materials-requirements planning.

- Improved customer order delivery performance. The subsystem's ability to establish integrity in the manufacturing order and purchase order due dates produces this improvement.

- Reduced overtime by using the MRP results in requirements for parts based on forecasts and actual customer orders. These requirements form production schedules that can be planned in advance, eliminating "hot lists" and unscheduled overtime.

- Reduced inventory and obsolescence. Requirements are generated only for parts that have been forecasted or have actual customer orders. Those requirements are also *time-phased*; that is, they specify *when* parts are needed, so that the parts are produced just before being used in the next level of the production process.

To achieve these benefits, an MRP subsystem requires data from a variety of sources. The data bases most often used by MRP include

1. *Part master,* which contains order planning parameters for each part
2. *Product structure,* which contains all parent and component relationships and is used in MRP
3. *Shop order component tracking,* which contains material components required to complete a shop order, representing a part demand in the MRP
4. *Stock location balance,* which contains inventory balances for each stockroom location of a part and is used to determine net requirements in the MRP process
5. *Customer order,* which contains customer part order quantities, representing a demand for that part in the MRP process

Capacity-Requirements Planning.   Manufacturing management needs accurate and timely work center load-versus-capacity information. This information helps management plan short-term labor requirements effectively, monitor utilization of available capacity, adjust resource capacities, and reschedule production to alternate work centers.

A CRP subsystem that supports the capacity planning function summarizes time-phased load requirements by work center. Planned orders generated in the MRP subsystem and released orders developed in the inventory control subsystem are back scheduled from their respective due dates. Load hours (machine and/or labor), capacity percentage, and cumulative available hours are calculated by time period, and overcapacity situations are highlighted. Detailed load reports provide work center load information by part, order, operation, and time period. This information is used to determine which orders should be rescheduled, rerouted, or sent to outside processors to correct capacity problems.

As a result of these features, the CRP subsystem provides management with timely load-versus-capacity information. This permits the economical planning and balancing of labor, machines, and other resources in conjunction with released and planned-order requirements.

The CRP subsystem is integrated with several production operations management subsystems. Design engineering provides part master data, manufacturing engineering provides routing and work center capacity information, shop floor control furnishes work-in-process data, and inventory control supplies order data. A conceptual overview illustrating the key elements of the CRP subsystem is shown in Fig. 19.16.

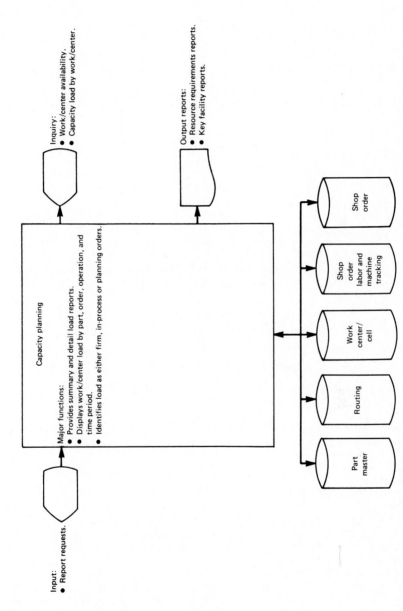

Input:
● Report requests.

Capacity planning

Major functions:
● Provides summary and detail load reports.
● Displays work/center load by part, order, operation, and time period.
● Identifies load as either firm, in-process or planning orders.

Inquiry:
● Work/center availability.
● Capacity load by work/center.

Output reports:
● Resource requirements reports.
● Key facility reports.

Part master

Routing

Work center/cell

Shop order labor and machine tracking

Shop order

FIG. 19.16 Capacity planning.

19.31

The users of a CRP subsystem include material control personnel, who are responsible for order planning, capacity planning, and order dispatching, and factory personnel, who are involved in capacity overload decisions. These users benefit from a CRP subsystem through

- Improved management planning and responsiveness to change. This improvement results from the subsystem's ability to perform on-line inquiries when accessing all critical information. Other reasons for the improvement include the subsystem's analysis of machine utilization based on changes in customer orders or work centers.

- Reduced overall lead times and minimal schedule delays. These reductions are possible through the subsystem's early identification of overloads at all work centers before an order is released to the floor. Another subsystem feature that leads to this improvement is its ability to provide on-line information regarding alternative machine availability.

- Improved operating efficiency. A CRP subsystem feature that supports proper planning of actual machines to be used eliminates NC tape and tool reworking. As a result, operating efficiency is improved.

- Improved delivery performance. This improvement results from management's ability to anticipate overload situations and prevent them by switching part of the production requirements to alternate work centers. Material then flows through the process more quickly.

- Reduced overtime. Early detection of overloads and alternate work centers and labor requirements leads to this important reduction.

To achieve these benefits, a CRP subsystem requires data from a variety of sources. These data bases are most often used by CRP:

1. *Part master*, which contains order planning parameters for each part.
2. *Work center or cell*, which contains information (for example, work center capacity and efficiency) used in capacity load projections.
3. *Shop order*, which contains data regarding a planned or released shop order, such as quantity and due date.
4. *Routing*, which details the process operations required to manufacture parts. CRP uses this information to determine which work centers will be used for each part.
5. *Shop order labor and machine tracking*, which contains information about orders that have been released to the shop floor.

Purchasing.   The prime responsibilities of the purchasing function are to obtain economic purchases and ensure timely receipts. Maintenance of vendor quotations, preparation of purchase order paperwork, and reporting on vendor performance assist in obtaining material at the lowest cost. Order status and exception reporting facilitates timely deliveries.

A purchasing subsystem supports this function by defining, organizing, and maintaining data on qualified vendors for each purchased part. The subsystem retains and summarizes actual vendor and buyer performance in terms of price, delivery, and quality. The subsystem enables buyers to convert purchasing requisitions (normally planned automatically through an MRP subsystem) to purchase orders on line, by selecting the appropriate vendor and combining or modifying requisitions to meet minimum order quantities and other provisions. The purchasing application also maintains contract and blanket-order information.

The purchasing subsystem interfaces with several other subsystems. It receives material requisitions for parts and any nonproduction items from inventory control and other nonproduction items from all departments. The purchasing subsystem also transmits the latest purchase costs to product costing and requisition status information to inventory control and maintenance. Accounts payable uses purchase order information to match and authorize payment of vendor invoices. Quality control also receives inspection information. A conceptual overview illustrating many elements of a purchasing subsystem is shown in Fig. 19.17.

The major users of a purchasing subsystem include material and maintenance planners, who create, maintain, and approve requisitions; cost accountants, who use purchase cost information to price products; and buyers, who purchase parts to fill requisitions and authorize vendors to develop supply contracts.

By using the purchasing subsystem, these users realize two important benefits. First, there is more accurate tracking of the status of requisitions. This improvement results from the subsystem's ability to create a single requisition file of all outstanding requisitions that provide status and due-date information. On-line inquiry for outstanding requisitions provides access to current status and due-date information. Requisition and status data can also be reported. Second, the time required to process a requisition is reduced. This time reduction results from purchasing's machine-generated requisition records and on-line maintenance and approval of requisitions.

To achieve these benefits, a purchasing subsystem requires data from a variety of sources. These data bases are used by the subsystem:

1. *Purchase requisition,* which contains information on quantity and other required data
2. *Vendor,* which contains financial information on supplies as well as performance history with respect to price, delivery, and quality
3. *Part master,* which provides the part specifications used in the purchase order
4. *Contract,* which contains key information on supply contracts, such as the items to be supplied, minimum quantities, and delivery requirements

Product Costing. All business organizations need accurate and timely product cost information to evaluate prices and profit margins, to value inventories, to establish budgets and measure performance, to identify variances for effective cost control, and to develop plans for future operations. A product costing subsystem satisfies this need by maintaining several cost types for each part: accounting standard, current standard, simulated, and latest engineering.

The *accounting standard cost* is used for inventory accounting and normally is not changed during the fiscal year. The *current standard cost* represents the cost calculated from the current manufacturing bills of materials and routings. It can be changed during each cost buildup to reflect current conditions. The current standard cost is also used for pricing and performance measurement. The *simulated cost,* is used to evaluate the impact on cost margins of anticipated increases in labor, overhead rates, or purchase prices. The *latest engineering cost* is used to monitor the cost of assemblies based on the latest (future) version of the bill of materials.

Product costing data are a natural by-product of maintaining the bills of materials and routing operations. This information, in conjunction with work center labor, burden rates, and purchased-part costs, is used to build up material, labor, and overhead costs for each part on a level-by-level basis.

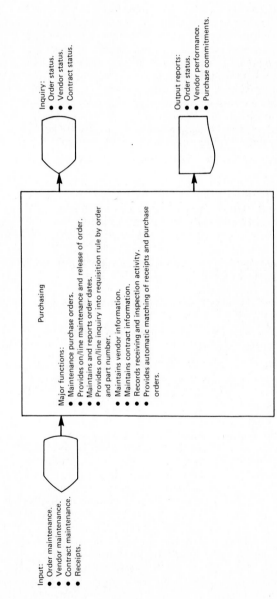

FIG. 19.17 Purchasing.

Input:
- Order maintenance.
- Vendor maintenance.
- Contract maintenance.
- Receipts.

Purchasing

Major functions:
- Maintenance purchase orders.
- Provides on/line maintenance and release of order.
- Maintains and reports order dates.
- Provides on/line inquiry into requisition rule by order and part number.
- Maintains vendor information.
- Maintains contract information.
- Records receiving and inspection activity.
- Provides automatic matching of receipts and purchase orders.

Inquiry:
- Order status.
- Vendor status.
- Contract status.

Output reports:
- Order status.
- Vendor performance.
- Purchase commitments.

19.34

A product costing subsystem is integrated with the CAED system through the design engineering and manufacturing engineering subsystems. Design engineering provides part master and component information, which is used by product costing to build up and update material costs. Manufacturing engineering creates and maintains the routing and work center information used to update labor costs. Both applications send messages to product costing whenever a change is made to part, bill of materials, routing, or work center data that impacts cost data. Also product costing provides inventory accounting with standard unit cost data. Figure 19.18 illustrates the key elements of a product costing subsystem.

The users of a product costing subsystem include pricing personnel, who estimate customer orders and determine list prices, and cost accountants, who use part standard cost data to cost shop orders and value inventory. These users reap many benefits:

- Reduced lead time required to develop, analyze, and revise estimates and standards. This reduction is possible through cost simulations, rolling costs up through all levels of the bill-of-materials structure, cost comparisons between different parts and cost types within a part, and on-line access to all costs.

- Less effort required to create a customer quote and less risk of giving an incorrect one. These reductions occur because the subsystem automatically recosts parts as a result of structure or routing changes.

- Improved cost control and more accurate costing of inventories. This is possible because of the ability to access on-line current cost information and therefore respond to cost changes quickly. Product costing provides the inventory subsystem with accurate cost information that aids in valuing inventories.

To achieve these benefits, data are needed from a variety of sources. The data bases most often used by product costing are

1. *Part master*, which contains all standard cost data for the part
2. *Product structure*, which contains all parent-component relationships and is required for cost roll-ups
3. *Routing*, which contains the process operations required to manufacture a part and which is needed to calculate standard labor rates
4. *Labor rate*, which contains labor rate data used to calculate standard costs
5. *Machine rate*, which contains current machine rate data used to calculate standard costs
6. *Work center or cell*, which contains work center overhead costs and which is used to calculate standard costs

Quality Reporting. A quality reporting subsystem receives basic inspection data from the inventory and shop floor control subsystems and captures additional rejection and disposition data for analysis. This subsystem tracks material throughout the disposition process and provides extensive analysis reports that aid in identifying quality trends and causes of quality problems. In addition to receiving reports, users can make on-line inquiries so that quality problems can be discovered quickly, thereby minimizing the amount of scrap produced.

Quality reporting is integrated with manufacturing engineering, which maintains part and routing information that determines inspection procedures for quality reporting. It is also integrated with the purchasing subsystem, which provides purchase order specifications. The shop floor control subsystem of the production

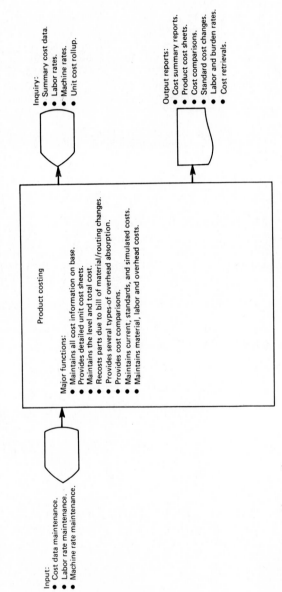

Input:
• Cost data maintenance.
• Labor rate maintenance.
• Machine rate maintenance.

Product costing

Major functions:
• Maintains all cost information on base.
• Provides detailed unit cost sheets.
• Maintains the level and total cost.
• Recosts parts due to bill of material/routing changes.
• Provides several types of overhead absorption.
• Provides cost comparisons.
• Maintains current, standards, and simulated costs.
• Maintains material, labor and overhead costs.

Inquiry:
• Summary cost data.
• Labor rates.
• Machine rates.
• Unit cost rollup.

Output reports:
• Cost summary reports.
• Product cost sheets.
• Cost comparisons.
• Standard cost changes.
• Labor and burden rates.
• Cost retrievals.

FIG. 19.18 Product costing.

operations management system transmits inspection operation results for further analysis and follow-up by quality reporting. Inspection results also may come directly from automated inspection and testing devices. Figure 19.19 is a conceptual overview of the key elements of the quality reporting subsystem.

Although the major users of a quality reporting subsystem are often inspection and quality control personnel, production workers, who increasingly are required to be their own inspectors, also need to have access to the system to report results and make inquiries to check performance. Additionally, production supervisors and managers need timely feedback on quality and often perform their own on-line analyses.

Quality reporting subsystems help improve quality control in the following ways:

- Timely review and disposition of discrepant material. The system tracks the location and status of material awaiting disposition and reports this information to the proper personnel.

- Identification of quality trends. The subsystem's rejection analysis reports are printed in a variety of sequences, including those by quality control personnel to uncover causes of quality problems that might otherwise be hidden.

- Quick correction of quality problems. Corrective action notices are automatically generated when the process is no longer in control. These notices allow production and maintenance personnel to correct the problem before large numbers of defective parts are produced.

- Improved supplier selection. Quality reports that analyze purchased-part quality and summarize vendors' quality performance provide buyers with better information for choosing vendors and making them accountable for quality.

A quality reporting subsystem requires certain pieces of information in order to function properly. The data bases used include

1. *Part master,* which contains basic quality data pertaining to a part
2. *Routing,* which contains inspection operation data
3. *Shop order labor and machine tracking,* which contains actual inspection operation results, such as quantity rejected, and reason codes that indicate why a part was rejected
4. *Nonconforming material,* which contains disposition information on rejected material
5. *Purchase order,* which contains the quality specifications and inspection results for purchased parts

Distribution and Shipping. Physical distribution is a major cost area for most businesses. Because of rising energy and labor costs, distribution costs have increased rapidly. Consequently, management must exert greater control over physical distribution costs.

Many companies employ a *two-tier distribution system,* which involves manufacturing plants shipping products to various distribution centers located near customers. The distribution centers, in turn, ship products to the customer. Although this approach improves customer service, it requires additional coordination because of the intermediate layer between seller and buyer. Warehouse operations come into play at either end of the manufacturing pipeline—at the beginning

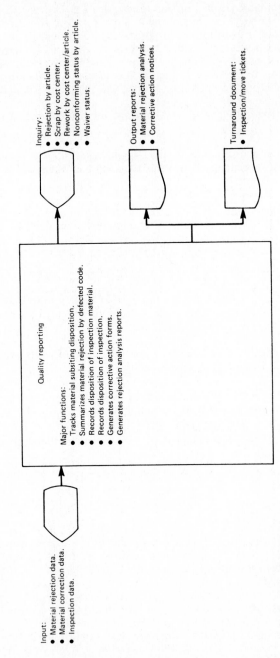

Input:
• Material rejection data.
• Material correction data.
• Inspection data.

Quality reporting

Major functions:
• Tracks material subsiting disposition.
• Summarizes material rejection by defected code.
• Records disposition of inspection material.
• Records disposition of inspection.
• Generates corrective action forms.
• Generates rejection analysis reports.

Inquiry:
• Rejection by article.
• Scrap by cost center.
• Rework by cost center/article.
• Nonconforming status by article.
• Waiver status.

Output reports:
• Material rejection analysis.
• Corrective action notices.

Turnaround document:
• Inspection/move tickets.

FIG. 19.19 Quality reporting.

19.38

as raw materials and purchased parts are received at the plant and at the end as finished products exit from the manufacturing process.

Distribution and shipping subsystems attempt to make receiving, storage, and shipping operations more productive through various means. Voice data-entry devices allow a receiving clerk to enter receipt information on-line without using a keyboard. Bar-code readers, which are used to read bar-coded receipt information from reusable containers, are often found in JIT environments. The subsystem can project labor requirements based on the number of incoming shipments, planned production from the floor, and planned shipments. Also, the system can dynamically assign locations to incoming material based on pallet size and anticipated storage time. It places high-turnover items in closer, more accessible locations and prints picking lists in an optimal picking sequence.

One feature that has a direct impact on costs is *truck building*. The distribution and shipping subsystem can accumulate replenishment orders for a warehouse until a truckload quantity is reached, thereby qualifying the shipment for a truck-load rate. The system also provides performance measurement tools that monitor space utilization, service levels, and labor performance against standards.

The data required for the distribution and shipping subsystem is maintained in several areas. Purchasing supplies information on incoming shipments. The inventory control subsystem transmits a profile of the amount of production that will need to be warehoused. Order-entry subsystems inform warehouse personnel as to what products will need to be shipped and when and allow the distribution and shipping subsystem to print shipping documents. Billing uses shipping information so that it can include the appropriate freight costs on customer invoices. Additionally, warehouse operations systems often interface with automated storage and retrieval systems, which mechanically store the material in the racks (most systems of this type do not even allow people to enter the storage area) and later pick it. A conceptual overview of many elements of a distribution and shipping subsystem is shown in Fig. 19.20.

Users of such systems include warehouse workers, who use the voice data entry terminals to enter receipts, and warehouse supervisors, who use the system's workload projection reports to schedule personnel and material-handling equipment. Warehouse management uses performance reports to plan and control the entire operation. The benefits that these users reap from a distribution and shipping subsystem include

- Reduced clerical effort. Voice data entry and bar-code devices speed data collection and improve accuracy by allowing data to be captured as the transaction occurs.
- Improved scheduling of personnel. Labor and equipment requirements can be projected from planned receipt and shipment data.
- Increased space utilization and improved picking productivity. Dynamic location of material based on size and usage requirements reduces wasted space and shortens travel distances for warehouse personnel who store and pick material.

To achieve these benefits, however, a distribution and shipping system requires certain types of information. The data bases used are

1. *Customer order*, which contains orders placed by customers and is used to generate picking lists
2. *Customer data*, which provides information needed to generate shipping documents

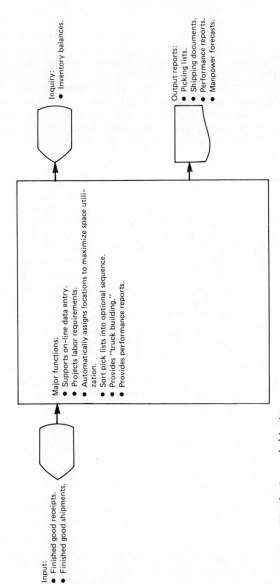

Input:
• Finished good receipts.
• Finished good shipments.

Major functions:
• Supports on-line data entry.
• Projects labor requirements.
• Automatically assigns locations to maximize space utili-
  zation.
• Sort pick lists into optional sequence.
• Provides "truck building."
• Provides performance reports.

Inquiry:
• Inventory balances.

Output reports:
• Picking lists.
• Shipping documents.
• Performance reports.
• Manpower forecasts.

FIG. 19.20 Distribution and shipping.

3. *Stock location balance,* which allows the subsystem to determine from where the material should be picked

4. *Shop order,* which contains the orders that are about to be completed

5. *Part master,* which contains data about the item (such as size, special storage, and packaging requirements).

Inventory Accounting.   The inventory accounting function is responsible for converting inventory activity to ledger entries. An inventory accounting subsystem supports this function by reconciling period beginning and ending inventory values. The activity for each inventory account is summarized and used to calculate the ending balance and net change for the period, including the impact of cost or account code changes.

Inventory accounting also summarizes the value of material and labor flowing into and out of work in process for each open production order. Material usage and labor performance variances are provided when orders are closed. The summary information is supported by optional detailed reports that contain information required by the accounting department to prepare period-end journal entries.

The inventory accounting subsystem interfaces with the inventory control and shop floor control subsystems when they send to inventory accounting material and labor transactions to be costed. In turn, inventory accounting sends material, labor, and overhead charges to be billed to the billing department. It also sends material, labor, and overhead transactions and associated variances to be posted to the general ledger.

Also inventory accounting is integrated with other subsystems that include product costing and purchasing. Product costing maintains standard material, labor, and overhead costs for each part, and purchasing maintains actual price data for material receipts. See Fig. 19.21.

The major users of an inventory accounting subsystem include cost accountants, who report variances between actual and planned costs, cost inventories to meet financial reporting requirements, and analyze costs by order. These users realize the following benefits:

- Reduced manual and clerical effort in the costing process. This reduction results from the automatic interfacing of cost information with the general ledger, the automatic allocation of job costs to each order, and the subsystem's on-line inquiry capabilities.

- More effective management through early detection of cost overruns. This is made possible through the timely comparison of actual costs against standards.

- Improved accuracy and integrity of all cost accounting information through the automatic allocation of inventory adjustments to orders.

To achieve these benefits, an inventory accounting subsystem requires data from a variety of sources. Data bases used by the subsystem include

1. *Part master,* which contains item descriptions and standard cost information

2. *Customer order,* which contains order data for each line item ordered by a customer

3. *Shop order component tracking,* which contains material cost information for in-process manufacturing orders

4. *Shop order labor and machine tracking,* which contains actual and planned machine and labor resources expended for in-process manufacturing orders

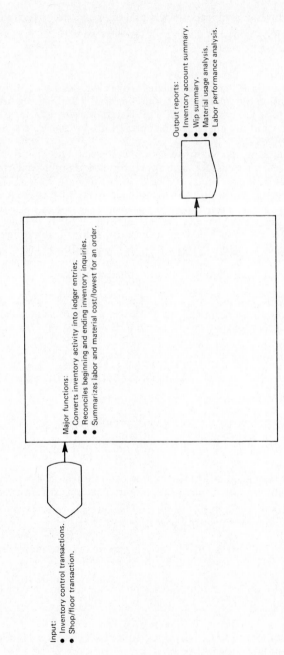

Input:
- Inventory control transactions.
- Shop/floor transaction.

Major functions:
- Converts inventory activity into ledger entries.
- Reconciles beginning and ending inventory inquiries.
- Summarizes labor and material cost/lowest for an order.

Output reports:
- Inventory account summary.
- Wip summary.
- Material usage analysis.
- Labor performance analysis.

FIG. 19.21 Inventory accounting.

19.42

5. *Labor rate,* which contains current and proposed labor rates for use in calculating actual manufacturing labor charges

6. *Machine rate,* which contains current and proposed cost rates by machine for use in calculating actual manufacturing cost for machine-paced operations

7. *Work center or cell,* which contains overhead rates for use in calculating actual manufacturing costs

8. *Purchase order,* which contains material prices for use in calculating amounts to be billed to customers for material purchases

Direct Numeric Control. A direct numeric control (DNC) subsystem maintains the library of NC programs and communicates NC program information to and from computer numeric control (CNC) machine tools according to schedules set by the shop floor control subsystem. Changes in priorities can, therefore, be instantly communicated directly to the machines performing the work. DNC itself provides machine utilization, failure, and status reporting. The same technology can be used to control similar programs for robots, inspection equipment, and other programmable devices. DNC also proves out NC programs, edits them from the shop floor, and creates postprocessed NC programs.

The DNC system is integrated with the CAED system, specifically with the CAM subsystem, which creates and maintains the NC programs distributed by DNC. The shop floor control subsystem provides DNC with continually updated order schedules through a factory supervisor computer. As mentioned earlier, DNC maintains interfaces with the various machine tools in the plant by sending operating instructions to them. The key elements of the DNC subsystem are shown in Fig. 19.22.

The major users of a DNC subsystem are NC programmers, who are responsible for proving out and editing the NC programs, and shop foremen, who are responsible for dispatching orders. Also using DNC, of course, are the machine tool operators, who run the CNC machines.

Two benefits are derived from a DNC subsystem. First, there is improved tape handling. The automated file and library management system eliminates the need for punched paper, Mylar tape, and existing tape verification and procedures for storage, retrieval, and handling. Second, NC program accuracy is improved. Tape errors are eliminated by verification checks.

The data required to operate a DNC subsystem are contained in the NC program data base. Included in this set of files are NC program instructions, such as cutter location data, and programs that have been postprocessed by the system.

Interfacing Systems

Although CIM is a concept that spans a seemingly limitless range of functions, the preceding sections described only the core CIM systems. What follows are brief descriptions of functions or systems that interface with CIM.

Decision Support. As information requirements become more complex and the number of end users increases, it becomes necessary to provide computer support for decision making. This support is typically in the form of information processing tools, which can be easily accessed and manipulated by users. These tools can include simulation languages, fourth-generation languages, such as FOCUS, generalized decision support systems, and application software packages. These decision support tools, no matter what form they take, use the existing data in the CIM data bases.

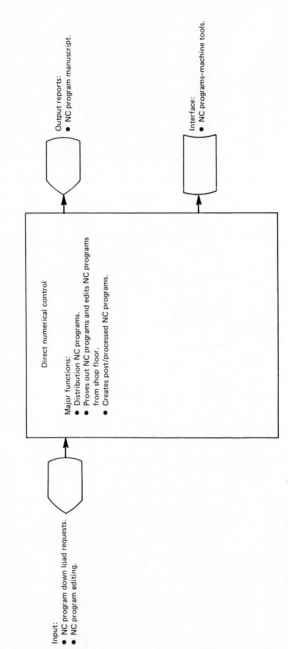

Input:
• NC program down load requests.
• NC program editing.

Direct numerical control

Major functions:
• Distribution NC programs.
• Proves out NC programs and edits NC programs from shop floor.
• Creates post/processed NC programs.

Output reports:
• NC program manuscript.

Interface:
• NC programs–machine tools.

FIG. 19.22 Direct numeric control.

19.44

General Ledger.   A general ledger subsystem controls financing and accounting operations and produces standards and user-defined reports for effective planning and decision making. This subsystem interfaces with inventory accounting to receive material, labor, and overhead costs; accounts payable to receive accounts payable entries; and billing to receive summary invoice data. Report-writer packages are often used to quickly provide ad hoc reports.

Order Entry.   An order-entry subsystem provides a high degree of contact with customers and important input to the master scheduling system. An order-entry clerk enters the customer order, using a display terminal which causes the system to display the necessary information, such as ship-to address, terms, calculated prices, and messages. At the same time, the system checks credit and inventory availability and, once the order is accepted, reserves inventory and generates a picking and shipping order at the warehouse. If the items are not available, the customer order can serve as an input to the MPS. The order-entry system also interfaces with accounts receivable to retrieve current information on a customer's credit standing.

Billing.   The purpose of a billing subsystem is to provide timely invoices to customers. To do this properly, it must interface with the shipping system to receive accurate information on what items have actually been shipped. Billing also interfaces with the order-entry system for customer order information. Included in these data are freight costs, which often are passed on to the customer. The billing system also sends transactions to the accounts receivable system so that customer balances can be updated.

Accounts Payable.   An automated accounts payable system is a tool for conserving and controlling cash in an organization. The accounts payable function is responsible for paying the company's bills in a timely manner, avoiding late fees and finance charges by paying on time, and maximizing the company's cash by remitting payments at the last possible time that does not involve penalty or interest fees. This function is also responsible for ensuring that only authorized payments are made.

   To fulfill these responsibilities, an accounts payable subsystem must be well integrated with the purchasing and general ledger subsystems. Purchasing provides data on purchase commitments made to vendors, and the general ledger subsystem uses payment information to update ledger accounts.

Accounts Receivable.   An accounts receivable system helps improve a business's cash flow by monitoring and controlling the money owed by its customers. A variety of reports and inquiry screens provide information on customer credit histories, open balances, and payments in order to speed up the collection of accounts receivable and avoid extending credit to customers who are poor credit risks. In an integrated financial system, the accounts receivable subsystem receives billing transactions from the shipping and billing systems and updates accounts in the general ledger.

Maintenance.   A maintenance subsystem stores equipment information and maintenance requirements as well as maintenance part inventory information. It controls maintenance activity by scheduling preventive maintenance and captures and tracks all maintenance and repair activity and costs by work order. The subsystem has a number of users, including general maintenance personnel, who maintain the equipment; facilities planners, who purchase equipment and maintain equipment master files; factory personnel, who inquire about the status of maintenance work orders; and methods and standards engineers, who inquire into the technical capabilities of machines found on the equipment master files.

A subsystem such as this helps reduce maintenance costs by automatically scheduling preventive maintenance at nondisruptive times rather than in response to machine breakdowns. Additionally, equipment history reports highlight malfunctioning equipment, and work orders can be automatically generated by the subsystem, thereby reducing clerical effort.

Maintenance subsystems can be integrated with the shop floor control subsystem to track machine usage information necessary to schedule preventive maintenance.

MAKE-TO-ORDER
AND DEFENSE CONTRACTOR CONSIDERATIONS

Manufacturers who build products specifically to customer orders are said to operate in a make-to-order environment. Labor and material costs and inventory may have to be tracked by individual customer order, even though the production process is most efficiently run in lot sizes that require orders and inventories to be commingled. Defense contractors are found at the end of the spectrum of make-to-order manufacturers, having to meet a multitude of government requirements for reporting cost and schedule status by contract.

A make-to-order environment complicates the manufacturing systems in several ways. Although orders and inventory should be controlled traditionally without regard to contract for efficiency purposes, contract allocation information must be maintained for progress payment and financial reporting purposes. This includes the tracking of inventory borrow and payback between contracts. Engineering changes often need to be tracked by serial number, and a history of the as-built configuration should be maintained.

JUST-IN-TIME REQUIREMENTS PLANNING

Manufacturers operating in a JIT production environment differ dramatically from those in traditional operations. Manufacturing lead times and lot sizes are a fraction of traditional ones, and production schedules are expressed in terms of rates per day rather than orders. Control and tracking of production are achieved more through the visibility of material as it flows through the process than by logging and reporting systems. Material movement is controlled through a "pull" system that requests parts only as they are needed, as opposed to a conventional "push" system that moves the parts according to a schedule.

In many aspects, a JIT environment simplifies manufacturing systems. The scope and complexity of shop floor control, capacity planning, and inventory accounting are reduced significantly. In other ways, it necessitates changes in the processing logic. Production must be scheduled by manufacturing cell rather than work center, to reflect the shop layout. Owing to the small lot sizes, production is reported without reference to an order number. Purchasing must process frequent vendor deliveries.

Kanban control is a new subsystem that is unique to a JIT environment. In some ways, it replaces shop floor control by using *kanbans*, or cards, to authorize the production and movement of containers of parts. Because the number of kanbans determines the amount of inventory on the floor, a system is needed to regulate the number of cards in existence, based on demand, production lead time, delivery lead time, and safety stock policies. Kanban control should also be able to print new kanbans that have bar codes for efficient transaction reporting.

PROCESS INDUSTRY CONSIDERATIONS

Manufacturers who produce material that is indistinguishable from other quantities of that material are said to operate in the process industry or to use process manufacturing techniques. An oil refinery is an extreme example, where one gallon of gasoline is physically indistinct from another gallon. Process industry manufacturers share some special systems needs with both make-to-order and JIT companies. They are similar to make-to-order environments in that production and inventories often need to be tracked by batches because of legal and regulatory requirements, just as make-to-order companies must track by contract. Just-in-time manufacturers try to emulate their counterparts in the process industry by moving material through the shops in a continuous flow, with a minimum of throughput time.

The process industry differs from discrete manufacturing, however, in that it is usually capacity-constrained rather than material-constrained. This has several additional manufacturing systems implications. Product structures must reflect quantities per batch rather than per parent. Yield factors and shelf life limitations are necessary. Routings typically require overlapping operations. Legal requirements may include inventory tracking by batch and expiration date. Labor may be a small portion of total costs and not charged against a manufacturing order.

BIBLIOGRAPHY

Arthur Andersen and Co.: *MAC-PAC Manufacturing Planning and Control System*, Chicago, 1982.

Hall, Robert: *Zero Inventories*, Dow Jones-Irwin, Homewood, Ill., 1983.

Martin, Andre: *DRP: Distribution Resource Planning*, Prentice-Hall, Englewood Cliffs, N.J., 1983.

Orlicky, Joseph: *Material Requirements Planning*, McGraw-Hill, New York, 1975.

Wight, Oliver: *Production and Inventory Management in the Computer Age*, CBI Publishing, Boston, 1974.

CHAPTER 20

Computers in Manufacturing

Editor

DONALD W. FOGARTY, Ph.D., CFPIM, Professor of Operations Management, Southern Illinois University, Edwardsville, Illinois

Contributors

TIMOTHY ALBERT, Engineer, Allied Automotive/Bendix Chassis and Brake Components Division, South Bend, Indiana

TIMOTHY J. GREENE, Ph.D., Associate Professor, Department of Industrial Engineering and Operations Research, Virginia Polytechnique University, Blacksburg, Virginia

O. JOHN HOWARD, Senior Manager, Technical Products, McCormick & Dodge, Irvin, Texas

KEITH R. PLOSSL, Vice President, George Plossl Educational Services, Inc., Atlanta, Georgia

RICHARD E. PUTNAM, Ph.D., System Analyst, Boeing Computer Services, Seattle, Washington

Applications of computer technology have changed manufacturing processes and manufacturing management. Most chapters in this book describe principles and techniques that are implemented by computerized systems. Material-requirements planning (MRP), forecasting, and capacity-requirements planning (CRP) are three examples. This chapter focuses on some uses of computers in manufacturing not covered in other chapters. It concerns robots, computer-aided design (CAD), computer-aided manufacturing (CAM), group technology (manufacturing cells and flexible manufacturing systems), loading and scheduling manufacturing cells, information system requirements, computer-integrated manufacturing, and software for training.

ROBOTS

A robot is an automatic device or apparatus that performs specific functions repetitively. In the first generation, robots repetitively performed fixed tasks without adapting to the environment. Because of primitive interfaces between the robot and its environment, cycles would be repeated regardless of whether items (material, parts, or assemblies) were in position. Present-generation robots can react to changes in the environment of their workspace as well as to other machinery around them.

A typical robot has three primary components: a manipulator, or arm, that performs the work; a power supply that may be pneumatic, hydraulic, or electric; and a controller that controls the other two units as well as peripheral devices when applicable. The control unit also may monitor the environment including the presence, properties, and orientation of items.

Classes

Robots are classified on the basis of the method in which the controller interfaces with the actuator. The three basic methods are non-servo-controlled, point-to-point servo-controlled, and continuous-path servo-controlled.

Non-servo-controlled robots use mechanical stops and limit switches to control the point-to-point movements of the manipulator in which only endpoint positions of the manipulator are specified and controlled. These robots follow a prescribed limited sequence repetitively. These generally are reliable, simple, and the least expensive to operate and maintain.

Point-to-point servo-controlled manipulators can move anywhere within a prescribed working envelope. The manipulator's positioning is very accurate and adjustable. Programming is done by manually moving the actuator through the desired work path. At each critical point the position is entered and recorded in the controller's memory. Operation is achieved by simply replaying the recorded points. The controller itself usually interpolates the path that the actuator follows. In most cases speed, acceleration, and deceleration can be programmed into the controller. The robot is controlled by a microcomputer control unit which can store a series of programs and can execute the programs upon command. These capabilities provide the point-to-point servo-controlled robot with much greater flexibility than the non-servo-controlled unit.

The continuous-path servo-controlled robot follows a precise path at specified speeds. Mechanical stops and limit switches are used to control the servo-controlled units and the non-servo controlled unit. But in the case of servo-controlled units, these stops and switches act more as safety features than as primary controls. Both the continuous-path and the point-to-point servo-controlled units have the ability to be taught and to play back the positional points of the manipulator. Thus the robot can position itself accurately. If the controller has sufficient capacity, the robot may be programmed by a "walk through" by the operator. By graphing the manipulator in the computer memory while moving it through a path in a teaching mode, the controller can be made to memorize the cycle so that it can repeat the cycle when switched to an operational mode.

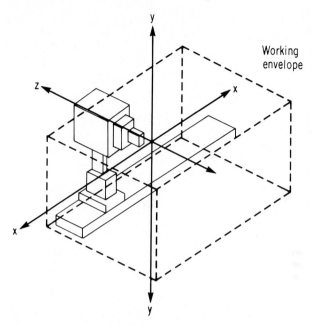

FIG. 20.1 Robot's area of work.

Arm Geometry

The robot's area of work (Fig. 20.1) is based on the envelope into which the manipulator can operate the wrist and hand assembly. A variety of possible geometric configurations can affect arm movement, but for the most part robot manufacturers use the following four types: cartesian coordinate, rectangular coordinate, spherical coordinate, and jointed coordinate geometries. See Fig. 20.2.

Each configuration has a different shape and volume depending on the arm linkage and its length. For different applications, various configurations are appropriate. A revolute arm might be best for reaching into a tub, while a cyclindrical arm is usually best for a straight thrust between the dies of a punch press. In every case the arm carries a wrist assembly to orient its hand according to the workpiece placement. The wrist provides three types of movement, *pitch, roll,* and *yaw.* These three movements provide universal orientation of the hand.

Hands

Robots have earned the reputation of being for general-purpose automation, but the hands are not as flexible and may have to be specially designed along with the special tooling requirements for a specific job. The method selected to grasp and handle an item depends mainly on its properties. Specifically, the type of hand and how hard it grasps the part depend on the type of material, weight of the part, friction between the part and hand, the speed at which the robot must move, and the relationship between the direction of movement and the hand's position at the beginning and endpoint. Hand options include mechanical grippers, hooks to grab

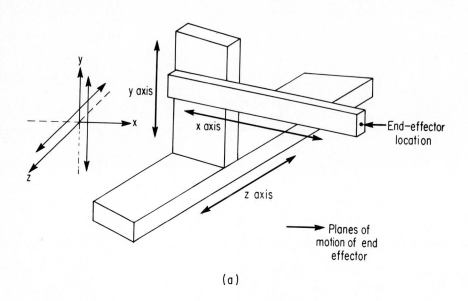

(a)

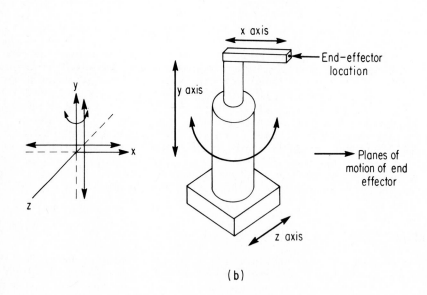

(b)

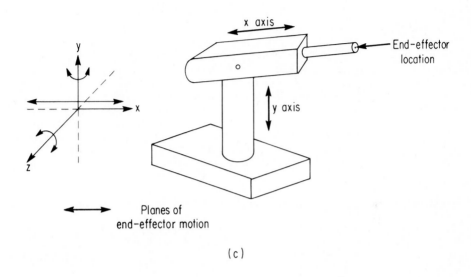

(c)

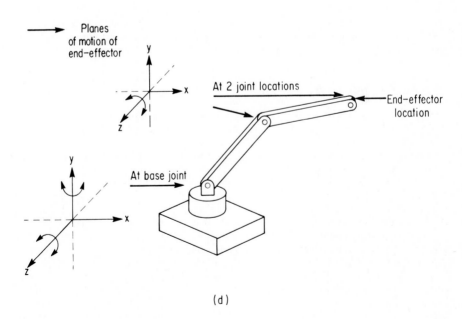

(d)

FIG. 20.2 Robot geometry: (a) cartesian coordinate geometry; (b) rectangular coordinate geometry; (c) spherical coordinate geometry; (d) jointed coordinate geometry.

a part, a spatula for lifting and transferring a part, scoop for ladling, electromagnets, vacuum cups, sticky adhesive-covered fingers, quick-disconnect bayonet sockets, and special-purpose tools such as welding guns and spray guns.

Drive Systems

Robot actuators can be driven by electric, pneumatic, hydraulic, or some combination of these systems, depending on the performance requirements. The simple limiter sequence robot usually has a pneumatic drive because it is less expensive and is inherently simple and easy to maintain. However, the pneumatic drive system does not have a method to easily control either speed or positioning. Electrically driven systems are fast, reliable, and accurate in simple applications. Hydraulic drives are used in the larger applications where greater weight-carrying capability is required. They are accurate and have a long life as well as being cost-efficient and safer for handling flammable material or where fumes are present.

Dynamic Performance and Accuracy

Emulating the human hand and arm motion is more difficult than it would appear. This difficulty stems from the human's ability to coordinate movement with the interplay of all motor skills and sensory perceptions in a dynamic way. Speed and accuracy are taken for granted in human movement. Speed combined with accuracy is mechanically difficult to achieve and robot design requires a balance between these two objectives. Robot's movements have distinctive mechanical characteristics that may be categorized into start time, accelerations, cruise time, deceleration, and stop. Equating the total robot time to human time would indicate the relative cost or saving possible if a robot were used.

Matching Robots to the Workplace

Part orientation, interlocks and sequence control, and workplace layout and limitations all figure prominently in determining a specific robot application.

Part Orientation.   Few robots have sight and touch capabilities because the technology is expensive to provide and consequently not cost-effective. To overcome this problem, robots need to have parts presented to them in a precise position. This position involves both the input and output of the workplace. When the robot reaches for a new workpiece to process, it reaches to a predetermined starting point. Parts being fed to the robot must be presented accurately in a predetermined place where the robot expects to find them. There can be one or more points. The positions can be predetermined, for instance, 24 separate points for a pallet containing 24 holes. The holes will be filled in a predetermined pattern. Limit switches or other devices can signal the robot when part orientation is inadequate. Robots generally cannot correctly select an item from a group of randomly piled parts.

Interlock and Sequence Control.   To establish a good working relationship between the robot and its associated equipment, interlocks and sensors have to be provided to replace the senses of a human operator. These are some examples of interlocks and sequence controls:

- Mechanically operated limit switches are clamped to machine slides, conveyors, or to any place where the position of a moving part is critical to starting or stopping the robot sequence.
- Microswitches are useful in conjunction with end stops to act as limit switches or to sense conditions such as pallet weight.
- Photoelectric devices can sense the presence of an object when that object interrupts a beam of light.
- Pressure switches can be arranged to monitor the pressure of air lines or hydraulic feeds to sense when an object has been properly grasped.
- Vacuum switches are used on robots with a vacuum-type pickup to indicate complete vacuum before the pickup is made.
- Infrared detectors are capable of detecting the presence or absence of hot material.
- Signals from other electronic control systems can activate the robot control system.

Because it is possible to both send and receive signals to and from associated equipment and to use this information at any desired point in the robot program (sequence of movements), a computer-controlled robot can accept complete control over any required sequence of operations. If all possible alternative actions are anticipated during the design process, the sophisticated industrial robot with a large memory is able to respond to a significant number of inputs with a full range of outputs. Thus it can nearly emulate the spontaneous behavior associated with human hands.

Workplace Layout. The ideal workplace configuration reflects the following:

1. Arrange work around the robot by placing the robot in a fixed position and arranging the work so as to accommodate the limits of the robot. This involves the least commitment and the least disruption of existing workplace arrangements.
2. Move the work past the robot by the addition of a computer control. The robot can be made to track a workpiece which is being carried on a conveyor, performing a task as the work passes.
3. Move the robot to the work when machining cycles are particularly long. A robot can be mounted on a track and thereby travel among more machines than can be grouped conveniently around a stationary robot. For instance, a robot mounted on an overhead track can travel back and forth to service several machines as their cycles require, and the entire installation can be controlled by a central computer which instructs both the machines and the robot.

The tracking function of a robot can be accomplished by either moving or stationary baseline tracking. *Moving baseline tracking* exists when the robot is mounted on some form of transportation system, such as a rail and carriage, which moves parallel to the line of work flow and at line speed. In *stationary baseline tracking* the robot is mounted in a fixed position relative to the line. This is a more economical installation.

Workplace Limitations. In installations where the robot hand has to enter hot and hostile environments, it is desirable to eliminate all electric and servo devices from the robot's extremities to reduce accidents and failures. Usually a robot is packaged as a self-contained unit. But when the robot is subject to severe vibrations, it is better to mount the control console on a shock-absorbing pad. Complete isolation of the robot arm from the power supply is necessary in explosive atmospheres such as paint rooms.

Robot joints are covered by rubber boots to protect them from abrasive dust or other contamination. Also, when hot metal is being handled, robot casing must be nonflammable. A partial answer to fire hazards is to use nonflammable fluids for lubrication and hydraulics. If the air is dirty, water cooling may be necessary.

The robot control unit should be protected from power line surges and electronic noise being picked up from surrounding equipment by the robot's communication links. If this is not done, incorrect cycling is likely.

Applications

Robots are particularly useful for performing hazardous, tedious, boring, or uncomfortable tasks. Robots are particularly well suited for pouring molten metal into molds and for loading and unloading presses. They also are used successfully in palletizing parts and removing parts from a conveyor. Their use in spot welding is widespread, especially in the automotive industry. Arc-welding robots can often double or triple the production rates of human workers. Also robots can be used for some machining operations such as drilling and in assembly operations that are standardized.

Continuous-path servo robots are useful for spray painting. Applications to spray painting require a constant paint delivery rate, proper and constant paint and air pressures, proper positioning of the item being painted, and a monitoring of these factors.

COMPUTER-AIDED DESIGN

CAD is the use of computers to help in the process of designing physical objects. Computer graphics, and particularly interactive computer graphics, is the backbone of CAD. Using CAD, a designer or engineer can create an image of an object and associated data describing the object and then use CAD's graphical capabilities to observe the object in different views, projections, rotations, magnifications, and cross sections.

Technology

A CAD system commonly employs a minicomputer, although a mainframe computer or a microcomputer may be used in some cases. A typical CAD workstation includes a graphics display unit that generates computer-drawn pictures or images; a number of interactive devices, such as alphanumeric keyboard, function keys, tablet, mouse, or joystick (cursor-moving devices); and a graphic digitizer as well as a plotter for hard-copy output. The CAD system requires sufficient memory and mass storage for the software and data. The system may have multiple workstations, each sharing the computer's processing resources, data storage, and hard-copy output devices.

Initially, the computers that supported CAD and interactive graphics were large-scale machines with complex hardware needs and channel-attached display consoles. These systems were rather expensive—one display console could cost $250,000. Aerospace companies, the automotive industry, government, and some universities were the few that could afford to buy and maintain these systems. Minicomputers provided the cost relief needed to get interactive graphics systems into more environments, and CAD software soon followed, The recent microcomputer revolution reveals a similar scenario. Microcomputer systems with graphics are being introduced into many new locations, and interactive capabilities are being added with joysticks, mouse cursor controls, tablets, and plotters. Already sophisticated CAD systems with three-dimensional geometry capabilities are available for desktop computer systems, and they cost much less than the earlier systems. Even simple CAD systems that can be run on home-type computers cost no more than a few thousand dollars.

Operation

A CAD system allows both geometric and nongeometric information to be created during an interactive design session with a designer using the computer and its related tools to define the information that represents an object. A designer, looking at the display screen and moving the cursor with one of the interactive devices, selects and invokes specific software functions to construct an image of the object to be designed. The construction and manipulation capabilities seem limitless and include two-dimensional, three-dimensional, surface, and solid-image constructs, often combining "primitives" such as lines, arcs, spheres, and cubes to create complex objects.

Data

Although the interactive graphics workstation is the heart of a CAD system, from the viewpoint of the designer sitting in front of the display screen, the true core of a productive CAD system is the data and data base that give meaning to the images produced by the CAD designer.

If there are no engineering data that coexist with the graphics,the benefits of the graphics are limited. The first attempts to give meaning to engineering-oriented computer graphic images involved putting annotations such as engineering dimensions and text on the pictures, to produce an engineering drawing. Thus drafting became one of the first applications of the interactive graphics computer systems. So the first meaning of CAD was computer-aided *drafting*, rather than computer-aided *design*. Over time, some systems that could do drafting were enhanced to perform other engineering functions, and it is appropriate to call these CAD systems true computer-aided design systems.

COMPUTER-AIDED MANUFACTURING

CAM means the use of computers to program, direct, and control manufacturing processing and handling equipment. The use of a computer to aid in manufacturing has developed from the use of numerical control (NC) machine tools, or NC machines. The first NC machines were controlled by electronic signals coming from controllers that read computer-punched paper tape. CAM today frequently involves some form of direct computer control. This may take many forms, but in general it ranges from providing extensive remote computing to a local computer attached directly to the machine tool. When significant computing power is at the machine tool itself, it is commonly referred to as computer numeric control (CNC); when the computer is some distance from the machine tool and is connected in some electronic way, it is usually called *direct numeric control* (DNC).

CNC is found in virtually all new machine tool controllers in some form. Usually CNC involves a microprocessor, some memory, and perhaps a more modern form of the paper tape, such as a floppy disk or magnetic-tape cassette.

DNC provides a direct link from a host computer to the machine tool. Thus the numeric instructions for the tool are sent electronically rather than via tape. Along with direct computer control of machine tools comes the concept of distributed numeric control whereby a computer of sufficient power feeds instructions to more than one machine tool at a time.

Numeric-control of machine tools and the modern derivations of this (CNC and DNC) all provide the potential for increasing productivity, but have also brought increasing requirements for computer accuracy, performance, and configuration control.

CAD/CAM Relationship

CAD and CAM have grown up rather independently. CAD is a product of engineering design and analysis, while CAM is in the domain of manufacturing. However, it is not unusual for CAD systems to be used in manufacturing engineering to design tooling for the manufacture of parts. But within engineering areas, automatically programmed tools (APT) programming, usually associated with programming of machine tools, has been used to advantage for the generation of engineering design drawings, particularly where complex or repetitive shapes are required.

It is only natural for there to be interest in providing some form of interaction and interfacing between the worlds of engineering and manufacturing. The interfacing that initially occurs is for some agreement on the form of the data used to represent the design of a product, so they can be used by the designer and by manufacturing. One simple way of doing this is by edict, where management decrees that the computer data generated by the engineering department can be read by the manufacturing personnel, such as tool designers and NC programmers.

A step above interfacing these areas is to provide some form of integration. Currently a number of terms connote this true merging of the minds of engineering and manufacturing: CAD/CAM when written as one word, computer-aided engineering (CAE), and computer-integrated manufacturing (CIM).

No matter what one calls it, the influx of the computer into the world of design and manufacturing will have greater impact than just interfacing CAD and CAM as defined here. That is, there is a great deal more than just providing parts drawings and computer data with CAD systems that can later be read by CAM systems. For example, the areas of part synthesis, analyses, part inspection, testing, quality control, inventory control, and ordering all become a part of a factory's global intergrated system.

As mentioned previously, the true center of the CAD process is the engineering graphics data that make the computer-generated drawings meaningful. In a similar way, the center of the CAD/CAM process is the data base that gives meaning to the design and manufacturing process. As shown in Fig. 20.3, this data base is at the hub of a wheel. This data base is a collection of all the information that describes the

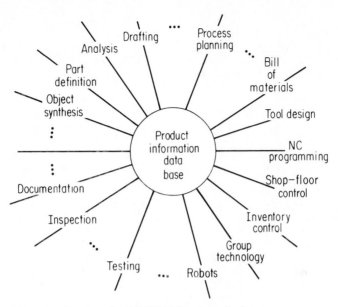

FIG. 20.3 Data base for CAD/CAM function wheel.

computer-designed products. The spokes of the wheel represent various engineering and manufacturing functions. These functions include object synthesis, part/object definition, analysis, drawing and drafting, process planning, bill of materials, tool and fixture design, NC programming, shop floor control, inventory control, group technology, assembly machines and robots, testing, inspection, technical documentation, and many others.

CAD/CAM Operations

The operation of this integrated system might be something like the scenario in Fig. 20.4. The design process starts with a concept being developed in rough sketch form and preliminary design and analysis being done by defining and manipulating two- or three-dimensional geometry by using a CAD system. These preliminary data, which are both geometric and nongeometric, are refined by the analysis group who might apply a mesh generation scheme to the three-dimensional geometry so that finite-element modeling could be done for heat transfer and stress analysis. This refinement and enhancing process will continue until certain "master dimensions and master characteristics" are established. At this point, preliminary manufacturing planning can take place, since the data base contains enough specific information for make-or-buy decisions and deciding whether CAD should be used for specific items. At this point, engineering work statements can be made along with development schedules and advanced material requests. The design process continues with the detailed design of the product, including initial tool and fixture designs, all done on the CAD system. As final drawings and/or computer data are officially released, the manufacturing groups begin to make final production and assembly plans, and the engineering data become officially available to the NC groups and part programmers.

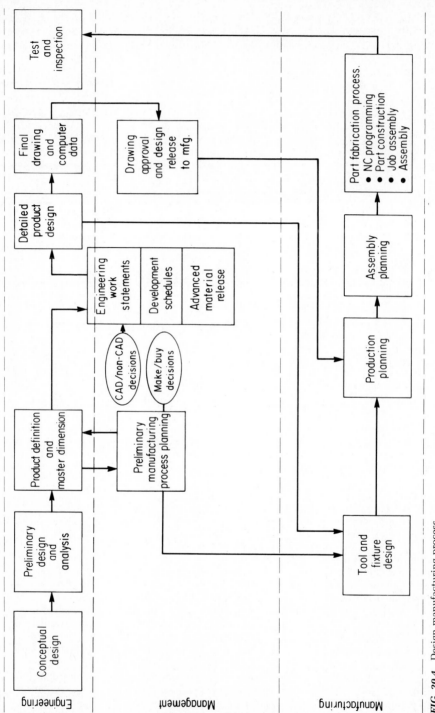

FIG. 20.4 Design manufacturing process.

The preceding description is a simplistic view of the design and manufacturing process; it leaves out most of the management and business operations that are taking place concurrently. However, the illustration of the process shown in Fig. 20.4 is reasonable from an engineering viewpoint. Note that the engineering data bases traditionally have not considered the needs of the manufacturing control system. It would be nice to be able to report that one of the prime outputs of all CAD systems is a structured parts list, but this is not true today. Certainly some CAD systems provide parts lists, but there is no provision for issuing a totally automated bill of materials.

Clearly one prerequisite for an effective MRP system is to have an accurate, timely bill of materials, but in many CAD systems this is done manually. First, the geometry of the object is created: then the computer operator manually attaches various "attribute tags" to this computer-based geometry data. These associated tags are carried along with but separate from the geometry data. One reason for doing this manually is that most CAD systems are, or were originally, just drafting systems intent on producing an engineering drawing. The drawing represents a real object, but the computer does not understand whether the collection of lines on the computer image represents surfaces or solid objects. The image is just an organized set of lines, curves, and text. Thus the data base cannot possibly know that certain lines represent a bolt and other lines represent a specific subassembly. The ongoing development of CAD systems is changing all this, but the established set of CAD systems in use today, for the most part, do not adequately handle bills of materials. Neither do they do a particularly good job of providing part numbers for individual parts or for assemblies. They also do not offer much in the way of computer support for engineering changes.

This is not to say that these capabilities are not being developed. Other computer programs have been, and are being, developed to cover some of the areas where CAD systems have been deficient. These programs are not thought of as CAD, but they certainly support CAD and support the entire design manufacturing process. For example, one computer system might support the control of engineering drawings by assigning numbers to drawings and drawing change notices and making sure that all outstanding drawing change notices are accounted for. Another computer system, or perhaps the same one, might be used interactively to "release" drawings and provide data on drawing revision levels. This system also might provide an interface to a parts-list computer system, by providing the date when the master file parts-list program is updated and then passing on the parts-list data to that system. Individual parts lists, when they are entered into an automated parts-list system, might then be the link between CAD systems and other business systems.

CAD systems of the future, capable of handling data that truly represent objects, will have many of these features. And these important functions will be supported in an automated and integrated way.

GROUP TECHNOLOGY

Group technology is an approach that identifies items with either similar design characteristics or similar manufacturing process characteristics and groups them into families of like items. Group technology is based on the premise that the number of substantially different processes are relatively small in comparison to the number of existing items.

Analysis of the designs of existing items frequently leads to the discovery of identical items, same design with different part number, and other items with very similar designs. Redundant designs can be eliminated, and similar designs can be combined on a single drawing. Analyzing manufacturing processes can lead to the discovery of many similar processes and the development of standardized processes and setups with minor modifications for each item, resulting in savings in engineering and manufacturing. Once similar manufacturing processes have been determined, the economic feasibility of one or more manufacturing cells can be evaluated. A *manufacturing cell* is a small group of workers and/or machines physically arranged in a repetitive production flow layout to manufacture a group of similar items. Use of such cells is known as *cellular manufacturing*.

Coding and Classification

The classification and coding systems are an essential element of group technology. It should provide for ready identification of those characteristics that define a group of parts and that are readily discernible from either an engineering drawing or the manufacturing process. Table 20.1 lists typical characteristics for classifying items. Initial coding may come from examining item descriptions. Many similar size cylindrical parts can be grouped in this manner, as illustrated in Fig. 20.5. Large castings, quite different in appearance but all requiring similar processing, may be easily recognized. Figure 20.6 is an example of such a grouping. Visual examination of shapes and part names is most useful but usually not sufficient for initiating a classification program.

A carefully planned and flexible coding system is essential for the initiation of a classification program and for the application of group technology to ongoing design and manufacturing engineering. Parts classification and coding systems usually are based on part design attributes, manufacturing process attributes, or both design and manufacturing process attributes.

Software packages for coding and classification are commercially available. Selection, or the internal development of such a system, should reflect future as well as present requirements and users.

Manufacturing Cells

A manufacturing cell may consist of a single machine, two or more machines, two or more operators using primarily small tools, or a combination of machines and operators. The essential characteristic is that the equipment be located in a process

TABLE 20.1 Typical Characteristics
for Group Technology Analysis

Design	Process
Geometry (shape)	Machine tools
Material	Major operation
Major dimensions	Minor operation
Minor dimensions	Operation sequence
Weight	Tooling
Width, maximum	Tolerances
Diameter, maximum	Surface finish
Function	Inspection requirements

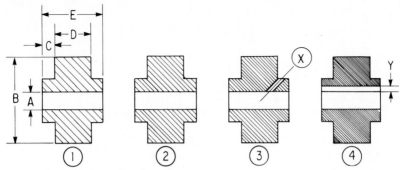

FIG. 20.5 Similar parts based on shape.

FIG. 20.6 Similar parts based on manufacturing process.

flow layout, dedicated to manufacturing a group of similar items. Combining modified equipment, special tooling, and joint orders can lead to reduced material handling, reduced work in process, reduced queues, reduced lead times, reduced setup times, and increased capacity. Figure 20.7 illustrates the difference between a typical functional layout and a manufacturing cell.

The manufacturing cell is arranged in a U configuration. This arrangement enables workers to perform more than one task, facilitates communications among workers, and provides immediate feedback should faulty products in one of the first operations be discovered at a downstream operation. U-shape lines are easier to balance, and the number of production workers can be varied as the load on a cell varies. Classification of manufacturing processes on the basis of machines, illustrated in Table 20.2, reveals rational manufacturing cell candidates.

Job shop
(Functional layout)
(Only a sample of paths included)

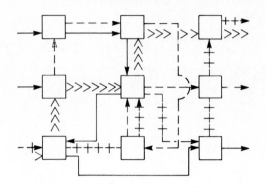

Manufacturing cell

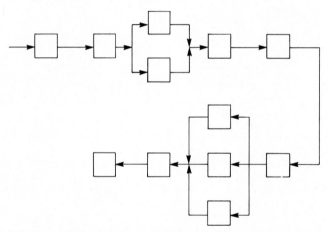

FIG. 20.7 Job shops versus manufacturing cell.

The degree of automation varies widely in manufacturing cells. The degree of computer-controlled machining and material handling (soft automation) usually is the basis for making the distinction between a manufacturing cell and a flexible manufacturing system.

FLEXIBLE MANUFACTURING SYSTEMS

A flexible manufacturing system is an automated cell with integrated material handling and machining equipment that is used to produce a group of parts. Although all the parts require similar manufacturing processes, the sequence of

TABLE 20.2 Classification of Manufacturing Cells

1. Manufacturing cells
    a. Operators set up the machine and perform a portion of the process.
    b. Operators set up the machines, the machine or transfer line is automatic (hard automation), and operators load parts.
2. Flexible manufacturing systems
    a. Computers control
        (1) Machine tools
        (2) Material-handling equipment
        (3) Integration of processing and handling equipment activities
    b. The operators
        (1) Perform emergency and preventive maintenance
        (2) Enter data, for example, part numbers
        (3) Enter new or revised part programs
    c. Either the operators or automated equipment may
        (1) Load materials, say rough castings, into the material-handling system
        (2) Unload completed parts from the material-handling system
        (3) Remove tools and add others to the tool magazines of the different machines

operations is not necessarily the same for each. Some systems consist of a single machine, a multifunction machining center, for example. Computers and software control the material handling and machining. Figure 20.8 is a schematic representation of a typical computer configuration and the information flow controlling a flexible manufacturing system. Operators enter data such as a part number and new or revised part processing programs.

A flexible manufacturing system is dedicated to manufacturing a family (group) of items. In an ideal situation, each item is designed with a standard set of mounting bosses, lugs, holes, and ears or is mounted on a standard plate or frame. Consequently, each item in a group is secured to the table, bed, or faceplate of a machine tool in the same manner as every other item in the group. So it is not necessary to change fixtures while switching from the machining of one part to another. There is no setup time; therefore, a lot size of 1 is economically feasible. In some situations, different mounting fixtures may be required for different parts. An automatic sensing device can recognize these variations and transmit the data so that the computer and software instruct the equipment to make the necessary adjustments.

In the traditional non-computer-controlled machine shop, setup time includes setting and adjusting various dials to control the parameters, such as the length and depth of the cut. This is not necessary in a flexible manufacturing system because each machine tool performs the prescribed operations according to the programmed instructions with an accuracy matching or surpassing that of the best operator. The computer controlling the machine's operation accesses and follows the computer program for machining a particular item. The machine also may have the capability of reading a bar-coded identification on an item and verify its identity. Thus the use of computers and software (soft automation) in a flexible manufacturing system is economical because many different items can be produced automatically and economically in small lot sizes. In contrast, hard automation is capable of producing one type of item in large quantities very efficiently.

Integration of Design and Manufacturing

Group technology through the coding of similar designs and similar processes is a natural focal point for integrating CAD/CAM, facility planning for manufacturing

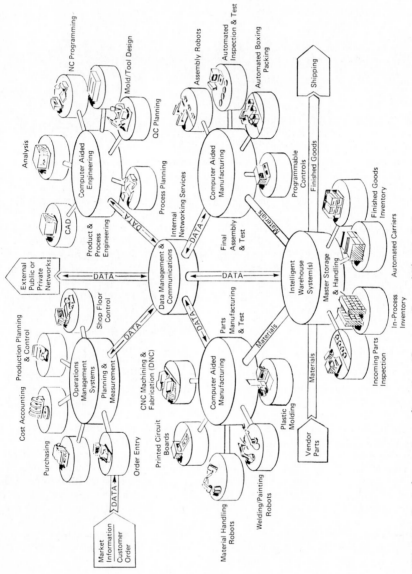

FIG. 20.8 Typical computer configuration. (*Courtesy: General Electric Co.*)

cells and flexible manufacturing systems, and manufacturing planning and control systems such as MRP. See Fig. 20.9. This integration requires the development of a data base accessible to design engineering, manufacturing engineering, and production control. Development of a data base is described later in this chapter.

LOADING AND SCHEDULING THE CELLULAR MANUFACTURING SYSTEM

Cellular manufacturing is the physical division of the manufacturing facility's machinery into production cells, where each cell is designed to produce a specific part family. A *part family* is a set of parts that require similar machinery, tooling, machining operations, and jigs and fixtures. Parts within a family normally are processed from raw material to finished parts within a single cell. Usually the entire manufacturing facility cannot be divided into specialized cells. Rather, a portion of the facility remains as a large, functional job shop, which has been termed the remainder cell. Multiple flexible manufacturing cells within a flexible manufacturing system are very similar to cellular manufacturing systems. Flexible manufacturing cells contain similar cell specializations and encounter similar loading and scheduling difficulties.

Controlling cellular manufacturing systems can be divided into two activities: cell loading and cell scheduling. *Cell loading* involves determining to which cell, among the feasible cells, the job will be assigned. *Cell scheduling* involves the internal control of the jobs within each cell. Scheduling, by definition, is the determination of both the order and the precise start and completion times of each job on each machine. In reality, most viable control schemes do not perform cell

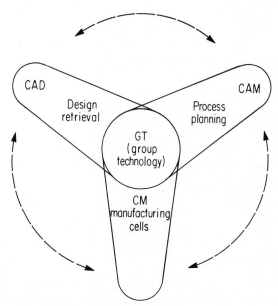

FIG. 20.9 Integrated design and manufacturing.

scheduling, but rather employ cell sequencing. Sequencing is limited to determining the order of the jobs placed on each machine and does not address timing.

The maximum benefits of cellular manufacturing—reduced material handling, setup, tooling, makespan, and in-process inventory—can be attained only if all the operations of a job are assigned to only one cell. If even one operation is assigned to another cell, some cellular manufacturing benefits are lost. Even though a manufacturing facility has well-designed cellular divisions, usually not all jobs can be completely machined in a specialized cell. These odd jobs are assigned to the remainder cell, and so all jobs can be assigned to at least one cell. The jobs that can be machined in one or more specialized cells can usually be machined in the remainder cell also. Hence, all jobs that can be assigned to a specialized cell usually can be assigned to a minimum of two cells. Thus it is imperative that jobs be assigned to the cells in the most efficient manner.

The problem of loading jobs into cells is directly related to system flexibility. *Flexibility* can be defined as the possibility of a job being assigned to more than one cell. With increasing flexibility, cell loading becomes more complex, but the capability of obtaining maximum cell and machine utilization with minimum work in process increases significantly. System flexibility is sometimes defined in terms of job density and machine density.

Cell Characteristics

Many system variables have an effect on cell loading or scheduling methods. These variables can be subdivided into two categories, cell and job characteristics, where the cell characteristics include number of cells, cell size, total number of machine types, cell composition, and remainder cell.

Number. There is no norm for the number of cells in a cellular manufacturing system. Small job shops might split two or three cells from the remainder of the shop. A larger facility might have dozens of cells. Experience has shown that 30 to 40 percent of a facility should remain as a job shop and should not be converted to cells.

A cellular manufacturing objective is to create specialized cells that can process a limited number of different job types. Although a job type should have more than one cell to which it can be assigned feasibly, it should not be capable of being processed in all cells. As the number of cells to which a job can be assigned increases, typical of the situation when the absolute number of cells increases, the loading problem becomes more complex.

In some facilities there is no dependence or interaction between specific groups of cells, thereby allowing analysis of a subset of the entire facility and reducing system complexity. This independence is significant in light of the complexity of the cell loading problem.

Size. The number of machine types per cell defines the cell size. Cell size typically is 3 to 15 machines with the mean number of machines per cell being approximately 6. Note that cell size is extremely user- and industry-specific, so it can vary greatly. As the number of machines in a cell increases beyond six, the advantages of cellular manufacturing appear to decrease. The material-handling problem increases rapidly, as does the effective control and scheduling problem. As the number of machines in a cell decreases below six, the advantages of cellular manufacturing remain, but the disadvantages become more apparent. The number of job types the cell can accept decreases rapidly with a decrease in cell size, thereby decreasing flexibility. With the decrease in the number of job types the cell can accept, the probability of the cell being extremely underutilized increases.

Total Number of Machine Types. The total number of machine types is the sum of the number of machines in the cell that have different capabilities. The total number of machine types directly affects the cell size and the cell composition. As this number increases, it appears that the cell size will increase or the composition of each cell will become more individualized. If the cell size increases, the loading and scheduling problems become more complex. If the cell becomes more individualized, the result is underutilized cells with reduced flexibility.

Cell Composition. Cell composition is a specific cell's machine content. Cell composition is a characteristic that is very difficult to quantify. A change in the composition of a specific cell can increase or decrease the number of feasible cells for several job types. In addition, a change in cell composition can, on one hand, eliminate the only feasible cell for a particular job type or, on the other hand, allow for a new job type.

Remainder Cell. The portion of the job shop that is not converted to a cellular system and comprises 30 to 40 percent of the total facility is the *remainder cell*. Many of the machine types in the remainder cell have very low utilization levels, cannot be moved, or otherwise require a specific facility location. Typically, the few jobs that require these machines are assigned to only the remainder cell. If a job must be diverted from a specialized cell to the remainder cell, then many cellular manufacturing advantages are lost. If the specialized cells have been designed successfully, the number of jobs assigned to the remainder cell compared to the total number of jobs is relatively small. Cell loading becomes more difficult as the number of jobs assigned to the remainder cell, or diverted to the remainder cell after initial machining in a specific cell, increases.

Job Characteristics

The characteristics which define the jobs that flow through the cellular manufacturing system are job routing, number of operations per job, number of different job types, and job mix.

Routing. The order of machines required to complete the job is job routing. For a cellular system it can vary from a flow shop to a modified flow shop to a job shop. When a cellular manufacturing system is designed, one objective is to create each cell as a small flow shop. Although this is an objective, not all the cells in a system are capable of being a flow shop when they are initially designed.

Number of Operations per Job. The ratio of number of operations per job to cell size directly affects and constrains the minimum cell size. As the number of operations per job increases, the number of machines in each cell typically increases. With an increase in cell size, the difficulty of cell loading and scheduling increases substantially.

Number of Different Job Types. A *job type* is defined as having a unique machine routing. The number of different job types is bounded by the job routing, number of operations per job, and total number of machine types. Although a large number of job types provide facility flexibility and capability, the complexity of the cell loading and scheduling problem is significantly increased.

Job Mix. The *job mix* is the composition by job type of the jobs in the system. Typically, a cellular manufacturing system is designed for a single job mix or for a very limited range of job mixes. The job mix can and does vary to some degree over time. And when the job mix does change, machine utilization can decrease while work in process and job lateness can increase. Because the imbalance between cells cannot be overcome, cell loading and scheduling are more difficult.

Cell Selection and Loading Concepts

Cell loading involves determining to which cell, among feasible cells, the job should be assigned. Cell loading is similar to capacity scheduling, capacity planning, shop loading, and workload balancing. The overall objectives of a cellular manufacturing system may vary from minimizing in-process inventory to minimizing lateness, to maximizing machine utilization. In general, to meet these objectives, the operational objective should be to balance the load throughout the system. *Load* can be defined as the total number of hours of work committed to a cell or to a specific machine within a cell. Balance indicates apportioning the load such that no one cell or machine is carrying an undue load. There are three pseudo objectives inherent to cell loading: (1) balance the cell loads among cells, (2) balance the machine loads within each cell, and (3) balance the proportion of jobs with large processing times and jobs with small processing times between and within cells.

By balancing the load between cells, no one cell is overburdened, thereby necessitating overtime, reducing employee morale, and causing excessive work in process. The same arguments hold for balancing the loads within each cell. The bottleneck effect of one overloaded machine within a cell becomes obvious very quickly. The concept of balancing large and small jobs is not so obvious. The appropriate analogy is trying to force large rocks versus sand through a funnel. The sand will conform easier than the rocks, and the rocks will interfere with each other and cause blockages. The same result holds for jobs going through a cellular manufacturing system. If a few large jobs are assigned to a cell or machine, their long processing times will cause multiple bottlenecks over time.

The cell loading process requires that two tasks be completed. First, determine which job should be loaded; second, determine which cell should be loaded. These two tasks can be accomplished in either order. If a job is identified first (task 1), then a cell should be selected, which is task 2. This assignment procedure is considered to have *job priority*. If the cell is identified first, which is task 1, and then a job selected, which is task 2, then the assignment procedure is considered to have *machine priority*.

Both jobs and cells possess attributes. A job's primary attributes are its routing, operation time, and processing time. *Processing time* is the sum of the operation times. An *operation time* is the production time required on a specific machine. A cell's primary attributes are its cell load and individual machine loads. The *cell load* is the sum of the individual machine loads divided by the number of machines in the cell. A *machine load* is the sum of operation times for all jobs assigned to a cell requiring a particular machine. Job and cell attributes are employed as criteria to determine the order and select the job or the cell.

The activity of assigning jobs to cells, be it job priority or machine priority, can be either a single- or multiple-pass activity. For a single-pass activity, once a job is assigned to a cell, the assignment does not change. For a multiple-pass activity, a job can be reassigned as many times as necessary. Typically, a multiple-pass activity assigns all jobs on the first pass, and then jobs are removed from the cells and reassigned so as to better balance the system. The criterion for reassignment does not have to be the same criterion employed for the first assignment. The multiple-pass activity usually gives a slightly better system load than a single-pass activity, but requires additional computation time.

In the following paragraphs we briefly discuss the two basic approaches to loading, job priority and machine priority. A job priority method first identifies a job to assign and then selects a cell to which the job could feasibly be assigned. From the job's attributes, criteria to identify a job can be established, and from the cell's attributes, criteria to select a cell can be established. Note that the cell selection criteria apply only to feasible cells.

The concept behind applying the job identification criteria is to determine those jobs that will have the largest impact when they are assigned. By assigning the job with the largest processing times, largest operation time(s), or largest difference in operation times to a cell first, the smaller jobs or jobs with more uniform operation times can be used to smooth and balance the cell and machine loads. Conversely, utilizing the cell selection criteria first enables one to find the least loaded cell or machine, or the cell with the largest difference in machine loads. By assigning jobs to these cells, the overall balance between cells and between machines can be improved.

For a job priority method, the job identification is static. By *static* it is meant that once the order of jobs to be assigned is established, it will not change as jobs are assigned. With the static method, the effort to identify the job is simplified, for it must be performed only once. Cell selection is dynamic, and a new cell must be determined after each job is assigned.

An advantage of the job priority method is that it is possible to ascertain the large or ungainly jobs and load them first because job identification precedes cell selection. A disadvantage is that the last jobs to be loaded might have to be assigned to a highly loaded cell or machine because of job/cell feasibility and because cell selection follows job identification.

The second basic method of cell loading is machine priority. A machine priority method first identifies a cell and then selects a job that could be feasibly assigned. From the cells' attributes, criteria can be determined to identify the cell which should be loaded. From the jobs' attributes, criteria to select the feasible job for assignment can be established. Again, note that the job selection criteria apply to feasible jobs only. Both the cell identification and job selection are dynamic for machine priority. Thus both cell identification and job selection must be determined each time a job is assigned.

The concept behind applying cell identification is to determine those cells and/or machines that have the least load or to identify the cell that has large differences between machine loads. Cells with these distinguishing characteristics should be loaded before the heavily loaded or balanced cells. Conversely, job selection is based on determining the job which will have the largest impact on the identified cell or machine. A job with large processing time, large operation times, or large differences in operation times might have a large impact on the identified cell.

An advantage of the machine priority method is that it is possible to ascertain the critical cell or machine and to load jobs to alleviate that critical situation, because cell identification precedes job selection. A disadvantage is that there might not be an available job to satisfy the critical cell or machine because job selection follows cell identification.

A Job Priority Loading Heuristic

The two useful loading heuristics, job priority loading (JPL) and machine priority loading (MPL), deserve a thorough definition. A job priority loading heuristic first identifies a job and then selects a cell to which to assign the job. Step 1 of the JPL method identifies and assigns those jobs that can go to one and only one cell. Step 1 also computes the cell and machine loads for those jobs.

Step 2 is to place in rank order those jobs that can go to more than one cell. The rank order should be in decreasing magnitude of each job's maximum operation time. In other words, find each job's maximum operation time and rank the job that has the largest operation time first; second largest, second; etc.

Step 3 is to select feasible cells for each job, proceeding in ranked order determined in step 2. The cell selected should be a feasible cell that has the minimum cell load. The cell load is the sum of the machine loads for the machines required by that job being loaded. The assignment progresses through the ranked order of jobs until all jobs have been assigned.

JPL is a very simple loading heuristic. The only inputs necessary are initial cell and job loads, jobs' operation times, jobs' routings, and job cell feasibility. In addition, once the job ranking is determined, it does not have to be recomputed. The cell loads are the only information that needs to be determined after each job is loaded.

A Machine Priority Loading Method

Machine priority loading (MPL) is a much more complex and time-consuming method than JPL. The MPL method first identifies a cell and then selects a job to which to assign that cell. MPL is similar to JPL in that step 1 assigns all jobs that can go to one and only one cell. MPL is also similar to JPL in that it is a single-pass activity method.

Step 2 is to identify the minimum loaded machine (key machine) within the minimum loaded cell (key cell). If all cells or machines are equally loaded, the heuristic picks the first cell as the key machine. With the key machine identified, MPL moves to step 3.

Step 3 determines the set, set A, of jobs that can be assigned feasibly to the key cell and that require the key machine. If set A is empty and there are no feasible jobs to be assigned, the method reverts to step 2 to find the next minimum loaded machine within the minimum loaded cell. This machine then becomes the key machine. If there is no feasible job for the key cell, the process selects the minimum loaded machine in the second lowest loaded cell as the key machine and key cell. If set A is not null, each job in set A is examined to determine which job, when assigned, minimizes the difference between maximum and minimum loaded machines within the key cell.

Step 4 assigns to the key cell the job that minimizes the maximum difference. With the job assigned, the loading heuristic reverts to step 2 to identify the next key cell and machine. Steps 2 through 4 are repeated until all jobs have been selected and assigned. As more and more jobs are assigned, the number of feasible jobs that could possibly be assigned to the key machine or key cell decreases. As the assignment process proceeds to the last job, iterations between steps 2 and 3 increase dramatically, requiring considerable computation time.

Cell Scheduling

Cellular manufacturing scheduling is nothing more than scheduling individual, small job shops or flow shops. Literally hundreds of documented scheduling techniques are available. In addition, there are thousands of industrial firms which have generated their own scheduling techniques of which there is no record.

The cellular manufacturing system can be modeled as either static or dynamic. For a static system, the jobs are pooled and scheduled at fixed time intervals. Once the jobs are scheduled, the schedule is set and fixed. For a dynamic system, jobs are scheduled as they arrive at the cell or at a machine. With this flexibility, the queue ordering in front of each machine can continually change.

If the cell is modeled as a static system, the available scheduling methods fall into three categories: combinatorial, mathematical programming, and Monte Carlo sampling. Combinatorial methods are based on changing from one permutation to the next by "switching around" jobs. Combinatorial methods are best suited for very small cells limited to three machines or less, because the factorial increase in permutations requires an exhaustive search of all combinations possible. Therefore, their applicability is severely limited.

The job shop (cell) scheduling problem has been formulated as an integer program for over 20 years, but the solution for realistic-size problems is still intractable. Tied closely to mathematical programming are enumeration and the associated branch-and-bound techniques. The consensus is that mathematical programming and enumeration fail to provide real-time control for even small-size problems because of the excessive computational requirements.

Monte Carlo sampling and simulation typically refers to the application of heuristic sequencing rules with analysis and validation via digital computer simulation. Because nearly all heuristic sequencing rules apply to both static and dynamic systems, these rules are discussed collectively under dynamic systems.

If the cell is modeled dynamically,the available scheduling methods fall into two categories: queuing theory and heuristic sequencing rules. Because of the cell's complexity, only limited queuing applications have been tried. In general, queuing theory has been useful only in scheduling large aggregate models and in planning models with limited success in cell sequencing.

Monte Carlo simulation with a digital computer has been the principle tool for analyzing heuristic sequencing rules, primarily because of the stochastic nature of the parameters associated with cells. Sequencing rules determine the order of jobs to be processed by individual machines. Most sequencing rules are based on a single job parameter (simple job rules) or on a combination of job parameters (complex job rules). Primarily these parameters are processing time, due date, number of operations, cost of job, setup time, arrival time, and next machine(s) or operation(s).

A few sequencing rules are not based on job parameters. Rather they are based on the state of the cell (machine rules). Some machine rules look at alternate routings to balance the cell load. Other machine rules "look ahead" to determine future cell bottlenecks or underutilization. Some machine rules become quite complex and time-consuming and begin to approach the problems associated with static scheduling methods.

Even with the considerable variation possible with cell parameters, certain priority rules yield consistent results. Among the simple job rules, shortest processing time (SPT) gives the smallest mean flow time and minimum work in process, but it gives a larger flow time variance than the first in shop/first out (FISFO) method. The due date, slack, and slack per operation all give good results for minimizing job tardiness.

In general, dispatching rules based on the processing time, operation time, or the operation time multiplied by the total processing time provided better results than the FISFO, first come first served (FCFS), or last in system/last out (LISLO) method. Improvements in SPT and shortest operation time (SOT) have been obtained by employing a dual sequencing rule. A dual sequencing rule changes from the primary sequencing rule (SPT, SOT) to a secondary sequencing rule (FISFO, FCFS) at predetermined time intervals. This change occurs for a fixed time, to force jobs with large operation times or processing times through the system, and then returns to the primary sequencing rule. A dual sequencing rule is called, in some instances, *truncation*. A dual sequencing rule gives a small mean flow time, as does SPT or SOT, and reduces the flow time variance. Futher sequencing information is given in other chapters.

INFORMATION SYSTEM REQUIREMENTS

The relationships among hardware, application software, and data base software are complex. The advent of plug-compatible (PC) machines, PC firmware with its hard-wired logic, background data base machines, and microlinks is part of the trend toward complete integration of complex data processing systems.

Computer Speed

The speed of computers today is measured in millions of instructions per second. Most computer manufacturers project that this speed will increase exponentially in the near future. Computer memory capacity is increasing and getting cheaper, and other hardware improvements seem unlimited.

The Bottleneck

Today, the computer's limiting factor is the speed of retrieving data that are in mass storage. Although a computer executes instructions at a speed rated in millions per second, it has to wait an average of $\frac{1}{25}$ second to access the mass storage for the data it needs. Fortunately multiprogramming allows one program to process while another waits for data. However, data retrieval time can cause the total elapsed time for the task to be excessive. This run time problem becomes painfully visible in some companies that have manufacturing control systems where material-requirements planning (MRP) runs are measured in days. The primary problem is the erratic distribution of the data throughout the files rather than the data base size. This deficiency can also lead to problems in query and reporting systems. The newer, more efficient disk subsystems or huge memory buffer pools may significantly alleviate this shortcoming.

Computer Hardware Developments

Large mainframe computers have had an advantage because of their greater data base capacity, system software, and numerous software applications. The speed of computers is increasing as the price is decreasing. Minicomputers and microcomputers are becoming the hardware equivalent of the large mainframe computers. Recent innovations include the microlink, wand readers, and distributed systems.

Microlink.　　The microlink is the software for microframe computer communications and data transfer. It provides greater flexibility for local information retrieval and reporting by supporting normal terminal functions. It also provides the intelligent analysis of a local data base which has been downloaded from the main data base.

Wand Readers.　　Wand readers are devices used to read data encoded on items, job tickets, and so on. In association with bar coding, wand readers, by giving timely and accurate reporting information, attempt to solve the factory floor communications and feedback problems.

Distributed Systems.　　Distributed data processing systems are networks in which some of or all the processing, storage, and control functions, in addition to input/output (I/O) functions, are dispersed among many terminals in the system. The intent is that, through a bus or other communication means, a transaction on a terminal may be processed by a selected central processing unit (CPU). Also data bases can be accessed by any CPU. This flexibility, with the required speed, would support any type of processing demand. Distributed systems have been discussed for years, but the current program architecture of several computer manufacturers is moving to CPU independence so that each one has access to every data base.

Data Base

It is important to understand what a data base is, both physically and logically, to comprehend the relationships of data. In its simplest terms, a *data base* is data stored in a mass storage device under the control of a software package called a *data base manager*. A data base exists both physically and logically.

Physical Data Base.　　Table 20.3 makes an analogy between a book structure and a data base structure. The data base structure can be equated to the outline of a book. It can be divided into areas, which are analogous to chapters, and can identify different themes or contents within each chapter. The basic physical unit of a data base is a page. The page contains a record cluster, such as a part master with its routings and product structures. A record cluster is analogous to a paragraph containing a group of words. The record is the basic logical unit similar to a sentence. Within a record there are fields, such as part master records with nomenclature, dimensions, descriptions, etc., analogous to words in a sentence. Graphically, the data base is physically divided into pages, where a page is a physical unit. Thus a physical data base size is defined, for example, as 10,000 pages of 2000 bytes each.

Physical Clustering.　　The next step is to decide the logical relationships of records and how to physically store them. Within a page one can have different records,

TABLE 20.3 Data Base Analogy

Data Base	Book
Areas (page range)	Chapters
Block per page	Page (basic physical unit)
Record cluster	Paragraph
Record	Sentence (basic logical unit)
Field	Word

which are groups of fields such as a part master, the routings, and the product structure. A different number of fields may be contained in different kinds of records. There are big pages and little pages to accommodate different size records. The data base is stored and retrieved one page at a time. A rule of thumb for a reasonable page size is somewhere between 2000 and 12,000 bytes. To avoid excessive processing time, the page should be large enough to contain the basic records such as part masters, routings, and product structures. If it is not, the logical page will consist of two or more physical pages connected by chains, or set pointers, described later. Remember, there is some overhead caused by the retrieval time for the chain or the set pointers.

Record Relationships.   Record relationships are illustrated in Fig. 20.10. Routing is owned (controlled) by part master, and the part master points to (references) the first routing. The first routing points to the alternate routing, and so on. That is why it is called a *chain*, or *set*. In a network-type data base, a record may be owned by any number of other record types, or it may own many other types of records. Each example is a set, or chain, where there is one owner and at least one owned type of record.

Some systems allow for *cluster reading*, which means that the buffer is filled any time a data base is read. If the buffer contains multiple pages, it will read multiple pages. Data buffers, managed by the data base management system (DBMS), contain blocks of data being transferred between the main data base memory and the system application memory. The DBMS changes the format of the data depending on the direction of flow to meet the requirements of the application or data base. This is a very valuable feature.

Networks.   A basic need of the factory of the future, especially if it is using group technology, is the integration of related data. Networks are one technique used for the integration of the systems.

The network relationships provide multiple accesses of the same data through the data base relationships. For example, in accessing the routings there are several options. Given the part number, all routings for parts may be accessed; or given the work center, all routings for parts routed through that work center may be accessed. A networking relationship is one basic way that a DBMS may establish data base relationships—and consequently integrate the data.

Data Storage.   Decisions concerning the storage of data in a computerized system are critical for manufacturing control systems. Inefficient placement of data in memory results in excessive input and output time as well as CPU time. The preferred technique is to cluster routings (Fig. 20.11) in the computer memory with the parts master so that they are physically near each other on the same data page. Thus, when master route sheets for releasing orders to the floor are printed and the work-in-process records are created, all routings are available on one data page. This minimizes the time for the relatively slow input and output of the mass storage.

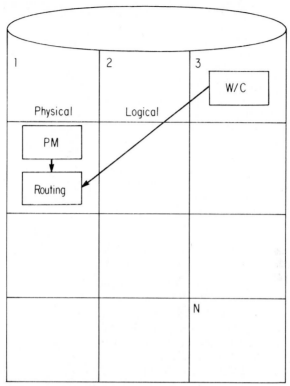

FIG. 20.10   Record cluster.

Since accessing the data base by work center is usually infrequent, the logical cluster need not be physical. Although the work center record is also a logical owner of the operations-performed record, it can be stored on some other page of the data base with a pointer to where the routing is stored. This is the preferred technique.

If this operation were reversed and the operation information were stored physically with the work center, the data processing time would be excessive. If the routing for a part were accessed, a physical input/output would be required for each work center in which the part was processed. For example, a file of 100,000 parts with each requiring an average of 10 work centers would have a total 1,000,000 operation-work center combinations. If the lead time were to be computed from these routings, it would take at least 10 hr to read the routings in this fashion, regardless of the size of the CPU. It would also take extensive CPU time to execute the estimated 1 to 10 billion instructions necessary to support all this input/output. If, on the other hand, the data base is designed properly, this operation requires approximately 20 min.

Input/Output

Physical input/output is the physical reading of the mass storage device. Normally one page at a time is read into memory. However, a new feature on some systems is *cluster reading.* This allows the reading of multiple pages with one I/O operation. This has limitations in that sufficient computer memory must be available for buffers. Also, with cluster reading one must consider the transfer rate, which in the

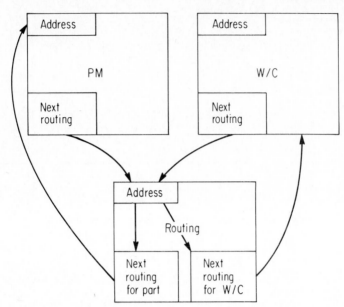

FIG. 20.11   Sets and chains: logical cluster.

past had not been a limiting factor. Regardless, this is still an I/O. The physical I/O is the critical data procesing path in most manufacturing environments.

Another term which should be understood is *logical I/O*, or *buffered I/O*. Once the data have been read from the data base into a buffer, one can access that same data over and over at memory speed, which is considerably faster than obtaining them from a disk or tape.

Effect of Overflow on Clustering

Clustering involves physically grouping data that will be processed with the same key such as a parts master with its bill-of-materials product structure. Thus if clustered, all the required data can be accessed with one I/O. If it takes two I/O operations, the I/O run time doubles. An inefficient data base design may increase the data processing time not by 10 to 50 percent but 1000 to 5000 percent. One basic problem in the present data base design is *data overflow*. This comes from two sources: system programmers and data base administrators who have an inadequate understanding of the production environment and production/inventory planning and control personnel who have an inadequate understanding of data base design and operation.

Various data base management software packages handle overflow differently. The data base design depends on the manufacturing environment and on the DBMS protocol for handling overflow. The variations in ordering policies, commonality of parts, number of work centers, work centers per routing, and the average and variance in the number of planned and released orders affect the data base design. Cluster readings compensate to some degree by allowing the reading of multiple pages with each read operation, assuming the buffers are large enough. This creates a trade-off in memory between the number of buffers allowed and the size of the buffers. Cluster readings can be a valuable aid.

An Example: Subfiling

Consider a file of 10,000 parts with an average of 10 routings per part, or 100,000 routings, that require 100 work centers. A good design practice would be to create two subfiles. Devote 5 pages of the data base to the information for work centers, and devote 10,000 pages to the parts and routings.

Devoting 5 pages to the work centers places a physical limitation on the number of work centers. The limitation is the number of pages, 5 times the page size divided by the work center record size. If the page size is 1000 bytes and each work center's record requires 100 bytes, then there is space for 50 work center records (1000 × 5/100). This would have to be discussed with the production people; and if 5 are not sufficient, additional pages would have to be added. Some limit should be specified. The objective is that anytime during processing, especially in batch logic where the work center records are used, a limited number of buffer pages is required to contain all work center records in memory without having to reread them. Thus, if a program were executed that read all routings and their work centers, it would require a limited number of physical I/O (one per page) to read or to update the work center records because they would be in computer memory. If the work centers were not concentrated in a small number of pages capable of being retained in memory, then 100,000 individual read and write operations would occur, one for each routing processed.

Design Issues

These factors influence the manufacturing control data base design: number of parts (items) master, number of bills of materials, ordering policies and techniques, number of released and planned orders, type of pegging, batch control requirements, distribution requirements, number of warehouses, and number of work centers. This list is only a partial one, and each situation must be analyzed.

Proper data base design requires certain statistics, and the data base designer, program user, and programmers should be involved in this analysis. Many questions concern the bill of materials. For example, if an end item is rescheduled, how many parts are affected? The distribution of parts in the parts list affects the number of buffers required because MRP logic explodes orders down to components. Many programmers do not foresee this requirement, so the systems and data processing personnel working with the production inventory management personnel must define the requirements.

Requirements and replenishments records are the most numerous and volatile records in an MRP data base. Consequently, master production scheduling policies and practices must be known to determine data base requirements.

The Problem with Relational Data Bases

Relational data bases are data bases in which all related items are equally accessible. They are the most desired form of data base, and they work very well in some environments. However, in most manufacturing environments they do not work well because key sizes are large, the relationships are many, and the volumes of data are large and erratic. The significant problem occurs because of the large number and size of the multiple indices required to have all related data equally accessible. The object is to store data by multiple keys, record identifiers, and have them all contained in the data base segment accessed. This approach could increase the number of indices to the point of requiring an excessive number of buffers to retain the keys. The result is *I/O thrashing*, which is bringing the keys in and out of the buffers as records are accessed or stored. In a static data base environment with a limited number of keys, relational data bases are very accommodating and programmer-friendly. However, in a system as volatile as a manufacturing environment, they can be disastrous.

Software Packages

The cost of programming talent is high, and the price of hardware continues to diminish. Therefore, using commercially available software packages is desirable because they reduce the time required for implementation. If a commercial package works, why change it? Analysts frequently attempt to create the perfect solution, which is a major reason for their delay and failure. The basic functions of many applications, such as the bill of materials, are fairly standard. Minimizing added features to those required reduces the delay in implementing solutions.

In summary, available hardware, software, and data bases, properly used, can support very large, sophisticated functions such as daily net change and MRP. This is the key: Do not overdesign, but stress basic data processing education for all personnel, including the users.

COMPUTER APPLICATIONS FOR TRAINING

Software can be used in conjunction with a formal educational program to cover the fundamentals of material control techniques and relationships. The software can demonstrate these relationships as systems are implemented and provide a foundation for problem solving to improve the plan execution. Educational software is an additional tool that can be an important part of an educational program.

There are two types of educational software: that designed for self-instruction and that designed for use in a classroom environment. Self-instructional software is used to tutor an individual in some skill. This type of software is useful where problems and solutions can be predetermined and programmed. However, few managerial decision-making problems have one correct answer. There are usually a number of possible answers to most management problems, and the most appropriate depends on management policies and objectives. Thus, individualized systems having predetermined correct answers are best used for subjects such as fundamental principles of inventory management. The other type of educational software is used in a classroom situation.

Classroom Situation Systems

Classroom manufacturing control programs are designed to be used by teams of students under the guidance of a knowledgeable instructor. In this application, the software provides data to be used for developing management decisions. The interaction between members of the team and between teams can provide a thorough exploration of many alternative decisions. The instructor guides this exploration to provide a range of potential decisions. This type of learning environment is best for teaching problem solving, especially the relationships of policies and objectives to decisions.

Computer Compatibility—Minicomputers and Mainframes

Educational software designed for use on either minicomputers or mainframes has two decided drawbacks: it consumes computer capacity needed for running the business, and usually it has limited access. In companies with a shortage of computer time, it is unlikely that education will have sufficient priority to get programs run. However, the manufacturing control system of the business and its educational software can be tailored to fit like hand and glove if they are written together and run on the same equipment. This tailored software can be very effective in training personnel to use an operating system. The integrated software system is available today because of the user orientation of most software suppliers.

Interactive-Type Software Systems with What-If Capability

Educational manufacturing control software is often looked to for its *interactive capability*, where interactivity is defined as the ability to do what-if explorations (simulation). The difficulty is that the complexity and size of such explorations can rival operating systems. Interactive educational systems offer many opportunities to explore parameter changes, but the size, complexity, and response times of the programs are frequently distinct liabilities. The major advantages of interactive capability are that numeric errors can be eliminated and all links within the system can be adjusted with changes in the input data.

In problem solving for manufacturing, the reverse of the normal planning procedure is used because problems are solved by working up (rather than down) the bill of materials. Interactive systems permit replanning when a problem-solving decision is made. Computers used for trial-and-error guesses of potential solutions may be harmful to the student when interactivity confuses replanning with execution, the real job of manufacturing. Replanning frequently involves the use of the existing lot size and scheduling rules, which may be the source of the problem. Interactive capability is useful when decisions are final and the system needs to be informed of the decisions made. Interactive systems are used in the same manner as locked data systems, to get the data needed to determine the best plan to follow, and so are best used to show the effect of decisions rather than to learn problem solving.

Locked Data Base Type of Software Systems

In a locked data base, the data do not change. And locked data base educational software can be used effectively to explore the way in which systems are used to solve problems. The data base can encompass many more types of problems than would normally be present at one time in operating or interactive systems. The reason is that the data and parameters can be inserted by design rather than being the existing data and parameters such as rules, costs, etc. Because the locked data cannot be changed, the same data are constantly available to explore problems; this allows the instructor's time to be used for guidance of discussion rather than keeping up to date on changing data. Problems can be developed with static data and thus the problems need not be revised to keep pace with dynamic, active systems. Given the speed advantage and small size of the programs needed for static data, small personal computers can be used for education. This reduces software development time and cost and provides a complete educational package for problem solving. Since the task of managerial education is to explore alternatives, locked data systems provide fast response, easy use, and minimum instructor data-review time. The major drawback is in the inability to show the system-generated results produced by the final decisions made.

Software Data Requirements

To make the best use of manufacturing control training software, all the files contained in a complete system are needed. This software must have all the elements needed, and the data must be interconnected as in normal operating systems. The following data should be available:

- MPS
- MRP
- Manufacturing routings
- Open-order status
- Dispatch lists
- Capacity-requirements plan
- RCCP requirements
- Bills of materials including where-used data
- Part specifications
- Work center listing
- Production machine asset records
- Engineering standards
- Work center and machine history
- Facilities and energy records
- Stock status including parts cost data
- Labor and material costs
- Maintenance schedules

These files provide a comprehensive data base for exploration and sufficient detail about a business that students can use the system to make educated managerial decisions. Although fewer pieces of data could be used for educational systems, part of the process of education is to determine what data are essential to operation and what additional data are needed to enhance student learning.

System Use.   The two biggest educational system requirements are speed of operation and ease of use. Educational software should provide nearly instant access to records by cathode-ray tube (CRT) terminal and in hard-copy form. Typically, response times should be less than 2 average with 5 a maximum. The software must also be easy to use, so that minimum instruction is needed to be able to access records. This dictates a completely menu-driven system with built-in help features. The software must be significantly easy to use so that learning instructions do not overshadow the manufacturing control education it is designed to facilitate. Static data systems hold a large advantage over interactive ones in both these categories because they are less complex and do less work by not having to reorganize data files. Although CRT access and printer data are not both required, an exploration of which medium is superior for problem solving has proved to be an interesting issue.

Documentation. Educational software requires thorough documentation because infrequent users must be able to follow simple step-by-step instructions. For most effective use in education, instructions should be a single typed page. System usage documentation should be fewer than five pages so that students spend most of their time using the system rather than reading the instructions. The documentation also must include step-by-step installation instructions written for users with little experience with computers. Single- or at most two-diskette systems for microcomputers are best for minimizing the instructions and operational difficulty.

System Test. Software should be completely tested in the environment in which it is to be used. Testing should be both on the hardware and in the educational environment. Untested software or software with minimal field use may have bugs which will confuse the educational process. Bugs in operating and interactive software are more difficult to eliminate than in static data systems, so more thorough testing is needed on these systems. As with manufacturing systems and personnel, a good track record is useful in determining the applicability of specific software packages for education.

Sample Problem Needs. Problems for college students using software should differ little from problems generally given to materials management students. The problems should be designed by professionals in materials management to be both realistic and representative of the real-world manufacturing environments. The problems should cover a wide range of materials concepts and be addressable on any level. For example, make-to-stock and make-to-order situations, flow process (continuous and repetitive), and job shop production should be covered. The software and problems should provide a challenge for the novice and experienced professional alike. The problems should be designed to foster thought and discussion among students and not simply to produce right or wrong answers.

The primary objective of providing or acquiring educational software is to remember that training is the acquisition of new facts and education is the process of learning to view already known facts from a different perspective. Software and problem-solving skills require education as well as training.

BIBLIOGRAPHY

Robots

Akagawa, Minuro: Introduction to Industrial Robots, Unpublished report, 1980.

————: Industrial Robot Handbook, vol. 2, Society of Manufacturing Engineers, Detroit, Mich., 1979.

Gerwin, Donald: "Do's and Don'ts of Computerized Manufacturing," *Harvard Business Review*, March-April, 1982, pp. 107–116.

Groover, Mikell P.: *Automation, Production Systems, and Computer Aided Manufacturing*, Prentice-Hall, Englewood Cliffs, N.J., 1980.

"Robots Join the Labor Force," *Business Week,* June 9, 1980, p. 62.

Susnjara, Ken: *A Manager's Guide to Industrial Robots,* Corinthian Press, Shaker Heights, Oh., 1982.

Group Technology

Baker, K. R.: *Introduction to Sequencing and Scheduling,* Wiley, New York, 1974.

Bestwick, P. T., and K. G. Lockyer: "A Practical Approach to Production Scheduling," *International Journal of Production Research,* vol. 17, no. 2, March-April, 1979, pp. 95–109.

Burbidge, J. L.: *The Introduction of Group Technology,* Wiley, New York, 1975.

————: "Production Flow Analysis," *The Production Engineer,* April-May, 1971, pp. 139–152.

Dannenbring, D. G.: "An Evaluation of Flow Shop Sequencing Heuristics," *Management Science,* vol. 23, no. 11, July, 1977, pp. 1174–1182.

Day, J. E., and M. P. Hottenstein: "Review of Sequencing Research," *Naval Research Logistics Quarterly,* March, 1970, pp. 11–39.

Eilon, S.: "Five Approaches to Aggregate Production Planning," *American Institute of Industrial Engineering (AIIE) Transactions,* vol, 7, no. 2, June, 1975, pp. 118–131.

Fogarty, Donald W.: "Manufacturing Cells and Flexible Manufacturing Systems: A New Ball Game," *First World Congress of Production and Inventory Control Presentations,* May 27–29, 1985, pp. 110–113.

Gere, Jr., W. S.: "Heuristics in Job Shop Scheduling," *Management Science,* vol. 13, no. 3, November, 1966, pp. 167–190.

Graves, S. C.: "A Review of Production Scheduling," *Operations Research,* vol. 29, no. 4, July-August, 1981, pp. 646–675.

Greene, T. J., and R. P. Sadowski: "A Review of Cellular Manufacturing Assumptions, Advantages, and Design Techniques," *Journal of Operations Management,* vol. 4, no. 2, February, 1984, pp. 85–97.

————: "Cellular Manufacturing Control," *Journal of Manufacturing Systems,* vol. 2, no. 2, 1983, pp. 137–146.

————: "Loading the Cellularly Divided Group-Technology Manufacturing System," *1980 Fall AIIE Conference Proceedings,* 1980, pp. 190–195.

Jackson, D.: *Cell System of Production,* Business Books, London, 1978, p. 169.

Mitfanov, S. P.: *Scientific Principles of Group Technology,* Boston Spa, England: National Lending Library for Science and Technology, translated from Nauchnye Osnovy Gruppovoi Tekhnologii (Leningrad: Lenizdat), 1966.

New, C. Colin: "MRP and GT: A New Strategy for Component Production," *Production and Inventory Management,* vol. 18, no. 3, 1977, pp. 50–62.

Petrov, V. A.: *Flowline Group Production Planning,* E. Bishop (trans.), Business Publications, London, 1968.

Warehouse and Distribution Operations

21

Physical Handling and Control of Inventory

Editors

JACK N. DURBEN, Director, Materials Management, Miles Laboratories, Inc., Elkhart, Indiana

CHRISTOPHER J. PIPER, CFPIM, Associate Professor, School of Business Administration, The University of Western Ontario, London, Ontario

SPAULDING SCHULTZ, P.E., P. ENG., Consultant to Management, Kingfield Farm, Gray, Maine

Inventories represent a substantial portion of the total assets of a company, and considerable effort is required to control the inventories. Once inventory is physically present, it is essential that it be handled and stored at minimum cost while at the same time allowing production schedules to be met.

Physical control of inventories is normally vested in the stores-keeping function. Stores-keeping involves the following basic activities:

- Receiving, holding, and protecting all materials and supplies until needed
- Issuing authorized materials and supplies to other departments and to agencies outside the company
- Controlling in-process material between production operations
- Maintaining the integrity of inventory records so that they accurately represent what is on hand

- Planning the layout of stores areas and the acquisition of appropriate stores equipment
- Maintaining the stores area in a neat and orderly manner

ORGANIZATIONAL ISSUES

In many manufacturing firms the stores-keeping function is organized as a discrete component of the materials management function. Sometimes this responsibility excludes the storage of spare parts and finished goods for distribution to customers, with these activities being the responsibility of a separate physical distribution organization. Occasionally, the stores-keeping function may be placed under the supervision of the purchasing agent or even the controller. Normally, there are peculiar circumstances that lead to these conditions, such as the need to coordinate purchasing of bulk materials with storage facilities, the policy of buying materials based on market conditions rather than current requirements, or the need to exercise closer controls over the allocation and location of finished goods to meet customer demands.

Regardless of where it is placed in the organization, however, the stores-keeping function is the guardian of company materials during and between production processes. This is the cardinal principle for controlling physical inventories: *No material is accepted, issued or moved without accompanying authorization.*

Administratively, materials are frequently grouped according to type, use, or condition. The same groupings are often used for accounting purposes as well as for storage and handling. The following are commonly designated inventory categories:

1. *Raw materials* are items that are received in basic forms requiring some type of chemical or physical transformation (e.g., refining, cutting, or shaping) prior to use. Common items are metals (roll stock, shapes), plastics (resins, films), papers, chemicals, and bulk materials.

2. *Component parts* are items that either have undergone some in-house processing or have been received ready for use as discrete components.

3. *Supplies* are expense items or nonproductive materials. They are used to support operations but do not normally enter or become part of the end product. Coolants, lubricants, cleaning materials, repair parts for equipment, maintenance materials, and processing supplies are examples.

4. *Work in process* consists of material that is either undergoing processing or temporarily being held between operations. Materials that have been processed and returned to storerooms prior to further processing or assembly are normally considered component parts.

5. *Finished goods* are complete units and assemblies carried in stock ready for delivery to customers or for transfer to other plants.

Not infrequently, one or two of these categories are combined. Process industries, for example, may place incoming raw materials into production so quickly that it makes sense to classify them as work in process as soon as they are received. Similarly, assembly plants may choose to treat certain purchased component parts in the same way under a just-in-time (JIT) mode of operation.

PLANNING THE PHYSICAL FACILITIES

Information Needs

The following information is needed to plan for handling and storage of materials: the basic materials data themselves and a materials classification scheme.

Basic Materials Data.   The basic data requirements are as follows:

1. Physical
    a. Size and shape of each item to be handled
    b. Weight of each item
    c. Number of units per pallet and pallet pattern
2. Movement
    a. Timing and volume of receipts
    b. Timing and volume of issues
3. Special characteristics
    a. Fragile, combustible, toxic, pilferable, refrigerated, radioactive, temperature- or humidity-sensitive

From the physical data, the volume, or cube, of an item can be calculated. When the cube is multiplied by the movement, the total cube, or total volume, moved in a given time is obtained. This basic information is used to determine equipment requirements.

Materials Classification.   After the basic materials data are obtained, the materials are separated into groups which have compatible characteristics. This step makes it much easier to select the right type of storage equipment. Generally speaking, like materials use like storage and materials handling equipment. For example, the grouping of materials by department or by vendor in a particular area is a typical example of materials classification.

In many cases, different combinations of characteristics are used to establish materials classifications. For example, all hi-cube items are together in one location, and all lo-cube items are in another location. However, within these groups there might be other important subclassifications (e.g., fast versus slow movers, high-value versus low-value items, heavy versus light items, odd versus symmetric shapes) which dictate special equipment or a special area. For example, grouping easily pilfered items facilitates the use of a security cage or locked cabinet within less secure areas.

In large distribution operations the inventory classification step may include the assignment of an *analysis code* to identify each product in a particular classification. The analysis code is a very useful tool when large amounts of data need to be sorted or ranked. The analysis code allows the analyst to assess the effect of various groupings without changing the data base. A three-position code has been found useful, with the first position used to indicate *cube*, the second position to indicate *movement*, and the third position used for *special considerations*. Alphanumeric codes offer the user maximum latitude in describing the many characteristics used to classify materials.

The three-position analysis code is a convenient way of describing a product's storage requirements. The three positions designate the following:

- Position 1 indicates the storage facility required as determined from the cubes moved in and out of storage daily and certain characteristics such as a full or repacked case.
- Position 2 of the code indicates whether a product has a high or low turnover rate, is used in spring or fall, is used only one time, or is obsolete.
- Position 3 indicates some special characteristic of the product.

When producing a code designator for a product, the following steps are used:

1. The number of cubes moved per day is determined and entered in column 1 of Table 1*a*. For example, a product has a "low" cube movement per day of .60. Reading across the table to the right, it can be seen that a space of 18 cubic feet should be allocated and that either a bin, flow rack, or pallet rack could be used.
2. The first position of the code is refined further by referring to the first column of Table 1*b* and deciding whether A, B, C, or D is appropriate.
3. The second position is determined from the turnover column (column 2) on Table 1*b*. For example, a product that is used only during the fall would have a D as a designator.
4. The third position is described in the column in Table 1*b*.

The third position, used to indicate additional characteristics, may by its very nature override the first two positions or may be used to supplement them. These additional specifications will prove helpful, not only in the final determination of materials handling and storage equipment, but also in locating the item within the equipment. The *one time* example on position 2 could be used to prevent the use of a prime location for items such as discontinued stock. Each company and each storeroom within a company will have to develop its own analysis-code structure to meet its particular situation.

TABLE 21.1a Cube Allocation

	Column 1	2	3	4	5
	Cube Movement per Day	A Bin	B and C Flow Rack	D and E Pallet Rack	F Floor Block
High	5.0	—	—	—	150 cu ft
	4.0	—	—	—	120 cu ft
	3.0	—	—	—	90 cu ft
	2.0	—	—	60 cu ft	60 cu ft
	1.0	—	—	30 cu ft	—
Medium	0.90	—	—	27 cu ft	—
	0.80	—	—	24 cu ft	—
	0.70	—	—	21 cu ft	—
	0.60	18 cu ft	18 cu ft	18 cu ft	—
	0.50	15 cu ft	15 cu ft	—	—
Low	0.40	12 cu ft	12 cu ft	—	—
	0.30	9 cu ft	9 cu ft	—	—
	0.20	6 cu ft	6 cu ft	—	—
	0.10	3 cu ft	3 cu ft	—	—

TABLE 21.1b   Three-Position Codes

Position 1 (Area or Cube)	Position 2 (Turnover Rate)	Position 3 (Special Conditions)
A Bin	A Hi turnover	A Bin—full shelf
B Cases on a flow rack	B Lo turnover	B Bin—½ shelf
C Repacked units on a flow rack	C Spring	C Bin—¼ shelf
D Cases on a pallet	D Fall	D Bin—⅛ shelf
E Repacked units on a pallet	E One time	E Heavy
F Floor storage	F Obsolete	F Flammable

Example: A product that has a low-cube movement of .60 requires 18 cubic ft of space to be set aside, which means that the first position of the code is either A, B, C, D, or E according to Table 1a.
   Since the product is a repacked item, C is the proper designator for the first position as shown in 1b.
   The product is used only in the fall, so the second designator would be D as shown under the second position column.
   One half of a shelf is required, so the third position of the code is B.
   Consequently the analysis code is C-D-B.

The analysis code tables may be produced to include more detail. Other considerations will also be discussed in the balance of this chapter.

Handling Methods and Equipment

Storeroom materials handling equipment must interface with the in-plant equipment; in some cases, they may be one and the same. As previously indicated, the planning effort requires the integration of materials handling equipment with the storage equipment, the layout, and the systems and procedures, all being influenced by the other.
   The most important consideration in materials handling is the size, shape, and weight of the material, or its container, and any auxiliary transport/storage unit, such as a pallet or skid.
   If all materials can be reduced to a simple standard transport/storage unit container, the materials handling equipment selection problem is greatly reduced.

Standard Unit Containers

A primary objective of stores operations is to minimize the handling of stores items. The most economical arrangement is for material to pass directly from the receiving point to the place of use. When this is not feasible, stores acts as a buffer by holding materials from the time of receipt until they are required by production. To minimize these handling costs which include shrinkages due to handling, the use of unit packaging or containers is widespread. Unit packaging consists of receiving, storing, and issuing items in standard-size containers containing several small parts or articles or a standard amount of bulk materials, such as drums of paint or bags of cement. Thus, materials can be delivered to the using department in the same containers in which they were received. This minimizes shrinkage and eliminates the need for unpacking and measuring bulk inventories and issues. Whenever possible, stores issues should be made in standard quantities based on the quantity per unit package and multiples thereof. Frequently, material can be stored more efficiently in unit containers rather than in bulk.

Unit containers should be specified on purchase orders. Dimensional limits of the unit load—pallet size and height—should be included to eliminate extra in-house work, such as breaking down pallets which are too high to fit in storeroom pallet racks or transferring material into bin boxes because the unit containers do not fit in assigned stock locations. The converse should be kept in mind when the storage equipment is laid out: Assign stock locations that will fit the supplier's standard pack; avoid adapting a location size which forces the breakdown of standard packs.

Storage Methods and Equipment

The cost of operation and the effectiveness of the storeroom are greatly influenced by the selection of proper storage equipment. The line between storage and handling equipment is becoming increasingly difficult to define since automatic storage/automatic retrieval (AS/AR) storage systems, as well as other types of automatic stocking and order-filling equipment, have become more widespread. When storage equipment is selected, these factors should be considered:

- Initial cost of equipment
- Operating costs
- Maintenance costs
- Flexibility, adjustability, expandability
- Training requirements

Generally speaking, there are several basic types of equipment that can be listed in order, from simple, lo-investment equipment used to store lo-cube items and accessed by storeroom personnel with little or no equipment, to increasingly higher-cube-capacity equipment requiring mechanized material-handling support and thus higher investment, to the most sophisticated equipment interfaced with computer control and a minimum of human interface. There are many special-purpose storage devices such as cantilever bar-stock racks, cable reel racks, drum racks, tool storage and lockup cabinets, and modular drawer units.

The basic types of equipment are bin-shelving units, flow racks, pallet racks, and mechanized automated storage equipment.

In each equipment diagram in this section, a small cube-movement matrix is shown in the upper left-hand corner as a legend to identify the general area of the cube-movement matrix being discussed. The shaded-area legend for Fig. 21.1 shows that this type of equipment is used in the lo-cube lo-movement portion of the matrix.

Bin-Shelving Units. The bin-shelving unit is a standard, universally used piece of storage equipment that costs little and is maintenance-free. As shown in the cube-movement matrix in Fig. 21.1b, bin shelving is used mainly for stock with lo-cube movement.

Difficulty of pick is recognized in several ways. Bin-shelving units are usually 1 to 2 ft deep to minimize the depth-reach problem, and normally they are not over 7 ft

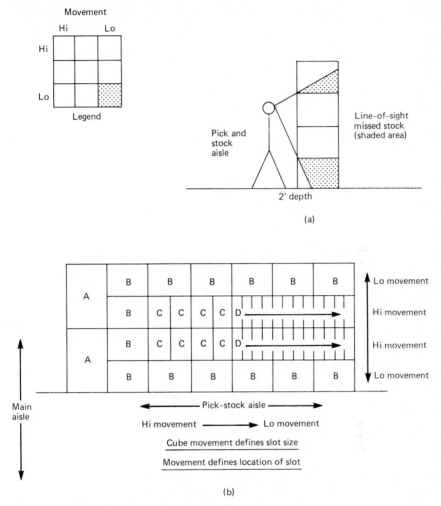

FIG. 21.1 Bin-shelving units—an equipment alternative.

high to minimize the reach problem. Figure 21.1 shows that the items stored on the top and bottom shelves are more difficult to see in the back of the bin. This leads to false stock-outs and a series of attendant paperwork adjustments. This problem can be alleviated by assigning hi-cube items to these hard-to-see slots. The small hard-to-see items are then assigned to the easy-to-see eye-level slots.

The cube-movement approach can be extended to every slot in the lo-cube movement stock area. Relatively hi-cube and lo-movement items are assigned to top or bottom, while lo-cube hi-movement items are assigned to center slots. Hi-movement items are at the head of an aisle, with lo-movement items at the end.

Another major consideration in a lo-cube-movement stock area is the grouping of materials by department (electrical, hydraulic, etc.) and manufacturer or vendor. This arrangement is helpful in lo-movement areas since floor stocks may be replenished on a department basis, increasing the probable demands for a group of similar products. By the same token, when the storeroom stock is replenished, orders tend to be filled out based on minimum-ship quantities—by weight and dollar value—which results in a number of items being received from one vendor. It is much easier to restock into a family or vendor area than at random.

Pallet Racks.   Along with bin-shelving units, pallet racks are by far the most popular storage devices. As indicated in the cube-movement legend on Fig. 21.2,

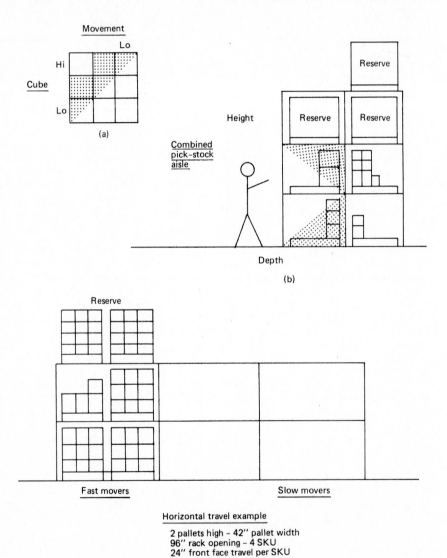

FIG. 21.2   Pallet racks—an equipment alternative.

the pallet racks are used for medium- to lo-cube-movement materials. The typical pallet slot, depending on pallet size and height, should range from about 5 up to 40 cubic feet (cu ft). With items of small cube or volume (as little as 5 cu ft, which may be the total stock or the picking stock quantity), the utilization of pallet cube can be as low as 12 percent, which is a very inefficient use of cube.

Significant savings can result from the reassignment of such stock from pallet-size slots to smaller slots, such as flow rack or bin-shelving units. Cube-capacity savings can be determined by reviewing cube-movement data and the selection of equipment which can be easily adjusted, not cut and rewelded, to provide different size slots for materials.

Several key factors to be considered in evaluating the use of pallet racks are shown in Fig. 21.2b. The diagram shows some of the negative aspects, such as reaching to the top level and bending for the bottom level. The higher the picking level, the greater the problem but also the greater the utilization of cubic space. The deeper the pallet slot, the greater the problem—but again, the better the utilization of the cube. Making the slot wider instead of deeper reduces reaching distance but increases the travel distance. Clearly pallet racks and every type of storage device have limiting factors, and adjusting one dimension may only create a problem in another place. In many companies the problem has been solved, for better or worse, by standardizing a pallet size already in use. This, in turn, limits storage and materials-handling alternatives.

Careful pallet size selection must be the prime consideration in planning the pallet area and selecting the rack. Once the pallet has been selected, it becomes the basic building block in establishing a series of cube modules for all other types of storage units that supplement the pallet rack. At this point operating costs are locked in.

Flow Racks.   Flow racks provide an alternative cube module size range for those cube modules which are space-inefficient in bin or pallet areas. The larger cube slots (full shelf) take up too much front face in bin-shelving units, while the smaller cube slots (5 to 10 cu ft) in the pallet rack lead to poor cube utilization and require a large amount of front face in relation to the cube of the slot. Also flow rack slots are modules of the larger-size slots in the bin-shelving units (full shelf, double shelf), and modules of smaller-size pallet slots (one-half and one-third pallet) consequently provide equipment alternatives (same cube in each type of equipment). The matrix legend in Fig. 21.3 shows that flow rack equipment is generally best for materials with medium- to lo-cube movement. The initial cost of flow racks is greater than either bin-shelving or pallet racks. The flow rack has some significant advantages, however, which can offset its cost. The flow rack provides adequate cubic capacity while at the same time reducing the front-face travel distance significantly. Order-picking aisles at the front of the rack and stocking aisles at the rear reduce worker interference and consequently operating costs. In addition, supervision is usually simplified when there are fewer aisles.

Figure 21.3 shows the reduced front face which is normal when flow racks are used. To maintain the cubic capacity, the depth of the rack is increased to offset the reduced front face; for example, a front face of 1 square foot (sq ft) with a depth of 10 ft will provide 10 cu ft of storage capacity. The greater depth will require a conveyor to bring the materials to the front of the rack. This makes it much easier to pick materials, since the stock always flows to the front of the rack. It also is easier to stock the flow rack since the conveyor carries the stock into the rack from the stocking face.

In addition to the case (original pack) flow rack just discussed, the *flow concept* can be utilized with pallet racks to increase cubic capacity. This step must be

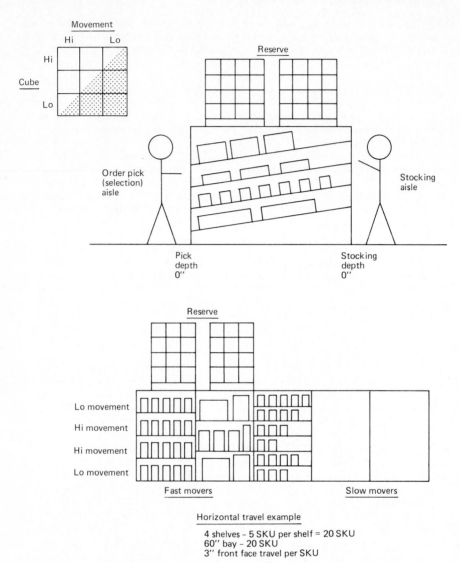

FIG. 21.3 Flow rack—an equipment alternative.

reviewed carefully, however, to be sure that only hi-cube hi-movement materials are assigned to take advantage of the flow idea. In contrast, the conventional case flow rack provides a much greater variety of cube-movement slots and so has the potential for improvement in cube utilization. A significant inventory management advantage of the flow rack is the forced first in/first out (FIFO) rotation of inventory.

Mechanized Automated Storage Handling Equipment. Cube movement has been a prime factor leading to development of mechanized and automatic storage handling equipment. Cube utilization has been a major factor in the development of narrow-aisle, high-rise storage units. These storage units are actually a combination of storage and handling equipment in one system. In most cases, the storage portion does not work without its handling equipment, and the handling equipment has limited usefulness and is economically unjustifiable without its associated storage equipment.

The combined systems have evolved over time, usually from modification of standard equipment to more specialized equipment. The progression in control of this equipment system has been from manual control to remote control, to computer control. When each of the many types of equipment is examined, it is interesting to note that they are upscaled sophistications of the old standbys, such as bin shelving, pallet, and flow racks. Carousel conveyors, storage retrieval systems, and flow rack order selection devices are some of the basic types of mechanized automated systems.

Carousel Conveyors.   In effect, carousel conveyors are a series of mechanized bin-shelving units. Carousels are also made to handle pallets. The prime advantage of these units is that the stock comes to the storeroom personnel—the carousel does the walking. In addition, space requirements can often be reduced since no picking or stocking aisle is required. Carousel units come in horizontal and vertical travel models with varying degrees of control from hand to computer. Examples of carousel conveyors are shown in Figs. 21.4 to 21.6.

FIG. 21.4   Carousel equipment. (*Source: White Storage and Retrieval Systems, Inc.*)

FIG. 21.5   Stock picking by using a carousel. (*Source: White Storage and Retrieval Systems, Inc.*)

FIG. 21.6   Assembly line and carousel. (*Source: White Storage and Retrieval Systems, Inc.*)

Storage Retrieval Systems.   The forerunner of mechanized storage retrieval systems was the stacker crane. From these rider-controlled units the array has expanded to fully automated computer-controlled units. The AS/AR system units are largely used for pallet-size loads and unit-load storage retrieval. Less than unit-load retrieval and storage can create system overloads, because of the system cycle time.

Normally, these units would be used for pallet items of low to medium movement. In effect, the AS/AR unit is a mechanized pallet rack which efficiently utilizes the cube of a building, minimizing aisle space and labor content. These systems are often referred to as *high-rise warehouses*. The greater the height, the greater the cube per unit of floorspace and the lower the cost. For some cases a high-rise warehouse may be the only means of providing the necessary storage capacity because of site limitations. AS/AR units are shown in Figs. 21.7 to 21.10.

Flow Rack Order Selection Device. This device has its counterpart in the AS/AR equipment ranging in sophistication from partial manual to computer control. The first step in sophistication is a regular flow rack outfitted with indicator light to signal which bay and pick slot requires a pick. The indicator also shows the amount of stock to pick. This type of equipment is shown in Figs. 21.11 and 21.12. Another step up is a computer-controlled rack which increments a feed to move the proper number of units from the pick slot onto a take-away conveyor that moves the stock to a pack station.

One early application of flow rack systems was the large grocery warehouse store-type flow racks with built-in depalletizers which feed stock to the unit and select stock automatically. This stock is then moved directly by conveyor to the shipping dock and into the waiting truck.

FIG. 21.7 High-rise storage retrieval system. (*Source: Eaton Kenway.*)

FIG. 21.8 Large high-rise storage retrieval system. *(Source: Eaton Kenway.)*

FIG. 21.9 Stocking with high-rise storage retrieval system. *(Source: Eaton Kenway.)*

FIG. 21.10 Material-handling and high-rise storage retrieval system. (*Source: Eaton Kenway.*)

FIG. 21.11 Flow rack equipment. (*Source: King-Way Order Selection Systems, The Kingston-Warren Corporation.*)

FIG. 21.12   Materials-handling equipment. (Source: King-Way Order Selection Systems, The Kingston-Warren Corporation.)

High-density mobile storage systems reduce storage space requirements by eliminating aisles. These systems are relatively expensive and best suited to lo-movement activities, such as record archives.

Still another mechanized system, used particularly in the garment industry, is the power and feed conveyor system to transport and store hanging garments. These systems are used primarily for transport and temporary storage. The inventory (or conveyor) movement must be high to justify the cost of the system.

In summary, the basic cube modules (slots) can be accommodated with basic types of equipment which optimize cube and operating costs (picking and stocking travel and reach effort). All systems are a combination of a storage device interfaced with materials-handling equipment and control of some type, from human to computer.

Cube-Movement Analysis

The efficient use of space (cube) and the effectiveness of the workforce are determined by the size and location of storage slots. Cube-movement analysis is used to determine this important function. Proper planning will reduce the high investment cost of physical facilities and, more importantly, the ongoing day-to-day operating costs. Before cube-movement data became available, slot sizes were often far too large, resulting in poor cube utilization and at the same time creating excess labor costs by increasing travel distance and effort needed to select stock from oversized locations.

A matrix explaining cube movement is shown in Fig. 21.13. This matrix shows some types of equipment, the storage unit, and location considerations for each particular combination of cube and movement. Hi-cube items that have hi-movement require a large amount of space. And a consistently hi-cube-movement item will require a large size picking slot in order to reduce stock-outs (picking slot being

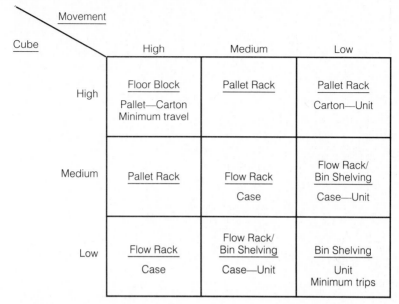

FIG. 21.13 Cube-movement matrix.

emptied too frequently), excess stock effort (less than unit load), and order picking delay (waiting for stock or interference in picking aisle).

Figure 21.13 also indicates the typical unit for picking—pallet, case, or unit for a particular storage device. A sufficiently wide range of different size storage slots is a major concern. The picking slot should vary in size all the way from floor-block drive-in racks for extremely hi-cube movement to individual case flow racks for medium- to lo-cube movement, to individual items such as broken cases in bin-shelving units for lo-cube movement.

Cube movement becomes both a convenient planning tool and a good means to test possible solutions. It forces comparison between widely divergent situations, say, hi-cube hi-movement versus lo-cube lo-movement situations.

Once the cube-movement concept is put into practice, it makes planning much easier and more accurate and offers a means to continually monitor cubic capacity. A sample cube-movement report is shown in Table 21.2.

The most important thing to do is to obtain the cube moved through each slot in a time period and the number of trips to the slot in that same period. Then the cube data are ranked in ascending order. The ranking of a large quantity of data makes the use of a computer all but mandatory. The cube data shown in the daily cube column are used to determine the storage picking slot size. Before that can be done, it is necessary to establish a series of standard slot sizes for each type of equipment.

The next decision involves the restocking interval to be used. From the inventory standpoint, determine how much inventory (cube) is to be stocked in each picking location. There are no hard-and-fast rules, but there are some basic guidelines. Generally the smaller the picking slot (bin-shelving unit), the greater the supply of stock; and the larger the slot (pallet), the smaller the supply. At a minimum, bin-shelving or flow racks should be sized to hold at least a 2-week stock and in most cases enough for a maximum of 6 to 8 weeks. The recent popularity of Kan Ban or JIT inventory control could reduce the slot sizing. If these concepts are in effect, the slot size, if a slot (stocking location) is required in a stockroom, would be sized

TABLE 21.2 Cube Movement/Hit Frequency Report

Report No. ABC0009.1 Computer Program XXXOOO			Order Inventory System Report as of 7/26/8X, Time 08:55				
Division and Warehouse	Product Code	Case or Repack Quantity	Order Hits*	Pallet Hits*	Daily Cube†	Case or Repack Flag	Description
1000	1002A	470	34	26	391.040	C	High speed
1000	1003A	284	23	20	205.332	C	High speed
1000	1004	424	27	21	120.416	C	High speed
1000	1004A	327	23	14	77.826	C	High speed
1000	1005	255	8	7	73.950	C	High speed
1000	1005B	108	23	14	68.688	C	High speed
1000	1005C	62	13	11	53.506	C	High speed
1000	1006	169	39	18	34.814	C	High speed
1000	1006A	10	1	2	34.810	C	
1000	1009	88	23	21	34.672	C	High speed
1000	1010A	50	7	5	33.500	C	
1000	1010D	160	4	4	32.960	C	High speed
1000	1011	31	12	8	32.860	C	
1000	1011A	148	7	6	32.856	C	High speed

* A hit is the number of times a picker goes to a particular storage area per work period.
† Number of cubic units (feet, inches, etc.) required.

21.20

according to the proposed on-hand quantity. Also, one must not forget the cost of purchase orders and receiving and handling costs for a large number of receipts.

Inventory policies are more appropriate in manufacturing and assembly operations where the product goes directly into production and bypasses the storerooms altogether. Inventory policies become much less appropriate in distribution-type operations, especially in finished-goods distribution, and those faced with unpredictable demand. Once the picking slot sizes have been determined, it is necessary to provide reserve storage slots for the stores that cannot be accommodated in the picking slot. Determining the number and size of reserve slots is a much more difficult task because of the unpredictable amount and frequency of incoming shipments. Changes in schedules coupled with minimum order quantities or special price breaks can create peaks and valleys in normal demands. Ideally there will be offsetting peaks and valleys on other items and reserve slots can be allocated on an overall basis considering the historical cube requirements based on current and forecasted inventory or inventory turnover rates.

Storeroom Configuration Guidelines

The layout of the storeroom equipment will determine whether the lowest cost of operation and highest effectiveness are achieved. Just as the cube-movement data were used to determine the type of equipment, they can also be used to make the storeroom layout.

In cube movement, movement determines location. Grouping frequently moved items together reduces travel time (horizontal movement), and locating them at waist to eye level reduces extra reaching and bending effort (vertical movement), as discussed earlier.

The following fundamentals should be considered when the layout is created:

1. Highest-activity items should be placed nearest to the point of use.
2. Basic flow pattern should be used in storeroom—straight through, U shape, etc.
3. Aisles should be straight, without dead ends.
4. Install mezzanines to utilize overhead cube.
5. Set up adequate incoming and outgoing marshaling areas.
6. Group parts by service windows to minimize traffic and time delays.
7. Group the parts for an assembly, to reduce travel and kitting time.
8. Provide for expansion space.

A well-designed layout is shown in Fig. 21.14. Bin-shelving storage is used for high-activity items on the first floor; slow, obsolete, and overstock bin-shelving units are on a mezzanine, to utilize cube. Pallet movement is confined to the rear portion of the storeroom with a wide center aisle for movement out to the factory floor as required. If a straight-through layout is not possible, the layout can be made into a U- or L-shaped flow.

Make certain the storeroom itself is in its proper location in the facility. Its location should be determined by its relationship to the other functions in the plant, i.e., receiving, machining, assembly, and the like. The relationships with these other areas are determined by the amount of materials and frequency of trips between them.

Stocking procedures should be carefully examined to make certain that the quantity and travel distance are reduced to the most economical level. For instance,

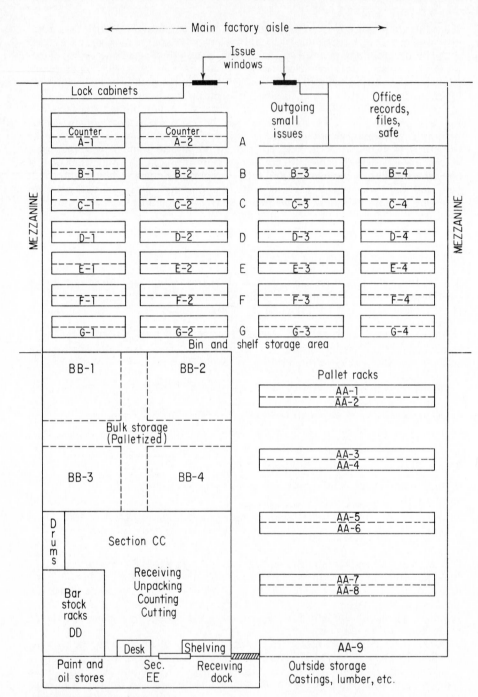

FIG. 21.14 Layout of storeroom.

stock stored on the plant floor can reduce the travel time to and from the storeroom. The benefits of increased use of floor stocks are accompanied, unfortunately, by the costs of reduced physical control. The most appropriate trade-off is situation-specific.

In a layout example of the type illustrated, it is impossible to give exact dimensions. There are, however, certain guidelines to follow in storeroom planning:

1. Main aisles should be wide enough to permit two-way traffic. They may be as wide as 10 to 12 ft.

2. Secondary aisles leading to pallet racks must be wide enough to allow fork trucks to turn and position loaded pallets on the racks. Aisles up to 11 ft wide may be required, depending on the mechanized equipment used.

3. Aisles between bins and shelves can be limited to one-way traffic and range in width from 2 to 3 ft.

4. The material being warehoused frequently dictates the practical height of the storage facility required, depending on its weight, bulk, and size and the capacity of material-handling equipment. Safety measures should also be considered.

OPERATING SYSTEMS AND PROCEDURES

The proper selection and placing of the storage or materials-handling equipment—or both—in a proper layout does not, in itself, guarantee optimum storeroom operation. Storeroom costs are also influenced by the systems and procedures used. Effective systems and procedures can often reduce the need for equipment and personnel. Therefore, a properly functioning stores-keeping operation requires both appropriate systems and procedures and well-planned physical facilities.

Control of Material Flow

Sound inventory management dictates that accurate records and physical control be maintained over all categories of inventories from the time they enter the plant until they are shipped. The flow diagram in Fig. 21.15 shows the flow of material and the control documents in a typical production and inventory control system. Note that every demand for material and material movement is accompanied by a corresponding transaction document which authorizes the release of a specified quantity of material, describes the operations to be performed, and indicates the destination of material and assemblies. Thus, inventories are controlled from the time they are received in the plant, throughout the production process, until they are shipped to a customer or transferred to another plant or division.

Identification Systems

A potential weak link in many operating systems is improperly identified material. As a general rule, the storeroom should not accept such materials until they have been properly identified by qualified personnel. The most current identification system practice is to identify materials, containers, and locations with machine-readable bar codes. These bar codes eliminate recording error and increase storeroom productivity. (See Chap. 28.)

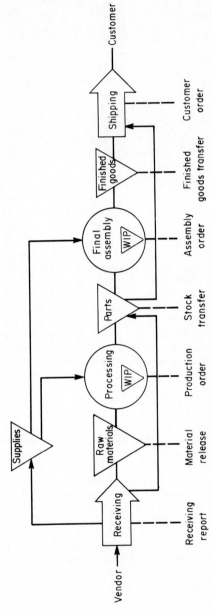

FIG. 21.15 Typical flow of material and associated transaction documents.

21.24

Stock Locator Systems

Inventory serves no purpose if it cannot be located. The most common waste of time in a storeroom is the hunt-and-search effort that goes into looking for lost or misplaced materials. To prevent this, there are three basic types of locator systems: generic stock location, stock number location, and stock by location.

Generic stock location systems are the oldest and most functional. Similar materials are stocked by name in the same general location. For example, nuts and bolts are kept together in the bin-shelving unit at the front of the stockroom. With this type of system, a few items can be readily handled, but it does entail a limited amount of hunt and search and the possibility of error. Thus, generic systems are appropriate only when there are relatively few items in each generic grouping and sufficiently few items in the overall system, so the generic group locations can be easily remembered.

It is sometimes convenient to have labels at each location showing part numbers and descriptions. When stock locations are so identified, however, it is absolutely essential to update the labels as location changes are made. Otherwise, utter chaos will result.

Stock number location systems put more order into intermediate-size store-rooms. When all materials have stock numbers, the storeroom can be set up in stock number sequence. Note, however, that such an arrangement is not normally consistent with the previously stated storeroom configuration guidelines. Stock numbers come and go, requiring space when they are added and creating space when they are deleted. Some stock numbers take lots of cube, and others need very little. If the stock numbering system has symbolic meaning, i.e., embedded product attributes such as voltage, horsepower, etc., then stock locations may not be readily apparent because the stock numbers will have gaps in the sequence. It is very difficult to rearrange stock-number-oriented storerooms. As a result, a progressive deterioration occurs which results in steady increases in both waste of space and stock selection travel time.

Stock by location is the most effective locator system for larger stockrooms. In this type of system, which is usually computer-based, each storage location (slot) is assigned a unique location code, typically composed of 6 to 12 alphanumeric characters. Upon entry to the storeroom, material is assigned to available slots, and two bookkeeping entries are made. First, the code numbers of the assigned slots are redesignated from "available" to "in use." Second, the slot code and the quantity received are recorded, either in a separate locator system file or in the inventory master file, depending on the overall system design. When material is removed from a slot, the entries are reversed.

This approach has the advantage that if the available slot types (floor, pallet rack, flow rack, etc.) become out of balance with storage requirements, then the empty slots can be reconfigured and recoded without affecting the integrity of the slots in use in any way. Similarly, if the cube or movement of an item changes, the item can be moved to a more appropriate available slot. Hence, the stockroom can be constantly updated and the layout kept at its optimum.

Inventory Verification Methods

Three key pieces of information need to be verified in order to maintain the integrity of stockroom operations: inventory count, inventory description, and inventory location. Accurate data for each are vital to any type of materials control system.

To detect the occurrence of bad data in the system, inventory records should be routinely compared and reconciled against actual holdings. This auditing process is called *physical inventory*.

There are two principal methods of taking physical inventories. The traditional method is performed annually, often under the supervision of the organization's auditors, as part of the annual financial reporting process. Being primarily a financial tool, the annual physical inventory is oriented toward verifying the firm's valuation of its assets in total dollars. Nonetheless, an important by-product of the annual physical inventory is the identification of individual record inaccuracies. This information should be used to identify and correct weaknesses in the inventory system.

Many manufacturing firms have found, however, that the annual physical inventory has not allowed them to attain the level of inventory record accuracy required by systems such as material-requirements planning (MRP). *Cycle counting* is a continuous sampling approach to inventory verification that can either replace or augment the annual physical inventory. Maximum benefits accrue when the annual physical inventory is eliminated. This move requires the approval of the firm's auditors, however, and it is recommended that preliminary discussions with them occur before a cycle-counting program is initiated. This will ensure that the system installed will be accepted without major modification.

Cycle Counting

The following section briefly summarizes the considerations that should go into the design of a cycle-counting procedure. For further detail, consult the American Production and Inventory Control Society (APICS) training aid by Henry H. Jordan, *Cycle Counting for Record Accuracy Training Aid*, 1977.

Justification for Cycle Counting.   Cycle counting has two advantages over the traditional annual physical inventory. First, since cycle counting occurs continuously during the year, it leads to more timely detection and resolution of inventory integrity problems. As the name implies, an annual physical inventory can only promise to uncover problems within a year of their occurrence. Second, it is generally believed that cycle counting is more accurate and less expensive. Unlike the annual physical inventory, which often requires that all operations cease, disruptions to production activities are minimal. This eliminates the rush conditions often associated with the annual physical inventory. Moreover, the counting can be accomplished by regular stockroom personnel who can be thoroughly trained in the technique. Otherwise, large numbers of untrained and sometimes poorly motivated employees will have to be used.

Prior to Implementation.   Before a cycle-counting program is begun, it is usually a good strategy to form a test group of 20 to 100 items broadly representative of the inventory holdings of the firm. Each item in the group should be counted once a week. This approach should quickly identify any major shortcomings of the current record-keeping practice. Full-scale implementation of cycle counting should be deferred until the shortcomings are corrected and near 100 percent record accuracy is attained for the test group. The most likely problem areas are inadequate transaction documentation, unauthorized stock movements, and imprecise locator systems. After the cycle-counting activity is implemented for all items, the test group can continue to provide an early warning should accuracy problems occur.

Cycle-Counting Sampling Plan.   Two interdependent decisions are required in designing a sampling plan: frequency of counts and grouping of counts. The procedure should provide for the counting of every item at least once a year. Beyond this, items with high value, frequent transaction errors, or high usage are candidates for more frequent counts. The ABC classification count schedule may also be used with high-value A items being counted once per month, medium-value B items once every 3 months, and low-value C items once a year. Items can be grouped for the daily counts in accordance with a number of criteria, including transaction-based triggers, such as after order release or after order receipt, and location-based checks (count all items in a given area) or randomly with each item's probability of selection being dependent on its count frequency.

Since many types of inventory record errors are associated with the inventory transaction, transaction-based schemes tend to maximize the likelihood of discovering transaction errors immediately after they occur. The counting time will be less if it is done when orders are received or released because the quantity will be at a minimum. Workloads can be further reduced with no loss in control by having stockroom personnel report zero balances.

The major benefits of counting all the holdings in a given location are ease of cutoff, reduced travel time during the count, and detection of "misplaced" stock, i.e., items that are in a location not shown on the inventory records.

Staffing for Cycle Counting.   The time required to perform the counts of the test group should be sufficient to yield information to determine labor requirements. For some firms, cycle-counting workloads will be sufficient to warrant a full-time cycle-counting staff. Others will elect to assign this task to the stockroom personnel. In either case, staff requirements are largest when the cycle-counting program is begun, and they can be expected to slowly decline as the underlying causes of record errors are detected and eliminated. Cycle counting can be utilized to keep personnel busy during slack periods.

Counting.   Counting can be facilitated if a worksheet is provided for the analyst(s) assigned to perform the day's cycle counts. Space should be provided for the analyst's name and the date of the count at the top of the worksheet. The remainder of the form can be set up with one line for each item to be counted and the following column headings:

- Item location
- Item number
- Order number (if work in process)
- Item description
- Unit of measure
- Quantity counted
- Time of count
- Reason for count

All this information, with the exception of quantity counted and time of count, can be entered by computer on the form in advance. Generally, the inventory record balance is not shown on the worksheet, to ensure that an independent count is taken. If a bar-code system is used, it may be possible to eliminate all handwritten input. In this case, the analyst simply scans each item's bar code and then records the quantity on hand on the scanning device.

To ensure that valid counts are taken, a system of inventory transaction cutoffs must exist. This prevents any movement of stock from occurring during the count that could change an item's on-hand balance. This need is particularly acute if the inventory records do not indicate on-hand quantities for specific locations. In this case, it may be impossible for the analyst to reconcile transactions, such as receiving, that would change an item's on-hand balance. The simplest cutoff method is to schedule the counts to occur after normal working hours. Because this is frequently impractical, however, an approach is required that effectively seals off the area(s) in which the count is being conducted and defers all updates of the records involved until the count is completed. It may be possible to relax the cutoff requirements and reconcile apparent inventory errors caused by unavoidable changes in physical holdings during the count if all transactions are stamped with the date and time.

Inventory Variance Reconciliation.   Once the counts have been completed, they should be compared with the inventory records. The record can be considered accurate if the count is within an acceptable tolerance. The APICS cycle-counting training aid recommends the following:

Inventory Class	Count Tolerance	Value Tolerance
A	0.2%	$100
B	1.0%	$100
C	5.0%	$100

Others have suggested that error tolerance should be based on achievable measurement accuracy. Following this line of reasoning suggests that hand counts be required to be exact and scale counts be as accurate as the measuring devices permit. Since different tolerances lead to different definitions of accuracy, care should be taken in comparing record accuracy between different organizations to ensure that measurement tolerances are comparable. In any event, if the count indicates that the record is in error, then the item should be recounted. Depending on the situation, it may be appropriate for the supervisor to perform the recount. If the error is confirmed, the inventory record should be adjusted accordingly, and action should be taken to identify the source of the error and to prevent its recurrence.

Cycle-Counting Control.   To ensure that the cycle-counting activity remains under control, the following administrative procedures are recommended:

1. Reconcile all variances between actual and recorded balances with approval by an appropriate level of management.
2. Train staff members to view each observed error as a valuable opportunity to detect and remove an underlying weakness in the inventory record system.
3. Regularly prepare an *inventory accuracy report* that tracks record accuracy, summarizes the major causes of record errors, and reports the status of efforts being undertaken to correct them. Reporting to management should be weekly at first and monthly once the system's overall record integrity has been satisfactorily verified.
4. Prepare a *cycle count status report* that compares planned and actual counts. This report can be used to monitor count progress and workloads.

5. Document the entire cycle-counting activity in a procedures manual, so that there can be no misunderstanding of criteria and so that new personnel can be quickly trained.

Taking the Annual Physical Inventory

The annual physical inventory procedure is discussed in two parts: physical inventory preparations and recording the physical inventory.

Physical Inventory Preparations.   Taking the annual physical inventory is a major task that requires careful planning. The larger the inventory, the greater the need for careful preparation. Inventory procedures should be formalized; detailed instructions should be given to each person participating in the inventory. The following points should be covered in preparing to take a physical inventory:

1. Set the starting date and target completion date.
2. Select personnel and assign them duties and responsibilities.
3. The scope of the inventory and categories of inventory, included with special instructions for each category, must be specified.
4. Forms to be used should be prepared and specific instruction issued governing their use.
5. Methods for measuring and counting inventories, including those that may be estimated because of the physical characteristics (e.g., weight counting), must be established.
6. Procedures for checking and reconciling the inventory records must be prepared.
7. Methods of tabulating the inventory, auditing the results, and releasing inventoried materials must be chosen.

Many firms have prepared physical inventory procedure manuals containing explicit instructions and detailed procedures. Thus, procedures are standardized and consistent from year to year; they are modified only when necessary to meet new conditions. Personnel assigned to inventory tasks become more skilled when procedures are standardized.

In preparation for the physical inventory, each department foreman and storekeeper should arrange the area so that like materials are grouped and properly identified. Likewise, a holding area should be set up in the receiving department, and any materials received during the inventory period should be held and excluded from the inventory count. Similarly, internal movements and shipments of material should be suspended for the duration of the inventory period except for emergencies.

Normally, the date for taking an inventory coincides with the end of an accounting period. The extent of the closedown for physical inventories depends on the amount and type of inventory. Careful planning for the physical inventory can minimize the extent of the plant shutdown.

In planning the physical inventory, procedures must be outlined to handle the following categories of material:

• Materials specifically excluded from the inventory
• Materials shipped or transferred during the course of the inventory

- Materials invoiced but not received from vendors
- Materials invoiced but not shipped to customers
- Materials supplied to vendors and subcontractors
- Rejected, salvaged, and scrap materials
- Supplies and perishable tools

Recording the Physical Inventory.   There are two basic forms generally used in taking physical inventories: the *inventory tag* and the *inventory summary sheet.* Previously, both forms were prepared manually. However, the advent of the computer permits preprinting primary data on the inventory tags and inventory summary sheets by machine. Bar coding is also gaining widespread use and is covered in Chap. 28.

The tag method for identifying and recording inventories is universally used and is considered the most convenient. Sample forms are shown in Figs. 21.16 and 21.17. The same basic data are recorded on both forms; however, one is a punched card with preprinted data such as the part of the stock code number, part name or description, unit of measure, unit cost, inventory account, and location. The tags are divided (perforated) so that the smaller portion can be detached and remain with the material after the count is completed. In some instances a two-part form is used, with the "flimsy" copy going to the inventory records section and the card copy directed to the accounting department.

All tags are serially numbered and controlled by a central department, normally the controller's office since the inventory is primarily a financial check. Tags should be issued in blocks of numbers and assigned to the person in charge of the inventory in each specific area. Normally, each department head should supervise the inventory in the area of responsibility. All inventory tags issued should be accounted for when the inventory is completed. Incorrectly marked tags should be voided and turned in with all unused inventory tags. Slow-moving items in stores may be inventoried a few days in advance of the regular inventory and any movement explained on the inventory tag.

Inventory teams normally consist of groups of two or more people. One person writes tags and places them on the materials, while the other team members count and check the materials identification. When the team completes its work, the department head should check the area to ensure that each lot of material is covered by an inventory tag. Before the tags are removed, personnel assigned to the area by the controller's office should spot-check the inventory for coverage, completeness, and accuracy. After they are satisfied with the inventory, the serial numbers should be checked to see that no tags are missing. If two-part tags are used, the top section of the tag remains with the material as a guide to locating lost tags and to facilitate recounts, when necessary. All tags should be accounted for before a department is authorized to resume production.

The perpetual inventory records and physical inventory should be reconciled from the inventory tags—the date, inventory tag number, and quantity should be posted to the inventory record. Then the inventory data from the tags should be transferred to the inventory summary sheets, grouping items by inventory category and materials accounts. The inventory verification sheet shown in Fig. 21.18 should include the quantity, part or stock number, inventory tag number, unit cost, and total value of inventory items. Thus, the total value can be calculated for each material control account, and the accounting records can be adjusted accordingly.

For the computer, the data that have been added manually to the preprinted card can be processed in either batch or on-line mode. The cards can be sorted and fed

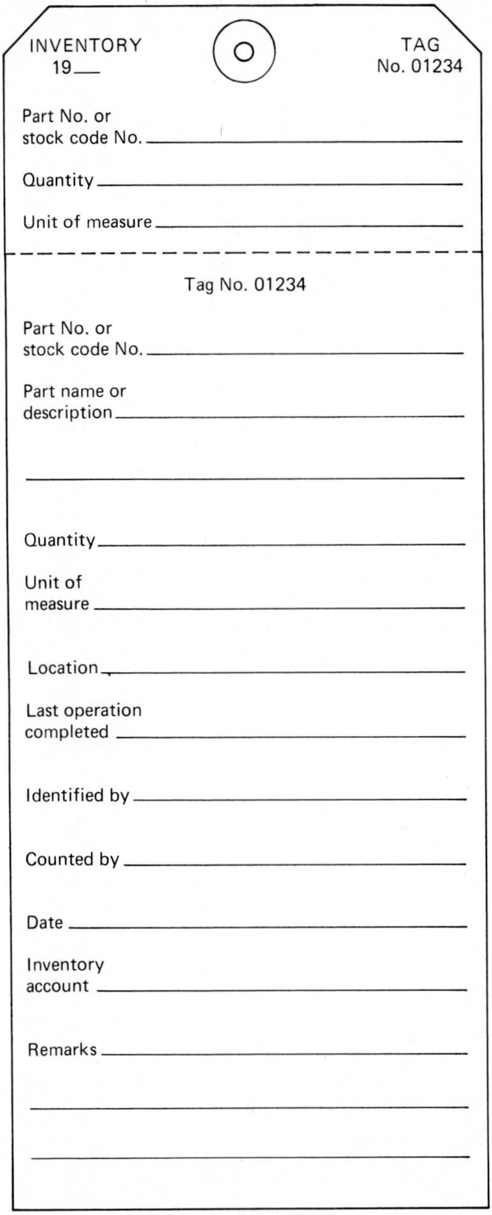

```
┌─────────────────────────────────────────┐
│ INVENTORY      ( O )         TAG          │
│    19___                     No. 01234    │
│                                           │
│  Part No. or                              │
│  stock code No. _____  │
│                                           │
│  Quantity _____   │
│                                           │
│  Unit of measure _____   │
│ ─ ─ ─ ─ ─ ─ ─ ─ ─ ─ ─ ─ ─ ─ ─ ─ ─ ─ ─ ─ │
│             Tag No. 01234                 │
│                                           │
│  Part No. or                              │
│  stock code No. _____  │
│                                           │
│  Part name or                             │
│  description _____   │
│                                           │
│           _____   │
│                                           │
│  Quantity _____   │
│                                           │
│  Unit of                                  │
│  measure _____   │
│                                           │
│  Location _____   │
│                                           │
│  Last operation                           │
│  completed _____   │
│                                           │
│  Identified by _____   │
│                                           │
│  Counted by _____   │
│                                           │
│  Date _____   │
│                                           │
│  Inventory                                │
│  account _____  │
│                                           │
│  Remarks _____   │
│                                           │
│           _____   │
│                                           │
│           _____   │
└─────────────────────────────────────────┘
```

FIG. 21.16   Inventory tag.

Part No./Stock code No.	Part name/Description	Unit meas.	Unit cost	Location		Part No./Stock code No.
				Date		Unit of measure
		INVENTORY 19__				
Inventory account	Last operation	Identified by:	Counted by	Quantity		Quantity
Remarks:						

Tag No. 00127

Inventory 19__
Tag No 00127

FIG. 21.17 Inventory tag—data processing.

INVENTORY VERIFICATION SHEET

Inventory category_____ Date_____

Item No.	Stock count	Record count	Part number stock code	Part name, description	Qty. adj.	Unit value	Adjustment $
1							
2							
3							
4							
5							
6							
7							
8							
9							
10							
11							
20							
21							
22							
23							
24							
25							

Total value of inventory adjustment $

Stores count_____

Inventory records corrected by_____

Inventory account No._____

Approved_____ Date_____   Approved_____ Date_____

FIG. 21.18 Inventory summary sheet.

into the computer for calculation and reconciliation of materials control accounts. Likewise, the inventory summary sheets, containing the same information as if prepared manually, can be printed by machine. Thus, the approved inventory adjustment updates the inventory record.

Work-in-process tags are used to check the open production orders and are then tabulated and used to reconcile the work-in-process inventory accounts.

SECURITY OF INVENTORIES

Security requirements vary widely within companies and depend on the nature of the material, its value, weight, size, application, and ability to be resold. As a rule of thumb, the more valuable a commodity, the greater the need for security, although there are exceptions. Items of low value that can be used for home or personal use require additional controls, while relatively expensive items such as raw gray iron castings require little or no protection because of their size, weight, and limited utility.

A company can take preventive measures to safeguard inventories by establishing and enforcing storeroom regulations and by periodically auditing the storeroom operation. The following measures apply to storeroom operations:

1. Prohibit general access to stores areas.
2. Keep storerooms locked except during normal working hours.
3. Count, weigh, or measure all receipts of incoming material, and carefully check them against purchase orders or other documents at the point of receipt.
4. Independently check material *entering storerooms* for quantity, condition, and identification.
5. Require requisitions for all material issued from stores.
3. Keep valuable articles in locked cabinets or in a safe, if necessary.

The following measures provide additional protection for inventories of the company:

1. Periodically spot-check inventories on hand against inventory records.
2. Review inventory procedures to ascertain that the system complies with policy and method of operation.
3. Investigate unusual consumption for improper usage, unauthorized usage, or possible theft.
4. Periodically check requisitions for authenticity of signatures.

Most companies, as a matter of policy, carry some form of indemnity insurance which protects against loss through improper or careless acts on the part of employees.

SUMMARY

The day-to-day physical handling and control of inventory is an essential part of the overall material management system. The most sophisticated forecasting models, inventory strategies, and information control will be of little value if the day-to-day handling and storage of inventory is performed ineffectively.

This chapter highlighted some major concerns that must be addressed to ensure handling and storing of inventory. Also this chapter reviewed some of the basic fundamentals used to plan the physical facilities, systems, and procedures to manage efficiently and effectively the physical handling and storage of inventories.

BIBLIOGRAPHY

Backes, R. W.: "Cycle Counting—A Better Method for Achieving Accurate Inventory Records," *Production and Inventory Management*, vol. 21, no. 2, 1980, pp. 36–44.

Burnham, J. M.: *Japanese Productivity*, American Production and Inventory Control Society (APICS), Falls Church, Va., 1983.

Candea, D., and A. C. Hax: *Production and Inventory Management*, Prentice-Hall, Englewood Cliffs, N.J., 1984.

Covin, S.: "Inventory Accuracy—One of Your First Hurdles," *Production and Inventory Management*, vol. 22, no. 2, 1981, pp. 13–22.

Fogarty, D. W., and T. A. Hoffman: *Production and Inventory Management*, South-Western Publishing, Cincinnati, 1983.

French, R. L.: "Accurate Work in Process Inventory—A Critical MRP System Requirement," *Production and Inventory Management*, vol. 21, no. 1, 1980, pp. 17–22.

Greene, J. H.: *Operations Management for Productivity and Profit*, Reston Publishing, Reston, Va., 1984.

————: *Production and Inventory Control*, 2d ed., Irwin, Homewood, Ill., 1974.

Hall, R. W.: *Zero Inventories*, Dow Jones-Irwin, Homewood, Ill., 1983.

Inventory Management Reprints, APICS, Falls Church, Va., 1984.

Jordon, H.: *Cycle Counting*, APICS training aid, APICS, Falls Church, Va., 1980.

Larson, S.: *Inventory Systems and Control Handbook*, Prentice-Hall, Englewood Cliffs, N.J., 1976.

Modern Materials Handling 1984 Casebook/Directory, vol. 38, no. 17, 1984. *Readings in Production and Inventory Control and Planning*, APICS, Falls Church, Va., 1984.

Shingo, Shigeo: *Study of Toyota Production System from Industrial Engineering Viewpoint*, Japanese Management Association, Tokyo, 1981.

Spechler, J.: *Administering the Company Warehouse and Inventory Function*, Prentice-Hall, Englewood Cliffs, N.J., 1975.

Vanesse, N. H.: "Parts Bank Locator Concepts", *Production and Inventory Management*, vol. 23, no. 4, 1982, pp. 68–86.

Vollmann, T., W. L. Berry, and D. Clay Whybark: *Manufacturing Planning and Control Systems*, Dow Jones-Irwin, Homewood, Ill., 1984.

Wolfmeyer, K.: "Effective Stockroom Control: Is It Possible?", *Production and Inventory Management*, vol. 22, no. 4, 1981, pp. 25–35.

22

Distribution Resource Planning*

Editor

ANDRÉ J. MARTIN, President, André Martin & Associates, Inc., Ste. Rose Station, Laval, Canada

WHAT IS DISTRIBUTION RESOURCE PLANNING?

The basic principles of distribution resource planning (DRP) are purely and simply the application of material-requirements planning (MRP) scheduling and time-phasing logic to the management of distribution inventories and transportation. These principles were first used in practice in 1975 in Abbott Laboratories, Montreal, Canada. Although the concept often referred to as *time-phased order point* had been known for some time, it was not until 1975 that it was actually used in industry for distribution. Since then DRP has evolved and has become a standard approach for managing distribution inventories and transportation. Today it is being used in a number of distribution and manufacturing companies.

This approach offers opportunities to use the same tools for managing inventories regardless of the nature or source of the inventories. Thus retailers, wholesalers, mass merchandisers, and manufacturers who maintain inventories for distribution

---

* Some material in this chapter was adapted from André J. Martin, *DRP—Distribution Resource Planning, Distribution Management's Most Powerful Tool*, 1983. Adapted by permission of Oliver Wight Limited Publications, Inc., Essex Junction, Vt.

can and do use the same tools. This eliminates the problems of using different systems in distribution and manufacturing which must then be interfaced to close the loop between the needs of distribution and the capabilities of manufacturing.

Functionality

Figure 22.1 illustrates a partial bill of materials used in manufacturing. This bill-of-materials structure shows one product (parent) calling for three components. To operate MRP, it is mandatory to structure bills of materials in that fashion. The same is true for operating DRP. Figure 22.2 illustrates a bill of materials for use by DRP. In this case, a bill of materials, sometimes called a *bill of distribution*, has been structured to show the flow of material from its supply source to three distribution centers that stock this product.

Depending on the applications, different configurations can be developed to show several various material flows. For example, not all products may be stocked in every distribution center. Some products may move from a plant location, regional center, or central supply source directly to the customer. Whatever the situation, the users must structure bills of materials specifying the material flow for each and every product to be handled by DRP.

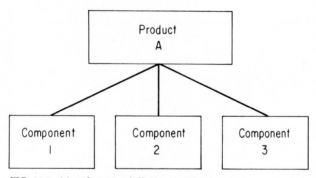

FIG. 22.1   Manufacturing bill of materials.

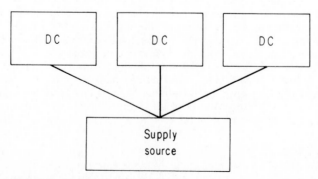

FIG. 22.2   Distribution bill of materials.

This method of structuring the flow of material from supply source to distribution points sets the stage for using DRP and at the same time has significant advantages in practice:

- Inventory interdependency is recognized between distribution and manufacturing inventories.
- A complete distribution network can be structured, thus giving users visibility up and down the network.
- DRP sets the framework for total logistics control from distribution to manufacturing to purchasing.
- DRP provides input for transportation planning and scheduling from the supply source to distribution points.

HOW DRP WORKS

DRP applies the same kind of calculation that is used to balance a checkbook or to develop a shortage list. Imagine that the distribution center manager has been asked to determine the need for a product. The first step is probably to find out the forecast quantity for the product. Then the on-hand inventory balance in the distribution center is used to calculate how long it will last. If a safety stock is desired, subtract it from the on-hand balance before calculating how long the inventory will last.

The date calculated is the date on which the inventory will be depleted or the date the inventory will drop below the safety stock if there is a safety stock. All this assumes there is nothing in transit. However, if something were in transit, the distribution center manager would add this to the on-hand balance to determine how long the inventory is projected to last. The date on which the sum of the on-hand balance and the quantity in transit will be used up is the best estimate of when to schedule the next delivery.

The shipping date from the supply source is the date needed, less the replenishment lead time. The replenishment lead time is the time it takes to ship the product from a supply source to the distribution center. That time includes the time required to do the paperwork for shipping and the time for picking, packing, shipping, and receiving the products at the distribution centers.

The distribution manager should go ahead and calculate the predicted shipping date for the next order, and the one after that, and so on for a year or so into the future. This will assist the planners for the product at the supply source. They will be able to see the projected sales for the product over the next year. This will allow them to have the product available when needed. These projections into the future become the forecast requirements from the distribution centers. As demand changes, DRP will replan and show the changes.

It might seem too much work to do all these calculations and make predictions. This is what a computer does to this type of calculation. It can calculate thousands of items in just a few hours. The power of a computer lies in its blinding speed in doing just this type of simple calculation and in doing it over and over.

A Los Angeles distribution center has 500 units of a product on hand, 200 units as safety stock, and a sales forecast that varies between 80 and 120 units per week. This is shown in Fig. 22.3. The projected on-hand balance is the calculation just shown as done by the manager of the distribution center. This logic reduces the on-hand balance by the quantities forecast for each week. For example, in the first

Vitamin C, 100-Tablet Bottles

On-hand balance: 500
Safety stock: 200

	Past Due	Week							
		1	2	3	4	5	6	7	8
Forecast		100	120	90	110	120	100	80	120
In transit									
Projected on hand	500	400	280	190	80	−40			

FIG. 22.3   Los Angeles distribution center.

week 500 units are on hand at the beginning of the week. Since 100 units are forecast to be sold during the week, they are subtracted, to give a projected on-hand balance of 400 units at the beginning of week 2. This continues. Note that the projected on-hand balance goes below the safety stock of 200 units in week 3 (projected on-hand balance of 190), and the distribution center will probably run out of stock and go on back order in week 5.

In this case, there is nothing in transit. However, if something were in transit, it would be added to the projected on-hand balance in the week that it is due to arrive. Some later examples include a quantity in transit.

The situation will occur as shown if nothing is shipped from the supply source. The distribution manager needs more of this product delivered in week 3, to keep from dropping below safety stock, and must have more units by week 5, to prevent a back order for this product. The replenishment lead time for this item is 2 weeks, and normally 300 units are shipped at a time. It takes 2 weeks to ship the product from the supply source to the distribution center. The order quantity of 300 represents two full pallet loads.

The manager of the distribution center wants a shipment of 300 units of this product to arrive in week 3. Otherwise, this item will drop below the safety stock. The shipment should be sent from the supply source in week 1. Figure 22.4 includes this planned shipment from the supply source in the two lines labeled *planned shipments*. The first, *planned shipments—receipt date* shows these planned shipments on the date they are due to arrive at the distribution center. The other line, *planned shipments—ship date*, shows the planned shipments on the date they are due to be shipped from the supply source.

Note that these planned shipments provide enough stock to last until week 8, although the distribution center will go below safety stock in week 6. Therefore, the manager of the distribution center wants another shipment to arrive in week 6, and this should be shipped from the supply source in week 4. Figure 22.5 gives the complete picture for this item at the distribution center.

As is clear from Fig. 22.5 the logic of DRP (1) calculates when the inventory on hand and in transit will be used up, (2) takes the order quantity supplied by the people using the system and creates planned shipments to the distribution center, (3) takes the planned replenishment lead time and calculates the shipping date for the planned shipments to the distribution center, and (4) includes these planned shipments in the projected on-hand balance calculations and continues this process to the end of the planning horizon. In the examples just used the planning horizon went out 8 weeks into the future. In an actual DRP system, the planning horizon would typically extend for a year or more.

Vitamin C, 100-Tablet Bottles

On-hand balance: 500
Safety stock: 200
Lead time: 2 wk
Order quantity: 300

	Past Due	Week							
		1	2	3	4	5	6	7	8
Forecast		100	120	90	110	120	100	80	120
In transit									
Projected on hand	500	400	280	490	380	260	160	80	−40
Planned shipments—receipt date				300					
Planned shipments—ship date		300							

FIG. 22.4 Los Angeles distribution center—planned shipments.

Vitamin C, 100-Tablet Bottles

On-hand balance: 500
Safety stock: 200
Lead time: 2 wk
Order quantity: 300

	Past Due	Week							
		1	2	3	4	5	6	7	8
Forecast		100	120	90	110	120	100	80	120
In transit									
Projected on hand	500	400	280	490	380	260	460	380	260
Planned shipments—receipt date				300			300		
Planned shipments—ship date		300			300				

FIG. 22.5 Los Angeles distribution center—considering safety stocks.

Now that it has been shown how DRP would work in one distribution center, let us extend it to all the distribution centers for this product. There are six distribution centers in total—Los Angeles, Montreal, New York, Vancouver, Toronto, and Chicago; the supply source is also in Chicago. The examples that follow, Figs. 22.6 to 22.11, are the DRP displays for the other five distribution centers and are similar to the DRP display shown before for the Los Angeles distribution center.

Figure 22.6 shows in the Montreal distribution center 150 units in transit. This order has just been shipped because the lead time is 2 weeks and it is due to arrive in week 2. Note that the in-transit quantity is added to the projected on-hand balance in the week in which the order is due to arrive. The manager of the distribution center can now see what material is in transit and when it can be expected.

In the New York distribution center (Fig. 22.7), a planned order is overdue for shipment. This is the planned shipment for 300 appearing in the past-due time period. There could be several reasons. Possibly sales were greater than forecast, so the product is needed in New York earlier than was originally planned. Another

Vitamin C, 100-Tablet Bottles

On-hand balance: 160
Safety stock: 75
Lead time: 2 wk
Order quantity: 150

	Past Due	Week							
		1	2	3	4	5	6	7	8
Forecast		40	50	45	50	40	45	40	50
In transit			150						
Projected on hand	160	120	220	175	125	85	190	150	100
Planned shipments—receipt date							150		
Planned shipment—ship date					150				

FIG. 22.6   Montreal distribution center.

Vitamin C, 100-Tablet Bottles

On-hand balance: 300
Safety stock: 100
Lead time: 2 wk
Order quantity: 300

	Past Due	Week							
		1	2	3	4	5	6	7	8
Forecast		120	130	115	125	140	110	125	105
In transit									
Projected on hand	300	180	350	235	110	270	160	335	230
Planned shipments—receipt date			300			300		300	
Planned shipments—ship date	300			300		300			

FIG. 22.7   New York distribution center.

possibility is that the shipment was not sent from the supply source on time. In this situation, the manager of the distribution center can find out if the supply source is failing to ship on time, and well before a stock-out.

The Vancouver, Toronto, and Chicago distribution centers shown in Figs. 22.8 to 22.10, respectively, are similar to the Los Angeles distribution center. There is nothing in transit, but there are several planned shipments from the supply source to the distribution centers. Because the Chicago distribution center is in the same city as the supply source, the lead time for Chicago is 1 day.

Note that the lead time, order quantities, and safety stocks are different for each distribution center. Each distribution center is an entity, and it can be scheduled independently of the others. In addition, the lead times, order quantities, and safety stocks can be different for different products at the same distribution center. This is not illustrated in the examples because only one of many products is shown. However, each product at each distribution center is scheduled independently. DRP gives the people running the system complete flexibility in scheduling any item at any distribution center.

The numbers shown in Fig. 22.11 are the planned shipments shown by shipping date. These numbers indicate when and what the supply source should ship to the

Vitamin C, 100-Tablet Bottles

On-hand balance: 140
Safety stock: 50
Lead time: 3 wk
Order quantity: 150

	Past Due	Week							
		1	2	3	4	5	6	7	8
Forecast		20	25	15	20	30	25	15	30
In transit									
Projected on hand	140	120	95	80	60	180	155	140	110
Planned shipments—receipt date						150			
Planned shipments—ship date			150						

FIG. 22.8   Vancouver distribution center.

Vitamin C, 100-Tablet Bottles

On-hand balance: 120
Safety stock: 50
Lead time: 1 wk
Order quantity: 150

	Past Due	Week							
		1	2	3	4	5	6	7	8
Forecast		25	15	20	25	20	20	25	15
In transit									
Projected on hand	120	95	80	60	185	165	145	120	105
Planned shipments—receipt date					150				
Planned shipments—ship date				150					

FIG. 22.9   Toronto distribution center.

Vitamin C, 100-Tablet Bottles

On-hand balance: 400
Safety stock: 150
Lead time: 1 day
Order quantity: 300

	Past Due	Week							
		1	2	3	4	5	6	7	8
Forecast		105	115	95	90	100	110	95	120
In transit									
Projected on hand	400	295	180	385	295	195	385	290	170
Planned shipments—receipt date				300			300		
Planned shipments—ship date				300			300		

FIG. 22.10   Chicago distribution center.

	Past Due	Week								
		1	2	3	4	5	6	7	8
Los Angeles		300			300				
Montreal					150				
New York	300			300		300			
Vancouver			150						
Toronto				150					
Chicago				300			300		
Totals	300	300	150	750	450	300	300	0	0

FIG. 22.11 Summary of planned shipments to the distribution centers.

different distribution centers to meet the forecast demands. They are not an average, an approximation, or a guess. They are the true needs of the distribution network.

This arrangement gives tremendous visibility into the distribution network. With this kind of information, a planner can truly foresee the needs of the distribution centers. The better a planner can predict the distribution center's future need, the better he or she will be able to meet those needs. This is the true meaning of planning: looking ahead, identifying problems, and solving them. The totals from DRP give this visibility for the first time. Yet DRP does not solve the problems. The people running the system must take this information and use it to solve the problems. It is similar to driving at night. Headlights give you the visibility to see where you are going, but someone still has to steer the car.

An important point about the summary of planned shipments is the lumpy demand from the distribution center. Note that the forecasts for all the distribution centers are fairly smooth over time. Thus one might expect the demand on the supply source to be smooth as well, with demand in any one week nearly the same as demands in other weeks. Yet, just the opposite is true. The demand on the supply source is lumpy. For example, in week 2 the demand is only 150, and in week 3 the demand is 750. This lumpy demand is an inherent characteristic of a distribution system that uses lot sizes.

This lumpy demand is one reason why it is so important to be able to see into the distribution network. Because the demand on the supply source can vary so much from week to week, a planner has to be able to see what is really needed and when, in order to meet the needs of the distribution centers. This lumpy demand is not the only reason that the type of visibility provided by DRP is needed, but it is an important one.

Some people hold that breaking down shipping requirements into lot sizes will create additional inventories. This is theoretically correct, but practicality supercedes theory in the real world. As many practitioners have learned, common sense and the particular environment must dominate in the establishment of shipping quantities. Each company's environment is different and must be taken into account. Some companies have fully automated warehouses that use computers and stacker cranes to put away and retrieve products. The lot size in that situation is determined by the type of material-handling system in use. Other companies have material-handling systems that are pallet-oriented. The lot size in this case is a function of how much of a product is stored on a pallet.

There are companies who have their own trucking fleet, or make use of common carriers, to ship products to their distribution centers based on specific shipping schedules. Typically, weight and cube to a given distribution location are planned and scheduled by the day or by the week. These are real issues. They can have an impact on how small or how large a shipping quantity must be to achieve the desired aggregate weight per cube and frequency of shipment to each distribution center.

DRP is a distribution system model which allows its users to represent their own environment, constraints, and differences in the system. And as these change, users must reflect these changes within DRP. The aim here is to simulate the real world.

A very important reason for needing the visibility which DRP offers is the ability to react to change. Distribution, like manufacturing, exists in a dynamic environment. The most apparent cause of change is sales that are different from the forecast. The forecast is only a guess, and what actually happens is not likely to agree exactly with the forecast. In many situations, sales do not even approximate the forecast. This is not to say that it is useless to try to improve the forecast. But regardless of how much effort is put into the forecast, the forecast will be wrong. Things will happen that are different from what was originally forecast.

In this kind of situation, what is needed is a system that can react to change. DRP is exactly such a system. Not only does DRP plan each item in each of the distribution centers, but also it replans them over and over. In a typical DRP system, each item in each distribution center is replanned at least once a week.

For example, consider the Los Angeles distribution center. The first display in Fig. 22.12 shows a forecast of 100 in week 1. Now assume that instead of selling the 100 that were forecast in the first week, 170 were actually sold. The following week the DRP display for this product at Los Angeles would change as shown in Fig. 22.13.

Notice that because the sales were greater than forecasted, the planned shipments moved up to earlier dates. The planned shipment of 300 due to arrive in week 6 is now needed in week 5, which is normal. In addition, a new planned shipment of 300 which did not exist last week has been created and is needed in week 8. In this case, the sales were so much greater than the forecast, that the planned shipment dates were changed. This does not happen in every case. It happens only when there is a significant difference between what was sold and what was forecast or when the projected on-hand balance is only slightly above the safety stock. Another change in the DRP display is the 300 in transit. This was a planned shipment last week. It was shipped to Los Angeles, and now it appears in transit under the week it is due to arrive.

As a result of these changes at the Los Angeles distribution center, the total demands on the supply source have changed. Shown in Fig. 22.14a are the total demands from last week, and the total demands for this week are seen in Fig. 22.14b. Comparison of the differences between the two reveals that the change in the total demands on the supply source went from 750 in week 3 to 1050, from 450 in week 4 to 150, and from 300 in week 6 to 600.

This is pure visibility. The distribution planner is able to see exactly the effect of the above forecast sales in Los Angeles. New demands on the supply source can be seen and plans made to supply these needs. DRP constantly replans, updates, and revises the plan based on the best available information. The true needs are kept up to date. Conventional inventory management systems do not have this ability to accurately look ahead and revise the plan based on the changes that have occurred. This forward visibility allows master schedulers and distribution planners to anticipate what may have to change in the future, as opposed to reacting to something that has actually happened.

Sales could have been less than forecast, rather than more. In that case, the planned shipments to the distribution centers would be rescheduled outward in

Vitamin C, 100-Tablet Bottles

Before Above-Forecast Sales
On-hand balance: 500
Safety stock: 200
Lead time: 2 wk
Order quantity: 300

	Past Due	Week							
		1	2	3	4	5	6	7	8
Forecast		100	120	90	110	120	100	80	120
In transit									
Projected on hand	500	400	280	490	380	260	460	380	260
Planned shipments—received date				300			300		
Planned shipments—ship date		300			300				

FIG. 22.12   Los Angeles distribution center, case 1.

Vitamin C, 100-Tablet Bottles

After Above-Forecast Sales
On-hand balance: 330
Safety stock: 200
Lead time: 2 wk
Order quantity: 300

	Past Due	Week						
		2	3	4	5	6	7	8
Forecast		120	90	110	120	100	80	120
In transit			300					
Projected on hand	330	210	420	310	490	390	310	490
Planned shipments—received date					300			300
Planned shipments—ship date			300			300		

FIG. 22.13   Los Angeles distribution center case 2.

time, rather than inward. This would be reflected in the total demands on the supply source.

In the last example, only one change to a planned shipment date occurred at one distribution center, Los Angeles. In actual practice, it is likely that changes to planned shipments would have occurred during the week at several distribution centers. It is even possible, although unlikely, that a change to the planned shipments would have occurred at all the distribution centers.

Sales that are greater or less than forecast are not the only reasons that the planned shipments change. Changes to the forecast quantities, safety stocks, lead times, and order quantities can cause the planned shipments to change. In other words, DRP picks up and reports any changes in the entire distribution network. It is a true simulation of a distribution network. It shows within the computer what is happening in the distribution system and what is predicted for the future.

Distribution Centers
Before   Above-Forecast Sales

	Past Due	Week							
		1	2	3	4	5	6	7	8
Los Angeles		300			300				
Montreal					150				
New York	300			300		300			
Vancouver			150						
Toronto				150					
Chicago				300			300		
Totals	300	300	150	750	450	300	300	0	0

(a)

After   Above-Forecast Sales

	Past Due	Week						
		2	3	4	5	6	7	8
Los Angeles			300			300		
Montreal				150				
New York			300		300			
Vancouver		150						
Toronto			150					
Chicago			300			300		
Total	0	150	1050	150	300	600	0	0

(b)

FIG. 22.14   Comparison of planned shipments.

The examples using DRP in six distribution centers that are supplied from one source are found frequently in practice. However, on occasion companies do business using networks that have more than one level of inventory in distribution. For example, a company might have one or several supply sources that distribute products to regional distribution centers which in turn distribute products to a number of satellite distribution centers. Figure 22.15 shows one such situation.

As previously stated, before attempting to apply DRP, one must configure the network, showing how material will flow from source to the ultimate point of distribution. There may be different material flows for different products, and DRP offers the flexibility of specifying material flow on a product-by-product basis.

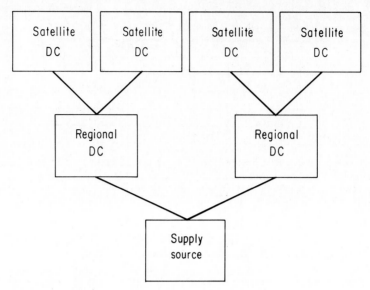

FIG. 22.15 Multilevel DRP system.

WHERE DOES DRP APPLY?

There are several applications in which DRP can be and is being used. From the standpoint of managing distribution inventories, DRP has universal applicability without any restriction. From a manufacturing standpoint, it obviously is applicable whenever a make-to-stock product is manufactured and distributed before it is sold to the end customer. DRP would not be applicable otherwise, as for make-to-order products, which typically are manufactured and then shipped directly to the customer.

Applicable Features

When DRP was first used, it found a home primarily with companies that manufactured and distributed the product through their own distribution network. Today DRP is being applied in pure distribution-type businesses that buy and sell products as opposed to manufacturers. DRP offers significant opportunities for distribution and manufacturing companies alike.

This latest trend is the next frontier; total materials logistics is now possible, with DRP as the key to its realization. Figure 22.16 represents the functions of DRP in a typical make-to-stock company. It is often called an integrated distribution/manufacturing system.

In this typical application, DRP is used to schedule distribution inventory needs (called *distribution demand* in the figure) and feeds the distribution demand to the master production schedule (MPS) as forecasts for manufacturing. Depending on the company, this forecast could be one of several forecasts that are summed to give a total requirement of needs that manufacturing must meet.

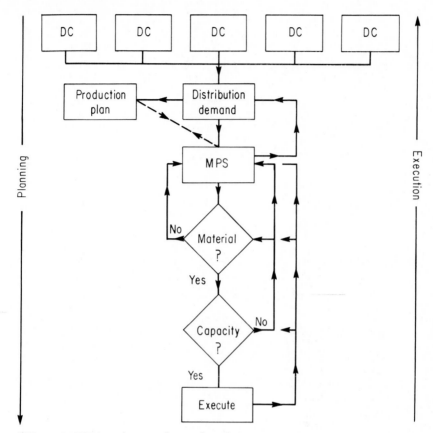

FIG. 22.16   DRP in make-to-stock manufacturing.

For example, a company might have requirements coming from export customers, bid and tender business, and large domestic customers. In such situations, the distribution demand coming from DRP is added to the other forecasts. The distribution demand is typically shown in a time-phased manner on a separate line of the MPS display. This allows users the visibility of distribution needs. The relative impact on manufacturing ability is thus clearly identified.

If DRP is applied to pure distribution types of businesses, the application is somewhat different in scope but not in function. Figure 22.17 shows the functions of DRP as it applies to retailers, wholesalers, and merchandisers. Note that the distribution demand becomes the input to the master purchase schedule—as opposed to an MPS in a manufacturing company, as indicated in Fig. 22.16.

Also note that in this case the distribution demand is an input to the purchase plan whereas in a manufacturing company it is the input to the production plan. Both of these conditions vary in scope and are covered in the section on features of DRP.

Once DRP is used to schedule inventory needs in the merchandising business, the focal point becomes the master purchase schedule function. Those responsible

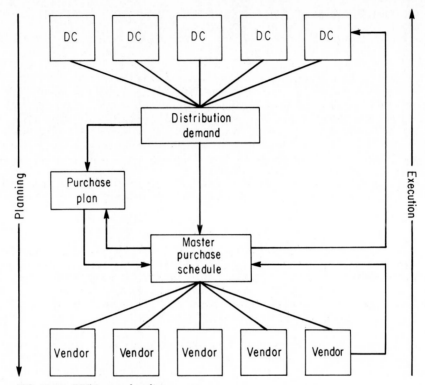

FIG. 22.17   DRP in merchandising.

for this function are essentially accountable for reconciling the needs of distribution with the capabilities of vendors.

In this environment the master purchase schedules are viewed as vendor schedules. Purchase releases to vendors are an integral part of this function.

FEATURES OF DRP

The totals from DRP represent the demands of the entire distribution network. In cases where DRP is used to integrate distribution with manufacturing, the job manufacturing personnel is to plan production such that the demands from distribution can be satisfied. In the merchandising business, the job of satisfying the demands from distribution rests with those responsible for releasing purchase orders to the vendors. This process is somewhat different in application, and both are covered here.

DRP in Manufacturing

Using DRP is a twofold process composed of production planning, which refers to families of products, and master scheduling, which refers to specific end items.

Production Planning

The production plan is a statement of production in gross terms. Typically, production plans are developed for families of products and for monthly periods. For
example, the production plan for vitamin C might be 100,000 tablets per month.
Other production plans might include the number of gallons per month of a certain
color of paint, the number of gallons per month of orange juice or ice cream, or the
quantity of a particular style of chair per month.

A production plan does not identify the specific package size in the case of
orange juice and paint or the specific model in the case of chairs. It is a statement of
production in terms of families of products, not the individual products themselves. The statement of production for specific package sizes and specific models
is the master schedule; this is explained later.

A family of products is a group that typically shares manufacturing facilities. For
example, the 1-pint, 0.5-gallon, 1-gallon, and 5-gallon containers of a particular
type of paint may use the same mixing tank and packaging line. So these products
are grouped in the same family for production planning. These manufacturing
families could be different from the marketing product groups.

The top management of a company is responsible for the accuracy and the
validity of the production plan. Some top managers say they are not concerned with
detailed planning. The production plan is not detailed planning; it is a broad
summarized statement of production rates. And the production plan has tremendous leverage over many things for which a top manager is held accountable. For
example, the production plan determines

- Whether the demands from distribution will be satisfied and, consequently, what
  customer service problems will result
- Whether the plant will be able to meet the production requirements and, if not,
  what other methods can be used to solve the problem
- What the staffing levels will be for the plant and how this fits with current labor
  contracts
- What the utilization of the plant and equipment will be and, consequently, what
  the overhead cost of the product will be
- What the inventory level will be over the course of the year and at the end of the
  year
- What the production cost will be and whether the cash flow will support the plan

All these things are determined directly or indirectly from the production plan.
It serves as the basic constraint on the MPS. The sum of the master schedule items
must be within the constraints of the production plan. In this way, the production
plan is management's single most powerful handle on the system. Because it is so
powerful and because it affects so many of the decisions for which top management
will be held responsible, the production plan must be revealed and approved by the
top manager. Typically, the production plan is developed and approved by the
president or the general manager and staff. It cannot be delegated to a lower level.

In developing a production plan for a family of products, basically three things
need to be considered:

1. What are the distribution demands that must be satisfied for the family of items?
2. What changes in inventory are planned for the family of items?
3. What are the manufacturing or purchasing constraints which could limit production for the family of items?

To illustrate, consider a family of paint products and see how a production plan would be developed. In this case, the production plan is to be developed so that the ending inventory is nearly the same as the starting inventory, the plan meets the demands from distribution, and the production rate does not exceed 2200 per month, which is the capacity for a three-shift operation. Table 22.1 shows the production plan that would be used for a family of products.

The distribution demands column is the total that comes from DRP. The total demands on the central supply facility for one product are added to the demands for the other products in a family. For example, the demands for the 1-pint, 0.5-gallon, 1-gallon, and 5-gallon sizes of this paint are added. In addition, the weekly demands for all these different sizes are added to give monthly totals. This is the demand that has to be satisfied to meet the requirements of the distribution centers.

The change-in-inventory column shows the planned increases and decreases in inventory. This is broken down into two rows; one is the monthly change in inventory, and the other is the cumulative change in inventory from the beginning of the year. These numbers are the sum of the inventories in all the distribution centers and the supply source. In the example, inventory is being built in anticipation of a peak selling season. The months of January, February, and March are used to build up 925 gallons in inventory. This is shown by the cumulative inventory in March, the starting inventory of 1580 in January, and the ending inventory of 2505 at the end of March. Then in April, May, and June, peak sales use up 920 of the 925 gallons in inventory. This is also shown by the cumulative-inventory numbers from March to June, the starting inventory of 2505 at the beginning of April, and the ending inventory of 1585 at the end of June.

Notice that the production plan is more stable than the distribution demands or the planned inventory levels. The distribution demands vary from a high of 2650 to a low of 1655. The inventory goes from a low of 1580 to a high of 2505. The production rate is more stable because manufacturing is unable to sustain a rate of production for this family of products of over 2200 per month. And if the production drops below 1900, there will have to be layoffs of skilled people, which is undesirable in this situation and should be avoided.

Typically, the production plan is reviewed once a month. Over the course of a month, there are usually changes. The distribution demands, for example, are likely to change based on sales that are greater or less than forecast or alterations in the forecast quantities, order quantities, methods of shipment that take more or less time, etc. In addition, there are other changes. There may no longer be the need to build as much inventory, or there may be a need to build more inventory. Manufacturing constraints may change and allow higher or lower rates of production than those used to develop the current production plan.

TABLE 22.1 Production Plan for High-Gloss Enamel Paint

	Distribution Demands	Change in Inventory		Inventory		Production Plan
		Monthly	Cumulative	Starting	Ending	
January	1655*	+345	+345	1580	1925	2000
February	1770	+230	+575	1925	2155	2000
March	1750	+350	+925	2155	2505	2100
April	2300	−200	+725	2505	2305	2100
May	2470	−270	+455	2305	2035	2200
June	2650	−450	+5	2035	1585	2200

*All numbers are in gallons.

The president, or the general manager, and staff review the production plan. This does not necessarily mean changing it. For example, if there were an increase in the sales forecast, probably the production plan would be changed provided that manufacturing could handle the increased rate of production. The production plan would not be changed, however, if things were happening as planned. Note that it is best to establish in advance the ground rules for when it is necessary or desirable to change the production plan. Then the discussion is focused on *solving the problem*, not on the rules for changing the plan.

Master Scheduling

The master schedule is the specific statement of what will be produced and when. The master schedule is in terms of specific items where the production plan is in terms of families of products. For example, individual master schedules would exist for the 1-pint, 0.5-gallon, 1-gallon, and 5-gallon sizes of paint. Each is an individual product and each has a master schedule.

Master schedules are developed based on the following information for an item: distribution demands, any other demands, inventory balance, safety stock, lead time, production lot size, and production plan for the family of items. For example, consider vitamin C in 100-tablet bottles which was used to show how DRP operates in the distribution centers. A master schedule display for this item is shown in Fig. 22.18.

The distribution demands are the totals from the distribution network. Figure 22.11 shows the sum of the distribution requirements for this product from all the different distribution centers. This is the same set of numbers that is shown in the distribution demands line. There are the demands that need to be satisfied to supply this product to the distribution centers.

The scheduled receipts line shows any released orders for this item at the date they are due into stock. If the item is manufactured, these are manufacturing orders that have been released to the shop. If the item is purchased, these are purchase orders that have been released to vendors.

The projected on-hand line is the same type of calculation as shown in the DRP display. The on-hand balance is reduced by the distribution demands and is increased by scheduled receipts and master schedule orders. This calculation

Vitamin C, 100-Tablet Bottles

On-hand balance: 1700
Safety stock: 0
Lead time: 3 wk
Order quantity: 1100

	Past Due	Week							
		1	2	3	4	5	6	7	8
Distribution demands	300	300	150	750	450	300	300	0	0
Scheduled receipts									
Projected on hand	1400	1100	950	200	850	550	250	250	250
Master schedule—receipt					1100				
Master schedule—start		1100							

FIG. 22.18 Supply source.

shows a projected inventory buildup or a stock-out, which is a projected on-hand balance of less than zero.

The master schedule is set and maintained manually by the master scheduler. The master schedule data in the display are not like the planned shipment data in the DRP display. Planned shipments at the distribution centers are generated by the computer, but in the master schedule they are not. The reason is that the master schedule can have a tremendous impact on the manufacturing facility. The master schedule is the source that is used to develop all supporting manufacturing schedules. Therefore, it must be managed carefully.

Master scheduling is a matter for human judgment and decision making. The management of a company and the master scheduler are responsible for developing and maintaining a master schedule which is the best estimation of what will be produced in the future. The kinds of judgments and decisions necessary to develop the master schedule cannot be made by a computer. The computer can only provide the master scheduler with information regarding demand for the item, inventory balance, ordering rules, lead time, etc., which can be used to develop and manage the master schedule.

A master scheduler, using the display shown, interprets the information and evaluates the situation for this product. The master scheduler may decide that more should be added to the master schedule or that the situation is all right and no changes are needed. The point is that a person is looking at the situation and evaluating it.

The production plan acts as a constraint on the master schedule. This means that the total for a family of items on the master schedule must equal the production plan for that family.

The Master Schedule, a Distribution and Manufacturing Interface. In DRP, the distribution demands end at the master schedule. The total demands from the distribution system for each product appear in the master schedule display.

In manufacturing, it all begins with the master schedule. All the supporting manufacturing schedules are based on the master schedule. The master schedule is exploded, and demands for components and raw materials are created. This is done in the same way that the planned shipments to distribution centers are shown as demands on the master schedule report. For example, consider the master schedule for vitamin C in 100-tablet bottles and see how it is exploded and posted as requirements to the components. The master schedule for this product is shown in Fig. 22.19 as well as the MRP display for the bottle, which is one of the component parts. The MRP display is used to plan these components and raw materials in the same way that the DRP display is used to plan an item in a distribution center.

Note that the gross requirements of 1100 in week 1 are coming from the master schedule for vitamin C in 100-tablet bottles. The gross requirements line shows the demands for this item. In this case, the other demands of 3300 in week 4, and 2100 in week 7 are coming from other products which use the same bottle.

The scheduled receipts line in the MRP display shows the released orders at the date on which they are due to arrive in stock. If the item is manufactured, these are the released manufactured orders. If the item is purchased, these are the released purchase orders. There is a purchase order for 6000 due in week 4.

The projected on-hand line is the same type of calculation shown in the DRP display and the master schedule display.

The planned-order releases line contains any planned orders for the item. These are the same as the planned shipments in the DRP display. They are created by the computer and shown at the release dates. The display does not show the planned orders at their receipt dates. This is just a convention; the planned orders could be

Vitamin C, 100-Tablet Bottles

	Past Due	Week							
		1	2	3	4	5	6	7	8
Master schedule—receipt					1100				
Master schedule—start		1100							

MRP Display / K391 Bottle

On-hand balance: 1500
Safety stock: 0
Lead time: 5 wk
Order quantity: 6000

	Past Due	Week							
		1	2	3	4	5	6	7	8
Gross requirements		1100	0	0	3300	0	0	2100	0
Scheduled receipts					6000				
Projected on hand	1500	400	400	400	3100	3100	3100	1000	1000
Planned-order releases									

FIG. 22.19 Master schedule and MRP display.

shown at their receipt dates if so desired. The MRP display explained here is a key element with a manufacturing resource planning system.

The point is that the master schedule is used to drive the schedules for all the components and raw materials. In addition, these schedules are used to calculate the capacity requirements by work center. The master schedule is the starting point for all scheduling in manufacturing.

Therefore, the master schedule is the focal point between distribution and manufacturing. Problems between the two areas tend to surface at the master schedule. In these situations the master schedule is not able to meet the distribution demands.

The solutions to these problems do not necessarily imply changing the master schedule, but the master schedule makes them visible. Sometimes problems can be solved in distribution, at other times they can be rectified in manufacturing, and at still other times they have to be solved by changing the master schedule. But the manager must realize that there are opportunities to solve problems in all three areas.

Problems can be eliminated in distribution by manipulating the distribution plan. If more of a product is needed than can be supplied, it is possible to reduce the demands. One way to do this is to reduce the quantity shipped to the distribution centers; another is to let the quantity on hand drop below the safety stock. Problems can also be solved in manufacturing by working overtime or extra shifts, using alternate equipment, splitting lot sizes, and reducing move and queue times. Finally, problems can be solved by changing the master schedule. However, this is generally the last resort. The objective is to meet the master schedule and change it only when there is no other choice.

The DRP display and the MRP display work in the same way. Manufacturing personnel can see and understand how distribution is run, and distribution personnel can see and understand how manufacturing is run. The same principles, the same methods, and even the same or similar reports are used for both distribution and manufacturing. Whether someone is looking for an item in a distribution center or a manufactured or purchased item, the same logic is used. The system provides visibility from manufacturing into distribution, and vice versa. This type of visibility and the utilization of a common system using common logic promote communication and a better appreciation of the other person's problems. Consequently, real teamwork will result. DRP is a common system that crosses organizational boundaries. It allows people to work together.

Note that DRP with production planning, master scheduling, and MRP tends to render obsolete some of the conventional ideas about inventory. Customer service objectives are no longer a function of finding the "correct" inventory levels or "target" inventories. Customer service is now a function of how well master scheduling, shop and vendor scheduling, and execution problems are identified and corrected. In some ways, this is a more difficult environment, but it is the environment of the real world. DRP does not enable people to sit back and pick a number, or use a formula, to eliminate problems. Results come from identifying problems and then solving them. DRP, with production planning, master scheduling, and MRP, makes it possible to identify these problems while there is still time to do something about them.

DRP in the Merchandising Business

DRP is ideal for the retail and wholesale business. The fundamental strength of DRP is found in the way it helps users manage and control inventories, which is precisely the major task in the merchandising business. These companies buy and sell products and, as a rule, that is their whole business. Therefore, distribution inventory management and merchandising is their game. In addition, profit margins in that business sector tend to be low. Thus greater emphasis must be placed on buying inventories in the most economical ways and moving them in the fastest way possible to minimize investment and maximize sales and profits.

This is easier said than done. Retailers tend to inventory a great number of products. Some are extremely seasonal, others are trendy, and still others have a normal distribution. The management of changes is constant in this type of business—much more than in a manufacturing environment.

The change variation that a manufacturer sees normally has been filtered many times before it affects production, and often it is not a true indication of what is happening at the retail level. Jay Forrester described that phenomenon very well in July 1958 in "Industrial Dynamics," *Harvard Business Review*.

Retailers and wholesalers are now turning to DRP to help in the management and buying of inventories. The scheduling and rescheduling capabilities of DRP are oriented toward the management of change. However there are differences in emphasis. Retailers and wholesalers tend to *pull* inventories away from their sources of supplies whereas in manufacturing the trend has been toward *pushing* inventories out of the plants to the distribution centers. At some point they meet, yet the approaches to inventory management vary on both sides.

Retailers, wholesalers, and manufacturers are discovering that much can be gained by all parties in a given channel of distribution if they can work closer and share information on inventory needs. In the future, retailers and wholesalers working with manufacturers will be able to accomplish much with DRP, such as by sharing the output of their DRP schedules with the manufacturers, thus eliminating uncertainty in the way vendors try to forecast the customer's needs. Also productivity will increase, safety stocks will be reduced, and customer service will improve for both retailers and manufacturers.

DRP is the natural extension of MRP in the management of inventories. The same scheduling logic is used up and down a distribution channel, and the magnitude of changes at the retail level is passed along quicker. This results in less overall inventory, and greater synchronization of supply and demand is achieved.

Figure 22.20 shows an integrated distribution channel where DRP is used to link members of the channel in managing inventories and ordering products from supply sources. In each step of the planning process required for purchases, DRP is used to summarize the purchases by product for all locations that stock it. The time-phased displays become the master purchase schedules. These master purchase schedules become the focal point of the interface between the needs of the customer and the capabilities of vendors to deliver.

The time-phased displays of the master purchase schedules showing the total purchase requirements show, in fact, the same information that is normally found in a blanket purchase contract with scheduled deliveries. The difference, however, is that DRP continually updates the information as conditions change.

Once purchase contracts are agreed on and delivery time fences are negotiated, customers and vendors can communicate this information electronically, thus accomplishing complete logistics planning from retailers to wholesalers to manufacturers.

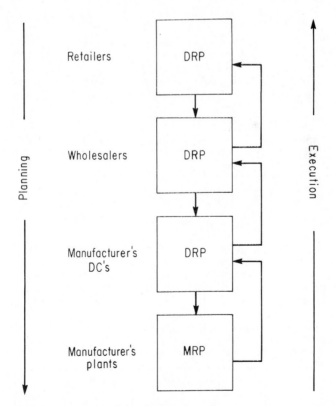

FIG. 22.20 Integrated distribution channel.

DRP/MRP Display

Since this is written for users of a production and inventory control (PIC) handbook, the format of the DRP display in the examples is modified. The display presented in this detailed section is a standardized display used by PIC practitioners. The standardized display is exactly the same for distribution center items, for manufactured items, or for purchased items. This standard format is also used in many software packages.

There are a number of reasons for adopting a standardized format for both manufacturing and distribution. One is that the logic of the system works in exactly the same way. Therefore, there is no need to make things look different with different displays. Another reason for a standardized display is that it makes the system easier to understand. Manufacturing and distribution personnel using the same display can communicate better and can understand better what the other person is doing.

Four things in the standardized display are different from the DRP displays shown earlier:

1. The term *gross requirements* is used instead of *forecast*. Gross requirements are the demands for an item. If the item is a product in a distribution center, gross requirements are the forecast. If the item is a manufactured or purchased item, gross requirements are what is needed to satisfy the master schedule.

2. The term *scheduled receipts* is used to replace *in transit*. Scheduled receipts are quantities scheduled to come into stock. If these items are products in a distribution center, scheduled receipts are in transit from the center supply facility. They may not actually be on the road. They could be in the process of being picked or packed and still be a scheduled receipt. If these are manufactured or purchased items, the scheduled receipts are either manufactured orders that have been released to manufacturing or purchase orders that have been released to vendors.

3. The term *planned orders* is used to replace *planned shipments—ship date*. Planned orders are not released. They are still in the planning stage, unlike scheduled receipts, which either have been shipped or are being worked on. If the item is a product in a distribution center, the planned orders are the schedule for future shipments from the supply source. If the item is a manufactured or purchased item, the planned orders are the schedule of what will be manufactured or purchased in the future. Planned orders are typically displayed by order start date. In the case of a distribution item, this is the shipment date from the supply source. For manufactured and purchased items, this is the date the order is released to the shop floor or the date the order is placed with the vendor.

4. The planned shipments shown by receipt date have been eliminated from the report. It is only necessary to see the planned orders at the start date. They are still added to the projected on-hand balance, just as they would be if the planned-order receipt line were on the display.

The DRP/MRP displays shown previously have two sections. One is the time-phased information composed of the gross requirements, scheduled receipts, etc., shown by date. This information has been discussed in the explanation of how DRP works and the standardized DRP/MRP display. The other section is the descriptive information—the on-hand balance, lead times, etc.

Descriptive Information.   The descriptive information in DRP includes the on-hand balance, safety stock, lead time, and order quantity.

On-Hand Balance The on-hand balance is the quantity in the stockroom or the distribution center. This does not include the quantity in transit or rejected material. For a finished-goods stockroom or a distribution center, the on-hand balance is the quantity available to ship. For a component-parts or raw-material stockroom, the on-hand balance is the quantity available to issue to manufacturing.

One thing that must be mentioned about the on-hand balance is the high level of accuracy needed. DRP does not work if the inventory records are not at least 95 percent accurate. The on-hand balance is the beginning of the DRP calculation. If it is incorrect, everything else for that item will be incorrect as well. Users should resist inaugurating a DRP system until 95 percent inventory accuracy has been achieved.

Safety Stock The second piece of descriptive information on the DRP display is the safety stock. This covers situations where the sales exceed what was forecast.

Note, however, that safety stock is handled differently in DRP than in statistical inventory management systems. According to the conventional wisdom of inventory management, the more safety stock, the better. The limitation was the amount that could be justified. Keeping all that safety stock was expensive, so studies were done to evaluate where safety stock was needed most, what items had the most forecast variance, etc. But the idea was still the same. The more safety stock that could be justified, the better the customer service would be.

In reality, this is not so. Too much safety stock does not improve customer service, but deteriorates it. The reason is that the system no longer tells the truth about *what* is needed and *when*. The strength of DRP is that it shows the true needs of the distribution system, both the quantities and the dates that items are needed. Putting a lot of safety stock into the system weakens this dynamic, and soon the system does not really tell what is needed and when.

This becomes a problem when there is a limited amount of manufacturing capacity or a limited amount of material. In these situations, one needs to be able to see the real demands from the distribution network. These demands should not be falsified by large and arbitrary safety stocks. Accurate information must be available that tells what is needed and when. Unfortunately, because of large safety stocks, the system fails when it is needed the most. As a result, some other system has to be created to tell what is really needed and when, so the scarce capacity or materials can be used to the best advantage.

To summarize, large safety stocks would not be a problem if a company had unlimited capacity, unlimited material availability, and enough space and cash to support the safety stocks. However, this is not the case. Companies do have limited and scarce manufacturing capacity and materials, so they need accurate information to make the best use of limited resources.

This is not to say that safety stocks should not be used. There is a legitimate use for safety stock with DRP. However, large safety stocks keep DRP from working well.

Often an argument can be made to keep safety stock at the supply source because then it can be shipped to any of the different distribution centers that need it. However, the supply source does not have the same uncertainty of demand as that at the distribution centers. Distribution resource planning will predict the distribution demands on the supply source resulting in less uncertainty in demand and, consequently, less need for safety stock. The net result of these two conflicting demands is that there is still some uncertainty of demand at the supply source, and any safety stock stored there could be used to supply any of the distribution centers. Therefore, most companies choose to keep some safety stock at the supply source.

Safety Stock Versus Safety Time Actually two techniques can be used to provide safety stock with DRP. One is to set a safety stock quantity, and this method has been used in all the examples so far. The other method is to set a safety time. Safety time schedules the planned orders and scheduled receipts into stock for a specified period before they are actually needed. Figure 22.21 shows how safety time versus safety stock works. The first display shows a safety time of 2 weeks. The second display shows a safety stock of 50.

Safety time works by calculating the planned-order due date based on the date on which the projected on-hand balance will be less than zero. In this case, the projected on-hand balance is negative in week 7. This is the planned-order due date. Then the system checks to see whether safety time is specified for this item. If so, the planned-order due date is backed off by the safety time. In this case, the planned-order due date is backed off from week 7 to week 5. Then the planned order is backed off by the lead time for the item.

Notice that, in this case, the planned-order dates are identical whether one uses a safety time of 2 weeks or a safety stock of 50. Basically, safety stock and safety time are different ways to express the same thing. However, safety time is easier to maintain since one can decide on 1 week, 2 weeks, etc., rather than calculating 50, 45, and so on. This compensates for changes in the forecast quantity. If, for example, the forecast doubles, the safety time does not have to be changed. However, a safety stock quantity has to be recalculated.

In some situations safety stock and safety time do not act in the same way. If an item has a very intermittent demand, for example, a demand of 500 this week, 0 for the next 9 weeks, and 500 in week 11, then the safety stock and safety time will act differently. A safety stock of 50 on this item requires 50 on hand all the time. A

Vitamin C, 100-Tablet Bottles
On-hand balance: 140
Safety time: 2 wk
Lead time: 3 wk
Order quantity: 150

	Past Due	Week							
		1	2	3	4	5	6	7	8
Gross requirements		20	25	15	20	30	25	15	30
Scheduled receipts									
Projected on hand	140	120	95	80	60	180	155	140	110
Planned orders			150						

On-hand balance: 140
Safety stock: 50
Lead time: 3 wk
Order quantity: 150

	Past Due	Week							
		1	2	3	4	5	6	7	8
Gross requirements		20	25	15	20	30	25	15	30
Scheduled receipts									
Projected on hand	140	120	95	80	60	180	155	140	110
Planned orders			150						

FIG. 22.21 Safety stock versus safety time.

safety time of 1 week does not require a quantity on-hand all the time, but allows the on-hand balance to drop to zero when there are no requirements. Safety time schedules the order 1 week before the demand.

Lead Time The time required from the release of an order to the time it is received in the stockroom or distribution center is the *lead time*. For distribution, lead time starts from the moment one determines the need for a replenishment to the time that the inventory need is replenished, and not from the time the order is given to central to be picked. This lead time for distribution is composed of several components:

1. *Order release and picking* This is the time required to release, pick, and pack the items to be shipped.
2. *Loading* This is the time needed to load the truck or rail car.
3. *In transit* This is the time required for transit, the time it takes to get from the supply source to the distribution center.
4. *Unloading* This is the time it takes to unload the truck or rail car and put the items away.

Two things about lead times are important to understand. First, lead times are only approximate, and sophisticated techniques for calculating and determining lead times do not help. Second, lead times for distribution are relatively fixed (more so than lead times for manufacturing or purchasing), although there are exceptions.

Lead times are just approximations of how long the different activities listed will take. For example, most companies are able to do their picking and loading in the same day. In such a situation, the lead time for these operations is 1 day. It does not make any sense to attempt to refine this.

The in-transit lead time depends on the type of transportation and how far the product has to go. For example, a rail car shipment from a supply source in Chicago to a New York distribution center generally takes 2 weeks. In this case, the in-transit part of the lead time is 2 weeks. Again, it does not make much sense to try to refine this to a more precise number. That is not to say that it is not important to keep an eye on the in-transit lead times and try to keep them short. It is important. However, putting a lot of effort into determining the exact lead time, to the fraction of a day, has little practical value.

In some situations the lead time can be compressed. These are exceptional situations where products are shipped via a faster, more expensive mode of transportation, such as when a product is badly needed (a planned shipment is delayed in transit, say). In these situations, the lead time is compressed. However, this shorter lead time is not used with DRP. The lead time used with DRP is based on the normal mode of transportation.

Order Quantity Four factors need to be considered in developing the order quantities for distribution items: frequency, economic order quantity, pallet size, and the total weight and cube.

The frequency of shipment to a distribution center has to be used to determine the order quantities for the items in that distribution center. If a distribution center receives only one shipment per month, then the order quantity for the items at that distribution center has to be in multiples of the quantity used each month, such as a 1-month supply, a 2-month supply, etc. If a distribution center receives a shipment every day, then the frequency of shipment is not really important in determining the order quantity.

The economic order quantity (EOQ) calculation is a way to theoretically determine the most economic order quantity given the ordering and carrying costs.

Under ideal circumstances, the EOQ will cost the least over the course of a year. However, several things need to be explained about EOQ.

First, the EOQ calculation is based on approximations. It assumes that the demand is the same each week and that there is a known cost for ordering and a known cost for carrying inventory, etc. These are just estimates, so any calculation based on those numbers is only an estimate.

Second, a precise calculation of the EOQ is not that important. Any quantity which is close to the EOQ will give nearly the same effect.

Third, too many people with blind faith in a formula assume that if each lot size is calculated correctly, the sum of the lot sizes will be correct. There is no reason why this should be true. In fact, the odds are very strong that it will not be. There may be a constraint such as the size of the warehouse. Economic lot sizes that would require buying a new warehouse would hardly be economical. There may be a limit to the amount of money that management wants to invest in inventory, and there is no reason why the individual lot sizes should total to this limit. The lot size also does not take into account shipping frequency, etc. And the lot-size formula itself has a fatal flaw. It assumes a linear relationship between the amount of inventory and holding costs. When a warehouse is filled, a new warehouse will be needed. Until the present warehouse gets so overcrowded that it is difficult to store material in it efficiently, there is no increase in the warehouse cost as inventory increases.

The perspective, then, is that EOQ is a helpful estimate to use in coming up with order quantities. It represents one factor: the balancing of ordering and carrying costs. However, it is just an estimate, and it is only one of the factors that have to be considered in developing order quantities for distribution.

Pallet size is an important factor. For most products, there is a shipping quantity that makes sense from a material handling and storage point of view. These are quantities such as the amount that will fit on a pallet, on a tray, in a storage container, etc. Any order quantity should be a multiple of these quantities. These shipping quantities are based on material handling and storage systems, and they are not necessarily the same as the selling quantities.

The total weight and cube (volume) is a critical factor in determining freight costs to the distribution centers. Freight rates for trucks and rail cars are based on weight, and the cube is limited. The goal is to get the best use of the car or truck by filling it with a mix of product which uses the available cube and, at the same time, gives the most weight.

Order quantities can be used to help do this. For example, say a small, heavy product is shipped every 2 weeks, and another product which is light and bulky is shipped every 6 weeks. The light, bulky product might take an entire rail car every 6 weeks because of the cube. Yet, the small heavy product does not utilize the entire cube of the rail car when it is shipped every 2 weeks. By changing the order quantity of the light, bulky product to once every 2 weeks, it can be used to fill the unused cube in the rail cars at no additional cost. In addition, this may eliminate the extra rail car needed every 6 weeks.

In situations, such as the one above, the solution is obvious. However, a number of other situations are not as easy to see. Distribution personnel need a tool to see and manage the mix of the products being shipped. DRP provides the ability to do this, and the details of how it is done are covered later.

Order Policies The examples so far have used a *fixed order policy*. Order policies are methods used to calculate the planned-order quantities. A fixed order policy means that an order quantity has been specified and the planned orders are made equal to that quantity. This is the most common order policy.

In a number of other order policies the quantity is recalculated for each planned order. Some are simple calculations, such as lot for lot. Lot for lot ordering means that the planned-order quantity is made equal to the unsatisfied requirements. If 20 are needed, the planned order is for 20. If 53 are needed, the planned order is for 53. This type of ordering makes sense where the setup and ordering costs are low. This is usually not used for distribution items since it means that the same item would be shipped to each distribution center each week. However, in some situations this type of ordering is used for fast-moving, bulky items.

Period order quantity is another order policy that can be used with DRP. With period order quantity, a time period is specified instead of a quantity. All the requirements over that time period are added to give the planned-order quantity. Use of the period order quantity creates planned orders which equal a specified number of weeks of demand. There are a number of situations in distribution where period order quantity could be used. Many times, the best way to specify the order quantity for a product in a distribution center is as a number of weeks of supply, say 6 or 10 weeks of supply. By using the period order quantity, the planned-order quantities equal the requirements over the specified number of weeks.

Other order policies include least total cost, part period balancing, least unit cost, and Wagner-Whitin algorithm. These order policies attempt to make up for some of the approximations in the EOQ calculation. They attempt to calculate the order quantity which balances the ordering and carrying costs for a demand that may be different from week to week (50 one week, 25 the next, etc.). To put it another way, these order policies would come up with nearly the same number as an EOQ calculation if the demand were the same in each week.

There are a number of problems with these order policies. One is that the balancing of ordering and carrying costs is only one of several factors that have to be considered in developing an order quantity. Another is that the order quantity is being calculated by the computer and this outside the control of the people using the system. Thus system users cannot really be held accountable for any ordering or rescheduling that occurs because the computer has recalculated the order quantity. For these reasons, the order policies for least total cost, part period balancing, least unit cost, and the Wagner-Whitin algorithm are not recommended for use in DRP.

It is easy to lose perspective in the order quantity calculations. Conventional inventory management systems pay an inappropriate amount of attention to how much to order. This was once considered one of the most critical questions. With DRP, the important thing is *what* is needed and *when* it is needed. The right order quantity is no good if it does not arrive when needed. The real benefits come from making a valid plan and then executing that plan.

Additional Descriptive Information The DRP/MRP displays in most companies include more descriptive information than the items explained so far. However, the items explained here are the most critical in running the system. Other information which may appear in the display as descriptive information can have a great deal of value to the planner, and most DRP/MRP displays contain this additional information. It often includes item description, unit of measure, costs (material cost, labor cost, overhead cost), shelf life, planner code, item type, inventory class, and so on.

Action Messages

In addition to the DRP/MRP display, the logic in the system will search for and detect conditions which may require some action from the planner. For example, the DRP/MRP logic will look for and highlight any planned orders that are due for release. These are the planned shipments to the distribution centers.

Action messages are also generated for shipments that are in transit and are scheduled to arrive rather too late or too early. In most cases, the planner does not act on these messages because there is generally no way to speed up or slow down the products in transit. However, these messages are available to the planner. And in some special cases, the planner may ship the product via a faster mode of transportation because the shipment in transit will not arrive in time. The DRP/MRP logic also generates a number of miscellaneous action messages. These are messages for a negative on-hand balance, an order quantity that is too large, an on-hand balance below safety stock, etc.

These messages are all useful, but the distribution planner does not use them to the same extent as the master scheduler or the planner in manufacturing. Master schedulers use the action messages to help change the master schedule. The planners in manufacturing and purchasing are usually able to speed up or slow down orders based on when the orders are needed. However, many distribution companies do not print the action messages for in-transit orders that are arriving too early or too late unless the stock-out is going to be serious, based on the length of time the stock-out is projected to last or the size of the projected negative on-hand balance.

One of the best, but sometimes frustrating, features of action messages is the fact that they never forget. Each time an item is planned with DRP, the item is examined for all the action messages. The system never forgets. The action messages continue to appear until the problem is solved. Net change systems do exist that can block the messages for several days.

The same types of action messages are generated with both the master schedule display and the DRP/MRP display. These are messages for master schedule orders that are due earlier or later than needed, messages for orders that are due for release, and miscellaneous exceptions.

In addition, the master scheduling logic includes an action message that does not appear with the DRP/MRP display. This is the message "not enough in the schedule to satisfy demands." With DRP or MRP, this message is not needed because the logic will create planned orders whenever there is not enough to satisfy the demands. The master schedule is manually set by the master scheduler, and planned orders are not created automatically. Therefore, an action message is needed to alert the master scheduler to consider adding more to the master schedule.

Planning Horizon

The planning horizon is not part of the descriptive information for an item. However, it is an important part of the system since it determines how far out into the future DRP looks. The planning horizon is the end of planning as far as DRP is concerned. Anything that goes on beyond the planning horizon is unknown to DRP. Thus if one wants information such as what is needed and when to predict inventory levels, space requirements, etc. from the DRP, then the planning horizon has to extend far into the future.

One approach is to extend the planning horizon very far, say 10 years. This will give planning information out that far, but there are some limitations. DRP is quite specific, and predicting events this far into the future is somewhat meaningless, since predictions are not that accurate several years ahead. Another limitation is that typically all this information is stored and manipulated each week. This storage and manipulation can be expensive, so most people face the option of a shorter planning horizon.

The shortest planning horizon that will work with DRP is based on the total cumulative lead time. The *total cumulative lead time* is the span from the date the first raw material or purchased items are ordered to the date finished products are delivered to the distribution centers for sale. This includes the lead time for raw materials and purchased items, the lead time for manufacturing, and the lead time for distribution.

Pegging. A distribution planner or master scheduler using the DRP/MRP or master schedule display often needs to know from where the demands are coming. For example, a master scheduler may have demands from the distribution centers which exceed the master schedule values. In such a situation, the master scheduler would like to be able to see from where these demands are coming. Likewise, a manufacturing planner using the DRP/MRP display for a manufactured or purchased item may have demands which exceed the manufacturing orders or the purchase orders. Again, under these circumstances, the planner would like to see from where these requirements are coming.

This information is called pegging in DRP. Pegging is a list of the distribution demands on an item that shows where the demands are coming from by date and quantity. In Fig. 22.22 the pegging information is shown for master schedule display. The pegging information is listed for the past-due week and the next 3 weeks. In most systems, pegging is listed for some part of the planning horizon. In some companies pegging is cut off beyond a specified number of weeks. In other companies, pegging is listed out to the end of the planning horizon. This is true for both distribution and manufacturing. In distribution, most people cut the pegging information off after 12 weeks or so. The reason is that the distribution planners rarely use this information very far into the future. In manufacturing, however, most

Vitamin C, 100-Tablet Bottles

On-hand balance: 1700
Safety stock: 0
Lead time: 3 wk
Order quantity: 1100

	Past Due	Week								
		1	2	3	4	5	6	7	8
Distribution demands	450	700	900	400	500	450	500	500	150
Scheduled receipts									
Projected on hand	1250	550	−350	350	−150	500	1100	600	450
Master schedule—receipt				1100		1100	1100		
Master schedule—start	1100		1100	1100					

Pegging Information

Week	Quantity	Location	Week	Quantity	Location
P.D.	400	New York	2	400	Montreal
P.D.	50	Toronto	2	500	Chicago
	450			900	
1	500	Los Angeles	3	400	New York
1	200	Vancouver		400	
	700				

FIG. 22.22 Pegging example.

companies display pegging further into the future. The reason is that the planners use pegging to plan manufactured and purchased items. Many times these items can have long lead times, and the planners are solving problems today on orders that are not due to arrive for some time.

It is also possible to display all the pegging information out to the end of the planning horizon. However, most people find that for the number of times pegging is used this far into the future, it is not worth displaying the information.

Pegging is a valuable tool and time saver for both master schedulers and distribution planners. They are able to get right at the source of problems. The alternative to pegging would be to look at each distribution center to see which caused the requirements.

Firm Planned Order.   In a number of situations a distribution planner or master scheduler would like a planned order to have a quantity or a date which is different from the quantity or date assigned by the order-planning logic of DRP. A master scheduler may not have enough of a product in the supply source and may want a smaller than normal lot size shipped to a distribution center. A distribution planner may want an item to be shipped to a distribution center before it is actually needed in order to fill a half-empty truck or rail car.

Regardless of the reason, the people using the system need a way to override the dates and quantities of planned orders. The *firm planned order* is one way to do this. A firm planned order is a planned order which a person manually maintains. The computer does not add, delete, or change firm planned orders in any way. People use them when they want an order to have a date or quantity different from the date or quantity which would be assigned by the normal order-planning logic.

Some things about firm planned orders are similar to both planned orders and scheduled receipts. Firm planned orders are like planned orders in that they are still in the planning stage and are not in transit. Firm planned orders have not been released to manufacturing or placed with vendors. They are similar to scheduled receipts in that they are not created or changed by the computer. People have to maintain them. Rescheduling action messages are given for firm planned orders and for scheduled receipts.

The firm planned order can be used to handle a number of situations in distribution. These situations include helping plan transportation scheduling and loading; allowing for stock buildups in distribution centers or other storage locations in advance of sales promotions, special sales offers, and seasonal sales; and allowing for stock buildups in distribution centers or other storage locations for anticipation of labor strikes, creating a new distribution center, and relocating or eliminating a distribution center.

TRANSPORTATION PLANNING AND SCHEDULING WITH DRP

Any distribution planning system that does not recognize the need and importance of scheduling both inventories and transportation from supply sources to distribution points is only half a system. In the world of physical distribution, there are fundamental requirements that must be satisfied. Given a network of distribution centers supplied from one or several sources, distribution personnel need to not only schedule and manage inventories in the network, but also schedule how to ship goods to the distribution centers.

In many companies, transportation is the largest cost element within distribution. In some companies, transportation costs represent more than half the total cost of distribution. For 10 years, transportation costs have been rising faster than any other element of cost within physical distribution. With transportation deregulation, opportunities have opened up to curb transportation costs. Without the proper tools to do an effective job of scheduling inventories and replenishments to distribution centers, companies will not be able to fully realize the savings that are possible.

In DRP, it is possible to do accurate transportation loading and scheduling. This is done for the shipments from the supply source to the distribution centers and from distribution center to distribution center. This scheduling and loading is possible because DRP is an accurate, detailed simulation of a distribution operation. As such, it can be used to show what items are planned to be shipped and when. This information can then be used to schedule and load transportation effectively.

However, most companies today do not have the tools needed for effective transportation planning. They are not able to predict what will be shipped to the different distribution centers in the future. If these companies were able to see what was to be shipped and when, they would be able to do some planning to take advantage of freight rates. For example, if they saw that in some week in the future they would be sending a half-full rail car or truck, they could begin to work on pulling some products up from a later week. By shipping some products earlier than planned, they could fill the rail car or truck. This would be done by pulling the right products up, products that will be used in the next few weeks, rather than just shipping any products that happen to be available at the time. Another example would be a company that has the scheduling visibility to utilize both the weight and the cube of a rail car or truck by adjusting the mix of product to be shipped.

One company, in a period of 2 years, went from a fill rate of 59.8 percent before DRP to a fill rate of 94.2 percent with DRP. These savings were achieved by distribution planners working with the transportation planning report. This is a very simple report that includes the information that already exists with DRP and displays it for the distribution planner. Table 22.2 is an example of this report.

The fundamental characteristic of this report is its simplicity. The report shown here requires very little in addition to what is already available with DRP. Now DRP contains the planned shipments by date and quantity for all the items to all the different distribution centers. These are the planned orders. All that has to be done to translate this information to a transportation planning report is to extend the

TABLE 22.2 Distribution Center Transportation Planning Report

Week	Distribution Center	Number of Pallets	Weight	Cube
1	Los Angeles	95	390,000	9,800
2	Los Angeles	80	340,000	8,040
3	Los Angeles	110	420,000	10,730
4	Los Angeles	98	405,000	10,380
5	Los Angeles	100	392,000	10,060
49	Los Angeles	90	370,000	9,475
50	Los Angeles	134	440,000	10,960
51	Los Angeles	115	425,000	10,785
52	Los Angeles	96	395,000	10,120

planned-order dates and quantities by some factors for weight, cube, and quantity per pallet. Then the information is displayed by distribution center by week. These factors are the weight of the product, usually in pounds; the volume of the packaged product, usually in cubic feet; and the quantity of the product that will fit on a pallet or other container. Many companies already have this information. For those that do not, the job of developing it is usually simple.

There are four significant advantages of DRP in transportation planning:

1. The distribution planners have the tools to plan transportation and loading.

2. The distribution planners and the master schedulers are put in a situation where they need to work closely together and help each other solve problems.

3. DRP is truly a simulation of what is going to happen. The planned and firm planned orders show what is going to be shipped and when. So this information is available for other uses.

4. Because the information is accurate, it can be used to develop transportation freight budgets, to negotiate freight rates, and to justify equipment such as trucks and railroad cars.

Recognizing Backhaul Opportunities

Many companies are in a situation where they are moving a lot of products to a distribution center which is near a supplier or several suppliers that are shipping to the distribution center supply source. This represents an opportunity for companies that operate or are close to justifying their own fleet of trucks.

If the transportation planners are aware of these backhaul opportunities, they can take advantage of them by having the trucks deliver products to the distribution center and then loading on purchased material or products from suppliers for the return haul to the supply source. But the transportation planners have to know when these opportunities exist. They have to know the approximate weight, cube, and timing of shipments from the suppliers.

DRP is a way to make these opportunities visible. As explained before, the planned shipments to the distribution centers are stored in the system. These are used to develop the transportation planning report. In addition, the planned shipments to the supply source also exist in the system. These are the planned orders for purchased material.

For example, suppose a particular material is purchased from a vendor located in the same city as one of the distribution centers. The planned orders to that distribution center represent the shipments from the supply source to that city. The planned orders for the purchased material represent the planned shipments from that city to the supply source.

By storing the weight and cube of the purchased material and coding the vendors located near distribution centers, the same type of transportation planning report could be developed as that for shipments to the distribution center. The only difference is that this report shows planned shipments to the supply source.

A planner can take these two reports and compare the planned weight and cube going to the distribution center and the planned weight and cube coming back. Looking at these two reports, a planner could determine whether the opportunity for backhauling exists. It would also be possible to combine the information from these two reports in a single report or CRT display. The weight and cube to and from one city can be listed side by side for the convenience of the planner.

Opportunities for Shipment Consolidations

Users of DRP are also taking advantage of the transportation planning information in situations where a given distribution center network is being supplied from several manufacturing facilities or supply sources. DRP is of great value in these situations in that consolidation opportunities can be planned and scheduled which take into consideration shipments from one or more supply source to the distribution centers.

DRP and Distribution Center Shipping Schedules

In a number of distribution companies, a shipment schedule has been established that states when shipments are to be made to the different distribution centers. For example, a shipping schedule might state that shipments to the Los Angeles distribution center are to be made every 3 weeks, shipments to Chicago every 2 weeks, and shipments to Montreal every week. Or it might specify certain days in a week.

Once the shipping schedules are set in the system, they must be adhered to religiously. If shipments are made to Dallas every Thursday and to Los Angeles every Friday, then those shipping dates must be adhered to. Any deviation will create more or less inventory in the pipeline, and reduce efficiency and credibility with the users.

Most forms of inventory have a common denominator—*time*. Inventory only exists, in most instances, because more or less time is required to ship, assemble, manufacture, or purchase something. If customers are willing to wait 2 weeks to get a product as opposed to 1 or 2 days, then one could do business with much less inventory. If a supplier's product were a phone call away, chances are that a company would carry little or no inventory. Efficient use of time requires that it be scheduled. Because inventory is affected so much by time, it must also be scheduled.

Shipping schedules deal with *shipping time*, so one must treat shipping schedule dates with respect if inventory levels are to be stabilized and users of the system are to believe the replenishment schedules. The shipping schedule is not generally changed from day to day or week to week. In fact, in many companies the shipping schedule is fairly rigid. There are a number of reasons:

1. A limited number of shipping doors or rail docks are available.
2. Loading dock space is limited.
3. Labor and equipment are limited.
4. The shipping schedule is dependent on the workload at the distribution centers.

The limitations in the number of doors, dock space, labor and equipment at either the shipping or receiving location cause many companies to prefer to level the load by assigning a fixed shipping schedule. However, there are other ways to do this. For example, a company might set its capacity at 40 trucks per day and not be concerned with where they are going or from where they are coming. In a number of cases, it is simpler and more convenient to set a fixed shipping schedule.

This is not to say that the fixed shipping schedule will not change from time to time. As the conditions change, the shipping schedule may be altered. However, the day-to-day or week-to-week shipping schedules are generally set and adhered to.

The planned orders created for shipping from the supply source to the distribution centers may not agree with the set shipping schedule. For example, DRP may plan an order that is due to be shipped in week 7, and the shipping schedule for Los Angeles is set for weeks 1, 5, and 9. This is shown in Fig. 22.23. In such a situation, the DRP is not a true simulation of reality because it does not truly represent what is going to happen. The planned order for 200 in week 7 will not actually be shipped in week 7. Instead, this product should be shipped in week 5. If this product is let go until the next shipment, which is in this case week 9, the Los Angeles distribution center will be out of stock and on back order.

However, if the planned order really will be shipped in week 5, then DRP should show it in week 5 and not in week 7, in order to create a valid simulation of what is really going to happen. By showing when the planned order will be shipped the DRP is correct for this item. The distribution demands will appear in the master schedule display in the correct week. The master scheduler will now see that the 200 items need to be on hand in week 5, which is 2 weeks earlier than the normal logic of DRP would calculate this product to be shipped to the distribution center.

In this situation, we have a conflict. To arrive in week 8, the product does not have to be shipped until week 7. However, the shipping schedule is for weeks 1, 5, and 9. Which is correct?

The correct schedule is what is actually going to happen. If the order is going to be shipped in week 5, then it should be shown in week 5. However, if something is going to be shipped earlier than normal logic would dictate, then the planner should be alerted. In this situation, the planned order should be moved to week 5, which is when it will be shipped. And an action message should be given to the planner to indicate that the order is due to be shipped earlier than absolutely needed. Thus the planner is able to see what the system is doing and maintain visibility into the system. The modified version of the DRP/MRP display for this item is shown in Fig. 22.24.

Some may question the need to generate an action message to show the planner that the logic of DRP has moved the planned order date. They fail to recognize that *people* are responsible for operating the system, not the computer. People are held accountable for running the system, and they need to be able to see both what the system has done and the real need dates for the orders. In some situations, there may not be enough stock to satisfy the distribution demands. When this happens, the planner needs to know for each distribution center what is really needed and when.

The best way to change the planned orders is by using the computer. It is possible for a person to make the changes, provided the number of changes is small enough

Green Beans, 16-oz Can

On-hand balance: 120
Safety stock: 40
Lead time: 1 wk
Order quantity: 200

	Past Due	Week							
		1	2	3	4	5	6	7	8
Gross requirements		40	40	40	40	40	40	40	40
Scheduled receipts		200							
Projected on hand	120	280	240	200	160	120	80	40	200
Planned orders								200	
Shipping Schedule		XX				XX			

FIG. 22.23 DRP and distribution center shipping schedules.

Green Beans, 16-oz Can

On-hand balance: 120
Safety stock: 40
Lead time: 1 wk
Order quantity: 200

	Past Due	Week							
		1	2	3	4	5	6	7	8
Gross requirements		40	40	40	40	40	40	40	40
Scheduled receipts		200							
Projected on hand	120	280	240	200	160	120	280	240	200
Planned orders						200			
Shipping Schedule		XX				XX			

Action Message   Planned order 200 wk 5 not needed for shipment until wk 7.

FIG. 22.24   Modified version of the DRP/MRP display.

to manage manually. However, in most situations, the number of changes is large enough to justify using the computer.

Regardless of whether the planned orders are changed by the computer or manually, the process is the same. The planned orders are calculated based on the date the items are needed at the distribution centers. Then the shipping schedule is considered, and any planned orders that are not scheduled to ship on one of the shipping dates are adjusted. The adjustment is to move the planned orders to the next earlier available shipping date.

However, there is a trade-off. Shipping earlier will create additional inventory in the distribution pipeline, and this must be evaluated. The results must be compared to the costs and advantages of maintaining a fixed shipping schedule. DRP can be used to simulate both conditions.

Two different methods could be used with the computer to adjust the planned-order dates to agree with the shipping schedule. One is to have the DRP logic plan orders and to take the shipping schedule into account before the planned orders are created and stored. The other method is to have a separate computer program which is run after DRP has created and stored the planned orders. This program adjusts the planned-order dates based on the shipping schedule and updates the distribution demands if they have been posted to the master schedule items.

Dos and Don'ts in Transportation Planning

A sound distribution system must schedule both inventories and transportation. However, there are pitfalls for the manager to avoid. Listed here are guidelines for taking full advantage of DRP in transportation from the supply sources to the distribution centers.

First, if shipments are made to distribution centers by using a shipping schedule, they should be planned and shown within the system. No one should go around the system. Otherwise, the users will lose faith in the system. It will lack credibility, and the informal system will take over.

Second, if it is company policy to ship only full truckloads to the distribution centers, then it must be planned for within the DRP system. Start by using DRP to tell how much weight and cube need to be shipped to the distribution centers. If it is not enough to fill a truck or rail car, use the information from the system to help advance the planned shipments. Remember that DRP has already calculated the next shipping priorities to the distribution centers. This information should be used.

Whatever decision is reached, it should be communicated to the system and the users. Planned shipments to the distribution centers should not be held back simply to get the weight and cube desired. This is the quickest way to destroy priorities and credibility with the distribution center personnel and the customers. If a transportation lead time of 1 week is used and is realistic, then stick to it and ship on time. Otherwise, one is playing with the transportation lead time, increasing inventories, and reducing reaction time. It is advisable to preselect high-volume products that will qualify for advanced shipments to make the weight and cube desired. Communicate this list to all interested users, and do not permit deviations from this list of "fillers" without prior approval. Otherwise, people will pick any product close at hand, ignore DRP priorities, and go around the system.

Third, any time future planned shipments are being advanced to make weight and cube requirements, it is vital that consideration be given to the possible impact on the master schedule. There is a distribution-manufacturing trade-off here, and it must be evaluated before the final decision is made.

Last, a manager with thousands of products in inventory to be shipped to multiple locations may need some computer support to help manage the transportation plan. The computer can do many things—sort the information, look for future planned shipments, and make recommendations. Take advantage of the massive data manipulation capabilities of the computer. Do not forget: *computers cannot make decisions.* They are incapable of thought, and cannot be held accountable for results, good or poor. The computer should only recommend action based on established parameters, but the manager must make the final decision. DRP has proved in practice to be a very powerful tool for transportation planning. Users of DRP have achieved excellent savings. A manager who uses DRP for transportation planning as recommended here and avoids the pitfalls cannot help but reduce transportation costs.

BIBLIOGRAPHY

Inventory Management Reprints, American Production and Inventory Control Society, Falls Church, Va., 1984.

Volmann, T., W. L. Berry, and Clay D. Whybark: *Manufacturing Planning and Control Systems*, Dow Jones-Irwin, Homewood, Ill., 1984.

Wight, O.: *MRP II, Unlocking America's Productivity Potential*, Oliver Wight Limited Publications, Williston, Vt., 1981.

23

Service Parts Management

Editors

WILLIAM B. LEE, Ph.D., CFPIM, Partner, Touche Ross & Co.,
Houston, Texas
EARLE STEINBERG, Ph.D., Partner, Touche Ross & Co., Houston,
Texas

Service, or spare, or repair, parts are used for the repair and/or maintenance of an assembled product. Typically service parts are ordered and shipped at a date later than the shipment of the product itself.

During the 1970s, there was a rapid explosion in knowledge concerning manufacturing and distribution control systems. Largely through the efforts of the American Production and Inventory Control Society (APICS), material-requirements planning (MRP) became an accepted method for managing dependent-demand inventory in the manufacturing environment.

This was followed closely by the development of manufacturing resource planning (MRP II), which is an approach for consolidating and coordinating manufacturing, distribution, financial, engineering, marketing, and other activities of the firm. Although these advances represent significant contributions to the state of the art of inventory management, similar progress has not been made in service parts management.

Although much of the literature developed during this period was concerned with inventory management for expendable or consumable items, little attention was paid to problems faced by those companies where major portions of the inventory investment consisted of service parts, which may move in a cycle from manufacturing through stages of installation, removal, repair or rework, stock storage, with in-transit and distribution states intertwined. The result is that service parts inventory represents a special problem in control.

Clearly, the problem of managing significant levels of inventory investment in service parts faces all companies selling assembled products that must be serviced or maintained. Yet several serious problems exist with service parts management as it is currently practiced in many companies.

First, in many companies the forecasts for service parts are loaded directly into the MRP system or the master production schedule (MPS) without any approval or review. Frequently, the forecast for service parts requirements is generated by demand for these parts as though such demand occurred on a regular basis and in easily predicted quantities. The forecasting approaches most often used for service parts requirements are those found commonly in determining future requirements for independent-demand inventory items. Yet it is clear that service parts, by their very nature, do not necessarily represent independent-demand inventory. Furthermore, in many companies, the service parts forecast for individual items is not related to the dollar amount projected for service parts sales. Therefore, companies often have one set of requirements which are generated by an aggregation of individually developed forecasts and another set of requirements which are measured in aggregate sales dollars. Significant differences frequently exist between the two.

Second, service parts often rank relatively low in terms of manufacturing priority. Faced with capacity problems and decisions about allocating capacity to end items or service parts, many companies report a high frequency of arbitrary decisions to allocate all capacity to the manufacture of end items. This approach consistently leads to customer complaints because of the nonavailability of service parts.

Third, requirements frequently exist for initial provisioning of service parts intended to provide customer service throughout a major portion of the product life cycle. Then at some point during the life of the product, another opportunity exists for a *last buy*, where manufacturing facilities produce service parts required to provide customer service throughout the remaining life of the product. Frequently very little thought is given in many companies to the fundamental trade-offs involved in initial provisioning as well as in last buys. In the absence of logical analysis, arbitrary decisions frequently are made without regard to the cost impact of inventory investment, appropriate levels of customer service, and manufacturing economics.

With these and other problems in mind, then, this chapter reports on how systems for managing service parts inventory are actually working in many firms. We identify some of the common and important elements in effectively managing service parts inventory as well as provide a common framework for understanding the different approaches which may prove effective in varying environments.

This chapter is concerned with the actual practice of service parts management. It seeks to define a common framework for looking at the problem in light of current practices of companies which operate in quite different environments.

BUSINESS PLANNING, STRATEGY, AND ORGANIZATION

Many firms believe that their competitive advantage in markets depends on the ability to service their equipment in the field. Some firms organize specifically to exploit opportunities for providing better service by elevating service parts to the level of a product line, complete with a management organization which exercises centralized control over inventory planning and distribution. Firms which do not have a service parts organization frequently report low priority given to manufacturing of service parts relative to end items shipped to customers.

Most firms whose philosophy reflects a high level of commitment to customer service realize that management of service parts is as important as delivery of finished goods to their customers.

Principle: *If service parts inventory constitutes a significant investment or if a strong commitment exists to high levels of customer service, then service parts should be treated as a separate product line.*

Many firms have managers of service parts whose place in the organizational structure is equal to that of other product-line managers.

In a firm that manufactures end items as well as service parts, capacity problems often lead manufacturing to view end items as "shippable goods" and service parts as "inventory goods." Therefore, service parts are manufactured only when excess capacity exists or when no significant conflict occurs with manufacturing schedules for end items. The service parts product-line manager concept helps alleviate this problem and raise the level of organizational visibility concerning the importance of service in the overall corporate strategy.

One company created a new product line—service and spare parts—headed by a product manager. The concept was to differentiate the company in the marketplace through superior service to customers. Traditionally, the availability of spare parts had not been strong among the company's major competitors. The improved after-the-sale support was intended to help influence new unit purchase decisions by customers and to mitigate the impact of cyclical market demand. One method used to market this pledge to customer support was a series of advertisements emphasizing the commitment to spares, service, and repair.

In another company, the material sales department is one of three major components of the service division. Other departments that report to the division's general manager include six regional service centers and a technical services department. The general manager of the service division reports directly to the president. This organization is the U.S. distributor of products produced by the parent company, which is based in Japan. The company has been in business for more than 100 years with production in over 40 highly automated factories throughout Japan. The U.S. annual sales are 3 million units per year, and 20 million units are operative in the United States after slightly more than 12 years of sales efforts. The company recognizes that after-sales service is as critical to sales success as any marketing and merchandising effort.

This success is due to the technical proficiency of the international engineering teams and to the artisans who create fashionable styles as well as others who merchandise the product. The merchandiser's efforts are enhanced by an aggressive group of independent distributors whose mutually exclusive territories cover all the United States. As "independents," the distributors have very high standards for the utilization of the newest and best technologies and require a very wide range of features and styles. In any of the two major selling seasons per year, as many as 100 new styles may be introduced.

The mission of the material sales department is to assist and enhance the marketability of products by providing service parts and technical information to the repair technicians within and without the organization.

A third company is a multinational corporation that manufactures and markets computers and peripheral equipment, terminals, and associated software and supplies. There are nine U.S. plants, four international plants, and over 1000 vendors which provide service parts. The company employs approximately 65,000 people worldwide and has sales in excess of $3 billion. Parts are distributed to service locations from the worldwide service parts center in Atlanta, Georgia; from service parts depots in Hong Kong and Schiphol, Holland; and from distribution centers located in Augsburg, Germany; Oiso, Japan; and Dundee, Scotland.

The vast majority of this company's customers are provided service through maintenance contracts. The parts that are required to perform service are provided to the customer as part of the maintenance agreement. Only customers who are serviced on a time-and-material basis or who are performing service themselves are actually charged for these items. The inventory management philosophy and service-level objectives are designed to minimize overall investment while providing satisfactory service.

To fully understand the nature of customer service at yet another company, it is critical to understand the customer service division's philosophy. The following statement of philosophy reflects the company's concern with the needs of its customers, the company, and its employees:

> To service all customers with concern and in a professional manner. To provide a working environment that is conducive to professional development and advancement for all service division personnel. To encourage service division employees to serve their community in a manner best fitting their skills and interests. To establish pricing and staff at levels that will allow the company a reasonable return on their investment.

The key to achieving this philosophy lies in providing trained people with quality parts at the right time. The following organizations support the service parts operations.

The *training* organization provides initial training of service engineers and upgrades training on new equipment or on a greater variety of equipment. The *technical support* organization analyzes new systems, develops maintenance philosophies, and provides technical assistance to engineers who require help on complex service problems. The *logistics* organization determines items to be stocked and locations to stock them and educates field personnel in inventory management. The *national repair center* repairs complex modules or systems and tests them before returning them to stock. *Outside equipment manufacturers'* (OEM) *support* is required if their equipment is used. This may be in the form of service maintenance training and the supply and/or repair of service parts. At another company, the vice president for customer service reports to the vice president of sales/marketing/service who in turn reports to the president. The staff of the vice president for customer service consists of the director of field service, international service coordinator, service operations manager, technical support and training manager, and logistics manager.

Field Service

This department has the direct responsibility for domestic field service. The nation is divided into eight regions, and each region's service manager reports to the director of field service. The eight service regions, which are organized to parallel the eight sales regions, have from three to five area offices, each of which has a supervisor with eight to fifteen field service engineers (FSEs) under direct control. To aid the regional service manager and area supervisor in parts administration, each region has a regional parts administrator to handle the ordering and tracking of parts within the region.

International Service Coordination

Until recently, service for the export market was handled as a function under the international department. But now it has been moved to the responsibility of the vice president of customer service. This department has the responsibility to oversee the integration of international service into a worldwide service support team, including the responsibility for worldwide site planning and installations.

Service Operations

The primary function of the service operations department is the operation of the customer product service center (CPSC) and the related management information center. The center receives the calls for service requests from product users and dispatches the FSE to the service call. In addition to the dispatch function, the management information center provides data to all service functions on the field-installed base (numbers of different pieces of equipment), parts usage history, and other important data for field service.

Technical Support and Training

This department has complete responsibility to train FSEs and to provide technical support to FSEs that need aid on a service call.

Logistics

The logistics department has the responsibility for processing worldwide orders for parts, planning of stock levels, central distribution warehousing, return-goods control, and repair center operations.

IDENTIFICATION OF SERVICE PARTS

Principle: *Identification of service parts should be based on engineering considerations balanced against projected customer requirements and capabilities.*

Often, relatively minor components will fail, but customers' and/or manufacturers' repair personnel will not have the technical skill or equipment to replace them without removing higher-level components. For example, it may be easier to replace an entire circuit board than an individual chip. Another consideration is the tool requirements for particular repair jobs. Although circuit boards often can be removed and replaced with relatively simple tools, the same may not be true of various components on the board. Obviously, this has implications for initial provisioning, inventory investment, stocking echelon decisions, and even repair personnel training. These decisions also interact with product design questions, such as redundancy and reliability, which must be addressed early in the product design process. Some products, in fact, are specifically designed to have a desired impact on serviceability as well as on service parts management.

Identification of service parts has a profound impact on inventory investment as well as customer service. A fundamental trade-off exists between the levels of components stocked as service parts versus the ease of replacement of those parts. Often, higher-level components (i.e., toward the top of the bill-of-materials structure) are easier to replace but more costly to stock.

Some firms develop specific service parts bills of materials for the field service organization. These bills of materials form the foundation for parts catalogs and technical guides as well as service kits carried by repair personnel. They may differ from standard manufacturing bills of materials in that only items which are selected as service parts are shown. Therefore, a manufacturing bill of materials quite probably will contain more levels and more items than a service parts bill of materials.

Part substitution and engineering change control are, of course, part of the process of maintaining service parts bills of materials. Some firms closely monitor engineering change orders for their impact on service parts inventories while others simply pass change orders to the service parts organization for any needed action. Many companies report serious concern with gradual phase-in of new parts, but some have tight controls to ensure that all old, serviceable parts are consumed before new ones are introduced.

Communications

Service parts information is communicated to field locations in several ways. Recommended spare-parts lists are used by field locations to order parts in preparation for installation of a new product and to adjust inventory levels to accommodate significant increases in the population of units installed. Translator file microfiche reports are used to identify equivalent part numbers. And parts reference file microfiche reports are used to identify primary part numbers, upgradeable part numbers, interchangeable part numbers, replacement part numbers, and bulletins that affect part numbers. Also on-line inquiry is available so field engineering organizations can have direct access to the service parts data base through remote terminals.

Dissemination of service parts and technical information is a job that requires technical expertise in product technology and, not surprisingly, expertise in library science. Communications to customers frequently reach every level of the industry and so represent an excellent public relations opportunity. Many companies continuously develop information packages in various formats aimed directly at different end users of service parts.

Companies frequently recognize that different "constituencies" have different information needs. An example is the technically proficient repair person who needs a basic sampler of information on different products. This need may be met by the development of a technical library complete with a general description of the theories behind the current technology.

Good communications are critical in light of the fact that many companies wish to continue to promote the utilization of the independent repair trade, which obviously is sizable and diverse but diminishing.

Besides the distribution of hard-copy technical guides and other catalogs, some companies actively market on microfiche the technical information that these texts provide. Acceptance by the trade in many industries has been surprisingly rapid, and the program has been expanded to the point where a repair person's references can be almost as complete as the factories' for a fraction of the cost of the hard-copy version. Through the use of the computer files from the factories, useful cross-references and other lists have been reproduced and distributed on computer output microfiche (COM) as a part of this microfiche sales program. Other formal methods of communicating technical or parts-related information are via newsletters and technical bulletins.

Old Products

The policy of many companies is to provide continuous service for any product ever manufactured by them, regardless of its age. This policy usually is supported by the manufacturing facilities which will maintain production capability for service demand. In addition, the engineering functions support this commitment throughout the product improvement process by providing for substitutions or alternative assemblies. Although component items ordered by customers frequently are inactive, typically every effort is made to ensure the availability of items that will satisfy the requirements of form, fit, and function.

New Models

In some companies, each manufacturing plant has a field engineering organization on the premises to participate in the new-product development process. This organization is responsible for developing the service philosophy at the earliest possible time in the product development cycle, in order to form the basis for maintenance plans and engineering trade-off studies. Formal statements of service philosophy include the strategies for local end-unit repair, rework sources for repairable assemblies, parts-stocking echelons, training requirements, and spare-parts requirements.

After new models are designed by engineering groups, they are tested by the various technical service groups. These groups identify whether components or assemblies should be carried in the parts manuals as service parts items. Generally, the parts manuals reference components rather than assemblies unless field repair of the component is too difficult or time-consuming. In such cases the assembly is listed in the parts manual with circuit boards, for example, being called out rather than the component parts.

Generally speaking, every part in the machine is listed in the manual either as a component or as an assembly and is given a part number. This means that personnel in the field can order these parts and expect delivery.

For new products, two types of service parts frequently are identified. The first is completely new parts. The second type is parts that are on current production systems but may have an increased base of use because of usage on the new product. Once these parts have been identified, the technical support group contacts material planning to arrange for stocking these parts.

In the case of parts used in current products, the material planner responsible for the part is notified of the expanded field-installed base and adjusts the forecast and inventory requirements for that line item. In the case of the completely new parts, the process is more complicated. New parts frequently are planned for various levels of stocking echelons and for a time horizon of a year or more. The quantities are developed by using the following typical guidelines:

1. To determine usage for the first year, the population of the units sold per quarter is multiplied by estimated failure rates to determine the quantities required of each service part. The failure rate usually is based on similar parts in similar systems but may be inflated for "infant mortality."

2. For parts that are needed for field stocking echelons, the number of pieces required per region and the number of pieces required for export are determined.

3. The total pieces required for usage and for each stocking echelon are added, and a stocking plan is developed. Then orders either are placed through purchase orders for those items made by outside vendors or are entered into the MPS for those items being secured from the company's manufacturing operations.

Another aspect of identifying service parts in new models is providing failure-rate data and a recommended parts list to dealers and others who stock parts. The failure-rate data may be expressed as demand per machine per month (DMM). Parts with a sufficiently high DMM are identified as *recommended* parts for stocking and perhaps as *custody* parts for service technicians. Such identification, along with knowledge of the marketing plan and technician training schedule, helps plan pipeline filling for new models.

Data relative to planned production schedules, estimated failure rates, probable product distribution, and installation density are used to determine the timing and quantities required initially as well as replenishment requirements for the first 12 to 24 months. This forecast is presented to manufacturing planning, which must either agree to provide the parts as presented or reach another mutually agreeable arrangement. The forecast is then provided to the service parts center for integration of these requirements into the inventory planning system. A continuous dialogue should be maintained among the service parts group, plant field engineering, and manufacturing. All these groups share the objective of providing satisfactory service. The service parts group has primary management responsibility after initial provisioning takes place.

A recommended service parts list is published to field locations to be used as a guide for ordering initial parts requirements. In addition, a parts manual is published which contains exploded-view illustrations of complete machines, major assemblies, components, and associated part numbers. It is used by the field engineer to order replacement parts.

Bills of Materials for Service Parts

In addition to the parts lists previously mentioned, technical guides which include the graphic explosions of each individual assembly and subassembly are widely available. Conceptually, therefore, a bill of materials can be represented simply by a product tree, but the information usually is formatted to facilitate repair as well as service parts planning and delivery.

Service parts bills of materials frequently fall into three areas: parts kits for FSEs, service kits for specialized product modules, and parts for production bills of materials. The contents of FSE parts kits are determined jointly by technical support, engineering, and logistics personnel. These kits either cover many product lines or are the components used only in a given product line, depending on the nature of the FSE's work.

One area of improvement for some companies has been the planning of service kits for certain types of equipment. Companies may seek to develop kits of service parts for their equipment that FSEs can use to repair the faulty unit. The kit contains all the parts required for a given type of repair job. These kits can be stocked at one of the regional offices and used within the region, or they can be stocked at the central warehouse and shipped to the site requiring the kit. In most instances kits are stocked at the regional level because that places the kit closer to the product site. After the kit has been used, the repairable defective component may be returned for repair.

Some companies use four types of bills of materials:

1. *Single-level bills* identify all components at the next lower level of assembly.
2. *Indented bills* are used in MRP systems to calculate dependent demands for lower-level assemblies and components.
3. *Single-level where-used bills* are inverted bills of materials and identify "parents" of the component.

4. *Indented where-used bills* are used extensively by field service organizations because they indicate the parents and link each to a top-level product identification. The identification of the top-level product is a key factor in component forecasting.

One of the biggest tasks of bill-of-materials maintenance, in which service planners may become involved, is the addition of OEM subassemblies to the company's product structure. OEM subassemblies may have a separate series of part numbers, and it is critical that these be linked to the parent and then to the final assembly.

Engineering Changes

Engineering modifications occur frequently and will continue to occur as a result of lack of availability of parts from vendors, product improvement and refinement, and patent protection. An engineering change request form usually classifies the change and stipulates disposition of existing parts along with the cost impact of the disposition. The engineering department usually reviews all requests and may classify each as a class 1 or class 2 change.

A class 1 change is any decision affecting interchangeability, performance, cost, customer warranty, contractual obligations, or manufacturing processes. Such changes require the use of new part numbers and approvals by engineering, product management, production planning, inventory control, manufacturing engineering, spare parts and service, purchasing, and quality assurance control.

A class 2 change includes design changes to new parts and assemblies during conceptual states prior to shipment, drawing errors, minor physical changes, tolerance revisions, field modifications, and omitted and additional information which does not conflict with class 1 changes. The only approval required on these changes is that of engineering.

If the change is a major product improvement, product management and engineering issue a product information bulletin which describes the modification and illustrates and lists the components affected. If the change is not major, existing inventory is depleted before the new item is made available to customers. Once stock is depleted, the customer is referred to the new part number.

Reusing of existing inventory by repairing defective parts and upgrading older configurations of parts to the latest configuration are primary objectives of engineering change management.

All engineering changes originated in the manufacturing plants and those originated by vendors generally are read and interpreted by the service parts center. These changes are issued to improve the function of a product or are a result of a cost reduction. Data concerning changes that affect service parts may be entered into two computer files. The first is called a *translator file*. It simply cross-references vendor part numbers and the company's part numbers. Translation to all part numbers is made if more than one had been assigned. To avoid ordering and stocking the same item under several part numbers, one is identified as the primary number. Several vendor numbers also may cross-reference to a single part number. The other file organizes parts into families and contains interchangeability and upgradeability information. It is known as the *parts reference file*.

The engineering design change is usually a permanent change, and the supply of the old part is either used up first or disposed of. If the change is made because of some large-scale problem, inventories of the old design are returned from the field warehouses or scrapped on site. However, usually the part with the old design is consumed before the new part can be ordered by the field, as in the case of a change for cost-reduction reasons. A *phase-out status* is entered on the old part in the inventory control system, and the new part number is referenced as its replacement. This approach prevents a reorder notice from being generated to purchase the old part. The new part is set up with a *phase-in status* and a reference to the part being replaced. When the old part reaches its reorder point, a reorder is generated for the new part based on the demand history of the old part. When inventory of the phased-out part is exhausted, orders are switched automatically to the new phased-in part number, and the customer is notified via a message on the order. If the service technicians carry inventory of the old part, that is used before the item is replaced by the new part.

The is the general rule: *If a design modification does not affect the function or fit of a part and if it is a direct substitution for the old part, then the part number is not changed.* Instead, the change is identified by a revision letter following the part number. This revision letter may be used internal to manufacturing and may not be communicated to field service personnel, since they are not affected by the change. The service parts center inventory system may not separate inventory by revision letters, so the various revisions become mixed in the warehouse bin. By using a first-in/first-out (FIFO) system of handling warehouse loads, the old parts tend to be used up first. This mixing of revisions may not be a problem because, by definition, both versions are acceptable for field service. If they were not, the new part would receive a new part number.

Official notification concerning design changes comes from the engineering department on a document usually called an *engineering change order* (ECO). The ECO has room for part numbers affected and instructions to the various groups involved for the proper disposition of the present and on-order inventory. The ECO also is used to announce a new part for an existing machine even when it does not replace an old part. The ECO usually must be approved by engineering, production, and quality assurance before it becomes an official action document.

Carrying the communication of a part number change a step further, the technical service group usually publishes parts-manual changes and field bulletins. If the change is a more significant one and will result in minimizing service costs, a special field publication called a *notice of field change* may be issued when the parts with the improved design are available.

Parts Substitution

A *parts family* frequently is defined as all the parts that are either interchangeable with or upgradeable to the current revision level or to a part number that is interchangeable. Parts family data are used in the replenishment ordering process as well as in the filling of field orders. The system permits substitution of a different part number from the one ordered by the field, provided it is directly interchangeable.

Parts tend to be upgraded in two ways:

1. Modifications are installed that affect reliability or function during a repair process performed by a rework center, vendor, or manufacturing plant. This includes both interchangeable and noninterchangeable modifications. Interchangeable modifications require a revision letter change to the part number, while noninterchangeable ones require a part number change.

2. Modification kits for formal retrofit programs usually are stocked under a unique part number series. Some are mandatory for all units within a range of serial numbers. Others are optional, depending on the application, the engineering, or the feature configuration of the end unit. They may be ordered by the field personnel as any other service part based on information published in a field upgrade bulletin, or mandatory changes may be sent automatically to all field locations.

Principle: *Parts substitution is best accomplished through a phase-in/phase-out process with minimum change in part numbers.*

As engineering changes occur, the impact on inventories of service parts can be more severe than the impact on work-in-process inventory in the factory. Service parts frequently are distributed throughout all echelons of the system, and engineering changes which result in substitution of one part for another can be extremely expensive if change control effectivity is not well managed.

FIELD SUPPLY

Design of the service parts distribution system varies widely depending on geographical coverage and responsibility for repair. Those firms that maintain a force of service repair personnel typically have more echelons in their distribution system than those who sell parts directly to customers.

To understand the flow of parts and the stocking echelons of a company, it is instructive to study a typical service call and to follow the options open to the FSE to secure the correct parts in the least time. The service call typically begins with a report of a need for service. Elements of the call usually include an identification of whether the equipment is fully operational, partially operational, or totally inoperative. This information may be critical because it frequently opens different avenues of parts availability if the equipment is down versus operational.

After the phone call, the service center pages the FSE who is assigned to the client's equipment. Part of the information commonly available to the FSE is a service history of the equipment and an indication of whether the problem is recurring or new.

At the product service site, the FSE examines the unit, using diagnostic tools routinely carried. Basic service components are used initially if possible. The parts which the FSE carries are the lowest echelon of stocking and tend to be both low-cost and transportable. These parts are reviewed frequently to determine which are really necessary for the FSE to carry.

If the unit cannot be fixed with the spares that are carried, then the FSE calls the regional parts administrator (RPA) with a request for parts. The RPA has a computer inventory of all the FSEs and area offices within the region. These area offices may represent the second echelon of stocking locations. Parts that have high usages usually are stocked within the region. The parts stocked within the area office are selected to fit the units which the office services. Each region also can have a third echelon of parts which have low usage within the region but which qualify for stocking. Parts that are stocked at the area office have a higher-usage history or are unique to products in the area. If the parts are available within the region, the RPA contacts the location that has the parts and arranges for shipment.

If the part is not available within the region, the RPA contacts the parts administration group at the service parts center and places the order. If the parts are for an emergency order (the unit is down) or an expedite order (the unit is partially operational), the order is phoned into the service parts center.

The fourth echelon of service spares is the central service parts warehouse which holds parts that have low national usage. When the RPA contacts the parts administration group, the RPA is told whether the parts are in stock, and they are shipped as quickly as possible. If the parts are not available, the order is turned over to the customer service expediters.

The expediters can exercise several options to secure the parts. One option is to determine whether defective parts are in the warehouse and whether they can be repaired and shipped to the FSE. If the option is not available, the expediters may secure the parts from the manufacturing divisions. The availability of parts from manufacturing depends on the stock on hand and the nature of the order. Under certain conditions, it is possible to remove a part from a unit of the finished product that is almost ready for shipment and send it to the FSE who needs the part. A third option may be to contact the other regions and see whether they have the parts. When the parts are needed for older models of equipment, this option usually is exercised before manufacturing is requested to supply the parts.

Once the parts are located and shipped to the FSE, the service call is completed and the FSE calls to perform the call close-out. The call close-out report includes the hours spent on the site, the nature of the problem, and the parts used. If the parts that have been removed from the equipment are repairable, the FSE returns them to defective inventory for repair.

Stocking Echelons

Principle: *Stocking echelon decisions should be based on inventory investment, customer requirements, and technical capabilities.*

For manufacturers who service and repair their own equipment, five stocking echelons generally have been identified.

Manufacturing Plant.   Some service parts may be maintained along with finished-goods inventory. Extremely expensive or very low usage parts which share some component commonality may be stocked at preassembly or component levels at the plant.

Service Parts Center.   Often this is a national or international stocking point which serves two purposes. First, it may be the receiving point for service parts which leave the plant and enter the distribution system. Second, it may be a consolidation point for very expensive or slow-moving parts.

Zone or Regional Warehouses.   These warehouses serve as main stocking locations for parts which are not carried by repair personnel or individual customers.

Service Technicians.   Manufacturers' service representatives and repair personnel usually carry standard kits which include numerous service parts. These kits provide parts needed to resolve common and/or routine equipment problems. Service parts included in the kit frequently are replaced from zone or regional warehouses on an as-used or periodic basis. For many companies, technicians' kits constitute a major inventory investment and are carefully designed to balance these costs against the technical capability of repair personnel.

Independent Dealers Who Maintain Their Own Inventory. Some manufacturers supply parts to independent dealers who provide customer service. Inventory investment at this echelon may be very high for a network of automotive parts dealers or lower for a network of independent jewelers. In most cases, the manufacturer does not own or control this inventory.

Identification of service parts as well as the echelon at which they are to be stocked, therefore, represents a balance between distribution system costs and the technical ability of personnel typically found at each echelon.

Principle: *A clear definition of the type of service performed is needed to plan service parts inventories properly at each echelon.*

If stocking decisions are made for each echelon, a definition of the type of service to be provided at various levels also is appropriate. A good example of such a definition follows:

- *Level 1*—replacement of the defective end item or unit. Examples are minor repairs such as replacing defective caps or knobs which require no special facilities, fixtures, tools, or equipment. Level 1 repairs often may be performed by repair personnel or, in some instances, by customers. Service parts for level 1 repairs often are maintained by customers or repair personnel as part of a recommended parts list.

- *Level 2*—module or subassembly replacements for repairing or modifying defective end items. This level of maintenance should be done by a trained repair person and may require specialized test equipment or other tools. These items typically are carried by technicians as part of a standard kit.

- *Level 3*—repairing defective modules by testing and troubleshooting and/or by replacing components. Level 3 maintenance usually is performed in a repair shop and requires special fixtures and equipment. Service parts for level 3 typically are found at the zone warehouse level or specialized maintenance and repair centers.

Allocation Approaches

Push-Pull. A *push system* of parts allocation typically is used to replenish the zone warehouses and the service technicians. Initial stocking for new models and restocking policies frequently are controlled by the service parts center. Other locations control their own inventories, such as independent dealers or corporate international subsidiaries. The service parts center typically issues a recommended parts list for new models, but customers are free to order the individual parts and quantities that they choose.

One exception is that individual service technicians usually can add parts to their own custody stock but must justify any additions to their supervisors. The parts and quantities stocked in the warehouse and in technician custody are determined from experience, from estimated failure rates for new models, and from demand history for ongoing products.

Limited-Supply Items. An automatic allocation routine frequently is activated whenever the inventory in the service parts center is less than the estimated lead-time demand for that part. A *critical ratio* for each stocking location's order is established based on the part's estimated lead-time demand. The lower the critical ratio, the higher the order priority. The system typically splits order quantities by allocating smaller numbers of items to avoid stock-out at all lower levels. Manual allocation of orders also can be done by appropriately coding the item master.

Priority Needs.   Not all parts orders need to be filled and shipped with the same priority. Various levels of service, therefore, have been established in most companies.

Principle: *A formal policy of service priorities is needed to manage service parts effectively.*

Nearly all firms have a clear understanding of priorities. Not all, however, have formal written policies to guide the scheduling of service repair personnel and allocation of parts in short supply. A typical formal priority scheme which would be useful would set both customer-call and order-fill priorities. Here is an example of such a policy:

- *Priority 1*—emergency order from field service personnel or direct from customer. This usually indicates either down equipment or problems in new equipment installation. This type of call moves to the top of a service person's schedule. If this results in an order to a regional or zone warehouse or to a higher echelon, this order takes priority over others and usually has a target shipping time of 24 hr or less.

- *Priority 2*—customer direct order for parts for nonemergency purposes. Appropriate target shipping date for this type of order frequently is 1 week or less.

- *Priority 3*—intercompany orders not for immediate customer needs. This may include shipments from one zone warehouse to another for satisfying inventory stocking policies or for channeling slow-moving items to other regions with higher demand. Typical shipping time targets for these orders is 2 weeks or less.

- *Priority 4*—major field retrofits or large spare-parts orders with new equipment. These are promised typically on a case-by-case basis.

Such a priority system is useful in allocating scarce parts as well as in managing the activity of parts storage facilities and service personnel in a way which provides effective customer service.

SUPPLIER INTERFACES

The materials control analyst typically is responsible for supplying a vendor source code when a new part is set up on the system. This code is used to identify the type of requisition to be generated with the reorder notice. While a product is being manufactured in a corporate plant, it is sufficient to identify the plant as the supplier. When the product goes out of production, the source of supply for service parts may be changed to indicate the specific outside vendor who produces the part. When production ceases, the plant may send the purchasing records to the service parts center, where the information is then retained on its system. The reorder notice contains a history of the last purchases so that vendor change information is available to the materials control analyst and the purchasing department. If the purchasing department has quotes on the part from other vendors, this information also is available on the reorder notice.

The vast majority of parts required to service products usually are supplied to field service locations by the service parts center. Local purchase by a service location may be encouraged for commonly available parts.

Each manufacturing plant provides data relative to parts manufactured, purchased, or assembled to make the end products. This information may include lead time, make-versus-buy decisions, and active or inactive status. These data serve as the basis for determining which plant is the source for spares. The actual selection may be generated by policy and may be included in the input by the selected plant. If the part is purchased from a vendor by a plant, the service parts center usually has the option of buying the part from the vendor or from the plant. The decision is influenced by quality, availability, and cost considerations. The business relationship between the spares procurement group and plants may be nearly the same as with vendors. Thus all transactions would be initiated through a purchase order or a change notice. This includes receipts, invoices, returns, or cancellations.

Most companies recognize that good vendor performance results in improved service and reduced expense in handling problems. Many firms, therefore, have established a team consisting of members from quality control, purchasing, materials management, and the main warehouse to work with vendors to achieve the following goals and others: on-time receipts, parts meeting print specifications, correct quantities received, and order priced according to quote.

Management of vendor lead times breaks down into three categories: (1) parts obtained from domestic vendors, (2) parts obtained from corporate manufacturing plants, and (3) parts obtained from international vendors. To handle the first category, a computerized quoting program can be used to anticipate reaching the reorder point and to generate a quotation request form, which is sent to purchasing. The intent is to correct lead times before the reorder point is reached. The second category may have the individual part lead times updated monthly by utilizing a computer comparison of lead times on the plant's system with those on the service parts center system. The third category generally has the lead times specified contractually, and these are updated only if the vendor requests a change. The subject of vendor lead-time updating should be covered in the parts contract with the vendor.

The best answer to minimizing conflict of priorities is frequent communication and always trying to maintain a spirit of mutual cooperation. Frequent trips should be made by service parts center personnel to the plants, and plant personnel should be encouraged to visit the service parts center. In addition, service parts centers frequently cooperate with the plants in supplying parts on an emergency basis to keep the manufacturing facilities running. Also, plant orders for parts used in remanufacturing may come to the service parts center for filling; therefore, the service parts center provides parts to keep the plant reconditioning line running also. This provides increased incentive for mutual cooperation.

The reorder notice should contain information necessary for the materials control analyst to decide whether to order the system-recommended quantity. If the order quantity is changed, this is noted on the reorder notice and its associated requisition. The requisition number, quantity, and so forth are entered in the system, and the paperwork goes to the purchasing department. Here a formal purchase order is created and sent to the vendor. A confirmation copy is returned, and the system is updated to indicate this information. Purchasing also inputs the purchase order information to the purchase order control system, which can be accessed via a remote terminal in the service parts center. Subsequent purchase order changes also are indicated on the system. When material is received, a receiving clerk updates the purchase order control system to indicate the receipt. The receipt of material updates the open-order files to indicate that the material has been received but not yet inspected or made available for allocation. After inspection, the material is put into stock, and the physical balances are updated on the system.

Replanning, Rescheduling, and Expediting

After an order has been placed with a vendor, conditions may change, requiring either expediting or deexpediting the order. The system usually handles this by issuing an expedite report in cases where delivery dates need pulling in and a deexpedite report for dates needing to be pushed out.

The expedite report frequently is issued to the purchasing department. It identifies purchase orders which require expediting to avoid stock-out or to relieve a back-order condition that currently exists. The date indicates when the system recommends that the material is needed. This *need date* is the date at which the system's unallocated balance will be at the safety stock level. A partial quantity is also frequently recommended to tell purchasing personnel the quantity required by the need date to keep the system's unallocated balance above the safety stock level until the original due date is reached. Other data on the report indicate whether a previously expedited part needs reexpediting. The expediter also may be able to enter a code to indicate that the order cannot be expedited any further.

The deexpedite report identifies orders which require either rescheduling delivery to a later date or actual order cancellation. The system may forecast the inventory balance at the time replenishment is due and then add the order quantity. If the result is greater than the safety stock plus the order quantity and if the order is not scheduled for immediate delivery, then the part may appear on the expedite report. In addition, the report may calculate the savings to be gained by delaying the order from the current due date to the actual need date. Frequently built into the system are features such as preventing orders from displaying a second time after action has been taken, monitoring previously dispositioned orders, and notifying the analyst of any significant change requiring more analysis.

Transfer Pricing

Interplant sales to the service parts division frequently are made at the supplying plant's total budgeted standard cost. A profit dividend may then be allocated back to the plant the month following the sale of the product to a customer. Profits may be allocated to the supplying location based on the profit margin on the sales of the products it supplied. The objective of this policy is to give the supplying plant an incentive to produce a cost-effective product, since its profit allocation is dependent on the profitability of the service parts division.

ORDERING AND STOCKING POLICIES

Most firms recognize the advantages of push over pull inventory systems at all but the lowest echelons (i.e., closest to customer) in the distribution system. Statistical methods and distribution-requirements planning approaches are widely used to determine order points and safety stocks, but initial provisioning approaches vary with the expected life of products. If a product has a long useful life, failure rates on similar items are used as the basis for initial provisioning, with service parts inventory projected to cover expected usage over a finite period. Products with shorter life cycles present more difficult problems in initial provisioning, chiefly because there are likely to be fewer production runs (often just one) and service parts must be planned carefully to cover projected usage over the entire market life of the product.

Principle: *Initial provisioning for service parts supporting products with long lifetimes should be accomplished on the basis of echelon stocking decisions.*

When new products are introduced, the manufacturer frequently supplies service parts for distribution to customers or repair personnel depending on the responsibility and organization for maintenance. A computer manufacturer, for example, often assumes responsibility for maintenance and repair through its own service organization. In this instance, initial provisioning is based on supplying repair personnel with appropriate parts for repair kits and with other more expensive or less frequently used components (based on projected mean times between failures), which are stocked at district, regional, or national service centers. However, if a manufacturer does not provide repair service, initial provisioning may be done on the basis of recommended parts kits to be given to the customer with the original equipment or on the basis of projected requirements to be stocked at various distribution points.

Principle: *If service parts are to be manufactured to support products which will be made in a one-time production run, initial provisioning must be accomplished on the basis of limited product lifetime expectations.*

The best way to understand this principle is to consider the product life cycle and stocking policy of companies that make numerous new products each year. Some companies may, in fact, introduce as many as 100 new products each year, each of which may be made in one large production run. Service parts which are intended to support each product throughout its life cycle may be manufactured at the same time. This initial provisioning is based on expected failure rates for various components over a limited product life. Although some opportunity may exist later for a last buy of service parts from the manufacturing facility, the quality of the initial provisioning decision has a significant impact on the manufacturer's reputation for quality and service.

Recycling and Reuse

It may be important to identify reconditionable parts that should not be scrapped by the service technician who removes them from the machine. Some companies have found that it is not enough to publish lists of parts on the reconditioning program. It also may be necessary to package the new part in a returnable carton, marked in a distinctive way to identify it as one that may replace a reconditionable part. The label tells the service technician to check whether the item is on the current reconditioning list before disposing of it. The reconditioning list is the official record of what may be returned. Periodically the reconditioning list is updated to include new items and to delete those parts whose reuse is no longer cost-effective.

Parts on the reconditioning list should be returned, and the service technicians usually are required to do this. However, since independent dealers cannot be forced to do so, they may be given a rebate as an incentive.

Repair of returned parts covered by the parts reconditioning program usually is done either by a manufacturing plant which has been set up to perform such jobs or by the vendor, whichever is most economical.

Another way of avoiding the purchase of new parts for models that are being phased out is to take parts from machines that are being scrapped. These are parts that can be used "as is" without reconditioning, such as cabinets, metal rollers, gears, sprockets, brackets, and so forth. They are given a minimum cleaning and are inspected only to see that they are functional. The idea is to hold down service costs, which is vital on an older piece of equipment.

A *quote and order on request (QOR) program* is another way to avoid routinely buying new parts for dying models. If a part for such a model has very slow movement and reordering new parts is expensive, the part is listed in the pricebook without a price and the notation QOR is added. If a customer orders the part, the materials control analyst involved with this program contacts the customer to verify the need and advises that the part is no longer available off the shelf but can be quoted from the vendor. In many cases, the order is canceled because either a wrong stock number was used or the customer finds a way around ordering a new part. If a new part is needed, the materials control analyst explores used parts or higher-level assemblies before a quotation of price and delivery information is obtained from the vendor and passed on to the customer. If the customer accepts the quote, the part is obtained in the quantity needed.

Surplus and Obsolete Parts

Materials generally are considered obsolete when there has been zero demand for a prespecified time. Exceptions, however, are made for certain product categories if their life-cycle patterns indicate that demand will develop at a later time. The issue of surplus materials typically is addressed on an item-by-item basis with each item reviewed with regard to pricing or other factors which can be altered to stimulate movement. Virtually all prudent marketing techniques are used by companies to correct an overstock position.

As production of a product ends or when an engineering change forces production termination of a part, it is necessary to assess long-term support capability and spare-parts requirements. Most companies have developed a systematic approach to the problem.

The process usually begins prior to production termination. A corporate strategy is created to reflect availability and impact of replacement products, the long-term customer need, and resulting estimated decline in field population. A bill of materials containing unique parts is supplied by manufacturing. All parts that have had activity as a service part are identified.

A future-requirements forecast is developed based on the demand that is expected to be required to support the field population during the remaining product life cycle. Additional input is obtained from the field engineering organization as well as manufacturing to ensure reasonableness and to identify additional items or change quantities based on information not apparent from historical activity. Those parts that can be readily obtained from vendors are eliminated from the analysis. Those whose requirements are minimal and are not practical to continue to produce are considered for a final buy or production run for stock. Manufacturing capability is retained for those parts that would require significant immediate investment as well as for high-risk parts.

Forecasting of Future Demand

Principle: *In managing the service parts inventory, care should be taken to plan specifically for demand which originates from separate sources.*

Some of these demands may be categorized as provisioning orders, usually based on the recommended spares list; replenishment orders, to replace parts that have been used to correct failures; and other orders such as modification kits. These distinctions are helpful in determining causes for significant fluctuations in item usage and offer help in understanding how much inventory should be stocked at each echelon in the distribution system.

Service parts planning cannot be done without some forecast of future requirements. Forecasts of individual item sales or usage are required for the operation of any inventory control system since the decisions about when to place an order, and for how much, for the replenishment of stock must be based on some estimate of future requirements. Forecasting of requirements for service parts is one of the primary concerns of those who are engaged in service parts management.

There are probably as many methods of forecasting as there are people who forecast. Many forecasting methods are good in certain situations; but, of course, no foolproof methodology exists. One common way to estimate future demand for a product is to determine the number of customers or users of the item, their uses of service parts, how much they need for each use, how and when each customer orders the material, and any other relevant information. Then a mathematical model can be developed to relate the demand for the item to the factors that cause that demand to occur.

Several problems are common in developing service parts forecasts, and most companies mention one or more of the following:

- Manufacturing or materials management feels that the service parts forecast they receive is never realistic, so they do not produce or procure items to forecast. They try to outguess the forecast and produce or procure more or fewer items than forecasted.

- The service parts forecast is loaded directly into the MRP system without any approval or review.

- Aggregated dollar values of the individual item forecasts differ widely from total sales projections. Often, the two are not reconciled.

- Capacity is often not checked to determine whether it is feasible to meet service parts forecast requirements as well as finished-goods manufacturing schedules.

Firms often cite problems in developing reliable forecasts for service parts because of the relatively high percentage of items which experience irregular, or "lumpy," demand. In some firms as many as 80 percent of the line items and as high as 90 percent of the inventory dollars experience lumpy demand. Obviously, the traditional averaging or smoothing type of mathematical models do not work well for lumpy-demand items.

Principle: *Lumpy-demand items are not forecastable with the same methodology suitable for other items.*

At least two separate forecasting methodologies are appropriate. Furthermore, each firm must develop appropriate diagnostics for separating lumpy-demand items from forecastable items. Clearly, all items must be categorized before forecasts are developed. Requirements for many items which experience fairly regular demand may be forecast by using standard techniques such as exponential smoothing. Forecasting models for lumpy-demand items may be developed to fit the particular needs of each company. These are some of the parameters which may be considered in such models:

- *Resupply or item lead time*—begins when an order to replenish stock is released and lasts until the item is delivered to stock and is ready for filling customer demands. This also may be thought of as being from the time of a reported failure until the item is delivered on site to the customer. This determines the minimum forecast horizon.

- *Systems or equipment operating hours*—the hours per day the customer is operating the equipment. Cumulative system operating hours frequently become one of the key components of forecasting methodologies.
- *Population of items in the field or in service*—the number of end items in service at the customer's sites.
- *Component consumption data*—the quantity by part number of the components consumed due to failure.
- *Mean time between failures*—the ratio, during a given period, of hours operated by equipment being measured to the number of confirmed failures.

Other factors which may influence the forecasts for service parts include engineering changes to improve product quality or reliability, marketing promotions, lead-time changes, distribution system changes which alter the number and/or location of stocking echelons, and any other fact which may cause future usage to be different from past patterns.

Inventory Planning

The following describes how one company plans for service parts inventory. Each part number is assigned to one of several inventory managers, who are grouped by the source of the item. However, several inventory managers may manage parts obtained from a single source, depending on the volume and complexity of the task. Each part is classified as either reworkable or nonreworkable and is grouped into one of four inventory categories.

Category	Number of Items	Percentage of Items	Percentage of Sales
A	923	1	73
B	2,651	3	20
C	3,887	4	5
D	91,518	92	2

The A, B, C, or D classification for a part determines the inventory ordering policy and the cycle count frequency. This classification is established annually and is recalculated monthly. A part may migrate to a higher classification during the year but can be downgraded only at the beginning of the year. Parts in the A, B, and C classifications are forecasted, while parts in the D classification use the reorder-point technique for replenishment ordering.

Nonreworkable parts are expensed upon usage by the field locations. Reworkable parts are recycled at predetermined repair points. Upon failure, the part is routed automatically to the correct repair point, such as local repair, regional rework center, finished equipment service center, manufacturing plant, and service parts center (production, vendor rework, and manufacturing plant).

All parts that leave a region require prior authorization and are controlled through the use of computer-generated authorization forms. Receipt transactions for parts returned to repair points are captured and become the basis for calculating a return rate, to be used in forecasting rework capacity requirements, and additional new items to be produced. Data required to make procurement decisions are contained in various computer files.

A *demand history file* is created for each part based on incoming customer orders, both normal and emergency.

Thirteen 4-week buckets comprise a year. One year of history is maintained on line and is used in the ordering and forecasting process. Demand is captured in the history file under several categories: provisioning orders, usually based on the recommended spares list; replenishment orders, to replace parts that have been used to correct failures; and orders such as modification kits. The distinction is helpful in determining causes for significant fluctuations. All demand is combined for forecasting purposes.

The *parts reference file* is used to pull together all related part numbers into a family. The *inventory master file* contains descriptive, essential business and asset information such as cost, source, lead time, inventory classification, ABCD category, quantity on hand, bin location, and so forth. The *customer order file* contains data relative to customer orders such as customer location, quantity, date ordered, and order status. The *forecast file* contains demand and rework forecasts as well as new build requirements. The *purchase order file* contains data relative to open purchase orders such as vendor name, price, delivery schedule, order number, and so forth. And the *field inventory file* contains on-hand and past-usage information for each service location within the United States. These data are summarized and used as supplementary information in the forecasting process.

The inventory manager receives summary reports covering approximately 25 percent of the active items each week. Each item is reviewed to ensure that the various descriptive data elements are reasonable and accurate, specifically, lead time, family structure codes, special handling codes, source, on-hand quantity and on-order quantity.

A review then is made of the customer ordering pattern to see how well it is tracking the current time-phased forecast. To facilitate the review, the system performs three calculations for each family member and the total family: single exponential smoothing, double exponential smoothing, and 6-month moving-average monthly demand.

If the actual demand is deviating significantly from the current forecast, an attempt is made to determine the cause. Field engineering personnel can supply information regarding new installations, design problems, or other technical events that impact spares. Manufacturing can supply information regarding process or reliability changes. If a new demand forecast is warranted, it is loaded into the forecast file.

The same process is followed in managing the rework forecast, except that instead of demand, a return rate times a yield percentage is forecasted. Then these data are combined to arrive at a projected on-hand amount for each period for the next eighteen 4-week periods as follows:

$$\text{Projected on hand} = \text{Current on hand} - \text{Back orders} - \text{Demand} \\ + \text{Due in new} + \text{Due in rework}$$

These data are reviewed by the inventory manager to determine action, such as expedite, reschedule, and so forth, necessary to maintain an acceptable service level.

The *safety stock level* is calculated by using the mean absolute deviation (MAD) combined with desired service levels. Demand deviations are typically smaller on parts that are ordered very frequently. When additional investment in safety stock is small compared to the volume and value of business, more safety stock is carried. The inventory manager also can establish safety stock at different levels, period by period, based on nonstatistical input.

The time-phased requirements planning system which permits communication of a requirements forecast is limited to A, B, and C category parts. These are 8 percent of the total items, representing 98 percent of sales. New orders are placed and forecasted, and new build requirements are adjusted to achieve the desired safety stock. Category D parts are ordered by the reorder-point technique. The order quantity for D items is generally 6 times the average monthly demand. However, policies regarding minimum order values sometimes result in larger quantities.

PERFORMANCE MEASUREMENT

Principle: *A formal performance measurement and reporting system is a key element of effective service parts management.*

A service parts system is intended to provide a needed service to customers while effectively managing cost. Performance should be measured at each echelon in the distribution system. Some of the most commonly used performance measures at different echelon levels are as follows:

1. Manufacturing plants
    a. Percentage of MPS achieved: measured as service parts actually produced (in dollars) divided by the amount scheduled (again in dollars) in a particular period
    b. Percentage of manufacturing lead time achieved: measured as actual manufacturing lead time for service parts divided by planned manufacturing lead time
2. Service parts center and zone warehouses
    a. Inventory turns: measured as cost of service parts shipped divided by average inventory of service parts (in cost dollars)
    b. First-pass fill rate: measured as percentage of orders from lower echelons which can be 100 percent filled with no back ordering
    c. Average fill rate: measured as average percentage of line items filled on orders
    d. Average age of back orders: measured in days or weeks
    e. Days of supply in inventory, usually based on usage of past 3 to 6 months

Targets for measures at zone warehouses typically will be different, of course, than for those at the service parts center.

3. Technicians and repair personnel
    a. First-call completion: measured as the percentage of service problems which can be solved on the first call
    b. Average age of problem calls: measured as the total time to solve repair and parts problems which cannot be solved on the first call
4. Independent dealers
    a. Inventory turns

b. Number of back orders

c. Average age of back orders

d. Down machine time resulting from service parts and repair problems

BIBLIOGRAPHY

Archer, Norman P.: *A Maintenance Inventory Control System for High Cost Items,* American Production and Inventory Control Society (APICS) Conference Proceedings, 1973.

Bertelsbeck, Robert: *Decentralized Service Parts Rework,* APICS, Service Parts Seminar Proceedings, 1983.

Borgendale, Mac: *Deciding What to Stock at Each Location,* APICS, Service Parts Seminar Proceedings, 1981.

Brown, R. G.: *Advanced Service Parts Inventory Control,* Materials Management Systems, Norwich, Vt., 1981.

Buffa, Frank P., and Tom R. Bryant: "Reflecting Logistics Costs in Customer Service Level Targets," *Production and Inventory Management,* first quarter, 1980.

Cook, Milt: *Service Parts Forecasting,* APICS, Service Parts Seminar Proceedings, 1981.

DeVries, Larry G: *Managing a Centralized Service Parts Inventory,* APICS, Service Parts Seminar Proceedings, 1983.

Domnick, Frederick A.: "When to Order? How Much to Order? Two Basic Questions Answered Using the Class Seasonal Approach," *Production and Inventory Management,* second quarter, 1977.

Giuntini, Ron: *Managing a Service Parts Business,* APICS, Conference Proceedings, 1983.

Glude, Terry L.: *Automated Service Parts Handling and Control,* APICS, Conference Proceedings, 1983.

Green, Donald J.: *Service Part Control Using Closed-Loop Manufacturing Techniques,* APICS, Conference Proceedings, 1983.

Kanet, John J.: *Inventory Planning Systems for Service/Spare Parts,* APICS, Conference Proceedings, 1983.

Lee, William B.: *Managing MRO Inventory in Large-Scale International Operations,* APICS MRO Stores Seminar Proceedings, May, 1984.

—— and Earle Steinberg: *Service Parts Management: Principles and Practices,* APICS, 1984.

Martin, A.: *Distribution Resource Planning,* Prentice-Hall, Englewood Cliffs, N.J., 1983.

Moody, Patricia E.: *Distribution Requirements Planning in the Spare Parts and Accessories Business,* APICS, Conference Proceedings, 1981.

Muir, James W.: *Forecasting Items with Irregular Demand,* APICS, Conference Proceedings, 1980.

O'Keefe, William. H.: *Resource Planning for Maintenance,* APICS, Conference Proceedings, 1980.

Peters, Judith K.: *A Case Study for Developing and Implementing a Spare Parts Department,* APICS, Conference Proceedings, 1983.

Pfunder, Robert K.: *Addressing Some Basic Problems that Plague MRO Operations,* APICS MRO Stores Seminar Proceedings, May, 1984.

Plossl, George W.: "Getting the Most from Forecasts," *Production and Inventory Management,* first quarter, 1973.

Prather, Kirk L.: *Turnaround of Spare Parts Inventory*, APICS, Service Parts Seminar Proceedings, 1981.

Smith, Bernard, T.: *Focus Forecasting—A New Level of Accuracy in Product Demand Forecasting*, APICS, Conference Proceedings, 1979.

Taylor, Paul A.: *Aggregate Inventory Management—Measurement and Control*, APICS, Service Parts Seminar Proceedings, 1981.

Winter, Omar E.: *Repairable/Replacement Material Inventory Management: "Inventory in Motion"*, APICS, Conference Proceedings, 1972.

Just-In-Time
Concepts and Applications

24

Just-in-Time Concepts

Editor

ROBERT W. HALL, Ph.D., CFPIM, Professor, Operations Management, Indiana School of Business at Indianapolis, Indiana

This chapter is a brief review of the planning and control of several kinds of production. The definitions come from a typology derived from condensing a framework of thought used by Harvard Business School faculty (Table 24.1).

DEFINITIONS

1. *Process industries or process manufacturing*—production which adds value by mixing, separating, forming, or chemical reactions. The product is often but not always a powder, liquid, or gas.
2. *Project production*—production in which each unit or small number of units is managed by a project team created especially for that purpose.
3. *Job shop production*—production of discrete units planned and executed in irregular-size lots. Material moves in integral lots through production. Both process production (batches) and fabrication and assembly (jobs) can be done by job shop methods.

TABLE 24.1   Types of Production

Production	Fabrication and Assembly	Process Industries
Project	Examples: construction, shipbuilding	Example: specialty chemicals
Job shop	Examples: custom machine shop, heavy generators	Examples: paint and pharmaceuticals
Flow shop	Repetitive manufacturing Examples: autos, appliances, (box wrenches)	Continuous-flow Examples: oil refining, rolling mill

4. *Repetitive manufacturing*—production of discrete units, planned and executed by rate, or schedule. Material moves in a flow, and production is *not* controlled by lots or work orders.

5. *Continuous-flow production*—production of nondiscrete material without interruption as in extrusion, distillation, or rolling operations. Production is *not* controlled by orders, but planning and control can differ substantially from the planning and control of discrete parts.

Although complete plants and even industries can be classified in these categories because a particular type of manufacturing prevails there, different kinds of production often occur under the same roof. The definitions may be used to classify different departments or operations which sometimes exist very close to each other. For example, a large batch operation in a brewery feeds a filling and packing operation which might be described as repetitive. Some classifications are hard to make by just thinking about the process, for example, coating turbine blades. A microphysical transformation takes place, but it is an advanced coating process which would be considered a normal part of fabrication and assembly if it were merely painting. From the point of view of production planning and control, an important distinction between job shop and repetitive operation is whether it is necessary to plan and control by using orders.

This chapter discusses process manufacturing, however planned and controlled, and repetitive manufacturing—the flow shop version of fabrication and assembly.

PROCESS INDUSTRIES

The process industries have considerable variety, but generally they tend to be capital-intensive, which means that capacity planning is often a major activity. Whether operated as a job shop (batch) or a continuous-flow production, in the process industry the capacity problem requires attention. Maintenance is one of the major areas requiring planning and control, and the process industries have been in the forefront of systems development of maintenance, repair, and operations (MRO) inventory. However, the management of MRO does not deviate substantially from the management of MRO in other industries.

Coproducts and By-Products

The process industries often have coproducts or by-products, and that leads to some unusual structures in what are called bills of materials for fabrication and assembly. Several products may emerge from combining the same set of ingredients in the formulation. If it is planned by material-requirements planning (MRP), this situation is handled by placing all the coproducts in the master schedule at the zero level, but using only one as the parent of the dependent materials. This requires alertness in master scheduling in those instances in which a change in process conditions (such as temperature) alters the mix of coproducts which may result.

Uncertain Composition of Raw Materials

Another problem common to process industries is the uncertainty of composition of the raw material. The primary purpose of many such industries is the conversion of raw material from the earth to homogeneous materials for use elsewhere. For example, the composition of oil from different locations differs enough that oil from a specific source can be run only in refineries designed for it. In addition, oil coming from the same location may differ in composition from day to day. That means, for example, that the yield of ethylene gas from a refinery varies somewhat from day to day, and the composition of the raw gas for polyethylene varies slightly. The process is adjusted for a "target" grade of output, but the results may be off target. The product is graded after it is made, a common practice in many process industries.

Often, the composition and grade of output depend on the technical conditions of a process itself, so that production control is almost inseparable from the technology. For example, the yields of different products from a distillation depend on the heat, pressure, and flow rate of the material being distilled. It becomes impossible to separate the details of production planning and control from the technical design and control of the process.

These factors create the uncertainty in the types and quantities of by-products and coproducts, all of which may be affected in a way interrelated to all the others. Some of the by-products may be wastes having high disposal costs. The bill of materials for such a process may be an inverted structure when compared with the type usually thought of for fabrication and assembly—there are more end products than starting materials, something which happens, for example, when different lengths of bar stock are cut. Production is analogous to a "disassembly process," or an overall product structure in which many end products come from one raw material (or a small set of raw materials combined in different proportions). Developing the material requirements comes from an explosion of the source materials for the different end products, which turns out to be a derivation by implosion to the raw materials. Much of the planning is forward planning.

Application of MRP to batch-mode processes may differ little from how it is applied to fabrication and assembly, but for many continuous-flow processes, little material may be held between steps of the process. Some processes may have no intermediate materials, nothing but raw material and end products. Others have material held at intermediate stages. Some processes may draw off material at intermediate stages or process it immediately.

All these conditions are plannable with MRP by using a little ingenuity in structuring the planning bills of materials. Where intermediate items can either be drawn off or processed further, they can be treated as pseudoitems in the bill structure for higher-level items. If it is planned to draw off the intermediates, they must be placed in the master schedule. By treating intermediates as pseudoitems, they can be time-offset without allowing for gross-to-net inventory calculations. Such items as catalysts can be treated as consumables.

The real problems in planning occur when production is not very predictable. Uncertainty in yields and decision points (whether to process materials further) creates problems in planning no matter what system is used.

Many process industries have products which must be packaged. MRP is used to back schedule the acquisition and preparation of containers and packaging material on one side of the bill of materials and the acquisition and processing of material to be filled on the other side (see Fig. 24.1). The two sides must meet at the master production schedule (MPS) level for filling and packaging. The MPS is derived from the requirements of the distribution system.

Capacity Planning

Most process industries are capital-intensive and sometimes energy-intensive, both of which put great stress on capacity planning. The uncertainty of the processes, as noted, makes capacity planning somewhat difficult. The mix of production which is planned may cause an unexpected shift in the bottleneck points in the processes, and adding to capacity for short-term overflows is usually impractical.

One way to improve capacity planning for process industries employs a bottom-up derivation of the items in an MPS by using a reverse MRP as follows:

1. Explode a first-cut master schedule but without updating all the files and creating the paperwork for execution purposes. Use the results of this explosion only for capacity planning.

2. Examine the capacity bottlenecks created by the proposed plan. Revise the timing and quantities of the intermediate processing steps as required. Hopefully, this is simplified by not having very many pieces of equipment which present bottleneck points. Adjust the timing and quantities of processing the materials at bottleneck points.

3. Put these revised quantities into a reverse MRP program to derive the master schedule which will give the desired result. That typically cannot be done by a standard MRP package, but requires a special simulator to do it.

4. Run the revised master schedule by using the full MRP program with all output.

This procedure is only an added data processing step in the usual logic for capacity planning with a capacity-requirements plan. It is very effective if capacity bottlenecks are predictable, but of course, no plan provides foresight for capacity problems which arise from processing failures, such as the complete failure of a fermentation process so that it must be restarted.

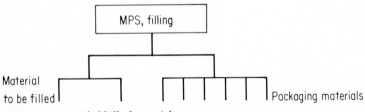

FIG. 24.1 Two-sided bill of materials.

Capacity costs usually force process industries to emphasize long-term capacity planning and aggregate planning because of the inability to run a plant in a "throttled back" condition. It is either up or down. Other problems which may affect production planning include environmental controls, safety, planning for downtime maintenance, finding optimum mixes, changeover scrap, and minimizing scrap from such operations as running bar stock of standard lengths and minimizing the loss of cutoff ends.

REPETITIVE MANUFACTURING: PUSH SYSTEM CONTROL

A job shop may begin moving toward repetitive manufacturing when it begins to have a number of job orders for the same part number on the shop floor at the same time. Unless excellent floor reporting is maintained, units will be completed for each of the different orders. If this continues, it may be decided to combine some orders and run parts straight through production on a single large work order, devising a way to report work against it. After a time, people discover that they are planning and controlling production according to the rate at which it moves.

If the runs are short, so all the parts can be moved at one time, lot integrity is preserved and with it the standard job order system. However, if the runs consume too much time for that, the shop floor operates without job orders. The output of MRP presented to the plant is to run given quantities at given times, usually as daily schedules. (In this kind of production, there is less tendency to refer to the plant as the "shop floor.")

Postdeduction Method of Inventory Relief

When material made in long runs is flowing through consecutive operations, a cumulative count of parts must be kept to know when to cut off one run and start another, although that is obvious if the operations run out of material. The type of floor reporting typically used in a repetitive manufacturing plant is the recording of parts counts at *count points* in the flow. Many of the count points are at assembly or subassembly operations. The counts are used to relieve work-in-process inventory by postdeduction, sometimes called *backflush*.

As an example, suppose socket wrench sets are packed and shipped on an assembly line. Some of the items are purchased, and these are issued in bulk to final assembly. Items fabricated in the plant may go to inventory and, in turn, be issued in bulk to final assembly, or they may pass directly from fabrication to final assembly with only a count being made. The counts and the bulk issues add material to the work-in-process inventory at final assembly.

The count of socket wrench sets packed is then multiplied by the bill of materials for each wrench set, and the result is deducted from the work-in-process inventory. Scrap and items removed from the floor for other reasons must be counted and deducted from the inventory by transaction.

Floor Schedules for MRP

Some repetitive manufacturers plan production with cumulative numbers, but others do not. However, the characteristic of all is to translate the plans to schedules for the shop floor. Feedback comes from comparing the counts against the schedules. To develop a simple schedule, the period requirements for an item are divided by the number of workdays in the period, to give a daily schedule rate. Sometimes this is done on an annual basis. For example, if 100,000 units of an item are required for a year containing 250 workdays, then a running rate of 400 units per day results and may be used, provided level, dedicated production is desirable.

However, situations are often not that simple. A shorter planning horizon and the need to allocate capacity to different items mean that more complex planning and replanning are usually necessary. The result is a plan for a series of runs, all timed to allow material to flow into a series of final-assembly runs.

Cumulative MRP

Systems which plan with cumulative MRP use the cumulative requirements in the master schedule, and these cumulative numbers are exploded through all dependent-demand levels for each period rather than using the noncumulative demand figures. Consider an example with only seven periods of demand shown in the MPS:

Period	1	2	3	4	5	6	7
Standard MPS	100	100	100	100	100	100	100
Cumulative MPS	100	200	300	400	500	600	700

Even without exploding this through several levels of dependent items, one advantage is immediately obvious for the case in which nearly identical demand appears in many consecutive periods. The cumulative figures provide an easier way to tell where you are in the schedule. They also provide easy checkpoints for comparison with cumulative counts of completed production.

The most frequent practice is to convert the cumulative planning figures to daily schedule requirements for shop floor workers. The cumulative figures are only used by production control to compare counts against requirements.

As can be detected by studying Table 24.2, planning and tracking by the cumulative system require exact definitions of the count points and highlight the progress of material flow. All inventory, stocked or in transit, existing between two different points in a flow of material is represented by the difference in the cumulative numbers tracked. In Table 24.2, cumulative requirements represent the target build schedule, but the schedule is different from the demand for shipping the product. For example, in period 11, 24,212 of item A have been completed, 212 more than cumulative requirements (schedule) and 912 more than have been shipped. The 912 items are somewhere between the end-of-line count point and the shipping count point taken during loading on the dock. Table 24.2 is a history of tracking and replanning the items shown.

Tracking Production

What to track is sometimes a problem. For example, is it worthwhile to show the cumulative usage for subassembly Y, or is it sufficient to allow the item to be controlled by feedback replanning the cumulative requirements? In general, it is better to select count points carefully, to maintain control without processing additional numbers.

TABLE 24.2 Cumulative Scheduling

Parent Item A: Annual Requirement (Forecast) of 100,000

	11	12	13	14
Assembly A				
Cumulative shipments	22,300	23,900	25,900	28,100
Cumulative requirements	24,000	26,000	28,000	30,400*
Cumulative completed	24,212	26,187	28,274	30,303
Subassembly X (purchased)				
Cumulative requirements	26,000	28,000	30,200†	32,600*
Cumulative used	24,212	26,187	28,484†	30,503
Cumulative received	26,400	26,400	29,500	32,100
Subassembly Y (fabricated)				
Cumulative requirements	28,000	30,000	32,000	34,400*
Cumulative complete (p. 5)	27,512	29,697	29,957	32,053
Cumulative through (p. 2)	28,288	30,905	31,118	33,233
Cumulative started	28,981	31,712	32,009	34,776

*Add 400 scrapped A's to the cumulative requirements. Explosion into the future adds the 400 to requirements for X and Y in period 14 and all subsequent periods.

†Add 200 scrapped X's to requirements for X in period 13 and all subsequent periods. X is time offset 1 week from A; Y is time offset 2 weeks from A.

Table 24.3 shows a simplified illustration of startup and cutoff of a production run based on the bill of materials diagramed. In the format of quantities shown for the four items, the use of cumulative planning provides a natural means for comparison with the cumulative numbers from tracking production.

Note also that the use of cumulative numbers lends itself to gross explosions. It is possible to reference the cumulative actual numbers and adjust the plan, and it is even possible to perform an MRP explosion with noncumulative numbers first and then convert the result to cumulative numbers. However, the major strength of cumulative MRP is the ease with which a gross explosion without netting inventory can be projected down through the bill of materials to create a plan in which the requirements at each level are simply time-offset from their need in final assembly. This simplicity is an advantage in a long-run, complex, fast-flow operation.

Advantages and Disadvantages of Cumulative MRP

Table 24.3 also shows the advantage of cumulative numbers for coordinating the startup and cutoff of material, especially for annual model runs. However, if item A were run for 5 weeks or so instead of 52, then the startup and cutoff would be coordinated in the same way. In fact, runs lasting only a few weeks can be planned and time-offset by noncumulative MRP. Then the master scheduler can combine the "orders" for each week into one planned run, which can then be tracked through production with cumulative quantities. If an order number is used, rather than just schedules, it can be called a *flow order*. This method does not require the volume of paperwork required by a large number of shop orders, and that is one of the major objectives.

Whether cumulative or noncumulative MRP is used, the major need of repetitive manufacturing is to simplify shop floor control by eliminating much of the paperwork needed by a lower-volume job shop. The major advantages of cumulative MRP are as follows:

TABLE 24.3   Startup and Cutoff with Cumulative System

Bill of Materials

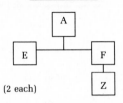

(2 each)

	1	2	3	. . .	50	51	52
Parent item A							
Plan	0	0	100	. . .	4,800	4,900	5,000
Actual	0	21	106	. . .	4,853	4,998	5,018
Component E							
Plan	0	200	400	. . .	9,800	10,000	10,000
Actual	58	237	413	. . .	9,753	10,002	10,036
Component F							
Plan	0	100	200	. . .	4,900	5,000	5,000
Actual	0	101	198	. . .	4,967	5,018	5,018
Component Z							
Plan	100	200	300	. . .	5,000	5,000	5,000
Actual	91	191	307	. . .	5,006	5,018	5,018

- Cumulative planning and tracking is a simple way to eliminate excess "nervousness" of gross-to-net planning in fast-flow operations.
- Cumulative numbers are easier to read in an extended, uniform schedule.
- Startups and cutoffs are easier to coordinate by simplifying tracking, even over long distances with minimum information. (The cumulative system seems to be in greatest use in companies with annual model changes.)

The *disadvantages* of cumulative MRP include

- The difference between two large numbers for inventory counts may seem psychologically to be a smaller amount than it really is.
- The system does not inherently provide the means for tight checks of data accuracy. One must be careful to account for scrap and other losses.

REPETITIVE MANUFACTURING WITH JUST-IN-TIME PRODUCTION

In the strict sense, being *just in time* means having *only* the correct part in the correct place at the correct time. This ideal is unattainable except by moving parts one at a time in a straight flow, as is literally done on a transfer line. In any case the ideal is to compress production lead time as much as possible.

Just-in-Time Production for Manufacturing Improvement

Just-in-time (JIT) *production* includes all the activities from design of the product to its delivery to the customer which permits JIT movement of material. JIT production has come to mean, in the broadest sense, a philosophy of manufacturing which strives to produce with the shortest possible lead time and the fewest possible mistakes.

The most basic approach is to examine *why* inventory is needed and to eliminate as many of the reasons for it as possible. With little or no inventory, material moves unimpeded from raw material to the finished state. Any impediment to the movement of material indicates that manufacturing has not been developed to as high a state as it could be.

The existence of inventory is an indicator of waste, and *waste* is defined as any unnecessary use of material, labor, space, equipment, or energy. Any activity which does not add value to the material is waste. Some of the impediments to the flow of material through production represent problems which cannot be solved with current technology, but many are solvable.

In a more practical vein, the basic idea is to slightly reduce inventory in selected areas by draining excess inventory, reducing lot sizes, and reducing lead time. Then examine how to change the methods of management to permit the same production to take place with less inventory. The most important part is to change the physical processes of production and to alter all kinds of management practices which require inventory or which add to lead time. Materials management is a part of this total effort, but only a part. Many of the corrective actions extend to such activities as plant layout, operator training, reduction of defect rates, reducing setup times, and so on. The idea is to improve the manufacturing process itself, both the physical process of production and the preparation activities for it.

It is the constant improvement which is the most important part of JIT production. And that applies to any kind of production, albeit through different methods for standardizing production according to what is possible.

This is really a management philosophy which impacts every aspect of manufacturing management, from marketing practice to supervision of the plant work force. Most of the subsequent discussion covers techniques used in repetitive manufacturing for JIT production. If it can be done, production is less wasteful if done repetitively. That can be seen just from thinking about the layout of a plant for streamlined flow of material as one might have for product-oriented production.

The materials management techniques associated with JIT production are intended to constantly force attention on identifying ways to improve manufacturing and to constantly direct action to make changes. The value of understanding the techniques is limited if one fails to keep in mind their purpose.

Pull System of Production Control

The operation of a repetitive-flow *pull system* depends on providing a pattern of flow beginning at final assembly that permits enough synchronization of production that the correct parts can be called for as needed by the using operations.

There are two essential differences between pull and push systems of material control. First, in the pull system, the work center making parts takes its cue from the users of the parts. The signal governing material movement comes from the user of the material, not from some central planning source. A work center does not receive a schedule as in push system repetitive manufacturing or a dispatch list as in job shops. Second, in the pull system, the parts made sit at the location where they were made. In the push system, the parts are moved to the next location immediately after completion.

Figure 24.2 shows an overview of a pull system of this type which could be based on a card system (or Kanban system) of material control or which could be operated by a type of signal other than cards. The "fishhooks" between the work centers denote that material is obtained only when needed.

Note that there are no stockrooms in either the overview or the detailed flow of cards in Fig. 24.3. All the work centers have been organized with inbound and outbound stock points at which parts are stocked in standard containers, a fixed number of parts in each container. The system does not work unless the plant floor has been developed somewhat as a stockroom, and it takes considerable time and effort to upgrade production processes to permit this. The pull system usually goes into place only as a result of considerable achievement in improving overall production practices.

The control system starts with the final-assembly schedule. The final-assembly line or stations must be capable of executing a *level final-assembly schedule*, that is, one which has a level distribution of requirements for all the materials which feed final assembly. Think of it as using a small, constant amount of all active parts every day. Then a level requirement for all materials can be anticipated by the work centers feeding the final-assembly area, some of which may be suppliers—work centers outside the plant.

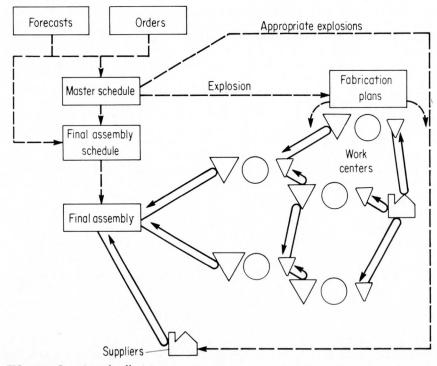

FIG. 24.2 Overview of pull system.

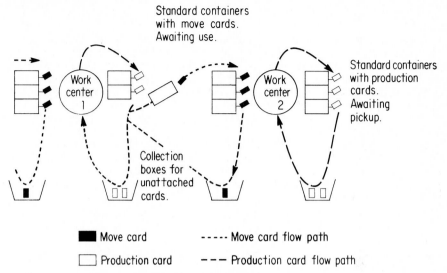

FIG. 24.3 Detailed flow path of cards at two work centers.

With the card system, there are two kinds of cards at the fabrication work centers, move cards and production cards. Each card goes on only one standard container having only one part number. Each move card is used to move one standard container of one part number between just two points. Each production card unattached to a full container is authorization to produce just one standard container of parts at the work center which produces that part number. Here are the work rules for using the cards in the way diagrammed in Fig. 24.3:

1. Always use standard containers.
2. Put only one card on a standard container.
3. Organize production into stock points with a fixed flow path (routing) for all material—one part number is found in one place.
4. Using work centers always send for material from producing work centers.
5. When parts are first removed from the container, remove the card also. Return the move card to the source stock point as authorization to move forward a full standard container of the same part number. Never move parts without the proper card.
6. When parts are taken from the work center which produces them, the production card is removed from the container taken and the move card is attached to it.
7. The unattached production card is authorization to make another container of that part number. Never make parts without authorization of an unattached production card.

Rule 4 is psychologically the most difficult. It is difficult to stop working or stop the machine if there is nothing currently desired by the work centers being supplied. A part of the overall system is to use this time for improving the process or preparing for future work. Never make parts that are not needed.

Pull Systems for Improvement

The emphasis is on constant improvement of the process, and the real purpose of this system is to provide a way to isolate problems by reducing inventory at key points. Since one card equals one standard container of one part number, limiting the number of cards limits the work-in-process inventory for that part number. This allows selective reduction of work-in-process inventory by the following procedure:

1. Start up a new schedule with extra cards to allow for startup problems. Final-assembly schedules are developed to operate at a level for finite periods—1 week to 1 month usually.
2. As startup problems are worked out, remove cards from the system (decrease pipeline inventories) until there is just barely enough pipeline inventory to function smoothly.
3. Pull cards at selected points to study problems. Pull move cards to study material-handling or transport problems and production cards to study problems at work centers.
4. Make changes to operate permanently with less inventory. Or, do not stop with improvement after the startup problems seem solved.
5. As soon as one improvement has stabilized, pull more cards and repeat the process.
6. If possible, keep going until no cards are needed—the operations are almost ready to be directly linked. When that is literally done, a transfer line has been created.

What has been described is a systematic method of inventory reduction to stimulate a major program of improvement in the basic production operations. The sources of defects have been identified and overcome. The layouts have been refined and compacted. The problem lies in the work required to do all this.

Estimates of how many cards to use in the system at various points can be made by production planning as it develops the schedule for a planning period. The cards (or inventory) may be reduced by production control personnel, but more often it is done by line management, the supervisors who have responsibility for identifying and overcoming the problems in production which require inventory to cover them. Line supervisors are the ones who must coordinate the improvement of production. By limiting the inventory, everyone must constantly be alert to the condition of the production process itself, including equipment, material, tooling, quality, maintenance, methods, and people.

The cards themselves are not necessary to the process. The production cards are seldom used, and frequently move cards are not used either. The part number and other basic information may be attached to a container. A limited number of marked containers circulate between two work centers, and when an empty container for a specific part number returns to the supplying work center, that is a directive to fill it up and make it ready for another pickup.

Tokens and markers may be substituted for cards. Electronic signals are sometimes used for this purpose. In cases where a very limited mix of parts is made, the outbound stock point may consist of only a restricted space for each part number. The supplying work center produces parts to fill the space provided for each part. If the space for all the parts to be demanded is full, work is stopped.

Conditions Necessary for Pull Systems

Two conditions are necessary for any system that replicates what has been described with cards. First, there must be a *repetitive, trackable flow of parts.* The supplying point must be able to anticipate what will be demanded by the using work center and be able to react. That is not possible if parts are customized, that is, in the case of parts which result from custom engineering. It is also not possible if there are drastic changes in overall rate and in the mix of parts demanded. It is possible to incorporate a large variety of optional items in this system provided their pattern of use can be anticipated.

Second, there must be *stable yields,* or *defect rates.* The ideal is to have 100 percent yield, or zero defects, but the system will work with actual performance somewhat less than that. It does not work very well if the production process is so poorly developed that large amounts of scrap can occur for unknown reasons. When that occurs, there is little recourse but to provide rework time in the planning or to hold extra inventory at various stages and plan production by using gross-to-net calculations on the inventory.

There is no magic in a pull system used only for production control. Such a system will work in repetitive manufacturing even if there are many problems with defects, machine breakdowns, etc. One only has to add inventory to the system to cover these problems. The system completely breaks down or is impossible to construct with nonrepetitive manufacturing.

The most important point is that the pull system keeps an upper limit on the inventory at all points in material flow and thereby maintains a self-induced pressure for faultless performance in every part of manufacturing. This, combined with the dictum that the feeding operations stop if there is no demand for their output, means that whenever any operation has trouble, the material does not stack up at that point. This makes the trouble points highly visible, and it forces attention on overcoming whatever problem has occurred.

This is a feedback system with emphasis on reducing the feedback reaction time. The reaction time is reduced, not just by a signal, but by reducing the inventory and developing the production process to respond quickly, thus keeping the inventory to a minimum. This is the purpose of the system. Its effectiveness depends on the fortitude of management to improve the flexibility and responsiveness of the production process.

An MRP system is sometimes described as a pull system because it provides clear priorities for job shop orders in queue or for runs planned in repetitive manufacturing. It uses feedback for systematic replanning. However, the pull system just described uses signaling directly from point of use to point of supply, not processed through a central control. The shop floor material movement system is still a push system if the material is moved immediately from where it is made to where it is used. The real benefit comes from restricting the work-in-process inventory between two points, doing this by a highly visible means. The objective is to make production problems visible and overcome them through fundamental changes in the production process. Limiting and controlling the inventory through a pull system is only one of the methods used to do that.

PLANNING AND SCHEDULING FOR A PULL SYSTEM

The final-assembly schedule is the key element. When executed, the final-assembly schedule initiates the flow of material through all production. There is a separate final-assembly schedule for each final-assembly line or station to which material is drawn. Each fabrication work center may feed many final-assembly centers, so the master schedule used to make up fabrication plans is the sum of the *expected* final-assembly schedules to be served. It is most commonly kept in daily time buckets. The master schedule is thus based on the development and refinement of final-assembly schedules through several revisions over the planning horizon.

Level Schedule

Leveling each final-assembly schedule is very important. The objective is to have an even-paced use of all material coming into final assembly. This is elementary if each final-assembly area is dedicated to only one product having only one bill of materials, but there are usually multiple models or options on one assembly line. In that case, the ideal is to run mixed models on the same assembly line or to come as close to that as possible.

Level Schedule and Line Balancing

Suppose three models are to be run on one assembly line each month: model A, 5000 units; model B, 3000 units; model C, 2000 units; for a total 10,000 units. This can be run as a repeating 5-3-2 proportional sequence:

A-B-A-C-A-B-A-B-A-C

In this simple example, it is easy to see how to organize the period requirements into a sequence. If many variations or options are run on the same line and the numbers do not round out, it is not so easy. But in many cases schedules can be prepared manually by using approximate sequences and distributing the "tag ends" throughout the resulting repeating cycles.

Before we go further, consider why the leveling is done. First, it improves the line balance in some kinds of assembly lines. Mixed models are almost always run on automotive assembly lines for reasons of balance. For example, if a station wagon is assembled only every eighth unit, the assemblers at the station which hangs tailgates can balance that activity with others performed on other types of vehicles, but it takes extra time to hang the tailgate. If two wagons were to appear together, they could not complete the two tailgates at line speed.

Second, if the subassembly of tailgates is done in synchronization with the assembly, and if two station wagons appear together, the subassembly work center might not be able to have the second tailgate prepared at the proper time. If much of the fabrication is done by methods that come close to being transfer lines in synchronization with assembly, much of the production work must be done in a balanced pattern. That is, the problem of line balance extends to the entire production network supporting assembly.

Finally, if there is a level workload in a repeating pattern at the work centers, there is also a level work pattern for material handling, for the toolrooms, for test operations, for maintenance, and so on. The benefits extend to the entire manufacturing organization. In considering line balancing, production-line cycle times must be used. A materials manager often thinks of cycle time as the time from when material enters a plant until it leaves, but in line balancing, cycle time is the time between the completion of units.

In the example of assembling three models, suppose there are 1000 working minutes each day to assemble 500 units each workday. Then a unit should finish every 2 minutes (min), or the cycle time equals 2 min per unit. The rate of production is the inverse, or 1 unit every 2 min, 30 units per hour.

Then refer to the mixed model sequence. The cycle time for model A is 4 min. For model C it is 10 min. For model B it is 6.67 min on the average. However, in the sequence shown, sometimes the interval is 8 min and sometimes it is 4 min, a range of actual cycle times, depending on whether there is 1 unit or 3 units between the B's.

In the more complex cases, the different models are sorted into a sequence which must abide by an upper and lower limit on cycle times for each model in the lineup. In other cases, usually those with shorter overall cycle times, balance may be achieved more easily by running models mixed in clusters.

There is another consideration—the ability to position or reposition material at assembly or subassembly in the correct sequence. A mixed sequence of small parts with short cycle times may be too difficult to execute, or space may not permit all the parts to be positioned as needed.

The upshot of all this is that the preparation of final-assembly schedules and sequences requires the scheduler to be aware of the various problems of balancing operations throughout assembly and fabrication. This may include considerations of tooling changes, equipment setups, and so on.

Another important consideration is the ability to change the schedule. To keep the overall process going smoothly, it is usually necessary to keep the overall rate of production nearly constant. That is, the cycle time between each unit cannot vary by more than ±10 percent cumulating in the same direction for very long before the balances begin to unravel—operator assignments and layouts require changes.

In discussing scheduling and planning for repetitive manufacturing, it is helpful to distinguish rate and mix. The *rate* is the overall rate at which all units are being produced. The *mix* is the proportion of models, options, and various materials required within the overall rate.

Option Mixes

The overall rate of production provides the supporting rhythm around which the variations of different models and options can be incorporated. Ideally, one would like to hold with the same mix of models and options for a time. However, that may not be possible, and the degree of mix change which is permissible is determined by the capability of the supporting fabrication network to develop the necessary flexibility. If a mix change at final assembly requires simple revision of a die setup at one operation and an insignificant work content change elsewhere, that is easily accomplished. But if the mix change calls for tools or materials which were not planned to be available, it cannot be accomplished.

Length of Level Schedule Period

In deciding how to schedule production to match market demand, the length of the level schedule period is important. The system runs smoothly if an identical rate and mix is sustained. This can be done if the schedule is fixed for a time, say 1 month; but allowing no changes for 1 month extends the lead time before a production change can respond to changes from the customers.

Scheduling for a pull system requires setting a fixed rate schedule for 5 to 25 work days and with it a target mix of models and options. In general, the target rate must be adhered to, especially if a large number of operations are closely synchronized. The balance of running rates between them is more difficult to preserve. If there are only three or four operations to link, the target rate is often less important, though it depends on the ability of each operation to run at different rates.

How long should the fixed period be? There are both physical problems and business problems to consider. The scheduling period is often 1 month only because it is a favorite business planning cycle the world over. The physical problems primarily concern the time needed to start up the production flow process and reconstitute the mix of parts in the pipelines. That may take an hour or two, or a day or two. It also takes some time to close out a period of fixed schedule, draining some old material from pipelines, if necessary, and revising the work areas in preparation for the new schedule.

In this system, engineering changes are normally concentrated at scheduled change times. Then the effects of a number of changes are worked through when the system starts up, and the system can operate free of engineering changes afterward. Once a repetitive manufacturing plant has been developed to operate in this way, material cutoffs can be done best at scheduled change times.

All the work-in-process inventory is usually counted at the end of a schedule period. By the time the plant is able to operate in this way, it should take only an hour or so for workers to perform this task.

These are some of the business problems which affect the length of a level schedule period:

- The length and timing of the business planning cycles of major customers.
- The length and timing of major planning cycles in the distribution of products.
- The payment methods worked out with customers, some of which may cause them to place orders and expect delivery inside limited time windows (for example, asking for delivery at the beginning of the month to maximize time before having to pay at the end of the month).
- Need for coordinated shipment of items to the same customers. An example is shipping a computer mainframe and various peripheral equipment from different plants timed to arrive at a customer location at the same time.

Master and Final—Assembly Schedules

In this kind of production the MPS is developed as a preliminary version of what is expected to be the final-assembly schedule at the time that it is actually run. Definite freeze points are established for rate and for mixes, so that preparation time is allowed. Figure 24.4 is a typical example of vehicle manufacture by this system. The MPS describes the expected mix in the final-assembly schedule, summarized in daily buckets. The daily schedule would reflect an identical rate for about a month at a time and usually for more time than that. The daily schedule would reflect the same mix for 7 or 8 workdays, or about one-third of a month.

The actual final-assembly schedule in this instance is the lineup of vehicles to be built in vehicle number sequence. This sequence is set 3 to 6 workdays in advance of running. The sequence may deviate somewhat from the mix actually used for planning purposes, but there are restrictions in selecting the actual vehicle orders to insert in the lineup, to prevent the actual production from drifting too far away from the planned mix.

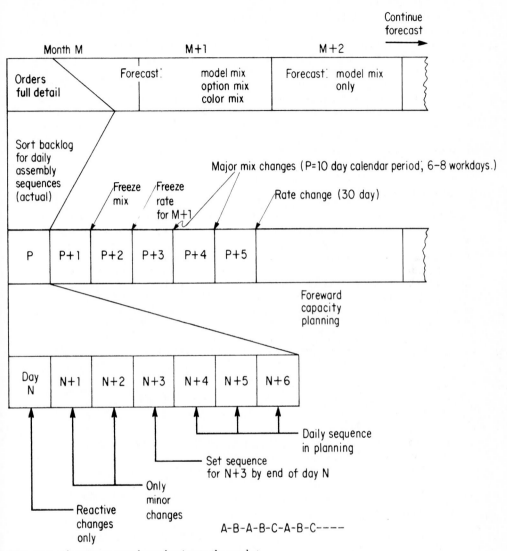

FIG. 24.4 Planning to match production to the market.

In the make-to-stock case, one of the first problems involves setting a level rate schedule for items that have high and low patterns in sales, or seasonal items. This is accommodated by changing the rate of output when the schedules are changed. The overall rate is stair-stepped up and stair-stepped down. It is not necessary to hold a level rate throughout a year, just long enough to allow the material flows to be established for fast-flow production. Level schedules are run in level rate segments.

The operation of a distribution system is affected. In the case of a seasonal product, it is still necessary to have a preseason buildup of finished goods if it is impractical to provide the capacity to meet demand at peak season. The risks associated with these buildups are well known.

Less seasonal items should see a reduction in finished-goods stock over time as capability is developed for JIT production. If setup times are greatly reduced and level schedules are adhered to, the large lot quantities which are moved into finished goods should almost disappear. New production of each end item enters finished goods at a steady rate. Therefore, most of the finished goods necessary in the distribution system exist only to provide distribution pipeline stock and buffer the normal variations in demand rates by customers. An additional amount is necessary to provide safety stock covering the time until the production output rate can be increased by the normal planning lead time.

Planning Fabrication Operations

The MPS is used with only a gross explosion for all the fabrication operations which can be controlled through a tight pull system. There is no inventory on record, so there is no gross-to-net requirements calculation. As each new schedule starts up, the pipelines of stock reconstitute themselves to accommodate the new rate and mix. If the throughput times for material are short relative to the length of the schedule period, all that is necessary is to provide a plan for fabrication work centers to prepare. The actual execution is in response to pull signals, not to a schedule issued from production control.

However, most complex products have parts or options which cannot be controlled by a pull system. It is necessary to commence the production process in advance of knowing exactly what will be required at final assembly. Consequently, inventory must be held, and sometimes operations are run with work orders, as in a job shop. For the long-lead-time operations and suppliers, a gross-to-net explosion with time offsetting is necessary just as in any other MRP system. Some actions must be taken based on only a forecast, for example, forward buying of long-lead-time raw material.

This kind of planning is a simplification of MRP. The explosion of the bill of materials for all items controlled by the pull system is done with a gross explosion and no time offsetting. The remaining items can be planned by the conventional MRP explosion with time offsetting and inventory netting. For most companies, the major operations which are not under pull system control are long-lead-time purchased items or items made in another plant which has its own independent planning system.

The planning bill of materials is simplified for the items controlled by a pull system. Some of the levels in the bill of materials can be eliminated if there is no reason to have inventory transactions. Other items can be coded as pseudoitems if they may be withdrawn occasionally as spare parts, but no inventory level has to be considered for planning higher-level items.

The output of this planning process is the planned part volumes for each work center and the cycle times at which those parts will be needed. This is the beginning point of the planning process in each fabrication department and for material handling inside the plant. The material-handling plan must provide for the movement of material at regular intervals without congestion in order for this plan to work.

Each supervisor develops detailed plans for her or his fabrication area or department. These are based on the *cycle times of need* (expected rates of use in final assembly) if the fabrication is operated virtually as a direct transfer close to final assembly. At a greater distance, this rate of use is cumulated by the times each day at which a pickup of material from that fabrication area is planned. It is also important to know the regular times at which material will be delivered. This is key information for determining when the fabrication operations are obligated to have material ready, although there will be some minor deviations from plan because of responding to what the using operations really want according to the feedback signals. Supervisor planning for each fabrication area must allow for

- The number of setups per day (or per week) for each part number.
- The approximate timing of tool changes and material changes.
- The pattern and timing of quality checks (gauging, control charting, etc.). These are almost always built in as part of the production process itself, or the system will not work.
- Preventive-maintenance schedule.
- Flow balance (line balance) between operations in that fabrication area. Fabrication may take place in cells or transfer lines of equipment.
- Improvement plans and changes in the department and plans for training of people.

An Overall Approach to Production

The preceding discussion has concentrated on materials management for JIT production in the repetitive manufacturing case. That is only one part of an overall program of activity necessary for the implementation of JIT production. Table 24.4 presents the elements of a JIT program somewhat in the order they are considered during implementation.

TABLE 24.4 Elements of Production

Elements Which Are Very Similar for Both Job Shop and Repetitive Manufacturing		
1. Workplace organization: housekeeping with a purpose		
2. Quality improvement through process capability improvement		
3. Reduced setup times; frequent setups		
4. Reduced lot sizes; small-lot material handling		
5. Preventive maintenance to sustain process capability		
6. Incremental inventory reduction to reveal problems		
7. Reduced space for less material travel distance and improved visibility; cell manufacturing when possible		
8. Multifunctional workers and multiperspective staff		
9. Excellent preparation for production		
Elements Which Are Most Different for Job Shop and Repetitive Manufacturing		
	Repetitive	Job Shop
10. Leveling the schedule	By material use	More limited
11. Balancing operations	Important	More limited
12. Material handling	Regular pattern	Irregular pattern

The purpose of Table 24.4 is to present the major elements of JIT production in a way that conveys some thought of how they all tie together. It is vital to see this as a cohesive program of manufacturing development, not as a set of disconnected parts.

The first nine elements presented are very similar for both repetitive and job shop manufacturing. The details are somewhat different even for these nine because of the lesser degree of standardization inherent in job shop production. This difference becomes more pronounced for the elements shown as most different for job shop and repetitive manufacturing. All the elements represent an effort to standardize production, something which can be done more completely in the case where the same parts can be made over and over. The elements are explained, one at a time, with emphasis on unifying the overall concept.

Workplace Organization: Housekeeping with a Purpose.   This element implies that nothing exists in the work areas except that which is required for production. All tools, materials, and supplies are kept in specific locations ready for use at any time. Developing the work force to do this is one of the first tasks. None of the other elements work without this one. Common sense says that defect-free quality, quick setups, and preventive maintenance are not accomplished without excellent workplace organization. Certainly the organization of stock points for a pull system does not work without it. Many problems are revealed by good housekeeping.

Quality Improvement through Process Capability Improvement.   To the maximum extent, the production process should be capable of producing items without defects. That implies not only statistical process control but also the incorporation of standard methods for preventing defects entering into the regular procedures. That is the essence of total quality control. There are several ways in which that is done:

Immediate Feedback. This method involves measuring items as quickly as possible after they are made and stopping to make corrections. That implies that the operation is so well known that immediate corrective action can be taken. Immediate feedback also occurs when the using operation informs the supplying operation of a defect. The shorter the time between production of a part and its use, the more likely it is to associate the discovery of a defect with its cause.

Fail-safe Methods. These are mostly methods of overcoming human errors. A check digit in data processing is an example of a fail-safe method.

Capability of Tools and Equipment Much Better than Required for Parts Made. If this is done, the assignable cause of nonstandard production can be found quickly.

Development of Excellent Methods for Isolating Causes of Defective Production and Other Production Problems. This includes systematic methods of using statistical tools, Pareto charts, cause-and-effect diagrams, and so on.

Again, these practices are easier if the same parts are made regularly, but they are still applicable on less replicable items in a job shop.

Reduced Setup Times: Frequent Setups.   Setup time refers to the machine downtime for preparing to produce a new part. When setup downtime is reduced, usually the labor time is also reduced.

Setup time reduction is related to quality and to proficiency in the production operations. A setup cannot be made quickly if people are fumbling trying to adjust equipment to bring the part into spec.

Setup time is reduced by making setup a standard, routine procedure. That requires practice, and practice comes through making setups regularly.

Setup times are not reduced just to provide small lot sizes. Short setup times are an indicator that everyone thoroughly understands how the production process works and is capable of doing any task at any time. If a machine is set up for a part rarely, the same people may never perform the setup twice in a row. They forget how between times. If the capability to do setups by standard methods is developed and maintained, small lot sizes will result.

There are four major steps in reducing setup times: organize to do as much as possible with the machine running, modify tools and equipment in simple ways, eliminate adjustments, and practice. Many people can do this if the setup problem is reduced to a finite problem—a set of parts, a set of tools and a specific machine. It is bringing the setup time reduction problem to this point which is often more difficult. The same setup does not always work on the same machine because of emergency reactions to schedule changes, breakdowns, and so on. Also, it is easier to see how setups can be standardized when the same parts are made repeatedly than in job shop operations for which many novel parts require novel setups. However, the setup reduction can be made more standard based on commonality of material, part geometry, and so on.

Setup time is a function of the total environment of production: process capability, schedule, layout, material handling, operator training, and other factors.

Reduced Lot Sizes: Small-Lot Material Handling. Small lot sizes follow from the practice of frequent setups. They aid the practice of immediate feedback for quality improvement. If production is defective, not so much is made, and it is easier to organize the work areas if very little material is present.

Small production lot sizes also call for small transport lot sizes. If material is left in the stock point from one setup when another one is started for the same part number, operators quickly see that the system is not as efficient as it could be.

Lot sizes are also a function of transport and handling, and that, in turn, is a function of travel distance inside a plant. The material-handling system must permit frequent pickups of material from outbound stock points—or direct transfer, if possible.

Sometimes small lot sizes are related only to the transport of material between plants. It is desirable to reduce the time between making and using a part, and that is facilitated by reducing both the lot sizes transported and the transport distance. However, many factors are involved in plant location besides these, and the main objective is to reduce the transport time—not necessarily transport distance—and to minimize the total effort and potential damage from material handling. The reasoning behind these changes needs to reflect all the factors involved.

A good example is the sheet-metal stampings which are painted later. Dirt, dings, and specks of rust are major causes of paint defects. The shorter the time between the origination of the sheet-metal stock and when the formed and fabricated part is painted, the fewer the defects in painting. With other kinds of material, these quality considerations may not be an important factor.

The idea is to think through why a small lot is useful given the considerations of the entire production process and to take action. The objective is to eliminate waste, not just to have small lot sizes.

Preventive Maintenance to Sustain Process Capability. Preventive maintenance is very important for both quality and reduced setup times—and for the rest of the production program. The purpose is to preserve the capability of the tools, instruments, and equipment. It is not to spend a little money on a regular basis to avoid having to spend a lot in a lump sum, as for an overhaul of equipment.

Time for preventive maintenance needs to be built into the schedule, and the practices become part of the daily routine.

Incremental Inventory Reduction to Reveal Problems. The major reason for reducing inventory is to reveal the problems which require the excess inventory. The reduction in inventory investment is a side benefit. Inventory is reduced only by large amounts and is permanently kept low only by having successful methods for attacking and overcoming the problems which surface.

The preceding discussion described some methods for incrementally reducing inventory after the procedure has been developed, but in the beginning, the incremental reduction is made by more approximate methods using the existing production control system. In any case, the most important point is to constantly attack the problems in quality, equipment, training, and elsewhere. Otherwise, the reduction in inventory is short-lived.

Reduced Space. The reduction in space by JIT production has benefits well beyond the obvious one of diminishing the need for brick and mortar. The reduction in space begins with the first steps of workplace organization and extends to major layout changes which reduce the distance between machines whenever possible.

Two of the major benefits are the reduced travel distance for material inside a plant and the improved visibility of operations. The more visible the users of material are to its suppliers, the less cumbersome the communications between them. Reduced material travel distance and greater visibility lead to possibilities for lower lot sizes, and this in turn leads to the potential for reducing space. One can easily go through a spiral of improvement.

One way to greatly reduce space is the use of cell manufacturing. There are two basic kinds of cells: (1) U-shaped transfer line in which equipment is positioned so that parts move one at a time in sequence and (2) flexible cell in which jobs are not processed in any particular machine sequence. Jobs are kept in a local work-in-process presetup inventory and are sent to the correct machine in the cell as it becomes open. The most common example is a flexible machining cell in which the workpieces are automatically transported and loaded and in which control is maintained by a computer dedicated to the cell. Obviously the U-shaped transfer line is much more likely to be used with repetitive manufacturing.

If operations can be grouped in a cell, the objectives of JIT production are realized with no intermediate stages by using cards or similar methods.

Multifunctional Workers and Multiperspective Staff. To accomplish all this, the workers must increase both the breadth and the depth of their skills. Rotating workers also requires them to constantly communicate the details of how to currently perform the jobs, something which incorporates quality work procedures into the "memory" of the organization if it is done with excellence.

Adherence to narrow job descriptions is the opposite of this approach, and the ways in which that reduces productivity are obvious to most managers. Less obvious is the effect of staff parochialism. JIT production cannot be developed by staffs who operate independently. Everyone must have a broad overview of the total context of production and operate as a team.

In fact, successful JIT production comes from a strong line management which coordinates the staff efforts. When the program is viewed as the specialty of any one staff, including materials management, it does not have the breadth to be successful. Line management and supervisor leadership are essential.

Excellent Preparation for Production. Active production in the plant is the test of whether adequate preparation was made for production. Many of the big problems which surface are in the functions that prepare for production. If engineering, purchasing, tool preparation, or software development is poorly done and is late, the material might as well not be on the plant floor.

A key to this for the plant floor is a willingness to stop production regularly and allow the improvement programs and preparations to take place. The managerial difficulty lies in the resistance to yield production time for purposes other than direct output. Likewise, if production time is to be used for plant floor improvement, quality improvement, setup time reduction, and other activities, specific programs must be in place.

Back in the offices, JIT production usually requires substantial revision in the procedures used and in the urgency and accuracy with which work is done. Some of the greatest managerial problems may arise in revising the preproduction and support work.

Leveling the Schedule.   The attempt to level the schedule assists in achieving all the other elements of stockless production, and vice versa. The leveling of production by equally distributing the production of all parts through time is possible only if there is a repeating pattern of parts and, beyond that, standardization of the production environment. Without the repeating pattern of parts, a pull system of control does not work.

Stockless production, that is, production without putting work-in-process into inventory, is conceivable in the job shop case. The work has to be standardized to a point where work can move through the shop in lot sizes which represent manageable blocks of time. Then one can hope to run work when it is desired by the schedule, not by selecting from the queue the jobs with highest priority.

Balancing Operations.   If the pattern of material use is uniform, then the pattern of work-cycle times at all supplying work centers can be established at repeating rates and times which balance. With a pull system of control, this is almost guaranteed through the production control system, but only if the work centers have been prepared for it.

More than just the work centers processing material are included in the balance. For example, the tools which come from toolrooms and the dies going to die shops also need to be on a balanced operating plan. Stockless production can perish from a bottleneck in a die shop just as readily as from a bottleneck at a work center which is not prepared.

The reduction of setup times and the revision of equipment selection enable a more balanced flow of material in the repetitive case. Balancing a U-shaped transfer line is much like balancing an assembly line. In fact, one can view the entire process on the basis of balancing the work rates through the entire production network. The existence of inventory is evidence that this balance has not been achieved.

Again, with a nonrepeating pattern of parts to be made, the degree to which a job shop can be standardized to do this is limited, but improvement is still possible.

Material Handling.   As stockless production develops, a regular pattern of material handling is important. The planning of the feeding operations keys on it. Expectations of when others want completed work are guided by it. At worst, if the material handling methods provided are inadequate because of either capacity or timing, the system must carry extra inventory as a result.

In the pull system of control, it is the obligation of every work center to have material ready on demand. In the routine case, the time of demand occurs when the material handler, or guided truck, or whatever, comes around to pick up what is wanted by the using operations. If material is picked up once a day, for example, the period of obligation is 1 day. The work center and all those supporting it work to be sure that material is ready at the end of each day. In contrast, many plants work more to meet shipping dates and billing obligations at the end of each month. A regular pattern of material handling provides the rhythm by which many of the feeding operations drive themselves.

Once again, with a nonrepeating sequence of parts to be made in the job shop, the ability to have a level workload for material handling is less possible.

Standardization

Repetitive manufacturing can be standardized to a high degree. The waste is eliminated from manufacturing chiefly by standardizing activities whenever possible. The problem is to determine the basis by which each plant can be standardized, no matter what it produces. Several factors are associated with the ability to standardize:

- Commonality of parts
- Modularity of design
- Interchangeability of options
- Life cycle of product
- Knowledge of design—causal reasons for design specifications
- Technical difficulty—ability to reproduce conditions
- Operations commonality—group technology considerations
- Workplace organization
- Ability to assign missions to equipment, broad or limited
- Stability of customer demand pattern

Starting a Program

Every program begins with people. Stockless production succeeds only when a large number of people understand what to do. Then the next steps are carried out on the plant floor, beginning with a detailed program to refine the layout and workplace organization.

During this time, people must learn to identify and overcome problems, especially quality problems. The existence of defects and the lack of knowledge of how to eliminate them can cause a JIT program to stall out early.

The workplace organization and quality improvements soon require the development of the outbound and inbound stock points if the pull system is to be used. The hard part is to overcome the breakdowns, revisions of schedule, and other problems which seem to require the presence of inventory.

The production planning and control system must plan and control a plant as it is. The system evolves as the other activities go on. Initially the changes include reducing both planned lot sizes and planned lead times. In general, it is better to work around an existing system, which is known, while great changes are taking place in the plant, than to try to change the production planning system too much in advance of knowing what kind of material flows can really be attained.

If a conversion from a push to pull system is made with repetitive manufacturing, the time of this change is very critical. A plant cannot live in a state of confusion halfway between those two systems for very long.

With suppliers, first reduce the excess inventory received from them and then work with them to improve the quality of parts or materials as necessary. The attempt to do this will reveal those suppliers capable of more long-term developments. In any case, there is no reason to expect performance from suppliers that cannot be attained internally in the customer company. If the suppliers can be given a stable schedule and good information about design specifications and can attain defect-free production, then perhaps the delivery of parts can be done just in time.

The evolution of production toward repetitive, or continuous-flow, production is evidence of the ability to standardize both product and production methods. JIT production is really a method which hurries that evolution.

BIBLIOGRAPHY

Bolander, Steven F., Richard C. Heard, Samuel M. Seward, and Sam G. Taylor: "Process Industry Production and Inventory Management Framework," *Production and Inventory Management*, first quarter, 1981, pp. 15−33.

――――, Samuel M. Seward, and Sam G. Taylor: "Why the Process Industries Are Different," *Production and Inventory Management*, fourth quarter, 1981, pp. 9−24.

Edwards, J. Nicholas: *MRP in a Mass Production Environment*, APICS 20th Annual Conference Proceedings, Nov., 1977, pp. 321−324.

Hall, Robert W.: *Zero Inventories*, Dow Jones-Irwin, Homewood, Ill., 1983 (also available from APICS).

――――: *Stockless Production for the United States*, APICS 25th Annual Conference Proceedings, Oct., 1982, pp. 314−418.

Heard, Richard: *Push Master Scheduling*, APICS Master Planning Seminar Proceedings, Las Vegas, March, 1982, pp. 77−88.

Monden, Yasuhiro: *Toyota Production System*, Institute of Industrial Engineers, Atlanta, 1983.

Novitsky, Michael P.: "Process Industry—Where Are You?" *Production and Inventory Management*, first quarter, 1983, pp. 118−120.

Powell, Cash: *Cumulative MRP—In a Repetitive Manufacturing Environment*, APICS 23d Annual Conference Proceedings, Oct., 1980, pp. 150−152.

Repetitive Manufacturing Group: *Master Scheduling for Repetitive Manufacturing*, Proceedings of Workshop, April, 1982 (available from APICS).

――――: *Purchasing for Repetitive Manufacturing*, Proceedings of Workshop, Nov. 4−5, 1982 (available from APICS).

Repetitive Manufacturing Group, "Repetitive Manufacturing," *Production and Inventory Management*, second quarter, 1982, pp. 78−86.

――――: *The Basis of Repetitive Manufacturing*, Proceedings of Workshops, June, 1981 (available from APICS).

Shingo, Shigeo: *Study of Toyota Production System*, Japan Management Association, Tokyo, 1981.

Shonberger, Richard: *Japanese Manufacturing Techniques*, Macmillan, New York, 1982.

Taylor, Sam G.: "Production and Inventory Management in the Process Industries: A State of the Art Survey," *Production and Inventory Management*, first quarter, 1979, pp. 1−16.

25

Just-in-Time Applications

Editor

ROBERT G. AMES, Vice President, Administration, California Industrial Products, Inc., Santa Fe Springs, California

Contributors

EARL W. HILDEBRANDT, Manager, Production Control, Deere & Company, Horicon, Wisconsin

MARK KORNHAUSER, Manager of Manufacturing Strategic Planning, Black & Decker, Professional Products Division, Hampstead, Maryland

ROBERT D. MILLER, Manager, Materials, FMC Corporation, Chicago, Illinois

MICHAEL J. ROWNEY, Ph.D., Director of Productivity and Technology, Omark Industries, Portland, Oregon

LEWIS E. STOWE, CPIM, Material Manager, Davidson Rubber Company, Ex-Cell-O Corporation, Dover, New Hampshire

During the late 1970s, manufacturing professionals began making excursions to Japan to investigate companies operating with unprecedented low levels of inventory and realizing exceptionally high levels of quality and productivity. These study missions came about primarily for two reasons. First, U.S. industry was painfully aware that they were losing markets to overseas competition; second, they began to realize that their once dominant role in manufacturing was eroding to the extent that entire industries were disappearing. Long the unchallenged authorities in manufacturing, U.S. industries became aware that other countries, specifically Japan, were accomplishing amazing results with manufacturing methods which were applied in many instances with completely different philosophies from those to which U.S. companies subscribed.

The revolutionary new production system studied so intently was the *Toyota production system*, pioneered and developed by Toyota Motor Company. It has received so much publicity, in both Japan and the rest of the world, that it has become known by many other generic names. Many refer to the system as the *Kanban system*, derived from the card used in the Toyota pull system, which unfortunately has received unwarranted and incorrect emphasis as the heart of the system and the essence of its success. In North America, *just-in-time (JIT) production* has become the most popular and most widely used name. The American Production and Inventory Control Society (APICS) chose to call it *zero inventory* (ZI) and many are now combining the two into ZI/JIT, for short. Yet others prefer to call it *stockless production, synchronous production, continuous-flow manufacturing*, etc. Some companies coined their own labels for their programs. Omark Industries calls theirs *zero-inventory production system* (ZIPS); IBM has chosen *continuous-flow manufacturing*; Harley Davidson calls their program *material as needed* (MAN); and Rolls-Royce calls theirs the *batch-of-one* system. Perhaps it is not so important what it is called, as long as the underlying principles for its successful operation are understood.

The objectives of ZI/JIT are frequently described as the need for survival, by eliminating waste and achieving the effects of automation. These are powerful motivating forces, but some companies may feel no threat at all and so may not see the necessity for changing their approaches to manufacturing so drastically. Perhaps it would be more universally appealing to define the objective as a desire to achieve a level of manufacturing excellence unparalleled in the company's history, one in which all impediments preventing smooth production are eliminated.

One impediment is waste, and focusing on eliminating waste has universal appeal. To achieve the effects of automation guarantees a smooth, uninterrupted flow of production.

ZI/JIT is often referred to as a philosophy of returning to basics or a new way of managing a business. To some degree each is true, but behind any philosophy there exist techniques, principles, and systems required to make it work. A comprehensive list follows:

Good housekeeping	High quality
Skill diversification	Setup time reduction
Focused worker involvement	Lot-size reduction
Control by visibility	Balanced flow
Supplier networks	Preventive maintenance
Pull systems	Cellular manufacturing
Uniform plant load	Compact plant layout

Each of these elements is important to the success of a ZI/JIT process. And in one form or another, each must be addressed in any manufacturing environment. Obviously, some will have greater impact than others. Where the implementation of this program is begun will depend on the situation in a given plant. Each department must assess its activities to determine which are the most significant.

All knowledgeable practitioners agree that there are several high-impact elements in every manufacturing concern which must be addressed in detail to ensure success of a ZI/JIT operation. The most important are

- Employee involvement
- Quality
- Setup time reduction (lot-size reduction)
- Leveling the schedule (converting to a pull system)
- Interface between material-requirements planning (MRP) and JIT
- Plant rearrangement, group technology
- Supplier relationships

Within each title lie a myriad of subelements, techniques, and concepts which enhance the main theme itself and contribute to the overall program. Study and use of ZI/JIT reveal the power of the synergistic interdependencies of these elements. As each element is addressed, it begins to stimulate other improvements or points out other problems which need to be solved to advance the program toward the ultimate goal of manufacturing excellence.

Several common themes run throughout the entire spectrum of these elements. Perhaps the most important element is people relationships, or employee involvement. No one task is immune from the impact of the social environment which exists within the organization's structure.

Another element is process quality improvement. This term encompasses quality in the traditional sense and includes a sense of quality execution in the entire production network. This brings more clearly into focus the necessity for the excellent execution of the numerous tasks and projects that all employees are doing, whether these employees are machine operators, clerks, repairmen, or accountants.

A final theme to keep in mind is the *system concept*. No magical formula, no mystical algorithms, no formal structure, and certainly no computer programs will lead to realizing the beneficial promises of ZI/JIT on the system. There is no secret or panacea to obtaining solutions. Nothing lies ahead but hard work, paying attention to the most minute details, studying the process and making improvements, then studying it again and again to find ways to make further improvements. Two principles stand out very clearly: The system must serve the process and the system must be kept as simple as possible.

One popular rationale for ZI/JIT success in Japan was attributed to the Japanese culture. The Japanese were somehow uniquely suited to this new way of conducting manufacturing. This myth has been dissipated by now, and any further attempt to use it as an excuse for failure to embark on the journey to excellence is discouraged.

The best teacher is experience, especially as it pertains to the ZI/JIT approach. There is only so much one can absorb from a classroom or a publication. The following case studies (shown in Table 25.1) from U.S. companies contribute their own experience in implementing ZI/JIT.

Through these five case studies, the uses of many ZI/JIT principles are clearly demonstrated. Careful examination reveals how these principles are universally applicable to all companies, how they can be used to address almost any project, and how they become synergistic in contributing to the success of the enterprise.

TABLE 25.1

Case Study	Company
Introducing zero-inventory systems	Omark Industries Portland, Oregon
Setup time reduction	FMC Corporation Chicago, Illinois
Level schedule/pull system	Deere & Company Horicon Works Horicon, Wisconsin
Integration of JIT and MRP	Black & Decker Professional Products Division Hampstead, Maryland
Purchasing interfaces	Davidson Rubber Company Ex-Cell-O Corporation Dover, New Hampshire

INTRODUCING ZERO-INVENTORY SYSTEMS

A serious effort to implement zero-inventory manufacturing in any company is a major challenge. Reports of failures even in Japan testify to this.

The endless journey toward zero-inventory manufacturing at Omark, a company of $300 million annual sales and 4000 employees, began in the fall of 1981 in a setting characterized by

- Five autonomous divisions with headquarters in various parts of the United States and one in Australia
- Twenty manufacturing plants, seven located in foreign countries or in Puerto Rico
- Extremely diverse product lines ranging from cutting chain for chain saws and sporting ammunition involving billions of units annually to heavy timber-harvesting equipment produced from tens to hundreds of units annually
- Essentially a nonunion work force, good employee-management relations, but no policy and a limited practice of involving shop floor personnel in problem solving and decision making
- Traditional batch manufacturing with respect to plant layouts, production control, and inventory management

Effective orientation and training have made a major contribution to Omark's progress in the direction of zero-inventory manufacturing. The company's accomplishments, although modest by Japanese standards, have received substantial recognition in North America.

This case study is essentially chronological, showing the sequence in which orientation and training needs were identified and met. Such an account should prove useful to organizations starting a zero-inventory manufacturing campaign, since many similarities in experience may be expected.

Much can be done by an enterprising manager aware of zero-inventory concepts to make significant improvements in a single plant. However, to change the entire company, Omark's top management had to be fully committed. Omark's experience is probably not representative of most companies, where change most often begins in the middle ranks, because the impetus came from observations made in Japan by the chief operating officer (COO). The report by the COO to the chief executive officer (CEO) and board of directors concluded that Japanese manufacturing success was the result of (1) unprecedented levels of employee training and involvement, (2) heavy emphasis on quality in all areas of the business, and (3) the revolutionary approach to the manufacturing system of the Toyota company.

A conviction that these three concepts would work at Omark led to the appointment of a joint corporate-division study team. The assignment was to confirm the CEO's conclusion and, if affirmative, to recommend an approach to implementation.

These ten managers made an in-depth study of all the articles, books, films, and videotapes they could find about employee involvement, quality, and the Toyota system. All the published material found was shared with corporate and division management. The study team visited many companies in the United States and Japan. Reports from these visits were widely disseminated. All employees were made aware of management's growing interest in Japanese manufacturing methods by articles written by senior managers for the company magazine. The study team also talked with consultants and arranged for them to present seminars to large audiences of management and staff.

After almost 5 months of study, the team issued an extensive report which confirmed the COO's conclusions and recommended that the concepts of employee involvement, quality, and ZIPS be implemented as a total integrated package. The team emphasized that ZIPS would not succeed without employee involvement or without a new approach to quality. Corporate and division management accepted the recommendation to implement the integrated package. This decision profoundly influenced the design of future orientation and training programs, since it required all three areas to be adequately addressed simultaneously. This underlying theme of the interdependence and mutual reinforcement of ZIPS, quality, and employee involvement is brought out in all Omark training material by the symbol of three overlapping circles, each containing one of the legends: ZIPS, total quality commitment (TQC), and employee involvement (EI).

To accomplish such a major transformation of the company, a vision of the future that would capture the imagination of all employees was required. Bound in booklet form, this document went out to all employees, shareholders, and others. Included was the objective of reducing total inventories by 50 percent in 3 years, which would have been an impossible task without the new tools of ZIPS.

To enlist true subscribers to the vision, the COO personally went to each North American and Puerto Rican operation, accompanied by the senior vice president responsible for the division and other corporate managers and staff. In a 2-day meeting, the vision was communicated face to face to all local managers and staff. In addition, seminars on people involvement, especially quality circles and ZIPS, were held and small group discussions addressed opportunities and problems.

This "roadshow" was the first formal exposure to the aims and concepts of ZIPS. The next challenge was to provide all key operating people with greater in-depth knowledge. Each plant management team was given the assignment of investigating thoroughly the potential application of ZIPS to the particular operation. If they concluded that ZIPS could be applied, they were to select a pilot project and develop an implementation plan.

The only study resource at that time, other than articles turned up by the original corporate study team, was a book by Shigeo Shingo.[1] The plant management teams formed study groups that met regularly to work through Shingo's book, chapter by chapter. Frequently one team member would study a chapter and summarize the knowledge for the whole team. This team study proved to be an extraordinarily effective learning tool.

The breadth and depth of new knowledge gained by the operation personnel down through first-line supervision were evident in the quality of the study team's reports and plans submitted to corporate headquarters. A great deal of employee involvement developed spontaneously before Omark's quality circle movement was launched. Quality circle activity has continued to grow steadily, to the point where there are about 100 circles involving about 20 percent of the work force. Many projects selected by the circle members themselves have directly addressed ZIPS improvements.

During the pilot project implementation, educational support from the corporate office took the following forms:

1. Purchase and distribution of books as they appeared in the market, such as that by Schonberger.[2]

2. Issuance of a weekly newsletter referencing key articles and featuring the experiences and accomplishments within Omark.

3. The distribution throughout the company of material developed on the initiative of an individual, plant, or division. A slide-audio tape program developed to introduce ZIPS to hourly employees turned out to be useful for a wider range of audiences including the board of directors and visitors from other companies. A videotaped skit developed by the Greeley, Colorado, division of Hewlett-Packard dramatizing the contrast between batch push and small-lot pull production inspired more than one division to enact its own skit along the same lines. In one division the actors were shop floor personnel.

4. Funding of study missions to Japan for division presidents, plant managers, and other key personnel. Over 60 key managers visited Japanese plants. Personal friendships have developed which facilitate the transfer of ideas.

5. A ZIPS conference to bring together corporate, division, and plant management to share experiences, listen to outside speakers, and compete for prizes for accomplishments in various aspects of ZIPS. Participants established contacts with their counterparts in other divisions. This reduced the problem of the corporate office becoming an information bootleneck. The ZIPS conference is now an annual event. It is the occasion for top management to set quantitative goals for the overall company.

6. A third roadshow to follow up on the progress in the operations and to present new ZIPS material.

The spread of ZIPS activities beyond the original pilot projects in all plants made it very evident that the part-time support of the divisions' do-it-yourself orientation and training efforts must be replaced by a broader, more systematic effort. A senior line vice president was given formal responsibility for internal communications and training. He assembled a full-time staff of three professionals. Their responsibilities are as follows:

1. Internal communications
   a. Publication of company magazine
   b. Publication of newsletter on ZIPS, TQC, and EI
   c. Preparation of annual report to employees
2. Technical training
   a. In-house development of videotape training programs on ZIPS and TQC
   b. Provision for value analysis training courses
   c. Outside training programs on specialized subjects, such as statistical process control

3. Personnel development
   a. Development of in-house training for quality circle facilitators, leaders, and members
   b. Administration of quality improvement training purchased from the Juran Institute[3]
   c. Team-building training
   d. Managerial and supervisory training
   e. Administration of the company's personnel development program (performance reviews, career guidance, etc.)
   f. In-house development of videotape program for new-employee orientation

This training team performed a thorough and systematic study of the training needs for the various groups of employees in ZIPS, TQC, and EI and developed an implementation plan.

In the case of ZIPS, no satisfactory training programs existed. Consequently, the training team planned 10 in-depth videotape training modules. The course lasts 5 hours (hr) and is given to small groups by a leader who conducts discussions between tape segments. Although intended primarily for shop floor employees, this course proved useful for all employees, including management. Following the completion of a TQC overview program, a series of ZIPS modules are planned on specialized subjects, such as small-lot production, set up time reduction, etc.

Omark's initial training strategy is to provide education in basic techniques of quality and ZIPS improvement to all employees through a three-part package consisting of quality circle problem-solving techniques, the ZIPS overview program, and a TQC overview. The target is to have 85 percent of all personnel trained. An additional target in the same time frame is to have 85 percent of all employees participating in some form of small-group activity. This may be a quality circle, ZIPS task force, quality improvement team, product development team, value analysis team, or a special task force.

The philosophy underlying Omark's training program is that a habit of constant improvement toward increasingly challenging goals is vital for the company's continuing prosperity. The route to prosperity is via ZIPS and TQC. These two movements cannot succeed without the intense involvement of all employees. The problems are too many, and management alone does not have all the solutions. To be involved effectively, each employee must be given the proper tools by an ongoing education program.

SETUP TIME REDUCTION

FMC Corporation is a highly diversified, multinational company with revenues of over $3.4 billion. It has 120 factory operations and mines in 45 states and 15 foreign countries organized into five major groups:

1. *Performance chemicals*—insecticides, herbicides, fertilizers, pharmaceuticals, marine colloids
2. *Industrial chemicals*—soda ash, phosphates, peroxide, natural resources (coal, silver, gold)
3. *Defense equipment and systems*—fighting vehicles, armored personnel carriers, naval gun turrets, and missile-launch systems
4. *Specialized machinery*—excavators. cable cranes, hydraulic cranes, beverage-carbonating equipment, citrus processing equipment, food processing equipment, packaging equipment, airline baggage handling equipment, vibratory

equipment, conveyors, automotive services equipment, street sweepers, and fire engines

5. *Petroleum equipment and services*—fluid control and wellhead equipment

About 50 of the manufacturing and mining operations account for the majority of the activity. All different types of operations are represented. Discrete manufacturers range from job shop to high-volume, repetitive factories. Chemical operations involve a combination of continuous-flow and batch processes. All discrete manufacturing operations have a computerized MRP system in place. Two are "class A" MRP users.

FMC feels that the JIT/TQC philosophy applies to all types of businesses, services, process as well as discrete manufacturing, job shops as well as high-volume repetitive operations. The principles may be applied to highly automated facilities or to those still using mostly manually controlled machines. The application of this philosophy provides a significant competitive advantage.

From a corporate point of view, FMC's approach to implementing JIT/TQC has been to first share the philosophy with the "trailblazer" operations, that is, those relatively few operations that like to try out new ideas. The corporate staff encouraged these operations to do something and then positively reinforced all successful actions. By recognizing and publicizing the successes of the trailblazers, other more cautious operations are motivated to start a JIT/TQC project.

The pre-JIT and JIT journey may be viewed in terms of the following 10 evolutionary stages:

	Stage	Typical Attitude and Activities
Pre-JIT	1	"We can't do any better."
	2	"We can do a little better."
	3	"We should do a little better each year" —there is some interest in JIT.
Developing commitment	4	"Let's try a JIT pilot(s) and start education."
	5	The pilot(s) has/have been successful; let's do more."
Breakthrough/enlightenment	6	"Let's become a class A JIT operation; JIT can be an enormous competitive advantage; JIT will enable us to survive." Usually the operation forms an operationwide steering committee to oversee the JIT process.
Degrees of implementation	7	JIT is integrated into the comprehensive, strategic operations plan, budget, and objectives.
	8	JIT is implemented on one product line.
	9	JIT is implemented on more than one product line.
	10	Class A JIT has been achieved throughout the organization; the operation is a world-class competitor

Note that movement from stage to stage does not have to be sequential or start at stage 1. Actually, an operation could start at stage 7; it is a matter of commitment, which is a mental decision. Most operations at FMC, however, have taken these steps sequentially.

The best way to understand the philosophy is to try it and learn by doing. Usually as a result of a number of pilot studies, an organization grows to understand the philosophy's tremendous potential and decides to become committed. It typically takes 6 to 9 months from the first exposure to the philosophy to commitment, stage 6.

Approaches to Setup Time Reduction

Setup time reduction is a prerequisite for many elements of the JIT/TQC philosophy. Faster setups allow improved customer response through shorter lead times, more flexibility for scheduling and product changes, and manufacturing in small lots. Reduced setup times enhance cellular manufacturing and allow rapid identification of the source of quality problems. If there is a quality problem, small lots minimize the amount of rework and scrap. At FMC the connection among quality, setup time, and lot-size reduction is emphasized. Secondary benefits include drastically reduced work-in-process inventories, reduced labor cost, and improved capacity utilization.

Elimination or reduction of setup time has been accomplished in the following ways at FMC:

1. Elimination of setup time by
   a. Eliminating the operation
   b. Dedicating equipment to run only one operation
   c. Better utilizing computer numerical control (CNC) equipment that has more than one worktable, to allow setups to be performed for one part while another part is being machined.
   d. Designing processes better, so that several operations may be combined into a single setup.
2. Reduction of setup time by
   a. Doing as much setup work as possible outside the machine while it is running
   b. Improving the setup method
   c. Eliminating or minimizing the need for adjustments
   d. Standardizing tooling and fixtures
   e. Having duplicate tooling and fixtures available
   f. Using quick-change tools
   g. Dedicating manufacturing cells to a family of parts
   h. Prekitting the tools needed for setups and using setup charts

Doing everything possible for the next setup while the machine is running has yielded very significant improvements—30 to 50 percent—without any capital investment by increasing machine capacity, reducing throughput time, and reducing direct labor costs.

Most of the equipment is operated by either numeric control (NC) or CNC, so once setup time reduction is emphasized, there is considerable opportunity for the operator to use the running time to prepare for the next setup while the present part is being machined. Workplace organization—i.e., a place for everything, and everything in its place and clean and ready for use—is probably the single best way to reduce setup time.

Before the decision is made of which setup time to reduce, it is important to consider the overall flow of products and product families. Once there is a fairly good idea of how the plant should be arranged, the appropriate approaches can be selected from the previous list. For example, there may be sufficient volume to justify dedicating equipment to run just one part, thereby eliminating the need to work on setup time reduction. Organizing the operation in its entirety will save an enormous amount of effort in the long run compared to an approach whereby like functional processes are grouped. Not only is machine utilization increased with production cells, but also the equipment required is often less complex than that needed in the traditional functional layout. For example, single-spindle drills might be used instead of multiple-spindle drills.

This holistic view is taken by the operations management staff and manufacturing engineering. Once the future concept of the operation has been defined sufficiently, the setup time reduction effort can start. All people, including shop floor personnel, must be involved to get the most out of the JIT/TQC philosophy. Shop floor personnel are anxious to participate in problem solving. Failing to consider their suggestions causes an enormous innovative resource to go untapped. Also the acceptance of change is much easier when those responsible for implementing the new setups are involved in designing them. Where the philosophy of employee involvement already exists, it is much easier to get the JIT/TQC concept going. Since this concept is best learned by doing, groups that are effective at problem solving can readily be given projects from which to learn. An objective is to create an atmosphere in which every machine operator consciously thinks about doing setups more efficiently.

After a "rough-cut" relayout or cell plan is developed, a factory must develop plantwide setup time reduction objectives. Table 25.2 is a typical format for controlling the reduction of setup times. Plantwide objectives must be shared by production, manufacturing, engineering, and material management personnel and be the basis for individual performance appraisals.

Examples of Setup Time Reduction

The following are examples of how the approaches discussed have been utilized.

South Carolina Plant. The production operations manager issued a setup time reduction challenge to the 11 work teams comprising all 140 production personnel. The Automotive Industry Action Group (AIAG) videotapes on JIT provided a strong motivation to move ahead. Each team picked a particularly troublesome setup operation. Results significantly exceeded expectations as reductions ranged from 60 to 75 percent with only minor expenditures. In this case manufacturing engineering was available as a resource and sounding board but not as a member of the team.

Much of the savings came from comparing notes among persons who had setup

TABLE 25.2

Setup Time	1984 Actual, %	1985, %		
		Objective	Actual	Variance
4−7 hr	15	0		
3−4 hr	35	25		
2−3 hr	25	25		
1−2 hr	20	35		
30 min−1 hr	5	10		
10 min−30 min	0	5		
Less than 10 min	0	0		

operations. They found that everyone did the setups differently. By standardizing and incorporating the best technique, large setup reductions were possible.

The next step was to reduce the setup times for all the operations required for fabricating a particular very large part. After setup times were reduced, a pull inventory system was implemented for this part, reducing work in progress from 150 to about 15 pieces and thereby eliminating a bad plant congestion problem.

California Plant.   The following are significant actions taken in the California plant:

1. Extensive operator training was undertaken to enable manual input of NC data. This eliminates the need to go back to the NC programmer for minor tape edits.
2. An increased use of indexing chucks eliminated setups and material queues.
3. Common tooling was located at the machine to reduce operator travel time and therefore the external setup time.
4. Tool locations were standardized for the two NC turret machines running similar parts. This eliminated tool adjustments and tool changes for those parts affected.
5. Changes were made from manual to hydraulic screw-tightening clamps on several inspection gauges to significantly reduce inspection fixturing time.
6. A polyurethane chuck, which is essentially a liner that fits into a standard holder, was developed. This eliminated the need for complex fixturing and extensive adjustment time caused by irregularities in raw material. Setup times were reduced from hours to minutes.

Texas Plant.   Manufacturing engineering in this plant initially focused on standardizing NC and CNC programs and setups. For example, now each tool has the same location in an automatic tool changer for all programs used for a given machine. A team was created to manage the total production of similar types of wellhead casings used for petroleum production. Machine operators and manufacturing engineers work together to reduce setup times on all operations required to manufacture casing heads. This team has been so successful that now all shop floor personnel want to participate in a manufacturing cell work team. The plant is taking a one-cell-at-a-time approach but at the same time is attacking all setups across the board.

Arkansas and Florida Plants.   Arkansas and Florida plants took advantage of the opportunity to replace worn-out machine tools with new machining centers having multiple worktables. By doing this, one job can be set up while another is running.

The initial setup reduction efforts combined the ideas of engineers, shop foremen, and machine operators. For example, the simple addition of a CNC package to an existing press brake eliminated enough setups to conserve $20,000 per year. By reprogramming frequently run production parts to alternate CNC machines and by utilizing universal tool blocks, queuing was reduced and throughput improved.

San Jose, California, Plant.   This plant probably had the most significant successes to date because of the development of a fixture using a ball-lock fastener and a standard baseplate. This baseplate can be mounted on the machine workstation in less than 2 min, resulting in a setup time reduction from 8 hr to 15 min. This has been facilitated by permanently mounting standard fixtures to the baseplate. The key to this method was the development of a ball-lock fastener, four of which join the standard baseplate to the workstation.

Stephenville, Texas, Plant.   This FMC operation first developed a strategic manufacturing plan for each of the three product lines. The plan essentially required three plants within the one plant building. For one product line, three assemblies accounted for approximately 67 percent of the total volume. So three manufacturing cells were designed, each dedicated to one of these three assemblies. This resulted in zero setup time.

In the second product line, the higher-volume lots were run on hard automation designed for large lot sizes. Small lot sizes were run on a machining center with two workplaces so that one could be set up while another part was being machined.

The third product line utilized a transfer line for one major component. The other major component was manufactured in a manufacturing cell that was being perfected.

One example of reducing setup times through a methods improvement was employed on a chucker machine. Instead of the six manually adjusted stops, one piece of metal was produced which would perform the same function. As a result, the time required to make the setup was reduced from hours to a few minutes.

LEVEL SCHEDULE/PULL SYSTEM

The John Deere Horicon Works, Horicon, Wisconsin, manufacture lawn-care equipment such as tractors, riding mowers, mower attachments, tillers, blades, and snowthrowers. They employ 1500 people and fabricate steel components and assemble products for independent retail outlets.

Traditional manufacturing techniques used in the factory were based on a batch system in which each product was scheduled and assembled monthly. The master production schedule (MPS) was developed by the factory based on marketing requirements and was seasonal.

The work-in-process and finished-goods inventories were high because of the monthly batch schedule and the high costs associated with changing the production line and other manufacturing processes from one model or part to another. The high inventories were also required by the ordering pattern of the retail dealers. They expected each shipment of finished products to contain a mix of all products assembled at the factory.

Parts and subassemblies were scheduled by production control scheduling personnel. Monthly quantities of all but the most bulky parts were produced and stored in work-in-process stores areas until needed by the next manufacturing process.

JIT Project

Horicon Works initiated a JIT project to evaluate the feasibility of pull-through production techniques and for possibly wider applications in Deere & Company. The project included one line of lawn tractors composed of seven models representing three different engines, three mowing widths, and two transmissions. This line accounted for about 20 percent of the factory's annual sales. The objectives of the project were to build a daily quantity of each of the seven models; to establish pull-through production techniques in the welding, subassembly, and final-assembly departments; and to start implementation of quick-change tooling in the parts fabrication departments.

The project very quickly broadened in focus from JIT inventory systems to waste elimination. The factory accepted the JIT definition as "the right amount of material in the right place at the right time." It became obvious to management and operating personnel that significant opportunities to reduce manufacturing costs were available if efforts in addition to the control of material were made. The emphasis was changed to waste elimination, which seeks to identify and to do away with all labor, material, and equipment costs not needed to support production.

Stabilized Schedule

A stabilized schedule with a constant rate of consumption was one of the most critical components of the JIT project. The traditional factory master scheduling technique was for a monthly batch. A typical monthly schedule for lawn tractors is shown in Table 25.3.

The JIT master schedule provided for building each model each day. A week of the same typical month is shown in Table 25.4. The same daily schedule was used each day of the month. This was developed by taking the monthly marketing requirement and dividing it by the number of production days in the month. The advantages of this master scheduling technique became apparent very quickly:

TABLE 25.3 Monthly Schedule

Model	Week 1	Week 2	Week 3	Week 4
A	120			
B	220			
C	180			
D	145	95		
E		240		
F		330	170	
G			495	665
Total	665	665	665	665

TABLE 25.4 Daily Schedule

Model	Mon.	Tues.	Wed.	Thurs.	Fri.	Total
A	6	6	6	6	6	30
B	11	11	11	11	11	55
C	9	9	9	9	9	45
D	12	12	12	12	12	60
E	12	12	12	12	12	60
F	25	25	25	25	25	125
G	58	58	58	58	58	290
Total	133	133	133	133	133	665

- Productivity increased slightly because the changeover time on the assembly lines and in support departments was reduced to zero and time previously spent on changeover was used to build product.
- Finished-goods inventory was reduced about 50 percent because each model was now available daily from the assembly line for shipment.
- The daily consumption of parts leveled the workload throughout the entire factory.

The factory and marketing reached the following agreements to facilitate implementation of the project and preserve marketing flexibility to meet customer needs:

1. The master schedule was frozen for 3 months in advance to ensure that vendors' lead times were met and factory stability was achieved.
2. Outside of the frozen period, any changes in model mix were acceptable, and a change in the monthly requirement (and therefore, daily requirement) was negotiable based on factory capacity.
3. The factory was to produce each of the seven models each day.

Seasonality requirements were met by changing daily output with the addition or removal of personnel from the assembly line and supporting manufacturing processes. The seasonal requirements had to be identified outside of the frozen period, and the factory had the option of leveling requirements. During the current year, for instance, the assembly line is staffed at three different levels—6 months at level A, 3 months at level B, and 3 months at level C—to meet seasonal requirements.

The agreements between marketing and the factory were an integral part of determining the effectiveness and eventual success of the project. The requirements of the frozen period were met, and seven models were produced each day. The schedule stability necessary to implement the project effectively and the marketing requirement to meet customer needs were also achieved.

Pull-Through Production

The daily build quantity for each tractor causes a level consumption of parts; makes possible the development of pull-through production techniques in the welding, subassembly, and final-assembly areas of the factory; and limits the amount of inventory at each stage of the manufacturing process. A succeeding process orders and withdraws parts from the preceding process only at the rate and the time at which it has consumed the parts. The method by which inventory is pulled from one process to another and eventually to the final-assembly line is referred to in the factory as a trigger. A trigger is an information device that controls or schedules the production of the necessary parts in the necessary quantities at the necessary time in every manufacturing process. Three types of triggers—paper, computerized, and container triggers—are used in the factory.

Paper Production Triggers. A paper production trigger withdraws purchased components from a stores area and authorizes their delivery to the assembly process as that process consumes parts. The paper trigger (Fig. 25.1) recirculates between the stores area and the assembly process. It is attached to a full container in the storeroom. Full containers weigh no more than 50 pounds (lb), so that handling is easy and no forklift trucks are required except to move a few bulky parts. The full container is transported to the assembly process on a trailer and unloaded directly

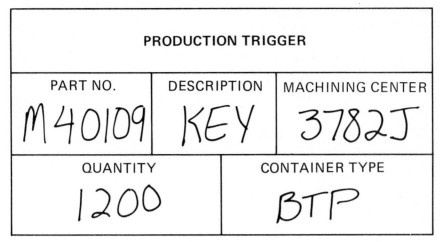

FIG. 25.1   Paper production trigger.

at the correct location of the assembly workstation. When the container is empty, the assembler removes the trigger and places it in a mailbox. Twice each shift a material handler removes triggers from each mailbox and takes them to the storeroom. In the storeroom a container is filled for each trigger. The material handler attaches a trigger to the full container and delivers it to the assembly location. Parts in the storage space are arranged in the same sequence as in the assembly stations so that travel time for the material handler is reduced.

Computerized Triggers.   A computerized trigger in the form of a move order performs the same functions as the paper production trigger and includes similar information. The basic difference is the addition of bar coding, which permits on-line allocation and recording of the movement of material in the factory's on-line material control system. The computerized triggers (Fig. 25.2) are used for parts made in the factory.

The computerized trigger is attached to a full container in the storage area. Full containers, which weigh no more than 50 lb, are transported to the welding or subassembly locations on a trailer and unloaded directly at the correct location for the using workstation. When the container is empty, the welder or subassembler removes the trigger and places it in a mailbox. A material handler removes the triggers from each mailbox hourly, takes them to the nearest on-line system terminal, and reads the bar code with a wand. This action causes an allocation of material in the material control system, and a duplicate trigger is printed and sent to the storage area. The old trigger is destroyed, and the new trigger is the authorization to fill another container and deliver it, with the new trigger attached, to the using workstation. Part of the trigger is removed in the stores area. The bar coding on this part is used to record the movement of material to the next department in the material control system.

Container Triggers.   The factory has found that containers are very effective as triggers for bulky or heavy parts which cannot be handled by the 50-lb-maximum containers used with paper or computerized triggers. Most containers used as triggers are steel containers or special racks mounted on wheels. These special

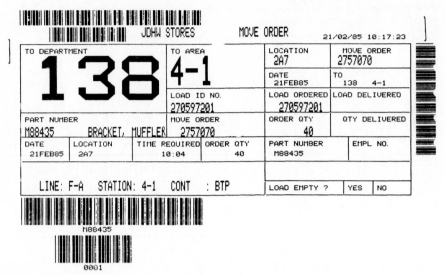

FIG 25.2 Move order.

containers on wheels enable the operator to push empty ones back to the workstation where the parts are produced. The employee then takes a full container back to the workstation where the parts are used. The empty container is an authorization to produce more parts and, just like the paper or computerized triggers, schedules the manufacturing process based on the consumption of parts at the succeeding process.

Pushing containers by employees over long distances is not very efficient. Consequently, it is advantageous to rearrange processes from the traditional layout in which all types of welding are done in one department, subassembly is done in another, and final assembly is done in still another. Mixing the processes to support one product so that welders, subassemblers, and final assemblers all work in one department or area reduces inventory and maximizes the efficiency of the flow of parts. Using containers as triggers minimizes the material-handling costs in these departments and, as with paper or computerized triggers, does away with the need for outside scheduling support.

Although this chapter addresses pull-through production, other elements of the JIT approach to manufacturing, such as reduced job setup times and rearrangement of processes, have contributed to improvements in quality and reductions in manufacturing cost.

Summary

The daily build schedule for each tractor and the pull-through production techniques of JIT resulted in a model mix that met customers' needs with significantly reduced finished-goods inventory, reduced indirect labor costs because of material-handling and changeover labor reductions, reduced work-in-process inventories, and no scheduling support. After 18 months, factory management decided to implement daily build schedules for all products and the pull-through production techniques in the welding, subassembly, and final assembly of all products. The efficiencies and cost reductions were significant enough to make a major contribution to the factory's goal of being the low-cost producer in its industry.

INTEGRATION OF JIT AND MRP

The Black & Decker Professional Products Division, Hampstead, Maryland, has a factory facility of slightly less than 1 million square feet (sq ft). Previously, the factory was organized in functional process groups to maximize the use of labor skills. All screw machines were in one department, and the other departments included steel machining, heat treating, injection molding, casting, assembly, and others.

The advanced manufacturing engineering group spent 6 months brainstorming how production could be improved. After proving to themselves the enormous benefits that must result from their ideas, they discovered that their concept was almost identical to the JIT concept. At the time, the JIT concept was in its infancy and commonly used as a buzz word.

The Black & Decker Corporation, the largest manufacturer of power tools in the world, reknowned for its manufacturing and business know-how, had to change its entire manufacturing philosophy. As the external environment changed, Black & Decker had to respond. At the root of the manufacturing strategy was the highly acclaimed MRP system, with one of the best class A systems in the world. Even today the Black & Decker manufacturing systems, developed in house, far surpass most, if not all, others. The challenge was to prove to upper management that the manufacturing strategy had to change, and Black & Decker had to reexamine its MRP system to change with the philosophy. The JIT concept had to be integrated within the existing MRP system.

To be a more effective producer of power tools, Black & Decker had to change its entire manufacturing strategy. The JIT concept had to be sold to upper management. The reasons cited for using JIT included increased quality, increased productivity, increased return on assets, and increased profitability. The strategy was implemented through the focused factory concept that required increased attention to detail, increased access to problem solving, increased dedication of personnel, increased teamwork of personnel, and increased product responsibility by personnel.

One of the main improvement measurements was inventory turns. High inventory levels are related to poor yields, excessive rework, production bottlenecks, quality problems, design problems, and excess overtime problems just to name a few. Management was determined to concentrate on inventory turns along with the other traditional forms of measurement.

Approximately 55,000 sq ft was cleared for the new focused factory area. The layout was designed for a flow process pattern with the machines required initially to manufacture 10 different units in 65 product variations. A few months after approval of the prototype plant, this "small-motors plant" was in operation. As a reference point, inventory turns of 4.7 for those 10 units were used just as if they had been manufactured under the original process layout.

Throughout the entire implementation and planning process, most of the production planning and inventory control community resisted this new manufacturing approach because of the inadequacies of the MRP system. Consequently, they did little to implement JIT production.

A materials group was formed to implement JIT by using some tools and techniques developed by the advanced manufacturing group. They were responsible for three activities: production planning and inventory control, production control, and purchasing. The strategy was to produce only what was required, without safety stocks or buffers. Attention focused on eliminating all the causes for carrying inventory in the first place. The materials organization became the disciplinarian of the JIT efforts. The approach was simple. The task was enormous. The results were outstanding.

Approach to Implementation

JIT was explained to upper management as a tool to achieve higher quality, greater productivity, and lower cost. The zero-inventory system prevents using inventory as a guarantee against defective parts, processes, and designs. The focused factory was given two goals: to shorten or eliminate setup times and to cross-train the work force. The shop floor was physically ready for JIT in terms of process flow layout and available capacity.

Task

At first, management did not fully understand the magnitude of the task. The first objective was to create and maintain a sound material plan. Marketing worked very closely with the materials group to create a valid master schedule that leveled labor hours for the entire plant. A technique was developed by using a query language to create planning bills of materials for labor and machine hours. This enabled simulation of each unit scheduled to achieve time-phased starting dates and shifts by part number and machine. This analysis gave an insight into assembly lot sequence, leveling of assembly hours, and scheduling of bottleneck equipment. This scheduling technique was one aspect of JIT that was contrary to traditional thinking. A sound schedule is not one that builds the same product or series of products every day. In fact, in a true JIT environment, the schedule should reflect actual customer demand, which is ever-changing. A sound schedule in the JIT framework does not mean an unchanging one; rather, it means a managed schedule. The schedule was never changed because of inefficiencies. The inefficiencies were corrected to make up the schedule.

Order planning was strict. No justification for inventory was acceptable. Production lot sizes, part-period balancing, and economic order quantities were not allowed. The lot-for-lot order quantity was the only acceptable rule. As a consequence, two things occurred. First, the shop immediately understood the need for cross-training and elimination of long setup times. Second, setup cost variances increased extensively.

Upper management immediately became disenchanted with JIT as it initially impacted the financial statement. The materials group was called in to explain the large setup cost. The answer to top management was, "The setup variance is not the problem; but setup time is."

The intense concentration on reducing the setup times became a way of life in the small-motors plant. As the factory operators set up jobs more often, they became more proficient. They also developed innovative techniques for substantially reducing setup times in a way that no others could. Process engineers also developed new methods for reducing setup times. Every capital appropriation request submitted had a major emphasis on setup cost reduction. Group technology techniques were also used. The result was a 50 percent decrease in total setup hours across the entire plant.

Another major task in JIT production was to significantly shorten throughput time. This was measured by calculating the planned lead time. MRP calculates throughput time as the summation for each operation 1 through N.

$$\sum_{N}^{1} (\text{Queue time} + \text{setup time} + \text{lot size x run time}) = \text{throughput time}$$

Setup times and lot sizes were being attacked continually and reduced. Run times were reduced by significantly increasing the planned overlapping from one operation to the next, as a true process flow would indicate.

Queue Formula Development

Queue times were part of the work-center records, but it was not clear how to use them in scheduling a work center. Past practice indicated that the queue time should be increased if that key machine group (KMG) displayed a constant backlog.

Through the use of the query language, a formula was developed to calculate predictable queues in front of machines based on the master schedule. Job A (Fig. 25.3) is in the KMG queue waiting until all the jobs ahead of it are finished (Job 4 is running on the machine):

Job A's waiting time = $SU_{\text{job 1}}$ + run time$_{\text{job 1}}$ + $SU_{\text{job 2}}$ + run time$_{\text{job 2}}$ + $SU_{\text{job 3}}$ + run time$_{\text{job 3}}$ + $SU_{\text{job 4}}$ + run time$_{\text{job 4}}$ remaining

where SU = setup time

$$\text{Queue time} = \frac{(\text{no. jobs} - 2) \times (\text{avg. job time}) + \frac{1}{2}\,\text{avg. job time}}{\text{no. machines in KMG}} \times \%\ \text{KMG load}$$

In this equation, -2 eliminates job A not in queue and job 4 on the machine. Therefore, the numerator encompasses jobs 1, 2, and 3 thus far. And half the average job time is used based on the assumption that on average the job on the machine (job 4) will be 50 percent finished, and so job 3 will wait for 50 percent of job 4 to be completed. This now completes the numerator for the total time that job A will wait. And the percentage of KMG load reflects the assumption that the probability that a job will be on the machine or waiting at the machine is directly proportional to its load.

Example: Calculate the queue time for KMG 955 with two machines. During the next 6 months (24 production weeks), 64 jobs have been scheduled.

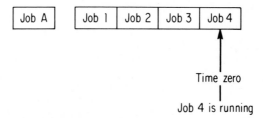

FIG 25.3 Queue illustration.

The total setup and run time for the 64 jobs is 1152 hr. The factory works three shifts per day, 7.5 hr per shift, 5 days a week.

Solution:

$$\text{Queue} = \frac{(N - 2) \times A + \frac{1}{2}A}{M} \times L$$

where N = number of jobs per week
 M = number of machines in KMG
 A = average time a job is on machine
 L = percentage of machine load during 6-month period

Thus

$$N = 64 \, \text{jobs}/24 \, \text{wk} = 2.67 \, \text{jobs/wk}$$
$$M = 2$$

and

$$A = \frac{\sum_{64}^{1} (\text{setup time/job} + \text{parts/job} \times \text{time/part})}{\text{no. jobs}}$$

$$= \frac{1152 \, \text{hr}}{64 \, \text{jobs}} = 18 \, \text{hr/job}$$

and

$$L = \frac{\text{hours used}}{\text{hours available}}$$

Since

Hours available = $(7\frac{1}{2}$ hr/shift$)$ $(3$ shifts/day$)$ $(5$ days/wk$)$ $(24$ wk/period$)$
 $(2$ machines$)$
 = 5400 hr/period

So

$$L = \frac{1152}{5400} = 21.33\%$$

Finally,

$$\text{Queue} = \frac{(2.67 \, \text{jobs} - 2 \, \text{jobs}) \, (18 \, \text{hr/job}) + (\frac{1}{2} \times 18 \, \text{hr/job})}{2 \, \text{machines}} \times 0.2133$$

$$= 2.25 \, \text{hr/machine}$$

By using the query language, the KMG queues were calculated for a 9-month period with actual schedules, and the results were amazingly accurate. The manufacturing lead times were reduced by 65 percent (see Fig. 25.4). Because weekly time buckets are used, lead times are stated in whole integers; so actually lead times were reduced by more than 65 percent.

A major factor in the success of JIT was the changes in production control. The plant personnel had to think in terms of units being assembled. Previously, all expediting was organized by department or functional area. Now each expediter was assigned an assembly line (i.e., product line) and was responsible for the assembly, its feeding manufacturing processes, and the required purchased parts. This style of control spread quickly throughout the plant. Supervisor and operators soon became accustomed to knowing the assembly schedule and the line rates. They learned to demand the information needed to schedule the manufactured components through their operations and into assembly.

Systems deficiencies were suddenly realized. The MRP system had some differences because weekly rather than daily buckets were used. Many query language programs were used for analysis and planning to supplement the normal MRP reports.

Dispatching is used only for the gating machines with several operations. In all other cases, shop personnel have become proficient in starting jobs to meet assembly dates.

Purchasing is handled in a similar fashion. Along with using blanket-order programs by commodity, products from nearby vendors are expedited by unit. Orders are also placed on a lot-for-lot basis. There were many obstacles to overcome including price increases and delivery problems. Prices have been decreased and many other problems overcome by working with the vendors in developing new purchasing techniques.

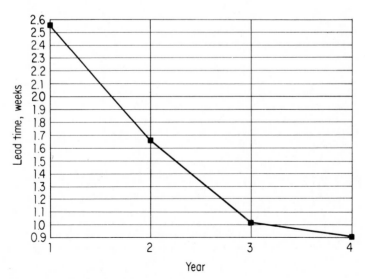

FIG 25.4   Leadtime reduction.

Results

The graphs display how well the integration of JIT and MRP was achieved. The number of units produced more than tripled, and the inventory investment was reduced dramatically (Fig. 25.5), thereby reducing the storeroom area required by over 65 percent (Fig. 25.6). Also note that while the output more than doubled, the number of direct employees increased by only 18 percent. And 40 inventory turns per year were achieved (Fig. 25.7) while output levels were dramatically increasing. Because of the decrease in storeroom floor space and work in process, the total plant square footage did not increase. Upper management was convinced that changing to the JIT strategy did increase the quality and decrease the operating cost.

PURCHASING IN A JIT ENVIRONMENT

Purchasing, as it is traditionally known, will never be the same under the JIT concept. Decentralizing the function to the lowest decision level is an essential policy, and timeliness of action, of information, and of decisions is the goal. It may seem like heresy to pass purchasing's responsibilities to manufacturing, but it is occurring; and within the Davidson Rubber Company, purchasing is the initiator of this change. Why is this occurring? JIT demands within the automotive industry have caused many drastic changes.

To understand how Davison Rubber is affected by the JIT concept, it is important to understand what it is. Davidson Rubber is the world's leading independent manufacturer of vinyl and urethane products for the automotive industry. It has five facilities in the United States with a total of 3500 employees. In addition, it has licensed technology manufacturers throughout the free world producing both exterior and interior component parts. The exterior components include front and rear

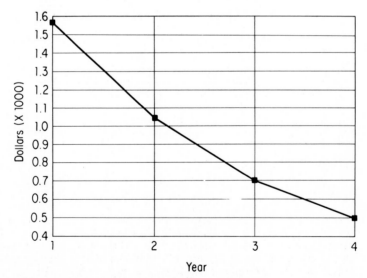

FIG 25.5 Inventory investment reduction.

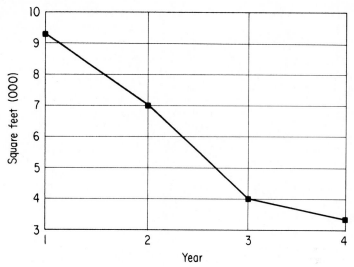

FIG 25.6 Storeroom area reduction.

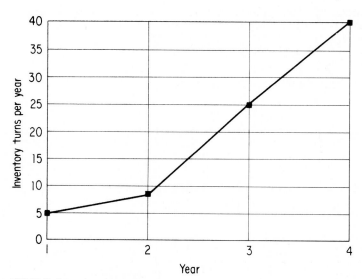

FIG 25.7 Inventory turns per year.

fascia, valance panels, woody trim, body side molding, and energy absorbers. Fascias are currently used on over 50 percent of the cars being manufactured in North America. The market position for Davidson Rubber is currently a 23 percent share of the North American rigid-injection-molding fascia market. It is the largest outside supplier to the automotive industry and has been a technical innovator since the first run of parts in 1974.

The interior components consist of instrument panels (commonly called crash pads), door-trim panels, armrests, glove-box doors, consoles, and headrests. The current market position on interior parts is as follows: Davidson Rubber has a 45 percent share of the North American armrest market, producing over 14 million parts per year. These are not considered JIT parts based on current automotive industry criteria. Davison Rubber currently has 30 percent of the North American instrument panel market, with 46 percent being projected for actual business already procured. This does not include the GM10 program which has been awarded. General Motors will produce this car at five of its assembly plants, and Davidson Rubber has been awarded the Oldsmobile and Chevy portion of the program, which is over 2 million currently with a projected 3.2 million in the future. Davidson Rubber will be producing between 14,000 and 16,000 instrument panels per day for the North American automobile manufacturers.

How did Davidson Rubber become a designated JIT supplier? The implementation of JIT manufacturing as a program within the company was initiated by top management. The JIT philosophy was embraced by all Davidson Rubber plants within a year, because it made common sense, not because of any desire to follow the competitors' programs. The company met the criteria of a JIT manufacturer on selected products by the following procedures:

- One-for-one production—repetitive: start to finish within 4 to 6 hr
- Quick tool changes: reduction per setup from 1 hr to 5 min
- Process changes: for example, changes were reduced from 8 hr to 20 min per change
- Employee involvement programs, such as ACE (a commitment to excellence) and SPC (statistical process control)

The definition of JIT developed by the Automotive Industry Action Group[4] is as follows:

> Just-In-Time is a disciplined approach to improving overall productivity and quality through respect for people and the elimination of *waste*. In the manufacturing and/or assembly of a product, Just-In-Time provides for the cost effective production and delivery of only the necessary quality parts in the right quantity, at the right time and place, while using a minimum of facilities, equipment, material and human resources. Just-In-Time is dependent upon the balance between the suppliers' manufacturing flexibility and the users' schedule stability and is accomplished through the application of specific elements which require total employee involvement and teamwork.

The purchasing department's goal of cost, delivery, and quality did not change, but the emphasis did. The manner in which cost related to both quality and delivery was important. Cost reduction is still the main goal, but what has changed is the sharing of responsibility with other departments. The decentralization of responsibility created direct involvement with the customer at all levels of the organization.

There is no purchasing decentralization at the plant level, but the lead function is the materials group. The introduction of a new-product program is done at the plant level through the coordination meetings of the materials group, where people with different responsibilities can discuss problems and select appropriate suppliers. The meetings are structured with an agenda and format, and the frequency of the meetings depends on the program. Group coordination meetings occur monthly or bimonthly and may take 2 to 3 days. The important objective is the elimination of adverse situations between the customer and supplier. Rather than having a single goal of cost, the materials group maintains a balance, when decisions are made relative to the product, by inclusion of the design engineer, production engineer, materials supervisor, and quality control supervisor. They are able to identify the true cost of the product. This occurs 2 years prior to production of the finished product.

The automotive industry has turned to its suppliers to implement design concepts for the finished product. The justification is the reduction of personnel, but also the supplier has the expertise to produce a quality part at the lowest cost. Sharing this knowledge requires credibility and confidence in each other. The supplier can design for the known future process specifications because only the supplier knows the processes, weaknesses and strengths, purchase price breaks for various quantities, facility capacity, first-run capability, and tool reliability. In the design phase, a difficulty may be encountered which prevents the manufacture of a product at the least cost. Under the old procedure, the supplier would not enter the review process until a year and a half prior to the car's manufacturing date. This would be too late to provide processing information that would affect the design of the product.

A product can be produced at the least cost by involving the supplier at an early stage, before final design and price quotations are made. To do this, purchasing departments must have suppliers who are qualified, approved, and credible. If these suppliers do not exist, they must be developed, encouraged, trained, and approved by the various acceptance levels within the organization. This is the way the purchasing department efforts are being redirected.

This system does not work with 100 percent efficiency. Davidson Rubber is weeding out its supplier network. Three major suppliers have dropped out because they could not step up to the JIT challenge. They are major suppliers for the automotive industry, but they refuse to see the reality of the situation. The reduction of the supplier network is a goal within the company as well as within the automotive business.

The Q-1 award is Ford Motor Company's way of recognizing the top 10 percent of its quality suppliers. Davidson Rubber has received the Q-1 award at two of its plants. General Motors gives the source evaluation and reporting award (SPEAR) to promote the control of quality at the point of manufacture. The Port Hope facility has received the SPEAR I and the Farmington plant has received the SPEAR II. Only those suppliers with a SPEAR II can bid on the GM10, Saturn, and any future programs. Obtaining a SPEAR I or II is a very difficult process. This is where credibility is developed during the evaluation process.

The purchasing departments within the automotive industry have implemented programs of target pricing. They state that they want a particular product at a certain cost. They have set the total car cost and ask the supplier to manufacture the components for a particular cost. They have the responsibility for controlling the costs. Elements of change that affect the cost are material, engineering, design, specification, timing, and volume changes. Each change can affect the price drastically or to only a minor degree and up or down. A company can improve its credibility by offering the customer a price decrease. It is not unusual for this to occur.

The key to gaining trust lies in the close coordination, implementation, and day-to-day dealing with the customer. With all the information available, changes can be implemented on a timely basis with complete assurance of acceptance by all members of the materials group. The automobile company's buyer deals no longer with the sales or marketing departments, but with the entire company.

An example of Davidson Rubber Company's involvement was the development of the Cadillac Deville instrument panel. It is one of the most complicated products made by the company. The initial involvement started in the third year during the design phase when the initial design decisions had been made and a major portion of the design was on paper. For more recent programs—the Eldorado, Seville, Chrysler P, and GM10—the company is involved in the initial design level.

This close coordination was accomplished simply by coordinating meetings on a scheduled basis of representatives from product engineering, purchasing, material control, quality assurance, and technical services of both Davidson Rubber and the vendor. These meetings were held initially every 2 months and then, as the program developed to its final stages, every month. The groups alternated for visits, and at all times the meetings were fully attended and the total agenda was covered. Open, frank discussions on the advantages and disadvantages of both the product and the groups were openly discussed. "You tell me your problems and I'll tell you mine" was the norm for the meetings, and solutions were derived on a timely basis. The atmosphere within the meetings was always open and friendly, and close relationships developed. Each group had the same goal, personal desires, and professionalism. The end product showed the results of this group effort.

There was a philosophy of free access to information and a bypassing of traditional barriers of communication at the meetings. The customary "do not quit until purchasing approves," maintaining security of proprietory information by the supplier, the organization divisions, and cost controls were nonexistent. This is not to say that rational decisions relative to cost were not made. The target price concept existed. The accountant was still there with the calculator determining the price—this goal was well established. The open discussions and frank responses were there. Ideas, once suppressed, were open for discussion and criticism, and the excellent end product was evident. This procedure was truly implementing employee involvement at higher levels.

This concept need not be restricted to the manufacturers of automotive parts. It is not a revolutionary style of management. The conservative nature of the Davidson Rubber Company still exists. Taking a concept such as JIT production and applying it throughout an organization, not only to manufacturing but also to the purchasing system, are a valid goal. This does not mean to just deliver the product on time. It does mean that the manufacturer must consider all the goals in developing a JIT system, a one-for-one manufacturing system, a repetitive process, the delivery of a product that eliminates the traditional waste. It will be a product created by a group of interested, involved, professional engineers and manufacturers.

The idea of the traditional quote procedure in purchasing is being replaced by a known final cost in target pricing. The product is known as to functionality, but the unknowns are resolved in a joint enterprise.

REFERENCES

1. Shigeo Shingo, *Study of Toyota Production System from the Industrial Engineering Viewpoint*, Japan Management Association, Tokyo, Japan, 1982.

2. Richard J. Schonberger, *Japanese Manufacturing Techniques*, Free Press, New York, 1982.

3. *Juran on Quality Improvement*, Juran Institute, Wilton, Conn., 1981.

4. Automotive Industry Action Group, *JIT Definition and Requirements*, AIAG, Southfield, Mich., 1984.

Managing the Function

26

Managing Concepts

Editors

GARY A. LANDIS, CFPIM, President, G. A. Landis and Associates, Pell City, Alabama

Assistant Editor

JULIE A. HEARD, Executive Vice President, Ed Heard & Associates, Columbia, South Carolina

Contributors

RALPH C. EDWARDS, Industrial Engineer, Leupold and Stevens, Inc., Beaverton, Oregon

RANDELL ELDRIDGE, CPIM, Superintendent of Material Control, ICI Americas, Inc., Charlestown, Indiana

ROBERT J. GREENE, Consulting Principal, A. S. Hansen, Inc., Lake Bluff, Illinois

MITCHELL LEVY, CPIM, Inventory Control Supervisor, Instromedix, Oregon

Production and inventory management can be defined as the management of the time, place, and physical facility of production. This means having the right materials, workers, and facilities at the right time and in a manner that both maximizes the service to the consumer and minimizes the investment of the company.

This chapter presents a background of the production and inventory control (PIC) function along with its basic organizational concepts. The duties and responsibilities of the various functions are described and highlighted. The types of development and training programs that should be used are emphasized. In addition, one section discusses how to evaluate performance and reward personnel accordingly.

It is imperative that PIC personnel be able to relate to the various functions as well as to various levels of management. These interfaces are described in detail in this chapter.

The computer's impact is significant and is becoming more vital each day. Therefore, one section discusses the use of the computer in PIC systems. Finally, a hint is given as to the future challenges of the profession. It is a dynamic field; to progress, one must be alert to future opportunities.

ORGANIZING THE FUNCTION

All organizations are supported by a structure consisting of the rules and regulations, policies and procedures, and operating methods employed by a business.

Defining Organizational Concepts

The basic concepts that define an organization are concerned with the manner in which it operates. Each individual organization must develop its own concepts. In essence, these concepts deal with planning and controlling the operation of the organization through the use of objectives, policies and procedures.

Objectives. Each organization and each manager within an organization must develop goals. Objectives deal with what is to be achieved by an organization, department, or individual. In most cases, objectives are specific and quantifiable. Examples include dollar or unit performance goals, efficiency goals, etc. Such objectives provide a sense of direction and motivation and form the framework for establishing policies and procedures.

Policies and Procedures. Once organizational objectives are established, a means of meeting those objectives must be developed. Policies and procedures focus attention on the "how to" aspects of meeting objectives. Policies are generally guidelines for employees to follow. Policies can be either explicit or implicit, and they allow management to make decisions once rather than every time a situation arises. Most policies are concerned with decision-making responsibilities, employee behavior and requirements, etc. Procedures, however, more often deal with the specific nature of how to accomplish an activity, such as paperwork routing, scheduling, personnel training, and promotion. Policies tend to be broader and more subject to interpretation, while procedures are generally more inflexible and detailed.

Rules. Rules are generally derived from policies and are often very specific. Rules are established to clarify for the personnel specific behavioral offenses and the resulting penalties.

Budgets and Plans. Budgeting and planning encompass many activities. Plans are specific operating guidelines for attaining the objectives and generally are established for the PIC activity in units of production and then translated to dollar terms for a budget.

Reporting Relationships

Reporting relationships within an organization depend on its structure to a great extent. Most often, line relationships exist, with each level reporting to the level above it. Authority and responsibility begin at the top of the organizational hierarchy and encompass ever-smaller areas farther down the organization chart. In most organizations, the "staff" serves in an advisory capacity.

Types of Structures

Organizational structures vary greatly from one corporation to another. Many are simple and straightforward; others are extremely complicated. The basic types are functionalized structures, line structures, line and staff structures, committee structures, and project teams.

Functionalized Structure.   Each individual function is a unit unto itself with its own specialized personnel and responsibilities. Generally, this type of structure has staff specialists with responsibility over line personnel. An example would be the quality control department that is empowered to directly command production personnel in the activities related to quality. The primary advantage of such a structure is the true utilization of specialized skills. The basic weaknesses are that reporting requirements and authority lines become fuzzy and lower-level personnel suffer from having to report to many bosses.

Line Structure.   Each functional area has a clear chain of command within the line structure. An example would be a corporation with marketing, manufacturing, and finance functions, each having a direct chain of command from top to bottom. Reporting relationships are generally simple and straightforward, as are responsibility and authority chains. Communication and decision making are generally quick processes. The primary disadvantage of this structure is the lack of specialized skills or knowledge that staff people often provide.

Line and Staff Structure.   This structure attempts to blend the two methods described above to provide a clear, concise, and quick chain of command as well as the specialized skills of staff personnel.

Committee Structure.   This structure attempts to use the skills and technical expertise of both line and staff personnel to solve problems and make decisions. The underlying theory is that two heads are better than one. Such committees may be standing or ad hoc and may be staffed permanently or temporarily. The committee process does allow input from many disciplines for decision making, and in some circles a decision by consensus is considered best. However, group decision making can often be a slow, painful process that does not necessarily produce the best decision. Rather, some feel that a group decision reflects the ideas of the most political, stubborn, or persistent member(s) of the group.

Project Teams.   Like the committee structure, project teams solicit information, ideas, and involvement from many functional areas of an organization. Such teams are often formed for selecting and implementing a specific system. A project team is often superimposed on the existing line or functional structure. The project team structure has the same basic advantages and disadvantages as the committee structure.

Each organization must develop its own "best" structure based on the type of industry, personnel, goals, reporting requirements, etc. Information about structure can be gained from observing other organizations, but in the final analysis the custom-tailored structure is often superior.

Management Direction

Delegation is a talent required of all managers which must be included from the beginning during the design of the first tentative organizational chart. It is often said that accountability and decision making should be delegated to a person at the lowest possible level of management. This will affect his training and will allow him to achieve and receive added responsibility.

Exceptions Principle.   A manager controls the actions of subordinates to a considerable degree through policy formulation and the scope of the authority delegated to them. In this way, the superior sets limits within which the subordinates act without further consultation. When a problem arises which is not routine and is outside the scope of a subordinate's authority, it is understood that he should refer the matter to his superior. If his superior does not have sufficient authority to decide, it is referred upward in the hierarchy to a manager having sufficient authority. This process is called the *exceptions principle.* When it is followed correctly, the exceptions principle frees the manager of excessive detail and those decisions more efficiently made at lower levels. Similarly, subordinates are not obliged to make decisions best made at higher echelons.

Span of Control.   The number of subordinates reporting to a manager is the *span of control.* The concept associated with the span of a manager is that there is a limit to its size. When this limit is reached, it is wise to break up the group into subgroups. Decreasing the spans of control will increase the number of levels required and could hinder effective communication between top and bottom organizational levels. However, the number of levels can be decreased only by widening the spans of control. There is a limit to the degree to which the spans can be increased before the manager's ability to coordinate subordinates is impaired, even if the manager uses such techniques as assistants, staff organizations, and committees.

Maximum spans of control for various organizational levels have been suggested, although there is some question about their validity. A better conclusion is that the limits depend on the manager's abilities, the types of activities to be managed, and the capabilities of the subordinates. Certainly an energetic, capable manager can accommodate a larger span than someone possessing these qualities to a lesser degree. If the activities of subordinates are routine and change very little, a larger span is possible, particularly if the subordinates have been adequately trained. This fact explains why larger spans of control tend to be found in the lower echelons. Finally, larger spans are justified if the subordinates are able and willing to carry out their duties with little supervision.

Employee Characteristics.   Managerial direction involves getting employees to effectively accomplish the tasks dictated, but the effectiveness of departmental employees depends on both their ability and their willingness to contribute. The strength of these two employee characteristics depends on several factors. These factors may be grouped according to the degree of influence that the manager has over them. There are at least six factors over which the manager has little direct control:

1. The number and quality of outside job alternatives perceived by the employee. If economic conditions are adverse or an employee's skills and experience are limited, the employer is likely to be very willing to contribute to the present organization.

2. The employees' attitudes, beliefs, and values which are formulated outside the work environment dramatically influence on-the-job behavior.

3. Group norms. The sanctions of informal groups exert enormous pressures on a member wishing to deviate from the norms of the group.

4. The emotional stability of subordinates.

5. The degree to which a manager can enlarge a subordinate's job to allow greater self-realization. Routine, uneventful jobs seldom evoke a strong loyalty and moral commitment on the part of an employee, yet the jobs must be done to achieve the economies of specialization.

6. The goals and expectations of employees as individuals and as a group. Yet the degree of compatability between these goals and the realities of the work environment materially affects employee behavior and willingness to contribute.

Do not conclude that the manager has no control over these six factors. These factors act as constraints which must be recognized in dealings with subordinates. Furthermore, there are four categories of factors over which the PIC manager has considerable control:

1. The plans, job activities, authority relationships, and job interrelationships formulated in earlier phases of the management process

2. The payment and promotion systems of the department and the degree to which these reward systems are linked operationally to effective behavior

3. The training and development programs available to departmental employees

4. Interpersonal relationships with subordinates, more precisely, leadership style, communication methods, and the manner in which the manager takes disciplinary action

Different aspects of some of these factors are discussed in greater detail, since few answers apply to all situations. Although the progress in the state of the art has been extensive, there is considerable room for differences of opinion. A policy which works in one department, company, or geographical region may not work in another. Much depends on the precise nature of the situation.

Work Force Requirements. To operate any functional area, workers are required. After the initial staffing of the department, one of the primary management tasks is to continually review worker requirements and availability. The effective manager does not simply staff a department, but also ensures that the right people in the right numbers are available at the right times and places to fulfill departmental responsibilities. A further responsibility of the manager is planning to ensure that personnel are trained and developed. By so doing, personnel can optimize the use of their talents and abilities and are less likely to suffer "burnout." In addition, with a well-trained (and cross-trained) staff, personnel replacement problems are less likely to disrupt department operations.

Ratios. Personnel or manpower ratios, based on dollar or unit sales volume, have been developed as a result of extensive surveys of PIC departments. Such surveys can serve as a guideline to the manager concerned with how many of each type are required. Such ratios often do not take into consideration aspects of PIC such as types, numbers, and kinds of equipment, physical processes, or space required. Thus, reliance on ratios alone could cause the manager to make incorrect, and difficult to correct, staffing decisions.

Clerical Skills.   As mentioned earlier, the PIC function was thought to be primarily clerical. Data collection and recording continues to be an important activity within the function. Without accurate data collection and recording procedures, decision making based on historical data would be impossible, financial accounting requirements would not be met, and product costing would be guesswork. The responsibility for such record keeping still falls within the PIC jurisdiction.

The purpose of record keeping is to provide accurate and timely information to decision makers and to offer input to the financial accounting system. Three basic types of records must be kept: availability records for material, equipment, and tooling; basic information records, such as bills of materials, stock sheets, routing sheets, and work orders; and performance records (actual versus planned performance, order progress, etc.).

The simplest system possible to collect the necessary data should be used to provide the shortest, simplest reports possible to convey the necessary information for future planning, decision making, and performance evaluation.

Management Skills.   Throughout this chapter, management skills are discussed. These skills include the ability to effectively recruit, train, motivate, and discipline personnel. Effective management requires a thorough knowledge of the function and the ability to perform the administrative details inherent in any managerial function. Most importantly, good management entails skillfully leading a staff in the performance of the required duties to attain organizational goals and objectives.

Organizational Inefficiences.   As in every organization, opportunities for inefficiency exist within PIC. Perhaps the most prevalent problem is functional-unit optimization. Each subsystem attempts to maximize the results of its activities but gives little consideration to the optimization need in other functional areas. The optimization of the entire system becomes less important than functional-unit optimization. As a result, each functional unit may appear to be prospering while the entire organization is faltering. Conflict in such situations can be resolved only when top-level management clearly identifies overall company goals and brings functional-unit goals into conformance in such a way that each unit's performance and the overall company performance are optimized.

As organizations become increasingly complex, so do information and communication flows between functional units. Faulty information from one unit to another is often cited as a cause of poor decision making, poor planning, and poor coordination. In structuring information and communication flows, the shortest and simplest path is often best. PIC professionals are often inundated with information, with much of it arriving in reports cluttered with needless detail and too late to be of much use for current problem correction and future planning. Again, the best solution is the simplest, fastest information format possible needed to convey data.

PIC Subsystems.   Several systems within the production control area support the primary system. Each functions somewhat independently of the primary system and the other subsystems. Each such subsystem is responsible for providing data to the primary system and to other subsystems. The two primary subsystems involved are materials handling and storage and indirect materials control. The materials-handling and storage subsystem is responsible for moving materials from internal and external sources to and from the storeroom and various work centers. It is responsible for record keeping regarding the storage and movement of such materials. The indirect materials control subsystem is responsible for purchasing, storing, controlling, handling, and issuing all indirect materials. These materials are essential for the manufacture of products but are not accounted for as raw materials. Examples are nails, screws, maintenance supplies, and perishable tools.

In addition to these two subsystems, many consider warehousing and/or shipping and purchasing to be PIC subsystems. However, they appear to have developed into systems that are related to, but independent of, PIC.

Recruiting.   One of the major responsibilities of managers is staffing their departments. Included in staffing is recruiting both from within the company and from external sources.

Generally, it is an accepted practice that promotions from within the organization, whenever possible, are most desirable. This attitude is based on the premise that promotions from within stimulate higher productivity, creativity, motivation, and commitment. In addition to their willingness to promote from within, most organizations have programs to actively train and educate employees to prepare for such promotions.

Despite the best efforts of a manager, sometimes promotion or recruiting from within is simply not possible. At that point, other likely sources include professional and trade societies, employment agencies, personnel consultants, and personal contacts. When a suitable candidate is located, care must be taken to promote a positive attitude on the part of current employees who will report to the new person.

Equal Employment Opportunity Commission.   Each department should provide a policy statement which prohibits discrimination because of age, sex, race, or national origin. Hiring and promotional considerations should be based on job performance, applicable experience, and demonstrated competence. Proper documentation should be maintained whenever hiring, promotions, or demotions are affected. Each manager or supervisor should maintain an employee file for each individual under her or his jurisdiction. All pertinent information should be placed in this file. In this manner, objectivity can be maintained.

Duties and Responsibilities

Many types of organizational structures are used in the materials management field. These vary from company to company and from plant to plant. In one company, the materials group may perform strictly clerical functions whereas in another company a similar group may perform significant staff work and have substantial line responsibility and accountability.

Organizational structures also vary greatly depending on the size of the company. When job descriptions are reviewed, functions rather than titles should be stressed. No matter how small the company, all functions must be performed to some degree. The foreman and clerk in a 25-employee shop may spend only a few minutes each week reviewing inventory while a large firm has a staff of several people perform the same basic task. As a company expands, the functions of the materials management group do not change; they simply receive more emphasis.

Many large corporations, even those that are very decentralized, have a corporate materials management group. The size and organization of these groups vary. As a result, their relationship with the plant-level materials management department varies widely from close daily control and supervision to providing primarily educational services. The most common corporate responsibility is purchase-contracts administration, typically the negotiation of contracts with major suppliers that service several corporate divisions or plants. In companies with several plants producing similar products, a central group might exist to develop long-range production plans and master production schedules. In that case, the plant materials group would focus on development and execution of short-range plans.

In spite of industry-to-industry variations and the many possible types of corporate structures, certain functions are generally accepted as the responsibility of materials management:

- Production control and inventory management, including master scheduling and physical stock control
- Distribution, including shipping, receiving, and traffic and frequently customer order entry and field warehousing
- Purchasing, including purchase-contract administration

Job Descriptions.   The job titles and short descriptions presented at the end of the chapter are representative of positions and functions generally found at the plant level in a manufacturing company. Their purpose is to aid in communication among materials management personnel, students, and others interested in the field. Fortunately, standardization of terminology for job titles and descriptions is underway. The title *master scheduler*, for example, is now used to describe people who share the same general range of duties and responsibilities in different industries.

The sample organizational charts shown in Figs. 26.1 and 26.2 illustrate job relationships and job progression. As mentioned earlier, job functions rather than job titles should be used in these charts and in a comparison of these jobs and those in a specific company.

Managerial, supervisory, and exempt positions are emphasized in these charts. Lower-level jobs such as those of stock clerks and material handlers tend to vary greatly between companies of different size and industry.

The sample job description shown in Table 26.1 represents the type of writeup that should be prepared for all the positions in a company as part of a formal wage and salary administration program. Information such as salary grade would be added by the company.

TABLE 26.1   Sample Job Description

Materials Management Executive   This is the top materials management position. This person is generally responsible for most of or all the following: production planning and control, inventory planning and control, distribution, and purchasing. This person reports to higher-level manufacturing or operations management.

Managerial Influence and Flexibility

The sample job descriptions make it clear that materials management personnel have considerable contact with other functional areas and, for many positions, considerable latitude in how they organize their own jobs and staffs. These are examples of contact and influence with other areas:

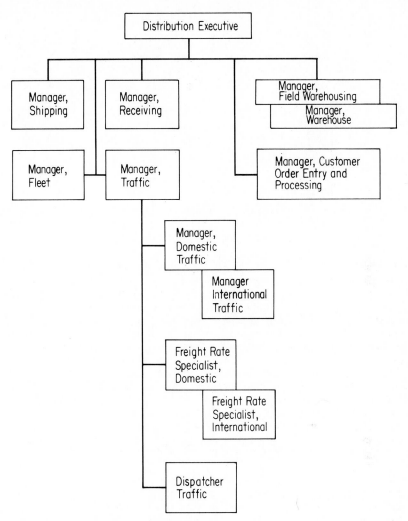

FIG. 26.1 Distribution organization chart.

1. Engineering
   a. Structuring of the product and its bills of materials to simplify production scheduling.
   b. Establishing schedules for new products and engineering changes.
2. Data processing
   a. Participation in the design and implementation of a variety of business systems.

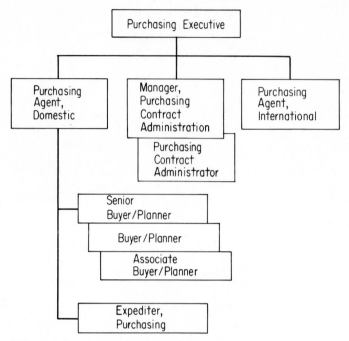

FIG. 26.2   Purchasing organization chart.

3. Cost accounting

    a. Stockroom and work-in-process inventories represent significant investments for most manufacturing companies.

    b. Changes in production schedules can have a major impact on the distribution of fixed costs.

4. Sales

    a. In many companies the materials management group has full responsibility for on-time delivery of finished products, from the time of entering the customer's order to shipment of the products.

Other groups can also have a major impact on the operation of a materials management group. For example, marketing provides the sales forecast that is the prime input to the master scheduling group. Cost accounting may prescribe requirements for auditing of various processes and records, e.g., cycle counting of inventory. The quality control group is important, too. Unexpected problems with product quality can undo months of careful planning. In addition, purchasing and traffic personnel typically support the entire company, not just manufacturing departments.

Materials management groups include, in general, a broader mix of hourly, exempt, and supervisory positions than other functions in manufacturing companies. This mixture allows for greater flexibility in job definition for individual employees. A data entry clerk, for example, can be prepared for eventual promotion by being taught to review input documents for reasonableness.

Employee Development and Training

As the PIC profession continues to grow, the employee development and training needs become greater. The process really entails four aspects. (1) A program should be created to offer guidance to the employee through career development. (2) A program for both management and personnel development should be generated. (3) Specific education, from both a generic and a company standpoint, should be provided. (4) Training specific to today's environment should be offered. This relates to systems software and the specific computer hardware.

Motivation.   Employees are willing to contribute to their departments only if they perceive that by doing so they gain more than they lose. This implies the need for a certain degree of congruency between individual and organizational goals. Understanding the goals of individual employees introduces the topic of motivation. The study of motivation begins with seeking out and cataloging the motivators of employees, to relate them to the reward system of the organization.

Perhaps the best of these cataloging schemes is called the *needs hierarchy*. Humans are said to be wanting animals that always seek to satisfy their needs. These needs exist in a hierarchy. As lower-level needs are satisfied, humans turn their attention and energies to higher-level needs, which become increasingly more difficult to satisfy. As humans attempt to satisfy their needs, they are motivated. It is interesting that a satisfied need is no longer a motivator.

Physiological and safety needs comprise the first and basic level of needs as humans seek protection from danger and threats. Being in a somewhat dependent relationship, an employee responds favorably to managerial behavior that is consistent and fair and that does not cause an undue amount of fear of discharge. The all-important payment system relates to this basic level of needs.

The next level of the hierarchy consists of *social needs*. Humans are social animals who seek a sense of belonging and acceptance. The prevalence of informal groups in the industrial setting gives adequate testimony to the human social requirement. Managerial action thwarting an employee's social needs may lead to behavior detrimental to the organization. To the extent that an employee is a social being, the manager should be aware of the employee's feelings and need to belong.

The highest rung of the needs hierarchy encompasses *egoistic and self-actualizing needs*. People seek autonomy, self-respect, status, and the experience of continual self-development. The manager is no longer the motivator and controller. Instead, the manager's role is to provide the framework and climate within which the employee's existing motivation and drives can be harnessed to serve organizational purposes.

Basing reward systems solely on one of these three simplified views of human needs would be naive. Humans are too complex to be described adequately as striving solely for one level of needs. People are highly variable; they are capable of acquiring new motives and needs. The PIC manager must, therefore, be capable of detecting the differing and changing needs of each subordinate. The manager has at hand a repertoire of behavior patterns, to facilitate adjustment to the needs of employees. The manager's behavior in motivating subordinates manifests itself along three dimensions: leadership, communication, and disciplinary practices.

Types of Education and Training.   Every PIC department should have a formally documented educational program. This program should be time-phased to focus the individual's education on specific functional responsibilities.

Education and training should be thought of as programs having different objectives. Education should teach concepts and theories, while training should provide hands-on practical instruction. Both are necessary for PIC personnel. Various types of education and training should be utilized. The best approach to use depends on the objectives of the program.

Independent Study. This is one of the least costly methods of educating and training, and it allows the individual to use time as it becomes available. This method should always be used in conjunction with other techniques.

APICS Certification Workshops. This approach is specifically oriented to the certification test. The curriculum thoroughly reviews the terminology and state of the art for specific manufacturing operations. This method is particularly important for new members of the department or old members who need a refresher course.

Consultants. Working with a professional automatically offers exposure to knowledge otherwise unavailable. In addition, this type of individual can offer formal educational programs on a specific subject tailored to the company's needs.

Seminars and Workshops. These are available throughout the country and cover every subject. Private consultants, educators, American Production and Inventory Control Society (APICS) chapters, and the APICS all offer programs of this nature. This type of education is suitable for new employees, seasoned professionals and anyone wanting more knowledge.

Tutorial Sessions. This approach uses videotapes, audiovisual presentations, and coordinators. As video equipment becomes more accessible, this type of technique will certainly be used more.

Software and Hardware Vendors. Almost all major software and hardware manufacturers publish literature on manufacturing control systems, and many offer training as part of the systems support. Once again, this method is good for every level of information required. But the reader or listener should be able to discriminate between fact and salesmanship.

Who Should Educate and Train.   Education and training can be accomplished by various types of individuals. Many companies hire training managers for their personnel departments. If properly informed, these individuals can be effective. Many new system implementations place a full-time project director in charge. This individual is usually qualified to satisfy any educational needs.

One untapped resource that most companies consider last is their own employees, managers or otherwise. As more of the staff become certified by APICS as a CPIM or CFPIM, their knowledge should be applied to training others. These individuals usually become good instructors.

External and Internal Training.   A balance of both external and internal education is most beneficial. External training helps the trainee assess what others are doing as well as apply these lessons specifically. External education gives the individual exposure to other companies' successes and failures. It also provides generic education and the understanding of basic principles and techniques. It shows how to use specific approaches to solving problems. Therefore, a blend of both the external and internal approaches is needed. Thus the employee learns to assess situations objectively.

Evaluating Performance

Performance evaluation is a commonplace activity in most organizations. Evaluations deal with individual, team or group, unit, and plant performance, and frequently they are based on how well a variety of goals, objectives, or standards are met.

Management by Objectives. All organizations have goals and objectives. Attainment of such goals and objectives is the responsibility of each employee. To meet organizational objectives, all employees must be actively involved. One method of increasing employee involvement is through management by objectives.

Management by objectives allows employees to set performance standards for their tasks and then to take an active part in measuring performance against those standards. These activities are involved in management by objectives:

- The employee and his or her direct supervisor discuss organizational objectives and the relationship between those objectives and specific goals for the employee's area of responsibility. Job content, major activities, relative priorities, and accountability are discussed and agreed upon.
- The employee sets performance targets and standards based on the decisions made.
- Employee and supervisor finalize the standards to be used to evaluate the employee.
- Performance checkpoints are established, as are performance measurements. The supervisor and employee meet regularly to review the employee's performance, discuss corrections and improvements, and consider modifications to future standards.

Management by objectives is not always a practical technique. But it often lessens employee resistance to control and increases motivation and involvement.

Discipline. An unfortunate fact of any superior-subordinate relationship is the need for occasional disciplinary action. When discipline is necessary, several factors are important in turning a potentially negative situation into a positive, constructive interaction that can reinforce established limits. Discipline should always be administered in a private discussion between the employee and the superior. It should take place virtually immediately after the action requiring discipline and should be applied both consistently and impersonally. To be effective, disciplinary action should involve only breaches of known, established standards and limits.

Lack of discrimination in applying discipline is critical to the future relationship between superior and subordinate, as is an impersonal attitude on the part of the superior. Only when discipline is administered fairly will the superior continue to be regarded as a source of help, encouragement, and motivation.

Audits. Personnel audits for each employee are beneficial in matching employees with jobs. Such an audit should cover a wide range of information about employees, including education, goals, outside interests, and abilities. Matching employees with jobs is difficult, but by relating job descriptions to personnel audits the task becomes easier. Promotion from within an organization is a valuable motivational tool accomplished most successfully through such matching.

Measuring Departmental Efficiency. A necessary step in improving systems and processes is evaluation based on past performance. Within the PIC area, such evaluation is a difficult process owing to the interaction with other disciplines. Performance and actions of those other disciplines can affect the ability of PIC to perform effectively and efficiently.

Care must be taken to evaluate both the department and the individual employees based on only those areas of responsibility over which they exercise adequate control. A major problem occurs when different functions do not share common objectives. For example, if purchasing is evaluated based on the purchase price of raw materials and PIC is evaluated based on inventory levels, a conflict is sure to arise, and one group is bound to have a negative evaluation. Such conflicts are, to some extent, unavoidable. However, every effort should be made to reduce the impact of such conflicts on departmental (and individual) performance evaluations. Each measure should be studied individually to determine the various factors that affect it. The objective of performance measurement—process system control and improvement—is admirable; the specific techniques used, however, are the source of many problems and conflicts.

Appraisals.   In performance evaluation activities, appraisals serve the same purpose as feedback systems in a closed-loop control system. The established reason for appraisals is to evaluate the employee's past performance and establish future criteria. Almost as an afterthought, the results of the appraisal are usually related verbally to the employee. Too often, employee appraisal meetings do not happen in that way. At times, such appraisals become nothing more than a general superior-subordinate conversation; at other times, they are a one-sided discussion of the past and future. Research has shown that employees resent their inability to affect the future course of their work.

Alternate processes, such as management by objectives, have been developed in the past several years. Because they involve the employee directly in planning and evaluating performance, these methods serve as a motivational tool rather than simply the annual appraisal that must be endured.

Promotion Systems.   Promotion systems exist in most organizations. Components of promotion programs are personnel audits, job descriptions, performance appraisals, etc. These elements tend to be very subjective and, as such, are apt to be criticized. Research has indicated that direct measures of performance, such as budgetary responsibility and specific performance standards and goals, are effective in rating employees.

Promotion policies can greatly affect employee motivation. The employee who sees management being hired from outside the organization will not be as performance- or goal-oriented as the employee who sees the link between job performance and career possibilities. Company policies and procedures related to promotion systems should be clearly stated, to encourage employees to set personal career goals and strive to attain them through superior performance.

Remuneration

For an organization to attract and retain the quality work force necessary to meet its business objectives, reward systems must be offered. To be effective, such reward systems must be equitable, competitive, legal and defensible, understandable and appealing, and efficient to administer. The manner in which such systems are designed and administered has a major impact on the ability to motivate employees to be productive and to contribute to the organization's success.

Every manager must ensure that the organization's reward systems are appropriate and adequate for the unit or function. The PIC function requires people with specific skills, although it is unlikely the organization will develop reward systems specifically for PIC. The responsible manager must ensure that these systems do not cause difficulties with recruiting, turnover, and employee motivation.

Reward systems include nonfinancial rewards such as recognition, challenging work, and a good environment as well as financial rewards. Frequently the absence of such nonfinancial incentives forces the employer to make up the difference with dollars. PIC management is responsible for ensuring that their employees receive adequate nonfinancial and financial rewards and that the balance between the two is appropriate.

Financial rewards consist of

- Direct pay, salary, and short-term incentives
- Long-term incentives such as capital-accumulation programs, retirement plans, stock-based programs, and profit sharing
- Employee benefits such as group health and life insurance and paid time off
- Employee services and perquisites such as education reimbursement, membership in professional organizations, and company-provided services

PIC management generally has control over and input to the determination of direct pay levels for employees, while benefits and other rewards are generally the same throughout the organization.

Direct pay for an employee is a function of both the nature and the relative value of the job performed. Typically job descriptions are used to classify employees and identify them with a specific job title based on the value of their work. Frequently job descriptions become a major input for organizational analysis and job/work team design efforts. The relative value of the job performed is measured by four universal factors:

1. Skill
    a. Knowledge (education and experience)
    b. Analytical
    c. Manual
    d. Interpersonal
2. Effort
    a. Mental
    b. Physical
3. Responsibility
    a. For assets and information
    b. For work of others
    c. For safety of others
    d. For internal and external contacts
    e. Latitude exercised and potential impact
4. Working conditions
    a. Adverse conditions
    b. Hazards

Employers must be able to defend the method of assigning relative job values both to employees and to government regulatory agencies. Employees are concerned about internal equity, which involves the relationship of one job to other jobs in the job-worth hierarchy; inequity is known to cause dissatisfaction and unwanted turnover.

The market rate for a job, in addition to being equitably valued within an organization, must compare with prevailing competitive rates in the relevant labor markets. Each organization must decide in which labor market it competes, who its competitors for personnel are, and what the competitive posture will be relative to prevailing pay levels.

The process of setting pay levels is complex because of differences in the rates for specific disciplines or jobs. New jobs constantly emerge as a result of technological change, for example, that of a robotics engineer. These new positions make the assessment of an organization's competitive ability even more difficult.

The Materials Management Association (MMA) has developed an annual materials management compensation survey for determining prevailing market rates for key jobs in the field. Included are job definitions for new or changing disciplines such as master scheduling, capacity planning, and manufacturing data administration as well as for the more traditional jobs in the stockroom, shipping, receiving, and traffic. By using the survey, current pay levels for materials management jobs can be compared with other jobs in the organization and with similar jobs in other organizations. Analysis of the materials management survey produces two pay relationship patterns which are similar to those widely found in other disciplines. See Tables 26.2 and 26.3.

Once an organization has determined the relative internal values of jobs, these jobs are usually grouped into job grades, each containing jobs of equal or similar value. The market values of the jobs are then used to establish pay ranges for each grade. A pay structure is the result, as shown in Fig. 26.3.

Pay ranges allow for the difference in rates between people on the same job. These rate differences are usually attributable to differences in one or more of the following: seniority, command of job-related skills, and performance. The profile shown by Table 26.4 describes a pay range and what each type of employee should be paid.

TABLE 26.2   Managerial Pay Relationshps at Corporate Level

Materials Management Executive	Percentage of Average Pay for Materials Management Executive
PIC, distribution, and purchasing executives	70–80
Manager of production planning, traffic, inventory planning, field warehousing, master scheduling, and fleet; purchasing agent; purchasing contract advisor	55–65

TABLE 26.3   Pay Relationships

Nonmanagerial Jobs within a Job Family*

Job Title	Pay Difference
Supervisor, quality control (QC)	Average difference between
Senior QC specialist	adjacent levels = 15%
QC specialist	
Associate QC specialist	

*A *job family* is a group of jobs involving work of the same nature but performed at different skill and responsibility levels.

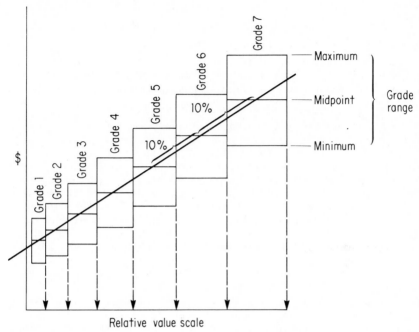

FIG. 26.3   Pay structure.

TABLE 26.4   Pay Range Profile

Pay Level	Time Frame	Type of Employee Who Should Be Paid at This Level
Maximum	4th Quarter	Employees whose performance is consistently outstanding and is sustained over extended period
Midpoint	3rd Quarter	Employees whose performance consistently exceeds standards
	2nd Quarter	Employees whose performance meets standards or who have acceptable performance but are still learning the remainder of the job
Minimum	1st Quarter	Employees whose performance occasionally meets standards or very new (minimally qualified) employees who are clearly in a learning capacity in the job

To administer pay rates within established pay ranges on the basis of performance, an organization must design and effectively administer a performance appraisal plan based on job-related results. A sound appraisal system has the following characteristics:

- Performance standards are defined in advance.
- Performance standards are communicated in advance.
- Performance standards are based on job-related results and are as objective as possible.
- Appraisals are performed by someone who knows the employee's work.
- Appraisals are performed by a trained person.
- Appraisals are written and reviewed with the employee.
- An appeals mechanism is available to employees.

Organizations are confronted by different economic conditions over time. Business cycles, technological change, competitive conditions, and government intervention may all affect the funds available for employee rewards. Pressure to maintain profit levels may precipitate cost-cutting programs, which typically affect the amount of money available for increasing direct pay levels. It is important that each manager ensure that an adequate share of the available funds goes to the employees in his or her organizational unit. Pay levels should be kept competitive so the organization does not find itself without the key employees needed for the organization's success.

Interfaces

To effectively fulfill assigned responsibilities, the PIC professional must interact with other company personnel from other disciplines. The key ingredients to successful interaction are communication and recognition of company-wide goals and objectives. Too often, one's own discipline appears to be the only important functional area of a business, and organizational goals are subjugated to area goals.

Human Relations. In the past decade, increased emphasis has been placed on the human relations aspects of the organization. Employee needs are given greater consideration. The result appears to be increased employee commitment and motivation. Effective leadership, good communication skills, and encouraging employee participation and motivation are all key elements in creating a positive atmosphere in the workplace. Employees need to feel that they are getting as much as they are giving. The company that maintains good human relations with its employees will have committed and loyal employees.

To be effective in their jobs, PIC personnel must be able to relate to peers, superiors, and subordinates. Special training and an understanding of human relations are imperative. PIC personnel act as the focal point or coordinating function for most of the operations with which they deal. They more than any others must be able to get other people to respond through persuasion. All people in staff positions must rely on behavioral techniques to accomplish tasks.

Top Management. Top management in many organizations is drawn from disciplines other than PIC. Frequently, top management comes from accounting, marketing, or the legal department. As a consequence, many top managers have relatively little understanding of the actual systems and processes in manufacturing and PIC. Despite their lack of understanding, they are ultimately responsible to stockholders for performance in both manufacturing and materials management.

The interaction between PIC and upper-level manufacturing and materials managers is generally easier because these positions are filled from the areas they represent. The practicing PIC professional deals with many details in day-to-day activities, and the top management for this activity is responsible for the overall company objectives, as well as the smooth performance of the area of responsibility. Thus, interaction with upper-level management is likely to be broad and general in nature rather than involving specific operating techniques.

An open-door policy on the part of upper-level management has become common. Such a policy encourages employees to channel information or grievances through the appropriate levels until they are satisfied with the outcome. Employees do not feel as cut off from the company when they are aware that such a channel is open to them.

Top management's primary responsibility is the overall operation of the organization. A key to ensuring the success of an organization is to keep all the players working as a team. Disputes between functional areas resulting from differing goals can be settled and eliminated only by top-management involvement.

Subordinates. The manager's relationship with his or her subordinates is critical. The responsibilities of management include providing leadership and motivation for employees, and good communication skills are required.

Employee motivation is a subject that has been discussed and debated widely. Current theory suggests that participation is a key element to motivation. When employees are involved in establishing organizational objectives, they take a more active interest and are committed to a much greater degree. Some participation techniques that stimulate motivation include management by objectives, quality circles, financial rewards for process or system improvements, etc.

Leadership styles abound, from democratic to authoritative and everywhere on the continuum between. Research indicates that the more democratic form of leadership encourages worker commitment, innovation, and self-fulfillment. This form of leadership is better accepted by employees and creates a more positive atmosphere.

Communication skills are essential in every aspect of life but perhaps nowhere more so than in creating positive superior-subordinate relationships. The ability to concisely convey instructions, relate necessary information, encourage, motivate, and discipline employees can be a manager's most effective tool and can have a most positive effect on overall objective attainment.

Relationships with Other Departments. PIC is frequently involved in disputes and/or conflicts with other departments. In part, such conflicts are the result of conflicting goals.

Each department should concentrate on overall organizational objectives rather than simply ignoring all but its own objectives. Communication and education are additional tools for strengthening organizational unity. Too frequently, the functions involved simply do not understand the objectives of others. Often when people from two departments do try to communicate, they cannot understand each other. As technology has made specialists of us all, separate languages have evolved which tend to be very specific. Learning about the other subjects involved in an organization is a difficult and often frustrating task, but one well worth the trouble because of the many positive results to be achieved.

Integration of New Techniques. The technological state of the art in PIC changes almost daily. Computer-aided design/computer-aided manufacturing (CAD/CAM), group technology, computer-integrated, manufacturing, (CIM), and Kanban all represent advances in the body of knowledge. Detailed explanations of these techniques are inappropriate here; however, each of these technological advances requires interdisciplinary cooperation and education. Once again, education and communication in the various techniques are the keys to maximizing the benefits.

Impact of the Computer

Technological developments in computer hardware and software have had an enormous impact on PIC in the past 10 years. As computers have become smaller and processing times shorter, computer terminals are seen more frequently in the manufacturing facility, both in the offices of PIC professionals and on the shop floor.

Systems Responsibilities.   Through an extended process of trial and error, it has been decided that responsibility for system implementation must rest with the user. In the early evolution of computerized systems, the entire responsibility for systems design, development, and installation rested with the data processing department.

Installation of a workable accounting system was a relatively easy task. Formal, written procedures existed based on the manual record-keeping system in use. In contrast to the ease of installing accounting software, PIC systems were difficult to design or purchase and nearly impossible to install. Historically, PIC worked primarily from informal systems which did not even perform well manually. Written documentation and procedures were scarce. The changing day-to-day activities and priorities made formal manual systems impractical.

Most inventory managers were not sure what they wanted or needed in a system. They were even less aware of the systems available to them. Each individual made decisions to keep supplies available and production running based on experience and knowledge. Thought processes used to make such decisions were, at best, vague and difficult to explain.

During this period, relatively few software packages were available to adapt to PIC use. Therefore, data processing was faced with the task of developing totally new systems for individuals who had little understanding of what they wanted. As a consequence, PIC systems were developed. However, they did not provide appropriate information for decision making, were difficult to use, and did not provide timely information. Thus, such systems soon deteriorated into informal systems which were less effective than the manual systems they replaced. During this evolution, it was determined that the only truly successful systems were those developed and installed by educated users of the system.

Successful system design and implementation depends on a person being held responsible for making it work. To ensure success, the end user must be involved and responsible. The user must be involved at all stages, including software selection, task force creation, management, implementation, test data preparation, etc.

To assist in a system installation, a task force should be established with members from all involved departments. The head of the task force should be the end user in the highest position within the company. At least one member of the task force should have full-time responsibility to work on the installation.

Importance of Change.   The installation of computers and computer systems has been one of the most significant changes in PIC management. Historically, the PIC function had been bogged down in routine paperwork, constantly fighting emergencies in order to keep the day-to-day activities going. The computer necessitated the development of formal, written procedures for inventory management. This procedure formalization process has been instrumental in speeding the emergence of the PIC body of knowledge.

Including the computer system in formal procedures leaves the inventory manager free to manage business more effectively. The result has been inventory reductions, improved customer service, and more efficient plant operations.

The computerization of the factory results in increased recognition of PIC as a profession. During recessions many companies are caught with excessive raw materials and finished-goods inventories. This results in layoffs, capital shortages, and inventory obsolescence. Membership in APICS increased by leaps and bounds as companies realized that properly trained and educated personnel were essential to prevent a resurgence of excess inventory after the recession ended.

Upgrading Skills. Changes brought about by the widespread use of computer systems necessitate numerous changes in the educational requirements of the PIC professional. Decisions must be made after careful analysis of the data and information provided by the computer. Such analysis requires a thorough understanding of the techniques and formulas used to manage inventory. Computer systems include sets of decision rules designed to make routine recommendations. With a thorough understanding the PIC professional will know which decisions require intervention and which decisions should be left to the computer.

Inventory affects every department of a company. Marketing must supply forecasts to plan material requirements, production must provide feedback on quantities produced, purchasing must provide order status, and sales must provide data on actual customer orders. To be effective, the PIC manager must have at least a working knowledge of all company functions and be able to analyze how they affect the decision-making process.

The PIC manager is affected now, as never before, by activities outside the company. Rapid changes in technology create a ripple effect throughout all industry. The PIC professional faces constant changes in customer demand for new products, government relations, economic conditions, and manufacturing methods. Remaining aware of such changes and staying technically abreast of those which affect one's industry are crucial.

Given the rapidly advancing state of the art and body of knowledge, constant reeducation becomes a prerequisite for success. New management techniques are being described in the APICS publication *Production and Inventory Management Journal*, in the *APICS News*, in other trade magazines, and in newsletters and publications by consultants. Most hardware and software vendors gladly supply material related to their products. Some of their literature is generic in design and offers an excellent, inexpensive way to stay abreast of the latest technology.

To be useful, education must be applied, and the ability to analyze data to determine the best course of action is of the highest priority. Also, the ability to communicate actions and justification of decisions is required.

Flexibility. The only constant in today's business environment is change. The computer provides the flexibility to deal with change in a timely manner, making good management decisions with confidence possible. Previously, all data were manipulated manually and could not be handled rapidly enough for decision making. Consequently, decisions were often made with partial, sometimes inaccurate information. Companies can no longer afford to make decisions based on partial information provided by manual systems.

Companies dealing with retail customers must react quickly to demand changes. Many retail stores now have point-of-sale terminals tied to a central data base for providing daily sale quantities of individual items. Customer demands are recognized immediately and have an immediate effect on orders sent to the manufacturer. The manufacturer must be able to react to new demands by ordering raw materials, scheduling, producing, and shipping to retail outlets. Conversely, a manufacturer must react to cancel raw-material orders and reschedule production capacity to produce salable products if necessary.

The emerging trend in building new or modernizing older factories is toward the development of a *flexible manufacturing system* (FMS). In an FMS, production equipment can be converted from producing one type of item or product line to another with little modification or loss of time. In addition, more operations are performed with a single machine, thus reducing queue and move times. Another feature built into some systems is computerized quality control. Flexible manufacturing systems contribute to lower in-process inventory, faster reaction to change, decreased manufacturing time, and production of higher-quality products.

Using the Computer as a Tool.   Computers manipulate large quantities of data in relatively short periods to provide information for decision making. Software systems should be evaluated based on this fact, and users must be trained and educated to ensure that the full advantage of such a tool capability is recognized.

Future Challenges

Technology is constantly changing, requiring upgrading the PIC function. To most PIC professionals, the challenge is to keep abreast of new technology and determine which is right for the particular manufacturing environment.

Systems Challenges.   Four rapidly developing technologies will have significant impacts on the PIC profession and the functions and responsibilities of PIC professional: microcomputers, input-output (I/O) devices, CIM, and robots.

Microcomputers. The microcomputer offers significant opportunities for the PIC professional to profit from the capabilities of a computer with little or no involvement of data processing personnel. Many have experienced the frustration of waiting for programming services, an especially difficult task for professionals in a discipline responsible for making things happen. Little time and training is required to learn how to program and operate a microcomputer which can provide usable information in a short time. Several advantages to user programming and operation are the shortened development time, increased user acceptance, changes being made without delay, and less reliance on other departments. All are large pluses to the PIC professional.

Properly regulated and used, microcomputers can play an ever-increasing role in inventory management. It is essential that developments occur in such a way that the necessary continuity of the PIC functions is maintained. Also, it is critical that the microcomputers use, address, and support overall business goals.

Input-Output Devices. Computers have been able to manipulate data at a much faster pace than input could be received or output could be generated. The rapid development and deployment of I/O devices will significantly enhance computer applications. Devices such as point-of-sale terminals, magnetic-tape readers, bar-code readers, laser scanners, and printers allow most input to be processed immediately, on line, without manual intervention. The PIC professional will receive timely information for making management decisions. Decisions will be made and actions taken at a more rapid pace than at present.

Computer-Integrated Manufacturing. With cheaper and more powerful computers, integration of all company activities can now be achieved. Manufacturing resource planning (MRP II) was a significant advance toward this aim. CIM goes beyond that and includes new technologies such as CAD, CAM, computer-aided engineering (CAE), and computer-aided process planning (CAPP).

Installation of a CIM system will lead to new opportunities and responsibilities for the PIC professional. One challenge will be to ensure that sufficient interfaces are established to provide the PIC professional with appropriate information to manage inventories. Therefore, one must stay abreast of the latest technologies and maintain a working knowledge of current capabilities.

Robots. The rapid deployment of robots is an inevitable development for the factory of the future. The use of robots will provide more reliable production quality and more dependable production rates.

In addition to the innovations mentioned above, various techniques and software packages have been available for many years but have not been implemented successfully. For example, in most companies, computer-controlled storage is not tied into the centralized data base, to obtain maximum use of the available capabilities.

The challenge to PIC is to fully utilize the available technology. All systems must be integrated and used to manage and further the overall goals of the company. Failure to properly implement such systems results in the further deterioration of the competitive posture in the world markets, resulting in slow economic growth of companies and the nation.

Management Involvement.   With the advent of the computer and the subsequent system opportunities, management must become more involved. Some managers have attempted to avoid this confrontation but have realized the advantages of these tools. Managers at higher levels will operate in teams without friction. They will be more supportive of the production plan and the master production schedule. They will be evaluated on the basis of their contribution in making and executing these plans.

Three significant developments should be expected in the future: (1) The trend toward simpler systems that users can understand should continue. (2) Better production plans need to be developed and executed. (3) Human resources need to improve. Problems must be solved by the priority of their importance.

It is obvious that PIC professionals have come of age. If they are to retain their leadership role, they must continue to be aware of new opportunities for improving inventory management techniques and be able to offer more efficient and effective methods of manufacturing.

Job Descriptions for Production and Inventory Management[1]

THE MATERIALS MANAGEMENT EXECUTIVE has the top materials management position. This person is generally responsible for all or most of the following: production planning and control, inventory planning and control, distribution, and purchasing. This executive reports to higher-level manufacturing or operations management.

THE PRODUCTION CONTROL AND INVENTORY MANAGEMENT EXECUTIVE is responsible for all or most of the following: production planning and control, inventory planning and control, warehousing, material handling, shipping, and receiving. This individual is not responsible for the distribution or purchasing functions and typically reports to the materials management executive.

THE DISTRIBUTION EXECUTIVE is responsible for all or most of the following: purchase of raw materials, component parts, equipment, services, and supplies. This person may also purchase supplies and services for nonproduction departments and typically reports to the materials management executive.

THE MATERIALS MANAGEMENT SYSTEMS COORDINATOR assists in the design, development, and implementation of data gathering and reporting methods and procedures within the materials management area. This person functions as a technical coordinator and internal consultant on data processing.

THE MANAGER OF PRODUCTION CONTROL is responsible for controlling the production schedule by directing the production planning and control activities. Responsibilities may include capacity planning, shop order releases, dispatch and shop scheduling, and the in-process expediting function. This person may supervise other managers or supervisors.

THE SUPERVISOR FOR CAPACITY PLANNING is responsible for determining, monitoring, and recommending adjustments to the limits of plant capacity to ensure coordination with the master production schedule (MPS). This employee supervises other capacity planners.

THE CAPACITY PLANNER is responsible for determining, monitoring, and recommending adjustments to the limits of capacity for work centers or departments to ensure consistency with the MPS. Normally 3 to 5 years of experience are required. This person reports to the supervisor for capacity planning.

THE SUPERVISOR OF SHOP ORDER RELEASE is responsible for preparation and release of documents (such as shop routings, picking lists, etc.) authorizing manufacture of specific parts or products in specific quantities.

THE OPERATIONS/SHOP SCHEDULER (DISPATCHER) is responsible for assignment of target start and/or completion dates and times for manufacturing or processing operations. The job also includes selection and sequencing of available processes and assignments to individual work centers or lines.

THE MANAGER OF MASTER SCHEDULING is responsible for all master scheduling and/or final-assembly scheduling activities. This person reports to the production control and inventory management executive and supervises master and/or final-assembly schedulers.

THE MASTER SCHEDULER is responsible for development of the production or manufacturing schedule at the highest level at which products will be stocked or planned, either prior to shipment (for made-to-stock operations) or prior to final assembly (for made-to-order operations). This person reports to the manager of master scheduling.

THE FINAL-ASSEMBLY SCHEDULER is responsible for schedule development for final assembly of finished goods and reports to the manager of master scheduling.

THE MANAGER OF INVENTORY CONTROL directs inventory planning and control activities and is responsible for all or most of the following: inventory planning, stockroom, material handling, and administrative controls for manufacturing and/or production records, documents, and files. This person supervises other managers or supervisors.

THE MANAGER OF INVENTORY PLANNING has overall responsibility for determining the required quantity and availability of materials needed to meet the MPS.

THE SENIOR MATERIAL PLANNER determines the quantity and order date for materials needed to meet the MPS, initiates purchase or production requisitions as appropriate, and may be expected to give direction and guidance to other material planners. Normally 5 or more years of experience are required. This person reports to the manager of inventory planning.

THE MATERIAL PLANNER has responsibility for determining the quantity and order date for materials needed to meet the MPS and initiates purchase or production requisitions as appropriate. Normally 2 to 3 years of experience are required. This person reports to the manager of inventory planning.

THE ASSOCIATE MATERIAL PLANNER assists in determining the quantity and order date for materials needed to meet the MPS. This is the entry-level materials planning position. This person reports to the manager of inventory planning.

THE STOCKROOM MANAGER is responsible for the physical custody and accuracy of inventory records for component items, assemblies, and/or finished goods within a manufacturing plant. This person may manage the supervisors of individual stockrooms.

THE STOCKROOM SUPERVISOR is responsible for the physical custody and accuracy of inventory records for component items, assemblies, and/or finished goods in a single stockroom area. This person supervises the activities of stockroom personnel.

THE SUPERVISOR OF CYCLE COUNTING is responsible for regular and systematic counting and verification of physical inventories to establish and/or maintain accuracy of inventory records. This person also determines causes of errors and assists in correction and may supervise the activities of cycle-counting personnel. (This does not include employees assigned to annual tag inventory on a temporary basis.)

THE SUPERVISOR OF MATERIALS HANDLING is responsible for physical movement of material within a manufacturing plant and supervises intraplant personnel including drivers, material handlers, etc.

THE MANAGER OF MANUFACTURING DATA ADMINISTRATION is responsible for monitoring the integrity and completeness of records, documents, and files for manufacturing and/or production activities. Normally this person coordinates the operational interface between inventory planning and control and computer-based systems.

THE TRANSACTION ANALYST is responsible for auditing the preparation of records and processing transactions that affect the inventory planning and control files.

THE BILL-OF-MATERIALS ANALYST develops, structures, and maintains bills of materials needed for producted and/or planning purposes.

THE ENGINEERING CHANGE NOTICE ANALYST is responsible for determining the impact of planned engineering changes on manufacturing and/or production activities and coordinates the implementation of change as appropriate.

THE MANAGER OF SHIPPING is responsible for the shipment of final or in-process product and other goods or materials as well as timely reporting of completed shipments. Typically this person reports to the distribution executive.

THE RECEIVING MANAGER is responsible for the initial physical receipt and timely reporting of materials received at a single facility. This can include responsibility for inspection, identification, and delivery to stocking locations. Typically this person reports to the distribution executive.

THE TRAFFIC MANAGER is responsible for the physical movement of material from a manufacturing and/or production facility. This typically includes shipments to both domestic and international customers and to plants within the same company. Typically included is the responsibility for incoming materials. This person may supervise other traffic managers and/or specialists and usually reports to the top distribution executive.

THE DOMESTIC TRAFFIC MANAGER is responsible for securing the most cost-efficient method of shipment both for incoming and outgoing materials and for products to and from domestic suppliers and customers. This person reports to the traffic manager.

THE INTERNATIONAL TRAFFIC MANAGER is responsible for securing the most cost-efficient method of shipment for both incoming and outgoing materials and products to and from foreign suppliers and customers. He or she reports to the traffic manager.

THE DOMESTIC FREIGHT RATE SPECIALIST is responsible for determining the appropriate domestic freight rate on incoming and outgoing materials and products. This person may audit freight invoices and reports to a traffic manager.

THE INTERNATIONAL FREIGHT RATE SPECIALIST is responsible for determining the appropriate international freight rate on incoming and outgoing materials and products. She or he may audit freight invoices and reports to a traffic manager.

THE TRAFFIC DISPATCHER assigns and schedules shipments with specific carriers and may trace lost or delayed shipments. This person typically reports to a traffic manager.

THE FLEET MANAGER is responsible for the control, maintenance, and scheduling of company trucks and vehicles assigned to a manufacturing and/or production facility (including facilities that are managed as one unit). Normally passenger vehicles and personal automobiles are not included. Typically this person reports to the distribution executive.

THE FIELD WAREHOUSING MANAGER (finished goods/product) is responsible for the physical custody and overall safeguarding of the finished inventory as well as operation of warehouse sites separate from the primary manufacturing and/or production facility. This person provides general direction for the managers and supervisors of individual warehouse sites and typically reports to the top distribution executive.

THE WAREHOUSE MANAGER is responsible for the physical custody and accuracy of finished-goods and/or product inventory records at a location removed from the manufacturing and/or production facility. He or she reports to the field warehousing manager (finished goods/product).

THE CUSTOMER ORDER ENTRY AND PROCESSING MANAGER is responsible for receiving, entering, and processing of orders and order changes from customers. This person supervises the activities of order entry personnel whose responsibilities include direct communication with customers regarding the feasibility of shipping orders as requested.

THE DOMESTIC PURCHASING AGENT is responsible for the purchase of goods and/or services used by the manufacturing and/or production facility. He or she approves and qualifies vendors, authorizes purchase orders, supervises the activities of buyer/planners and expediters (purchasing), and usually reports to the purchasing executive.

THE SENIOR BUYER/PLANNER determines the quantity and order date for purchased materials needed to meet the MPS, selects and negotiates with approved vendors, and places purchase orders. This person may give guidance and direction to other buyer/planners. Normally 5 or more years of experience are needed. She or he reports to the purchasing agent or purchasing executive.

THE BUYER/PLANNER determines the quantity and order date for purchased materials needed to meet the MPS, negotiates with approved vendors, and places purchase orders. Normally 2 to 4 years of experience are needed. This person reports to the purchasing agent or purchasing executive.

THE ASSOCIATE BUYER/PLANNER, under direct supervision, assists in determining material needed to meet the MPS and assists in planning and placing purchase orders. This may follow up with vendors regarding order status. This is the entry-level buyer/planner position. This person reports to the purchasing agent or purchasing executive.

THE EXPEDITER (purchasing), a top-level specialist, with minimal direction, is responsible for resolving vendor-related problems with regard to specifications, timing, quality, quantity, and delivery. This person reports to the purchasing agent or purchasing executive.

THE INTERNATIONAL PURCHASING AGENT is responsible for the purchase of goods and/or services from foreign suppliers. This person approves and qualifies vendors, authorizes purchase orders, may supervise the activities of buyer/planners and expediters (purchasing), and reports to the purchasing executive.

THE MANAGER OF PURCHASING CONTRACT ADMINISTRATION is responsible for the review and administration of long-term and/or blanket purchase contracts. This person may supervise other purchasing contract administrators and reports to the purchasing executive.

THE PURCHASING CONTRACT ADMINISTRATOR reviews and administers one or more long-term and/or blanket purchase contracts. She or he reports to the manager of purchasing contract administration or to the purchasing executive.

REFERENCES

1. *Standard Job Titles and Descriptions for Materials Management Positions*, Portland, Oregon, chapter of APICS and A. S. Hansen, Inc., 1983.

BIBLIOGRAPHY

Approaches to MRP Education and Training, Auerbach Publishers, Penssauken, N.J., 1981.

Fogarty, D. W., and T. R. Hoffman: *Production and Inventory Management*. South-Western Publishing, Cincinnati, 1983.

"How Your Job Is Changing: Part Nine," *Purchasing*, Mar. 29, 1984, p. 47.

Plossl, George W.: *What We've Had and What's Ahead*, Proceedings of 21st Annual International Conference of APICS, Oct., 1978.

———— and O. W. Wight: *Production and Inventory Control: Principles and Techniques*. Prentice-Hall, Englewood Cliffs, N.J., 1967.

Powell, Cash, Jr.: *MRP System—MRP Organization*, Proceedings of 24th Annual International Conference of APICS, Oct., 1981.

Standard Job Titles and Descriptions for Materials Management Positions, Portland, Oregon, chapter of APICS and A. S. Hansen, Inc., 1983.

Testa, Nicholas M., Jr., CFPIM: *Career Growth in Production and Inventory Control,* Proceedings of 25th Annual International Conference of APICS, Oct., 1982.

Thierauf, Robert J., Robert C. Klekamp, and Daniel W. Geeding: *Management Principles and Practices,* Wiley, New York, 1977.

Wight, O. W.: *Production and Inventory Management in the Computer Age,* Cahners Books International, Boston, 1974.

CHAPTER 27

Performance Evaluation

Editor

GUS BERGER, CPIM, President, The Gus Berger Group, Inc., Anaheim, California

Contributors

SHARON B. ALLEN, M.A., Instructor, Rancho Santiago Community College, Santiago, California

DAVID W. BUKER, President, David W. Buker, Inc., Antioch, Illinois

DENNIS FISHER, CPIM, Senior Consultant, The Gus Berger Group, Inc., Anaheim, California

PAUL FUNK, CPIM, Director of Education, The Gus Berger Group, Inc., Anaheim, California

ELIYAHU M. GOLDRATT, Ph.D., Chairman, Creative Output, Milford, Connecticut

JAMES A. JACOBS, CPIM, Executive Vice President, The Gus Berger Group, Inc., Anaheim, California

MICHAEL J. STICKLER, CPIM, Vice President, David W. Buker, Inc., Antioch, Illinois

With the advent of unstable economies and declining profits, the need to improve productivity spawned a new era of interest in formal performance evaluation and measurement for individuals, departments, and corporations. This chapter offers guidance for evaluating and measuring performance in a significant number of manufacturing and/or distribution functions and in related activities. Performance evaluation and measurement techniques common to manual systems, manufacturing resource planning (MRP II), material-requirements planning (MRP), optimized production technology (OPT), zero inventory, and just-in-time (JIT) systems are presented. Readers are encouraged to look for "best fit" concepts as opposed to perfect solutions. The techniques of performance evaluation and measurement must relate directly to the specific user's situation.

Performance evaluation and measurement often fail not because of the measurement techniques, but because of the lack of a firm foundation for measurement. The company lacking strategic business planning, stable master schedules, good business practices, and timely, accurate communication will find the implementation of performance evaluation and measurement to be very difficult, with results often less than satisfactory. This chapter must be used not as a stand-alone guide but rather in conjunction with other chapters which describe in detail the foundation necessary for the successful application of performance evaluations and measurement.

PREREQUISITES

The prerequisites for the evaluation and measurement of performance to some predetermined expectation include

- Clearly defined statements of work
- Clearly defined time elements for performance
- Delegation of authority adequate to perform the task(s) to be measured
- Unrestricted access to any tools necessary to perform the task(s)
- Mutual agreement between the person(s) performing the task(s) and the person measuring the performance that the task is doable as stated.

RESPONSIBILITY AND ACCOUNTABILITY

It is management's responsibility to measure the performance of its direct personnel. Since the manager measures the employee's performance based on certain functions and activities, the employee must be given the authority to control those functions and activities. To hold someone accountable for an activity over which that person has insufficient control is perhaps the greatest mistake made in performance measurement. Typical examples of unrealistic evaluations include the measurement of the director of marketing's performance as a function of the sales-dollar volume when product quality is so poor that customers are reluctant to buy the product. Another example is the inventory control manager being held accountable for minimizing inventory while untrained executive management continually juggle the master schedule, thus producing levels of unused inventory beyond the control of the inventory control manager.

Perhaps the best definition of responsibility and authority for performance evaluation and measurement is provided within the guidelines of OPT, which defines the three basic tasks of performance measurements:

1. The evaluation of individual peformance in a manner resulting in the motivation of the work force

2. An evaluation of the overall assumptions used as a basis for performance measures, assumptions that are really an estimate of overall capabilities

3. An evaluation of the system as a whole, recognizing that performance measures are based on an estimate and that the overall performance of the system may require a restating of the original goals

The last two statements provide a missing link in the typical application of performance evaluation and measure. It is critical to recognize two things: (1) Performance measures are typically based on an estimate of capabilities, and an estimate is no better than the knowledge and experience of the individual developing the estimate. (2) The total system must be considered as a part of the performance evaluation and measurement process. Extremes in total system performance, either positive or negative, can seriously disrupt the assumptions on which the original performance measures were based.

Therefore, it is the responsibility of the evaluator not only to use past performance history but also to develop sound assumptions concerning future performance capabilities within the anticipated operating parameters. What may appear today as a reasonable set of objectives may, at the actual time of measurement, be distorted. This distortion may be caused by errors in the capability estimate or unexpected deviation in the operating system's performance.

REFERENCE BASES

Whether an individual or a department or a company is measured, there must be a reference base from which to compare future performance. The reference base must begin with the migration of the strategic business plan to the particular function or individual being measured. Historical performance, when available, should be used to moderate or temper anticipated performance based on the new strategic business plan. A typical reference base for the management of finished-goods inventory might include

- The last 1- or 2-year history including trends and seasonality
- The planned development of new products
- The current definitions of customer service
- Anticipated future definitions of customer service
- A comparison with industry inventory trends
- The position of current products in their life cycle

This list displays several of the total closed-loop system characteristics that are responsible for confusing the apparent simplicity of a task such as projecting the finished-goods inventory level. Although a half-dozen elements that complicate the projection of finished-goods inventory have been defined, it is easily possible to identify many more.

If reference bases were established for the measurement of the purchase price variance (PPV), a few of the factors to be considered would include

- Prior purchase price history
- National economic trends

- Local economic trends
- Product life-cycle influence on production run sizes
- Competitive product influence on production run sizes
- Anticipated new-customer influence on production run sizes
- Any specific changes in inventory management policies including changes in inventory management policies such as changing from order point to MRP, a movement from MRP to OPT, changing from MRP to the zero-inventory concept, and changes in financial management policies toward minimizing asset value or minimizing purchase-price variance

Understanding the stability of reference bases is critical in the management of performance evaluation and measurement. Any shift of direction in any related reference base, even well outside the responsibility and authority of the individual or department being measured, can produce a drastic shift in the expected results of the performance evaluation and measure.

CUSTOMER SERVICE LEVEL

A critical measure of any manufacturing or distribution company's performance is its customer service level. The customer service level describes the company's ability to deliver a product to the customer on schedule as promised. It is not a measure of any individual department such as sales or production control; rather, it measures company's performance as a whole within the closed-loop system. To measure customer service is to measure the effectiveness of the ability of the chief executive officer (CEO) to develop an integrated business system entity, featuring respect for others and mutual cooperation throughout. The equation for measuring *customer service* is

$$\left(\begin{array}{c} \text{Total units delivered} \\ \text{on time in a} \\ \text{particular period} \end{array} \div \begin{array}{c} \text{Total units scheduled} \\ \text{for delivery in} \\ \text{the same period} \end{array} \right) \times 100 = \_\_\_\_\_\ \%$$

Most companies target 90 to 95 percent customer service an an acceptable delivery performance objective. Failure to meet this target must not be looked at simply in terms of a manufacturing performance failure or production control performance failure without first evaluating the entire system. Key measurable departmental requirements or objectives for the successful attainment of customer service levels are listed by departments:

1. Material and production control
   a. Create and maintain total end-item product lead-time analysis including both purchased and fabricated assembled items.
   b. Convey lead-time information to the sales department in a timely manner.
   c. Maintain purchased-part delivery status.
   d. Maintain fabricated and assembled item open-order status.
   e. Follow up and expedite to ensure performance to purchasing and fabrication and/or assembly schedules.

Material and production control presents a difficult challenge for accurate performance evaluation and measurement. Since it is at the center of the closed-loop business process, apparent performance is distorted by almost every business system fluctuation.

2. Sales and marketing

   a. The sales and marketing staff must understand the significance of lead-time data provided by material and production control functions.

   b. Sales and marketing must respect lead times, with deviations from lead times agreed to in advance with the material and production control function. In case of scheduled overloads, sales and marketing must decide to use premium time and expedited costs or agree to change previously scheduled delivery dates to allow the rational utilization of critical or bottleneck resources.

   c. Sales and marketing is responsible for maintaining both short- and long-range sales forecasts.

   d. Sales and marketing is responsible for evaluating, obtaining, and conveying "acceptable marketplace lead time" information for key products.

   e. Sales and marketing is responsible for negotiating delivery dates on all items "in excess of forecasts" if coverage is not available.

The evaluation and measure of customer service are of critical importance to the company's well-being. It is the CEO's responsibility to ensure that the evaluation and measurement are performed on time and accurately. Rescheduled promised dates, if changed at the customer's request, should be treated as an original promised date. Otherwise, on-time delivery to a rescheduled date caused by the manufacturer should be treated in the measurement as a missed target commitment. If deliveries are promised free on board (FOB) to the customer's dock, performance must be measured to final delivery at the customer's dock.

PURCHASING SERVICE LEVELS

Purchasing presents many opportunities for performance measurement. As a vital "front-end" element of the material flow cycle, purchasing performance must be monitored for several key indicators including on-time delivery, purchase-part quality, and purchase price variances.

On-Time Delivery

The equation for measuring on-time delivery is

$$\left(\begin{array}{c}\text{Total purchase order} \\ \text{line items received} \\ \text{on time}\end{array} \div \begin{array}{c}\text{Total purchase order} \\ \text{line items received}\end{array}\right) \times 100 = \underline{\qquad}\%$$

The measurement of on-time delivery must be subjected to critical evaluation. This formula should not be used until purchase requisitions are analyzed for acceptable lead time. The formula for measuring purchase requisitions with acceptable lead time is

$$\left(\begin{array}{c}\text{Total purchase requisitions} \\ \text{received with acceptable} \\ \text{lead time}\end{array} \div \begin{array}{c}\text{Total purchase} \\ \text{requisitions received}\end{array}\right) \times 100 = \underline{\qquad}\%$$

Purchase-Parts Quality

The formula for measuring purchased-parts receipt quality is

$$\left(\begin{array}{c}\text{Total purchased} \\ \text{items accepted}\end{array} \div \begin{array}{c}\text{Total items} \\ \text{received}\end{array}\right) \times 100 = \underline{\hspace{1cm}} \%$$

The purchase-parts quality (PPQ) should be evaluated by vendor, defect classification, ABC classification, and buyer; and defect prevention programs should be developed and implemented based on the direction provided by the PPQ measurements.

Favorable Purchase Price Variance

The measure of purchase price variance (PPV) must be handled with caution, particularly during installation of any time-phased material planning system. Excessive emphasis on PPV may cause purchasing to buy in excess of the quantity required per time frame to obtain lower costs based on quantity ordered/delivered. The formula for PPV measurement is

$$\left(\begin{array}{c}\text{Total purchased} \\ \text{items with an} \\ \text{unfavorable PPV}\end{array} \div \begin{array}{c}\text{Total purchased} \\ \text{items}\end{array}\right) \times 100 = \underline{\hspace{1cm}} \%$$

SERVICE LEVELS OF PRODUCTION STORES

The measure of the service level of the production stores directly indicates the ability to provide raw material, fabricated parts, and subassemblies to production in support of the master schedule. Again, however, it must be used not as a stand-alone measurement of material and production control or any other individual department, but rather as an indicator of the total closed-loop system operation. It only becomes a measure of the material and production control planning capability when sales forecasts used to generate the long-range material plan convert to actual sold orders while still within adequate procurement and/or manufacturing lead times. The production and inventory control (PIC) planning processes, including MRP, are totally subject to master schedule stability and to the ability to schedule new sales production requirements within adequate lead-time constraints as defined by material and production control. The formula for measuring the service level of the production stores is

$$\left(\begin{array}{c}\text{Total line items} \\ \text{filled per scheduled} \\ \text{requirements}\end{array} \div \begin{array}{c}\text{Total line items} \\ \text{requested}\end{array}\right) \times 100 = \underline{\hspace{1cm}} \%$$

The problem of determining the customer service level is difficult to solve since it varies by industry, but the following example indicates the importance of a very high production store service level. A 95 percent service level indicates that 95 times out of 100 when a part is requested from the production stores, it is available for issue. Yet by applying a basic law of statistics, an attempt to pull a kit of six parts or an order of six items simultaneously from the 95 percent service-level production store produces the following likelihood of a complete parts issue:

$$95\% \times 95\% \times 95\% \times 95\% \times 95\% \times 95\% = 73\% \text{ service level}$$

As this example indicates, a performance measurement of the production stores service level is one more vital tool in the measurement of the total closed-loop system and should become a part of the weekly or monthly performance reports to executive management.

FIELD SERVICE AND SPARES SERVICE LEVELS

Although customers often rate the company's ability to provide replacement parts as equally important to delivering the original product on time, few companies apply performance measures to service parts replenishment equal to those applied to the delivery of the finished products. In fact, a service part is often "pushed back" in priority in favor of completing the "higher shipping dollar" end-item product. The extreme emphasis often placed on shipping dollars creates a misprioritization of resources supporting the spares and field service replenishment parts. The measurement of spares and field service replacement parts performance then becomes entangled with the internal system's ability to properly prioritize all production jobs. The formula for measuring field service and spares support stores inventory service level is

$$\left(\frac{\text{Total service part}}{\text{demands filled complete}} \div \frac{\text{Total service}}{\text{part demands}} \right) \times 100 = \underline{\hspace{1cm}} \%$$

It is obvious that the field service and spares replenishment service level measurement is complex and dependent on many items often considered unrelated. To measure field service and spares support parts performance requires an in-depth understanding of the closed-loop business system and all the related performing functions.

INVENTORY TURNOVER

Inventory turnover is a measure of the velocity of material flow through a manufacturing or distribution operation. The general formula is

$$\left(\frac{\text{Total material content}}{\text{of annual sales (\$)}} \div \frac{\text{Total of all inventories}}{\text{now on hand (\$)}} \right) = \text{inventory turns rate}$$

The inventory turns rate is easy to calculate but, in most companies, very difficult to analyze for cause and effect. The inventory turns rate is affected by more unrelated actions than almost any other measured element of company operations. Departments usually held accountable for inventory turns—production control, inventory control, material control—normally control less than 50 percent of the factors influencing the inventory level. The major controlling element for inventory turns is the master schedule.

Many companies attempt to compare their inventory turns performance to averages obtained from financial community publications. Although the averages may be quite accurate, it is unrealistic to measure a given company's turns rate to the printed averages without first understanding those items influencing the inventory turns rate. The single most critical item is the company's customer service objective. The difference in inventory turns rate created between "immediate service at any cost" and "balancing customer service against the cost to provide it" may exceed two or three to one.

An unstable master schedule with constant changes in production rates and quantities within lead times has a very serious impact on the inventory turns rate. Inventory turns are managed successfully only when they become a total company objective to manage both inventory turns and customer service as an integrated objective.

PRODUCTION PRODUCTIVITY

Probably the single most often measured operation in any company is the *production activity*. This includes measures of people productivity, machine productivity, and performance to budget. Although many companies fail to realize it, measuring the productivity of the production operation without having a thorough understanding of the operational environment might be likened to measuring the fuel economy of an automobile without regard to whether it was operating in the city or in the country. In fact, the measurement of production productivity in many cases contributes directly to the failure of time-phased production planning systems such as MRP. It is necessary to understand the philosophies of OPT, JIT production, and zero inventories to understand the problems created by current production performance measures. Typical production measurement techniques revolve on the accomplishment of previously calculated setup and run times usually based on optimum run size or lot quantities. The various lot-sizing techniques often result in production ignoring small work order/job order run quantities in favor of the larger orders that generate favorable production time variances. Because so much emphasis is placed on production productivity, the production manager must often violate policies supporting overall company inventory and customer service objectives in order to meet productivity objectives upon which jobs depend!

As the concepts of OPT, zero inventory, and JIT production management are embraced by the manufacturing community, it will become necessary to totally rethink the roles of the standards engineer, cost accountant, and those responsible for productivity measurement. The thrust of manufacturing control is moving from the measurement of elemental workplace performance to one of creating a smooth flow of small quantities of work through the production workplace.

Performance measures must change from an emphasis on compliance to individual operation time standards to an emphasis on the reduction of setup times, a flexibility of the work force, and the ability of the production function to produce a high-quality product by the specified completion date. Although we do not advocate the total elimination of operation time measurements, it becomes necessary to create a new performance measurement objective based on compliance to scheduled completion dates and quantities with a very high-quality product output.

Unless industry is willing to change the production evaluation and measurement concept as applied today, in favor of recognizing performance to operational objectives, it will be virtually impossible to implement the concepts of OPT, zero inventory, or JIT production.

ADMINISTRATIVE PRODUCTIVITY
(MANAGEMENT AND INDIRECT LABOR)

Overhead, general and administrative, and other indirect labor expenses are constant targets for cost reduction and are often used as a measurement of effectiveness for the directly responsible management. Unfortunately, in many cases, indirect labor levels are, in reality, a measurement of master schedule stability and executive management direction. As an example, the unstable master schedule and its "instantly created shortages" create requirements for additional material and production control personnel, purchasing personnel, receiving personnel, receiving inspection personnel, stores personnel, and supervisory manufacturing personnel to provide adequate support for a never-ending series of "fire drills."

Improperly designed or applied ABC inventory management criteria also create additional requirements for the same group of indirect personnel. An excessive amount of C-level inventory procurement creates additional demands on indirect labor resources and raises total operating costs substantially and out of proportion to the return on the inventory savings. With the exception of C-level inventory replenishment that competes for bottleneck resource capacity, procurement quantities should represent a substantial number of months' demand to avoid the "whiplashing" of indirect labor resources.

Management by objectives (MBO) is one of the more common techniques for evaluating and measuring white-collar personnel. The prerequisites mentioned earlier are critical to this concept. MBO seeks to orient the management team to results rather than "process" maintenance. There is a strong tendency among managers to overemphasize procedures and methods—simply because methods are easier to observe and control. Task accomplishment and performance review are more difficult. The MBO approach encourages subordinates to set their own goals, to test their own performance, and to be stimulated by expected payoffs for results, not just for "process" compliance. Care must be taken to integrate major goals and subgoals into a logically developed overall company program. If this is not accomplished, the results cannot be measured clearly and the feedback to the employee may even lessen his or her motivation.

Assumptions of MBO

The underlying assumptions of MBO must be addressed in order to properly obtain the true motivational effects available from the use of this technique. First, the tendency in developing MBO tasks and objectives is to view the employees as people to be manipulated since they are not being given additional ownership in the plans that they are expected to support. Second, the interdependency of individuals in the larger group is at least as important as their own capabilities; thus both objectives and methods of appraisals must be developed within the group. The basic reason for having an organization is to achieve more as a group than each member could accomplish alone. Both horizontal and vertical goal formulations for peers and superior-subordinate relationships create a more integrated network than the typical vertical structure commonly applied in MBO applications. Finally, the tools and skills used for performance appraisals are generally hierarchical. This top-down orientation is generally a communications inhibiter. The superior is responsible for the performance of the subordinate; in fact, the single most important factor often affecting an employee's performance is his or her supervisor. Management by objectives tends to generate competition and conflicts based on these three assumptions. The closed-loop concept of performance appraisal is most effective. Both superior and subordinate should together appraise their performances to mutual and individual goals. The subordinate may evaluate the superior on the basis of how well the superior was able to help in accomplishing the job.

The key to using the MBO concepts effectively is to carefully analyze the expected from the appraisal interviews. Knowledge gained from these interviews is critical to the periodic reassessment of the overall goals. Table 27.1 is an example of

TABLE 27.1 Performance Review Worksheet for Interviewee

Company Objectives: List those objectives that comply with the definitions of assumptions of MBO.

- *Note:* The reviewer must carefully explore the objectives with the interviewee to determine whether they agree with management's objectives.

Objectives for the Review Cycle: List previously determined objectives for this review time interval. Include all items in sufficient detail to allow effective analysis.

Successes: List all activities that you perceive as successes since the last review cycle.

- *Note:* The reviewer should also create a list of items.

Shortcomings: List all activities in which you perceive that you may not have lived up to your own, your superior's, or your peer's expectations.

- *Note:* The reviewer should also create a list of items but allow the interviewees to identify specific items. A joint effort should be conducted to keep these items to specific details.

Problems: List any items which you feel have kept you from doing your job as originally defined. These may include tools, policies, procedures, training, peers, etc.

- *Note:* The reviewer may encounter a tendency to blame people or "things." Attention to detail in support of generalities is essential for a clear definition of the problems that may be inhibiting the employee's performance to objectives.

Personal Objectives: List any personal actions that you may take that will help you achieve those special goals in your life.

Refined Objectives for Next Review Cycle: List the objectives that you perceive as appropriate for the next review cycle. Objectives should be aggressive, doable, and within the framework of the company's objectives.

- *Note:* The reviewer must encourage the attainment of personal goals which tend in the direction of the company's goals. Those goals not in a reasonably parallel direction with the company's may require further inquiry to determine whether the interviewee is moving away from the company's established direction.

---

an easy-to-apply review sheet. It is filled out by the individual being reviewed and includes techniques which help to resolve the biases typically associated with the appraisal interviews.

INFORMATION SYSTEMS PRODUCTIVITY

The past few years have created a rapid evolution in manufacturing systems application software. With system emphasis shifting from the keypunch environments to on-line, real-time, interactive concepts, it has become mandatory that hardware and software function correctly—virtually 100 percent of the workday. To control any system of this magnitude, certain performance measurements must be made. Information systems performance evaluation and measure are often difficult to develop and understand; however, they are as important as the formal performance measurements used to manage the running of the business. To understand more easily information systems performance evaluation and measurement, the analysis is divided into two areas, user measurements and technical measurements.

1. *User evaluation and measurement of information systems.* The user, as defined for this section, includes the employees who enter data and employees who receive printed reports or information on a video display terminal or cathode-ray tube (CRT). Users are concerned with several basic performance measurements:

   a. Up time—the time the system is available for use. The formula is

   $$\left(\begin{array}{c} \text{Actual time} \\ \text{available} \end{array} \div \begin{array}{c} \text{Scheduled time} \\ \text{available} \end{array} \right) \times 100 = \underline{\hspace{2cm}} \% \, \text{uptime}$$

   b. Response time—the time it takes the system to respond to a CRT inquiry. Depending on the processing necessary to compile the needed information, the response time could range from virtually instantaneous to several minutes. The measurement most commonly used involves selecting several transactions and inquiries, establishing a standard or expected response time for each, and then measuring these activities several times daily. The measurement should be taken during both low and peak load times. Generally, accepted response time is less than 10 seconds for video access, data-entry response, or a simple CRT inquiry. Sorted information or complex inquiries and reports may take a substantially longer time.

   c. Processing accuracy—correct report of inquiry responses. This evaluation is difficult to measure because of the levels of program complexity and accuracy of furnished data. Data must be carefully audited during the pilot-test phase and sampled on a periodic ongoing basis.

2. *Technical measurements of information systems.* Technical measurements refer to an area normally invisible to the end user. With the development of complex, integrated, on-line, real-time systems, the need to measure the performance of the newest asset, information processing, has become critical. Areas to evaluate include

   a. *Processing time or input-output (I/O) time.* I/O time is system time required to write and execute instructions from one system device to another [i.e., from the CRT inquiry to the computer's central processing unit (CPU), to the actual display of the system's response]. This measurement can provide insight regarding data base efficiency, file structure efficiency, and the application software's efficiency with the hardware/software system combination.

b. *System load test.*   The system load test indicates what percentage of the time the CPU is being used to actually process information. A high-CPU-use load factor is often an early warning of future system overload conditions.

c. *Application software.*   Application software is defined as user modules such as MRP, purchasing, or shop floor control. Performance measures should be established by using a standard to which a given application is compared. Measurement criteria include file size and design, amount of memory and disk space required, and user friendliness.

d. *Information system management.*   A set of performance targets should be established for the information system manager. Measurement criteria include system uptime, response time, and processing accuracy so that one can ensure the management information system (MIS) function supports the needs of the end user.

e. *Information systems cost to sales ratio.*   Another factor used to evaluate information systems is the ratio of the total cost of the information system services to total company sales. This is an exceptionally misleading measure, unless it can be compared to a group of virtually identical companies with virtually identical sales volumes, customer service objectives, numbers of parts and finished goods, and similar computer hardware and software report generators. The hardware-software combinations, with their unique support staff requirements, may create a valid total operating cost differential in excess of 500 percent!

In summary, it is necessary to measure the information system function, identifying deficiencies, understanding their cause, and developing the means to correct the problems. As business becomes more dependent on information system processing, performance evaluation and measure must be in place to ensure timely system response to company needs.

CONCLUSIONS

Performance evaluation and measurement must be performed by knowledgeable, qualified individuals with a technical understanding of what is to be measured, valid assumptions of capabilities, and valid assumptions of the closed-loop system behavior during the measurement interval. Too often, performance evaluation and measurement prove to be an evaluation of the evaluator's capabilities rather than of those of the performer. The performer becomes the victim of the evaluator's level of competency!

Properly applied, performance evaluation and measurement become a tool for motivation as well as a technique for measurement. The evaluator, in establishing the basis for performance measurement, has both technical and ethical responsibilities to be knowledgeable in the areas to be evaluated. The evaluator must be in a position to predict future closed-loop system deviations from normal occurrences, making provision for modification to the measures in case of substantial change in the assumptions. It is also a responsibility of the evaluator, in conjunction with the individual or entity to be evaluated, to achieve agreement on the doability of objectives in both the time frame and actions required to achieve the objective of the performance evaluation and measurements.

Although many companies restrict performance evaluation to a semiannual or annual occurrence, it is important that more periodic, informal discussions be held to review progress toward objectives. Informal progress reviews assist those evaluated in achieving their objectives, thus acting as a motivator, a reward, and insurance to avoid a tragic surprise at the end of a formal evaluation period.

BIBLIOGRAPHY

Alter, Stewart: "One Step at a Time," *Computer Decisions*, June 15, 1984, pp. 14–24.

Barnett, E. M., and E. L. Barnett: *Making Your Working Styles More Effective*, Proceedings of the 26th Annual Conference, American Production and Inventory Control Society, APICS, New Orleans, 1983.

Bushnell, Jon L.: *Improving Manufacturing Performance through Human Resources Accounting and Management*, Proceedings of the 26th Annual Conference, APICS, New Orleans, 1983.

Crow, Rufus C., Jr.: *Bottom-Line Results Using Performance Management*, Proceedings of the 26th Annual Conference, APICS, New Orleans, 1983.

Edson, Norris W.: *Measuring MRP System Effectiveness*, Proceedings of the 24th Annual Conference, APICS, Boston, 1981.

Edwards, J. Nicholas: *Measuring the Effectiveness of P&IC*, Proceedings of the 24th Annual Conference, APICS, Boston, 1981.

Gozzo, Michael, and Robert E. Olson: *Balancing the Three-Legged Stool*, Proceedings of the 24th Annual Conference, APICS, Boston, 1981.

Halverson, Robert A.: *Survival Strategies for Managing in a Changing Environment*, Proceedings of the 24th Annual Conference, APICS, Boston, 1981.

Jacobs, James A.: *Profitable Business Disciplines, or How to Avoid the MRP Failure Loop*, Proceedings of the 26th Annual Conference, APICS, New Orleans, 1983.

Janson, Robert L.: *Key Indicators for Production and Inventory Control*, Proceedings of the 24th Annual Conference, APICS, Boston, 1981.

Kaiser, Rich: *Manufacturing and Marketing—Resolving the Conflict*, Proceedings of the 24th Annual Conference, APICS, Boston, 1981.

Ling, Richard C.: *Marketing and Manufacturing—Being More Competitive Together*, Proceedings of the 24th Annual Conference, APICS, Boston, 1981.

McGuire, Kenneth J.: *Impressions from Our Most Worthy Competitor*, Proceedings of the 26th Annual Conference, APICS, New Orleans, 1983.

Riggs, James L.: *Production Systems: Planning, Analysis and Control*, Wiley, New York, 1976.

Stickler, M. J.: *Performance Measurements for Productive Management*, Proceedings of the 26th Annual Conference, APICS, New Orleans, 1983.

Tucker, S.: *Production Standards for Profit Planning*, Van Nostrand Reinhold, New York, 1982.

———: *Handbook of Business Formulas and Controls*, McGraw-Hill, New York, 1979.

Techniques and Models

28

Bar Coding

Editor

EUGENE F. BAKER, CMC, E. F. Baker & Associates, Inc., North-brook, Illinois

From the initial data processing systems before World War II to the present, there has been an evolution of better and faster data entry systems. Four major systems—optical character recognition (OCR), magnetic-strip coding, voice coding, and bar codes—have competed for top position.

Optical character reading has been used in retail businesses such as Sears. One version of OCR with magnetic ink is used in the Federal Reserve and bank clearing-house operations. Another version, embossed credit cards, is used by credit card and oil companies. The major advantage of OCR is that the characters are easily read, but the major disadvantage is that they are fragile and easily damaged.

Magnetic-stripe coding, as used on the back of bank credit cards, has the advantage that it can be densely packed with information. The code cannot be read without being processed, which is a major disadvantage. At one time IBM applied the magnetic stripe to the back of unit-record cards for some applications. They have abandoned magnetic stripes in favor of bar codes.

Voice-entry systems have not proved satisfactory because the technology is not well enough developed to accommodate the differences in voices. Although it would be more convenient for the operator not to punch keys or scan with a wand, this method is still subject to many of the human errors of omission and word transposition.

Although the data entry systems described have proved satisfactory for some applications, they are not suitable for factory applications. The bar code has the advantage of durability because it can be read even if it is partially damaged. There is redundancy because of the bar code's height. The accuracy is excellent because of built-in self-checking features. Its major disadvantage is that it must be interpreted before it is readable. This difficulty is overcome by printing the information adjacent to the code. Bar codes are used for identifying anything that can have a letter, number, or alphanumeric designator assigned to it.

Bar codes used for identifying objects are a configuration of dark and light spaces, preferably black and white, that represent numerals, letters, and symbols (Fig. 28.1). Various light sources are used to determine the presence or absence of a black or white bar. There are different methods of reading codes, but basically all direct a light beam on the bar code which is either absorbed or reflected to a sensor in the light source instrument. The white areas reflect the light, and the black bars absorb the light. It is this detection of the absorbing and reflecting surfaces which constitutes the signals which are in turn interpreted as a number or letter. For this reason, the contrast between the dark and light areas is very important.

The bar-code readers either are in a fixed location or are movable, such as a wand (Fig. 28.2), which is a pencil-like device that is passed across the bar code. The basic sequence in using the bar code, shown in Fig. 28.3, consists of applying the code, reading the code, processing the code in a computer, and storing the data for use or output reports or for mechanical or electrical machine instructions.

Probably nothing has come on the production and inventory control (PIC) scene as rapidly and with such momentum as bar coding. In fact, the bar-coding equipment and related technology have been advancing at a faster pace than the development of microcomputers and personal computers. Since bar-coding improvements are increasing almost geometrically, it is difficult to predict the state of the art a few years from now. However, certain fundamentals in bar coding and OCR will guide the hardware and software developments for many years to come. Therefore, in this chapter, particular attention is paid to the basic functional requirements of bar coding and the available equipment which, no doubt, will be greatly enhanced in years to come. A considerable part of the discussion dwells on the application of bar coding, not only to provide information on how to use it but also to serve as a catalyst for individuals processing applications for specific uses. Remember that every system must be designed for the individual company's application despite the fact that software may be purchased to perform the operations. To meet industrial requirements, most computer software has been modified as much as 50 percent over the years. Similar experiences can be expected with computer software for the bar-code systems.

Bar coding will not cure existing systems ills. If the system is presently producing the wrong information, bar coding will not improve it, but will merely produce it faster. To change this, basic system improvements should be made prior to the installation of a bar-coding system.

The advent of bar coding has made it necessary to rethink the fundamental systems and learn what can be accomplished at a reasonable cost. Therefore, an analysis of the individual and integrated systems should be made before one dives into the application and selection of bar-coding equipment and software. With these precautions in mind, bar coding, OCR, and magnetic stripes are discussed.

MANAGEMENT CONTROLS AND THE CHANGING SCENE

In recent years, there have been major changes in both the data collection equipment and systems used in the production environment. Consequently, many pro-

Possible trace
of a scanning
beam through the
symbol

FIG. 28.1   Typical bar-code symbol.

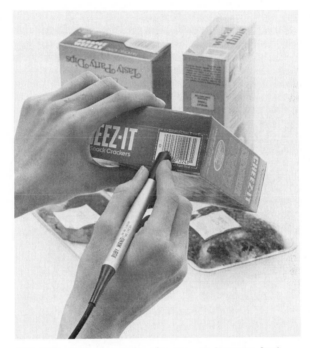

FIG. 28.2   Bar-code wand reader. *(Source: Intermec, Inc.)*

duction workers are performing semiclerical operations in various manufacturing
and warehousing environments. A few of the key changes are worth considering.

   Considerable effort has been made to reduce clerical functions on the shop floor,
particularly those performed by timekeepers and shop clerks. To do this, data
retrieval equipment of various types has been placed in the shop for simple tasks
such as timekeeping, job tracking, inventory control, and such sophisticated procedures as reject analysis, rework instructions, job costing, and indirect cost accumulation. This action has required employees with jobs not normally requiring clerical
skills to perform semiclerical operations. Consequently the input speed has increased, but the accuracy of the data input to the computer has decreased because it
is neither properly edited nor properly entered.

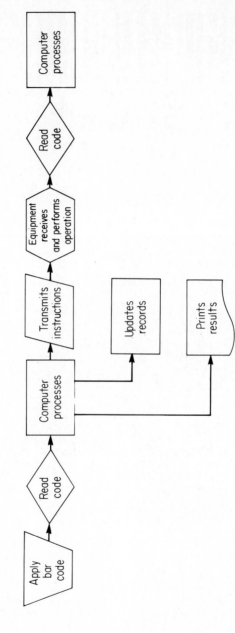

FIG. 28.3 Basic use of bar codes. (*Source: E. F. Baker & Associates, Inc.*)

The computer terminal with its cathode-ray tube (CRT) is being used by the operating personnel of many production processes, warehouses, and shipping and receiving departments. The worker is often not skilled in using the computer terminal and consequently makes entry errors. The data content is no better than would be obtained if it had been entered on handwritten documents.

The minicomputer has become a major tool in the production and inventory management environment of many companies. The microcomputer and personal computers are also moving into these areas rapidly. Again the same speed and accuracy problems as previously mentioned exist. Nonclerical workers are inaccurately performing semiclerical duties at a comparatively slow speed.

Foreign competition, particularly the Japanese, is forcing the adoption of the just-in-time (JIT) system to meet manufacturing and cost-reduction requirements. The Japanese-style Kanban system is not adaptable to most domestic companies with their computerized operations that place a high priority on rapid and accurate data input requirements from on-line systems operating in the real-time mode for scheduling, order releases, order tracking, and inventory transacting.

Over half of the domestic production is in small or medium companies making a wide variety of products in small quantities. For these companies to become more efficient and meet the ever-growing foreign competition, flexible manufacturing management systems must be introduced so that small quantities can be produced as efficiently as mass-produced items. Flexible manufacturing and JIT inventory control require efficient, rapid, and accurate data input into the date processing system if information is to be available instantly for management decisions and control.

The introduction of robots and more flexible automation systems has made a sizable impact on production operations. These improvements have also brought with them some new requirements and problems. Approximately 40 percent of the robots must be scheduled and given instructions. If the robots are the variable-use type, the individual operations to be performed must be identified through some input procedure.

Numeric control (NC) processes and their materials-handling systems frequently require the same information as needed for other materials-handling and transfer systems. The items must be easily identified by bar codes or other methods to determine what action or process is to be performed. In addition, instructions must be included with appropriate lead times in the routing in the same manner and sequence as for any operation. The materials-handling and transfer operations are frequently loaded in the capacity plan in the same manner as operations for individual fabrication machines or processing equipment.

To reduce costs, many U.S. companies have resorted to setting up manufacturing operations outside the continental limits of the United States. The integration of the activities of these various remote sites with those within the continental United States has become a problem. This is especially true if parts, components, and subassemblies are shipped to the United States for final assembly. The two major problems experienced in this type of operation are communicating instructions and maintaining the appropriate inventory. Many inherent cost advantages from an offshore operation are being partially lost because of mistakes that result from a lack of communication and understanding. Excess inventory, which is caused by lack of information, is a problem. Information about shipments, their location, and the expected date of arrival is often lacking or inaccurate. Consequently, inventory investments may increase as much as 50 percent. Improved integration, reliability, and speed of communication must be achieved if high productivity with minimum inventory investment is to be attained.

In 1982 the Department of Defense (DOD) made it mandatory that all vendors' shipments conform to Military Standards 129H and 1189 for bar-code labeling. In effect, this order says that everything that is sold and shipped to the DOD must carry the appropriate identification or part number in bar code or, in certain cases, OCR, which can be deleted in the future. In addition, the General Services Administration (GSA) has incorporated a requirement in their regulations that all items purchased by them have a bar code. The GSA requirements may have a greater effect on the manufacturer than the DOD requirements since the GSA procures a variety of common products ranging from rubber bands and paper clips to office furniture. The National Aeronautics and Space Agency (NASA) will also be using bar coding because a considerable amount of its procurement is performed by the Air Force. For example, the space shuttle program has included bar coding in its procurement procedure. Studies are underway in many other agencies such as Customs, Immigration, the Food and Drug Administration, the Justice Department, the Agriculture Department, and the Treasury Department, to determine the feasibility of applying bar coding.

Real-time computer systems are firmly in place and can now be cost-justified. Their expansion in the future will be extensive and will play a major role in the factory of the future. Real-time computer systems will require rapid and accurate identification of products. Bar coding can help minimize the work-in-process inventory and reduce the lead-time investment.

ADVANTAGES OF BAR CODES FOR DATA ENTRY

To operate efficiently, all production systems must have accurate data. Otherwise the system is of little value and can cause major planning and control decision errors. Integrity of the data must exist in original data, such as engineering specifications, bills of materials, routings, costs, etc. It must also exist in the information fed into the system on a continuing basis as a result of activities which have been planned or accomplished. Unreliable data cause the users to lose confidence in the system and start private "bottom drawer" systems to meet individual needs.

Information entered into the system by people is subject to transposition and omission of individual digits. The more digits, the greater the impact of transposition errors.

An accounting firm's study has found that once an entry number becomes longer than eight digits, the error rate goes up significantly, in fact, almost geometrically. A comparision of the accuracy of various methods follows. Data recording by hand depends on the individual's background, experience, and aptitude and is subject to transpositions and long-number errors. The error rate for operators familiar with making keyboard entries is approximately 4 errors per 1000 entry strokes. Magnetic-character and OCR label-reading tests have shown that approximately 1 character error occurs out of every 10,000 characters scanned. This figure is based on actual characters accepted by the reading device, not on the number of passes made over a label in order to get a satisfactory reading. Magnetic-stripe reading tests have shown a high accuracy equivalent to that of bar coding. The problem is to obtain correct information on the first reading or any information at all when it is used in the production environment.

The particular density of the bar code and the particular code being read will cause some variation in the accuracy of bar-code reading. However, one test on commercial-quality labels, using code 39, showed that the error rate was approximately 1 for every 3,379,000 scans. A more recent study reported 1 error per 10,000,000 scans.

Just about anyone can be taught to pass a bar-code reading wand across a label or use one of the other types of scanners. In fact, in some geographical areas, U.S. companies have incorporated bar coding in the manufacturing operation for the express purpose of overcoming the language barrier. Bar-code wanding by an individual is at least twice as fast as that of a trained keypunch operator, approximately four digits per second. Automated bar-code scanners, such as lasers, scan at a considerably higher rate. Items on a moving conveyor belt can be scanned at a rate of 400 to 600 feet per minute. The OCR scanning rate is slower than scanning the bar code but may be up to 50 percent faster than entering data by the keystroke method.

The ever-increasing volume of data entered to record the events for tracking production on the shop floor makes it imperative that a real-time system have a method of rapid data entry. Terminals for making such entries are so expensive that companies can afford only one for every one, two, three, or even four people. However, it is important that the entries be made as rapidly as possible so that the equipment can be shared and workers do not have to stand in line. The newer bar-coding equipment allows inexpensive terminals to have satellite wand readers which are available to employees at their workplace.

For managers to obtain the proper information for instructions and answers today, a common data base is required which is updated with fast, accurate, and timely entries for all events in the integrated production system. Without that, a current, balanced, up-to-date picture of production is not available to give proper instructions to perform operations or to issue requisitions for tooling, materials, and parts. Without correct information, orders would be given, only to be changed later because some component in the production plan was not available.

Computers are frequently used on the modern shop floor for running simulations of the activities to determine which course of action is best at a particular moment. Such capability is required on the shop floor so that, given the actual factory conditions, the best possible decisions can be made to optimize the use of the plant resources. This is not possible if the shop data for the simulation process are not current, and bar codes are one way of obtaining current data.

Shortening the lead time, with the resulting reduction of work-in-process inventory, is one of the major requirements for improving the productivity of the manufacturing operations. To accomplish this, detailed information must be entered frequently into the system, so that supervisory and management personnel can ensure the proper flow of orders through the plant by accurately tracking positions for continuous processing with minimum queues.

The JIT and zero-inventory practices depend on information for planning; so with proper control all the production factors, materials, parts, and labor come together at the proper location and time. No stockpiling of parts and materials at an operation or assembly point is envisioned in JIT systems. Rather they depend on computer information for synchronizing all the activities leading to the actual production. To do this, accurate, frequent, and timely information, which can be derived from bar codes, is a must for the system.

The flexible manufacturing management system needs to know the manufacturing position at any time, to enable quick production changes and remedy breakdowns. It requires the ability to make a quick run-through of components needed for a particular job to determine availability. It also includes a routing simulation capability to determine which particular method should be used based on the quantity to be produced given the present load in the plant. In addition, a certain amount of shift overlapping occurs in flexible manufacturing systems. This requires timely information at every moment for planning the various operations and adjusting the schedule for the overtime required to have a flexible capacity capability.

The cost of data collection contributes to the cost of the product and the reduction of profits. Frequently shop clerks, who contribute to the overhead, have been eliminated by installing more efficient data collection systems. However, having direct labor operators perform clerical tasks can be very costly because of their ineptness and lack of desire to keep accurate records. Wand scanning of bar codes requires minimal operator training and can reduce the time required for direct labor operators to perform clerical duties. If automatic scanning can be used, no human operator is required at all. Another advantage is that more data can be accumulated at little cost, which can thus improve the productivity. With a fully integrated data collection system, frequently the shop clerical function can be eliminated with an improvement in data accuracy.

Productivity can be increased if workers do not have to wait in line to record their operations while tools, parts, etc., are recorded and delivered. These costs can be reduced by the use of modern data entry equipment such as bar coding.

Communication costs from using bar-coding or similar equipment depend on the distance and type of equipment required. Bar-code signals can be transmitted over standard telephone lines if a modem is used and directly over digital lines in many areas. In some cases today bar coding is transmitted by radio through the proper interface equipment. Communication is not normally a major cost factor in bar-coding equipment.

DEVELOPMENT OF BAR-CODE TECHNIQUES

As far as is known, bar coding is a post-World War II development and did not come from any wartime research or system. In 1949 a patent for a circular bar code was filed by New Jersey Woodland et al. That appears to be the first recorded activity in this direction. In 1960 the color coding for railroad freight cars was developed by Sylvania Manufacturing Company and was operable for many years. Its primary problem was not with the system's operation, but rather the railroad's maintenance of clean, readable bars on the freight cars.

About this same time a group considered and made some initial tests using black dots instead of punched holes in paper tape for optical scanning. This development never became commercially feasible and was dropped.

The advent of the supermarkets, with their large sales volume, caused that industry to investigate a means of cutting down the workload at the checkout counter, in shelf stocking, and in the stockroom areas. In 1970 a committee was formed by the supermarket industry in the United States for the express purpose of developing a universal product code. As a result of this investigation, the universal product code (UPC) symbol was adopted as an industry standard in 1973. In 1971 the Plessey code was developed in Europe and became widely used in the European libraries. In 1972 the CODABAR patent application was made. The code was basically an interleaved two-of-five system. The full alphanumeric capability appeared in 1974 in the form of the *three-of-nine code*, also known as *code 39*. This particular coding symbology remains one of the major formats and is becoming more widely used. In 1982 code 39 became the standard for the Department of Defense. In 1977 CODABAR was adopted as the American Blood Commission's standard, and it continues to be used.

In 1981 the Automated Identification Manufacturers (AIM) and American National Standards Institute (ANSI II) draft standards were released, and many codes, including interleaved two-of-five and code 39, meet these standards. Both codes became official standards in 1984.

Several new standards have been developed recently, such as code 93 and code 128, but they appear to have limited usage. However, their format is such that they can sometimes be read with code 39 equipment. Although many other codes have been developed during the last 10 to 15 years, they are not in wide use and were primarily beneficial in the development of new codes that more nearly met the user's specific requirements.

BAR-CODING TERMS

As in any technical field, there are unique terms which must be mastered. The following are required for any one working with bar codes:

ACTION NUMBER. The bar-coded number that describes what happened to a base number, for example, operations completed, employee placed on direct labor, or inspection information.

BAR-CODE SYMBOL. A graphic (printed or photographically reproduced) code composed of parallel bars and spaces of various widths as illustrated previously.

BASE NUMBER. The bar-coded number such as a part number or employee number to which action, location, or results are applied.

BIDIRECTIONAL CODE. A code format which permits a right-to-left or left-to-right reading.

CHARACTER SET (CODE CAPACITY). Those characters available for encoding within the bar code. For example, code 39 has a character set of 10 digits, 26 letters of the alphabet, 7 symbols, and start/stop signals.

CHECK DIGIT. A character included within a code used for error detection.

CODE DENSITY. Number of characters per inch permitted by the code specifications.

CONTINUOUS CODE. In a continuous code the intercharacter space between bars is part of the code.

CONTRAST AND BAR DEFINITION. Since bar-code reading is based on the absorption and reflection of light, it is important that there be a distinct contrast between the dark, absorbed-light areas and the white, reflective areas. The definition of the printed bar is important and is the key element in how dense a code is printed as well as reading accuracy. Note that the lower the intensity of the printed code, the lower the definition quality. The key to code definition is the straightness of the bar edges and the darkness and consistency of the color.

DENSITY. This term, as used in bar coding, refers to how close the individual bars are to each other, which in turn determines how many characters can be recorded in a prescribed space. The degree of the density obtained depends on the method of printing the bar code and the type of code being used. Scanning equipment for dense codes is usually expensive, and wand scanning is not suitable. Some characteristics and recommendations for the sizes of codes are shown in Fig. 28.4

DEPTH OF FIELD. This is the maximum distance the label may be from the light source and still have the entire label within the light until it can be scanned.

DISCRETE CODE. The intercharacter space is not part of the code and may be allowed to vary freely.

FIRST-READ RATE. The number of correct reads divided by the number of attempted reads.

FOCAL POINT. This is the ideal distance at which the system is placed to read the bar code. Generally the label can be read some distance farther away and closer than this point.

FIG. 28.4 Bar-code characteristics and recommendations. (*Courtesy: Bar Code Symbology.*)

INFORMATION NUMBER. The bar-coded number that provides information about the base or action number, for example, location and time.

INTERCHARACTER GAP. The space between the last element of one character and the first element of the adjacent character of a discrete bar-code symbol.

MENU. A group of bar codes placed together and read consecutively. Each bar code can be for a different application such as a part number or customer order number. The bar codes may be applied in a number of ways, such as a preprinted card or as a series of labels.

MESSAGE LENGTH. The number of characters contained in a single encoded message.

NONREAD. Absence of data output after the scanning of the code owing to either an operator error, such as wanding too slowly or not holding the wand tip in contact through the entire message, or a defect in the code's printing.

OVERHEAD. The fixed amount of a bar-code message consumed by the start/stop and message-checking character(s). For example, code 11 requires a start/stop and 2 check digits, or 4 characters of overhead. Thus a 3-digit message requires 7 digits of space; a 20-digit message requires 24 digits of space. The primary purpose of the overhead is to make it possible to read codes in either direction, to provide a reading check mechanism to improve reliability, and to provide special instructions either to the scanning equipment or to the computer receiving the signal.

OPTICAL THROW. This term refers to the distance over which the light source is required to transmit an effective beam.

PITCH. This term is used to determine the degree of permissible tilt of the label away from the ideal position, in the vertical plane. It can generally be as much as 45 degrees away from the ideal reading position.

PREAMBLE. A code fixed to a specific scanning device to identify the unit. The scanning device may be associated with a department, work center, or particular activity. An application program entry can change the code.

PRINT CONTRAST. The comparison between reflectance of the bars versus the background. Specifically, the print contrast signal (PSC) is

$$PCS = \frac{100\%(\text{Background reflectance} - \text{Bar reflectance})}{\text{Background reflectance}}$$

QUIET AREA. This is the blank area on the left and the right end of the code, as shown in Fig. 28.4 just before the start and after the stop symbol bars. These white areas are necessary to adjust and inform the scanning equipment that it is starting and stopping a new read.

RESOLUTION. The dimension of the smallest code element that can be printed by a bar-code printer or identified by a scanner.

SELF-CHECKING ALGORITHM. Some codes contain a self-checking algorithm to ensure that there has been a proper reading of all the characters. This is usually represented by a series of bars forming a particular digit which may or may not be printed out for reading. This is also considered a part of the overhead.

SELF-CHECKING BAR CODE. A bar code that uses an algorithm which checks each character so that errors can occur only if two or more independent printing defects appear within a single character.

SELF-CLOCKING CODE. A self-clocking code is designed for reading with a single-aperture reader over a range of velocities and usually has a reasonable allowance for changes in velocity after the reading has commenced.

SKEW. This term describes how far the label can be turned in the horizontal plane away from being at a direct right angle to the light source. Usually the label can be turned as much as 45 degrees and still obtain a perfect read.

SPACE. The lighter element of a bar code.

START AND STOP CODES. Start and stop codes are used at the beginning and end of each bar-code message to provide initial timing references and direction of read information to the decoding logic. The start code is a series of narrow and wide bars at the left side, or beginning printed part, of the label; the stop code is a series of narrow and wide bars at the very end, or right-hand edge, of the bar code indicating the end of the sequence of characters.

UNIT. The narrowest bar or space in the code. Wider bars or spaces are usually specified as multiples of one unit.

BAR CODES USED IN INDUSTRY

The following discussion will familiarize the reader with some of the codes that have been developed.

Two-of-Five and Interleaved Two-of-Five Codes

These two codes were the first used to any great extent in industry. The basic characteristic, and the reason for their names, is that two out of every five bars are wide regardless of whether they are black or white. The original code was made up of five black bars of which two were wide. In all the various configurations, the numbers are expressed by a binary system.

In the original code, the spaces between the bars were the same regardless of whether they were between two wide bars, two narrow bars, or a combination of the two. Later it was decided to use the spaces between the dark bars to represent additional numerals, and thus it became the *interleaved two-of-five code*. In this system the white spaces are of the same width as wide and narrow bars and are placed in the same sequence for developing the particular normal and binary code. In reading a sequence of numbers (Fig. 28.5), the first or odd number is represented by the black bars, and the second position or even number is represented by the white bars. This method is continued throughout the entire coding sequence. This coding method permits information to be packed densely in a particular bar-code ratio, but the limitation is that it is confined strictly to numeric coding and a few special characters.

UPC and EAN Codes

The UPC, the *European article number* (EAN) *code*, and several others used in other countries were developed primarily for the fast checkout systems of the supermarket. The UPC symbol is actually two bar codes, one on the left and the other on the right. The five numerals on the left side are assigned to a specific manufacturer while the five characters on the right side are assigned to a generic product such as a food name. Start and stop symbols are in addition to these codes. How these symbols are formed is somewhat involved, and it is not necessary for the average user to understand them since all codes are assigned by the UPC Committee, Dayton, Ohio. There are different versions of the code, each developed to meet a specific need. For example, more recently an *add-on code* has been used by publishing companies for their own control situation which could not be included in the original UPC format. Abbreviated UPC formats composed of just the right-hand side of the full code have been installed for some applications. The UPC has been successful in supermarkets and other retail establishments, but its use is primarily limited to computerized checkout, pricing procedures, and the identification and control of inventory items.

Code 39, or Three-of-Nine Code

This code was originally developed to expand the basic two-of-five code to include alphanumeric capability. The designation 39 initially came from the fact that the original set had 39 characters in it. But today it has been expanded, so the entire 128 characters of the American Standard Code for Information Interchange (ASCII) can be represented. In addition there are three wide bars for a total of nine dark and light bars for a particular character. In every character there are two wide black bars and one wide white bar (Fig. 28.6). In addition, there are five dark bars and four light bars or spaces to represent each character. This particular coding system is by far the most popular in industry today and appears to be rapidly becoming the world standard. There are many other codes, some of which are illustrated in Fig. 28.7, that are presently used to varying degrees.

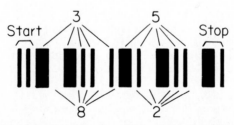

FIG. 28.5   Interleaved two-of-five code. (*Courtesy: Bar Code Symbology.*)

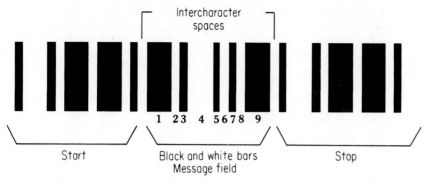

FIG. 28.6   Code 39. (*Courtesy: Bar Code Symbology.*)

FIG. 28.7   Assorted bar-code symbols. (*Courtesy: Bar Code Symbology.*)

Continuous Code

In a *continuous-code system*, the spaces between the black bars and between the characters are used as part of the coding. Although this code permits a greater number of characters to be packed into a prescribed length, it is not possible to check each character to determine whether it is read properly, which is possible in code 39.

Discrete Code

The *discrete code* is the opposite of the continuous code in that each character stands alone with a distinct separation between each set of bars representing a character. Improved checking is possible in this system since the code can be validated character by character and not just on one composite code or by a separate check digit.

BAR-CODE EQUIPMENT

A company acquiring bar-code equipment must consider the method of printing or attaching the bar-code symbol to the item, the printing process, the scanning device to be used, and the computer and other devices interfacing with the bar-code equipment.

Bar-Code Printing Requirements

Printing of bar codes is quite exacting. The proper configuration of the bars, the spacing between the bars, and the definition of the black and white areas are all important. The successful use of bar codes is based on the quality of the printing, regardless of the technique used. The following key points should be remembered and checked during the production of the bar code whether it is printed on a label or on some other form.

Tolerance.   There is a total permissible tolerance between the printed code and the scanning equipment. If the printed code consumes most of the tolerance, then the scanning equipment can have little tolerance. The scanner and the label must work together. So prior to finalizing either the printing method or the scanning equipment, it should be determined whether they function together efficiently.

Printing Accuracy.   Printing accuracy is essential for the success of bar codes. It is this accuracy that contributes to the total success of bar code systems. The lines and spaces must be proportioned accurately in accordance with the particular bar-code specifications. The definition between the black and white areas is extremely important. The print of a high-density code must have a better definition than one of a low-density code.

Optical Characteristics.   The optical characteristics of the environment in which the printed code is going to be used must be considered in the printing. The contrast between dark and light areas is most important. Another important point is the type of light used in the reading process. If the light is in the infrared spectrum, the label must be printed with carbon-black ink to obtain the proper readability. Laser, white, and other light sources must also be taken into consideration if the most satisfactory type of label is to be printed.

Defects.   One advantage of bar coding is that code defects usually do not prohibit the reading of the code unless they extend the entire height of the bar. In the printing of codes, conditions should be controlled to minimize the occurrences of defects, such as varying the intensity of the black printing, ragged bar edges, ink bleeding into the white spaces, and white spaces in the dark bar.

Printing Media

There are various ways of applying the bar code to the desired item. The code can be imprinted directly on a product or imprinted on a label or tag which is attached to the item.

Labels.   Label stock is made of many materials, from ordinary paper to aluminum and special types of paper stock resistant to particular environmental conditions.

Bar-code label stock may be a simple label of 1 inch or less in length or as large as card format approximately the size of the data processing card. In the case of matrix printing, regular computer paper stock is generally used. Certain protective and laminating processes are also available for labels. The selection of the proper label to meet individual conditions is important in developing the bar-code system to be introduced and implemented in a manufacturing or distribution situation.

Tags. Some products do not have the form or size suitable for attaching a label. Therefore, tags are necessary which can be printed directly with the bar code or to which labels are attached.

Direct Application. As everyone is aware, bar codes may be imprinted directly on the product. It is not uncommon to see a bar code imprinted on a box of cereal, dog food, cigarettes, or other items sold in a retail store.

Inks. Good-quality ink is very important in any printing. The flow of ink must be controlled so it will not cause a "bleeding" situation owing to slow drying or soft paper. The ink must not deteriorate as a result of light or other adverse conditions. For dense codes, reusable ribbons must be reinked frequently with a high-quality product. Otherwise, a low-density code will have to be used because of the poor definition between the end of the dark areas and the beginning of the white areas.

Label Covering. At times security requires that a code not be read by personnel. It can be printed with an intensely black carbon ink which is then covered with a black film.

Printing Techniques

Lexographic and Flexographic Processes. These processes offer a very good quality with high reliability when large quantities of identical codes are needed. Of course, commercially printed coded material pays off only in large quantities.

Letterpress. This is also another good process for printing bar codes in quantities, and the same general conditions apply as in the lexographic and flexographic processes.

Continuous-Form Presses. In this process, as well as those mentioned previously, consecutive numbers expressed in bar codes are introduced. The cost of the printing equipment for the continuous process is quite expensive. The reliability and accuracy of such printed codes are good. If a quantity of coded forms are required, this process is excellent.

Form or Impact Printers. See Fig. 28.8. The quality of these printed codes is excellent since each code is engraved on a cylinder which prints the bar code. The definition on the cylinder is exact; and if the ribbon is new, excellent-quality bar codes are obtained. These types of printers are quite expensive because of the quality of the printing unit and the cost of making the cylinder.

Dot-Matrix Printers. Matrix printers are the most flexible printers available. They can produce both a bar code and regular printed text on the same form. These printers use computers which are controlled by programs to print the particular

FIG. 28.8   Impact printer. *(Source: Intermec, Inc.)*

documents being prepared. Since the bars are made by the overlapping of dots, the definition of the bars is not as good as with impact printing. Therefore, the code must have a lower density than that created by several other processes.

   Serial Printers.   These printers form the characters through the use of a moving printing head. Their application is limited to printing labels or pages.

   Line Printers.   Matrix line printer codes are prepared under the control of a computer program in the same manner as the dot-matrix serial printers and are formed by a series of overlapping dots. They are subject to the same problems as the dot-matrix serial printer of precise alignment and ragged edges. The actual operation or formation of the code is made as the computer makes line sweeps from right to left and left to right, rather than by moving the printing head in several directions to form the character.

Thermal Printers.   This printer is probably the cheapest available, but it operates at a low speed. It creates a black bar on special label stock by burning an image. The wide and narrow bars are created by the alignment of a succession of bars. The square-matrix thermal printer illustrated in Fig. 28.9 is more versatile.

Ink-Jet Printers.   The basis of this system is a series of tiny nozzles through which ink is controlled as it is sprayed onto the paper to form the code. One big problem is maintenance to ensure that the individual jets are kept open for the ink to pass through. There is also the problem of cleanup. Although this process holds considerable promise, it requires further development if it is to be used for bar codes for the average manufacturer.

Laser Printers.   Laser etching has had considerable use in developing special bar-coded plates that are to be placed on products. However, the laser printer, as a bar-code printing device for producing labels, is not used extensively. As with ink-jet printers, this system holds considerable promise, but more development is required before it will become profitable for general use.

FIG. 28.9 Square-matrix thermal printer. *(Source: Intermec, Inc.)*

Other Printers. Various other types of printers have been developed and are on the market, but they have not proved to be of major importance for bar-code printing. The common computer printers with special programs have been used in a manner similar to the dot-matrix or line-matrix printers. The density and quality of the print are very poor compared to the specialized printers discussed.

Ribbons. The selection of the ribbon for the printing is important for good quality and if a high first-read rate from the scanning is to be obtained. In addition, the ribbon should be maintained in satisfactory condition and not permitted to become a light gray or worn out. High-carbon-content ribbons are required for infrared scanning.

Bar-Code Scanning

The surface and ease of attaching a label often determine the scanning method employed. Rough surfaces cannot be read effectively with a wand, so they must be read by a laser beam or through some other noncontact method. Another surface consideration is whether an adhesive will hold the label to the surface given the period of time, environment, and process.

Retro-optics bar-code reading works primarily from the light beam reflected from the bar-code target which is sensed for the reflection of spaces and the absorption by bars. The signal from sensing the bar code is the original input of bar-code scanning. In all cases the system works on the presence or absence of a dark bar, its size, and a white space and, in some cases, its size.

The reflected or read signal wave must be conditioned in the scanning instrument from the proper digital binary-code format. The digital signal is transmitted to the processor in binary code which is then interpreted to form the proper character for storage, processing, or printing or for an application that has been programmed.

One group of scanning equipment, which includes wands and card slot equipment (Fig. 28.10), actually makes contact with the label or printed bar to read the code. Noncontact readers can identify and read the bar code from just a short distance to as far away as 3 or 4 ft.

Laser Scanners.   The laser reader depends on the application of a laser beam. However, it still reads on the basis of white and dark area definition. A handheld unit which can be used with either a fixed or a portable reader is illustrated in Fig. 28.11.

FIG. 28.10   Card slot scanner. (*Source: Intermec, Inc.*)

FIG. 28.11   Handheld laser scanner. (*Source: Scope, Inc.*)

Wand Scanners.   A wand is a small pencil-like device which makes contact with a label as it is passed across the bar code. Wands are connected directly to fixed or portable reading equipment or are of the remote or satellite variety, feeding into a piece of scanning equipment from a distant point. Wands usually are constructed in two types. One type has a hard point, such as a ruby. The other has a recessed light in the casing. The light source is usually either ordinary light or infrared light. In some cases, the latter is used with special types of scanning equipment. Some wands do not have to make contact but travel slightly above the surface of the reading area.

Portable Scanners.   Portable units (Fig. 28.12) that can be easily carried by the operator are usually attached to the operator's belt or to a shoulder strap. They are powered by a battery that can be recharged. The wands on these units may be the same as those used with a fixed-position unit, but laser guns can also be attached to portable units. These units have memories to retain the scanned information. Some portable scanners also have special built-in computation programs and memory.

Fixed-Head Moving Laser Beam.   The beam is swept back and forth across the bar code in a movement undiscernible to the eye as the bar code is moved past the scanner. This scanner is used for high-speed applications such as controlling or sorting items on a conveyor line. Conveyor speeds of 500 feet per minute have been attained.

FIG. 28.12   Portable scanner with wrist menu. (Source: Intermec, Inc.)

Bar-Code Interfaces

Except for a small mainframe computer, it is generally not practical or economical to interface bar-coding devices directly. It will delay the computer's operations because of the slow input-output speeds of the bar-code equipment.

A study of the existing computer's capability and its capacity for handling the volume of data required for bar coding is one of the first steps to be taken. Since there will be more devices used than for any existing data collection system, adequate computer entry ports or a port concentrator must be considered. Generally this unit handles up to 16 scanners or printers. In addition, bar coding generally works best in the real-time mode, and it should be determined whether such operations are feasible. If they are not, other methods should be studied to obtain the equivalent so that bar coding can be used effectively. The planned configuration of new equipment should be studied, and the basic methods of bar-code system operations reviewed completely so the operating scheme, software, and hardware requirements can be developed.

Computer networks allow greater flexibility by providing a greater amount of data storage to accommodate the large amount of information to be entered into the system. Generally they function better in a real-time environment. However, a study has to be made.

Minicomputers are generally larger than microcomputers but often have microcomputer networks feeding into them. Bar-code equipment may be interfaced directly with the microcomputers or with CRTs which are in turn interfaced with the minicomputers.

Microcomputers and their networks may be used along with higher-level computers and are ideal for real-time, on-line bar-code systems. Since these micro units can be programmed to transmit data by the network to higher-level computers with their buffered storage areas, they should definitely be considered in any expanded bar-code operations.

The largest equipment problem of new bar-coding users is that the computers do not have a sufficient number of ports for direct entry of the scanning equipment or enough exit ports for outputting to printing devices. Therefore, an interface such as the port concentrator is used which accepts up to 16 ports but requires only 1 computer port. This device generally contains a memory from 64K to 128K. Some have overflow disk systems and perform editing and buffering functions. In many cases this equipment eliminates the need for a larger or more extensive computer memory. In addition, many users find that by using port concentrators and microcomputers, they can convert from a batch-oriented system to a real-time, on-line procedure without changing their mainframe computer.

The interface equipment mentioned meets the AIEE, RS 232 or 422 standards. However, many of the larger mainframe manufacturers have developed or are developing other special equipment for interfacing between scanning devices and an output function, such as NC equipment.

A number of companies design their equipment with bar-code entry or exit features. There are weighing scales on the market that read a bar code and create a new label which includes the code and weight. Machine counters are being produced that identify the incoming bar code and create a new label which includes the part number and quantity. Bar-code printers are available that laminate the label and apply it, all in one operation.

Software Systems

The condition of a company's computer software determines how much benefit will be obtained from the introduction of bar coding. The degree of modularity and how these modules are linked in the software system are of major concern in determining the immediate benefits that can be obtained from a bar-code system. Some points need to be checked:

Modules. Since the bar code is primarily for identification purposes, the I/O modules must have sufficient capacity to handle the new bar-code technique in lieu of present reading or output methods.

Hardware and Software Linkage. A problem sometimes encountered involves linking the bar-code hardware components into the existing software. Check to ensure that components or modules can be substituted as necessary and still maintain the integrity of the software program. In most software packages, the introduction of bar coding does not cause major problems.

Data Base. The organization of the data base is most important when bar codes are used. It should be one that can be easily updated by an efficient management system. The data base should be capable of handling a large volume of different records and structure trees. The update of the data base by the I/O bar-code system is most effective when a single or comparatively few inputs can update a quantity of information through the retracing of the output tree. To facilitate data retrieval and data base updating, a unique index number is assigned to the structure and master used to produce the output.

Operating System. The operating system needs to be thoroughly reviewed to determine whether it can handle, on a real-time basis, the volume of information expected with the new system. In addition to processing larger volumes of information, the system will poll the port concentrators or other storage locations on a frequent and rapid basis, so that the most current information can be transmitted to smaller computers or to the CRTs directly.

The basic method of operation should be defined first, and then the software requirements should be developed and programs selected. Many improved system changes are possible and will have a major effect on the type of software procured.

BAR-CODE APPLICATIONS

Bar coding allows the entire production system to be kept current and the entire system tightly integrated. Some of the various ways that this can be done are presented in this section.

Purchasing and Receiving

Constant usage and updating of inventory and order status can be maintained by bar coding for immediate use by the purchasing department or other concerned personnel. This enables buyers to place orders with up-to-date information.

The bar code is imprinted on the purchase order. If the code is placed on the product and the packing slip is sent by the supplier, this greatly improves the efficiency of identifying shipments on the receiving dock (Fig. 28.13). At the receiving operations, a portable bar-code reader can be used for checking in material (Fig. 28.14). From this input an immediate update entry is made in the stock status file, and the necessary labels for the products can be printed right at the receiving dock or at the inspection and stocking areas. The integrated system can

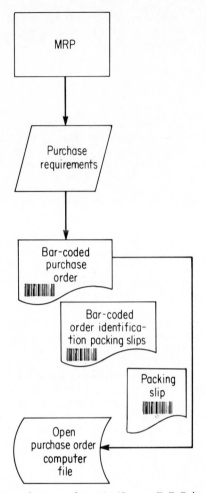

FIG. 28.13 Puchasing application schematic. (*Source: E. F. Baker & Associates, Inc.*)

also immediately transmit the receipt to the accounts payable department for processing.

Materials Handling

Materials handling equipment can be classified in two categories: employee-controlled and automated. In both cases bar codes can make a significant improvement in the handling and control of the material. Employee-handled material, such as that on a forklift truck or in a railroad car, can be scanned for a bar code as it passes a particular point. Bar-code identification numbers placed on skids, containers, or the material itself can be detected by a wand directly by the materials handler where it is picked up or dropped off.

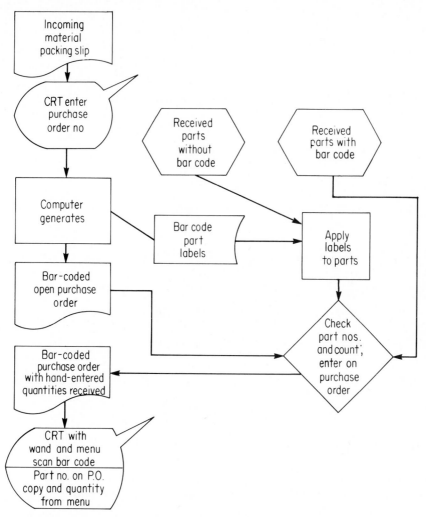

FIG. 28.14   Receiving application schematic. *(Source: E. F. Baker & Associates, Inc.)*

On a materials-handling conveyor system (Fig. 28.15), the laser scanner can read the bar-coded items (Fig. 28.16). According to a pre-prepared computer program, the laser scanner causes gates to be opened or makes other adjustments so the items are delivered to the proper point, such as a stockroom or work center. The increase in inventory activities caused by JIT inventory procedures means that a greater number of deliveries have to be made to the shop floor. There will also probably be an increase in the type and use of materials-handling equipment, particularly overhead conveyors which deliver materials right to the work center. The bar-code system can be readily used in this application to improve productivity and to reduce costs. Some automatic stackers and other types of equipment have bar-code scanners on the equipment that sense the exact adjustments needed for alignment to

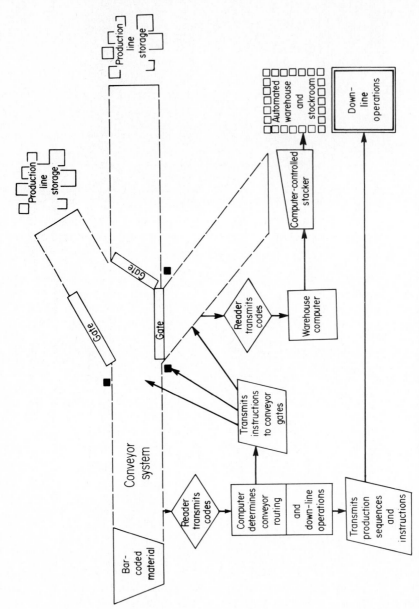

FIG. 28.15 Conveyor application schematic. (*Source: E. F. Baker & Associates, Inc.*)

FIG. 28.16   Fixed-head laser scanner monitoring production line. *(Source: Scope, Inc.)*

a particular shelf location. They may also scan the part number or container number to determine that it is the correct one.

Automated Processing

On some production lines, the kinds of items are not always the same or even grouped by lots. In these situations, necessary selections are made by a sensor device. In other cases, each item is identified so proper instructions can be given to change the processing machinery. This makes for greater flexibility in the total manufacturing process. An even simpler method is to have a bar code on an item that is read as it moves to the automated process. Thus the item is identified, and information is sent to the computer where the prearranged program transmits instructions to the processing machine, telling it what is to be done to the particular item. A reading of the item's bar-code label as the product leaves the process can be used to count each item and the time involved.

Numeric Control

One bar-code application which is not so common is the selection of the proper program to be brought into the numeric control (NC) machines. With the use of integrated systems and a single computer to do the shop functions, NC processes are frequently being performed by the same computer as that used in the production control department.

When the work schedule is entered into the computer system by production control, those items to be processed by NC machinery are immediately checked to determine whether there is an NC program available in the computer's memory or in the equipment itself. If the answer is negative, a message is transmitted to production control immediately to withhold the scheduled operation, and another notice is sent to the process engineering organization to prepare the needed program. When the floor manager does issue the work order to the operator and the NC program is available, the program is moved into position in the equipment from the computer's general storage area or is brought into the operating mode in the computer for computer-controlled machine operations.

Shop Floor Control

A study for job shops shows that only 15 percent of the time is something being done to the work in process, such as fabricating, assembling, inspecting, or moving. These studies indicate further that the problem is one of sufficient planning and coordination by management and control personnel. The control system generally uses the shop orders with batch control and a dispatch system. Bar coding can completely change the method of controlling the work in process including supporting a paperless system (Fig. 28.17). Instructions can be printed directly on an operation ticket by a bar-code printer on the shop floor or can be transmitted to a CRT in front of the workplace. Consequently, the shop schedule does not have to be printed on hard copy but can be displayed on a CRT, from which the individual operations can be directed as needed by the shop floor manager.

Starting to work on a new job, the employee passes his individual bar-coded badge and the job ticket through scanning equipment, so no job time tickets are needed. At the completion of the job, the job ticket with a bar-coding entry of the quantity completed is scanned and entered into the computer. This immediately updates the work-in-process inventory, the shop load, and the efficiency report of the operator and process.

Studies show that 85 percent to 95 percent of the work-in-process inventory is stored or in queue on the shop floor. Also some reports have shown that in some industries as much as 46 percent of the annualized inventory carrying costs are incurred for the work-in-process inventory. Therefore, it is important that this inventory be reduced. One reason for having a large work-in-process inventory is to build up a safety stock in case some unexpected circumstance develops. Another reason it is produced early is to level production or hedge against an unexpected demand. This condition cannot remain if managers move to JIT inventory procedures with the zero-inventory concept. With this system, timing the operations is most important in helping to reduce safety stocks. Bar codes provide an excellent input of information to control the flow of inventory on the shop floor if zero-inventory procedures are used.

Inventory builds up on the shop floor when no decision has been made about scrapping material. With bar codes such rejects can be tracked and a decision forced to either rework or dispose of the material, so it does not remain in the inventory.

The integration of materials-handling and other activities is important for an efficient shop floor production system. Through the use of bar-coded information, materials-handling equipment can be coordinated between work centers, stockroom locations, etc. As a result, a considerable reduction is realized in the amount of handling and the accumulation of materials on the factory floor in advance of the actual time needed.

Lead time needs to be reduced in all manufacturing activities since it causes a buildup of work in process. Studies have shown that in a number of cases the reason for long lead times is that detailed events planning has not been performed to ensure that the processes are ready when the product shows up. Integration of the stockroom, manufacturing operations, tooling, and other manufacturing support systems allows a manager to obtain adequate coordination and planning, so there are no processing false starts. When an order is issued to start an operation, all the requirements, such as materials, parts, tools, gauges, prints, and others, are available. This is an application of bar coding with great potential savings.

Stockroom Control

Bar coding was originally used for inventory control. The stockroom use of bar coding is well known, but its integration into the total system for production

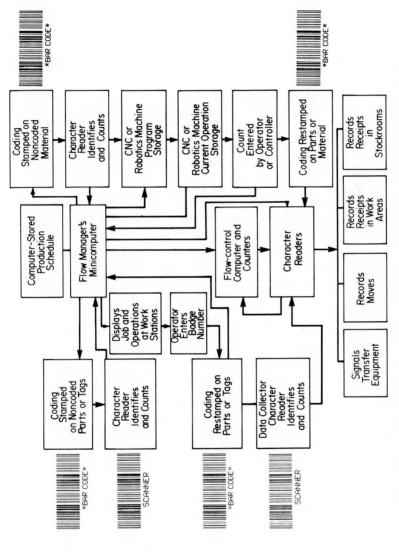

FIG. 28.17 Paperless shop floor control system schematic. (*Source: E. F. Baker & Associates, Inc.*)

processing, maintenance distribution, and the shop floor management have not been as well explored. When a stockroom system is prepared, it is wise to consider all bar-code applications so they can be integrated into a total system.

Stock picking was one of the early applications of bar coding and continues to remain a very important one. However, some new methods are being employed. If the picking list has the bar code printed on it, the stock picker can "wand" the picking list and the stock label to ensure selection of the proper item. Each individual item may be scanned to obtain a count, or a menu may be used to introduce to the system the quantity withdrawn. The bar-code equipment for this operation may be portable or fixed. More efficient picking is possible now since the quantity and location are updated immediately once a pick is made or material is stored in a new location. Also a picker can be guided through the most efficient routes for material selection.

A new development in stock picking is the portable bar-coding unit programmed for the best stock-picking sequence. Information about the items to be picked is loaded from the computer terminal into the portable unit, which then directs the inventory clerk to the location of the items to be picked. This ensures that all locations have been included. Wanding the items for bar-code identification ensures that the proper item is being picked. After completing the picking at each location, the clerk is directed to the next location. Upon completion of all the stock picking, the information is loaded back into the computer system, and the stock status is updated immediately.

Other bar-code innovations are being used in the stockroom. Stockroom locations and shelves are being bar-coded. When items are stored, the location and quantity are recorded in the computer. This assists in the stock-picking program, allowing random storage and first-in/first-out stock removal. Several large auditing firms have accepted bar-coding systems in the stockroom as a substitute for cycle or physical inventory counts.

Robot Control

As in automated processing and materials-handling conveyor systems, robots need to receive frequent instructions. Many recently developed robots do multiprocessing and handling and are not necessarily limited to one specific act. Therefore, they must be instructed. Approximately 40 percent of robots require some instruction other than that from a "sensing" or "feeling" type of input. This offers an excellent opportunity to use bar coding (Fig. 28.18). As a part is moving toward the robot, a bar-code scanner determines its identity and transmits the message to the computer controlling the robot. The computer, in turn, sends the necessary placement and operation instruments to the robot.

Robots are also used in materials handling. They are programmed to move through an area and stop to deliver an item, go "home," or perform some other operation. While robots are performing their activities, their location and instructions are frequently conveyed by reading the bar codes printed along the aisles with a laser scanner.

Costing

Bar-code data collection systems in the production environment permit very accurate and current processing costs. The monthly closings of accounts are made in a matter of hours in plants using on-line, real-time systems with bar codes. At any instant the cost of the work in process can be determined. When material is introduced to work in process, its point of entry and quantity are recorded through

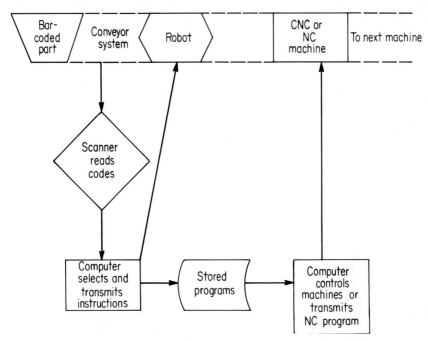

FIG. 28.18   Robot and CNC application schematic. *(Source: E. F. Baker & Associates, Inc.)*

the bar-code system. Labor costs can be accumulated from time cards that have been bar-coded. As the product moves through the plant, each operation is reported and recorded in the cost sheets as to quantity, cost, and location.

The amounts of material and labor introduced and recorded through the bar-code system can be compared with the standards contained in the bills of materials and routing file. The standard costs and their variances can be determined immediately as well as their causes. Rejects and scrap information can be introduced immediately by bar coding. The accounts are updated, and material is written off. Costs of rejects are also controlled through this method.

Maintenance

The maintenance department's transactions (Fig. 28.19) have proved a very effective application of bar codes since craftsmen's waiting time should be minimized to reduce costs. Bar coding used at the maintenance department store's distribution window has materially speeded up the process of withdrawing material and allows quick employee service.

The maintenance stockroom can update the material inventory upon receipt of the bar-coded transaction, and replenishment stock, if necessary, can be ordered immediately. This enables maintenance stock to be reduced since it provides a fast-acting system for critical maintenance items. Bar codes on items or packages ensure the issuance of the proper parts. This is particularly useful when many parts are similar. This reduces the necessity of returning improper items.

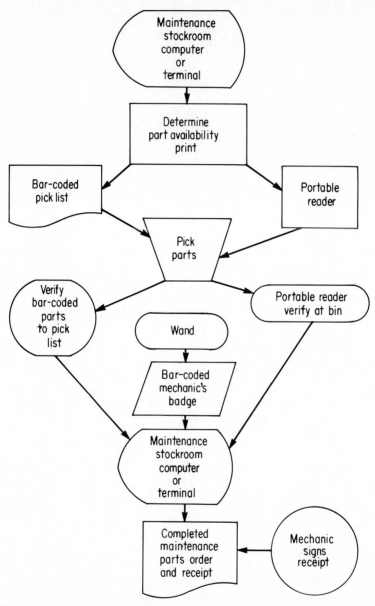

FIG. 28.19 Maintenance stockroom application schematic. (*Source: E. F. Baker & Associates, Inc.*)

In industries where departments are far apart, bar codes can be used to read a part number on a machine list which is then transmitted by phone or radio to the maintenance storeroom for immediate action, so it can be available when the requesting department's personnel arrive (Fig. 28.20).

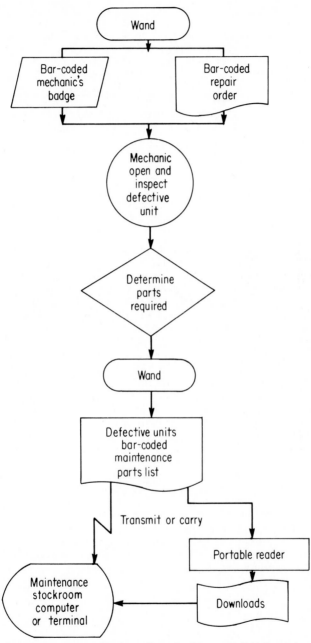

FIG. 28.20 Emergency repair application schematic. (Source: E. F. Baker & Associates, Inc.)

Tool and Gauge Control

Many of the applications mentioned for maintenance planning and control apply to the tool, die, fixture, and gauge activities. In addition the information, if kept on a computer system, can be available to the production planning department. The shop floor manager can determine whether the necessary tools, dies, and fixtures are available for a particular operation before the shop order is issued. A record of usage can be readily maintained to determine when tools, dies, and gauges should be reworked to avoid producing poor-quality products. The location of tools, dies, fixtures, and gauges is always known, which prevents tool hoarding by shop floor personnel.

CONCLUSION

A few companies in the United States today have a paperless shop floor operation. These are well-integrated systems in which a great deal of thought was given to the equipment planning and software. All items entering the plant are bar-coded if they have not already been coded. Weighing and counting equipment translates information to bar codes. The storage locations are also bar-coded together with the part number in that location. CRTs, in front of the worker, have instructions projected on their screen for items previously identified by bar codes. The bar codes are read at the completion of each shop floor operation, and labor is added. Material quantities are also added according to the bill of materials. If errors are found later, they are entered at that time.

Conveyor systems are controlled as described previously. The stock status in the computer is updated from receipts, issues, and stock returns. All outgoing items are selected from stock by the bar-code method, and the shipping papers are produced from bar-code input. Shipments are checked by scanning equipment as they are loaded onto commercial carriers.

At present there appears to be no limit to bar-code applications. The extent of its use in any particular company is completely up to the imagination of its personnel. Other input devices such as OCR and magnetic-stripe devices will continue to be used in certain business applications, but their use in the manufacturing environment appears limited. However, in such applications as credit cards used in retailing, they will probably be around for considerable time.

The number of standardized bar codes appear to have settled down to a relatively few. And one or two, probably code 39 and the interleaved two-of-five code, have become a complete U.S. (and eventually worldwide) standard. From the equipment point of view, one can expect improvements in speed, ease of use, and the performance of related functions. Bar coding will be one vehicle in the drive to improve productivity and profits.

BIBLIOGRAPHY

Allais, David C.: *Bar Code Symbology—Some Observations on Theory and Practices*, Intermac Corp., Lynwood, Wash., Dec. 1,1984.

Baker, Eugene F.: *Industry Shows Its Stripes—A New Role for Bar Coding*, American Management Association, New York, March, 1985.

————: Bar Code—The Catalyst: The Opportunity for Obtaining Maximum Production Benefits, Readings in Productivity Improvements, American Production and Inventory Control Society (APICS), 27th Annual International Conference Proceedings, Oct. 9–10, 1984, Las Vegas.

————: "The Changing Scene on the Production Floor," Management Review, January, 1983, pp. 8–11.

————: "Management Giving Production Planning Bigger Role in Shop Floor Operations," Management Review, July, 1980, pp. 34–35.

Bar Code Seminar Proceedings, TDA Publications, Inc., Hollywood, Fla., Sept. 13–14, 1982.

Buffa, Elwood S.: Meeting the Competitive Challenge, Dow Jones-Irwin, Homewood, Ill., 1984.

Burke, Harry, E.: Handbook on Bar Code Systems, Van Nostrand and Reinhold, New York, 1984.

29

Inventory Theory*

Editor

ROBERT G. BROWN, CFPIM, President, Materials Management
Systems, Inc., Thetford Center, Vermont

An inventory *control* system is a set of procedures that suggest when to reorder stock and how much to order. The procedures may be implemented in ways that range from using no records whatsoever, or manually posted records, to very elaborate computer systems. All such systems keep track of *stock status*—what is on hand, what is due in, and what is owed to customers. All such systems also have provisions for stating *requirements*, which include a forecast of demand during a replenishment lead time and some sort of safety stock.

In the simplest environment, it is sufficient to keep track of stock status and requirements for each stock-keeping unit (SKU), or product in a particular location, and make replenishment decisions for each SKU on its own merits. Merchant wholesalers frequently decide to replenish a list of products supplied from one source on the basis of the stock status and requirements for all products from that supplier. In a multiechelon distribution system, decisions to replenish one SKU may be affected by stock status and requirements for that product at all stocking locations.

*All the material in this chapter is taken from R. G. Brown, *Advanced Service Parts Inventory Control*, Materials Management Systems, Thetford Center, Vt., 1981.

29.1

Status Control

If the records are posted manually (or if stock status is "recorded" by the physical stock itself), the stock status can be represented by *available stock*—the amount on hand, plus what is due in, less what is owed to customers. A customer demand reduces the available balance. A replenishment order at the source increases the available balance. Receipt from the source becomes a transfer from stock due in to stock on hand (Fig. 29.1).

The requirements in such a system are represented by an *order point*, which is the sum of the forecast over the replenishment lead time and a safety stock. Later sections of this chapter discuss methods of forecasting and ways of computing safety stock.

The replenishment procedure compares available stock with the order point. If available stock is below the order point, either order a predetermined quantity or order enough to bring the available stock up to some predetermined maximum stocking objective. Later sections of this chapter discuss methods of computing the economical order quantity (EOQ).

The decision to order more stock cannot be made more frequently than the records are posted with transactions. If it is possible to order after any demand transaction is posted, the lead time is as short as possible. If orders can be generated only at fixed intervals, the length of that interval must be added to the lead time for computing order points.

Source	J.B. Bigley 930 Third Ave. NYC 10020			Cost 3.07	Unit Each	Package 200	
				Order up to 2800		Reorder point 2000	
Date	To/from reference	Comp date	Due date	Quantity in	Quantity out	On hand	Available stock
Dec. 30	Physical inventory	12/30				2675	2675
Jan. 3	5-11279 Jones	1/3			600	2075	2075
Jan 4	5-11283 Smith	1/4			319	1756	1756
Jan 5	P-88357 Bigley	3/8	Mar.	1000		1756	2756
Feb 11	5-11306 Harris	2/11			350	1406	2406
Feb 18	5-11511 Jones	2/18			350	1056	2056
Mar 8	P-88357	3/8		1000		2056	2056
Mar 9	5-11382 Jackson	3/9			400	1656	1656
Mar 10	P-88402 Bigley		May	1200		1656	2856
Mar 17	5-11497 Smith	3/17			373	1283	2483
Part no. .T0061	Description Sprockets					Buyer 20	Class A

FIG. 29.1 Manual record of transactions with available balance.

TIME-PHASED CONTROL

When the inventory control system is implemented on a modern computer, it is possible to keep track of both requirements and available stock over time. The added information, as in material-requirements planning (MRP), makes it possible to anticipate, rather than react, and to offer better service to customers with a lower inventory investment.

The graph in Fig. 29.2 is a convenient way of representing the relationships. The horizontal axis represents time, starting from the most recent posting of stock on hand and extending to a planning horizon much beyond any replenishment lead time. The vertical axis is in *cumulative* units. The cumulative forecast is a straight line for uniform forecast, but has an S shape for seasonal demand. If there are scheduled orders for large amounts at infrequent intervals, the cumulative forecast may look like a staircase. The *cumulative gross requirements* include either a safety stock or a safety time added to the cumulative forecast. Safety stock and safety time may also vary over time.

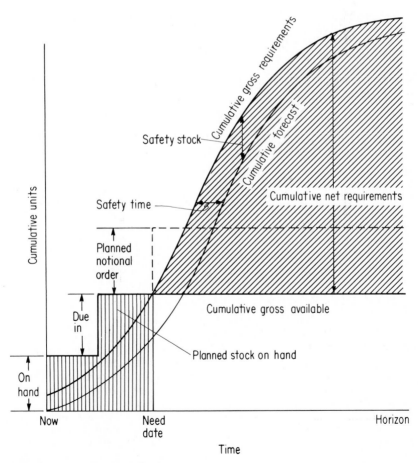

FIG. 29.2 Time-phased control.

Cumulative gross available stock starts at current time with the net stock on hand (which might be negative if there are customer back orders) and increases each time that stock is due to be received from the source. The cumulative gross available stock will remain flat for an indefinite time after the due date for the last order now open on the supplier.

The time at which the cumulative gross available stock is exceeded by the cumulative gross requirements is the *need date*. Insofar as possible, replenishment orders should be generated so that the material arrives on or before that need date. If the need date is beyond the lead time, it is practical to order slightly in advance of need. When the need date is within lead time, replenishment orders may have to be expedited to maintain customer service.

An order for any quantity will increase the available stock, which moves the need date further into the future. It is practical to simulate a succession of notional replenishment orders out to the planning horizon, to give suppliers information about their "lumpy" demand.

In the process industries, "orders" can be represented by production *rates* for successive planning periods rather than order quantities. In Fig. 29.3, these rates are represented as a series of line segments for cumulative gross available stock. Note that these rates are planned always to exceed cumulative gross requirements. The shaded area represents an investment in *stabilization stock*.

In either Fig. 29.2 or Fig. 29.3, the excess of cumulative gross requirements over the cumulative gross available is the *cumulative net requirements*, starting with the need date. The excess of cumulative gross available over cumulative gross requirements, before the need date, represents the current expectation for what stock will be on hand at any future time.

ORDERING STRATEGY

The time-phased control system permits greater flexibility in the choice of a procedure for deciding when and how much to order (Fig. 29.4). The quantity to order could be a predetermined quantity, just as in the status control system, or an amount sufficient to bring available stock up to some maximum stock level. If there is any difference between the two approaches, ordering up to a maximum level will generally give somewhat better service with lower inventory. There may be external constraints that force one to order in particular quantities.

The time-phased control system makes it possible to generate an order when the need date falls within a window of time beyond the lead time and thus to anticipate requirements slightly.

Suppose several items are to be ordered jointly from the same supplier. There is usually a total order quantity, such as $10,000 worth of material or a truckload of 35,000 pounds or perhaps a railroad car with 42 pallets. Translate the cumulative net requirements for each product supplied from that source into dollars, pounds, or pallets; then accumulate the total net requirements over all products. The quantity to be ordered will cover those net requirements through some period (Fig. 29.5). The quantity to order for each product is given by the net requirements for that product through that period. Products with need dates beyond the coverage time are not included on this order.

Another variation on the same theme occurs when a manufacturer supplies the same product to several regional distribution centers or warehouses. The total amount that can be used to replenish warehouses is what is on hand or is coming in the immediate future from production (Fig. 29.6). That quantity will cover the

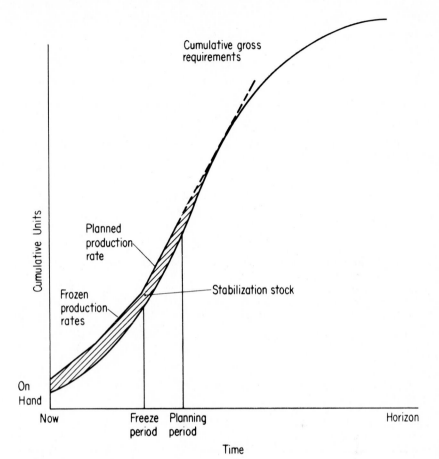

FIG. 29.3 Production rates.

How much to order

	Preset quantity	Difference between operating level and available
Compare available with order point	(1) Simplest system, small demand continual posting	(2) Lumpy demand or long intervals between posting
Compare ordering date with calendar	(3) Not feasible	(4) Coordinate orders for many items

When to order

FIG. 29.4 Ordering rules.

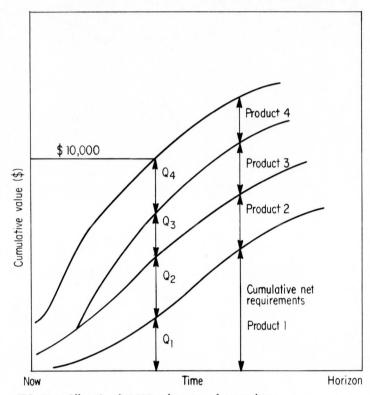

FIG. 29.5 Allocating $10,000 order among four products.

cumulative net requirements for that product summed over all stocking locations for a period. The *fair-share quantity* to be sent to any particular location is that location's cumulative net requirements through that coverage period. In this case, however, the quantity does not need to be sent to all locations—until the need date falls within one shipping interval of the transit lead time.

INVENTORY MANAGEMENT

Figure 29.7 illustrates the inputs and outputs of the inventory management system.

Economic Order Quantities

The concept of the economic order quantity (EOQ) is to balance the expected *cost of acquisition* for stock against the expected *costs to hold* the stock. There are five principal elements to be considered in selecting the proper formula. Since there are many alternative assumptions about the operating environment under each of these five headings, a very large variety of different formulas exist. As long as the formula is derived from assumptions that match the operating environment, it will produce useful results.

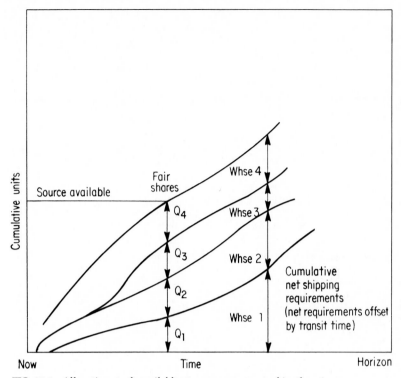

FIG. 29.6 Allocating stock available at source among stocking locations.

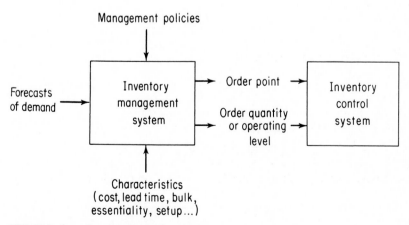

FIG. 29.7 Inventory management systems.

The EOQ may be used to determine a preset quantity to be ordered whenever more stock is required. Alternatively, one may set a maximum stocking objective as the order point plus one standard EOQ, and thus generate actual orders based on available stock whenever an order is triggered.

Order-quantity formulas are very robust (Fig. 29.8). As a general rule, if the value of any factor considered were to double or halve, the total annual costs would rise by only 6 percent. Thus it pays to interpret the computed values pragmatically and round them to vendor minimums and increments and to practical handling quantities. Probably the computed values should be recorded to no more than two significant digits—15, 160, 3400, 55,000, and so on.

Theoretically there is an interaction between the order quantity and safety stock. If the quantities are small, there are many opportunities per year to run short, so more safety stock is needed to maintain customer service. In practice, if the order quantity is at least as large as the standard deviation used to compute safety stocks, that interaction is negligible. The academic approach would be to try to solve a pair of nonlinear equations to find the optimum balance between order quantities (and therefore frequency) and the safety stock. In practice, round the computed order quantity, if necessary, upward to be at least as large as the standard deviation. Then you can safely ignore the interaction. That increase will be effective usually for expensive, slow-moving products. These items tend to have large standard deviations and small EOQs.

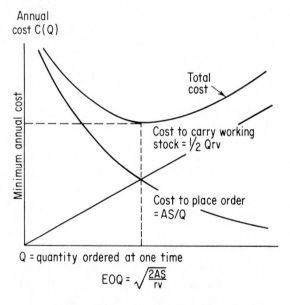

Annual cost C(Q)

Minimum annual cost

Total cost

Cost to carry working stock = 1/2 Qrv

Cost to place order = AS/Q

Q = quantity ordered at one time

$$EOQ = \sqrt{\frac{2AS}{rv}}$$

S = annualized rate of usage (units per year)
A = cost to process an order (dollars per order)
v = unit cost (dollars per unit)
r = carrying charge (dollars per dollars per year)
Q = quantity ordered at one time (units per order)

FIG. 29.8 Economic order quantities.

Base Case. The simplest case is to assume that

S = annualized usage (pieces per year), to continue at same rate for an indefinitely
     long time
Q = quantity delivered to stock (pieces), delivered all at same time
v = unit value (dollars per piece), the same at any time in future for any reasonable
     order quantity
A = acquisition cost (dollars per order), applies to each product individually;
     sometimes called setup cost
r = carrying charge (dollars per dollar per year), applies to extended value of
     working stock, at unit cost v

Then the economic order quantity Q (Fig. 29.4) that minimizes the sum of annual
holding and acquisition costs is given by

$$Q = \sqrt{\frac{2AS}{rv}}$$

Usage Rate. The usage rate S is provided by some sort of forecast, which can range
from a statistical forecast derived from past usage to a time-phased schedule of
dependent demand. If the usage rate varies unpredictably with a standard deviation
σ (pieces per lead time), then increase the computed Q (if necessary) to be at least as
large as σ.
   If there are irregular patterns of dependent demand, or significant trends and
seasonal patterns, compute the order quantity Q on the basis of annualized demand
S, and convert the result to a time supply $T = S/Q$ (years). The actual quantity to
order at any time would be the forecast during the next period T.
   If demand continues for only a finite period or a finite amount, clearly never
order more than will be used. If demand can cease unexpectedly, so that any stock
left on hand must be scrapped, then increase the carrying charge to represent the
risk of that sort of write-off.

Delivery Quantity. If the product is delivered to stock at a finite rate P (pieces per
year) while it is being produced, then increase the order quantity to reflect the
reduction in stock by usage during the production cycle, shown in Fig. 29.9:

$$Q = \sqrt{\frac{2AS}{rv(1 - S/P)}}$$

This correction is justified only if $S < P < 2S$. If $P >> S$, the base case will give
results acceptably close to the best you can do.

Unit Value. When there are quantity discounts (Fig. 29.10), evaluate the expected
annual costs of acquisition (AS/q_i) and the cost of holding the working stock
$(\frac{1}{2}rv_iq_i)$ for each of the quantities q_1 where there is a different unit cost v_i. Select
$Q = q_i{}^*$ for which the total expected annual cost is the smallest.
   If the unit price is expected to be larger when it is time to order the next time (as
after a promotion, with noncurrent tooling, or when the supplier announces a price
increase, then it is economical to buy a larger quantity at the current price, to defer
subsequent purchases. If subscript 1 refers to current quantities and prices and 2
refers to the quantities and prices on subsequent purchases, then

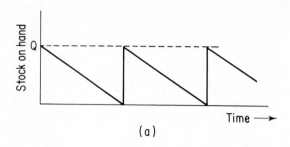

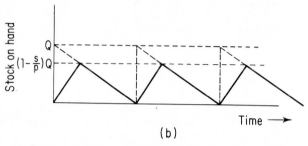

FIG. 29.9 Delivery rate. (a) Instantaneous delivery; (b) finite delivery.

$$\frac{Q_1v_1 - Q_2v_2}{Sv_1} = \frac{v_2 - v_1}{rv_1}$$

The left-hand side expresses the extra quantity, in years of supply over what will be economical in the future. The right-hand side is the percentage price increase, divided by the carrying charge.

Acquisition Cost. For a list of products supplied from the same vendor there may be a *header cost* A for the order, with additional line costs *a* for each additional product on the same order. The same situation occurs in manufacturing where there is a major setup cost A for a family of items with minor changeover costs *a* from one member to another within the family. In that case, the economical time supply for the family is computed by

$$T = \sqrt{\frac{2(A + na)}{r\Sigma S_i v_i}}$$

where there are *n* items in the family. The quantity to be ordered for each item should last T years (usually a fraction), given current available stock. If the current stock already exceeds that coverage, the item can be omitted from the current order.

We can refine the calculation by computing a multiple k_i for the *i*th item

$$k_i = \frac{1}{TS_i}\sqrt{\frac{2a_i}{rS_iv_i}}$$

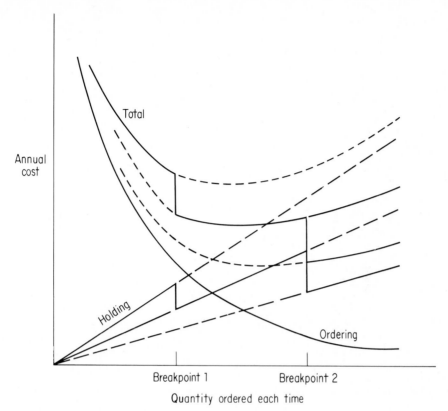

FIG. 29.10 Quantity discounts.

and rounding to the nearest integer (1 or greater). Note that the right-hand side involves an EOQ based on the marginal line cost a_i of adding the ith item to the order. The multiple will be larger than 1 for the slow-moving items in the family. Then the economical time supply is

$$T = \sqrt{\frac{2(A + \Sigma a_i/K_i)}{r\Sigma k_i S_i v_i}}$$

Carrying Charge. The starting point for setting a carrying charge for inventory management is the current corporate return on assets employed. If money weren't tied up in inventory, it could be invested to earn that return elsewhere in the business. Increase the carrying charge if you believe that inventories are more risky, or less liquid, than the typical investment.

The carrying charge can be used as a management policy variable (Fig. 29.11): increase it to decrease working stock and increase the number of orders processed. There is a practical limit to the maximum carrying charge that has any effect. For larger values, the safety stock increases (because of increased exposure to the risk of a shortage) by more than the working stock decreases.

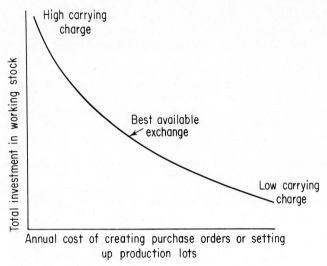

FIG. 29.11   Exchange curve.

If the carrying charge is used as a management policy variable, make *large* changes and expect a very slow response in actual inventories to that change.

The carrying charge should be increased for analyzing the proper quantity to buy in anticipation of a price rise, to reflect the added risk that demand may change during that time. The proper value would be the value used in analyzing the present value of discounted cash flow for risky projects.

If space is at a premium for bulky products, you may want to set up a second carrying charge *w* (dollars per cubic foot per year) and take account of the size (as packed for storage) of the product *c* (cubic feet per piece);

$$Q = \sqrt{\frac{2AS}{rv + wc}}$$

It is obvious how to combine the formulas when several variants on the base case are important in your operations.

Forecasting

A statistical forecast can describe only what has already happened in historical demand, in terms of a level, trends, and seasonal profiles. (See also Chap. 9.) Explanatory forecasts introduce intelligence about such requirements as dependent demand, exploded from higher levels of assembly; large orders booked for future delivery; and market intelligence about the change in demand that may result from changes in the marketplace or changes in marketing policy.

If each warehouse plans its own time-phased requirements, then they can be offset by the transit lead time and accumulated at the source as a special kind of dependent demand, called *net shipping requirements*.

The ideal forecasting system provides for statistical forecasting of the going rate, with effective ways of adding information from other sources. When there are large scheduled orders, this demand must be segregated from the history used for statistical forecasting.

A market intelligence group has its own source of information about changes in demand (Fig. 29.12). The statistical forecasting procedures can facilitate incorporation of this information both by feedback that evaluates the improvement due to such intelligence, and by exception reports such as demand filters and tracking signals that focus attention on the critical few products where the statistical forecast is not tracking demand well.

Statistical Forecasting. A statistical forecast describes the pattern of demand in terms of a level—the current deseasonalized rate of demand; a trend—the rate of change of the level from period to period; and a seasonal profile, if necessary (Fig. 29.13). The seasonal profile may be specified as a string of values, one for each period of the year, to be added to (or multiplied by) the deseasonalized forecast. If the swing from high to low point of the year is large, there is an inherent instability in trying to estimate that profile from historical data. A library of typical profiles has no guarantee of including the pattern required for the next product.

An alternative is to describe the seasonal profile as a linear combination of orthogonal fitting functions, such as a Fourier series of sines and cosines. A small library of standard patterns (no more than one per observation per year) is guaran-

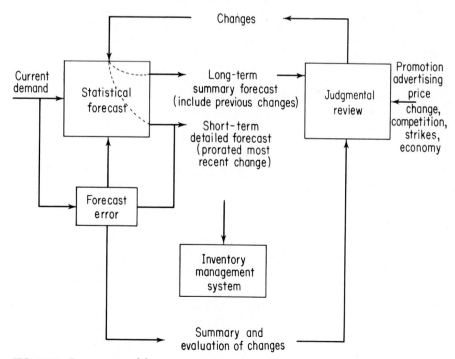

FIG. 29.12 Exogenous model.

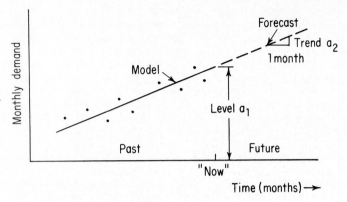

FIG. 29.13 Forecasting model.

teed to represent any possible profile, and the coefficients in the model can be calculated by regression or least squares.

A statistical forecasting procedure must provide for initial model selection and usually provides for forecast revision at regular intervals (weekly, monthly, or quarterly) on the basis of current information. The process of revising the forecast is called *smoothing*.

Model Selection. A model can be fitted to historical demand data by least squares, to estimate current values of the coefficients in that model (see Chap. 30). That model can be evaluated backward in time. The differences between the model and the actual history are called *residuals*. The average of the residuals must be zero, so the *variance* of the residuals is the average of their squared values, taking account of the loss of degrees of freedom because of the coefficients calculated for the model. That is, if there are $N = 48$ observations of history and the model has $m = 4$ terms with coefficients estimated by least squares, then the degrees of freedom for error will be $N - m = 44$ in computing the average squared error. The *standard deviation* of the residuals is the square root of the variance.

Check that no single residual is larger than about 4 standard deviations. If there are a few outliers, assign those periods of history weight zero, and recompute the coefficients by least squares for the remaining observations.

The variance is the average of the squares of the residuals—each residual multiplied by itself. The serial correlation uses the product of a residual for one period by the residual from the preceding period. If these products are sometimes for values of the same sign and sometimes for values of opposite sign, the average value will be close to zero. If the average product of lagged residuals is close to the mean square error, that is evidence of significant *serial correlation*. Thus the model chosen does not describe the demand history well. Consider alternative models: a multiplicative seasonal pattern instead of an additive one; presence or absence of seasonality; logarithmic growth; or, what is most likely with demand data, the pattern of demand has shifted abruptly so that only the more recent observations are relevant to current forecasts. The Box-Jenkins technique of forecasting has quite elaborate ways of interpreting the serial correlation to see how to transform the data (find a better model). The ideal of any forecast model selection process is to find uncorrelated residuals.

If the seasonal profile is described by a Fourier series, it is practical to test for the significance of the amplitude (power or information) at any frequency and to eliminate terms in the model which are not significant. That increases the degrees of freedom available for error and may reduce the mean square error and thus the standard deviation.

A great many forecasting procedures in use tend to overlook some of these key points about finding the right model in the first place.

Forecast Revision: Smoothing. As an additional period elapses, there is more information about the model. Smoothing calculations are quite a bit less expensive than model selection, so that when there are a great many products in an inventory, it pays to revise forecasts, as opposed to continually going through the whole process of finding a model from history to date for each period.

Every smoothing process available is equivalent to a weighted least-squares fit of the chosen model to the history now available. The differences among techniques can be completely described by the series of weights used. It is not necessary to go through extensive simulations with "real data" to compare techniques. You can find the set of weights used in any process by starting with a history which is all zero, so that all the coefficients in the model are zero. Then simulate smoothing where the "actual" demand is 1 in the first period and then returns to zero. The forecasts are the *impulse responses* which are in turn exactly the weights used in that smoothing process.

Two techniques that have the same weights, or the same impulse responses, will produce the same forecast accuracy. In practice, with the kind of short histories available for stocked products, the weights from any technique most often reduce to an exponentially declining series—hence the popularity and effectiveness of exponential smoothing. The difference in effect between an "optimum" smoothing constant—which can be computed only from very long series—and a standard value is usually unimportant for the forecasts used in inventory control.

Exception Reports. A *demand filter* exception report will flag any SKU for which the current demand differs from the current forecast by more than some threshold, on the order of 4 to 10 standard deviations. That should give the market intelligence group an opportunity to find the assignable cause and to correct either the demand or the forecast before smoothing unusual data.

A *tracking signal* exception report flags any forecast that shows a potential bias—the demand is consistently high (or low). Various techniques of smoothing the error tend to lag behind changes in the pattern of demand. The cumulative sum of the forecast errors will react more quickly when there are changes. Control limits on the cumulative sum may be expressed as some multiple of the current estimate of the standard deviation. There are also parabolic masks and V masks, derived from Wald's technique of sequential analysis, which are more powerful but also require more effort to compute.

Interpolation. If two-thirds of the first period has passed, one image of demand is that the remaining forecast is for one-third of the original forecast. That is probably true for hotel rooms and demand for service parts. Another image is that if the original forecast for the first period was 1000 units and 800 have been sold, the remaining forecast is for 200 units, regardless of the elapsed time. That is often nearly true in industries where the sales department works to a quota evaluated for each forecast period. It is important to know which is a better model of how your business operates and to be sure that your forecasting procedures are designed accordingly.

Forecast Interval. Demand is measured at regular intervals, when the forecast is revised, and the forecast is recorded for similar intervals into the future. As a rule, the forecast interval should be on the order of one-third to one-tenth of the replenishment lead time (you do not measure consumption of pulp wood by the hour, nor do you track an orbiting astronaut once a week). Results are not sensitive to the length of the forecast interval, which should be selected as a week, a month, an accounting period, or a quarter, whichever makes sense in the general conduct of your business. With modern computers there is no reason why forecast intervals have to be of equal length (they can be calendar months) or why they have to bear any relation to the production planning calendar. It is practical on today's computers to interpolate forecasts from the forecast calendar to any different production calendar.

Forecast Error. The forecast error is measured each period as the difference between current actual demand and the forecast made at the end of the previous period. The estimate of the mean square error (MSE) can be revised by simple exponential smoothing

$$MSE = \beta MSE + (1 - \beta)(error^2)$$

where β is a discount rate on the order of 0.9. [In the 1950s data processing equipment could not handle squares and square roots, and it was necessary to use the mean absolute deviation (MAD) and then estimate the standard deviation as 1.25 (MAD). That factor is true only for a strictly normal distribution of forecast errors, and in practice it may range from 1 to 1.5. There is no excuse on modern computers for using MAD any longer.]

For a lead time of L forecast intervals, the standard deviation to use in computing safety stocks is $\sigma = \sqrt{L \times MSE}$. The lead time L may be a fraction of one forecast interval or several intervals. It should encompass order processing time, including the interval between posting stock status records; transit time to deliver material from the source to the destination, including manufacturing lead time if the source does not stock the product; administrative time to post the receipt to stock status; and the interval between opportunities to ship.

If lead times vary unpredictably, there is no adequate model of that variation which can be used to estimate the standard deviation of demand during a lead time. The best procedure, given that it is impossible to eliminate the source of the variation, is to measure demand during a lead time directly and to measure the standard deviation of errors in forecasting that statistic.

Whenever a replenishment order is triggered, by definition that is the beginning of a lead time. Record the actual demand year to date then, along with other information about the order. When material is received in response to that order, that is the end of the lead time. Compare current demand year to date with the recorded value. The difference is the (variable) demand that occurred during the (variable) lead time. Use those differences as the history for forecasting and error measurement.

Probability Distributions. (See Chap. 30.) If forecast intervals are short compared with replenishment lead times, and if demand is the result of a large number of customers ordering the same product, then the probability distribution of the forecast errors can likely be described well enough by the normal distribution (Fig. 29.14), which is symmetric about the average error zero.

When the forecast interval is the same length as the replenishment lead time, and demand comes from a fairly small population of customers in any one period, the forecast errors may be better described by one of the skewed distributions such as Poisson, exponential, or log-normal (Fig. 29.15). It is important to verify what sort of a probability distribution adequately describes the environment. Safety stock decisions made from a table for the wrong form of the distribution may be seriously different from what is really required to achieve a specified level of customer service. Table 29.1 summarizes the relevant formulas.

Component = Normal
200 Observations have range 120, mean 103.1, and sigma of 23.83
Median = 104, MAD = 19.34
Coefficient of variation = 0.2313
Distribution function = 1

Normal

```
  O         *
  oooooooo      *
  oooooooooo    *
  oooooooooooo    *
  oooooooooooooo     *
P oooooooooooooooooo*
R oooooooooooooooooo*
O ooooooooooooooooooo*
B ooooooooooooooooooooo*
A oooooooooooooooooooooo*
B oooooooooooooooooooooooo*
I oooooooooooooooooooooooooo*
L ooooooooooooooooooooooooooo*
I ooooooooooooooooooooooooooooo*
T ooooooooooooooooooooooooooooo*
Y oooooooooooooooooooooooooooooooo*
  ooooooooooooooooooooooooooooooooo  *
  oooooooooooooooooooooooooooooooooooo   *
  ooooooooooooooooooooooooooooooooooooooo    *
  oooooooooooooooooooooooooooooooooooooooooo
```

Data

		Empirical		Theoretical	
Safety Factor	Order Point	Shortage Probability	Partial Expectation	Shortage Probability	Partial Expectation
0.00	103.06	0.51500	0.40430	0.50000	0.39894
0.25	109.02	0.40500	0.28612	0.40224	0.28611
0.50	114.97	0.34000	0.19424	0.30988	0.19713
0.75	120.93	0.24500	0.12534	0.22769	0.13037
1.00	126.89	0.15000	0.07938	0.15912	0.08285
1.25	132.85	0.11000	0.04939	0.10561	0.05063
1.50	138.80	0.07000	0.02764	0.06657	0.02966
1.75	144.76	0.04500	0.01405	0.03987	0.01651
2.00	150.72	0.02500	0.00701	0.02267	0.00864
2.25	156.68	0.01500	0.00293	0.01223	0.00423
2.50	162.63	0.00500	0.00029	0.00623	0.00194
2.75	168.59			0.00299	0.00086
3.00	174.55			0.00135	0.00038

FIG. 29.14 Normal distribution.

Component = Log 1
200 Observations have range 108, mean 19.05, and sigma of 19.57
Median = 12, MAD = 12.36
Coefficient of variation = 1.028
Distribution function = 4

Log-Normal

```
  o*
  oo*
  ooo*
  oooo*
  oooo*
P ooooo*
R oooooo*
O ooooooo*
B ooooooo  *
A oooooooo  *
B ooooooooo  *
I  oooooooooo  *
L  oooooooooooo  *
I  ooooooooooooo  *
T ooooooooooooooooo*
Y ooooooooooooooooooo*
   oooooooooooooooooooooo    *
   ooooooooooooooooooooooooo      *
   oooooooooooooooooooooooooooooooooooo      *
   oooooooooooooooooooooooooooooooooooooooooo
```

Data

| Safety Factor | Order Point | Empirical | | Theoretical | |
		Shortage Probability	Partial Expectation	Shortage Probability	Partial Expectation
0.00	19.04	0.32500	0.34709	0.33694	0.31747
0.25	23.94	0.28000	0.27106	0.24511	0.24622
0.50	28.83	0.19500	0.21436	0.18137	0.19492
0.75	33.72	0.13000	0.17515	0.13647	0.15687
1.00	38.61	0.11500	0.14491	0.10433	0.12784
1.25	43.50	0.10500	0.11744	0.08094	0.10519
1.50	48.39	0.07500	0.09357	0.06363	0.08720
1.75	53.28	0.06000	0.07734	0.05064	0.07276
2.00	58.17	0.04500	0.06554	0.04074	0.06105
2.25	63.06	0.04500	0.05429	0.03309	0.05150
2.50	67.95	0.03500	0.04429	0.02712	0.04366
2.75	72.85	0.03000	0.03576	0.02241	0.03719
3.00	77.74	0.03000	0.02826	0.01865	0.03813

FIG. 29.15 Log-normal distribution.

TABLE 29.1 Probability Distributions

If the order point OP, or planning level, is expressed as OP = mean + k standard deviations, then the relations among the probability of a shortage $F(k)$, the partial expectation $E(k)$, and these functions of the order point are as follows.

Distribution		Probability	Partial Expectation
Normal		$F(OP) = F(k)$ $F(k) = \int_k^\infty p(t)dt$	$E(OP) = \sigma E(k)$ $E(k) = \int_k^\infty (t - k)p(t)\, dt$
	Density	$p(t) = \dfrac{1}{\sqrt{2\pi}}\, e^{-t^2/2}$	
Exponential		$F(OP) = F(k)$ $F(k) = e^{-(1+k)}$	$E(OP) = E(k)$ $E(k) = e^{-(1+k)}$
Uniform from A to B		$F(OP) = \dfrac{B - OP}{B - A}$	$E(OP) = \sqrt{3}\left(\dfrac{B - OP}{B - A}\right)^2$
		$F(k) = \dfrac{0.5 - k}{\sqrt{12}}$	$E(k) = \sqrt{3}\left(\dfrac{0.5 - k}{\sqrt{12}}\right)^2$
Log-normal		Let the demand, in pieces, be $X = \sigma_x + k\mu_x$ Let $Y = \ln X = \sigma_y + T\mu_y$ Covariance $\text{cov} = \dfrac{\sigma_x}{\mu_x}$ Parameter $\sigma_Y^2 = \ln(1 + \text{cov}^2)$ Parameter $T = \left(\dfrac{1}{\sigma_y}\right)\ln e^{\sigma^2/2}(1 + k\,\text{cov})$ Use the normal distribution for $F(T)$ and $E(T)$.	

Safety Stocks

The order point, or the cumulative gross requirements, includes provision for a safety stock to manage the trade-off between customer service and the investment in inventory. Safety stock (Fig. 29.16) can always be expressed as $k\sigma$ pieces, where k is a safety factor that might vary over time in a selling season and σ is the standard deviation of errors in forecasting demand over a lead time. Its value may also vary over time in a seasonal industry or where there are significant promotions. The standard deviation is computed (and revised at regular intervals) in the forecasting procedures. The safety factor k can be computed from any of several alternative decision rules.

Table 29.2 summarizes five alternative safety stock decision rules, ranked in sequence by the amount of information about the product required to compute a value for the safety factor. The rules can be named by the objective, in the left-hand column.

The second column gives the mathematical formula for computing the safety factor (the symbols are described in the table footnote). The third column identifies the management policy variable. This value is somewhat arbitrary, but a common value applies to a homogeneous class of products (critical, captive, current parts, for

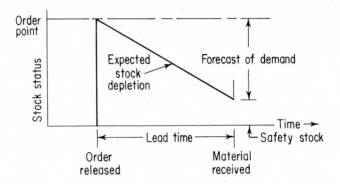

Forecast = sum of forecasts for each month in lead time
+ Safety stock = (safety factor) X (standard deviation over lead time)
= Order point

FIG. 29.16 Safety stocks and order points.

example, versus trim, commercial, standard parts for noncurrent machines). A large value implies more inventory and better service.

The next column indicates briefly the relative sizes of the safety factor for class A and class C products. The next-to-the-right column lists all the item characteristics taken into account in the formula. Note that on each line the formula takes account of all characteristics for formulas above it, plus something additional.

The rightmost column suggests the circumstances in which each formula might be appropriate. The acronym *SCOOT* stands for serve customers out of town and implies a search-and-find operation which makes it practical to fill an order quickly from an alternative location when the facing warehouse is out of stock.

Measures versus Controls. Customer service can be *measured* in a variety of ways—products out of stock, dollars back ordered, lines not filled completely, orders not filled completely, time required to fill an order completely, first-pass service versus system fill, demand for stocked products versus nonstocked products. There is a danger in discussing service as a percentage, because different people may be using different implicit measures. One cannot average percentages by adding percentage values and dividing by the number of values used. It is necessary to add the values in the numerators and the values in the denominators and then compute the percentage from the ratios of those sums.

There are only two primary *controls* on customer service which can be reliably predicted in advance under varying conditions. One is based on the *probability* that demand will exceed the order-point quantity during the next replenishment lead time. The other is based on the *expected quantity* by which demand will exceed the order point. Some decision rules tend to favor one control over the other. Action that will improve either of these controls will also improve the other measures of service. The relationship can be inferred by measuring both over time.

Exchange Curves. Apply a particular decision rule to every product in some homogeneous class of items, using any arbitrary value for the management policy variable. Then the total investment in safety stock (SS) is

TABLE 29.2   Summary of Safety Stock Decision Rules

Objective	Formula	Management Policy Variable	Effect on Safety Factor	Item Characteristics	Recommended
Simplicity	$k = \text{MPV}$	Safety factor	All equal	Standard deviation σ	Simple systems
Equal service	$E(k) = (1 - \text{MPV})\dfrac{Q}{\sigma}$	Fraction filled from stock	Class A: large Class C: small	σ, replenishment frequency N	Not recommended
Minimum back orders	$F(k) = \dfrac{1}{\text{MPV}} \times N$	Expected time between shortages	Class A: large Class C: small	σ, N, budget I	Facing ultimate customer
Minimum expediting	$p(k) = \dfrac{rv\sigma}{\text{MPV} \times N}$	Imputed marginal cost of shortage	Class A: small Class C: large	σ, N, I, cost v	Intermediate echelon if expediting effective
Minimum total cost	$F(k) = \dfrac{rv}{N(c_2 w + c_1/b)}$	Carrying charge	Large for: heavy, cheap, class C, few pieces per demand	σ, N, I, v, weight w, pieces per demand b	Multiple warehouses with SCOOT

k = safety factor (safety stock = $k\sigma$)
σ = standard deviation of lead-time errors
Q = replenishment lot, equivalent to S/N pieces
S = annual sales, pieces per year
N = number of replenishment lots per year
MPV = management policy variable, definition according to rule used
v = unit cost, dollars per piece
b = pieces per demand transaction

w = unit weight, pounds per piece
c_1 = cost per SCOOT transaction
c_2 = cost per pound SCOOTed
I = inventory budget, totaled over safety stocks for all items
$p(k)$ = density function
$F(k)$ = probability
$E(k)$ = partial expectation
r = carrying charge, \$/\$/year

$$SS = \Sigma v_i k_i \sigma_i$$

where v = unit value (dollars per piece)
       k = safety factor resulting from rule
       σ = standard deviation of forecast errors

The expected number of shortage occurrences SO is

$$SO = \Sigma N_i F(k_i)$$

where N is the number of replenishment orders per year and $F(k)$ is the probability that demand during the next lead time will exceed the forecast by more than $k\sigma$ pieces. The value of this probability can be looked up in a table for the appropriate form of the distribution. And the expected dollar value of back-ordered demand is

$$BO = \Sigma N_i v_i \sigma_i E(k_i)$$

where $E(k)$ is the *partial expectation*, sometimes called the *linear loss function* (Raiffa) or the *service function* (IBM). It is not commonly tabulated in classical statistics texts. It is the integral of the probability function $F(k)$.

Since the values of the safety factors k_i depend on the rule analyzed and the value assumed for the management policy variable, also the safety stock, shortage occurrences, and back orders depend on that rule and the management policy variable. Repeat the analysis several times for the same rule but different assumptions about the value for the management policy variable. Larger values lead to more safety stock and lower shortages and back orders.

The curve that relates investment to either measure of service is called an *exchange curve* (Fig. 29.17). Comparison of alternative values with current investment and service gives some guidance as to the value of the management policy variable that will be like current operations or that will achieve some degree of improvement as perceived by management.

Exchange curves can be developed for two different decision rules and applied to the same homogeneous class of inventory. Then comparison of the strategic differences between rules enables one to select the rule that gives performance which improves the measure of service important in the business.

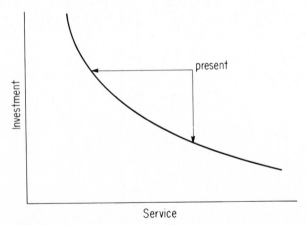

FIG. 29.17 Exchange curve.

BIBLIOGRAPHY

Armstrong, J. Scott: *Long-Range Forecasting*, Wiley, New York, 1978.

Box, G. E. P., and G. W. Jenkins: *Time Series Analysis Forecasting and Control*, Holden-Day, San Francisco, 1982.

Brown, R. G.: *Advanced Service Parts Inventory Control*, Materials Management Systems, Thetford Center, Vt., 1978.

Makridakis, S., and S. Wheelwright: *Forecasting Methods and Applications*, Wiley, New York, 1978.

CHAPTER

Statistics*

Editors:

TZVI RAZ, Assistant Professor, College of Engineering, Department of Industrial and Management Engineering, The University of Iowa, Iowa City, Iowa

STEPHEN D. ROBERTS, Professor of Industrial Engineering, School of Industrial Engineering, Purdue University, Lafayette, Indiana

Statistics deals with the collection, display, and characterization of data and with the use of data to draw conclusions and make decisions. The word *data*, the plural of the Latin word *datum*, means facts. Statistics is concerned with facts about events and entities and the processes that generate or affect them. The relevant characteristics of the events of interest are represented by variables which are either qualitative or quantitative. A *quantitative variable* may take on numerical values, while a *qualitative variable* takes on categorical values. For example, part size, stated as small, medium, or large, is a qualitative variable, while part weight, measured in pounds, is a quantitative variable. If a quantitative variable assumes only certain values such as integers, it is referred to as a *discrete variable*. If the variable can assume any value in a given range, then it is referred to as a *continuous variable*.

The value of a variable is not known until it is actually measured or determined in some way. The process of determining the value of a variable may be conceived of as an experiment whose outcome is uncertain or subject to chance and so is referred to as a *random variable*. A variable that can assume a single value is no longer

*Parts of this chapter were included in the first edition in Chap. 28, "Statistical Theory," edited by Dr. Warren H. Thomas, Chairman, Department of Industrial Engineering, State University of New York at Buffalo, Buffalo, New York.

random and is actually a constant. Here, the concern is mainly with the use and analysis of data in the form of numerical random variables.

The term *population* denotes the set of entities about which conclusions are being drawn, and the term *sample* indicates the part of the population for which data were actually collected. For instance, one may take a sample of 20 units and measure the weight in pounds to draw a conclusion regarding the weight of the population of units in a particular production run.

A population can be finite or infinite. Very large populations, even though finite, may be considered infinite for practical purposes. Most statistical techniques assume that data were collected from a *random sample*, which is a sample selected such that all members of the population are equally likely to be included.

It is randomness in the sample which allows inferences to be made from statistics to population parameters. The sample must be not only random but also representative. This means that one must be careful that the sample taken is in fact characteristic of the population. Hence, the sample must be large enough to adequately reveal the population characteristics. Sometimes special schemes such as stratification, proportionality, and so forth are used to ensure proper representation. These schemes form the foundation of sampling theory and statistical inference.

From a set of sample observations one can calculate *statistics*, which are numerical values that characterize the sample. In a similar manner, a population is characterized by a set of descriptive measures known as *parameters*. The techniques used to draw conclusions about the parameters of a population based on the values of sample statistics are referred collectively to as *statistical inference*. The underlying theory that allows one to draw these conclusions is known as *probability theory*.

DESCRIPTIVE STATISTICS

There are many methods of obtaining information, from personal observations to elaborate automated systems. Important internal sources of data for production control include such reports as the production records, sales forecasts, routings, material supply schedules, budgets, scrap reports, etc. This information can be collected by hand (manually), by electronic data processing equipment, by a key-sort system, and by many other methods. Most management information systems provide means of collection and storage of data. Therefore, familiarization with these modes of collection can greatly aid in obtaining information.

Frequently, external data sources must be consulted. This is especially true in forecasting. In this case one might consult such publications as *Survey of Current Business* or other external sources.

Display of Data

After data are collected, it is helpful to display them in some insightful fashion. This display can often reveal useful properties about data and imply important characteristics, presenting data which can be understood with a minimum of explanation. In general, there are two methods of display: tabular and graphical.

Tabular Displays.   These displays of numerical values emphasize some relevant fact. The three displays of primary interest are the historical table, the research table, and the frequency table.

Historical Table. The historical, or reference, table is a means of collecting concise reference material. It generally takes the form shown in Table 30.1. This specific table illustrates the number of employees for each department for 3 separate years. The basic parts indicated in Table 30.1 should be used as a guide in the preparation of such tables. It is important that emphasis be placed where most desired. People have a tendency to read from left to right and from top to bottom, so the data in the upper left-hand corner should be most prominent. In general, the arrangement should be easily understood and yet provide sufficient information to effectively communicate valuable ideas. Footnotes should provide additional explanation, and the information source should be acknowledged.

Research Table. The research table, sometimes called the *analytical*, or *cross-reference, table*, serves as an aid for more specific analysis of data. An example of this kind of table is shown in Table 30.2. This table presents the effects of machine speeds, feeds, and material types on scrap rates and the interrelationships among the variables. Since the table contains three variables—speed, feed, and material—it is sometimes called a *three-way table.*

Frequency Table. Of primary importance in descriptive statistics is the *frequency table*. This is described best with an illustration. Suppose one is interested in customer orders outstanding which are late. Table 30.3 presents the data as they are collected. There are 40 tardy orders. Obviously the data, as collected, are difficult to understand in present form, so one would like to present them in a more

TABLE 30.1 Average Number of Employees per Department

Department	Year 1	Year 2	Year 3
Stock	3	4	5
Plating	7	7	8
Screw machine	8	9	10
Milling	10	12	12
Drilling	5	5	6
Miscellaneous parts	15	15	17
Stores	5	5	6
Assembly	20	22	23
Warehousing	6	7	7

TABLE 30.2 Effects of Machine Speed, Feed, and Material on Scrap Rates

Speedy ft/min	Material A Feed, in/rev 0.005	0.010	Material B Feed, in/rev 0.005	0.010	Material C Feed, in/rev 0.005	0.010
200	0.05	0.06	0.04	0.08	0.08	0.02
250	0.04	0.07	0.05	0.07	0.06	0.03
300	0.02	0.06	0.07	0.07	0.05	0.03
350	0.01	0.05	0.09	0.08	0.06	0.04

usable and effective manner. In their original form the data are often referred to as *raw data*

For this case, the data may be ordered according to the degree of tardiness, as presented in Table 30.4. This is sometimes called a *frequency array*, since the number of times, or frequency, of a particular number of days tardy is presented as well as the days tardy. However, reduction to a frequency array usually does not greatly improve the compactness of the presentation. Consequently, it is often convenient to group the data into classes, or groups, of specified intervals. For this case it could be accomplished by using a class size of 5. These grouped data are then tabulated in Table 30.5. Such a tabulation is called a *frequency distribution. A class* refers to the designation of information within a given interval, while the interval itself is called a *class interval*. For this case there are five classes, each with an interval of 5. The boundaries of the classes, 0, 4, 5, 9, etc., are referred to as the *class limits.*

Note, however, that while this presentation does give a clear and concise picture of tardiness, it was achieved through some loss of information. This is illustrated by the fact that one cannot decipher from the table which orders are more than 19 days late. To obtain this information, one must refer to the raw data.

TABLE 30.3   Tardiness of Orders (Days)

10	11	20	1	0
9	12	16	6	17
16	15	9	31	19
12	12	11	15	2
8	4	6	14	8
7	13	3	2	7
5	17	10	11	18
13	14	12	5	22

TABLE 30.4   Frequency Array of Tardiness

Days Tardy	Frequency	Days Tardy	Frequency
0	1	11	3
1	1	12	4
2	2	13	2
3	1	14	2
4	1	15	2
5	2	16	2
6	2	17	2
7	2	18	1
8	2	19	1
9	2	20	1
10	2	22	1
		31	1

TABLE 30.5 Frequency
Distribution of Tardiness

Days Tardy	Number of Orders
0–4	6
5–9	10
10–14	13
15–19	8
Over 20	3
	40

Consequently, the reduction of the data to a more concise form depends directly on the number of classes chosen. This is not easy to determine and requires much insight. If there are too many classes, the resulting frequency distribution becomes bulky, and the concentrations of the data are difficult to ascertain. If there are too few classes, much of the information is concealed within the class intervals, and the frequency distribution becomes so compact that an important pattern may be completely grouped within a class. A good rule of thumb states that the number of classes should range between 5 and 15. Obviously in some special situations 15 may be too few or 5 too many, but without any other insight the rule has proved very useful.

Selection of the class interval and class limits is also difficult. The class limits should not be overlapping but should be exclusive. If, for example, the class limits were 0 to 5 for the first class and 5 to 10 for the second, an order having a tardiness of 5 could be placed in either the first or second class. If the class interval and limits are established before the data are collected, this consequence should be considered so that accurate data are obtained. To make the table easy to understand and construct, the class intervals should be equal. This was done in constructing Table 30.5, and the reasons should be clear.

For discrete data it is not difficult to define class limits because the data can assume only certain values. Consequently, the limits were 0 to 4, 5 to 9, 10 to 14, and so forth, since this guaranteed that all data would be contained in mutually exclusive classes. However, this is difficult to do if the data are continuous. Suppose, for example, that the tardiness were measured in half-days. A tardiness of 4.5 would not lie within the limits of any class boundary. Thus the class limits would have to be revised. To avoid this ambiguity, one usually represents the class limits to one decimal point more than that of the data. For example, the class limits could be revised to the following: 0.00 to 4.54, 4.55, to 9.54, 9.55 to 14.54. Since the data are measured to only one decimal place, the new class limits will be nonoverlapping, and the class intervals remain equal. Note that this may always be done, since any time data are collected, they are made discrete to some extent; thus class limits may be constructed, so that all information will fall within a class.

Hence it is important that there be no separation between classes. Often this is difficult to avoid without using too few classes. Therefore, it is sometimes convenient to utilize *open-ended classes*. This is, in fact, what the fifth class is in the table. An open-ended class has only one class limit. It is useful when part of the data appears far away from the major concentration of the information. In the tardiness example, the use of an open-ended class avoided the use of an empty class (25 to 29). Notice that open-ended classes can occur at the beginning of a frequency distribution as well as at the end. The disadvantage of such classes is that they cover an extremely large range and do not provide any magnitude information such as how many days over 20 are the orders late.

In addition to the class intervals, limits, size, and so forth, the *midpoints* of the classes are important. The midpoint is merely the sum of the class limits divided by 2, or just the average of the class limits. The midpoint of the classes should be of such a magnitude that its value can actually be obtained. For continuous data this presents no problems. However, for discrete data the values of the data are restricted to a certain set of values. The midpoint is important since data within a class are often represented by their value, and the data should tend to cluster about this point. Thus the use of the classes in the table appears satisfactory.

An important type of frequency table is called the *percentage table*. This table represents the proportion, or percentage, of data which may be found in a certain class. Thus it is merely the frequency table transformed to percentage data. An illustration of this for the tardiness example is given in Table 30.6. This table indicates, for example, that 25 percent of the orders are 5 to 9 days late. If these 40 orders were a random sample of some larger population, we might use the percentage table to reflect the tardiness character of the population itself.

Sometimes it is even useful to collect cumulative data. For example, suppose we wanted the number of orders less than or equal to 9 days late. Table 30.7 supplies this type of information. This is sometimes called a "less than" table. Note that this may also be presented in percentage form, as indicated by Table 30.6. One may construct an equivalent "more than" cumulative table. The less-than table *begins* with zero, while the more-than table *ends* with zero. Often the *cumulative frequency table* (of the less-than type) is referred to as the *cumulative distribution*, and it represents an important concept in descriptive statistics.

TABLE 30.6   Percentage Table

Days Tardy	Percentage
0−4	15.0
5−9	25.0
10−14	32.5
15−19	20.0
Over 20	7.5
	100.0

TABLE 30.7   Cumulative Frequency Table

Days Tardy	Cumulative No. of Orders	Cumulative Percentage
0−4	6	15.0
5−9	16	40.0
10−14	29	72.5
15−19	37	92.5
Over 20	40	100.0

Graphical Display.   As with the tabular display, the graphical display is used to emphasize some particular aspect of the data, but through a visual or pictorial medium. Graphical presentations may be used to highlight certain significant facts and are often used in conjunction with tabular results. Management appreciates graphical displays which present, at a glance, simple and clearly significant points. Often graphical displays are used for presentation of information to a group of people where a large display can provide a persuasive exhibit. There are many types of graphical displays, but among the most important are bar charts, line charts, pie charts, pictograms, histograms, and frequency polygons.

Bar Charts.   The *bar chart* is one of the most popular of the graphical displays. It is simple to construct and easy to understand. The basic characteristic of the bar chart is that it is strictly one-dimensional. In other words, only the lengths of the bars vary. An example of a bar chart is given in Fig. 30.1. This presents the distribution of people during the year for the plant departments. Notice that the bars are separated for ease of identification, and normally the bars are placed in increasing or decreasing order unless they are fixed by something such as time. The height of the bar represents the number of people. More specifically, this bar chart is called a *simple vertical-bar chart*, or *column chart*. This chart may be turned on its side and then is called a *simple horizontal-bar chart*. The preference for vertical or horizontal is simply a question of which makes the most effective presentation and which is simplest to construct.

In addition to the simple bar charts there exist other types of bar charts. Among the most widely used are the component-part bar chart, the grouped bar chart, and the two-directional bar chart. These charts are illustrated in a horizontal fashion in Figs. 30.2, 30.3, and 30.4.

The *component-part bar chart* is recognized because the bars themselves are composed of components. This type of chart permits a visual comparison of the

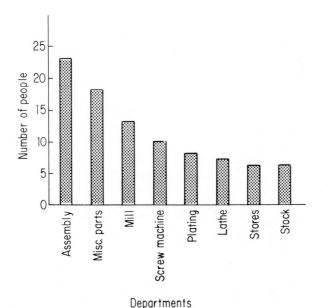

Departments

FIG. 30.1   Distribution of people during the year for plant department.

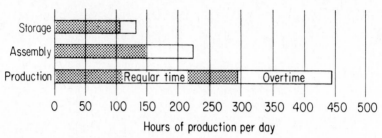

FIG. 30.2   Component chart—breakdown of production hours.

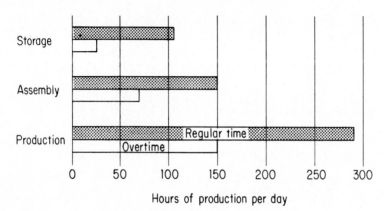

FIG. 30.3   Grouped bar chart—breakdown of production hours.

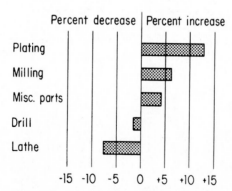

FIG. 30.4   Two-directional chart: percentage change in department performance for 2 years.

contribution of regular time and overtime to the total production hours per day for each departmental group. However, all overtime components have different origins on the scale, and so it is difficult to compare the overtime among the departmental groups.

This disadvantage is overcome by the *grouped bar chart*. In this chart, both overtime and regular time may be compared with each other and also with those of the other departmental groups. But this chart has a disadvantage which the component-part chart does not possess. Comparisons are difficult between the total production hours for each departmental group when a total includes the sum of overtime and regular time.

When relative gains and losses are desired, the *two-directional chart* emphasizes the characteristics. The percentage change in departmental performance for 2 years is presented. The departments are ranked from the most positive to the most negative, so analysis is simplified. Note that component-type bars may be used as well as grouped bars. These types of charts are extremely useful to indicate improvements or losses on the same chart around a common base of zero. In the example one is able to pinpoint which department's performance is deteriorating or improving.

In constructing bar charts, it is important that direct labeling be used, as illustrated, so that they are easily read. For the component-part or grouped charts, the bars should be shaded, crosshatched, or colored so that each bar is distinct. Also the bars should be spaced, for ease in identification. Grouped bars of the grouped bar chart are, however, often side by side. The central theme in construction should be clarity and ease of presentation and identification.

Line Chart.   *Line charts* are particularly useful whenever the variable is a function of or depends on time. Sales forecasts are examples of this type of need. Normally time is plotted on the horizontal axis while the quantity of interest is plotted on the vertical. Line charts may be *simple* or of the *component-part type* similar to bar charts. Figure 30.5 illustrates the simple line chart for the personnel requirements of three major departmental groups—assembly, production, and storage. The vertical axis could be of the same form as in Fig. 30.2, except the line segments connect components of the data, thus forming a component-part line chart. The series of connecting lines is called a *curve* and represents the variable of interest as the time varies. The major advantage of such a chart is the ability to visualize the character of the data as they change with respect to time.

Pie Charts.   *Pie charts* or *circle charts* are used to portray components of a total. The pie chart is particularly eye-catching, but application is limited to component-type characteristics. An example is presented in Fig. 30.6. In constructing the pie

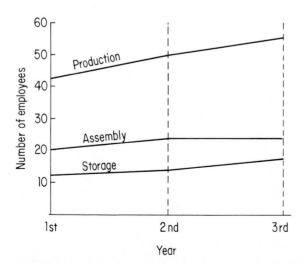

FIG. 30.5   Personnel requirements for departmental groups.

chart, a protractor is useful to obtain the desired proportions. Also it is desirable to arrange the sectors according to their magnitude. Colors can produce a more striking appearance. Pie-chart suitability lies in its eye-catching appeal, and so it is useful for public presentation. However, it lacks the accuracy of other charts.

Pictograms. Like the pie chart, the *pictogram* is used because of eye appeal and is particularly useful for a wide range of audiences. The pictogram is simply a bar chart constructed from symbols which serve the same purpose as the bars in the bar chart. A typical pictogram is shown in Fig. 30.7, denoting the number of employees for each shift. Note that in constructing such a chart the symbol has a numerical relationship with the data, and thus each symbol represents a certain segment of the data. Sometimes the size of the symbol represents the data, and often fractional symbols are used. The pictogram should illustrate the data clearly and should not distract from the importance of the result. In constructing such a chart, avoid the pitfall of displaying too much information, thus confusing the viewer.

Histograms. The *histogram* is a means of graphically illustrating a frequency distribution. In many ways it is similar to a vertical bar chart; however, it is two-dimensional in that both the width and height of the bars are variables. Consider the frequency distribution of Table 30.8, which depicts the distribution of daily demand for stock over a period of 160 days. Figure 30.8 illustrates the histogram constructed from this frequency distribution and using the class limits and frequency. The frequency for each class is represented by the height of the bar, while the width of the bar for each class is governed by the class limits. The bars are

FIG. 30.6 Pie chart for proportion of inventory.

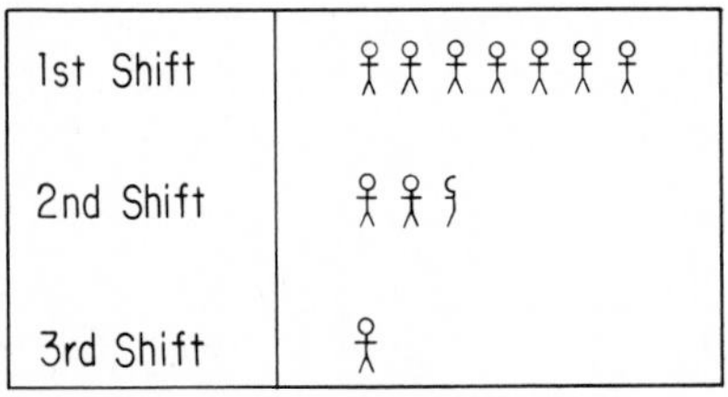

FIG. 30.7 Pictogram of number of employees per shift.

usually not separated, so the numbers on the horizontal axis practically form a continuous span.

Note that a histogram cannot be constructed for distributions which have open-ended classes. One should also avoid using a histogram for distributions when classes are not equal. The histogram may be altered if classes are unequal but closed by making the frequency within each interval proportional to the area of the bar for the class. For example, if one class interval is twice as wide as the rest, then the height of the bar for this particular class should be reduced by one-half. In general, however, one cannot use the histogram for cases involving open-ended classes, and care must be used if the class intervals are unequal.

TABLE 30.8 Frequency Distribution of Bar-Stock Demand

No. of Bars Demanded	Frequency of Demand
30–34	1
35–39	4
40–44	13
45–49	26
50–54	50
55–59	39
60–64	20
65–69	5
70–74	2
	160

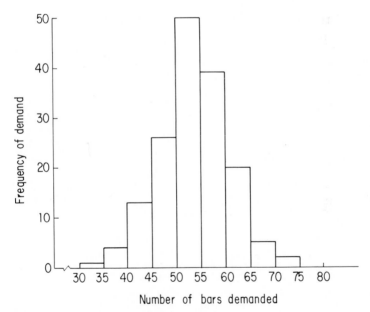

FIG. 30.8 Distribution of bar-stock demand.

Frequency Polygons.   The *frequency polygon* is an alternative method for graphically illustrating the frequency distribution and performs a function similar to that of the histogram. The frequency polygon for the data in Table 30.8 is shown in Fig. 30.9. The frequency polygon is formed by letting the midpoints of the classes assume the frequency of the class. Then these points are connected by a set of line segments, thus forming a type of curve. Note that the extra classes with zero frequency are artificially augmented at both ends of the distribution so that the curve will meet the horizontal axis on both ends, thus enclosing the frequency within the polygon.

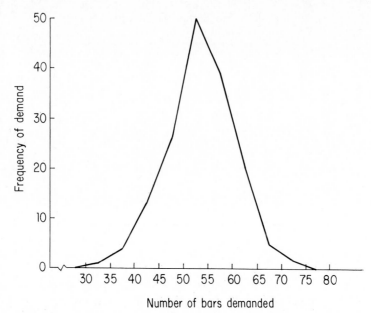

FIG. 30.9 Frequency polygon of distribution of bar-stock demand.

As with the histogram, the frequency polygon cannot be constructed if one of the classes is open-ended. If the class intervals are unequal, the same adjustment must be made for the frequency polygon as has to be done for the histogram.

The choice of whether a frequency distribution is to be represented by a frequency polygon or histogram is a matter of personal preference. The only advantage of a frequency polygon lies in comparing two or more distributions plotted on the same chart, but the histogram seems to be preferable when a discrete set of data is presented.

Cumulative Frequency Representation. Like the frequency table, the frequency polygon or the histogram may be represented in cumulative form. For example, if the less-than distribution were to be graphed for Table 30.8, its cumulative frequency representation in polygon form would look like Fig. 30.10. Note that the vertical axis may be represented by frequency or by percentage.

Sometimes these types of curves are called *ogives.* Note that the ogive differs from the frequency polygon in that the cumulative frequency is plotted at the upper class limit (or between the upper limit of the class and the lower limit of the next class), so that the less-than notion agrees with the graphed display.

Naturally a cumulative histogram could be constructed in the same manner. Cumulative representations tend to be S-shaped, rising from zero at the lower left to the maximum at the upper right. These curves allow interpolation and are very similar to their continuous counterpart, the distribution functions. These are widely used in simulation studies, particularly those of the Monte Carlo variety.

MEASURES OF LOCATION

The frequency distribution is useful to characterize the pattern of variation of variables. The frequency table provides a tabular form of the distribution, while the

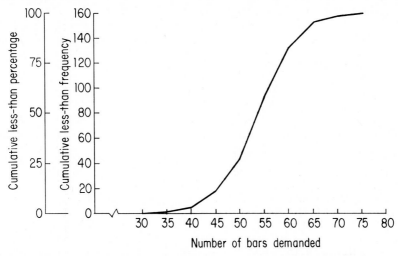

FIG. 30.10 Cumulative bar-stock demand.

frequency polygon presents a graphical display. However, working directly with the frequency distribution is quite cumbersome, and one may wish to investigate the data by summarizing some of the more important properties. This discussion is directed particularly to developing measures of the location, or position, of the distribution. Specifically, one wishes to know about what point the distribution seems to be concentrated. Methods of measuring such a point are referred to as *measures of location*. Sometimes they are called *measures of position, measures of central tendency*, and *measures of central values*. In general, the measures of location tend to summarize the distribution in the sense that they characterize by a single value the location, or position, of the frequency distribution.

Mean

This first measure of location is called the *average*, or *mean*, or, more accurately, the *arithmetic mean*. Consider n observations whose values are $x_1, x_2, x_3, \ldots x_n$. The mean is defined as follows:

$$\text{Mean} = \frac{x_1 + x_2 + \ldots + x_n}{n} = \frac{\sum_{i=1}^{n} x_i}{n}$$

where $\sum_{i=1}^{n} x_i = x_1 + x_2 + \ldots + x_n$.

To illustrate this computational method, suppose in a particular shop there are five screw machines whose production capabilities are as follows (in parts per hour): 255, 215, 157, 230, and 188. By the above formula, the mean production capability of the screw machines is

$$\frac{255 + 215 + 157 + 230 + 188}{5} = \frac{1045}{5} = 209$$

If the mean is calculated from the entire population, it is denoted by the Greek letter μ (mu) and thus represents a population parameter. However, if the calculation is made for a sample, the mean is denoted by $\bar{x}$ (x bar) and is thus a statistic. For a particular population, μ is a constant; however, $\bar{x}$ for the same population is a variable, since the sample mean will depend on the values of the sample chosen. Hence for different samples from the same population, there will probably be a different mean.

Mean of the Frequency Distribution

The mean may be computed from the frequency distribution as well as the raw data or data array. Consider the frequency distribution of Table 30.8 concerning the demand of bar stock. Obviously, one cannot work with the individual demands in this case, since they have been grouped into classes. Consequently, one must make an assumption regarding the distribution. It is assumed, usually validly, that all frequencies located within each class may be represented by the midpoint. Hence, this emphasizes the necessity for selecting the classes and their midpoints with care. For most distributions found in production and inventory control, the errors introduced by this assumption tend to cancel themselves eventually. However, the formula for calculating the mean must be modified:

$$\text{Mean from a frequency distribution} = \frac{\sum_{i=1}^{k} x_i f_i}{\sum_{i=1}^{k} f_i} = \frac{\sum_{i=1}^{k} x_i f_i}{N}$$

where $\sum_{i=1}^{k} f_i = N$ and f_i is the number of observations in class i.

An illustration of this calculation for the mean bar-stock demand of Table 30.8 is given in Table 30.9. Since these are results from a sample (and this is always the case

TABLE 30.9 Calculation of Mean of Bar-Stock Demand

Class	Bar Demand	Midpoint x_i	Frequency f_i	$x_i f_i$
1	30–34	32	1	32
2	35–39	37	4	148
3	40–44	42	13	546
4	45–49	47	26	1222
5	50–54	52	50	2600
6	55–59	57	39	2223
7	60–64	62	20	1240
8	65–69	67	5	335
9	70–74	72	2	144
			$\sum_{i=1}^{9} f_i = 160$	$\sum_{i=1}^{9} x_i f_i = 8490$

unless it is indicated otherwise), one may assert that $\bar{x}$ = 8490/160 = 53.0625, upon application of the previous formula. The table includes the general method for accomplishing the calculation. Of major importance are the columns containing x_i, f_i, and $x_i f_i$, since they form the basis of the calculation. The first four columns are taken from Table 30.8, while the last column is simply the product of the midpoints and frequencies.

Weighted Mean

Suppose one wishes the average space utilization in all three storage areas—rough stock, in-process stock, and finish stock. The arithmetic average of the utilization in each of the three areas is inappropriate, since more than likely each store occupies a different area. Suppose the utilization in rough stock is 21 percent, 33 percent in in-process stock, and 47 percent in finish stock; and the area of rough stock is 700 square feet (sq ft), in-process stock is 400 sq ft, and finish stock occupies 1050 sq ft. Therefore, the overall space-utilization mean for all stores is

$$\frac{(0.21)(700) + (0.33)(400) + (0.47)(1050)}{700 + 400 + 1050} = 0.359, \text{ or } 35.9\%$$

Thus by weighting each utilization with the proper area, a more representative mean is calculated. In this way the size of the area is incorporated along with its utilization.

In general, suppose we have a set of n values $x_1, x_2, \ldots, x_n$, whose importance is reflected by the weights $w_1, w_2, \ldots, w_n$. Thus the *weighted mean* may be defined as

$$\text{Weighted mean} = \frac{\sum\limits_{i=1}^{n} w_i x_i}{\sum\limits_{i=1}^{n} w_i}$$

Another application of the weighted mean utilizes the combination of several means. For example, suppose one knows the mean number of personnel in each of n departments. Let $\bar{x}_1, \bar{x}_2, \ldots, \bar{x}_n$ be the mean number of people in each of the n departments. Suppose the sizes of the departments are given by $m_1, m_2, \ldots, m_n$. Then the overall (sample) mean number of people in the n departments is

$$\bar{\bar{x}} = \frac{\sum\limits_{i=1}^{n} m_i \bar{x}_i}{\sum\limits_{i=1}^{n} m_i}$$

Hence one may use the above formula to calculate overall means, which are in essence a form of the weighted means. Consequently, overall means may be formulated from the means of several sets of data.

Properties of the Mean

The following are among the most important characteristics of the mean:

1. The mean is a concept of general familiarity and is easily understood.
2. The mean always exists and so always may be calculated.
3. For a given set of values, only one mean can be calculated. Thus the mean is unique.
4. The mean is influenced by every value in the sample. If the data are classified by a frequency distribution, then all midpoints and class frequencies affect the mean.
5. The unit of measure of the mean is identical to the unit of measure describing the data; i.e., if the data are in units of demand, then the mean is described in units of demand.
6. The algebraic sum of the differences between the mean and the data is zero. Expressed mathematically, this is

$$\sum_{i=1}^{n} (x_i - \bar{x}) = 0$$

7. The sum of the squares of the differences between the mean and the data is a minimum. In other words, the sum of the squares of the differences between the data and any point other than the mean will produce a larger value. This property may be demonstrated by merely calculating the sum of the squared difference first about the mean and then about any other value. The interested reader may verify this for Table 30.9, utilizing the mean and any other values. This characteristic has a special significance in computing a measure of the variation called the standard deviation, which is discussed later.

Median and Other Quartiles

In a series of ordered data (either increasing or decreasing) the *median* is the middle value, or the value which divides the total frequency in half. If the number n in the ordered series is an odd number, then the median is merely the $(n + 1)/2$ value, counting from either end. For example, consider the following ordered series composed of five numbers:

15   17   23   24   26

Since the number of values in the series is odd, the median is $(5 + 1)/2$, or the third number from either end. Thus the median of the above series is 23. If the n values of the ordered series are odd, then the median is the mean of the middle values. To illustrate, consider the following ordered series composed of six numbers:

12   17   18   22   26   28

Since 18 and 22 are the middle two values, the median is $(18 + 22)/2 = 20$. Hence the median is a positional measure, since the values of the numbers in the series do not, in general, have a critical effect on the median. For example, one may change 12, 17, 26, and 28, and the value of the median will be unaffected *as long as the order in the series is maintained.*

Quartiles, Deciles, and Percentiles

If the total frequency is divided into 4 equal proportions, the 3 values at the division are called *quartiles*. If the frequency is divided into 10 equal proportions, the 9 dividers are referred to as *deciles*. Likewise, if the frequency is divided into 100 equal parts, the 99 dividers are called *percentiles*. Note that the number of dividers is always 1 less than the number of parts, because both ends of the frequency are not counted.

The quartiles in general are determined in a manner similar to the median. Again, interpolation is required when data come from the frequency distribution.

Properties of the Median

The following are among the most important characteristics of the median:

1. The median is simple to calculate and always exists for any set of data.
2. For any set of data, it is a unique value.
3. It is relatively unaffected by extremes in the data and is influenced by the position rather than by the actual value of each data entry.
4. It can be calculated from a frequency distribution with open classes or unequal intervals (as long as the median does not fall in an open interval).
5. The sum of the absolute value of the differences between a set of values and the median is a minimum. The interested reader may verify this for a series of values.

Mode

The *mode*, which as a measure of location, is the value most frequently found in a set of data. Consequently, if is often referred to as the most "probable" value in the set of data, since it occurs the most often. Many times, in every day usage, the mode is the most "typical" value. For example, the typical grade received by a student is a C.

To demonstrate how to locate the mode in a data array, consider the following list of numbers:

$$9 \quad 11 \quad 10 \quad 8 \quad 12 \quad 10 \quad 9 \quad 13 \quad 9 \quad 7$$

The most frequently repeated number in this set is 9, and it is repeated three times. Thus 9 is the mode for this set of data.

Mode of the Frequency Distribution. The mode may be determined from a frequency distribution by first noting which class has the highest frequency of occurrence. This class is commonly called the *modal class*. If two adjacent classes have the highest (equal) frequency, then the mode is merely the boundary between the two classes.

Properties of the Mode.   The following are among the most important characteristics of the mode:

1. It is extremely easy to calculate and enjoys a meaningful interpretation as a typical value.
2. It is unaffected by extremes in the data and may be computed from distributions involving open classes or classes having unequal intervals.
3. It may not be unique in that the maximum frequency may be attained by more than one value. Also if all values have equal frequency, it does not exist at all.

Comparison of the Mean, Median, and Mode

For distribution whose general shape is perfectly symmetric, the mean, median, and mode are identical (Fig. 30.11). If the shape of the distribution is not symmetric and the mass of the data tends to be concentrated toward the high numbers, tailing off slowly with lower numbers, then the mean will have the lowest number, followed by the median and then the mode. If the concentration of the data appears skewed toward lower values, then the mode will be the smallest number, followed by the median and then the mean.

For distributions which are moderately skewed, there exists an approximate relationship among the mean, median, and mode. These are roughly related as follows:

$$\text{Mode} = \text{Mean} - 3(\text{Mean} - \text{Median})$$

In general, the mean, median, and mode each measure the location of the frequency distribution. The mean represents the average, or center of gravity, while the

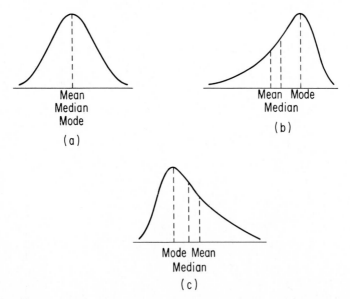

FIG. 30.11   Examples of symmetric and skewed frequency distributions.

median indicates a central, or middle, value and the mode indicates the most typical value. The question as to which should be used depends on the application and interpretation required of the results.

MEASURES OF VARIATION

It is a characteristic of frequency distributions and variables to contain *variation*, or *variability*. Sometimes this variation is referred to as *dispersion*. Variables such as the mean, median, and mode measure the position or central tendency; however, these measures do not adequately describe the degree of scatter often encountered.

Variation, or dispersion, in a frequency distribution is very important in decision making, especially in production and inventory control. Consider the demand of bar stock given in Table 30.8. Because of the variation in this demand, one cannot merely stock the average demand required (where average may be mean, median, mode, etc.) because the demand may be very high in certain periods and an "average" value of stock on hand will not suffice. This was illustrated by the frequency distribution of Table 30.8. Thus the degree of variation determines the amount of safety stock carried for the bar stock. Consequently, the variation in the frequency distribution can be very important, and to describe this characteristic, one must determine measures which reflect this variation, or dispersion.

Range

The simplest and most easily obtained measure of variation is the *range*. It is calculated as the difference between the highest and lowest values in a group of data. For example, consider the following data:

$$15 \quad 5 \quad 17 \quad 18 \quad 9 \quad 13 \quad 15$$

The range for this example is merely $18 - 5 = 13$. Although easiest to calculate, the range is normally not a satisfactory method to measure variation. It reflects only the extremes in the data and does not account for the dispersion throughout the remaining data. Its main advantage is that it is simple to calculate and may be most useful when a rough, quick measure of the variation is required.

Interquartile and Interdecile Range

Sometimes it is common to eliminate extreme values in computing ranges. If the upper and lower quarters of the data are removed, the resulting range is called the *interquartile range*. This measure reflects the range in which 50 percent of the data is contained. If one lets Q_1, be the first quartile and Q_3 the third, the interquartile range is simply the difference between Q_3 and Q_1, or $Q_3 - Q_1$.

If one calculates the first decile D_1 and the ninth decile D_9, then the *interdecile range* is merely $D_9 - D_1$. This range includes 80 percent of the values and so describes more of the data than the interquartile range.

Interquartile and interdecile ranges are better than simple ranges because they are location-based. This refers to the fact that their bases stem from the median and are thus related, to some extent, to a representation of the position, or location, of the data. Hence, in general, they reflect more of the dispersion of the data and are less subject to extremes. Also interquartile and interdecile ranges are quickly obtained from frequency distributions even if there are open classes.

Average Deviation

In an effort to overcome the disadvantage of the range measure of variation, one might consider the deviation of individual values from some positional value such as the mean or median. This would allow all items in the data to influence the measure of variation. A method for accomplishing this scheme is to calculate the average of the absolute values of the deviations about the mean. This measure of variation is commonly referred to as the *average deviation*. For lists of data, it may be expressed as

$$\text{Average deviation} = \frac{\displaystyle\sum_{i=1}^{I} |x_i - \bar{x}|}{n}$$

where $\bar{x}$ is the mean of the data under consideration.

Therefore, for data which tend to be concentrated about the mean, the average deviation is low. As the dispersion in the data becomes more pronounced, the average deviation *increases* to reflect this increased variability.

For data which are grouped into a frequency distribution, the deviations are calculated from the class midpoints. Thus, for calculating the average deviation from a frequency distribution,

$$\text{Average deviation} = \frac{\displaystyle\sum_{i=1}^{k} (|x_i - \bar{x}|f_i)}{N}$$

where x_i = midpoint of the ith class
f_i = class frequency
k = number of classes
N = total frequency

For the bar-stock example of Table 30.8, the computation of the average deviation is given in Table 30.10. The average deviation is shown to be

$$\text{Average deviation of bar-stock demand} = \frac{879.7500}{160} = 5.498$$

It might be preferable to sum the absolute deviations about the median rather than the mean since it is a minimum (see property 5 of the median); however, it has been common practice to use the mean. Although the average deviation does represent an improvement as a measure of variation over the range, it is used very infrequently. The main reason is that more mathematically complex analysis cannot be performed because of the use of absolute values.

TABLE 30.10 Calculation of Average Deviation of Bar Stock

Class	Midpoint x_i	f_i	$\lvert x_i - \bar{x} \rvert$*	$f_i \lvert x_i - \bar{x} \rvert$
1	32	1	21.0625	21.0625
2	37	4	16.0625	64.2500
3	42	13	11.0625	143.8125
4	47	26	6.0625	157.6250
5	52	50	1.0625	53.1250
6	57	39	3.9375	153.5625
7	62	20	8.9375	178.7500
8	67	5	13.9375	69.6875
9	72	2	18.9375	37.8750
		160		879.7500

* $\bar{x} = 53.0625$.

Variance and Standard Deviation

Another commonly used measure of dispersion is the *variance*, s^2, which is defined as the mean squared deviation from the mean value:

$$s^2 = \frac{\sum_{i=1}^{n} (x_i - \bar{x})^2}{n - 1}$$

Notice that the denominator is $n - 1$ rather than n. This is due to some theoretical considerations which are not discussed here.

The units of s^2 are the square of the units of x. For instance, if x is measured in pounds, s^2 is given in square pounds. In many cases it is more meaningful to consider the square root of the variance, which has the same units as the original variable. This quantity, referred to as the *standard deviation*, is calculated as follows:

$$s = \sqrt{\frac{\sum_{i=1}^{n} (x_i - \bar{x})^2}{n - 1}}$$

Frequently this formula is awkward to use and is especially subject to rounding errors. An alternative formula, which gives identical results, is

$$\text{Standard deviation} = \sqrt{\frac{\sum_{i=1}^{n} x^2 - \left(\sum_{i=1}^{n} x \right)^2 / n}{n - 1}}$$

Table 30.11 illustrates the calculation of the standard deviation of an array of six x values. For this table,

$$s = \sqrt{\frac{46}{5}} = \sqrt{9.2} = 3.033$$

Some General Aspects of the Standard Deviation.   The following are among the most important aspects of the standard deviation as a measure of variation:

1. For many of the distributions found in production and inventory control, about 68 percent of all values in a particular distribution do not deviate from the mean by more than 1 standard deviation; about 95 percent of the values do not deviate from the mean by more than 2 standard deviations; and about 99 percent of the values do not deviate from the mean by more than 3 standard deviations. In general, at the very worst, $1 - 1/k$ of the values will not deviate from the mean by more than k standard deviations.

2. The standard deviation provides a measure of variability such that statistical tests regarding properties of the data can be analyzed. For example, one may wish to know if the production rates on two screw machines are statistically different.

3. The standard deviation provides a basis for inference regarding a population parameter. For example, one may calculate an interval in which he is almost sure the average bar-stock demand will lie.

4. Use of the standard deviation and variance establishes the groundwork for more sophisticated statistical analysis of data such as regression analysis, correlation analysis, analysis of variance, etc.

Relative Measures of Variation.   The previously discussed measures of variation deal with an absolute measure of variation in the sense that the magnitudes of the units are not considered. For example, suppose one is interested in the variation in departmental sizes. Suppose from historical records department A has a standard deviation of 2.3 men, while that of department B has more variation than department A. However, the mean number of men in department A is 10, while that of B is

TABLE 30.11   Calculation of the Standard Deviation

	Array		
x_i	$(x_i - \bar{x})^*$	$(x - \bar{x})^2$	x_i^2
6	-5	25	36
10	-1	1	100
11	0	0	121
11	0	0	121
13	2	4	169
15	4	16	225
66		46	772

$^*\ \bar{x} = {}^{66}\!/_{6} = 11$

20. Since the magnitude of the means is not similar, this suggests the use of some relative measure of variation.

Perhaps the most popular of the relative measures is one which simply expresses the standard deviation as a percentage of the mean. The measure called the *coefficient of variation* may be expressed as follows:

$$\text{Coefficient of variation} = \left(\frac{\text{Standard deviation}}{\text{Mean}}\right) 100$$

The advantage of such a measure is that variation is expressed as a percentage. Hence not only can variation involving different magnitudes be compared, but also the variation in data involving different units of measure such as time and distance may be compared.

Another measure of relative variation is called the *coefficient of quartile deviation*. This is especially useful for relative measures of variation involving open-end distributions. It is defined simply as the interquartile range as a percentage of the sum of Q_1 and Q_3, as follows:

$$\text{Coefficient of quartile deviation} = \left(\frac{Q_3 - Q_1}{Q_3 + Q_1}\right) 100$$

This again reduces the variation to a percentage, making comparisons possible. The coefficient of quartile deviation is simply calculated through the use of quartiles, as discussed earlier.

MEASURES OF THE SHAPE OF THE FREQUENCY DISTRIBUTION

Although measures of variation and location indicate two of the most important characteristics of the frequency distribution, they do not indicate completely its shape. Although applications of measures of shape are found infrequently, they are important as a further description of the frequency distribution.

Skewness and Symmetry

The *skewness* in a distribution refers to the position of the concentration of the mass of the data with respect to the total distribution. In general, whenever the mean, median, and mode are not identical, skewness is present in the distribution. A distribution is said to be *symmetric* if the shape of the distribution above the mean is a *reflection* of the distribution below the mean. Whenever symmetry is present, the mean, median, and mode of the distribution are identical. Figure 30.11*a* illustrates a symmetric distribution.

A distribution such as that in Fig. 30.11*b* is said to be *skewed to the left* when there is a prominent "tail" to the left. In general, for this type of skewness the mean will be exceeded by the median, which in turn will be exceeded by the mode. Figure 30.11*c* illustrates a distribution skewed to the right and the typical positions for the mean, median, and mode.

Kurtosis, or Peakedness

Kurtosis refers to the peakedness of the distribution. A distribution possessing relatively flat tails but very peaked is called *leptokurtic*. This type of shape is illustrated in Fig. 30.12a. Figure 30.12b indicates a *platykurtic* distribution, distinguished by very thin tails and a long broad hump.

ELEMENTS OF PROBABILITY THEORY

The purpose of this section is to provide an elementary foundation in probability theory sufficient to make meaningful the subsequent consideration of statistical methods. The treatment of probability is brief and is clearly oriented toward the particular use that will be made of it in this chapter.

Probability Distributions

Although there are several definitions for the term *probability*, the "frequency" definition is the most common. It embodies the notion that as the number of times an experiment is rerun (trials) increases toward infinity, the probability of an occurrence of a certain value for the random variable equals the fraction of trials in which that value would occur.

It is convenient to discuss separately the probability distributions of discrete and continuous random variables. However, the basic concepts are similar.

Discrete Random Variables. Let x_i denote a particular value which can be assumed by a discrete random variable. For example, roll two dice and define a random variable equal to the sum of the two faces. This variable takes on values

$$x_i = 2, 3, 4, \ldots, 12$$

Next let $p(x_i)$ represent the probability that the random variable takes on value x_i. This is known as the *probability distribution function* of x_i.

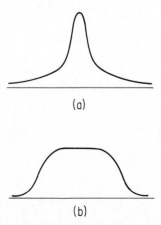

(a)

(b)

FIG. 30.12 Leptokurtic and platykurtic distributions.

TABLE 30.12 Probability Distribution Function: Sum of
Two Dice

x_i	2	3	4	5	6	7	8	9	10	11	12
$p(x_i)$	$\frac{1}{36}$	$\frac{2}{36}$	$\frac{3}{36}$	$\frac{4}{36}$	$\frac{5}{36}$	$\frac{6}{36}$	$\frac{5}{36}$	$\frac{4}{36}$	$\frac{3}{36}$	$\frac{2}{36}$	$\frac{1}{36}$

Given unbiased dice in which all face values are equally probable, the probability distribution function for the random variable equal to the sum of two faces is as shown in Table 30.12. This random variable is now completely defined. All values that it might take on are specified, as are the probabilities that each of these might occur.

It is often convenient to describe the probability distribution functions graphically with a line on the x axis corresponding to the probability of occurrence of each value of x. Table 30.12 thus gives rise to Fig. 30.13.

Two properties must be satisfied by every discrete random variable:

1. The range of the probability function must be 0 to 1:

$$0 \leqslant p(x_i) \leqslant 1$$

2. The sum of all probabilities is equal to 1:

$$\sum_{\text{all } x_i} p(x_i) = 1$$

The first property specifies that the probability of occurrence of any value x_i must be nonnegative and cannot exceed 1. The second property specifies that the sum of the probabilities over all values of x_i must equal 1. These are useful checks in attempting to enumerate all possible values of x_i and $p(x_i)$. Note that the random variable defined in Table 30.12 satisfies both these requirements.

It is often of interest to have available the probability that a random variable takes on values less than or equal to a specified value. For this we define the *cumulative distribution function*. Let $F(b)$ equal the probability that the random variable takes on values less than or equal to b. Hence

$$F(b) = \sum_{x_i \leqslant b} p(x_i)$$

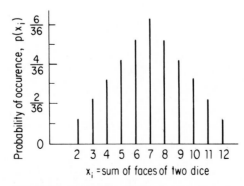

FIG. 30.13 Probability distribution function of a discrete random variable.

TABLE 30.13 Cumulative Distribution Function

x	2	3	4	5	6	7	8	9	10	11	12
F(x)	$\frac{1}{36}$	$\frac{3}{36}$	$\frac{6}{36}$	$\frac{10}{36}$	$\frac{15}{36}$	$\frac{21}{36}$	$\frac{26}{36}$	$\frac{30}{36}$	$\frac{33}{36}$	$\frac{35}{36}$	$\frac{36}{36}$

The cumulative distribution function for the random variable defined in Table 30.12 is listed in Table 30.13. Note that $F(b)$ is necessarily a nondecreasing function. A graphical interpretation is frequently useful and is shown for the example in Fig. 30.14. This is a *step function*, since only discrete x_i values may occur. The probability that the random variable takes on values less than or equal to 3.4, for example, is equal to $p(2) + p(3)$. Hence $F(b)$ is the same for all values of b from 3 to, but not including, 4.

Continuous Random Variables. A continuous random variable is one which may take on any value within a range of possible values. Therefore, it conceptually may take any one of an infinite number of possible values in the range. It is meaningless to consider the probability of a particular value occurring. We therefore deal with the probability that the random variable takes on a value within some specified interval.

The probability that the random variable (RV) takes on values in the interval [x, x + dx] for a very small value dx (see Fig. 30.15) is

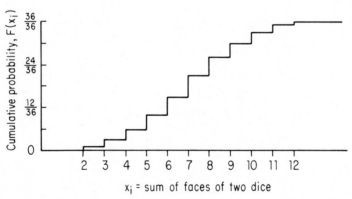

x_i = sum of faces of two dice

FIG. 30.14 Cumulative distribution function of a discrete random variable.

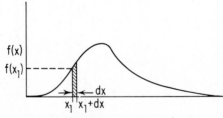

x = a continuous random variable

FIG. 30.15 Probability density function of a continuous random variable.

$$\Pr\{x_i < RV < x_i + dx\} = f(x_i)dx$$

where $f(x)$ is the probability density function. And $f(x)$ is most conveniently interpreted when it is plotted as in the figure. The area of the slice of height $f(x_i)$ and width dx corresponds to the probability of the random variable taking on values in that particular interval.

The probability that the random variable takes on a value between any two values a and b can be obtained by measuring the area under $f(x)$ from a to b, as represented by the shaded portion in Fig. 30.16. This area can be found mathematically by integrating $f(x)$ from a to b:

$$\Pr\{a < x < b\} = \int_b^a f(x)dx$$

For $f(x)$ to be a probability density function, it must satisfy the conditions

and
$$f(x) \leqslant 0 \qquad \text{for all } x$$

$$\int_{-\infty}^{\infty} f(x)dx = 1$$

As with discrete random variables, it is frequently of interest to find the probability that the variable takes on a value less than or equal to a specific value, say, b. This can be found by

$$\Pr\{x < b\} = \int_{-\infty}^{b} f(x)dx$$

This is defined as the *cumulative distribution function* $F(b)$.

Note that this is analogous to the discrete case discussed previously with the summation replaced by the integration operation. The probability that x falls between a and b can now be rewritten in terms of the difference in two values of the cumulative distribution function as

$$\Pr\{a < x < b\} = \Pr\{x < b\} - \Pr\{x < a\}$$

$$= \int_{-\infty}^{b} f(x)dx - \int_{-\infty}^{a} f(x)dx = F(b) - F(a)$$

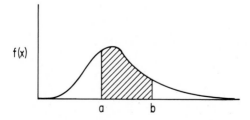

x = a continuous random variable

FIG. 30.16 Probability that $a < x < b$.

The cumulative distribution function can be evaluated for all possible values of x and plotted as shown in Fig. 30.17. This figure illustrates two basic properties. First, $f(x)$ must start at zero on the left-hand end and second, it must reach 1 on the right-hand side.

Consider as a specific example the uniform distribution in which the probability density function is constant in the interval 0 to a. The density function is shown in Fig. 30.18a. Note that

$$f(x) = \begin{cases} 1/a & \text{for } 0 \leq x \leq a \\ 0 & \text{elsewhere} \end{cases}$$

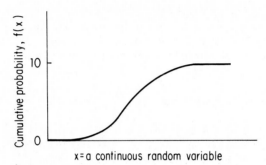

FIG. 30.17   Cumulative distribution function of a continuous random function.

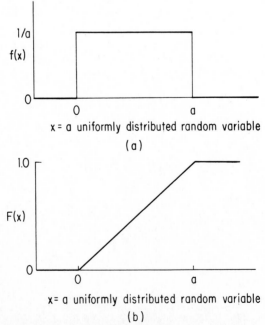

FIG. 30.18   A uniformly distributed random variable.

which follows from the requirement that the area under the curve equal 1. It can be found by solving

$$\int_0^a K\, dx = 1$$

for the constant K.

The cumulative distribution function is found by

$$F(x) = \int_0^x \frac{1}{a}\, dx = \frac{x}{a}$$

which is plotted in Fig. 30.18b.

Note that the slope of $F(x)$ at any point x corresponds to the height of $f(x)$ at that point. In this case the slope $F(x)$ is constant everywhere on the interval $(0,a)$ corresponding to the uniform density function in the interval.

POPULATION PARAMETERS

The mean and variance of a sample have been defined. In a similar manner, one may define the mean (or expected value) and variance of a particular population described in terms of a probability distribution (or density, in the continuous case) function.

By denoting the mean by μ and the variance by σ^2, the following equations are obtained for a discrete distribution:

$$\mu = \sum_{i=1}^{n} x_i p(x_i)$$

$$\sigma^2 = \sum_{i=1}^{n} (x_i - \mu)^2 p(x_i)$$

For the continuous case,

$$\mu = \int_x x f(x)\, dx$$

$$\sigma^2 = \int_x (x - \mu)^2 f(x)\, dx$$

The standard deviation of a population is equal to the square root of the variance and is denoted by σ. Notice that μ and σ^2 are constant for a given population while $\bar{x}$ and s^2 depend on the specific values included in the sample and may vary among different samples taken from the same population.

Normal Distribution

The most common distribution encountered in statistical work is the *normal distribution*. A normally distributed random variable x is a continuous random variable whose probability density function $f(x)$ is given by

$$f(x) = \frac{1}{\sqrt{2\pi}\sigma}e^{-(x-\mu)^2/(2\sigma^2)}$$

where μ is the mean and σ the standard deviation. For convenience we occasionally use here the shorthand notation $N(\mu, \sigma^2)$ to represent a normally distributed random variable with mean μ and variance σ^2.

When it is graphed, the *density function* appears as shown in Fig. 30.19a. Note that the distribution is symmetrically centered about the mean μ. Knowledge of μ and σ is sufficient to completely define the distribution. It is therefore referred to as a *two-parameter distribution*.

The cumulative distribution function

$$F(x) = \int_{-\infty}^{x} f(x)\, dx$$

appears, when plotted, as depicted in Fig. 30.19b. One frequently needs to evaluate the area under the density function to determine relevant probabilities. For example, given μ and σ, what is the probability that the random variable x exceeds b? Mathematically it is given by

$$\Pr(x > b) = \int_{b}^{\infty} f(x)\, dx$$

which is equivalent to finding the shaded area of Fig. 30.20.

The normal density function is unfortunately a function which cannot be easily evaluated. In practice, the scheme is to use a table of the cumulative area. However,

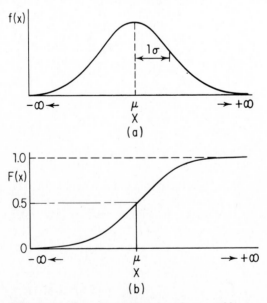

FIG. 30.19 Normally distributed random variable.

we would need a separate table for all combinations of μ and σ—clearly an impossibility. Instead we use a table of the *standardized normal distribution* and use a simple transformation to relate it to the particular problem at hand. Let z represent the standardized normal variate:

$$z = \frac{x - \mu}{\sigma}$$

This is the appropriate transformation relating the distribution of x to the z distribution.

The standardized normal variate has a mean of 0 and a variance of 1 [N, (0, 1)]. The density function is

$$f(z) = \frac{1}{\sqrt{2\pi}} \, e^{-z^2/2}$$

In the example below, let z_α represent the value of z for which

$$\Pr\{z > z_\alpha\} = \int_{z_\alpha}^{\infty} \frac{1}{\sqrt{2\pi}} \, e^{-z^2/2} \, dz = \alpha$$

Graphically this is equivalent to the shaded area in Fig. 30.21. For example, Table 1 in the Appendix shows that

$$\Pr\{z > 1\} = 0.1587$$

and
$$\Pr\{z > 1.645\} = 0.05$$

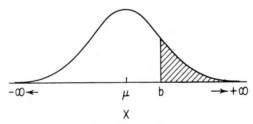

FIG. 30.20 Probability that $x > b$.

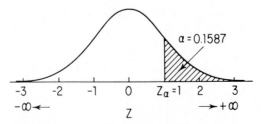

FIG. 30.21 Standardized normal distribution.

The probability is 0.1587 that z will take on a value greater than 1 and 0.05 that it will take on a value greater than 1.645.

Our interest is, however, not in z but in x, which is $N(\mu, \sigma^2)$. Given b a particular value in the distribution of μ, and recalling that $z = (x - \mu)/\sigma$, we find

$$Pr\{x > b\} = Pr\left\{z > \frac{b - \mu}{\sigma}\right\} = Pr\{z > z_\alpha\} = \alpha$$

This is represented graphically in Fig. 30.22. For example, given x which is $N(10,4)$, the probability that x will take on a value greater than 12 can be found as follows. Let

$$z_\alpha = \frac{b - \mu}{\sigma} = \frac{12 - 10}{\sqrt{4}} = 1$$

Then

$$Pr\{x > 12\} = Pr\{z > 1\} = 0.1587$$

Instead of seeking the probability that x takes on a value greater than b, the problem might be to find b such that the probability that $x > b$ is equal to a given α. For example, given x as $N(10,4)$, what is b for which

$$Pr\{x > b\} = 0.05$$

We solve this by finding z_α corresponding to $\alpha = 0.05$. From the tables we found above $z_\alpha = 1.645$ satisfies this requirement; that is

$$Pr\{z > 1.645\} = 0.05$$

Set

$$z_\alpha = \frac{b - \mu}{\sigma}$$

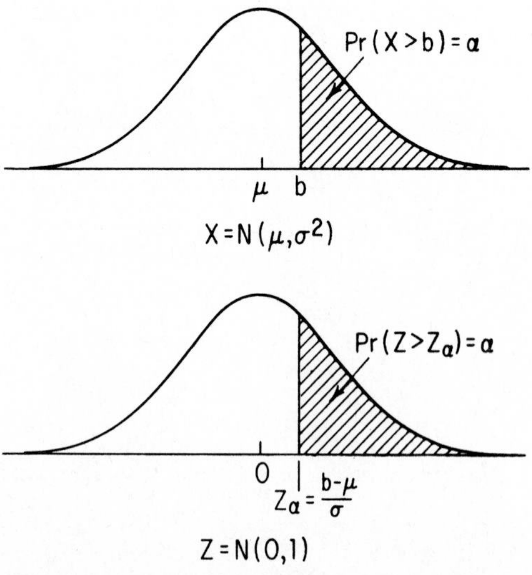

FIG. 30.22 Area under normal curve of interest.

and solve for b.

$$1.645 = \frac{b - 10}{2}$$

from which we obtain

$$b = 13.29$$

Hence

$$\text{Pr}\{x > 13.29\} = 0.05$$

By utilizing the fact that the area under the entire curve from $-\infty$ to $+\infty$ equals 1, one can find

$$\text{Pr}\{x < b\} = 1 - \text{Pr}\{x > b\}$$

or
$$\text{Pr}\{z < z_\alpha\} = 1 - \text{Pr}\{z > z_\alpha\}$$

Again using the above example,

$$\text{Pr}\{x < 12\} = 1 - \text{Pr}\{x > 12\} = 1 - 0.1587 = 0.8413$$

Since the function is symmetric, tables contain entries only for the right-hand half (i.e., > 0). Because of this symmetry and since the standardized normal has a zero mean,

$$\text{Pr}\{z < -z_\alpha\} = \text{Pr}\{z > +z_\alpha\}$$

Consider the task of finding

$$\text{Pr}\{x > 8\}$$

given that x is N(10,4). First find

$$z_\alpha = \frac{8 - 10}{2} = -1$$

$$\text{Pr}\{z_\alpha > -1\} = \text{Pr}\{z_\alpha < +1\} = 1 - \text{Pr}\{z_\alpha > +1\} = 1 - 0.1587 = 0.8413$$

The above can be combined to yield answers to questions of the form

$$\text{Pr}\{a < x < b\}$$

STATISTICAL INFERENCE

Statistical inference consists of drawing conclusions about a population based on the results of a sample. Even though the actual probability distribution of the population may not be known, the central limit theorem allows one to use the normal distribution or one of its derivatives to develop statistical techniques for drawing conclusions. The central limit theorem states that the means of samples of size n, drawn from any population of mean μ and finite variance σ^2, have a distribution that tends to the normal distribution as n is increased. The mean of the distribution is μ, and its variance is σ^2/n.

In addition to the normal distribution, discussed to some extent in the previous section, two other distributions are often used in statistical inference: the t distribution and the χ^2 (chi-square) distribution. Both, are in effect, a family of distributions, indexed according to a quantity known as *degrees of freedom*, which is related to the number of observations in the sample used for inference.

HYPOTHESIS TESTING

The purpose of hypothesis testing is to examine the reasonableness of a statement regarding a population parameter in the light of sampling results. Although the details of hypothesis testing are beyond the scope of this book, the procedure involves specifying two complementary hypotheses: a null hypothesis, denoted by H_0, and an alternative hypothesis, denoted by H_1. The null hypothesis is assumed to be true, and the results of sampling are examined to see whether they refute this assumption. If such is the case, then H_0 is rejected and H_1 is accepted as true. Most often, the null hypothesis H_0 is the one for which erroneous rejection has more serious consequences.

The fact that a hypothesis is accepted may be the result of one of two reasons. First, the hypothesis may be, in fact, true. Second, there may be such a large degree of variability inherent in the data that any actual difference between the hypothesized parameters and the actual population parameters may be masked. Additional data from a larger sample may enable one to remove some of the masking due to chance variation, thus possibly leading to rejection of the hypothesis where at first acceptance was the only possible conclusion. It is not possible to completely remove the effect of this inherent chance variation without examining the entire population. However, then the problem would no longer be one of statistical inference, for complete information would be available.

Typical Applications

Quite frequently one wishes to compare two populations to ascertain whether they are different. For example, one may want to find out whether there is a difference in the mean production rate for two machines.

The test of a proportion is useful when one wishes to draw conclusions about a proportion such as the fraction of tardy orders or the proportion of defective units in a production batch.

The theory of hypothesis testing and its applications may be found in many statistical books, some of which are referenced at the end of the chapter.

ESTIMATION

Estimation consists of determining the likely values of the population parameter(s) based on sample results. An estimator is a function of sample values that provides an estimate of a population parameter. There are two basic types of estimates: point estimates and interval estimates.

Point Estimation

A *point estimate* is a single value used to estimate the population parameter of interest. In each case a random sample is taken from the population of concern. A statistic is then calculated which provides an estimate of a corresponding population parameter. Several estimators of interest are presented here. These have been shown to provide quality estimates, a discussion of which, however, is beyond the scope of this chapter.

1. To estimate the population mean μ, use the sample mean $\bar{x}$ computed by

$$\bar{x} = \frac{\displaystyle\sum_{i=1}^{n} x_i}{n}$$

2. To estimate the variance of a population σ^2, use

$$s^2 = \frac{\displaystyle\sum_{i=1}^{n} (x_i - \bar{x})^2}{n - 1}$$

3. In estimating the population proportion ρ of a binomial population, use

$$\rho = \frac{k}{n}$$

where ρ = estimate of π, true proportion of population
      k = number of occurrences
      n = sample size

Interval Estimates

Estimation by point estimates does not permit the inclusion of information about the degree of variability associated with the variable used in the estimates. For example, a sample may yield a point estimate that the true production rate for a process is 50 units per minute. It may be important, however, to know whether the true value is between 49 and 51 or 40 and 60. To provide this type of information, interval estimates are employed.

An *interval estimate*, sometimes called a *confidence interval*, is the specification of two values obtained from a single sample between which a parameter of interest is estimated to lie with a prescribed degree of confidence. Procedures are described in the references for establishing confidence limits for several parameters. Although the details may differ, every interval estimation follows the same general approach:

1. A sample is drawn from the population of interest.
2. A sample statistic is calculated from the sample.
3. Upper and lower limits are established for the appropriate population parameter.

REGRESSION AND CORRELATION

Often it is of interest to examine the effects that some variables exert (or appear to exert) on others. The techniques of regression and correlation are useful in this examination.

In regression we wish to establish a relationship whereby the value of one variable can be predicted, given knowledge of other variables. Let x represent an *independent variable* which can be set to either a desired value, such as months for forecasts, or values that can be observed but not controlled (such as business indexes or competitive prices). This is used to predict a *dependent*, or response, variable y as product demand.

In simple linear regression, one seeks to determine the coefficients a and b of the linear function

$$y = a + bx$$

where a is the y axis intercept and b is the slope. Given a value of the independent variable x, a prediction can be made about the value of the dependent variable. For example, one may wish to predict sales on the basis of knowledge of some general index of business activity.

Simple linear regression analysis makes the prediction with a single independent variable. Correlation analysis also is used to examine relationships. Instead of deriving a prediction equation, correlation analysis provides a measure of the degree to which variables are associated.

Development of Regression Equations

Given a set of n data pairs in which values for the independent variable x and the dependent variable y are simultaneously measured for each of n observations, establish a linear relationship. Consider as an example the data of Table 30.14 in which for each of 8 years a particular industry's domestic sales are recorded along with the consumer disposable income. With an estimate of disposable income it should be possible to predict domestic sales for the industry. Disposable income, in this case, is the independent variable x, and domestic sales is the dependent variable y.

TABLE 30.14 Domestic Sales versus Disposable Income

Disposable Income x (Billions of Dollars)	Domestic Sales y (Billions of Dollars)
181.6	0.435
206.1	0.621
226.1	0.819
236.7	0.879
250.4	0.933
254.8	0.970
274.0	1.070
284.0	1.180

The first step in the analysis is to construct a *scatter diagram* of the sample data to provide a visual portrayal. The procedure is to plot for each value of x a point corresponding to the value of y (Fig. 30.23). Hence, there will be n data points, each representing an (x, y) pair of observations.

Clearly an apparent linear relationship exists. The scatter diagram is particularly useful in the detection of nonlinear relationships. The techniques for linear regression may be accepted to fit a best-fitting straight line even though the relationship might actually be nonlinear. Hence, visual examination of the relationships displayed by the data is desirable.

Given the n data points, we want to determine a straight line of the form y = a + bx through these points. One method is to simply establish visually a line of reasonable fit. For some purposes such a scheme might be satisfactory. However, usually it is not. As dispersion of the points from the line increases, visual fitting becomes more difficult. Hence there is need for a quantitative method.

Underlying the method of linear regression is the existence of a true (although unknown) relationship between each x_1 and y_i described by the model

$$y_i = \alpha + \beta x_i + \epsilon_i$$

where α is the true value of the y intercept and β is the true slope of the straight (or regression) line describing the relationship.

If all data points lie on a straight line, one has the equation of a straight line $y_i = \alpha + \beta x_i$. Inasmuch as not all observations lie on such a line, an additional term

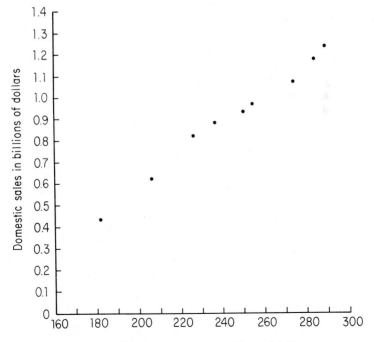

FIG. 30.23 Scatter diagram.

must also be present. This term is defined as the error ϵ_i that identifies the error associated with the ith observation and enters the model in an additive manner:

$$y_i = \alpha + \beta x_i + \epsilon_i$$

Since the true regression coefficients α and β are not known, we wish to obtain estimates of them based on the information contained in the sample of n data points generated by the true model. Let a be an *estimate* of the true intercept and b be an *estimate* of the true slope such that the line

$$y_i = a + b x_i$$

determined from the data produces an estimate of the true linear relationship

$$y_i = \alpha + \beta x_i$$

The objective of the regression analysis is to find a and b such that some function of the error is minimized. The minimization of the sum of errors is unsatisfactory inasmuch as positive and negative errors cancel in the sum. Moreover, minimizing the sum of the absolute deviations, while theoretically satisfactory, is characterized by significant computational difficulties. However, if the errors are squared, the problem of cancellation in the sum is overcome, yielding a tractable computational problem. Hence the *method of least squares* determines the coefficients a and b of the best-fitting straight line such that the sum of the squares of the deviations of the observations from the line is a minimum.

Minimizing the sum of error squares results in the following equations for a and b:

$$b = \frac{\displaystyle\sum_{i=1}^{n} x_i y_i - \left(\displaystyle\sum_{i=1}^{n} x_i \displaystyle\sum_{i=1}^{n} y_i \right) \Big/ n}{\displaystyle\sum_{i=1}^{n} x_i^2 - \left(\displaystyle\sum_{i=1}^{n} x_i \right)^2 \Big/ n}$$

and

$$a = \frac{\displaystyle\sum_{i=1}^{n} y_i}{n} - b \frac{\displaystyle\sum_{i=1}^{n} x_i}{n} = \bar{y} - b\bar{x}$$

Table 30.15 shows the calculations of the various sums and sums of squares and products required to compute a and b for the sample data. This table yields

$$n = 8 \qquad \Sigma xy = 1709.2985$$
$$\Sigma x = 1913.7 \qquad \Sigma x^2 = 465{,}959.09$$
$$\Sigma y = 6.907 \qquad \Sigma y^2 = 6.366957$$

from which

$$\bar{x} = 239.21 \qquad \text{and} \qquad \bar{y} = 0.8634$$

TABLE 30.15 Details of Calculations

x	y	x^2	xy	y^2
181.6	0.435	32,978.56	78.9960	0.189225
206.1	0.621	42,477.21	127.9881	0.385641
226.1	0.819	51,121.21	185.1759	0.670761
236.7	0.879	56,026.89	208.0593	0.772641
250.4	0.933	62,700.16	233.6232	0.870489
254.8	0.970	64,923.04	247.1560	0.940900
274.0	1.070	75,076.00	293.1800	1.114900
284.0	1.180	80,656.00	335.1200	1.392400
1,913.7	6.907	465,959.07	1,709.2985	6.366957

The slope is found to be

$$b = \frac{1709.2985 - (1913.7 \times 6.907)/8}{465,959.09 - (1913.7)^2/8} = 0.00698$$

and the intercept

$$a = \frac{6.907}{8} - (0.00698)(1913.7) = -0.8056$$

The estimate of the regression line is

$$y = -0.8056 + 0.00698x$$

where y is the domestic sales and x is disposable income, both in billions of dollars. This line is plotted in Fig. 30.24.

For larger data sets, it becomes quite cumbersome to perform the various calculations manually. Extensive computer software is available to assist in these types of analysis. A selected list appears at the end of this chapter.

Correlation

In correlation the interest lies in determining the *degree of relationship* between the two variables rather than predicting one from the other. Correlation differs theoretically from regression in the manner in which the observations are measured. In regression, the independent variable x is assumed measured without error, whereas the dependent variable y is measured with error. In correlation both variables x and y are assumed to be measured with error, there being no differentiation between independent and dependent variables.

Clearly a least-squares straight line can be fitted to any set of data whether or not the data really follow a linear relationship. We therefore desire some measure which reflects the degree of joint behavior of two factors. This measure is the unitless coefficient of correlation r, computed by

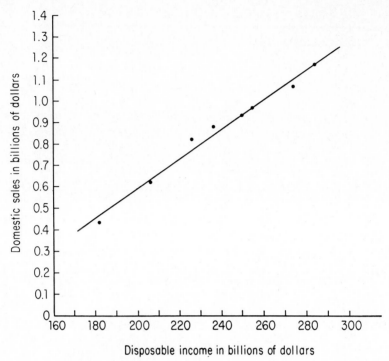

FIG. 30.24   Sales forecast by regression.

$$r = \frac{\displaystyle\sum_{i=1}^{n}\sum_{j=1}^{n} x_i y_j - \left(\sum_{i=1}^{n} x_i \sum_{j=1}^{n} y_j\right)\Big/ n}{\sqrt{\left[\displaystyle\sum_{i=1}^{n} x_i^2 - \frac{\left(\sum_{i=1}^{n} x_i\right)^2}{n}\right]\left[\displaystyle\sum_{j=1}^{n} y_j^2 - \frac{\left(\sum_{j=1}^{n} y_j\right)^2}{n}\right]}}$$

The coefficient of correlation lies between -1 and 1.

Interpretation of Correlation Coefficient.   The magnitude or absolute value of r, denoted by $|r|$, reflects the quality of the relationship. A high value indicates a good relationship; a low one, a poor relationship. The sign of r specifies the direction. A plus means that y increases with increasing x, while a minus sign shows that y decreases with increasing x.

Now $|r| = 1$ would indicate a perfect fit, whereas $|r| = 0$ would result if there were no relationship whatsoever. Figure 30.25 provides graphical interpretation of the coefficient of correlation.

Another useful measure is the *coefficient of determination*, defined as r^2. Obviously, r^2 is always positive and falls in the range between 0 and 1. It may be

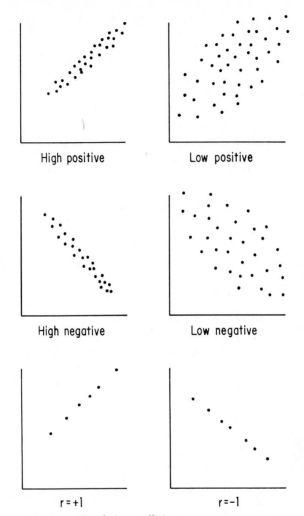

High positive   Low positive

High negative   Low negative

$r = +1$ $r = -1$

FIG. 30.25   Correlation coefficient.

interpreted as the percentage of variation in y that is explained by x. Thus, a high value of r^2 indicates that x is related to y and actually explains its variation. For a test of hypotheses related to regression and correlation coefficients, refer to the literature listed at the end of the chapter.

It is possible to perform regression and correlation analysis on data with more than one independent variable. The calculations, however, become quite voluminous. Therefore, it is recommended to utilize statistical software, some of which is listed next.

STATISTICAL SOFTWARE PACKAGES

Mainframe Computers

BMDP—Biomedical Computer Programs, P series, programs for advanced statistical techniques.

> BMDP Statistical Software
> Los Angeles, Calif.

IDA—Interactive Data Analysis and forecasting system, a general-purpose statistical package.

> IDA Marketing Manager
> SPSS, Inc.
> Chicago, Ill.

IMSL—International Mathematical and Statistical Library covers statistics, mathematics, and numerical analysis.

> IMSL Customer Relations
> Houston, Tex.

LISREL—analysis of linear structural relationships.

> University of Uppsala
> Department of Statistics
> Uppsala, Sweden

MINITAB—General-purpose statistical package.

> The Pennsylvania State University
> Department of Statistics
> University Park, Pa.

SAS—Statistical analysis system.

> SAS Institute, Inc.
> Cary, N.C.

SPSS—General-purpose statistical package.

> SPSS, Inc.
> Chicago, Ill.

Microcomputers

PC FIT

> William P. Smith
> Environmental Protection Agency
> Washington, D.C.

INSTAT-P

> Mikel Aickin
> Statistical Consulting Services
> Tempe, Ariz.

STAN version II.O

> David M. Allen

Statistical Consultants, Inc.
Lexington, Ky.

SYSTAT—General-purpose statistical package.

SYSTAT, Inc.
Evanston, Ill.

BMDP-PC—Microversion of BMDP.

BMDP Statistical Software
Los Angeles, Calif.

SPSS/PC—Comprehensive statistics and reporting package.

Lucy Saunders
SPSS, Inc.
Chicago, Ill.

ABSTAT—An interactive statistical package.

Anderson Bell Company
Canon City, Colo.

CRISP—The crunch interactive statistical package is simple to learn and offers good quality.

Crunch Software
San Francisco, Calif.

STATPRO/PC—Wide range of statistical capabilities and excellent graphics.

Wadsworth Professional Software
Boston, Mass.

BIBLIOGRAPHY

Berger, James O., and Robert L. Wolpert: *The Likelihood Principle*, Institute of Mathematical Statistics, Haywood, Calif., 1984.

Boot, J. C. G., and E. B. Cox: *Statistical Analysis for Managerial Decisions*, 2d ed., McGraw-Hill, New York, 1974.

Canavos, George: *Applied Probability and Statistical Methods*, Little, Brown, Boston, 1984.

Chase, Clinton: *Elementary Statistical Procedures*, McGraw-Hill, New York, 1984.

Chou, Y.: *Statistical Analysis*, 2d ed., Holt, Rinehart & Winston, New York, 1975.

Dixon, J., and F. J. Massey, Jr.: *Introduction to Statistical Analysis*, 4th ed., McGraw-Hill, New York, 1983.

Elzey, Freeman: *Introductory Statistics—A Microcomputer Approach*, Brooks/Cole, Belmont, Calif., 1984.

Freund, J. E.: *College Mathematics with Business Application*, 2d ed., Prentice-Hall, Englewood Cliffs, N.J., 1975.

Goldman, Robert, and Joel Weinberg: *Statistics—An Introduction*, Prentice-Hall, Englewood Cliffs, N.J., 1985.

Hettmansperger, Thomas P.: *Statistical Inference Based on Ranks*, Wiley, New York, 1984.

Hoel, P. F.: *Introduction to Mathematical Statistics*, 4th ed., Wiley, New York, 1971.

Johnson, Richard A., and G. K. Bhattacharya: *Statistics—Principles and Methods*, Wiley, New York, 1985.

McGhee, John: *Introductory Statistics*, West, St. Paul, Minn., 1985.

McLean, Robert A.: *Applied Factorial and Fractional Design*, Marcel Dekker, New York, 1984.

Revesz, P.: *Limit Theorems in Probability and Statistics*, vols. 1 and 2, Elsevier, New York.

Rustagi, Jagdish S.: *Introduction to Statistical Methods*, Rowman and Allanheld, Totawa, N.J., 1985.

Sheskin, David: *Guide Book of Statistical Tests and Experimental Design*, Gardner Press, New York, 1984.

31

Quantitative Methods

Editor

STEPHEN A. DeLURGIO, PH.D., CFPIM, Professor of Operations
Management, University of Missouri, Kansas City, Missouri

The term *quantitative methods (QM)* has several meanings, including the synonyms *operations research (OR)* and *management science (MS)*. Simply defined, QM is the application of the scientific method to solutions of managerial problems. Historically, OR/MS became a recognized discipline during World War II. It has since grown to include many techniques that can be effective in planning, executing, and controlling operations. In the past, there have been some technical and behavioral problems in using QM.[1-7] Fortunately, more help is now available to both managers and analysts because (1) comprehensive and accessible QM textbooks exist, (2) knowledge has improved on how to apply QM successfully,[8-10] and (3) the effectiveness of computers and software has improved greatly.

This chapter illustrates quantitative methods that solve production and inventory control (PIC) problems and discusses QM's assumptions, limitations, benefits, and disadvantages. Its objective is to provide enough information so that managers will be receptive to quantitative methods, be able to recognize when they are applicable, and know where to find additional information about them. Because this chapter cannot present all the methods, many references are included for further study.[1-10,16-24]

CHARACTERISTICS OF QUANTITATIVE METHODS

In general, the purpose of QM is to assist managers in solving problems by using models, and the fundamental objective of QM is to provide information for better decisions. Information is derived through the collection of data, the formulation of hypotheses, and the construction, validation, and implementation of models. Modeling is an essential part of QM because both the modeling process and the model assist problem solvers in analyzing, predicting, and controlling real world systems better.[13]

Because models are abstractions of the essentials of real systems, the process of modeling is one requiring both art and science. Too often, those responsible for modeling and decision making ignore the interaction of QM science and art.

While many forms of models exist, such as physical, schematic, graphical, mathematical, analog, and digital, this chapter only discusses the mathematical and logical models implemented by digital computers. Some people mistakenly believe that the only purpose of QM is to provide optimal solutions; although this is certainly an important purpose, much modeling activity in QM is directed to providing insightful information for better decisions.[14] The reduction of uncertainty through simulation and experimentation is one of the most important purposes of modeling. In practice, the best measure of a model's validity is its ability to improve the decisions of management.

Solution Methods

Two types of solution methods exist for solving quantitative problems: *deductive* and *inductive*. Deductive methods, such as economic order quantity (EOQ) formulas, derive solutions directly from mathematical techniques, such as the maxima-minima theorem of calculus. In contrast, inductive methods employ iterative procedures to search for good solutions to problems. Because larger and more realistic problems are solvable using inductive methods, they are applied more frequently. The procedures of decision theory, mathematical programming, simulation, part-period balancing, computer spreadsheet models, and MRP "what if" analysis are inductive procedures.

Sometimes problems are forced to fit a familiar, easy, or optimal solution procedure. However, a good solution to a realistic model is sought, not an optimal solution to an unrealistic model. Therefore, solution procedure should be selected after problem formulation and modeling, not before.

Types of Models

Two types of models exist: *deterministic* and *probabilistic*. In a deterministic model, the values of all factors are known with certainty. In contrast, a probabilistic model includes variables which are randomly distributed and which are therefore described by appropriate probability distributions.

Deterministic Models. If a system has mathematical relationships that are known with certainty (deterministic), then powerful mathematical methods can be used to achieve optimal solutions. For example, in scheduling production with known demands, capacities, and materials, a deterministic model can be used. Deterministic solution methods include linear programming and the continuous mathematical optimization methods of calculus, as used in EOQ.

If the deterministic assumption is valid, then deterministic techniques provide insightful information about the behavior of the system. However, if the deterministic assumption is invalid, then the model may be meaningless or misleading. One should always critically evaluate the assumptions of a quantitative model. However, frequently the assumptions of a model do not have to be perfectly accurate because its solutions may be insensitive to violations of assumptions, a condition called *robustness*. For example, the EOQ model has been found to be valid in a variety of situations that violate its assumptions.

Most often, systems are not perfectly deterministic. If a system is dominated by deterministic events, certainty may be assumed or "what if" experiments can be used to explore the effects of minor uncertainties in a procedure called *sensitivity analysis*.[16-29] However, if sensitivity analysis shows that the uncertain events greatly affect system behavior then a probabilistic model should be used.

Probabilistic Models.   Systems that possess one or more random variables may have to be modeled using frequency or probability distributions. In general, probabilistic systems are more difficult to model than are deterministic systems. However, most systems exist in uncertain environments. For example, if considerable uncertainty exists in demand, it may be necessary to use probability distributions to describe demand. Consider the following probabilistic model.

A manufacturer sells a product under two different retail brand names, A and B. The brand A forecast yields two possible order quantities and probabilities, a 40 percent chance of 100 and a 60 percent chance of 140, while the brand B forecast yields a 50 percent chance of 200 and 50 percent chance of 300. What is the mean (expected) demand for the product?

$$\text{Let } P_{A,1} = \text{probability that brand } A \text{ demand equals quantity 1 } (Q_{A,1})$$
$$P_{A,2} = \text{probability that brand } A \text{ demand equals quantity 2 } (Q_{A,2})$$
$$P_{B,1} = \text{probability that brand } B \text{ demand equals quantity 1 } (Q_{B,1})$$
$$P_{B,2} = \text{probability that brand } B \text{ demand equals quantity 2 } (Q_{B,2})$$

Assuming that the demands for each brand are independent of each other, the laws of probability and statistics yield the following forecasts:

$$\text{Expected sales } A = P_{A,1}(Q_{A,1}) + P_{A,2}(Q_{A,2})$$
$$= 0.40(100) + 0.60(140) = 124$$
$$\text{Expected sales } B = P_{B,1}(Q_{B,1}) + P_{B,2}(Q_{B,2})$$
$$= 0.50(200) + 0.50(300) = 250$$
$$\text{Expected sales } (A + B) = \text{expected sales } A + \text{expected sales } B$$
$$= 124 + 250 = 374 \text{ units}$$

In this simple example, only two random variables exist; however, when the number of random variables increases to more than a few, it may be necessary to use simulation, one of the most powerful analytical tools of management (discussed in the following section, "Probabilistic Methods").

Essentials of Quantitative Methods

The QM approach to managerial problem-solving has three essential characteristics: a systemwide perspective, the use of an interdisciplinary team, and the use of the scientific method.

Systemwide Perspective.   A problem must be identified, modeled, and solved in the context of the specific environment in which it exists. In solving systems problems, one must study the system, its environment, its parts, and their interrelationships, interactions, and purposes.

Interdisciplinary Teams.   Many complex managerial problems require a variety of perspectives, skills, and knowledge. A proper mix of managers and analysts will achieve more effective results than will specialized groups. It is always important to have an interdisciplinary perspective when solving complex problems.

The Scientific Method.   The essential characteristic of the scientific method is the systematic and objective repetition of observation, measurement, experimentation, and hypothesis testing. Through these activities, one can define valid models of essential system behavior. Figure 31.1 illustrates the scientific method and the steps of QM, of which the most important step is the problem formulation—from

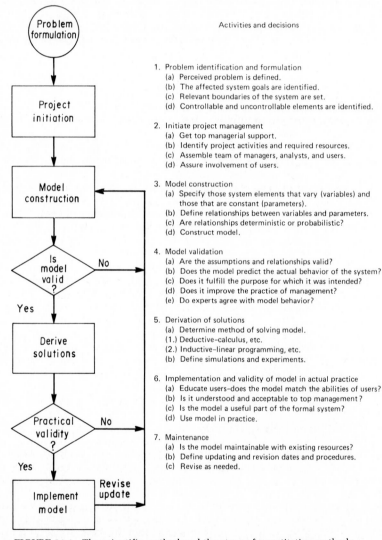

FIGURE 31.1   The scientific method and the steps of quantitative methods.

which all other activities follow. While the scientific method is shown sequentially, the steps are executed somewhat simultaneously and repetitively.

Utilization of Quantitative Methods

Surveys have shown that over a span of 20 years, the percentage of firms using QM increased from 51 to 90 percent, while the percentage of firms using QM in production increased from 24 to 85 percent.[8-12] Table 31.1 shows that the quantitative methods most utilized in production and inventory control are inventory models, exponential smoothing, regression analysis, linear and mathematical programming, program evaluation review techniques and the critical-path method (PERT/CPM), simulation, heuristics, and (with considerably less frequency) queueing theory, dynamic programming, decision theory, game theory, and Markov analysis. This table presents survey results of 250 directors of OR/MS of the largest industrial firms in the United States.[12] These percentages are based on 73 responses from 86 firms returning questionnaires.

This chapter presents in an accessible manner the most popular QM of production and inventory control (PIC). Accessibility is a primary objective here because research has shown that many managers lack a basic knowledge of QM; it is this, not the inapplicability of QM, which is the major reason for few QM applications.

PROBABILISTIC METHODS

Because simulation models are the most flexible and comprehensive of all QM, they have been one of the most widely used techniques in PIC.[25-29] The recent increase in the availability of computers has resulted in even more applications.

Simulation

Simulation is the process of seeking (usually through the use of computers) the optimal solutions to complex problems through dynamic experimentation with system models.[30-36] The term *dynamic* has particular importance, denoting that models are experimented with as time or other system elements are varied. Dynamic behavior can be induced manually through computer spreadsheet programs or through "what if" analysis in material requirements planning (MRP) and distribution-resource planning (DRP);[37-39] however, the most powerful method of experimenting is a technique called *Monte Carlo sampling*.

Monte Carlo Sampling. Monte Carlo sampling is the use of a chance process, such as the spin of a roulette wheel or the use of a random-number generator, to simulate the uncertain behavior of a system. Table 31.2 defines the Monte Carlo method for randomly generating the expected weekly demand for a product having a 2-week lead time. The weekly demand for this product during the last 96 weeks has been uniformly and randomly distributed, as shown in column 2. The demand has been 1 to 6 units per week, each with a probability of 1/6, or 0.167. As shown in the table, each interval of random numbers has been chosen so that each demand has a probability of being selected equal to 1/6. If a randomly selected number has a value of 888 (see column 4), a weekly demand of 6 occurs. Actual random numbers from 001 to 996 are generated by chance processes so that all numbers have an equal probability of being selected (see Table 4 in the Appendix).

TABLE 31.1 Utilization of OR Techniques in Various Production Applications

Application Area	N*	OR Techniques							
		Linear Programming	Simulation	Network Models	Regression Analysis	Queuing Theory	Dynamic Programming	Game Theory	Other
Production scheduling	56	53.6† (41.1)	46.4 (35.6)	10.7 (8.2)	8.9 (6.8)	16.1 (12.3)	12.5 (9.6)	0.0 (0.0)	17.9 (13.7)
Inventory analysis/control	47	23.4 (15.1)	57.4 (37.0)	6.4 (4.1)	25.5 (16.4)	8.5 (5.5)	6.4 (4.1)	2.1 (1.4)	14.9 (9.6)
Plant location	43	74.4 (43.8)	53.5 (31.5)	18.6 (11.0)	11.6 (6.8)	2.3 (1.4)	4.7 (2.7)	0.0 (0.0)	9.3 (5.5)
Logistics	41	65.9 (37.0)	58.5 (32.9)	19.5 (11.0)	14.6 (8.2)	7.3 (4.1)	2.4 (1.4)	4.9 (2.7)	4.9 (2.7)
Project planning/control	40	25.0 (13.7)	22.5 (12.3)	70.0 (38.4)	0.0 (0.0)	5.0 (2.7)	2.5 (1.4)	0.0 (0.0)	7.5 (4.1)
Production planning/control	37	51.4 (26.0)	48.6 (24.7)	18.9 (9.6)	8.1 (4.1)	10.8 (5.5)	8.1 (4.1)	0.0 (0.0)	8.1 (4.1)
Blending	34	94.1 (43.8)	17.6 (8.2)	2.9 (1.4)	8.8 (4.1)	2.9 (1.4)	0.0 (0.0)	0.0 (0.0)	2.9 (1.4)
Plant layout	32	40.6 (17.8)	59.4 (26.0)	15.6 (6.8)	6.3 (2.7)	15.6 (6.8)	0.0 (0.0)	3.1 (1.4)	9.4 (4.1)
Quality control	27	7.4 (2.7)	7.4 (2.7)	3.7 (4.1)	55.6 (20.5)	0.0 (0.0)	0.0 (0.0)	0.0 (0.0)	33.3 (12.3)
Equipment acquisition/replacement	22	18.2 (5.5)	50.0 (15.1)	4.5 (1.4)	0.0 (0.0)	4.5 (1.4)	0.0 (0.0)	0.0 (0.0)	31.8 (9.6)
Maintenance and Repair	16	0.0 (0.0)	50.0 (11.0)	18.8 (4.1)	25.5 (5.5)	18.8 (4.1)	6.3 (1.4)	6.3 (1.4)	25.0 (4.4)

* This figure represents the number of respondents to each specific production application area.

† These percentage figures in each table cell are the proportion of those responding to a given area who indicated the use of the technique for that area. The figures sum to more than 100%, since some respondents indicated the use of more than one technique for a given area.

Numbers in parentheses represent the percentage of the 73 respondents to the production applications portion of the questionnaire who indicated that they used a particular technique in a given application area. The percentage figures do not total 100%, since many respondents indicated that they used more than one technique in a given application area.

Source: W. N. Ledbetter and James F. Cox, "Operations Research in Production Management: An Investigation of Past and Present Utilization," *Production and Inventory Management,* third quarter, 1977, pp. 84–92.

31.6

Table 31.3, which is derived from a microcomputer random-number generator, uses the random-number relationships of Table 31.2 to simulate 10,000 two-week lead times. It shows the randomly generated numbers and the corresponding demand. The table's results, which in a manual simulation could have been generated from a random-number table or a toss of dice, took less than 1 min to generate on a microcomputer. They were used to produce Table 31.4.

Because random sampling is used in Monte Carlo simulation, the laws of probability apply in making statistical inferences. For example, using the percentage frequencies of 10,000 lead times of Table 31.4, column 3, one can forecast that demand during the lead time will exceed 10 units only 8.3 (5.6 + 2.7) percent of the time. It is possible to make many other statistical inferences using these results.

The validity of the above probability statement can be illustrated by comparing the simulated results of column 3 to the known, theoretical results of column 4 in

TABLE 31.2 Random Numbers to Simulate Demand per Week

Demand (Units per Week) (1)	Frequency (n = 96) (2)	Probability ($\frac{1}{6}$) (3)	Random-Number Interval (4)
1	16	0.167	001−166
2	16	0.167	167−332
3	16	0.167	333−498
4	16	0.167	499−664
5	16	0.167	665−830
6	16	0.167	831−996
Total	96	1.00	

TABLE 31.3 Simulation of Demand during 10,000 Two-Week Lead Times

Random Number, Week 1	Demand, Week 1	Random Number, Week 2	Demand, Week 2	(Weeks 1 + 2) Demand during Lead Time
158	1	483	3	4
092	1	741	5	6
099	1	070	1	2
724	5	648	4	9
674	5	956	6	11
.	.	.	.	.
.	.	.	.	.
.	.	.	.	.
066	1	319	2	3
597	4	093	1	5
467	3	222	2	5
543	4	296	2	6
041	1	014	1	2

Table 31.4. As shown in column 3, the frequencies of the 10,000 simulated lead times differ only slightly from the theoretical probabilities of column 4. Because random processes are used in Monte Carlo simulation, the variations of the simulated results from the theoretical (that is, the joint-probability-rule) results can be described by statistical sampling error and probability statements. This is one of the simulation's greatest advantages.[35,40–42]

An Inventory Management Simulation Example.[22]   A paper company that supplies large rolls of paper to newspaper publishers is interested in determining whether a different order quantity or reorder point would reduce inventory investment while at the same time maintaining customer delivery schedules.

The current decision rule is to order 35 rolls of paper whenever the sum of on-hand and on-order paper reaches 35 rolls. An analyst has examined the past demands and receipts and has found that both the demand per week and the lead time are randomly distributed, as shown in Tables 31.5 and 31.6. The demand has varied from 4 to 9 rolls per week, and the lead times have varied from 1 to 7 weeks. Each table also gives the random numbers used to simulate these occurrences. The simultaneous variation in demand and in lead times can result in significant shortages or in too much inventory; therefore, the potential benefits from modeling this system's behavior are substantial.

Table 31.7 shows a 40-week simulation for this example. In week 1, column 2, a typical beginning inventory of 60 was chosen as a starting condition for the simulation.[43] A random number, 12, was selected to yield a demand in week 1 of 5 rolls. The ending inventory is the beginning inventory of the following week. Using the basic inventory equation, the beginning inventory of week 2 is 55.

$$\text{Beg. inv. (wk. 2)} = \text{end. inv. (wk. 1)} = \text{beg. inv. (wk. 1)}$$
$$- \text{demand (wk. 1)} + \text{receipts (wk. 1)}$$
$$= 55 = 60 - 5 + 0$$

TABLE 31.4   Simulation of Demand during Lead Time

Demand during Lead Time (1)	Frequency (n = 10,000) (2)	Percentage Frequency* (n = 10,000) (3)	Expected Theoretical Probability[†] (4)
2	270	2.7	2.8
3	550	5.5	5.6
4	840	8.4	8.3
5	1120	11.2	11.1
6	1360	13.6	13.8
7	1680	16.8	16.7
8	1400	14.0	13.8
9	1110	11.1	11.1
10	830	8.3	8.3
11	560	5.6	5.6
12	270	2.7	2.8
	100	100.0	100.0

* Based on 10,000 simulated lead times.

[†] Generated using the joint probability law.

TABLE 31.5 Probabilities and Random Numbers of Weekly Demand

X No. of Rolls per Week	Past Frequency	Probability P(X)	Random Numbers Assigned
4	10	0.05	00−04
5	30	0.15	05−19
6	60	0.30	20−49
7	40	0.20	50−69
8	40	0.20	70−89
9	20	0.10	90−99
$\bar{X} = 6.65$	200	1.00	

TABLE 31.6 Probabilities and Random Numbers of Lead Times

Length of Lead Times L (Weeks)	Past Frequency	Probability P(L)	Random Numbers Assigned
1	70	0.35	00−34
2	50	0.25	35−59
3	40	0.20	60−79
4	20	0.10	80−89
5	10	0.05	90−94
6	6	0.03	95−97
7	4	0.02	98−99
$\bar{L} = 2.42$	200	1.00	

The ending inventory of week 1 becomes the beginning inventory of week 2. The reorder point has not been reached, and no additional inventory is ordered. Another random number is selected to simulate week 2's demand. This procedure is repeated until week 4, when the ending-inventory quantity equals the reorder point quantity and an order is placed. A random number, 11 (in column 7), is selected to determine the length of the lead time. As shown in Table 31.6, a random number of 11 denotes that the lead time is 1 week. Therefore, the order placed in week 4 is received in week 5. These procedures are repeated for another 35 weeks.

To validate this model, one can simulate the current decision rules of the firm and then compare the simulated results to those actually experienced.[44] If the simulated model behaves as the real system and meets statistical goodness-of-fit tests, then the model is most likely valid and can be used in experiments to achieve better decision rules. Assume here that the model reproduced the system's behavior and is therefore valid.

Given a valid model, one can simulate different decision rules to improve the system. In this case, the main decision rules are the reorder point (R) and the order quantity (Q). The results of Table 31.7, where R = 35 and Q = 35, assist in determining how to change the decision rules. As shown at the bottom of the table, the average beginning inventory is 40.73 units and the average ending inventory is 34.20 units; therefore, the average inventory is (40.73 + 34.20)/2, or 37.47.

TABLE 31.7 Inventory Simulation with Q = 35, R = 35

Week (1)	Beg. Inv. (2)	Demand Random Number (3)	Demand X (4)	Ending Inv. (5)	Order Qty. Q (6)	Lead-Time Random Number (7)	Lead Time L (8)	Receipts (9)
1	60	12	5	55	0			
2	55	64	7	48	0			
3	48	09	5	43	0			
4	43	82	8	35	35	11	1	
5	35	23	6	29	0			35
6	64	51	7	57	0			
7	57	29	6	51	0			
8	51	10	5	46	0			
9	46	56	7	39	0			
10	39	28	6	33	35	97	6	
11	33	42	6	27	0			
12	27	05	5	22	0			
13	22	45	6	16	0			
14	16	62	7	9	0			
15	9	34	6	3	0			
16	3	86	8	−5	35	57	2	35
17	30	18	5	25	0			
18	25	22	6	19	0			35
19	54	75	8	46	0			
20	46	16	5	41	0			
21	41	52	7	34	35	28	1	
22	34	60	7	27	0			35
23	62	93	9	53	0			

24	53	38	6	47	0			
25	47	94	9	38	0			
26	38	45	6	32	35	70	3	
27	32	48	6	26	0			
28	26	74	8	18	0			
29	18	85	8	10	0			35
30	45	73	8	37	0			
31	37	57	7	30	35	33	1	35
32	30	19	5	25	0			
33	60	48	6	54	0			
34	54	99	9	45	0			
35	45	00	4	41	0			
36	41	68	7	34	35	21	1	35
37	34	63	7	27	0			
38	62	15	5	57	0			
39	57	53	7	50	0			
40	50	29	6	44	0			
	1629	Totals	261	1368			15	
	40.73	Means	6.53	34.20			2.14	

* A negative ending-inventory value denotes a back order filled later.
† Amount received is available as beginning inventory for the next period.

31.11

This is a turnover rate of approximately 261/37.47, or 6.97. During one of seven simulated lead times, a back order occurred; it was in period 16. Approximately 98 percent of demand [(261 demanded − 6 back orders)/261] was supplied directly from stock, probably an acceptable customer-service level. Based upon these results, one could experiment with other decision rules (such as R = 35 and Q = 30).

This inventory simulation could have been made more complex by including the costs, revenues, and profits of different decision rules. Then, through experimentation, improved decision rules could be identified. Even though this is a simple example, one can appreciate the power and versatility of simulation.

Advantages of Simulation:

Experimental Optimization.   Simulation allows experimentation with systems without disrupting the actual system. Managers can use models in an automated or manual "what if" search procedure to find good system designs and decision rules.[45] The ability to seek better solutions to complex probabilistic problems makes simulation extremely powerful.

Model Flexibility and Validity.   A simulation model can provide a realism unequaled by other methods. Complex systems with large numbers of logical, mathematical, and probabilistic relationships can be modeled because simulation is not limited by mathematical or logical assumptions concerning variables and their relationships.

Modeling Ease and Software Availability.   General-purpose simulation languages exist to make computer formulations of relatively complex models easier for individuals who have little programming experience. All popular simulation languages are now available for microcomputers, and small- to medium-size models can be simulated by using BASIC and spreadsheets.

Statistical Inferences.   As a statistical sampling procedure, simulation is a powerful approach to solving problems and making inferences in a probabilistic environment.

Disadvantages of Simulation:

Costly and Time-Consuming.   Because there is no general simulation model, it can be more costly to implement a simulation. It can require significantly more development and solution time and resources than other QM approaches.

Nonoptimality of Solutions.   In general, simulation only provides better decisions, not optimal decisions. However, offsetting this disadvantage is the decision maker's desire for better decisions, not mathematically optimal solutions to unrealistic problems.

Simulation Methodology.   Simulation models differ almost as much in their structure and complexity as do the systems they represent. The methodology follows the general steps of QM shown previously. There are several other considerations in simulation, including the choice of computer language, the construction of probability distributions, decision-rule selection, the choice of starting conditions, the length of simulation runs, the search procedure for optimality, and the choice of relevant statistical tests. These are relatively simple considerations for simple models, but they may be complex decisions for complex models.

Computer Simulation Languages.   Special-purpose simulation languages simplify the formulation and execution of simulations and have distinct advantages not found in general-purpose languages such as FORTRAN, BASIC, COBOL, PL/1, or

APL. These advantages are (1) ease of model construction; (2) ease in programming; (3) better input, output, and documentation procedures; (4) good error diagnostics; and (5) ease of revision and maintenance of the model.

In general, there are three types of simulation languages: discrete, continuous, and combined continuous-discrete languages. The distinction between *discrete* and *continuous* may be explained by comparing the differences in digital and analog watches. The digital displays of clocks and watches are discrete occurrences, while the sweep hands of analog watches are continuous. The daily, weekly, monthly, and annual reports of businesses are all discrete reporting procedures. Consequently, discrete languages are the most popular in business and economic applications. In a continuous system, the state of the system is measured and represented by variables that change continuously over time. Continuous systems are modeled using differential equations, but the user does not have to be a mathematician to use continuous simulation languages.

- *Discrete simulation languages* include GPSS,[46] Q-GERT,[47] and SIMSCRIPT.[48]
- *Continuous languages* include DYNAMO[49] and CSMP III.[50]
- *Combined discrete-continuous languages* include SIMAN,[51] GASP IV[52] and SLAM.[53]

These languages greatly increase the effectiveness and productivity of computer simulation methods.

Decision Analysis

Production and inventory managers must often make decisions under uncertain conditions. This section introduces QM for making decisions in ill-structured, nonroutine situations under risk and uncertainty.[54-56] Risk describes a situation in which alternative events and their probabilities are known; for example, risk was illustrated when the sales of products A and B were calculated using probability estimates. In contrast, *uncertainty* describes a situation in which events can be identified but probabilities cannot be estimated. Uncertainty is the most difficult situation under which to make good decisions. The purpose of *decision analysis* is to optimize the outcomes of decisions while facing risk or uncertainty.

A manufacturer/distributor is currently medium in size and complexity, which will increase or decrease as the sales volume and the number of products, production facilities, and distribution centers increase or decrease. The manufacturer/distributor is deciding which of two production information control systems to purchase. System 1 is currently more desirable, but it is not as easily expanded as system 2. Forecasting has provided three scenarios concerning the company's complexity levels and their probabilities. Table 31.8, shows low, medium, and high company complexity and the returns on investments in percentages of each production information control (PIC) system. Based on this information, the company must decide which system to purchase.

Elements of Decision Problems.   There are five common elements to most decision problems. Each will be considered in this solution.

Goals.   Assume that the goal of this firm is to maximize the expected (mean) return on investment (ROI). The laws of probability denote that the expected value (EV) of a decision alternative d_i is

$$EV(d_i) = \text{sum of } [P(x_j)O(d_i,x_j)] \qquad i = 1 \text{ to } n \qquad j = 1 \text{ to } m$$

where
$$n = \text{number of alternative decisions}$$
$$m = \text{number of different events}$$
$$P(x_j) = \text{probability of event } x_j \text{ occurring}$$
$$O(d_{i,xj}) = \text{value of decision } d_i \text{ when event } x_j \text{ occurs}$$

For example, the expected value of a gamble with a 60 percent chance of winning $10 and a 40 percent chance of losing $10 is $2:

$$EV(\text{gamble}) = 0.60(\$10) + 0.40(-\$10) = \$2$$

Courses of Action (Alternative Decision). In this case, the decision maker has two alternative actions: purchase system 1, d_1 or system 2, d_2.

Random Events. Depending on sales, one of three possible company complexities will occur: x_1 = low, x_2 = medium, or x_3 = high.

Probabilities of Events $P(x_j)$. The probabilities in the table were forecasted using historical and subjective data.

Outcomes of Decision-Event Combinations $O(d_i,x_j)$. The returns on investments associated with decision-event combinations are shown in the table. Assume that these were determined using a spreadsheet model.

Optimal Decisions Using Expected Values. A frequent criterion used to select optimal decisions is the maximization of the expected values (EV). The following describes the expected returns on investments of each decision:

System 1
$$
\begin{aligned}
\text{Expected ROI}(d_1) &= P(x_1)O(d_1,x_1) + P(x_2)O(d_1,x_2) + P(x_3)O(d_1,x_3) \\
&= 0.3(12) \qquad\quad + 0.5(18) \qquad\quad + 0.2(15) \qquad\quad = 15.6\%
\end{aligned}
$$

System 2
$$
\begin{aligned}
\text{Expected ROI}(d_2) &= P(x_1)O(d_2,x_1) + P(x_2)O(d_2,x_2) + P(x_3)O(d_2,x_3) \\
&= 0.3(-2) \qquad\quad + 0.5(18) \qquad\quad + 0.2(24) \qquad\quad = 13.2\%
\end{aligned}
$$

The best decision is to purchase system 1 because it yields the highest expected return on investment. Highest *expected* means that over the long run, with repeated trials, this decision will yield the highest *average* return on investment. The

TABLE 31.8 PIC Systems, Events, Probabilities, Decisions, and Outcomes

			Decision	
			System 1, d_1	System 2, d_2
	Event		Outcomes	
	Company Complexity	*Event Probability*		
j	x_j	$P(x_j)$	$O(d_1, x_j)$	$O(d_2, x_j)$
1	Low, x_1	0.3	12	-2
2	Medium, x_2	0.5	18	18
3	High, x_3	0.2	15	24
Expected ROI			15.6	13.2

assumption of repeated trials is an important one, meaning that this or similar decisions are frequently made. In repeating similar decisions, one achieves the highest profit by selecting that decision which has the highest average profit. The highest average profit yields the highest total long-run profit. In contrast, if such a decision were made only once in a lifetime, then maximizing the expected value might not be the best criterion.

Limitations of Expected Values. In general, the expected value is the most rational decision criterion when probability estimates exist. However, there are several situations in which expected values are not desirable.

Infrequent Decisions. When a decision is made very infrequently and therefore the repeated-trials assumption is not true, the expected-value criterion may be invalid. A decision maker may see an opportunity in one action that may not ever be available again. Seizing or avoiding an opportunity despite its lower or higher expected value may take precedence over the expected-value criterion.

The Whole Distribution Is Important. Because it does not describe the whole distribution of possible outcomes, the expected value ignores important information concerning extreme value. Therefore, when a decision yields extremely undesirable outcomes (such as bankruptcy, loss of job, or death), one might not choose the decision with the highest expected value. In such situations, those decision alternatives with unacceptable outcomes might be ignored.

In contrast, one might face a situation in which a decision with a low expected value has an outcome that is very desirable. Given a choice between the following alternatives, different executives may react differently: Decision 1 yields a 50 percent chance of $10 million and a 50 percent chance of −$15 million; decision 2 yields a 70 percent chance of $2 million and a 30 percent chance of −$1 million. The expected values of each are

$$\text{Expected value}(d_1) = 0.50(10,000,000) + 0.50(-15,000,000) = -\$2,500,000$$
$$\text{Expected value}(d_2) = 0.70(2,000,000) + 0.30(-1,000,000) = \$1,100,000$$

Decision 2 has the highest expected value. However, some individuals might have a preference for decision 1 after considering the whole distribution of outcomes; they might therefore choose decision 1. A more formal approach to making decisions using such personal preferences is available through the use of utility functions.

Utility Functions. One desires outcomes from decisions because of their *utility* (their inherent, personal value). Utility is simply a way of representing the intrinsic value of money.[57] While the utility that one receives from money is greater for higher sums than for lower sums, the utility may not be proportionate throughout all possible monetary sums. For example, a company may view a potential loss of $1 million as quite different than just double the loss of $500,000 if the larger loss will result in bankruptcy.

While the construction of utility functions is beyond the scope of this discussion, they are not difficult to arrive at through an interview process. Assume that three executives have been interviewed concerning the utility of the monetary values of column 1, Table 31.9. Utility scales are commonly chosen to run from 0 to 1. In this case, a 1.0 utility is associated with a $20 million gain, while a 0.0 utility is associated with a $20 million loss.

Expected Utility. To calculate the expected utility of the previous decisions, simply substitute the utility values of Table 31.9 for monetary sums in the expected-

TABLE 31.9 Utility Values for Three Executives

Value of Sum Equal to (dollars)	Individual 1 (risk avoider) Utility	Individual 2 (risk neutral) Utility	Individual 3 (risk seeker) Utility
−20,000,000	0	0	0
−15,000,000	0.250	0.125	0.100
−1,000,000	0.500	0.475	0.300
2,000,000	0.560	0.550	0.400
10,000,000	0.775	0.750	0.725
20,000,000	1.000	1.000	1.000

value formulas. Let U_i ($X) represent the utility that individual i receives from the monetary sum of $X.

Individual 1, the risk avoider, chooses decision 2 because its expected utility is highest:

$$\text{Expected utility } (d_1) = 0.50U_1 (10{,}000{,}000) + 0.50U_1 (-15{,}000{,}000)$$
$$= 0.50(0.775) + 0.50(0.250) = 0.512$$
$$\text{Expected utility } (d_2) = 0.70U_1(2{,}000{,}000) + 0.30U_1(-1{,}000{,}000)$$
$$= 0.70(0.560) + 0.30(0.500) = 0.542$$

Individual 2, the risk neutral, will by definition always choose that decision which is best by using expected monetary values; therefore, the risk neutral executive chooses decision 2:

$$\text{Expected utility } d_1 = 0.50(0.750) + 0.50(0.125) = 0.4375$$
$$\text{Expected utility } d_2 = 0.70(0.550) + 0.30(0.475) = 0.5275$$

Individual 3, the risk seeker, chooses decision 1 because of the relatively high utility of $10 million as opposed to the relatively low utility of the $2 million gain of decision 2:

$$\text{Expected utility } d_1 = 0.50(0.725) + 0.50(0.100) = 0.4125$$
$$\text{Expected utility } d_2 = 0.70(0.400) + 0.30(0.300) = 0.370$$

Utility functions can be valuable decision aids, yet there are some problems in their use: (1) A derived utility function is only valid for the given decision maker; (2) the shape of the utility function for an individual may change over time, therefore making periodic revisions necessary; (3) it is very difficult to determine reliable utility functions for groups of individuals.

Offsetting these disadvantages are several advantages: (1) Utility functions do express the intrinsic value associated with alternatives, (2) utility functions can be useful in measuring the value of trade-offs between monetary and nonmonetary alternatives, (3) multiattribute utility functions provide a method for evaluating several different measures of goals and outcomes (loss of occupation, bankruptcy, pollution, etc).[58−60]

Decision Criteria under Uncertainty. While uncertainties (unknown event probabilities) make decision making more difficult than under conditions of risk, decision criteria do exist to assist the executive.

The *equally likely criterion* assumes that when probabilities are unknown, each outcome has an equal probability of occurring. One chooses that decision having the highest expected value, assuming that all events have equal probability. Using this criterion, reconsider the problem concerning the production information control (PIC) system in Table 31.8. Assume that each of the three events has a $\frac{1}{3}$ probability of occurring:

$$d_1 \text{ yields } \tfrac{1}{3}(12) + \tfrac{1}{3}(18) + \tfrac{1}{3}(15) = 15\%$$
$$d_2 \text{ yields } \tfrac{1}{3}(-2) + \tfrac{1}{3}(18) + \tfrac{1}{3}(24) = 13.33\%$$

Therefore, d_1 is the best decision.

The *maximin* (maximum of the minimums) criterion directs one to choose that decision which has the maximum of all possible minimum outcomes d_1 with a 12 percent ROI. This is a conservative approach that has general relevance.

The *maximum likelihood* criterion states that one should choose that decision which is best with the most frequent event. In this case, the most frequently occurring event is "medium complexity"; both d_1 and d_2 yield 18 percent. Therefore, this criterion leaves one indifferent between d_1 and d_2.

The *maximax* (maximum of the maximums) criterion identifies the best decision as that which yields the outcome with the maximum value, regardless of the probability of the outcome. In this case, d_2 yields the maximum of the maximum ROIs, 24 percent. However, d_2 also yields the lowest ROI, -2 percent. This criterion will normally be illogical because it ignores the probabilities of negative events. Yet if the probabilities are unknown and the decision maker is a "gambler," this rule may be relevant.

These may be useful decision guides under uncertainty. In general, if the event probabilities are known, then the equally likely, maximum likelihood, and maximax criteria become less relevant. But even if the probabilities are known, maximin is often relevant because organizational decision makers are normally risk avoiders. As discussed later, these criteria are also very important in game theory, in which intelligent competitors react to each other's decisions.

Decision Trees for Sequential Decisions. Frequently, one faces sequential decisions that are influenced by random events.[61] In this situation, decision trees (such as Fig. 31.2) are valuable. Reconsider the selection of the best PIC system in Table 31.8. In selecting decision 1, management was concerned about the low return on investment (15 percent) if the company's size and complexity were high. As shown, in Fig. 31.2, management has determined that a second decision can be made to expand system 1 if the company's complexity is high. This system expansion has an 80 percent probability of being successful and yielding a 26 percent ROI; it has a 20 percent probability of being unsuccessful, in which case the ROI of system 1, given high system complexity, would be only 12 percent.

Consider the main elements of a decision tree by referring to Fig. 31.2. *Decision nodes* are shown as squares and represent points at which decisions must be made. *Random-event nodes* are shown as circles. After constructing a decision tree, an optimal solution is found by working backward from each decision node and trimming or slashing (///) those decisions with lower expected values. The values shown in the squares and circles are the expected values of decisions or events. The sequence of decisions that remains after trimming is optimum. The company's management thus determines that its optimal decisions are to purchase system 1 and to expand it if the complexity increases.

Decision analysis and decision trees are particularly powerful tools for complex, ill-structured situations. Decisions such as acquisition and development of a com-

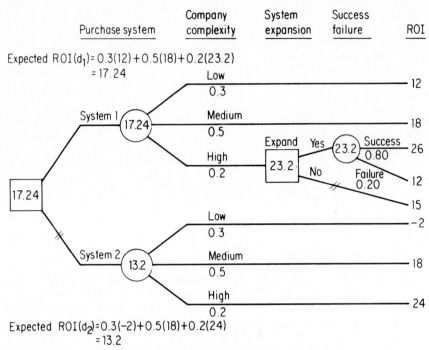

FIGURE 31.2 Decision tree for PIC system acquisition and expansion.

puter-based information system, facility planning, and location analysis are candidates for decision analysis.

Only a few of the decision-analysis tools available to the production and inventory professional have been presented in the above discussions.

Applications of decision analysis have not been reported in the literature as much as one would infer from its relative ease of application, low computational costs, and potential benefits. As improvements in information and decision-support systems continue, the number of reported applications should increase.

Queueing Models

Typical queues (waiting lines) include calls at a telephone switchboard, trucks waiting at docks, jobs waiting in a job shop, orders arriving at a distribution center, machinists waiting at tool cribs, customers waiting at service counters, and interactive users of computers. Many of these systems could be designed or controlled more effectively by using queueing models.[62-66]

Queueing theory was originated by the Danish mathematician and engineer A. K. Erlang in 1909 as he designed and configured telephone switching equipment. The basic purpose of queueing theory is to design a service facility so as to maximize the profit or ROI from serving and having individuals (such as parts, products, paperwork, or people) wait. Providing service usually requires both a fixed cost (such as adding more machines or docks) and a variable cost (such as the hourly wage of workers), while the cost of waiting includes having individuals idle (as a result, for instance, of late orders, poor customer service, or poor efficiency).

Only the simplest queueing model, the single-server single-phase system, is presented here. This is typified by a single-server retail counter, a single-person tool crib, or a single machine. One should note that the concepts illustrated here are very useful in describing systems for analyses using a variety of methods, including simulation. In addition, the basic concepts of queueing models assist in better management and analysis of a variety system. Simple queueing systems have simple equations for modeling system behavior. In contrast, complex queueing systems require much more complex mathematical formulas and may be impossible to model using queueing formulas; consequently, Monte Carlo simulation may be needed in order to model complex queueing systems.[67,68]

Queueing-System Structure.   A single-server single-phase queueing system is shown in Fig. 31.3a. The *number of servers, or channels,* refers to the number of servers at each phase of the system. Figure 31.3b illustrates a single-server multiphase queueing system. As shown, two servers exist in the system, but they provide only a single path (or channel) for service; therefore, this is referred to as a single-server, or single-channel, queueing system. In contrast, a multiserver single-phase system has several servers to provide only one service (Fig. 31.3c); an example of this is a multiserver retail counter where patrons either take a number or wait in a single line. Figure 31.3d is a multiserver multiphase queueing model. Figure 31.4 summarizes some common assumptions concerning queueing models.

Population Size.   A system serving a very small population behaves differently than one serving a large population. For example, the probability of one machine needing repair from a large population of machines is easily described by using simple probability statements; however, if the population consists of only eight machines, two of which are in the shop for repair, the probability distribution of breakdowns becomes more complex. Frequently, it is possible to assume that the system serves an infinitely large population. If the population is relatively small (such as 50), then special queueing tables must be used to describe the system.

Arrival Rate.   Probability distributions are used to describe the arrival patterns of individuals entering a queueing system. Many theoretical and empirical distributions can be used to describe arrivals; these include constant, Poisson, random, Erlang, hyperexponential, and general distributions. One of the most common is the Poisson distribution (see Fig. 31.5a and 5b for examples).

Poisson/Exponential Distributions.   The Poisson distribution describes the *rate* of occurrences of a random event. The concept of rate is important. It measures occurrences per unit of space or time, such as the number of phone calls at a switchboard per hour or the number of orders received per week. If the rate of an event is the result of a relatively large number of minor, independent chance influences, if the probability of the event in any one unit of time or space is very low, and if the number of possible points of occurrences is very large, then the events will follow a Poisson distribution. For example, the probability of a phone call arriving at a switchboard during the next second is very low, but the number of seconds per hour is quite large; therefore, the arrival rate may follow a Poisson distribution. The other characteristics of the Poisson distribution are that it describes discrete events that are independent of each other and possess a constant mean.

If the rate of an event follows a Poisson distribution, then the *time* between occurrences follows an exponential distribution. The exponential distribution has a mean equal to the inverse of the mean of the Poisson distribution. Therefore, the *rate of arrivals* is described by the Poisson distribution and the *time between arrivals* is described by the exponential distribution.

Statistical goodness-of-fit methods can be used to identify the theoretical distri-

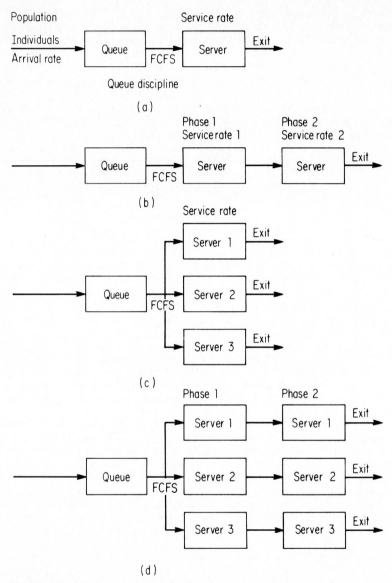

FIGURE 31.3 Basic queueing-system structure.

bution of the actual arrival rate of a system. If the pattern of arrivals does not follow a known theoretical distribution like the Poisson, it can be modeled as a general empirical distribution; or, when queuing formulas fail, Monte Carlo simulation methods can be used.

Queue Length. If a service facility (for example, a conveyor) has a limited number of spaces in its queue, then it will behave differently than if there were no limit. Models exist for both infinite and finite queue lengths. How the system

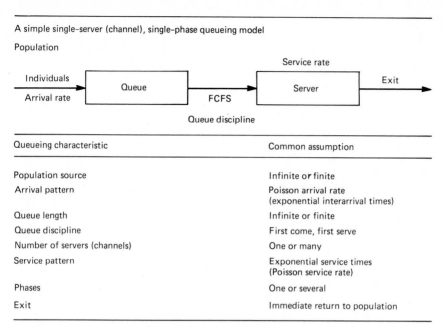

FIGURE 31.4   Characteristics of typical queueing systems.

behaves with a full queue may not be easily modeled. If individuals balk (that is, do not enter) when the queue is full, then this may be modeled easily, but if individuals behave differently, then the model may be too complex for queuing analysis.

Queue Priority.   This describes the order in which individuals are served. The most common queue discipline is the first-come first-served rule.

Service Rate.   The time spent serving an individual includes only the time spent with him or her. If this *time* follows an exponential distribution, then the service *rate* is a Poisson distribution. As with arrival rates, queueing formulas can model several different probability distributions for service rates.

Exit.   There are different exits that an individual can make from the system. After leaving the system, the individual might be eligible to reenter the queue or might enter a different population that might not enter the service system for some time. For example, the probability of a machine needing service immediately after an overhaul should be lower than that of one which is due for an overhaul.

Shop-Load Queueing Example.   A work center has been exhibiting excessive lead times. While the average input to the work center (7.75 jobs per day) has been less than the average output (8 jobs per day), the work center's lead times and backlogs seem excessive. Even though the average input is less than the average output, the variability of each causes large backlogs and long lead times. To understand better how the backlog could increase under these conditions, a queueing model is selected to model the system.

The input to the work center has the frequency distribution shown in the Poisson distribution (Fig. 31.5*a*). The mean input rate is 7.75 jobs per day. A chi-square goodness-of-fit statistical test reveals that the distribution is consistent with the Poisson. The output rate (Fig. 31.5*b*) is also a random variable described by a Poisson distribution with a mean of 8 jobs per day.

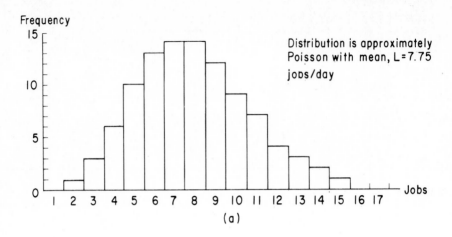

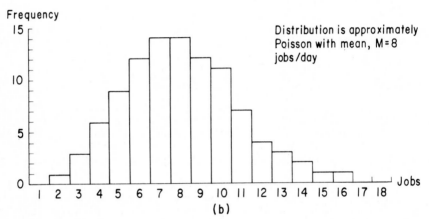

FIGURE 31.5 Poisson distributions: (a) daily input rates to the shop for 100 days and (b) daily output rates of the shop for 100 days.

The scheduling system uses a first-come first-served (FCFS) queue discipline. The number of jobs that can wait in the work center is large; therefore, the queue length is assumed to be infinite, and the population of possible jobs is also infinitely large. These characteristics describe a single-server single-phase queueing system with a Poisson arrival rate, a Poisson service rate, an FCFS queue discipline, an infinite queue length, and an infinite population size. This model is often noted using Kendall's notation M/M/1, where the first M denotes a Poisson arrival rate, the second M denotes a Poisson service rate, and the 1 denotes the number of servers. The M notation refers to a Markovian (Poisson) process.

Queueing Formulas.   The mathematical formulas of an M/M/1 model are given in Table 31.10. The derivation of these formulas is beyond the scope of this handbook. One does not need to know how these formulas were developed to apply queueing models properly, but one *does* have to understand the assumptions underlying the formulas. After confirming that the assumptions are valid, the system is analyzed using the formulas of Table 31.10.

TABLE 31.10 Single-Channel (Single-Server) Queueing (M/M/1) Formulas

Queueing assumptions: Poisson arrivals; Poisson service; one server; infinite population; infinite queue; FCFS
Arrival rate = L
Service rate = M

Utilization of the system: $p = \dfrac{L}{M}$ (1)

Mean number in the queue: $\bar{n}_q = \dfrac{L^2}{M(M - L)}$ (2)

Mean number in the system: $\bar{n}_s = \dfrac{L}{M - L}$ (3)

Mean time in the queue: $\bar{t}_q = \dfrac{L}{M(M - L)}$ (4)

Mean time in the system: $\bar{t}_s = \dfrac{1}{M - L}$ (5)

Probability of n individuals
in the system: $P_n = \left(1 - \dfrac{L}{M}\right)\left(\dfrac{L}{M}\right)^n$ (6)

The behavior of the shop is described by the following:

Utilization of System: $p = \dfrac{L}{M} = \dfrac{7.75}{8.00} = 97\%$ utilized   (1)

Because the average input to the system is less than the average output, the system is utilized 97 (idle 3) percent of the time. It may seem illogical that the system is sometimes idle and at other times has long backlogs.

Mean number in queue: $\bar{n}_q = \dfrac{L^2}{M(M - L)} = \dfrac{7.75^2}{8(8 - 7.75)} = 30.03$ jobs   (2)

Even though the work center's average input is less than its average output, there is an average backlog of 30.03 jobs waiting in the system. Also, the backlog frequently exceeds 30.03 jobs.

Mean number in system: $\bar{n}_s = \dfrac{L}{M - L} = \dfrac{7.75}{(8 - 7.75)} = 31$ jobs   (3)

The average number of jobs in the system is 31. As shown above in Eq. (1), the system is 97 percent utilized. Consequently, on the average, there is 0.97 of a job at the server plus 30.03 jobs in the queue, and therefore 31 jobs in the system.

Mean time in queue: $\bar{t}_q = \dfrac{L}{M(M - L)} = \dfrac{7.75}{8(8 - 7.75)} = 3.875$ days   (4)

The average job waits 3.875 days before being worked on.

Mean time in system: $\bar{t}_s = \dfrac{1}{M - L} = \dfrac{1}{8 - 7.75} = 4.0$ days   (5)

The average job takes 4.0 days to be completed, 3 days 7 hr (or 3.875 days) waiting, and 1 hr being processed.

Probability of 40 jobs in the shop: $P_n = \left(1 - \dfrac{L}{M}\right)\left(\dfrac{L}{M}\right)^n$

$$P_{40} = \left(1 - \dfrac{7.75}{8}\right)\left(\dfrac{7.75}{8}\right)^{40} = 0.00877 \qquad (6)$$

While the probability that there will be exactly 40 jobs in the shop is quite low (0.00877), the probability that there may be 40 or more jobs in the shop is quite high. Figure 31.6 illustrates the cumulative probabilities of different backlogs. For example, there is approximately a 27 percent probability of more than a 40-job load in the shop; that is, the shop will have more than 40 jobs waiting 27 percent of the time.

While the results of this analysis may be counterintuitive, they are accurate when the assumptions of the model are valid. The interaction of the random arrival and service rates results in large backlogs in some periods and idle times in others. This situation plagues many systems that cannot or do not control their input and output. However, management can design systems to preclude these random influ-

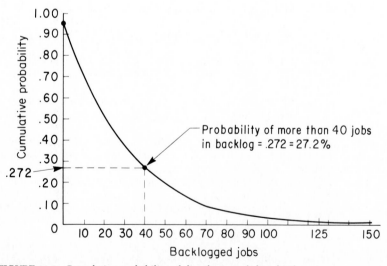

FIGURE 31.6 Cumulative probability of distribution of shop load.

ences. For example, if the arrival rate and the service rate were constant, then a work center could operate with a 100 percent utilization and no backlogs.

Limitations of Simple Analytical Models. While queueing models are very useful, there are limitations to their applicability. First, queueing formulas describe the behavior of the service system after reaching a steady state. If the actual system never reaches a steady state or if one is interested in describing the dynamics of reaching a steady state, than queueing models are less applicable. Second, formulas for complex queueing applications may not exist, and simulation procedures may therefore be needed.

Queueing models have been successfully used in a variety of applications, most recently in the design of computer and communications systems,[63,68] having become an important aid in the management of complex information systems. They will become more important in PIC as managers become more knowledgeable of QM's advantages and limitations and as production systems become more automated.

DETERMINISTIC METHODS

Linear Programming

Linear programming (LP) methods are a subset of mathematical programming (MP) methods. LP and MP provide optimal solutions and insights when allocating scarce resources in many deterministic environments. They are applicable in determining where, when, and how limited resources should be allocated so as to achieve the highest level of effectiveness (maximum profit, minimum cost, shortest time, smallest square footage, etc.). The term *programming* may be misleading here, for LP does not necessarily involve computer programming. Most LP applications are implemented using programs that facilitate problem formulation and model construction but do not require programming expertise.

Some people have the misconception that LP is a tool only for the process industries. This is not so. LP methods are general and are effective in managing manufacturing operations. While the dimensions of a complex MRP system may be too large for the cost-effective use of LP, there are many other complex problems that are solvable by LP. In fact, the forte of LP models is their ability within very little computer time to find optimal solutions to extremely large problems.

Typical Applications of LP. LP has been used in almost every conceivable environment.[69-72] In several surveys, LP has emerged as one of the most frequently applied quantitative methods in PIC.

Production Distribution and Logistics. LP can be very useful in determining the lowest-cost shipment routes from existing distribution centers (DCs) to retail outlets or from factories to DCs.[73,74] In addition, LP is useful in determining the best location for DCs given the existing or future locations of factories or retail outlets.[75,76] Also, LP has been used to plan the production, inventory, and distribution of parts for shipment between plants and distribution centers. These applications do not eliminate MRP or distribution-resource planning (DRP) systems, but they enhance them through rough-cut capacity planning.[70,76]

Aggregate Production Planning. LP has been used in scheduling the lowest-cost or highest-profit production rates for product groups over finite planning horizons. The OR/MS literature is abundant in the areas of "production smoothing" or aggregate production planning and scheduling.[77,78] The benefits of LP have increased through the widespread use of time fences, "frozen" master schedules, rough-cut capacity-planning procedures, planning bills, and the analysis of bottleneck work centers. These approaches remove the uncertainty and instability of production plans and master schedules, and therefore enhance the effectiveness of LP in manufacturing.

Product-Mix, Blending, and Cutting-Stock Problems. Associated with master scheduling and production planning is *product-mix planning*, which is the determination of the optimal mix of products, given constraints on labor, materials, and sales. LP has been used to solve product-mix problems in a variety of manufacturing and process industries.[70,79]

Blending problems in the process industries are ideally suited for solution by MP procedures. The lowest-cost (highest-profit) blend of ingredients must meet technological, chemical, nutritional, or palatability requirements. The blending of human and animal food, of petroleum products, and of menus are a few examples.

The cutting-stock problem is one in which a mill desires to minimize the waste in cutting and trimming stock for a variety of products (which have different widths, lengths, and thicknesses, for instance), subject to the available stock of materials, to technical specifications, and to demands for the final product.[80]

Hierarchical Applications. While LP can be used to solve extremely large problems in operations, many situations have exceedingly large dimensions. A medium to large manufacturing planning and control system is a good example. For such systems, LP procedures have been embodied in a larger system of models arranged in a hierarchical or sequential manner. The hierarchical approach recognizes the top-down and bottom-up relationships and feedback loops that exist in most systems. When a system is very complex, it may be impossible to model the effects of decisions at all levels simultaneously, but it is possible to solve problems systematically and sequentially—much as is done iteratively and heuristically in an MRP system. In the hierarchical approach, an LP model can be used for medium- to long-term planning, and a simulation or MRP model can be used for immediate- to short-term planning.[81-83]

Other Applications. Other applications of LP are too many to mention; Table 31.1 lists a few.[69-72,84,85]

Important Assumptions of LP. The term *linear* means that LP relationships are assumed to be linear. For example, in maximizing the profits from manufacturing, linearity denotes that if twice as many products are produced, the costs will double. In contrast, the costs might be more or less than double in a nonlinear relationship. The linearity assumption does not significantly reduce LP's applicability, because linearity is often valid and it is possible to include some nonlinearities in LP models by using approximations of nonlinear functions. When these approaches fail, nonlinear programming (NLP) can be used.

Another assumption of LP is that the environment being modeled is relatively certain (that is, deterministic). Costs, demands, priorities, and capacities are assumed to be known with certainty. When a few uncertainties exist, "what if" procedures (called sensitivity analyses) can be used to explore the effects of uncertainty. Consider these assumptions in the example below.

Production Planning Example of LP. A firm desires to maximize its profit by selling all the gas-powered (G) and wind-powered (W) turbines it can produce. However, it is constrained by capacity in two departments: fabrication and assembly. Each G sold yields a profit contribution of $70; each W, $50. The profit contribution is the difference between the selling price and the cost per unit. Each G requires 5 fabrication hours and 20 assembly hours; each W, 1 fabrication hour and 30 assembly hours. There are 200 and 2400 hr of capacity available in the fabrication and assembly departments, respectively. Using this information, an LP model is formulated and solved for the maximum profit.

Step 1: Objective Function. The most important step in a problem formulation is the identification of the related system objective, such as to maximize profits, to maximize the ROI, or to minimize costs. This *objective function* measures the optimality of different decisions. In this situation, the objective has been clearly defined: Maximize the profit Z from producing G's and W's. Mathematically, this is

Maximize: Profit (Z) = \$70 for each G + \$50 for each W
$$= \$70G + \$50W$$

Step 2: Constraint Formulation. Identify constraints that limit the upper or lower values of variables (such as G's and W's). In general, *constraints* are technical, regulatory, economic, or policy limits on that number of units of a variable which can exist in the solution. The constraints of the example are:

Lathe constraint: 5 hr for each G plus 1 hr for each W must be less than or equal to the 200 hr available in the lathe department.

$$5G + 1W \leq 200 \tag{7}$$

Assembly constraint: 20 hr for G plus 30 hr for each W must be less than or equal to the 2400 hr available in the assembly department.

$$20G + 30W \leq 2400 \tag{8}$$

Nonnegativity constraint: In addition to the above constraints, it is mathematically necessary to eliminate negative values of G and W as solutions. That is, all variables in LP are restricted to be nonnegative.

$$G \text{ and } W \geq 0 \tag{9}$$

Definitions. The constants on the right side of the inequality sign are called *right-hand sides (RHSs)*. The variables G and W are called *decision variables*, and the numeric constants or multipliers (that is, 70 and 50, and 5, 1, 20, and 30) are referred to as *objective-function coefficients* and *constraint coefficients* respectively. Now that this problem has been formulated, which is normally the most difficult step, consider the graphical solution in Fig. 31.7.

Step 3: Solution. In Fig. 31.7, the vertical axis represents the number of W's produced and the horizontal axis the number of G's produced. Also plotted are an objective-function line, the fabrication constraint, and the assembly constraint. The "less than" portion of the constraints lies below and to the left of each line. The shaded area (*ABCD*) of the figure outlines the region, called the *feasible region*, of all possible combinations of G's and W's that meet the requirements of all constraints, that is, do not exceed the capacities of the fabrication and assembly departments.

As points move up and to the right of the origin, where G = 0 and W = 0, the values of G and W increase, and therefore the profit increases (that is, 70G + 50W increases). To calculate the profit at any point, just find the values of W and G at that point and substitute them into the objective-function equation. The plotted objective function is one of many possible profit lines. It was chosen to display the slope of the objective function. In this case, a profit of \$3,500 yields two convenient points on the W and G axis. Given Z = 70G + 50W = \$3,500: When G = 0, then W = 70, and when W = 0, then G = 50.

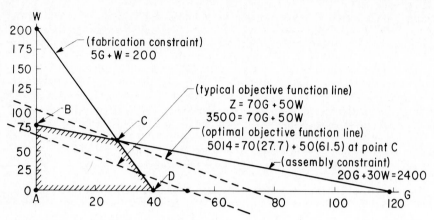

FIGURE 31.7 Feasible region and optimal solution at point C.

When written in standard algebraic form, with the vertical variable on the left-hand side of the equal sign, the objective-function equation is

$$W = Z/50 - 70/50(G)$$

where $-70/50$ is the slope (that is, the change in W resulting from a one-unit change in G) and $Z/50$ is any conveniently chosen value of the objective function (such as $3,500) in the figure.

The slope of the objective function is important in determining the optimal combination of G's and W's. A graphical solution is obtained by moving the objective-function line as far away from the origin as possible while still touching the feasible region and without exceeding any of the constraints. This is done by taking a ruler and moving the objective-function lines parallel to the original line and as far from the origin as possible in the feasible region. In this case, point C is the farthest point; therefore, given the current objective-function slope and constraints, C yields the highest profit. As shown on the graph, at the optimal point (C)

$$G = 27.7 \tag{10}$$
$$W = 61.5 \tag{11}$$
$$\text{Maximum profit} = \$70(27.7) + \$50(61.5) = \$5,014 \tag{12}$$
$$\text{Lathe utilization} = 5(27.7) + 1(61.5) = 200 \text{ hr} \tag{13}$$
$$\text{Assembly utilization} = 20(27.7) + 30(61.5) = 2400 \text{ hr} \tag{14}$$

This is the highest-profit combination of all feasible G's and W's. In this solution, both departments' constraints were fully utilized, but in the general problem, some departments will be fully utilized while others will be underutilized. In addition to the information given above, LP solutions provide planning information called *postoptimality analysis*.

Postoptimality Analysis. One of the benefits of LP is the "what if" planning information it provides. How these data are derived will not be obvious from our discussion, but they are a standard output of commercially available mathematical programming software.[86-90] The postoptimality analysis for this problem is as follows:

Marginal Values.   As shown in Eq. (13), the lathe department is fully utilized (that is, its load is 200 hr). Logically, additional profit could be achieved by increasing its capacity. Postoptimality analysis provides a variable called a *marginal value* (also known as the *dual price, shadow price,* or *imputed value*) for every constraint in the model. In this case, the marginal value of the fabrication department denotes that a 1-hr increase in capacity (from 200 to 201 hr) will increase profits by $8.46. The marginal value for the assembly department is $1.38; thus, the profit could be increased to $1.38 for each added assembly hour. These incremental profits are generated by producing additional G's and W's. Clearly, if additional resources were available, it would be most profitable to allocate them to the fabrication department ($8.46/hr versus $1.38/hr).

In addition to answering questions concerning increases in capacity, the marginal values are useful in simulating reductions in capacity. The values also denote that if the available capacity of the fabrication or assembly departments were reduced by 1 hr, then the profit would go down by $8.46 and $1.38, respectively.

Ranges.   Marginal values are only valid over a finite range of increases or decreases. In this case, postoptimality analysis yields the following: The fabrication capacity could increase to 600 hr or decrease to 80 hr and the profit would increase or decrease, respectively, by $8.46 for each 1-hr change; the assembly capacity could increase to 6000 hr or decrease to 800 hr and the profit would increase or decrease, respectively, by $1.38 for each hour of capacity change.

Postoptimality analysis also yields other planning information. The current solution ($G = 27.7$ and $W = 61.5$) is the optimum with respect to the slope of the objective function ($-70/50$). The slope will change if the profit coefficients of G and W change. If the coefficients of G and W change, will the optimal solution ($G = 27.7$ and $W = 61.5$) change? To answer such a question, ranges are available for the objective-function coefficients; these ranges show when the solution will change as a result of changes in the coefficients. In this case, if the profit for G remains in the range of $34 to $250, then this solution remains optimum; and if the profit for each W remains from $14 to $105, then the current solution is still optimum. These ranges can be determined graphically on the figure by rotating the objective-function line at C until it touches point D, then B. These two slopes set the ranges quoted above.

The Simplex Method.   It is impossible to solve realistic problems graphically because three dimensions are insufficient to represent multidimensional problems. Each decision variable (such as G and W) in a realistic problem adds a dimension to the graph. Fortunately, the simplex procedure quickly solves LP problems with large numbers of decision variables (30,000 to 100,000) and constraints (16,000).[91,92] The method is very efficient because the optimal solution to constrained resource problems will always be at a corner point of the feasible region when the objective function and the constraints are linear; this is called the *simplex theorem*. The simplex method only evaluates a fraction of the corner points of the feasible region to determine the optimal solution. Note that point C in Fig. 31.7 is a corner point representing the intersection of two linear equations in two unknowns. In general, at corner points there are n linear equations of n unknowns, an easily solved system of equations.

The simplex method does algebraically what is done graphically in Fig. 31.7. It efficiently moves the objective function from corner point to corner point until it finds that corner point at which the profits of all adjacent corner points are lower. For example, the profit at point C is higher than at the adjacent corner points of B and D.

Linearity is a necessary assumption of LP and the simplex method because it yields a feasible region that is a convex polygon. *Simplex* is a mathematical term meaning a multidimensional convex polygon. Figure 31.8 illustrates convex and concave polygons. Because of its shape, a convex polygon ensures that a corner point is optimum when all of its adjacent corner points have lower profits (maximization) or higher costs (minimization). The simplex procedure locates the optimum solution to large problems by evaluating only a few corner points; often the number of points evaluated equals the number of constraints.

Whereas a convex polygon has all internal angles less than or equal to 180°, a concave polygon has one or more internal angles greater than 180°. These large internal angles give the concave polygon the "caved-in" shape that makes it difficult to find an optimal solution.

Each of the figures in Fig. 31.8 illustrates two objective-function lines. Given these two polygons and objective lines, the optimal solutions are at points C and E, respectively. When the simplex method is used, it evaluates one corner point on either side of C (Fig. 31.8a) and finds that the profit decreases at B and D; therefore, C is the optimal solution and the search stops. In contrast, if nonlinearities exist, a concave polygon (Fig. 31.8b) might describe the feasible region. Because the simplex procedure does not have a graph as an aid, when it is used it may mistakenly converge on C as the optimal solution because the profits are lower at B and D; however, point E is the optimum. Mathematically, the simplex method cannot look ahead more than one corner point; therefore, concavity hides optimal points that are more than one point away from a corner point. Point C of the concave polygon is called a *local optimum*, while point E is the *global optimum*.

Production Planning Using Dynamic LP.   To consider a more complex LP application, a firm desires to schedule production to maximize the profits from selling two product lines, wagons (W) and bicycles (B). The firm must minimize regular production, overtime production, and inventory holding costs while meeting known demands. Using a rough-cut bill of capacity, the firm has estimates of the fabrication (F) and assembly (A) times for each product. Also, the planning horizon consists of two periods. While this problem has been contrived to have two periods, two products, and two work centers, the general case of many products, periods, and work centers is a simple extension of this problem and is practical in many firms [although an extremely large problem (with more then 20,000 constraints, for example) might be too costly to implement]. To formulate this LP model, consider the price, cost, demand, and capacity requirements provided in Table 31.11.

To solve this problem, express the profit function as the total revenue minus the total cost. Table 31.12 provides definitions of the variables used in this problem in order to facilitate its formulation and solution. From this information, formulate this problem as a linear programming problem.

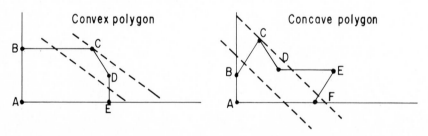

FIGURE 31.8   (a) Convex and (b) concave polygons.

TABLE 31.11 Prices, Costs, Demands, and Capacities

	Wagons	Bicycles
Price ($/unit)	20	25
Cost of fabrication ($/unit):		
Regular time	3	4
Overtime	4.5	6
Cost of assembly ($/unit):		
Regular time	6	8
Overtime	9	12
Cost of holding ($/unit/month)	1	1
Bill of capacity (hr/unit):		
Fabrication	2	2.67
Assembly	1	1.33
Demand (unit/period):		
Period 1	25	15
Period 2	15	25

Departmental Capacity (hr/period)	Fabrication	Assembly
Period 1:		
Regular time	80	40
Overtime	20	10
Period 2:		
Regular time	80	40
Overtime	20	10

TABLE 31.12 Definition of Variables

Period 1 Terms
WFR1 = Wagons fabricated on regular time in period 1
WFO1 = Wagons fabricated on overtime in period 1
WAR1 = Wagons assembled on regular time in period 1
WAO1 = Wagons assembled on overtime in period 1
EIW1 = Ending inventory of wagons in period 1
BFR1 = Bicycles fabricated on regular time in period 1
BFO1 = Bicycles fabricated on overtime in period 1
BAR1 = Bicycles assembled on regular time in period 1
BAO1 = Bicycles assembled on overtime in period 1
EIB1 = Ending inventory for bicycles in period 1
DB1 = Demand for bicycles in period 1
DW1 = Demand for wagons in period 1

Period 2 terms are identical in definition to those of period 1.

Model Formulation. Now that the decision variables and coefficients of the problem are defined, the LP formulation is given below:

Objective function. Maximize the profit:

$$
\begin{aligned}
Z = {} & 20(DW1) + 25(DB1) + 20(DW2) + 25(DB2) - 3(WFR1) - 4.5(WFO1) \\
& - 4(BFR1) - 6(BFO1) - 6(WAR1) - 9(WAO1) - 8(BAR1) - 12(BAO1) \\
& - 1(EIW1) - 1(EIB1) - 3(WFR2) - 4.5(WFO2) - 4(BFR2) - 6(BFO2) \\
& - 6(WAR2) - 9(WAO2) - 8(BAR2) - 12(BAO2) - 1(EIW2) - 1(EIB2)
\end{aligned}
$$

subject to:

Period 1 fabrication constraints. Production in period 1 = demand 1 + ending inventory 1 − ending inventory 0. That is, produce enough at least to meet the demand of period 1. Also assume that the ending inventory of period 0 is 0.

$$WFR1 + WFO1 = DW1 + EIW1$$
$$BFR1 + BFO1 = DB1 + EIB1$$

Period 1 assembly constraints. Assembly quantities are forced to equal fabrication quantities.

$$WAR1 + WAO1 = WFR1 + WFO1$$
$$BAR1 + BAO1 = BFR1 + BFO1$$

Period 1 capacity constraints. Input to work centers must be less than or equal to capacity.

$$2WFR1 + 2.67BFR1 \leq 80$$
$$2WFO1 + 2.67BFO1 \leq 20$$
$$1WAR1 + 1.33BAR1 \leq 40$$
$$1WAO1 + 1.33BAO1 \leq 10$$

Period 2 fabrication constraints. Production 2 = demand 2 + ending inventory 2 − ending inventory 1. That is, produce enough at least to meet the demand of period 2.

$$WFR2 + WFO2 = DW2 + EIW2 - EIW1$$
$$BFR2 + BFO2 = DB2 + EIB2 - EIB1$$

Period 2 assembly constraints. Assembly quantities are forced to equal fabrication quantities.

$$WAR2 + WAO2 = WFR2 + WFO2$$
$$BAR2 + BAO2 = DFR2 + BFO2$$

Period 2 capacity constraints. Input to work centers must be less than or equal to capacity

$$2WFR2 + 2.67BFR2 \leq 80$$
$$2WFO2 + 2.67BFO2 \leq 20$$
$$1WAR2 + 1.33BAR2 \leq 40$$
$$1WAO2 + 1.33BAO2 \leq 10$$

Period 1 and 2 demand constraints. Demand is shown as a variable to facilitate planning and "what if" analyses. These values are for the next two periods; future planning can use different values.

$$DW1 = 25$$
$$DB1 = 15$$
$$DW2 = 15$$
$$DB2 = 25$$

Nonnegativity constraint. No variable can be negative.

Assumptions of This Model:

- Prices, costs, demands, and capacities are known constants.
- Holding costs are $1 per unit per period of ending inventory.
- Shortages or back orders are not allowed.
- Linear relationships adequately define the system.

The optimal solution is illustrated in Table 31.13. Like all LP solutions, it has fractional values for the decision variables. This is a consequence of the continuous, linear assumption. In this application, one can round the results to achieve a good integer solution. However, no integer solution can have a profit that exceeds the continuous, linear solution. Postoptimality analyses of constraints and variables

TABLE 31.13 Optimal Solution to Dynamic LP Problem When Total Profit $Z = \$900.01$

Period 1	Period 2
Wagons	
Fabrication:	
WFR1 = 25	WFR2 = 15
WFO1 = 0	WFO2 = 0
Assembly:	
WAR1 = 20.0	WAR2 = 6.67
WAO1 = 5.0	WAO2 = 8.33
Inventory:	
EIW1 = 0	EIW2 = 0
Bicycles	
Fabrication:	
BFR1 = 11.24	BFR2 = 18.75
BFO1 = 3.76	BFO2 = 6.25
Assembly:	
BAR1 = 15.0	BAR2 = 25
BAO1 = 0	BAO2 = 0
Inventory:	
EIB1 = 0	EIB2 = 0
Demands	
DWI = 25	DW2 = 15
DB1 = 15	DB2 = 25

are not presented here; however, these are available as output of LP computer software packages.

Now that this problem has been solved and validated, it is very easy to update the demands by using a rolling planning horizon. That is, to plan production for months 2 and 3, only the forecasted demands and beginning inventory need be changed. Thus, the plan can be rolled over each month.

Summary of LP.   The purpose of LP is to maximize or minimize some linear objective function subject to linear constraints. Its assumes that certain, linear, and continuous relationships exist. *Certain* means that the constants and relationships are known with certainty (deterministic). *Linear* denotes, for example, that doubling the inputs yields a doubling of output. However, if slight nonlinearities exist, there are methods of approximating nonlinear functions by using piecewise separable methods. *Continuous* denotes that variables can equal fractional values. However, if the values of variables are large, then rounding may be a valid approach to integer solutions: otherwise, integer programming may be necessary.

The simplex algorithm finds solutions to very large problems in a short time on a computer and guarantees that an optimal solution has been achieved. Software packages are capable of routinely solving and maintaining LP models with tens of thousands of variables and constraints.[91-93] The simplex theorem states that the optimal solution occurs at a corner point of a convex polygon; at a corner point there are n linear equations in n unknowns, a deterministic and easily solved system of equations.

Postoptimality information is provided by commercial software. This information is important in exploring "what if" analysis under conditions of uncertainty. The marginal values measure the increases or decreases in the objective function as the right-hand-side coefficients are changed.

Finally, LP has been widely applied in PIC and will become even more widely used in future PIC applications.

Network Models

The transportation method (TM) and assignment method (AM) are special cases of LP referred to as *network models*. While they solve problems similar to those discussed in the preceding section, they are simpler models and are computationally more efficient, making possible the solution of exceedingly large problems with hundreds of thousands of relationships.[94-96] In addition to efficiency, these methods always guarantee an optimal integer solution.

Besides these two approaches, there are many other network methods. The transportation and assignment methods will be briefly reviewed below.

Transportation Method.   TM optimally allocates scarce resources from many sources to many destinations, given a linear objective function (such as to maximize profits, minimize costs, or minimize travel distance). Its applicability should be obvious after an example.

A Distribution Example.   International Tire Inc. operates two distribution centers (Kansas City and Toronto), from which it ships unit loads of tires to three warehouses. Transportation costs are a significant determinant of profitability, and the distribution centers have limited supplies of tires. Orders from the three warehouses (in Quebec, Los Angeles, and New York) are received weekly at a central distribution office. During a typical week, Quebec orders 12 unit loads, Los Angeles 10, and New York 22. What is the minimum shipment cost, given the supply of 22 units at both Kansas City and Toronto?

The general transportation problem is described by Figure 31.9. The unit shipping costs are given in the coefficient cells (smaller squares), the supply at each source in the right-hand column, and the demands in the bottom row. The circled values are the optimal shipment quantities, while the values with + signs are the marginal values (explained shortly). The solution procedure, although not illustrated here, is very straightforward. Study the solution of how the supply and demand for each location is met: The 12 units demanded in Quebec are shipped from Toronto, the 22 units demanded in New York are met from Kansas City and Toronto, and the 10 units demanded in Los Angeles are shipped from Kansas City. The minimum shipment cost totals $249.00. Table 31.14 illustrates this solution using a different format.

There are a number of different algorithms for solving general transportation problems. These include the *stepping-stone procedure*, which is frequently used with the *northwest-corner method* and *Vogel's approximation method (VAM)*. Other, more efficient algorithms include the *SHARE out-of-kilter code* and the *transshipment code*. The transshipment code is efficient for solving very large problems. Fortunately (and thus not discussed here), the basics of all solution methods are easily learned by users with little mathematical background.[16-23,94-96]

Postoptimality Information. Postoptimality information is a by-product of the transportation method, just as it is for the simplex method. Alternative solution costs are given by the noncircled numbers in the allocation cells of the Fig. 31.9. These *marginal values* are the increased costs of shipping from nonoptimal locations instead of from optimal locations. For example, shipping one unit from Toronto to Los Angeles will increase the total cost by $6.50. Each unit shipped from Kansas City to Quebec will increase the cost of the schedule by $5. Because a

From	To						Supply
	Quebec		Los Angeles		New York		
Kansas City	$10	+5.0	$9.0	⑩	$8.0	⑫	22
Toronto	$1.5	⑫	$12.0	+6.5	$4.5	⑩	22
Demand	12		10		22		44 = 44

FIGURE 31.9 Optimal shipment schedule by transportation method.

TABLE 31.14 Costs and Allocations of the Optimal Solution

Units	From	To	Unit Cost	Total Cost
10	Kansas City	Los Angeles	$9.00	$ 90.00
12	Kansas City	New York	8.00	96.00
12	Toronto	Quebec	1.50	18.00
10	Toronto	New York	4.50	45.00
44				$249.00

shipment from Kansas City to Los Angeles is an optimal shipment route, its marginal value (while not shown) is zero.

By using marginal values, one can consider alternative shipping schedules. Table 31.15 is an alternative schedule that forces a shipment from Toronto to Los Angeles. As shown, it costs $6.50 more (or $255.50) to ship by this schedule than by the optimal schedule, even though the number of units shipped is 44 in each plan.

While not obvious from this presentation, TM is a special case of LP. If one were to formulate and solve this problem using the simplex method, it would be seen that the assumptions and form of TM are the same as those of the general LP model except that the left-hand-side constraint coefficients are all 1s or 0s.

A Production-Planning Example. TM can be useful in production and distribution planning. Table 31.16 illustrates the demands, costs, and capacity facing a firm. The firm desires to minimize its regular and overtime production costs, inventory holding costs, and back-order costs for the next three periods.

The optimal solution to this problem is given in Fig. 31.10. Explanations of the cost coefficients are given in the footnotes.

There are many applications in which TM can provide effective solutions. Its structure and solution method are easily understood, and when TM is applicable, it provides important information. In addition, TM has the advantage of providing integer solutions to extremely large problems by using fast algorithms. For example, one can easily combine the production-planning example with the distribution example to form a single, integrated production-distribution optimization model.

Assignment Method. The assignment method optimally allocates scarce resources when n supply sources are to be assigned to m demands and only one resource assignment is made from supply to demand (such as assigning 12 jobs to 12

TABLE 31.15 Nonoptimal Alternative Solution

Units	From	To	Unit Cost	Total Cost
9	Kansas City	Los Angeles	$ 9.00	$ 81.00
13	Kansas City	New York	8.00	104.00
1	Toronto	Los Angeles	12.00	12.00
12	Toronto	Quebec	1.50	18.00
9	Toronto	New York	4.50	40.50
44				$255.50

TABLE 31.16 Demands, Costs, and Capacity in Production Planning

	Period 1	Period 2	Period 3
Demand (units)	180	250	220
Regular-time capacity (units)	200	220	240
Overtime capacity (units)	80	88	96
Regular costs	$10/unit		
Overtime costs	$15/unit		
Inventory holding costs	$2/unit/month		
Back-order costs	$6/unit/month		

From	To: Demand for:			Supply
	Period 1	Period 2	Period 3	
Regular time 1	$10.0* (180)	$12.0+ (20)	$14.0	200
Overtime 1	$15.0∓	$17.0	$19.0	80
Regular time 2	$16.0§	$10.0 (220)	$12.0	220
Overtime 2	$21.0	$15.0 (10)	$17.0	88
Regular time 3	$22.0	$16.0	$10.0 (220)	240
Overtime 3	$27.0	$21.0	$15.0	96
Demand	180	250	220	650/924

* Regular time cost of $10/unit.
\+ Regular time cost plus $2/unit/month holding cost from period 1
  to period 2.
∓ Overtime cost of $15/unit.
§ Regular time cost plus $6/unit/month backorder cost.

FIGURE 31.10 Production planning by the transportation method.

machines). The efficiencies, times, costs, or profits from each assignment are
known, and the objective is to find the optimal assignment of all jobs, such as the
lowest cost or highest profit.

Figure 31.11 illustrates a simple minimum-cost assignment problem with the
optimal solution shown circled. While not illustrated here, the manual and computer solution methods are very straightforward. If one were to formulate and solve
this problem using the simplex method, one would see that the assumptions and
form of AM are the same as those of the general LP model except that the left-hand-
side constraint coefficients and the right-hand-side constants are all 1s or 0s.

The importance of AM and TM is their ability to find optimal solutions to very
large allocation problems. If a problem possesses the structures illustrated above,
then significant improvements in costs and profits are possible through the use of
AM or TM. In addition, the simplicity and efficiency of these approaches make
them effective algorithms of more complex planning and allocation systems.

Other Network Algorithms.   In addition to TM and AM, several other network
methods exist. These include the shortest-path problem, the longest-path problem,
the maximal-flow problem, and the critical-path method.[94-99]

There have been several computational improvements in network models in
recent years. These techniques represent methods that can be very useful in routing
vehicles, in scheduling and tracking thousands of jobs in a job-shop environment, and in other specialized problems.[94,95]

jobs	Machine			
	A	B	C	D
1	20	15	(12)	35
2	(10)	5	7	22
3	45	(24)	30	47
4	12	75	44	(22)

FIGURE 31.11   Optimal assignment of jobs (1−4) to machines (A−D.)

Project Planning and Scheduling Using PERT/CPM.   Large projects can be managed with specialized network algorithms and software. In recent years there has been a rapid growth of project management systems with the popularity of micro-computers.[97−102] (See Chapter 17 for further discussion.)

Advanced Mathematical Programming

Goal Progamming (GP).   Decision makers often face problems which have multiple goals that must be considered in achieving good solutions. The standard LP approach optimizes only a single-objective function and may therefore not be useful in finding a good solution if there are conflicting goals. Fortunately, GP methods exist to solve such problems. GP is a special case of LP which is no more difficult to solve than an LP problem and which has many applications in PIC.[59−60,103−105]

Integer Programming.   LP methods solve continuous, linearly constrained problems very efficiently, and the fractional values of a continuous solution frequently cause no problems. For example, if in a production-planning problem the optimal number of units to be produced on regular time is 1000.5, then little loss of optimality exists in rounding the solution to 1000 or 1001. But if in a facility-planning problem the optimal solution is to build 3.4 distribution centers with 13.3 loading docks supplied by 2.8 factories, then there can be considerable difference in the optimality of rounded solutions. In such cases, integer programming (IP) methods are necessary.[86−90,106,107]

A simple example of an integer programming problem is the production planning of gas and wind turbines. The optimal integer solution arrived at through enumeration is as follows (the continuous LP values are given in parentheses):

Integer	Continuous LP
G = 27	(27.7)
W = 62	(61.5)
Maximum profit = $70(27) + $50(62) = $4,990.00	($5,014)
Lathe utilization = 5(27) + 1(62) = 197 hr	(200)
Assembly utilization = 20(27) + 30(62) = 2400 hr	(2400)

The optimal integer solution ($4,990) is always lower than the optimal continuous solution ($5,014); consequently, the continuous solution always provides a benchmark in judging alternative integer solutions. In addition, the search for integer solutions can provide insights to alternative solutions. For instance, during the enumeration process of this example, it was noted that $40 additional profit could be generated by adding 5 hr of capacity to the fabrication department. This alternative solution is:

Integer
G = 29, W = 60
Maximum profit = $70(29) + $50(60) = $5,030.00
Lathe utilization = 5(29) + 1(60) = 205 hr
Assembly utilization = 20(29) + 30(60) = 2380 hr

This solution illustrates the ability to undertake "what if" analysis by using LP and IP methods. Such explorations can be insightful even if the model does not perfectly fit the environment.

There are several types of IP problems: integer problems in which all variables are integers [pure integer programming (PIP)]; mixed integer programming (MIP) problems, in which both continuous and integer values are in the solution; and zero-one integer programming (0-1P), which can be mixed or pure integer. A number of IP methods work very well with these problems if the model does not possess more than a thousand integer variables; these methods include the cutting-plane, branch-and-bound, and implicit-enumeration methods of IP. By far the most popular solution method is the branch-and-bound method. The cutting-plane method has not been found to be of value in practice, and the implicit-enumeration method works best with integer variables that have only values of 0 or 1.[91-92]

Nonlinear Programming.   Nonlinear functions frequently occur in business and economics. Costs, revenues, and productivity may be nonlinear because of the law of diminishing returns, geometric growth, the time value of money, etc. Often these can be modeled using linear approximations of the nonlinear function; that is, a nonlinear curve can be separated into a number of linear line segments and solved as an LP problem; this is called *separable programming*. When this is not possible, nonlinear programming (NLP) methods may often, but not always, solve the problem.[108,109]

Because there is an infinite variety of nonlinear forms of equations, the NLP problem may be considerably more difficult to solve than the LP problem. There is not one nonlinear method, but many different methods; consequently, NLP methods solve only one subclass of nonlinear problems. Also, the formulation and solution of nonlinear problems may be quite difficult, very often requiring skills not available to many manufacturers. These limitations reduce the importance of NLP in solving the general problems facing PIC managers.

Dynamic Programming. Dynamic programming (DP) is a general approach to determining the optimal solution to sequences of decisions made over time or space. There is no standard mathematical formulation or procedure for solving dynamic programming problems; different solution techniques (such as linear programming or differential calculus) are used to find optimal solutions.

The familiar Wagner-Whitin algorithm is a good example of a forward DP method, and the solution procedure used in the decision tree of Fig. 31.2 is an example of a backward DP algorithm.[20,22,110-112] While DP may appear to be very complex, there are several situations in which DP can be easily and effectively applied.

Other Quantitative Methods

There are many quantitative methods. Those not discussed in this chapter include statistical and probability methods, forecasting methods, inventory models, and project planning methods, all of which are discussed in other chapters. In addition, the game theory and Markov processes are only briefly mentioned below because they are not widely applicable in production and inventory management. Also worthy of mention are heuristic procedures, which are embodied in most PIC systems, and techniques such as the part-period balancing method.

Game Theory. Game theory is used to model the relationship between two competing entities, such as individuals, corporations, or governments. These competing entities anticipate and react to each other's decisions. While it is not widely used at the operational (tactical) level, game theory is an important tool at the strategic level.[16-23]

Markov Processes. These are useful in describing how the state of a system changes over time. A *Markov process* is a probabilistic process for which the future state depends only on the immediately preceding state. Markov processes have been used in marketing to model "brand switching" and in PIC to study equipment adjustment, maintenance, and quality control. Like queueing analysis, Markov models can become very complex and difficult to solve in the general case—but if the specific situation fits a Markovian process, then considerable benefit can be achieved from Markov analysis.[16-23]

Heuristic Procedures. These use intuitive rules to achieve good solutions to complex problems. They are used whenever an optimal procedure is too costly, impossible to use, or unavailable. There have been many applications of heuristics in PIC, including the part-period balancing and least-total-cost methods of inventory control. The future growth of *expert systems* and *artificial intelligence* will yield more sophisticated and useful heuristic procedures. A study of these two topics will assist those desiring more knowledge of heuristics.

REFERENCES

General QM Implementation and Survey References

These references discuss either the role of QM in business, the problems and proper methods of implementing QM, or surveys of actual applications of QM.

1. H. M. Wagner, "The ABC's of OR," *Operations Research*, vol. 19, Oct. 1971, pp. 1259–1281.
2. F. Zahedi, "A Survey of Issues in the OR/MS Field," *Interfaces*, vol. 14, Mar.–Apr. 1984, pp. 57–68.
3. W. J. Duncan, "The Researcher and the Manager: A Comparative View of the Need for Mutual Understanding," *Management Science*, vol. 20, Apr. 1974, pp. 1157–1163.
4. G. J. Feeney, "The Role of the Professional in Operations Research and Management Science," *Interfaces*, vol. 1, no. 6, 1971, pp. 1–4.
5. J. S. Hammond, "The Role of the Manager and Management Scientist in Successful Implementation," *Sloan Management Review*, vol. 15, Winter 1974, pp. 1–24.
6. C. J. Grayson, Jr., "Management Science and Business Practice," *Harvard University Review*, vol. 51, July–Aug. 1973, pp. 41–48.
7. S. Eilon, "The Role of Management Science," *Journal of the Operational Research Society*, vol. 31, no. 1, 1980.
8. R. L. Schultz and D. P. Slevin (eds.), *Implementing Operations Research/Management Science*, American Elsevier, New York, 1975.
9. R. K. Wysocki, "OR/MS Implementation Research: A Bibliography," Interfaces, vol. 9, 1979, pp. 37–41.
10. N. Gaither, "The Adoption of Operations Research Techniques by Manufacturing Organizations," *Decision Sciences*, vol. 6, Oct. 1975, pp. 797–813.
11. J. A. DaCosta and G. Thomas, "A Sample Survey of Corporate Operations Research," *Interfaces*, vol. 9, no. 4, Aug. 1979, pp. 102–111.
12. W. N. Ledbetter and J. F. Cox, "Operation Research in Production Management: An Investigation of Past and Present Utilization," *Production and Inventory Management*, vol. 18, third quarter, 1977, pp. 84–91.
13. A. F. Grum and R. Hesse, "It's the Process, Not the Product (Most of the Time)," *Interfaces*, vol. 13, no. 5, Oct. 1983, pp. 89–93.
14. A. M. Geoffrion, "The Purpose of Mathematical Programming is Insight, Not Numbers," *Interfaces*, vol. 7, no. 1, 1976, pp. 81–92.
15. T. B. Green, W. B. Newsom, and S. R. Jones, "A Survey of the Application of Quantitative Techniques to Production/Operations Management in Large Corporations," *Academy of Management Journal*, vol. 20, no. 4, 1977, pp. 669–676.

Comprehensive Introductory Quantitative Methods Textbooks

16. D. R. Anderson, T. A. Williams, and D. J. Sweeney, *An Introduction to Management Science: Quantitative Approach to Decision Making*, 2d ed., West Publishing, St. Paul, Minn., 1979.
17. F. S. Hillier and G. J. Lieberman, *Introduction to Operations Research*, 3d ed., Holden-Day, San Francisco, 1980.
18. H. Bierman, Jr., C. P. Bonini, and W. H. Hausman, *Quantitative Analysis for Business Decision*, 7th ed., Irwin, Homewood, Ill., 1986.

19. R. E. Markland, *Topics in Management Science*, 2d ed., Wiley, New York, 1983.

20. H. M. Wagner, *Principles of Operations Research*, 2d ed., Prentice-Hall, Englewood Cliffs, N.J., 1975.

21. E. S. Buffa, and J. S. Dyer, *Management Science−Operations Research: Model Formulation and Solution Methods*, Wiley, New York, 1977.

22. N. K. Kwak and S. A. De Lurgio, *Quantitative Models for Business Decisions*, Duxbury Publishing, North Scituate, Mass., 1980.

23. J. J. Moder and S. E. Elmaghraby, *Handbook of Operations Research*, Van Nostrand Rheinhold, New York, 1978.

24. E. Turban, and N. P. Loomba (eds.), *Cases and Readings in Management Sciences*, rev. ed., Business Publications, Plano, Tex. 1982.

Simulation

25. H. Bekiroglu (ed.), *Computer Models for Production and Inventory Control*, Simulation Councils, La Jolla, Calif., 1984.

26. W. Lee and C. McLaughlin, "Corporate Simulation Models for Aggregate Materials Management," *Production and Inventory Management*, vol. 15, no. 1, 1974, pp. 55−67.

27. R. Markland, *Distribution Systems Analysis and Design: A Simulation Methodology*, APICS Conference Proceedings, 1971.

28. H. Shycon and R. Maffei, "Simulation—Tool for Better Distribution," *Harvard Business Review*, Nov.−Dec. 1960, pp. 65−75.

29. D. P. Christy and H. J. Watson, "The Application of Simulation: A Survey of Industry Practice," *Interfaces*, Oct. 1983, 47−52.

30. R. E. Shannon, *Systems Simulation, The Art and Science*, Prentice-Hall, Englewood Cliffs, N.J., 1975.

31. J. A. Payne, *Introduction to Simulation*, McGraw-Hill, New York, 1982.

32. D. W. Fogarty, "Simulation: A Decision-Making Technique," *Production and Inventory Management*, Oct. 1967, pp. 69−82.

33. G. Gordon, *System Simulation*, Prentice-Hall, Englewood Cliffs, N.J., 1969.

34. H. Maisel and G. Gnufnoli, *Simulation of Discrete Stochastic Systems*, Science Research Associates, Chicago, 1972.

35. A. M. Law and W. D. Kelton, *Simulation Modeling and Analysis*, McGraw-Hill, New York, 1982.

36. J. R. Emshoff and R. L. Sisson, *Design and Use of Computer Simulation Models*, Macmillan, New York, 1970.

37. O. Wight, *MRP II*, Oliver Wight, Williston, Vt., 1983.

38. G.W. Plossl, *Production and Inventory Control*, 2d ed., Prentice-Hall, Englewood Cliffs, N.J., 1985.

39. A. Martin, *Distribution Resource Planning*, Oliver Wight, Williston, Vt., 1983.

40. A. M. Law, "Statistical Analysis of Simulation Output Data," *Operations Research*, vol. 31, 1983, pp. 983−1029.

41. J. P. Kleijnem, *Statistical Techniques in Simulation*, Dekker, New York, 1974.

42. G. S. Fishman, "Achieving Specific Accuracy in Simulation Output Analysis," *Communications of the ACM*, vol. 20, 1977, pp. 310−315.

43. J. R. Wilson and A. A. B. Pritsker, "A Survey of Research on the Simulation Startup Problem," *Simulation*, vol. 31, 1978, pp. 55−58.

44. R. L. Van Horn, "Validation of Simulation Results, *Management Science*, vol. 17, 1971, pp. 247–258.
45. W. Farrell, *Literature Review and Bibliography of Simulation Optimization*, Winter Simulation Conference Proceedings, 1977, pp. 116–124.
46. G. Gordon, *The Application of GPSS V to Discrete Systems Simulation*, Prentice-Hall, Englewood Cliffs, N.J., 1975.
47. A. A. B. Pritsker, *Modeling and Analysis Using Q-GERT Networks*, Halstead Press, New York, 1979.
48. E. C. Russell, *Building Simulation Models with SIMSCRIPT II.5*, CACI, Los Angeles, 1983.
49. J. W. Forrester, *Industrial Dynamics*, Wiley, New York, 1961.
50. H. Speckhart and W. H. Green, *A Guide to Using CSMP*, Prentice-Hall, Englewood Cliffs, N.J., 1976.
51. C. D. Pegden, *Introduction to SIMAN*, System Modeling Corporation, State College, Pa., 1985.
52. A. A. B. Pritsker, *The GASP IV Simulation Language*, Wiley, New York, 1974.
53. A. A. B. Pritsker, *Introduction to Simulation and SLAM II*, Wiley, New York, 1984.

Decision Analysis

54. C. A. Holloway, *Decision Making under Uncertainty: Models and Choices*, Prentice-Hall, Englewood Cliffs, N.J., 1979.
55. E. F. Harrison, *The Managerial Decision-Making Process*, Houghton Mifflin, Boston, 1975.
56. W. T. Morris, *Decision Analysis*, Grid Publishing, Columbus, Ohio, 1977.
57. R. O. Swalm, "Utility Theory—Insights into Risk Taking," *Harvard Business Review*, Nov.–Dec. 1966, pp. 123–136.
58. R. Keeney and H. Raiffa, *Decision with Multiple Objectives: Preferences and Value Trade-offs*, Wiley, New York, 1976.
59. C. L. Hwang et al., *Multiple Objective Decision Making—Methods and Applications: A State-of-the-Art Survey*, Springer-Verlag, New York, 1979.
60. M. K. Starr and M. Zeleney (eds.), *Multiple-Criteria Decision Making*, Elsevier, New York, 1977.
61. J. F. Magee, "Decision Trees for Decision Making," *Harvard Business Review*, July–Aug. 1964, pp. 126–138.

Queueing

62. Len Gorney, *Queueing Theory: A Solving Approach*, Petrocelli, Princeton, N.J., 1981.
63. C. Saur and K. Chandy, *Computer System Performance Evaluation*, Prentice-Hall, Englewood Ciffs, N.J., 1981.
64. G. F. Newell, *Application of Queueing Theory*, Chapman and Hall, N.Y., 1982.
65. D. Gross and C. M. Harris, *Fundamentals of Queueing Theory*, 2d ed., Wiley, N.Y., 1985.
66. R. B. Cooper, *Introduction to Queueing Theory*, 2d ed., Elsevier, New York, 1981.
67. S. L. Solomon, *Simulation of Waiting Lines*, Prentice-Hall, Englewood Cliffs, N.J., 1983.
68. L. Kleinrock, *Queueing Systems*, vols. 1 and 2, Wiley, New York, 1976.

Mathematical Programming

69. F. J. Fabozzi and J. Valente, "Mathematical Programming in American Companies: A Sample Survey," *Interfaces*, vol. 7, no. 1, Nov. 1976, pp. 93−98.

70. K. D. Lawrence and S. H. Zanakis, *Production Planning and Scheduling: Mathematical Programming Applications*, Industrial Engineering and Management Press, Norcross, Ga., 1984.

71. H. M. Salkin and J. Saha, *Studies in Linear Programming*, Elsevier, New York, 1975.

72. P. Gray and C. Cullinan-James, "Applied Optimization—A Survey," *Interfaces*, vol. 6, no. 3, May 1976, pp. 24−41.

73. A. M. Geoffrion, "A Guide to Computer-Assisted Methods for Distribution Systems Planning," *Sloan Management Review*, Winter 1975, pp. 17−41.

74. T. K. Ziere, W. A. Mitchell, and T. R. White, "Practical Applications of Linear Programming to Shell's Distribution Problems," *Interfaces*, vol. 6, Aug. 1976, pp. 13−26.

75. A. M. Geoffrion and R. F. Powers, "Facility Location Analysis Is Just the Beginning," *Interfaces*, vol. 10, no. 2, Apr. 1980, pp. 13−21.

76. R. E. Markland and R. J. Newett, "Production-Distribution Planning in a Large-Scale Commodity Processing Network," *Decision Sciences*, Oct. 1976, pp. 579−594.

77. S. Eilon, "Five Approaches to Aggregate Production Planning," *AIIE Transactions*, vol. 7, 1975, pp. 118−131.

78. E. S. Buffa and J. G. Miller, *Production-Inventory Systems: Planning and Control*, 3d ed., Irwin, Homewood, Ill., 1979.

79. J. Byrd, Jr., and L. T. Moore, "The Application of a Product Mix Linear Programming Model in Corporate Policy-Making," *Management Science*, vol. 24, no. 13, 1978, pp. 1342−1350.

80. M. A. Vonderembse, "Selecting Master Slab Width(s) for Continuous Steel Casting," *Journal of Operations Management*, Vol. 4, May 1984, pp. 231−244.

81. A. C. Hax and H. C. Meal, "Hierarchical Integration of Production Planning and Scheduling," in M. A. Geisler (ed.), *Studies in the Management Sciences*, vol. 1, Logistics, North Holland-Elsevier, Amsterdam, 1975.

82. G. Bitran, E. Haas, and A. Hax, "Hierarchical Production Planning: A Two-Stage System," *Operations Research*, vol. 30, no. 2, Mar.−Apr., pp. 232−251.

83. T. Vollmann, W. Berry, and D. C. Whybark, *Manufacturing Planning and Control Systems*, Dow Jones-Irwin, Homewood, Ill., 1984.

84. N. K. Kwak and M. J. Schiederjans, *Managerial Applications of Operations Research*, University Press of America, Washington, D.C., 1982.

85. N. J. Driebeek, *Applied Linear Programming*, Addison-Wesley, Reading, Mass., 1969.

86. G. P. Dantzig, *Linear Programming and Extensions*, Princeton University Press, Princeton, N.J., 1963.

87. S. P. Bradley, A. C. Hax, and T. L. Magnanti, *Applied Mathematical Programming*, Addison-Wesley, Reading, Mass., 1977.

88. S. I. Gass, *Linear Programming*, 4th ed., McGraw-Hill, New York, 1975.

89. N. K. Kwak, *Mathematical Programming with Business Application*, McGraw-Hill, New York, 1973.

90. C. McMillan, Jr., *Mathematical Programming*, 2d ed., Wiley, New York, 1975.

91. W. W. White, "A Status Report on Computing Algorithms for Mathematical Programming," *Computing Surveys*, vol. 5, no. 3, 1973, pp. 135−166.

92. W. Orchard-Hays, "History of Mathematical Programming Systems," in H. J. Greenberg (ed.), *Design and Implementation of Optimization Software*, Sijthoff and Noordhoff, Alphen aan den Rijn, The Netherlands, 1978.

93. Ramesh Sharda, "Linear Programming on Microcomputers: A Survey," *Interfaces*, vol. 14, no. 6, Nov.−Dec. 1984, pp. 27−38.

Network Models and PERT/CPM

94. D. Klingman and J. M. Mulvey (eds.), *Network Models and Associated Applications*, Elsevier, New York, 1981.

95. F. Glover and D. Klingman, "Network Applications in Industry and Government," *AIIE Transactions*, Dec. 1977, pp. 363–376.

96. S. K. Shatnagar, *Network Analysis Techniques*, Wiley, New York, 1985.

97. E. S. Buffa and G. Miller, *Production-Inventory Systems: Planning and Control*, 3d ed., Irwin, Homewood, Ill., 1979.

98. N. J. Aquilano and D. E. Smith: "A Formal Set of Algorithms for Project Scheduling with Critical Path Scheduling–Material Requirements Planning," *Journal of Operations Management*, Nov. 1980, pp. 57–67.

99. R. E. D. Woolsey and H. S. Swanson, *Operations Research for Immediate Applications—A Quick and Dirty Manual*, Harper & Row, New York, 1975.

100. D.I. Cleland and W. R. King, *Project Management Handbook*, Van Nostrand Rheinhold, New York, 1983.

101. E. W. Davis, "Project Scheduling under Resource Constraints—Historical Review and Categorization of Procedures," *AIIE Transactions*, Dec. 1973, pp. 297–313.

102. L. J. Goodman and R. N. Love, *Project Planning and Management: An Integrated Approach*, Pergamon Press, New York, 1980.

Advanced Mathematical Programming

103. J. P. Ignizio, *Linear Programming in Single & Multiple Objective Systems*, Prentice-Hall, Englewood Cliffs, N.J., 1982.

104. S. M. Lee, *Goal Programming for Decision Analysis*, Auerbach, Philadelphia, 1972.

105. J. P. Ignizio, *Goal Programming and Extensions*, Lexington Books, Lexington, Mass., 1976.

106. H. M. Salkin, *Integer Programming*, Addison-Wesley, Reading, Mass., 1975.

107. S. Zionts, *Linear and Integer Programming*, Prentice-Hall, Englewood Cliffs, N.J., 1974.

108. D. G. Luenberger, *Introduction to Linear and Nonlinear Programming*, Addison-Wesley, Reading, Mass., 1973.

109. M. Avriel, *Nonlinear Programming: Analysis and Methods*, Prentice-Hall, Englewood Cliffs, N.J., 1976.

110. B. Glass, *An Elementary Introduction to Dynamic Programming*, Allyn & Bacon, Boston, 1972.

111. H. M. Wagner and T. M. Whitin, "Dynamic Version of the Economic Lot-Size Model," *Management Science*, vol. 5, 1958, pp. 89–96.

112. R. E. Bellman, *Dynamic Programming*, Princeton University Press, Princeton, N.J., 1957.

Periodicals Featuring QM in PIC

AIIE Transactions
Computers and Industrial Engineering
Computers and Operations Research
Decision Sciences
Harvard Business Review
Industrial Engineering
Interfaces
International Journal of Operations and Production Management
International Journal of Production Research

Journal of Operations Management
Journal of the Operational Research Society
Management Science
Operations Management Review
Operations Research
Production and Inventory Management
Project Management Journal
Project Management Quarterly
Simulation
Sloan Management Review

Abstract Services Reviewing PICS Applications of QM

APICS Bibliography, American Production and Inventory Society, Falls Church, Va.
Applied Science and Technology Index, H. W. Wilson, N.Y.
Business Periodicals Index, H. W. Wilson, New York.
Dissertation Abstracts, University Microfilm, Ann Arbor, Mich.
Engineering Index, Engineering Information, Inc., N.Y.
Government Reports Index, National Technical Information Service, Springfield, Va.
Information Services in Mechanical Engineering, Data Courier, Louisville, Ky.
International Abstracts in Operations Research, Operations Research Society of America, Baltimore, Md.
Operations Research/Management Science (OR/MS) Abstracts, Executive Sciences Institute, Whippany, N.J.
Quality Control/Applied Statistics (QC/AS) Abstracts, Executive Sciences Institute, Whippany, N.J.
Science Citation Index, Institute for Scientific Information, Philadelphia, Pa.

Appendix

Greek Alphabet

A α	....	alpha	N ν	....	nu
B β	....	beta	Ξ ξ	....	xi
Γ γ	....	gamma	O o	....	omicron
Δ δ	....	delta	Π π	....	pi
E ϵ	....	epsilon	P ρ	....	rho
Z ζ	....	zeta	Σ σ	....	sigma
H η	....	eta	T τ	....	tau
Θ θ	....	theta	Υ υ	....	upsilon
I ι	....	iota	Φ ϕ	....	phi
K κ	....	kappa	X χ	....	chi
Λ λ	....	lambda	Ψ ψ	....	psi
M μ	....	mu	Ω ω	....	omega

TABLE 1 Normal Distribution

This Table Gives the Area α under the Standard Normal Curve from z_α to $+\infty$

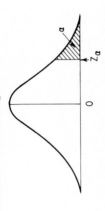

z_α	.00	.01	.02	.03	.04	.05	.06	.07	.08	.09
0.0	.5000	.4960	.4920	.4880	.4840	.4801	.4761	.4721	.4681	.4641
0.1	.4602	.4562	.4522	.4483	.4443	.4404	.4364	.4325	.4286	.4247
0.2	.4207	.4168	.4129	.4090	.4052	.4013	.3974	.3936	.3897	.3859
0.3	.3821	.3783	.3745	.3707	.3669	.3632	.3594	.3557	.3520	.3483
0.4	.3446	.3409	.3372	.3336	.3300	.3264	.3228	.3192	.3156	.3121
0.5	.3085	.3050	.3015	.2981	.2946	.2912	.2877	.2843	.2810	.2776
0.6	.2743	.2709	.2676	.2643	.2611	.2578	.2546	.2514	.2483	.2451
0.7	.2420	.2389	.2358	.2327	.2296	.2266	.2236	.2206	.2177	.2148
0.8	.2119	.2090	.2061	.2033	.2005	.1977	.1949	.1922	.1894	.1867
0.9	.1841	.1814	.1788	.1762	.1736	.1711	.1685	.1660	.1635	.1611
1.0	.1587	.1562	.1539	.1515	.1492	.1469	.1446	.1423	.1401	.1379
1.1	.1357	.1335	.1314	.1292	.1271	.1251	.1230	.1210	.1190	.1170
1.2	.1151	.1131	.1112	.1093	.1075	.1056	.1038	.1020	.1003	.0985
1.3	.0968	.0951	.0934	.0918	.0901	.0885	.0869	.0853	.0838	.0823
1.4	.0808	.0793	.0778	.0764	.0749	.0735	.0721	.0708	.0694	.0681

	.0	.1	.2	.3	.4	.5	.6	.7	.8	.9
1.5	.0668	.0655	.0643	.0630	.0618	.0606	.0594	.0582	.0571	.0559
1.6	.0548	.0537	.0526	.0516	.0505	.0495	.0485	.0475	.0465	.0455
1.7	.0446	.0436	.0427	.0418	.0409	.0401	.0392	.0384	.0375	.0367
1.8	.0359	.0351	.0344	.0336	.0329	.0322	.0314	.0307	.0301	.0294
1.9	.0287	.0281	.0274	.0268	.0262	.0256	.0250	.0244	.0239	.0233
2.0	.0228	.0222	.0217	.0212	.0207	.0202	.0197	.0192	.0188	.0183
2.1	.0179	.0174	.0170	.0166	.0162	.0158	.0154	.0150	.0146	.0143
2.2	.0139	.0136	.0132	.0129	.0125	.0122	.0119	.0116	.0113	.0110
2.3	.0107	.0104	.0102	.00990	.00964	.00939	.00914	.00889	.00866	.00842
2.4	.00820	.00798	.00776	.00755	.00734	.00714	.00695	.00676	.00657	.00639
2.5	.00621	.00604	.00587	.00570	.00554	.00539	.00523	.00508	.00494	.00480
2.6	.00466	.00453	.00440	.00427	.00415	.00402	.00391	.00379	.00368	.00357
2.7	.00347	.00336	.00326	.00317	.00307	.00298	.00289	.00280	.00272	.00264
2.8	.00256	.00248	.00240	.00233	.00226	.00219	.00212	.00205	.00199	.00193
2.9	.00187	.00181	.00175	.00169	.00164	.00159	.00154	.00149	.00144	.00139
z_α	.0	.1	.2	.3	.4	.5	.6	.7	.8	.9
3	.00135	$.0^3968$	$.0^3687$	$.0^3483$	$.0^3337$	$.0^3233$	$.0^3159$	$.0^3108$	$.0^4723$	$.0^4481$
4	$.0^4317$	$.0^4207$	$.0^4133$	$.0^5854$	$.0^5541$	$.0^5340$	$.0^5211$	$.0^5130$	$.0^6793$	$.0^6479$
5	$.0^6287$	$.0^6170$	$.0^7996$	$.0^7579$	$.0^7333$	$.0^7190$	$.0^7107$	$.0^8599$	$.0^8332$	$.0^8182$
6	$.0^9987$	$.0^9530$	$.0^9282$	$.0^9149$	$.0^{10}777$	$.0^{10}402$	$.0^{10}206$	$.0^{10}104$	$.0^{11}523$	$.0^{11}260$

SOURCE: Reproduced by consent of publisher from Frederick E. Croxton, *Elementary Statistics with Applications in Medicine*, Prentice-Hall, Englewood Cliffs, N.J., 1953, p. 323.

A.3

TABLE 2 t Distribution

This Table Gives Specified Value of t for d Degrees of Freedom and a One-Tail Area of α

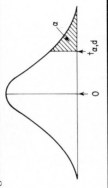

Value of α

d	.40	.30	.20	.10	.05	.025	.01	.005	.001	.0005
1	.325	.727	1.376	3.078	6.314	12.71	31.82	63.66	318.3	636.6
2	.289	.617	1.061	1.886	2.920	4.303	6.965	9.925	22.33	31.60
3	.277	.584	.978	1.638	2.353	3.182	4.541	5.841	10.22	12.94
4	.271	.569	.941	1.533	2.132	2.776	3.747	4.604	7.173	8.610
5	.267	.559	.920	1.476	2.015	2.571	3.365	4.032	5.893	6.859
6	.265	.553	.906	1.440	1.943	2.447	3.143	3.707	5.208	5.959
7	.263	.549	.896	1.415	1.895	2.365	2.998	3.499	4.785	5.405
8	.262	.546	.889	1.397	1.860	2.306	2.896	3.355	4.501	5.041
9	.261	.543	.883	1.383	1.833	2.262	2.821	3.250	4.297	4.781
10	.260	.542	.879	1.372	1.812	2.228	2.764	3.169	4.144	4.587
11	.260	.540	.876	1.363	1.796	2.201	2.718	3.106	4.025	4.437
12	.259	.539	.873	1.356	1.782	2.179	2.681	3.055	3.930	4.318
13	.259	.538	.870	1.350	1.771	2.160	2.650	3.012	3.852	4.221
14	.258	.537	.868	1.345	1.761	2.145	2.624	2.977	3.787	4.140
15	.258	.536	.866	1.341	1.753	2.131	2.602	2.947	3.733	4.073
16	.258	.535	.865	1.337	1.740	2.120	2.583	2.921	3.686	4.015
17	.257	.534	.863	1.333	1.734	2.110	2.567	2.898	3.646	3.965
18	.257	.534	.862	1.330	1.734	2.101	2.552	2.878	3.611	3.922
19	.257	.533	.861	1.328	1.729	2.093	2.539	2.861	3.579	3.883

A.4

20	.257	.533	.860	1.325	1.725	2.086	2.528	2.845	3.552	3.850
21	.257	.532	.859	1.323	1.721	2.080	2.518	2.831	3.527	3.819
22	.256	.532	.858	1.321	1.717	2.074	2.508	2.819	3.505	3.792
23	.256	.532	.858	1.319	1.714	2.069	2.500	2.807	3.485	3.767
24	.256	.531	.857	1.318	1.711	2.064	2.492	2.797	3.467	3.745
25	.256	.531	.856	1.316	1.708	2.060	2.485	2.787	3.450	3.725
26	.256	.531	.856	1.315	1.706	2.056	2.479	2.779	3.435	3.707
27	.256	.531	.855	1.314	1.703	2.052	2.473	2.771	3.421	3.690
28	.256	.530	.855	1.313	1.701	2.048	2.467	2.763	3.408	3.674
29	.256	.530	.854	1.311	1.699	2.045	2.462	2.756	3.396	3.659
30	.256	.530	.854	1.310	1.697	2.042	2.457	2.750	3.385	3.646
40	.255	.529	.851	1.303	1.684	2.021	2.423	2.704	3.307	3.551
50	.255	.528	.849	1.298	1.676	2.009	2.403	2.678	3.262	3.495
60	.254	.527	.848	1.296	1.671	2.000	2.390	2.660	3.232	3.460
80	.254	.527	.846	1.292	1.664	1.990	2.374	2.639	3.195	3.415
100	.254	.526	.845	1.290	1.660	1.984	2.365	2.626	3.174	3.389
200	.254	.525	.843	1.286	1.653	1.972	2.345	2.601	3.131	3.339
500	.253	.525	.842	1.283	1.648	1.965	2.334	2.586	3.106	3.310
∞	.253	.524	.842	1.282	1.645	1.960	2.326	2.576	3.090	3.291

TABLE 3 Chi-Square Distribution

This Table Gives Specified Value of X_α^2 for d Degrees of Freedom and a Tail Area of α

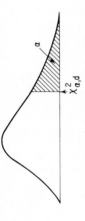

Value of α

d	.995	.99	.98	.975	.95	.90	.80	.75	.70	.50
1	$.0^4393$	$.0^5157$	$.0^3628$	$.0^3982$	.00393	.0158	.0642	.102	.148	.455
2	.0100	.0201	.0404	.0506	.103	.211	.446	.575	.713	1.386
3	.0717	.115	.185	.216	.352	.584	1.005	1.213	1.424	2.366
4	.207	.297	.429	.484	.711	1.064	1.649	1.923	2.195	3.357
5	.412	.554	.752	.831	1.145	1.610	2.343	2.675	3.000	4.351
6	.676	.872	1.134	1.237	1.635	2.204	3.070	3.455	3.828	5.348
7	.989	1.239	1.564	1.690	2.167	2.833	3.822	4.255	4.671	6.346
8	1.344	1.646	2.032	2.180	2.733	3.490	4.594	5.071	5.527	7.344
9	1.735	2.088	2.532	2.700	3.325	4.168	5.380	5.899	6.393	8.343
10	2.156	2.558	3.059	3.247	3.940	4.865	6.179	6.737	7.267	9.342
11	2.603	3.053	3.609	3.816	4.575	5.578	6.989	7.584	8.148	10.341
12	3.074	3.571	4.178	4.404	5.226	6.304	7.807	8.438	9.034	11.340
13	3.565	4.107	4.765	5.009	5.892	7.042	8.634	9.299	9.926	12.340
14	4.075	4.660	5.368	5.629	6.571	7.790	9.467	10.165	10.821	13.339
15	4.601	5.229	5.985	6.262	7.261	8.547	10.307	11.036	11.721	14.339
16	5.142	5.812	6.614	6.908	7.962	9.312	11.152	11.912	12.624	15.338
17	5.697	6.408	7.255	7.564	8.672	10.085	12.002	12.792	13.531	16.338
18	6.265	7.015	7.906	8.231	9.390	10.865	12.857	13.675	14.440	17.338
19	6.844	7.633	8.567	8.907	10.117	11.651	13.716	14.562	15.352	18.338
20	7.434	8.260	9.237	9.591	10.851	12.443	14.578	15.452	16.266	19.337
21	8.034	8.897	9.915	10.283	11.591	13.240	15.445	16.344	17.182	20.337
22	8.643	9.542	10.600	10.982	12.338	14.041	16.314	17.240	18.101	21.337
23	9.260	10.196	11.293	11.688	13.091	14.848	17.187	18.137	19.021	22.337
24	9.886	10.856	11.992	12.401	13.848	15.659	18.062	19.037	19.943	23.337
25	10.520	11.524	12.697	13.120	14.611	16.473	18.940	19.939	20.867	24.337

d										
26	11.160	12.198	13.409	13.844	15.379	17.292	19.820	20.843	21.792	25.336
27	11.808	12.879	14.125	14.573	16.151	18.114	20.703	21.749	22.719	26.336
28	12.461	13.565	14.847	15.308	16.928	18.939	21.588	22.657	23.647	27.336
29	13.121	14.256	15.574	16.047	17.708	19.768	22.475	23.567	24.577	28.336
30	13.787	14.953	16.306	16.791	18.493	20.599	23.364	24.478	25.508	29.336

Value of α

d	.30	.25	.20	.10	.05	.025	.02	.01	.005	.001
1	1.074	1.323	1.642	2.706	3.841	5.024	5.412	6.635	7.879	10.827
2	2.408	2.773	3.219	4.605	5.991	7.378	7.824	9.210	10.597	13.815
3	3.665	4.108	4.642	6.251	7.815	9.348	9.837	11.345	12.838	16.268
4	4.878	5.385	5.989	7.779	9.488	11.143	11.668	13.277	14.860	18.465
5	6.064	6.626	7.289	9.236	11.070	12.832	13.388	15.086	16.750	20.517
6	7.231	7.841	8.558	10.645	12.592	14.449	15.033	16.812	18.548	22.457
7	8.383	9.037	9.803	12.017	14.067	16.013	16.622	18.475	20.278	24.322
8	9.524	10.219	11.030	13.362	15.507	17.535	18.168	20.090	21.955	26.125
9	10.656	11.389	12.242	14.684	16.919	19.023	19.679	21.666	23.589	27.877
10	11.781	12.549	13.442	15.987	18.307	20.483	21.161	23.209	25.188	29.588
11	12.899	13.701	14.631	17.275	19.675	21.920	22.618	24.725	26.757	31.264
12	14.011	14.845	15.812	18.549	21.026	23.337	24.054	26.217	28.300	32.909
13	15.119	15.984	16.985	19.812	22.362	24.736	25.472	27.688	29.819	34.528
14	16.222	17.117	18.151	21.064	23.685	26.119	26.873	29.141	31.319	36.123
15	17.322	18.245	19.311	22.307	24.996	27.488	28.259	30.578	32.801	37.697
16	18.418	19.369	20.465	23.542	26.296	28.845	29.633	32.000	34.267	39.252
17	19.511	20.489	21.615	24.769	27.587	30.191	30.995	33.409	35.718	40.790
18	20.601	21.605	22.760	25.989	28.869	31.526	32.346	34.805	37.156	42.312
19	21.689	22.718	23.900	27.204	30.144	32.852	33.687	36.191	38.582	43.820
20	22.775	23.828	25.038	28.412	31.410	34.170	35.020	37.566	39.997	45.315
21	23.858	24.935	26.171	29.615	32.671	35.479	36.343	38.932	41.401	46.797
22	24.939	26.039	27.301	30.813	33.924	36.781	37.659	40.289	42.796	48.268
23	26.018	27.141	28.429	32.007	35.172	38.076	38.968	41.638	44.181	49.728
24	27.096	28.241	29.553	33.196	36.415	39.364	40.270	42.980	45.558	51.179
25	28.172	29.339	30.675	34.382	37.652	40.646	41.566	44.314	46.928	52.620
26	29.246	30.434	31.795	35.563	38.885	41.923	42.856	45.642	48.290	54.052
27	30.319	31.528	32.912	36.741	40.113	43.194	44.140	46.963	49.645	55.476
28	31.391	32.620	34.027	37.916	41.337	44.461	45.419	48.278	50.993	56.893
29	32.461	33.711	35.139	39.087	42.557	45.722	46.693	49.588	52.336	58.302
30	33.530	34.800	36.250	40.256	43.773	46.979	47.962	50.892	53.672	59.703

Reproduced by consent of publisher from Frederick E. Croxton, Elementary Statistics with Applications in Medicine, Prentice-Hall, Englewood Cliffs, N.J., 1953, pp. 328–329.

TABLE 4 Table of Random Digits

2380	4072	3008	1403	1341	5417	0429	2183
1100	0011	0163	0876	3790	4854	5012	6793
3056	4643	0353	0324	8766	9682	9196	5561
3596	3171	6664	1438	8653	8974	5965	5347
7054	0858	1663	2252	8541	0973	8965	2839
0932	5976	7465	1000	8810	3864	3891	7094
2586	2239	156	0779	3270	2610	6227	7875
3300	1457	9042	1136	5435	2379	5360	2489
7794	6527	9013	5338	0907	7399	6226	0850
7761	6076	6604	4934	0167	6590	8035	8335
9340	7971	3762	0827	1103	9175	5124	2922
3617	3321	7369	4324	9618	8791	6179	6110
6654	2553	5427	9580	8636	5595	5847	4881
2305	0902	4666	9875	7255	4653	2628	6974
0891	7370	6201	0871	9413	8637	7107	4457
9978	5992	6144	2937	2324	7506	4124	3677
2205	4959	9903	4788	9595	4481	0526	5784
0642	2127	6986	2767	3726	7450	1164	6878
2687	4597	3392	8976	3333	9208	5249	4190
8033	2356	1841	9836	2445	6147	4872	1725
0236	5882	3172	6088	7979	3084	6690	3820
9055	9955	8230	9779	4607	9625	6288	6388
3216	1799	1854	4927	2873	2897	1521	8034
5440	0327	3002	5066	3378	4667	7600	5022
6444	3467	2802	5606	8420	0065	4607	5035
9523	1816	5194	4815	2139	9497	7735	8564
6365	1116	9403	6377	3633	4400	3697	3864
7140	8066	4131	2196	5990	6177	3149	0751
6259	0797	8446	3501	4987	8410	5582	0765
8551	4419	9560	7380	9443	8433	5610	8901
1088	6418	8721	4560	8866	2152	3119	8163
2864	3715	6513	5614	5227	589	6487	7956
2124	1140	7718	6047	6817	6473	7486	4725
5729	1844	9502	415	6974	8109	5881	3885
9655	2965	0890	8657	3933	5677	8664	4906
5471	8666	2756	8542	6441	1771	2653	7186
5998	1310	3875	1453	3846	9997	5363	2828
2228	7915	7436	3379	3349	9686	7969	9936
9139	5404	0172	2394	2820	5370	6836	8621
4480	9288	5408	8852	4436	6947	1760	3907

Index